TEACHER'S ANNOTATED EDITION

LAND of LIBERTY

A UNITED STATES HISTORY

James J. Rawls
Diablo Valley College
Pleasant Hill, California

Philip Weeks
University of Akron
Akron, Ohio

Holt, Rinehart and Winston, Publishers

New York Toronto Mexico City London Sydney Tokyo

AUTHORS

James J. Rawls
Diablo Valley College
Pleasant Hill, California

Philip Weeks
The University of Akron
Akron, Ohio

CONTRIBUTING WRITERS

TEACHER'S ANNOTATED EDITION

Danton Ponzol
Southern Lehigh School District
Center Valley, Pennsylvania

Margaret Steneck
Dumont High School
Dumont, New Jersey

Contributing writers and consultants for the pupil edition are listed on page 3 of the pupil edition.

STAFF CREDITS

EDITORIAL DEVELOPMENT

Alice Trimmer
Lynn M. Lustberg
Mary Jean Katz

PRODUCT MANAGER

W. Christopher Elliott

FIELD ADVISORY BOARD

John Eskew
Sam Sherwood
Gary Crump
Keith Hogle
Stu Natof
Jean Slankard
Dennis Spurgeon

MARKETING RESEARCH

Erica S. Felman

EDITORIAL PROCESSING

Margaret M. Byrne
Holly L. Massey

ART AND DESIGN

Carol Steinberg
Paula Darmofal

PRODUCTION

Bev Silver
Joan McNeil
Heidi Henney

PHOTO RESOURCES

Linda Sykes
Rita Longabucco

Printed in the United States of America

ISBN: 0-03-064227-2
56789 039 98765432

Table of Contents

LAND OF LIBERTY FIELD TEST

During the time that *Land of Liberty* was under development, a portion of the book was field-tested by 95 teachers in 29 states. These teachers used the material in the classroom, and both students and teachers returned questionnaires commenting on both the content and the graphic design. These comments provided valuable feedback to us, and many of the suggestions were incorporated into the text and supplementary materials.

The text was found to be at an appropriate level of difficulty for the eighth grade student, although seventh-grade teachers found that their students could use the book with ease as well. Teachers were very positive about the interest level of the writing, the clear explanation of concepts, and the page design and layout. They expressed particular appreciation for the reading helps in the student text.

Our thanks and appreciation go to the following teachers who used our field test materials in their classrooms.

Arizona

Mary Ann Butler
Madison #1 School
Phoenix

Ray Davies
Vail J.H.S.
Tucson

Alan C. Little
Pistor J.H.S.
Tucson

Jolene McGowan
Bethune School
Phoenix

Rolando Mauro
Ann Ott School
Phoenix

Chip Parsons
Chaparral J.H.S.
Tucson

Harlan Peckham
Chaparral J.H.S.
Tucson

Phyllis Skelley
McKemy J.H.S.
Tempe

California

Seymour Baybrook
Sylvandale I.S.
San Jose

Mary Beebe
Gage Middle School
Huntington Park

Patricia Cain
Most Holy Trinity School
San Jose

Sr. Helen Keane
Holy Angels School
Colmer

Gary Moore
Casimir Middle School
Torrance

Sr. Peter Joseph Navone
Saint Lucy's School
Campbell

Colorado

Helen Dounas-Frazer
Merritt Hutton J.H.S.
Thornton

Diane K. Marino
Northeast J.H.S.
Northglenn

Patricia Miller
Northeast J.H.S.
Northglenn

Phillip Perry
Kepner Middle School
Denver

Donald D. Trickel
Horace Mann Middle School
Denver

Connecticut

Barbara Maybin
Fox Middle School
Hartford

Jessie Meyers
John F. Kennedy J.H.S.
Enfield

William Weatherby
Read Middle School
Bridgeport

Florida

Robert Gosling
Bradenton Middle School
Bradenton

Illinois

Thomas O. Jewett
Wolf Branch School
Belleville

John Moline
North J.H.S.
Crystal Lake

Myron T. Shannon
Rock Falls J.H.S.
Rock Falls

Iowa

Mark Caputo
Sioux City North H.S.
Sioux City

Maryland

Ralph Doyle
Johnnycake J.H.S.
Baltimore

Ruby L. Fuller
Mount Royal Middle School
Baltimore

Cynthia Higgins
Pimlico J.H.S.
Baltimore

Addie C. Ruffin
Hamilton J.H.S.
Baltimore

Massachusetts

James J. Collins
Vernon Hill School
Worcester

Elaine Nigro
Milford Catholic
Elementary School
Milford

Michigan

Margaret Berian
Mount Morris J.H.S.
Mount Morris

Jerome W. Roulo
Holmes Middle School
Livonia

Ken Tesauro
Swan Valley Schools
Saginaw

Merida Eddie Whitfield
North I.S.
Saginaw

Mark Zink
Hampton Middle School
Detroit

Minnesota

Michael Bosanko
Oak Grove J.H.S.
Bloomington

Imogene K. Hoff
Carl Sandburg J.H.S.
Golden Valley

Cheryl Martens
Oak Grove J.H.S.
Bloomington

Janet Moberg
Carl Sandburg J.H.S.
Golden Valley

Russell Olson
Hosterman J.H.S.
Minneapolis

Mary Shasky
Hosterman J.H.S.
Minneapolis

Missouri

Sherry E. Beyers
Saint Angela Merici School
Florissant

Lea Hardcastle
Nipher Middle School
Kirkwood

New Hampshire

Sandra Axton
Spring Street J.H.S.
Nashua

Paul Tumas
Amherst School District
Amherst

New Jersey

Barbara Maier
Churchill J.H.S.
East Brunswick

Gerad Maier
Churchill J.H.S.
East Brunswick

Mary C. Tomchuk
Woodrow Wilson J.H.S.
Edison

New Mexico

Mary M. Arrowsmith
Taylor Middle School
Albuquerque

P. Blake
Picacho J.H.S.
Las Cruces

Gerad Kaye
McKinley Middle School
Albuquerque

Susan Keefe
Cleveland Middle School
Albuquerque

Robert Sanchez
Washington Middle School
Albuquerque

Michael D. Shepherd
McKinley Middle School
Albuquerque

Michael R. Smith
Grant Middle School
Albuquerque

New York

Robert C. Novarro
St. Robert Bellarmine
Bayside

Gene Reese
Resurrection-Ascension
Rego Park

North Carolina

Bill Demke
Papillion J.H.S.
Papillion

North Dakota

J. Belcher
Schroeder J.H.S.
Grand Forks

Donn Feldner
Erik Ramstad J.H.S.
Minot

Carrie Gibson
Nathan Twining J.H.S.
Grand Forks

Gordon Johnson
Valley J.H.S.
Grand Forks

John Moritz
South J.H.S.
Grand Forks

Anita L. Row
Wachter J.H.S.
Bismarck

Ohio

Saundra Gerber
Colerain J.H.S.
Cincinnati

Bobby M. Herren
Northmont J.H.S.
Clayton

Louis M. O'Neill
Saint Bernadette School
Amelia

Joseph H. Putnam
Robert A. Taft Middle School
Canton

Steve Schreiner
Princeton J.H.S.
Cincinnati

D. Senior
Sycamore J.H.S.
Cincinnati

Richard L. Smith
Innes J.H.S.
Akron

Richard P. Worron
Litchfield Middle School
Akron

Oregon

Marvin D. Binegar
Moss J.H.S.
Oregon City

Joan Kent
Whitaker Middle School
Portland

Pennsylvania

James C. Dallessandro
North East J.H.S.
Reading

Michael O'Hara
John Reynolds J.H.S.
Lancaster

Joseph T. Sanquilli
St. Huberts Catholic H.S.
for Girls
Philadelphia

Rhode Island

Mary K. Burke
Cranston Johnston
Catholic Regional
Cranston

Raymond S. Dalton, Jr.
St. Leo the Great School
Pawtucket

Sandy Gasbarro
St. Mary's School
Cranston

Margaret M. Manchester
Mount Saint Charles Academy
Woonsocket

South Dakota

Diana L. Herman
Dakota J.H.S.
Rapid City

Texas

Jane Haley
Quail Valley J.H.S.
Sugar Land

Utah

Robert James Gardner
Brockbank J.H.S.
Magna

John C. Parks
North Layton J.H.S.
Layton

Annette Weber
Oquirrh Hills Middle School
Riverton

Virginia

Winfred C. Shuping
Breckinridge J.H.S.
Roanoke

Lois W. Switzer
Botetourt I.S.
Fincastle

Washington

Pete Jarvis
Naches Valley Middle School
Naches

Wisconsin

Melinda Skrade
Immaculate Conception School
Milwaukee

Wyoming

Nathan Breen
McCormick J.H.S.
Cheyenne

Craig Wilson
Carey J.H.S.
Cheyenne

Our thanks also go to the following teachers and administrators who reviewed the field test chapter.

Howard Brokate, Jr.
Guillen I.S.
El Paso, Texas

Frederick D. Cole
New Bedford High School
New Bedford, Massachusetts

Malcolm L. Cook
Laramie Country School
District #1
Cheyenne, Wyoming

Joan L. Dobzanski
St. Josephs J.H.S.
Manchester, New Hampshire

Margie Eustice
Perkins Middle School
Akron, Ohio

William Gabrielson
Public Schools of Edison
Township
Edison, New Jersey

Donald E. Jones
South J.H.S.
Brockton, Massachusetts

Sr. Mary Judith Korte
Diocese of Belleville
Belleville, Illinois

Larry S. Krieger
East Brunswick Public Schools
East Brunswick, New Jersey

Patricia Marmaduke
Akron Public Schools
Akron, Ohio

Florence B. Misselwitz
Hartford Board of Education
Hartford, Connecticut

Richard Rattan
Martin Luther King J.H.S.
Germantown, Maryland

Bruce C. Ross
Winthrop High School
Winthrop, Massachusetts

Ann B. Seddon
Cave Spring J.H.S.
Roanoke, Virginia

Gary Shiffman
Heard Middle School
Phoenix, Arizona

Thomas Smallridge
Raytown Public School
Raytown, Missouri

Betty Goodwin Watkins
Decatur P.S. District 61
Decatur, Illinois

Robert Weiner
Manalapan-Englishtown
Regional Schools
Englishtown, New Jersey

Jack Winn
El Paso Public Schools
El Paso, Texas

INTRODUCTION

Land of Liberty is a comprehensive, chronological history of the United States written with the special needs and capabilities of the junior high school student in mind. The student text provides comprehensive coverage of events, dates, and facts set within a narrative that is coherent, engaging, and full of concrete details. The student text also contains a sequential skills strand to aid comprehension.

Students' mastery of basic **social studies skills**, particularly those related to geography and chronology, varies widely in the average junior high classroom. *Land of Liberty* begins with a section entitled "Using Social Studies Skills" that helps students review the tools needed to study American history. Skill-building continues in each unit with the "Social Studies Skills" features. These are sequentially developed skill lessons that tie into the content of the chapter while providing the student with step-by-step instruction in how to master the skill. In addition, skill reinforcement is carried out in chapter review timelines and in the "Sharpening Your Skills" section of the unit reviews. Each map in the text has a caption question that requires the student to use mapping skills.

Students become involved in **critical thinking** throughout the text. The last question in each section review is a critical thinking question; in addition, the "Analyzing the Facts" segments in both chapter and unit reviews give students an opportunity to draw new conclusions from what they have learned.

Land of Liberty also contains a **reading methodology** based on the idea that organized previews, knowledge-based objectives, guide questions, summaries and reviews will enhance student comprehension. Each unit opener is structured as an advance organizer that provides a capsule overview of each chapter in the unit. Each chapter opener includes a list of knowledge and skill objectives, and each section within the chapter begins with a prereading question, labeled "Before you read." Reading comprehension is checked in the section review, where the "Before you read" question is the first question in the section review.

In addition, in the narrative itself, scrupulous attention has been given to maintaining an appropriate level of readability, both in control of sentence length and vocabulary and in attention to maintaining a logical, well-supported sequence of ideas. Important social studies terms are bold-faced and defined on the page.

Of course, the content, skill and reading structure of a book needs an appealing framework to keep students motivated to learn. In *Land of Liberty*, **special features** unique to this book have been included to capture student interest. The "Famous Americans" are biographical sketches of less well-known Americans whose achievements have made a difference in myriad areas of American life. "Famous Americans" features demonstrate to students that the achievements of individuals matter and that individual initiative is important. The "Eureka!" feature focuses on American inventions and scientific breakthroughs that have had a major impact on the American way of life.

In the front of the **Teacher's Annotated Edition** is a section entitled "Resource Materials." This section contains two levels of classroom activities and the answers to all questions in the Pupil Edition.

The Teacher Resource Book contains chapter and unit **tests** and **worksheets** for each chapter. These are printed in blackline master form with answer keys. The worksheets encompass three types of activities for each chapter: factual review, skill-building, and critical thinking. Comprehensive chapter and unit tests are criterion referenced to the objectives listed in the pupil edition.

Pacing Your History Course

Land of Liberty has thirty-four chapters and is designed for flexible use. For a course covering pre-colonial times to the present day, the class should cover about one chapter per week. The solid arrows on the chart below suggest how to schedule this type of course. The dotted arrows show suggested pacing for a course that ends with the Reconstruction era.

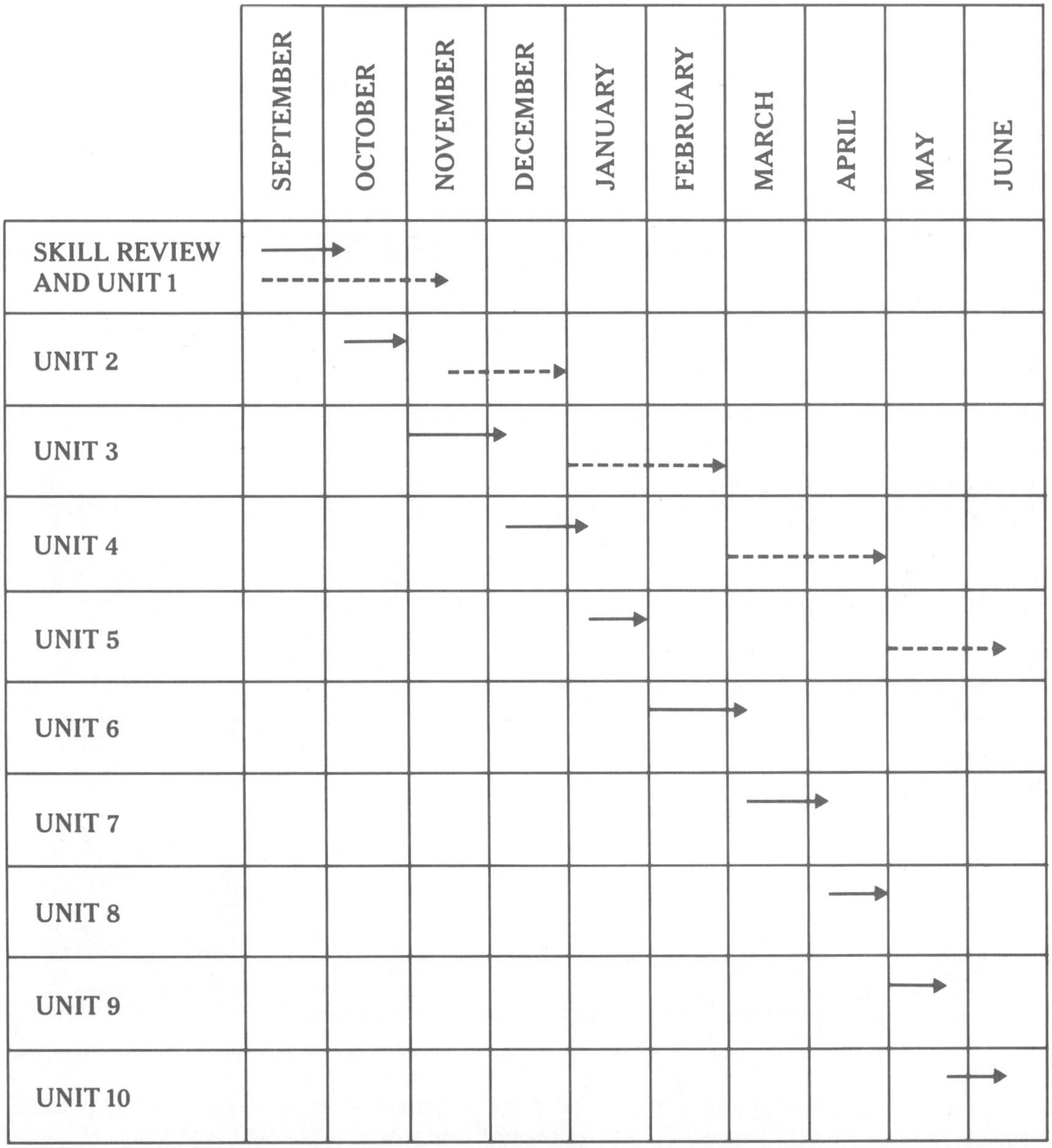

SEPTEMBER
OCTOBER
NOVEMBER
DECEMBER
JANUARY
FEBRUARY
MARCH
APRIL
MAY
JUNE
SKILL REVIEW AND UNIT 1
UNIT 2
UNIT 3
UNIT 4
UNIT 5
UNIT 6
UNIT 7
UNIT 8
UNIT 9
UNIT 10

HIGHLIGHTS OF

LAND OF LIBERTY

FINALLY

a book students will read!
a book that helps students learn!

Unit

1 The New World's Settlers

1 Scientists believe that ancestors of the American Indians arrived in America over 25,000 years ago. The Indian population grew from the first small groups of prehistoric hunters to millions of people. These people developed rich and complex societies in America.

34

2 In the 1400's, Europeans began to explore the world for new trade routes. These explorers found two continents they did not know existed—North and South America. By 1500, Europeans had begun the exploration of this New World.

3 The English began to establish permanent colonies in North America in the early 1600's. Within a short period of time, these English colonies grew and prospered. Eventually, individuals no longer thought of themselves as English colonists but as Americans who lived in English America.

35

Unit openers serve as **advance organizers** by providing both visual and verbal previews of each chapter's content.

Lively chapter **introductions** set the stage for the narrative of the chapter.

Objectives for each section let students know what they can expect to gain from reading the chapter.

Knowledge objectives

Skill objectives

Chapter ***10***

A Changing America

The United States changed dramatically during the early nineteenth century. A major cause for the change was the development of new manufacturing methods and the growth of industry. Changes in manufacturing led to the growth of American cities. During those same years, the United States experienced rapid changes in transportation and communication. Westward expansion and the growth of industry forced the nation to improve its methods of travel. The nation built roads, dug a vast network of canals, and began linking the country together by means of railroads and telegraph lines.

After you read this chapter, you will be able to:

1. Explain the causes of industrial growth in the early 1800's.
2. Identify the major developments in transportation and communication in the early 1800's.

☐ Read a bar graph.

248

Chapter **content** is divided into short sections written in an engaging, readable style.

A **Before you read** question is provided to help focus student attention on the main idea of the section.

New **vocabulary** is defined in context and in a vocabulary insert at the end of the paragraph. All vocabulary words appear in the **glossary.**

2. Domestic Affairs

BEFORE YOU READ: *What new groups began to organize for their civil rights?*

On July 20, 1969, the American spacecraft *Eagle* landed on the moon. Neil Armstrong, commander of the three-member flight crew, was the first person ever to walk on the moon's surface. His first step, he said, was "one small step for a man, one giant leap for mankind."

The lunar landing was an event that drew the nation together. Other events during the late 1960's and early 1970's, however, emphasized the continuing differences among Americans.

Civil Rights

President Nixon was not a strong supporter of the civil rights movement. The President, for example, opposed **busing**, or the transportation of students to a school to achieve desegregation. Nevertheless, in 1971 the Supreme Court ruled in favor of busing.

busing the transportation of students to a school to achieve desegregation

The continued successes of the black civil rights movement encouraged other minority groups to organize. American Indians were one such group. American Indians are among the nation's poorest people. The unemployment rate among Indians in the 1960's was ten times the national rate. For those Indians living on reservations, housing, health care, and job opportunities were very poor.

In 1968, the American Indian Movement (AIM) was organized. AIM and other American Indian rights groups called for improved conditions and better opportunities for Indian people. To make Americans aware of their situation and demands, the members of AIM staged a number of protests. In 1972, nearly one thousand Indian demonstrators held a six-day sit-in at the Bureau of Indian Affairs in Washington, D. C. At the town of Wounded Knee, South Dakota, Indian protestors clashed with federal officials. One Indian was killed and another wounded.

Indian protests in the late 1960's and early 1970's were successful in bringing about public and government awareness of Indian issues and problems.

695

COMPREHENSIVE SKILL DEVELOPMENT

An **introductory skills chapter** reviews the basic skills needed to study history: reading maps, charts, and graphs; working with chronology; reading for understanding; and study techniques.

1. Map and Geography Skills

Geography is a branch of social studies that describes the land, sea, air, and plant and animal life of the earth. Geography, in other words, can tell us about the places where history has occurred.

Directions on a Map

In 1603, the French explorer, Samuel de Champlain, traveled up the St. Lawrence River. He hoped to sail across Canada and reach the riches of the Orient. But Champlain came upon rapids, or fast-moving waters, which blocked his way. Neither Champlain nor his crew knew how to cross the rapids or what lay beyond them. The explorer went to a nearby Indian camp for information. Unfortunately, Champlain only spoke French, and the Indians did not understand him.

Champlain's Birch Bark Drawing

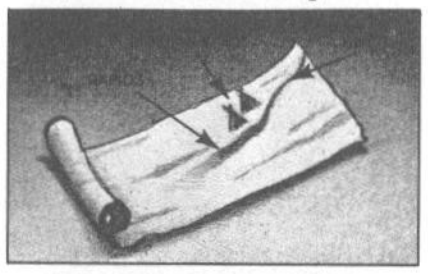

Drawing Completed by the Indians

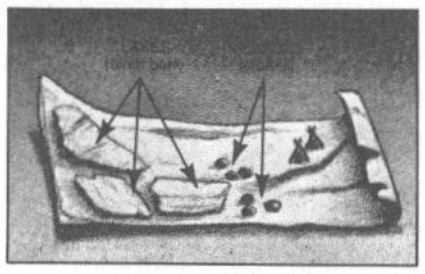

Champlain cut a piece of bark from a birch tree. On the bark he drew a picture of the river, the rapids, and the Indian camp. Then Champlain pointed to the part of the drawing that had nothing on it. The Indians understood that the explorer wanted them to complete the drawing and show him what the river was like beyond the rapids. They picked up a few stones and put them on the bark drawing. They used the stones to show where other Indian villages were. Then they cut up smaller pieces of birch bark to represent lakes.

Together, Champlain and the Indians had drawn a map. It proved to be a good map because Champlain was able to learn what lay beyond the rapids.

Today we have maps of every part of North America, as well as the rest of the world. But maps are not very useful if you cannot read them. Regardless of whether you are an explorer, an airline pilot, or a person planning a trip, you need to be able to read a map in order to locate your destination.

On a map, north means toward the North Pole. If you travel from any point on the earth toward the North Pole, you are heading north. On most maps, a direction finder, such as a **compass rose** or an arrow, indicates the direction of north. South, the direction of the South Pole, is always opposite north. East is to the right, and west is to the left. These four directions are called the **cardinal**

16

Skill features in each unit highlight particular social studies skills for more detailed study.

Social Studies Skills

Using a Map Scale

Samuel de Champlain explored the St. Lawrence River from its mouth to the Great Lakes. The distance he actually traveled can be measured by using a map scale. Distances on maps are drawn in proportion to distances in the real world. The map scale shows this ratio. To measure the distance between Quebec and Montreal, follow these steps:

1. Mark off on the edge of a strip of paper the space between the dot marking Quebec and the dot marking Montreal.
2. Place your paper strip on the map scale so that your first mark is at zero. Notice that your second mark falls at approximately 250 kilometers (155 miles). This means that the distance between these two points is about 250 kilometers (155 miles).

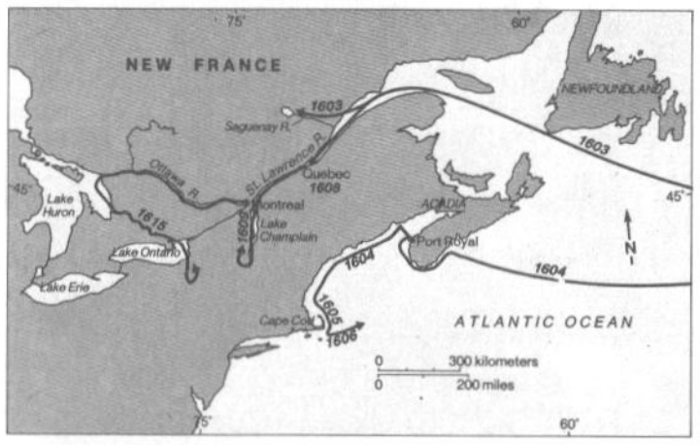

1. How many kilometers is Quebec from Port Royal?
2. What is the distance in miles between Quebec and Port Royal?
3. About how long is Lake Champlain?
4. How many kilometers is it from Montreal to the southern tip of Lake Huron?
5. How would you measure the distance between two points if the space between them were greater than the length of the map scale?

70

All maps have **caption questions** to encourage student involvement.

Victory in Europe

North Africa gave the Allies a solid base from which to attack southern Europe. In January 1943, President Roosevelt flew across the Atlantic to Casablanca for a strategy meeting with Prime Minister Churchill. Roosevelt and Churchill made plans for the invasion of Europe. The invasion would begin on the island of Sicily, off the southern coast of Italy. From there, the Allied forces could move onto the Italian peninsula.

At the Casablanca conference, President Roosevelt made a historic declaration of Allied war aims. He declared that the Axis Powers would have to surrender on whatever terms the Allies set. President Roosevelt, in other words, demanded the **unconditional surrender** of the Axis Powers.

unconditional surrender the surrender of a defeated nation on the terms set by the victors

World War II in Europe and North Africa

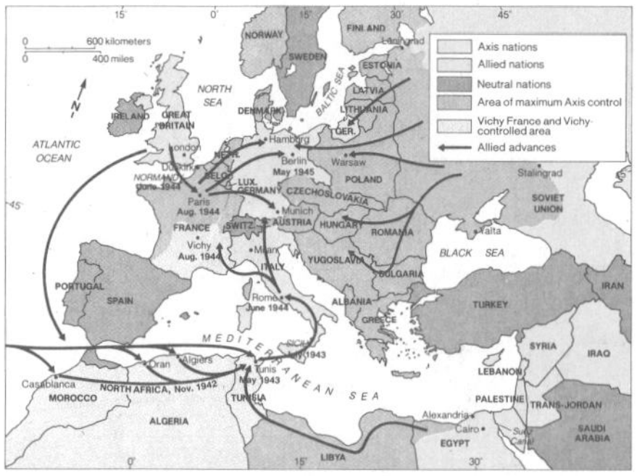

Where did the Allied armies in Africa go after defeating the Axis forces in Tunis? In what direction and through which countries did Soviet forces advance?

610

Outstanding **photographs** bring each era to life.

This picture shows the reception following Jackson's inauguration in 1829. What does it suggest about the kind of people who attended?

the affair in a letter to her relatives. "But what a scene did we witness!" she wrote. "The majesty of the People had disappeared. . . . [It had become] a mob, scrambling, fighting, romping. . . . Ladies fainted, men were seen with bloody noses." Mrs. Smith concluded, "What a pity, what a pity!"

John Quincy Adams ended his term as President in the same fashion as his father. He left the White House the night before the inauguration. Adams refused to attend the ceremonies for the "barbarian," as he called Jackson. As Jackson began his term as the new President, one Supreme Court justice expressed the fear that this was the beginning of the reign of "King Mob."

Frequent **Section Reviews** give a thorough review of the content of the section.

The first question reviews the central idea raised in the **Before you read** question.

The final question invites students to **think critically** about what they have learned.

Section Review

1. How did Andrew Jackson rise to political power?
2. How was sectionalism demonstrated in the election of 1824?
3. What was Henry Clay's American System?
4. What events led to the establishment of the Democratic party?
5. Why do you think Andrew Jackson won the election of 1828?

273

HIGH-INTEREST FEATURES

Eureka! features celebrate American ingenuity through close examination of technological breakthroughs or new inventions.

EUREKA!

The Submarine

Credit for building the first submarine is usually given to Cornelius Drebbel, a Dutch inventor. Drebbel launched a leather-covered craft in 1620. But it was an American named David Bushnell who first thought of using the submarine as a weapon of war.

Bushnell built his first submarine, which was known as the *Turtle*, in 1776. The *Turtle* was a clumsy contraption. Made of wood, it resembled a lemon with two propellers and a rudder, which the pilot cranked by hand. The pilot steered the submarine alongside an enemy ship and drilled a hole in the ship's side. Into the hole he fitted a gunpowder mine. Then he and the *Turtle* got as far away from the ship as possible. At least, that was the idea.

In 1776, Sergeant Ezra Lee used the *Turtle* to attack the British ship *Eagle*, in New York harbor. But the submarine's drill was too weak to pierce the ship's copper side.

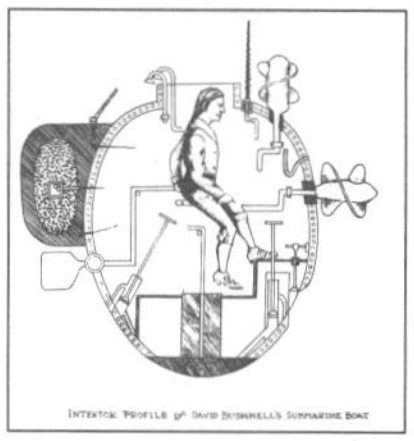

Near the end of his life, David Bushnell built another submarine, which was used in the War of 1812. But his second design was no more successful than the *Turtle*. Other attempts to perfect underwater vessels followed. Only with the development of powerful electric motors in the 1880's did submarines find a permanent place in the world's navies.

hired by Great Britain to fight in the colonies. Hiring mercenaries was not an unusual practice at this time. Most of the mercenaries were from the German state of Hesse. Americans referred to all the German mercenaries as Hessians.

mercenary a professional soldier hired to serve in a foreign army

The Fall of New York City

Great Britain hoped it would not have to use its huge attack force. The British thought that merely the show of such superior strength would make the rebels back down. General Howe even sent a message to the Continental Congress in late summer. It said that the colonists would be pardoned by the king if

131

Famous Americans features give biographical sketches of persons who "made a difference" in American life.

Famous Americans

SEIJI OZAWA

Seiji Ozawa, the conductor of the Boston Symphony Orchestra, was born in 1935. His love of music developed early. He learned to enjoy Western music through the hymns he heard in church. Ozawa also enjoyed the Japanese music that surrounded him.

Ozawa's family was very poor, but they did all they could to help develop Seiji's exceptional musical talent. By the age of seven, Ozawa was playing the music of the great nineteenth-century Western composers. His career as a concert pianist seemed certain. But he broke a few fingers playing rugby at school, and his hands never healed properly for piano playing.

For a time, Ozawa decided that composing was the field he should go into. But his teachers at the Toho School of Music in Tokyo thought he would be a good conductor. Ozawa graduated from the Toho School and went to Paris to study conducting.

Ozawa progressed rapidly in his profession. He was engaged as an assistant conductor of the New York Philharmonic for the 1961–1962 season. In 1964, he was invited to return to the New York Philharmonic. During the 1960's, Ozawa served as the conductor of the Toronto Symphony of Canada and music director of the San Francisco Symphony. In 1973, he became the youngest permanent conductor and music director of the Boston Symphony Orchestra.

What makes Ozawa such a great conductor is his ability to conduct classical, romantic, and modern works equally well. He conducts difficult works with ease, and all works are conducted from memory.

In recent years, Ozawa traveled with the Boston Symphony to Japan where he was warmly greeted.

697

THOROUGH REVIEWS

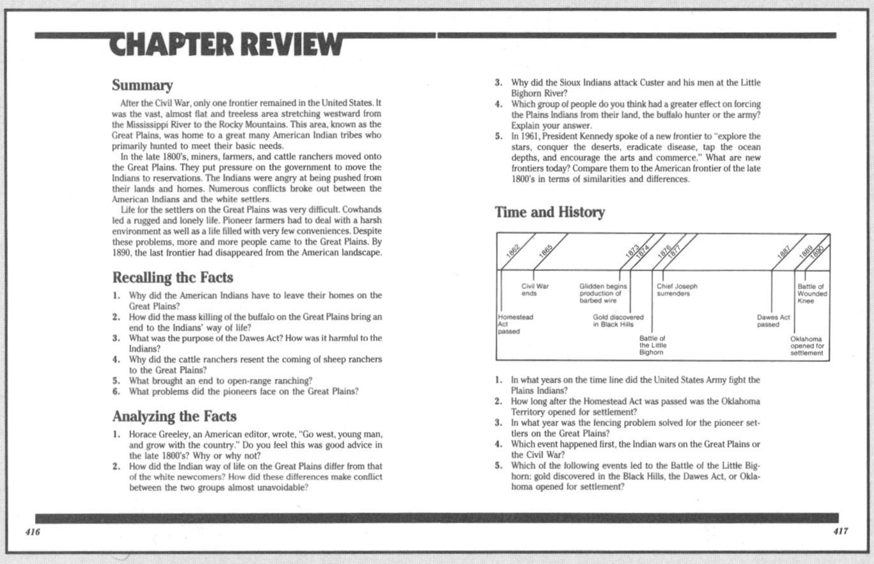

CHAPTER REVIEW

Summary

After the Civil War, only one frontier remained in the United States. It was the vast, almost flat and treeless area stretching westward from the Mississippi River to the Rocky Mountains. This area, known as the Great Plains, was home to a great many American Indian tribes who primarily hunted to meet their basic needs.

In the late 1800's, miners, farmers, and cattle ranchers moved onto the Great Plains. They put pressure on the government to move the Indians to reservations. The Indians were angry at being pushed from their lands and homes. Numerous conflicts broke out between the American Indians and the white settlers.

Life for the settlers on the Great Plains was very difficult. Cowhands led a rugged and lonely life. Pioneer farmers had to deal with a harsh environment as well as a life filled with very few conveniences. Despite these problems, more and more people came to the Great Plains. By 1890, the last frontier had disappeared from the American landscape.

Recalling the Facts

1. Why did the American Indians have to leave their homes on the Great Plains?
2. How did the mass killing of the buffalo on the Great Plains bring an end to the Indians' way of life?
3. What was the purpose of the Dawes Act? How was it harmful to the Indians?
4. Why did the cattle ranchers resent the coming of sheep ranchers to the Great Plains?
5. What brought an end to open-range ranching?
6. What problems did the pioneers face on the Great Plains?

Analyzing the Facts

1. Horace Greeley, an American editor, wrote, "Go west, young man, and grow with the country." Do you feel this was good advice in the late 1800's? Why or why not?
2. How did the Indian way of life on the Great Plains differ from that of the white newcomers? How did these differences make conflict between the two groups almost unavoidable?
3. Why did the Sioux Indians attack Custer and his men at the Little Bighorn River?
4. Which group of people do you think had a greater effect on forcing the Plains Indians from their land, the buffalo hunter or the army? Explain your answer.
5. In 1961, President Kennedy spoke of a new frontier to "explore the stars, conquer the deserts, eradicate disease, tap the ocean depths, and encourage the arts and commerce." What are new frontiers today? Compare them to the American frontier of the late 1800's in terms of similarities and differences.

Time and History

1. In what years on the time line did the United States Army fight the Plains Indians?
2. How long after the Homestead Act was passed was the Oklahoma Territory opened for settlement?
3. In what year was the fencing problem solved for the pioneer settlers on the Great Plains?
4. Which event happened first, the Indian wars on the Great Plains or the Civil War?
5. Which of the following events led to the Battle of the Little Bighorn: gold discovered in the Black Hills, the Dawes Act, or Oklahoma opened for settlement?

416 417

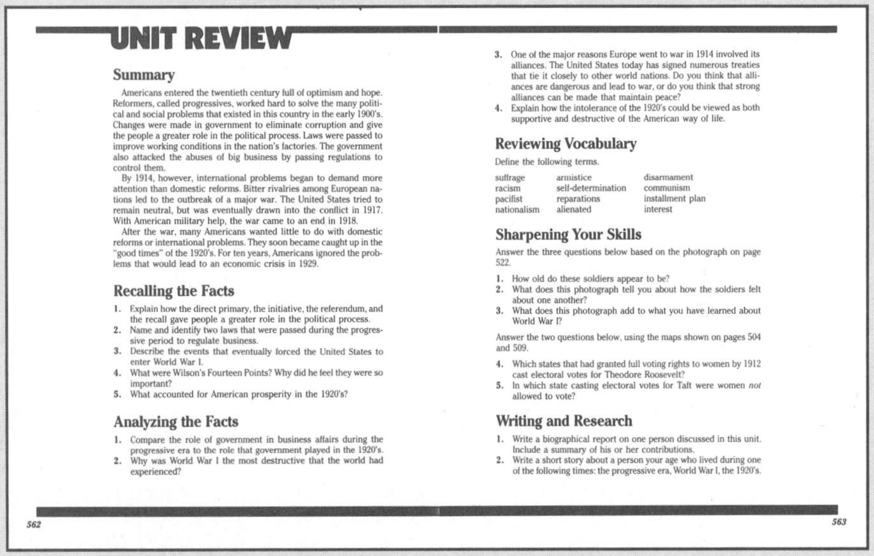

UNIT REVIEW

Summary

Americans entered the twentieth century full of optimism and hope. Reformers, called progressives, worked hard to solve the many political and social problems that existed in this country in the early 1900's. Changes were made in government to eliminate corruption and give the people a greater role in the political process. Laws were passed to improve working conditions in the nation's factories. The government also attacked the abuses of big business by passing regulations to control them.

By 1914, however, international problems began to demand more attention than domestic reforms. Bitter rivalries among European nations led to the outbreak of a major war. The United States tried to remain neutral, but was eventually drawn into the conflict in 1917. With American military help, the war came to an end in 1918.

After the war, many Americans wanted little to do with domestic reforms or international problems. They soon became caught up in the "good times" of the 1920's. For ten years, Americans ignored the problems that would lead to an economic crisis in 1929.

Recalling the Facts

1. Explain how the direct primary, the initiative, the referendum, and the recall gave people a greater role in the political process.
2. Name and identify two laws that were passed during the progressive period to regulate business.
3. Describe the events that eventually forced the United States to enter World War I.
4. What were Wilson's Fourteen Points? Why did he feel they were so important?
5. What accounted for American prosperity in the 1920's?

Analyzing the Facts

1. Compare the role of government in business affairs during the progressive era to the role that government played in the 1920's.
2. Why was World War I the most destructive that the world had experienced?
3. One of the major reasons Europe went to war in 1914 involved its alliances. The United States today has signed numerous treaties that tie it closely to other world nations. Do you think that alliances are dangerous and lead to war, or do you think that strong alliances can be made that maintain peace?
4. Explain how the intolerance of the 1920's could be viewed as both supportive and destructive of the American way of life.

Reviewing Vocabulary

Define the following terms.

suffrage	armistice	disarmament
racism	self-determination	communism
pacifist	reparations	installment plan
nationalism	alienated	interest

Sharpening Your Skills

Answer the three questions below based on the photograph on page 522.

1. How old do these soldiers appear to be?
2. What does this photograph tell you about how the soldiers felt about one another?
3. What does this photograph add to what you have learned about World War I?

Answer the two questions below, using the maps shown on pages 504 and 509.

4. Which states that had granted full voting rights to women by 1912 cast electoral votes for Theodore Roosevelt?
5. In which state casting electoral votes for Taft were women *not* allowed to vote?

Writing and Research

1. Write a biographical report on one person discussed in this unit. Include a summary of his or her contributions.
2. Write a short story about a person your age who lived during one of the following times: the progressive era, World War I, the 1920's.

562 563

All chapter and unit reviews contain:

A **Summary** of the content
Recalling the Facts questions
Analyzing the Facts for critical thinking

Chapter reviews contain a **Time and History** feature consisting of a timeline and questions that strengthen understanding of chronology.

Unit Reviews contain **Reviewing Vocabulary and Sharpening Your Skills** questions as well as **Writing and Research** activities.

Resource Materials for the teacher include a choice of enrichment activities for students of varying abilities.

A activities require more advanced thinking and independent work.

B activities focus on skill building and developing a sense of achievement in students.

All answers to review questions in the student text are provided.

RESOURCE MATERIALS

Activities and Answers to Questions

Unit 1: THE NEW WORLD'S SETTLERS

Chapter 1
The American Indians *pp. 36–53*

ACTIVITIES

Level A: Have students select and research the culture of a specific Indian tribe or nation. Reports should include information on shelters, clothing, food, forms of travel, religious beliefs, work done by the men and women, recreation, and special characteristics of the group. Students can make posters showing the most distinguishing characteristics of their Indian group. Have students share the information from their reports with the class. Display posters around the room.
Level B: Divide the class into groups with the task of developing their own sign language as a form of universal communication. Each group must work out a system that can be understood by others. Have the groups then present to the whole class a simple message. Students who are observing should write down what they think the message means. After all groups have done this, compare what the class has written down and what the group was trying to say. See which groups were the most successful in conveying their messages to others. Then discuss the difficulties encountered in developing a universal language.

ANSWERS

Section 1 Review *p. 42*

1. Many scientists believe the first people to migrate to America did so by using the Bering Strait land bridge during the Ice Age. (p. 37)
2. Farming changed early Indian societies by providing a more dependable food supply. It was no longer necessary for them to wander in search of food. (p. 39)
3. An anthropologist is a scientist who studies human culture and development. Technology is the knowledge, skills, and objects necessary for human survival and comfort. (pp. 37–38)
4. They were used as burial places and for religious ceremonies. (p. 41)
5. Answers will vary, but should include the influence of climate on food, clothing, and shelter.

Section 2 Review *p. 51*

1. They differed in their ways of obtaining food, their clothing and shelter, the languages they spoke, and their forms of political organization. (pp. 43–51)
2. No. In 1500, the Indian population numbered approximately 110 million people. This was larger than the population of Europe at the time. (p. 43)
3. An alliance is a close association for a common objective. The Iroquois Confederacy, made up of five separate Iroquoian tribes in upper New York State, became a powerful intertribal alliance ruled by a council of 50 tribal leaders. (p. 46)
4. Answers will vary, but should include the idea that people who think or behave differently are often considered inferior. Respect for nations with different cultures is frequently lacking in countries where this attitude exists.

T16

Teacher **annotations** are labelled for teaching convenience.

Background—information to clarify and augment material in the student text

Discuss—questions to help students think and speak about what they are learning

Vocabulary—suggestions to define and clarify words in the text that might be unfamiliar to students

For extra interest—ideas to help motivate students through extra projects in and out of class

advancing army at the little town of Gettysburg. Between July 1 and July 3, a battle raged in and around the town.

On the first day of the battle, Meade's troops were pushed back through Gettysburg. They finally took up a position on a series of hills, called Cemetery Ridge, just to the south of the town.

On the second day, Lee sent troops to attack the right and left flanks of the Union line. The fighting lasted all day. By dusk, Meade's army still held its ground.

On the third day, after bombarding Union troops for nearly one hour, General Lee ordered his army to charge the center of the Union troops on Cemetery Ridge. The Confederates reached the Union troops but were thrown back. The charge had failed.

The Confederate troops returned to the woods. Some 7,000 Confederates had died during the charge. The battle of Gettysburg was over. It was the bloodiest battle of the Civil War. In the three days of fighting, the two armies suffered more than 51,000 casualties. Lee had lost roughly 28,000 men. Meade had lost some 23,000.

Lee and his troops retreated into Virginia. Lee's invasion of the North had begun with great hopes and had ended in disaster. The Confederate losses at Vicksburg and Gettysburg in early July crushed the South's hopes, especially for assistance from Great Britain.

During Pickett's Charge, Confederate General Lewis Armistead led a brigade that accomplished the farthest penetration of the Union lines. Armistead was mortally wounded in the battle. He is shown on a horse to the right of three Confederate flags.

365

TEACHER'S RESOURCE BOOK

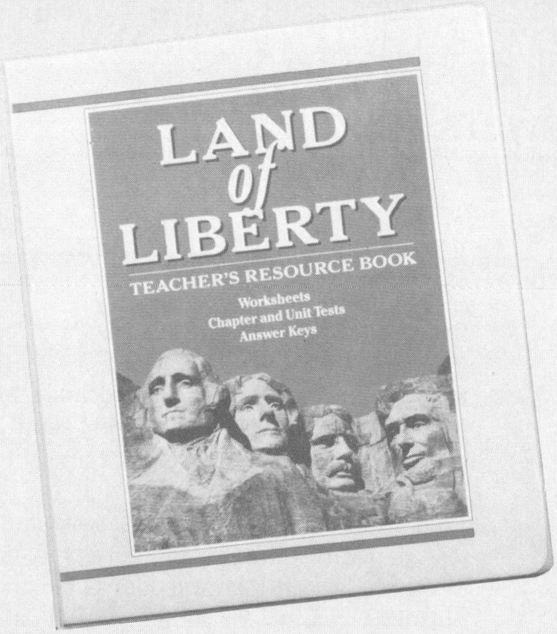

Worksheets for each chapter contain challenging activities to reinforce and supplement information in the pupil text.

Review of information in the chapter
Skill-building activities
Critical thinking

Chapter and Unit Tests provide a combination of multiple choice, short answer, and essay questions. All chapter objectives, including skill objectives, are tested.

Answer keys are provided. The *Teacher's Resource Book* is packaged in an attractive 3-ring binder.

SOFTWARE

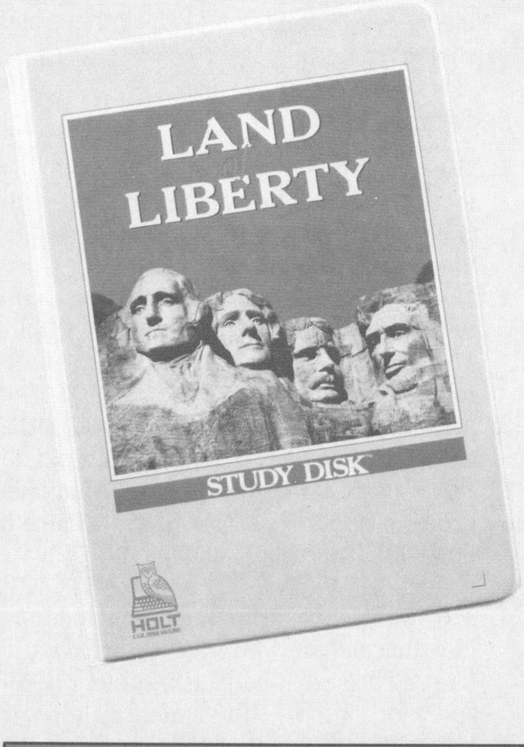

The LAND OF LIBERTY Study Disk™ is available to help students review for tests. This computerized study guide provides twenty questions per chapter. Students have the option to study alone or in pairs, and they can choose the question format (true-false, multiple choice, or short answer). Page references to the correct answer in the student text are provided to encourage further study and reinforcement.

RESOURCE MATERIALS

Activities and Answers to Questions

Unit 1: THE NEW WORLD'S SETTLERS

Chapter 1
The American Indians *pp. 36–53*

ACTIVITIES

Level A: Have students select and research the culture of a specific Indian tribe or nation. Reports should include information on shelters, clothing, food, forms of travel, religious beliefs, work done by the men and women, recreation, and special characteristics of the group. Students can make posters showing the most distinguishing characteristics of their Indian group. Have students share the information from their reports with the class. Display posters around the room.

Level B: Divide the class into groups with the task of developing their own sign language as a form of universal communication. Each group must work out a system that can be understood by others. Have the groups then present to the whole class a simple message. Students who are observing should write down what they think the message means. After all groups have done this, compare what the class has written down and what the group was trying to say. See which groups were the most successful in conveying their messages to others. Then discuss the difficulties encountered in developing a universal language.

ANSWERS

Section 1 Review *p. 42*

1. Many scientists believe the first people to migrate to America did so by using the Bering Strait land bridge during the Ice Age. (p. 37)
2. Farming changed early Indian societies by providing a more dependable food supply. It was no longer necessary for them to wander in search of food. (p. 39)
3. An anthropologist is a scientist who studies human culture and development. Technology is the knowledge, skills, and objects necessary for human survival and comfort. (pp. 37–38)
4. They were used as burial places and for religious ceremonies. (p. 41)
5. Answers will vary, but should include the influence of climate on food, clothing, and shelter.

Section 2 Review *p. 51*

1. They differed in their ways of obtaining food, their clothing and shelter, the languages they spoke, and their forms of political organization. (pp. 43–51)
2. No. In 1500, the Indian population numbered approximately 110 million people. This was larger than the population of Europe at the time. (p. 43)
3. An alliance is a close association for a common objective. The Iroquois Confederacy, made up of five separate Iroquoian tribes in upper New York State, became a powerful intertribal alliance ruled by a council of 50 tribal leaders. (p. 46)
4. Answers will vary, but should include the idea that people who think or behave differently are often considered inferior. Respect for nations with different cultures is frequently lacking in countries where this attitude exists.

Chapter Review *pp. 52–53*

Recalling the Facts

1. Many scientists believe that the first humans to come to North America walked across the Bering Strait land bridge. (p. 37)
2. The Hohokam. (p. 39)
3. Kivas were large circular rooms built underground and used for religious ceremonies; they were built by the Anasazi. (p. 41)
4. The term sedentary village means a settled, permanent village inhabited by people who do not move from place to place. (p. 43)
5. Corn. (p. 46)
6. By hunting buffalo. (p. 48)

Analyzing the Facts

1. The term Ice Age is appropriate because it was a time when large sheets of ice covered much of North America.
2. The development of agriculture was important because it allowed people to establish sedentary villages.
3. Sign language was a necessity for the early Indians because as many as 2,000 different languages were spoken among the tribes, and they needed a way to communicate.
4. They were affected by different environmental conditions.
5. Answers will vary, but should include that the Pueblo Indians believed peaceful behavior would bring rewards, and since they were farmers, they had no need to raid other villages.

Time and History

1. Mogollon **2.** Mound Builder **3.** Archaic period **4.** 15,000 years **5.** 8000 B.C.

Chapter 2 Exploration and Settlement

pp. 54–77

ACTIVITIES

Level A: Have students prepare a bulletin board map showing the routes of the various explorers discussed in this chapter. Labels for the seven continents and four oceans should be made and affixed to the map. Geographic areas and points relevant to exploration, such as the East Indies, the Mississippi River, and the Cape of Good Hope, should also be labeled. Have students, using different colored yarn or markers, trace and label the routes of the European explorers. Have students make a key to explain the colors used to represent each explorer and the flag he sailed under. Finally, give the map a title.

Level B: Have the students write a letter to the King and Queen of Spain in favor of sending Columbus on his westward voyage to Asia. The purpose of the letter is to help the monarchs reach a speedy decision by presenting all the reasons such a voyage would benefit Spain. When students have completed their letters, have them present them to the class. Have the class discuss which letter or letters were the most convincing and why.

ANSWERS

Section 1 Review *p. 59*

1. The rise of powerful national monarchs, the desire to find a new trade route to the Far East, and improvements in navigational and sailing technologies. (p. 56)
2. The Vikings were superb sailors and shipbuilders from Denmark, Norway, and Sweden. Archeologists unearthed a Viking settlement in Newfoundland in 1961. This proved that the Vikings had explored a part of North America. (p. 55)
3. To get Eastern goods more quickly and cheaply. They did not like being dependent on Arab and Italian traders who controlled the overland trade routes. (p. 56)
4. The astrolabe, magnetic compass, and improved mapmaking. (pp. 56–57)
5. He had been unable to find a sea route to the Orient. Answers should include the idea that many people's achievements are overlooked in their lifetimes because the importance of their achievements is not immediately recognized.

Section 2 Review *p. 64*

1. The three goals were to find gold, to convert the Indians to Christianity, and to win glory for themselves and their country. (p. 60)
2. A conquistador was a Spanish explorer who explored and conquered much of Spain's New World empire. An isthmus is a narrow neck of land that separates two bodies of water and connects two large land regions. Circumnavigate means to sail completely around something. (pp. 60–61)
3. Father Junípero Serra established a chain of Spanish missions in California. He instructed the Indians in Catholicism and taught them Spanish ways. He was the first and most famous of the missionaries in California. (p. 63)
4. In 1598, Don Juan Oñate led a group of soldiers, settlers, and missionaries into New Mexico. In 1680, the Indians in New Mexico organized an army to revolt against the harsh treatment of the Spanish. The governor and citizens of Santa Fe were forced to flee. By 1695, Spanish troops had completed the job of reconquering the Indians of New Mexico. (p. 64)
5. Answers will vary. Answers may include the following: although the Spanish took a great deal of gold from Indians they conquered, they were unsuccessful in finding as much gold as they sought; they established a chain of missions in the New World for the purpose of converting the Indians to Christianity, and they created one of the largest and most long-lasting empires in the Western Hemisphere.

Section 3 Review *p. 69*

1. Colonization of New France was begun by Samuel Champlain, who founded Quebec in 1608. In 1682, Robert de La Salle claimed the entire Mississippi Valley for France. Two areas of settlement in New France developed—one along the St. Lawrence River and the other at the mouth of the Mississippi River in New Orleans. New Netherland was established by the Dutch West India Company in 1621 and was run to make profits for a small group of wealthy people. (pp. 65–68)
2. The Northwest Passage was an imaginary water passage that early explorers believed would lead through North America to Asia. (p. 65)
3. The fur trade. (pp. 66–67)
4. The French and Dutch were unable to attract many settlers to their colonies because settlers were given few rights and had no voice in how their colony would be run. Few people wanted to come to work on a noble's estate. Giving their colonists a voice in their government and free land grants might have attracted more colonists to New France and New Netherland.

Social Studies Skills *p. 70*

1. 500 km
2. 312 mi.
3. 172 km (107 mi.)
4. 760 km
5. Mark the distance on a sheet of paper. Place the paper on the scale with one point at zero. Make a second mark at the end of the scale and record the distance. Move the second mark to zero, and repeat the process until the total distance has been measured. Finally, add the measurements to get the total distance.

Section 4 Review *p. 75*

1. Religious intolerance in England, the desire of many English people to improve their lives, opportunities for economic profit, and a desire for adventure and glory. (pp. 73–74)
2. Sea dogs were English pirates who raided Spanish ships and towns in the late 1500's. Mercantilism was an economic system designed to increase the wealth of a country by discouraging imports and encouraging exports. Colonies helped to serve this purpose. (pp. 72, 74)

3. Joint-stock companies raised the money necessary to establish colonies. They established the first three permanent colonies: Virginia, Plymouth, and Massachusetts Bay. (p. 73)
4. Answers will vary.

Chapter Review *pp. 76–77*

Recalling the Facts

1. The development of the astrolabe and the magnetic compass. (p. 57)
2. Vasco da Gama. The route went around the tip of Africa and across the Indian Ocean. (p. 58)
3. Cortes' goal was to conquer the Aztec Empire and take its vast riches. (p. 61)
4. Settlements in New France developed along the St. Lawrence River, including Nova Scotia, and at the mouth of the Mississippi River in New Orleans. (p. 66)
5. Hudson was looking for a water route through the continent. (p. 67)
6. England was caught up in religious disagreements between English Catholics and Protestants, which nearly brought the country to war. Also, much of England's energy was focused on a long and bitter war with Spain. (p. 71)

Analyzing the Facts

1. Relations between the Vikings and the American Indians were poor. Neither side trusted the other, although some trading between them did occur. The Vikings treated the Indians with cruelty. Eventually, the Indians destroyed the Viking settlement.
2. Strong national monarchs were necessary because only powerful monarchs could accumulate the large sums of money needed for long voyages.
3. Answers will vary, but should include the idea that sailors could sail in sight of land.
4. Explorers were looking for an all-water route through America to the East. A Northwest Passage would save time by eliminating the need to sail around the tip of South America.
5. No great mineral wealth had been discovered there. Few wished to come to New France to be workers on the nobles' estates. Bitter winter weather in the north also discouraged settlement.
6. Answers will vary, but should include the idea that many colonists probably resented mercantilism because it was an economic system that benefited the home country and restricted colonial trade.

Time and History

1. Magellan's **2.** 1664 **3.** Magellan **4.** Raleigh **5.** 15 years **6.** four **7.** 519 years

Chapter 3
The English Colonies
pp. 78–101

ACTIVITIES

Level A: Hold a mock town meeting in class. Divide the class into the following groups: small farmers, merchants, religious leaders, and wealthy landowners. The problem to be discussed is: Several orphan families, whose parents have died of smallpox, have been stealing food from farmers and merchants. What should be done about this?

Give the groups time to decide the stand they will take on this problem. Select a chairperson to preside over the meeting. The chairperson should keep order, make sure each group has an equal amount of time to present its views, and make a list of the different suggestions made.

Tell the students that there will be no debate, only a presentation of positions. When all is over, have the chairperson write the suggestions made during the presentations on the board, and have the class discuss the merits and weaknesses of each suggestion. At the end of the discussion, have students vote for the position they support. Afterward, discuss with the students their feelings as to the fairness of the system they just took part in.

Level B: Have students work in groups to

prepare 2-to-4 page newspapers commemorating significant events relating to colonization and life in the New World during the seventeenth century. Each group should prepare news stories, advertisements and cartoons, or comic strips for their newspaper. Have examples of newspapers available for students to look at for ideas on headlines and style. Stress the fact that everything in the paper must have occurred during the 100-year span between 1600 and 1700. When all are completed, have the class put them on display.

ANSWERS

Section 1 Review *p. 82*

1. Massachusetts Bay settlers were well prepared for settlement, and the colony was successful from the outset. It experienced no period of starvation, and it was able to attract many more settlers than had the other colonies. (pp. 79, 81–82)
2. The headright system offered free land as a way to bring new settlers to the Virginia colony. It enticed people to settle in America by offering them free land. (p. 80)
3. It was the beginning of self-government in America. (p. 80)
4. The Pilgrims were English religious dissenters who had separated from the Church of England. Because of religious persecution in England, they went to Holland. Fearful that their children were losing their English culture, they went to Massachusetts, where they established the Plymouth colony. (p. 80)
5. Answers will vary, but should include careful planning and smart leadership.

Social Studies Skills *p. 83*

1. Primary sources are produced or written during the time period being studied. Secondary sources are written or produced in a later time period.
2. Primary source material allows a person to see the past through the eyes of people who lived during a particular period of time. Answers will vary for disadvantages. Possible answers are: primary sources may not be accurate, they may be biased, or they may be difficult to read or understand.
3. The ship was crowded, the seas were rough, and many people became ill. The food was often dirty, and hot food was served only three times a week.
4. Answers will vary. Accounts should mention that the sea voyage was difficult; passengers were crowded and often tossed from side to side in rough weather; illness and death on board; bad food.

Section 2 Review *p. 89*

1. The steady population growth in Massachusetts and the narrow-mindedness of the Puritan leaders in Massachusetts led to the establishment of other colonies in New England. (p. 84)
2. Williams had to leave Massachusetts because he disagreed with Puritan leaders on two issues: a) the Puritans had not purchased the colony's land from the Indians, and b) he felt that Christians of any faith should be allowed to worship in peace. He went to Rhode Island. (p. 84)
3. Life centered around towns, which had almost complete control over local affairs. Citizens became involved in local government through town meetings. Family life and religious activities were very important. (pp. 85–86)
4. Answers will vary, but should include a connection between the student's community (state) and the following contributions of the Puritans: democratic town government; the Puritans' belief in public education, hard work, and striving to better oneself.

Section 3 Review *p. 94*

1. In the middle colonies, many different religions were practiced freely and colonists came from many different countries in Europe. (p. 90)
2. Quakers were persecuted because they

did not feel there was a need for ministers, priests, or religious ceremonies. They believed in complete equality of people, and they refused to serve in the military or take part in wars. (p. 91)

3. King Charles II gave Penn title to the land that became Pennsylvania in order to pay off a debt owed to the Penn family. (pp. 91–92)
4. Answers will vary.

Section 4 Review *p. 99*

1. Many Catholics settled in Maryland, where tobacco farming was important. Some landowners in the Carolinas started large rice and indigo plantations and led relatively luxurious lives. Many of Georgia's early colonists were debtors. (pp. 95–97)
2. A proprietary colony was a colony granted by an English king to a person, family, or group of people who governed the colony in the name of the king. (p. 95)
3. They sold their labor (usually for a term of four to seven years) in exchange for passage. These individuals were called indentured servants. (p. 98)
4. The competition for profits in the southern colonies favored larger farms and plantations. The large planters needed a steady supply of forced labor to work on their lands. Unlike indentured servants, slaves worked for someone else for life, and slavery was an inherited condition. (pp. 98–99)
5. Answers will vary, but could include the idea that separating black familes would further break the black's spirit.

Chapter Review *pp. 100–101*

Recalling the Facts

1. Tobacco. (p. 80)
2. Squanto was an Indian who helped the Pilgrims survive in the New World. (p. 81)
3. Franklin established the first fire department in the colonies, started the first library and hospital in Philadelphia, helped improve the postal system, and established a school that later became the University of Pennsylvania. (p. 94)
4. Maryland. (p. 95)
5. The Middle Passage was the journey of slaves from Africa to America. (p. 99)

Analyzing the Facts

1. Its poor location and "gentlemen" settlers who refused to work caused the near failure of Jamestown in its first year.
2. By building a settlement outside of English territory, they could do as they wished without concern for English or Virginian laws.
3. The Great Awakening renewed the colonists' interest in religion. It also broke down some of the barriers between the classes in the colonies.
4. Settlers of all religions and nationalities would be attracted to Pennsylvania because all religions and nationalities were welcomed there.
5. Answers will vary, but should include the idea that people living on the frontier were more concerned with the problems of survival. A willingness to work hard and the ability to handle a gun might have been important to them.

Time and History

1. Jamestown; **2.** 10 years; **3.** Philadelphia; **4.** 24 years; **5.** 120 years; **6.** 57 years

Unit Review *pp. 102–103*

Recalling the Facts

1. Many scientists believe the Indians walked across the Bering Strait land bridge during the Ice Age. (p. 37).
2. The Vikings. Archeologists have unearthed a Viking settlement in Newfoundland. (p. 55)
3. They wanted to find new trade routes to the Far East. (p. 56).
4. Spain, France, the Netherlands, and Great Britain established colonies. Spain controlled almost all of Mexico, Central America, and the southwestern part of the present-day United States. France controlled

the land around the St. Lawrence River and the Mississippi River valley. The Netherlands established a colony around present-day New York. Great Britain controlled the area along the eastern coast of North America between present-day New England and Florida. (pp. 60–69, 98)

5. Europeans settled in the English colonies in America for religious freedom, to make profits, for adventure and glory, and to better their lives. The Puritans—religious freedom. (pp. 73, 81–82)

Analyzing the Facts

1. Early people might have crossed the land bridge following herds of migrating animals, which they hunted for meat.
2. Agriculture is almost always needed before true civilization can begin because people who must wander in search of food have little time to spend developing the elements of civilization.
3. Answers will vary, but should include the idea that people of Columbus' time were not convinced the earth was round. Also, da Gama had already discovered an all-water route to the Far East by sailing around Africa.
4. The settlers in Jamestown were not as well prepared for settlement as the Puritans, who came with adequate supplies and a willingness to work.
5. Answers will vary, but should include the idea that the French were primarily fur traders who were helped by the Indians. Also, the plantations that did exist were worked by European peasants.

Reviewing Vocabulary

anthropologist, p. 37; extinct, p. 38; kiva, p. 41; wickiup, p. 45; archeologist, p. 55; astrolabe, p. 57; charter, p. 67; joint-stock company, p. 73; mercantilism, p. 74; cash crop, p. 80; covenant, p. 82; religious toleration, p. 96

Sharpening Your Skills

1. Approximately 125 km (78 mi.)
2. Approximately 1,975 km (1,227 mi.)
3. Scientists probably studied weapons, tools, and other artifacts to determine the Indians' early migration routes.
4. Answers will vary. Sample answer: Puritan boys wore short pants, stockings, and shoes with large buckles. They also wore bow ties and long coats that extended to midcalf. Their clothing was more formal than that worn by children today.

Unit 2: CREATING THE AMERICAN REPUBLIC

Chapter 4
Great Britain Under Strain
pp. 106–127

ACTIVITIES

Level A: Have students present one side of a debate on one of the following issues:

1. Mercantilism is/is not a fair system of trade.
2. Parliament has the right/does not have the right to tax the colonies.
3. Colonists should/should not be allowed to move west of the Appalachian Mountains in 1763.

Tell students to use arguments that British and colonial citizens might have used. At the conclusion of each debate, have the class discuss which arguments were the most convincing.

Level B: To reinforce students' knowledge of European land claims, have them reproduce the two maps on page 110. Hand out two outline maps of North America to each student. Have them draw in and/or label the Appalachian Mountains, the Mississippi River, the St. Lawrence River, Florida, the Ohio Valley, and Canada. Students should title one map "European Land Claims in North America, 1713" and the other map "European Land Claims in North America, 1763." Have the students color in the areas belonging to Spain, France, Great Britain, and Russia using different colored crayons or pens. Then have students make a key to explain the colors on each map.

ANSWERS

Section 1 Review *p. 111*

1. The English tightened their control over the American colonies through the passage of laws that restricted colonial trade. The Navigation Acts prevented the colonists from trading with countries other than England. The English also sent officials to the colonies to make sure that the Navigation Acts were obeyed. (pp. 107–108)
2. A monopoly is exclusive control over a product or business. (p. 108) A rebellion is armed resistance or opposition to one's government. (p. 108) A militia is an army made up of citizens rather than professional soldiers. (p. 110)
3. The Ohio Country was claimed by both Britain and France. When the French began to build forts to protect their claim, the British and the colonists organized an army to stop them. Warfare erupted, and the French and Indian War began. (p. 109)
4. Possible answers include: the War for Independence, the Civil War, the war in Vietnam, and Watergate. All of these were periods when disagreements among the leaders of government led to uncertainty and disunity in the nation as a whole.

Social Studies Skills *p. 112*

1. About 1200 km (746 mi.)
2. About 825 km (513 mi.), 375 km (233 mi.)
3. About 350 km (217 mi.)

Section 2 Review *p. 117*

1. The colonists were not allowed to elect representatives to the British Parliament. They had no voice in matters that directly affected them, such as taxes. (p. 114)
2. A boycott is a refusal to buy from or deal with a foe so as to punish or bring about change. (p. 116) To repeal is to do away with or take back. (p. 117)
3. The Proclamation prevented them from settling the territory west of the Appalachian Mountains. (p. 114)
4. The colonists called for a Stamp Act Congress to coordinate and organize colonial opposition to the Stamp Act. This was the first time the colonies pulled together for their own interests. (p. 116)
5. Boycotts are used today by the government as well as by citizens to bring about change both at home and abroad. In 1979, President Carter called for a boycott of the 1980 Olympic Games in Moscow to protest the Soviet invasion of Afghanistan. Consumers boycotted California table grapes in the 1960's to force growers to recognize the right of workers to unionize.

Section 3 Review *p. 125*

1. The Tea Act, the Coercive Acts, the Quebec Act, British attempts to seize colonists' war supplies and capture rebel leaders, and the attack at Breed's Hill. (pp. 120–125)
2. Radical colonists believed that Great Britain would never give Americans a voice in Parliament. They were determined to create a new nation, even if it meant revolution. Moderate colonists wanted self-government for the colonies while still remaining loyal to the king. The moderates did not want a revolution, only a greater share of independence. (p. 119)
3. A minuteman was a colonial soldier who could be prepared to fight at a minute's notice. (p. 122)
4. The formation of the Continental army and the appointment of George Washington as its commander-in-chief, and the Declaration of Independence. (pp. 124–125)
5. Answers will vary. Answers may focus on the need for law and order, loyalty to one's government, or the right of revolution.

Chapter Review *pp. 126–127*

Recalling the Facts

1. The colonies could supply the home country with cheap raw materials, and they could buy finished products from the home country. (p. 107)
2. He was the prime minister of Great Britain who sent more soldiers and money for supplies to North America and enlarged the British navy to help the British win the French and Indian War. (p. 111)
3. France gave Canada and all land east of the Mississippi River to Great Britain. France gave New Orleans and the Louisiana Territory to Spain. (p. 111)
4. They made speeches, attacked people who sold the stamps, and formed the Stamp Act Congress. The Stamp Act Congress requested that the king remove the tax. The Congress also organized a boycott of British goods. (p. 116)
5. They planned to arrest Samuel Adams and John Hancock in Lexington and capture the colonists' war supplies in Concord. (p. 122)
6. Declare their independence. (pp. 124–125)

Analyzing the Facts

1. Without competition, the colonies would be forced to pay whatever Britain charged for finished goods and accept whatever Britain wanted to pay for raw materials.
2. The colonists no longer had to fear French or French-supported Indian attacks on their settlements. They became much less dependent on British military protection.
3. In 1765, the British backed down and repealed the Stamp Act. In 1773, Britain refused to back down and passed laws to punish the Massachusetts colonists for the Boston Tea Party.
4. The opening shots of the American Revolution confirmed the colonists' willingness to fight for their rights. Many people in Europe and the Americas realized that the outcome of this rebellion would significantly influence the course of world colonization.
5. Answers will vary. Possible answers are: yes, the colonies had become prosperous and no longer needed to maintain colonial ties with Britain; no, the colonists were not united or prepared for war at this time.

Time and History

1. 1760's **2.** 5 years **3.** the fighting at Lexington **4.** 74 years **5.** 1 year

Chapter 5
The War for Independence
pp. 128–147

ACTIVITIES

Level A: Assign half the students in the class to the role of a news reporter who has gone back in time to the War for Independence. Have them write questions for an interview with one of the following people: George Washington after he had been named commander-in-chief of the Continental army; General Burgoyne after his defeat at Saratoga; General Howe as he made plans to attack New York City, General Cornwallis after his defeat at Yorktown, a black soldier who had joined the Continental army; Molly Hays after the battle at Monmouth; and so on. Assign the remaining class members to the role of one of the historical figures above. Students playing the roles of the historical figures should be encouraged to do additional research. When all students are ready, hold the interviews in front of the class. Students may be encouraged to dress appropriately for their presentations. Follow up the interviews with a short discussion of which historical characters seemed to be portrayed most accurately and which interviewers were the most effective.
Level B: Have students pretend that the date is October 19, 1781, and they have just witnessed Cornwallis' surrender at Yorktown. Have them write two letters—one as an American soldier and one as a British soldier—describing the events that led up to this day and the day of the surrender itself. Also have

them describe in each letter how they feel about those events. Encourage students to write from two different points of view. Display the best letters on the bulletin board.

ANSWERS

Section 1 Review *p. 134*

1. The colonists were not united in their opposition to Great Britain. The Continental Congress lacked the power to tax and could not raise the money needed to fight the war. American Indians sided with Great Britain during the war. The Continental army was small and undisciplined. (p. 129)
2. A mercenary is a professional soldier hired to serve in a foreign army. The British. (pp. 130–131)
3. They bolstered the Continental army's low morale and convinced the American soldiers that they might be able to defeat the British after all. (p. 133)
4. Fighting on one's own territory makes it easier to keep troops supplied. The army is more familiar with the land and can count on the support of citizens. People are fighting to defend their homes, farms, and businesses. On the other hand, fighting on one's own land can result in the destruction of property and civilian casualties.

Section 2 Review *p. 140*

1. Soon after the American victory at Saratoga, France entered the war on the side of the Americans, providing much-needed support. (p. 136)
2. Severe shortages of food and supplies, crude housing, a lack of blankets, clothing, and medicine. (pp. 136–137)
3. Pulaski helped in the training of American troops. Kosciusko helped design the fortifications at West Point. Von Steuben drilled and trained American troops, making them into an efficient fighting force. (pp. 138–139)
4. Women formed associations that collected money to purchase supplies for the soldiers. Other women traveled with the army serving as nurses and cooks. Some women took up arms to protect their homes, and a few fought in battles. Many managed farms and businesses while their fathers or husbands were away. (p. 139)
5. Answers will vary. Answers may reflect the idea that some Americans believed slaves were inferior to white Americans because of the color of their skin. Other Americans regarded slavery as an economic necessity.

Section 3 Review *p. 145*

1. The United States was able to achieve victory and independence from Great Britain because of British losses in battles in the South. After Cornwallis' surrender at Yorktown, many British leaders and citizens pressured the king to begin peace negotiations. The Treaty of Paris recognized American independence. (pp. 142–144)
2. Guerrilla warfare is a method of warfare used by small bands of revolutionary fighters. Guerrilla warfare was used in the South Carolina backcountry. Francis Marion and his troops attacked the British in "hit-and-run" fashion. (p. 142)
3. The French and Americans planned to surround the British at Yorktown by both land and sea. The British were trapped and forced to surrender. (p. 143)
4. The Treaty of Paris recognized American independence. The 13 colonies were recognized as 13 independent states, joined together as the United States of America. The boundaries of the United States extended from the southern border of Canada to the northern boundary of Florida, and from the Atlantic Ocean to the Mississippi River. (p. 144)
5. Answers will vary. The United States extends military aid to Israel, El Salvador, Egypt, Greece, Brazil, Kenya, and many other countries. Military aid is given to these countries to help them defend themselves from aggressive neighbors and rev-

olutionary threats from within, and to protect American business and political interests.

Chapter Review *pp. 146–147*

Recalling the Facts

1. Soldiers in the Continental army could shoot better than the British, were more familiar with the land they were fighting on, were fighting for a cause, and had a well-respected commanding general. (pp. 129–130)
2. He strongly believed in representative government, and he felt that the British had been taking rights and powers away from colonial assemblies. (p. 130)
3. Howe failed to march north from New York City to join Burgoyne. St. Leger's forces were defeated and never reached Albany. Also, Burgoyne's forces were defeated at Saratoga. (pp. 135–136)
4. Southerners were frightened and upset to see black Americans in the military. They felt that this might encourage southern slaves to revolt. For a time, blacks were not allowed to serve in the army. (p. 140)
5. The French fleet encircled Yorktown by sea. Lafayette led his troops closer to Yorktown. Rochambeau's troops moved southward to join up with Lafayette. The French forces helped to trap Cornwallis by land and by sea. (p. 143)

Analyzing the Facts

1. Answers will vary. Possible answers are: honesty, ability to make good decisions, persuasive, fair, and dignified. Any or all could be applied to Washington.
2. They were familiar with the land and could shoot better than the British.
3. They did not want to lose to their old enemy Great Britain.
4. Answers will vary. Possible answers are: they were unfamiliar with the land; they had poor leadership; or they had to rely on supplies transported from Britain.
5. Answers will vary. Possible answers are: the fourth of July would be just another day, Washington's birthday would not be celebrated, we would be British citizens singing "God Save the Queen" instead of "The Star-Spangled Banner."

Time and History

1. 7 years **2.** 1778 **3.** Yorktown **4.** Saratoga **5.** 2 years. Answers will vary. Possible answers are that communication was slow and the treaty had to be approved by both countries before it went into effect.

Chapter 6
Forming a New Nation
pp. 148–195

ACTIVITIES

Level A: Have each student write an essay to persuade an uncommitted reader to support ratification of the Constitution. Students should use information from the chapter to formulate arguments that this new plan of government would solve problems the United States had experienced under the Articles of Confederation. They should also explain how the Constitution was designed to prevent problems from occurring in the future. Read the best essay to the class.

Level B: Have students make three charts outlining the compromises made at the Constitutional Convention: the Great Compromise, the Three-Fifths Compromise, and the slave trade compromise. On each chart, have students state the opposing viewpoints to the compromise to show that the compromise was a combination of the two conflicting ideas. Display the finished charts in the classroom.

ANSWERS

Section 1 Review *p. 154*

1. The national government was unable to repay its war debts or maintain an army or navy. It could not prevent states from

passing tariffs that hurt trade with other states. It failed to convince Spain to reopen the Mississippi River. It failed in its attempts to force British troops off American soil. It could not maintain peace and order within the nation. (pp. 151–154)

2. To ratify is to approve officially. (p. 149) A bill of rights is a legal document outlining the rights and privileges of citizens that are to be protected by law. (p. 153)
3. Few small farmers had the $640 needed to buy a section, the minimum sale permitted. They were forced to buy smaller parcels at higher prices from wealthy investors who had bought the land from the government. (p. 153)
4. When a territory's population reached 60,000, the area would be admitted as a state. Ohio, Indiana, Illinois, Michigan, and Wisconsin. (p. 153)
5. The federal government can prevent states from crippling the trade of other states through the unfair use of tariffs.

Section 2 Review *p. 158*

1. The Great Compromise, the Three-Fifths Compromise, and the slave trade compromise. (pp. 157–158)
2. The Virginia Plan recommended a government made up of three branches: the executive branch, the judicial branch, and the legislative branch. It also proposed that each state be represented in Congress according to its population. The Great Compromise. (p. 157)
3. The Three-Fifths Compromise provided that each slave would be counted as three-fifths of a person for both taxation and representation. (p. 158)
4. Without compromise, politicians and government officials would never be able to reach agreements on issues where they held differing opinions.

Section 3 Review *p. 163*

1. The legislative branch has the power to tax and collect taxes, declare war, establish post offices, coin money, regulate trade, raise revenue for the government, and approve treaties made with foreign governments. The executive branch has the power to command the nation's armed forces, conduct foreign affairs, veto legislation, enforce federal laws, and appoint federal judges, ambassadors, and other government officials. The judicial branch has the power to hear cases involving the Constitution and national laws, handle disputes between states, and handle lawsuits involving foreign citizens. (pp. 159–160)
2. A federal system is a system of government that divides power between the national government and individual states. (p. 159) To veto is to refuse to approve. (p. 160) To amend is to change or add to. (p. 161)
3. It is a system by which each branch of government can limit the powers of the other two branches. This prevents each branch from becoming too powerful. The President's power in conducting foreign affairs can be checked by Congress' power to declare war. The Supreme Court can check the power of the President with its power to decide whether the policies of the executive branch are in accordance with the Constitution. (p. 160)
4. Answers will vary.

Social Studies Skills *p. 164*

1. Advantage—it makes information easier to understand without much reading; disadvantage—it is shortened for easier reference and may not give all the information needed.
2. Any of the following: to tax, to borrow money, to build roads, to charter banks, to establish courts
3. Federal government
4. State governments

Chapter Review *pp. 194–195*

Recalling the Facts

1. Americans distrusted power and authority

because of their experience with British rule. (p. 150)

2. The power to tax and the power to regulate trade and commerce. It had to rely on voluntary contributions from the states, which often refused to send money. The states tried to cripple the trade of other states by using tariffs. (p. 151)
3. Madison played a key role in calling the convention, took a leading role in the debates, and took careful notes of the proceedings. (p. 156)
4. The legislative branch makes the laws, the executive branch enforces the laws, and the judicial branch interprets, or explains, the national laws. (p. 157)
5. The system of checks and balances; possible examples are: the President can veto laws passed by Congress; only Congress can declare war; the courts can rule that laws are unconstitutional. (p. 160)

Analyzing the Facts

1. Answers will vary. Possible answers are: it was probably the best way to solve problems and maintain union.
2. It was fair because the large states got representation by population in the House of Representatives, and the small states got equal representation in the Senate.
3. Some states still feared that a strong national government might take away the rights of the people if those rights were not protected in the Constitution.
4. Answers will vary. Possible answers are: agree—resistance keeps the government responsive to what the people want; disagree—resistance could lead to arguments that would cause the country to break up.
5. Answers will vary, but most probably the states would not have remained united as one country. They might have become 13 independent nations.

Time and History

1. 2 years **2.** 1784 **3.** 4 years **4.** the Articles of Confederation **5.** Spain closed the Mississippi River to American shipping in 1784.

Chapter 7
The Early Republic *pp. 196–213*

ACTIVITIES

Level A: Have students pretend that they are newspaper editors covering the Whiskey Rebellion in 1794. Allow students time to research the topic, and then have them write an editorial that might have appeared in a newspaper of the day. Have them decide either to support or oppose the Whiskey Rebellion and to write their editorials based on the positions they take. Be sure the class is aware that, depending on which side they support, they are either in favor of a strong central government or strong states' rights. When students are finished, collect the editorials and read the best ones to the class. Be sure to read several editorials in support of each side. After the editorials have been read, see which side most of the class supports and discuss reasons why.

Level B: Discuss with the class the purpose of a political campaign poster. Be sure that students know what a slogan is and how it can be used to associate a candidate with a particular idea in the minds of the voters. Following the discussion, have each member of the class design a campaign poster to inspire support for either John Adams or Thomas Jefferson in the election of 1800. The ideas of the Federalist and Republican parties should be incorporated into the poster to give the voter a feeling of what the candidate stands for. When students are finished, display the posters in the classroom. Have students decide which posters they think are the most effective and discuss reasons why.

ANSWERS

Section 1 Review *p. 200*

1. As he was the nation's first President, he had no one to model himself after. His actions in office would set precedents for future Presidents. (p. 197)

2. A revenue tax is a tax that raises income for the government, while an excise tax is a tax placed only on goods produced within a country. (p. 199)
3. He meant that there were powers belonging to the federal government that were suggested by the wording of the Constitution. He was referring to Section 8 of the Constitution, or the elastic clause, which says that the government can pass all laws that are necessary and proper to help the nation. (p. 200)
4. Our government today extends aid to businesses by making loans, reducing taxes, and granting assistance through measures such as oil depletion allowances. Our government also believes in a strong military, as evidenced by our growing defense budget.

Section 2 Review *p. 206*

1. The Federalists represented bankers, merchants, manufacturers, and large landowners. They believed that the government should be run by the educated and the wealthy. They favored supporting Great Britain in its war with France because they did not want to hurt American trade with Great Britain. The Republicans represented small farmers and the skilled working class. They believed in the ability of the common person to govern wisely. They favored supporting France in its war with Great Britain to repay the French for their help in the American Revolution. (pp. 201–203)
2. Impressment is the practice of forcing people into public service, especially into a navy. The British practice of impressment upset the United States because innocent Americans were being seized along with the British deserters. (p. 204)
3. The Pinckney Treaty was a treaty negotiated between the United States and Spain in 1795. Under the terms of the treaty, the United States was permitted to use the Mississippi River and the port of New Orleans without fear of interference. The treaty was a major triumph for the government, and it also satisfied westerners' needs. (p. 205)
4. Answers will vary.

Section 3 Review *p. 211*

1. The Federalists that Adams appointed to his Cabinet were not loyal to him. Relations with France worsened because of the XYZ Affair. The French and American navies clashed in an undeclared war lasting from 1798 until 1800. Adams faced strong opposition to the Alien and Sedition Acts from the Republicans. (pp. 208, 210)
2. In the XYZ Affair, agents of the French government demanded a huge bribe as the price of negotiating a treaty of friendship and trade with the United States. Americans were furious. Congress repealed the Treaty of 1778 with France and authorized American ships to attack those of the French. From 1798 to 1800, the French and American navies clashed in an undeclared war. (p. 208)
3. They were passed to restrict criticism of and opposition to the undeclared war with France. Jefferson and Madison opposed them because they believed the acts were unconstitutional. (pp. 208–210)
4. Answers will vary. Possible answers include: American defenses were not strong enough to wage a war with France, the American people were not united in their desire for war.

Chapter Review *pp. 212–213*

Recalling the Facts

1. His actions would set a precedent for all future Presidents to follow. (p. 197)
2. Republicans—small farmers and the skilled working class; Federalists—bankers, merchants, manufacturers, and large landowners (p. 201)
3. The Republicans felt we owed France a great debt for their help in the American Revolution. In addition, the French were fighting for many of the same ideals fought

for in the American Revolution. The Federalists did not want to hurt trade with Great Britain. They were also shocked and disgusted by the violent nature of the French Revolution. (pp. 202–203)

4. Jay's demands were: leave the Northwest Territory, stop impressment, and accept America's right to freedom of the seas. Britain agreed to leave the Northwest Territory. (p. 204)
5. Each member of the electoral college cast two votes. The members did not specify which vote was for President and which was for Vice-President. Adams received the most electoral votes, and Jefferson received the second-largest number of votes. (p. 207)

Analyzing the Facts

1. Answers will vary. Possible answers are: yes, because France had helped the Americans in the American Revolution, and the people of France were fighting for some of the same ideals; no, because helping France would have hurt the American economy, and the United States had to look out for its own interests.
2. The British navy kidnapped any sailor from American ships that they *suspected* of being a deserter from their navy. Americans felt that the British had no right to do this.
3. The President and the Vice-President must work closely together in leading the country. If they frequently disagree over issues, the government would appear weak and indecisive.
4. Amendment I guarantees freedom of speech; the Sedition Act said that Americans could be jailed or fined if they criticized the government. Amendment V guarantees due process of law; the Alien Act gave the President the power to order *suspicious* persons to leave the country.

Time and History

1. John Adams **2.** 3 years **3.** 1798 to 1800 **4.** 1791 **5.** Washington, D.C., did not become the nation's capital until 1800. George Washington was inaugurated in 1789 and 1793.

Unit Review *pp. 214–215*

Recalling the Facts

1. Many colonists did not think that the British government had the right to tax them, since they were not allowed to send representatives to Parliament. Other colonists simply resented having to pay taxes that they previously had been able to avoid. (p. 114)
2. Great Britain was the world's richest nation. It had a well-equipped and well-trained army. It had a powerful navy. Britain also had the help of American Indian allies. (p. 129)
3. The American victory at Saratoga persuaded the French to send money and soldiers to support the Americans. The Battle of Yorktown was the last significant battle of the war. British troops surrendered to the Americans. (pp. 136, 143–144)
4. The Federal government lacked the power to tax and regulate trade. Problems arose among the states that the federal government was powerless to solve. (p. 151)
5. They disagreed over the existence of "implied powers" in the Constitution, the establishment of a national bank, which country the United States should support in the war between France and Great Britain, and whether common people should have a role in government. (pp. 200–203)

Analyzing the Facts

1. The war strained relations between the colonies and Great Britain. After the French and Indian War, Parliament started to tax the colonies in order to pay off British war debts.
2. Answers will vary. Possible answers are: the Sons of Liberty—they organized colonial resistance and consistently urged the colonists to declare their independence; the British Parliament—if it had not passed and attempted to enforce laws that ran counter to colonial interests, then the

colonists would not have felt it necessary to declare their independence; the Continental Congress—it made the decision to declare independence.

3. Answers will vary. Possible answers are: they did not want to break with Britain for patriotic and or economic reasons; they were looking out for their own well-being.
4. Answers will vary. Possible answers are: the Constitution gave the federal government the power to tax and regulate trade, created an executive branch, and it included a Bill of Rights.
5. He led the Continental army. He presided over the Constitutional Convention and was the first President of the United States. His leadership contributed to the establishment of the United States.

Vocabulary Review

monopoly, p. 108; rebellion, p. 108; militia, p. 110; mercenary, p. 131; guerrilla warfare, p. 142; confederation, p. 149; compromise, p. 157; federal system, p. 159; precedent, p. 197; jurisdiction, p. 198; implied powers, p. 200; neutrality, p. 203

Sharpening Your Skills

1. About 217 km (135 mi.)
2. About 112 km (70 mi.)
3. The Supreme Court can declare laws unconstitutional.
4. Congress
5. Congress can override a veto by a two-thirds vote.

Unit 3: THE NATION GROWS

Chapter 8
The Age of Jefferson
pp. 218–233

ACTIVITIES

Level A: Have the class design posters to recruit explorers for the Lewis and Clark expedition. The posters should communicate something about the journey and appeal to a motive for exploration, such as adventure, or fame. To prepare for this activity, show the class examples of travel advertisements and posters. Discuss the information given and the motives for travel each advertisement appeals to.

Display the completed posters. Have the class discuss which posters are the most appealing and how they would have been effective in recruiting explorers to accompany Lewis and Clark in 1804.

Level B: Have students create a bulletin board display entitled "The Contributions of Thomas Jefferson." Divide a bulletin board into three sections and assign one third of the class to work on each section. Section 1 should be devoted to Jefferson's political contributions before 1800. Section 2 should show the contributions of Jefferson as President, and Section 3 should cover Jefferson's accomplishments after 1808 as well as his inventions. Have students make a list of Jefferson's contributions in each of their assigned areas using reference materials. Have them decide as a group how best to show the information they have found.

ANSWERS

Section 1 Review *p. 222*

1. Jefferson wanted to prevent the government from becoming a burden to the American public. To accomplish this, he lowered taxes, repealed the excise tax on whiskey, cut spending for defense, reduced the size of the army, and dismantled many ships. (p. 221)
2. The Twelfth Amendment requires that the President and Vice-President be elected by separate ballots. It was passed to avoid

a crisis similar to the one that had occurred in the election of 1800. The Republicans won the presidency in that election, but the Republican ticket did not specify which candidate, Jefferson or Burr, was the presidential candidate. (p. 219)

3. Civil liberties are rights guaranteed to a person by law or custom, such as freedom of speech. (p. 219) Judicial review is the right of the Supreme Court to declare an act of Congress unconstitutional. (p. 222)
4. Jefferson wanted to reduce the government's role in the economy and reduce government spending. To do this, he lowered taxes and repealed the excise tax on whiskey as well as cut defense spending. Hamilton favored expanding the role of the government in the economy through increased taxes, the whiskey tax, and increased military spending.

Section 2 Review *p. 226*

1. The United States purchased the Louisiana Territory from France for $15 million. (p. 223)
2. Thomas Jefferson did not want France controlling Louisiana, the Mississippi River, and New Orleans. He was afraid the French might interfere with the transportation and trade of western farmers. Napoleon needed a large sum of money to renew his war against Great Britain. The Louisiana Purchase solved both leaders' problems by giving Jefferson the Louisiana Territory and Napoleon $15 million. (p. 223)
3. Meriwether Lewis was an experienced explorer and soldier who commanded the expedition that explored the Louisiana Territory. (p. 224) Sacajawea was a Shoshone Indian who served as a guide and interpreter for the Lewis and Clark expedition. (p. 225) Zebulon Pike led an expedition that explored central and southwest Louisiana Territory. (p. 226)
4. Their careful descriptions gave people an idea of what the land was like. This was important for the future settlement of the region. Their descriptions also were of great value to scientists and future explorers.

Section 3 Review *p. 231*

1. Napoleon issued orders that said the United States could no longer trade with Great Britain. He also declared that certain American vessels would be seized. Great Britain pursued a similar course of action. The French and British actions violated American neutral rights and created problems for Americans involved in trade and the shipbuilding business. (pp. 227–228)
2. The British ship *Leopard* opened fire on the American ship *Chesapeake* after the commander of the American ship signaled that his ship had no deserters on board and that he would not permit a search. Three sailors were killed, 18 were wounded, and the *Chesapeake* was badly damaged. Many Americans saw this incident as a direct attack on the United States and called for a declaration of war on Great Britain. (pp. 229–230)
3. He wanted to pressure France and Great Britain into recognizing American neutral rights. Jefferson assumed that the embargo would be effective because he thought Europeans needed our trade more than we needed theirs. The embargo, however, hurt the American economy badly, and many businesses were ruined. (p. 230)
4. Both used economic measures to try to effect change and protect American rights. Jefferson's embargo was designed to hurt European trade to such an extent that violations of American neutral rights would end. The colonists boycotted the purchase of British goods, such as tea, hoping that the economic impact of the boycott would convince the British to stop taxing the colonists unfairly.

Chapter Review *pp. 232–233*

Recalling the Facts

1. The transfer of power from one political

party to another could take place in the United States without violence. (pp. 219–220)

2. Federalists appointed to judgeships by Adams on his last day in office; Republicans were convinced that the Federalist judges would declare Republican legislation unconstitutional. (p. 221)
3. He needed money to pay for a war with Britain. (p. 223)
4. Lewis and Clark were to study American Indian tribes and their languages; assure the Indians that the United States would be friendly; study the region's plants, animals, soil, and geography; and keep detailed records of their experiences. (p. 224)
5. Both sides wanted to cut off their enemy's trade in the hope of starving their enemy into surrender. (p. 227)

Analyzing the Facts

1. Answers will vary. Possible answers are: yes, because all of the appointees were Federalists—if they declared Republican legislation unconstitutional, this would disrupt the balance of power; no, the Constitution gives the President the power to appoint federal judges—if the Republicans were displeased, they could have blocked the appointments in the Senate.
2. The Supreme Court can do away with laws made by Congress and approved by the President if it judges them to be in conflict with the Constitution.
3. Lewis and Clark kept detailed records; Pike was a less careful observer.
4. Britain wanted to starve France into surrender. Shipments of food and other nonmilitary items from America would allow France to hold out longer.
5. The British continued to kidnap American sailors from American ships despite demands from the United States that this be stopped. The British knew that the United States was militarily powerless to stop them and did not take American demands seriously.

Time and History

1. 2 years **2.** Louisiana Purchase **3.** 4 years **4.** 1803 **5.** 15 months

Chapter 9
The Republic Survives
pp. 234–247

ACTIVITIES

Level A: Give each student an outline map of Latin America showing present-day national boundaries. Have them label the countries of Central and South America. Direct the students to use reference materials to find out when each of the countries became independent. Have them label the dates on their maps: Mexico (1821), Guatemala (1821), El Salvador (1821), Honduras (1821), Nicaragua (1821), Costa Rica (1821), Colombia (1819), Venezuela (1811), Ecuador (1822), Peru (1824), Brazil (1822), Bolivia (1825), Chile (1818), Argentina (1816), Paraguay (1811), Uruguay (1825), Haiti (1804), and the Dominican Republic (1821). (Note: In 1825, Panama was a part of Colombia.) Cuba, Jamaica, Puerto Rico, British Honduras, and the Guianas were still controlled by European powers in 1825. Have students color the colonies of European nations one color; all nations that were independent by 1825 should be shaded another color. Have students make a key explaining the colors used on the map, and give the map a title. When the maps are completed, discuss with the class how the political situation in Latin America in the early 1800's influenced the United States to issue the Monroe Doctrine in 1823.

Level B: Divide the class into three groups. Each group should be responsible for researching and presenting a report to the class on one of the following topics related to "The Star-Spangled Banner": (1) the circumstances under which the poem was written, (2) all of the verses of the poem, and (3) the design of the flag that inspired the poem. Students assigned to the third topic should work together to prepare a picture of the flag.

ANSWERS

Section 1 Review *p. 240*

1. The war was caused by Britain's refusal to recognize America's right to freedom of the seas, Britain's blockade of New York harbor, its increased impressment of American sailors, and the election of many young politicians in 1810 who were eager for war with Great Britain. (pp. 235–236)
2. A stalemate is a deadlock in which neither side seems able to gain an advantage. (pp. 238–239) The War of 1812 was a stalemate because neither side was able to win a clear-cut victory. (pp. 237–240)
3. The Battle of New Orleans was Great Britain's last attempt to invade the United States. It took place after the peace treaty ending the war had been signed. (p. 240)
4. Answers will vary. Possible answers are: yes, Britain had repealed the Orders in Council two days before Congress declared war; if communications had been faster, Congress might not have declared war; no, the War Hawks were elected by Americans who were angry at the nation's failure to respond to British aggression. War fever was too strong to avoid a war.

Section 2 Review *p. 244*

1. The years 1817–1824 were a time when there was a strong sense of unity and harmony in the nation. (p. 241)
2. The Monroe Doctrine stated that the United States would not permit any new colonization in the Americas. Any European interference in the affairs of the Americas would be viewed "as dangerous to our peace and safety." In exchange, the United States would stay out of the affairs of Europe. (p. 243)
3. The protective tariff and the government's land-sale policy. (pp. 243–244)
4. A strong government in Washington could someday move to end slavery.

Social Studies Skills *p. 245*

1. Outlining is a method of organizing information using a set pattern.
2. Outlines can be valuable tools for studying or preparing reports.
3. The topic or main idea is located at the far left and is labeled with a Roman numeral.
4. They would go under "1" and would be marked with lower-case letters of the alphabet.
5. The outline would help in organizing ideas so they can be expressed clearly and in an organized manner.

Chapter Review *pp. 246–247*

Recalling the Facts

1. This law reopened trade with both France and Great Britain. It also said that when either nation recognized America's right to freedom of the seas, Congress would cut off trade with the other. It was unsuccessful because France had no intention of keeping its promise to stop seizing American ships; in retaliation for the cut-off of American trade, Great Britain blockaded New York harbor and increased its impressment of American sailors. (p. 235)
2. The American Indians wanted to stop Americans from further settling on Indian land. They also wished to recover the Northwest Territory, making the Ohio River the boundary between the United States and Indian Country. (p. 235)
3. British and American troops were unaware that a peace treaty had been signed. (p. 240)
4. Many Americans regarded them as traitors after the war because the Federalists had organized opposition to it. (p. 240)
5. People in the West wanted government land sold in large-sized lots at low prices to encourage settlement. Southern planters did not want the government to sell the land at all because they did not want competition. Other southerners wanted land sold cheaply and in large quantities so they could buy land and become cotton

growers. In the North, industrial workers wanted government land sold cheaply so they could escape from factory life. Factory owners, fearing the loss of their labor supply, did not want the land sold at all. (p. 244)

Analyzing the Facts

1. It is doubtful that they could have succeeded. The Indians lacked the weapons necessary to keep white settlers off their lands for long.
2. In the early 1800's, news from Europe had to be sent on sailing ships, which took many weeks to reach America. Today we have the telegraph, telephone, and communications satellites.
3. Washington, D.C., was the seat of the federal government in the United States. Destroying it would disrupt the American war effort and create confusion in the country. The American people would feel they had weak leaders.
4. Answers will vary. Possible answers are: Britain did not want to fight another war with the United States; the War of 1812 taught Great Britain to respect the United States and firmly established American independence.

Time and History

1. 2½ years **2.** James Madison **3.** Battle of New Orleans **4.** 4 years **5.** second

Chapter 10
A Changing America *pp. 248–261*

ACTIVITIES

Level A: Hold a mock press conference. Have one group of students assume the roles of people who contributed to the American industrial revolution, such as Samuel Slater, Eli Whitney, Francis Cabot Lowell, Robert Fulton, and Samuel Morse. Students should be given time to do additional research on these people. The rest of the class will pretend to be reporters and should prepare a list of questions to ask at the press conference. A second press conference can be held with one group of students playing the following roles: a worker in a Lowell factory, a city resident in 1840, a passenger on an early railroad, a western farmer in favor of an improved transportation network, and an eastern manufacturer in favor of an improved transportation network.

Level B: Distribute copies of the Morse code to the class. (It can be found in unabridged dictionaries under the heading "Morse Code.") Have students encode any proper noun from the chapter. Ask the students to exchange papers and decode each other's words. Then, if possible, obtain a basic telegraph sounder and a number 6 dry cell battery. The school science laboratory might have these. Use the equipment to send a message to the students, such as "Close your eyes" or "Raise your left hand."

ANSWERS

Section 1 Review *p. 252*

1. Samuel Slater, a British mechanic, memorized the details of the spinning machine and then came to the United States. He built a model of the British spinning machine in Providence, Rhode Island. It was the first successful full-time factory in America. (pp. 249–250)
2. Eli Whitney invented the cotton gin in 1793. The gin was a machine that quickly separated cotton fibers from cottonseeds. Whitney also developed a system of interchangeable parts for the assembly of rifles. This technique was applied to many other goods. (p. 250)
3. The Lowell system's labor force consisted of young, unmarried New England farmwomen. Other factory systems employed entire families in a mill and preferred to use as many child laborers as possible because children could be paid lower wages. (pp. 250–251)
4. Yes. Cities grew without any planning, much like a wilderness area. Cities were

congested with people and traffic, much like a wilderness area that is dense with trees and forests. Cities lacked essential services, such as garbage collection, as does a wilderness area.

Social Studies Skills *p. 253*

1. Cotton production in the United States from 1800 to 1850
2. 80,000 bales
3. 2,130,000 bales
4. 1840–1850

Section 2 Review *p. 259*

1. People traveling westward looking for work or new homes wanted better roads. Western farmers wanted faster and better routes to get their crops to eastern markets. Eastern manufacturers wanted better routes to get their products to western markets. (p. 254)
2. Internal improvements are the upgrading of a transportation network: roads, canals, and/or railroads. (p. 254) To lobby is to engage in activities aimed at influencing public officials toward a desired action. (p. 258)
3. The canals reduced the cost of shipping goods dramatically. Because shipping costs declined, the prices of the shipped goods fell. The canals also stimulated the growth of cities connected by the canal system. (pp. 255–256)
4. Answers will vary. Possible answers include: the supersonic transport plane (SST), the space shuttle, and communications satellites.

Chapter Review *pp. 260–261*

Recalling the Facts

1. Power to drive the machines was provided by running water. (p. 250)
2. Machines could produce goods more quickly and cheaply. Goods produced by machines also tended to be of higher quality than homemade goods. (p. 249)
3. Cities were densely populated, congested, and noisy. Fires were a constant problem. Cities were also dirty and extremely unhealthy. People threw their garbage into the streets, and contagious diseases swept through urban areas. (pp. 251–252)
4. Eastern manufacturers wanted better routes to get their products to western markets. (p. 254)
5. Railroads could be built almost anywhere. They were faster, and they could operate year-round. (p. 259)

Analyzing the Facts

1. Most probably they were not sorry because many had come to escape starvation caused by a long-lasting potato famine in Ireland. Conditions in Ireland at this time were worse than in America.
2. Canals, because canals reduced the cost of shipping goods dramatically; in 1830 there were only 21 km. (13 mi.) of railroad track, and steamboats were used primarily on western rivers.
3. A canal has no current, so it is easy for vessels to travel up and down. A river could be too shallow for a vessel to navigate. Canals can be built in some areas where natural waterways do not exist.
4. Cities grew up along transportation routes. They became trade centers.
5. In 1840, more and cheaper goods were available to more people than ever before. Many Americans worked in factories in 1840; in 1800, most Americans had been farmers or craftspeople. Roads, canals, and railroads had been built by 1840.

Time and History

1. Slater's spinning machine **2.** improved roads **3.** eighteenth century **4.** 7 years **5.** 1842

Unit Review *pp. 262–263*

Recalling the Facts

1. The Louisiana Purchase doubled the size of the United States, thus providing more land for a rapidly growing American population. Also, the United States gained con-

trol of the Mississippi River and the port of New Orleans. (p. 223)
2. Americans were angry at Jefferson because the Embargo Act hurt the American economy badly. All areas of the country were affected by the loss of European trade. Also, this act did not force France or Great Britain to recognize America's right to freedom of the seas. (pp. 230–231)
3. Great Britain refused to recognize America's right to freedom of the seas, the British blockaded New York harbor, and the British impressment of American sailors. (p. 235)
4. Many Americans left their farms to move to the cities to work in the factories. Factory hours were long, and wages were low. The factories themselves were often dirty and unhealthy places to work. Cities were congested, noisy, dirty, and unhealthy places to live. (pp. 249, 250–252)
5. New and improved roads were constructed, canals were built, the steamboat was invented, and railroads were constructed. (pp. 254–259)

Analyzing the Facts

1. Answers will vary. Possible answers are: the arms race and communist aggression.
2. It resolved a number of old problems with Great Britain peacefully. Both nations pledged that they would not keep warships on the Great Lakes. This reduced the threat that either nation would start a war in that area. It was a step in the direction of arms reduction.
3. They probably would not have taken it seriously because the United States had not demonstrated that it had the strength to enforce it. The War of 1812 won the United States the respect of the European powers.
4. Yes, food for industrial workers and the goods produced in the factories must be transported quickly and cheaply.

Vocabulary Review

judicial review, p. 222; Continental Divide, p. 225; embargo, p. 230; stalemate, p. 239; goodwill tour, p. 241; doctrine, p. 243; industrial revolution, p. 249; mass production, p. 249; urban, p. 252; slum, p. 252; internal improvements, p. 254; lobby, p. 258

Sharpening Your Skills

1. Answers will vary.
2. 1835
3. False (decreased in 1830)
4. 1835
5. Total immigration increased with significant increases in 1830, 1835, and 1840.

Unit 4: THE NATION DIVIDING

Chapter 11
The Jacksonian Era *pp. 266–285*

ACTIVITIES

Level A: Have students make an election map for the presidential election of 1832. Students should research the electoral votes cast by each state. Direct students to look at an historical atlas of the United States. Provide students with an outline map of the United States as it existed in 1832, or have them draw their own.

Level B: Have the class make a list of Andrew Jackson's accomplishments during his first term in office and a list of what leadership traits Jackson possessed. Put both lists on the board. Then, have each student write a paragraph explaining why he or she would have voted for Andrew Jackson in 1832. Encourage students to refer to the lists on the board for ideas.

ANSWERS

Section 1 Review *p. 269*

1. It permitted slavery in Missouri while admitting Maine as a free state. Slavery

was forbidden in territories north of a line drawn from Missouri's southern border westward across the Louisiana Purchase. Slavery was permitted in territories to the south of the line. (p. 269)

2. Sectionalism is a concern for one's own region that ignores the well-being of the country as a whole. (p. 267) Missouri applied for statehood in 1818 and wished to enter the Union as a slave state. Northerners opposed to slavery wanted to make sure that slavery did not remain a permanent practice in Missouri. Southerners felt that Northerners were trying to deny them their property. (pp. 267–268)
3. The amendment stated that bringing any new slaves into Missouri would be a crime. It also said that all slaves born in Missouri after it became a state would be freed when they reached the age of 25. The amendment upset Southerners more than Northerners. Southerners felt that they were being denied the right to move from one state to another with their property. (pp. 267–268)
4. Answers will vary. Jefferson may have perceived the debate as a warning signal of how sectional differences could threaten national unity.

Section 2 Review *p. 273*

1. After losing the election of 1824, Jackson organized strong opposition to President Adams in Congress. He and his supporters formed a new political party and Jackson became its leader. Jackson campaigned hard and won in 1828. (pp. 271–272)
2. Each section of the country ran at least one candidate for the presidency. (p. 270)
3. It was a program of vast economic and internal improvements. It called for the construction of more roads and canals, paid for by the federal government. It also called for high tariffs and for a national banking system. (p. 270)
4. Andrew Jackson felt that he had been unfairly denied the presidency in the election of 1824. Jackson and his supporters formed the Democratic party in order to fight Adams and win the presidency in 1828. (pp. 271–272)
5. Answers will vary. Answers may include that Jackson had succeeded in convincing Americans that Adams was a weak President or that Jackson was perceived as the common people's candidate and thus had wide support.

Social Studies Skills *p. 274*

1. It visually shows how electoral votes are distributed.
2. Mississippi, Alabama, Tennessee, South Carolina, North Carolina, Indiana, Pennsylvania, and New Jersey
3. Henry Clay; Missouri, Kentucky, Ohio, New York
4. The New England states and eastern New York all cast their electoral votes for John Q. Adams. Jackson was very strong in the South.

Section 3 Review *p. 278*

1. The tariffs of 1828 and 1832 were protective tariffs. Southerners opposed the tariffs because they feared foreign nations would retaliate by placing tariffs on Southern cotton and rice. Southerners argued that if a law passed by Congress gave the national government powers not specifically stated in the Constitution, a state could declare the law nullified. South Carolina challenged the President and Congress to enforce the law. (pp. 276–278)
2. Nullification is an action taken by a state that declares a law of Congress not valid within the borders of that state. (p. 276) To secede is to withdraw formally from membership in a group. (p. 278)
3. Most of Jackson's Cabinet members were not highly qualified people. They had been appointed for political purposes. Jackson formed a group of informal advisers whose opinions he trusted. They came to be called the "Kitchen Cabinet." (p. 275)

4. Answers will vary. Elected officials might reward supporters who had paid them money to secure a government position. They could place people in positions where there might be a conflict of interest.

Section 4 Review *p. 283*

1. In the early 1800's, the government began forcibly removing eastern tribes to lands west of the Mississippi River. The Cherokees appealed the government's action in the federal courts. The Supreme Court upheld the rights of the Cherokee nation to their land. But Georgia ignored the court's decision, and President Jackson refused to enforce the decision. In April 1838, the army rounded up the Cherokees and forced them to march west to Oklahoma. (pp. 279–280)
2. In vetoing the Second Bank's application for a new charter, Jackson argued that the President, not Congress, was truly the voice of the people. Jackson's attitude strengthened the role of the President. (p. 282)
3. The Whigs were a political party formed in 1834 by people who opposed the administration of Andrew Jackson. The Northern Cotton Whigs supported the extension of slavery into the territories. The Southern Cotton Whigs and the Northern Conscience Whigs opposed the extension of slavery into the territories. The Union Whigs wanted to ignore the slavery question because it could lead to division within the nation. (pp. 282–283)
4. Answers will vary. Indian removal might have been prevented if Congress had taken action to enforce the Supreme Court's decision. However, most Americans were not concerned with Indian rights at this time.

Chapter Review *pp. 284–285*

Recalling the Facts

1. It contained the Tallmadge Amendment, which would have eventually eliminated slavery in Missouri. Southerners objected to any restrictions on what they could do with their property. (pp. 267–268)
2. Jackson failed to receive enough electoral votes to win. The House of Representatives chose John Quincy Adams. (p. 271)
3. Kitchen Cabinet—a group of informal advisers to the President; Jackson appointed members to his official Cabinet for political purposes. Most were not the most qualified people. (p. 275)
4. Southerners feared that foreign nations would respond with their own protective tariffs. This would cause Southerners to lose a great deal of business. (p. 276)
5. They adopted many American ways. They appealed their case in the federal courts. (p. 280)
6. It was formed to oppose Jackson and his policies. (p. 282)

Analyzing the Facts

1. Adams' election caused Andrew Jackson to organize the Democratic party to oppose Adams' programs and policies.
2. Differences—Jackson was from the West, used the spoils system more freely, relied on his Kitchen Cabinet for advice, and believed in a strong presidency; similarities—He was a wealthy slave owner, a war hero, and he started a new political party.
3. South Carolina could have lobbied in Congress against the tariffs. They could have also appealed to the Supreme Court.
4. During the nullification crisis, Jackson threatened to send troops to South Carolina to enforce the tariff laws. Jackson refused to take any action to enforce the Supreme Court's decision in the case of the Cherokees.
5. Answers will vary. Possible answers are: Jackson's victory at the Battle of New Orleans, the formation of the Democratic party, his handling of the nullification crisis, and so on.

Time and History

1. John Quincy Adams **2.** 9 years **3.** no **4.** one **5.** 3 years

Chapter 12

Slavery and the Old South

pp. 286–299

ACTIVITIES

Level A: Have students pretend they are Northerners visiting the South in 1835. Tell them that on their trip they will visit a large plantation, the cities of Charleston and New Orleans, and a frontier settlement in Mississippi. Have the students write a letter to their families back home. The main emphasis of the letter should be a description of what was seen or experienced while traveling. For example, students might describe a slave auction or a house raising.

Level B: Have the class make a model of a wealthy planter's estate. Divide the class into groups. Have each group research what plantations looked like. Have them include the main house, the fields, slave quarters, stables, and workplaces for a blacksmith, woodworker, and so on. Have each group prepare a small poster to serve as a key to the buildings and areas included on the model. When done, have each group explain their model to the class.

ANSWERS

Section 1 Review *p. 291*

1. Planters needed a steady supply of labor to work the cotton fields. They came to rely on the forced labor of slaves, and the slave population grew. (p. 288)
2. At the top of the South's social pyramid were the planters who owned the largest plantations and the largest number of slaves (50 to 100). Beneath this group were the planters who owned 10 to 50 slaves. Beneath this class were farmers who owned nine or fewer slaves. Below this were white farmers who owned no slaves at all. Manufacturers and merchants made up a separate class as did professionals. (pp. 289–290)
3. Southern society was held together by race. All white Southerners thought themselves superior to any black person. (p. 291)
4. Southerners were content with their society as it was. Southerners would not tolerate criticism of their society, especially slavery. (p. 291)
5. Answers will vary. Students may mention the Middle East and oil, various Latin American nations and the coffee bean. This dependence could ruin a region's economy if the resource runs out or weather destroys a crop. There would be no other product or crop to fall back on.

Section 2 Review *p. 297*

1. Most free blacks lived in cities and worked at unskilled jobs. Their wages were low. Although they were free, their freedom was limited by local laws. Most agricultural slaves worked long hours and lived in miserable conditions. Urban slaves lived under fewer restrictions than agricultural slaves. All slaves had no legal rights. Slave codes kept their activities under tight control. (pp. 292, 294–296)
2. He meant that even though life could be very hard as a free black, it was much better than life as a slave. (p. 292)
3. It was the most serious slave revolt in the South. Turner and his followers brutally murdered 57 white people before the revolt was put down. The Nat Turner revolt caused the southern states to strengthen their slave codes, restricting the movements of slaves even further. (p. 297)
4. Answers will vary. By keeping slaves ignorant, slaves feelings of inferiority and dependence were reinforced. Slaves would also have a difficult time communicating with slaves on other plantations, reducing the risk of a large-scale revolt.

Chapter Review *pp. 298–299*

Recalling the Facts

1. Northern society—characterized by in-

dustry, growing cities, rapidly increasing population, large railroad network, openness to change, growing opposition to slavery. Southern society—rural, smaller population, agricultural, valued tradition more than change, supported slavery. (p. 287)

2. About 25 percent (p. 289)
3. They could not travel freely, they could not testify against whites in court, and they could not vote. (p. 292)
4. The children of slaves and the Upper South (p. 293)
5. The master (p. 295)
6. The slave codes were strengthened, which further restricted the movements of slaves. (p. 297)

Analyzing the Facts

1. There were few factories in the South, so few immigrants went there. Also, few Southerners hired workers for agricultural labor.
2. The cotton gin and the increase in demand for cotton. The number of slaves increased.
3. The Southern social structure placed all whites, even the poorest, above all blacks. The poor whites were afraid that any changes might lower their social standing.
4. Slaves were expensive. If a slave was severely harmed when disciplined or mistreated, it would cost a slave owner money in lost hours of labor. Economic considerations may have placed a restraining hand on acts of excessive brutality and neglect.
5. To serve as an example to other slaves of the risk in running away.
6. Slaves were not allowed to meet in large groups unless a white person was present; they could not read or write; they could not travel without a pass; they were not allowed to carry firearms. Fear of severe punishment may have kept many slaves from participating.

Time and History

1. 1808 **2.** 15 years **3.** 30 years **4.** Nat Turner's revolt **5.** Ohio; 1821

Chapter 13
The Changing North *pp. 300–313*

ACTIVITIES

Level A: Have students create a small pamphlet that could have been distributed in the 1830's on one of the reform issues discussed in the chapter. Allow time for students to research conditions prior to 1830. Encourage students to use the reference books and research methods discussed in this chapter's skill feature. Completed pamphlets should include both writings and illustrations.

Level B: Have students write a short story about the journey of a fictional group of slaves on the Underground Railroad. Stories should be based on historical fact. All stories should include the role played by abolitionists who helped the slaves escape. You may wish to review with the class some of the mechanics of story writing before they begin.

ANSWERS

Section 1 Review *p. 303*

1. The upper class was made up of bankers, shippers, merchants, and manufacturers. The middle class was made up of small business people and manufacturers, religious leaders, doctors, lawyers, and farm owners. The lower class consisted of agricultural workers and workers who lived in the cities. (pp. 302–303)
2. Immigration accounted for much of the growth. Also, thousands of Americans left their farms to work in the cities' factories. (p. 301)
3. The steel plow allowed farmers to plow the hard prairie sod of the West. The mechanical reaper enabled farmers to harvest their crops with more efficiency. Both machines enabled farmers to grow more crops. (pp. 301–302)
4. Lower-class agricultural workers—drifted from one job to another, little money, and poor diets. Lower-class city workers—did

manual labor or factory work, worked long hours, received low wages, workplaces were unsafe, children were forced to work to help support the family. (p. 303)

5. Answers will vary. Jobs were available in Northern factories; the South had few factories at this time, and Southern agricultural work was done by slave labor; many immigrants probably did not have enough money to buy land in the West.

Section 2 Review *p. 310*

1. Access to education, prison conditions, the treatment of the mentally ill, alcohol abuse, equal rights for women, and slavery (pp. 304–308)
2. He led the modern public education movement. He set up an improved and expanded system of free public education in Massachusetts that many other states soon copied. He also established the first teacher training schools. (p. 304)
3. It was a declaration adopted by women's rights supporters at the Seneca Falls Convention in 1848 that called for equal rights for women in work, in politics, and under the law. Women wanted the right to vote, the right to hold office, property rights, and equal rights in decisions involving their children. They also wanted access to higher education and the right to sue in a court of law. (pp. 306–307)
4. It was a radical antislavery movement that wanted slavery abolished immediately, without compensation for slave owners. Southerners reacted harshly to the movement. (pp. 308, 310)
5. Answers will vary. The Industrial Revolution helped to make Northern society more willing to experiment with changes that held out the hope of improving society. Unlikely, Southerners were content with their society as it was.

Social Studies Skills *p. 311*

1. The index or table of contents
2. It tells what books are available in the library and where they can be found on the shelves.
3. 920.073 B
4. Probably, because William Lloyd Garrison is listed on the card as part of the content summary.

Chapter Review *pp. 312–313*

Recalling the Facts

1. Upper class—10 percent; middle class—35 percent; lower class—50 percent (pp. 302–303)
2. They had to go to work to help support their families. They were unable to acquire the training or skills that would get them out of the lower class. (p. 303)
3. Young offenders were separated from older, hardened criminals. Prisoners were taught trades. Harsh punishments were halted. Some prisons were built with separate cells for each prisoner. (p. 305)
4. It worked to get Americans to moderate their drinking of alcohol or do without it completely. It also tried to win passage of laws that would outlaw alcohol. Over one million Americans gave up alcohol. The demands of the temperance groups prompted a few states to pass prohibition laws. (pp. 305–306)
5. They published abolitionist newspapers, and they helped slaves escape on the Underground Railroad. (pp. 308–309)

Analyzing the Facts

1. Similarities are: the lower class contained the bulk of the population, and crop production increased due to new inventions. Differences are: Northern society developed around industry and was open to change; Southern society was agriculturally based and valued tradition. Also, Northern society was free, while slavery existed in the South.
2. The McCormick reaper cut wheat. Very little wheat was grown in the South. The steel plow was useful in breaking hard sod. The South had no problem breaking its soil.

3. Similarities are: both were poor, and most slaves were agricultural workers. Differences are: farm laborers were free and had rights that were protected by law.
4. The Industrial Revolution brought changes to the North. Northern society developed a positive attitude toward change because it came to be associated with progress and advancement. The South saw change as destructive to its way of life.
5. Advantages: all children would have the opportunity to better themselves; children would no longer be exposed to dangerous working conditions. Disadvantages: there would be less income in families.

Time and History

1. 1830's mechanical reaper and the steel plow **2.** 1817 **3.** Dorothea Dix worked to improve the treatment of prisoners and mental patients beginning in 1841, and the Seneca Falls convention of women's rights took place in 1848. **4.** 8 years **5.** Oberlin College

Chapter 14
Westward Expansion *pp. 314–331*

ACTIVITIES

Level A: Have students construct maps showing the major trails traveled by settlers moving west from 1835–1850. All maps should show the Oregon Trail, the Mormon Trail, and the California Trail. If students have access to an historical atlas of the United States, you may wish to have them shade in and key the extent of the settled area in 1850.
Level B: Have students design a poster to encourage settlement in either Texas or Oregon. Posters should give special emphasis to what the area has to offer. Information intended to dispel the fears of would-be settlers can also be included. Encourage students to make their posters visually attractive by using art as well as writing. Display the finished posters in the classroom.

ANSWERS

Section 1 Review *p. 319*

1. Americans began to settle in Texas after the Spanish granted land there to Moses Austin in 1821. After Mexico gained its independence from Spain, the Mexicans encouraged other Americans to settle in Texas. The first Americans to settle Oregon were missionaries. Some missionaries worked actively to bring American settlers to Oregon. Thousands of settlers eventually crossed the plains on their way to Oregon. (pp. 315, 317, 319)
2. It seemed dry, barren, and inhospitable to them. (p. 315)
3. If Texas was admitted as a slave state, it would have upset the balance of free and slave states in the Senate, causing another sectional crisis. (p. 317)
4. The missionaries' descriptions of the land in reports and letters, Whitman's efforts to bring more settlers to Oregon, the successful journey of the settlers of 1843. (pp. 317, 319)
5. Answers will vary. Yes—the settlers had no desire to disturb the Plains Indians. No—the settlers had frightened the buffalo off some tribes' lands completely. The settlers also carried new diseases against which the Indians had no natural defenses.

Section 2 Review *p. 324*

1. The war was caused by a border dispute. Texas claimed that its border with Mexico was the Rio Grande. Mexico claimed that the border lay at the Nueces River. The Mexicans refused to negotiate the border issue. When Mexican troops crossed the Rio Grande and attacked an American mounted patrol, the war began. (pp. 321–322)
2. The Mormons were members of a religious group known as the Church of Jesus Christ of Latter-Day Saints. They had to flee the United States because they were victims of persecution and hostility. (p. 321)

3. To annex is to attach a country or other territory, making it part of a nation. Texas was annexed in 1845 when Northern Democrats felt sure that President Polk and the Southern Democrats would bring Oregon in as a free state. (p. 320)
4. Lands in the Southwest including the present-day states of Arizona, New Mexico, California, Nevada, Utah, and parts of Colorado and Wyoming. (p. 324)
5. They both declared that the United States was to be the dominant power in the Western Hemisphere.

Section 3 Review *p. 329*

1. California's request upset the balance of free and slave states. (p. 328)
2. Should Congress open the new lands acquired by the treaty to slavery or should it ban slavery there? (p. 325)
3. A forty-niner was a person who took part in the rush to California for gold in 1849. (pp. 327–328) A Fire-Eater was a Southern radical who wanted the South to secede from the Union. (p. 328) A fugitive is a person who flees or tries to escape. (p. 329)
4. California was admitted as a free state. The question of slavery in the territory acquired from Mexico would be decided by the settlers who lived there. The slave trade in the District of Columbia was prohibited. However, slavery would still be permitted to exist there. Finally, Congress would pass a new and tougher fugitive slave law. (pp. 328–329)
5. Answers will vary. The expansion of slavery was such a volatile issue that neither political party wanted to risk losing votes by taking a stand on it.

Chapter Review *pp. 330–331*

Recalling the Facts

1. American settlers ignored Mexican laws. Mexico's attempt to enforce its laws and prohibit further American settlement in Texas produced the conflict. (p. 315)
2. It frightened the buffalo off of some tribes' lands completely. Western settlers brought new diseases against which the Indians had no natural defenses. (p. 319)
3. That the United States would take control, by force if necessary, of the Oregon Country up to the 54°40′ parallel
4. In the valley of the Great Salt Lake in Utah (p. 321)
5. Southerners hoped that land won from Mexico would be organized into slave states. Many Southerners also had family ties with people in Texas. Many Northerners opposed the war because they saw it as a war to spread slavery. (p. 322)
6. This would open most of the new territories to slavery because most of the new territories were below this line. (p. 327)

Analyzing the Facts

1. The admission of Texas was delayed for almost 10 years because it would upset the balance of slave and free states. California was admitted as a free state only after a compromise was worked out.
2. They believed in Manifest Destiny.
3. They both left their homelands to escape religious persecution.
4. Answers will vary. Yes—the Mexican government refused to negotiate the Texas border dispute; no—Polk wanted Mexican land and war was a way to get it.
5. North—California was admitted as a free state, and the slave trade was prohibited in the District of Columbia; South—a stronger fugitive slave law was passed, and slavery continued to exist in the District of Columbia; both—the question of slavery in the new territories would be decided by the settlers who lived there.

Time and History

1. 1846–1848; James K. Polk **2.** 17 years **3.** Mexico's prohibition of slavery in its provinces **4.** 1849 **5.** Millard Fillmore

Unit Review *pp. 332–333*

Recalling the Facts

1. The tariffs of 1828 and 1832. Jackson or-

dered the army to prepare troops to enforce the law in South Carolina. He also worked behind the scenes to get a lower tariff passed. (pp. 277–278)

2. Jackson organized the Democratic party after his defeat in the election of 1824. Those who opposed Jackson's policies as President formed the Whig party in 1834. (pp. 272, 282)
3. The cotton gin made raising cotton more profitable. More land was converted to cotton production. This increased the demand for slaves. (pp. 287–288)
4. Industry developed and factories were built. The population of Northern cities grew rapidly due to the arrival of large numbers of immigrants and rural Americans. New farm machinery increased crop production. Reformers worked to improve social conditions. (pp. 301–302, 304–309)
5. Manifest Destiny was the belief that the United States was intended to spread from the Atlantic to the Pacific oceans. Manifest Destiny was the underlying cause of the Mexican War. (pp. 320, 322)

Analyzing the Facts

1. Answers will vary. Advantages: an elected candidate can reward supporters with government jobs; those who run the government will probably work toward common goals. Disadvantages: qualified people may lose their jobs, incompetent people may be appointed.
2. The treatment and care of slaves was left almost entirely to those who owned them.
3. Answers will vary. Possible alternatives are: free all blacks and pay them to work on plantations; hire poor whites to work on plantations. These alternatives would be less profitable and would disrupt the social structure that placed the planters in the upper class.
4. The Great Plains, Rocky Mountains, and the Southwest. Answers will vary. Possible answers are: Indians died from diseases brought by whites; Indians were forcibly removed as white settlers demanded more of their land.

Reviewing Vocabulary

emancipate, p. 269; spoils system, p. 275; Indian Country, p. 279; Cotton Belt, p. 288; hiring-out system, p. 295; slave codes, p. 296; reform, p. 305; gag rule, p. 310; abolitionist, p. 308; annex, p. 322; fugitive, p. 329; forty-niner, p. 328.

Sharpening Your Skills

1. Author, title, subject
2. Copy the call number onto a sheet of paper, and then look for the book on the shelves.
3. New York had 36 electoral votes; 16 were cast for John Q. Adams, and 20 were cast for Andrew Jackson.
4. New England
5. 95

Unit 5: DIVISION AND REUNION

Chapter 15
The Breaking of the Union

pp. 336–353

ACTIVITIES

Level A: Have students write a campaign speech for one of the candidates in the election of 1860. The speech should focus on the candidate's position on the extension of slavery into western territories. Its purpose should be to convince voters to accept the candidate's position on this issue. Read the best speeches to the class.

Level B: Have students write a news article describing one important event of the 1850's. Suggested topics include the attack on Fort Sumter, the publication of *Uncle Tom's Cabin,* John Brown's execution, and the Kansas-Nebraska Act. Background information and sectional reactions to the event should be included. Each article should be accompanied by a picture. Display the completed articles in the classroom.

ANSWERS

Section 1 Review *p. 341*

1. The act stated that the slavery issue would be decided by the people of these territories. This effectively repealed the Missouri Compromise. Slavery could now exist in any territory or state if the people voted for it. (p. 340)
2. The Fugitive Slave Act was part of the Compromise of 1850. It made it easier for slave catchers to get convictions against alleged runaway slaves. The act also provided stiff penalties for any citizen who interfered with its enforcement. Black Northerners were frightened by the act. Some white Northerners supported it. Others refused to obey it. (pp. 337–339)
3. Popular sovereignty is the belief that the people of a territory should have the right to decide whether their territory would permit slavery. (p. 340) Southerners, Southern Whigs, and Democrats (p. 341)
4. It opposed the expansion of slavery and demanded the repeal of the Kansas-Nebraska Act and the Fugitive Slave Act. Southerners believed that the Republicans wanted to free all slaves and destroy Southern society. (p. 341)
5. Answers will vary. It could help the settlers get their farm products to eastern and western markets quicker. It could hurt by attracting more settlers to the plains. This would cause the price of land to rise and reduce Indian landholdings.

Section 2 Review *p. 346*

1. The Supreme Court ruled that slavery could exist anywhere in the territories. The Missouri Compromise, therefore, was unconstitutional. (p. 344)
2. Northerners and Southerners organized settlers who held the "right" views on slavery to move into Kansas. Some of the settlers came prepared to fight for their beliefs. By 1856, violence and bloodshed were sweeping across Kansas. (p. 342)
3. Buchanan had been out of the country during the trouble over the Kansas-Nebraska Act. He had not taken a public stand on the law, so he had made few enemies. (p. 343)
4. He believed that the Union could not continue to exist half slave and half free. This probably caused some Southerners to worry that he would work to abolish slavery.

Social Studies Skills *p. 347*

1. The North and the South
2. It represents the explosive issue of slavery expansion into western territories. By pushing the cannonball, the men are trying to impose their views on the other side.
3. The largeness of the cannonball symbolizes the importance of this issue.
4. Both the North and the South were pushing hard to have their way on the issue of the expansion of slavery into the western territories.

Section 3 Review *p. 351*

1. Lincoln was perceived as a symbol of Northern hostility toward the South. (p. 349)
2. Brown planned to arm the slaves who would then lead a widespread slave revolt to end slavery. (p. 348)
3. Fort Sumter was a Union fort located in a seceded state and surrounded by Confederate troops. The Confederates wanted to gain control of the fort. They demanded Fort Sumter's surrender. The demand was rejected, and fighting broke out. The Civil War had begun. (pp. 350–351)
4. Answers will vary. Students may mention the different political situations that existed during the two time periods. The col-

onies had no say in their government. Southerners had a say in government and the right to alter laws through the legislative and amendment processes.

Chapter Review *pp. 352–353*

Recalling the Facts

1. Settlers wanted the land organized in preparation for statehood. Railroad planners wanted the land organized so that a transcontinental railroad could be built. The transcontinental railroad would increase the value of the land that Douglas owned, which he could sell for enormous profits. (p. 339)
2. The Whig party split along sectional lines and eventually disappeared. Northern Whigs joined with others who opposed the expansion of slavery and formed the Republican party. Southern Whigs joined the Democrats because they supported the expansion of slavery. Democrats who opposed the Kansas-Nebraska Act joined the Republican party. (p. 341)
3. Scott had lived with his master in the free state of Illinois and the free Wisconsin Territory. Scott asked the court to set him free on the grounds that he had become free when taken into free territory. (p. 344)
4. Stephen A. Douglas (Northern Democratic)—supported popular sovereignty; John C. Breckinridge (Southern Democratic)—favored the expansion of slavery; Abraham Lincoln (Republican)—against the expansion of slavery; John Bell (Constitutional Union)—recommended that the issue be ignored. (pp. 348–349)
5. The states of the Upper South had threatened to secede if any force was used to bring the seceded states back into the Union. (p. 350)

Analyzing the Facts

1. The Kansas and Nebraska territories were part of what had been the Louisiana Territory. The issue of slavery in the Louisiana Territory had previously been settled by the Missouri Compromise.
2. The Democrats supported popular sovereignty. The Republicans opposed it.
3. *Uncle Tom's Cabin* attacked slavery as a moral wrong. Helper's book attacked slavery because slavery hurt Southerners who owned no slaves. Both books were very popular in the North and produced outrage in the South.
4. Southerners probably felt more threatened because the Northerners who admired Brown favored ending slavery in the South, by force if necessary.
5. Answers will vary. Possible answers are: it was Union territory, and Lincoln was not willing to give it up; Lincoln wanted to provoke an attack so that the Confederates would be forced back into the Union.

Time and History

1. Franklin Pierce **2.** 6 years **3.** 1861 **4.** *Uncle Tom's Cabin* and *The Impending Crisis of the South* **5.** The 1858 Illinois Senate race. Douglas.

Chapter 16
The Civil War *pp. 354–377*

ACTIVITIES

Level A: Have students role-play the following individuals at a mock press conference following the surrender at Appomattox in 1865: Ulysses S. Grant, Robert E. Lee, Abraham Lincoln, Jefferson Davis, Stand Watie, Robert Smalls, and Clara Barton. Additional figures from the chapter can be added if desired. Class members who are not role-playing should prepare questions that can be answered from the information presented in the chapter. Arrange the classroom so that those students playing roles face the "press."

Level B: Have students make a bulletin board map showing the major battle sites of the Civil War. One group of students can be assigned to draw a map of the eastern half of the United States. Have other students mark and label the sites of battles. Union victories,

Confederate victories, and battles that ended in a draw should be color-coded and a map key attached. Individual students should be assigned to write a short paragraph describing a particular battle. Have students use yarn to connect the paragraphs with the appropriate battle site on the map.

ANSWERS

Section 1 Review *p. 358*

1. Both sides planned to capture their enemy's capital and bring the war to a quick close. (pp. 357–358)
2. Northern advantages—larger population, greater reserves of money, more industrial power, larger railroad network, larger navy, more commercial ships. Southern advantages—fighting a defensive war, high quality of military leaders, a strong wartime President. (pp. 356–357)
3. Each side realized that the Civil War would not be ended by one battle. (p. 358)
4. Answers will vary. Students should recognize that the North's advantages would become more significant in a longer war. The South would fare better in a short war where its military superiority could be directed towards winning a quick victory.

Social Studies Skills *p. 359*

1. Choose a topic. Compare the amount of information available on a particular topic with the desired length of the report.
2. Any quoted information
3. Organization ensures that the information will be presented in a logical and concise manner.
4. It gives the reader an idea of what the report is going to be about.
5. In the bibliography

Section 2 Review *p. 366*

1. To bring the war to a quicker end, to give the Union a moral cause, to keep Great Britain out of the war, to provide the Union with more troops (p. 362)
2. Blockading the entire coastline of the Confederacy to create supply problems for the Confederate army, splitting the South in order to weaken it, and inflicting as many casualties as possible (p. 360)
3. The Confederate army failed to take Gettysburg. Lee's plan for invasion of the North had ended in disaster. The South's hopes for assistance from Great Britain were crushed. (p. 365)
4. Grant won major victories that gave the Union control of the Mississippi River and cut the South in half. (pp. 363–364)
5. Answers will vary. Britain's textile industry was dependent on Southern cotton. But the British people opposed slavery and, after Southern losses at Vicksburg and Gettysburg, did not want to support a losing cause.

Section 3 Review *p. 371*

1. Training was brief; fighting was ferocious; spare time was spent washing clothes, cleaning weapons, playing cards or writing letters; food was poor; medical care was inadequate. (p. 367)
2. Fewer white Northerners were enlisting. Many came to believe that blacks should share the burden of dying for the Union. The government decided to permit blacks to join the army. (p. 369)
3. Women replaced men in the factories. Women took over the running of farms, plantations, and businesses. Many women served as nurses. Some women ran hospitals or transported supplies. (pp. 369–370)
4. Answers will vary. Southerners were fighting for the same cause, the protection of property, and would therefore live up to their promise at the war's end.

Section 4 Review *p. 375*

1. Grant finally defeated Lee in April 1865 with a successful attack on Petersburg and Richmond. (p. 374)
2. Major defeats at Vicksburg and at Gettysburg in 1863 caused morale to sink. The

Union naval blockade of the South created shortages of goods, and Southern industry could not provide all that was needed. Fewer men joined the army, and thousands in the army deserted. (p. 372)

3. Northern victories at Mobile, Alabama and at Atlanta, Georgia (p. 373)
4. Lee's army had to lay down its weapons. Every Confederate soldier was permitted to go home. Confederate soldiers were allowed to take their horses and mules with them for spring planting. (pp. 374–375)
5. Answers will vary. Yes—it is an effective tactic for destroying an enemy's morale, agriculture, and industrial resources. No—it is unnecessarily destructive. Wars can be won without total destruction.

Chapter Review *pp. 376–377*

Recalling the Facts

1. Virginia, North Carolina, Tennessee, and Arkansas joined the Confederacy. The people of western Virginia formed their own state and joined the Union. Delaware, Kentucky, Missouri, and Maryland remained in the Union. (pp. 355–356)
2. McDowell was removed following the defeat at Bull Run. McClellan was removed after he failed to defeat Lee's army at Richmond and Antietam. (pp. 360–362)
3. The number of volunteers began to dwindle and the number of desertions increased. Many Southerners opposed the draft because they felt that the Confederate government was exercising too much authority. Many Northerners opposed it because the draft was not in the spirit of the American tradition of freedom. (pp. 367–368)
4. Prior to 1862, the Union army had refused to accept blacks. By 1862, fewer white Northerners were enlisting. Many came to believe that blacks should share the burden of dying for the Union. (p. 369)
5. Grant's army broke through Lee's defenses at Petersburg and captured Richmond. Lee's army fled westward. Grant's men pursued Lee. Union General Philip Sheridan's cavalry swept down from the north. Lee was trapped. Lee surrendered on April 9, 1865. (p. 374)

Analyzing the Facts

1. The side with more specie can buy more materials needed to win the war.
2. The Emancipation Proclamation freed only those slaves living in the states that had seceded. Slaves living in the border states were not included. Lincoln also said that he would cancel the Proclamation if the South returned to the Union.
3. It was hoped that having Johnson on the ticket would improve Lincoln's chances for getting votes in the border states.
4. The President is commander in chief of the armed forces. He appoints the generals who make the military decisions. He can also fire them if he feels they are not doing a good job.

Time and History

1. Battle of Bull Run **2.** 4 years **3.** Antietam, Gettysburg, Atlanta **4.** Richmond **5.** West Virginia, 1863

Chapter 17
The Problems of Peace
pp. 378–393

ACTIVITIES

Level A: Have students write an editorial in support of one of the plans for Reconstruction: Lincoln's "Ten Percent Plan," Johnson's "Presidential Restoration," the Wade-Davis Bill, or the Reconstruction Act. The editorials should concentrate on the advantages of the plan as well as the disadvantages of the rival plans. Encourage students to outline their ideas before writing.

Level B: Have students construct a chart comparing the various plans for Reconstruction. The chart should show the requirements for readmission as well as any other methods for reconstructing Southern society. This could be a group or individual project.

ANSWERS

Section 1 Review *p. 382*

1. Cities, railroad tracks, and factories were in ruins. Farm fields were overgrown. The economy was bankrupt. (p. 379)
2. Most blacks lacked money, a home, and a job. Most were uneducated. Many were unfamiliar with the rights they had. They faced white hostility. (pp. 380–381)
3. It was a federal agency that provided aid to former slaves and any Southerner who needed help. It distributed food, medicine, and supplies. It established hospitals and schools. (pp. 380–381)
4. Sharecropping is a system in which people who cannot afford to buy land can rent land to farm and pay their rent from the profits made from their crops. (p. 382) A crop-lien system is a system by which farmers borrow money to run their farms and repay the loan with crops. (p. 382)
5. Answers will vary. Union leaders might not have wanted to create more bad feelings between the North and South. They may have recognized that some of their officers were also guilty of war crimes.

Section 2 Review *p. 385*

1. Presidential plan—a former Confederate state would be readmitted when 10 percent of those who had voted in the 1860 presidential election had taken an oath of loyalty to the Union. The state would also have to outlaw slavery. Congressional plan—required 50 percent to take an oath of loyalty before readmission. (p. 383)
2. Johnson's plan required the Southern states to ratify the Thirteenth Amendment before they could be permitted to rejoin the Union. (p. 384)
3. It granted citizenship to blacks and said that if any state prevented citizens from voting, that state would lose a number of seats in the House proportionate to the number of voters excluded. (pp. 384–385)
4. Answers will vary. The battle between Congress and the President might have been avoided due to Lincoln's abilities as a politician.

Section 3 Review *p. 391*

1. Blacks gained the right to vote and hold public office. As a result, blacks took an active role in Southern state governments. They also voted in large numbers. (p. 387)
2. Johnson was frustrating the administration of the reconstruction acts. Senators and representatives wanted to stop him. They decided that Johnson should be removed from office. (p. 386)
3. Scalawags were Southern whites who joined or supported the Republican party during Reconstruction. Carpetbaggers were Northerners who moved to the South after the Civil War. Scalawags and carpetbaggers become involved in the new Southern governments. (p. 388)
4. The results of the election of 1876 were in dispute. The Democrats agreed to accept the Republican Hayes as the winner if Hayes guaranteed that he would end Reconstruction and remove all federal troops from the South. (pp. 390–391)
5. Answers will vary. Black rights were guaranteed through the Thirteenth, Fourteenth, and Fifteenth amendments, and black participation in government was encouraged. But freedom did not mean equality. Once Reconstruction ended, the South resumed its practice of segregation.

Chapter Review *pp. 392–393*

Recalling the Facts

1. The Democrats were viewed as the party that caused the Civil War; the Republicans as the party that saved the Union. (p. 379)
2. Steps required for readmitting Southern states, whether to give blacks equal rights, and who was to be in charge of Reconstruction (p. 383)

3. The Senate failed to convict Johnson of the impeachment charges. (p. 386)
4. They used threats and violence to prevent blacks from voting. They frightened white Southern Republicans to keep them from supporting carpetbagger governments. (p. 390)
5. Black Americans had to accept low wages, unfair treatment by the legal system, and white violence. The South resumed its practice of segregation. (p. 391)

Analyzing the Facts

1. Answers will vary. Possible answers are: Confederate veterans—the South had been destroyed, the economy was bankrupt, many veterans were in poor physical condition, and they had to adjust to black freedom; Southern blacks—most were penniless, homeless, uneducated, and unskilled.
2. The Republicans were seen as the party that freed them from slavery, and the Republicans passed amendments that guaranteed blacks basic rights.
3. The legislative branch—it impeached President Johnson and overrode many of his vetoes. Congressional Reconstruction was the program that was ultimately implemented.
4. Answers will vary. Yes—blacks had the right to vote and they had their freedom; no—many blacks lacked skills and were being terrorized by white Southerners to keep them from voting.
5. It prevented them from participating in the dominant culture of the country.

Time and History

1. 5 years **2.** 12 years **3.** Ulysses S. Grant **4.** Ten Percent Plan **5.** 3 years

Unit Review *pp. 394–395*

Recalling the Facts

1. Southerners felt threatened by John Brown's raid and Northerners' reactions to it. Northerners believed that *Uncle Tom's Cabin* presented a true picture of slavery, while Southerners saw it as exaggerated. Northerners were angered by the Dred Scott decision, while Southerners rejoiced over it. (pp. 344, 346, 348)
2. With the fall of Vicksburg, the Union gained control over the Mississippi River, and the Confederacy was split in half. Lee's defeat at Gettysburg halted the Confederate advance into Northern territory. The fall of Richmond led to the surrender of Lee's army at Appomattox and the end of the war. (pp. 363–365, 372–375)
3. The radical Republicans were instrumental in getting Congress to pass the Wade-Davis Bill, which was a harsher program of Reconstruction than that proposed by Lincoln. They pushed the Reconstruction Act through Congress in 1867. They were also the force behind Andrew Johnson's impeachment. (pp. 383–386)
4. In the disputed election of 1876, Rutherford B. Hayes was allowed to become President in exchange for the removal of federal troops from the South. Many Northerners were tired of fighting the Reconstruction battle. Many were no longer committed to helping Southern blacks. (pp. 390–391)

Analyzing the Facts

1. Douglas was anxious to organize the territories so that a transcontinental railroad could be built across them. He may have seen popular sovereignty as the quickest way to get the North and the South to approve the organization of Kansas and Nebraska.
2. In the Civil War, Americans fought against each other. The casualties on both sides were American.
3. Southerners resented being a part of the United States again. Northerners blamed the South for causing the war and for all war deaths. White Southerners threatened and committed violent acts against blacks and Republicans in the South.
4. The Bill of Rights lists rights that cannot be taken away by the federal government.

The Fourteenth Amendment stipulates that rights cannot be taken away by state governments either.

Reviewing Vocabulary
land speculator, pp. 339–340; blockade, p. 360; war of attrition, p. 360; gunboat, p. 361; draft, p. 368; war crime, p. 379; bankrupt, p. 379; Reconstruction, p. 382; black code, p. 384; impeach, p. 386; graft, p. 389; segregation, p. 391.

Sharpening Your Skills
1. Organization
2. A bibliography is a list of sources used in preparing a report. It should be placed on a separate page at the end of the report.
3. The main ideas and supporting details; a summary of the main ideas.
4. Possible answers include death or the defeat of the Confederacy.
5. Antiblack groups, such as the White League and the Ku Klux Klan, terrorized blacks to the extent that conditions for blacks were worse than they had been under slavery.

Unit 6: AGE OF INDUSTRY

Chapter 18
The Last Frontier
pp. 398–417

ACTIVITIES

Level A: Ask students to assume the roles of the various people who lived on the Great Plains (Indians, cattle ranchers, farmers, and sheepherders). Have other students assume the roles of government officials.

Each group should try to convince the government officials that it should be allowed to pursue its own way of life. Each group should also take a position on the removal of the Indians from the Great Plains. Government officials should then choose an appropriate course of action based on the arguments.

Level B: Assign students to work in small groups or individually to create a bulletin board display of aspects of frontier life. The students could depict Indians, ranching life, cowhands, pioneer homes, pioneer farms, cow towns, and quilting bees.

ANSWERS

Section 1 Review *p. 404*

1. White settlers wanted to use the land for ranching and farming, and gold was discovered on their lands. (p. 399)
2. Blankets, moccasins, clothing, tepees, farming tools, cups and spoons, water bottles, hairbrushes, and fuel (p. 399)
3. Chief Joseph was a Nez Perce leader. He led his people on a long trek in an unsuccessful attempt to escape from soldiers sent to move the Nez Perce to a reservation. Wovoka was a Paiute Indian. He was the prophet of the Ghost Dance movement. (pp. 401, 403)
4. It divided up the reservation lands into individual sections, which could be farmed by Indian families. (pp. 403–404)
5. Answers will vary but could include the idea that if whites had not moved onto Indian lands, conflict would have been avoided.

Section 2 Review *p. 409*

1. Cattle ranchers claimed free government land, built small houses on their claims, and raised calves. As they became more successful, they built larger houses and hired more cowhands. Cowhands lived out on the open range for months at a time. They worked at line riding, roundups, branding, and herding cattle on the "long drives." (pp. 406–407)

2. Vaqueros were Mexican cattle herders; the basic skills of the trade. (p. 408)
3. They made an annual "long drive" to the railroad. The railroad then took the cattle to eastern markets. (pp. 405–406)
4. Answers will vary. Possible answers are: books, movies, and television shows with western themes; rodeos; toys; and "dude ranches."

Section 3 Review *p. 415*

1. Water problems were solved by windmills and "dry farming." Farming problems were solved by improvements in farm machinery. The fencing problem was solved by the invention of barbed wire. Fuel problems were solved by burning dried buffalo and cow manure; the invention of stoves that burned bundles of hay, corncobs, or cornstalks; and supplies of coal and wood brought by railroads from the East. The housing problem was solved by building dugouts and sod houses. (pp. 410–412)
2. Literacy rate is the percentage of people in a specific population group who can read and write; Kansas and Nebraska. (p. 413)
3. Pioneer women had a very difficult time keeping sod houses clean, washing clothes, and cooking. The hard work of the frontier left women with little time for visiting or for having fun. (pp. 411–413)
4. They were people who acquired land in the hopes of selling it later at a great profit. They often hired others to claim land for them; built very small houses on the land, which they described to the government in a deceptive way; and rolled houses from claim to claim. (p. 414)
5. Answers will vary. Possible answers are: yes, once the problems were solved, life on the Great Plains became easier and profitable; no, the hardships were too great and the solutions too costly.

Chapter Review *pp. 416–417*

Recalling the Facts

1. The government moved the Indians so that farmers, ranchers, and miners could have more land. (p. 399)
2. The Indians relied on the buffalo for many things, including food, clothing, and shelter. (pp. 399, 402)
3. To assimilate the Indians by having them become farmers on individually owned plots of land; millions of acres of reservation land that was not given to individual Indians was sold to white settlers by the government. (pp. 403–404)
4. Ranchers feared that the sheep would ruin the plains by biting off the grass too close to the ground. Less grass would be available as food for their cattle. (p. 409)
5. Overgrazing, droughts and blizzards, competition for land from the sheepherders, and pioneer farmers who plowed the grasslands under and fenced in the land (pp. 408–409)
6. Problems of water; fuel; housing; tough, dry soil; difficult living conditions; harsh weather; and insects (pp. 410–412)

Analyzing the Facts

1. Answers will vary. This would be good advice for someone who was willing to endure hardships in order to become prosperous; it would not be good advice for someone who was content with what they had.
2. The newcomers were farmers, ranchers, and miners. Most of the Indians on the plains were nomadic hunters and gatherers. Both groups wanted to use the same land for different and incompatible purposes.
3. The Sioux did not wish to return to the reservation. The United States government was not protecting the Sioux's land and was not providing the Indians with decent food.
4. Answers will vary. Buffalo hunters destroyed the buffalo that was the basis of the Indians' way of life. The army physically forced the Indians to move.
5. Answers will vary. New frontiers today include space, the oceans, Antarctica, and various areas of scientific research. These

new frontiers hold out the prospects of a better life for many people. Early pioneers can expect to encounter many difficulties and disappointments. They differ from the frontier of the late 1800's in that they are not all land areas.

Time and History

1. 1876, 1877, 1890 **2.** 27 years **3.** 1873 **4.** the Civil War **5.** gold discovered in the Black Hills

Chapter 19 The Rise of American Industry

pp. 418–437

ACTIVITIES

Level A: Using magazines and newspapers, have students make a scrapbook of products that use electricity. Label each product (light bulb, refrigerator, can opener, and so on). Have students research and write a brief description of what people did before each of these electrical devices was developed. Then have students evaluate which electrical items in their scrapbooks are essential to their daily lives and which are not.

Level B: Have students use the information in the chapter to complete a chart entitled "Inventors and Inventions." The chart should include the following five headings: Inventor, Invention, Year, Purpose of Use, In Use Today (yes or no). If students do not know if a certain invention is still in use, have them use reference materials to locate the information.

ANSWERS

Section 1 Review *p. 422*

1. Abundant natural resources, a large work force, talented entrepreneurs, the formation of corporations, methods of mass production, and help from the government (pp. 419–422)
2. Former soldiers, farm workers who had left their farms as a result of improvements in farm equipment, women, and new immigrants (p. 420)
3. Entrepreneurs were people who organized and managed businesses. They were able to identify the need for new types of goods or services, start businesses and keep them operating, locate and obtain needed resources, and manage the labor of many other people. (pp. 420–421)
4. A corporation is a business organization formed by individuals who pool their money and become stockholders in the business. An assembly line is a method of producing goods in which workers put together a product as it goes pass them on a moving belt. *Laissez-faire* is a government policy of not interfering in the affairs of business. (pp. 421–422)
5. Answers will vary. New opportunities exist in the fields of computers and high technology.

Social Studies Skills *p. 423*

1. It is round and its pieces are similar to slices of pie.
2. To show visually how percentages compare to each other and to the whole.
3. 63 percent; 37 percent
4. 35 percent; 35 percent

Section 2 Review *p. 427*

1. Their inventions improved the lives of millions of people. (pp. 426–427)
2. A patent is a government license that gives someone the right to make and to sell an invention for a certain number of years. (p. 424)
3. The typewriter, cash register, adding machine, air brake, telephone and electric lighting system (pp. 424–427)
4. Answers will vary. The phonograph, motion picture machine, telephone, and electric light may seem especially important.

Section 3 Review *p. 432*

1. By combining businesses. By forming pools and trusts, businesses could agree

on common prices. (pp. 430, 432)

2. Railroad construction created a demand for products such as rails and locomotives. The railroads carried the raw materials needed by industry and expanded America's transportation network thereby creating a nationwide market for the products of industry. (pp. 428–429)
3. By using the most modern equipment and methods of steelmaking, paying low wages, and becoming the owner of every aspect of the production process (pp. 430–431)
4. A rebate is a refund of part of the rate charged for goods or services. Rockefeller won rebates from the railroads. By shipping his oil more cheaply, Rockefeller was able to lower the price of his oil. This allowed him to take more customers away from other oil companies. (pp. 431–432)
5. Answers will vary. Advantage—companies that belong to a trust can make large profits; disadvantage—trusts destroy competition, which results in high consumer prices.

Section 4 Review *p. 435*

1. The government passed the Interstate Commerce Act to regulate the railroads and the Sherman Antitrust Act to break up trusts. (pp. 433–435)
2. The Supreme Court ruled that the ICC could not set shipping rates for the railroads. (p. 435)
3. A holding company is a corporation that owns enough stock in other companies to control them. (p. 435)
4. Answers will vary. The government regulates health and safety, sets minimum wages for workers, and sets environmental impact standards.

Chapter Review *pp. 436–437*

Recalling the Facts

1. Improving America's transportation network made it easier for businesses to transport raw materials and products to market. Tariffs on foreign goods raised the price of foreign goods and encouraged Americans to buy goods made in the United States. The government also allowed businesses to develop and grow with very little interference. (p. 422)
2. Goods move through a factory on a slowly moving belt or track. As the goods pass by, each worker completes one part of the process. (p. 421)
3. Gas lighting was expensive and kerosene lamps were a fire hazard. (p. 426)
4. A corporation is a business organization formed by people who pool their money and become stockholders in the business. A rebate is a refund of part of the rate charged for goods or services. A trust is a group of businesses that unite to control production and prices of their goods and make larger profits. A holding company is a corporation that owns enough stock in other companies to control them. (pp. 421, 432, 435)
5. The act required railroads to charge reasonable rates, prohibited the formation of pools, and prohibited rebates. This law showed that the government was willing to regulate the activities of business. (pp. 433–434)

Analyzing the Facts

1. Answers will vary. All six factors (abundant natural resources, a large work force, talented entrepreneurs, corporations, mass production methods, and help from the government) were important for various reasons. Answers should be supported by logical reasoning.
2. Any product that has interchangeable parts can be made on an assembly line. An assembly line is one method of mass production. Mass production involves using machines to produce goods quickly and cheaply.
3. With electric light, people have more hours each day for reading, visiting, working, or playing; steel has made possible the construction of bridges and tall buildings.

4. Answers will vary. Possible answers are: the government should have no control—people who invest in a business should be able to run it in any way they want; the government should pass laws that are fair to business owners, yet protect the public.
5. Answers will vary. People today may feel the same emotions. Some people worry that computers may eliminate their jobs.

Time and History

1. typewriter **2.** 8 years **3.** 1870's **4.** No, the long-lasting light bulb was invented in 1879, three years after the Centennial Exposition took place. **5.** 18 years

Chapter 20
New Ways of Life Begin
pp. 438–457

ACTIVITIES

Level A: Have each student pretend to be an immigrant from a southern or eastern European country, or from China. In diary form, have each explain why he or she left their native land, what the journey was like, and what it is like to settle in a new country. Encourage students to describe any problems they have had and what new and exciting things they have found in America. Students should be encouraged to talk with family members, who have immigrated to America, about their experiences in order to get ideas for their diary entries.

Level B: Invite two people who have immigrated to America to come and speak to the class about their experiences. One of the speakers should be an older American who came to this country before World War II. The other speaker should be a more recent immigrant, preferably someone who arrived after 1970. Have the speakers tell why they left their native lands, what their journeys were like, and any problems or unusual events they experienced in settling in America. Follow up this presentation the next day by leading a discussion on the similarities and differences between the experiences of the two speakers and how their experiences compare to those of nineteenth century immigrants.

ANSWERS

Section 1 Review *p. 444*

1. Some were attracted by the democratic way of life and the economic opportunities. Others were recruited by employers. Unfair laws and religious persecution encouraged many immigrants to leave. The steamship made the passage to America easier and cheaper. (pp. 439–441)
2. They were immigrants from southern and eastern Europe who began coming to America in large numbers in the late 1800's. Before the 1890's, most immigrants to the United States had come from northern and western Europe. (p. 441)
3. Nativists are people who believe that native-born Americans are superior to immigrants. People objected to the crowding caused by increased immigration. Some feared that immigrants would take jobs away from American workers. Others wrongly believed that the New Immigrants could never become good Americans because they were so "different." (pp. 442–443)
4. The Chinese Exclusion Act of 1882 stopped immigration from China for ten years. The Foran Act of 1885 stated that employers could no longer recruit skilled foreigners to work in American industry. A literacy test measures the ability of a person to read and write. (p. 444)
5. Answers will vary. Many immigrants today are coming from Southeast Asia, Mexico, and Latin America. Problems are similar to the problems faced by immigrants in the late 1800's.

Section 2 Review *p. 449*

1. They made improvements in housing, water systems, and sewage-disposal sys-

tems. Transportation problems were solved by paving streets with asphalt and the development of the cable car, electric streetcar, and subway. (pp. 448–449)

2. The expansion of industry created more jobs in the cities. (p. 445)
3. Ethnic refers to anything having to do with a group of people who share the same customs, language, and culture. A tenement is an apartment house that is run-down, very crowded, or poorly built. (pp. 446–447)
4. Answers will vary. Poverty and crime are major problems. Possible solutions include: public works projects, improved education, and better law enforcement.

Section 3 Review *p. 455*

1. The Knights of Labor, the American Federation of Labor (AFL), the American Railway Union (ARU), and the Socialist party (pp. 451–455)
2. Not all workers shared equally in the benefits of employment. Working conditions were poor. Assembly line work was dull. The opportunity of becoming one's own boss was not as great as it once was. (pp. 450–451)
3. Craft unions are groups of workers sharing the same craft or skill who have joined together to improve wages and working conditions. Unions used collective bargaining, strikes, and boycotts. (pp. 452–453)
4. An injunction is an order from a court stopping an individual or group from carrying out some action. Employers hired strikebreakers, fired workers who joined a union, required new employees to sign yellow-dog contracts, and blacklisted workers who were active in union organizing. (p. 454)
5. Answers will vary. Advantage—workers may win higher wages or improved working conditions; disadvantage—workers may lose income during the strike, and if they lose the strike, they may lose their jobs.

Chapter Review *pp. 456–457*

Recalling the Facts

1. The democratic way of life and job opportunities (p. 439)
2. They feared that immigrants, who were often willing to work for low wages, would take jobs away from American workers. (pp. 442–443)
3. Poor quality housing, inadequate water supplies and sewage disposal, and transportation. Laws were passed to raise housing standards; cities began to filter and purify their water supplies; sewage disposal systems were improved; roads were paved; and cable cars, electric streetcars, and subways were developed. (pp. 447–449)
4. Wages were low and frequently depended on the worker's sex, race, or length of residence in the United States. Hours were long. Accidents on the job were common. Thousands of workers died from diseases caused by poor working conditions. (p. 450)
5. Collective bargaining involves discussions between members of a union and their employers over work-related issues. A strike is a refusal by employees to work until their demands are met. In a boycott, workers and their supporters refuse to buy the products of a business until the business owners grant the demands of the employees. (p. 453)

Analyzing the Facts

1. Many immigrants settled in the cities to get jobs in industry. The population of the cities grew. Labor unions formed to help protect the American worker.
2. Answers will vary. Possible answers are: Agree—shortage of low-cost housing, crowded city streets, and inefficient public transportation; Disagree—higher housing standards, water and sewage treatment plants, and efficient public transportation.
3. The poem encourages and welcomes immigration. American workers demanded restrictions on immigration.

4. Answers will vary. For—allowing groups like police officers and firefighters to strike would endanger the public. Against—everyone, regardless of occupation, should have the right to strike. Students may mention doctors, nurses, sanitation workers, farmers, or teachers.

Time and History
1. cable cars, electric streetcars, subways
2. 21 years 3. 17 years 4. 1882
5. The Socialist party was formed three years after the Pullman Strike.

Chapter 21
Political Machines and Parties
pp. 458–475

ACTIVITIES

Level A: Divide the class into four groups. Have each group prepare one side of a panel debate on one of the following issues.

1. All government jobs, with the exception of elected offices, should be filled by civil service candidates.
2. High tariffs are necessary to protect American jobs and manufactured goods.

Level B: Have students do a class research project on today's Democratic and Republican parties. Divide the class into four groups and assign each group one of the following tasks.

1. Write to the party's headquarters in your city or state requesting information about the party. Also ask for pictures of public officials from each party.
2. Use library materials to research the origins of each political party, and make a chart outlining important events relating to the establishment of each party.
3. Obtain and label pictures of Democratic and Republican Presidents since the Civil War.
4. Using an almanac, prepare a graph or chart showing membership increases and/or decreases since the Civil War.

When all work has been completed, have students make a bulletin board display of the materials they have collected and prepared.

ANSWERS

Section 1 Review *p. 462*

1. New immigrants, the unemployed, the poor, and city residents were helped by the corrupt city governments. Members of the political machines made fortunes through bribes and kickbacks. The corruption, however, cost the cities' taxpayers enormous amounts of money. (pp. 460–461)
2. Rapid city growth, the failure to provide basic services, the confusing organization of city governments, voter apathy, and the attitude of some wealthy residents that city politics was beneath them (p. 459)
3. Kickbacks are monies received as payment that are illegally returned to a corrupt official. Bribes are illegal payments given in return for an expected favor. (pp. 460–461)
4. The newspapers strongly criticized Boss Tweed's corrupt activities. Newspapers today can expose corruption through investigative reporting. Reporters can be assigned to cover government affairs, political conventions, and elections.

Section 2 Review *p. 467*

1. Both parties depended on local political machines, lacked unity, had about the same number of supporters, tried to avoid taking clear stands on the issues, and received large contributions from businesses. The Republican party was strongest in New England and among Protestant voters and older American families. The Democratic party was strongest in the South and among Catholic, Jewish, and New Immigrant voters. (pp. 463–464)
2. The Pendleton Act of 1883 said that ability

would be the basis for federal employment. Civil service is government jobs filled by persons who pass competitive public exams. (p. 466)

3. High tariffs encouraged American consumers to buy goods made in the United States and allowed American manufacturers to charge higher prices and make larger profits. (p. 467)
4. Answers will vary. Students should be guided in analyzing the strength or weakness of each President by considering major foreign policy decisions, willingness to take an unpopular stand on an issue, and ability to win legislative approval for domestic programs.

Section 3 Review *p. 473*

1. It would raise the price of their crops and thus allow them to make more profit. It also would lower the value of their debts. (p. 470)
2. They were laws passed in the farm states of Illinois, Wisconsin, Iowa, and Minnesota to regulate the railroads and grain elevators. (p. 468)
3. They advocated government ownership of the railroads, government warehouses to store farm products, lowering of property taxes, and the adoption of an income tax. (p. 469)
4. William Jennings Bryan (Populist and Democratic) and William McKinley (Republican). McKinley was the winner. Bryan's defeat was a defeat for farmers and the Populist party. (pp. 472–473)
5. Answers will vary. People might want to form a new party if they believe the existing parties are not responding to their needs.

Chapter Review *pp. 474–475*

Recalling the Facts

1. Cities grew rapidly and often failed to provide basic services. The organization of city governments was confusing and offered opportunities for corruption. Many honest and industrious citizens took no interest in city government. (p. 459)
2. Political machines are political groups that organize to control policy or officials in power. Political machines provided services to city residents in return for votes. (p. 460)
3. The two parties shared near equal voter support. The parties were afraid they might offend voters. If even a few voters were offended, the other party might win the election. (p. 463)
4. Under the spoils system, government jobs were given out by elected officials to their supporters. Under the civil service system, people had to pass tests to show they were qualified for the positions. (pp. 464, 466)
5. High shipping rates, high fees to "go-betweens," high property taxes, expensive new farm machinery, and falling prices for farm products (p. 468)
6. Government ownership of the railroads, a federal income tax, the direct election of United States senators, the people's right to initiate laws, and the unlimited coinage of silver (pp. 470–471)

Analyzing the Facts

1. Answers will vary. Possible answers are: vote, run for office, and keep informed of what officeholders are doing.
2. Answers will vary. Choices could be based on ethnic or religious background, area of the country in which the student lives, or party philosophies in the late 1800's.
3. It could prevent any one candidate from receiving enough electoral votes to win, or it could draw voters away from one of the major parties, giving a victory to the other major party.
4. Answers will vary. Possible answers are: the Presidents were generally weak leaders; industry dominated American life, and the government did not interfere with business; it is hard to think of anything specific to associate with each President of this time.
5. Answers will vary. Inflation would raise

wages, and debts could be paid off in dollars with less value than those borrowed. But it would raise the price of food, housing, and so on.

Time and History
1. Republican party **2.** James Garfield served only four months. **3.** Benjamin Harrison **4.** 3 years **5.** Grover Cleveland

Chapter 22
A Show of Strength
pp. 476–495

ACTIVITIES

Level A: Have students design the front page of a newspaper in the style of yellow journalism. Students should select one event from the chapter and exaggerate the events to make them descriptive and vivid.
Level B: On an outline map of the world, have students color in the areas where the United States became politically involved in the late 1800's. Those areas that became possessions of the United States should be colored green. Areas of American involvement should be colored red. Have students put dates on their maps to indicate when the United States took possession of the area or when the United States became involved in the affairs of the area.

ANSWERS

Section 1 Review *p. 481*

1. Owners of America's farms and factories (p. 477)
2. Expansionists are people who believe a nation should expand its territory or power. (p. 477)
3. Cuba, Greenland, Iceland, the Danish West Indies, the Midway Islands, Alaska. He was successful in acquiring the Midway Islands and Alaska. (p. 478)
4. To keep China open for American traders (pp. 480–481)
5. Answers will vary. Alaska has valuable supplies of petroleum, fish, and wood products. Hawaii produces sugar, fruits and vegetables, and clothing.

Section 2 Review *p. 487*

1. Cuba was freed from Spanish control, and Spain ceded the Philippine Islands, Puerto Rico, and Guam to the United States for $20 million. (pp. 486–487)
2. Yellow journalism is the use of exciting but exaggerated news stories to make a newspaper more popular. (p. 482)
3. To free Cuba from Spanish control because of the destruction of the *Maine* (pp. 482–483)
4. Commodore George Dewey and Theodore Roosevelt (pp. 484–485, 487)
5. Answers will vary. Possible answers are: annex the territories to the United States or grant them independence.

Social Studies Skills *p. 488*

1. Propaganda is the spreading of information for the purpose of furthering one's own cause or damaging an opposing one.
2. Answers will vary. Possible answers are: Card stacking—"Naval Officers Unanimous That the Ship Was Destroyed on Purpose;" Name-calling—enemy, criminals; Bandwagon—everyone thinks the destruction of the *Maine* was the work of an enemy.
3. Transfer
4. So that propaganda is not confused with objective factual information

Section 3 Review *p. 493*

1. The Roosevelt Corollary, the acquisition of the Panama Canal Zone, the agreement with Japan to limit Japanese immigration, and the negotiation of a peace settlement ending the Russo-Japanese War. Roosevelt pushed the United States to the center of world affairs. (pp. 490–493)
2. It would reduce the travel time from one coast of the United States to the other. It

would also make trade much easier between the eastern United States and Asia. (p. 490)

3. Intervene means to interfere by military force in the internal affairs of another nation. The United States took over the collection of taxes on imported goods in the Dominican Republic. This prevented European governments from intervening to collect money owed to their citizens. (p. 491)
4. Answers will vary. Roosevelt was weak as a child and was teased by older bullies. As President, Roosevelt took forceful action in obtaining the Panama Canal Zone. He announced the Roosevelt Corollary to protect Latin American countries from European "bullying."

Chapter Review *pp. 494–495*

Recalling the Facts

1. Owners of America's farms and factories. They were producing more goods than they could sell to American consumers. They needed other markets. (p. 477)
2. For better defense. Naval patrols from the bases also could protect American shipping. (p. 478)
3. To stop the bloodshed in Cuba, to get revenge for the *Maine* (pp. 482–483)
4. The United States helped the Panamanians become independent. The new nation of Panama leased the canal zone to the United States. (p. 490)
5. The Midway Islands, Alaska, the Hawaiian Islands, Puerto Rico, Guam, and the Philippine Islands (pp. 478, 480, 486)

Analyzing the Facts

1. The war lasted only ten weeks, there were few casualties, and the United States gained control of new territories.
2. They still serve as defense bases, markets for manufactured goods, sources of raw materials and agricultural products.
3. It means that words should be backed up with military force, if necessary. Answers will vary. Yes—it would show other countries that the United States backs its words with military action. No—it could lead to war. (p. 491)
4. Roosevelt took an active role in international affairs, and he was an expansionist.
5. Answers will vary. Possible answers are: No—the canal is still important to American defense; Yes—the canal is no longer vital to American defense, and it is too costly to operate.

Time and History

1. Alaska and the Midway Islands **2.** Theodore Roosevelt **3.** Gentlemen's Agreement **4.** 1 year **5.** He worked to end the war between Russia and Japan.

Unit Review *pp. 496–497*

Recalling the Facts

1. Farmers, ranchers, and miners moved onto the plains in large numbers, and the Plains Indians were removed to reservations. (pp. 399, 405, 410)
2. Abundant natural resources, a large work force, talented entrepreneurs, corporations, mass production methods, and help from the government (pp. 419–422)
3. They were attracted by the democratic way of life and job opportunities. The New Immigrants came from southern and eastern Europe. (pp. 439–441)
4. A desire among workers for higher wages, shorter working hours, and better working conditions (pp. 450–451)
5. Owners of American farms and factories (p. 477)

Analyzing the Facts

1. Big businesses often lowered their prices to such an extent that small businesses were unable to compete.
2. Immigrants in both periods came to escape religious persecution and to make a better life for themselves.
3. People may believe that their interests and concerns are not being met within the two-party system.
4. Prior to the war, America took little inter-

est in world affairs. The Spanish-American War was the first time America assumed a leadership role in world affairs.

Reviewing Vocabulary
assimilate, p. 403; homesteader, p. 414; speculator, p. 414; stock, p. 420; *laissez-faire,* p. 422; entrepreneur, p. 420; ethnic, p. 446; collective bargaining, p. 453; injunction, p. 455; inflation, p. 470; sphere of influence, p. 481; yellow journalism, p. 482.

Sharpening Your Skills
1. 16.8 percent
2. 1860
3. The percentage living in rural areas decreased by 16.8 percent from 1860 to 1900.
4. name calling; that the Spanish treated Cubans brutally
5. They were written to arouse public opinion against the Spanish in Cuba. They presented only one side of the picture.

Unit 7: REFORM, WAR, REACTION

Chapter 23
Reform in America
pp. 500–521

ACTIVITIES

Level A: Have students write a letter to their state or congressional representative about a national problem they would like to see solved. Have them briefly describe the problem and suggest solutions. Make sure students are sufficiently informed about the problem before they write their letters. Encourage them to read the newspaper and/or listen to the news prior to this activity.
Level B: During the progressive era, many people, like Jane Addams, worked to help the needy. Have students organize a school-wide project to help a group of needy citizens. Contact a local charitable organization, hospital, or nursing home for suggestions of how your class could be of help. When the project is completed, ask students to share their feelings on their involvement in this type of activity.

ANSWERS

Section 1 Review *p. 505*

1. They were journalists who uncovered corruption and poverty in America in the early 1900's. They made millions of people aware of the need for reform. (p. 501)
2. A direct primary is an election to nominate candidates to run in the general election. The initiative is a process by which people can propose a law and submit it for approval by the voters or the legislature. The referendum is a process by which people can approve or reject a law. The recall is a petition signed by voters calling for a special election in which the voters would decide if an official should remain in office. (p. 503)
3. Suffrage is the right to vote. (p. 504) In 1920, the Nineteenth Amendment was ratified, giving all women the right to vote. (p. 505)
4. Answers will vary. Possible answers include: industrial pollution, corruption in government, false advertising, poverty in the cities. Modern-day muckrakers include: investigative reporters, insiders who leak information to the press, and special interest groups.

Social Studies Skills *p. 506*

1. 10 years old
2. The South, because the mill appears to be well-lighted, large, and has many windows.
3. Yes, her clothing appears to be in poor condition. She is working while other girls her age, who came from wealthier families, would probably be in school.
4. It makes the written description clearer

and more vivid.

Section 2 Review *p. 510*

1. Solving social problems, getting new laws passed to regulate big business, working for greater federal control over the railroads, and conserving the nation's natural resources (p. 507)
2. The Elkins Railroad Act made rebates illegal. The Hepburn Act gave the ICC the power to set maximum shipping rates. The Mann-Elkins Act extended the power of the ICC to regulate telephone and telegraph rates. (pp. 507–508)
3. The regulation of corporations and a minimum wage for all workers (p. 509)
4. The Federal Trade Commission and the Clayton Antitrust Act. The FTC could stop businesses from engaging in unfair methods of competition. The Clayton Antitrust Act outlawed business combinations that destroyed competition or controlled an industry. (p. 510)
5. Answers will vary. Students should be reminded that a President depends upon the cooperation of Congress to help achieve national goals.

Section 3 Review *p. 514*

1. The progressives ignored the problems of the New Immigrants and of black Americans. (p. 511)
2. Racism is the belief that people of one race are, by nature, inferior to people of another race. (p. 511) Nativism is similar because it is the belief that people who are immigrants are inferior to people who are native-born citizens of a country. (p. 443)
3. Washington was born a slave in the South. He believed that it was foolish and dangerous for blacks to try to fight the system of segregation. He believed that blacks should concentrate on learning better agricultural and industrial skills. Du Bois was born free in the North. He urged blacks to protest and fight segregation. He believed blacks should demand full equality of opportunity in all things. Du Bois also believed that higher education should be available to black students. (p. 513)
4. Answers will vary. Although racial discrimination is illegal today in almost every area of American life, patterns of segregation continue in housing and public education. Unemployment is highest among young blacks. Income levels for blacks are lower than for whites.

Section 4 Review *p. 519*

1. Literature and painting focused on describing the experiences of the common people. A greater attempt was made to portray people and life as they actually were. (pp. 515–517)
2. He suggested that the outward form of a building should express the building's function. (p. 517)
3. John Dewey. A proper education was learning to understand the problems of society and becoming able to solve them. Dewey also believed that children could best "learn by doing." (p. 517)
4. Americans enjoyed spectator sports such as professional baseball, amusement parks, and motion pictures. (p. 519)
5. Answers will vary. Home video games are one new form of entertainment. Entertainment can be harmful if it distracts people from other important activities and responsibilities.

Chapter Review *pp. 520–521*

Recalling the Facts

1. Tarbell—Rockefeller's use of rebates and cut-throat competition; Steffens—the practice of paying bribes and kickbacks to corrupt city bosses; Sinclair—the unsanitary conditions in the Chicago stockyards and meat-packing industry; Norris—how the Southern Pacific Railroad was strangling California wheat farmers (p. 501)
2. Galveston—city commission form; Staunton—city manager form (p. 502)
3. Two major concerns of women during the

progressive era were winning the right to vote and greater rights as workers. (pp. 504–505)

4. Roosevelt lost the Republican nomination to Taft. He refused to accept defeat; he and his Republican followers formed the Progressive Party. (p. 509)
5. Many progressives believed that the new immigrants from southern and eastern Europe were "inferior." Also, immigrants benefited from the services of the city bosses whom the progressives attacked. Many immigrants voted for the bosses' candidates. (p. 511)
6. Steel-beam construction and electric elevators made it possible to build skyscrapers. (p. 517)

Analyzing the Facts

1. The direct election of U.S. senators, an income tax, and the initiative
2. Roosevelt felt that most business combinations should be regulated. Taft believed that many large business combinations should be broken up. Roosevelt set aside millions of hectares (acres) of forest land as national forests. Under Taft, some of these lands were removed from federal protection.
3. The "Bull Moose" Party split the Republican vote which helped Wilson to win. Wilson received the full support of the Democratic party.
4. Answers will vary. Possible answers are: Washington's methods—When whites realized that blacks were as skilled and educated as the white population, whites would have to recognize equality and end segregation; Du Bois' methods—The only way to achieve equality is through protest and legal action.
5. Sullivan's buildings reflected the *real* purpose or function of the building. Art and architecture both reflected reality.

Time and History

1. 12 years **2.** Oregon **3.** Mann-Elkins Act **4.** 4 years **5.** baseball and motion pictures **6.** Theodore Roosevelt

Chapter 24 World War I

pp. 522–541

ACTIVITIES

Level A: Have each student design a poster that might have appeared during World War I encouraging Americans to enlist in the armed forces or to buy Liberty Bonds. Review the propaganda techniques discussed in the skill feature in Chapter 22. Direct students to use one or more of these techniques in designing their posters. Display the finished posters in the classroom. Have students choose the posters they think are the most effective and discuss why.

Level B: Divide the class into three groups. Assign each group the task of preparing one-third of a bulletin board display on World War I. Group 1 should prepare a display of new weapons that were introduced during World War I. Group 2 should prepare a display of military uniforms worn during World War I. Group 3 should prepare pictures of what people on the home-front did to support the war effort.

ANSWERS

Section 1 Review *p. 528*

1. They were competing for control of foreign territory and markets in Asia and Africa. People were becoming more nationalistic. Each nation was building up its military forces. (p. 525)
2. A pacifist is a person who believes that international disputes should be settled by peaceful means rather than by force or violence. Bryan helped negotiate a series of "cooling-off" treaties among 30 nations of the world. These treaties provided that disputes among the nations be submitted to an international commission for peaceful solutions. (p. 523)
3. A blockade is the isolation of a country at

war to prevent the passage and delivery of goods. (p. 360) The British blockade effectively reduced trade between the United States and the Central Powers. At the same time, American trade with the Allies soared. (p. 528)

4. Many Americans were immigrants or the children of immigrants from the nations engaged in the war. Allied propaganda aroused American sympathies for the Allies. American trade with the warring nations made neutrality difficult, especially as trade came to be almost entirely with the Allies. (pp. 527–528)
5. Answers will vary. Some recent wars include: the Falkland Islands war, the war between Iran and Iraq, and the Arab-Israeli wars. Propaganda, economic interests, political interests, and ethnic ties may make neutrality difficult.

Section 2 Review *p. 534*

1. American fighting forces gave the Allies the added strength they needed to defeat the Central Powers. American naval vessels provided protection for merchant ships carrying needed supplies to the Allies. American industry organized and expanded to produce the military goods needed for an Allied victory. (pp. 529–533)
2. In 1917, the Germans resumed unrestricted submarine warfare, the Zimmermann note was intercepted by the British, German submarines sank four American ships, and the United States declared war on Germany and entered World War I. (pp. 529–530)
3. A convoy is a protective escort for ships or troops. (p. 533) An armistice is a truce that stops the fighting of a war. (p. 534)
4. Airplanes, the rapid-firing machine gun, barbed wire, poison gas, tanks (pp. 532–533)
5. Answers will vary. Probably the most important reason was the German decision to resume submarine warfare. This was a threat to American neutrality and safety.

Section 3 Review *p. 538*

1. All people should be guaranteed the right to live under a government of their own choosing. Freedom of the seas and the removal of trading barriers should be guaranteed. Treaties should be openly negotiated. Each nation should reduce its stockpiles of weapons. A general association of nation's should be formed to guarantee the independence and security of all nations and to settle disputes among nations peacefully. (p. 535)
2. He did not choose any senators or prominent Republicans to serve on the peace commission. The Republican-controlled Senate would have to approve any treaty negotiated at Versailles. (p. 535)
3. Reparations are payments by a defeated nation for damages caused during a war. Germany was required to pay $56 billion in reparations. (p. 536)
4. Some Americans opposed the treaty because it violated so many of the Fourteen Points. Other Americans opposed it because it included the League of Nations. They feared that if the United States joined the League, it would become permanently involved in the disputes of Europe. (p. 537)
5. Answers will vary. Some may blame the Republican senators who were reservationists or irreconcilables. Others may blame Wilson for his mistakes in picking members of the peace commission. Wilson could also be blamed for his unwillingness to compromise. Lodge's actions could also be mentioned.

Social Studies Skills *p. 539*

1. Austria, Hungary, Czechoslovakia, Estonia, Latvia, Lithuania, Poland, Yugoslavia
2. Serbia, Montenegro, Austria-Hungary
3. Russia, Germany, Austria-Hungary
4. They were neutral nations during the war.

Chapter Review *pp. 540–541*

Recalling the Facts

1. To keep peace in the world. They agreed

to submit disputes to an international commission. In the meantime, they promised not to go to war. (p. 523)

2. Allied Powers—Great Britain, France, Russia, Italy; Central Powers—Germany, Austria-Hungary, Turkey (p. 525)
3. The message was sent from the German foreign minister to Mexico. It proposed that Mexico join Germany in war against the United States in exchange for "lost territory in Texas, New Mexico, and Arizona" when the war was over. The American people were outraged. (p. 529)
4. Americans bought Liberty Bonds and paid extra taxes. Many women took jobs in factories. The government organized the nation's industries to produce more. (pp. 530–532)
5. The treaty violated many of Wilson's Fourteen Points. But he was proud of it because: (1) the newly drawn borders of the European nations left fewer people on "foreign soil" than at any other time in history; (2) Germany's former colonies were to be prepared for independence; and (3) it included a provision for a League of Nations. (pp. 536–537)

Analyzing the Facts

1. Unrest had been building in Europe for years as a result of imperialism, nationalism, the build up of military forces, and the forming of alliances. The assassination caused these hostilities to erupt into a world war.
2. Free trade was important to the economic well-being of the country.
3. Answers will vary. Possible answers are: Yes, Americans had been killed long before the United States declared war; No, many more Americans would have died if the United States had entered earlier.
4. Answers will vary. Possible answers are: The group that supported Wilson—The United States was a world power and should assume its share of responsibility for preserving world peace; Reservationists—The United States should take military action only if such action is supported by the American people; Irreconcilables—The United States should not become involved in the affairs of other nations.
5. Answers will vary. Possible answers are: war would have come regardless, because the Versailles Treaty was so harsh. Also, the United Nations has not been very effective in preventing wars in the last 40 years. If the United States had joined, the League might have been able to prevent war by organizing worldwide opposition toward aggressor nations.

Time and History

1. 4 years **2.** 3 years **3.** German U-boat sinks *Lusitania;* 1915 **4.** The Zimmermann Message **5.** Russia had made a separate peace with the Central Powers in 1918 before the armistice ending World War I was signed.

Chapter 25
The Roaring Twenties
pp. 542–561

ACTIVITIES

Level A: Divide the class in half, and have one group research the Sacco and Vanzetti trial while the other group researches the Scopes trial. Students should then reenact the trials by role-playing. Each group should choose students to play the parts of the judge, the defendant(s), the lawyer(s) for the accused, the prosecutor, and the witnesses. Each group will present their case to the other half of the class who will act as jurors. A discussion can be held following the role plays on how these trials were reflective of American attitudes during the 1920's.
Level B: Divide the class into three groups. Have each group prepare a 3 to 5 minute radio broadcast on one of the following: Lindbergh's departure from Roosevelt Field, Lindbergh's return from Paris, the world premiere of the first talking motion picture.

In addition, have students create a 30-second commercial for an imaginary company selling one of the new labor-saving appliances of the 1920's. Have the students tape-record their scripts. Play the recordings for the entire class the next day.

ANSWERS

Section 1 Review *p. 547*

1. American industries expanded to supply the goods needed by Europe as it recovered from the war. There was an increased demand for goods among Americans after the war. Government policies and the growth of new industries also contributed to prosperity. (pp. 543–544)
2. The automobile contributed to the growth of the steel, rubber, oil, glass, and paint industries. More roadways were paved. Restaurants, motels, gas stations, and the tourist industry all expanded to provide for the needs of American drivers. (p. 544)
3. A consumer society is a society in which people buy goods for the pleasure of buying them rather than because of need. Many residents of America's cities came to regard as necessities goods that earlier had been luxuries. Household appliances were purchased in great quantities. Advertisers created other needs by boosting the virtues of other "consumer goods." (p. 545)
4. Many American writers believed that American society was becoming too concerned with material wealth and was losing sight of its ideals. (p. 547)
5. Americans had had enough of war and international crises. They were also tired of idealism and reform.

Section 2 Review *p. 551*

1. They wanted to avoid becoming involved in another war after experiencing the horror of World War I. (p. 548)
2. Communism is an economic system in which all property, in theory, is owned by the people and managed by the national government. Federal agents arrested suspected radicals and deported some of them. Two Italian radicals, Nicola Sacco and Bartolomeo Vanzetti, were executed for murder. (p. 549)
3. The Ku Klux Klan opposed blacks, new immigrants from southern and eastern Europe, Catholics, and Jews. (p. 550)
4. Good effects: It reduced the amount of alcohol consumed by the average American. Bad effects: It contributed to the rise of organized crime. (p. 551)
5. Answers will vary. The differences of the 1920's may be less today than then. New issues, however, continue to divide Americans of the cities and the countryside.

Section 3 Review *p. 555*

1. Attorney General Harry Daugherty sold pardons and paroles to criminals. Veterans Bureau Director Charles R. Forbes demanded and received kickbacks from businesses selling goods to the Bureau. Secretary of the Interior Albert B. Fall accepted bribes for allowing private oil companies to lease government oil reserves. (pp. 553–554)
2. Coolidge believed that the government should interfere as little as possible with business or other activities of the nation. Coolidge, himself, was a man of little action and few words. (p. 554)
3. Taxes on corporations were cut by more than half. Tariffs were raised to protect industries from foreign competition. Businesses were encouraged to cooperate with each other by exchanging information about products and markets. Business leaders were appointed to serve on the Interstate Commerce Commission, the Federal Trade Commission, and the Federal Reserve Board. (p. 554)
4. The biggest factor in Hoover's victory was the Republican record of prosperity. Other factors were that many voters in the countryside rejected Smith because he was a

New Yorker and an opponent of prohibition. Other people voted against Smith because he was a Catholic. (p. 555)

5. Answers will vary. Students should recognize that of the three Presidents, Hoover had the most extensive background in serving the government.

Section 4 Review *p. 559*

1. The coal industry declined as many factories switched from coal to oil as their primary fuel. The cotton and wool cloth industries declined as many Americans began buying clothing made from synthetic fabrics. The construction and automobile industries had expanded too rapidly. As the demand for automobiles fell and auto production declined, industries related to the automobile also declined. (p. 556)
2. Overproduction. Improvements in farm machinery and farming methods. (p. 557)
3. In the 1920's, workers and farmers were not earning enough to buy the products of American industry. The installment plan enabled Americans to buy goods by only paying a small part of the total price of the items. (p. 558)
4. Most daily newspapers in major cities print the prices of stocks on the New York Stock Exchange. If prices are up, it is a "bull market." If prices are going down, it is a "bear market."

Chapter Review *pp. 560–561*

Recalling the Facts

1. It ended the isolation of many rural areas. It spurred the growth of suburbs. (p. 545)
2. Women began to enter the labor force in large numbers. They also began to have more social freedom. (p. 547)
3. Possible answers are: unjustified arrest of immigrant citizens during the Red Scare, race riots, rebirth of the KKK, new laws limiting the immigration of "undesirable" groups. (pp. 549–550)
4. Support for Prohibition was strongest in the countryside and weakest in the cities. Many people in the countryside agreed with the law that caused Scopes' arrest. Many city newspapers ridiculed the law. (p. 551)
5. They believed that government should play a limited role in the nation's affairs. (p. 552)
6. Farmers—Farm prices dropped because too much food was being produced; Workers—Their increases in wages were far below the increases in profits for the business owners; government did little to help either group. (pp. 557–558)

Analyzing the Facts

1. Americans were tired of war, idealism, and reform. They longed for "good times." He offered no new ideals or reforms, and he called for a "return to normalcy."
2. There were no means to enforce the promises made in the treaties.
3. Most black Americans had been born in the United States and considered it home. Also, by the 1920's, most of Africa had been colonized by Europeans.
4. Answers will vary. Possible answers are: He recognized his own limits and chose many talented people to serve in his administration; he did not try to cover up the scandals in his administration.

Time and History

1. 1923–1929 **2.** 6 years **3.** 1920
4. 1921 and 1924 **5.** Fitzgerald

Unit Review *pp. 562–563*

Recalling the Facts

1. Direct primary—all citizens could vote in a special election to select their party's candidate; Initiative—people could propose laws; Referendum—a process by which people can approve or reject a law; Recall—allows people to challenge any elected official at any time and possibly remove him or her from office (p. 503)
2. Any of the following: Elkins Railroad Act—made the giving and receiving of rebates

illegal; Hepburn Act—gave the ICC the power to set maximum shipping rates charged by the railroads; Mann-Elkins Act—extended the power of the ICC to regulate telephone and telegraph rates; the Federal Trade Commission—stopped businesses from engaging in unfair methods of competition; Clayton Antitrust Act—outlawed business combinations that destroyed competition or that controlled an industry. (pp. 507–508, 510)

3. In March 1917, German U-boats sank four American merchant ships killing many Americans. (p. 529)
4. They were the principles upon which Wilson believed the peace should be based. They included the right of self-determination for all people, freedom of the seas, the removal of trade barriers, the reduction of weapons stockpiles, and the formation of a League of Nations. Wilson saw the Fourteen Points as a way to avoid future wars. (p. 535)
5. United States industries expanded to supply the goods needed by Europe as it recovered from the war and to meet the American demand for goods of all kinds, high tariffs; lower taxes on corporation profits; and the growth of new industries. (p. 543)

Analyzing the Facts

1. During the progressive era, government attempted to regulate business affairs. In the 1920's, government returned to a *laissez-faire* policy toward business.
2. The war was fought over a large land area, new and more destructive weapons were used, and millions of civilians and military personnel were involved in the fighting.
3. Answers will vary. Possible answers are: Alliances lead to war—If one member of an alliance is attacked, all members are obligated to become involved; Alliances do not lead to war—They may keep nations from attacking because of the threat of so much opposition.
4. Supportive—It protects the United States from potentially troublesome people like revolutionaries. Destructive—It does not allow people to think or act freely, and goes against the principles of the nation.

Reviewing Vocabulary

suffrage, p. 504; racism, p. 511; pacifist, p. 523; nationalism, p. 525; armistice, p. 534; self-determination, p. 535; reparations, p. 536; alienated, p. 547; disarmament, p. 549; installment plan, p. 558; interest, p. 558

Sharpening Your Skills

1. About 17 to 35 years old
2. There was a comraderie among the soldiers.
3. Answers will vary.
4. Washington and California
5. Vermont

Unit 8: DEPRESSION AND WAR

Chapter 26
The Great Depression
pp. 566–585

ACTIVITIES

Level A: Have students prepare a chart of the New Deal legislation. The chart should show the name of the act, the date it was passed, its basic purpose, and whether it was intended to provide relief, recovery, and/or reform. A final column should list any unusual features of the act, such as if it was declared unconstitutional.

Level B: Have students pretend they are American workers living during the Great Depression. Ask them to write three diary entries describing their lives (a) just after the stock market crash in 1929; (b) in the fall of 1932, telling who they will vote for in the presidential election and why; and (c) after

Roosevelt's election when the economy begins to recover. Each diary entry should describe what life was like for workers and their families, what problems they had, what they worried about, and so on.

ANSWERS

Section 1 Review *p. 571*

1. He urged voluntary cooperation from business and farmers. He encouraged Congress to pass the Agricultural Marketing Act that provided loans to farm cooperatives to buy surplus crops. He supported passage of the Hawley-Smoot Tariff that raised the tariff on most foreign manufactured goods and farm products. He persuaded Congress to create the Reconstruction Finance Corporation that loaned money to banks, railroads, and other businesses. (pp. 569–570)
2. A depression is a period in which business activity slows, prices and wages decline, and many workers lose their jobs. (p. 567) The unemployment rate is the percentage of workers who are jobless. (p. 569)
3. The stock market crash; the "drying up" of investment money; the poor distribution of wealth; overproduction; insufficient government regulation of business; high tariffs (pp. 567–568)
4. Answers will vary. Hoover supported and identified himself with the Republican economic policies of the 1920's, which contributed to the depression. Hoover alone, however, was not to blame. The causes of the depression were the deep weaknesses in the American economy.

Section 2 Review *p. 577*

1. Farmers—Agricultural Adjustment Act; business—National Industrial Recovery Act, Federal Housing Administration; workers—National Recovery Administration, Public Works Administration, Civilian Conservation Corps, Federal Emergency Relief Administration, Works Progress Administration (pp. 573–577)
2. A bank holiday is a temporary closing of the nation's banks. (p. 572) A devaluation is a reduction in value. (p. 573) Parity is the equality of value of current farm products with the value of farm products in another period. (p. 573)
3. FDIC—the Federal Deposit Insurance Corporation insured bank deposits up to $5,000 for each depositor. (p. 572) PWA—the Public Works Administration increased federal spending for large construction projects that would benefit the public. (p. 574) CCC—the Civilian Conservation Corps recruited young men to work on projects in the countryside. (pp. 575–576) TVA—the Tennessee Valley Authority bought, built, and operated dams in the Tennessee Valley to provide flood control and cheap electricity to the people in this region. (p. 577)
4. Answers will vary. Students might identify areas of the rural South, the central cities across the nation, Indian reservations in the Southwest or Far West, or areas close to their own communities.

Section 3 Review *p. 583*

1. The New Deal expanded the role and responsibilities of the federal government in economic hard times. The New Deal affected the lives of many Americans. (pp. 582–583)
2. An industrial union is an organization of all workers of an industry in a single union. (p. 579) Deficit spending is a government policy of spending more money each year than is collected in taxes. (pp. 582–583) A coalition is an alliance of several groups of supporters behind a political candidate or party. (p. 583)
3. Under the Indian Reorganization Act passed in 1934, the federal government began acquiring more land for American Indians. The IRA also gave American Indians a greater role in government on the reservations. Seventy-two CCC projects were set aside for unemployed Indians in 15 western states. Other New Deal pro-

grams brought work to the reservations. (p. 582)

4. Answers will vary. Many of the regulatory commissions and programs created by the New Deal are still in existence, such as the SEC, the NLRB, Social Security, the FDIC, and the TVA. Deficit spending continues. Unions remain protected by federal guarantees.

Chapter Review *pp. 584–585*

Recalling the Facts

1. As stock prices began to drop, shareholders feared they would not be able to pay their debts. People rushed to sell their stocks. Their selling of stock caused prices to drop more rapidly. (p. 567)
2. Banks had not been properly regulated by the government in the 1920's. Many had made poor use of their depositors' money. When people came to withdraw their money, the banks were unable to pay them. (p. 568)
3. Communities of homeless people, living in crude shelters, were called "Hoovervilles." Unemployed men who slept on park benches called their newspaper bedsheets "Hoover blankets." People with no money wore "Hoover flags," empty pockets turned inside out. (p. 570)
4. The CCC created federal jobs for unemployed men, ages 18 to 25. These men worked on projects that conserved the nation's natural resources. The WPA provided jobs for unemployed workers by putting them to work building hospitals, post offices, schools, and bridges. (pp. 575–577)
5. The Supreme Court had declared seven major programs or agencies of the New Deal unconstitutional. Roosevelt wanted to be able to appoint justices to the Supreme Court who would be sympathetic to the New Deal. (p. 580)

Analyzing the Facts

1. Americans who had invested in the stock market had little or no money to buy factory products; as a result, factories closed and many workers lost their jobs.
2. Answers will vary, but should include the idea that the need was too great for charitable organizations to handle, and contributions to such organizations probably decreased because fewer people could afford to give to charity.
3. Roosevelt's confidence gave many Americans hope. Fireside chats and frequent press conferences boosted the nation's spirits. He was willing to listen to others and to change his plans, if necessary.
4. Answers will vary. Possible answers are: Agree—Too many people have become dependent on the government for handouts. People do not save enough for retirement because they know they will receive Social Security from the government; Disagree—The government should be responsible for helping those truly in need. It would be a disgrace for the government, which has the ability to help, to allow people to suffer needlessly.

Time and History

1. 4 years **2.** Hawley-Smoot Tariff **3.** 3 years **4.** No years; alphabet agencies were created in the same year Roosevelt became President **5.** Farm Tenancy Act

Chapter 27
Seeds of Conflict *pp. 586–604*

ACTIVITIES

Level A: Hold a congressional debate over the kind and amount of aid the United States should give the Allies in 1940. Have half of the class represent and argue the isolationist position in 1940; the other half will take Roosevelt's position. Appoint one student to preside over the Congress. The presiding officer will recognize persons to speak and will keep order. When the debate is over, have students write two brief paragraphs summarizing the main arguments of each side.

Level B: Have students make a timeline

showing the years 1931–1941. Have them label the timeline with the events that led to World War II and the events of the first two years of the war. Direct students to show all dated events in Chapter 27, or you may wish to prepare a list of events to be shown for them.

ANSWERS

Section 1 Review *p. 593*

1. They created their own private armed forces or secret police; they used propaganda; they brutally treated opponents; they outlawed political parties that opposed them; they preached an intense nationalism; they followed a policy of aggression. (p. 587)
2. Aggression is unprovoked attack or invasion. (p. 587) Appeasement is the policy of giving in to the demands of an aggressor in an attempt to avoid further trouble. (p. 593)
3. Adolf Hitler believed that Germany should expand its borders over all territories where German-speaking people lived. Hitler maintained that all lands taken from Germany under the Treaty of Versailles should be restored to Germany. Hitler also believed that the German people were a "superior race" and therefore *deserved* more living space. (p. 591)
4. Answers will vary. An alternative would have been for the Allies to hold firm against Hitler. This policy might have discouraged Hitler from further aggressive acts. However, students should recall that most Europeans were anxious to avoid another war, and this led to the policy of appeasement.

Section 2 Review *p. 597*

1. Germany—the invasion and occupation of western Poland; the invasion of Denmark, Norway, Luxembourg, the Netherlands, and Belgium; the invasion and occupation of northern France; air attacks on Great Britain; the recapture of Libya; the defeat of Greece and Yugoslavia; the invasion of the Soviet Union. Italy—the invasion and occupation of southern France, the invasion of Greece, attacks on the British in Egypt. Japan—continued assaults on China (pp. 594–597)
2. An underground is a secret movement organized to overthrow a government or the occupation forces of an enemy. (p. 595) Radar is an electronic device that detects objects at long distance. (p. 596)
3. Yes. The Germans were unsuccessful in the battle of Britain. The Italians were forced out of Greece and suffered some setbacks in North Africa. The Germans failed to capture Moscow and were driven back by the Soviets. (pp. 596–597)
4. Answers will vary. Possible answers include that when people saw their homes, businesses, and public buildings destroyed as well as friends, family, and neighbors wounded or killed, it made them more determined to resist the Germans.

Section 3 Review *p. 602*

1. The American response was to pursue a policy of neutrality. (p. 599)
2. Diplomatic recognition is the formal acceptance or recognition by one nation of the government of another. (p. 599) To quarantine is to separate a diseased person or group from the rest of the population to keep the disease from spreading. (p. 600)
3. The Neutrality Act of 1935 prohibited the sale of military supplies or weapons to any nation engaged in war. The act also warned Americans that if they traveled on the ships of a warring nation, they did so at their own risk. The Neutrality Act of 1937 provided that any nation at war could buy nonmilitary goods from the United States only by paying cash. The warring nation would also have to transport the goods from the United States on its own ships. The neutrality acts were designed to

keep the United States out of war. No loans would be made to either side, and no American ships would be sunk. (p. 599)

4. No. In 1939, the United States allowed the Allies to buy military supplies on a "cash and carry" basis. In 1941, the "cash and carry" portions of the neutrality acts were replaced by the Lend-Lease Act that loaned the Allies $50 billion worth of military supplies. American warships began accompanying vessels carrying military supplies to Great Britain. (pp. 600–601)
5. Answers will vary. Students should focus on the main points of the national debate in their answers: Hitler was not just a threat to the Allied nations but to the entire human race; American involvement would only result in a defeat at the hands of the powerful Axis nations.

Social Studies Skills *p. 603*

1. Roosevelt thought that the United States should send military supplies to the Allies to help them defeat the Axis Powers.
2. Lindbergh did not believe that England could win the war even with the type of assistance Roosevelt proposed.
3. Lindbergh thought that the United States should maintain its armed forces so that the Western Hemisphere could defend itself in the event of an attack.
4. Answers will vary.

Chapter Review *pp. 604–605*

Recalling the Facts

1. Dissatisfaction with the Treaty of Versailles and the worldwide depression of the 1930's (p. 587)
2. Japan invaded the Chinese province of Manchuria in 1931 and began an invasion of the rest of China in 1937. Italy attacked Ethiopia in 1935 and Albania in 1939. Germany moved troops into the Rhineland in 1933 and Austria in 1938. In 1938, Germany also took over the Sudetenland and seized the rest of Czechoslovakia in March 1939. (pp. 590–593)
3. World War II began on September 3, 1939, two days after the German army invaded Poland. (p. 593)
4. More than 900 British vessels went across the English Channel to rescue Allied soldiers being pushed toward the channel by the advancing German armies. About 338,000 men were rescued. (p. 595)
5. The United States agreed not to interfere in the internal or external affairs of Latin American nations. This was a reversal of the Roosevelt Corollary, announced by Theodore Roosevelt in 1904. (p. 598)

Analyzing the Facts

1. Yes. Power in the United States government is divided among three branches. Each branch checks and balances the power of the other two.
2. This was probably not wise because it forced Germany to fight the war on two fronts.
3. Hitler signed a nonaggression pact with the Soviet Union because he wanted to avoid having to fight a war on two fronts. In this pact, the two nations agreed not to attack each other. Later, Hitler broke the pact by attacking the Soviet Union.
4. Answers will vary. Possible answers are: The United States, a major world power, was not a member; the League had no power to force nations to take action against aggressors; the member nations could not agree on what action to take.

Time and History

1. 20 years **2.** Japan; Manchuria in 1931
3. 12 years **4.** Good Neighbor policy
5. 1 year

Chapter 28
World War II *pp. 606–625*

ACTIVITIES

Level A: Have students prepare a bulletin board display on World War II. Divide the bulletin board into three sections. Label the sections "The European Front," "The Pacific Front," and "The Home Front." Divide the class into three groups, and assign each group to prepare one section of the bulletin board. Suggested items include sketches, maps, pictures, posters, charts, and graphs. **Level B:** Invite three people with first-hand knowledge of the United States' involvement in World War II to speak to the class about their experiences. Each of the three speakers should represent one of the three war fronts—the Pacific front, the European front, and the home front. Have each speaker give a brief account of his or her experiences during the war. Allow time following the presentations for a general question and answer period.

ANSWERS

Section 1 Review *p. 613*

1. Battle of Coral Sea, battle of Midway, battle of El Alamein, defeat of French and German forces in North Africa, defeat of the German forces in Italy and France, island-hopping victories on Guadalcanal, the Marshall Islands, the Marianas, the Carolines, the Philippines, Iwo Jima, and Okinawa (pp. 607–613)
2. Unconditional surrender is the surrender of a defeated nation on the terms set by the victors. (p. 610) Island hopping was an American military strategy during World War II to force the Japanese to give up their conquered islands by fighting on each one. (p. 613)
3. Victory in North Africa gave the Allies a solid base from which to attack southern Europe. Victory in Italy meant that an important area of southern Europe was securely under Allied control. (pp. 610, 611)
4. Isoroku Yamamoto—the commander of the Japanese fleet (p. 608); Bernard L. Montgomery—a British general, in charge of British forces in Egypt, who stopped the German advance at the battle of El Alamein (p. 608); Douglas MacArthur—the commander of American forces in the Philippines (p. 607)
5. Answers will vary. Students may express shock, outrage, anger, sadness, foreboding, or determination.

Section 2 Review *p. 618*

1. Enormous spending for national defense ended the depression. The number of people in the work force grew by nearly 7 million. Manufacturing output nearly doubled between 1939 and 1945. War-related industries expanded greatly. Farm production increased by more than 20 percent. GNP nearly doubled. (p. 614)
2. To ration is to limit the portion or share of scarce goods. (p. 614) A conscientious objector is a person who refuses to participate in a war for moral or religious reasons. (p. 615) Espionage is spying. (p. 616)
3. Many people on the West Coast feared that Japanese immigrants would take their jobs. Many held the mistaken view that the Japanese were an inferior race. After the attack on Pearl Harbor, many people imagined that the Japanese Americans were disloyal. Japanese Americans were removed from the West Coast and sent to relocation camps in the Far West. (pp. 616–617)
4. Answers will vary. Students should mention the Democratic arguments regarding the danger of changing leaders in the middle of the war and the need for an experienced person to lead the nation through the war. The latter argument was probably the most compelling.

Social Studies Skills *p. 619*

1. Highest—1932, 23.6%; lowest—1944, 1.2%
2. Unemployment rose significantly from 1930 to 1932 (14.9%). This was followed by a gradual decline from 1932 to 1936. Between 1936 and 1938, unemployment increased by 2.1%. From 1938 to 1940 unemployment gradually declined again.
3. 9.9%
4. Unemployment in the United States rose after the war.

Section 3 Review *p. 623*

1. The United States dropped atomic bombs on the Japanese cities of Hiroshima and Nagasaki. (pp. 622–623)
2. Physicists researched and developed the atomic bomb. (pp. 621–622)
3. General Assembly—a governing body of the UN in which any member can bring matters before the assembly for debate and action. The assembly elects the secretary-general. Security Council—investigates disputes between nations and has the power to order action against aggressors. Trusteeship Council—oversees various colonial matters. (p. 621)
4. Answers will vary. Students might argue that the United States had learned the perils of isolation following World War I. By not taking early action to stop the aggressions of the Axis Powers, the greater conflict of World War II resulted. International cooperation, rather than isolation, seemed more likely to preserve the future peace.

Chapter Review *pp. 624–625*

Recalling the Facts

1. December 8, 1941, because the Japanese bombed the United States naval base at Pearl Harbor, Hawaii. (p. 607)
2. Australia was saved from Japanese invasion by the battle of Coral Sea, and the battle of Midway was a turning point in the war in the Pacific; Allied forces were on the offensive after this battle. (pp. 607–608)
3. In June 1944, the Allied army captured Rome. Shortly after that, the Allies landed in France, pushing the Germans out of almost all of France and Belgium. In March 1945, the Allies crossed onto German soil. On May 7, Germany signed an unconditional surrender. (p. 611)
4. The government borrowed money by selling war bonds to the American people. Taxes were placed on amusements and luxuries. The tax rate was raised on large incomes and on wartime profits of businesses. The income tax was extended to more Americans. (pp. 614–615)
5. Large numbers of women volunteered for the armed forces. Millions of American women also became workers in industry. More than one million black Americans entered the armed forces. Charles Drew discovered a way to preserve and store blood for use in transfusions. About 25,000 American Indians joined the armed forces. The Navajo language was used as a secret code for military communications. Thousands of other Indians worked in defense industries. A higher percentage of Mexican Americans volunteered for military service than did any other group of Americans. They also received the highest percentage of Congressional Medals of Honor. The 442nd Regimental Combat Team, made up entirely of Japanese Americans, received the most medals in the war. The unit participated in the Allied invasion of Italy. (pp. 615–616)
6. It set forth the terms for the unconditional surrender of Japan. Japanese military leaders opposed surrender. (p. 622)

Analyzing the Facts

1. It marked the beginning of the final Allied assault on Germany.
2. Enormous spending by the federal government for national defense
3. The British had to concentrate their forces in Europe for most of the war to fight the Germans. The United States was the major power in the best geographic position to fight the Japanese.
4. A nation holding veto power could stop any action directed against it by the Security Council. This severely weakens the Council's ability to prevent aggressive action by any of the Big Five nations.
5. Pros—Its use would probably shorten the war and save many American lives that would be lost in an invasion of Japan. Cons—Thousands of Japanese civilians would be killed, the damage would be tremendous, and a nuclear arms race might follow the use of the bomb.

Time and History

1. 4 years **2.** 1 year **3.** 1945 **4.** 3 years **5.** Philippine Islands

Unit Review *p. 626–627*

Recalling the Facts

1. Overproduction and the poor distribution of wealth in the 1920's; insufficient government regulation of business; high tariffs; the "drying up" of investment money, and the stock market crash (pp. 567–568)
2. The New Deal was Roosevelt's program to bring reform, recovery, and relief to the United States during the depression. (p. 572)
3. They created their own private armed forces or secret police, used propaganda, brutally treated their opponents, outlawed political parties that opposed them, preached an intense nationalism, and followed a policy of aggression. (p. 587)
4. World War II started in Europe on September 3, 1939, following the German invasion of Poland on September 1. The United States entered the war on December 8, 1941, after the Japanese air attack on Pearl Harbor, Hawaii, on December 7. (pp. 593, 606–607)
5. This was the code name given to a top-secret group of scientists and engineers who worked on developing an atom bomb from 1943 to 1945. This group successfully produced the atomic bombs that were dropped on Japan in August 1945. Japan surrendered quickly after the second bomb was dropped. (pp. 622–623)

Analyzing the Facts

1. Unlike Hoover, who felt that charitable organizations and state and local governments should bear the burden of relief, Roosevelt made the federal government responsible for providing relief. Hoover also relied on voluntary cooperation to help the economy recover, while Roosevelt sponsored legislation to promote recovery.
2. The New Deal expanded the role of the federal government. Today people can get welfare, food stamps, social security, home loans, and unemployment compensation from the government. The federal government also supervises the stock market, insures bank deposits, and sets minimum wages and maximum hours for workers.
3. Answers will vary. Possible answers are: No—The Allies would have been defeated without the aid of American military forces, and the Axis Powers would have eventually turned their attack on the United States. Also, the trend from 1939 to 1941 was of increased American involvement in the war on the side of the Allies.
4. Answers will vary. Possible answers are: No—If economic hard times ever hit Japan again or if its trade were disrupted, Japan might choose to use its military to take what it needs. Yes—The burden of defending Japan is too costly, and if Japan was attacked, the United States would be forced to become involved.

Reviewing Vocabulary

depression, p. 567; Fireside Chat, p. 572; devaluation, p. 573; deficit spending, p. 583; aggression, p. 587; fascist, p. 587; appeasement, p. 593; underground, p. 595; island hopping, p. 613; gross national product (GNP), p. 614; sabotage, p. 616; physicist, p. 622

Sharpening Your Skills

1. Hoover did not believe in direct federal aid for the poor. He felt that people would become permanently dependent on the federal government. Roosevelt believed that the federal government should take direct action to provide relief for the poor.
2. Some scientists opposed any use of the bomb whatsoever. Many of them recommended that the bomb be dropped on a barren island or in a desert. Once the Japanese saw the power of the bomb, they would surely surrender.
3. 1938
4. 1933, 1934, 1936
5. \$49.51 billion; \$28.08 billion; \$21.43 billion

Chapter 29
Postwar America *pp. 630–647*

ACTIVITIES

Level A: Put a list of 20 to 30 occupations on the board. Include jobs that produce goods (such as baker, factory worker, author) and jobs that produce services (such as doctor, nurse, teacher, banker) on the list. Have students identify which jobs produce goods and which produce services. Then have students identify as many other service jobs as they can. List these on the board.

Follow up this activity by inviting people who hold service jobs in your community to speak to the class about their jobs. Each speaker should describe the educational preparation needed and the future outlook for jobs in his or her field. Allow time for students to ask questions following the presentations.

Level B: Have students pretend they are one of the following three people living in the United States in the years following World War II: (a) a war veteran who had been drafted after completing high school, (b) a black junior high school student in the South in the early 1950's, (c) a young married man or woman living in a large city (the husband works in a factory and is a member of a union that has just decided to strike; the couple is expecting their first child). Have students write a diary entry for one of these people expressing his or her current concerns and expectations for the future.

ANSWERS

Section 1 Review *p. 635*

1. Continued spending by the federal government for national defense, increased foreign trade, and increased demand for goods from American consumers (p. 632)
2. Low-interest loans to former GIs for businesses, homes, and farms; unemployment relief for veterans who had problems finding jobs; $500 a year to pay for education or job-training (p. 631)
3. Productivity is the ability of a worker or business to produce more goods with the same or fewer inputs of land, labor, or capital. Increased productivity meant that fewer workers were needed to produce the nation's goods. More workers went into service jobs. Work hours were reduced. (p. 633)
4. Answers will vary. Students should consider the positive contributions of television mentioned in the text as well as some of the more familiar criticisms of television. (It is a passive activity; it has led to a decline in reading; most programming is of poor quality; and so on.)

Social Studies Skills *p. 636*

1. Almost 4,000,000
2. 1950–1955
3. It is difficult to estimate symbol fractions precisely.
4. The information would be added between the data given for 1965 and 1970. Five and a half symbols would be shown.

Section 2 Review *p. 640*

1. An expanded social security program, a higher minimum wage, continued wage and price controls, guaranteed "full employment," federal aid to education, national health insurance, a public-works program, and new public-housing projects. (p. 637)
2. A liberal is a person who believes that government should take action to regulate the economy and promote the greater welfare and liberties of the people. A conservative is a person who believes that government regulation of the economy should be kept at a minimum and that progress can best be achieved by allowing business the greatest possible freedom. (p. 638)

3. Business interests and the suburban middle class (p. 640)
4. George Washington, Andrew Jackson, William Henry Harrison, Zachary Taylor, and Ulysses S. Grant. Answers will vary. Recent American wars did not produce popular heroes who pursued political careers.

Section 3 Review *p. 645*

1. Discrimination against and poverty among immigrants and blacks, inflation, and labor strikes (pp. 641, 643)
2. It prohibited closed-shop agreements and limited the amount of money that unions could contribute to political candidates. It allowed the government to impose a 60-day "cooling-off period" on unions before they could go on strike. (p. 642)
3. Civil rights are rights guaranteed to individuals by the Constitution. (p. 642) To desegregate is to end racial segregation. (p. 643)
4. Racial discrimination in federal employment and segregation in the armed forces ended. The Supreme Court ordered the nation's public schools to desegregate in 1954. The Civil Rights Acts of 1957 and 1960 gave more protection and help to blacks who were being prevented from voting. (pp. 642–645)
5. Answers will vary. In both periods, the federal government passed laws that extended more rights to blacks and protected other civil rights. The federal government intervened with the aid of the military to see that the laws were obeyed. In both periods, federal action stirred Southern resistance and resentment. One major difference was that the South was under military occupation by the federal government during Reconstruction. In the 1960's, such extreme measures were not necessary.

Chapter Review *pp. 646–647*

Recalling the Facts

1. GI—a man or woman who had served in the armed forces. 52–20 Club—veterans who collected unemployment benefits of $20 per week for a maximum of 52 weeks; baby boom—the large number of children born in the postwar years. (p. 631)
2. Fewer workers were needed to produce the nation's goods. More workers were thus available for jobs in service industries. It also allowed businesses to reduce the number of hours they required their employees to work. (p. 633)
3. Television and recording (pp. 633–635)
4. He did not exert strong leadership, and he was unable to inspire the kind of loyalty that Roosevelt had enjoyed. (p. 637)
5. Segregation in public schools was unconstitutional. Many southern communities disobeyed the court's order. Some governors called out the National Guard or threatened to close schools. Federal troops had to be called out in some cases to protect the students and ensure that the court order would be obeyed. (pp. 643–644)
6. A black Baptist minister from Atlanta, Georgia, who became the national leader of the civil rights movement; peaceful demonstration (p. 645)

Analyzing the Facts

1. Answers will vary. Possible answers are: Yes, because they risk their lives for the defense of the nation; No, military service is a duty.
2. The nation had elected Republican majorities to Congress in 1946, which seemed to indicate dissatisfaction with Democratic policies. Liberals and conservatives were critical of Truman. The Democratic party split—Southern and liberal Democrats ran their own candidates. All public opinion polls showed that Dewey would win.
3. Answers will vary. Possible answers are: Eisenhower because Eisenhower had proved to be a strong leader during World War II; Stevenson because Stevenson was very intelligent.
4. Winning teams mean more money to the

teams' owners. If a black player could help a team win, the color of his skin became secondary.

5. Similarities: staged by groups who felt they were not being treated equally; lasted about a year; were successful. Differences: the bus boycott was local and the boycott of British goods involved all the colonies; the specific issues of the boycotts were different.

Time and History

1. 8 years **2.** 8 years **3.** Eisenhower **4.** 11 years **5.** Servicemen's Readjustment Act

Chapter 30
The Cold War *pp. 648–665*

ACTIVITIES

Level A: Give each student an outline map of the world. Using reference materials, such as almanacs or atlases, have them label and color red all nations that have communist governments today. Then have them label and use different designs to mark the nations that are NATO members (vertical lines), SEATO members (dots), and Warsaw Pact members (horizontal lines). Direct students to make a map key. Finally, have students suggest a title for the map. Display the completed maps in the classroom.

Level B: Have students read and summarize at least one current newspaper article that deals with some aspect of American-Soviet relations. You may wish to have students share the information from their summaries with the class. Follow up this activity with a discussion of how current relations between the two superpowers compare with their relations during the Cold War.

ANSWERS

Section 1 Review *p. 651*

1. Soviet Union—controlled by a single political party; few political freedoms; limited private property; government ownership of all industries and natural resources; government control of all types of economic activity. United States—a democracy; guaranteed political freedoms; private ownership of property; a capitalist economy (pp. 649–650)
2. To secure their western border against attack, to secure a warm-water port on the Mediterranean Sea, to destroy capitalism and western imperialism, to promote communism (p. 650)
3. Ideology is a basic belief or theory of government and society. (p. 649) Capitalism is an economic system in which the production and distribution of the nation's goods are privately owned and operated for profit. (p. 650) A cold war is a war fought with propaganda, economic pressure, and military threats. (p. 651) A satellite is a small nation that is dominated by another larger and more powerful nation. (p. 651)
4. Answers will vary. Students should be able to cite examples to support their answers.

Section 2 Review *p. 658*

1. Gave aid to Greece and Turkey, approved the Marshall Plan, sent airlifted supplies to West Berlin, joined Western European nations in forming NATO, sent armed forces to South Korea, sent aid and military advisers to South Vietnam, and joined SEATO (pp. 652–658)
2. To help restore the ruined economies of Western Europe and thereby prevent Communist parties from gaining control of these countries; The Marshall Plan restored the economies of Western Europe, and the strength of European Communist parties declined. (pp. 652–653)
3. Eisenhower believed that it was important to help the Saigon government. He convinced Congress to send military aid and military advisers to South Vietnam. He was opposed, however, to the sending of American combat forces. (pp. 657–658)
4. Massive retaliation was the American

policy of responding to any aggressive act by launching a counterattack of nuclear weapons. (p. 656) An intercontinental ballistic missile is a missile capable of carrying a nuclear weapon accurately over long distances. (p. 657) A protectorate is a dependent nation over which another nation assumes protection and exercises great influence. (p. 657)

5. Truman was angered that MacArthur continued to disagree publicly with national policy in Korea. Truman was upholding the constitutional principle of civilian control of the military.

Social Studies Skills *p. 659*

1. A fact is something known to be true or to have really happened. An opinion is a belief or a person's point of view about something.
2. The United States received an appeal from the Greek government for financial and economic assistance. Reports from the American Economic Mission and the American ambassador in Greece support Greece's need for assistance.
3. Truman's belief that the American people do not wish to ignore Greece's appeal.
4. Answers will vary. Possible answers are: Send assistance because there is evidence that Greece needs it; do not send aid because there is no evidence that the aid would keep communism out of Greece.

Section 3 Review *p. 663*

1. The expansion of Communist power around the world, Soviet espionage, and irrational fears (p. 660)
2. Alger Hiss had been an official in the State Department during both the Roosevelt and the Truman administrations. He was accused of giving secret government information to the Soviet Union. The Republicans could charge that the Democrats were "soft on communism." (p. 661)
3. A subversive is a person who works from within a nation to undermine and eventually overthrow the government. (p. 661) Perjury is lying while under oath to tell the truth. (p. 661) A demagogue is a leader who, to boost his or her own popularity, stirs the people by appealing to their worst emotions. (p. 662)
4. Answers will vary. Students may choose any of the three factors mentioned in the text.

Chapter Review *pp. 664–665*

Recalling the Facts

1. Soviet domination was seen as a threat to the freedom of Poland. The Soviet action in Poland was also a direct violation of the promise Stalin had made at the Yalta Conference concerning free elections in Poland. (p. 651)
2. MacArthur ignored Truman's warning to cease his public disagreement with national policy over the war in Korea. (pp. 655–656)
3. Korea remained divided near the 38th parallel. North Korea was under Communist control, and South Korea remained free. (p. 656)
4. McCarthy wanted to increase his popularity to ensure his reelection to the Senate. (p. 662)
5. Khrushchev and Eisenhower both expressed the desire of their nations to live together in peace. The two leaders agreed to a summit conference to be held in Paris in 1960. In May 1960, the Soviets shot down an American U-2 spy plane. The United States refused to apologize for the incident, and the summit conference collapsed. (p. 663)

Analyzing the Facts

1. The Soviet Union was committed to the overthrow of capitalism and Western imperialism and to controlling its neighbors in order to maintain its security. Americans saw the expansion of communism as a threat to their way of life.
2. Answers will vary. Possible answers are: Yes—Millions of Russians had been killed

during the German invasions, and the Soviet Union had almost been conquered; No—The people living in Eastern Europe should have had the right to choose their own form of government.

3. Answers will vary. Possible answers are: Yes—Threatening to use nuclear weapons would have shown the Soviet Union that the United States intended to stop Soviet aggression; No—Threatening to use nuclear power might have led to a nuclear war.
4. Answers will vary. Possible answers are: Yes—American aid to Greece and Turkey in 1947 and the Marshall Plan are evidence of its effectiveness; No—American aid to China and Vietnam was not effective in stopping the spread of communism.
5. Yes, because Americans' fears contributed to a panic that caused many innocent people to suffer needlessly.

Time and History

1. 3 years, 1950 to 1953 **2.** 1957, U.S.S.R. **3.** 4 years **4.** (a) The U-2 incident happened the year after Khrushchev visited the United States. (b) The Soviet Union did not test its first hydrogen bomb until 4 years after the Communists gained control of mainland China.

Chapter 31 Years of Challenge *pp. 666–685*

ACTIVITIES

Level A: Have each student write a letter to the editor expressing his or her opinion on American involvement in the Vietnam War. Letters should clearly reflect a 1960's hawk or dove position. Students should support their positions with historically accurate facts. You may wish to present additional material, or have students do additional research on the war before they write their letters.

Level B: Have students interview parents or relatives about life and events in the 1960's. Students should work together in groups to prepare a list of questions to ask on the following topics: the Bay of Pigs invasion, the Cuban missile crisis, Kennedy's assassination, the civil rights movement, Martin Luther King, Jr.'s assassination, the Vietnam War protests, Johnson's administration, the counterculture, and so on. Students should conclude their interviews by asking the person they interview how they view the 1960's now. You may wish to have the interviews placed in the school library, as examples of oral history.

ANSWERS

Section 1 Review *p. 671*

1. Foreign issues: combatting Communist guerrillas, improving relations with Third World nations, the Bay of Pigs disaster, the construction of the Berlin Wall, the Cuban missile crisis. Domestic issues: civil rights, the enforcement of federal laws and federal court orders dealing with desegregation (pp. 668–671)
2. He developed the Special Forces, he created the Peace Corps and proposed the formation of the Alliance for Progress, he tried to overthrow the Communist government in Cuba, and he blockaded Cuba during the missile crisis. (pp. 668–669)
3. A sit-in is an organized protest in which protesters occupy a business until it agrees to grant their demands. To force Woolworth's to serve blacks as well as whites at its lunch counter (p. 669)
4. Answers will vary. Both crises involved Cuba and the United States. The placing of the missiles in Cuba may be seen as a response to the earlier American-backed invasion of Cuba at the Bay of Pigs.

Section 2 Review *p. 676*

1. The Civil Rights Act of 1964 and the Voting Rights Act of 1965; students may also include the 24th Amendment, although it was not legislation, that abolished poll taxes in all federal elections. (pp. 673, 675)
2. Poll taxes, literacy tests, and tests requiring knowledge of the Constitution (pp. 673–674)

3. A ghetto is a section of a city occupied by members of a single racial or ethnic minority group. In the ghettos of America's cities (p. 675)
4. Answers will vary. Students may mention Jesse Jackson, Andrew Young, Tom Bradley, Julian Bond, Barbara Jordan, and others. Modern leaders share the same ideals and goals as King but are working in the field of politics rather than organizing mass demonstrations to bring about change.

Section 3 Review *p. 680*

1. Johnson won passage of the Tonkin Gulf Resolution. As a result of this resolution, Johnson ordered American warplanes to bomb North Vietnam. He ordered American combat troops to Vietnam. (p. 678)
2. The Communists were supported by many people in South Vietnam. An effective military strategy for defeating the Communists was never developed. Pacification and relocation proved to be ineffective. Also, the United States was unable to decide whether to expand or reduce its role in the war. (pp. 678–680)
3. To defoliate is to strip the leaves from trees and other plants by using a chemical spray. (p. 679) A dilemma is a situation in which one has to choose between unpleasant alternatives. (p. 680)
4. The hawks believed that the war in Vietnam was caused by Communist aggression. They felt that the United States had to contain communism by defending South Vietnam. The doves argued that the war was essentially a civil war between different groups of Vietnamese. They felt that the United States had no business interfering in Vietnam. Answers will vary.

Section 4 Review *p. 683*

1. The emergence of a counterculture was, in part, a result of the baby boom. The counterculture was also a direct response to the dominant consumer culture and a result of the larger issues troubling American society, such as civil rights and the Vietnam War. (p. 683)
2. Racial discrimination, American involvement in Vietnam, the draft, and college policies that restricted students' political activities (p. 683)
3. Popular music became a unifying force of the counterculture generation, speaking for the counterculture by expressing themes of alienation and protest. (p. 682)
4. Answers will vary. Students should consider such topics as popular attitudes and values, dress styles, music, and political opinions.

Chapter Review *pp. 684–685*

Recalling the Facts

1. Nixon—more experienced, familiar to more voters, associated with Eisenhower (advantages). Eisenhower gave Nixon's candidacy only lukewarm support, and Nixon appeared stiff and nervous during the debates (disadvantages). Kennedy—better public speaker, appeared relaxed and confident in the debates (advantages). Kennedy was a Catholic and was less well known (disadvantages). (p. 667)
2. He ordered the desegregation of all bus and train stations, sent federal troops to the University of Mississippi to enforce the court's desegregation order, and introduced to Congress a major civil rights act. (pp. 670–671)
3. He won passage of the Economic Opportunity Act, the Medicare and Medicaid programs, and the Elementary and Secondary Education Act. The Department of Housing and Urban Development and the Model Cities program were created. (p. 673)
4. Pacification and relocation. Neither strategy was very successful. (p. 679)
5. The counterculture rejected the values and life styles of the majority of Americans. In place of hard work and achievement, the counterculture emphasized "self-fulfillment." The counterculture was strongly linked to political and social pro-

test and was especially strong on college campuses. (pp. 682–683)

Analyzing the Facts

1. He personally knew many members of Congress. He knew how Congress worked and when and how to apply pressure to get laws he favored passed.
2. Southern states created other means besides race, such as poll taxes and literacy tests, to keep blacks from voting.
3. Blacks who could not vote had no say in who represented them or what laws were passed.
4. King supported nonviolence as the way to end racial segregation. Malcolm X urged blacks to build their own society, and he rejected the philosophy of nonviolence.
5. Answers will vary. Possible answers are: fight an all-out war in Vietnam to win because pulling out would encourage Communist aggression elsewhere; end American involvement in Vietnam because the war was a civil war in which the United States had no right to interfere.
6. Television was more powerful than other forms of media in bringing the horrors of the war to the attention of the American people. Many Americans began to question American involvement in the war. Opposition to the war steadily grew.

Time and History

1. 5 years **2.** Johnson; 1965 **3.** 1 year **4.** President Kennedy was assassinated, and Vice-President Johnson became President. **5.** 1964

Unit Review *pp. 686–687*

Recalling the Facts

1. Continued government spending for defense, an increase in foreign trade, and increased demand for housing and goods by American consumers (p. 632)
2. Containment of communism (p. 652)
3. (a.) 1954 Supreme Court decision in the case of *Brown* v. *Board of Education of Topeka* (b.) Civil Rights Act passed in 1964 (pp. 643, 673)
4. Johnson feared that further escalation would bring direct intervention by China or the Soviet Union; he believed that abandoning Vietnam would encourage the Communists to take over other countries. (p. 680)
5. Berlin airlift (June 1948 to May 1949)—Truman; Korean War begins (June 25, 1950)—Truman; U-2 incident (May 1, 1960)—Eisenhower; Bay of Pigs invasion (April 17, 1961)—Kennedy; civil rights demonstration in Washington (August 1963)—Kennedy; Tonkin Gulf Resolution (August 1964)—Johnson (pp. 655, 656, 663, 668, 671, 678)

Analyzing the Facts

1. To keep communism from spreading into these countries and because the ideologies to which the United States had objected no longer governed these countries
2. Communist rebels were trying to overthrow government in South Vietnam. The United States sent help to Vietnam as part of its containment policy.
3. Answers will vary. Possible answers are: Yes—Other nations would hesitate to attack a nation with nuclear weapons out of fear of retaliation; No—Mistakes can occur, or the possession of nuclear weapons may not prevent another nation from attacking.
4. King preached nonviolence, yet he died a violent death (assassination).

Reviewing Vocabulary

liberal, p. 638; conservative, p. 638; civil rights, p. 642; ideology, p. 649; capitalism, p. 650; cold war, p. 651; massive retaliation, p. 656; subversive, p. 661; demagogue, p. 662; poll tax, p. 673; ghetto, p. 675; defoliate, p. 679

Sharpening Your Skills

1. Opinion—it cannot be verified without looking at statistics
2. Facts—the events can be proven to have happened
3. 1,500,000
4. 1945–1946
5. 1950

Unit 10: CONTEMPORARY AMERICA

Chapter 32
Years of Crisis *pp. 690–703*

ACTIVITIES

Level A: Organize a debate around one of the following resolutions: Gerald Ford made a wise decision in pardoning former President Richard Nixon; the United States made the right decision in ending its involvement in Vietnam. At the end of the debate, have students cast votes indicating which side of the issue they support.

Level B: Have students design a campaign poster for one of the 1968 presidential candidates: Kennedy, McCarthy, Humphrey, Wallace, or Nixon. Each poster should be designed around an actual or fictional slogan that identifies the candidate with a particular issue. Encourage students to use writing, pictures, and art on their posters. Display the finished posters in the classroom.

ANSWERS

Section 1 Review *p. 694*

1. The United States signed a peace agreement with North Vietnam in 1973 and withdrew its troops. Fighting resumed among the Vietnamese. In April 1975, the Communists took control of Saigon, and the war was over. (p. 692)
2. Vietnamization was the planned withdrawal of American forces from Vietnam with the goal of turning all fighting over to the South Vietnamese. It called for a cease-fire and a return by North Vietnam of several hundred American prisoners of war. It also said that all remaining American forces would leave Vietnam. (p. 692)
3. Equilibrium is a state of balance between opposing forces. (p. 693) Détente is a relaxation of tensions between nations. (p. 694) Nixon made efforts to establish relations with the People's Republic of China in the hope that this would serve as a balance to Soviet power. Nixon also tried to reduce tensions with the Soviet Union by negotiating SALT I. (p. 694)
4. Answers will vary. Students could argue either side of the question, supporting their answers with evidence from the section.

Section 2 Review *p. 698*

1. American Indians, Hispanic Americans, and women (pp. 695–696)
2. Barrio is a Spanish word meaning district or neighborhood. (p. 696) A feminist is a supporter of equal rights for women. (p. 696) The consumer price index is the average price of a selected group of consumer goods purchased by a typical family. (p. 698)
3. Massive federal spending for the Vietnam War and domestic social programs, and a rise in prices of raw materials purchased overseas, especially oil.
4. Answers will vary. Families might have to consider doing without certain items or postponing the purchase of items they might otherwise be able to afford.

Section 3 Review *p. 701*

1. President Nixon tried to cover up the reelection committee's involvement in the planning of the burglary. He secretly ordered the CIA to ask the FBI not to investigate the crime. (p. 699)
2. In addition to planning the Watergate break-in, members of the Nixon administration gathered information about the President's critics, opened critics' mail illegally, illegally tapped critics' telephones, gathered illegal campaign contributions, and played dirty tricks on Nixon's Democratic opponents. (p. 699)
3. President Nixon resigned because the House judiciary committee voted to recommend that he be impeached, and the

White House tapes proved that the President had tried to stop the investigation of the Watergate burglary. Nixon faced almost certain impeachment by the House and conviction by the Senate. He resigned to avoid being removed from office. Obstruction of justice is an illegal attempt to stop the investigation of a crime. (p. 700)

4. During the Ford administration, prices continued to rise while economic activity remained stagnant. The economy entered the worst recession since the 1930's as production fell and unemployment rose. (p. 701)
5. Answers will vary. Students should assess the impact of a trial on the nation and possible imprisonment of a former President. This impact should be weighed against the concept of "equal justice for all."

Chapter Review *pp. 702–703*

Recalling the Facts

1. In 1972, Nixon became the first American President to visit China. Agreements were made to establish scientific and cultural exchanges; plans were made for trade to resume between the two nations; and steps were taken toward eventual diplomatic recognition of the People's Republic. Negotiations with the Soviet Union resulted in the SALT I agreement. (p. 694)
2. The Equal Pay Act of 1963 barred employers from paying workers of one sex more than they paid workers of the other sex for equal work. The Civil Rights Act of 1964 prohibited job discrimination based on sex. In 1971, Congress expanded its affirmative action standards to include women. Employers were thus encouraged to seek qualified women for available jobs. (p. 696)
3. Nixon first tried to curb inflation by reducing the nation's money supply. This "tight money" policy had little effect. Nixon then ordered a 90-day freeze on all wages and prices. Under Phase II, Nixon established standards for future wage and price increases. The standards were enforced by a new federal agency. Phase II slowed inflation, but it also caused many businesses to cut back production resulting in increased unemployment. Phase III included more flexible and voluntary wage and price guidelines. The voluntary plan failed, and inflation rose even higher. (p. 698)
4. Tapes of conversations recorded at the White House on June 23, 1972, proved the President had tried to stop the investigation of the Watergate burglary. (p. 700)
5. The lunar landing in 1969 and the bicentennial in 1976 (pp. 695, 701)

Analyzing the Facts

1. Blacks, American Indians, American Hispanics, and women all faced discrimination. Many blacks, Indians, and Hispanics lived in poverty. All of these groups organized to demand equal rights and an end to conditions that kept them from achieving equality. They staged demonstrations and strikes.
2. International trade can hurt the American economy by increasing competition. If American consumers prefer foreign products over products made in the United States, domestic businesses are forced to cut back and unemployment increases. International trade can help the American economy by opening up foreign markets to American products.
3. Answers will vary. Possible answers are: No—Americans would not want to reelect a President whose staff or campaign organization had been involved in illegal activities; Yes—Nixon won a landslide victory in 1972. Although some people might choose not to vote for Nixon, he would probably still have won the election.
4. When Nixon ordered the FBI not to investigate the Watergate burglary and later refused to turn over White House tape recordings requested by the congressional investigation committee, he was disrupting the system of checks and balances. He was trying to prevent the other branches from checking the power of the presidency.

Time and History
1. 1 year **2.** 2 years **3.** China and the Soviet Union **4.** 2 years **5.** Answers will vary.

Chapter 33
The Era of Limits *pp. 704–713*

ACTIVITIES

Level A: Invite guest speakers to talk to the class on the pros and cons of nuclear energy. Allow for a question and answer period following the presentations. Follow up this activity by having students write letters to their congressional representatives indicating their support for or opposition to nuclear power plants.
Level B: Have students obtain a road map of your state. Choose five to ten points of interest, and ask students to trace the route they would take if traveling by car to all of these points on a vacation. Have them calculate the total distance traveled using the scale in kilometers or miles. Help students calculate how many liters (or gallons) of gasoline such a trip would require (assuming all vehicles have the same fuel efficiency), and how much that gasoline would cost at current prices.

ANSWERS

Section 1 Review *p. 707*

1. President Carter supported the deregulation of domestic oil and gas prices. He supported tax credits for homeowners who put energy-saving insulation in their homes. He supported setting fuel-efficiency standards for American automakers. Carter also supported the development of new energy sources, such as solar energy, synthetic fuels, and nuclear energy. (pp. 706–707)
2. At first, Carter took steps to ease the recession. But as the recession began to disappear, inflation increased. Carter then moved to fight inflation. The Federal Reserve Board raised interest rates in response to rising inflation. Businesses and individuals did less borrowing; the demand for many goods fell. Prices fell as demand fell, and inflation eased. But the economy slipped back into recession, and unemployment rose sharply. Carter's efforts were not very successful. (p. 706)
3. Solar energy is energy obtained directly from sunlight. Synthetic fuels are liquid fuels made from coal or natural gas. Nuclear energy is energy released from an atom in a nuclear reaction or by radioactive decay. (p. 707)
4. After Watergate, many Americans had lost faith in government. Carter was pledging to restore honesty to the office of the President.

Social Studies Skills *p. 708*

1. The more factual evidence upon which an inference or conclusion is based, the greater the likelihood that it will be valid or correct.
2. Rosalynn Carter played an active role in political affairs during her husband's administration.
3. He regarded her as a key adviser and his personal representative. He sent her to visit Latin America on his behalf. She made campaign speeches for him.
4. Answers will vary. Possible answers are: Yes, she has had experience in government and has visited foreign nations on behalf of the President. No, she may not know the language of the country she is sent to or there is not enough evidence on which to form an opinion.
5. It allows you to expand the factual information you have at hand by making educated guesses based on evidence.

Section 2 Review *p. 711*

1. He worked out a pair of treaties with Panama that transferred control of the Panama Canal to Panama. Carter helped Egypt and Israel work out a comprehensive

peace treaty at Camp David, Maryland. He improved American relations with the People's Republic of China by beginning formal diplomatic relations. Carter signed the SALT II treaty with the Soviet Union that placed limits on the strategic arms each country could possess. (p. 709)

2. A hostage is a person held prisoner until a demand is granted. (p. 711) In November 1979, a mob of Iranian students invaded the United States Embassy in Teheran and took more than 50 diplomats and other Americans, who were in the embassy, hostage. President Carter's diplomatic efforts to free the hostages failed. As a result, he ordered the marines to attempt to rescue the hostages. (pp. 710–711)
3. He ordered an embargo on the sale of American grain and other products to the Soviet Union; he refused to allow American athletes to participate in the 1980 Summer Olympic Games to be held in Moscow; he withdrew the Salt II treaty from debate by the Senate; and he announced that the United States would defend any nation in the Persian Gulf area against Soviet aggression. (p. 711)
4. Answers will vary. The Iranian crisis was more of a direct challenge to the United States. The invasion of Afghanistan was a major act of aggression by the Soviet Union. Hostilities between the United States and the Soviet Union pose the gravest danger to world peace.

Chapter Review *pp. 712–713*

Recalling the Facts

1. He hosted radio "call-in" programs in which Americans could talk to the President. He attended town meetings across the country and even visited with Americans in their homes. (pp. 705–706)
2. The Federal Reserve Board tried to reduce inflation by raising interest rates. High interest rates led to reduced borrowing by businesses and individuals. The demand for goods fell causing a decline in prices. Inflation eased, but the nation's economy slipped back into recession. (p. 706)
3. Supporters of nuclear energy see it as a source for generating electricity. Opponents charge that there is no way to dispose of deadly wastes from nuclear plants. They also fear the danger of nuclear plant accidents. (p. 707)
4. Khomeini condemned the United States because of its support for the shah. (p. 707)
5. The United States was the most powerful country on earth, and yet it was unable to force the Iranians to free the hostages. (p. 711)

Analyzing the Facts

1. As governor of Georgia, Jimmy Carter had supported equal rights for blacks in his state.
2. The worldwide demand for oil was very high. Nations dependent on foreign oil had to pay what OPEC asked. In response to high prices, the United States began to develop policies for energy conservation and to look for new energy sources.
3. Advantages are: improved relations with Panama and other Latin American nations; the United States is no longer responsible for its maintenance or defense. Disadvantages are: the possibility exists that the canal could be closed to American ships; it may not be properly maintained.
4. Answers will vary. Possible answers are: Yes—Returning the shah would have improved American relations with the new Iranian government and freed the hostages faster; No—By refusing to give in, the United States showed the Iranian government that it would not pay ransom; it would not have been honorable to return the shah to Iran when he had been admitted to the United States as a guest of the government.

Time and History

1. 1979 **2.** 2 years **3.** Camp David Agreement **4.** 1977; Department of Energy **5.** 1980

Chapter 34
Realities and Possibilities
pp. 716–729

ACTIVITIES

Level A: Have students make a map showing how the population of each state has changed in recent years. An almanac or other source of current statistics should be used to obtain population figures for the years 1960 and 1980. Population change should be shown in percentage increases or decreases. If the source used does not give figures in percentages, help students calculate the percentages on a calculator or by long division. Once the percentages have been calculated, direct students to make a five-color key as follows: −10 to 0%, 0 to 10%, 10 to 20%, 20 to 30%, 30 to 40%. A sixth color may be added as needed for percentages over 40%. Have students label each state with its name and percentage of change. Each state should then be shaded with the color in the key that corresponds to its percentage of change. Finally, have students give their maps a title. Display the completed maps in the classroom.

Level B: Have students clip and summarize two current newspaper articles that deal with American involvement in world affairs. You may wish to specify that the articles relate to a single area of involvement or two different areas. Summaries should include the reason(s) for involvement, the form of involvement, and the anticipated outcome of American involvement.

ANSWERS

Section 1 Review *p. 717*

1. Reagan ordered the removal of hundreds of government regulations affecting business. He asked Congress for cuts in government spending in almost every area of the federal budget except defense. Reagan also proposed a huge reduction in federal taxes. As the federal deficit grew, Reagan changed his tax policy and convinced Congress to pass a federal tax increase. (pp. 716–717)
2. Reagan said that he would improve the nation's economy by reducing taxes and government spending. He promised to free business from government regulation. (p. 715)
3. Supply-side economics is an economic theory that says cutting taxes will lead to economic growth and higher government revenues. (p. 716) The budget deficit is the difference between government spending and revenues when spending exceeds revenues. (p. 717)
4. Answers will vary. His acting career contributed to his skills as a communicator. This proved to be very important in an age when television plays such an important role in politics. His acting career also contributed to his name recognition among Americans. Also the glamour of being a Hollywood actor added to his attractiveness.

Section 2 Review *p. 720*

1. President Reagan ordered the CIA to train and arm a "secret army" of anti-Sandinista guerrillas. He also ordered increased American military aid to the government of El Salvador. Salvadoran soldiers were brought to the United States for training. American military advisers went to Honduras to train other Salvadoran forces and to provide further aid. (pp. 718–719)
2. President Reagan took steps to increase defense spending. New and more powerful weapons were supplied to the armed forces. Additional nuclear missiles were installed at American bases in Europe. Reagan also supported development of the MX missile. (p. 718)
3. Martial law is temporary military rule over a civilian population. To nationalize is to transfer control of land, resources, or industries to the national government. (p. 718)
4. Answers will vary. In both cases, American

military advisers were sent to help train local soldiers to fight Communist guerrillas. In both cases, American Presidents pledged not to send American combat troops to join the fighting. Both situations were viewed as part of the global pattern of Communist expansion. Differences exist in the level of American commitment to Vietnam and El Salvador. Differences also exist because many Americans want to avoid becoming involved in "another Vietnam" in El Salvador.

Section 3 Review *p. 723*

1. The Southeast and Southwest have been growing much more rapidly than the Northeast and Midwest. (p. 721)
2. Life expectancy is the average number of years that a person can expect to live. As Americans live longer, the number of older Americans has increased. This has created problems for the Social Security system, which has become overburdened as the over-65 population increases. (pp. 721–722)
3. Sandra Day O'Connor became the first woman justice of the Supreme Court in 1981. Sally K. Ride became the nation's first woman astronaut in space in 1983. (p. 722)
4. Answers will vary. Students should note that more representatives in the House will come from the Sunbelt states with their growing populations. Also, presidential and vice-presidential candidates will likely come from the Sunbelt.

Social Studies Skills *p. 724*

1. West
2. South and West
3. 1910–1919, 1920–1929, 1930–1939
4. Missouri
5. 1850–1859, 1870–1879

Section 4 Review *p. 727*

1. A postindustrial society relies on high technology; it is marked by increased productivity in industry and agriculture; increasing emphasis is placed on the importance of technology in education. (p. 725)
2. Organ transplants, electronic pacemakers, and genetic research (p. 725)
3. Toxic wastes are harmful or deadly waste products from factories or chemical plants. (p. 726) Biomass energy is energy generated from organic materials. (p. 727) Geothermal energy is energy from the earth's core, obtained from hot water or steam near the earth's surface. (p. 727)
4. Answers will vary. Historical knowledge can allow for the formation of generalizations about cause and effect, thus guiding policy formation. Historical knowledge can help us avoid some of the errors we have made in the past. It can also help us realize the depth of current problems by giving us an understanding of their origin. Knowledge of American history can provide Americans with a sense of strength to overcome present difficulties. From a knowledge of past accomplishments, Americans can gain confidence to face the challenges and opportunities of the future.

Chapter Review *pp. 728–729*

Recalling the Facts

1. Many Americans were frustrated by Carter's failure to secure the release of the American hostages in Iran and his inability to solve the nation's economic problems. Others were unhappy with the way Carter handled the crisis in Afghanistan. (p. 715)
2. In 1981, the Soviet Union pressured the Polish government to crack down on Solidarity, an independent labor movement that called for major reforms from the Communist government of Poland. In response, the Polish government imposed martial law in Poland and arrested the leaders of Solidarity. President Reagan denounced the establishment of martial law. Relations between the two superpowers worsened. (p. 718)

3. Reagan feared that the new modern jet airport being built in Grenada with the help of the Cubans would be used for long-range military aircraft. After the assassination of government leaders on the island, the President was also concerned about the safety of American citizens there. Tensions increased between the two superpowers. Reagan blamed the events in Grenada on the Soviet Union. (pp. 719–720)
4. The population has been shifting to the Southeast and Southwest. People have moved to the Sunbelt because of its milder climate and its growing economic opportunities. (p. 721)
5. Hispanics. The Hispanic population faces severe problems of low income and high unemployment. One out of every four Hispanic families lives in poverty, compared to one out of ten non-Hispanic white families. (p. 723)
6. Computer-based "video games" have transformed television watching into a more active pastime. Cable television has introduced a broader range of programs. Video-tape and video-disc players have brought to television a variety of new entertainment options. (p. 725)
7. In 1970, Congress created the Environmental Protection Agency. The EPA has adopted regulations to control the future dumping of toxic wastes and has taken action to clean up existing dumps. Congress also passed the Clean Air Act in 1970. This act requires that new automobiles be equipped with antipollution devices. (pp. 726–727)

Analyzing the Facts

1. If the election appears close, it might prompt more westerners to vote. However, if one candidate appears to be winning a landslide victory, it might prompt fewer westerners to vote because they might feel that their votes would have no effect on the outcome of the election.
2. Reagan believed that the development of this missile system would keep the Soviet Union from using its nuclear weapons out of fear of retaliation by the United States and thus preserve peace.
3. As the population of a minority group increases, so does its political power. More minority group members will be elected to political office. Pressure for programs to aid minority group members will increase.
4. Education and training will become more important because jobs in a postindustrial society will require skilled workers. Unskilled labor will be performed by robots. Workers will also need to upgrade their skills or education constantly in order to compete in the labor force.

Time and History

1. 1983 **2.** 2 years **3.** 2 years **4.** 10 years **5.** a terrorist bombing

Unit Review *pp. 730–731*

Recalling the Facts

1. Hubert Humphrey was the Democratic candidate and Richard Nixon was the Republican candidate. Nixon won. He promised to bring the war in Vietnam to an end by achieving "peace with honor" and to restore order and stability to the United States. (p. 691)
2. Ford was appointed Vice-President following the resignation of Vice-President Spiro Agnew. When Nixon resigned in 1974 over the Watergate scandal, Ford became President. (p. 700)
3. President Carter tried many forms of diplomacy to free the hostages. When his efforts failed, he ordered a rescue attempt. The rescue attempt also failed. (p. 711)
4. One-third of all black Americans are part of the American middle class. The percentage of black high-school graduates going on to college is almost the same as that of white graduates. Blacks have also gained more political power. Black mayors head 30 of the nation's largest cities in both the North and the South.
5. As the earth's population continues to grow and more nations become industrial-

ized, the demand for oil will rise sharply. The best long-range hope for solving the energy crisis remains the conservation of existing energy supplies and the development of new sources. (p. 727)

Analyzing the Facts

1. Nixon had lied to the American people about the involvement of his staff in the Watergate burglary. It was also discovered that Nixon's campaign organization had engaged in illegal activities and "dirty tricks." Many people who had trusted the President were shocked and angry when they discovered that their trust had been misplaced. They became hesitant to trust politicians again.
2. Many people must borrow money to purchase an automobile or a house. When interest rates are high, many people can no longer afford to borrow money. As demand for automobiles and housing decreases, business activity in these industries falls off.
3. Answers will vary. Possible answers are: Soviet-American relations because of the threat of nuclear war; the energy crisis because of its potential to cripple the American economy; pollution because of its damaging effects.
4. Answers will vary. Possible answers are: medical advances that will increase life expectancy and improve the quality of life; advances in computer technology that will make work more efficient; space exploration that will add to knowledge.

Reviewing Vocabulary

détente, p. 694; busing, p. 695; stagnant, p. 701; recession, p. 701; cartel, p. 706; deregulation, p. 706; nuclear energy, p. 707; supply-side economics, p. 716; budget deficit, p. 717; nationalize, p. 718; Sunbelt, p. 721; postindustrial society, p. 725

Sharpening Your Skills

1. It can be inferred that the United States was heavily dependent on foreign oil. When imports were cut back in 1979, there was not enough gasoline to meet the demand.
2. It could be inferred that they felt disappointment and frustration. Many Americans had to cancel their vacation plans. Those who wished to purchase gasoline had to wait in long lines to fill their tanks.
3. The population of Arizona increased.
4. North Dakota, Iowa, Wisconsin, Ohio, Tennessee, Alabama, West Virginia, Pennsylvania, Connecticut, and New York
5. California and Florida; California is located in the West, and Florida is located in the South.

Bibliography of Books and Audiovisual Aids

Books suitable for student use are marked with an asterisk.

Unit 1: THE NEW WORLD'S SETTLERS

BOOKS

Catton, Bruce, and Catton, William B. *The Bold and Magnificent Dream: America's Founding Years, 1492–1815.* Garden City, N.Y.: Doubleday, 1978.

*Clark, William. *Explorers of the World.* New York: Natural History Press, 1964.

Morison, Samuel E. *The European Discovery of America: The Northern and Southern Voyages.* New York: Oxford University Press, 1974.

*Palmer, Ann. *Growing Up in Colonial America.* East Sussex: Wayland Ltd., 1978.

AUDIOVISUAL AIDS

Age of Discovery—English, French, and Dutch by Coronet Instructional Media. 11 min./ color film

Christopher Columbus by Churchill Films. 16 min./color film

Indians in the Americas by BFA Educational Media, a division of Phoenix Films, Inc. 15 min./ color film

Puritan Experience—Making of a New World by Learning Corporation of America. 31 min./color film

Unit 2: CREATING A REPUBLIC

BOOKS

*Dobler, Lavina, and Toppin, Edgar. *Pioneers and Patriots.* Garden City, N.Y.: Doubleday, 1974.

*Forbes, Esther. *Johnny Tremain.* Boston: Houghton-Mifflin, 1943.

Pearson, Michael. *Those Damned Rebels: The American Revolution As Seen Through British Eyes.* New York: G.P. Putnam's Sons, 1972.

Quarles, Benjamin. *The Negro in the American Revolution.* New York: Norton, 1973.

*Sanderlin, George. *A Hoop to the Barrel: The Making of the American Constitution.* New York: Coward, McCann, and Geoghegan, Inc., 1974.

AUDIOVISUAL AIDS

American Revolution—Background Period by Coronet Instructional Media. 10 min./ color film

Boston Tea Party by Walt Disney. 30 min./color film

Constitution by Encyclopedia Britannica Educational Corporation. 19 min./color film

Independence by National Audiovisual Center. 30 min./color film

How a Bill Becomes Law by Mar/Chuck Films. 18 min./color film

Shot Heard Round the World by Walt Disney. 32 min./color film

Unit 3: THE NATION GROWS

BOOKS

*Breton, Pierre. *Flames Across the Border.* Boston: Little, Brown & Co., 1981.

DeVoto, Bernard. *The Journals of Lewis and Clark.* Boston: Houghton-Mifflin, 1953.

*Sprague, Marshall. *So Vast, So Beautiful a Land: Louisiana and the Purchase.* Boston: Little, Brown & Co., 1974.

*Tucker, Glenn. *Tecumseh: Vision of Glory.* New York: Atheneum, 1973.

AUDIOVISUAL AIDS

Lewis and Clark Journey by Coronet Instructional Media. 16 min./color film

Life in America—1800 by Aims Instructional Media. 15 min./color film

Marbury v. Madison by McGraw-Hill. 36 min./color film

War of 1812 by Coronet Instructional Media. 13½ min./color film.

Unit 4: THE NATION DIVIDING

BOOKS

*Bontemps, Arna. *Frederick Douglass: Slave, Fighter, Freeman.* New York: Alfred A. Knopf, Inc., 1974.

*Clark, Electa. *Cherokee Chief; The Life of John Ross.* New York: Macmillan Inc., 1970.

Franklin, John Hope. *From Slavery to Freedom.* New York: Alfred A. Knopf, Inc., 1974.

*Meltzer, Milton. *Bound for the Rio Grande: The Mexican Struggle, 1845–1850.* New York: Alfred A. Knopf, Inc., 1974.

Rieger, Robert, and Athearn, Robert. *America Moves West.* New York: Holt, Rinehart and Winston, 1971.

AUDIOVISUAL AIDS

Goldrush and the 49er's by BFA Educational Media, a division of Phoenix Films, Inc. 20 min./color film

Jackson Years—The New Americans by Learning Corporation of America. 28 min./color film

Oregon Trail by Kaw Valley Films. 31 min./color film

Plantation South by Encyclopedia Britannica Educational Corporation. 17 min./color film

United States Expansion—Texas and the Far Southwest by Coronet Films. 16 min./color film

Unit 5: DIVISION AND REUNION

BOOKS

Catton, Bruce. *This Hallowed Ground.* New York: Pocket, 1961.

*Hunt, Irene. *Across Five Aprils.* Chicago: Follet Publishing Co., 1964.

Katz, William L. *Eyewitness: The Negro in American History.* Garden City, N.Y.: Doubleday, 1973.

*Keith, Harold. *Rifles for Watie.* New York: Harper & Row, 1957.

Stampp, Kenneth M. *The Era of Reconstruction, 1865–1877.* New York: Alfred A. Knopf, Inc., 1965.

AUDIOVISUAL AIDS

Abraham Lincoln—A New Birth of Freedom by Handel Films. 30 min./color film

Autobiography of Miss Jane Pittman by Learning Corporation of America. 111 min./color film

Civil War—Promise of Reconstruction by Learning Corporation of America. 28 min./color film

Gettysburg—1863 by Centron Films. 19 min./color film

Years of Reconstruction—1865–1877 by McGraw-Hill. 25 min./color film

Unit 6: THE AGE OF INDUSTRY

BOOKS

Chu, Daniel and Samuel. *Passage to the Golden Gate: A History of the Chinese in America to 1910.* Garden City, N.Y.: Doubleday, 1967.

*Latham, Frank. *Panic of 1893: A Time of Strikes, Riots, Hobo Camps, Coxey's Army, Starvation, Withering Droughts, and the Fears of Revolution.* New York: Franklin Watts, Inc., 1971.

*Moskin, Marietta. *Waiting for Mama.* New York: Coward-McCann, 1975.

Schlesinger, Arthur M., Jr., and Fow, Dixon R. *Rise of the City, 1878–1898.* New York: Franklin Watts, Inc., 1971.

Washburn, Wilcomb E. *The Indian in America.* New York: Harper & Row, 1975.

AUDIOVISUAL AIDS

I Will Fight No More Forever by Films, Inc. 108 min./color film

Inventors and America's Industrial Revolution by Churchill Films. 14 min./color film

Land of Immigrants by Churchill Films. 16 min./color film

Lure of Empire—America Debates Imperialism by Learning Corporation of America. 27 min./color film

Masses and the Millionaires—The Homestead Strike by Learning Corporation of America. 27 min./color film

Unit 7: REFORM, WAR, REACTION

BOOKS

Allen, Frederick Lewis. *Only Yesterday.* New York: Harper & Row, 1957.

*Gurney, Gene. *Flying Aces of World War I.* New York: Random House, Inc., 1965.

*Jantzen, Steven. *Hooray for Peace, Hurrah for War: The U.S. in World War I.* New York: Alfred A. Knopf, Inc., 1978.

*Lardner, Rex. *Ten Heroes of the Twenties.* New York: Putnam, 1966.

AUDIOVISUAL AIDS

Jazz Age by McGraw-Hill. 52 min/B&W film

Progressives by McGraw-Hill. 25 min./color film

Teddy Roosevelt—The Right Man at the Right Time by Learning Corporation of America. 28 min./color film

Twenties by McGraw-Hill. 25 min./color film

Wilson—The Road to War by Films Inc. 24 min./B&W film

Unit 8: DEPRESSION AND WAR

BOOKS

*Davis, Daniel S. *Behind Barbed Wire: The Imprisonment of Japanese Americans During World War II.* New York: Dutton, 1982.

Esposito, Vincent, J., ed. *A Concise History of World War II.* New York: Praeger, 1964.

*Frank, Anne. *The Diary of a Young Girl.* Garden City, N.Y.: Doubleday, 1958.

*Hunt, Irene. *No Promises in the Wind.* New York: Grosset & Dunlap (Tempo Books), 1970.

AUDIOVISUAL AIDS

American People in World War II by McGraw-Hill. 24 min./color film

Great Depression by BFA Educational Media, a division of Phoenix Films, Inc. 33 min./color film

New Deal by McGraw-Hill. 25 min./color film

Truman and the Atomic Bomb by Learning Corporation of America. 15 min./B&W film

Unit 9: AMERICA'S CHANGING ROLE

BOOKS

*Barton, Thomas. *LBJ, Young Texan.* Indianapolis: Bobbs-Merrill, 1973.

Chafe, William Henry. *The American Woman: Her Changing Social, Economic and Political Roles, 1920–1970.* New York: Oxford University Press, 1974.

*Preston, Edward. *Martin Luther King, Fighter for Freedom.* Garden City, N.Y.: Doubleday, 1970.

*Tregarski, Richard. *John F. Kennedy and PT-109.* New York: Random House, 1962.

AUDIOVISUAL AIDS

Age of Kennedy—The Presidency by McGraw-Hill. 52 min./B&W film

Focus on 1954 by Screen Digest News. 15 min./B&W film

Troubled Neighbors by Screen Digest News. 14 min./color film

Truman and the Korean War by Learning Corporation of America. 16 min./B&W film

Vietnam—An Historical Document by Carousel Films. 52 min./color film.

Unit 10: CONTEMPORARY AMERICA

BOOKS

*Gersh, Harry. *Women Who Made America Great.* New York: J. B. Lippincott Co., 1972.

Rothchild, E. *Richard Nixon and Détente, 1969–1972.* Sanford, N.C.: Microfilming Corp., 1979.

White, Theodore. *Breach of Faith: The Fall of Richard Nixon.* New York: Atheneum, 1975.

AUDIOVISUAL AIDS

After Oil What? by International Film Bureau. 25 min./color film

America's First Women Astronauts by Screen News Digest. 14 min./color film

Inflation—Passing the Buck by Carousel Films. 25 min./B&W film

Educating the Exceptional Student in the Regular Classroom

Federal Law PL 94–142

Mainstreaming has come to mean the integration of persons with handicapping conditions into the regular classroom wherever feasible. Some students with handicapping conditions have always been mainstreamed; others have attended special education classes or received special services. Federal Law PL 94–142 states that handicapped children are to be educated in the "least restrictive environment." For some this means education in special schools. For others it means partial or full integration into regular school programs with nonhandicapped peers. In classes in which handicapped students are mainstreamed, the following information will be useful to the teacher.

Identification and Placement

Federal Law PL 94–142 requires all students with handicapping conditions to be identified, tested, and evaluated by the appropriate agencies or school services. (If you suspect that a student has a handicap not previously identified, contact the school health department.

The school service, in agreement with the teacher, the student, and the student's parents, selects the most appropriate and least environmentally restrictive educational plan. The plan can include total integration with related special services or partial integration with enrollment in selected courses and with the remainder of the day spent in special education courses.

Handicapping Conditions

Physical impairments include those of an orthopedic nature, other health impairments, visual impairments, and blindness.

Communicative handicaps are conditions that adversely affect a student's communicative ability or effective use of language: hearing impairments, deafness, speech impairments, and specific learning disabilities. The term "specific learning disabilities" refers to dysfunction in one or more of the basic psychological and physiological processes involved in understanding or using language. Specific learning disabilities include dyslexia, minimal brain injury, perceptual impairments, and developmental aphasia.

Mild mental retardation refers to slowed intellectual functioning. Emotional disturbance refers to an emotional condition that handicaps a student's overall functioning.

Instructional Management Systems

Be aware of the educational plan selected for each handicapped student in your class. If a student is partially integrated and returns to the special education teacher or resource teacher for supportive and additional instruction, the resource teacher writes an Individualized Education Plan (IEP) with input from the classroom teacher. Use the chapter objectives in the Pupil Edition as a basis for choosing goals for each student.

The gifted student is well above average in academic ability. Many gifted students benefit from independent activities such as those suggested in the "Writing and Research" feature in the unit review. The bibliographies in the Teacher's Annotated Edition give additional suggestions for resource material. The Level A activities in the Resource Materials section of the Teacher's Edition and the "For Extra Interest" annotations in the Teacher's Annotated Edition offer additional projects that gifted students might undertake either independently or as group leaders. Finally, the gifted members of the class should be encouraged to answer the critical thinking questions in the section, chapter, and unit reviews in the Pupil Edition with depth and creativity.

Helping the Exceptional Student

In January 1978, *Instructor* magazine published an annotated bibliography of national nonprofit groups to contact for help with special children in the classroom. The list below is taken from *Instructor*'s bibliography. The help provided varies from group to group. Some groups are referral agencies; some provide pamphlets, packets, films, and other teaching aids; some provide diagnostic information. For details, contact the group at the address and/or telephone number given here.

GENERAL

The Council for Exceptional Children
1920 Association Drive
Reston, VA 22091
Call toll-free 800-336-3728

National Information Center of the Handicapped
PO Box 1492
Washington, DC 20013

Division of School Information National Foundation March of Dimes
1275 Mamaroneck Avenue
White Plains, NY 10606
914-428-7100

MENTALLY RETARDED

National Association for Retarded Citizens
2709 Avenue E East
PO Box 6109
Arlington, TX 76011
817-261-4961

American Association on Mental Deficiency
5101 Wisconsin Avenue, NW
Washington, DC 20016
202-686-5400 or
Call toll-free 800-424-3688

HARD-OF-HEARING AND DEAF

International Association of Parents of the Deaf, Inc.
814 Thayer Avenue
Silver Spring, MD 20910
301-585-5400

Alexander Graham Bell Association for the Deaf
3417 Volta Place
Washington, DC 20007
202-337-5220

Convention of American Instructors of the Deaf
814 Thayer Avenue
Silver Spring, MD 20910
301-585-4363

VISUALLY HANDICAPPED

National Association for Visually Handicapped
305 East 24 Street, 17-C
New York, NY 10010
212-889-3141

American Foundation for the Blind
15 W. 16 Street
New York, NY 10011
212-924-0420

Instructional Materials Reference Center
P.O. Box 6085
American Printing House for the Blind
1839 Frankfort Avenue
Louisville, KY 40206
502-895-2405

PHYSICALLY IMPAIRED

Information Center National Easter Seal Society
2023 W. Ogden Avenue
Chicago, IL 60612
312-243-8400

Muscular Dystrophy Association
810 Seventh Avenue
New York, NY 10019
212-586-0808

United Cerebral Palsy Association
Program Services Department
66 E. 34 Street
New York, NY 10016
212-481-6350

OTHER HEALTH IMPAIRED

Epilepsy Foundation of America
1828 L Street, NW, Suite 406
Washington, DC 20036
202-293-2930

Greater New York City Chapter, EFA
225 Park Avenue South
New York, NY 10003
212-677-8550

EMOTIONALLY DISTURBED

Mental Health Association
1800 N. Kent Street
Roslyn, VA 22209
703-528-6405

National Institute of Mental Health
Printing and Publications Section
5600 Fisher Lane, Room 6-105
Rockville, MD 20857
301-443-5480

LEARNING DISABILITIES

Association for Children with Learning Disabilities
4156 Library Road
Pittsburgh, PA 15234
412-341-1515

New York Association for the Learning Disabled and its Associations for Brain Injured Children
Room 276, Richardson Hall
SUNY-Albany
Albany, NY 12222
518-472-7110

International Reading Association
800 Barksdale Road
Newark, DE 19711
302-731-1600

GIFTED OR TALENTED

National-State Leadership Training Institute on Gifted and Talented
316 W. Second Street
Suite PH-C
Los Angeles, CA 90012
213-489-7470

National Association for Gifted Children
217 Gregory Drive
Hot Springs, AR 71901
501-767-6933

LAND *of* LIBERTY

A UNITED STATES HISTORY

James J. Rawls
Diablo Valley College
Pleasant Hill, California

Philip Weeks
University of Akron
Akron, Ohio

Holt, Rinehart and Winston, Publishers

New York Toronto Mexico City London Sydney Tokyo

JAMES J. RAWLS a native of Washington, D.C., received a B.A. from Stanford University and a Ph.D. from the University of California, Berkeley. Since 1975, Rawls has been an instructor of history at Diablo Valley College. His articles and reviews have appeared in such publications as *The Journal of American History, The Wilson Quarterly, The American West,* and *California History.* He is the author of *Indians of California: The Changing Image* and coauthor of *California: An Interpretative History.* Rawls has served as an historical consultant on numerous films and a series of television programs funded by the National Endowment for the Humanities.

PHILIP WEEKS teaches United States history and American Indian studies, and serves as an academic counselor at The University of Akron. His undergraduate and graduate degrees were awarded to him by Kent State University. Weeks has also taught at Kent State University and at Lorain County Community College, Ohio. His articles and reviews have appeared in such publications as *Ohio History, The History Teacher,* and *The Indian Historian.* Weeks' books include *Subjugation and Dishonor, The American Indian Experience,* and *Farewell, My Nation.* He has appeared on a number of television and radio programs to discuss topics of historical interest.

ACKNOWLEDGMENTS

For Elizabeth Jane Kathleen and for Jeanette and Michael.

Photo and art credits are on pages 767–768.
Additional acknowledgments appear with the material used.

ISBN: 0-03-064226-4
56789 039 98765432

CONTRIBUTING WRITERS

BIOGRAPHICAL FEATURES

Fay Metcalf
Boulder High School
Boulder, Colorado

TECHNOLOGY FEATURES

Carla Reiter
Science writer
New York, New York

SKILL DEVELOPMENT MATERIALS

Vivian Grano, Ed.D.
New York City Board of Education
New York, New York

REVIEW MATERIALS

Danton Ponzol
Southern Lehigh School District
Center Valley, Pennsylvania

Margaret Steneck
Dumont High School
Dumont, New Jersey

CONSULTANTS

TEACHER CONSULTANTS

Sallie Pipes Blackwell
Hand Middle School
Columbia, South Carolina

Carol D. Lambiotte
Huntington Middle School
Newport News, Virginia

SPECIAL INTEREST CONSULTANTS

Joseph D. Baca
New Mexico Department of Education
Santa Fe, New Mexico

Norman McRae, Ph.D.
Detroit Public Schools
Detroit, Michigan

MaryJo Wagner
University of Oregon
Eugene, Oregon

GEOGRAPHY CONSULTANT

Pamela Edwards
E. H. White Senior High School
Jacksonville, Florida

CONTENT CONSULTANTS

Jon Butler
University of Illinois at Chicago
Chicago, Illinois

Diane Lindstrom
University of Wisconsin—Madison
Madison, Wisconsin

Shaw Livermore, Jr.
University of Michigan
Ann Arbor, Michigan

Walter Nugent, Ph.D.
Indiana University
Bloomington, Indiana

Around the globe, political, social, and economic events are changing and shaping the world in which we live. These are events that we, as Americans, can influence. But deciding how our nation should respond requires knowledge of the past as well as the present.

No event occurs in isolation. No one situation or crisis develops because of current conditions alone. The past provides us with clues that make the present more understandable.

Why is the United States engaged in an arms race with the Soviet Union? Why is the United States involved in the affairs of other nations? Why is the United States in the kind of economic shape it is in today? These are some of the questions that surface as you read the newspaper or watch the evening news. The answers to these questions can be found by studying our nation's history.

To tell you the truth, I only learned this a little late in life. When I was in junior high, all that stuff that happened years ago couldn't have seemed further from what was actually going on in the world. But later I found out that I had been wrong. There was *nothing* going on that didn't have its roots in history. By studying our history, we can learn how our nation was formed, how it grew, and how it took its place among the nations of the world. We can discover the traditions and beliefs that have made us the kinds of people that we are. We can learn what steps our leaders have taken in the past to help solve the problems facing our nation. This knowledge will help us to decide how we want to exert our influence as voters and as citizens in tomorrow's world.

Table of Contents

THE EXTREME CLIPPER SHIP
OCEAN EXPRESS

Unit 6 The Age of Industry 396

Life
10¢

Unit
9 America's Changing Role 628

Unit
10 Contemporary America 688

MAPS

CHARTS AND GRAPHS

Social Studies Skills Review

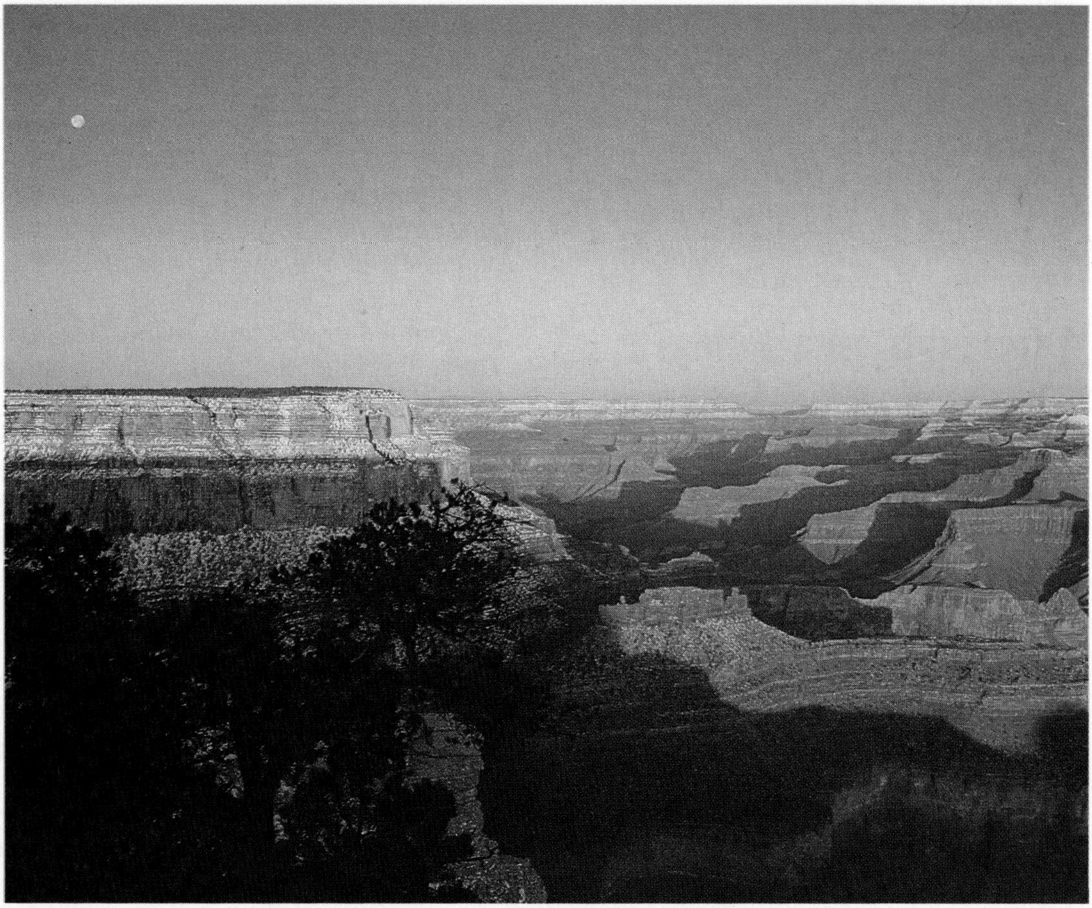

***H**istory is a branch of knowledge that records and explains past events. This year you are going to learn about the history of our nation. You will learn about the people and events that have influenced our past and shaped our present. Like an explorer leaving on a journey through unfamiliar territory, your journey through American history will be made easier if you have the proper equipment. The equipment for studying history is made up of social studies skills. Social studies skills range from reading maps to reading paragraphs. They are skills that can help you read more effectively and remember what you read. This section of your book covers five major areas of social studies skills. Reviewing this section will help you as you begin your study of American history.*

1. Map and Geography Skills

Geography is a branch of social studies that describes the land, sea, air, and plant and animal life of the earth. Geography, in other words, can tell us about the places where history has occurred.

Directions on a Map

In 1603, the French explorer, Samuel de Champlain, traveled up the St. Lawrence River. He hoped to sail across Canada and reach the riches of the Orient. But Champlain came upon rapids, or fast-moving waters, which blocked his way. Neither Champlain nor his crew knew how to cross the rapids or what lay beyond them. The explorer went to a nearby Indian camp for information. Unfortunately, Champlain only spoke French, and the Indians did not understand him.

Champlain's Birch Bark Drawing

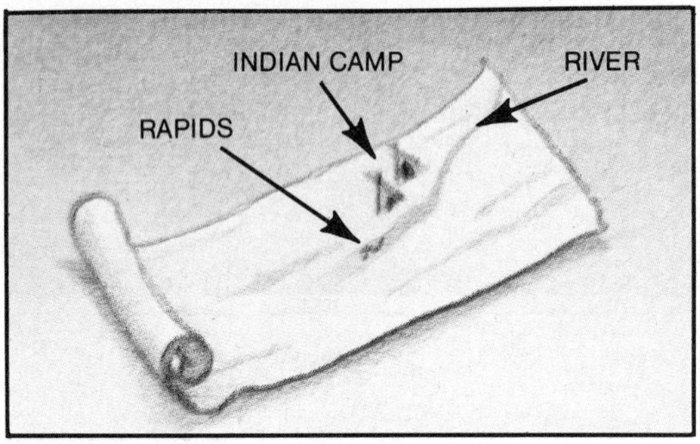

Drawing Completed by the Indians

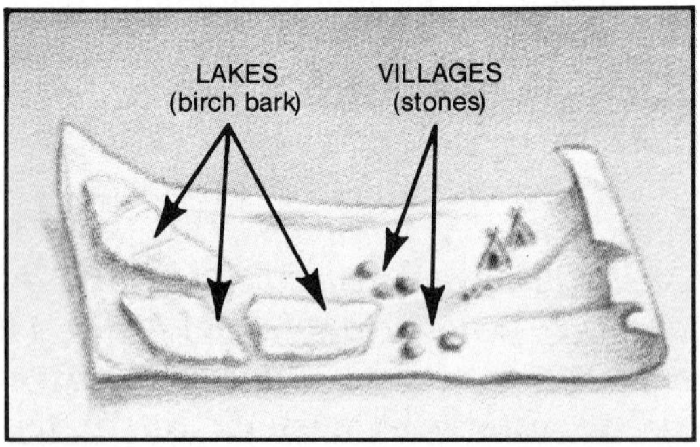

Champlain cut a piece of bark from a birch tree. On the bark he drew a picture of the river, the rapids, and the Indian camp. Then Champlain pointed to the part of the drawing that had nothing on it. The Indians understood that the explorer wanted them to complete the drawing and show him what the river was like beyond the rapids. They picked up a few stones and put them on the bark drawing. They used the stones to show where other Indian villages were. Then they cut up smaller pieces of birch bark to represent lakes.

Together, Champlain and the Indians had drawn a map. It proved to be a good map because Champlain was able to learn what lay beyond the rapids.

Today we have maps of every part of North America, as well as the rest of the world. But maps are not very useful if you cannot read them. Regardless of whether you are an explorer, an airline pilot, or a person planning a trip, you need to be able to read a map in order to locate your destination.

On a map, north means toward the North Pole. If you travel from any point on the earth toward the North Pole, you are heading north. On most maps, a direction finder, such as a **compass rose** or an arrow, indicates the direction of north. South, the direction of the South Pole, is always opposite north. East is to the right, and west is to the left. These four directions are called the **cardinal**

Compass Rose

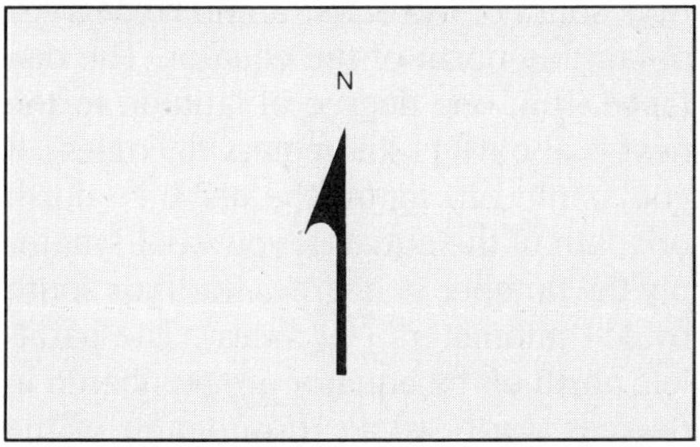

Cardinal Directions

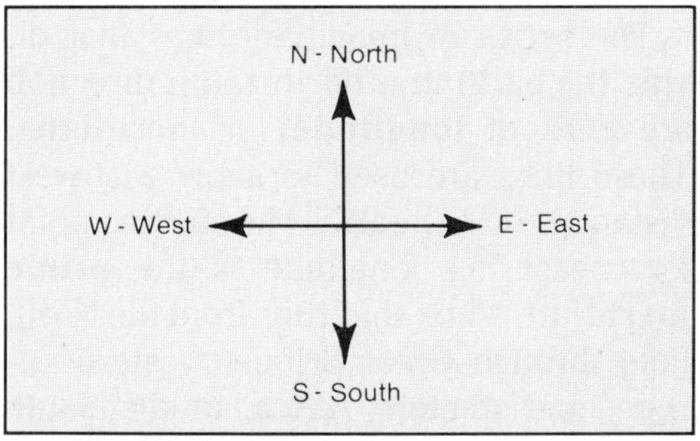

Intermediate Directions

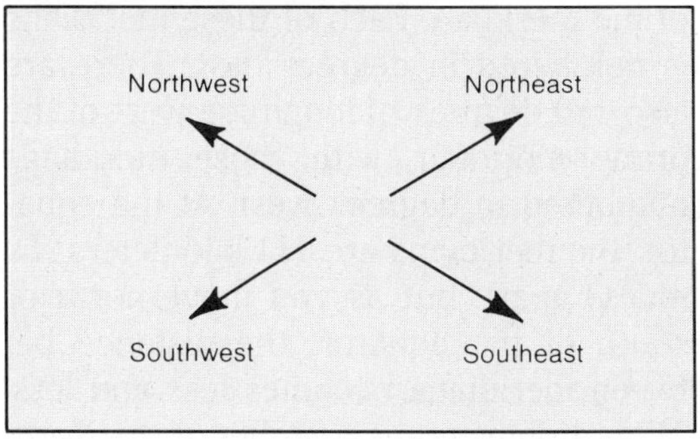

directions. The **intermediate directions,** or in-between directions, are northeast, northwest, southeast, and southwest.

On most maps, north is at the top of the page. To be sure where north is, check the direction finder. If there is no direction finder, assume north is at the top.

Using a Map Key

The first thing to look for in reading a map is the title or caption. This describes the subject or purpose of the map. The title tells you the kind of information you will find on the map. In order to provide more information about the land, a map contains symbols. Symbols are signs that stand for something else. On the map that Champlain and the Indians made, the Indians used stones to stand for the Indian villages and small pieces of birch bark to represent the lakes.

Color is often used as a symbol. The maps in this book, for example, use the color blue to represent water. The symbol for a national boundary is frequently a solid line, while dots and stars usually represent cities and capitals.

To unlock the meaning of the symbols on a map, find the **key** or **legend.** The map key identifies the meaning of the symbols.

Latitude and Longitude

The earth is a large solid body shaped like a ball. Your classroom globe is a model of the earth. Cartographers, or mapmakers, use lines of **latitude** and lines of **longitude** to locate places on the earth's surface.

The east-west lines are called lines of **latitude,** or **parallels.** Each parallel is numbered in degrees. These imaginary lines, like circles drawn around a ball, show distance north and south of the equator. The **equator** lies at 0° latitude. It is an imaginary line that circles the earth and lies halfway between the North and

Latitude

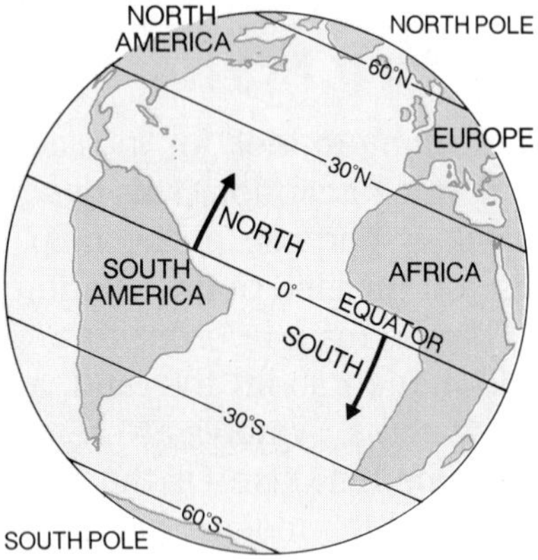

Longitude

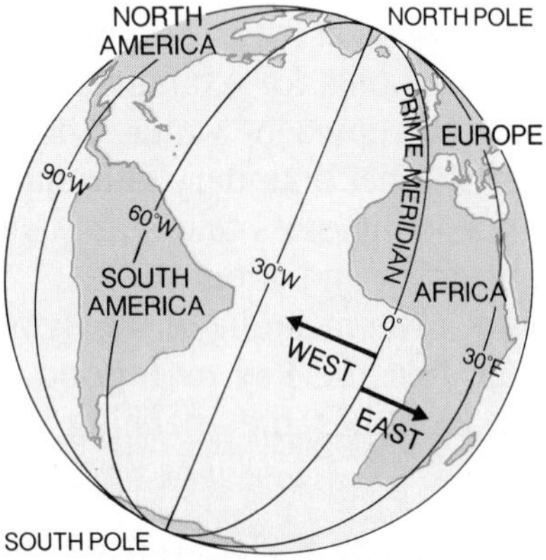

Latitude and Longitude

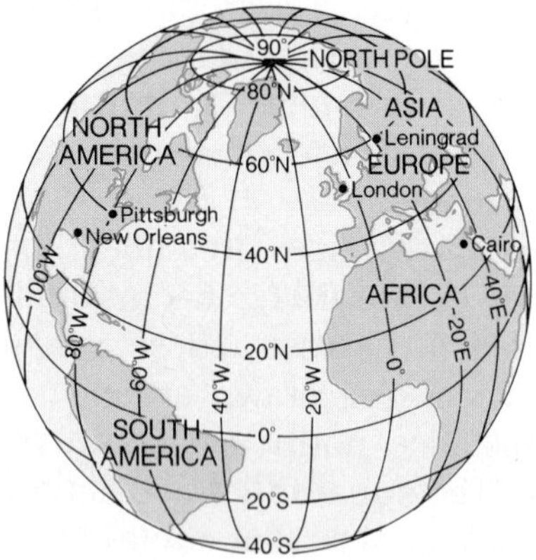

South poles. There are 90 degrees of latitude south of the equator and 90 degrees of latitude north of the equator. The distance from one degree of latitude to the next is about 111 kilometers (69 miles). If you wanted to figure the distance north or south of the equator, you would multiply the number of degrees north or south by 111 kilometers (69 miles). The parallels north of the equator are numbered in degrees north, while those south of the equator are numbered in degrees south. Therefore the North Pole is at 90° N.

The series of imaginary lines that divide the earth in a north-south direction are lines of **longitude,** or **meridians.** These lines are used to show east-west distances on the earth. The starting point for measuring longitude is the **prime meridian,** a line that runs from the North Pole through Great Britain, western Europe, and western Africa, to the South Pole. The prime meridian lies at 0°. There are 180 degrees of longitude east of the prime meridian. Each of these meridians is numbered in degrees east. There are also 180 degrees of longitude west of the prime meridian, with those meridians numbered in degrees west. At the equator, the meridians are 111 kilometers (69 miles) apart, but as you move north or south of the equator, the distance between meridians becomes less and less. All meridians come together at the North and South poles.

Each line of latitude intersects each line of longitude at only one place. Any spot on the earth can be located by finding the place where a line of latitude and a line of longitude meet. Think of latitude and longitude as streets or avenues that help you find a location in the same way that you might ask a friend to meet you on a street corner. For example, Pittsburgh is located where the 40th parallel north meets the 80th meridian west. To describe Pittsburgh's location, you would give the numbers, or **coordinates,** of these lines. Therefore, Pittsburgh is located at 40° N, 80° W.

When you study the earth, it is convenient to think of it in halves or **hemispheres.** "Hemi" comes from a Greek word meaning "half of." The equator divides the earth into the Northern Hemisphere and the Southern Hemisphere. Since we live north of the equator, the United States is in the Northern Hemisphere.

The division of the earth into Eastern and Western hemispheres is made at 20° W. Thus, Europe is in the Eastern Hemisphere, while the United States is in the Western Hemisphere.

Hemispheres

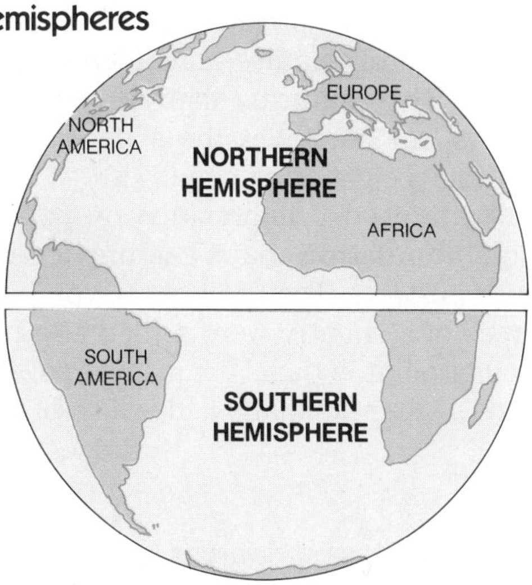

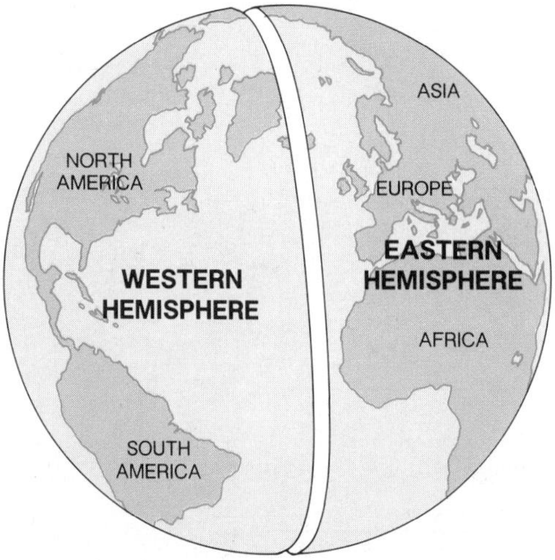

Types of Maps

No one map can show everything about an area. For that reason, this book contains many different kinds of maps. Each provides different kinds of information about the area shown.

A **physical map** is one that specializes in showing the **topography,** or natural features, of a place or region. Natural features are made by nature. They include landforms such as mountains, valleys, and deserts, and bodies of water such as oceans, rivers, and lakes.

The map on page 33 shows the topography of the United States. Shades of color are used to indicate mountains, highlands, plains, and other types of land found in the United States. You can identify the type of land found in each area by matching the color on the map to the color on the map key. For example, northwestern Alaska is colored light green. The map key indicates that areas colored light green are plains.

If you wanted to know where the United States is located, or what countries are our neighbors, a **political map** will provide the answers. A political map illustrates the boundaries of nations, states, cities, counties, and other political units. The political map on page 32 shows our 50 states, the state capitals, and our neighboring countries.

If you needed information on population, **population maps** can provide you with answers. They can show you what areas of a country were settled at a particular point in time. The map on page 31 shows the population density of the United States today. The map uses color to show how thickly populated each area of the country is.

If you wanted to know the climate of a particular area, you could consult a **climate regions map.** The map below, for example, divides the United States into eight climate regions. By consulting the map key, you can learn the climate of each region. The map indicates that Hawaii, which is colored yellow, has the

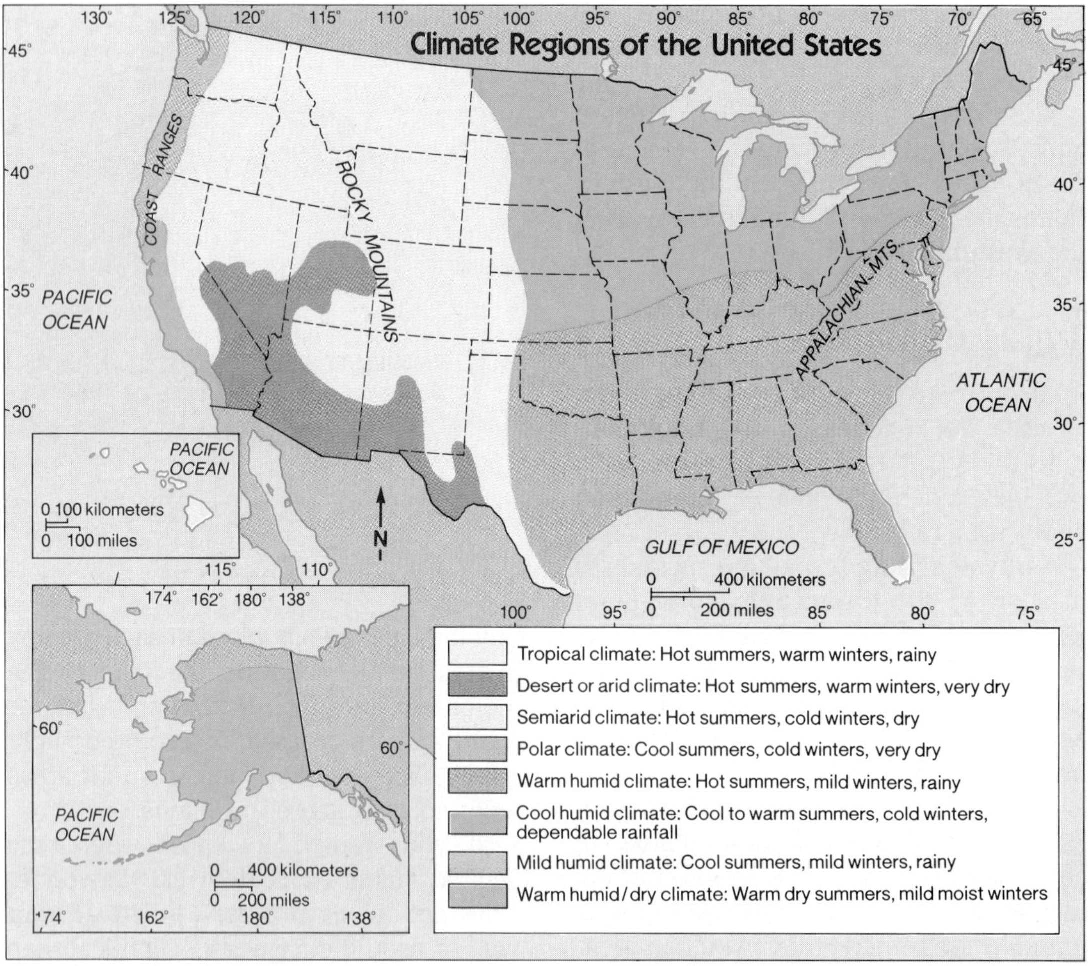

warmest climate. The coolest climate is found in northern Alaska, which is colored lavender.

Knowing how to read and use maps can make the rest of the textbook easier to understand. It can help you better remember what you have learned.

CHECK YOUR SKILLS

1. Define geography and compass rose.
2. Explain the purpose of a map key or legend.
3. Using the political map of the United States on page 32, what direction is Washington, D.C., from Baton Rouge, Louisiana?
4. What are the lines on a globe called that measure distance north and south of the equator?
5. List the four hemispheres. In what hemispheres is the United States found?
6. Using the climate map on page 20, describe the climate where you live.

2. Understanding Time

American history covers an enormous span of time, beginning with the arrival of the first people on this continent thousands of years ago. To make all of the events that have occurred since that time more understandable, it is helpful to have a system for organizing and arranging events. One such system is **chronological order.** Chronological order is based on time. It arranges events in the order in which they occurred, starting with the earliest events and ending with the most recent ones.

Chronological order uses dates to determine the order of events. Dates tell us when events took place. Chronological order also uses longer spans of time to organize events. A **century** is a period of 100 years. Centuries are counted starting with the year 1 A.D., the year that officially marks the birth of Jesus Christ. The 100 years between 1 and 100 are called the first century. The years from 101 to 200 are called the second century, and so on.

A **decade** is a one tenth of a century, or ten years. The 1960's, for example, was a decade. This decade covered the years from 1960 through 1969. A **generation** is the average time between the birth of parents and the birth of their children. In our country, about 30 years is considered a generation. How long is a **lifetime?** In our country today, it is considered to be about 70 years. In earlier times, a lifetime was much shorter.

A **timeline** is a chart that shows how events are related in time. On a timeline dates and events are arranged in chronological order. Some timelines represent hundreds or thousands of years; others show only a short span of time. The timeline on page 22 gives you the dates and the basic facts needed to understand the sequence of some important events in American history. You read a horizontal timeline from left to right. The earliest date is at the left and the most recent date is at the right.

CHECK YOUR SKILLS

1. Why is it useful to arrange events in chronological order?
2. Define century and generation.

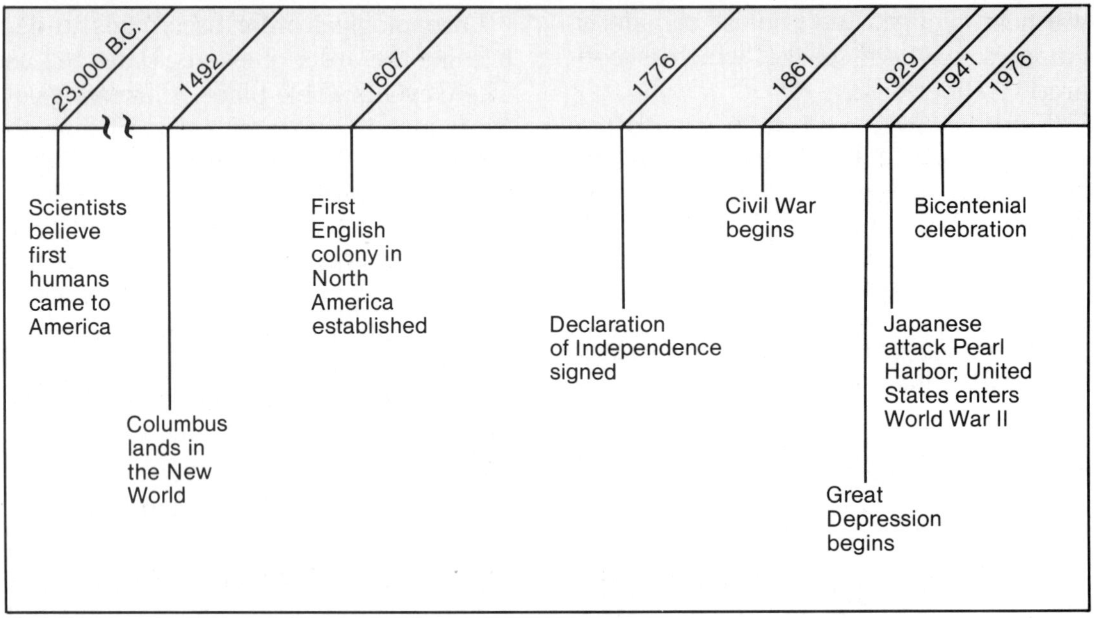

3. Draw a timeline for the twentieth century. Mark off the timeline in decades. Look in Units 7, 8, 9, and 10 of the text, and find five events that occurred during the twentieth century. Put these events on your timeline.

3. Using Historical Information

The task of researching a specific event or time period from the past is something like putting the pieces of a jigsaw puzzle together. The historian's "puzzle pieces" are sources. These sources come from a variety of different places and are fitted together to form a picture of the event or time period.

Primary Sources

One of the most important sources of information to the historian is what is known as **primary source material.** Primary source materials are first-hand accounts or objects that were created by people who lived during the time period under study.

An examination of a town's tax rolls will reveal information about population and family size. People's wills provide information about how people lived by describing the things they owned. Letters, diaries, and newspapers describe day-to-day life and give an idea of issues that concerned people most. Paintings and photographs show dress and life styles. Furniture, implements, tools, and weapons can indicate the level of technology. Business records and cargo lists can provide information on occupations and the standard of living. All of these sources of information are used by the historian in creating a picture of the past.

Putting the pieces of an historical "puzzle" together is no easy task. Two historians researching the same event can very well come up with different conclusions because the information left by our ancestors is often incomplete.

Using Statistics

Historians also use a variety of **statistics** to complete their picture of the past. Statistics are facts or data assembled and organized so as to present significant information about a particular subject. Historians often make extensive use of two types of statistics. These are **economic statistics** and **demographic statistics.**

Economic statistics are used to determine the relative well-being of industry, agriculture, and labor at a particular point in time. Historians look at such statistics as the earnings of workers, the output of industry, and the level of prices to determine how well-off people may have been at a specific point in history.

Demographic statistics consist of data collected about the population itself. Historians use demographic statistics to determine characteristics of the population, such as race, sex, age, religion, level of education, and so on. **Vital statistics** are data related to births, deaths, marriages, health, and disease. These statistics are a good indicator of the quality of a society's food, shelter, clothing, and medical care.

Historians use economic and demographic statistics to look for changes that have taken place in the economy and population over time. Figures showing **trends,** or the general direction in which a population is changing, are studied to determine their relationship to historical events. Statistical trends can provide clues to the causes and effects of many events in history.

One of the most useful statistical sources of information about American history is the U.S. **Census.** The census gathers data on the population size, income, housing, education, race, marital status, and a variety of other information about Americans. The first census was taken in 1790, and one has been taken every ten years since.

Ways to Organize Statistics

A history book usually includes several different types of graphics, or pictures, to display statistical information. **Charts, graphs,** and **tables** are used to summarize information and make it more easily understood.

Charts can be used to show sequence, organization, comparison, and development. They summarize important information in a visual manner. To read a chart, first look at the title to determine what kind of chart it is. Also look at any column headings to determine what information is being presented.

A statistical table is a shortcut to reading pages and pages of facts and figures. It presents a great deal of information in a compact form for easy reference.

Tables are easy to read if you follow these steps:

1. Read the title to determine the purpose or subject of the table.
2. Note the units of measurement that are being used.

3. Look for a label at the top of each column.
4. Read across the columns from left to right.
5. Note any special explanations or footnotes.
6. Finally, ask yourself, "What is the significance of the data in the table?"

You may have noticed that tables and charts are very similar in purpose and composition. The major difference between them is that tables tend to have more numbers than words.

Read the table below, and decide which city you would like best to live in. Let the questions below guide you:

1. What is the title of the table?
2. What three factors of city life are shown in the table?
3. How many cities are in the table?
4. What years are compared?
5. How is change between the years shown?

One of the ways to illustrate trends is through the use of a graph. A graph indicates what has happened over a period of time. For example, it might show whether there has been an increase, or a decrease in births, prices, and so on. In reading a line graph, follow these steps:

1. Read the title of the graph.
2. Look at the vertical and horizontal axes. Read any words or numbers that go along with them.
3. Check to see where the line begins and where it ends. Does the line go up or down?
4. Ask yourself what conclusions can be drawn from the graph.

Look at the graph of American trade with Europe on page 528 to see if trade with the nations of Europe was increasing or decreasing in the early 1900's. Do you see a trend?

CHECK YOUR SKILLS

1. What kinds of sources does an historian use in recreating past events?
2. What is the difference between economic statistics and demographic statistics?
3. What is a trend?

City Life

City	Population Density (Persons per square km)			Crime (Serious crimes per 1,000 persons)			Taxes (Local taxes per person)		
	1970	1980	Change	1970	1982	Change	1970	1981	Change
New York	68,234	60,748	−11%	66	97	+47%	$383	$1,053	+175%
Chicago	39,202	34,121	−13%	38	61	+61%	$113	$ 263	+133%
Los Angeles	15,695	16,535	+ 5%	62	108	+74%	$110	$ 255	+132%
Philadelphia	39,303	32,150	−18%	23	56	+143%	$183	$ 500	+173%
Houston	7,358	7,426	+ 1%	49	104	+112%	$ 82	$ 253	+209%
Detroit	28,407	22,984	−19%	84	128	+52%	$148	$ 300	+103%
Dallas	8,234	7,032	−15%	60	128	+113%	$106	$ 260	+145%

4. What is the purpose of putting information in graphic form?

4. Reading Skills

Your social studies text is filled with information about the people and events that have shaped our nation's history. However, you cannot read a textbook as you would read a novel. Reading a textbook requires a different set of reading skills.

The Parts of the Book

Before you begin to read, it is helpful to familiarize yourself with the scope and contents of your textbook. You can do this by examining certain parts of the book. The **table of contents** allows you to see the scope of the material included in the book as well as the order of the specific topics. The table of contents on pages 5–14 indicates that this book traces United States history from the arrival of the first people on this continent up to the present time. The table of contents contains a list of all maps, charts, and graphs found in your book. The table of contents also tells you that this book begins with a review of skills and ends with a **glossary** and **index.** The table of contents can help you find things in your book quickly and efficiently.

The glossary on pages 738 through 748 is a dictionary of the unfamiliar social studies terms you will be learning in this book. A textbook glossary is very helpful if you are unsure of a word and do not have a dictionary at hand.

The index is an alphabetical listing of all of the main topics discussed in your book. It provides you with page numbers where information on each topic may be found. The index of this book is on pages 749–766.

This textbook is organized into units, chapters, and sections. Each unit begins with a brief preview of the chapters found in the unit. By reading these previews, you can get an idea of the main topics that will be covered. Each chapter begins with a list of objectives. These objectives tell you what the most important topics and skills are in the chapter. Each section of the book begins with a question called "Before you read." The purpose of this question is to help you focus on the main topic in the section as you begin your reading.

Getting the Most Out of Your Reading

Most textbooks are filled with facts and details. If you can connect all the facts to a main idea, or topic, you will find the information easier to read and remember.

Some clues to the main topics are frequently found in chapter titles, section headings, and subsection headings. Look at Chapter 1. It is entitled: "The American Indians." Section headings in that chapter include: "The New World Prehistory" and "Indian Societies and Civilizations." The chapter titles and section headings clearly tell you what the topics are.

After you have identified the topic, the next step is to find the main idea. The main idea is the most important fact or concept that relates to the topic. Sometimes the main idea is given in the first sentence of a paragraph. At other times it is at the end or in the middle. Occasionally the main idea is not directly stated but merely suggested.

Related ideas and facts, or details, grow out of the main idea and tell about it. Often these details support and illustrate the main idea. A key to being a good reader is to keep track of the main idea and to recognize that details are only important insofar as they explain and illustrate the main idea.

Functions of Paragraphs

Paragraphs tend to have some common patterns. Recognizing these patterns can help you understand and remember what you read.

1. *Central Thought Supported by Details.* In this form of a paragraph, the main idea is stated in the first or last sentence. The other sentences of the paragraph give additional information about the main idea. An example is shown below:

> **main idea** [The buffalo provided the Plains Indians with almost everything they needed to survive.] **details** [The Indians ate fresh buffalo meat and dried what was left. From the buffalo skin they made blankets, moccasins, clothing, and tepees.]

2. *Paragraphs of Definition.* These paragraphs define an idea or technical term. They provide background for further information and understanding. Here is a paragraph of definition.

> **technical term** In 1887, Congress passed [the Dawes Act.] **definition** [This act divided the Indian reservations into individual sections of land. Each head of an Indian family was to be given 65 hectares (160 acres). Any reservation lands leftover were sold by the government.]

A paragraph of definition explains the meaning of one or more words, phrases, or clauses. In reading such paragraphs from your textbook, you should ask yourself two questions:

1. What is being defined?
2. What does it mean?

3. *Paragraphs of Comparison.* Describing likenesses and differences is a pattern that is often used in history texts. Authors frequently compare people, eras, and events. In reading such paragraphs, you should ask yourself two questions:

1. What or who is being compared?
2. What likenesses or differences are being compared and contrasted?

Certain words signal this pattern. Words that signal likenesses include: also, like, too, as well as, besides, and as much as. Some words that signal differences are: in contrast, on the other hand, although, but, and however. The paragraph below illustrates comparison.

> **comparison** [Great Britain had a well-equipped and well-trained army.] **clue word** [Besides its army, Great Britain had [also] a powerful navy.] It was capable of dominating American waters and the ocean shipping lanes.

4. *Paragraphs of Cause and Effect.* Social studies textbooks contain many paragraphs with cause and effect patterns. A cause is something that makes something else happen. What happens, or the result, is the effect. Historians frequently research to find the causes of wars or movements, and then they explore the effects.

Watch for words that may signal cause/effect patterns such as: because, since, therefore, thus, and as a result.

The following paragraph is an example of the cause and effect pattern. Does a cause and effect pattern always have to have a signal word? Read the following paragraph and decide.

> **cause** [The coming of the Europeans to America changed the lives of American Indians forever.] **effect** [Many Indians died in battles fought against the newcomers. Even more died from diseases, like smallpox, which the Europeans brought with them.]

5. *Paragraphs of Sequence.* Frequently historians describe a sequence of events—one thing happening after another in time. Time order relationships are easy to spot because they are often signaled by dates or clue words such as: first, next, then, later, finally, before, after, during, soon, and since. Read the following paragraph and notice the sequence of events presented in the paragraph.

> The relationship between the Vikings and the Indians was tense. The Vikings treated the natives with cruelty. **sequence clue** [Finally,] the tense relationship erupted into warfare. The Viking settlement was destroyed. The Vikings escaped with their lives but the experience convinced them to give up and go home. **sequence clue** It would be almost 500 years [before] Europeans and Indians met again.

Paragraphs have specific functions. Some explain a cause and effect, some compare and contrast, some tell you time order. Not all patterns are clearly visible, and some may be mixed or combined. Even so, looking for a pattern in a paragraph will help you in understanding the main ideas of the writers and in remembering what they said.

Scanning and Skimming

When you read social studies material, your reading usually has one of two purposes. One purpose may be to find specific information. The other purpose is to learn all important points and the facts that support them.

Two useful reading tools that can help you to read social studies material more effectively are **scanning** and **skimming.** Scanning involves reading material rapidly for the purpose of finding some specific information. It is similar to scanning a crowd of people when you are trying to locate a friend. In reading history, you can use scanning to find a date, a name, or a specific block of information.

See how long it takes you to scan the following paragraph for the number of people living in New Netherland.

> The Dutch West India Company ran New Netherland to make profits for a small group of wealthy people. The company granted large estates along the Hudson River to wealthy lords or "patroons." Each patroon was required to bring fifty colonists to America. These colonists were to farm the

patroon's estate. The colonists were allowed to build their own villages, but they had to live by the patroon's rules. Other Dutch settlers were given no voice in running the colony either. As a result, few people were attracted to New Netherland. By the mid 1660's, only about 10,000 people had settled there.

Skimming is used to get a general idea of the material, to alert you to the author's purpose, and to help you when you are reviewing for a test or writing a report. Skimming involves looking for key words and phrases.

The following passage shows how to skim effectively. The words in bold type are those that you might read if you were skimming the paragraph.

> **Scientists think** the **first people** came to **America** at least **25,000 years ago during the Ice Age.** These early settlers were the **ancestors** of the **American Indians.** There was **never** a **large or continuous migration** of the early settlers to America. They **came** to this new world in **small groups** over a **period** of **thousands** of **years. Anthropologists** who have **studied** the early Indians' material **culture** (pots, tools, weapons, and the like) **estimate** that the **migrations ended only about 2,000 years ago.**

Using Vocabulary Clues

There are many clues in this textbook to the meaning of unfamiliar words. New social studies terms can be found in bold print as you read. These words are defined in phrases or sentences that come before or after them. You can also find a formal definition of these words at the end of the paragraph in which they appear. The glossary in the back of your book contains all of these social studies terms.

Writers often provide you with the meaning of an unfamiliar word within the same sentence. There are three punctuation marks that are used to signal that an explanation of the word will follow. These punctuation marks are commas, parentheses, and dashes. Here is an example:

> In or near each settlement was a **kiva,** an underground building used for religious purposes.

The words following the comma explain what the word **kiva** means. Authors also use certain words to signal that a definition of an unfamiliar word is being provided. Such signal words include; or, who is, that is, called, meaning, and which is.

Here is an example;

> They lived in permanent, or sedentary, villages.

CHECK YOUR SKILLS

1. On what pages in this book is there information about Ronald Reagan?
2. What is the glossary definition of the word suffrage?
3. Look at the first paragraph in the righthand column on page 505 of your text. What kind of organization is used in this paragraph?
4. Explain the difference between scanning and skimming.

5. In the sentence that follows, use context clues to write a definition of the underlined word: The nomadic people of this region lived in small brush shelters called hogans.

5. Study Skills

In order to get the most out of your social studies reading, it is important to develop a study schedule and stick to it. Find a quiet spot away from people and the television, and begin your reading.

Previewing

To help you concentrate, comprehend better, and remember more, a system of studying is needed. First, preview the chapter so that you can better anticipate what the authors are going to tell you. The better you can predict the message of the authors, the more you will understand and remember. This textbook makes it particularly easy for you to look ahead, because the unit opening pages provide capsule previews of each chapter in the unit. Read the unit previews, and then read the paragraphs that introduce the chapter you will be studying. Note the chapter objectives to see what you should be able to do after reading the chapter. Quickly skim all of the subheadings, the graphics, and the final paragraph of the chapter. The final paragraph will give you an idea of where the authors are headed. Then read the chapter summary located on the chapter review pages. The chapter summary contains a brief review of the important concepts and events in the chapter.

Question and Read

As you read each section or subsection, you should stop and ask yourself, "What are the authors going to tell me?" Apply the question technique by taking the section and subsection headings and turning them into questions. In reading "Great Britain Under Strain," you might form the question:

Why was Great Britain under strain?

Then, when you finish the section or subsection, check to see that you have found the answer to your question.

As you read, try to make mental pictures of what you are reading about. If the passage is about Indians, try to visualize the Indians and their style of life. Making your own mental pictures helps bring what you are reading into sharp focus.

Look at the graphics—the maps, charts, and tables—as carefully as you read the rest of the textbook. The graphics help you understand what you are reading about. One map, chart, or table, may make hundreds of words instantly clear.

Review

After you are through reading, check to see if you have understood what you read. See if you can state the main idea and some of the important details that support the main idea. If you find that you cannot do this, that is a sign that you need to do some rereading.

Studies show that students remember much more of what they have studied if they review the material. To help you review, you will find section review questions, chapter reviews, and unit reviews throughout your book. These questions help to let you know what you have learned and what you may need to relearn. When reviewing, you should turn back to the chapter objectives found on the first page of each chapter. Check to see if you can accomplish them. See if you can answer the "Before you read" questions found at the beginning of each section. The best time to review is within a day or two of questioning and reading.

Studying for a Test

The most important way to prepare for a test is to study every day. Paying attention in class and completing your daily assignments will help you to be well-prepared when test day comes. There are other things you can do, in addition to daily study, to help improve your performance on tests.

1. Review the answers to the questions in the chapter and unit reviews. Many teachers use these questions, or similar ones, as items on their tests.
2. Ask yourself: What kind of questions will my teacher include in the test? Then, see if you can answer those questions. If possible, find out whether the test will be an essay or objective test or a combination of both. Look at previous exams you have taken in class for clues as to the kinds of questions your teacher tends to put on exams.
3. Write a one-page summary of the main ideas of the chapter or unit.
4. Recite the most important names, places, dates, and terms discussed in each chapter.
5. Compare and contrast the terms, issues, and ideas discussed in the reading.
6. Recite the causes and effects of the most significant events discussed in each chapter.
7. Look over the graphics, and write out the main idea of each.

Taking a Test

Be sure to write clearly. Your teacher will appreciate an answer that is easy to read. If the test involves essay questions, carefully organize your answers. Many students make the mistake of putting down everything they know with little thought about how the ideas connect to each other.

1. Begin your essay with an introductory statement in the first paragraph.
2. In the next paragraph, make your first major point, and supply some details to explain your idea.
3. Assuming that your essay has a second major point, develop that in a third paragraph. Again, offer a few details or examples.
4. End your essay with a concluding paragraph which sums up your essay.

CHECK YOUR SKILLS

1. What are some ways to preview the material in a chapter?
2. Apply the "question and read" technique to the subsection "The First Americans" found on page 37.
3. Why is it important to review material you have read?
4. How should an essay be organized?

Population of the United States

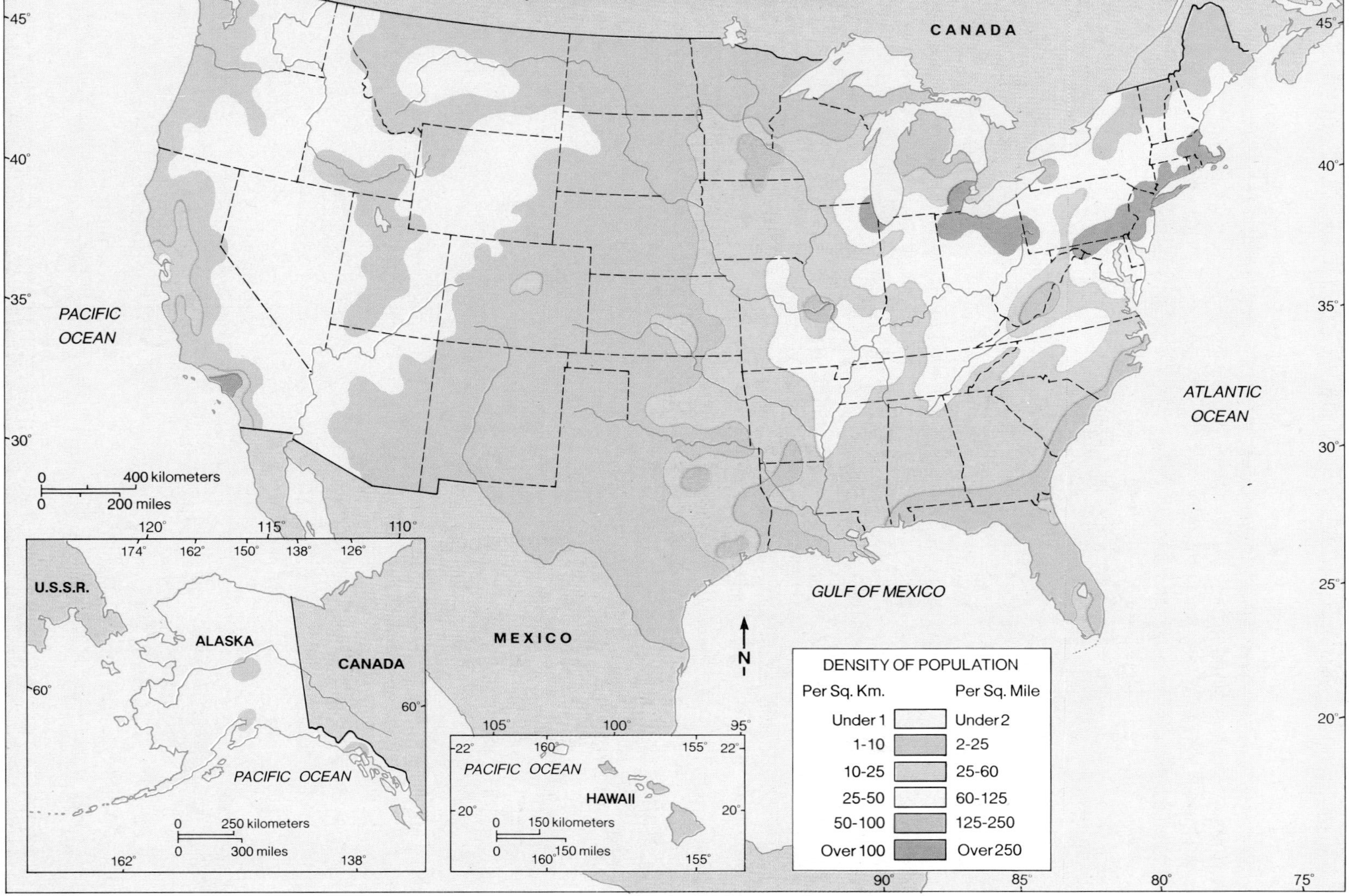
CANADA
PACIFIC OCEAN
ATLANTIC OCEAN
GULF OF MEXICO
MEXICO
N
400 kilometers
200 miles
U.S.S.R.
ALASKA
CANADA
PACIFIC OCEAN
250 kilometers
300 miles
PACIFIC OCEAN
HAWAII
150 kilometers
150 miles
DENSITY OF POPULATION
Per Sq. Km. Per Sq. Mile
Under 1 Under 2
1-10 2-25
10-25 25-60
25-50 60-125
50-100 125-250
Over 100 Over 250

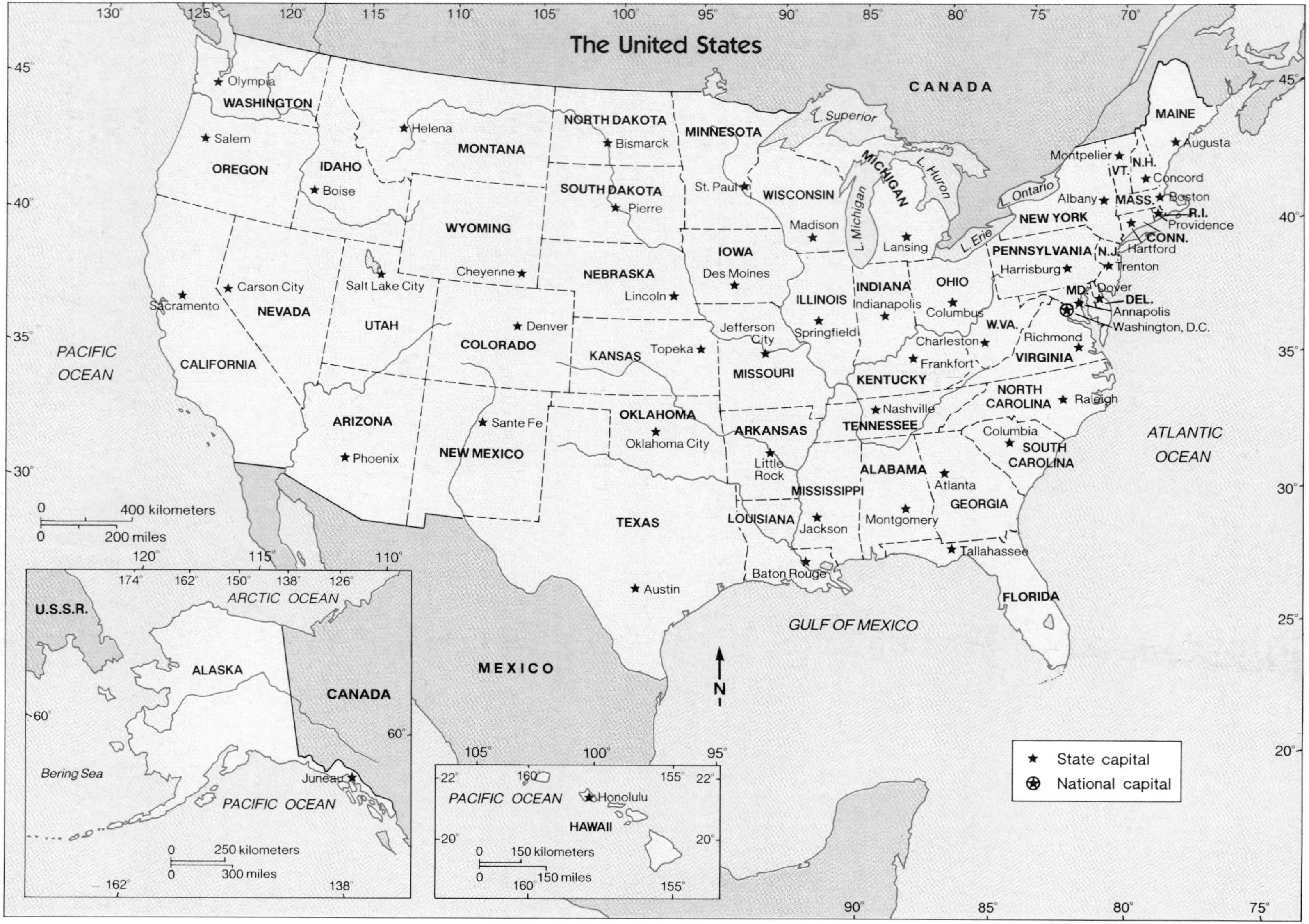
The United States
CANADA
PACIFIC OCEAN
ATLANTIC OCEAN
GULF OF MEXICO
MEXICO
WASHINGTON
★ Olympia
OREGON
★ Salem
CALIFORNIA
★ Sacramento
NEVADA
★ Carson City
IDAHO
★ Boise
MONTANA
★ Helena
WYOMING
Cheyenne ★
UTAH
Salt Lake City
ARIZONA
★ Phoenix
COLORADO
★ Denver
NEW MEXICO
★ Sante Fe
NORTH DAKOTA
★ Bismarck
SOUTH DAKOTA
★ Pierre
NEBRASKA
Lincoln ★
KANSAS
Topeka ★
OKLAHOMA
Oklahoma City
TEXAS
★ Austin
MINNESOTA
St. Paul ★
IOWA
Des Moines
MISSOURI
Jefferson City
ARKANSAS
Little Rock
LOUISIANA
Baton Rouge
WISCONSIN
Madison
ILLINOIS
Springfield
MICHIGAN
Lansing
INDIANA
Indianapolis
OHIO
Columbus
KENTUCKY
Frankfort
TENNESSEE
Nashville
MISSISSIPPI
Jackson
ALABAMA
Montgomery
GEORGIA
Atlanta
FLORIDA
★ Tallahassee
SOUTH CAROLINA
Columbia
NORTH CAROLINA
★ Raleigh
VIRGINIA
Richmond
W.VA.
Charleston
PENNSYLVANIA
Harrisburg
NEW YORK
Albany
N.J.
Trenton
MD.
Annapolis
DEL.
Dover
Washington, D.C.
CONN.
Hartford
R.I.
Providence
MASS.
Boston
VT.
Montpelier
N.H.
Concord
MAINE
Augusta
L. Superior
L. Michigan
L. Huron
L. Erie
L. Ontario
0 400 kilometers
0 200 miles
N
130° 125° 120° 115° 110° 105° 100° 95° 90° 85° 80° 75° 70°
45° 40° 35° 30° 25° 20°
U.S.S.R.
ALASKA
CANADA
ARCTIC OCEAN
PACIFIC OCEAN
Bering Sea
Juneau
174° 162° 150° 138° 126°
60°
0 250 kilometers
0 300 miles
PACIFIC OCEAN
HAWAII
★ Honolulu
22° 20° 160° 155°
0 150 kilometers
0 150 miles
★ State capital
⊛ National capital

Landforms of the United States

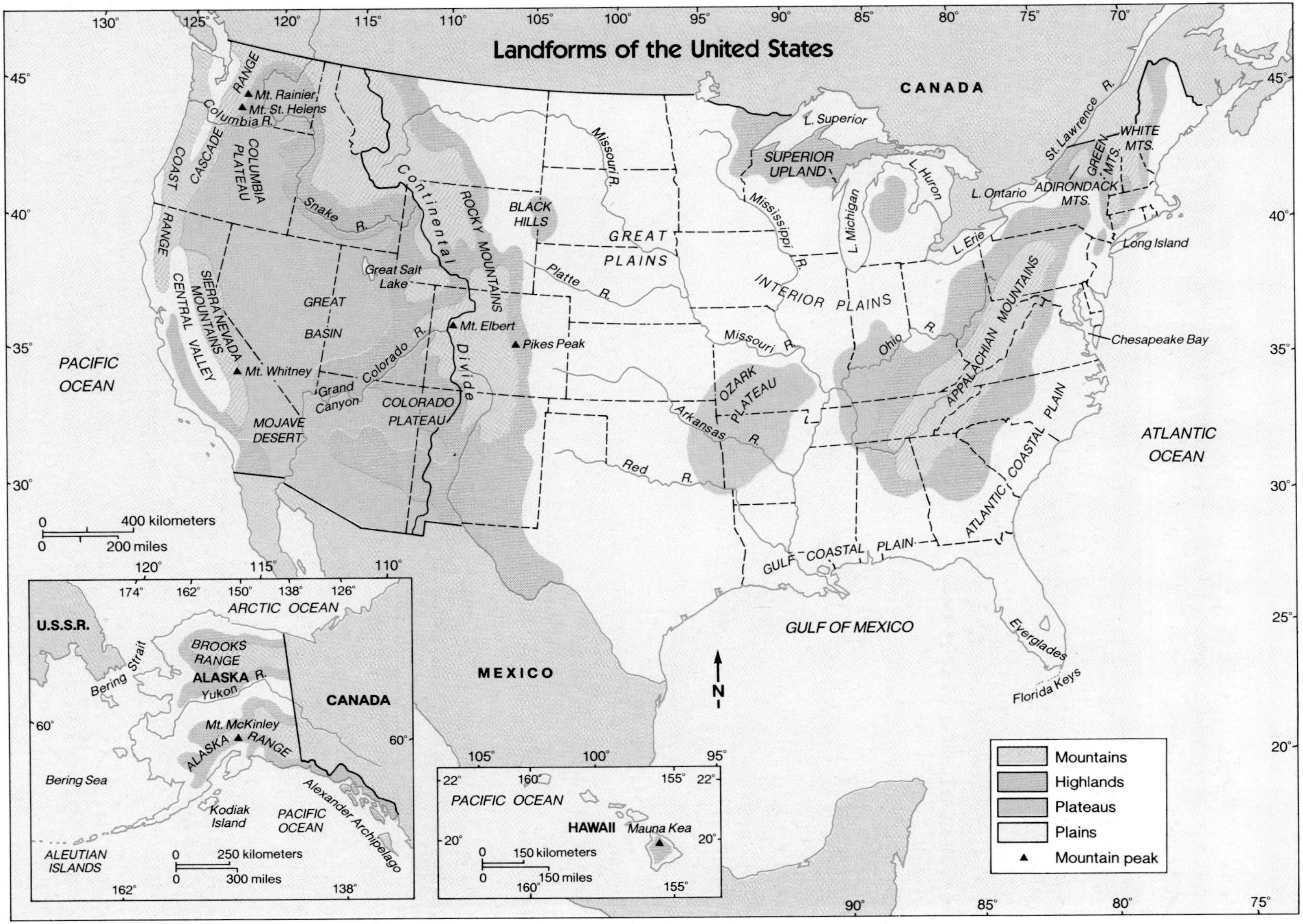
CANADA
PACIFIC OCEAN
ATLANTIC OCEAN
GULF OF MEXICO
MEXICO
COAST RANGE
CASCADE RANGE
Mt. Rainier
Mt. St. Helens
Columbia R.
COLUMBIA PLATEAU
Snake R.
SIERRA NEVADA MOUNTAINS
CENTRAL VALLEY
Mt. Whitney
MOJAVE DESERT
GREAT BASIN
Great Salt Lake
Grand Canyon
Colorado R.
COLORADO PLATEAU
Continental Divide
ROCKY MOUNTAINS
Mt. Elbert
Pikes Peak
BLACK HILLS
Missouri R.
GREAT PLAINS
Platte R.
Red R.
Arkansas R.
OZARK PLATEAU
INTERIOR PLAINS
Mississippi R.
Ohio R.
L. Superior
SUPERIOR UPLAND
L. Michigan
L. Huron
L. Erie
L. Ontario
St. Lawrence R.
ADIRONDACK MTS.
GREEN MTS.
WHITE MTS.
Long Island
Chesapeake Bay
APPALACHIAN MOUNTAINS
ATLANTIC COASTAL PLAIN
GULF COASTAL PLAIN
Everglades
Florida Keys
N
0 400 kilometers
0 200 miles
U.S.S.R.
ARCTIC OCEAN
Bering Strait
BROOKS RANGE
ALASKA
Yukon R.
CANADA
Mt. McKinley
ALASKA RANGE
Bering Sea
Kodiak Island
PACIFIC OCEAN
Alexander Archipelago
ALEUTIAN ISLANDS
0 250 kilometers
0 300 miles
PACIFIC OCEAN
HAWAII
Mauna Kea
0 150 kilometers
0 150 miles
Mountains
Highlands
Plateaus
Plains
Mountain peak

Unit 1 The New World's Settlers

1 *Scientists believe that ancestors of the American Indians arrived in America over 25,000 years ago. The Indian population grew from the first small groups of prehistoric hunters to millions of people. These people developed rich and complex societies in America.*

2 *In the 1400's, Europeans began to explore the world for new trade routes. These explorers found two continents they did not know existed—North and South America. By 1500, Europeans had begun the exploration of this New World.*

3 *The English began to establish permanent colonies in North America in the early 1600's. Within a short period of time, these English colonies grew and prospered. Eventually, individuals no longer thought of themselves as English colonists but as Americans who lived in English America.*

Chapter
1

The American Indians

One of the most interesting parts of history is the story of the first Americans and their descendants. For centuries people have been fascinated by how the ancestors of the American Indians migrated to America. The story of how their many different societies developed is a remarkable one. In this chapter, you will read about the American Indians and the cultures and life styles they developed.

After you read this chapter, you will be able to:

1. Describe how the first humans might have come to America and what their lives were like.
2. Identify and explain major differences among the seven American Indian cultural groups.

Background: It is correct to refer to the native American populations as Indians even though the name is actually a misnomer that refers to Columbus' mistaken impression that he had made contact with the inhabitants of the East Indies.

1. The New World Prehistory

BEFORE YOU READ: *How did the first people reach North America, and what were their lives like after they arrived?*

Scientists think the first people came to America at least 25,000 years ago during the Ice Age. These early settlers were the ancestors of the American Indians. There was never a large or continuous migration of the early settlers to America. They came to this continent in small groups over a period of thousands of years. **Anthropologists** who have studied the early Indians' material culture (pots, tools, weapons, and the like) estimate that the migrations ended only about 2,000 years ago.

anthropologist a scientist who studies human culture and development

The First Americans

The Ice Age began long before the first people came to North America. Scientists estimate that it started some 3 million years ago and ended about 10,000 years ago. During this period, glaciers, which are huge sheets of slowly moving ice, covered much of North America. Temperatures were so cold that sea water froze and turned into glaciers. As sea water froze, the water level dropped, sometimes by as much as 100 meters (330 feet). The Bering Strait, which today separates Asia from North America, became a wide stretch of dry land during the Ice Age.

Possible Migration Routes

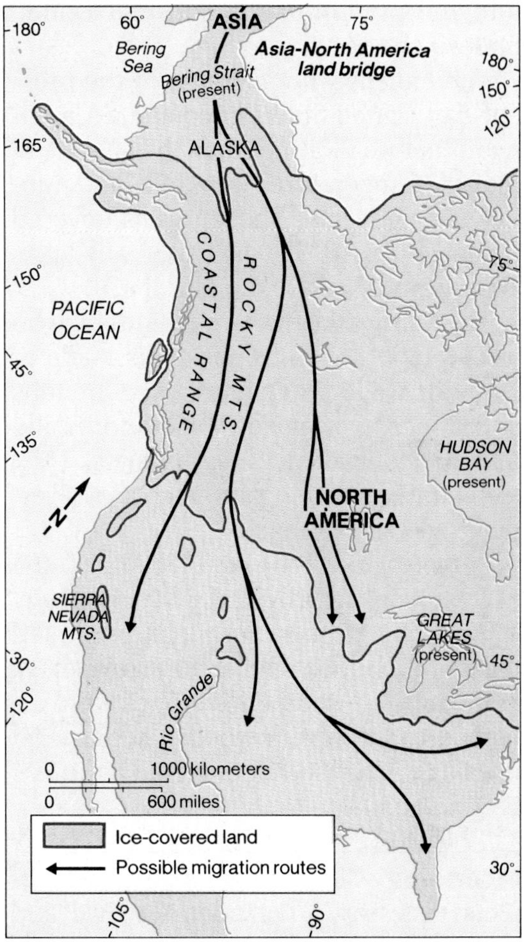

According to this map, in what general direction did the Indians travel?

Many scientists believe the first people to migrate to America did so by using this Bering Strait land bridge.

Scientists think the newcomers settled in present-day Alaska for a long time. Then, slowly, the newcomers began to follow the game herds southward through ice-free routes along the slopes of the Rocky Mountains. These early Indians eventually passed below the southern

For Extra Interest: Ask the class if they can think of any areas of the world that have glaciers today. Have them name and locate specific areas or countries on a wall map, if one is available. Assign a class project in the library to research the historical movement of glaciers.

Background: Some scientists suggest that we may yet experience another ice age. They point to a trend toward cooler temperatures. Other scientists believe that a "greenhouse effect," owing to pollution, will counteract the cooler temperatures.

edge of the glaciers. They were crossing into the present-day continental United States.

The Indians who migrated to the present-day United States encountered a climate that was warmer than the climate of Alaska. Temperatures were mild and rainfall was abundant. The land was covered by dense forests, tall grasses, many lakes and swamps, and lush plant life.

The early Indians were hunters who used simple weapons and tools made of stone or wood. They used wooden clubs and stones to bring down mammoths and mastodons, giant Ice Age animals. They also hunted smaller game such as wolves, deer, elk, and rabbits.

Between 25,000 B.C. and 8000 B.C., the early Indians improved their **technology** by carving stones into sharp-pointed darts, which look similar to arrowheads. Some of these sharpened stones were attached to the tips of wooden spears and used as weapons. Others served as knives to skin animals.

---

technology knowledge, skills, and objects necessary for human survival and comfort

---

About 8000 B.C., the Ice Age ended. The weather became warmer and the glaciers melted. America's climate changed, too, and the weather patterns that we know today began to emerge. The eastern portion of the country remained humid and rainy. In the southwest, however, dry plains and deserts began to appear. Some scientists believe the great Ice Age animals could not adapt to the newer climate and environment, and soon became **extinct**.

---

extinct no longer living

The early Indians faced major problems as well. They needed to change their way of life to survive in the new environment. They had to locate new food sources. During this period of prehistory, called the Archaic Age, they met these challenges with determination and remarkable ability.

Archaic Age Indians

The Archaic Age lasted from about 8000 B.C. to about 1200 B.C. During this era, Indians worked hard adjusting to the changing environment. They looked for new sources of food and developed better technology.

Western Archaic Indians lived in a dry and barren region where animal and plant resources were in short supply. They were nomadic, or wandering, people who never lived long in one place. Traveling in small groups, they had to move continuously to find enough food. Life for them was hard and demanding.

Eastern Archaic Indians, on the other hand, had a far easier existence. In fact, they prospered throughout this era. They lived and developed cultures in a region that was full of forests and lakes. Fish, animals, and plants were plentiful. Men did the hunting and women prepared the animal hides for clothing. The Indian population in the East grew much larger than that of the West.

Archaic Indians lived in small, mobile family groups. The group selected their leaders from among those adult males who were considered to be the best hunters and providers. It was not uncommon

For Extra Interest: Ask the class to solve the problem of making stone tools, using nothing except other stones or pieces of wood. List the solutions that the students propose on the board. Have the class comment on the practicality of each solution.

for the Indians to choose leaders who were closely related, such as brothers. In this way, they hoped, leaders would cooperate for the good of the entire group.

Archaic Indians in both the east and the west struggled hard to improve the life style inherited from their ancestors. Archaic Indians became more than just hunters. They fished when possible. They also gathered items such as seeds, nuts, berries, and roots that were fit to eat. They learned how to catch animals with nets, traps, and pits dug in the ground. To assist them with hunting and to help guard their camps, they began to train wolves. They learned how to use fire for cooking and for warmth.

Archaic Indians also began to use a variety of materials to make tools, weapons, and utensils. In addition to stone and wood, they crafted items from bone, horns, shells, hide, and copper.

However, the most important and far-reaching advancement the Indians made was farming. They adapted wild plants, such as corn, to home cultivation. Farming changed their way of life dramatically. Those Indians who learned how to grow crops no longer had to wander in search of food. Farming provided a more dependable source of food than had hunting or gathering.

Early Indians of the West

The spread of agriculture across the Southwest gave rise to three great early Indian cultures—Mogollon (MOE-go-yon), Hohokam (hoe-hoe-KAM), and Anasazi (an-ah-SAH-zee).

Mogollon society developed first, sometime around 300 B.C. It was centered in the mountain region of southwestern New Mexico and eastern Arizona. The Mogollon were skilled craftspeople who made beautiful pottery and fine bows and arrows. They relied on hunting, gathering, and farming. Mogollon farmers raised corn, beans, and squash.

Hohokam society, located in present-day southern Arizona, emerged around 300 B.C. Most Hohokam were farmers. But their land received little rainfall. The soil there was dry, and farming was difficult. To solve this problem, they came up with a clever solution—the Hohokam developed a system of irrigating their land. Large work crews built and maintained a network of canals that directed river-water and floodwater to crops in the field. The canals were almost 2 meters (6 feet) deep, 9 meters (30 feet) wide, and often 16 kilometers (10 miles) long.

For recreation, the Hohokam people played a game similar to basketball on outdoor ball courts. Some of their ball courts were almost as large as modern football fields. Sometimes the game was played for more than recreation. It was used as a way to settle arguments

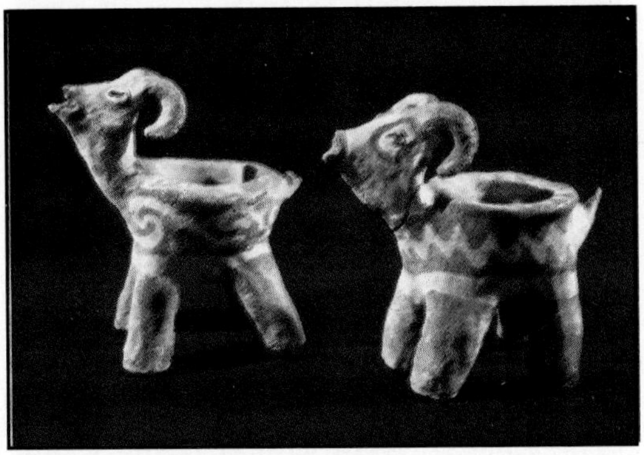

What do you think these Hohokam vessels were used for?

Prehistoric Indian Cultures in North America

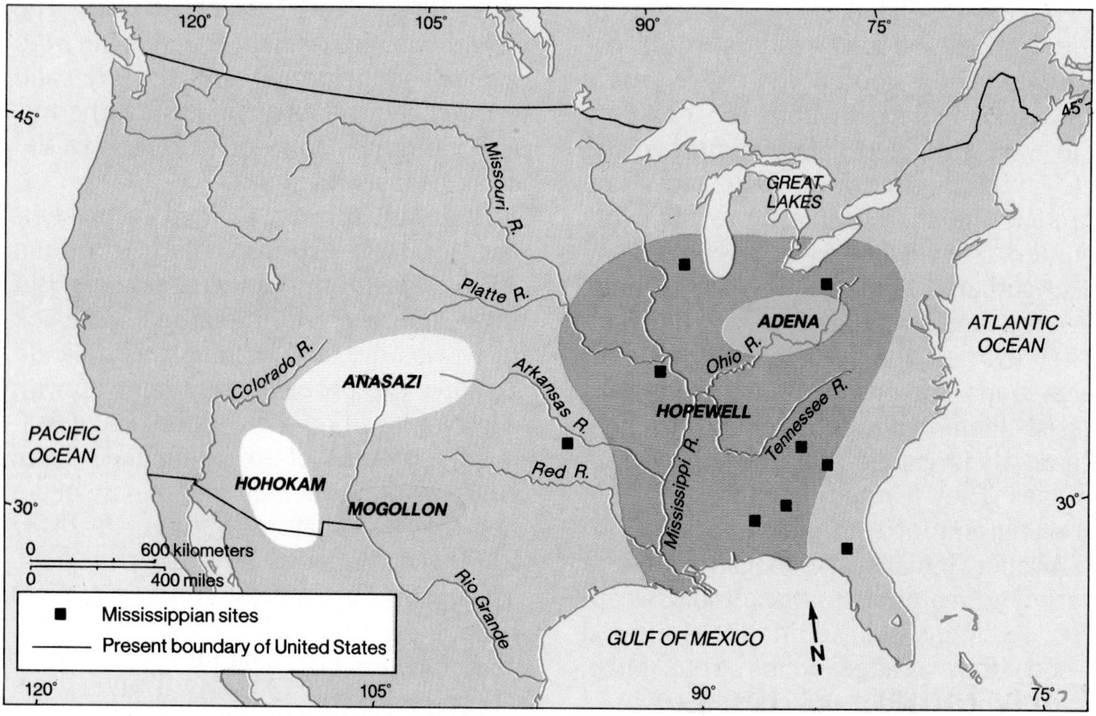

Were any prehistoric Indian cultures located in your state? If so, which cultures?

between Indian villages. Whichever side won the match also won the argument. This made more sense than warfare to the Hohokam people.

The last great western culture was the Anasazi, or the "old ones." The Anasazi lived in the four corners region where the borders of the present-day states of Utah, Colorado, Arizona, and New Mexico meet. They were the ancestors of the modern Pueblo (pu-EB-loe), Hopi, Zuñi, and Tewa Indians. The Anasazi had the most advanced culture in the West during this time period.

The Anasazi were skilled farmers and basketmakers as well as excellent designers and builders. Their settlements were built high above river valleys along the walls of canyons. Here, safely protected from their enemies, the Anasazi lived in tall, apartmentlike buildings. Some of their buildings were five stories high and contained up to 800 rooms. Ground-level dwellings were built without doors. The upper levels were reached by ladders that could be pulled up in case of an enemy attack. Within each building were a number of rooms in which family members lived, worked, and slept.

The Anasazi practiced the domestication, or taming, of animals. They used dogs to guard households. They found that turkeys were easy to tame and breed as a source for food.

The Anasazi were a deeply religious people who believed in supernatural beings or spirits. In or near each settlement was a **kiva**, an underground building used for religious purposes. The Anasazi only allowed men to enter this sacred location. The Anasazi believed that spirits from within the earth could appear to them in the kiva.

---

kiva a circular room built underground and used for religious ceremonies

---

The great Anasazi buildings were in use from about 900 A.D. to about 1300 A.D. We are not sure why they were abandoned. We do know that the buildings were vacated quickly in some cases. The Anasazi left behind rooms filled with food, tools, and various personal articles.

The ruins of these Anasazi kivas were found in Colorado.

Early Indians of the East

Three advanced cultures also emerged in the East during the period between 800 B.C. and 1250 A.D. These cultures were centered near the Mississippi, Missouri, and Ohio rivers. The Adena (ah-DEE-nah) culture arose first, followed by the Hopewell and the Mississippian cultures. Although these three cultures developed during different time periods, they shared many similar qualities.

All three cultures lived in large, permanent villages. Adena, Hopewell, and Mississippian peoples were skilled at making pottery. They used pottery to store food and other objects of value. They also were able craftspeople who fashioned beautiful ornaments for personal and ceremonial use. All three cultures were traders. They exchanged their goods with those of other Indians who lived in distant places to the east and west.

What the Adena, Hopewell, and Mississippian people are best remembered for are the great ceremonial mounds they constructed. For this reason, the three societies are often referred to by a single name: the Mound Builders.

Like many ancient peoples, the Mound Builders were sun worshippers. Their religious beliefs and ceremonies focused upon death and an afterlife. Anthropologists believe that the huge mounds were built for religious use. Some mounds were hollow. They served as burial places. Often, valuable objects were put beside the bodies in the tombs. Other mounds were solid, earthen structures built high into the air. Temples were built upon these mounds to be used for religious ceremonies. Another group of Mound Builders built mounds in the shapes of animals.

Background: The remains of Indian mounds were not recognized as humanmade until the nineteenth century. Plant growth had so completely covered the mounds that they could not be recognized as anything other than hills.

Background: The mounds built in the shapes of animals, birds, or reptiles are called "effigy mounds."

The Giant Serpent Mound in Adams County, Ohio, curls for more than 390 meters (1,300 feet) from tail to open jaws.

The Mound Builder cultures prospered for about 2,000 years. They began to vanish around 1250 A.D. Anthropologists are not sure why this happened. They do know that other, less-developed Indian groups, who were more warlike, lived in the same region. The Mound Builders feared these groups. They took great care to strengthen their villages against attack. It is possible that, in the end, the Mound Builders were unable to defend themselves and thus were destroyed. Another theory is that bitter arguments and fighting in their societies tore them apart. Perhaps this is what caused their downfall. We may never be sure of the answer because the Mound Builders left no oral or written records.

Section Review

1. How do many scientists think people were first able to migrate to North America?
2. How did the development of farming change early Indian societies?
3. Define anthropologist and technology.
4. What were the mounds of the eastern Indians used for?
5. How does climate influence the ways in which people and societies develop? How do modern people respond to climate?

Background: A culture that has not developed a written language is termed *preliterate*. Some Indian cultures developed sophisticated architecture and art forms without developing a written language.

2. Indian Societies and Civilizations

BEFORE YOU READ: *What differences existed among American Indian tribes in terms of life style and culture?*

It is a common belief that the Americas were thinly populated at the time the Europeans first explored and settled there. Actually, the opposite is true. In 1500, the Indian population numbered approximately 110 million people. This was larger than the population of Europe at that time. About 10–12 million Indians lived north of Mexico. About 30–35 million lived in Mexico and Central America. The rest lived in South America and on the islands in the Caribbean Sea.

Variety Among the Indians

The Indian societies living in what is now the United States varied greatly in culture and way of life. Many were farmers who grew a wide variety of crops. Others engaged in fishing. Some hunted to obtain food. Still others combined hunting, gathering, and farming.

There was wide variety in the forms of Indian political organization, too. The Plains Indians, for example, were organized into small tribal groups. Others, like the Indians of the Southeast, often organized their tribes into **confederacies**, or unions of independent groups or societies. Some, like the Iroquois of New York State, were **democratic** in some of their governmental activities. Members of the tribe were treated as equals in making any decisions that affected the tribe. The Natchez of Louisiana, on the other hand, were ruled by their religious leaders.

---

confederacy a union of independent groups, societies, or states

democratic treating all persons in the same way

The languages spoken by Indians were equally varied. As many as 2,000 separate languages were spoken among tribes of both North and South America. These languages were as different as English, French, and Spanish. They were not simply variations of one "Indian" language. The Sioux Indians, for example, spoke a language completely different from that of the Cheyenne of the same region.

American Indian Cultural Regions

The American Indian societies in the United States can be divided into at least seven groups, according to the geographic area they occupied.

Eastern Woodland Indians lived in the great forests of the northeastern United States, east of the Mississippi River, and north of Tennessee and North Carolina. They lived in permanent or **sedentary villages**. Their way of life was based primarily upon farming. Plenty of forests, fertile farmlands, lakes and rivers, and game allowed these people to develop stable, sedentary communities.

---

sedentary village a settled, permanent village inhabited by people who do not move from place to place

---

Background: Over 100 Indian languages are still spoken in the United States, but most Indians in the United States today also use English.

EUREKA!

Medicinal Uses of Plants

Illness, aches, and pains have plagued the human race since humans first appeared. For almost that long, people have been devising remedies to combat what ails them. The American Indians were no exception. They used the landscape in which they lived as their "drugstore." The Indians developed treatments for illnesses ranging from the sniffles to heart disease.

Colds were a problem for all American Indian tribes, and they had many cold remedies. A tea made from the needles of the balsam fir tree was especially popular. In the western United States, the Indians taught European settlers to chew the leaves of clematis flowers to relieve sore throats. The Paiute and Shoshone tribes drank a tea made of twigs and berries from the juniper tree for their colds.

Onions were a particularly useful cold and flu remedy. They were used raw, cooked, and as a watery cereal to treat these illnesses. Some tribes covered flu sufferers with ground-up onions, then wrapped them in blankets so that they would absorb the juice and vapors.

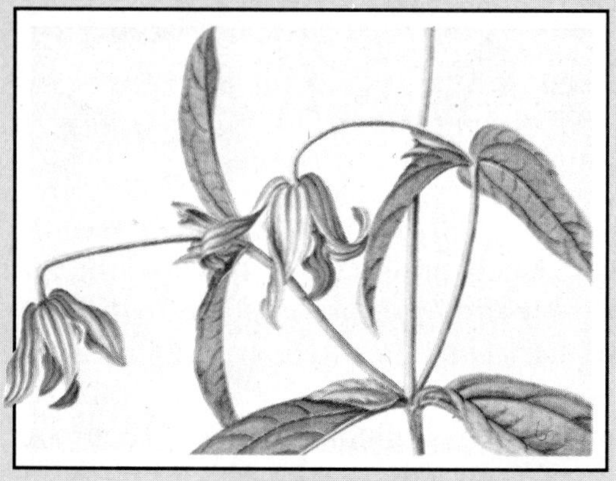

Many desert tribes relied on the creosote bush for a whole medicine chest of remedies. Creosote tea mixed with badger oil was an ointment for burns. A weak tea made from creosote bark was good for stomach trouble. The tops of the bush were made into a hot pack for treating rheumatism.

Modern science has learned the chemical reasons for the success of some Indian remedies. A few of the remedies have become part of today's medical practice. Indians used the foxglove plant to treat heart ailments, for example. Today, scientists know that the foxglove contains the chemical digitalis. Digitalis is one of the most widely used modern treatments for heart attacks.

The Southeastern Indians lived south of the Eastern Woodland tribes in the southern part of the country. The Southeastern Indians developed stable, sedentary communities based upon an agricultural economy. Many Indian tribes of this thickly populated region were organized into confederacies.

The homeland of the Plains Indians was the central portion of the country. Although some tribes were sedentary, the majority were wandering buffalo hunters.

The Indians of the Southwest made their homes in the desert areas of what is today Arizona, New Mexico, western Texas, and parts of Utah, Colorado, and northern Mexico. Most of the Pueblos were farmers. Others were hunters and gatherers. The Navajo (NAH-vah-hoe) became successful sheepherders after the Spanish brought sheep to America in the 1700's. Many Southwest Indians lived in large villages, and their homes were made of adobe, or sun-dried bricks. Most of the nomadic peoples of this region lived in small, brush-covered shelters called **wickiups**.

wickiup a brush-covered hut built by the nomadic Indians of the Southwest

John White, a settler at Roanoke, recorded in watercolors his impressions of an Indian village.

The Great Basin and Plateau Indians lived in the arid and semiarid lands between the Rocky Mountains on the east and the Sierra Nevada on the west. Because of the harsh environment, the region had a small population. The Shoshone who lived there fished, hunted, and gathered. But plant and animal life were sparse. Life was very difficult for these Indians.

The lands along the Pacific coast were home for people called the California Indians. The climate was temperate and there was plenty of food—acorns, game, fish, fowl, and various wild plants. California Indians lived in a land of plenty.

Finally, the Northwest Coast Indians lived along the Pacific coast in the area of northern California, Oregon, western Washington, and the southwest corner of Canada. They relied primarily on fishing for salmon and halibut, and hunting seals for their food supply. Northwest Coast Indians were skilled at working with wood. They crafted beautifully carved totem poles. They also made wooden boats that were as much as 18.3 meters (60 feet) long.

Indian societies living in what became the United States were varied. By looking at three groups—Eastern Woodland, Great Plains, and Southwestern—the variety of Indians can be seen more clearly.

Eastern Woodland Indians

Dense forests covered the northeastern section of the country. Its rolling hills and valleys were well supplied with lakes, rivers, and streams. Except in the most northern regions, the soil was rich and

Discuss: The Northwest Coast Indians were able to live in sedentary villages even though they did not practice agriculture. Have students identify and discuss the environmental conditions that made this possible.

Discuss: Why did five Iroquois tribes form a confederacy? What are some of the advantages and disadvantages of making alliances?

the climate satisfactory for intensive agriculture. Wild animals, birds, and plants were in abundance.

Most Eastern Woodland Indians were farmers and hunters. Some also fished and traded. Most of the region's tribes were Algonquian (al-GAHN-kee-un). However, many of the Iroquois (IH-ruh-kwoi) had penetrated the Algonquians' country and lived in its central region. The Iroquois settled in upper New York State, in Pennsylvania, and along the shores of the eastern Great Lakes. A few Iroquoian people, like the Cherokee, lived in the Southeast.

The Algonquians of the eastern woodlands depended only partly on farming for survival. They established their villages and farm fields on rich land along rivers. The villages were occupied only during the growing season. After the harvest, Algonquians left their summer villages and separated into smaller bands for the winter.

For summer travel, the Algonquians used birchbark canoes. These were light and efficient craft, easily carried on land. They used snowshoes in the winter to travel or to pursue animals. Algonquians lived in wigwams. These were bark-covered lodges with rounded roofs and wooden frames.

The Iroquois, who were fierce warriors, dominated the eastern woodlands. Their strength also came from uniting to form a confederacy. Five separate Iroquoian tribes in upper New York State had united to form the Iroquois Confederacy. This became a powerful intertribal **alliance** ruled by a council of 50 *sachems* or tribal leaders. The council decided on matters that affected all five member tribes. However, the council did not interfere in the affairs of a member tribe.

---

alliance a close association for a common objective

Women had influence, and their views were respected in the Iroquois Confederacy. Sachems were always men. Women within each member tribe always selected the successor to a sachem who had died.

The name *Iroquois* means "The People of the Longhouse." The Iroquois lived in long, wooden, rectangular lodges with rounded edges. Longhouses were community dwellings in which up to 20 families lived.

The Iroquois longhouses were located in large towns. Often, hundreds of hectares (acres) of cultivated farmland surrounded each town. The men cleared the fields of trees and brush. The women did the farming.

Most Iroquoian religious ceremonies centered on the agricultural cycle. The Green Corn ceremony was the most important. It was performed annually when the first of the corn crop was ready to harvest. The ceremony gave the Iroquois the opportunity to give thanks for their chief food crop and to ask for a bountiful harvest the next year.

Indians of the Great Plains

Across the center of the nation are the Great Plains. It is a vast region of grasslands stretching from mid-North Dakota down to Texas. The Great Plains extend from the Mississippi River to the foothills of the Rocky Mountains. The plains are

Background: Early weapons of the Iroquois included bows and arrows, clubs, and shields of wood or bark. Body armor made of wooden slats tied with a cord was often used.

Famous Americans

HIAWATHA

Hiawatha was a Mohawk *sachem* or chief who lived in central New York State in the 1500's. One day, he wandered off into the wilderness. There he met Deganawida (day-gah-nah-WEE-dah), who was either a supernatural creature or a real man. Deganawida told Hiawatha of a vision he had. He saw all Iroquois Indians living together in peace. For this to happen, the five tribes that made up the Iroquois—the Cayuga, Mohawk, Seneca, Oneida, and Onondaga—had to unite and join in a league of peace. They had to give up fighting among themselves and had to respect the power of the League. Hiawatha carried this message to all the tribes. He was a persuasive speaker. He had no trouble convincing the tribes to join the League until he came to the Onondaga. Their chief did not want to give up his power. Hiawatha proposed a solution. The Onondaga must join the League and follow its rules. But the Onondaga would become the keepers of the "central fire" of the League. This meant that their village would be the Iroquois capital and site for the annual meetings of the League. The Onondaga agreed and joined the League.

The League that Hiawatha helped create was one of the first democratic governments in America. Power came from the small local units and all member tribes were given a representative voice. The League existed at a time when kings and nobility ruled Europe. Most Europeans had no voice in their own government. Benjamin Franklin later used the Iroquois League as one of the models for the new government of the United States. Hiawatha was a true American hero.

---

treeless except for the river valleys. Enormous herds of buffalo and antelope once grazed here. Other game—deer, elk, rabbits, grizzly bears—also lived on the plains.

Two different Indian groups lived on the Great Plains. One group were sedentary farmers. The other were nomadic buffalo hunters. The farming people settled the area first. They settled in the river valleys of the eastern Great Plains and raised corn, beans, and squash.

The Plains farmers lived in large, permanent villages. Their houses were circular in shape, built of poles and heavy timber, and covered with a thick layer of dirt. The dirt covering kept them warm during the winter months. The earth lodges were also large, holding as many as 40 people. Most lodges were about 9 meters (30 feet) in diameter. Some, however, were as wide as 17 meters (55 feet).

This oil painting, completed by George Catlin in 1836, shows Indian women playing a ball game.

Most Plains Indians were nomadic buffalo hunters, not village dwellers. These Indians were expert horseriders, hunters, and daring warriors.

Some 30 nomadic tribes dominated the Great Plains. Because these tribes used so many different languages, most tribes were unable to speak with one another. To overcome this, the Plains Indians developed sign language. Making signs with their hands and fingers, Plains Indians learned to express complex thoughts and exchange useful information and ideas without speaking a word.

Buffalo was the chief source of food for the nomadic tribes. But the Plains Indians also used the buffalo for many other things. The hides were used for clothing, robes, rawhide ropes, and even bedding for the winter months. The hooves were made into glue, horns were carved into spoons, and muscle tendon was made into bowstrings.

The buffalo-hunting tribes, because of their nomadic existence, had little use for permanent homes. For shelter they used the tepee, a portable cone-shaped tent usually covered with buffalo skins. A fire was built in the center of the tepee, and beds were placed around the edge. The tepees were always made, set up, and cared for by the women.

Vocabulary Help: tendon—white, tough, fibrous tissue that connects muscles to bones, also called sinew. It was perfect for use as a cordlike material in a society in which cord and string were not produced.

Background: Much Indian religion involved sympathetic magic. This is the belief that by acting out a hunt or drawing a picture of an animal, the hunter controls the animal's spirit and can capture the animal.

The men of the tribe were hunters and warriors in times of conflict. Becoming a skilled and respected warrior was important to the men of the tribe. It was necessary to establish a record of feats during battle to earn the respect of the tribe. Recognition was given for taking a scalp or killing an enemy. Those warriors exposing themselves to the greatest danger received the greatest honors. For example, a warrior was honored if he touched a live enemy in battle without receiving any wounds himself.

The Plains tribes were highly religious. Many of their ceremonies were dedicated to helping hunters catch buffalo. Perhaps the most important ceremony was the Sun Dance, which took place in the middle of the summer. The purpose of the Sun Dance was to ask God, or the Great Spirit, to bless the tribe during the coming year.

Indians of the Southwest

The Southwest has a desert climate. Little rain falls in this area each year. Most Indians here were forced to rely upon wild vegetation for food—berries, nuts, fruits, roots, seeds. When game was available, they hunted. One group of Southwestern Indians, however, used agriculture successfully.

The agricultural tribes can be divided into two groups. The first, the Pueblo Indians, lived in villages with stone and adobe apartmentlike dwellings. Today, 30 such dwellings remain in Arizona and New Mexico.

The second group, the Riparian people, did not live like the Pueblos. Tribes such as the Pima resided in large, single-room pit houses. The pit houses were constructed of thick layers of dirt. The floor was located below ground level. This kept the houses cool in summer and warm in the winter.

The Pueblo Indians grew corn, squash, beans, tobacco, and cotton. Eastern Pueblos, located in north central New Mexico, planted their crops on lands near the Rio Grande and Chama rivers. They watered their crops using an irrigation system. Western Pueblos living in the deserts of the Southwest planted crops that were drought-resistant. They grew certain hearty types of corn. They were unable to use irrigation because water was so scarce.

Pueblo men did most of the farming. They were assisted by women only at planting and harvesting time. In addition to being excellent farmers, the Pueblo Indians were skilled craftspeople and traders. Pueblo women excelled in making fine pottery, baskets, cotton cloth, and blankets. The Pueblos exchanged **surplus**, or extra, goods and crops with Indians of other western regions.

---

surplus an extra supply

The Pueblo Indians believed that the object of life was to live in harmony with one another. They encouraged cooperation and succeeded in creating a peaceful and orderly society. If they achieved harmony, they believed that the spirits of the dead would permit the rain to fall, the harvest to be good, and the people to be healthy.

There was a second major group of Southwestern Indians. They were nomadic hunters and gatherers who arrived

Discuss: In most Indian cultures that practiced agriculture, the women did the farming. Why do you think that women generally performed this task? Why do you think that farming was principally done by the men of the Pueblo Indian tribes?

Indian Cultural Regions of North America

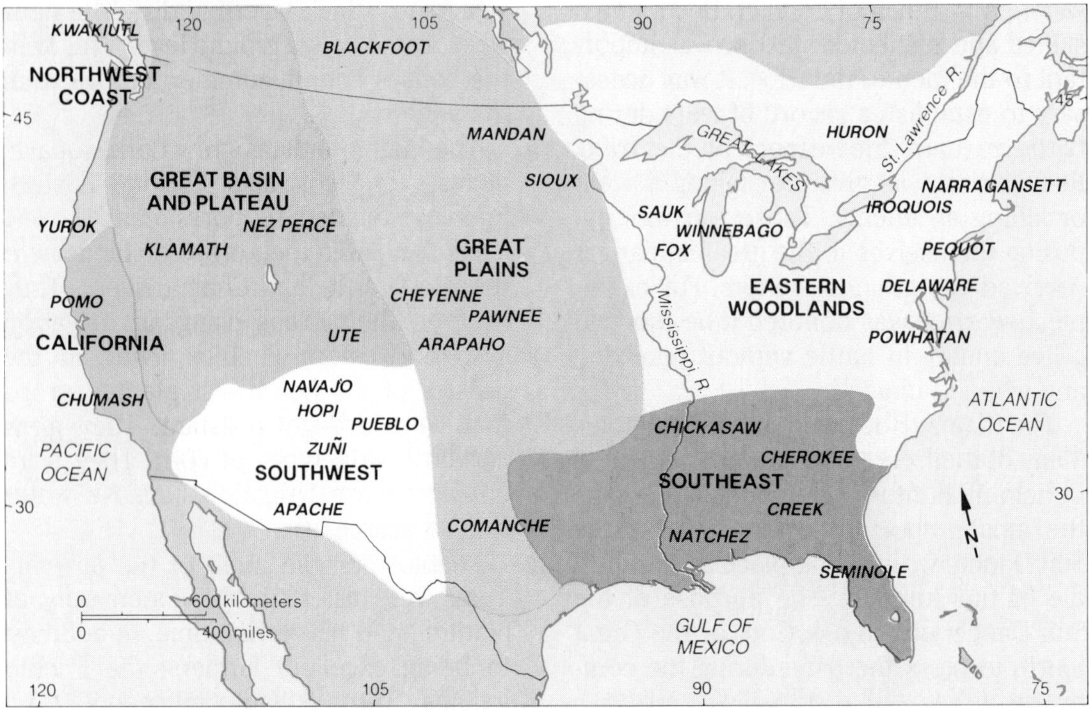

In which Indian cultural region is your state located? Which tribes lived in this region?

in the Southwest between 900 and 1500 A.D. In time, they separated into two groups: the Apaches (uh-PATCH-ees) and the Navajos (NAV-uh-hoes).

The Apaches and Navajos were good hunters and brave fighters. They attacked the Pueblo Indians, raiding their villages, crops, and animal herds. In fact, the two tribes received their present names because of such activity. The Pueblos called them *Apache de Navajo*, "Raiders and Burners of Our Crops." The two tribes called themselves "Diné," or "the People."

The Pueblos took measures to protect themselves from these attacks. They walled up the first-floor windows and doorways of their homes. Some northern Pueblos apparently abandoned their villages in the face of these raids. Other villages were made larger to take in those who had fled. When Spanish and Mexican settlers began to pour into the Southwest, the Apaches and Navajos raided their settlements too.

The Apaches' and Navajos' ways of life changed after their arrival in the Southwest. At first, they were a nomadic people who relied on hunting and gathering. Because they were constantly on the move, the Apaches and Navajos had few possessions, and their crafts were limited. In time, some picked up farming from their agricultural neighbors. They raised small crops of corn, squash, and beans.

Discuss: Why do you think the Apaches and the Navajos attacked the Pueblo Indians? Why did the Navajo eventually abandon their fighting tradition?

Background: Smallpox, a viral disease, was introduced to the Western Hemisphere by the Spanish in the sixteenth century. Because the Indians had no previous contact with the disease, they had developed no immunity to it.

As time went on, the Navajos dropped their nomadic way of life and became expert sheepherders and weavers. The Apaches, on the other hand, continued in the more traditional way of life. In contrast to other American Indian groups, most of the Indians of the Southwest today live in many of the same places as their ancestors.

George Catlin painted this picture of a 12-year-old Indian girl in 1832.

The Beginning of the End

The coming of the Europeans to America changed the lives of American Indians forever. Many Indians died in battles fought against the newcomers. Even more died from diseases, such as smallpox, which the Europeans brought with them. From 33–50 percent of the American Indian population died from exposure to European diseases.

The way of life of American Indians in each of the seven cultural areas declined during the next period of history. This was the period of exploration and settlement of America by Europeans. The Indians' reaction to the newcomers is summed up well by Chief Hiamovi: "Then came strangers from across the Great Water. No land had they; we gave them our land. No food had they; we gave them of our corn. The strangers [have] become many and they fill our country. . . . There are two roads, the white man's road and the Indian's road. . . . [In] a little while, the old Indians will no longer be."

Section Review

1. In what ways did American Indian groups differ in life style and culture?
2. Is it correct to say that America was thinly populated in 1500? Explain your answer.
3. Define alliance and explain how it can be used to describe the Iroquois Confederacy.
4. Indians of one geographic region often did not respect the culture and people of a different region. Why do you think this was so? Do modern people respect other nations which have different cultures? Explain your answer.

Discuss: What do you think Chief Hiamovi meant by "the white man's road" and "the Indian's road"?

CHAPTER REVIEW

Summary

America was populated by humans long before the Europeans arrived in the eleventh century. Scientists believe that Native Americans, now called Indians, existed as far back as 25,000 years ago. At that time, the earth was in an Ice Age, and the level of the seas was much lower than it is today. A narrow bridge of dry land connected Asia to North America where the Bering Strait is today. It was across this land bridge that early people migrated into America. The Indians spread slowly out and across North and South America until they occupied almost every section of both continents.

These groups occupied very different land areas, and developed different ways of life. The rich soil and favorable climate in eastern North America encouraged the Eastern Woodland Indians to practice agriculture. The majority of the Plains Indians, however, depended primarily on the buffalo as a source of food. Their existence was nomadic as they followed the great herds. Many of the Indians living along the Pacific Coast relied mainly on fish for food.

The Indian cultures that developed in America began to change with the arrival of Europeans, and the period of American prehistory came to an end.

Recalling the Facts

1. How do many scientists believe the first humans came to North America?
2. Who were the earliest people in North America to use irrigation?
3. What were kivas, and who built them?
4. What does the term *sedentary village* mean?
5. What was the chief food crop of the Iroquois Indians?
6. How did the majority of the Plains Indians get their food?

Analyzing the Facts

1. Why is the term *Ice Age* appropriate in describing the period when humans arrived in America?
2. Why was the development of agriculture so important?

3. Was the development of sign language a necessity for the early Indians? Explain your answer.
4. Why did Indian groups living in different parts of America develop different cultures?
5. Why do you think the Pueblo culture was a peaceful one?

Time and History

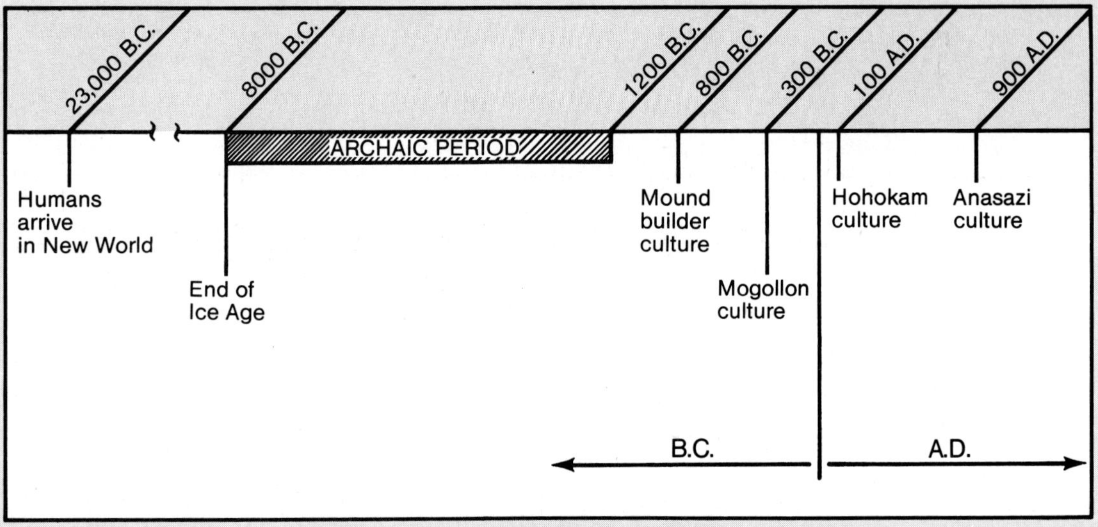

1. Which is the oldest culture on the timeline: the Hohokam culture or the Mogollon culture?
2. Which was the first Indian culture to begin after the end of the Ice Age?
3. What was the first period after the Ice Age?
4. How long were humans in the New World before the Ice Age ended?
5. Which date is the earliest in time: 8000 B.C., 1250 A.D., 300 B.C., or 100 A.D.?

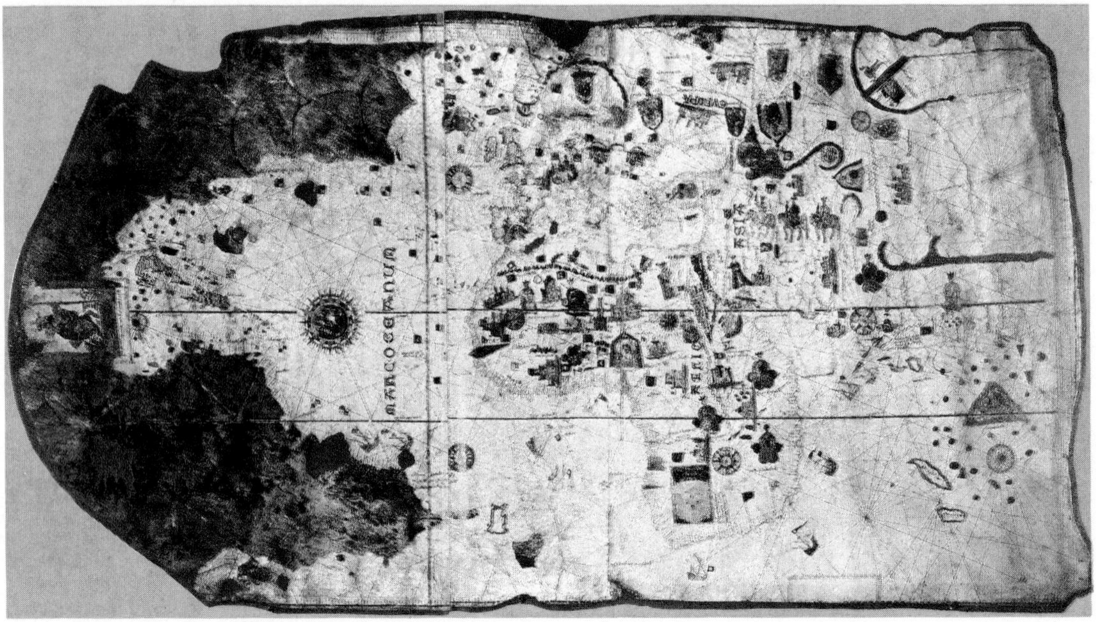

Chapter
2

Exploration and Settlement

On the morning of October 12, 1492, three ships were anchored off an island in the Bahamas. Europeans had reached the New World, although they did not yet realize it. Christopher Columbus had sailed westward from Spain to reach the Orient. According to his calculations, he was off the coast of Japan. In time, Europeans realized that Columbus had reached two new continents. The nations of western Europe took advantage of this discovery and tried to conquer the land.

After you read this chapter, you will be able to:

1. Explain why the nations of western Europe became interested in exploration in the 1400's.
2. Identify significant Spanish explorers and their achievements.
3. Describe how the Spanish, Dutch, and French settlements in America differed from each other.
4. Explain the reasons for English settlement in America.

☐ Use a map scale.

Background: Greenland is still a colony of Denmark. Iceland, a former Danish colony, gained complete independence in 1944.

1. The Awakening of Western Europe

BEFORE YOU READ: *What three developments propelled western Europe into an age of exploration?*

The first Europeans to reach North America were the Vikings. They came at the beginning of the eleventh century. The Vikings were superb sailors and shipbuilders. They were among the first to build ships sturdy enough to cross the ocean.

Viking Exploration

From bases in their homelands of Denmark, Norway, and Sweden, the Vikings searched for new lands to conquer. They colonized Iceland in 870 A.D. and Greenland a century later.

In the 900's, a Viking named Biarni Heriulfson (BYAHR-nee hur-YOOHLF-son) sailed west from Greenland. He saw the coast of eastern Canada but did not go ashore. His descriptions of the land he saw inspired Leif Ericson to repeat the voyage. Around the year 1000, Ericson landed on the eastern shore of Canada and sailed southward to Newfoundland. The Vikings set up a base there and explored the area. They found timber that they could use in shipbuilding and berries from which wine could be made. Ericson named the land "Vinland," or wine-land.

Thorvald, Ericson's brother, led a second expedition, which spent the winter of 1004–1005 in Vinland. Other expeditions soon followed. The Vikings constructed a group of buildings in Newfoundland. **Archaeologists**, or scientists who study ancient peoples, unearthed this settlement in 1961. This proved that the Vikings had explored a part of America. The archaeologists also found evidence of an ironworks in which small metal objects could be made. They also found utensils that were not Indian in origin.

---

archaeologist a scientist who studies the way of life of ancient peoples by examining artifacts and remains

---

The relationship between the Vikings and the Indians was tense. Neither side trusted the other, although some trading between them did occur. The Vikings treated the natives with cruelty. Finally, the tense relationship broke into open warfare. The Viking settlement was destroyed. The Vikings escaped with their lives, but the experience convinced them to give up and go home. It would be almost 500 years before Europeans and Indians met again.

The Vikings later recorded the story of their experiences in North America in a series of legends called the *Greenlander's Saga*. The legends were widely known in Scandinavia, Greenland, and Iceland. Other Europeans who knew of the legends claimed that they were only made-up stories.

Christopher Columbus was one of the next voyagers to come to America. Columbus can be given credit for starting the large-scale movement of Europeans to America. However, Columbus could not have made his voyages unless his European supporters were ready and able to help him.

Discuss: Why do you think the Vikings left North America after hostile contacts with the Indians? The Vikings were in possession of superior weapons, organization, and seafaring techniques. Why do you think they did not simply overwhelm the Indians?

Background: Christians fought against the Muslims in Spain for many years. In 1469, Ferdinand of Aragon married Isabella of Castile. Their marriage united the Christian kingdoms. The complete unification of Spain was completed in 1492, when Christian forces drove the Muslims out of Spain.

Developments in Western Europe

During the 1400's, three developments combined to propel the nations of western Europe into an age of exploration. The first development was political.

For centuries, the monarchs of western Europe had struggled to unite their kingdoms. These struggles ended around 1450 when the monarchs of England, Spain, Portugal, and France were able to take control of their countries. The monarchs at last ruled their states with complete authority.

Only powerful monarchs had the large amounts of money needed for long voyages. Spain was a good example of this. There, the marriage of Ferdinand and Isabella united Spain under one rule. Ferdinand and Isabella were then able to raise the money needed for Columbus to make his voyages.

A second development that led to voyages of exploration was the desire to find new trade routes to the Far East. Between roughly 1100 and 1300, merchants began bringing into Europe costly luxuries from the Far East. The far eastern, or Oriental, trade supplied Europeans with silks, perfume, tapestries, jewels, and spices. But these items were expensive and time-consuming to obtain.

The Oriental trade was controlled by Arab and Italian merchants. The Arabs transported the goods overland from China, across Asia, to the Mediterranean Sea. The goods were then sold to the Italians, who then transported them across the Mediterranean Sea to Europe.

By the time goods reached the countries of western Europe, their prices were outrageously high. Arab and Italian merchants charged a commission on the goods as they were traded from the Orient to Europe. Various rulers also charged taxes and fees.

Europeans were not pleased with the situation. Monarchs of the newly united kingdoms of western Europe did not like being so dependent on Arab and Italian traders. Wealthy nobles were angry over the high prices they had to pay. Local merchants wanted some of the enormous profits the Arab and Italian merchants were making. All three groups wanted to find an alternative. They wanted to find a route that would take them directly to the source of the Oriental trade.

Almost by coincidence a book was written that provided Europeans with the information they were seeking. The book was Marco Polo's *Travels*, which appeared in 1477. Polo was an Italian merchant who dealt in the Oriental trade. He had lived in China between 1274 and 1292. His descriptions of China as a land of fabulous wealth excited Europeans. Polo also reported that China was bounded on the east by an ocean. This was the information that convinced many Europeans that the Far East could somehow be reached by ship.

The third development to promote exploration was improvements in navigational and sailing technologies. The first improvement was in ship design and construction. The Portuguese developed a new kind of ship, called a caravel. Caravels were small, wooden ships that could sail against the wind better than earlier ships could. These swift ships greatly reduced the time it took to get to distant lands.

Background: The astrolabe only allowed for the determination of latitude. The sextant, which replaced the astrolabe as a navigational instrument in the eighteenth century, was able to determine both latitude and longitude.

Several tools that aided in navigation were developed in the fifteenth century. The magnetic compass helped to tell direction. The **astrolabe** helped a ship's navigator to locate certain stars and obtain the ship's latitude.

---

astrolabe a device used by navigators in the 1400's to determine the position of a ship at sea by locating certain stars

---

Mapmaking improved during this century. Sailors carefully mapped the shorelines along which they sailed. By the late 1400's, the coastal areas of most of the known world had been mapped. Some people realized the earth was round. But they thought it was much smaller than its actual size. In 1492, the same year that Columbus made his first voyage, the first globe was produced in Nuremberg, Germany. It showed one ocean separating western Europe from Asia.

These three developments in politics, economics, and technology created the conditions necessary to support large-scale exploration. The people of western Europe now had both the reasons and the means to explore for a sea route to the Far East. The nation that took the first steps along this path was Portugal.

Portugal Leads the Way

The age of exploration began with Portuguese voyages made under the leadership of Prince Henry the Navigator. He

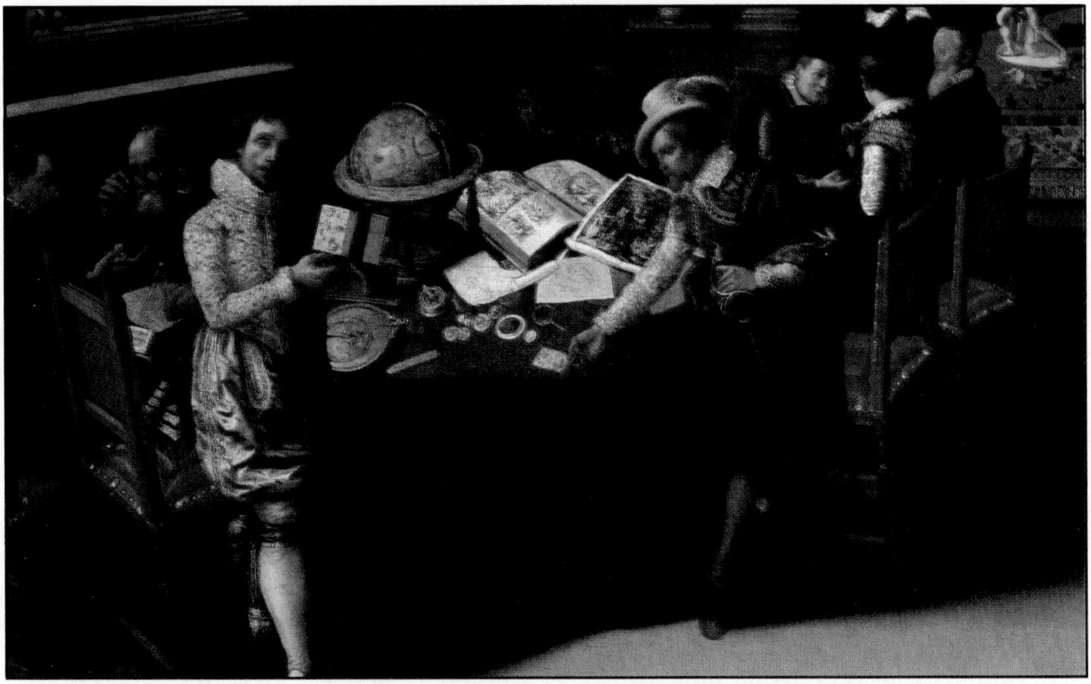

In this painting of English explorers, the large disc-shaped object in front of the globe is an astrolabe. What other navigational aids can you identify?

Discuss: What were the advantages of looking for an all-water route west after Portugal had proven that India could be reached by sailing around Africa? For what reasons might Spain have decided to pursue this idea?

The Four Voyages of Columbus

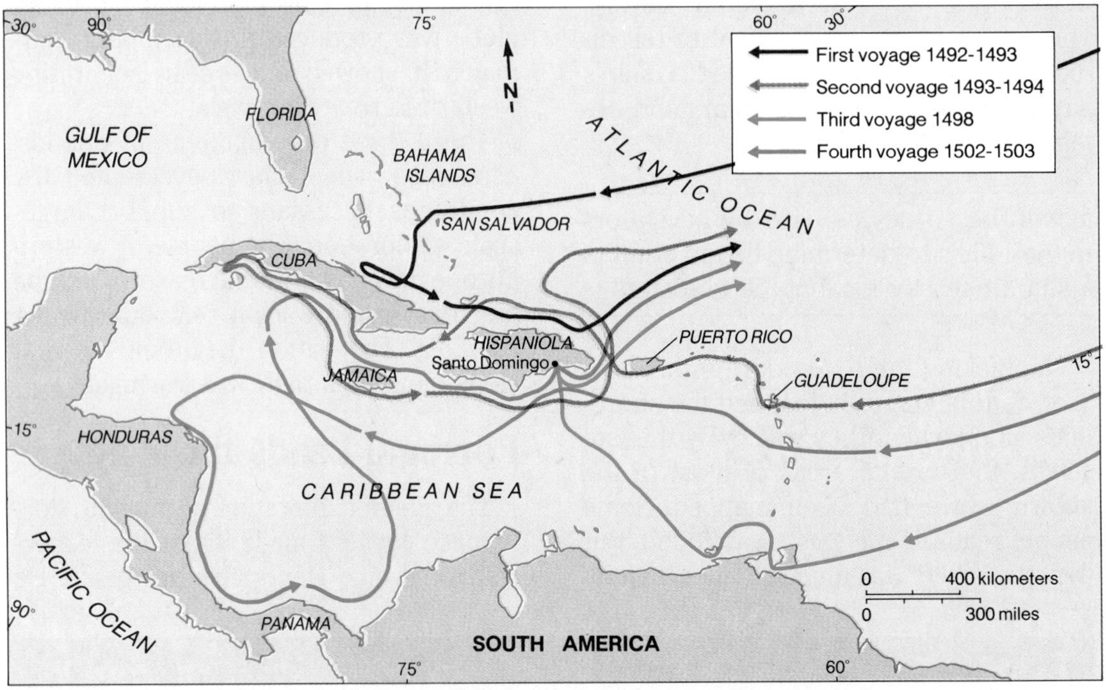

On which voyages did Columbus sail along the coast of South America?

founded a school of navigation in Portugal. The school trained sailors and sponsored research in navigation. The prince also sent his ships out along the western coast of Africa. He hoped to expand trade and find a passage to the Orient.

Following Prince Henry's death in 1460, his work was carried on by other explorers. In 1488 Bartholomew Dias (DEE-ahs) sailed around the Cape of Good Hope (then called the Cape of Storms), which is located at the southern tip of Africa. Dias wanted to sail farther, but his crew would not allow it. They were terrified because they thought that the waters beyond the Cape were filled with sea monsters.

Another important voyage occurred a decade later. Vasco da Gama, after sailing for three months without seeing any land, rounded the tip of Africa and sailed on to India. At last, an all-water route to the East had been found!

The Voyages of Columbus

Christopher Columbus was born in the busy seaport of Genoa, Italy, around 1451. His father was a weaver. He received his early sailing training on voyages along the Italian coast and on the Mediterranean Sea.

At the age of 25, Columbus went to Lisbon, Portugal. There he became a crew member on ships that were trying to find

Background: Remind the class that at this time, no one suspected that two huge land masses lay to the west between Europe and Asia. It was, therefore, perfectly rational to expect to find an all-water route to the East by sailing west.

Discuss: Why did it take the Spanish monarchs several years to make up their minds to support Columbus' request for funds for a westward voyage to India? Ask the class to give reasons why they think the government hesitated before giving Columbus the money he asked for.

a sea route to Asia. He believed that a route around the Cape of Good Hope was possible. He proposed that a faster and easier route to the Orient would be westward across the Atlantic Ocean. The Portuguese king rejected his plan. In 1486, Columbus approached King Ferdinand and Queen Isabella of Spain with the same plan. After several years of discussions, the Spanish rulers agreed to sponsor his voyage.

It took Columbus months to convince 90 sailors to travel with him across the "Sea of Darkness." Finally, at sunrise on August 3, 1492, the *Niña,* the *Pinta,* and the *Santa María* set sail from Palos, Spain. Their destination was Asia, which Columbus believed lay 4,400 kilometers (2,400 nautical miles) to the west. After sailing for ten days, sailors began to talk of mutiny. They were frightened of what lay ahead. Finally, in the early morning of October 12, land was spotted. The crew was overjoyed. Columbus' calculations were correct. The ships had sailed some 4,400 kilometers (2,400 nautical miles), and now here was land. Columbus thought he had reached Asia. Instead, his ship was offshore of a small island in the Bahamas. Columbus named this island San Salvador.

Columbus explored San Salvador and then sailed on to other islands in the Caribbean. He gave the island of present-day Haiti and the Dominican Republic the name "Hispaniola," or Little Spain.

At each stop Columbus made contact with the Indians living there. The first tribe Columbus met were the Arawaks. Since Columbus believed he had arrived in the East Indies, he called the natives *Indios*. This word became "Indians" in English.

Columbus established the first Spanish colony, La Navidad, on Christmas Day, 1492. The following month he returned to Spain. He reported to the Spanish monarchs that he had found the islands that lay off the coast of Asia.

Columbus made four voyages in all to the land he thought was Asia. His last voyage was made in 1502. When he died in 1506, Columbus had still failed to find a sea route to the Orient. Few realized the importance of the lands he had found.

In spite of Columbus' failure, the Spanish monarchy continued to believe a sea route to Asia could be found.

Section Review

1. Identify three developments that led to the age of exploration.
2. Who were the Vikings, and how do we know that they had settlements in North America?
3. Why did the nations of western Europe wish to find a sea route to the Orient?
4. What contributions in navigation did the Portuguese make?
5. Columbus' voyages to America were judged a failure during his lifetime. Why? Why do you think many people's achievements are overlooked in their lifetimes?

Discuss: Compare Spanish goals for exploration in the fifteenth century with our goals today for exploration of such areas as the sea, Antarctica, and space. Are our goals the same or different from Spain's?

2. Spanish Exploration and Settlement

BEFORE YOU READ: *What were the three goals of the early Spanish explorers?*

The Spanish at first believed that Columbus had found the Orient. After 1500, many realized that the lands Columbus had visited were not the Orient. Instead of abandoning these lands, the Spanish developed plans for their use. Spanish explorers were sent to the New World to accomplish what can be summed up as "Gold, God, and Glory."

Gold, God, and Glory

Many of the early Spanish explorers were sent to the New World to find gold. They had heard tales of Indian towns so rich that homes were built of gold. They also knew the tales of the fabulous "Seven Cities of Gold," supposedly located in the American Southwest.

Also of importance to the Spanish was missionary work. The Spaniards wanted to convert, or change, the natives' beliefs to those of Christianity, specifically Roman Catholicism. The Spanish monarchs sent priests to the New World to teach the Indians Christian and European ways.

Finally, Spanish explorers saw an opportunity to win glory for themselves and for their country by going to the New World. These explorers came to be called **conquistadors** (con-KEES-tuh-dorz), or conquerors.

---

conquistador a Spanish explorer who explored and conquered much of Spain's New World empire

---

Major Explorations

By 1500, around 6,000 Spaniards had settled in the New World. From settlements on Hispaniola and Cuba, explorers set out for the other Caribbean islands and the American mainland.

One such explorer was Juan Ponce de León (HWAN ponss duh lee-ON), an experienced soldier and explorer. In 1512, Ponce de León was made governor of the new Spanish colony on Puerto Rico. Anxious to investigate the region, he led an expedition to what is now Florida in 1513. Ponce de León was struck by the beauty of the land and claimed it for Spain.

At about the same time, Vasco Núñez de Balboa (VASS-koe NOON-yezz day bal-BO-ah) was making his way across the **isthmus**, or narrow strip of land, at Panama. Balboa pushed his men across the isthmus on an exhausting 23-day march through tropical forests. At the end of their march, they became the first Europeans to see the Pacific Ocean.

---

isthmus a narrow neck of land that separates two bodies of water and connects two larger land regions

---

In 1519, yet another sailor set out to find the westward sea route to the Orient. Ferdinand Magellan (muh-JELL-un) reached the southern end of South America in October 1520, where he came upon a strait that today bears his name. Hoping that the strait would provide a passage

Vocabulary Help: strait—a narrow body of water connecting two larger bodies of water; it corresponds to the land designation isthmus. Have students use a wall map to name and locate straits.

Background: In 1494, the Pope drew an imaginary line of demarcation through a map of the Americas. Anything discovered to the west of this line would belong to Spain, while anything east of the line would belong to Portugal. Show students the line on a wall map.

Spanish Explorations in the New World

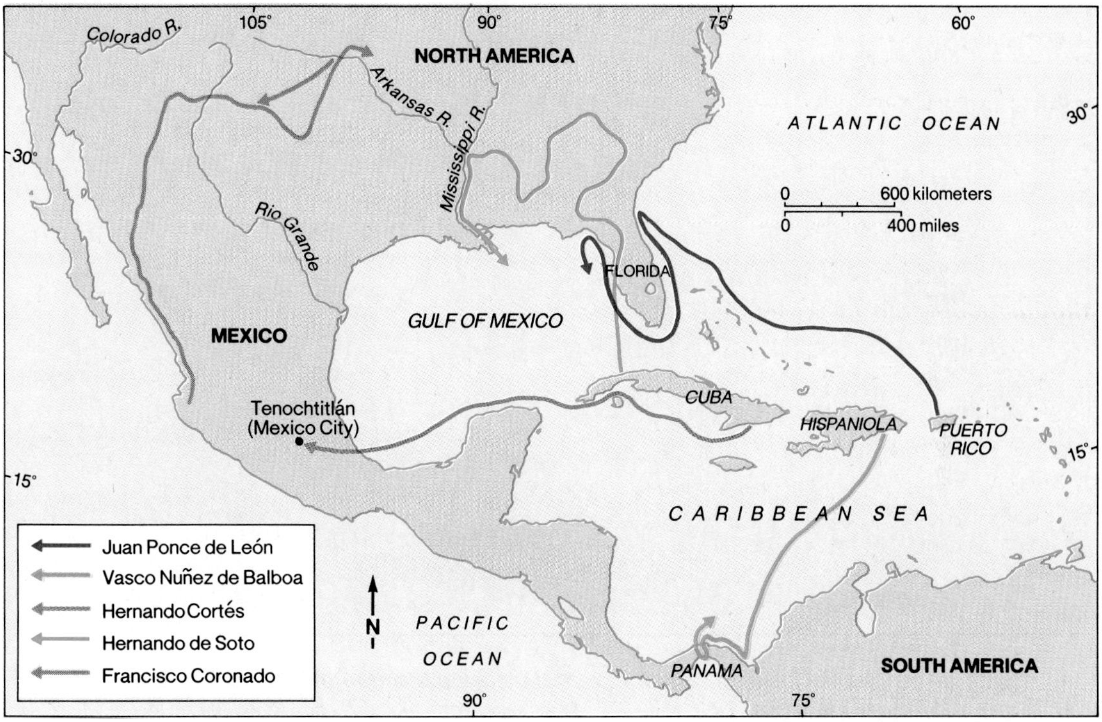

Which two explorers were able to gain information about Florida? How far did Coronado travel in search of the Seven Cities of Gold?

around the continent, Magellan pressed onward. His fleet struggled through the rough waters of the strait and reached the Pacific Ocean. Magellan sailed westward to the Philippines, where he was killed in a battle with the Filipinos. The rest of his fleet sailed on and arrived back in Spain in 1522. Only 18 of the original crew of 270 had survived. But the fleet of Ferdinand Magellan had been the first to **circumnavigate**, or sail around, the world.

---

circumnavigate to sail completely around something

The Conquest of the Aztecs

While Magellan was beginning his voyage around the world, Hernando Cortés (hur-NAN-doe kor-TEZZ) landed on the gulf coast of Mexico with an army of 500 men. His goal was to conquer the Aztec (AZZ-teck) Empire and take its vast riches.

The Aztecs ruled much of central and southern Mexico. Their capital was Tenochtitlán (tay-nawk-tee-TLAHN), a busy city with a population of at least 100,000.

The Aztecs were a well-educated people. All children were taught history,

Background: Not all Aztec sacrificial victims were prisoners. Sometimes a victim would be selected from among the town's leading citizens. It was a great personal and family honor to volunteer.

Why do you think Cortés is shown here not wearing a suit of armor, as he leads his army to meet the Aztecs?

crafts, and Aztec traditions. The Aztecs had a system of writing and kept written records of important events. They were also expert craftspeople.

Religion influenced almost every aspect of Aztec life. The Aztecs worshipped many gods and believed that human sacrifice was necessary in order to please the gods. The Aztecs sacrificed young men and women captured from neighboring villages.

The Aztecs under Emperor Montezuma (mon-tuh-ZOO-muh) II were at the height of their power in 1519. But Aztec priests warned Montezuma of signs of future trouble. They reminded him of the ancient legend of Quetzalcoátl (ket-sahl-KWAT'l). Quetzalcoátl was a god who had been rejected by humans. His sons vowed to return from the east someday to punish the Aztecs. When they returned, the legend claimed, they would appear as light-skinned, bearded men.

Shortly after Cortés' landing, word reached Montezuma that bearded, light-skinned men had landed to the east. Montezuma thought that Quetzalcoátl's sons had returned. Cortés and his men could be no one else. The conquistadors attacked Tenochtitlán. They captured Montezuma and raided Aztec supplies of gold and silver. By 1521, Aztec power was broken forever.

The Aztecs' wealth encouraged other conquistadors to come to America in search of gold. Hernando de Soto was one

Background: The Aztecs owned large quantities of gold. The metal had a religious significance and was often used as decoration. The excessive demand the Spanish had for gold amazed the Indians, who thought the Spanish used it as food.

Background: There were never enough Spanish soldiers to control their massive territory effectively. In some areas, Spanish rule was in name only, and the Spanish administrator would acknowledge the receipt of official orders with the words, "I understand, but cannot enforce."

such gold hunter. Between 1539 and 1542, he led an expedition throughout Florida and most of the southeastern United States to look for gold. He treated the Indians with great cruelty. De Soto seized them, put them in chains, burned their villages, and killed hundreds of people. De Soto and his men found no gold, but they were the first Europeans to see the Mississippi River. In 1540, Francisco Vásquez de Coronado (frahn-SISS-koe vahs-KEZZ day koe-rah-NAH-doe) explored the American Southwest as far north as Kansas for the Seven Cities of Gold. One of Coronado's assistants happened upon the Grand Canyon. He was the first European to view this magnificent natural wonder.

Settling Spanish America

Spanish settlement took four forms: land grants, *presidios* (pray-SEED-ee-os), *villas* (VEE-yass), and missions. Land grants were given to conquistadors by the king. These land grants usually included an Indian village or a group of villages. The conquistador was responsible for protecting and educating the Indians. The conquistadors were given the power to demand labor from the Indians and to receive a part of the crops they grew.

The *presidio* was the frontier military post. It provided protection for settlers and maintained control of Indian tribes. The *presidio* also guarded the Spanish missions that were often built nearby.

Villas or towns were established by civilian settlers. Some settlers raised animals or farmed. Others were traders, trappers, and miners.

Missions were small settlements built around a church. Catholic priests ran the missions. Each mission contained living quarters, classrooms, warehouses, barns, and other buildings to serve the community. Indians were either persuaded or forced to live in the missions.

The missionaries had many responsibilities. Their first duty was to instruct Indians in Roman Catholicism. Next, the missionaries taught the Indians skills such as working with metals, carpentry, blacksmithing, and plastering.

In the eighteenth century, Spanish settlers pushed northward into what is now California. The coast of California had first been explored in 1542 by the Portuguese explorer Juan Rodriguez Cabrillo. Cabrillo served the Spanish king. However, it was not until about 200 years later that the Spanish king ordered settlement to begin in California.

A man who helped lead this settlement was Father Junípero Serra (hoo-NEEP-uh-roe SERR-uh). He was the first and the most famous of the missionaries in California. Father Serra's first work as a missionary was in Mexico. He spent years in Mexico, during which time he impressed many people with his dedication.

During the 1760's, officials of New Spain decided to establish settlements in California. Father Serra was given the job of establishing missions there. Spanish settlement began in 1769 when soldiers founded a *presidio* at present-day San Diego. Father Serra and other missionaries established a mission nearby.

For the next 15 years, Father Serra worked with the Indians. He instructed them in Catholicism and taught them Spanish ways and customs. Nine missions were founded during his lifetime. After Father Serra's death in 1784, other priests

For Extra Interest: Divide the class into four groups and assign each one of the four Spanish colonial settlement patterns: land grants, presidios, villas, and missions. Have each group describe and give advantages of its pattern as a form of colonial government for New Spain.

carried on his work. By 1834, they founded 12 more missions between San Diego and San Francisco bays.

An Expanding Empire

Spanish settlers built settlements in all parts of the empire. St. Augustine was built in 1565 as a fort in northeastern Florida. It guarded Spanish ships, loaded with gold and silver, that sailed from Mexico to Spain.

In 1598, Don Juan Oñate, a Spanish explorer, helped colonize the area now called New Mexico. The Spanish government sent Oñate to New Mexico to look for gold and to prevent any other country from making claims on the land. Oñate led a group of soldiers, settlers, and missionaries into New Mexico. Soon, other settlers arrived, and Spanish settlements dotted the New Mexico frontier. The region's capital became San Gabriel. In 1610, the capital was changed to Santa Fe.

Spanish rule was harsh on the local Indians. At the time of Oñate's arrival, New Mexico's 66 Indian villages had a population of over 40,000 people. By 1800, their numbers had declined to less than 10,000.

The harsh treatment eventually sparked a revolt among the Indians. The Indians organized an army in 1680 under the leadership of Popé, a San Juan Indian. The Indian army crushed the settlers and attacked the capital at Santa Fe. The governor and the town's citizens were forced to flee. In 1689, Spanish troops began to reconquer the Indians of New Mexico. By 1695, their job was completed.

Spanish settlement also extended into an area called Pimeria Alta. Today, this district includes parts of northern Mexico and southern Arizona. Beginning in 1690, Jesuit missionaries settled there to work among the Indians. Father Eusebio Francisco Kino, an Italian, established 24 missions in Pimeria Alta, seven of which were in Arizona. Father Kino introduced cattle, sheep, goats, horses, and wheat to the region.

By the early 1700's, the Spanish had built missions in Texas. The Alamo, constructed in 1718, was a mission in San Antonio, Texas. Spain created one of the largest and most long-lasting empires in the Western Hemisphere. By 1800, the Spanish flag flew from the Straits of Magellan at the southern tip of South America to San Francisco.

Section Review

1. What were three goals of Spanish explorers in the New World?
2. Define conquistador, isthmus, and circumnavigate.
3. Who was Father Junípero Serra?
4. Describe the important events in Spanish settlements of New Mexico.
5. Which of the three goals described as "God, Gold, and Glory" do you think the Spanish were most successful in achieving? Why?

Background: A Northwest Passage was sought as late as 1969 by the American icebreaker tanker *Manhattan* as a way to bring Alaskan oil to the East Coast. Although the tanker made it to Alaska without major difficulties, the venture proved to be too costly for commercial use.

3. The French and Dutch in America

BEFORE YOU READ: *How were New France and New Netherland colonized?*

France entered the race for New World colonies in the early 1500's. As early as 1503, French fishers had sailed to the coast of Newfoundland. They built huts near the shore and fished for codfish. They were successful at their work, but the king of France, King Francis I, hoped to gain more than fish from Canada.

In 1524, the French king selected an Italian navigator, Giovanni da Verrazano (veh-rah-TSAN-oh), and sent him to the New World to explore for France. Verrazano was to look for gold and a **Northwest Passage**, the hoped-for water route through North America to Asia.

Northwest Passage an imaginary water passage that early explorers believed would lead through North America to Asia

---

Verrazano sailed along the East Coast of North America from the Carolinas to Newfoundland. Verrazano passed in and out of 50 unknown harbors, but none led to the Northwest Passage.

Verrazano and his crew got acquainted with the Eastern Woodland Indians. Their first encounter was a friendly one. Anchoring off the Carolina coast, where he believed he was very close to China, Verrazano sent a boat ashore. He recorded that the Indians came to meet the boat and welcomed the European sailors.

Further north, Verrazano and his crew tried to land again, but the waves were too violent. Indians who had gathered on the shore seemed eager to welcome them. As an act of friendliness, Verrazano ordered a young sailor to swim ashore. The sailor nearly drowned in the rough surf. Upon reaching the beach, he collapsed. The Indians stripped him and then built a great fire. His shipmates expected him to be roasted and eaten. But to their surprise, the sailor was warmed, fed, and helped to rejoin the ship.

Verrazano returned to France, enthusiastic about his voyage. The king felt differently. Verrazano had failed to find any gold. He also had failed to find the Northwest Passage.

France Explores Farther

Verrazano's explorations were followed by those of Jacques Cartier (zhahk khar-TYAY). Cartier found the mouth of the St. Lawrence River in 1534. Sailing up the river the following year, Cartier visited the future sites of Quebec and Montreal. He also hoped to find the Northwest Passage. In fact, he thought he had found it in the St. Lawrence River. However, beyond Montreal he saw a stretch of rapids so violent that nothing bigger than a canoe could get through them. The St. Lawrence River was not the Northwest Passage either.

Cartier made three voyages in all to the New World. On the basis of his voyages, France claimed the right to colonize Canada.

In 1603, French exploration of Canada continued with the voyages of Samuel de Champlain (duh sham-PLANE). First he

Vocabulary Help: rapids—a term applied to the parts of a river where the current is unusually swift. They are typically shallow, and the current is often broken by exposed rocks. Have students research how rapids are formed.

What does this painting of Quebec from 1642 tell you about life in the early settlements of New France?

explored the St. Lawrence River Valley. In July 1608, Champlain founded Quebec on the cliffs overlooking the St. Lawrence River. Quebec became the capital of "New France," the name of France's empire in America. Champlain later became the governor of New France.

By the middle of the 1600's, French explorers with the help of Indian guides had explored much of the Great Lakes region. It was there that they discovered rivers flowing southward.

In 1673, Jacques Marquette (mahr-KETT), a missionary, and Louis Joliet (zhole-YAY), a fur trader, canoed down the Mississippi River. They ended their trip at the junction of the Arkansas River, about 563 kilometers (350 miles) north of the Gulf of Mexico. In 1682, Robert de La Salle (duh luh-SAL) led an expedition down the entire length of the Mississippi River. He planted the French flag and claimed the entire Mississippi Valley for France. He named it Louisiana, after King Louis XIV of France.

Together, Louisiana and New France (Canada) provided France with an immense empire in North America. It stretched from Hudson's Bay in Canada to the Gulf of Mexico.

Settlement in New France

The population of New France was never very large. In 1688, the population numbered about 11,000 people. Only two major areas of settlement developed.

One area of settlement included Nova Scotia and the land along the St. Lawrence River. Here powerful French nobles built great estates. Their land was farmed by peasants, who had few rights.

The second settlement grew up in the south at the mouth of the Mississippi River. This area was made up of plantations that lined the Mississippi. The center of social and business activity was New Orleans.

The fur trade became the major economic activity of New France. It was conducted by trappers and traders called *coureurs de bois* (koo-RUR duh BWAH). The name meant "runners of the woods." They hiked and canoed over a large part of the interior of North America to trap and trade for furs with the Indians. The French traded hatchets, knives, tools, and cloth in return for pelts the Indians trapped for them.

On the whole, New France offered little that would attract settlers. No great mineral wealth had been discovered there. Few wished to come to New France to be workers on the nobles' estates. In the north, the bitter winter weather discour-

Discuss: Why were the Indians willing to trade for tools and weapons when they had been making them for centuries before the Europeans came to the New World?

Background: During his fourth voyage of exploration, a mutinous crew put Henry Hudson and some of his men to sea. They disappeared forever. Hudson became a legendary figure in Washington Irving's short story "Rip Van Winkle."

aged settlement. France had created an enormous empire in terms of size. However, it was never able to convince large numbers of people to **emigrate**, or leave France, to settle there.

emigrate to leave one country and settle in another

The Dutch in America

The Dutch also controlled a colony in North America, the colony of New Netherland. New Netherland consisted of the future states of New York, New Jersey, and Delaware. Dutch holdings of land were small, and they ruled for only a brief time—between 1609 and 1664.

Dutch claims to land in North America dated from 1609 when a group of Dutch spice traders hired Henry Hudson, an English navigator, to find a route to the Orient. Hudson was asked to explore the North American coast for a water route through the continent.

When Hudson reached North America, he sailed along the coast from Newfoundland to the Carolinas. He entered Delaware Bay. Later, he explored the river that was named for him: the Hudson. Hudson failed to discover the Northwest Passage, but he did establish a Dutch claim to land in America.

In 1621, the parliament of the Netherlands gave a **charter**, or grant of rights, to the Dutch West India Company. The company was given total control over New Netherland's fur trade. The Dutch West India Company was also given the power to govern New Netherland and appoint the colony's governor.

This painting shows coureurs de bois in New France canoeing down a waterway to trade for furs with the Indians.

charter a written grant of rights made by a government or ruler to a person or a company

By the 1630's, the Dutch had opened up several fur trading posts. The two most important posts were located at Fort Orange (now Albany, New York) and New Amsterdam (now New York City).

The New Netherland Colony

New Netherland could have become a colony that attracted many settlers. The wide and deep harbor at New Amsterdam

Discuss: The fur trade of North America encouraged the exploration and settlement of new areas. Ask the class why furs were so much in demand during this time period.

The French and Dutch in North America

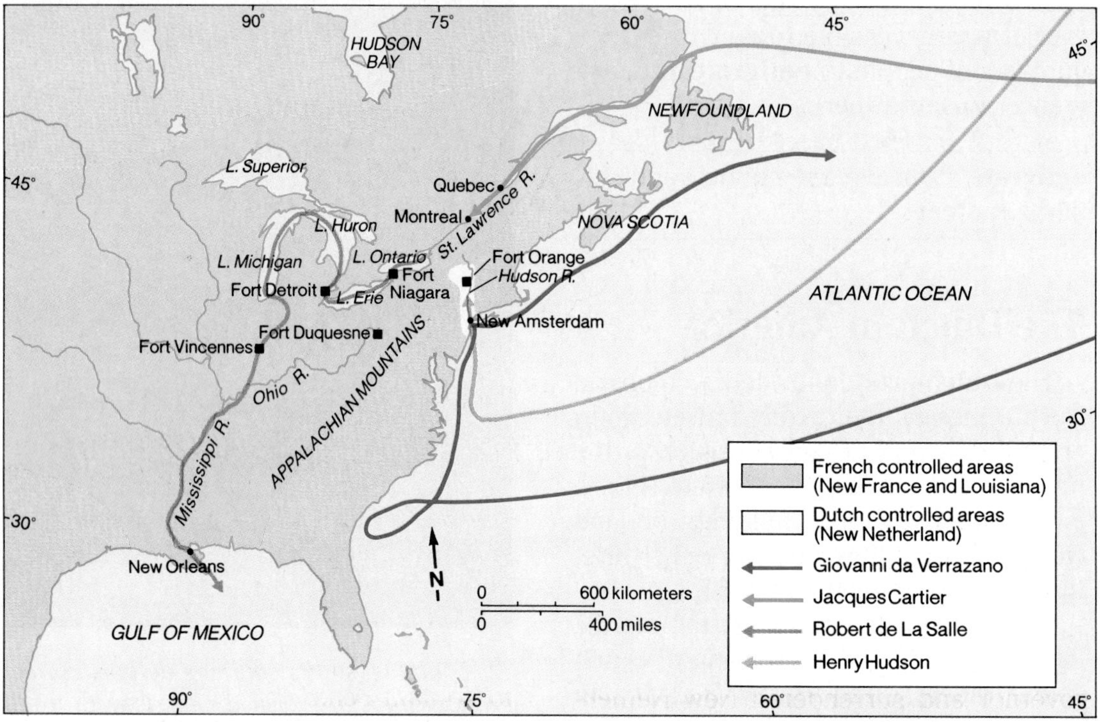

Through which Great Lakes did Robert de La Salle sail while exploring New France and Louisiana? About how long was his journey down the Mississippi River?

could have made the colony a great shipping and trading center. The Hudson River passed through the heart of the fur country before emptying at New Amsterdam. The land in the colony was rich and fertile.

The Dutch West India Company ran New Netherland to make profits for a small group of wealthy people. The company granted large estates along the Hudson River to rich lords or "patroons." Each patroon was required to bring 50 colonists to America. These colonists were to farm the patroon's estate. The colonists were allowed to build their own villages, but they had to live by the patroon's rules. Other Dutch settlers who came were given no voice in running the colony either. As a result, few people were attracted to New Netherland. By the mid-1660's, only about 10,000 people had settled there.

The governors of New Netherland were strict. They enforced the orders of the Dutch West India Company with an iron hand. Two such governors were Peter Minuit, who became governor in 1626, and Peter Stuyvesant, who became governor in 1647. Both men were known for their fiery tempers and strict rule.

Vocabulary Help: The Netherlands, as Holland came to be known after the Middle Ages, is located on the coast of the North Sea. Much of its land is at or below sea level. The word *nether* means below or under.

Discuss: Why were the inhabitants of New Amsterdam not as willing to fight the English as their government was? How might the manner in which the Dutch colonies operated influence the attitude of the colonists?

The Dutch and English were commercial rivals and bitter enemies in the 1600's. England recognized the wealth that New Netherland had to offer. England felt its people could develop this region better than the Dutch. England also hoped to drive the Dutch out of North America. In 1664, King Charles II of England granted the Dutch colony to his brother, James. James, who was the Duke of York, renamed the colony New York. Then he sent four English warships to take possession of New Netherland.

In August 1664, the English fleet sailed into New Amsterdam harbor. The captain demanded that the Dutch surrender their colony. Governor Stuyvesant angrily refused. He said that he would fight to the end before surrendering. However, many citizens were not as willing to put up a fight. On September 8, they overruled the governor and surrendered New Netherland to the English.

James took control of his new territory and divided it up. He kept New York for himself and gave the land across the Hudson to friends. That land became New Jersey. Later, the areas that became Pennsylvania and Delaware were granted to William Penn.

This is an early view of New Amsterdam, which later became Manhattan.

The Netherlands had lost its chance to build a strong base in North America. England's prospects for greater power and profit from its colonies seemed brighter than ever.

Section Review

1. How were New France and New Netherland colonized?
2. What was the Northwest Passage?
3. What were the chief economic activities of New France and New Netherland?
4. Why were the French and Dutch unable to attract settlers to their colonies? What could the French and Dutch have done to attract settlers to their colonies?

Social Studies Skills

Using a Map Scale

Samuel de Champlain explored the St. Lawrence River from its mouth to the Great Lakes. The distance he actually traveled can be measured by using a map scale. Distances on maps are drawn in proportion to distances in the real world. The map scale shows this ratio. To measure the distance between Quebec and Montreal, follow these steps:

1. Mark off on the edge of a strip of paper the space between the dot marking Quebec and the dot marking Montreal.
2. Place your paper strip on the map scale so that your first mark is at zero. Notice that your second mark falls at approximately 250 kilometers (155 miles). This means that the distance between these two points is about 250 kilometers (155 miles).

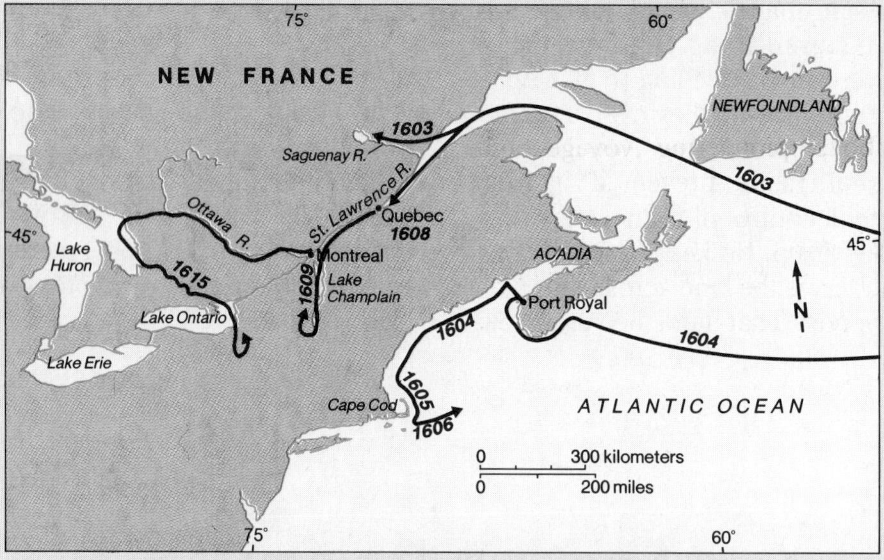

1. How many kilometers is Quebec from Port Royal?
2. What is the distance in miles between Quebec and Port Royal?
3. About how long is Lake Champlain?
4. How many kilometers is it from Montreal to the southern tip of Lake Huron?
5. How would you measure the distance between two points if the space between them were greater than the length of the map scale?

Background: Only with the defeat of the Spanish Armada in 1588 was England able to extend its power over the seas. After the Spanish defeat, English ships were able to send people and supplies to the New World with little fear of attack.

4. The Background of English Settlement

BEFORE YOU READ: *What were the reasons for English settlement in America?*

No permanent English colony in North America was established until 1607. Yet, England had been among the first to explore this New World. In 1497, King Henry VII sent John Cabot to explore North America. Cabot reached Newfoundland, where he stayed for a month. Then he sailed southward along the coast, perhaps as far as Virginia. Cabot was the first European to reach North America since the Vikings. Within a decade, Europeans from many countries were sailing to Newfoundland each year to fish off its coast.

England planned to explore farther after Cabot's pioneering voyage, but problems at home prevented it from doing so. England was caught up in religious disagreements between English Catholics and Protestants. These disputes nearly brought the country to war. Secondly, much of England's energy was focused on a long and bitter war with Spain.

It was not until Elizabeth I became queen in 1558 that England again showed an interest in overseas adventure. Queen Elizabeth I was eager to establish English colonies in America. She actively pursued this goal.

The Elizabethan Era

During the reign of Elizabeth I (1558–1603), England changed from a farming country to a leader in trade. A new merchant class developed that soon became wealthy and powerful. English shipyards were busy building a fleet that would take English goods to the markets of the world. Pride in being English increased.

But the Elizabethan era was not a prosperous time for everyone. The common people suffered most from changes in society. Thousands of rent-paying tenant farmers were thrown off the land so that owners could use their farmland to raise sheep. The wool from the sheep was the resource upon which the English textile, or woven cloth, industry was based. The displaced farmers wandered in gangs around England searching for food and

This painting shows Queen Elizabeth, age 25, at her coronation.

Background: Piracy in the Caribbean Sea area had been a long-standing occupation for unemployed sailors. England gave tacit support to these pirates when it served its national interest to do so.

charity. They alarmed those who still had houses, land, and jobs. These events were recorded in a well-known nursery rhyme: "Hark, hark! The dogs do bark; the beggars are coming to town."

The population of England grew from 3 million to 4 million people between 1485 and 1603. Because more and more land was being used to raise sheep, not enough food could be grown to support the increasing population.

Exploration Begins Again

Amidst the widespread growth and troubles of Elizabethan England, English adventurers set to sea once again. Beginning in the 1570's, English pirates known as **sea dogs** began hunting Spanish ships.

Sir Walter Raleigh established the first English colony in America at Roanoke.

Under leaders like Francis Drake and John Hawkins, the sea dogs attacked Spanish ships that were carrying gold and silver. Queen Elizabeth did not openly give approval to these pirates, but neither did she stop them. The sea dogs prowled the Caribbean Sea looking for Spanish treasure ships to ambush. Spain objected to this illegal activity and declared war against England. English adventurers realized the urgent need to establish bases of operation in the New World. From these bases, strikes against Spanish ships and towns in America would be easier. What was needed was a permanent settlement in America.

sea dogs English pirates who raided Spanish ships and towns in the late 1500's

One sea dog, Sir Walter Raleigh, approached the Queen. He asked permission to establish a permanent settlement in America. Elizabeth agreed, granting Raleigh all land north of Florida. He named this territory Virginia.

In 1585, Raleigh established a colony on Roanoke (ROE-uh-noke) Island, off the northeastern coast of North Carolina. The spot was sandy and deserted, and the settlers, a small group of men, had a difficult time. The colony was abandoned the following year. Raleigh was not ready to give up, however. He organized a second group of people who wished to go to America. They started their colony at Roanoke in 1587. The second group of settlers included women and children as well as men. Raleigh hoped that this would help make the colony permanent. There were 10 children and 17 women at Roanoke, as well as about 100 men.

Vocabulary Help: "Sea dog" was also used to refer to experienced sailors after piratical activity had come to an end. Sea dogs were, in effect, privateers, that is, private citizens using their own ships in fighting their nations' enemies.

The Roanoke colony was dependent for its survival on English supply ships. But for three years no ships came. One finally arrived in 1590, and a party of soldiers was quickly sent ashore. To their bewilderment, they found no one. The entire colony had vanished without a trace. There were no bodies, no dwellings, not even a sign of struggle. The soldiers searched without success for the colonists. All that they found was the word *Croatan* carved on a tree. What was this? The name of local Indians? The name of a location where the colonists moved the settlement? What Croatan meant, or what happened to this "Lost Colony" of Roanoke, remains a mystery to this day.

The failure of the Lost Colony revealed major problems that would have to be corrected if more permanent colonies were to be established. First, a supply link with England had to be maintained. Second, a better site for a colony was needed, and settlers with the necessary skills to set up and maintain a colony had to be found.

In 1603, King James I succeeded Elizabeth to the throne of England. Under his leadership, England prepared to establish colonies overseas again. While James I was monarch (1603–1625), colonies that eventually became the United States were started.

Why Go to America?

What prompted English colonists to leave their homes, sail across a treacherous ocean, and settle in an unknown land? They were drawn to America by a dream. It was not a simple dream but one as complex as the number of people who made the dangerous crossing. The earliest colonists looked upon America as a land of opportunity. Like the Spanish looking for gold, and the French and Dutch trading in furs, some English were also seeking riches. Others came seeking religious freedom or hoping for adventure. But the greatest pull came from the dream of a fresh start. America provided the hope of a new beginning for colonists.

Many English people hoped to profit from going to America. Merchants and businessmen made up one group. They knew the New World was rich in furs, fish, good farmland, lumber, and many other raw materials. Enormous profits were possible from trade. But to tap the resources available in America, large-scale settlement was necessary. New colonies would have to be organized.

Establishing a colony took more money than any merchant or small company possessed. To overcome this obstacle, merchants and businessmen formed a new type of business called a **joint-stock company**. Interested people contributed money to a company whose job it was to start a colony. Joint-stock companies established the first three permanent colonies: Virginia in 1607, Plymouth in 1620, and Massachusetts Bay in 1630.

---

joint-stock company a company that is formed through the pooling of many people's money. Any profits made by the company are shared among those who have invested in it.

The English government also hoped to profit from the colonies being established in America. The government believed

Discuss: What do you think happened to the colonists of the Roanoke colony? What kinds of evidence might have been left that would tell more about their fate?

Vocabulary Help: Raw materials are the basic unprocessed materials obtained from nature and used in the manufacturing of finished products. Have students make a list of 5–10 raw materials.

that the purpose of the colonies was to benefit the home country. This belief about the role of colonies was called **mercantilism**. According to this theory, England should establish colonies to supply it with raw materials. In turn, the raw materials would be made into goods in England. The colonies were not permitted to buy manufactured goods from any country except England. Mercantilism would make England wealthier, and it would provide more jobs for English workers.

---

mercantilism an economic system designed to increase the wealth of a country by discouraging imports and encouraging exports. Colonies, with their raw materials, help to serve this purpose.

A third group seeking wealth in America was a segment of English society called the "underclass." These people were the common folk, comprising about 40 percent of the English population. They were ordinary farmers and workers who came from the upper part of the lower class and the middle class. They were ambitious and eager to work hard. They wanted to improve the lives of their families. Most early English colonists to America were from this ambitious underclass. Other English people came, too, of course, but in much smaller numbers. The poorer members of the lower class were unable to raise enough money to pay for passage to America. The wealthy English of the upper class were already living comfortable lives and had no reason to leave England.

By 1600, religious persecution was driving many English people to America. The only religion that people were permitted to practice in England was Anglicanism. It was a state religion with the monarch as the head of the church. Other Protestants and Roman Catholics were persecuted by the king and the leaders of the Church of England. Many religious groups felt it would be better to leave England for America.

Religious groups from England established four colonies: Maryland by Catholics, Plymouth by Pilgrims or Separatists, Pennsylvania by Quakers, and Massachusetts Bay by Puritans.

For some English people, the attraction of America was the prospect of adventure. Colonies in America would provide a base for striking at Spanish colonies and ships.

The Journey and Arrival

Whatever the reason was that caused an individual to leave England, he or she faced a journey that was difficult and dangerous. Getting to America was as hard as surviving once a person arrived.

Most English citizens had little if any experience with ships. Once people decided to go to America, they had to overcome their fear of ships and sailing. In addition, settlers faced the sadness of leaving home. Most of them had roots that went back for centuries in a particular area. Everything around them was familiar. They had their families, friends, churches, animals, gardens, streams, and schools. All of these things gave meaning and identity to their lives. The decision to go to America forced people to give many of these things up, usually forever.

Background: Most nations in Europe at this time supported a state religion. Religious toleration was not a widely honored concept. In many cases, a person who did not support the state religion was considered a traitor to his or her state.

For Extra Interest: Show pictures of sailing ships and pictures of modern ocean liners. Have students identify the apparent differences between the two types of ships, and tell how these differences might influence the length of a voyage or the comfort of the passengers.

The ships that brought colonists to America were small and unsanitary. Passengers were crowded together below decks for most of the voyage. If the weather was good, the trip might take 10 to 13 weeks. If the weather was stormy, the journey could take as long as five months.

With passengers jammed together, the ship headed westward across the Atlantic Ocean. Sickness was common on many trips. Typhus, spread by lice, was a major killer. Yellow fever and smallpox took the lives of many passengers, too. Frequently, the passengers faced starvation. In order to cut costs, the ship's owner or the ship's captain often did not supply enough food for the voyage. Because a child was treated as half a passenger, children received only half portions of food. Parents were helpless to keep their children from dying of starvation. The death rate on some ships reached 60 percent.

Finally, when land was seen the ships would dock, and the passengers would go ashore. They had arrived in America.

What did the earliest colonists see upon arrival? They found a land covered by vast forests. Like many Europeans, the English were afraid of forests. They believed forests held "beasts" that would destroy them if given the chance. They knew the forests were also full of Indians who they had heard were wild and vicious people.

A great many English who arrived in America were disappointed with what they found. Yet, they were terrified to make the return voyage back home. So they stayed and made the best of things. There was no time to recuperate from the voyage, either. Once they arrived, they had to attend to immediate needs like food and housing.

Two Waves of Immigration

There were two waves of European immigration to America during the colonial period. The first group was English. They came in their largest numbers from 1607 until 1715. In that period, all of the original 13 colonies, except Georgia, were established.

The second wave of immigrants arrived from 1715 onward until the first shots of the American Revolution in 1775. This group was made up largely of non-English Europeans who settled in all of the English colonies.

Section Review

1. What were the reasons for English settlement in America?
2. Define sea dogs and mercantilism.
3. Explain how joint-stock companies helped to establish colonies in America.
4. It was hard for colonists to leave those things that were familiar to them in their homelands. What things in your community give meaning to your life and help you identify who you are?

Background: Scurvy, a disease caused by a lack of vitamin C, was another hazard on long ocean voyages. To combat this condition, British sailors of the nineteenth century drank lime juice. From this practice, the slang term *limey*, referring to someone British, originated.

CHAPTER REVIEW

Summary

The first Europeans to sail to the New World were the Vikings. They arrived in America around 1000 A.D. The Vikings stayed only a short time because of conflicts with the Indians. It was almost 500 years before Europeans again landed in America.

What brought Europeans back to America was the growing demand for luxury items from the East. Many European nations began to explore for the fastest route to the East. Portugal took the lead in exploration with the discovery of an all-water route east around Africa. Not to be outdone, Spain sent Columbus on a voyage westward across the Atlantic. Instead of finding the Far East, he landed in America in 1492. The race for colonies began.

All European countries looked to the New World as a source of power and wealth. Soon Spain, Portugal, France, the Netherlands, and England were in competition for New World territory.

European settlers came to America for religious reasons, in search of profits, and for glory and adventure. By the early seventeenth century, permanent English settlements had been established in America.

Recalling the Facts

1. What improvements in navigation occurred during the 1400's?
2. Who found the first all-water route east? Where was it?
3. What was the goal of Cortés when he landed in Mexico?
4. In what two areas of New France did settlements develop?
5. What was Hudson seeking in North America?
6. Why did English exploration halt for a time after Cabot?

Analyzing the Facts

1. What conclusions can be drawn about the relationship between the Vikings and the American Indians?
2. Why were strong national monarchs necessary before European exploration of the world could begin?

3. Explain why you think the Portuguese took the eastern route around Africa in attempting to reach the Far East.
4. Why did explorers try to find a Northwest Passage?
5. Why was New France unable to attract many settlers?
6. How do you think the colonists felt about mercantilism?

Time and History

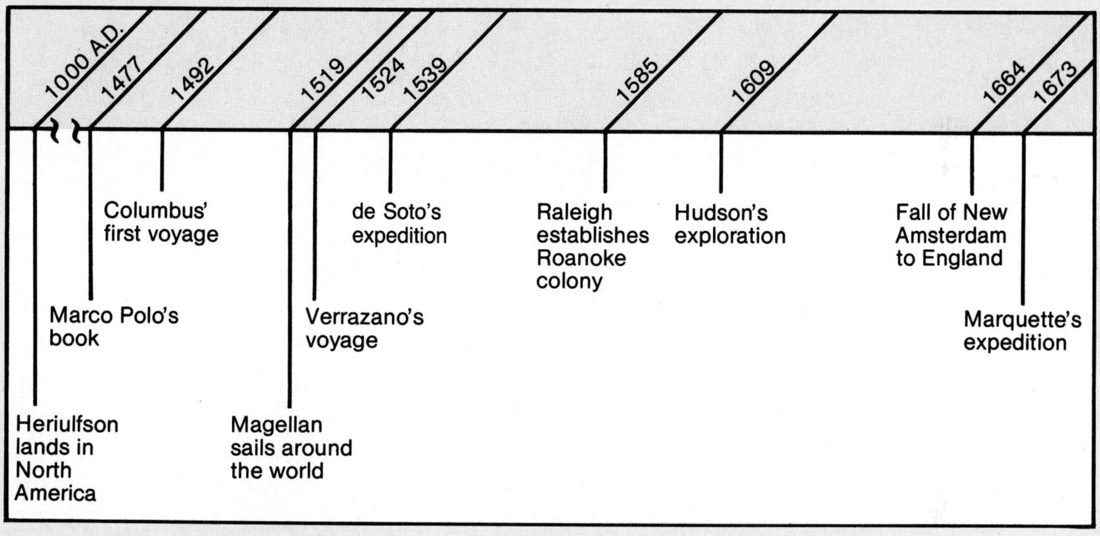

1. Which expedition came first: de Soto's, Hudson's, or Magellan's?
2. In what year did the Dutch lose their main colony in America?
3. Who was the first person to circumnavigate the world?
4. Who established the first English colony at Roanoke?
5. How many years after Marco Polo's book did Columbus make his first voyage to the New World?
6. How many expeditions on the timeline occurred during the sixteenth century?
7. About how many years passed between the time the first European set foot in the New World and the first trip around the world?

Chapter 3

The English Colonies

The city of London was filled with the joy of the Christmas season as three small ships made their way down the Thames River on December 20, 1606. Their destination was America. The 144 men and boys aboard the *Godspeed, Susan Constant,* and *Discovery* had no idea how important their journey would be. Following a rough crossing of the Atlantic Ocean, 104 survivors of the trip came ashore in mid-May 1607. They established a colony in Virginia, which they named Jamestown. It became the first permanent English colony in America. In this chapter, you will read about the founding of 13 English colonies in America and how they grew during the colonial era.

After you read this chapter, you will be able to:

1. Explain where and why the first permanent English colonies were established in America.
2. List the New England colonies and explain why each was settled.
3. Identify the differences between life in the New England colonies and life in the middle colonies.
4. Describe the different classes in colonial society.

- Distinguish between primary and secondary sources.

Vocabulary Help: Malaria is a parasitic disease transmitted by the bite of a mosquito. The disease is characterized by periodic attacks of chills and fever. In the sixteenth and seventeenth centuries, the cause of the disease was unknown, and many people died.

1. English Beginnings in America

BEFORE YOU READ: *In what ways was Massachusetts Bay colony different from the Virginia and Plymouth colonies?*

The colony of Virginia was founded by the London Company. This was a group of London merchants who were interested in starting a settlement in North America. The London Company's first settlement was established in 1607 at Jamestown.

From the start, everything seemed to go wrong at Jamestown. The colonists had chosen a poor location for their settlement. The ground around the colony was swampy. Malaria killed many people. The colonists themselves proved to be a problem. Many of them were "gentlemen" who felt it was not their job to do hard work like chopping wood, building houses, or planting crops. As a result Jamestown did not have enough food stored for the winter. By the next spring, over half of the colony were dead.

One colonist, John Smith, was determined to prevent the colony from failing. He ordered *all* colonists to clear fields, plant crops, and build houses. Smith's policy of "no work, no food" angered the gentlemen but saved the colony.

During this first year, Smith also made contact with Powhatan (pou-uh-TAN), the 60-year-old chief of the area's Algonquian tribes. Powhatan was friendly toward Smith and the newcomers. The chief offered food to some of the colonists to help them through the hard times.

The Jamestown Colony

New settlers and supplies arrived from the London Company in 1608 and 1609. Smith left for England in October 1609, satisfied that the colony was doing better. No sooner had he left than the colonists fell back into their lazy habits. Almost no attention was paid to the crops. During the winter, they paid a heavy price: the colony's population dropped from 500 to 60 settlers. Food supplies were so low that some colonists ate rats, dogs, insects, frogs, and snakes.

The survivors were ready to head back to England in June 1610, when relief ships arrived. Aboard were 300 new colonists and fresh supplies. The survivors remained in Jamestown.

In 1611, Thomas Dale was made the colony's governor. Dale was a stern leader who believed that the hard times were caused by the colonists' laziness. He ordered everyone to work, and he put the colony on a daily schedule. Settlers arrived for work in the fields at six each morning, went to prayer meetings at ten, and ate dinner at noon. Then they returned to the fields at two. The governor demanded obedience to all laws. Although Dale was a harsh governor, under his rule the colony began to expand.

The London Company was eager for the colonists to develop a crop that would bring in profits. That crop was tobacco. The Virginia settlers found the native tobacco that grew in North America too bitter. In 1612, one settler, John Rolfe, experimented with some tobacco brought from Trinidad. He found it grew well in Virginia's soil. It was also milder than the native tobacco. Rolfe's discovery

Background: Powhatan's daughter, Pocahontas, is said to have saved the life of John Smith. He was captured by the Pamunkey Indians, who had become angry over the loss of their land to the Europeans. Smith claimed that as a result of Pocahontas' pleadings, his life was spared.

Discuss: Why do you think it was important to the success of a colony that all the colonists owned their own land? How was this different from being an employee of a colonizing company?

meant that the colony had found its **cash crop**, or crop that could be sold for profits. Soon, Virginia was exporting thousands of kilograms (pounds) of tobacco to England each year.

cash crop a crop that is grown to be sold, rather than used by the farmer

In 1618, the London Company decided to permit private ownership of land in order to attract new settlers. A new arrangement, called the **headright system**, gave each settler 40 hectares (100 acres) of land, plus another 20 hectares (50 acres) to the head of each family. The headright system brought thousands of settlers to Virginia.

headright system a system in which land was offered free as a way to bring new settlers to the Virginia colony

The London Company also ordered the election of representatives from each of the 11 settlements in Virginia. This group, called the House of Burgesses, advised the governor. However, the House of Burgesses was soon making laws for the colony. The House of Burgesses was the beginning of self-government in America.

As the colony of Virginia slowly grew, settlers ignored the Indians' rights to their own land. In 1622, the Indians attacked the Virginia settlements, killing 347 colonists. Many colonists lost hope, and the London Company fell on financial hard times. In 1624, James I took back the company's charter and placed Virginia under his control.

The Pilgrims

All English citizens were required by law to belong to the Anglican Church. The Church was a national church, so it was also called the Church of England. Its head was the king or queen. Those who refused to join the Church of England were subject to arrest and jail.

In eastern England was the small town of Scrooby. Some of its citizens had separated from the Church of England and formed their own religious congregation. They became known as Separatists. The English treated them so badly that the Separatists fled England in 1608. They settled in the Netherlands. But the Separatists began to fear that their children were losing their English culture and traditions. The Separatists wanted to live in an English land. They decided that an English colony in America might be the solution to their problem. The group obtained permission to settle in Virginia.

Calling themselves "Pilgrims" (homeless travelers), they left for America on September 16, 1620. Land was sighted on November 9, and the *Mayflower*, the Pilgrim's old and leaky ship, put down its anchor. The Pilgrims were not in Virginia, however. They were hundreds of kilometers (miles) north of Virginia.

The Pilgrims realized that some sort of rules were needed for their settlement. They drew up the Mayflower Compact. This was an agreement, or set of rules, that all would live by.

After the Pilgrims came ashore, they came upon an abandoned Indian village and selected it as the site for their settlement. They named the settlement Plymouth. The Pilgrims were not prepared for

Background: The Mayflower Compact may be considered the earliest European expression of democratic principles in America. While it did not establish a true government, the Compact was an agreement that all would abide by the laws that they would make.

Discuss: Many of the first European-Indian contacts were quite friendly; hostile acts seem to have occurred later in the colonization process. What kinds of things might have produced the later conflict between the two groups?

their first winter. They had few supplies, poor housing, and no time to plant any crops. About half the settlers died.

The following spring, the survivors met two Indians, Samoset and Squanto. Squanto was a great help to the Pilgrims. The Governor of Plymouth, William Bradford, gratefully recorded: "He [Squanto] directed them how to set their corn, where to take fish, and to procure [get] other commodities [useful items]. . . . [He] never left them [the Pilgrims] till he died."

Plymouth colony never became very large. By the 1630's, another English religious group, the Puritans, came to America for reasons very similar to those of the Pilgrims.

The Puritans

The Puritans, while they lived in England, were members of the Church of England. But they were unhappy with the Church. They argued that its ceremonies and beliefs were too similar to those of the Roman Catholic Church, which the Puritans had rejected. They believed the Church should sweep away all that reminded them of Catholicism. Neither the king nor church officials approved of the Puritans' beliefs. When Charles I became King in 1625, he began to persecute the Puritans. Puritans in government lost their positions. Puritan ministers were expelled from their churches. All across England, Puritans were jailed.

This painting depicts the Pilgrims being rowed out to the sailing ships that will take them to America.

For Extra Interest: Show a map of Boston and have students comment on why the Puritans might have chosen to settle on this site.

In August 1629, the Puritans decided to emigrate to America. More than 1,000 persons arrived in Massachusetts Bay in the summer of 1630. The Puritans, unlike earlier colonists, were well prepared for settlement. They brought livestock, supplies, and food. The Puritan colony spread rapidly and soon included eight towns. The largest town was Boston.

Once settled in America, the Puritans established the Congregational Church as the religion of Massachusetts Bay Colony. All colonists were required to attend services and give the church financial support. Every other faith was prevented from practicing its beliefs.

The Puritan leaders demanded complete obedience to their rules. They believed the Bay Colony represented a **covenant**, or an agreement, between the people and God. Under the agreement, people of the colony must promise to lead good lives based upon God's will as expressed in the Bible. In turn, they believed, God would bless the colony.

covenant an agreement entered into very seriously, to do a specific thing

Puritan children, painted around 1770.

The Puritan experience was unique in many ways. The Puritans were able to attract many more settlers than the other early colonies in America. The Massachusetts Bay Colony never experienced hard times like Virginia and Plymouth had. The Puritan leaders were well-educated people. They provided careful planning and smart leadership. As a result, Massachusetts Bay was successful from the start.

Section Review

1. Identify two ways in which Massachusetts Bay Colony was different from Virginia and Plymouth colonies.
2. Define headright system. How did it help to settle America?
3. What was the importance of the Virginia House of Burgesses?
4. Who were the Pilgrims, and why did they come to America?
5. What do you think contributed to the success of the Puritan colony in Massachusetts Bay?

Social Studies Skills

Primary and Secondary Sources

When historians study the past, they often use primary sources. Primary sources include documents, letters, maps, drawings, artifacts, and other items that were written or produced during the time period being studied.

Secondary sources are written or produced in a later time period. This textbook is an example of a secondary source. Much of the information in a secondary source comes from primary source material. Some secondary sources are based on other secondary sources.

Studying primary source material allows a person to see the past through the eyes of people who lived during a particular time period. It is a record of what people in the past said, wrote, made, or saw.

Read the following primary source account of a German who traveled from Europe to America in 1756:

> In the course of a storm, the sea begins to surge and rage so that waves often seem to rise up like high mountains, sometimes sweeping over the ship. Tossed by the storm and the waves, the ship rolls from side to side. The tightly packed people, the sick as well as the healthy, are thrown every which way.
>
> Children between the ages of one and seven seldom survive the sea voyage. Parents must watch their children suffer miserably, die, and then be thrown into the sea.
>
> It is not surprising that many people become ill, because in addition to all the other troubles and miseries, warm food is served only three times a week, and at that it is very bad. Also, there is very little of it, and it is so dirty you can hardly eat it. (From G. Mittelberger, *Journey to Pennsylvania*).

1. What is the difference between primary and secondary source material?
2. What is the advantage of using primary over secondary source material? What might be a disadvantage?
3. From the primary source material on the sea voyage, why was the trip from Europe to America so uncomfortable and unhealthy for the passengers?
4. Write a secondary source account of the sea voyage based on the information given in the primary source.

Discuss: Why do you think the Puritans, who left England for religious freedom, denied this freedom to others in their colony? What does this suggest about religious ideas at that time? How did this affect the establishment of other colonies?

2. The New England Colonies

BEFORE YOU READ: *Why were other colonies established in New England?*

Soon after Massachusetts Bay Colony was settled, people began leaving it to establish other colonies. One reason for this was the steady population growth in Massachusetts. Another was the narrow-mindedness of the Puritan leaders. The New England colonies came to include Connecticut, Rhode Island, and New Hampshire, as well as Massachusetts.

The Growth of New England

The Puritans refused to allow anyone in their colony to disagree with them about religion and the colony's government. As a result, many people left.

The first migration away from Massachusetts was southward. In 1636, Reverend Thomas Hooker led 35 families into the Connecticut River valley and founded Hartford, Connecticut. Hooker believed that the right to vote belonged to all free men, no matter what their religious beliefs were. In Massachusetts Bay, only church members could vote and select the government. Hooker was followed by others, and various towns sprung up in Connecticut.

Other people left Massachusetts for Rhode Island, which was founded by Roger Williams in 1636. Williams had been a minister in Salem, Massachusetts, before coming into conflict with Puritan leaders. Williams charged that Puritans illegally occupied their colony, since they had never purchased the land from the Indians. Williams believed that Christian settlers should purchase all land at fair prices from the Indians. Williams was also angry about the Puritans' rejection of other religious beliefs. Williams believed that any Christian, regardless of faith, should be able to worship in peace.

Anne Hutchinson preaching in her home.

Puritan leaders forced Williams to leave the Bay Colony in 1636. Williams purchased some of the Narragansett Indians' land and founded the town of Providence. The colony of Rhode Island became the home of other persons who fled from Puritan rule.

Anne Hutchinson aroused the Puritans' anger, too. Women were not supposed to take an active role in religious matters. Hutchinson, a woman of strong opinions, stated that individuals could communicate with God and be saved without the help of churches. Her beliefs challenged the authority of the Puritan Church. Hutchinson was tried and convicted of holding wrong religious views. As a result, she was forced to leave Massachu-

Background: The strict religious regulations of the Puritan settlements caused dissenters to move away from the first centers of colonization. In this way, settlements were distributed throughout much of the New England area.

For Extra Interest: Have interested students research and report on the Salem witchcraft trials of 1692.

Famous Americans

LADY DEBORAH MOODY

Lady Deborah Moody was the founder of the colony that was to become Brooklyn, New York. Lady Moody came to the American colonies in 1639 from England, where she was known for her devotion to religious and individual rights.

For a time her life was comfortable. Lady Moody purchased a large farm in Salem, Massachusetts. Soon, however, she began to disagree with the religious leaders of the colony. In 1643, she was scolded by the church for her views. Lady Moody left Massachusetts with several followers and moved to an area of the New Netherland colony called Long Island. The Dutch granted Lady Moody's group complete religious freedom and the right of self-government. Under Lady Moody's leadership, the colonists made an impressive beginning. They drew up a plan for the town and began town meetings. They paid the Indians for the land they settled on and insisted that no liquor be sold to the Indians in the area.

In 1657, Quaker missionaries arrived in New Netherland. They held one of their first meetings in America in Lady Moody's house. It is not known if she became a Quaker. Some historians believe she may have been attracted to the Quaker religion because of its belief in equality for women. Whether she converted or not, Lady Moody insisted on the Quakers' right to preach their own religion. Lady Deborah Moody proved that she believed in religious freedom for all. She also demonstrated that women could be able leaders in the New World.

setts. She and her followers fled to Rhode Island.

Two other areas in New England were settled at this time, although neither was heavily populated. A small number of persons went north of Massachusetts in the 1620's and settled in what is now New Hampshire. Other people settled along the rugged coast of Maine. Massachusetts Bay Colony bought Maine in 1677 and it remained a part of Massachusetts until 1820.

The New England Community

The Puritans originally intended to form one settlement in their colony. This settlement was to be Boston. However, the arrival of some 20,000 English people between 1630 and 1643 forced the Puritans to alter this plan.

A common plan was developed to establish new towns. Colonial governments

Background: In the Puritan communities, there was little opportunity for social activities. Religious meetings, prayer gatherings, and church services thus took on social as well as religious meaning to the people in these colonies.

The plentiful New England lumber provided work for sawyers, or people who saw wood into planks.

in New England granted land in 93-square-kilometer (36-square-mile) blocks called townships. At the center of each township was the village. The village consisted of a meetinghouse, or church, and an open land area called the green. The green was a place for people to walk, gather, and graze their animals.

The village also contained a plot of land for each family. These plots were large enough for a house and vegetable garden. The land surrounding the village was used for farming.

All town matters and decisions were discussed at town meetings. However, while all villagers were allowed to participate at meetings, only property owners were allowed to vote.

The family played an important role in New England life. No one was permitted to live alone. All unmarried people were required to live with a family. A young man could not marry before he had become a landowner. A young woman needed a gift or dowry of household goods to give to her future husband before she could marry. Most married couples had between six and eight children. The father was the absolute head of the family. All members of the household had to obey him.

Puritans came to America for religious reasons, and it was expected that village life would center around the church. While villagers were expected to follow religious rules each day, the Sabbath day was reserved for religious activities. Sabbath began at six in the evening on Saturday and lasted until sundown on Sunday. Sundays were spent at the meetinghouse attending church services. Every member of the village was required to attend. There the congregation listened to sermons and sang.

The New England Economy

Fishing and farming became the major occupations of colonists. Many varieties of fish could be found in the rivers and along the coast of New England. Whaling was a very profitable industry in this region because whale oil was widely used as a fuel for lamps. Farming, while widespread, was difficult. The soil in most areas of New England is hard, rocky, and not very fertile.

Many people who came to the colonies were skilled in crafts. They made their living as carpenters, masons, black-

Background: The early Puritans saw themselves as fulfilling a mission by setting up a colony in the New World. Their colony would serve as an example to others as the right and just way to live.

Triangular Trade Routes

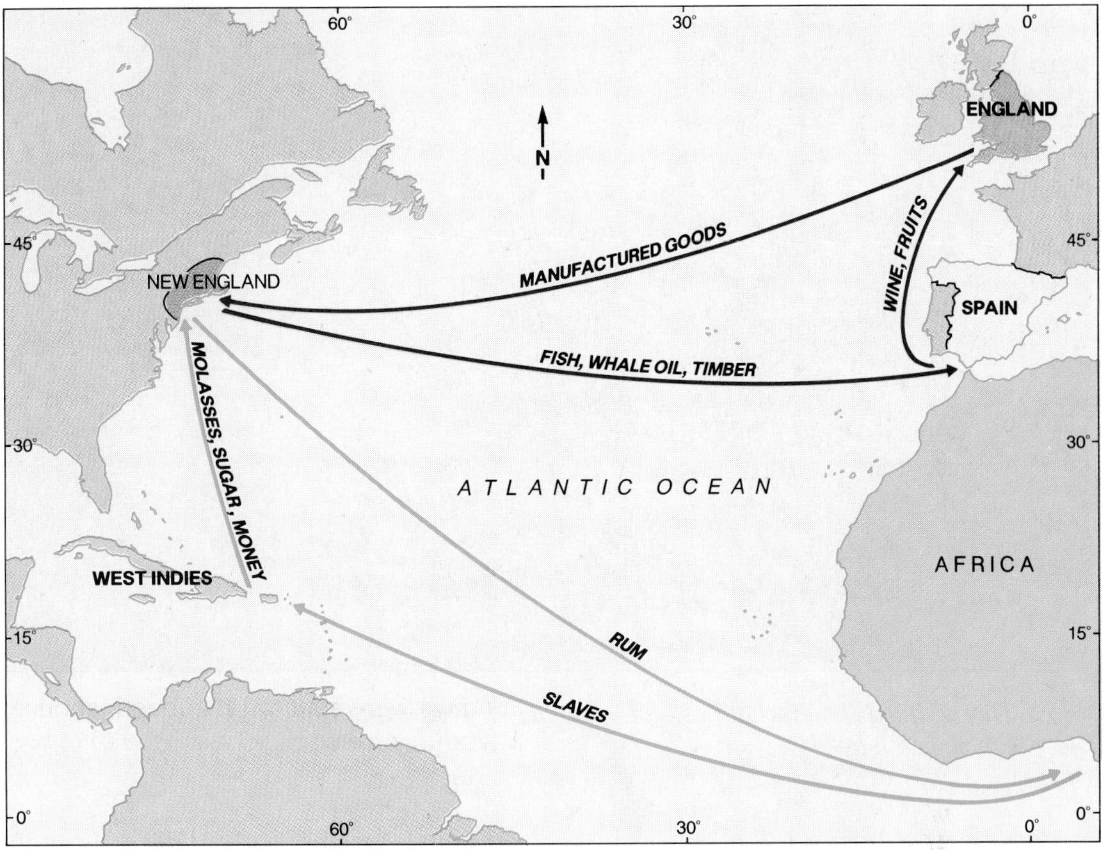

How does this map help you to explain why England needed to import wine and fruits?

smiths, tailors, and weavers. By the late 1600's, some towns began to specialize in making certain types of goods. Lynn, Massachusetts, for example, became known for its shoes.

The colonists who became the wealthiest were those who worked in overseas trade. New England merchants developed close ties with English and European merchants. By 1660, a complex network of overseas trade had emerged. This network became known as the triangular trade because the routes formed triangles. New England merchants sent fish, whale oil, and timber to Spanish ports. These items were traded for wine and fruits bound for England. In England, the fruits and wine were traded for manufactured goods like linens, furniture, china, and tools. The New Englanders also shipped rum made from molasses and sugar to Africa. There the rum was traded for slaves, who were shipped to the West Indies. The slaves were traded in the West Indies for sugar, molasses, and money. These were the things the New England

Background: Whales were hunted from open rowing boats and killed by hand harpoons. The whale was then towed to shore, where the blubber was removed and the oil extracted.

Background: The English navy needed tall, straight trees for the masts on their sailing vessels. Since the supply of such trees was almost exhausted at home, the English took an active interest in preserving such trees in the colonies for mast construction.

This painting shows what Boston looked like in 1765. What aspects of colonial life are shown here?

traders brought home.

The growth of trade helped New England's shipbuilding industry to develop. Timber was plentiful in New England. This made shipbuilding costs 20 to 50 percent lower than in England. New England became one of the great shipbuilding centers in the world.

Trade stimulated the growth of cities. Boston remained the largest city in New England. By 1690, Boston's population had reached about 7,000.

The Great Awakening

In all the colonies, including New England, religious activity and interest was declining by the early 1700's. Church membership and attendance dropped steadily as colonists became more interested in business activities. Ministers tried without success to stop this trend. But many people thought their sermons and messages bland and uninspiring.

Toward the middle of the 1700's, a religious revival swept across America. Intense religious feelings became common again. Many people believe this revival started with Jonathan Edwards and George Whitefield (WITT-feeld). Edwards, a minister, gave rousing sermons throughout New England. He sparked new interest in religious matters. Whitefield was an English minister who came to the

Background: While the Great Awakening was successful in bringing the colonists back to their religion, the initial enthusiasm did not last long.

Discuss: Why do you think that the only subjects taught in the first Puritan schools were reading, writing, arithmetic, and religious studies? If you were going to add any other subjects to the curriculum, what would they be? Why would you choose them?

colonies in 1738. Whitefield drew huge crowds as he traveled throughout the colonies. In October 1740, for example, he spoke before 19,000 people in Boston. Whitefield's sermons were so moving that thousands of colonists returned to leading deeply religious lives. The movement of people back to their faith was called the Great Awakening.

The Great Awakening did much more than renew interest in religion. It broke down some of the barriers between the classes in the colonies. Rich and poor, planters and small farmers, big merchants and small shopkeepers were all caught up in the Great Awakening.

New England Education

Education was highly valued in New England. The Puritans were well educated before coming to America. They were determined that their children would also be educated. Puritans also wanted to make sure that their children knew how to read the Bible. As a result, they started schools.

By 1647, the Massachusetts Bay Colony had passed laws requiring every town with 50 or more families to establish a free public school. Schools emphasized the learning of Puritan religious beliefs and instruction in the basic skills of reading, writing, and arithmetic.

New England also had the first American college. Harvard College was founded near Boston in 1636, before Massachusetts Bay Colony was 10 years old. Harvard was established to train Congregational ministers. The second New England college, Yale, was established in 1701. The students at both Harvard and Yale were all men. At that time, only men were admitted to colleges.

The Puritan Contributions

By the 1700's, power and authority in New England were slipping away from the Puritans. Still, the Puritans left us with many values that have played major roles in our history. From the Puritan's system of town government came the seeds of democracy. Also, the Puritans' belief in free public education slowly spread throughout the land. Their belief in hard work and striving to better oneself formed the basis of American attitudes toward work.

By the mid-1700's, the New England colonies had developed into a populated and prosperous society. Many of the characteristics of their way of life became common throughout America.

Section Review

1. Why were other colonies established in New England?
2. Why did Roger Williams have to leave Massachusetts? Where did he go?
3. What was life like in the New England community?
4. Describe how the various Puritan contributions can be seen today in your town or state.

For Extra Interest: Have students name and locate other large American cities that have grown up at river mouths. Have them discuss why they think a city develops at the mouth of a river.

3. The Middle Colonies

BEFORE YOU READ: *How did life in the middle colonies differ from life in the New England colonies?*

New York, New Jersey, Delaware, and Pennsylvania were called the middle colonies. They were located between the New England colonies and the southern colonies. No other set of English colonies was so varied. Many different religions were practiced in the middle colonies. The people who settled there came from many different countries in Europe. Because of this variety, the middle colonies were the melting pot of colonial America.

New York and New Jersey

The population of New York under English rule grew much faster than it had under the Dutch. By 1685, about 30,000 people lived in the colony. Most settlements were located near the Hudson River. The largest was situated at the river's mouth in the city of New York.

New York City became one of the great centers of commerce in colonial America. Merchants traded furs, agricultural products, and forest products. The manufacture of flour and bread became the city's chief industry. As the city grew, New York harbor filled with ships flying the flags of many countries.

At the same time, immigrants from Europe continued to come to America in

Dutch cottages in New Amsterdam were built mostly of brick and stone. The cottage pictured here dates from 1679.

Background: Quakers could not sanction war because of their religious beliefs. They therefore became suspect in Europe as subversives. This suspicion was carried to the American colonies.

large numbers. Many decided to make their home in New York colony. Those that did not settle in New York City pushed out into the Hudson Valley. The excellent soil and climate made their farms thrive. They grew wheat, rye, corn, oats, and barley. New York, along with the other middle colonies, was known as the "bread basket" of the American colonies.

New Jersey, once also a part of New Netherland, was awarded by the Duke of York to two of his friends. To attract settlers these two men permitted freedom of religion and sold land at low prices. Many Puritans from New England and Long Island were attracted to New Jersey.

What does this picture of a Quaker meeting tell you about the role women took in the Quaker religion?

The Quakers' Experiment

The only middle colony to be formed for religious reasons was Pennsylvania. Its founders were the Quakers, or Society of Friends.

In 1649, George Fox, a shoemaker, founded the Society of Friends in England. His followers became known as the Quakers from Fox's warning to them to "tremble at the name of the Lord." According to the Quakers, God gives us guidance through our consciences. For this reason, Quakers did not feel there was a need for ministers, priests, or religious ceremonies. They also believed in complete equality among people. However, although they believed in equality, many of the Quakers who settled in America owned slaves down to the mid-1750's. The Quakers also stressed that Christians must live peaceful lives. They refused to serve in the military or take part in wars.

The Quakers were very unpopular in England because of their beliefs and practices. They became the most persecuted Christian group in England. Eventually, some Quakers came to America in search of safety. Some settled in New England, where they were often fined, whipped, and told to leave. Four Quakers who refused to leave were put to death. The Quakers realized that they needed a colony of their own. But no company or wealthy person in England was willing to help them. Then a wealthy young man named William Penn became a Quaker.

William Penn's father was Admiral William Penn, a close friend of kings Charles II and James II. As luck would have it, King Charles II owed a large amount of money to the Penn family. Not wishing to part with his money to pay off the debt, the

Background: It was not unusual during this period of history for wealthy individuals to make loans to the monarch of their country. For this reason, it should not be surprising that the king owed the Penn family a large debt.

This hand-colored etching shows a productive agricultural settlement in Bethlehem, Pennsylvania, in 1757.

king instead gave William Penn title to the land between New York and Maryland. Penn named the area "Sylvania," or Woodland. The king, however, insisted on adding the prefix "Penn" to honor his friend Admiral Penn. The colony's name thus became Pennsylvania.

William Penn wished to make his colony a model of peace and harmony. Penn saw to it that religious freedom was guaranteed, that individual rights were protected, and that all Indians were treated fairly by settlers. The colony became an attractive place to settle, and it grew rapidly.

All religions and nationalities were welcomed in Pennsylvania. French, German, Swedish, Dutch, Welsh, Irish, and English settlers came there. By 1700, Pennsylvania was the largest and most prosperous colony in America.

Pennsylvania's Economy

Pennsylvania's economy was not dependent upon a single crop or one particular manufactured good. Pennsylvania produced wheat, corn, rye, oats, and barley. Fruits and vegetables were grown. Yet the colony could also boast of its fame as a business center.

The most important city in Pennsylvania was Philadelphia. William Penn founded Philadelphia in 1682. Penn selected the Greek name *Philadelphia*, which means "brotherly love," for his town. He was determined that this city would grow in an organized fashion. Philadelphia was laid out with a well-de-

Background: Town planning was unknown in the seventeenth century. In Europe, most cities grew in a haphazard manner. Designing a city to provide comfortable, healthy living conditions and to accommodate growth is called urban planning today.

EUREKA!

The Lightning Rod

On a stormy night in 1752, Benjamin Franklin performed a famous experiment with a kite. The experiment showed for the first time that lightning was a form of electricity. It also gave Franklin the information he needed to develop the lightning rod. The lightning rod is a metal device that has saved thousands of buildings from fires caused by lightning.

Franklin's kite experiment was simple but very dangerous. He already knew that electricity was attracted to metal points. He hung a metal key from his kite string and flew the kite into a storm cloud. When lightning struck the kite, the key became electrified.

Franklin now knew that lightning was a form of electricity. His experiment also showed that an electric current would flow through metal, the key, and be carried into the ground.

Franklin cleverly put these pieces of information together. He attached a pointed metal rod to a building and had the rod run down into the earth. Any lightning that struck was drawn to the rod rather than to the building. The lightning would move through the rod and be conducted harmlessly into the ground.

In 1753, Franklin wrote an essay called "How to Secure Houses, etc., from Lightning." Soon lightning rods began appearing on buildings all over the world. They were one of the ways that people first harnessed electricity. Though their designs have changed, lightning rods are still in use today.

signed street plan. In each of the four corners of the town, a park was built for the enjoyment of citizens.

Philadelphia's streets were filled with shops and business establishments. Merchants did a brisk overseas trade in lumber, furs, and foods. By the 1720's, over 10,000 people lived in this prosperous community.

Benjamin Franklin

One of the most famous residents of Philadelphia was Benjamin Franklin. Franklin came to Philadelphia at the age of 17. He became a printer and learned his craft well. Between 1729 and 1766, he owned and published a leading newspaper, the *Pennsylvania Gazette.* Franklin

Vocabulary Help: bifocal glasses—glasses designed with a dual lens system that allows the user to view objects that are both near and far with clarity. Prior to this, people had to change back and forth between two pairs of glasses.

Illustration from Poor Richard's Almanack.

also wrote and published *Poor Richard's Almanack*, a book of facts about the weather and stars plus other information. The almanac also contained proverbs, or sayings, that stressed the importance of thrift and self-discipline. Many of his sayings are still quoted today: "A stitch in time saves nine."

At the age of 42, Franklin retired from business to devote himself to writing, public service, and scientific investigation. In each field, he excelled. Franklin experimented with the nature of electricity. He also developed many useful inventions, such as the lightning rod, bifocal glasses, and an improved stove.

His contributions did not stop there. The first fire department in the colonies was started by Franklin in Philadelphia. He also built the town's first library and hospital, and improved the colonies' postal service. In 1749, he helped establish a school that later became the University of Pennsylvania. Benjamin Franklin later played an important role as a founding father of the United States.

Section Review

1. How did life in the middle colonies differ from life in the New England colonies?
2. Why were the Quakers persecuted for their beliefs and practices?
3. How did William Penn acquire the land that became the Pennsylvania colony?
4. Select a modern American who has made a contribution to American life. How does her or his contribution compare with the contributions of Benjamin Franklin?

Vocabulary Help: university—an institute of higher learning with a college of liberal arts and a graduate school attached to it.

4. The Southern Colonies

BEFORE YOU READ: *How did the people who settled in each of the southern colonies differ from one another?*

The five southern colonies were Virginia, Maryland, North Carolina, South Carolina, and Georgia. All of the southern colonies, except Virginia, were created by a grant from an English king to a person, family, or group of people. Those who received such grants were known as the owners or proprietors. The colonies established by the proprietors were called **proprietary colonies**.

---

proprietary colony a colony granted by an English king to a person, family, or group of people who governed the colony in the name of the king

---

The Founding of Maryland

In June of 1632, Cecilius Calvert, whose title was Lord Baltimore, received a grant from Charles I of 4,046,856 hectares (10 million acres) between the Chesapeake and Delaware bays. Calvert named the colony Maryland. It was established as a refuge or shelter for persecuted English Catholics. Calvert also hoped the colony would increase his family's fortune. Calvert was given total political authority over the colony. He could appoint the governor and judges, grant land to others, coin money, and make all laws. In time, Calvert allowed the Maryland settlers to elect their own legislature.

The first group of settlers, numbering about 300 people, arrived in Maryland in 1634. They established the settlement of St. Mary's near the mouth of the Potomac River. Tobacco grew well in the region's soil. Like Virginia, Maryland established a profitable tobacco trade with England.

Cecilius Calvert, the founder of Maryland, and his son.

Background: The Maryland Act of Religious Toleration actually narrowed the formerly broad toleration practiced in the colony. Non-Christians, who had previously been allowed to live in peace, were now looked upon unkindly.

Although the Calvert family had established the colony as a refuge for Catholics, most of Maryland's settlers were Protestants. Because the Catholics were so outnumbered, Lord Baltimore feared that his Catholic colonists would be persecuted. To prevent this, he persuaded the Maryland legislature to pass a law in 1649 declaring **religious toleration**. This would allow all Christians to worship according to their own beliefs.

---

religious toleration recognition of the right to worship according to one's own beliefs

---

Throughout the 1600's, the Calvert family lost much of its political power in the colony. The people of Maryland came to own their own property and gained in political power.

The Carolina Grant

In 1663, Charles II issued a grant of land to eight friends. The grant was very large, covering the area from the south of Virginia to Spanish Florida. The area granted to the eight proprietors was given the name Carolina.

Only two areas of settlement developed in Carolina during the colonial period. One was established in the 1670's around Albemarle Sound in the northeastern section of Carolina. Few settlers came, however. The land there was too swampy and sandy to be productive.

The settlement of present-day Charleston, called Charles Town until the mid-1700's, began in 1680. Many of its first residents had come from English islands in the West Indies. There, large sugar plantations worked by slave labor had driven

This drawing shows indigo processing on a South Carolina plantation in the eighteenth century. Indigo is a plant used to make a blue dye.

Vocabulary Help: indigo—a blue dye that was obtained from plants. It was much in demand in colonial times to make blue-colored cloth.

Background: It was hoped that the colonists in Georgia could cultivate mulberry trees upon which silkworms feed. The production of silk in Georgia would reduce British dependence on silk from the Far East. Unfortunately, however, silk could not be produced profitably in Georgia.

out small, independent farmers. These farmers migrated to Carolina in search of a fresh start.

By the 1700's, farmers had begun growing rice and indigo on plantations in the surrounding countryside. These plantations made huge fortunes for their owners, but the weather in the area made them unpleasant places to live. Many planters left their swampy fields to be managed by caretakers. They came to Charleston, built splendid mansions, and lived a pleasant life.

In the Southern colonies, love of music was widespread. Villagers would bring out fiddles and other instruments for festive occasions. Charleston became a musical center. Public concerts were given there as early as 1733.

In 1712, the Carolina grant was split into two colonies: North and South Carolina. In 1729, the king placed North and South Carolina under his control. They became royal colonies.

Georgia

The last English colony to be established in America was Georgia. In 1732, James Oglethorpe received a grant from King George II to organize a colony south of the Carolinas. Georgia was expected to serve two purposes. First, it was supposed to serve as a barrier, protecting the Carolinas from attack by the Spanish in Florida. Second, some of the debtors who were filling the jails of England were to be sent to Georgia.

Oglethorpe and the 19 other proprietors of Georgia selected settlers with care. Those picked to go to Georgia were given free passage, 20 hectares (50 acres) of land, tools, and seeds. The proprietors set down strict rules for the settlers.

Georgia was successful in growing rice and indigo, as well as wheat, corn, and livestock. The forests produced lumber, tar, and pitch.

Georgia's growth was disappointingly slow. Those who settled there refused to live by the proprietors' strict rules. The proprietors gave up and asked the king to take over the colony. Georgia became a royal colony in 1752.

American Society Takes Form

Both the English government and the colonists had assumed that society in America would resemble that of England. But the developing American colonies were not England. English customs changed continuously in America to meet the needs of the new land. The result was the development of a new culture and a new system of social class.

Most Americans of 1750 believed that people were not equal. They felt that society should consist of separate social classes in order to reflect this inequality.

At the top of the social ladder was the upper class. In England, the upper class consisted of nobles whose social position came from titles and lands they inherited. In America, the upper class was made up of large landowners, successful business people, and plantation owners. Their status could be earned and was chiefly the result of their own efforts.

The upper class in all parts of the colonies paid close attention to dress, manners, polite speech, and education. Members of the upper class did not want

Vocabulary Help: pitch—a thick, black, sticky substance formed in the distillation of coal tar, wood tar, or petroleum. It was used primarily for waterproofing ships in colonial times. Similar substances that are liquid at room temperature are usually called tars.

Background: Indentured servants were not slaves, and being an indentured servant was not looked upon as a humiliation. In indentured servitude, the only item sold was a fixed amount of the person's labor, not his or her entire person as in the case of a slave.

anyone outside their class to look or act like them.

The colonial middle class consisted of owners of businesses, small farmers, and skilled laborers. The middle class believed that America was the land of opportunity. They hoped that with hard work and luck they, too, could become members of the upper class.

Near the bottom of the social ladder was the underclass. Some members of the underclass were poor white farmers. Other members of the underclass lived in cities, where they performed backbreaking jobs that others refused to do.

The underclass also included white workers employed under contract for a specific number of years. They were called **indentured servants**. Lacking money to buy passage to the colonies, these people made a contract with a ship's captain. They sold their labor, usually for a period of four to seven years, to the captain who brought them to America. Upon landing, the contract was sold by the captain to a colonist needing workers. The new settlers, now indentured servants, were obliged to work for the colonist without pay for the time stated in the contract. When the term was up, the indentured servants were freed and given their "freedom dues": seeds, farming tools, and a small piece of land. Up until 1715, indentured servitude was the most common way in which people came to the American colonies.

indentured servant a person who worked for someone for a specified period of time to pay off the cost of passage to another country

The Thirteen English Colonies

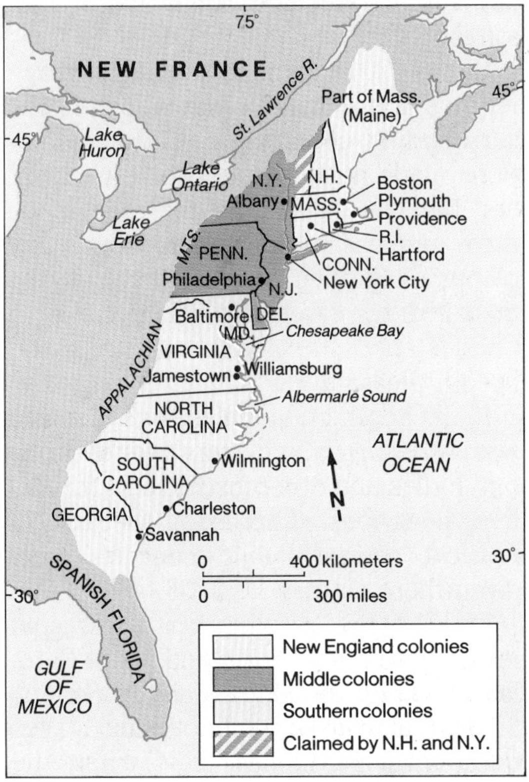

What formed the western boundary of the Thirteen Colonies?

Blacks in Colonial America

At the very bottom of American society were blacks, the first of whom had arrived in 1619. Little is known of their first arrival except that a Dutch pirate named Jope brought 20 blacks to Jamestown, where he offered them for sale. The Virginia colonists, short of workers, bought them. Early colonial blacks were treated as indentured servants. But the position of most blacks gradually changed. The competition for profits in the southern

Background: Blacks from Africa were considered an improvement over previously enslaved American Indians. Fewer blacks died from exposure to European diseases, and their lack of familiarity with the land and the native languages made it more difficult for them to escape.

Background: It is possible that almost half of the blacks that left Africa as slaves either died from diseases, committed suicide by jumping overboard, or were permanently maimed from their struggles against the chains.

colonies favored larger farms and plantations. The large planters needed to find a steady supply of forced labor to work on their lands. These factors pushed the southern colonies steadily toward a system of slavery. By the 1640's, some blacks were considered slaves for life, not indentured servants. Local laws were passed in the 1660's making slavery an inherited condition. This meant that a child born to a slave was a slave, too.

Once a system of slavery developed in the South, the slave trade became a big business. European traders went to Africa where they bought slaves at auctions.

The slaves' journey from Africa to America was called the Middle Passage. Slaves were herded onto overcrowded ships. They were allowed up on deck only in good weather. No sanitation facilities were provided. The death rate of slaves ran as high as 60 percent.

Upon arrival in America, the slaves were prepared to be resold. First, the black person's spirit was broken. The most common methods used to achieve this were whippings and starvation. Once broken, the slaves were cleaned up, fed hearty meals, and otherwise made to look good so that someone would purchase them. The auction block was the typical method for selling slaves. Little effort was made to keep black families together. In fact, family members were often purposely sold to different owners.

Slavery existed both in the northern and southern colonies during the 1600's. In 1700, there were around 25,000 slaves in the American colonies. By 1760, about 400,000 slaves were here, at least three-fourths of whom resided in the southern colonies. Most Southern slaves worked on the big plantations.

By 1750, the colonies were populated and thriving. They had grown from their struggling start in 1607 into something in which both the American colonists and the British government took great pride. Few people in 1750 would have believed that the close relationship between the colonies and Great Britain would last less than 30 more years.

Section Review

1. How did the people who settled in each of the southern colonies differ from one another?
2. Define proprietary colony.
3. Explain how Europeans who lacked money for passage to America were able to come.
4. Why did a system of slavery develop in the American colonies? How was slavery different from indentured servitude?
5. Why do you think that black families were often purposely broken up and sold to different owners upon their arrival in America?

Discuss: Why were many more slaves needed in the southern colonies than in the New England colonies? Why didn't the North ever become as large a buyer of slaves as the South?

CHAPTER REVIEW

Summary

The colonies in North America were established for a variety of reasons. Some were established to protect certain religious groups from persecution. Others were founded to make money for private companies in Europe. Still others were set up to make money for the monarch. In a short period of time, England was able to dominate the East Coast of North America from Maine to Georgia.

The early settlers in the colonies faced many hardships, such as starvation, disease, and harsh environments. However, as more colonists came to the New World, life became more than just a struggle to exist. The population slowly expanded to fill up most of New England. Manufacturing and trade developed there, while the southern colonies continued with agriculture as their main occupation. The middle colonies prospered from both trade and agriculture. In most areas, the people had a voice in governing their colony. The practice of self-government dated back to the Mayflower Compact and was the principle behind the New England town meeting.

With growing cities, colleges, and wealth, the American colonies had become a model of colonial growth. Few people could imagine that in a few short years, the English colonies would rebel and break away from England.

Recalling the Facts

1. What crop made Jamestown a profitable colony?
2. Who was Squanto?
3. What contributions did Franklin make to his community?
4. Which colony was originally established as a refuge for Roman Catholics?
5. What was the Middle Passage?

Analyzing the Facts

1. What caused the near failure of Jamestown in its first year?
2. Some historians believe the Pilgrims intended to land many miles north of their original destination in Virginia. Why might they have wanted to build their settlement outside of Virginia's borders?

3. How did the Great Awakening affect the colonists?
4. What kinds of settlers would have been attracted to the colony of Pennsylvania? Why?
5. Class distinctions were of little importance to colonists living on the frontier. Why do you think this was so? What personal characteristics do you think would have been important to them?

Time and History

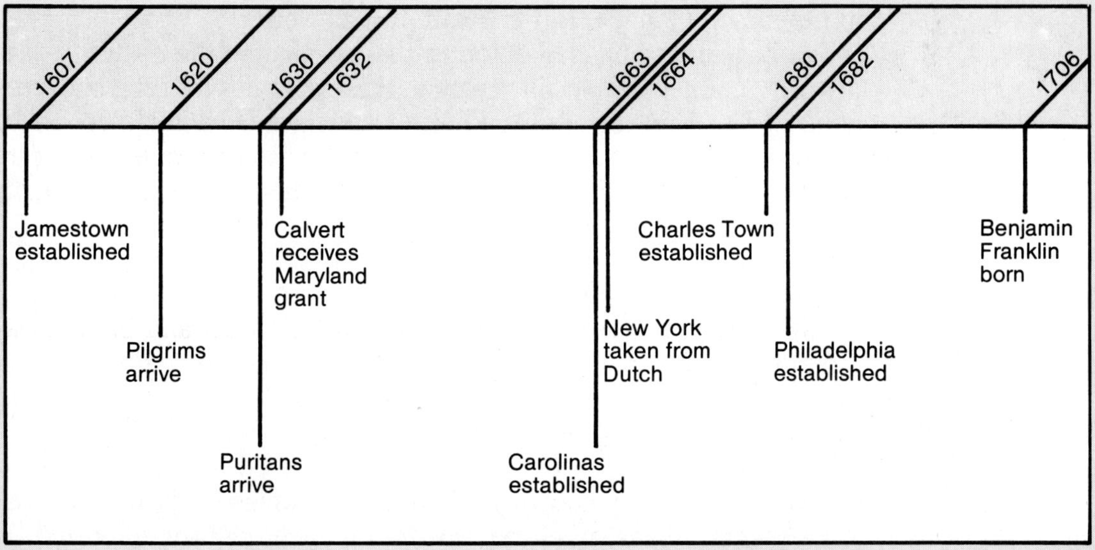

1. Which town is oldest: Philadelphia, Jamestown, or Charles Town?
2. How many years passed between the arrival of the Puritans and the Pilgrims?
3. What colonial city was founded last according to the timeline?
4. How many years before Franklin was born was the city of Philadelphia established?
5. How many years passed between the establishment of Jamestown and the arrival of the Pilgrims?
6. How many years separate the founding of Jamestown and the capture of New York?

UNIT REVIEW

Summary

The first people to come to America walked across the Bering Sea land bridge during the last Ice Age. These natives, called Indians, skillfully adapted to the wide variety of environments found in both North and South America.

Around A.D. 1000, the Vikings became the first Europeans to set foot in America. However, it was not until 1492, when Columbus made a landing in the New World, that the long period of European exploration and colonization of America began. Spain, Portugal, France, the Netherlands, and England rushed to claim territory and establish colonies in the hope of gaining more wealth and power.

The English established colonies that dominated the eastern coast of North America. Europeans came to these colonies for religious freedom, profits, and adventure. England supported colonial growth to increase the flow of raw materials to its factories and to provide markets for its manufactured goods. By 1750, the English colonies in North America were populated and thriving.

Recalling the Facts

1. How do many scientists believe the Indians got to North America?
2. Who were the first Europeans to come to America? How do we know that they were here?
3. Why were Europeans in the 1400's interested in exploration?
4. What European countries established colonies in North America? Describe the areas of the New World each country colonized.
5. Give reasons why Europeans settled in the English colonies in America. Which one of these reasons applies to the Puritans?

Analyzing the Facts

1. Why would early people have crossed the land bridge into North America?
2. Explain why agriculture is almost always needed before true civilization can begin.
3. Why do you think it took Columbus several years to convince the Spanish monarchs to finance his voyage westward?
4. Compare the preparations made by the London Company for the

settlement of Jamestown with those made by the Puritans for the establishment of their colony in Massachusetts.

5. Why do you think slave labor was less frequently used in New France than in the English colonies in North America?

Reviewing Vocabulary

Define the following terms:

anthropologist	archaeologist	mercantilism
extinct	astrolabe	cash crop
kiva	charter	covenant
wickiup	joint-stock company	religious toleration

Sharpening Your Skills

Answer the first two questions, using the map, "The Thirteen English Colonies," on page 98.

1. How far is it from Philadelphia to New York City?
2. How far is it from the northern tip of New Hampshire to the southern tip of Georgia?
3. Scientists have theorized that the first Americans moved southward from Alaska along several paths of migration. What primary source materials do you think they used to determine these migration routes?
4. Look at the painting of the two Puritan children on page 82. Based on this picture, write a secondary source description of the clothing worn by Puritan children.

Writing and Research

1. Pretend that you are one of the Pilgrims living in the Plymouth colony in the spring of 1621. Write a letter to a friend in England describing your voyage, the establishment of the colony, contacts with the American Indians, and the hardships of the past winter.
2. Research and write a brief biographical report on someone associated with the early exploration and settlement of the New World.

Unit 2

Creating a Republic

4 *Great Britain's rule over her American colonies was weak during the early colonial years. But between 1660 and 1688, and again after 1763, Britain tightened control. This created great tensions between the colonies and Great Britain. In April 1775, mounting tensions erupted into open warfare.*

5 *The War for Independence lasted from April 1775 to September 1783. The American troops were led by George Washington. Struggling against the best army in the world, Washington led his army to victory over Great Britain.*

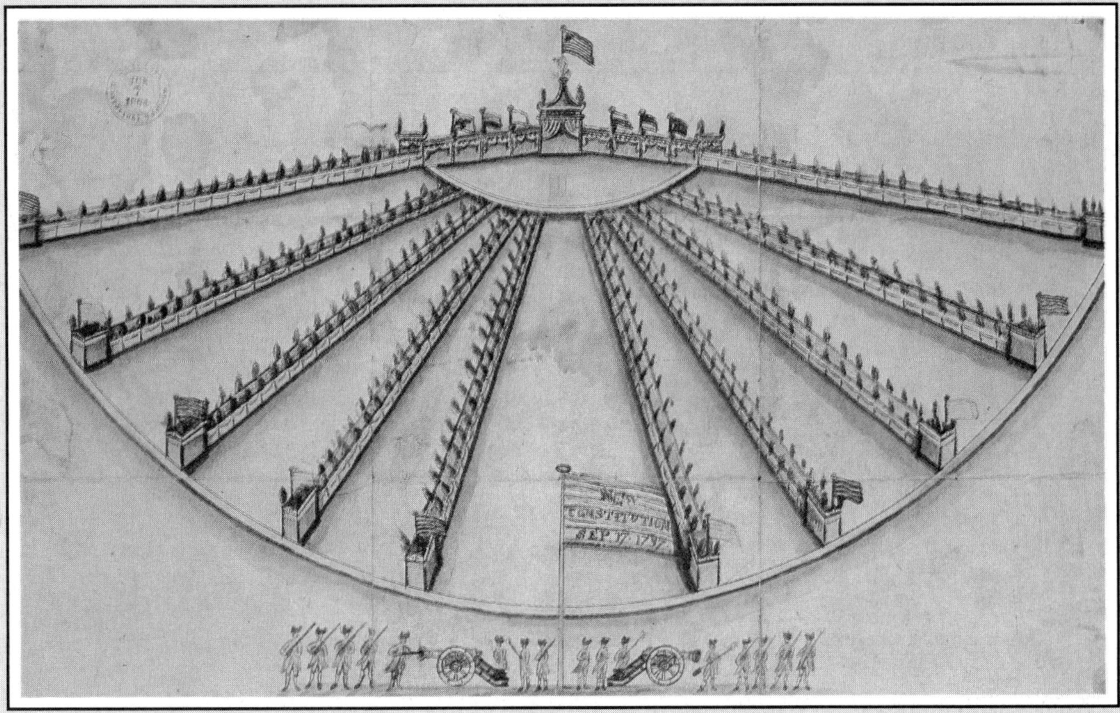

6 *After gaining independence, the United States faced the difficult task of organizing a government. The first government, the Confederation, lasted less than ten years, from 1781 to 1789. The second government was formed under the Constitution of the United States.*

7 *The first two American Presidents were George Washington and John Adams. They faced two critical problems: seeing to it that the new republic ran smoothly at home and guaranteeing that the nation survived in a world filled with enemies.*

Chapter 4

Great Britain Under Strain

Throughout the night of April 18, 1775, riders desperately crisscrossed the Massachusetts countryside. The riders broadcast an alarming message: British troops were coming. The British troops had left Boston late that evening, marching under orders of General William Howe. The next morning, the troops reached their first destination, the town of Lexington. There they were met by a colonial army of 70 soldiers. Each soldier examined his foe across Lexington Green. All anxiously fingered the triggers of their muskets. A few seconds more and the first shot of the War for Independence would ring out.

After you read this chapter, you will be able to:

1. Describe how the British came to rule much of North America.
2. Explain why the colonists found British rule between 1763 and 1774 objectionable.
3. Identify the events following the Boston "Tea Party" that led to the Declaration of Independence.

☐ Trace routes on a map.

Background: Under mercantilism the home country exports more goods than it imports. This brings more money into the country's treasury because more goods are sold than are bought.

1. America and the British Empire

BEFORE YOU READ: *How did the British tighten their control over the American colonies?*

For almost 170 years following the founding of Jamestown in 1607, England's rule of the American colonies was weak. At various times, however, English authorities would become uneasy about their lack of control. It was at these times that England would attempt to tighten its rule over the colonies. Such attempts generally created confusion and anger in the colonies.

The English Colonial System

During the early days of settlement, the colonies depended upon England for many needed supplies. In time, the colonies grew more prosperous and less dependent on England. England, both because of distance and because of political trouble at home, permitted the colonists a great deal of freedom. In fact, England's rule up until 1660 was very weak.

England permitted the colonies to run their own local affairs. As a result, the colonists became used to self-government, and they came to believe it was their right. This belief was bound to create problems with the government in England.

Problems began with the reign of King Charles II. During his reign, which lasted from 1660 to 1685, England's neglect of its American colonies ended. Charles II interfered with the colonies by trying to control their economy. His brother James II, who ruled from 1685 to 1688, followed Charles' policies.

Mercantilism

The English believed that the American colonies existed primarily to benefit the home country. This belief was based on the theory called mercantilism. According to the theory, colonies could help the home country become wealthy and strong in two ways. First, colonies could supply the home country with cheap raw materials. Second, the colonies could buy finished products from the home country. Mercantilism could also free England from having to purchase raw materials from its enemies. For example, England could break its dependence on Spain by purchasing all the rice and tobacco it needed from South Carolina and Virginia.

The English government and English merchants recognized that trade with the colonies was the path that would lead to riches. England began to put mercantilism into effect through a series of laws known as the Navigation Acts. The major Navigation Acts were passed by Parliament, the British law-making body, in 1660, 1663, and 1673. Other similar laws were passed up to the mid-1700's. All of these laws were designed to direct the flow of colonial raw materials into England. They were also designed to keep foreign goods and ships from reaching the colonies.

Under the first three Navigation Acts, goods being shipped to the American colonies had to be transported on English vessels. This gave England control of

Discuss: Why did the colonists dislike the Navigation Acts? Why do you think the colonists in New England were especially opposed to these laws? How would free trade have provided greater profits to the colonists?

Discuss: Many students will be familiar with the board game "Monopoly." What is the goal of this game? How does the goal of this game relate to British attempts to control colonial trade in the seventeenth century?

shipping and trade with the American colonies. Complete control of this kind is called a **monopoly**. Certain colonial goods such as cotton, sugar, and tobacco could be shipped only to Great Britain or its other colonies around the world.

monopoly exclusive control over a product or business

A Time of Uncertainty

To enforce the Navigation Acts, England sent officials to the colonies. The colonists were not pleased. They had become used to running their own affairs without interference from England. The colonists looked for ways to avoid both the Navigation Acts and the officials. Smuggling, or the taking of goods in or out of a country illegally, was one way. There was widespread trading with foreign nations, which was illegal under the Navigation Acts. Colonists also discovered that English officials were willing to look the other way, if they were given a bribe.

At the same time that the Navigation Acts were passed, serious conflict arose in New England between the Indians and the colonists. The Wampanoag Indians lived in southeastern Massachusetts. By 1670, their lands were completely surrounded by the settlements of the land-hungry colonists. The leader of the Wampanoags was Metacomet, known to the colonists as King Philip. King Philip began to fear that all of his people's land would soon be taken away by the settlers. He convinced his tribe to fight for their land. The Wampanoags were joined by two other tribes of the region.

King Philip

Warfare broke out in late June 1675. By the spring of 1676, the Indians had destroyed 12 settlements and attacked 40 others. But the tide turned in 1676. The Wampanoags ran out of food and ammunition. King Philip was killed, and New England troops defeated his followers.

In that same year, armed resistance, or **rebellion**, broke out in Virginia. The leader of the rebels was Nathaniel Bacon, a planter who had arrived in the colony only a few years earlier.

rebellion armed resistance or opposition to one's government

Bacon and his supporters lived along the western frontier of Virginia. They demanded that Sir William Berkeley, the

Background: The Indians were unable to make guns or ammunition. They had to rely on Europeans to supply them with weapons. It was hard for the Indians to win a prolonged war against the whites because they often ran out of ammunition.

Discuss: Bacon's Rebellion and Metacomet's War both involved conflict between the Indians and the whites. How were these conflicts similar? How were they different?

royal governor, permit colonists to settle on Indian land. The governor refused, stating that earlier treaties had reserved this land for Indian use. Berkeley also hoped to avoid starting a major war like King Philip's War in New England. Bacon and his supporters did not believe Berkeley's explanation. They charged that the true reason was the governor's desire to preserve his profitable fur-trading business with the Indians.

Trouble broke out when Doeg Indians killed the servant of one settler. Bacon and his supporters used this as an excuse to attack not only the Doegs but the Susquehannocks. The Susquehannocks, in turn, began to raid frontier plantations.

Berkeley and Bacon soon clashed. Bacon formed an army of frontiersmen to take the Indians' land by force. Berkeley organized his own army to crush the rebellion. Rebels, Indians, and the governor's troops battled during the summer of 1676. In September, the rebels, led by Bacon, marched on Jamestown and burned the city to the ground. Bacon contracted an illness and died a few weeks later. As a result the rebellion collapsed.

Even though Bacon's Rebellion failed, Bacon had been able to unify many settlers against the government. At the same time, the American Indians learned that guarantees of the right to own their land meant little if settlers desired it.

Wars with France

For hundreds of years, Britain and France had been bitter enemies. They argued over land in France that Britain claimed. There was rivalry over foreign trade and other economic matters. Numerous wars had been fought between them in Europe. After both established colonies in North America, the fighting spread there as well. Americans fought willingly on Britain's side because they considered themselves British citizens.

From 1689 to 1763, Britain fought four wars against France. None of the first three conflicts produced a clear-cut winner. Both France and Great Britain realized that victory would come to the nation which gained control of North America. Both sides began to focus their attention on the land west of the Appalachian Mountains and north of the Ohio River. This region was called the Ohio Country. Both Britain and France laid claim to the Ohio Country.

In 1752, the French began to build forts along the western Pennsylvania border to serve as a barrier to British and American expansion. In 1754, the French took control of the strategic point—now Pittsburgh—where the Allegheny and Monongahela rivers meet to form the Ohio River. At this site they built Fort Duquesne.

In 1754, Governor Robert Dinwiddie of Virginia sent a small group of citizen soldiers, or **militia**, to seize Fort Duquesne and order the French to leave. The militia was led by a young, inexperienced commander by the name of George Washington. The French pushed Washington's troops back into the southwestern corner of Pennsylvania, below Fort Duquesne. Washington had his soldiers build a fort, which they named Fort Necessity. However, the French soon surrounded the Virginians and gave them a sound beating. This was the first battle of the war the colonists called the "French and Indian War."

Background: Britain based its claim to the Ohio Valley on the exploration and claims of John Cabot. France based its claim to the region on the explorations and claims of Jacques Marquette, Louis Joliet, and Robert de La Salle.

Background: Virginia claimed ownership of the land where the French were building forts.

militia an army made up of citizens rather than professional soldiers

Following the battle at Fort Necessity, most of the Indians of the Ohio Country joined the French side. Washington's loss had convinced them that the British and the Americans were not going to win the war.

The French and Indian War

In 1755, Great Britain sent General Edward Braddock to take command of the British army in America. That spring, Braddock led British and American troops back to capture Fort Duquesne. The general was not wise in the ways of wilderness fighting. He marched his men in straight lines, which was the accepted European formation. He expected to fight the enemy in European battle style. This called for two armies to fire at each other with muskets from 45 to 90 meters (50 to 100 yards) away. But, the Indians and the French did not fight this way. Braddock lay exposed to attack from an enemy firing from behind bushes, trees, and any other hiding places. Braddock and his troops were ambushed a few kilometers (miles) south of the fort. The combined

European Land Claims in 1713

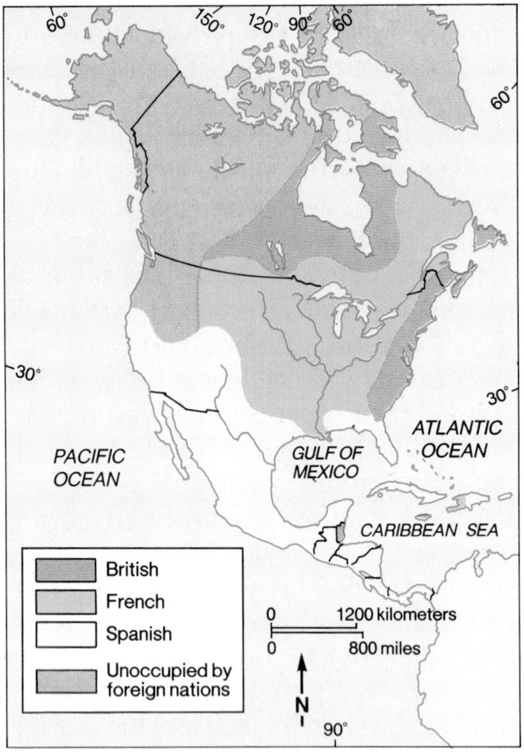

European Land Claims in 1763

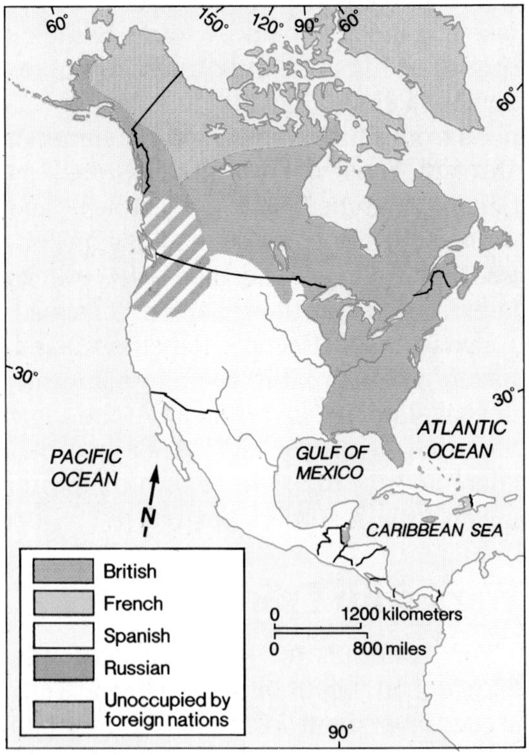

What territory did France lose in North America by 1763?

Background: The colonists had told Braddock about the style of fighting used in the American wilderness. Braddock, however, ignored his colonial advisers and was badly defeated. The colonists were angry over Braddock's defeat because his stubbornness had cost many American lives.

French and Indian force killed Braddock and a large number of his troops.

Panic spread across the frontier. Many settlers, fearing for their lives, abandoned their homes and retreated eastward across the Appalachian Mountains.

The French and Indian forces continued to pound the British and their colonial allies. One defeat followed another over the next three years, and American spirits sank.

William Pitt became the British prime minister in 1757. Pitt was determined to drive the French out of North America. Pitt sent more soldiers and more money for supplies, and he enlarged the British navy.

The British and American forces scored victory after victory. In 1758, British and colonial troops under General John Forbes cut their way through the wilderness of Pennsylvania. The French blew up Fort Duquesne with black powder and then fled. Forbes built Fort Pitt on its ruins. The following summer, Fort Niagara fell to the British. Pitt turned his attention next to Quebec, the capital of New France.

In September 1759, the British general, James Wolfe, moved his troops into position below Quebec. Quebec is located atop towering cliffs overlooking the St. Lawrence River. In a surprise night attack, Wolfe's forces scaled the cliffs using a hidden ravine. The British stormed across the Plains of Abraham and captured Quebec. A year later, the British captured Montreal, the last French fort.

In September 1760, the governor of New France surrendered all of Canada. The war in America was over.

The Treaty of Paris

A peace treaty ending the conflict was signed at Paris in 1763. Under the terms of the treaty, France gave Canada to Great Britain. France also gave Great Britain all French territory east of the Mississippi River except the port of New Orleans. New Orleans and the Louisiana Territory went to Spain.

Thus, France lost all its territory on the mainland of North America. The American colonies no longer had to worry about a French threat in America. But difficulties in America did not end with the Treaty of Paris.

Section Review

1. In what ways did the English tighten their control over the American colonies?
2. Define monopoly, rebellion, and militia.
3. What did the Ohio Country have to do with the start of the French and Indian War?
4. In what other periods of American history have events in government created a time of uncertainty? Explain your answer.

Background: During the French and Indian War, the colonists objected to the forced recruitment of soldiers, attempts to commandeer supplies, and the housing of troops in private homes. Pitt changed some of these policies, and American enlistment and enthusiasm for the war increased.

Social Studies Skills

Tracing Routes on a Map

In 1756, the French and Indian War broke out in North America. The French and the Indians fought together against the British and the American colonists. The French had built a string of forts along the St. Lawrence River and into the Ohio River valley. The map on this page shows the routes followed by the British generals as they led their troops in attacks on various French forts. The map also shows the locations of battles.

The routes taken by the British are not straight lines, yet it is possible to measure the distance of such routes by using something flexible, like a piece of string. Lay the string on the route to be measured, and mark off the space between the beginning and the end of the route. Then use the map scale to calculate the length of the route.

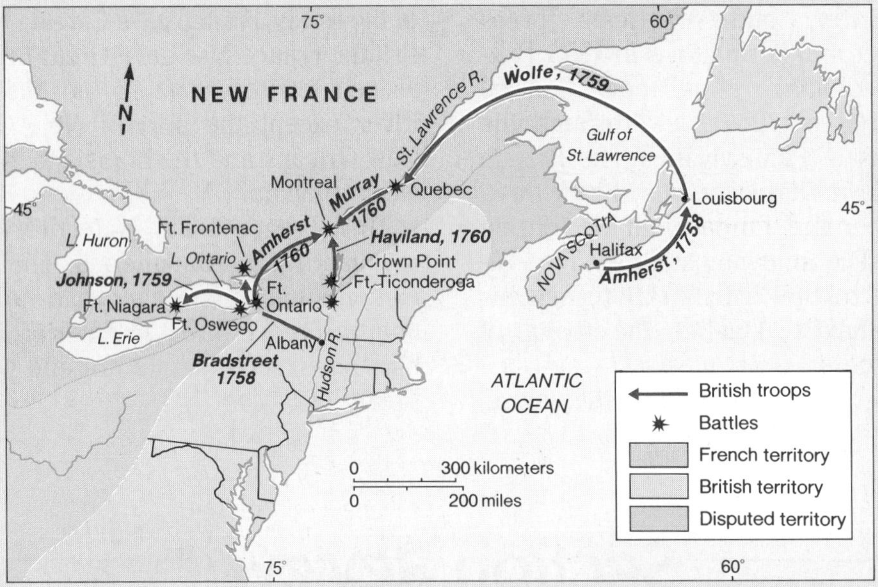

1. How far did General Wolfe travel from Louisbourg to Quebec in 1759?
2. How far would Wolfe have had to travel if he had gone from Louisbourg to Quebec in a straight line? How much shorter would this route have been?
3. How far did General Amherst travel from Fort Ontario to Montreal in 1760?

Discuss: Why did Great Britain only weakly enforce its will in the colonies during its wars with France? Why do you think this was a sensible policy for Great Britain to follow at that time?

2. Changing Policies and Building Tensions

BEFORE YOU READ: *Why did the colonists feel that Great Britain had no right to tax them?*

Great Britain faced two major problems once the French and Indian War ended in 1763. The first was how to rule its vast new empire in North America. Britain had to develop policies to govern both American colonists and French Canadians. It also had to keep relations peaceful between the colonists and the Indians.

Secondly, the war had left Britain with huge debts of nearly half a billion dollars. Victory over the French had been achieved because of British money and the strength of the British army and navy. Britain had paid for ships, food, guns, ammunition, and military salaries both for itself and the colonies. The British people themselves were already heavily taxed. Great Britain felt strongly that the colonies must pay their fair share of the war debt. After all, the British reasoned, British troops had freed the colonies from the threat of the French.

Great Britain's policy after the war had three basic aims. First, Britain wanted to keep relations between the colonists and both the Indians and the conquered French Canadians peaceful. The second aim was to raise taxes to help pay off the war debt from the French and Indian War. The third aim was to assert British authority over its American colonies.

Americans did not agree with the new British policy, especially its third aim. Once the wars with France had begun in 1689, Britain had only weakly enforced its will in the colonies. By 1763, Americans had become quite used to being rather independent. Now the colonists found the British trying to assert their authority and power over the colonies.

Pontiac's Stand

The Treaty of Paris placed the American Indians in a difficult situation. Their French allies were gone, and their land in the Ohio Country now "belonged" to Great Britain. Soon after the treaty was signed, settlers poured into the Indian lands of western Pennsylvania, and some settlers even pushed into Ohio. Traders moved into the Indian villages and cheated the people outrageously, selling them poorly made British goods. The Indians found it harder to obtain powder and shot at the British forts. Indians needed them to hunt game. The Indians' distress increased daily.

Pontiac, an Ottawa chief, believed it was time to take a stand. Many other tribes agreed, and they offered Pontiac their support. The Indians hoped to drive every soldier and settler out of the Indians' homeland and back over the mountains. The Indians almost succeeded. In the spring of 1763, Pontiac's forces attacked British forts in the Great Lakes region. They struck as far north as the Straits of Mackinac in northern Michigan, and as far east as the Niagara River above Buffalo, New York. They captured every western fort except forts Detroit, Pitt, and Niagara. By fall, the Indians were tired from the continuous fighting, and Pontiac's movement collapsed.

Background: The biggest factor working against the success of an Indian war was the inability of the tribes to stick together for long periods of time. Pontiac had to break off his siege of Detroit in October 1763 because most of his warriors had returned to their villages.

Background: Great Britain intended to allow the colonists to move west of the Appalachian Mountains as soon as Indian claims had been satisfied and an orderly system of land sale and settlement had been worked out.

British officials wanted to put an end to this frontier warfare between the Indians and the colonists. To prevent future wars, Britain had to stop white settlers from moving onto Indian land. In October 1763, the British government issued an official announcement, or proclamation. The Proclamation of 1763 stated that no colonists were permitted to settle west of the Appalachian Mountains.

The colonists were upset. They did not see the proclamation as Britain's way of preventing frontier warfare. Rather, it seemed to be a way of stopping westward settlement. Colonists generally ignored the proclamation and moved into Ohio and Kentucky. Perhaps the most famous of these settlers was Daniel Boone, who led settlers through the Cumberland Gap to the bluegrass country of Kentucky.

Grenville's Tax Program

George Grenville became Britain's prime minister in 1763. He was the top adviser to King George III. Grenville wanted American colonists to share the cost of running the empire.

Grenville asked Parliament to pass new tax laws that would raise money from the colonies. He also planned to get strict with those colonists who avoided paying taxes on imported goods. Grenville would now use the British navy to catch and punish smugglers. Grenville also sent a new group of tax collectors to America. These people were both loyal and honest. Grenville hoped they would not take bribes from the colonists.

Grenville's first tax law was the Sugar Act of 1764. Colonial merchants would now pay a tax on all sugar, coffee, wines, and other products imported from places outside the British empire. Grenville hoped this law would stop colonists from buying French and Dutch sugar. Instead, he wanted sugar growers in the British West Indies to profit from the colonists' business.

The Sugar Act also reduced the tax on foreign molasses by half. Molasses was an important part of the triangular trade and was used in the production of American rum. The British thought that cutting the tax in half would please the colonists. It did not. The old tax was seldom collected. So this new tax, although cut in half, meant that colonists would now have to pay something to Great Britain.

The colonists were upset by Grenville's program, especially the taxes. Many colonists believed that Parliament did not have the right to tax Americans, even though they were British subjects. The colonists had no elected representatives in Parliament. Therefore, they considered taxation without representation unjust. They complained bitterly to Parliament. Colonists explained that without representation they had no voice in matters affecting them, such as the sugar tax. The issue of taxation without representation became a major colonial concern.

Another new law of Parliament that alarmed colonists was the Quartering Act. It had been requested by General Thomas Gage, commander of the British forces in America. The act required colonists to house and feed British troops. This was a common practice in Britain. Inns, taverns, and unoccupied dwellings were commonly used, not private homes. However, Americans resented using private property in this way. The Quartering

Background: George Grenville was the head of the Tory party in Great Britain. Unlike the Whigs, who had accepted the validity of colonial self-government in local affairs, Grenville and the Tories had little use for colonial claims to self-rule.

Background: Explain to the class that the money used to buy postage stamps is not a stamp tax. It is a fee for the service of delivering the mailed item.

In March 1766, Benjamin Franklin appeared before the British Lords in Council to argue against the Stamp Act. He warned that any attempt to enforce it might bring on rebellion.

Act added fuel to the rising fire of American resentment.

The Stamp Act

If colonists had been upset by the Sugar Act, they were furious about Grenville's next plan to raise money. This was the Stamp Act, passed by Parliament in 1765. It put a tax on almost all printed material in the colonies. Anyone selling items such as newspapers, pamphlets, insurance papers, and even playing cards had to affix a tax stamp. A stamp tax was required on important legal documents, too, such as birth certificates, marriage licenses, and death certificates. Merchants paid the tax and then passed it along to consumers in the form of higher prices.

The purpose of the stamp tax was reasonable. The money collected from the tax was used by the British government for the defense of the colonies. The money helped pay soldiers' salaries and buy weapons, food, clothing, and other supplies. But this was the first time that Parliament taxed colonists directly. It was for this reason that the Stamp Act caused a storm of protest in America.

Discuss: Do you think Parliament had the right to tax the colonists as it did through the Sugar Act and the Stamp Act? Why or why not?

Background: In October 1765, an organized crowd in Charleston shouting "Liberty Liberty and stamp'd paper" forced the South Carolina stamp distributor to resign. In January 1766, white resistance leaders were horrified when slaves paraded in the streets similarly crying "Liberty."

At first, protest took the form of speeches. In the Virginia House of Burgesses, a young man named Patrick Henry made a fiery speech, calling for open resistance to the Stamp Act. Some colonial merchants turned to a traditional form of protest, one used frequently in Britain. They hired mobs to take the law into their own hands and riot. In Boston, a mob calling themselves the "Sons of Liberty" attacked all people who sold the hated tax stamps. They succeeded in preventing collection of the tax. The Sons of Liberty even broke into Royal Governor Thomas Hutchinson's house on August 26, 1765, and destroyed furniture, broke dishes, damaged the interior, and burned some of his papers.

The Stamp Act Congress

Many colonists felt that a more sensible approach was needed. A meeting of delegates from most of the colonies was scheduled. The delegates met in New York in October 1765. This was an important occasion. It marked the first time the colonies pulled together for their own interests.

The delegates were careful to express their loyalty to King George III. Then, after much discussion, the Stamp Act Congress adopted a number of statements and requests to send to the king. The Congress declared that colonists *did not* have to pay any tax that was passed without their consent. "No taxation without representation" became their motto.

The Stamp Act Congress knew it needed to back up its beliefs with action. The members of the Congress decided that no more British goods should be purchased by the colonists. They hoped that this tactic, called a **boycott**, would make the British do away with the Stamp Act. The Stamp Act Congress called upon colonial merchants to boycott British goods.

Opposition to the Stamp Act was so strong in the colonies that people bought teapots and other articles containing slogans that expressed their feelings.

---

boycott a refusal to buy from or deal with a foe so as to punish or bring about change

---

Nearly 1,000 colonial merchants agreed to join in the boycott. The effects were soon felt in Great Britain, as Americans refused to buy any British goods. In January 1766, British merchants frantically demanded that Parliament do away with, or **repeal**, the Stamp Act. Grenville, however, wanted to use the British army to enforce the law. Parliament, after long debate, sided against him. In March 1766, the Stamp Act was repealed. William Pitt had sided with the colonial demands during the long debate. He was partly re-

Discuss: How effective do you think a boycott would be today in bringing about change? Explain your answer.

Background: The Townshend Acts also said that part of the money raised from the new taxes would be used to pay governors' salaries. This threatened the colonial assemblies because an independent salary would eliminate the only power the assemblies had over the governors.

sponsible for the repeal of the Stamp Act. To honor him, South Carolina erected a statue of him in Charleston. It was the first statue of a public official to be built in America.

repeal to do away with, take back

Americans rejoiced at news of the repeal. They immediately ended their boycott. However, Parliament was not through. Immediately after the repeal of the Stamp Act, Parliament passed the Declaratory Act. This act stated that Great Britain had an absolute right to tax the colonies and enact any law it wished.

More Colonial Defiance

Early in 1766, the Massachusetts Assembly disobeyed the Quartering Act. The Assembly refused to house or feed British troops stationed in the colony. In November, the New York Assembly did the same thing. New York and Massachusetts had not only disobeyed the Quartering Act, they had also ignored the Declaratory Act. The colonies were again challenging Parliament's authority to pass laws affecting them.

By then the prime minister was William Pitt, the individual who had sided with the colonies in their fight to repeal the Stamp Act. However, illness kept Pitt from being an active leader. The king's financial minister, Charles Townshend, ran the government in Pitt's place.

Charles Townshend felt it was time to show the colonies that Parliament's laws must be obeyed. At his request, Parliament passed a new and tougher set of laws in June 1767. These laws were called the Townshend Acts. The laws suspended the New York Assembly indefinitely. The laws stated that the Assembly could meet again when New York obeyed the Quartering Act. In addition, the Townshend Acts put a new tax on lead, paint, paper, and tea. On the surface this tax looked similar to the Sugar Act. But there was one important difference. The newest tax was placed on items imported *from within the British empire.*

Americans were stunned by the Townshend Acts. The fate of the empire rested on whether the colonists would obey or whether they would resist. The question now was, what would the colonists do? And if the colonists resisted, what would Great Britain's next move be?

Section Review

1. Why did the colonists feel that Great Britain had no right to tax them?
2. Define boycott and repeal.
3. Why did the colonists object to the Proclamation of 1763?
4. Why did the colonists call for a Stamp Act Congress? Why was this meeting significant?
5. How are boycotts used today to bring about change? Give some examples.

Background: The name "redcoats" came from the British army uniform of the day, which included a bright red coat over a white tunic.

3. The Road to Revolution

BEFORE YOU READ: *What events led to the Declaration of Independence?*

During the summer of 1767, Boston merchants began another boycott against all British goods to protest the Townshend Acts. The protest spread, and by 1768 merchants in Philadelphia and New York had joined in the boycott. Next, some of the southern merchants and planters agreed to boycott the British. Between 1768 and 1769, British goods were boycotted throughout the colonies. British merchants soon felt the pinch in their pocketbooks, as exports from Great Britain to America dropped by half.

Colonial Unrest

The Sons of Liberty played an important role in organizing the boycott. Women also took part in the resistance by organizing a group called the Daughters of Liberty. They boycotted British cloth. The Daughters of Liberty made their own homespun cloth, often spinning it in public as an insult to Great Britain.

Nowhere was American unrest greater than in Boston. Mobs harassed merchants who refused to join the boycott. The mobs also interfered with the work of the British tax collectors. These unlucky men stopped collecting taxes in Boston when the taunts and threats became too great. Some frightened collectors sought safety at Castle William, a fortress located on a small island in Boston harbor.

The British reaction was stern. Two regiments of troops were brought in from the frontier to Boston. The presence of "redcoats" patrolling the streets and protecting the tax collectors made colonists even angrier. Many townspeople insulted and attacked the soldiers.

On March 5, 1770, the lawless behavior of a colonial mob erupted into tragic violence. A crowd of boys and men confronted some British soldiers, jeering and throwing snowballs at them. The soldiers panicked and opened fire on the crowd. Five colonists were killed, and six were wounded. Samuel Adams, a leader of the Sons of Liberty and the Boston mob, called the incident a massacre. A massacre is the killing of innocent people.

The British Back Down

Late in January 1770, Lord Frederick North became the new British prime minister. He recommended repealing the Townshend Acts because they were hurting British trade severely.

In April 1770, one month after the Boston Massacre, Parliament repealed all of the Townshend Acts except the tax on tea. The tax was left on tea as a symbol of Britain's right to tax the colonies. This did not initially cause a strong reaction in the colonies. Colonists smuggled in most of their tea from the Netherlands.

The years between 1770 and 1773 were generally peaceful. Colonists were pleased because Great Britain had backed down on almost all of the taxes. Great Britain did not even make much of an effort to collect the tea tax. During this calm period, colonists debated the question of what their status should be in the British empire.

Background: The first person to be killed in the Boston Massacre was Crispus Attucks, a black sailor and fugitive slave. His death contributed to a change in attitude among some white colonists. They came to believe that slaves had as much right to freedom as they had.

Vocabulary Help: revolution—overthrow of a government usually by forceful means. Have students look in newspapers or magazines to discover where revolutions are occurring today.

Some colonists took a moderate position on this question. They wanted self-government for the colonies while still remaining loyal to the king. The moderates did not want a revolution, only a greater share of independence. The most famous moderate was Benjamin Franklin. A small number of colonists took a more radical, or extreme, position, however. The three most well-known radicals in 1770 were Patrick Henry, John Hancock, and Samuel Adams. The radicals believed that Great Britain would never give Americans a voice in Parliament. Britain was corrupt, in their opinion. The radicals were determined to create a new nation, even if it meant revolution.

Another small group of colonists wanted no change. These colonists were called loyalists. They believed all British subjects were equal, whether they lived in Great Britain or America. All shared the same rights and responsibilities. Because they were equal, all British subjects were required to obey the laws of Parliament. The American loyalists would not support a revolution.

Other colonists were uncommitted or undecided. In fact, most colonists in 1770 were probably among this group. They thought of themselves as good citizens. They did not like British taxation, but they accepted it as Great Britain's right. Most were busy just leading their own lives. It is unlikely that they thought about revolution.

The Radicals and Tea

Revolutions do not just happen. They are planned out and organized. The radicals realized this. Shortly after the Boston Massacre, the radicals in that city met to make plans. Their leader, Samuel Adams, declared, "It is high time for the people of this country . . . to declare whether they will be Freemen or Slaves." He went on, "Let it be the topic of conversation. . . . Let Associations . . . be everywhere set up to recover our just rights."

In 1772, Adams organized Committees of Correspondence in all the towns of Massachusetts. Their purpose was to keep Massachusetts' radicals in touch with Boston's radical leaders. The following year, Virginia radicals, including Thomas Jefferson, helped organize a network of committees in all the colonies.

The radicals waited patiently for the British government to assert its authority

By the 1770's, colonists were so opposed to British taxes that they removed British flags and began to recruit an army.

Background: It was not unusual then nor is it now for the government to help a company in economic trouble if that trouble could affect the economy of the whole nation. An example in our time is the recent government aid to the Chrysler Corporation.

once again. They planned to use this event as the spark that would set off a revolution. The radicals did not have to wait long. The spark came in 1773 when King George III and Lord North assisted one of Britain's big companies.

The British East India Company was a joint stock company chartered by Parliament in 1600 to conquer, govern, and exploit India. The company had a monopoly on all trade between India and Britain. By the spring of 1773, it was in deep financial trouble. In today's dollars, the company was $600 million in debt, and it had 6.8 million kilograms (17 million pounds) of unsold tea stored in British warehouses. Many of the company's officials spent their energy making themselves rich rather than attending to business. The result was that the company was at the point of financial collapse. Parliament passed the Tea Act in 1773 to help the company. The act gave the East India Company a monopoly on tea shipped to America.

Americans were furious when they learned of the Tea Act. The Tea Act forced them to buy only British tea, and British tea was the one good still being taxed. Colonial authorities in New York and Philadelphia refused to let the tea ships dock. The ships were sent back to Great Britain without unloading any tea. Trouble over tea also developed at Charleston, South Carolina, and Annapolis, Maryland. But it was in Boston that the Tea Act produced the greatest confrontation.

In Boston the royal governor, Thomas Hutchinson, allowed the tea ship *Dartmouth* to anchor in Boston harbor. Samuel Adams and other members of the Committee of Correspondence objected. The ship should not be allowed to unload its tea, stated the Committee. Governor Hutchinson disagreed; the tea would be sold and the tax would be collected.

Many people in Boston were angry. But it was the more radical townspeople who did something about it. On the night of December 16, 1773, a group of men dressed as Indians boarded the *Dartmouth* and dumped the hated tea into the harbor. A large crowd watching from the wharf cheered them on.

The men who carried out the "Tea Party" were sending a message to Great Britain: We are committing a serious crime by destroying private property. We defy you to do anything about it! Great Britain could not back down. Massachusetts had gone too far.

The Coercive Acts

George III, Lord North, and Parliament were furious about the Boston Tea Party. They were determined to restore law and order and to assert British authority in the colonies. They also wanted to see that Massachusetts, specifically, was punished. Between March and June 1774, Parliament passed the Coercive Acts.

One of the Coercive Acts closed Boston harbor until the townspeople paid for the destroyed tea. A second act placed Massachusetts under military rule. The royal governor would rule with the aid of some 10,000 troops. Citizens of the colony were only permitted to hold one town meeting per year. A third act renewed the old Quartering Act. This would help feed and house the thousands of British soldiers in Massachusetts.

The Coercive Acts created a sense of

Vocabulary Help: coercive—intended to force people to do something against their will. Explain why you think Great Britain called the laws passed after the Boston Tea Party the Coercive Acts.

unity among the colonists. The colonists believed the Coercive Acts threatened all Americans' liberties. Many colonists sent supplies and food to help the people of Boston while their port was closed. Angry colonists cried, "[These Acts are] unjust, illegal, and oppressive [severe]. . . . We scorn the chains of slavery; we are the sons of freedom!" Americans thought these laws were so unfair that they called them the "Intolerable Acts."

The Quebec Act

On May 20, 1774, Parliament passed the Quebec Act. Its purpose was to improve relations with French Canadians. The Quebec Act extended the boundaries of Quebec province to include the Ohio Country. It also placed the Ohio Country Indians under the authority of the French Canadians.

Americans resented the Quebec Act for a number of reasons. First, they had fought in the French and Indian War so that Americans could move into the Ohio Country. They now believed it was being taken from them. Secondly, Americans wanted the Indians to leave the Ohio Country. With the French Canadians in control of the Indians, the Americans could not be sure that the Indians would leave. The Quebec Act added to the colonists' anger toward Great Britain.

The First Continental Congress

The crisis in the colonies grew after the passage of the Coercive Acts. On May 13, 1774, the British general, Thomas Gage, arrived in Boston to become the military governor. Within two weeks, calls for a meeting of all the colonies came from the Committees of Correspondence of Providence, Philadelphia, and New York City. The Massachusetts House of Representatives urged that the colonies meet in Philadelphia that autumn to plan a united protest.

The meeting of the colonies was held at Carpenters' Hall on September 5, 1774. Fifty-five delegates representing all the colonies except Georgia were in attendance. The group called itself the Continental Congress and met in secret out of fear of the British. The delegates agreed that the Coercive Acts were a major threat to colonial self-rule. If Great Britain could deny Massachusetts self-rule, delegates stated, then Great Britain could deny self-rule to all the colonies.

The Continental Congress expressed disapproval of all British laws since 1763. It called upon George III to repeal the Coercive Acts. The delegates agreed that the colonies must boycott all British goods to put pressure on the British. If this was not effective, then colonial exports to Great Britain would be halted, too. Before adjourning, the Congress agreed to meet again in May 1775 if Great Britain had not yet backed down.

During the winter, Parliament tried to find a means to calm the colonists. William Pitt recommended that British troops be removed from the colonies. Lord North wanted to appeal for support from moderates and loyalists. Other members of Parliament suggested that the Coercive Acts be repealed.

The situation in Massachusetts bordered on war. Farmers and townspeople

Background: When colonial delegates spoke of self-rule, they were referring to the individual rule of each colony by its people. They were not talking about united rule of the colonies as one country.

For Extra Interest: Have students make a chart showing all the laws Great Britain passed from 1763 to 1775 to which the colonists objected. Have them show the date each law was passed, why it was passed, why the colonists objected to it, and how the colonists protested it.

were gathering arms and ammunition. Bands of **minutemen** drilled endlessly, so that they would be ready to fight the British at a minute's notice. They paid close attention to the British troops in Boston, watching for any sign that a showdown was coming.

minuteman a colonial soldier who could be prepared to fight at a minute's notice

"The Shot Heard Round the World"

Upon hearing of the meeting of the Continental Congress, George III declared, "The New England Governments are in a State of Rebellion. Blows must decide whether they are to be subject to this Country or Independent." The showdown came on April 18, 1775.

Late in the evening of April 18, General Gage, acting upon orders from the British Secretary of State for the Colonies, sent nearly 1,000 soldiers marching from Boston. The British troops had two objectives. First, they were to seize the colonists' war supplies at Concord, about 32 kilometers (20 miles) northwest of Boston. Second, they were to capture the rebel leaders Samuel Adams and John Hancock. Adams and Hancock were thought to be hiding at Lexington, a town halfway between Boston and Concord.

The patriots learned of the British plan. Two messengers on horseback, Paul Revere and William Dawes, galloped across the countryside spreading the news. The British were coming! Revere reached Lexington at midnight and warned Adams

Lexington and Concord, 1775

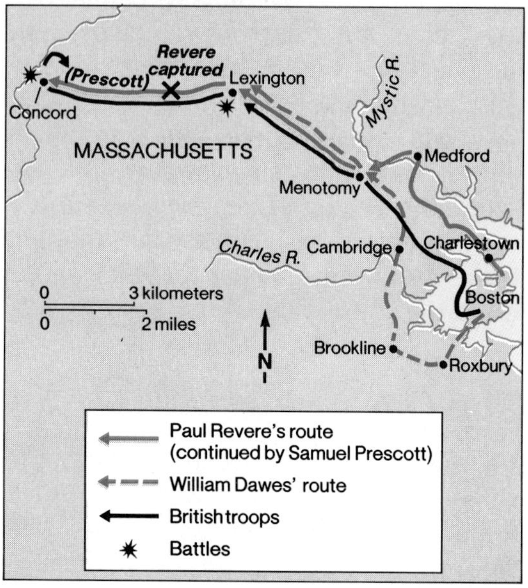

About how long was Paul Revere's ride? About how long was William Dawes' ride?

and Hancock. Then as Revere left Lexington for Concord, he was captured by the British. Dawes avoided capture and continued to warn the colonists. Dawes was later joined in his ride by Dr. Samuel Prescott. Church bells tolled throughout the night warning everyone, including the British, to expect trouble.

At dawn on April 19, the British soldiers approached Lexington. Facing them were 70 minutemen. Realizing how badly the minutemen were outnumbered, the minutemen's commander, John Parker, ordered a retreat. Then a shot rang out. Whether the shot was from a British or an American musket, no one knew. But the British troops opened fire, killing eight Americans and wounding another ten. The surviving minutemen fled. The British were unable to find Adams or Hancock, who were hiding in a nearby marsh.

For Extra Interest: Due largely to Henry Wadsworth Longfellow's poem, "The Midnight Ride of Paul Revere," Paul Revere became a legendary figure in American history. Distribute copies of this poem to the class and have the students take turns reading portions of it aloud.

Background: Many members of the American militia who gathered around Boston in April 1775 did not stay long since they were needed at home for spring planting.

The British gave up their search and marched on to Concord. There they destroyed what few weapons the colonists had left behind.

The long march back to Boston was hazardous for the British redcoats. Thousands of Americans fired at them from behind trees, houses, bushes, and stone walls. By the time the British troops arrived back in Boston, they had lost nearly 275 men. The first day of the War for Independence was over. Neither side could back down now.

The Battle of Breed's Hill

Armed men from all over the New England colonies headed for Boston. By April 20, over 16,000 colonists had gathered around Boston. Within a few days they had encircled the city. Early in June, a British ship arrived in Boston harbor. It brought more soldiers and three new generals, including Sir William Howe, to assist General Gage.

Howe did not wait long before moving into action. On June 17, he tried to drive the American militia off the hills north of Boston. The British attacked the militiamen on Breed's Hill three times. This occurred near Bunker Hill, which is the name often given to the battle. The Americans answered each British attack with a hail of bullets until they ran out of ammunition. In the end, the Americans were forced to abandon the hill. One hundred and forty Americans had been killed, and over 250 had been wounded.

The British organized their troops into columns to storm the colonists defending Breed's Hill. This fighting strategy cost the lives of many British soldiers.

Discuss: Why do you think the Battle of Bunker Hill is often considered an American victory even though the colonists were forced to retreat?

Discuss: The olive branch is a symbol of peaceful intentions. Why do you think the moderates at the Second Continental Congress chose to name their petition after this symbol?

The victory was General Howe's, but the cost had been high. Over 800 British troops were wounded and 226 had been killed. The British army was so weakened that it was unable to pursue the militiamen as they fled. One of Howe's generals wrote, "Another such victory would have ruined us."

The Second Continental Congress

On May 10, 1775, the Second Continental Congress met in Philadelphia. Many radicals were in attendance, as were many moderates. Events of the preceding month had caused many moderates like Benjamin Franklin to change their position. Many new faces were there, too. One such delegate was from Virginia. His name was Thomas Jefferson. Virginia also sent George Washington. He arrived wearing a blue colonel's uniform to indicate his willingness to help the army. The Adams cousins, John and Samuel, arrived from Massachusetts. The Boston merchant, John Hancock, was chosen to be president of the Continental Congress.

One of the first actions taken by the Second Continental Congress was the formation of the Continental army. George Washington was appointed its commander-in-chief. Washington was selected because of his military experience and because he was a Virginian. Congress believed that choosing a Virginian as the army's commander in chief would symbolize the unity of all the colonies in their support of Massachusetts.

In June, the Continental Congress issued the Olive Branch Petition and the Declaration of the Causes of Taking-Up Arms. The first, written by John Dickinson, stated the colonies' loyalty to King George III, and asked him to end the hostilities. It was issued to satisfy moderates who hoped peace could be restored. The declaration, written by Dickinson and Jefferson, defended the colonies' revolt against Great Britain. "Our cause is just. Our union is perfect," wrote Jefferson. "We . . . [are] resolved to die Freemen rather than to live [as] Slaves."

Great Britain was taking an equally tough stand. Parliament voted to send 25,000 additional soldiers to America. The king hired German troops to assist in crushing the rebellion. Later, in December, Parliament cut off all British trade with the colonies.

Toward Independence

Initially the colonists believed that they were rebelling to defend their rights as British subjects. Over the winter months of 1775–1776, this belief began changing. More and more people talked of independence from Great Britain. They saw independence as the only way to protect Americans' rights.

More colonists began to believe in the cause of independence when Thomas Paine published a pamphlet called *Common Sense.* Paine's *Common Sense* first appeared in Philadelphia in January 1776. Thomas Paine's message was very clear. Independence was America's destiny. Like a child who has grown to maturity, he reasoned, America was ready to separate from Great Britain, its home country. Paine did not attack Parliament so much as King George III, whom he called the

Background: Recruitment in Great Britain lagged, forcing Parliament to hire German mercenaries. The British did not want to deplete their own divisions of soldiers stationed in other areas of the British empire to fight the war.

Background: The Declaration of Independence explained to the world why the colonists felt they had the right to use force to change their government. A copy of the document can be found on pages 736–737.

"Royal Brute." Paine called upon the American people to free themselves from this cruel ruler.

Soon demands for independence swelled throughout the colonies. On June 7 in Philadelphia, Richard Henry Lee of Virginia asked Congress to consider the following resolution: "That these United Colonies are, and of right ought to be, free and independent States; that they are absolved [forgiven] from all allegiance to the British Crown; and that all political connection between them and the State of Great Britain is, and ought to be, totally dissolved." It was a call to proclaim independence from Great Britain.

Congress did not pass the resolution at once but appointed a committee to write a formal declaration of independence. The committee was composed of five delegates: Thomas Jefferson, Benjamin Franklin, John Adams, Robert R. Livingston of New York, and Roger Sherman of Connecticut.

Thomas Jefferson, at 33, was the youngest member of the Continental Congress. The committee gave Jefferson the task of writing the declaration of independence. "Why?" asked Jefferson. John Adams replied, because "you can write ten times better than I can."

Jefferson labored hard for about two weeks, perfecting the phrases to justify the people's right to revolution. He presented the Declaration of Independence to Congress on June 28. With a few changes, it was adopted on July 4, 1776.

The Declaration of Independence was a masterful piece of work. On August 2 it was formally signed. The first to sign was John Hancock, the president of the Continental Congress. He wrote his name in bold, large letters so that George III could read it without putting on his glasses. Following the ceremony, Hancock is said to have warned the other delegates: "We must be unanimous; there must be no pulling different ways; we must hang together." Benjamin Franklin turned and replied, "Yes, we must, indeed, all hang together, or most assuredly we shall all hang separately." He meant that if the revolution failed, Great Britain would hang them all as traitors.

Independence from Great Britain had been declared. The difficult task of winning independence on the battlefield still awaited.

Section Review

1. What events led to the Declaration of Independence?
2. Describe the major differences in the views held by colonists who were radicals and those who were moderates.
3. Define minuteman.
4. What were two important actions taken by the Second Continental Congress?
5. If you had lived during the early 1770's, do you think you would have been a "moderate," a "loyalist," or a "radical"? Explain the reasons for your answer.

Discuss: In the Declaration of Independence, Jefferson states "that all men are created equal." What do you think this statement meant in 1776?

CHAPTER REVIEW

Summary

Before 1660, the colonists had largely ignored the weak attempts of the British government to regulate colonial affairs. However, in 1660 Britain adopted a more mercantilistic attitude. In that year, Parliament began to pass the Navigation Acts. Many colonists resented these new laws because they favored Britain over the colonies by restricting the colonies' trade.

Resentment in the colonies steadily grew as Britain tried to increase its control over colonial affairs. After the end of the French and Indian War in 1763, Britain passed a series of tax laws designed to pay off its war debts. The colonists felt that Britain had no right to tax them because they were not represented in Parliament. As the British pressured them to obey these and other laws, the colonists became angrier. They organized boycotts of British goods, harassed the soldiers sent to enforce the laws, and practiced military drills on village greens.

Fighting broke out in 1775 at Lexington, Massachusetts. One year later, the colonists declared their independence from Britain. Over the next five years, the colonists would struggle to win it.

Recalling the Facts

1. According to the theory of mercantilism, in what two ways could colonies help the home country become wealthy?
2. Who was William Pitt, and what did he do to help the British win the French and Indian War?
3. Explain how the European land claims in North America were changed by the Treaty of Paris in 1763.
4. How did the colonists protest the Stamp Act?
5. Why were British troops going to Lexington and Concord in 1775?
6. In his pamphlet *Common Sense,* what did Thomas Paine urge the colonists to do?

Analyzing the Facts

1. How would the practice of mercantilism hurt the colonies?
2. How do you think the removal of the French from the North American mainland in 1763 affected colonial military dependence on Great Britain?

3. How did the British response to colonial protests over the Stamp Act in 1765 differ from their response to protests over the Tea Act in 1773?
4. The expression "the shot heard round the world" is an example of figurative language. It does not mean exactly what it says—people around the world did not actually hear the shot. What does this expression mean?
5. Do you think the colonies should have declared their independence from Britain in 1776? Explain your answer.

Time and History

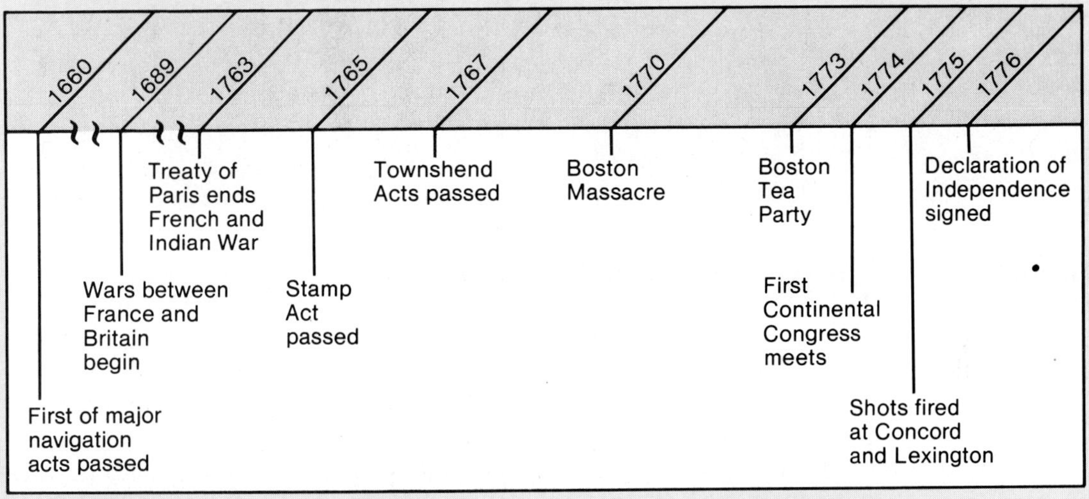

1. In which decade did Parliament pass laws that taxed the colonists?
2. How many years after the Boston Massacre did the first actual battle of the American Revolution occur?
3. Which of the following events could not have been discussed at the First Continental Congress: the Stamp Act, the fighting at Lexington, the Boston Tea Party?
4. For how many years did France and Britain fight wars for the control of North America?
5. How many years after the fighting began at Concord and Lexington did the colonists declare their independence?

Chapter 5 The War for Independence

On the fourth day of July 1776, the Congress of the United Colonies was debating the final form of a document called the "Declaration of Independence." Its main author, Thomas Jefferson, sat quietly amidst the commotion, saying nothing, only taking notes. In the evening, the debate ended at last. Solemnly, all except one statesman took their turn signing the momentous document. The United Colonies had declared that they were free and independent states.

After you read this chapter, you will be able to:

1. Describe the disadvantages faced by the colonies in the War for Independence.
2. Explain which battle was the turning point for the colonies during the war.
3. Discuss how America achieved victory and independence from Great Britain.

1. Early Years of the War

BEFORE YOU READ: *What factors made people think that the American colonies could not defeat the British?*

Few people in 1776 thought the colonies could win their War for Independence. The colonies were fighting Great Britain, the world's richest nation. Great Britain had a well-equipped and well-trained army. Besides its army, Great Britain also had a powerful navy. It was capable of dominating American waters and the ocean shipping lanes. However, having to transport soldiers and supplies over 4,800 kilometers (3,000 miles) of rough ocean caused Great Britain severe problems.

Colonial Disadvantages

The colonies' chances for victory did not look very promising. Many factors seemed to indicate that the colonies would lose.

First, and perhaps most important, the colonists were not united. The Declaration of Independence had been signed by a handful of Americans. The question now was whether the American people would support it. About 20 percent of the population were Loyalists who did not want to separate from Great Britain. Loyalists were opposed to the war. Active patriots accounted for only about 40 percent of the American people. In addition, a large number of the colonists (perhaps 40 percent) were uncommitted. When it was to their advantage to support the revolution, they did so. When it appeared that Great Britain was winning, these people supported the British.

The weakness of the Continental Congress was a second disadvantage. The Congress lacked the power to tax. Without the power to tax, colonists had great difficulty raising the money they needed to fight the war.

Another disadvantage the colonists faced was the American Indian. Most American Indians favored the British because the colonists had treated them roughly and unfairly.

Finally, the colonists were at a disadvantage because of their army. The Continental army was a small army, averaging about 10,000 men and a few women. It was never more than 18,500 strong during the war. The British had around 40,000 troops. The term of service in the Continental army was short, in some cases as short as three months. Many Americans did not fight at all in the spring and fall. They had to return home for harvesting. There was also a high desertion rate in the Continental army. Troops became discouraged and left for home. Those who stayed were highly undisciplined and did not take orders well.

After considering all of the disadvantages, most people thought the colonies had little chance of victory. But the Continental army did have some advantages. American soldiers could shoot better than the British. The American rifle was more accurate and could hit a target at a greater range than the British musket. Also, American soldiers were more familiar with the land they were fighting on. Perhaps of greatest importance, the soldiers in the Continental army knew

Background: The Americans also had problems supplying the army. There were many fine gunsmiths in the colonies, but they produced so many types and sizes of weapons that providing the proper ammunition was difficult.

that they were fighting for a cause—independence. They also had a well-respected commanding general, George Washington.

The Commanding General

George Washington's presence gave hope to the rebel cause. He was well over 183 centimeters (6 feet) tall, and he carried himself in a dignified manner. He was friendly to his troops, but he was always aware that he was the soldiers' leader. Washington demanded and received respect. His honesty was beyond question. He was the type of person that people naturally look up to.

George Washington was born in 1732, the youngest son of a Virginia planter. His older brothers inherited the family's wealth and lands, so Washington became a surveyor to make a living. It was not until his half-brother Lawrence's death in 1752 that George Washington inherited the estate at Mt. Vernon. In 1759, Washington married a wealthy widow, Martha Dandridge Custis.

George Washington was a moderate, not a radical. But he accepted the leadership of the Continental army because he believed so strongly in representative government. He felt that the British had been taking rights and powers away from the colonial assemblies.

Shortly after the Battle of Breed's Hill, Washington arrived in Massachusetts. He took command of the Continental army on July 3, 1775.

Washington tightened his grip around Boston during the winter of 1775–1776. His army formed a strong line of defense around the British troops. The Continental army slowly moved forward, taking strategic hills around Boston. Early in March 1776, Washington seized Dorchester Heights, overlooking Boston. The British general, William Howe, finally gave up his attempt to hold Boston. On March 17, 1776, the British withdrew to Halifax, a town in eastern Canada. For the first time since hostilities broke out, there were no British troops on the American colonies' soil.

The Invasion of New York

George Washington knew that Howe would not be gone for long. Washington studied his maps and decided that Howe would attempt to take New York City. New York would make an excellent base of operations for the British. The harbor would serve as an excellent port for British naval vessels. From New York, British troops could attack New England to the north and the remaining colonies to the south. Washington left some of his troops to guard Boston. He moved the rest to the New York area in the spring of 1776. If Howe tried to take New York, Washington hoped to drive him out.

In June 1776, General William Howe brought his army down from Halifax. His 10,000 soldiers landed on Staten Island in New York harbor on July 2. Soon after, a huge British fleet arrived in the waters around New York. The fleet was under the command of Admiral Lord Richard Howe, the general's brother.

By early August, some 32,000 troops were ready to attack New York City. Among those fighting with the British were 9,000 German **mercenaries**. The mercenaries were professional soldiers

EUREKA!

The Submarine

Credit for building the first submarine is usually given to Cornelius Drebbel, a Dutch inventor. Drebbel launched a leather-covered craft in 1620. But it was an American named David Bushnell who first thought of using the submarine as a weapon of war.

Bushnell built his first submarine, which was known as the *Turtle,* in 1776. The *Turtle* was a clumsy contraption. Made of wood, it resembled a lemon with two propellers and a rudder, which the pilot cranked by hand. The pilot steered the submarine alongside an enemy ship and drilled a hole in the ship's side. Into the hole he fitted a gunpowder mine. Then he and the *Turtle* got as far away from the ship as possible. At least, that was the idea.

In 1776, Sergeant Ezra Lee used the *Turtle* to attack the British ship *Eagle*, in New York harbor. But the submarine's drill was too weak to pierce the ship's copper side.

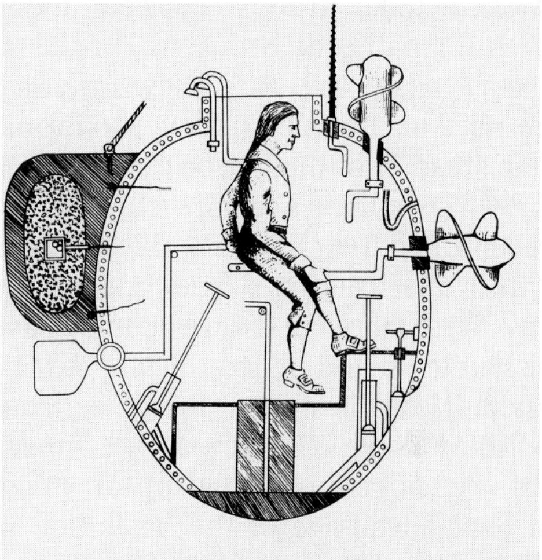

INTERIOR PROFILE of DAVID BUSHNELL'S SUBMARINE BOAT

Near the end of his life, David Bushnell built another submarine, which was used in the War of 1812. But his second design was no more successful than the *Turtle.* Other attempts to perfect underwater vessels followed. Only with the development of powerful electric motors in the 1880's did submarines find a permanent place in the world's navies.

---

hired by Great Britain to fight in the colonies. Hiring mercenaries was not an unusual practice at this time. Most of the mercenaries were from the German state of Hesse. Americans referred to all the German mercenaries as Hessians.

mercenary a professional soldier hired to serve in a foreign army

The Fall of New York City

Great Britain hoped it would not have to use its huge attack force. The British thought that merely the show of such superior strength would make the rebels back down. General Howe even sent a message to the Continental Congress in late summer. It said that the colonists would be pardoned by the king if

Vocabulary Help: pardon—to cancel the penalty for an offense. Ask students why they think the Continental Congress refused the pardon offered by Howe.

For Extra Interest: Have students pretend that they are a British, Hessian, or colonial soldier who has just fought in the battle for New York City. Have them write letters home describing their experiences and feelings during this battle.

they abandoned the Declaration of Independence. Congress refused to accept Howe's peace offer.

Washington's troops readied themselves for battle at Brooklyn Heights, a series of hills to the east of New York City. Howe had his troops cross over to Brooklyn. Instead of hitting hardest at the center of Washington's troops, the British concentrated their attack at the two ends of the American line. The Continental army was trapped. Howe could have crushed them and ended the war, but he waited. He still hoped the Americans would lay down their arms. The Americans were not about to give up. Washington took advantage of the hesitation to withdraw his troops to Manhattan Island.

Howe pursued the Americans. He captured New York City at the southern tip of Manhattan Island. The Americans were pushed farther up the island.

Throughout October and early November, Washington tried to hold the American forts along the Hudson River. However, he was unsuccessful as Howe's superior forces pushed the Americans back. Finally, the dwindling Continental army retreated to New Jersey. The army crossed the state with the British at its heels. Arriving at Trenton, New Jersey, the Americans took the last available boats across the Delaware River to Pennsylvania. Minutes later, Hessian troops reached Trenton.

Trenton and Princeton

The situation looked bleak for the Americans. The Continental army had dwindled to about 3,000 soldiers. Many discouraged soldiers had returned to their homes. The soldiers who remained were weary. Congress, fearing a British attack on Philadelphia, fled to Baltimore. George Washington wrote, "I think the game is pretty well up." Thomas Paine echoed Washington's feelings when he wrote from the gloomy American camp, "These are the times that try men's souls."

Washington, however, planned a counterattack. On Christmas night 1776, Washington and 2,500 soldiers recrossed the ice-filled Delaware River and headed for Trenton. A sleet storm raged about them. Following holiday celebrations, the Hessians at Trenton were sleeping. The Americans took them by surprise. Nine hundred Hessians were captured, and

Washington's Retreat, 1776

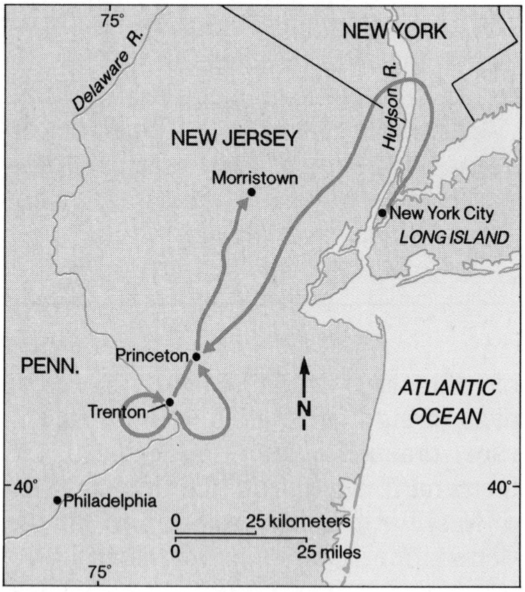

Describe George Washington's retreat from New York City, using cardinal and intermediate directions.

Background: "These are the times that try men's souls" opens the first of "The Crisis" pamphlets published by Paine between 1776 and 1783. Washington had this pamphlet read to his dispirited soldiers, and it is believed to have inspired the courage needed to win the battle at Trenton.

Washington planned to have three forces of soldiers cross the Delaware river and attack the Hessians at Trenton. Only the force led by Washington himself made it across the river.

their commander was killed. A few escaped to warn the British in New York.

The British general, Lord Charles Cornwallis, moved his troops out of New York and headed for Trenton. In a daring night move, Washington left his camp fires burning to deceive the British. He marched his troops around Cornwallis' army by a side road and attacked Princeton. On January 3, 1777, the Americans captured the entire enemy base at Princeton and burned all its supplies. Cornwallis retreated back to New York.

The excited American troops marched farther into New Jersey, as far as Morristown. There the weary soldiers encamped for the winter. They were only some 48 kilometers (30 miles) west of New York City.

The victories at Trenton and Princeton were not big in a military sense. But they did wonders for the Continental army's low morale. The victories also convinced the American soldiers that they might be able to defeat the British after all.

The New British Strategy

That winter, leaders in London developed a new strategy. Their plan called for conquering the state of New York. By doing this the British would isolate New England, and the other states would be unable to help. After defeating New England, the British could then crush the other states easily.

The British strategy called for a two-pronged attack. One army was to attack

Discuss: Why do you think the British were interested in isolating the New England colonies? Do you think this was a good strategy to use to win the war? Why or why not?

For Extra Interest: Have students calculate the distance from New York City to Philadelphia using a map scale. Ask students why they think it took Howe two months to move his troops from one city to the other.

from the north, while another attacked from the south. General John Burgoyne was to lead the attack from Canada. His large army would invade northern New York, then move south to Albany, New York. General Howe was to lead the other half of the attack. From New York City, Howe's army would move north to join Burgoyne in Albany.

General Howe was aware that Burgoyne would get most of the glory for this plan. He came up with a plan of his own that would keep Britain's attention on him. His plan was to capture the rebel capital of Philadelphia. If time allowed, he would hurry back and help Burgoyne.

It took Howe two months to move his troops by sea and then by land from New York to Philadelphia. George Washington used this time to move his troops into a position to block Howe and defend Philadelphia. On September 11, 1777, the two armies clashed at Brandywine Creek. Howe was able to push past Washington and drive his troops toward the rebel capital. Philadelphia fell to General Howe.

Washington was determined to attack the British once more before the winter set in. On October 4, the Continental army hit the British hard at Germantown, Pennsylvania. Washington's troops were almost successful, but Howe finally drove them off. Washington's army went into winter quarters at Valley Forge, Pennsylvania, battered but with spirits intact.

George Washington as a young man

Howe's decision to capture Philadelphia should have earned him praise from London. Instead, critics charged that Howe's behavior was treasonous. They claimed that Howe had intentionally tried to lose the war by failing to meet up with Burgoyne in New York.

Section Review

1. What disadvantages did the colonies face in fighting the War for Independence?
2. Define mercenary. Which side used mercenaries in the War for Independence?
3. Why were the American victories at Trenton and Princeton important to the American cause?
4. How can fighting a war on one's own territory be both helpful and harmful?

2. The Turning Point

BEFORE YOU READ: *How did Burgoyne's defeat at Saratoga change the course of the War for Independence?*

While Howe chose to move his troops down to Philadelphia, the invasion of New York State was getting under way. Two forces of British troops moved into New York from Canada. The first wing, led by General John Burgoyne, was the main invasion force. According to the plan, Burgoyne was to march southward and link up with Howe at Albany. Colonel Barry St. Leger led the second wing. It was composed of both British and Indian troops. They were to attack Albany from the west, by way of the Mohawk River valley.

The Invasion of New York State

St. Leger left Canada on June 23, 1777. He and his Indian allies quickly moved up the St. Lawrence, crossed Lake Ontario, and started moving east across New York.

Meanwhile, General Burgoyne's army of almost 8,000 soldiers had set out from Montreal on June 17. They easily passed through northern New York and floated down Lake Champlain. Burgoyne wondered why Washington had not yet attacked him. He did not know that Washington was far to the south preparing to defend Philadelphia against Howe.

Burgoyne's forces took Fort Ticonderoga in early July and headed into the woodlands of New York. The going became difficult and slow. Americans chopped down trees to block the roads and paths. Americans also fired their muskets from unseen hiding places within the forests. British cannons and supply wagons fell farther and farther behind the main body of troops. A few kilometers (miles) to the south, American troops under generals Horatio Gates and Benedict Arnold waited for the redcoats.

Burgoyne neared Albany by mid-September. He knew that his troops were in deep trouble. The Americans had completely cut them off from their supply wagons. It was also clear that Howe was not coming to help. Then the Americans struck. Troops led by Horatio Gates moved in and surrounded the British.

Saratoga Campaign, 1777

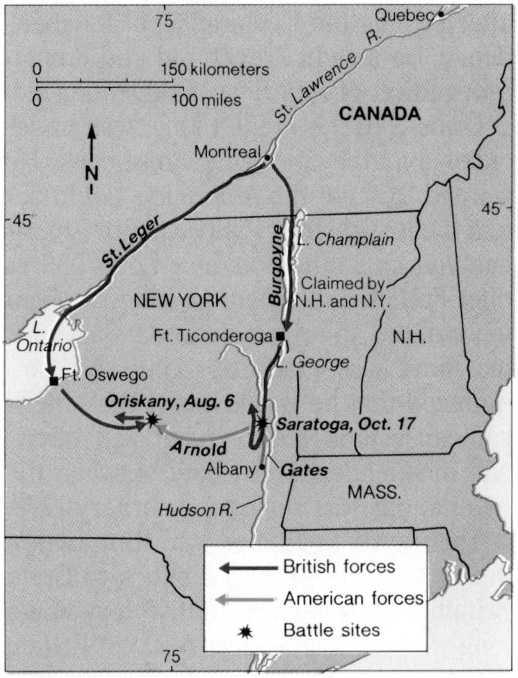

Why was St. Leger unable to meet Burgoyne at Albany?

Background: In May 1775, Ethan Allen and the Green Mountain Boys had seized Fort Ticonderoga and Crown Point from the British without a struggle.

Discuss: Who do you think was responsible for the British failure to capture New York and isolate New England? Explain your answer.

After several bloody clashes, Burgoyne retreated to Saratoga, just north of Albany. He realized all was hopeless. Only about 5,700 of his troops were still alive. On October 17, 1777, Burgoyne ordered his troops to lay down their weapons and surrender.

To the west, St. Leger had been no more successful. On August 6, American troops had stopped him at the Battle of Oriskany, New York.

The American victories in New York, especially at Saratoga, were a turning point in the war. Soon after, France entered the war on the side of the Americans, providing much-needed support.

The French Enter the War

Benjamin Franklin had traveled to Paris after signing the Declaration of Independence. He sought French aid and French recognition of American independence.

Louis XVI, the French king, was undecided about helping the Americans. He wanted to see if the Americans could defeat the British army. Only a major American victory would convince Louis XVI to offer French aid. When the king received news of the American victory at Saratoga, his mind was made up. Louis XVI announced that he would assist the American cause. France also recognized American independence. A treaty between the two nations was signed in February 1778.

This news, combined with Burgoyne's defeat at Saratoga, was a shock to Great Britain. It now seemed that victory was a long way off. The leaders of Great Britain decided to make a peace offer to the Americans in the hope that this would end the war. Prime Minister Lord North said that Britain would repeal the Coercive Acts and the Tea Act. If the Americans wanted more, he was ready to repeal every act passed since 1763. Lord North even said that the American colonies would never be taxed again by Great Britain. In return, the American colonies would remain a part of Great Britain. However, the British government would retain control only over foreign relations and defense.

A Royal Peace Commission was sent to America to present the British peace offer. The Americans rejected it. They told the British that Congress would discuss only two matters: the British evacuation of Philadelphia and British recognition of American independence. The two sides were deadlocked. The Royal Peace Commission returned to London, its mission a failure. The War for Independence continued.

Valley Forge

During the winter of 1777–1778, George Washington and his troops camped at Valley Forge. From Valley Forge, the Americans could keep watch on the British in Philadelphia. Valley Forge was only about 32 kilometers (about 20 miles) northwest of Philadelphia.

The army spent a dreadful winter at Valley Forge. Little food could be found in the area. Civilians were supposed to aid the troops, but few sent them any food or supplies. Throughout the winter, supplies were painfully short. Crude housing had to serve the troops. The huts they built from trees and odd pieces of wood were incapable of keeping out the cold. Blankets, clothing, and medicine were lacking.

Discuss: Why do you think the French waited until after the colonists won a major victory before siding with them against the British? What did France have to gain and lose by entering this conflict?

Famous Americans

LYDIA BARRINGTON DARRAGH

Lydia Barrington Darragh was a skilled nurse who cared for sick and wounded American soldiers during the War for Independence. But she is best remembered for one particular act during the war that demanded great cleverness and courage.

In the winter of 1777, Philadelphia was occupied by British soldiers. The British used Darragh's home as a meeting place for British officers. They believed she would not become involved in the war because of her Quaker religion.

On the night of December 2, 1777, the British officers held a meeting in her home. Darragh listened at the door of their meeting room. She overheard the British plotting a surprise attack on one of General Washington's camps near the city. She decided she had to warn the American army. Early on the morning of December 4, Darragh left her house carrying an empty sack. She told a British guard that she was going to the countryside to buy some flour. Once she was beyond the British lines, Darragh changed course and headed for the American camp, which lay 21 kilometers (13 miles) away. She met Thomas Craig, an American soldier and friend. She gave her message to Craig, who rode off to warn Washington.

Darragh's action gave the Americans time to prepare for the British attack, which came that night. After a few days of unsuccessful fighting, the British returned to Philadelphia. Darragh had helped to prevent a British victory. Perhaps her walk was as important as Paul Revere's ride.

Thousands of soldiers were unfit for combat because they had no shoes.

Washington's army became smaller and smaller. Thousands of soldiers gave up. Some returned to their homes and families. Others made their way to Philadelphia to join the British army. Washington kept pleading with Congress to send supplies. But none came.

In contrast to the situation at Valley Forge, the British spent a comfortable winter in Philadelphia. General Howe and his officers went to many parties and balls. These social events were given by the townspeople of Philadelphia. The regular British soldiers were not permitted to attend these functions. But they ate well and rested in warm winter quarters.

General Howe was urged to attack Washington at Valley Forge. The British could have easily crushed Washington's forces. Except for a skirmish in the early

Background: On December 23, 1777, Washington wrote, "We have this day no less than 2,873 men in camp unfit for duty because they are barefooted and otherwise naked." More than 3,000 soldiers died during the winter at Valley Forge.

This painting shows Washington and Lafayette inspecting American troops during the bitterly cold winter at Valley Forge.

part of December at Whitemarsh, Howe did not move. He still hoped the Americans would surrender. Authorities in Great Britain were furious with Howe. Sir William Howe resigned. He was replaced as British commander by General Sir Henry Clinton.

Foreign Assistance

Some Europeans with military experience believed in the American cause of independence. Among the first to offer their help were Casimir Pulaski (puh-LASS-kee) and Thaddeus Kosciusko (koss-ee-USS-koe). Both were Polish officers. Pulaski helped in the training of American troops. Kosciusko was a great military engineer. He helped design the fortifications at West Point, which guarded the Hudson River in New York.

The Marquis de Lafayette (mahr-KEE duh lah-fee-ETT), a young French aristocrat, also wished to help. He enlisted in the American revolutionary army in 1777. Lafayette and Washington became the best of friends. Lafayette was a symbol as well as a military leader. He symbolized the bonds of friendship between France and America.

Friedrich von Steuben (STOO-ben) arrived at Valley Forge during the terrible winter of 1777–1778. Von Steuben was a veteran of the Prussian (German) army. He drilled the American army daily. He trained the American soldiers to reload their guns in half the time it had taken them previously. By spring, the Continental army was becoming an efficient fight-

Discuss: Why do you think General Howe was replaced as the British commander in 1778? Do you think the British decision to replace Howe was wise? Why or why not?

Background: In 1780, Esther Reed headed a committee of 39 Philadelphia women who raised $7,500 for Washington's army. When told that the money could best be spent on shirts, the women purchased linen. They sewed over 2,000 shirts, which were delivered by year's end.

ing force. Von Steuben's drills also helped keep the soldiers' minds off their misery.

Women and the War Effort

Women played key roles in the War for Independence. In many states, women formed Ladies Associations. These associations collected money to purchase clothing and other supplies for the soldiers. Other women traveled with the army. Most were the wives or widows of soldiers. They performed important and necessary tasks about the camps. Some served as nurses, others as cooks, still others washed and mended clothing. The women received little or no wages for their work. Many frontier women took up arms to protect their homes and settlements from attack.

These were not the only ways in which women made a contribution. While thousands of men were involved in fighting or serving in government, many women took over the management of farms and businesses. One such woman was Abigail Adams, who was married to John Adams. She successfully managed the family farm in Massachusetts while her husband was away serving as a delegate to the Continental Congress.

Some women even found themselves caught in the heat of battle. One of the more famous experiences was that of Molly Hays. In June 1778, American soldiers were fighting the British at Monmouth Courthouse in New Jersey. Molly Hays was there assisting her husband John and the other soldiers during the battle. Molly Hays brought buckets of fresh water to the soldiers during the battle. They jokingly called her "Molly Pitcher." At one point in the battle, British shots tore through the American lines. John Hays was wounded. Molly Hays bravely took his place at the cannon.

Not all female patriots became as famous as Abigail Adams or Molly Hays. However, thousands made important contributions during the war.

Slavery and the War

The issue of slavery raised many difficult questions during the War for Independence. How could Americans justify slavery, while at the same time fight for freedom from Great Britain? How could a nation that believed in liberty for all justify human slavery?

For some patriots slavery was seen as an economic necessity. This was especially true for southern planters who needed slave labor to produce crops such as rice and tobacco. Slavery was also an accepted part of life in both the North and South. Slaves cooked, drove carriages, cared for children, and did carpentry. Yet slavery could not be justified, especially by the Americans' definition of freedom. American leaders decided to ignore the slavery issue for fear that it might divide the American people even more. The problem was never solved during the Revolution.

For some slaves the War for Independence offered an opportunity to gain their freedom. The British tried to attract black Americans into the military with promises of freedom. All slaves who aided the British would be freed when the war was over. For many black Americans a British victory seemed the best chance of gaining freedom. Many slaves ran away from

Discuss: Why do you think the question of slavery did not become a major issue between the North and the South during the War for Independence?

Background: Of the 300,000 soldiers who fought for American independence, approximately 5,000 were black. Although a few separate black companies were established, the majority of blacks served in fighting groups made up primarily of whites.

their masters and joined the British army or navy.

Not all black Americans served with the British. About 5,000, both slave and free, joined the Continental army. They supported the cause of American independence. More slaves served in the American than the British army. Their owners promised them money, land, and the opportunity to earn their freedom.

At the beginning of the war, black volunteers flocked to join George Washington. As long as the fighting stayed in the northern states, blacks were accepted by the army, although most were not permitted to carry arms. They were assigned to other jobs in the army.

This policy changed when the fighting moved to the southern states. White southerners were frightened and upset to see black Americans in the military. Slaveowners were angered at seeing armed blacks in their states. They felt that this might encourage their own slaves to revolt. The army's policy toward accepting black Americans was changed. No longer would they be allowed to volunteer for the army. Those already in the army were ordered to leave.

The Continental army badly needed new troops during the final years of the war. Reluctantly, black Americans were again accepted into the military. They were promised their freedom when the war was over. They helped the American forces defeat the British. Black Americans took great pride in their contribution to the war effort.

Gains for Black Americans

Black Americans made some gains because of their role in the war. Starting with Pennsylvania in 1780, northern states passed laws that gradually freed slaves in their states. Smaller but still important gains were made in the South, too. Some southerners believed slavery and freedom could not exist side by side. They voluntarily freed their slaves. Much of this occurred in Virginia. Over 10,000 black slaves were given their freedom in Virginia between 1782 and 1790.

Section Review

1. How did Burgoyne's defeat at Saratoga change the course of the War for Independence?
2. What problems did Washington and his troops face at Valley Forge?
3. How did Europeans like Pulaski, Kosciusko, and Von Steuben help the Americans during the war?
4. Explain the ways in which women played important roles in the War for Independence.
5. The Declaration of Independence declared that all Americans are equal. Why then would some Americans continue to own slaves?

Background: Benedict Arnold was put in charge of American troops in reoccupied Philadelphia. In 1780, Arnold secretly agreed to turn over West Point to the British in return for money and an army commission. Fortunately, his plan was discovered. Arnold escaped and became a British general.

3. Victory and Independence

BEFORE YOU READ: *How did Americans achieve victory and independence from Great Britain?*

In the spring of 1778, a French fleet set sail for America. Aboard the French warships were French troops sent by King Louis XVI to assist the Americans.

The British general, Henry Clinton, felt he did not have the troops to defend Philadelphia and the surrounding area. Philadelphia was evacuated on June 18. Clinton moved his 17,000 soldiers across the New Jersey countryside and headed for New York.

Washington and the Continental army left Valley Forge on June 19 and pursued Clinton. The long line of British forces made the British an easy target. American troops attacked them at Monmouth Courthouse, New Jersey. Neither side was able to gain the advantage. The battle raged for one full day and ended in a draw. Washington claimed victory, since his troops had not been repelled by the British. Monmouth Courthouse was the last major battle fought in the North. The main focus of the war shifted to the South after this.

Clinton and his troops made their way to New York City. For the next two years American and French troops hemmed in part of the British army at New York.

A Southern Strategy

The British government developed a new war strategy in 1778. The British had not been able to bring the war to an end in the North. Great Britain felt it might have more success in the South. Loyalist sympathy was thought to be stronger in that region. If American troops could be forced out of the South, then the British would have a base from which the North could be attacked again.

The first British targets in the South were Georgia and South Carolina. General Henry Clinton ordered 3,500 soldiers to sail from New York to Georgia. In December 1778, the troops landed in Savannah, defeated the American defenders, and occupied the city. The rest of Georgia fell to British troops within the following year.

In early 1780, General Clinton personally led a huge British army to Charleston, South Carolina. Charleston was the most important American city in the South. If captured, it would be a major victory for Great Britain. The British attacked with determination. American soldiers under General Benjamin Lincoln tried desperately to save Charleston. They held out for six weeks with no new food or supplies. But Clinton's army proved too strong. Lincoln surrendered Charleston in May 1780, along with the entire southern army of some 5,500 soldiers.

From Charleston, British troops spread out into the interior of South Carolina. Victory came quickly. All seemed to be going according to plan for the British. General Clinton returned to his headquarters at New York City. He left General Charles Cornwallis to command the British army.

The conquered patriots were treated roughly in both South Carolina and Georgia. Their crops were destroyed, and their

Background: The new British strategy in 1778 was to "roll up" (south to north) the colonies.

Background: While the fighting raged in the South, George Rogers Clark led a group of Kentuckians against the British in the Ohio River valley. When the war ended, the British controlled the Ohio River valley, and the Americans controlled the frontier south of the Ohio River.

homes and farms were burned. The patriots themselves were arrested and thrown into jail. These British actions only made the patriots more determined.

Individuals like Francis Marion, nicknamed the "Swamp Fox," organized resistance in the South. He fought from hideouts deep within the swampy South Carolina backcountry. His band of patriot fighters was small and quick-moving. Marion and his troops would attack in a "hit-and-run" fashion. They hit the British hard when they were least expecting it and then dashed away to hide and wait for another opportunity. They waged **guerrilla warfare**. These patriot bands tormented the British and the Loyalists. The guerrilla bands never had a chance of winning. But they did keep the enemy off balance.

---

guerrilla warfare a method of warfare, used by small bands of revolutionary fighters

---

Setbacks and Victories

Congress acted quickly to send aid to the South. It selected Horatio Gates, the hero of Saratoga, to be the new commander in the South. Gates headed into South Carolina. On August 16, 1780, he encountered Cornwallis at Camden. The battle was an American disaster. Cornwallis ordered his troops to attack. The Americans fled in panic. Many of the American troops were killed as they retreated. The Battle of Camden became the worst defeat of the war.

Congress desperately needed to find a general who could stop the British in the South. Congress turned to Nathanael Greene. Next to Washington, who was tied down directing operations in New York, Greene was the best general in the army.

Before Greene took over, the tide of the war in the South began turning. Soldiers and guerrilla fighters from the Carolinas took on a Loyalist force at King's Mountain, located near the border of North and South Carolina. All of the Loyalists were either killed, wounded, or captured.

Greene arrived shortly after the battle at King's Mountain. He and his trusted assistant, General Daniel Morgan, forced Cornwallis to chase them through the woods of North Carolina. The patriots hit the British in swift strikes, then retreated and waited for another opening. In January 1781, the two sides battled at Cowpens, in northwestern South Carolina. General Morgan brilliantly defeated some of the best troops in the British army.

Cornwallis frantically pursued Greene and Morgan. In a battle at Guilford, North Carolina, the two armies fought to a draw. Cornwallis badly needed more supplies and fresh troops. He retreated to the coast of North Carolina to await their arrival from New York.

Greene and Morgan did not sit still. With Cornwallis away, they swept the Loyalist and British forces out of South Carolina, except for those at Charleston.

The End Draws Near

General Cornwallis was desperate for a victory. Disobeying Clinton's orders, Cornwallis left the Carolinas and marched north to conquer Virginia. He spent the summer raiding Virginia. On August 1, Cornwallis retired to Yorktown,

Background: Cornwallis felt compelled to obtain a clear-cut victory on the battlefield. This was not always possible because of the tactics used by the colonists in wilderness warfare. As a result, he wasted and frustrated his troops in his vain pursuit of the colonists.

Discuss: How was Cornwallis' decision to attack Virginia in 1781 similar to Howe's decision to capture Philadelphia in 1777? Why do you think both commanders decided to do what they did?

Virginia, near Chesapeake Bay. From this base, he could keep in contact with General Clinton in New York.

Meanwhile, Washington was meeting with the French general, Count de Rochambeau (roe-sham-BOW), in Connecticut. Rochambeau commanded some 7,000 French troops sent by Louis XVI to help the Americans. The two generals agreed to make a joint attack against New York City. Just before the attack began, Washington learned of Cornwallis' base at Yorktown. Washington also received a letter from the French Admiral De Grasse. His fleet with 7,000 French troops aboard would be in American waters in August. Washington saw his chance to trap and destroy Cornwallis.

A daring plan was devised to defeat Cornwallis. The American and French armies would surround him on land. The French fleet would encircle Yorktown by sea.

The plan was set in motion in August 1781. First, Lafayette's soldiers in Virginia moved closer to Yorktown. Next, De Grasse's fleet sailed into Chesapeake Bay. In early September, a British fleet rushed to help Cornwallis. The French and British navies clashed in a sea battle. Neither fleet won, but the damaged British ships had to return to New York for repairs. De Grasse was now in control of the waters off Yorktown.

Washington and Rochambeau led their troops southward and joined up with Lafayette. There were now nearly 17,000 French and American soldiers surrounding Yorktown. They were more than twice the size of the British force at Yorktown. Cornwallis was helpless. He was trapped by land and by sea. The American and

Yorktown Campaign, 1781

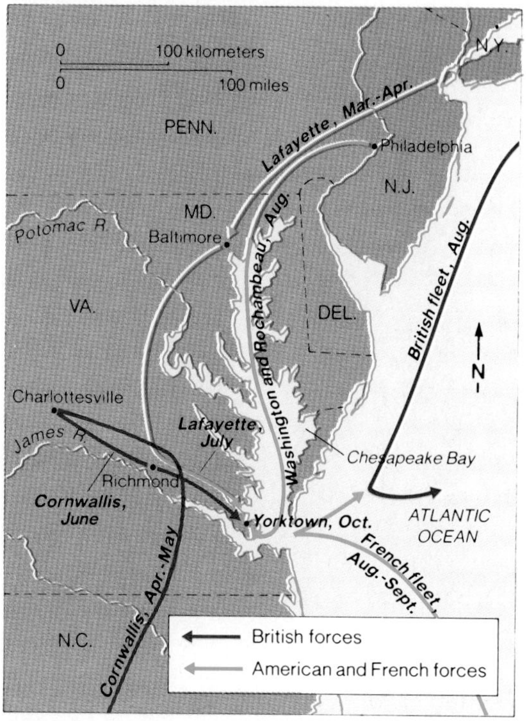

Why was the British fleet unable to help Cornwallis at Yorktown?

French troops attacked again and again, driving the British back toward the sea. Cornwallis held out until October 17. He was outnumbered and running out of food. Cornwallis decided that it would be "wanton [reckless] and inhuman to sacrifice the lives of this small body of gallant soldiers."

On October 19, 1781, Cornwallis surrendered his army of 7,200 soldiers, plus 850 sailors. That afternoon his troops marched out to the surrender area and laid down their weapons. The British band played an old army marching song, "The World Turned Upside Down." The

For Extra Interest: Have students create a bulletin board display entitled "Who's Who in the American Revolution."

Discuss: Why did the battle of Yorktown signal the end of the war? The British still had a large concentration of troops in the North and were not really defeated there. Why do you think the British did not adopt a new strategy to continue the war in the North?

General Charles Cornwallis surrendered his army to Washington at Yorktown on October 19, 1781.

American and French soldiers watched the surrender with pride and delight.

Washington and his American troops returned to the New York area. Rochambeau's troops spent the winter in Virginia. Then they returned to France. The war dragged on for another year, but Yorktown was the last significant battle of the War for Independence. With the capture of Cornwallis' entire army, British hopes for victory collapsed.

The War Winds Down

In London, King George III demanded that the war against the American rebels continue. He ran into strong opposition, both in the government and from his subjects. The king was forced to back down. In April 1782, Great Britain sent Richard Oswald to Paris on a secret mission. He was to consult with Benjamin Franklin about peace terms. John Adams and John Jay went to Paris to join in the discussions. Seven months later, an agreement was reached. Congress approved the terms and on April 11, 1783, it issued an order that fighting be halted.

The peace treaty ending the War of Independence was signed in Paris in September 1783. The terms of the Treaty of Paris were highly favorable to the United States. Of most importance, the treaty recognized American independence. The 13 colonies were recognized by Great Britain as 13 independent states, joined together as the United States of America. The treaty also provided generous boundaries for the country. The United States would extend from the southern border of Canada to the northern boundary of Florida, and from the Atlantic Ocean to the Mississippi River.

Washington Bids Farewell

The last British troops left the United States on November 25, 1783. It was a day of national rejoicing. In New York City, Washington agreed to participate in a victory parade. It was both a joyous and a sad occasion. New York was bleak and battered from the British occupation. The townspeople looked tired and strained from what they had endured. But they cheered their commanding general with grateful hearts.

On December 4, George Washington came to Fraunces Tavern in New York

For Extra Interest: Have students draw a map of the United States as it existed in 1783. Have them draw in and label the 13 states as well as major geographic features.

Discuss: What do you think was the most important reason why the colonists won the War for Independence? Explain your answer.

City to bid farewell to his officers. They toasted one another for the last time. Washington finally rose from his table. With tears streaming down his face, he embraced each officer separately. Then George Washington walked from the room.

Washington traveled from New York to Annapolis, Maryland, where Congress was meeting. He appeared before all the members to thank them and resign his commission as commander-in-chief. Now, like the rest of his soldiers, Washington was free after nine long, hard years of war. Washington headed south through Virginia toward his home there at Mount Vernon.

Why America Won

Few people in 1776 had given the colonies much chance of winning the War for Independence. They had faced the best army in the world. The Continental army and the colonies had survived hard times and many defeats. The British had won more victories than the Americans. Why, in 1783, was the United States free? Part of the reason was American desire and determination. The American people wanted independence more than Great Britain was willing to fight to prevent it.

Two other factors were important in the American victory. The first was France. The United States could not have won without French assistance. France provided troops, a navy, weapons, and money.

The second factor was George Washington. It is fair to say that, without Washington, America would not have won the War for Independence. George Washington was a man with a very special appeal. Washington was the sort of person whom people trusted. So long as George Washington led the Continental army, no matter how dark things looked, Americans had hope.

Section Review

1. How did the United States achieve victory and independence from Great Britain?
2. Define guerilla warfare. How was guerilla warfare used during the American Revolution?
3. Describe the strategy used by the Americans and the French to defeat Cornwallis at Yorktown.
4. What were the terms of the Treaty of Paris?
5. France came to the aid of the United States during the War for Independence. Name some countries that the United States gives military aid to today. Why does the United States do this?

Discuss: Why do you think people placed so much trust in George Washington? What type of person would you trust? What do you expect from the people you trust?

CHAPTER REVIEW

Summary

In 1776, few people thought the American colonists had much chance of winning their War for Independence. Although they had some advantages, including familiarity with the land and the excellent military leadership of George Washington, the odds of winning the war were heavily in favor of the British.

In September 1776, British troops captured New York City. By September 1777, Philadelphia was taken. A month later the Americans won an important battle at Saratoga, New York, which convinced the French to come to the aid of the Americans. Having failed to isolate New England, the British decided to try a different strategy. Fighting shifted to the South, where the British were initially successful. However, the Americans soon frustrated the British commander, Cornwallis, with their hit-and-run style of fighting. The last significant battle of the war was fought at Yorktown, Virginia. French and American forces surrounded Cornwallis and his army and forced the British general to surrender on October 19, 1781. The colonists had won the war, and Great Britain formally recognized American independence in the Treaty of Paris signed in 1783.

Recalling the Facts

1. What advantages did the American colonists have in the War for Independence?
2. Why did Washington accept command of the Continental army when he himself was not a radical?
3. Why did the plan to capture New York State and isolate the New England colonies fail?
4. Why did the policy concerning blacks in the Continental army change when the fighting moved to the southern states? How was the policy changed?
5. How did the French help to trap Cornwallis at Yorktown?

Analyzing the Facts

1. What do you think are the characteristics of a good leader? Which of these characteristics did George Washington have?

2. Why do you think the Americans were better at hit-and-run fighting than the British?
3. Why do you think the French waited until after the American victory at Saratoga to help the colonists?
4. Why do you think the British lost the War for Independence?
5. What things in your life would be different if the colonists had not won the War for Independence?

Time and History

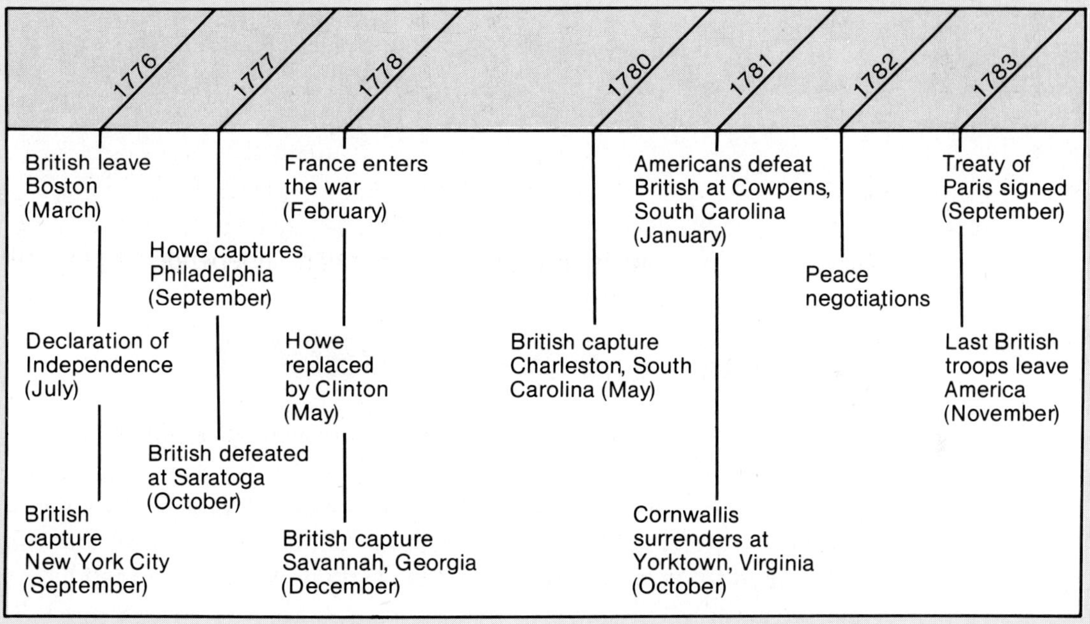

1. How many years after the colonists declared their independence did they achieve it?
2. In what year did the fighting shift to the South?
3. What was the last battle of the War for Independence?
4. After which American victory did the French decide to aid the colonists?
5. How many years after Cornwallis surrendered did the war officially end? Why do you think it took so long?

Chapter
6

Forming a New Nation

In 1787, for the second time since the Declaration of Independence, American political leaders gathered to try to establish a lasting government. Their first effort was the Articles of Confederation. Their second effort was the federal Constitution. James Madison of Virginia maintained that the Constitution of the United States was "intended to last for ages."

After you read this chapter, you will be able to:

1. Identify the major problems facing the national government under the Articles of Confederation.
2. Describe the compromises that resulted in the Constitution of the United States.
3. Explain how the government is organized under the Constitution.

☐ Read an organizational chart.

Background: Be sure students understand the basic differences and similarities between a national government and state governments.

1. The First Government

BEFORE YOU READ: *What were the major problems facing the national government under the Articles of Confederation?*

In June 1776, Richard Henry Lee, a Virginian, proposed to the Continental Congress that the 13 colonies form a union for governing themselves. The Continental Congress appointed a committee to develop a plan of union. The committee presented John Dickinson's draft of a plan to the Congress. The plan called for a loose union of the 13 states in which each member state would retain many powers of government. The plan was called the Articles of **Confederation**. The Continental Congress was so busy with military matters at that time that it took over a year to debate and rewrite the Articles. In November 1777, Congress approved the Articles of Confederation.

confederation a loose union of states in which each member state retains many powers of government

Accepting a Plan of Government

Congress still had to obtain the approval of all 13 states before the Articles of Confederation could become law. Agreement from the states did not come quickly or easily. It took four years before all gave their approval.

The cause of the delay had to do with the land west of the Appalachian Mountains. Before the American Revolution, this vast region belonged to the British king. In fact, the Proclamation of 1763 had forbidden American colonists to settle there. Once the Revolution began, Americans did not feel these western lands belonged to the king any longer. Larger states like Virginia, New York, Massachusetts, and the Carolinas said the lands belonged to them. They based their claims on their colonial charters, which said their borders ran from "sea to sea," or as far west as the land extended. The smaller states, led by Maryland, refused to **ratify**, or officially approve, the Articles of Confederation. Their charters did not give them "sea to sea" rights. The smaller states felt that because all states were fighting Great Britain, all should be entitled to share the western lands.

ratify to approve officially

The new government had not even been formed, and the states were already fighting among themselves! The smaller states at first stubbornly stuck to their demand. They would not ratify the Articles unless the western lands were turned over to the national government. Eventually, all backed down except Maryland. After four years of arguing, the larger states gave in. The western lands would be controlled by Congress. Maryland then ratified the Articles of Confederation. The Articles of Confederation created a confederacy called "The United States of America."

The new government became effective on March 1, 1781. It was called the "Confederation." It was the first government of the United States.

Discuss: Do you think land west of the Appalachian Mountains and east of the Mississippi River should have been given to the large states based on their colonial charters, or should it have been turned over to the national government to be shared by all the states? Explain your answer.

State Claims to Western Lands, 1781

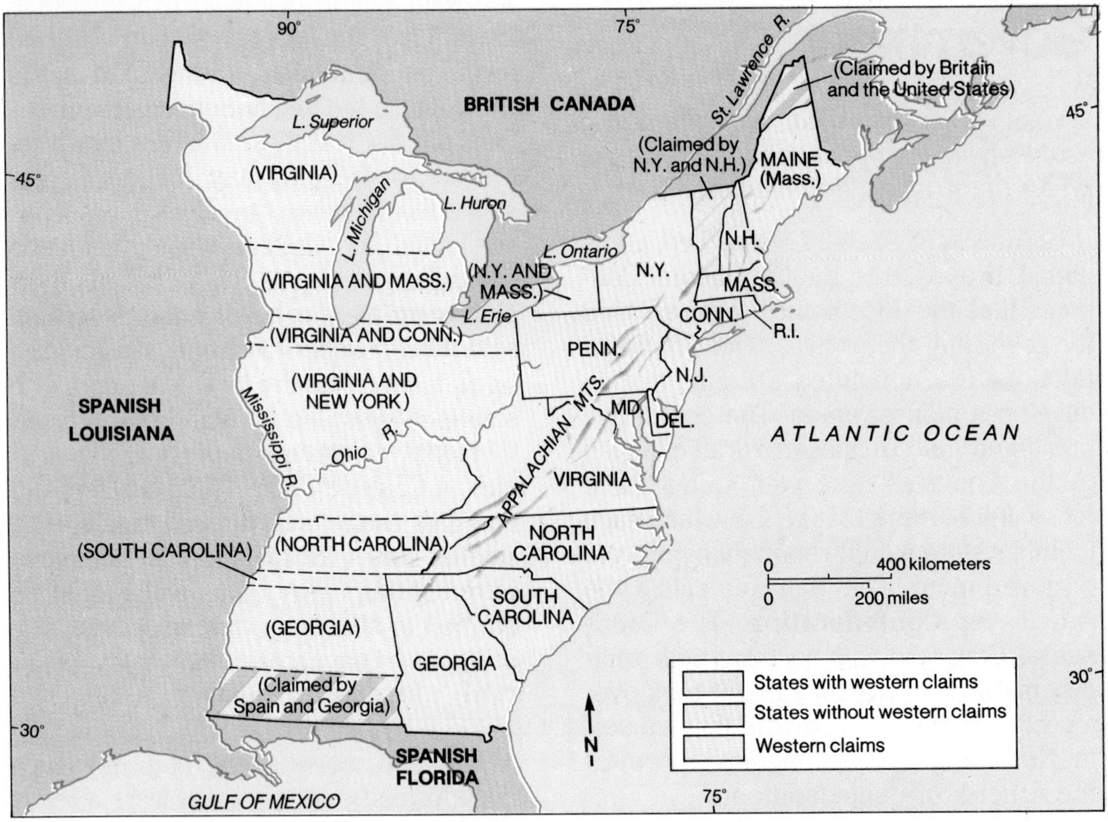

Which state had claims to the largest amount of land in the West?

The national government that the Articles of Confederation created was not at all like the one we have today. What the Articles created was a "League of Friendship." All 13 states remained free to act like independent nations. The new national government, the Confederation, existed only to help, not to rule them.

Americans distrusted power and authority because of their experience with Great Britain. Americans wanted a weak national government. This is what the Articles of Confederation created.

The Articles of Confederation

The national government under the Articles of Confederation was made up of one lawmaking, or **legislative**, group. This group was the Congress.

---

legislative having to do with the making of laws

All states were to have equal representation in Congress. Each state had the

Discuss: Do you think each state should have equal representation in Congress regardless of its size? Explain your answer.

Background: Congress tried to amend the Articles of Confederation to allow the national government to place a 5 percent tax on all imports. Amending the Articles, however, required unanimous consent of the states, and Rhode Island refused to ratify the amendment.

same single vote in Congress regardless of its size or population. The larger states were bitter about this arrangement. To the larger states, the Articles gave the smaller states more influence in government than they deserved. But to the smaller states, the Articles protected them from being dominated by the larger states.

The Articles of Confederation gave Congress very little power. Congress could only propose laws. All legislation had to be approved by nine of the 13 states before it became law.

The Articles of Confederation denied Congress two other important powers. First, Congress had no power to tax. Taxes are the principle means by which governments raise money to run themselves. If the Confederation government needed money, it had to request it from the states. In most cases, the states refused to send any money. As a result, the Confederation government could not pay its officials and its diplomats, or maintain its army and navy. It could not repay its war debts to France or to its own citizens.

Congress also had no power to regulate commerce or trade. It had no control over trade among the states or with foreign nations. Each state set up its own rules and regulations regarding trade and commerce. It could place a **tariff**, or tax on any goods coming into the state, either from abroad or from other states.

---

tariff a tax imposed by a government on imported goods

Problems quickly developed. Some states tried to cripple the trade of other states through the use of tariffs. The Confederation government was powerless to do anything.

Evaluating the Confederation Government

By 1787, Americans felt that government under the Articles of Confederation was a failure. In many respects, the government was too weak to run the nation effectively. The government was able to handle some of the young nation's problems very well. With most problems, however, its weakness led to failure.

One such problem arose with Spain. In the 1780's, Spain still had an empire in North America. Spain controlled the Mississippi River and the land west of the river, called the Louisiana Territory.

After the War for Independence, thousands of Americans moved onto lands west of the Appalachian Mountains and south of the Ohio River. This area eventually became Kentucky and Tennessee. Spain was alarmed. It refused to recognize any American claims to land between the Ohio River and Florida. Spain feared that the Americans would cross the Mississippi and try to settle the Spanish territory.

To prevent this Spain put pressure on the American settlers. In 1784, Spain closed the Mississippi River to American shipping. This was disastrous to the growing western settlements. The settlers' major trade route with the rest of the nation and the world was closed. Spain hoped this action would make the settlers ally themselves with the Spanish. Instead, western settlers turned to the Confederation government to help them.

The Confederation tried to end the

Background: On June 21, 1779, Spain had declared war on Great Britain, but refused to recognize American independence. The Spanish government was fearful that an independent United States would threaten its American possessions.

For Extra Interest: Have students calculate the distance from Louisville to Philadelphia. Compare this to the distance between these cities via the Mississippi River. Ask students why they think western farmers preferred to ship their goods by the water route rather than the more direct land route.

crisis by negotiating a treaty with Spain in 1786. Southern states rejected it, however, because it did not provide for free navigation of the Mississippi. The treaty was never ratified. A major weakness of the Confederation showed itself.

A similar problem developed with Great Britain. The Treaty of Paris called for all British troops to leave American soil. Troops in the eastern United States left, but in the west they refused. British troops still occupied a chain of forts and fur-trading posts along the Great Lakes. All were in American territory.

The Confederation demanded that the posts be evacuated. Great Britain refused to do so until Americans had paid off debts owed to British banks and merchants. These debts had existed before the Revolution began. In fact, some Americans supported the Revolution in the hope that an American victory would cancel their debts. The Confederation was unable to make its citizens pay back their debts to Britain. The government could not force the British out.

The Confederation's one success was in organizing the western lands. The Treaty of Paris had given the United States a huge region called the Northwest Territory. The Northwest Territory was bounded by the Mississippi River, the Great Lakes, and the Ohio River.

Congress had to find a way to organize the Northwest Territory for settlement. More was involved than just permitting settlers to move in. Congress needed a policy for selling land and for setting up governments. Congress also had to determine whether new states formed out of the territory would be equal to the original states. Laws, or **ordinances**, were passed by Congress in 1784, 1785, and 1787 to deal with these matters.

---

ordinance a rule or law of government

The Land Ordinances

In 1784, Thomas Jefferson drafted the first plan for organizing the western lands. His plan specified that new states would be established from the Northwest Territory. However, the exact number of new states to be formed out of the Northwest Territory was not specified. The Land Ordinance of 1784 also declared that all the new states were to be absolutely equal with the 13 original states.

In 1785, Congress came up with a plan for dividing the land of the Northwest Territory. The Northwest Territory would be divided into squares, called townships. Each township would be a 9.6 kilometer (6 mile) square. The township would then

Diagram of a Township

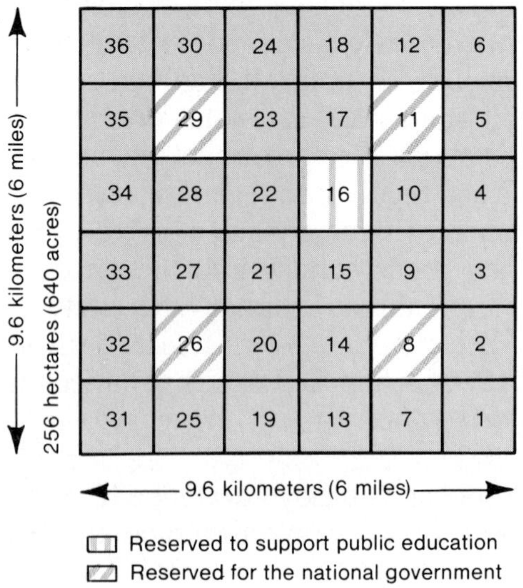

Discuss: Why do you think Americans would have been reluctant to move into the Northwest Territory if they were not assured that the states to be created there would have equal status with the other 13 states?

be subdivided into 36 sections, each consisting of about 256 hectares (640 acres) of land. Four of the 36 sections were reserved for the national government. One section near the center of the township, section 16, was set aside to support public education. The land was to be used as a site for a school. All other sections were to be sold at an auction for no less than $1 per .4 hectare (one acre). The minimum amount of land that a person could buy was one section. All money received from the sale of the land would go to the national government.

The Land Ordinance was supposed to help small farmers settle in the Northwest. However, very few had the $640 needed to buy a section. The Land Ordinance favored wealthy investors. Most of the Northwest Territory was purchased by these investors. They, in turn, resold the land in smaller parcels to small farmers, making a handsome profit on the deal.

The Northwest Ordinance

The Northwest Ordinance created a system of government and the means for making states out of the Northwest Territory. Congress appointed one governor and three judges to preside over the territory. When a part of the territory's population reached 5,000 adult males, a legislature could be established. A delegate could also be sent to Congress, but this delegate could not vote. When a part of the territory's population reached 60,000, the area would be admitted as a state. Congress said that no less than three and no more than five states could be created from the Northwest Territory. Eventually, five states were formed: Ohio, Indiana, Illinois, Michigan, and Wisconsin.

The Northwest Ordinance also included a **bill of rights**. This was a legal document that outlined the rights of all citizens. All citizens of the Northwest Territory were guaranteed freedom of religion, freedom of speech, freedom of the press, and the right to a trial before a jury. In addition, the ordinance stated that the Indians of the Northwest Territory would be treated with fairness. Their lands were not to be taken from them without their consent. Finally, slavery was prohibited north of the Ohio River.

bill of rights a legal document outlining the rights and privileges of citizens that are to be protected by law

Debts and Daniel Shays

The Confederation was successful in dealing with some problems. But more often than not, it was too weak to govern effectively. Its weakness became all too clear in its failure to maintain peace and order within the nation.

The War for Independence had damaged America's economy. In the South, crops such as rice and tobacco were destroyed during the war. After the war, business activity in New England suffered badly. Merchants lost many of their trading partners in the British West Indies. Farmers also lost many of their markets. Many people were out of work. Money was in short supply. But the most severe problem seemed to be with debts. Many people had borrowed money to buy land, farms, and houses. During these hard

Discuss: Why do you think Congress said that at least three and no more than five states could be created in the Northwest Territory?

Background: Following the War for Independence, both Britain and France restricted American trade with their colonies. The British West Indies had been a prime market for surplus goods from America. After the war, this market was closed to American trade.

On August 31, 1786, armed men in Massachusetts kept their land from being seized by preventing the court from holding session.

times, people who had loaned them the money demanded repayment. Those in debt were unable to pay. State governments raised taxes, which the debt-ridden farmers were unable to pay. Soon, those who could not pay their loans or taxes had their property seized and were jailed.

Riots began to break out. Groups of angry farmers tried to prevent the collection of debts and the seizure of property. In Massachusetts, the farmers were led by Daniel Shays, a former captain in the Continental army. Shays and his 1,500 followers interrupted court sessions to prevent debt collection. They broke into jails filled with debtors and freed the prisoners. The governor of Massachusetts called out the state militia, which sent the farmers running. Shays and some of his followers fled to Vermont.

People called the events in Massachusetts "Shays' Rebellion." Some charged that "Liberty had run mad." What they meant was that the nation under the Articles of Confederation was weak, and people were taking advantage of it. Many feared that mobs would next try to take over state governments.

Shays' actions had shown that the Confederation was too weak to maintain order. The only way to give the national government more authority was to change the Articles of Confederation.

Section Review

1. What were the major problems facing the national government under the Articles of Confederation?
2. Define ratify and bill of rights.
3. How did the Land Ordinance of 1785 work against small farmers?
4. How did a territory become a state under the Northwest Ordinance? Which states were formed under these terms?
5. Why is it important for the federal government to have the power to regulate trade among the states?

Discuss: Samuel Adams, a former revolutionary leader himself, demanded the death penalty for Shays' followers. Why do you think he called for such a harsh penalty for Shays and his followers when they were acting in the same way Adams had urged people to act during the revolution?

Discuss: What is the danger in having a national government that is too weak? What is the danger in having a national government that is too strong?

2. Creating the Constitution

BEFORE YOU READ: *What compromises were made in creating the Constitution?*

By the middle of the 1780's, Americans were seriously discussing whether to modify or discard the Articles of Confederation. Many citizens believed that Americans' liberties could only be protected by a strong national government. Other Americans felt that weak government would be less able to take away the liberties of the American people.

Both groups wanted the type of government that would best protect liberty and maintain order in society. Each had a different view as to what that government should be like.

James Madison

Calls for a Convention

The movement to create a new government began in an unlikely way. An agreement over oysters set the movement in motion.

The richest oyster beds in the United States were found in the Chesapeake Bay. Both Maryland and Virginia bordered on the Chesapeake Bay. Both claimed the right to harvest oysters there. The disagreement between the two states became bitter. A national court could have easily solved this disagreement. But the Confederation government had no court system. Maryland and Virginia finally took it upon themselves to solve the issue. Representatives of both states met in Alexandria, Virginia, in 1785. They worked out a peaceful agreement regarding the use of the Chesapeake Bay and the Potomac River.

Attending the meeting in Alexandria was James Madison of Virginia. Madison pointed out to those at the meeting that the Confederation was ineffective. It could not solve easy problems like a debate over an oyster bed. Nor could it solve difficult problems like trade among the states. Madison suggested that all the states meet to solve the major problems facing the nation.

One person who strongly agreed with Madison was Alexander Hamilton. Hamilton, who served as Washington's aide during the American Revolution, was a young New York lawyer. At a meeting in Virginia in 1786, he and Madison suggested that all 13 states meet to alter the Articles of Confederation. Their suggestion was quickly accepted. A call was issued for delegates from all states to meet in Philadelphia the following spring.

For Extra Interest: Show students a large-scale map of the Chesapeake Bay area. Compare the area shown on the large-scale map to the same area on a small-scale map. Ask students when it would be most useful to use each map.

The Constitutional Convention was held in the State House in Philadelphia beginning in May 1787.

The Philadelphia Convention

In May 1787, the Convention assembled at the State House in Philadelphia. All states except Rhode Island sent a delegation. In all, 55 delegates gathered in the city of Philadelphia.

The delegates to the Convention were an able group. They were fairly young, averaging about 40 years of age. They were well educated. Many were lawyers. Most were war veterans or leaders in the cause of American independence. All were experts on governmental matters, since they had gained much experience during the Revolution.

Perhaps the two most important delegates were George Washington and James Madison. Washington had been hesitant to come to the Convention at first. But Madison convinced him that his presence would show the nation that he approved of the Convention and its task. Washington was selected as the Convention's president.

James Madison is often called the "Father of the Constitution." He played a key role in calling for the Convention. His quick mind grasped the troublesome issues the delegates faced. Madison took a leading role in the debates. He also took careful notes of the proceedings. His journal provides the most complete record of activities at the Convention.

The delegates decided that the Convention would be held in secret. The public would not be told anything until the Convention was over. Such secrecy would permit the delegates to speak their minds freely and openly. They could

Background: James Madison, at 26, was one of the youngest delegates to the Constitutional Convention. He prepared for the Convention by buying and studying more than 200 books on history and government.

Background: Benjamin Franklin, a delegate to the Convention from Pennsylvania, has often been called the "Peacemaker of the Convention." Whenever tempers rose during a discussion, Franklin's well-chosen words often helped to calm the other delegates.

change their position if they wished. No one would have to worry about criticism in the newspapers or the pressure of public opinion.

Conflicting Plans

Every delegate at the Convention had the same goal—to create a stronger national government. Early in their deliberations, the delegates agreed to abandon the Articles of Confederation. An entirely new plan of government would be created. For nearly four months, from May to September 1787, the delegates discussed what form the new government would take.

James Madison drafted a plan called the "Virginia Plan." It recommended a government made up of three branches. One branch would be the **executive**, or law-enforcing, branch of government. Another branch would be the **judicial**, or law-examining, branch of government. The third branch would be the legislative, or lawmaking, branch.

---

executive having the authority to enforce laws and administer government affairs

judicial having the authority to examine the laws of a government

---

The Virginia Plan also contained a proposal for determining representation in Congress, the legislative branch of government. Each state would be represented in Congress according to its population. Larger states would be permitted more representatives in Congress. The Virginia Plan clearly favored the larger, more populous states.

The smaller states would not accept the Virginia Plan. They feared that Congress would be dominated by the larger states. For example, the largest state, Virginia, would have about ten times more representatives than the smallest state, Delaware.

New Jersey proposed a different plan. The "New Jersey Plan" called for equal representation in Congress for all states, regardless of population size. This plan was supported by the smaller states. Now the larger states were dissatisfied. They believed that the smaller states would have more influence in government than their size justified.

Day after day the delegates argued over the two plans. The debates were so fierce that many feared the Convention would break up in failure. Finally, in mid-July, Oliver Ellsworth and Roger Sherman of Connecticut introduced an acceptable **compromise**, or plan in which both sides gave up something. It has become known as the "Connecticut Plan," or the "Great Compromise."

---

compromise a settlement in which each side gives up some demands

---

The Great Compromise called for a Congress made up of two houses. One house would be called the Senate. The other house would be called the House of Representatives. Each state would have two senators in the Senate. Equal representation would favor the smaller states. In the House of Representatives, the number of representatives from each state would be based on population. This would favor the larger, more populous states. Both sides were satisfied by this.

For Extra Interest: The Constitution guarantees each state at least one representative in the House of Representatives regardless of population. Have students find out which states today are entitled to send only one representative to the House.

Discuss: How could a nation founded on the concept of liberty and the equality of its citizens accept the institution of slavery?

Compromises Over Slavery

Another problem developed centering on how slaves would be counted in the population. Northerners felt that slaves should be counted in the population of a state when determining that state's share of federal taxes. The federal tax that a state had to pay was based on the size of a state's population. Naturally, southerners did not agree with this. Southerners wanted slaves counted in the population only when determining the number of representatives a state would send to the House. In this way, the South's slaves would give them more members in Congress. The North rejected this idea.

This problem was resolved by another compromise. It was called the "Three-Fifths Compromise." Each slave would be counted as three-fifths of a person for *both* taxation and representation.

The Three-Fifths Compromise still left the delegates with the question of what to do about slavery in America. Most Americans did not think slavery was wrong, although some people were opposed to it.

Most Americans, whether they supported or opposed it, believed slavery would die out. Slavery by the 1780's existed primarily in the South. The delegates agreed that slavery should not be tampered with where it already existed.

The delegates had to deal with one final slavery issue. This was the African slave trade. Delegates who wished to see slavery end wanted to put a halt to the slave trade. This would prevent new slaves from entering the country. The slave-owning states would not hear of this. To win southern support for the Constitution, another compromise was reached. The African slave trade could continue for 20 more years, until 1808. Congress would then decide its fate.

The Constitution is Ready

By mid-September 1787, all issues had been resolved, and the Constitution was ready for signing. The document turned out to be a series of compromises. It did not entirely satisfy any of the delegates. But the majority, 39 in all, signed it.

The work of the Convention was finally over. The Constitution was submitted to Congress for approval. Congress, in turn, sent it to the individual states. According to Article VII of the Constitution, nine of the 13 states needed to ratify it before the Constitution went into effect; and then only in the states that had ratified it.

Section Review

1. What compromises were made in creating the Constitution?
2. Describe the Virginia Plan. Which compromise solved the problem between the large states and the small states?
3. Explain the Three-Fifths Compromise.
4. Why is compromise necessary in the work of politicians and government officials?

Background: Benjamin Franklin expressed the general attitude of the delegates on the completed Constitution when he said, "There are several parts of the Constitution which I do not presently approve, but I am not sure that I shall never approve them."

Vocabulary Help: Have students look up the word "preamble" in the dictionary. Ask them how the origin of the word compares to its definition. Review with the class how the structure of a word may give a clue to its meaning.

3. The Organization of Government

BEFORE YOU READ: *What powers does the Constitution give to each branch of the national government?*

The Constitution

The Constitution defines the roles and responsibilities of citizens, the states, and the national government. The Constitution has survived for nearly 200 years because it is flexible. It was written in a way that enables it to bend with the times. It guides us today and helps us to preserve our democratic way of life.

The Constitution of the United States begins with a preamble, or introductory statement. The preamble explains why the Constitution was written. The preamble also stresses that the government is based upon the will of the people.

The preamble is followed by seven articles. The articles explain the relationship between the states and the national government. They also describe the structure of the national government.

Relations with the States

The Constitution created a **federal system**. Government in our nation exists at both the national level and state level. Power is divided between the national and state governments.

federal system a system of government that divides power between the national government and individual states

The Constitution and all laws and treaties made under it were to be the "supreme law" of the land. Broad powers were granted to the federal government. Only the federal government can make treaties with foreign governments, coin money, and place tariffs on imports.

The Constitution gives some powers to both the states and the federal government. These are called "shared powers." Both the states and the federal government can levy taxes. Each has its own court system. State courts deal with violations of the laws of that particular state. The federal courts deal with disputes between states and violations of federal law. Federal laws are those passed by the United States Congress.

The Constitution does not specifically outline the powers granted to the states alone. Instead, the Tenth Amendment to the Constitution says that powers not given to the federal government are reserved for the states. One such power is the power to manage education.

Separation of Powers

The first three articles of the Constitution describe the structure of the national government. These articles also clearly define the powers of the three branches of government.

The legislative branch, or Congress, makes the nation's laws. It is composed of the Senate and the House of Representatives. Senators are elected for six-year terms. Representatives are elected for two-year terms. Congress is provided with specific powers. Congress has the power to tax and collect taxes. It has the power to declare war. Congress can

Background: Article 6 makes the Constitution the supreme law of the United States.

For Extra Interest: A complete list of the powers of Congress can be found in Article 1, Section 8 of the Constitution. Have students locate the clause in this section that gives Congress the power to adopt the metric system as the system of weights and measures for the United States.

establish post offices, coin money, and regulate trade. The House is responsible for originating all laws that raise revenue, or income, for the government. The Senate has the responsibility of approving treaties made with foreign governments. Those who wrote the Constitution were careful to ensure that Congress can expand its powers to meet new needs. Section 8, clause 18, of Article I is often referred to as the elastic clause. The elastic clause gives Congress the power "to make all laws which shall be necessary and proper for carrying into execution the foregoing powers."

The executive branch consists of the offices of President and Vice-President. Both are elected for a four-year term. The executive branch also includes all officials and advisers who assist the President in executing the duties of the office.

The President is commander in chief of the nation's armed forces. The President also conducts foreign affairs. The President may **veto**, or refuse to approve, all laws of Congress. The President executes or enforces federal law. Finally, the President appoints all federal judges, ambassadors, and other important officials within the government.

veto refuse to approve

The Vice-President presides over the Senate. Besides this, the office is given no other specific power. The Vice-President often serves as an adviser to the President. If the President dies while in office, the Vice-President becomes President.

The judicial branch, or the Supreme Court and other federal courts, hears cases that involve the Constitution and national laws. The judicial branch handles disputes between states and lawsuits involving foreign citizens. Justices of the Supreme Court hold office for life.

The Constitution did not give total power to just one branch of government. Power is divided among all three branches. This prevents one branch from becoming stronger than the others. A balance was created among the legislative, executive, and judicial branches by separating their powers.

Checks and Balances

The Constitution also created a system by which each branch of government could limit the powers of the other two branches. This was done to prevent one branch from becoming too powerful. Each branch was given certain powers that enabled it to "check" every other branch.

The President, for example, can check Congress by vetoing, or refusing to sign, bills passed by both houses. The President can check the Supreme Court through the power to appoint its members. As a check upon the President's powers, only Congress may declare war, and only the Senate may ratify a treaty. Congress can check the Supreme Court through its power to approve all judicial appointments made by the President. The Supreme Court can check the other branches. It determines whether the laws passed by Congress are in agreement with the Constitution. The Supreme Court also decides whether the policies of the executive branch are in accordance with the Constitution.

Discuss: Why do you think that all elected officials in the federal government (senators, representatives, the President, and the Vice-President) do not serve for equal periods of time? What is the benefit of having different officials elected at different times?

Discuss: Do you think it is easy or difficult to amend the Constitution? Explain your answer.

Checks and Balances

Checks on the Congress	Checks on the President	Checks on the Supreme Court

• President can veto laws. • Supreme Court can declare laws unconstitutional.	• Congress can override a veto by a two-thirds vote. • Congress can impeach and remove a President from office. • Congress can refuse to approve presidential appointees or treaties.	• Justices are appointed by the President. • Congress can impeach and remove a Justice from office. • Congress can amend the Constitution if the Justices rule a law unconstitutional.

Changing the Constitution

The writers of the Constitution felt that the document had to be flexible. It had to be able to change as times and the nation changed. Therefore, Article V provides a means for changing, or **amending**, the Constitution.

---

amend to change or add to

There are two ways in which an amendment can be added to the Constitution. First, Congress can propose an amendment by a two-thirds vote. Then Congress sends the proposed amendment to the states, which may accept or reject it. If three-fourths of the states accept it, the amendment becomes part of the Constitution.

The second way to amend the Constitution begins with the states. If two-thirds of the states call for a convention to propose an amendment, Congress must honor their wishes.

The Bill of Rights

Many states criticized the Constitution because it did not contain laws that protected important rights. The states wanted guarantees of certain freedoms and the protection of certain rights to be written into the Constitution.

The first ten amendments to the Constitution are called the Bill of Rights. The Bill of Rights forbids the federal government from interfering with freedom of religion, freedom of speech, and freedom of the press, plus some other freedoms. It guarantees citizens a trial by jury. It forbids cruel punishment imposed by a court for crimes committed. These are rights and freedoms that the government

Background: George Mason of Virginia had proposed adding a bill of rights to the Constitution just before it was signed in September 1787. The surprised and weary delegates rejected the idea at the time.

For Extra Interest: Have each student write a letter to the editor of a newspaper in 1787 expressing either Federalist or Anti-Federalist views about the Constitution.

can never take away from the people.

The Bill of Rights was added to the original Constitution during the first session of Congress in 1791. These rights are so important that the first ten amendments are often viewed as part of the original constitution.

Federalists and Anti-Federalists

When the time came to ratify the Constitution, Americans were divided. Those who supported the Constitution called themselves Federalists. They approved of a strong national, or federal, government. Those who opposed the Constitution were called Anti-Federalists. They believed in a weaker national government, like the Confederation. The Anti-Federalists believed the Constitution would take too much power from the people and the states. Both the Federalists and the Anti-Federalists were patriotic. Each group had the welfare of the nation at heart. The key difference between them was their position on adopting the Constitution.

Alexander Hamilton

The Federalists had the support of seven states. The approval of Delaware, Pennsylvania, New Jersey, Georgia, Connecticut, Maryland, and South Carolina was never in doubt. The new government was only two states short of being accepted. The Federalists were confident they could win two of the six remaining states.

The Anti-Federalists mounted a strong effort in three key states—New York, Virginia, and Massachusetts. The debate in the key states took place in newspapers, pamphlets, and at the state conventions. If either New York, Virginia, or Massachusetts rejected the Constitution, it was doubtful that the new government would be accepted. If they all rejected it, the new government was doomed for sure.

The Federalists set to work trying to win ratification in the key states. James Madison, Alexander Hamilton, and John Jay concentrated their efforts in New York. They wrote a series of brilliant essays for the state's newspapers. The three men carefully explained all aspects of the Constitution. They stressed the weaknesses of the Confederation and the need for a strong national government to pre-

Discuss: Why would the new government probably have failed if it had not been approved by Massachusetts, New York, and Virginia?

For Extra Interest: Have students design posters commemorating the 200th anniversary of the ratification of the Constitution in 1788.

serve order and harmony within the country. The essays were eventually collected and published as a book called *The Federalist*.

Ratifying the Constitution

In February 1788, Massachusetts was the first key state to ratify the Constitution. The margin of victory was slim: 187 in favor and 168 opposed. Like many states, Massachusetts criticized the Constitution because it lacked a bill of rights. Only when Massachusetts Federalists promised they would seek a bill of rights for the Constitution was it approved. By May 1788, Maryland and South Carolina had met and ratified the Constitution. In June, New Hampshire became the ninth state to ratify it. The new government now would go into effect in nine of the thirteen states.

New York and Virginia were still undecided. In both states, opposition to the Constitution was very strong. Like Massachusetts, Virginia would not ratify unless a bill of rights was added to the Constitution. When this had been agreed to by Virginia Federalists, Virginia ratified the Constitution on June 25, 1788. The next month, New York ratified the Constitution by a margin of just three votes. The victory in New York was the result of public pressure to follow Virginia's lead.

Two states still remained opposed, Rhode Island and North Carolina. Both states had voted against the Constitution. They did not join the Union until after the new government was in operation. They realized they could not exist as independent nations.

What was there about the Constitution that made the nation support it? First, the Constitution created a strong and stable government for the nation. Enough Americans realized this to make it the law of the land. Second, it guaranteed Americans' basic liberties through the addition of the Bill of Rights. In addition, the Constitution protected and strengthened the nation's business system. It created a sound government that would honor its financial obligations, support economic development, and provide for a stable economy. The most respected man of his generation, George Washington, supported it. But above all, the Constitution met the needs of the American people.

Section Review

1. What powers does the Constitution give to each branch of the national government?
2. Define federal system, veto, and amend.
3. What is the system of checks and balances? Name two checks upon the President's powers.
4. Which rights guaranteed in the Bill of Rights do you consider most important? Why?

Reading an Organizational Chart

The Constitution gives state governments certain powers and the federal government certain powers. It also gives some powers to both the states and the federal government. The chart below shows the division of some of these important powers.

Charts give a great deal of information in a brief form. They make information available without a long written description. When information is presented in a chart, it is shortened for easier reference. To read the chart below, follow these steps:

1. Study the title of the chart.
2. Look at the heading above each column.
3. Read down the column.

By looking at this chart, you can see at a glance those powers given to and shared by the federal and state governments.

DIVISION OF POWERS

POWERS GIVEN TO THE FEDERAL GOVERNMENT	SHARED POWERS	POWERS GIVEN TO THE STATE GOVERNMENTS
regulate interstate and foreign trade	tax	regulate voting
declare war	borrow money	maintain a system of public education
coin money	build roads	establish marriage and divorce laws
control the postal system	charter banks	establish traffic laws
establish and support the armed forces	establish courts	regulate trade within the state

1. What is the advantage of using a chart to get information? What disadvantages might there be in using a chart?
2. Name three powers shared by the state and federal governments.
3. Which government(s) has (have) the power to regulate foreign trade?
4. Which government(s) has (have) the power to set up schools?

The Constitution of the United States

(Portions of the text within brackets have been changed by amendment or are no longer in effect. The text of the Constitution appears in black; explanations appear in blue.)

Preamble

We, the people of the United States, in order to form a more perfect Union, establish justice, insure domestic tranquility, provide for the common defense, promote the general welfare, and secure the blessings of liberty to ourselves and our posterity, do ordain and establish this Constitution for the United States of America.

The Preamble. The opening is called the *Preamble.* It states the purpose of the Constitution. Note that it begins, "We, the people," not "We, the states. . . ."

Article 1. The Legislative Branch

Section 1. Congress

All legislative powers herein granted shall be vested in a Congress of the United States, which shall consist of a Senate and House of Representatives.

Section 1. This section states how Congress shall be organized and that it will have the power to make all federal laws. This clause has been modified in practice so that regulations made by certain federal agencies can function as federal laws.

Section 2. House of Representatives

1. Election and Term of Members. The House of Representatives shall be composed of members chosen every second year by the people of the several states, and the electors in each state shall have the qualifications requisite for electors of the most numerous branch of the state legislature.

Clause 1. Members of the House serve two-year terms. The term *electors* refers to voters.

2. Qualifications. No person shall be a Representative who shall not have attained to the age of twenty-five years, and been seven years a citizen of the United States, and who shall not, when elected, be an inhabitant of that state in which he shall be chosen.

Clause 2. A representative must be at least 25 years old, must have been a United States citizen for at least 7 years, and must be a resident of the state from which he or she is elected. The states are divided into congressional districts, each of which elects a representative.

3. Apportionment of Representatives. Representatives [and direct taxes] shall be apportioned among the several states which may be included within this Union, according to their

Clause 3. The number of members in the House of Representatives was to be determined by the number of "free persons" in each state, plus "three-fifths of all other persons." This meant that states could count only three-fifths of their respective numbers [which shall be determined by adding to the whole number of free persons, including those bound to service for a term of years, and excluding Indians not taxed, three fifths of all other persons]. The actual enumeration shall be made within three years after the first meeting of the Congress of the United States, and within every subsequent term of ten years, in such manner as they shall by law direct. The number of Representatives shall not exceed 1 for every 30,000, but each state shall have at least 1 Representative; [and until such enumeration shall be made, the state of New Hampshire shall be entitled to choose 3; Massachusetts, 8; Rhode Island and Providence Plantations, 1; Connecticut, 5; New York, 6; New Jersey, 4; Pennsylvania, 8; Delaware, 1; Maryland, 6; Virginia, 10; North Carolina, 5; South Carolina, 5; and Georgia, 3].

Black slaves. This provision was overruled by the 13th Amendment (1865) and Section 2 of the 14th Amendment (1868).

Because representation is based on population, the Constitution provides for a national head count, or census, every ten years. The United States was the first nation to conduct a regular census. Every representative represents at least 30,000 people, but each state is entitled to at least one representative. In 1929, in order to prevent the House of Representatives from growing too large, Congress limited the membership of the House to 435.

4. Vacancies. When vacancies happen in the representation from any state, the executive authority thereof shall issue writs of election to fill such vacancies.

Clause 4. If a member of the House of Representatives dies or resigns, the governor of the state orders a special election to fill the vacant seat.

5. Impeachment. The House of Representatives shall choose their Speaker and other officers; and shall have the sole power of impeachment.

Clause 5. By majority vote, the House can impeach, or accuse, officers of the executive branch or federal judges. The Senate tries all impeachment cases.

Section 3. Senate

1. Number of Members and Terms of Office. The Senate of the United States shall be composed of two Senators from each state [chosen by the legislatures thereof], for six years, and each Senator shall have one vote.

Clause 1. Each state legislature was to elect two members to the Senate. Senators represent states, not people. This system was changed by the 17th Amendment in 1913. Senators are now elected directly by the voters of each state.

2. Classification; Vacancies. [Immediately after they shall be assembled in consequence of the first election, they shall be divided as equally as may be into three classes. The seats of the Senators of the first class shall be vacated at the expiration of the second year, of the second class at the expiration of the fourth year, and of the third class at the expiration of the sixth year, so that one-third may be chosen every second year; and if vacancies happen by resignation, or otherwise, during the recess of the legislature of any state, the executive thereof may make temporary appointments until the next meeting of the legislature, which shall then fill such vacancies.]

Clause 2. Senators serve six-year terms. The paragraph defining "classes" of senators sets up a staggered system, whereby one third of the Senate comes up for reelection every two years. If a Senator resigns or dies, the 17th Amendment provides for the governor to call a special election to fill the vacancy or to appoint a temporary successor.

3. Qualifications. No person shall be a Senator who shall not have attained the age of thirty years, and been nine years a citizen of the United States, and who shall not, when elected, be an inhabitant of that state for which he shall be chosen.

4. The President of the Senate. The Vice-President of the United States shall be president of the Senate, but shall have no vote, unless they be equally divided.

Clauses 4 and 5. The Vice-President serves as the President of the Senate and votes only to break a tie. This is the only vice-presidential duty specified in the Constitution. If the Vice-President is absent or becomes President, the Senate elects a temporary president (pro tempore) to preside over its meetings.

5. Other Officers. The Senate shall choose their other officers, and also a president pro tempore, in the absence of the Vice-President, or when he shall exercise the office of the President of the United States.

6. Impeachments. The Senate shall have the sole power to try all impeachments. When sitting for that purpose, they shall be on oath or affirmation. When the President of the United States is tried, the Chief Justice shall preside; and no person shall be convicted without the concurrence of two-thirds of the members present.

Clauses 6 and 7. The trial of members of the executive or the judiciary accused by the House of Representatives is conducted by the Senate. A vote of two-thirds of the Senate is necessary for conviction. If convicted, the person is removed from office and is then subject to indictment and criminal proceedings according to the law. Andrew Johnson is the only President who was impeached (1868). He was not convicted. Conviction failed by one vote. Richard M. Nixon was the first President to resign from office. He did so in 1974, when the Judiciary Committee of the House of Representatives recommended that he be impeached. Following his resignation he was granted a presidential pardon, which spared him from possible prosecution.

7. Penalty for Conviction. Judgment in cases of impeachment shall not extend further than to removal from office, and disqualification to hold and enjoy any office of honor, trust, or profit under the United States; but the party convicted shall nevertheless be liable and subject to indictment, trial, judgment, and punishment, according to law.

Section 4. Elections and Meetings

1. Holding Elections. The times, places, and manner of holding elections for Senators and Representatives shall be prescribed in each state by the legislature thereof; but the Congress may at any time by law make or alter such regulations, except as to the places of choosing Senators.

Clause 1. The states set the conditions of congressional elections, determining who can vote. This was modified by the 15th Amendment (1870), which prevents the states from interfering with the right of Blacks to vote; the 19th Amendment (1920), which extends voting rights to women, the 24th Amendment (1964), which bans the poll tax as a condition for voting, and the 26th Amendment (1971), which lowers the voting age to 18.

2. Meetings. The Congress shall assemble at least once in every year, [and such meeting shall be on the first Monday in December,] unless they shall by law appoint a different day.

Clause 2. The date for Congress to assemble was changed by the 20th Amendment (1933). Congress now convenes on January 3.

Section 5. Procedure

1. Organization. Each house shall be the judge of the elections, returns, and qualifications of its own members, and a majority of each shall constitute a quorum to do business; but a smaller number may adjourn from day to day, and may be authorized to compel the attendance of absent members, in such manner, and under such penalties, as each house may provide.

Clause 1. Both houses have the right to refuse to seat members. A *quorum* is a majority of members of each house of Congress and is the minimum number required to be present to carry out business. In practice, however, business can be and often is transacted without a quorum as long as no member objects. Each house can compel the attendance of its members when their presence is needed.

2. Proceedings. Each house may determine the rules of its proceedings, punish its members for disorderly behavior, and with the concurrence of two-thirds, expel a member.

3. The Journal. Each house shall keep a journal of its proceedings, and from time to time publish the same, excepting such parts as may in their judgment require secrecy; and the yeas and nays of the members of either house on any question shall, at the desire of one-fifth of those present, be entered on the journal.

Clause 3. The framers of the Constitution wanted the voters to be kept informed of the activities of Congress. Such a record would also enable the people to find out how their representatives had voted on particular issues. Such openness in government was unknown in Europe at the time the Constitution was written. The *House Journal* and the *Senate Journal* are published at the end of each session of Congress. The *Congressional Record* is published for every day Congress is in session. It records the action of both houses.

4. Adjournment. Neither house, during the session of Congress, shall, without the consent of the other, adjourn for more than three days, nor to any other place than that in which the two houses shall be sitting.

Clause 4. Once Congress is in session, the House and the Senate must remain at work until both agree on a time to adjourn. Because they work together, they must both work in the same place.

Section 6. Privileges and Restrictions

1. Pay and Privileges. The Senators and Representatives shall receive a compensation for their services, to be ascertained by law and paid out of the Treasury of the United States. They shall in all cases, except treason, felony, and breach of the peace, be privileged from arrest during their attendance at the session of their respective houses, and in going to and returning from the same; and for any speech or debate in either house, they shall not be questioned in any other place.

Clause 1. This clause permits members to speak freely by providing *congressional immunity* from prosecution or arrest for things they say in speeches and debates in Congress. Members of Congress set their own pay.

2. Restrictions. No Senator or Representative shall, during the time for which he was elected, be appointed to any civil office under the authority of the United States, which shall have been created, or the emoluments whereof shall have been increased, during such time; and no

Clause 2. This clause underscores the principle of separation of powers. No member of Congress can hold any other government office. If Congress creates an office or raises the salary of an old one, no member of Congress may fill that office until his or her term expires. This provision was made to prevent the executive, or the President, from controlling Conperson holding any office under the United States shall be a member of either house during his continuance in office.

gress. In Britain in the 18th century, the king and his ministers controlled Parliament by promising offices as bribes.

Section 7. Passing Laws

1. Revenue Bills. All bills for raising revenue shall originate in the House of Representatives; but the Senate may propose or concur with amendments as on other bills.

Clause 1. Bills for raising money by taxes must be introduced in the House of Representatives. This was part of the compromise between the large states and the small states. The large states received proportional representation in one house, and that house was also given first authority over money and tax measures. This provision has little practical importance, however, because the Senate can amend such bills.

2. How a Bill Becomes a Law. Every bill which shall have passed the House of Representatives and the Senate shall, before it becomes a law, be presented to the President of the United States; if he approves, he shall sign it, but if not, he shall return it, with his objections, to that house in which it shall have originated, who shall enter the objections at large on their journal, and proceed to reconsider it. If after such reconsideration two-thirds of that house shall agree to pass the bill, it shall be sent, together with the objections, to the other house, by which it shall likewise be reconsidered and, if approved by two-thirds of that house, it shall become a law. But in all such cases the votes of both houses shall be determined by yeas and nays, and the names of the persons voting for and against the bill shall be entered on the journal of each house respectively. If any bill shall not be returned by the President within ten days (Sunday excepted) after it shall have been presented to him, the same bill shall be a law, in like manner as if he had signed it, unless the Congress by their adjournment prevent its return, in which case it shall not be a law.

Clause 2. Every bill that passes both houses of Congress is sent to the President. If the President approves the bill and signs it, it becomes law. The refusal to sign is called a *veto.* A vetoed bill is sent back to Congress with a written statement of the President's objections. If both houses can pass the bill by two thirds majority (usually very difficult to obtain), Congress can *override* the President's veto and the bill becomes law. If not, the veto is *sustained* and the bill dies. If the President receives a bill and keeps it ten days without acting on it, it automatically becomes law. If Congress adjourns within those ten days, the bill must be introduced again in the next congressional session. This is called a *pocket veto.*

The Presidential veto is an important check of the executive branch of the government on the legislative branch. Congress checks the President when it overrides a veto.

3. Presidential Approval or Veto. Every order, resolution, or vote to which the concurrence of the Senate and House of Representatives may be necessary (except on a question of adjournment) shall be presented to the President of the United States; and before the same shall take effect, shall be approved by him, or being disapproved by him, shall be repassed by two-thirds of the Senate and House of Representatives, according to the rules and limitations prescribed in the case of a bill.

Section 8. Powers Delegated to Congress

The Congress shall have power

Section 8. This section lists the 18 *delegated* or *enumerated* powers granted to Congress. The first 17 specify areas in which Congress has authority and are called *expressed* powers. The 18th power is the elastic clause. The doctrine of *implied* powers developed from this clause.

1. To lay and collect taxes, duties, imposts, and excises, to pay the debts and provide for the common defense and general welfare of the United States; but all duties, imposts, and excises shall be uniform through the United States;

Clause 1. Congress has the power to levy taxes to pay the nation's debts and to provide for national defense and for the general welfare of the people. All federal taxes must be the same throughout the country.

2. To borrow money on the credit of the United States;

Clause 2. The Constitution sets no limit on the amount Congress can borrow—Congress itself sets the national debt.

3. To regulate commerce with foreign nations, and among the several states, [and with the Indian tribes];

Clause 3. Congress has the power to regulate trade with foreign nations. It also has direct control over interstate commerce. This phrase is so broad that it permits Congress to regulate transportation, the stock market, and the broadcasting industry.

4. To establish a uniform rule of naturalization, and uniform laws on the subject of bankruptcies throughout the United States;

Clause 4. Congress can decide how immigrants may become citizens. It can also make laws about procedures involved in business failures.

5. To coin money, regulate the value thereof, and of foreign coin, and fix the standard of weights and measures;

Clause 5. Congress can mint coins, print paper money, and set the value of both American money and foreign currency within this country. It can also set standard measurements for the nation.

6. To provide for the punishment of counterfeiting the securities and current coin of the United States.

Clause 6. Congress can make laws fixing the punishment for counterfeiting currency, bonds, or stamps.

7. To establish post offices and post roads;

Clause 7. Congress can designate which highways should be used to transport mail.

8. To promote the progress of science and useful arts by securing for limited times to authors and inventors the exclusive right to their respective writings and discoveries;

Clause 8. Congress can pass patent and copyright laws to give to inventors and artists sole rights to their works for a number of years. Anyone who uses patented inventions or copyrighted material without permission may be punished.

9. To constitute tribunals inferior to the Supreme Court;

Clause 9. All federal courts except the Supreme Court are established by acts of Congress.

10. To define and punish piracies and felonies committed on the high seas and offenses against the law of nations;

Clause 10. Congress can decide what acts committed on American ships are crimes and how such acts should be punished. It can also decide how American citizens who break international laws shall be punished.

11. To declare war, [grant letters of marque and reprisal,] and make rules concerning captures on land and water;

Clause 11. Only Congress may declare war. However, American forces have engaged in combat in some instances without congressional declarations of war—for example, in Korea and Vietnam. *Letters of marque and reprisal* refer to permission granted to American merchant ships to attack enemy ships, a practice common in early wars. This practice has been outlawed by international agreement.

12. To raise and support armies, but no appropriation of money to that use shall be for a longer term than two years;

Clause 12. All money for the army comes from Congress. However, Congress may not grant such money for longer than a two-year period. This is to make sure that civilians exercise financial control over the army.

13. To provide and maintain a navy;

Clause 13. There is no two-year limit on naval appropriations because the navy was not considered a threat to liberty.

14. To make rules for the government and regulation of the land and naval forces;

Clause 14. Because Congress can create the armed forces, it has power to make rules for the services. Such rules now include the air force.

15. To provide for calling forth the militia to execute the laws of the Union, suppress insurrections, and repel invasions;

Clause 15. Congress can call into federal service the state militia forces (citizen-soldiers now referred to as the National Guard) to enforce federal laws and defend life and property. Congress can empower the President to call out the militia, but only for the reasons named here.

16. To provide for organizing, arming, and disciplining the militia, and for governing such part of them as may be employed in the service of the United States, reserving to the states, respectively, the appointment of the officers, and the authority of training the militia according to the discipline prescribed by Congress;

Clause 16. The states may appoint officers for the militia, but Congress establishes rules for training the militia.

17. To exercise exclusive legislation in all cases whatsoever, over such district (not exceeding ten miles square) as may, by cession of particular states, and the acceptance of Congress, become the seat of government of the United States, and to exercise like authority over all places purchased by the consent of the legislature of the state in which the same shall be, for the erection of forts, magazines, arsenals, dockyards, and other needful buildings;—and

Clause 17. Congress has control over the District of Columbia as well as all forts, arsenals, dockyards, federal courthouses, and other places owned and operated by the federal government.

18. To make all laws which shall be necessary and proper for carrying into execution the foregoing powers, and all other powers vested by this Constitution in the government of the United States, or in any department or officer thereof.

Clause 18. The framers were very careful to ensure that Congress would be able to meet the needs of a changing society. Sometimes called the elastic clause of the Constitution, this clause enables Congress to frame laws that are related to specific powers listed in the Constitution. For instance, as part of its power "to raise and support armies,"

Congress can undertake the construction of roads. Such roads are "necessary and proper" for transporting, or maintaining, an army.

This elastic clause has enabled Congress to meet the changing needs of society over two centuries. The power that has become the most expandable is the power to regulate interstate trade and commerce. In the 20th century, Congress has used this power to pass Civil Rights Acts (protecting the free movement of people and trade) and labor legislation that guards the right of unions to organize (strikes interfere with interstate commerce).

Section 9. Powers Denied to the Federal Government

1. [The migration or importation of such persons as any of the states now existing shall think proper to admit shall not be prohibited by the Congress prior to the year 1808; but a tax or duty may be imposed on such importation, not exceeding $10 for each person.]

Clause 1. "Such persons" refers to slaves. This clause was the result of a compromise between northern merchants and southern planters. The Constitutional Convention gave Congress powers to regulate commerce and to tax imports, while also providing that the importation of slaves would not be prohibited prior to 1808 and that there would not be an import tax of more than $10 per person. The importation of slaves was prohibited in 1808.

2. The privilege of the writ of *habeas corpus* shall not be suspended, unless when in cases of rebellion or invasion the public safety may require it.

Clause 2. A *writ of habeas corpus* protects citizens from arbitrary arrest. It is an order demanding that a person who has been arrested be brought before a court so that a judge can decide if he or she is being held lawfully.

3. No bill of attainder or *ex post facto* law shall be passed.

Clause 3. A *bill of attainder* is a law that declares an individual guilty of a crime without a court trial. An *ex post facto* law makes an act a crime after the act has been committed.

4. [No capitation or other direct tax shall be laid, unless in proportion to the census herein before directed to be taken.]

Clause 4. Congress must allocate direct taxes among the states according to their populations. This provision was included to keep Congress from abolishing slavery by taxing slaves. The 16th Amendment (1913) makes it possible for Congress to levy a tax on individual incomes without regard to state population.

5. No tax or duty shall be laid on articles exported from any state.

Clause 5. Southern delegates to the Constitutional Convention opposed a tax on exports because they exported goods, such as tobacco and cotton, to Europe. The Constitution permitted Congress to tax imports for revenue, but not exports.

6. No preference shall be given any regulation of commerce or revenue to the ports of one state over those of another; nor shall vessels bound to, or from, one state, be obliged to enter, clear, or pay duties in another.

Clause 6. No port in any state is to have preference over any other. Ships going from state to state may not be taxed by Congress.

7. No money shall be drawn from the Treasury, but in consequence of appropriations made by law; and a regular statement and account of the receipts and expenditures of all public money shall be published from time to time.

Clause 7. Only Congress can grant permission for money to be spent from the Treasury. This provision permits Congress to limit the power of the President by controlling the amount of money to be spent to run the executive branch of government.

8. No title of nobility shall be granted by the United States; and no person holding any office of profit or trust under them, shall, without the consent of the Congress, accept of any present, emolument, office, or title, of any kind whatever, from any king, prince, or foreign state.

Clause 8. This clause prohibits the establishment of a noble class and discourages bribery of American officials by foreign governments.

Section 10. Powers Denied to the States

1. No state shall enter into any treaty, alliance, or confederation; grant letters of marque and reprisal; coin money; emit bills of credit; make anything but gold and silver coin a tender in payment of debts; pass any bill of attainder, *ex post facto* law, or law impairing the obligation of contracts, or grant any title of nobility.

Clause 1. The clauses in this section limit the powers of the states. Most of these limitations stemmed from complaints the nationalists had made against the states during the Confederation period. The prohibition of laws "impairing the obligations of contracts" was intended to prevent the kind of relief laws the states had passed during the hard times of the 1780's (the time of Shays' Rebellion). These laws protected debtors against lawsuits. A debt or other obligation was a contract, and a state could not interfere with it.

2. No state shall, without the consent of the Congress, lay any imposts or duties on imports or exports, except what may be absolutely necessary for executing its inspection laws; and the net produce of all duties and imposts, laid by any state on imports or exports, shall be for the use of the Treasury of the United States; and all such laws shall be subject to the revision and control of the Congress.

Clause 2. States cannot interfere with commerce by taxing goods, although they may charge fees for inspecting such goods. Any such inspection fee must be paid into the Treasury of the United States. Also, all tariff revenue goes to the national government and not to the states.

3. No states shall, without the consent of Congress, lay any duty of tonnage, keep troops, or ships of war in time of peace, enter into any agreement or compact with another state, or with a foreign power, or engage in war, unless actually invaded, or in such imminent danger as will not admit of delay.

Article 2. The Executive Branch

Section 1. President and Vice-President

1. Term of Office. The executive power shall be vested in a President of the United States of America. He shall hold his office during the term of four years, and together with the Vice-President, chosen for the same term, be elected as follows:

2. Electoral System. Each state shall appoint, in such manner as the legislature thereof may direct, a number of electors, equal to the whole number of Senators and Representatives to which the state may be entitled in the Congress; but no Senator or Representative, or person holding an office of trust or profit under the United States, shall be appointed an elector.

3. Former Method of the Electoral System. [The electors shall meet in their respective states, and vote by ballot for two persons, of whom one at least shall not be an inhabitant of the same state with themselves. And they shall make a list of all the persons voted for, and of the number of votes for each; which list they shall sign and certify, and transmit sealed to the seat of the government of the United States, directed to the president of the Senate. The president of the Senate shall, in the presence of the Senate and House of Representatives, open all the certificates, and the votes shall then be counted. The person having the greatest number of votes shall be the President, if such number be a majority of the whole number of electors appointed; and if there be more than one who have such majority, and have an equal number of votes, then the House of Representatives shall immediately choose by ballot one of them for President; and if no person have a majority, then from the five highest on the list the said House shall in like manner choose the President. But in choosing the President the votes shall be taken by states, the representation from each state having one vote. A quorum for this purpose shall consist of a member or members from two-thirds of the states, and a majority of all the states shall be necessary to a choice. In every case, after the choice of the President, the person having the greatest number of votes of the electors shall be the Vice-President. But if there should remain two or more who have equal votes, the Senate shall choose from them by ballot the Vice-President.]

Clauses 2 and 3. The framers of the Constitution did not want the President to be chosen directly by the people. They thought the voters would not become familiar with the qualifications of leaders living in distant states. Therefore they devised an electoral college. The electors, it was hoped, would be prominent individuals acquainted with leaders in other states. They would thus be able to make a wise choice for President. Originally, the state legislatures chose the electors, but since 1828 they have been nominated by the political parties and elected by the people. The electors from all the states make up the electoral college. Each state has as many electors as it has senators and representatives.

This system provided that each elector vote for two candidates, with the person receiving the largest number of votes (provided it was a majority) becoming President and the one who was runner-up becoming Vice-President. In 1800 the two top candidates tied, making it necessary for the House to choose the President. The 12th Amendment (1804) was passed to prevent a situation of this kind.

4. Time of Elections. The Congress may determine the time of choosing the electors, and

Clause 4. Elections for President are held on the first Tuesday after the first Monday in November. The electors cast the day on which they shall give their votes; which day shall be the same throughout the United States.

their votes on the first Monday after the second Wednesday in December.

5. Qualifications for President. No person except a natural-born citizen [or a citizen of the United States, at the time of the adoption of this Constitution], shall be eligible to the office of the President; neither shall any person be eligible to that office who shall not have attained to the age of thirty-five years, and been fourteen years a resident within the United States.

6. Filling Vacancies. In the case of the removal of the President from office, or of his death, resignation, or inability to discharge the powers and duties of the said office, the same shall devolve on the Vice-President, and the Congress may by law provide for the case of removal, death, resignation, or inability, both of the President and Vice-President, declaring what officer shall then act as President, and such officer shall act accordingly, until the disability be removed, or a President shall be elected.

Clause 6. If the presidency becomes vacant, then the Vice-President takes the office. Congress may decide by law who will become President when neither the President nor the Vice-President is able to serve. In the present succession law, the Speaker of the House is next in line, followed by the President pro tempore of the Senate. The 25th Amendment (1967) deals with the inability of Presidents to discharge their duties.

7. Salary. The President shall, at stated times, receive for his services, a compensation, which shall neither be increased nor diminished during the period for which he shall have been elected, and he shall not receive within that period any other emolument from the United States, or any of them.

8. Oath of Office. Before he enter on the execution of his office, he shall take the following oath or affirmation:—"I do solemnly swear (or affirm) that I will faithfully execute the office of President of the United States, and will to the best of my ability, preserve, protect, and defend the Constitution of the United States."

Section 2. Powers of the President

1. Military Powers. The President shall be Commander in Chief of the Army and Navy of the United States, and of the militia of the several states, when called into the actual service of the United States; he may require the opinion in writing, of the principal officer in each of the executive departments, upon any subject relating to the duties of their respective offices, and

Clause 1. The President, who cannot be a member of the military, heads the armed forces. This clause places the armed forces under civilian control. The President can ask the heads of executive departments for written opinions about matters related to their departments. This clause provides the constitutional basis for the cabinet.

he shall have power to grant reprieves and pardons for offenses against the United States, except in cases of impeachment.

2. Treaties and Appointments. He shall have power, by and with the advice and consent of the Senate, to make treaties, provided two-thirds of the Senators present concur; and he shall nominate, and by and with the advice and consent of the Senate, shall appoint ambassadors, other public ministers and consuls, judges of the Supreme Court, and all other officers of the United States, whose appointments are not herein otherwise provided for, and which shall be established by law; but the Congress may by law vest the appointment of such inferior officers, as they think proper, in the President alone, in the courts of law, or in the heads of departments.

Clause 2. The President can make treaties with foreign countries, but they must be approved by two thirds of those present at a session of the Senate. Note that this is a power given to the Senate but not to the House and is a part of the checks and balances system.

The Senate must also approve the appointment of American representatives abroad, judges of the Supreme Court, and any other government official not provided for in the Constitution. However, Congress may make laws allowing the President, the courts, or heads of departments to appoint minor government officials.

3. Filling Vacancies. The President shall have power to fill up all vacancies that may happen during the recess of the Senate, by granting commissions which shall expire at the end of their next session.

Clause 3. If vacancies occur in appointive federal offices when the Senate is not in session, the President may make temporary appointments.

Section 3. Duties of the President

He shall from time to time give to the Congress information of the state of the Union, and recommend to their consideration such measures as he shall judge necessary and expedient; he may, on extraordinary occasions, convene both houses, or either of them, and in case of disagreement between them, with respect to the time of adjournment, he may adjourn them to such time as he shall think proper; he shall receive ambassadors and other public ministers; he shall take care that the laws be faithfully executed, and shall commission all the officers of the United States.

Section 3. The President must give Congress information about the condition of the country. It has become customary for the President to deliver a "State of the Union" message to Congress every January. If the need arises, the President may call either or both houses of Congress into special session. The President has the power to end a session of Congress if the two houses cannot agree on an adjournment date. The President is to receive foreign representatives, see that the laws of the federal government are carried out, and commission all officers of the armed forces.

Section 4. Impeachment

The President, Vice-President, and all civil officers of the United States, shall be removed from office on impeachment for, and conviction of, treason, bribery, or other high crimes and misdemeanors.

Section 4. (See annotation for Article 1, Section 2, Clause 5, and Section 3, Clauses 6 and 7.)

Article 3. The Judicial Branch

Section 1. Federal Courts

The judicial power of the United States shall be vested in one Supreme Court, and in such inferior courts as the Congress may from time to time ordain and establish. The judges, both of the Supreme and inferior courts, shall hold their offices during good behavior, and shall, at stated times, receive for their services a compensation, which shall not be diminished during their continuance in office.

Section 1. The framers of the Constitution sought to control the power of the federal government with a system of checks and balances. Each branch of government—legislative, executive, and judicial—has certain checks against the other two. The President can veto acts of Congress, but Congress can override vetoes. In particular, the Senate must approve the President's appointments and consent to the President's treaties. The judiciary is an extremely important part of this system of balanced government.

Section 1 authorizes a Supreme Court and such lower courts as Congress shall establish. Both the President and Congress have checks on the courts. Congress determines the number of judges on the Supreme Court and creates by law all other courts. The President, with the consent of the Senate, appoints all federal judges. Federal judges hold office for life and may be removed only by impeachment.

Section 2. Jurisdiction of Federal Courts

1. General Jurisdiction. The judicial power shall extend to all cases, in law and equity, arising under this Constitution, the laws of the United States, and treaties made or which shall be made, under their authority; to all cases affecting ambassadors, other public ministers and consuls; to all cases of admiralty and maritime jurisdiction; to controversies to which the United States shall be a party; to controversies between two or more states; [between a state and citizens of another state;] between citizens of the same state claiming lands under grants of different states, and between a state or the citizens thereof, and foreign states, citizens, or subjects.

Clause 1. Over the years the courts have defined their jurisdiction and established some checks of their own. In 1803 Supreme Court Chief Justice John Marshall asserted the power of the Court to determine the constitutionality of acts of Congress. If the Court finds a law unconstitutional, it is of no effect. Through Marshall's ruling, the Court made itself the interpreter of the Constitution. The Supreme Court has several times declared that the President is "under the law" as interpreted by the Court. Only once was there the threat of an open confrontation. In 1952 President Truman, acting in the emergency of the Korean War, seized the nation's steel mills. The Supreme Court, declaring that he had exceeded his constitutional powers, ordered him to return them to their owners. He did.

2. Supreme Court. In all cases affecting ambassadors, other public ministers and consuls, and those in which a state shall be a party, the Supreme Court shall have original jurisdiction. In all the other cases before mentioned, the Supreme Court shall have appellate jurisdiction, both as to law and fact, with such exceptions, and under such regulations as the Congress shall make.

Clause 2. "Original jurisdiction" refers to the right to try a case before any other court hears it. Actually, very few cases come directly to the Supreme Court. Most federal court cases begin in the district courts. They can be appealed to the circuit courts and may finally be carried up to the Supreme Court. "Appellate jurisdiction" refers to the right to review cases appealed from lower courts. Most cases reaching the Supreme Court are taken to it on appeal. The Supreme Court has original jurisdiction in cases involving foreign representatives or in cases involving disputes between states. Congress determines appellate jurisdiction of the Supreme Court.

3. Conduct of Trials. The trial of all crimes, except in cases of impeachment, shall be by jury; and such trial shall be held in the state where the said crimes shall have been committed; but when not committed within any state,

Clause 3. Except for impeachment cases, anyone accused of a federal crime has the right to a trial by jury. The trial must be held in the state where the crime was committed.

On July 23, 1788, a parade was held in lower Manhattan in celebration of the Constitution's ratification. The "federal ship," named in Hamilton's honor, was pulled along this New York street "with floating sheets and full sails."

the trial shall be at such place or places as the Congress may by law have directed.

Section 3. Treason

1. Definition. Treason against the United States shall consist only in levying war against them, or in adhering to their enemies, giving them aid and comfort. No person shall be convicted of treason unless on the testimony of two witnesses to the same overt act, or on confession in open court.

Clause 1. Treason is the only crime defined by the Constitution. Notice how strict the requirements are—there must be two witnesses to the same overt (open) act. The framers did not want anyone tried for treason merely for criticizing the government.

2. Punishment. The Congress shall have power to declare the punishment of treason, but no attainder of treason shall work corruption of blood or forfeiture except during the life of the person attained.

Clause 2. Congress has the power to fix the punishment for treason. But the families and descendants of a person found guilty of treason cannot be punished for his or her crime.

Article 4. Relations Among States

Section 1. Official Acts

Full faith and credit shall be given in each state to the public acts, records, and judicial proceedings of every other state. And the Congress may by general laws prescribe the manner in which such acts, records, and proceedings shall be proved, and the effect thereof.

Section 1. Each state must respect the laws, records, and court decisions of other states. If this were not the case, a person might move to another state to avoid legal punishment imposed by another state. The "full faith and credit" clause avoids much of the confusion arising from different state regulations.

Section 2. Privileges of Citizens

1. Privileges. The citizens of each state shall be entitled to all privileges and immunities of citizens in the several states.

Clause 1. This clause gives a person moving into a state the same rights the state gives to its own citizens. The state may still require a person to meet its own residency requirements for voting in elections and holding state office.

2. Extradition. A person charged in any state with treason, felony, or other crime, who shall flee from justice, and be found in another state, shall on demand of the executive authority of the state from which he fled, be delivered up, to be removed to the state having jurisdiction of the crime.

Clause 2. If a person charged with a crime flees to another state, the governor of the state where the crime was committed may request that he or she be returned. Sending back such persons for trial is called *extradition*. In the vast majority of cases, the return is automatic, but in a very few cases state governors have refused to return the fugitives.

3. Fugitive Slaves. [No person held in service or labor in one state, under the laws thereof, escaping into another, shall in consequence of any law or regulation therein, be discharged from such service or labor, but shall be delivered up on claim of the party to whom such service or labor may be due.]

Clause 3. This clause provided the constitutional basis for slave owners to have their escaped slaves returned to them. The 13th Amendment (1865) ended slavery, making this clause obsolete.

Section 3. New States and Territories

1. Admission of New States. New states may be admitted by the Congress into this Union; but no new state shall be formed or erected within the jurisdiction of any other state; nor any state be formed by the junction of two or more states, or parts of states, without the consent of the legislatures of the states concerned as well as of the Congress.

Clause 1. The Constitution specifically gave Congress power to govern the western territories. It can admit new states to the Union but cannot subdivide states without their consent. Subdivision has happened only three times. Kentucky was separated from Virginia in 1792. Maine was split off from Massachusetts in 1820. And during the Civil War (1863), West Virginia separated from Virginia and joined the northern Union.

2. Powers of Congress over Territories and Other Property. The Congress shall have power to dispose of and make all needful rules and regulations respecting the territory or other property belonging to the United States; and nothing in this Constitution shall be so construed as to prejudice any claims of the United States, or of any particular state.

Clause 2. Congress may govern and make regulations for the territories and properties of the United States. "Territories" here refers to lands not under the control of any state.

Section 4. Guarantees to the States

The United States shall guarantee to every state in this Union a republican form of government, and shall protect each of them against invasion; and on application of the legislature or of the executive (when the legislature cannot be convened) against domestic violence.

Section 4. In practice, Congress determines whether a state has a republican form of government. The Constitution also requires the federal government to protect a state against invasion and, upon request of the proper state authorities, to protect it against rioting and violence. Sometimes Presidents have ordered federal intervention without request from states when federal laws were being violated.

Article 5. Methods of Amendment

The Congress, whenever two-thirds of both houses shall deem it necessary, shall propose amendments to this Constitution, or, on the application of the legislatures of two-thirds of the several states, shall call a convention for proposing amendments, which, in either case, shall be valid to all intents and purposes, as part of this Constitution, when ratified by the legislatures of three-fourths of the several states, or by conventions in three-fourths thereof, as the one or the other mode of ratification may be proposed by the Congress; provided that [no amendments which may be made prior to the year 1808 shall in any manner affect the first and fourth clauses in the Ninth Section of the First Article; and that] no state, without its consent, shall be deprived of its equal suffrage in the Senate.

Article 5. The framers of the Constitution recognized that later generations would need to make some changes in the Constitution. However, they wanted to make the process of change difficult so that the Constitution would not be battered by every popular trend. According to Article 5, Congress can propose an amendment by a two thirds vote of both houses. Or, if two thirds of the state legislatures request it, Congress calls a convention to propose an amendment. So far, all amendments have been proposed by Congress. An amendment must be approved by three fourths of the state legislatures or by conventions in three fourths of the states.

Considering the enormous changes in American society, there have been remarkably few amendments to the Constitution. The first ten (known as the Bill of Rights) were approved within two years, but there were only two more amendments before the Civil War. There has been a total of 26 amendments.

Article 6. General Provisions

1. Public Debts. All debts contracted and engagements entered into, before the adoption of this Constitution, shall be as valid against the United States under this Constitution, as under the Confederation.

Clause 1. All debts and treaties made under the Articles of Confederation were recognized by the United States. This action was favored by Alexander Hamilton and was one of several steps taken by Congress to establish the credit of the new government.

2. The Supreme Law. This Constitution, and the laws of the United States which shall be made in pursuance thereof, and all treaties made, or which shall be made, under the authority of the United States, shall be the supreme law of the land; and the judges in every state shall be bound thereby, anything in the constitution or laws of any state to the contrary notwithstanding.

Clause 2. This clause is the basic, constitutional statement of national authority. It makes the Constitution and federal laws, rather than state laws, supreme. Many years—even a Civil War—intervened before the precise relationship between the federal government and the states was worked out.

3. Oaths of Office. The Senators and Representatives before mentioned, and the members of the several state legislatures, and all executive

Clause 3. All the officials listed must pledge themselves to support the Constitution. But such a pledge, or oath, cannot include any religious test or requirement that a person be-

and judicial officers, both of the United States and of the several states, shall be bound by oath or affirmation, to support this Constitution; but no religious test shall ever be required as a qualification to any office or public trust under the United States.

long to a particular religious faith. This provision results from the principle of separation of church and state in the United States.

Article 7. Ratification

The ratification of the convention of nine states shall be sufficient for the establishment of the Constitution between the states so ratifying the same.

DONE in Convention by the unanimous consent of the States present the seventeenth day of September in the year of our Lord one thousand seven hundred and eight-seven and of the independence of the United States of America the twelfth. In witness whereof we have hereunto subscribed our names,
G. Washington—President and deputy from Virginia

Article 7. The final article sets up the process of ratification. The framers knew they had to submit their document for popular approval. But they wished to avoid the state legislatures, which might resent the powers of the federal government. As a result, they provided for specially elected ratifying conventions, one in each state. And when nine states approved, the Constitution would be considered in effect. Of the 55 people who attended the Constitutional Convention in the summer of 1787, 39 signed the Constitution.

NEW HAMPSHIRE
John Langdon
Nicholas Gilman

NEW YORK
Alexander Hamilton

DELAWARE
George Read
Gunning Bedford
John Dickinson
Richard Bassett
Jacob Broom

NORTH CAROLINA
William Blount
Richard Dobbs Spaight
Hugh Williamson

MASSACHUSETTS
Nathaniel Gorham
Rufus King

NEW JERSEY
William Livingston
David Brearley
William Paterson
Jonathan Dayton

MARYLAND
James McHenry
Daniel of St. Thomas Jenifer
Daniel Carroll

SOUTH CAROLINA
John Rutledge
Charles Cotesworth Pinckney
Charles Pinckney
Pierce Butler

CONNECTICUT
William Samuel Johnson
Roger Sherman

PENNSYLVANIA
Benjamin Franklin
Thomas Mifflin
Robert Morris
George Clymer
Thomas FitzSimons
Jared Ingersoll
James Wilson
Gouverneur Morris

VIRGINIA
John Blair
James Madison

GEORGIA
William Few
Abraham Baldwin

Amendments to the Constitution

(The first ten amendments constitute the Bill of Rights. They became an official part of the Constitution in 1791. They limit the powers of the federal government but not the powers of the states.)

Amendment 1. Freedom of Religion, Speech, Press, Assembly, and Petition (1791)

Congress shall make no law respecting an establishment of religion, or prohibiting the free exercise thereof; or abridging the freedom of speech, or of the press; or the right of the people peaceably to assemble, and to petition the government for a redress of grievances.

Amendment 1. This amendment guarantees to Americans the most essential freedoms. Freedom of religion guarantees the right to worship as one chooses without interference from Congress. The Supreme Court has interpreted this amendment as a guarantee of the separation of church and state. Freedoms of speech and press are limited only when they involve slander and libel (false and malicious statements) or statements that might be injurious to the general welfare of the nation. The First Amendment also entitles the people to hold meetings and to request the government to respond to their grievances.

Amendment 2. Right to Bear Arms (1791)

A well-regulated militia, being necessary to the security of a free state, the right of the people to keep and bear arms shall not be infringed.

Amendment 2. The states have the right to maintain armed militias for their protection. However, the rights of private citizens to own guns can be, and are, regulated by federal and state legislation.

Amendment 3. Housing of Troops (1791)

No soldier shall, in time of peace, be quartered in any house, without the consent of the owner; nor in time of war, but in a manner to be prescribed by law.

Amendment 3. One source of bitter complaint in the colonies had been the British practice of housing their troops in American homes. The Third Amendment guarantees that no soldier will be quartered in a private residence during peacetime or in wartime without specific congressional authorization.

Amendment 4. Searches and Seizures (1791)

The right of the people to be secure in their persons, houses, papers, and effects, against unreasonable searches and seizures, shall not be violated; and no warrants shall issue but upon probable cause, supported by oath or affirmation, and particularly describing the place to be searched, and the persons or things to be seized.

Amendment 4. This amendment was proposed and ratified in response to the British writs of assistance—blanket search warrants permitting officers to search any house at any time. For an American home to be searched, a warrant must be issued by a judge, and it must state precisely what the official expects fo find.

Amendment 5. Rights of Accused Persons (1791)

No person shall be held to answer for a capital, or otherwise infamous, crime, unless on a presentment or indictment of a grand jury, except in cases arising in the land or naval forces, or in the militia, when in actual service in time of war or public danger; nor shall any person be subject for the same offense to be twice put in jeopardy of life and limb; nor shall be compelled, in any criminal case, to be a witness against himself; nor be deprived of life, liberty, or property, without due process of law; nor shall private property be taken for public use, without just compensation.

Amendment 5. No person can be tried for a serious crime in a federal court unless indicted, or charged, by a grand jury. A grand jury is a group of 23 persons who hear in secret accusations against a person and then decide whether the person should be tried in court. "Twice put in jeopardy," or double jeopardy, means that no person can be tried twice in a federal court for the same crime.

People cannot be forced to give evidence against themselves that will help prove their guilt. This clause allows people on trial to refuse to answer questions, without paying penalties.

"Due process of law" has become quite complicated, but the framers wished to guarantee proper judicial procedures for a person accused of a crime (see Amendment 6). The taking of private property for public use is called the right of *eminent domain.* The government cannot take such property without giving owners fair prices for their property. The price is determined by a court.

Amendment 6. Right to a Speedy, Fair Trial (1791)

In all criminal prosecutions, the accused shall enjoy the right to a speedy and public trial, by an impartial jury of the state and district wherein the crime shall have been committed, which district shall have been previously ascertained by law, and to be informed of the nature and cause of the accusation; to be confronted with the witnesses against him; to have compulsory process for obtaining witnesses in his favor, and to have the assistance of counsel for his defense.

Amendment 6. This amendment defines the rights of the accused under due process of law. A person has the right to be informed of the charges against him or her and to a speedy and public trial by jury. Witnesses for and against the accused may be compelled to appear in court to give evidence. The accused is entitled to confront these witnesses and to be represented by a lawyer at all stages of the criminal proceedings.

Amendment 7. Civil Suits (1791)

In suits at common law, where the value in controversy shall exceed $20, the right of trial by jury shall be preserved, and no fact tried by a jury shall be otherwise reexamined in any court of the United States than according to the rules of the common law.

Amendment 7. If a sum of money larger than $20 is the object of dispute, the people involved may insist on a jury trial. However, in actual practice, cases do not reach federal courts unless much larger sums are involved.

Amendment 8. Bails, Fines, Punishments (1791)

Excessive bail shall not be required, nor excessive fines imposed, nor cruel and unusual punishments inflicted.

Amendment 8. The Eighth Amendment continues the enumeration of the rights of the accused. Before a criminal trial, the accused may remain free on payment to the court of a sum of money called bail. Bail is returned if the person appears for trial as ordered. Neither the amount of bail set nor the punishment inflicted should be excessive. The Supreme

Court has the final say in determining what is "excessive," "cruel," and "unusual" in any case.

Amendment 9. Powers Reserved to the People (1791)

The enumeration in the Constitution, of certain rights, shall not be construed to deny or disparage others retained by the people.

Amendment 9. This means that the rights listed in the Constitution are not necessarily the only rights that exist. Other rights shall not be denied to the people simply because they are not enumerated in the Constitution.

Amendment 10. Powers Reserved to the States (1791)

The powers not delegated to the United States by the Constitution, nor prohibited by it to the states, are reserved to the states respectively, or to the people.

Amendment 10. In the same vein as the previous amendment, the Tenth Amendment stipulates that those powers not given to the federal government are reserved to the states or to the people.

Amendment 11. Suits Against States (1798)

The judicial power of the United States shall not be construed to extend to any suit in law or equity, commenced or prosecuted against one of the United States, by citizens of another state, or by citizens or subjects of any foreign state.

Amendment 11. A state cannot be sued in any court other than the courts of the state. This amendment overruled a Supreme Court decision (*Chisholm* v. *Georgia,* 1793) that allowed two citizens of South Carolina to sue Georgia in a federal court.

Amendment 12. Electing the President and Vice-President (1804)

The electors shall meet in their respective states, and vote by ballot for President and Vice-President, one of whom, at least, shall not be an inhabitant of the same state with themselves; they shall name in their ballots the person voted for as President, and in distinct ballots the person voted for as Vice-President, and they shall make distinct lists of all persons voted for as President, and of all persons voted for as Vice-President, and of the number of votes for each, which lists they shall sign and certify, and transmit, sealed, to the seat of government of the United States, directed to the President of the Senate; the President of the Senate shall, in the

Amendment 12. This amendment nullifies Article 2, Section 1, Clause 3. At first the electors voted for President and Vice-President without specifying which person they wanted for each office. After the election of 1796, in which the people elected a Federalist President and a Republican Vice-President, and the election of 1800, which was a tie, the 12th Amendment was passed to require each elector to cast two ballots—one for President, one for Vice-President. Electors are nominated by the political parties and elected by the people. Each state has as many electors as it has senators and representatives in Congress. The electors of the party with the most *popular votes*—that is, votes cast by the people of the state—get to cast all the state's electoral votes for the party's candidates. The electoral votes are counted by the President of the Senate in the presence of both houses of Congress. Each candidate for President and Vice-President must receive a majority of electoral votes to be elected.

Political parties are not mentioned in the Constitution—the framers considered them unnecessary as well as harmful to national unity. The 12th Amendment recognized the fact that presence of the Senate and House of Representatives, open all the certificates and the votes shall then be counted; the person having the greatest number of votes for President shall be the President, if such number be a majority of the whole number of electors appointed; and if no person have such majority, then from the persons having the highest numbers not exceeding three on the list of those voted for as President, the House of Representatives shall choose immediately, by ballot, the President. But in choosing the President, the votes shall be taken by states, the representation from each state having one vote; a quorum for this purpose shall consist of a member or members from two-thirds of the states, and a majority of all the states shall be necessary to a choice. [And if the House of Representatives shall not choose a President whenever the right of choice shall devolve upon them, before the fourth day of March next following, then the Vice-President shall act as President, as in the case of the death or other constitutional disability of the President.] The person having the greatest number of votes as Vice-President, shall be the Vice-President, if such number be a majority of the whole number of electors appointed, and if no person have a majority, then, from the two highest numbers on the list, the Senate shall choose the Vice-President; a quorum for the purpose shall consist of two-thirds of the whole number of Senators, and a majority of the whole number shall be necessary to a choice. But no person constitutionally ineligible to the office of President shall be eligible to that of Vice-President of the United States.

political parties had developed since the Constitution was ratified.

Amendment 13. Abolition of Slavery (1865)

Section 1. Neither slavery nor involuntary servitude, except as a punishment for crime whereof the party shall have been duly convicted, shall exist within the United States, or any place subject to their jurisdiction.

Section 2. Congress shall have power to enforce this article by appropriate legislation.

Amendment 13. The 13th, 14th, and 15th Amendments were passed after the Civil War. The 13th Amendment abolished slavery and gave Congress the right to enforce the law.

Amendment 14. Citizenship (1868)

Section 1. Citizenship Defined. All persons born or naturalized in the United States and subject to the jurisdiction thereof, are citizens of the United States and of the state wherein they reside. No state shall make or enforce any law which shall abridge the privileges or immunities of citizens of the United States; nor shall any state deprive any person of life, liberty, or property, without due process of law; nor deny to any person within its jurisdiction the equal protection of the laws.

Section 1. The main purpose of this amendment was to give Blacks equal rights. The first sentence, by definition, gives Black Americans citizenship. The second sentence prohibits the states from interfering with any citizen's right to equal protection under the law or with the right of due process of law. In recent years the Supreme Court has interpreted the phrase "due process" to mean that the states must respect the judicial rights guaranteed by the Bill of Rights.

Section 2. Apportionment of Representatives. Representatives shall be apportioned among the several states according to their respective numbers, counting the whole number of persons in each state, [excluding Indians not taxed]. But when the right to vote at any election for the choice of electors for President and Vice-President of the United States, Representatives in Congress, the executive and judicial officers of a state, or the members of the legislature thereof, is denied to any of the [male] inhabitants of such state, [being twenty-one years of age] and citizens of the United States, or in any way abridged, except for participation in rebellion, or other crime, the basis of representation therein shall be reduced in the proportion which the number of such [male] citizens shall bear to the whole number of [male] citizens [twenty-one years of age] in such state.

Section 2. This section nullified the three fifths compromise and declared every man over the age of 21 to be entitled to one vote. Notice that Indians and women were still excluded. This section provides for a punishment against any state preventing its eligible citizens from voting. This penalty has never been imposed.

Section 3. Disability for Engaging in Insurrection. No person shall be a Senator or Representative in Congress, or elector of President and Vice-President, or hold any office, civil or military, under the United States, or under any state, who, having previously taken an oath, as a member of Congress, or as an officer of the United States, or as a member of any state legislature, or as an executive or judicial officer of any state, to support the Constitution of the United States, shall have engaged in insurrection or rebellion against the same, or given aid or comfort to the enemies thereof. But Congress may, by vote of two-thirds of each house, remove such disability.

Section 3. This section was designed to punish the leaders of the Confederacy for breaking their oaths to support the Constitution. Many southern leaders were excluded from public office by this amendment, but by 1872 most were permitted to return to public life. In 1898 all the Confederates were pardoned.

Section 4. Public Debt. The validity of the public debt of the United States, authorized by law, including debts incurred for payment of pensions and bounties for services in suppressing insurrection or rebellion, shall not be questioned. But neither the United States nor any state shall assume or pay any debt or obligation incurred in aid of insurrection or rebellion against the United States [or any claim for the loss or emancipation of any slave]; but all such debts, obligations, and claims shall be held illegal and void.

Section 4. This section dealt a harsh financial blow to the South. The war debt of the Union was declared valid; the war debt of the Confederacy was declared void. There would be no reimbursement on Confederate bonds and no payment for the loss of slaves.

Section 5. Enforcement. The Congress shall have power to enforce, by appropriate legislation, the provisions of this article.

Amendment 15. Right to Vote (1870)

Amendment 15. This amendment prohibits federal or state governments from preventing any citizen from voting because of "race, color, or previous condition of servitude." It was designed to guarantee voting rights to Black American men.

Section 1. The right of citizens of the United States to vote shall not be denied or abridged by the United States or any state on account of race, color, or previous condition of servitude.

Section 2. The Congress shall have power to enforce this article by appropriate legislation.

Amendment 16. Income Tax (1913)

Amendment 16. This amendment permits Congress to tax individual incomes without basing the tax on state populations. The income tax is now the major source of revenue for the federal government.

The Congress shall have power to lay and collect taxes on incomes, from whatever source derived, without apportionment among the several states, and without regard to any census or enumeration.

Amendment 17. Electing Senators (1913)

Amendment 17. This amendment gave the people the right to elect senators directly. Before this, senators were elected by the state legislatures. If a senator dies or leaves office during his or her term of office, the governor of the state can either order an election for a successor or appoint a temporary successor.

Section 1. Method of Election. The Senate of the United States shall be composed of two Senators from each state, elected by the people thereof, for six years; and each Senator shall have one vote. The electors in each state shall have the qualifications requisite for electors of the most numerous branch of the state legislatures.

Section 2. Filling Vacancies. When vacancies happen in the representation of any state in the Senate, the executive authority of such state shall issue writs of election to fill such vacancies: *Provided* that the legislatures of any state may empower the executive thereof to make temporary appointments until the people fill the vacancies by election as the legislature may direct.

[**Section 3. Not Retroactive.** This amendment shall not be so construed as to affect the election or term of any Senator chosen before it becomes valid as part of the Constitution.]

Amendment 18. Prohibition (1919)

Amendment 18. This amendment forbade the manufacture, sale, and shipment of alcoholic beverages. It was repealed by the 21st Amendment.

[**Section 1.** After one year from the ratification of this article the manufacture, sale, or transportation of intoxicating liquors within, the importation thereof into, or the exportation thereof from, the United States and all territory subject to the jurisdiction thereof for beverage purposes is hereby prohibited.

Section 2. The Congress and the several states shall have concurrent power to enforce this article by appropriate legislation.

Section 3. This article shall be inoperative unless it shall have been ratified as an amendment to the Constitution by the legislatures of the several states, as provided in the Constitution, within seven years from the date of the submission hereof to the states by the Congress.]

Amendment 19. Women's Suffrage (1920)

Amendment 19. This amendment gave women the right to vote.

Section 1. The right of citizens of the United States to vote shall not be denied or abridged by the United States or by any state on account of sex.

Section 2. Congress shall have power to enforce this article by appropriate legislation.

Amendment 20. "Lame Duck" Amendment (1933)

Section 1. Beginning of Terms. The terms of the President and Vice-President shall end at noon on the 20th day of January, and the terms of Senators and Representatives at noon on the 3rd day of January, of the years in which such terms would have ended if this article had not been ratified; and the terms of their successors shall then begin.

Section 2. Beginning of Congressional Sessions. The Congress shall assemble at least once in every year, and such meeting shall begin at noon on the third day of January, unless they shall by law appoint a different day.

Section 3. Presidential succession. If at the time fixed for the beginning of the term of the President, the President-elect shall have died, the Vice-President-elect shall become President. If a President shall not have been chosen before the time fixed for the beginning of his term, or if the President-elect shall have failed to qualify, then the Vice-President-elect shall act as President until a President shall have qualified; and the Congress may by law provide for the case wherein neither a President-elect nor a Vice-President-elect shall have qualified, declaring who shall then act as President, or the manner in which one who is to act shall be selected, and such person shall act accordingly until a President or Vice-President shall have qualified.

Section 4. Filling Presidential Vacancy. The Congress may by law provide for the case of the death of any of the persons from whom the House of Representatives may choose a President whenever the right of choice shall have devolved upon them, and for the case of the death of any of the persons from whom the Senate may choose a Vice-President whenever the right of choice shall have devolved upon them.

[**Section 5. Effective Date.** Sections 1 and 2 shall take effect on the 15th day of October following the ratification of this article.

Section 6. Time Limit for Ratification. This article shall be inoperative unless it shall

Amendment 20. This amendment moved the President's inaugural day from March 4 to January 20. Members of Congress take office on January 3 instead of the following December. The date of congressional sessions was also moved to January. Transportation and communication were so slow when the Constitution was written that it would have been almost impossible for officials elected in November to reach the capital in January. Hence newly elected representatives did not "sit" until the next congressional session began, 13 months later. The expression "lame duck" was used to refer to the defeated or retired officeholder still serving during the period between the election and the inauguration.

Section 3. This section provides for succession to the Presidency when a President-elect dies or fails to qualify.

have been ratified as an amendment to the Constitution by the legislatures of three-fourths of the several states within the seven years from the date of its submission.]

Amendment 21. Repeal of Prohibition (1933)

Amendment 21. This repealed the 18th Amendment.

Section 1. The eighteenth article of amendment of the Constitution of the United States is hereby repealed.

Section 2. The transportation or importation into any state, territory, or possession of the United States for delivery or use therein of intoxicating liquors, in violation of the laws thereof, is hereby prohibited.

[**Section 3.** This article shall be inoperative unless it shall have been ratified as an amendment to the Constitution by conventions in the several states, as provided in the Constitution, within seven years from the date of the submission hereof to the states by the Congress.]

Amendment 22. Two-Term Limit for Presidents (1951)

Amendment 22. This amendment was passed because many feared that President Franklin D. Roosevelt's four terms had set a dangerous precedent. Prior to his election to a third term in 1940, Presidents had followed the tradition of serving no more than two terms.

Section 1. No person shall be elected to the office of the President more than twice, and no person who has held the office of President, or acted as President, for more than two years of a term to which some other person was elected President shall be elected to the office of the President more than once. [But this Article shall not apply to any person holding the office of President when this Article was proposed by the Congress, and shall not prevent any person who may be holding the office of President, or acting as President, during the term within which this Article becomes operative from holding the office of President or acting as President during the remainder of such term.]

[**Section 2.** This Article shall be inoperative unless it shall have been ratified as an amendment to the Constitution by the legislatures of three-fourths of the several states within seven years from the date of its submission to the states by the Congress.]

Amendment 23. Presidential Electors for District of Columbia (1961)

Amendment 23. This amendment gave the residents of Washington, D.C., three members in the electoral college and hence the right to vote for President and Vice-President.

Section 1. The District constituting the seat of Government of the United States shall appoint in such manner as the Congress may direct:

A number of electors of President and Vice-President equal to the whole number of Senators and Representatives in Congress to which the District would be entitled if it were a state, but in no event more than the least populous state; they shall be in addition to those appointed by the states, but they shall be considered, for the purposes of the election of President and Vice-President, to be electors appointed by a state; and they shall meet in the District and perform such duties as provided by the twelfth article of amendment.

Section 2. The Congress shall have power to enforce this article by appropriate legislation.

Amendment 24. Poll Taxes (1964)

Amendment 24. When this amendment was passed, five southern states used the poll tax as a means of discouraging Blacks from voting. This amendment applies only to national elections.

Section 1. The right of citizens of the United States to vote in any primary or other election for President or Vice-President, for electors for President or Vice-President, or for Senator or Representative in Congress, shall not be denied or abridged by the United States or any state by reason of failure to pay any poll tax or other tax.

Section 2. The Congress shall have the power to enforce this article by appropriate legislation.

Amendment 25. Presidential Disability and Succession (1967)

1. In case of the removal of the President from office or his death or resignation, the Vice-President shall become President.

2. Whenever there is a vacancy in the office of the Vice-President, the President shall nominate a Vice-President who shall take the office upon confirmation by a majority vote of both houses of Congress.

3. Whenever the President transmits to the President pro tempore of the Senate and the Speaker of the House of Representatives his written declaration that he is unable to discharge the powers and duties of his office, and until he transmits to them a written declaration to the contrary, such powers and duties shall be discharged by the Vice-President as Acting President.

4. Whenever the Vice-President and a majority of either the principal officers of the executive departments or of such other body as Congress may by law provide, transmit to the President pro tempore of the Senate and the Speaker of the House of Representatives their written declaration that the President is unable to discharge the powers and duties of his office, the Vice-President shall immediately assume the powers and duties of the office as Acting President.

Thereafter, when the President transmits to the President pro tempore of the Senate and the Speaker of the House of Representatives his written declaration that no inability exists, he shall resume the powers and duties of his office unless the Vice-President and a majority of either the principal officers of the executive department or of such other body as Congress may by law provide, transmit within four days to the President pro tempore of the Senate and the Speaker of the House of Representatives their written declaration that the President is unable to discharge the powers and duties of his office. Thereupon Congress shall decide the issue, assembling within 48 hours for that purpose if not in session. If the Congress, within 21 days after receipt of the latter written declaration, or, if Congress is not in session, within 21 days after Congress is required to assemble, determines by two-thirds vote of both houses the President is

Amendment 25. This amendment clarifies Article 2, Section 1, Clause 6. The Vice-President becomes President when the President dies, resigns, or is removed from office. The new President then nominates a Vice-President, who must be approved by a majority of Congress. If a President is unable to perform the duties of the office, Congress must be informed of this fact in writing by the President or by the Vice-President and a majority of the cabinet. In this case, the Vice-President performs as acting President until the elected President is once again able to function.

This amendment was first used in a case in which Presidential disability was not a factor. In 1973 Vice-President Spiro T. Agnew resigned; President Richard M. Nixon filled the vacancy, according to Section 2 of this amendment, by naming Gerald R. Ford, a member of the House of Representatives, the Vice-President. Mr. Ford was approved by a majority of both houses of Congress. In 1974 Nixon became the first President to resign from office. Ford, in succeeding Nixon, became the first President not elected to that office or to the Vice-Presidency. To fill the Vice-Presidential vacancy, Ford appointed Nelson A. Rockefeller, who was then approved by a majority of both houses of Congress.

unable to discharge the powers and duties of his office, the Vice-President shall continue to discharge the same as Acting President; otherwise, the President shall assume the powers and duties of his office.

Amendment 26. Voting Age Lowered to 18 (1971)

Amendment 26. This amendment lowered the minimum voting age to 18.

Section 1. The right of citizens of the United States, who are 18 years of age or older, to vote shall not be denied or abridged by the United States or any state on account of age.

Section 2. The Congress shall have the power to enforce this article by appropriate legislation.

The Constitution was written at the Constitutional Convention in 1787. Delaware was the first and Rhode Island was the last of the original thirteen states to ratify the Constitution.

CHAPTER REVIEW

Summary

Long before Britain recognized American independence, the colonists were designing a plan of government to replace British rule. In 1781, the Articles of Confederation were adopted. This plan severely restricted the power of the national government by granting the powers to tax and regulate trade to the state governments. By 1787, many people believed that the Articles of Confederation should be revised or discarded.

The delegates who met in Philadelphia in 1787 to revise the Confederation decided to discard it and write a new plan of government. Their work was marked by many compromises and resulted in the Constitution.

The Constitution outlines the structure and powers of the national government. The three branches of the government each have separate powers and duties designed to prevent one branch from becoming too powerful. People who opposed the Constitution felt that it gave too much power to the national government. However, its supporters succeeded in persuading enough states to ratify the Constitution in 1788 to have it adopted as the law of the land.

Recalling the Facts

1. Why did the Articles of Confederation so severely limit the power of the national government?
2. What were the two major powers that the national government lacked under the Articles of Confederation? Why was the lack of these powers a problem?
3. Why is James Madison called the "Father of the Constitution"?
4. Briefly explain the purpose of each of the three branches of government as outlined in the Constitution.
5. Explain by using examples how the Constitution prevents one branch of the government from becoming too powerful.

Analyzing the Facts

1. Why do you think it was important that the delegates to the Constitutional Convention were willing to compromise?
2. How was the Great Compromise fair to both the large and small states?

3. Why do you think that some states insisted that a bill of rights be added to the Constitution before they agreed to ratify it?
4. Jefferson wrote, "a little resistance now and then is a good thing, and as necessary in the political world as storms in the physical." Do you agree or disagree with this idea? Explain your answer.
5. What do you think would have happened to the United States if the Articles of Confederation had not been discarded or revised?

Time and History

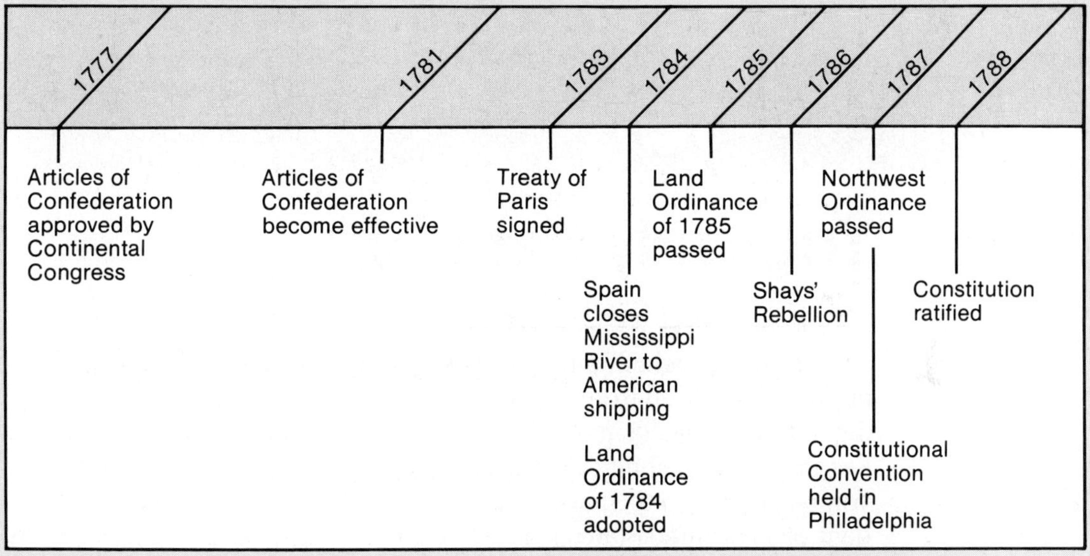

1. How many years before the United States became independent were the Articles of Confederation in effect?
2. In what year was the first Land Ordinance passed?
3. How many years after the United States acquired the Ohio Country was the Northwest Ordinance passed?
4. Which of the following topics might have been discussed when the Treaty of Paris was signed: Shays' Rebellion, the Constitutional Convention, the Articles of Confederation?
5. Why would farmers who bought land in the Northwest Territory in 1785 have difficulty transporting their goods to New Orleans?

Chapter 7 The Early Republic

On the morning of April 30, 1789, a crowd gathered outside the New York home in which George Washington was staying. Shortly after noon, a delegation from Congress arrived. Their task was to escort the first President-elect to Federal Hall. Later, standing on the porch of Federal Hall, Washington put his hand on a Bible. He was asked, "Do you solemnly swear that you will faithfully execute the office of President of the United States, and will to the best of your ability, preserve, protect and defend the Constitution of the United States?" "I solemnly swear," replied Washington. With that, the first President of the United States took office, and a new era in the nation's history began.

After you read this chapter, you will be able to:

1. Identify the challenges facing George Washington as the nation's first President.
2. Discuss the origins of the first political parties.
3. Explain the problems faced by John Adams during his presidency.

Background: The President is not elected directly by the people. Electors are chosen from each state. The number of electors each state is entitled to is equal to the number of representatives and senators that state has in Congress. The electors unanimously elected Washington.

1. The First Presidency

BEFORE YOU READ: *What challenges faced George Washington as the nation's first President?*

In July 1788, Congress called for elections to set up the new government. Elections were held during January and February 1789. George Washington was the unanimous choice for President. John Adams won the vice-presidency.

Washington the President

On April 14, George Washington received notification of his election. He set out from his home in Virginia, for New York City, the temporary capital of the United States. He was nervous, feeling "more anxious and painful sensations than I have words to express." It cheered him to see crowds of supporters all along the route to New York. Washington's arrival in New York caused great excitement. Cannons boomed, crowds cheered, and flags flew from every building. On April 30, 1789, Washington was installed in office, or **inaugurated**.

---

inaugurate to install in office with a formal ceremony

The responsibilities facing the first President were enormous. Because Washington was the first President, he had no one to model himself after. He had to set policy and direct the nation using his best judgment alone. He knew everyone was watching him closely. "The eyes [of Americans] . . . are upon me," Washington complained, "and no slip will pass unnoticed." Washington knew that his actions as President would set an example, or **precedent**, for all future Presidents to follow.

---

precedent an act or statement that serves as an example for a later one

---

Washington wanted to fill government positions with people who were "friends of the Constitution." He selected trusted associates to head each department in the executive branch. He picked Alexander Hamilton, his friend from New York, to be Secretary of the Treasury. Hamilton would handle financial matters for the government. General Henry Knox of Massachusetts was chosen to handle military affairs as Secretary of War. Washington picked the former governor of Virginia, Edmund Randolph, as Attorney General. Randolph would be advising the President on matters of law. Finally, Thomas Jefferson would look after foreign affairs as Secretary of State.

Washington quickly established the practice of calling his department heads together for advice. They came to be known as the President's Cabinet. The Constitution says nothing about forming a group of presidential advisers. The Cabinet, then, was a precedent established by President Washington.

Organizing the Judicial Branch

Congress also faced new and important responsibilities. One of its first tasks was to organize the federal court system. The

Background: The British government had long had a group of advisers called the Cabinet who met from time to time to advise the king on important matters.

Vocabulary Help: circuit—a periodic journey through a given area or territory to perform certain legal duties. Until 1891, when Congress created the circuit courts of appeals, Supreme Court justices "rode the circuit" to hear appeals from district courts.

Constitution in Article III had provided the outline: "The judicial power of the United States shall be vested in one Supreme Court, and in such inferior courts as the Congress may from time to time ordain and establish."

Congress acted to fill in the outline. In September 1789, it passed the Judiciary Act, which created two levels of federal courts. At the top level was the Supreme Court. The Supreme Court consisted of six members—a Chief Justice and five associate justices. John Jay was appointed the first Chief Justice. Jay had been a lawyer and had much experience in government service. He had been a member of the First and Second Continental Congresses and had helped negotiate the peace treaty with Great Britain at the end of the War for Independence. Few Americans could claim to know as much about the new Constitution.

The Judiciary Act established two other federal court systems below the Supreme Court. It divided the nation into 13 judicial areas, called Federal District Courts. One judge was assigned to each area to hear cases. The Judiciary Act also established three circuit courts. Each circuit court had three judges, two from the Supreme Court and one from the particular district. When the Supreme Court was not in session, the justices were expected to visit the different districts, or "ride the circuit." At appointed stops they would preside over the circuit courts.

The legal power of the Supreme Court, or its **jurisdiction**, was also clarified. The Supreme Court could act on three kinds of cases: those involving the Constitution, those involving treaties made by the federal government, and those dealing with state laws that conflict with federal laws.

---

jurisdiction authority or legal power to hear and decide cases

---

A New Economic Program

A workable federal court system was now in place. Another major job for the government was establishing an economic program for the nation. The job fell to Alexander Hamilton. Hamilton was a genius in financial matters.

Hamilton believed that a nation could only be politically stable if it was economically stable. And economic stability depended on the willingness of the government to aid businesses. Hamilton also believed that the United States had to have a strong military.

The government was deeply in debt from the War for Independence. It faced a national debt of $54 million. More than $11 million of the debt was owed to foreign bankers. The rest was owed to Americans for money loaned to fight the war. Hamilton began an economic program to help the nation. Between 1790 and 1792, he made recommendations that became known as the "Hamiltonian System."

Hamilton recommended that the government reduce the huge national debt by paying off all debts owed by the Continental Congress and the Confederation. He proposed that the federal government also take over payment of the debts the states had accumulated while fighting the War for Independence. His plan had two purposes. It would prove to the world that the United States honored its obligations. It would also increase the states' loyalty to the new federal government.

Discuss: The national debt today is over $1 trillion. Do you think this debt will ever be paid off? Why or why not?

Background: Western farmers had difficulty selling their grain to eastern customers because of high overland transportation costs. It was cheaper to distill the grain into whiskey, which could be carried over bad roads more easily than bulky farm products.

Hamilton next dealt with ways of raising money to run the government. He suggested that the government sell any lands it owned, such as the Northwest Territory, to raise large sums of money quickly. He also recommended that the government place taxes on certain goods as a way to raise income, or revenue, for the government. Hamilton proposed placing a **revenue tax** on all imports. In addition, Hamilton recommended that the government tax goods produced within the country. Hamilton wanted an **excise tax** placed on the manufacture of liquor. The purpose of the excise tax went beyond raising money. Hamilton wanted to make western farmers feel the power of the federal government. Western farmers were an independent group whose loyalties were to their region, not to the new federal government. The farmers' surplus grain often went to market in liquid form as whiskey. The excise tax would leave no doubt that the new government was a strong one.

revenue tax a tax that raises income for the government

excise tax a tax placed on goods produced within a country

The Bank of the United States

Alexander Hamilton also proposed the establishment of a national bank to help collect and pay out the government's funds. The Bank of the United States was a national banking system. It was made

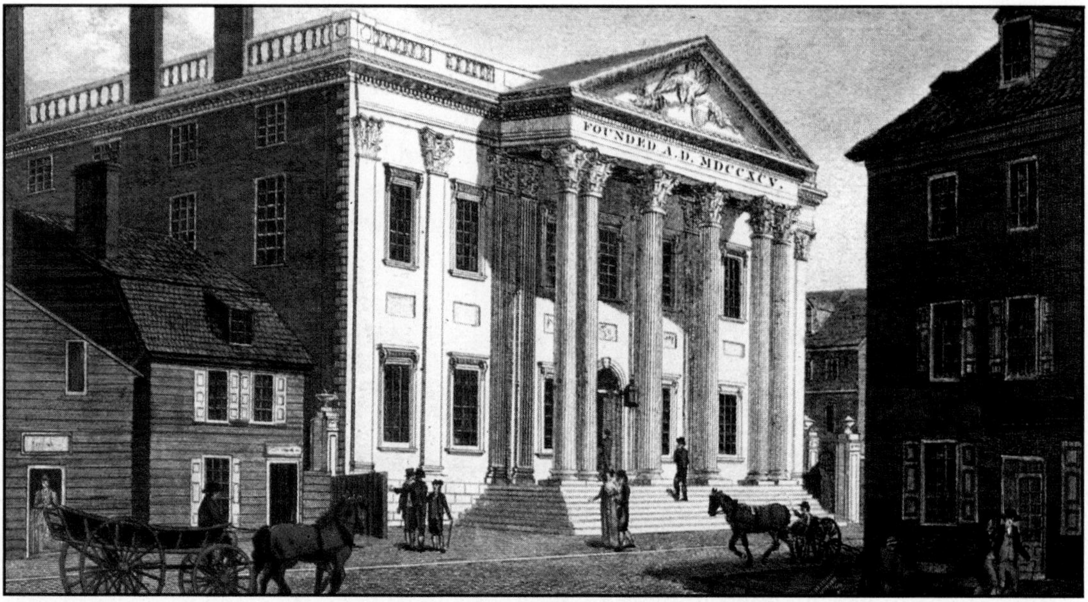

This engraving shows the Bank of the United States in Philadelphia as it looked in 1799.

Background: There were almost no banks of any kind in the United States in 1790. Hamilton felt that a national bank would allow businesses to grow more rapidly by loaning them money to expand their operations.

For Extra Interest: Invite a loan officer from a local bank to speak to the class on how individuals can obtain loans, how loans benefit the bank, and how they stimulate the growth of business.

up of a large central bank and branch banks in major cities. The Bank of the United States could print money, and it would hold the government's funds. The Bank also could make loans from these funds to help stimulate business and commerce.

Many influential government leaders opposed Hamilton's proposal for the Bank. They objected to the Bank because the Constitution did not specifically authorize the creation of a national bank. Hamilton argued that the Constitution gave two types of powers to the government. Some powers were specific powers. These were powers the Constitution described in detail, like the power to raise and collect taxes. Other powers were **implied powers**. These were powers that were not described in detail but were suggested by the wording of the Constitution. To prove his argument, Hamilton pointed to Section 8 of the Constitution. This was the elastic clause. It said that the government can pass all laws that are necessary and proper to help the nation. The Bank of the United States was constitutional under the elastic clause, Hamilton claimed. The Bank was needed to strengthen the nation's money system.

implied powers powers that are not clearly stated in the Constitution but are suggested because of the way the Constitution is worded

Thomas Jefferson and James Madison strongly disagreed. They charged that the Constitution contained no implied powers. The government could only exercise those powers specifically described in the Constitution. Because of this, they reasoned, the Bank of the United States was **unconstitutional**, or not in agreement with the highest law of the land.

unconstitutional not in agreement with the highest law of the land

In spite of these strong objections, Congress gave its approval to the Bank in 1791. It chartered the Bank of the United States for a 20-year period.

But a serious split was developing among some of the members of Washington's Cabinet. The President hoped the division would end, but it did not. Distrust and anger continued to grow between those who agreed with Hamilton and those who agreed with Jefferson and Madison.

Section Review

1. What challenges faced George Washington as the nation's first President?
2. What is the difference between a revenue tax and an excise tax?
3. What did Alexander Hamilton mean when he said that the Constitution contained implied powers?
4. Give an example of how Alexander Hamilton's beliefs are accepted and applied by our government today.

Background: Point out to the students that the Republicans of the 1790's are in no way connected to the Republican party today. Although called Republicans for short, the opponents of Hamilton were also known as the Democratic-Republicans.

2. Problems for the Federalists

BEFORE YOU READ: *What were the differences between the Federalists and the Republicans?*

By the spring of 1791, opposition to Hamilton's Federalist policies was increasing. Thomas Jefferson and James Madison emerged as leaders of the opposition. The opposition began calling themselves the "Republicans."

The rise of political parties alarmed many Americans, including Washington and Adams. It was believed that parties would divide the American people, making them more interested in the good of the party than the good of the nation. Vice-President Adams declared that the "division of the republic into two great parties . . . is to be dreaded as the greatest political evil." The two parties that emerged rallied around two men—Jefferson and Hamilton. The views of each man became the views of his party.

Jefferson Versus Hamilton

Jefferson spoke for the small farmers and the skilled working class. Hamilton represented the bankers, merchants, manufacturers, and large landowners. Jefferson, who believed in the ability of the common person to govern wisely, said, "I am not among those who fear the people. They, and not the rich, are our dependence for continued freedom." Hamilton believed government should be left to the educated and the wealthy. "Take mankind as they are, and what are they governed by? Their passions."

In the fall of 1791, Jefferson and Madison established the *National Gazette*. They started this newspaper to acquaint the public with the Republicans' views on government. It competed with the Federalists' newspaper, the *United States Gazette*, which was already being published.

Washington's Second Term

By 1792, George Washington strongly wished to retire to his home in Mount Vernon. He was tired after nearly 20 years in government service. Washington told Jefferson "that he really felt himself growing old; his bodily health less firm; his memory—always bad—becoming worse. . . . Business, therefore, [became] more irksome, and tranquility and retirement became an irresistible passion." Both Hamilton and Jefferson pleaded with him to accept reelection. The young nation still needed him as a symbol of strength and unity.

Washington reluctantly agreed to continue as President. On February 13, 1793, Washington was again the choice of the electors. The Federalist John Adams received 77 votes for Vice-President against 50 for George Clinton, the Republican party's candidate.

No sooner had Washington been elected than a new and dangerous problem arose in Europe. The French Revolution had broken out in 1789. The French overthrew the monarchy and established a republic. In 1793, the French government beheaded the king and queen, and it declared war on Great Britain and other European countries. Soon war engulfed all of Europe.

Vocabulary Help: political party—a group of people who have the same or similar ideas on how the government should direct the affairs of the nation. Have students name the first two political parties formed in the United States and identify the issues they disagreed on.

EUREKA!

Interchangeable Parts

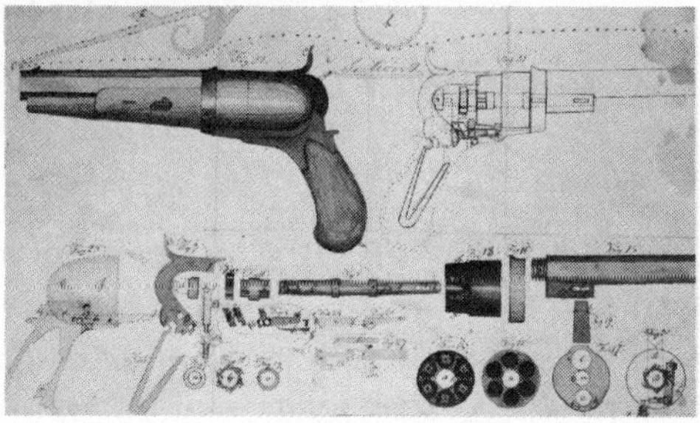

In 1798, Eli Whitney received a contract from the federal government to produce 10,000 muskets for the United States Army. He was supposed to deliver them in only 15 months. Whitney failed to meet his deadline. But in the process of trying, he invented a new method of manufacturing. This method of manufacturing laid the groundwork for the production methods of today.

The traditional way of making guns was for a skilled craftsperson to build each one by hand. Whitney realized that if he stuck to this time-consuming practice, he would never be able to deliver the muskets on time. So he invented machines and tools that would manufacture the different parts of the guns. For example, one machine produced triggers, while another made the gun barrels. Complete guns were then assembled from the parts.

Whitney called his method "the uniformity system." In order for the guns to fit together, all of the parts had to be identical and interchangeable.

Whitney demonstrated his method for officials at the treasury office in Philadelphia in 1800. They chose parts at random from parcels that Whitney had brought with him. Then Whitney assembled a perfect musket before their eyes.

Despite the success of the system, Whitney was several years late delivering his muskets to the army. It took time to set up the machinery for his factory. But the military recognized how efficient the system of interchangeable parts was. Soon after this, the army required all of its guns to be made by the uniformity system. It was the beginning of modern manufacturing methods.

The United States was caught in the middle as France and Great Britain battled. The United States wanted to trade with both sides. However, the American people were divided over what position their country should take. Some Americans wished to remain completely uninvolved. Some wanted to remain uninvolved but give nonmilitary help to France, our old ally from the American Revolution. Jefferson and the Republicans supported France. The Republicans felt the United States owed France a great debt for its help in the American Revolution. In addition, the French were fighting for many of the same ideals fought for in

Background: The United States depended heavily on import tariffs as a source of revenue. Since America's imports came primarily from Great Britain, the United States could not afford to jeopardize trade relations with Britain by siding with France.

the American Revolution. Others wanted to remain uninvolved but give help to Great Britain, with whom the United States had deeper ties. Hamilton and the Federalists were part of this group. The Federalists did not want to hurt American trade with Great Britain. The United States traded more goods with Great Britain than with France. The Federalists also were shocked and disgusted by the violent nature of the French Revolution.

Most Americans held strong views about the French Revolution and the war in Europe. Unfortunately, there was deep disagreement over what position the United States should take.

Problems developed at home for the new government in 1794 because of the excise tax on whiskey. This tax hit western farmers in Pennsylvania, Virginia, and North Carolina most heavily. Opposition to the whiskey tax became violent in western Pennsylvania. Farmers defied the government and refused to pay the tax. They also attacked tax collectors, pouring hot tar and feathers on some. Washington remembered Daniel Shays and feared that history was repeating itself. Washington personally marched an army into Pennsylvania to crush the "Whiskey Rebellion." The angry farmers, learning that troops were on the way, scattered before Washington arrived. The federal government had shown that it meant to have its laws obeyed, even if force had to be used.

Trouble All Around

Foreign affairs became the most important concern of Washington's second term in office. Washington wanted to avoid getting involved in the European war. He also wanted to maintain trade with all of the warring nations of Europe. America's right to **freedom of the seas**, or freedom to trade with any nation, had to be protected.

---

freedom of the seas the right of any nation's merchant ships to travel in any waters in order to trade with any nation

---

Washington was also concerned with protecting American territory from foreign interference. The British still controlled forts in the Northwest Territory. Spain still would not permit Americans to ship goods down the Mississippi River. American Indians who lived in the Northwest Territory demanded that the United States give up all claim to the Northwest Territory. Washington faced many difficult problems.

By the early 1790's, France was putting enormous pressure on the United States to join in its war against Great Britain. The French declared that the Americans owed it to France to help them. Washington was determined to avoid involvement at all costs. On April 22, 1793, he issued a Proclamation of **Neutrality**, or noninvolvement. The Federalists cheered the action. The Republicans complained that France and freedom had been betrayed. Relations with France grew worse. Washington stuck to his position. He forbade American citizens from participating in the war.

---

neutrality a position of not participating directly or indirectly in a war between other nations

---

Discuss: Compare the government's response to the Whiskey Rebellion in 1794 to its response to Shays' Rebellion in 1786–1787. What does this tell you about the strength of the government in 1794 compared to 1786–1787?

Background: American settlers in the Northwest Territory claimed that the British outposts were supplying the Indians in the area with guns to use against them. These settlers demanded that the government force the British out of the territory.

This picture shows the impressment of American sailors by the British.

Treaties with Britain and Spain

In the spring of 1794, John Jay was sent to Great Britain to work out differences and improve relations. He asked the British to leave the forts in the Northwest Territory. He called for a halt to the British practice of **impressment**. The British had been stopping American ships and kidnapping American sailors to force them into the British navy. The reason for this was that the British navy treated its sailors harshly. British sailors would often desert when their ships reached a foreign port. Many times they got jobs on American ships. Great Britain felt justified in stopping American ships and taking off anyone suspected of being a deserter. Unfortunately, many innocent Americans were seized along with the British deserters. Jay also insisted that Great Britain accept America's right to freedom of the seas.

---

impressment the practice of forcing people into public service, especially into a navy

---

In November 1794, Jay concluded a treaty with Great Britain. Under the terms of the treaty, Great Britain agreed to leave the Northwest Territory. But Great Britain refused to stop its policy of impressment. Great Britain also refused to accept America's right to freedom of the seas.

Background: The British navy had always used impressment on sailors since their navy was the least desirable of their armed services. Although Americans considered military service a duty, they felt that the British should not enforce it in a manner that violated American rights.

Background: Although extremely unpopular with the Republicans, the Jay Treaty did avert war with Great Britain. In 1793, the United States lacked an effective navy and could not have hoped to win a conflict with Britain.

When the terms of the treaty were made known in America, few people were pleased. Both President Washington and John Jay came under heavy criticism by Americans.

Some of the criticism of Washington diminished in October 1795, when Thomas Pinckney negotiated an important treaty with Spain. Under the terms of the Pinckney Treaty, the United States was permitted to use the Mississippi River and the port of New Orleans without fear of interference. This treaty was a major triumph for the government, and it also satisfied westerners' needs.

Securing the Nation's Borders

The Indians in the more remote areas of the Northwest Territory and the South were determined to hold onto their lands at all costs. Washington said that he wanted "to advance the happiness of the Indians and to attach them firmly to the United States." But Washington and Secretary of War Knox soon realized that force would have to be used to bring the Indians to the bargaining table. The American Indians were determined to resist the American army.

General Wayne is shown here dictating the terms of the Treaty of Greenville after defeating the Indians at the Battle of Fallen Timbers.

Background: Spanish officials suspected that the Jay Treaty contained an unpublished clause outlining a joint attack by American and British troops. They readily signed the Pinckney Treaty in 1795 hoping that friendly relations with the United States would prevent such an attack.

Background: The defeat of American forces in the Ohio Country in 1791 was among the worst defeats suffered by whites in the entire history of warfare between whites and American Indians. Over 600 whites were killed and another 250 were wounded.

As early as the 1790's, two groups of American militia marched into the western part of the Ohio Country to conquer Shawnees, Miamis, Ottawas, Chippewas, and others. The Americans were badly defeated.

President Washington called on General Anthony Wayne to lead a new attack against the Indians in the Ohio Country. At the Battle of Fallen Timbers near Toledo, Wayne defeated the Indians in August 1794. In the Treaty of Greenville, signed the following summer, the American Indians abandoned their claims to much of the Northwest Territory. Many of the Indians, especially the Shawnee, were very bitter about the treaty.

Washington's Farewell Address

As the election of 1796 approached, Washington was determined to step down. He issued a Farewell Address, written with the aid of Hamilton, on September 19, 1796. Washington offered his advice on foreign and domestic matters. He urged Americans to remain true to the Union and the representative form of government. He warned against "permanent alliances" with foreign nations, by which he meant France. Alliances might pull the United States into wars in which it did not belong. Washington also warned against political parties, by which he meant the Republicans. Parties could only create enemies, drive Americans apart, and threaten the Union, in his opinion. Washington told Americans to work against the slowly emerging sectional hostility. He was referring to the three sections of the nation—the North, South, and West. Each section seemed to be showing more concern for itself and its problems than for the country as a whole.

George Washington had given shape and direction to the presidency. He established a workable executive branch and, with the aid of Hamilton, a sound economic plan. He was able to resolve problems with Spain. With France, Great Britain, and the American Indians, he was less successful.

George Washington returned to his home at Mount Vernon, where he spent the remaining years of his life enjoying his plantation and his family. He died peacefully on December 14, 1799.

Section Review

1. What were the differences between the Federalist party and the Republican party?
2. Define impressment and explain why it upset the United States.
3. What was the Pinckney Treaty? Why was it important?
4. Which of the concerns raised by George Washington in his Farewell Address seems most significant to you? Explain your answer.

Background: Mount Vernon, Washington's home, lies about 21 km (13 mi) south of Washington, D.C. on the Potomac River. In 1799, the estate totaled more than 3,240 hectares (8,000 acres) and supported about 240 people, free and slave.

Background: Many delegates to the Constitutional Convention had favored the idea of having the President elected by the Congress. Other delegates favored direct election by the people. The electoral college system that emerged was a compromise.

3. The Second Presidency

BEFORE YOU READ: *What problems faced John Adams during his administration?*

The United States had two well-established political parties by the time Washington left office, the Federalists and the Republicans. The founders of the nation had never foreseen political parties. They had not planned for them when they wrote the Constitution.

According to the Constitution, members of the electoral college were to cast two votes in a presidential election. The electors did not specify which vote was for a President and which was for a Vice-President. They simply chose from a list of qualified candidates, none of whom was supposed to belong to a political party. The candidate with the largest number of votes and also a majority was elected President. The candidate with the second largest number of votes became Vice-President. This is how President Washington and his Vice-President, John Adams, were elected in 1788 and 1792.

The rise of political parties in the 1790's altered this process. By 1796, the Federalists and the Republicans each planned to support two candidates, one for the presidency and one for the vice-presidency. This made for a confusing situation in the elections of 1796 and 1800.

The Election of 1796

In 1796, John Adams and Thomas Jefferson were the presidential candidates of the rival parties. Adams' partner on the Federalist ticket was Thomas Pinckney. Jefferson's partner on the Republican ticket was Aaron Burr. Adams received 71 electoral votes to 68 for Jefferson. They were followed by Pinckney with 59 and Burr with 30 votes. The Federalists had won the presidency but not the vice-presidency. Adams, the Federalist, became President because he received the most votes. The Republican, Thomas Jefferson, became Vice-President because he received the second largest number of votes. The nation faced the possibility of

John Adams

Background: Although bribing officials was a more accepted practice then than it is today, Talleyrand demanded $250,000. This was a huge sum and, at today's prices, would amount to several million dollars.

very real problems. Adams and Jefferson disagreed on just about every issue.

John Adams' presidency was not a smooth one. John Adams was intelligent, hardworking, and patriotic. He also was headstrong and outspoken. Benjamin Franklin once said of Adams that he was "always an honest man, often a wise one, but sometimes, and in some things, absolutely out of his senses." Many of the Federalists Adams appointed to his Cabinet were not loyal to him. These advisers openly took their orders from Alexander Hamilton. Hamilton thought he could run the government from New York, where he was the leader of that state's Federalist party.

Relations with France Worsen

France felt betrayed when the United States began negotiating a treaty with the British. The French navy started seizing American vessels on the high seas in revenge. By the time Adams became President, nearly 300 American ships had been seized. The President still wanted peace. In May 1797, Adams sent a delegation of Americans to France to work out a treaty of friendship and trade. The American delegates were Elbridge Gerry of Massachusetts, Charles Pinckney of South Carolina, and John Marshall, a well-known lawyer and Federalist from Virginia.

The three Americans arrived in France in October. Upon their arrival they were visited by three agents of the French government. The agents gave the Americans a message. The French foreign minister, Talleyrand, demanded a huge bribe as the price of negotiating a treaty. Although this was a common practice among European nations, the Americans were outraged. The talks broke off, and Marshall and Pinckney came home. In their report of the incident, the Americans referred to the three French agents as X, Y, and Z. Thus the incident became known as the XYZ Affair. In April 1798, President Adams released the delegates' report to the American public. Americans were furious. War hysteria swept the nation.

John Adams refused to declare war, but he ordered Congress to prepare for it just the same. Congress passed measures to strengthen the army and create a navy. Several warships were rapidly built. Congress also repealed the Treaty of 1778 with France and authorized American ships to attack those of the French. Congress was determined to defend the nation's right to freedom of the seas.

For the next two years, from 1798 to 1800, the French and American navies clashed in an undeclared war. France had more sailors and more guns than the United States. Neither side proved itself the victor, although Americans captured some 80 French vessels.

The Alien and Sedition Acts

In 1798, the Federalists passed four laws designed to restrict criticism of and opposition to the undeclared war with France. The laws were called the Alien and Sedition Acts. The Alien Act gave the President the power to order suspicious persons who were not citizens of the United States to leave the country. The Sedition Act said that Americans could be fined or jailed if they criticized the Presi-

Background: Despite the furor over the XYZ Affair, the Republicans remained strong supporters of the French and the ideals of the French Revolution. The Alien and Sedition Acts were passed by the Federalist-controlled Congress to silence the Republicans.

Famous Americans

BENJAMIN BANNEKER

Benjamin Banneker was born a free black in Maryland in 1731. Although he had very little formal schooling, Banneker was especially good in mathematics and the sciences. During his lifetime, he learned enough astronomy to predict an eclipse of the sun. In 1789, Banneker completed work on an almanac for the year 1790. It contained predictions for the weather and information about the tides, moons, crops, and sun. Thomas Jefferson saw the almanac and was very impressed. He asked President Washington to appoint Banneker to the committee that was planning the new capital, Washington, D.C.

The committee that planned Washington, D.C., was made up of three people. Major Pierre Charles L'Enfant, a French engineer and architect, had been chosen to design the city. Major Andrew George Ellicott, an American, and Banneker were to survey the land and establish the city's boundaries. L'Enfant was a stubborn and temperamental man. He insisted on going ahead with his plans in spite of budget problems and land claim disputes. President Washington finally dismissed L'Enfant in 1792. L'Enfant left the United States in anger. He took with him the plans for the city. President Washington turned to Banneker and Ellicott to complete the work. The two men were able to reconstruct the plans for the city from memory, and work continued. Banneker was to consider his participation in the project as his greatest accomplishment. James Henry, Secretary of War, agreed. He said that Banneker's achievements were "fresh proof that the powers of the mind were disconnected with the color of the skin."

But Banneker felt that more than compliments were due to black Americans. In a letter to Jefferson, Banneker wrote several pages on the injustice of slavery. He reminded Jefferson of his own words, "that all men are created equal."

Banneker's last years were spent defending the cause of world peace. He suggested that all children should be educated in the goals of peace. These concerns made Banneker known and respected world wide.

dent or members of Congress. This act was aimed at silencing Republican opposition to the undeclared war. Over the next two years, 25 Republicans were brought to trial for violating the Sedition Act. Ten were convicted, fined, and jailed.

Vocabulary Help: theory—an idea or plan of how something might be done. Ask students how the Compact Theory proposed that the constitutionality of laws be determined.

This picture shows the Executive Mansion in 1799.

The other two laws included in the Alien and Sedition Acts restricted people's freedoms in similar ways. With these Alien and Sedition Acts, the Federalists were chipping away at the basic liberties of the American people.

Jefferson and Madison led the Republican opposition to the Alien and Sedition Acts. They condemned the acts in writing. Jefferson wrote the Kentucky Resolutions. Madison wrote the Virginia Resolutions. These resolutions said that the Alien and Sedition Acts were unconstitutional. The resolutions also set forth a theory about the Constitution called the "*Compact*" or "*States' Rights Theory*." This theory says that the actions of the states formed the federal government. The states gave the federal government specific powers in the Constitution. All laws that go beyond these powers can be judged by the states to be unconstitutional. The states, not the courts, were the final judge of the federal government's actions. The legislatures of Kentucky and Virginia adopted these resolutions. The Compact Theory raised a serious question about the nature of the relationship between the states and the federal government.

Northern states rejected the Compact Theory, while southern states largely agreed with Jefferson and Madison. The Alien and Sedition Acts themselves either were repealed or expired between 1801 and 1802.

In 1800, as Adams' first term was ending, the President sent William Vans Murray to Paris to talk with Napoleon Bonaparte, who had seized power in France. In September 1800, an agreement was reached that ended the undeclared naval

Vocabulary Help: theory—an idea or plan of how something might be done. Ask students how the Compact Theory proposed that the constitutionality of laws be determined.

Background: Pierre Charles L'Enfant had come to America in 1777 to serve in the Continental army. In 1789, he remodeled Federal Hall in New York City. His design for Washington, D.C. included broad avenues with generous space for parks.

war between France and the United States.

A New Capital

In November 1790, the nation's capital had moved from New York to Philadelphia. Washington and Adams governed the nation from there. But plans were already being made to build a new capital, one that would serve as the permanent capital city.

Both the North and the South wanted the nation's capital to be built in their region. A deal was made in 1790 to build the capital in the South. Presiding over the deal were Thomas Jefferson and Alexander Hamilton. Jefferson promised enough southern votes in Congress to pass part of Hamilton's economic program. Hamilton, in turn, promised enough northern votes to put the capital in the South. In July 1790, Congress established the District of Columbia along the banks of the Potomac River. The site was selected by George Washington. In March 1791, Washington appointed the French engineer and architect, Pierre Charles L'Enfant, to plan the town. The executive mansion, begun in 1792, was first occupied by John Adams in 1800. In that year, the government moved with the President to the new federal capital. By then, many were calling it "Washington."

The small town of Washington seemed dull when compared to the excitement of New York and Philadelphia. Washington was a swampy, mosquito-ridden place that was terribly hot and humid in the summer. Washington's muddy streets were lined with creaky wooden boardinghouses. This was where members of Congress stayed. The President's mansion was located at the northwestern end of Pennsylvania Avenue. The unfinished Capitol building was located at the southeastern end of the same road. The new capital city had little appeal for members of Congress. It was many years before members of Congress did not dash back to their home states when Congress recessed. It was still more years before they brought their families with them to come and live in Washington.

Section Review

1. What problems faced John Adams during his administration?
2. How did the XYZ Affair lead to an undeclared naval war with France?
3. Why were the Alien and Sedition Acts passed? Why were Jefferson and Madison opposed to them?
4. Why do you think the undeclared war with France never became a full-fledged war?

Discuss: Congressional representatives now stay in Washington, D.C., almost year-round. What changes have taken place in the past 200 years that have made Washington a more pleasant place to live and work?

CHAPTER REVIEW

Summary

With ratification of the Constitution in 1788 came the task of putting its principles into action. In 1789, George Washington was inaugurated as the first President, and the structure of the federal court system was established. From 1790 to 1792, Alexander Hamilton proposed several controversial measures to strengthen the financial structure of the new nation.

The arguments that erupted over Hamilton's program led to the establishment of the first political parties in the United States: the Republican party and the Federalist party. These two parties held opposing views on many issues.

In 1793, Washington began his second term of office with foreign affairs as his most important concern. Under his strong yet careful leadership, the United States avoided military involvement in the war between France and Great Britain. In 1795, a treaty with Spain opened the Mississippi River to American shipping, and in that same year American Indians gave up their claims to the Northwest Territory. By the time John Adams became President in 1797, the United States had succeeded in establishing a strong and stable government.

Recalling the Facts

1. Why did Washington, as the first President, have to be particularly careful about what he did in office?
2. What groups of Americans did the Republicans represent? What groups were represented by the Federalists?
3. Why did the Republicans feel that the United States should support France in its war with Great Britain? Why did the Federalists favor supporting Great Britain?
4. What were the three demands that John Jay made of Great Britain in 1794? To which of these demands did Britain agree?
5. How did it happen that Adams, a Federalist, and Jefferson, a Republican, became President and Vice-President in the election of 1800?

Analyzing the Facts

1. Do you think that the United States should have supported France in its war against Great Britain? Explain your answer.
2. Why did the British practice of impressment anger Americans?
3. Why do you think it is important for the President and the Vice-President to be members of the same political party?
4. Compare the provisions of the Alien and Sedition Acts to the rights guaranteed by Amendments I and V of the Constitution. Why do you think that Jefferson and Madison considered the acts to be unconstitutional?

Time and History

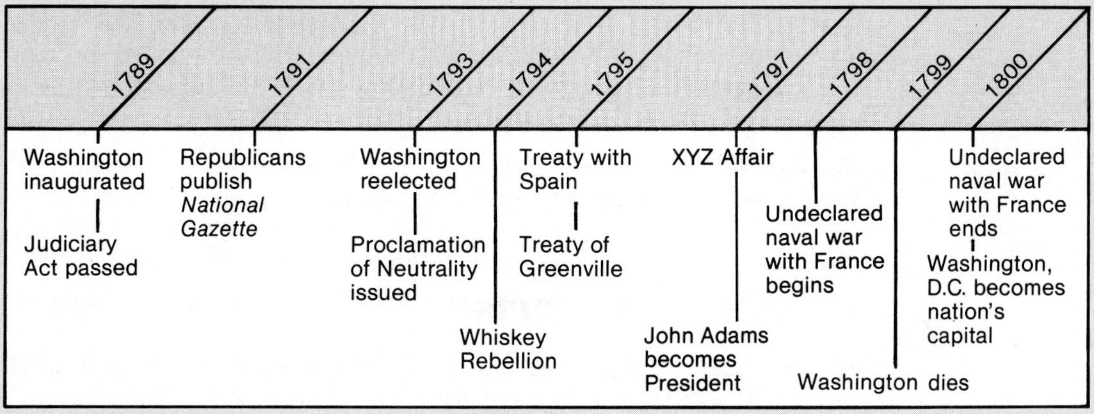

1. Who was the President during the XYZ Affair?
2. How many years after he retired from public service did Washington die?
3. During what years did the United States fight an undeclared naval war with France?
4. In what year did the Republican party begin to publish the *National Gazette*?
5. Why was George Washington never inaugurated in Washington, D.C.?

UNIT REVIEW

Summary

In the late seventeenth century, the British government changed its colonial policy from one of neglect to one of increased regulation. This new policy caused resentment in the colonies, which ultimately led to the Declaration of Independence and war. In the War for Independence, George Washington's small and inexperienced Continental army defeated the more powerful British forces. A new nation, the United States, was born.

The United States first governed itself under the Articles of Confederation. When this form of government proved incapable of solving the problems faced by the new nation, it was discarded. A new plan of government, the Constitution, was approved in 1788.

In the 1790's, under the leadership of Presidents Washington and Adams, the United States worked to resolve conflicts with Great Britain, Spain, France, and the American Indians. By the turn of the century, the United States had successfully met the challenge of establishing a stable and democratic government.

Recalling the Facts

1. Why did the colonists resist British efforts to tax them?
2. What advantages did the British have in the War for Independence?
3. Why were the battles at Saratoga and Yorktown important battles in the War for Independence?
4. Why was government under the Articles of Confederation weak?
5. Over what issues did Jefferson and Hamilton disagree in the 1790's?

Analyzing the Facts

1. What effect did the French and Indian War have on the relationship between Great Britain and the colonies? Explain your answer.
2. Which of the following do you think did the most to advance the cause of American independence: the Sons of Liberty, the British Parliament, or the Continental Congress? Explain your answer.
3. Why do you think that many colonists remained uncommitted to the Revolution?

4. Explain three ways in which the Constitution differed from the Articles of Confederation.
5. What did George Washington do to earn him the title "Father of His Country"?

Vocabulary Review

Define the following terms.

monopoly	guerilla warfare	precedent
rebellion	confederation	jurisdiction
militia	compromise	implied powers
mercenary	federal system	neutrality

Sharpening Your Skills

Answer the two questions below based on the map of Washington's retreat on page 132.

1. How far did Washington's forces travel from New York City to Trenton, New Jersey?
2. How far did Washington's army travel from Trenton to Morristown, New Jersey?

Answer the three questions below based on the chart of Checks and Balances on page 161.

3. How can the Supreme Court check the power of Congress?
4. What group has more checks on presidential power, the Congress or the Supreme Court?
5. How can the Congress check the President's power to veto laws?

Writing and Research

1. Research one of the following colonial crafts: soap making, candle making, spinning, weaving, dyeing, barrel making, silver or pewter making, printing and bookbinding, cabinetmaking, iron forging, quilting, flour milling, shoemaking, gunmaking, and so on. Write a report or give an oral presentation describing how the craft was practiced during colonial times.
2. Make a list of all the rights and freedoms guaranteed to Americans in the Bill of Rights. From your list choose the one that you feel is the most important, and write a paragraph explaining why.

Unit 3

The Nation Grows

8 *Thomas Jefferson was President from 1801 to 1809. During his first term in office, he purchased the Louisiana Territory, which doubled the size of the United States. Jefferson's second term was troubled by growing conflicts between the United States, Great Britain, and France.*

9 Between 1812 and 1815, the United States fought another war with Great Britain, the War of 1812. There was no clear winner in the War of 1812, but it caused the nation to enter into a brief period of harmony and pride called the "Era of Good Feelings."

10 The American Industrial Revolution began in the 1790's. Machines were invented that sped production of all kinds of goods. Faster production also meant lower costs for consumers. As consumers demanded more goods, a need developed for better systems of transportation and communication.

Chapter 8
The Age of Jefferson

Thomas Jefferson was a widely admired man by the time he became President in 1801. He had been the governor of Virginia, a member of the Continental Congress, secretary of state, and Vice-President. He was the author of the Declaration of Independence and the founder of the University of Virginia. Thomas Jefferson played many roles in the early years of the nation. Jefferson achieved what few others have—he stamped his name forever on an era in United States history.

After you read this chapter, you will be able to:

1. Summarize the major political programs of Thomas Jefferson's first term as President.
2. Explain the importance of the Louisiana Purchase.
3. Describe how problems in foreign affairs threatened to draw the United States into war with Great Britain and France.

Background: Jefferson was finally elected President by the House of Representatives on the 36th ballot. His election was largely due to the influence of Alexander Hamilton. Burr and Hamilton, both lawyers in New York City, were long-standing and bitter competitors.

1. "The Revolution of 1800"

BEFORE YOU READ: *What were the major goals and programs of Jefferson's first term in office?*

The Federalists were losing supporters as the election of 1800 drew near. The party's policies and actions over the past 12 years had angered and upset many Americans. Matters such as heavy taxes, the Whiskey Rebellion, Jay's Treaty, and the Alien and Sedition Acts added to the Federalists' troubles. They were also split among themselves. In spite of these problems, however, John Adams chose to run for reelection.

The Republicans again selected Thomas Jefferson to run against Adams. Jefferson's running mate was Aaron Burr. The Republicans attacked the Federalists' policies, especially the Alien and Sedition Acts. The Republicans believed these acts were a serious threat to rights guaranteed to Americans by law. They made **civil liberties** the main issue of the campaign.

---

civil liberties rights guaranteed to a person by law or custom, such as freedom of speech

---

When all the votes were counted, the Republicans had won. Adams received 65 electoral votes while Jefferson and Burr each received 73 votes. The Republicans had won the presidency. But which Republican candidate was the new President—Jefferson or Burr? In the case of a tie, the Constitution said the House of Representatives must choose between the two candidates. Each state's delegation in the House would cast one vote. A candidate needed a majority of these votes to be declared the winner.

Jefferson had the support of eight of the nation's 16 state delegations. Burr could count on the votes of six. One more vote would give Jefferson the majority, and thus the presidency.

The battle in the House between the supporters of Jefferson and Burr dragged on into 1801. Inauguration day, on March 4, drew closer, and still no President had been chosen. Finally, on February 17, the House chose Jefferson. Aaron Burr would be the Vice-President.

To prevent a similar crisis from occurring again, the Twelfth Amendment to the Constitution was passed in 1804. It requires that the President and Vice-President be elected by separate ballots.

A New President

On March 4, 1801, Thomas Jefferson walked from his boardinghouse to the Capitol. There he took the presidential oath and delivered his inaugural address. He began his address with an attempt to restore harmony in the nation: "We are all Republicans—we are all Federalists." Jefferson meant that Americans shared the same democratic beliefs even though they might have different opinions about how the nation should be run or how it should grow and prosper.

The presidential transition from John Adams to Thomas Jefferson was an important moment for the United States. Power had passed peacefully from one political party to another. Jefferson later said that "the revolution of 1800 . . . was

Background: Inauguration Day was changed from March 4 to January 20 by the 20th Amendment passed in 1933. Elections for President are held on the first Tuesday after the first Monday in November.

Famous Americans

AARON BURR

Aaron Burr is one of the most complex figures in American history. He was a brilliant attorney, a hero of the American Revolution, and a dedicated Vice-President. Yet he was also a man of great pride and a schemer.

Burr was born in Newark, New Jersey, in 1756. Both of his parents died by the time Burr was three years old. Burr was then raised by an uncle, who found Burr to be a bright but rebellious child. Burr entered Princeton University at the age of 13 and studied law.

During the War for Independence, Burr served under many generals and became a regiment commander. He fought bravely in the battle of Monmouth.

After the war, Burr became active in New York politics. He was appointed attorney general of New York, elected to the United States Senate, and later became a member of the New York Assembly. Then, in 1800, Burr tied Thomas Jefferson in the race for the presidency. The House of Representatives chose Jefferson to be President. Burr became the third Vice-President of the United States.

Before he finished his term as Vice-President, Burr decided to run against Alexander Hamilton for governor of New York. Burr lost the election. During the campaign, Hamilton is said to have remarked that Burr was a "dangerous man and one who ought not to be trusted with the reins of government." Burr responded to this by challenging Hamilton to a duel. On July 11, 1804, after the election was over, the two men met at Weehawken, New Jersey. Opinions differ as to whether Hamilton ever fired at Burr, but Hamilton was shot and fatally wounded.

Burr was never punished for the shooting. He returned to Washington, D.C., and finished out his term as Vice-President.

In 1806, Burr got involved in a scheme to seize Spanish America. It is not clear whether he intended to make an independent nation of this land or make it into an American colony. Burr's plans were betrayed to the American government, and he was put on trial for treason. Burr was brought to Richmond, Virginia, for his trial. Burr was declared innocent by Chief Justice John Marshall because he did not have any actual plans to overthrow the government. In addition, two witnesses could not be found who would support the treason charge.

Even though he was declared innocent, Burr's reputation was ruined. He left the United States and lived in Europe for four years. He then returned to New York City, where he practiced law until his death in 1836.

Discuss: Do you think it would be a good idea for the current President to encourage people to stop by and visit? Why or why not?

as real a revolution in the principles of our government as that of 1776 was in its form; not effected indeed by the sword, . . . but by the [vote] of the people." Change could take place in the United States without violence.

The new President brought a new style to the office. Jefferson abandoned the coach and six horses used by Washington and Adams. Instead, he rode on horseback or walked about in the streets of Washington, D.C. Jefferson also abandoned the formal weekly presidential receptions for officials and foreign dignitaries. He encouraged all people to stop by and visit.

The President preferred to handle political discussions in a casual atmosphere. He held dinners at the Executive Mansion three times a week for members of Congress. At these dinners Jefferson raised matters such as taxes, the economy, or foreign affairs. The President usually found his guests willing to discuss them.

Jefferson's Presidential Program

In 1801, the world was at peace. The war between France and Great Britain had ended temporarily. When Jefferson took office, he did not have to worry about involving the United States in foreign policy matters. During his first term, Jefferson was free to concentrate on issues and problems at home.

Unlike the Federalists, Thomas Jefferson had always believed in a weak federal government. According to Jefferson, the government should not be a burden to the American public. In putting his beliefs into action, Jefferson lowered taxes and repealed the excise tax on whiskey. To save money, he cut spending for defense. Jefferson reduced the size of the army from 4,000 to 2,500 soldiers. He sold or dismantled many of the navy's ships. Jefferson also ordered that no new naval vessels be built. The money saved from Jefferson's program reduced the national debt by nearly half. President Jefferson was remarkably successful in keeping his pledge to run "a wise and frugal [not wasteful] government."

The Federalists were powerless to prevent Jefferson from implementing his program because they were greatly outnumbered in Congress. However, the Federalists still controlled the judicial branch of government. During the 1790's, not a single Republican was appointed to a federal court judgeship. In February 1801, one month before Jefferson's inauguration, the Federalists pushed the Judiciary Act through Congress. The act created 16 new federal judgeships, which John Adams immediately filled with Federalists. Some of the new judges were nicknamed "midnight judges." Late into the evening of his last day in office, John Adams sat up signing the papers making these people judges.

Jefferson and the Republicans were convinced that the Federalist judges would declare Republican legislation unconstitutional. Jefferson was determined to fight the Judiciary Act of 1801. First, he sent word to those "midnight judges" whose appointment papers had not yet been delivered. Jefferson told them to consider themselves without a job. Then, in 1802, the President had Congress repeal the Judiciary Act of 1801.

Background: In 1801, the War Department consisted of only the secretary, an accountant, 14 clerks, and two messengers. The attorney general did not even have a clerk. Yet to Jefferson's eyes, this tiny bureaucracy had become "too complicated, too expensive."

Chief Justice John Marshall

The structure of the judicial branch would return to its original form as outlined in the Judiciary Act of 1789.

William Marbury, one of Adams' "midnight judges," was angry with Jefferson. Marbury's papers had been signed and sealed by Adams. By accident Adams had not delivered them before he left office. Marbury's papers still sat on the desk of Jefferson's secretary of state, James Madison. Marbury wanted the papers to prove that he could hold his new judgeship. Jefferson ordered Madison to withhold delivery. Marbury filed suit in court. He asked the court, based on section 13 of the Judiciary Act of 1789, to order Madison to deliver the papers. The suit, *Marbury v. Madison*, came before the Supreme Court in February 1803.

The Chief Justice of the Supreme Court was John Marshall. Chief Justice Marshall refused to issue a court order forcing Madison to deliver Marbury's appointment papers. Marshall said that section 13 of the Judiciary Act of 1789 did give the Chief Justice the right to issue a court order. But, he continued, no such right was granted by the Constitution. Since the Constitution is the supreme law of the land, Marshall declared section 13 of the Judiciary Act of 1789 unconstitutional. Marshall's decision was the first time the Supreme Court declared an act of Congress, or part of one, unconstitutional. Marshall's action established the Supreme Court as the final authority in determining the constitutionality of laws. This is called the principle of **judicial review**. Marshall's decision expanded the power of the Supreme Court.

judicial review the right of the Supreme Court to declare an act of Congress unconstitutional

Section Review

1. What were the major goals and programs of Jefferson's first term as President?
2. What is the Twelfth Amendment to the Constitution? Why was it passed?
3. Define civil liberties and judicial review.
4. How did Jefferson's economic program differ from that of Alexander Hamilton?

 Discuss: How can Congress check the power of the Supreme Court to declare laws unconstitutional?

Background: France never took military possession of the Louisiana Territory. On November 30, 1803, Spain turned the colony over to a representative of the French government, and on December 20 the French transferred the colony to the United States.

2. Gaining a Western Empire

BEFORE YOU READ: *How was the Louisiana Territory obtained by the United States?*

Ever since the United States gained its independence from Great Britain in 1783, many American leaders had been interested in making the Louisiana Territory part of the United States. The Louisiana Territory was huge. It was about 3,219 kilometers (2,000 miles) wide, stretching from the Mississippi River to the Rocky Mountains. It was about the same distance in length, stretching from Canada to the region's southernmost point at the mouth of the Mississippi River. The Louisiana Territory could provide more land for a growing American population.

American control of the Louisiana Territory would also mean control of the Mississippi River and the port of New Orleans. For the Americans who lived west of the Appalachian Mountains, the Mississippi River was their most important trade route. Westerners could ship their products easily and cheaply down this waterway to New Orleans. There, the goods could be sold, shipped to commercial centers on the Atlantic, or sent overseas. It was important for Americans to have access to the Mississippi River and New Orleans.

The Louisiana Territory was owned by Spain, who had acquired it in 1763 from France. In 1800, Spain was a weak nation. As long as Spain controlled the Louisiana Territory, there seemed little threat to the United States or westerners.

This situation changed when Napoleon Bonaparte came to power in France in 1799. Under his rule France became the greatest military power in the world. Early in his rule, Napoleon decided he wanted to create a French empire in America. Spain was terrified of Napoleon. On October 1, 1800, Spain signed a secret treaty with France giving up the Louisiana Territory.

Word of the treaty reached President Jefferson late in 1801. The President recognized the grave danger facing the United States. No longer was the land west of the United States controlled by a weak Spain. Now France, a powerful nation, controlled Louisiana and with it the Mississippi River and New Orleans.

Jefferson hoped to solve the problem peacefully. Perhaps Napoleon would sell New Orleans to the United States. The President sent his trusted friend, James Monroe, to negotiate with France. Monroe and Robert R. Livingston, the American minister (ambassador) to France, were authorized to offer up to $10 million for New Orleans.

Even before Monroe arrived in Paris, Napoleon had changed his plans. Louisiana was no longer his main concern. Napoleon was planning to renew his war against Great Britain. But first he needed to find a large sum of money to pay for the war. Napoleon offered to sell the entire Louisiana Territory to the United States for $15 million.

Napoleon's offer was accepted. The possibility of conflict with France disappeared. Jefferson's Louisiana Purchase doubled the size of the United States, adding to it about 2,144,510 square kilometers (828,000 square miles) of land.

Background: The United States paid approximately $1.00 for 14 1/3 hectares (about 36 acres) of land in the Louisiana Territory, or approximately $.07 per hectare.

Explorations of the Louisiana Purchase

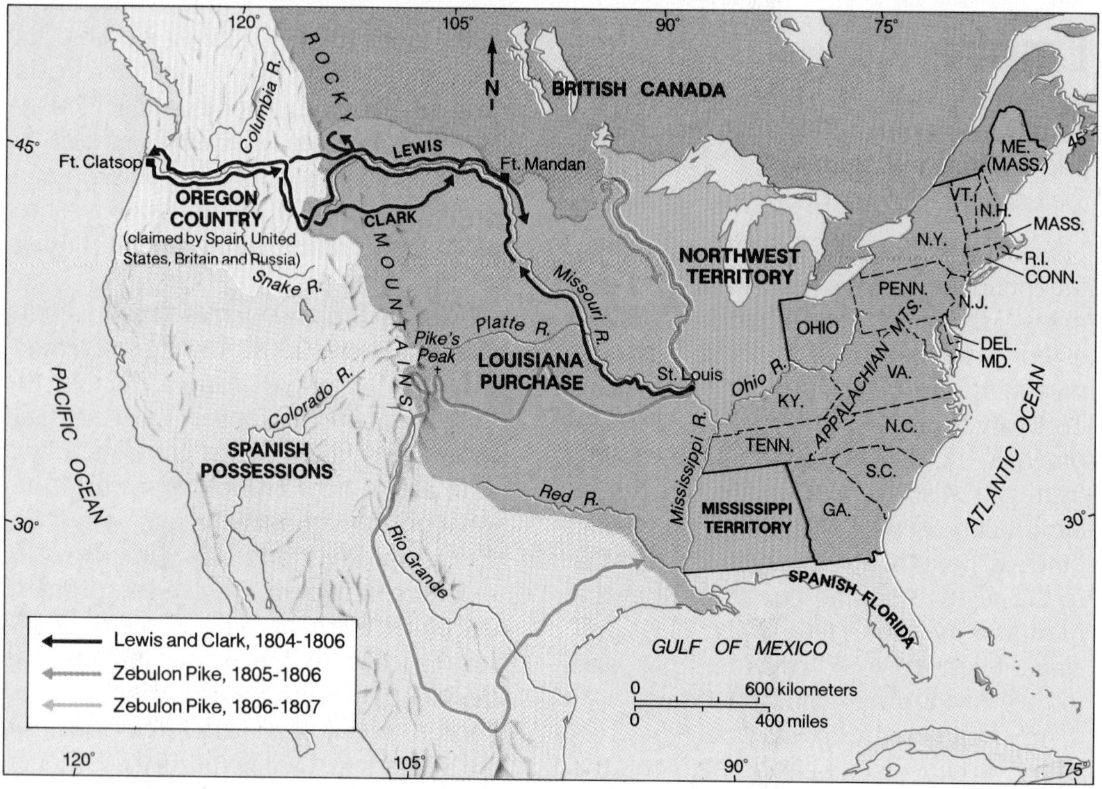

How many kilometers did Lewis and Clark travel to reach Fort Clatsop?

Exploring the Louisiana Territory

The Louisiana Territory excited widespread curiosity. What kinds of animals lived there? What was the land like? Americans had no sure answers.

Thomas Jefferson was interested in finding out more about the vast region he had just purchased. In 1803, he obtained money from Congress to send explorers across the territory to the Pacific coast. To command the expedition Jefferson selected Meriwether Lewis, an experienced explorer and soldier. Lewis' assistant was William Clark, a woodsman and veteran of the army.

President Jefferson instructed Lewis and Clark to study the American Indian tribes and their languages. They were to assure the Indians that "they will find in us faithful friends and protectors." The expedition was also instructed to study the region's animals and plants. Jefferson further asked them to study the soil and the region's geography. Finally, the President requested that they keep a detailed record of their experiences. Both Lewis

Background: William Clark's slave, Ben York, was also among the group of explorers sent to explore the Louisiana Purchase. York's willingness to assist the exploring party, and not just Clark, was greatly valued by the group.

Vocabulary Help: keelboat—a long, narrow, shallow craft. It was pointed at one or both ends and was built on a keel (a large piece of timber that ran the length of the boat) and ribs. Ask students why this type of boat was appropriate for the Lewis and Clark Expedition.

and Clark turned out to be excellent observers. Their accounts, later published as *The Journals of Lewis and Clark*, provide an exciting description of one of the greatest explorations in history.

Lewis and Clark selected and trained a group of experienced explorers, frontier dwellers, and soldiers for their exploring party. Lewis and Clark's "Corps of Discovery" embarked from St. Louis in May 1804. Nearly 50 strong, they traveled in a keelboat and two dugout canoes. For nearly six months, they pushed up the Missouri River as far as the Mandan Indian villages in North Dakota.

By this time it was November. Lewis and Clark decided that the Corps of Discovery would stay near one of the Mandan villages for the winter. The explorers built their shelters and prepared for the winter months ahead.

In the spring, the explorers were joined by an Indian woman named Sacajawea (SACK-uh-juh-WEE-uh). Sacajawea was immensely valuable to the Corps as a guide and an interpreter. Sacajawea had been born to the Shoshone Indians of the Rocky Mountains. At a young age, she had been captured by a Minitari Sioux war party. Sacajawea hoped that the expedition would return her to the Shoshones.

On April 7, 1805, the explorers headed westward, guided by Sacajawea out into the unknown. In June, the expedition reached the Great Falls of the Missouri River. "We proceeded up the river . . . to the Falls, which we had heard for several miles, making a deadly sound," wrote Clark in his journal. "I beheld those cataracts [waterfalls] with astonishment . . . . From the foot of the Falls rises a continued mist which is extended for 150 yards." Passing the Great Falls, they traveled over the **Continental Divide** at Lemhi Pass in southwestern Montana.

Continental Divide a ridge of the Rocky Mountains that separates the rivers flowing in an easterly direction from those flowing in a westerly direction

---

By August, they neared the foothills of the Rocky Mountains. Sacajawea recognized this area as her homeland. The explorers were as excited as she was. Their food supply was running dangerously low. They needed horses to be able to cross the rugged Rockies. They hoped they could obtain the food and horses they needed from Sacajawea's people. Sacajawea was reunited with the Shoshones and their chief, Cameahwait (kuh-MAY-uh-wate). She recognized him as one of her two brothers who had survived the Sioux raid. According to Clark, "She instantly jumped up, and ran and embraced him . . . ."

The Shoshones sold horses to the explorers. They also made sure that Lewis and Clark were given good directions. By the end of August, the Corps of Discovery left for the last part of the journey. They climbed the Rockies, finding their way through the dangerous mountain passes. They emerged at the Clearwater River, where friendly Flathead Indians gave them food.

Traveling was easier now as they descended to the Pacific by boat on the Columbia River. Many American Indians crowded the banks to see if the Corps could successfully navigate the swift river. They did, reaching the Pacific

Background: The name "Flathead" was applied by whites to the Indians living near the Clearwater River. When whites first met them, the tribe might have included some members of coastal tribes that artificially flattened their foreheads. When the children were small, their heads were placed between boards.

Background: The area of the Louisiana Purchase eventually became the states of Louisiana, Arkansas, Missouri, Iowa, Nebraska, Oklahoma, South Dakota, much of North Dakota, Kansas, Minnesota, Colorado, Montana, Wyoming, and part of Texas and Arizona.

Lewis and Clark meet the Chinook Indians in the Pacific Northwest.

Ocean in November. There, William Clark excitedly carved a record of their achievement on a tree: "By land from the United States in 1804 & 5." The Corps spent the winter near present-day Astoria, Oregon.

In the spring, the explorers headed homeward, following approximately the same rugged route. Their journey ended on September 23, 1806, when they docked at St. Louis. Lewis and Clark brought back volumes of information. Their maps and descriptions were of great value to scientists, future explorers, and settlers.

Exploring the Southwest

While Lewis and Clark explored the northern Louisiana Territory, Jefferson sent Lieutenant Zebulon Pike to explore central Louisiana. On his first expedition in 1805, Pike followed the Mississippi River almost to its source in present-day northern Minnesota. Later, in 1806, he explored the Colorado region. Pike observed the tall peak south of Denver that now bears his name. He headed toward Santa Fe in Spanish Territory. Spanish soldiers stopped Pike, questioned him, and eventually escorted him out of Spanish Territory and into the Louisiana Territory at Natchitoches. The reports that Pike wrote describing his journey gave the United States an idea of what the Southwest was like. However, Zebulon Pike was not nearly as careful or accurate an observer as either Lewis or Clark.

Thanks to these early explorers, Louisiana was no longer completely unknown to Americans. By the time Thomas Jefferson left office in 1809, settlers had begun to move into the Territory.

Section Review

1. How was the Louisiana Territory obtained by the United States?
2. How did the Louisiana Purchase solve the problems of both Thomas Jefferson and Napoleon Bonaparte?
3. Identify Meriwether Lewis, Sacajawea, and Zebulon Pike.
4. Why do you think it was important for the explorers of the Louisiana Territory to make careful descriptions of the land, animal life, and plant life they encountered?

Discuss: Do you think that France and Great Britain were justified in disrupting each other's trade during the war in the early 1800's? Why or why not?

3. Problems in Foreign Affairs

BEFORE YOU READ: *What problems did the United States face with Great Britain and France in foreign affairs?*

Thomas Jefferson was very successful during his first term as President. He had peacefully doubled the size of the United States through the Louisiana Purchase. He had lowered taxes and reduced the national debt. Congress had passed almost all the legislation he supported.

As Jefferson's first term drew to a close, he was very popular. In the 1804 presidential election, he easily defeated the Federalist candidate, Charles C. Pinckney. Jefferson won every state except Connecticut and Delaware. However, his popularity declined during his second term. Foreign affairs were once again going to plague the nation.

The War in Europe Resumes

In 1803, Napoleon resumed the battle for control of Europe. By 1806, all of France's enemies except Great Britain had been defeated. At first, the war benefited the United States. Both sides needed American goods and American vessels to deliver the goods to them. Foreign trade increased tremendously. The American shipbuilding industry boomed.

As the war continued, however, the threat to American security increased. The greatest danger arose over America's **neutral rights**, or freedom of the seas. Americans were determined to trade with both sides. Americans saw freedom of the seas as their right as a neutral nation. But both Great Britain and France felt their war with each other was a fight for survival. Neither looked kindly upon American trade with its enemy.

---

neutral rights the right of a country at peace to sail on any sea or ocean and trade with any nation

---

Serious problems began in 1806 for the United States. The war had come to a standstill. Napoleon controlled the European continent, while Great Britain controlled the high seas. Neither nation was able to strike the winning blow.

Both nations, therefore, tried to strike indirectly at one another. Each turned to **economic warfare**. Each nation would try to cut off its enemy's trade in the hope of starving its enemy into surrender. The United States was a major trading partner with both France and Great Britain. It was caught in the middle.

---

economic warfare the action of waging a war by damaging an enemy's trade, commerce, or economy

---

Napoleon wanted to prevent any foreign goods from reaching Great Britain. He issued orders which said that the United States could no longer trade with Great Britain. He also declared that American vessels stopping at British ports before sailing to the European mainland would be seized. These orders angered Americans because they violated American neutral rights.

The British government responded

Discuss: Is economic warfare only effective if accompanied by military fighting, or can it be an effective weapon alone?

Background: Although the French were busy seizing American ships in 1807, American anger was directed against Great Britain. The British were more successful in capturing American ships and had humiliated the United States with its impressment.

with its own orders, called the Orders in Council. The Orders in Council had two parts. First, all American trade with French-controlled ports in Europe was forbidden. Also, all American ships stopping at European ports not controlled by France had to stop first at a British port. There, a tax had to be paid before the ship could go on to the European mainland. Great Britain did this because it needed money to pay for the war. Even so, the United States was insulted by this second part of the Orders in Council. Great Britain was treating America as if it was still a British colony.

The United States was caught between Napoleon's orders and Great Britain's orders. American vessels risked capture by the British navy on the high seas. They also risked seizure by the French in European ports. Although Americans were annoyed by the French actions, it was Great Britain's actions that made Americans especially angry. The British began to seize American trading vessels. Relations with Great Britain steadily grew worse.

Increasing Tensions

Not only were the British seizing American trading ships, they also began to resume their policy of impressment. As far back as the War for Independence, the British navy had been kidnapping American sailors. Living conditions in the British navy were very bad. Sailors were whipped, poorly fed, and paid next to nothing. They lived in dirty and dangerous conditions aboard the ship. At their first chance many British sailors deserted. Many signed aboard American vessels and asked to become American citizens. The British were determined to stop this. Their warships would swoop down on American ships. British troops would come aboard and check for deserters. The terrified sailors waited to see if they would be impressed. To the unfortunate sailors picked and placed upon the British ships, impressment was little better than slavery. Thousands of sailors, many of whom were American citizens, were kidnapped in this way.

Americans were outraged by the British resumption of impressment. But the United States was too weak to do anything about it. Secretary of State James Madison demanded that the British abandon impressment immediately. "The [argument] advanced by Mr. Madison that the American Flag should protect every Individual sailing under it," the British replied, "is too extravagant to require any serious [reply]."

President Jefferson was firm about America's policy of freedom of the seas. "We have principles from which we shall never depart," Jefferson stated. "Our neutrality should be respected." But then he added, "On the other hand, we do not want war, and all this is very embarrassing." The President refused to rebuild the American navy. He preferred to rely upon a small fleet of ships, which was practically powerless against the mighty British navy.

Then, in the summer of 1807, the British navy acted more aggressively than ever. On June 22, 1807, the USS *Chesapeake*, an American warship, set sail from Norfolk, Virginia. Its destination was the Mediterranean Sea, where it would take over patrol duty from the USS *Constitu-*

Discuss: What alternatives did the British have other than impressment to secure more sailors for its navy?

EUREKA!

The Dental Drill

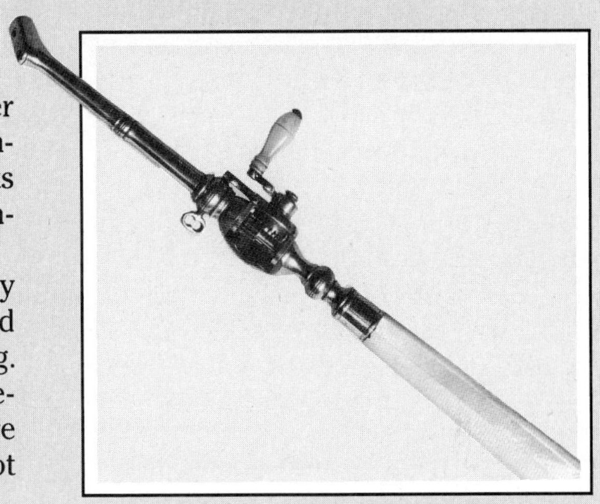

The occasional pains one may suffer in a modern dentist's chair cannot compare with the agony dental patients faced before the invention of the high-speed dental drill.

Early dentists used drills powered by bowstrings. The bowstrings were twisted and released to set the drill bit spinning. The drills were tricky to use and, because they turned very slowly, were quite painful for the patient who had not been put to sleep.

By the 1700's, most dentists had graduated to crank-turned drills resembling those used by carpenters. These were slightly better than the old type but not a major improvement.

The first foot-powered dental drill was made by an American named John Greenwood. In the eighteenth century, becoming a dentist did not require the extensive schooling it does today, and Greenwood turned to dentistry after a career as a sailor. Among his patients was George Washington, for whom he carved an impressive set of false teeth from hippopotamus teeth and elephant tusks.

In 1785, Greenwood borrowed his mother's spinning wheel and adapted the foot-pedaled device to turn a drill. He called his invention a "dental tool engine."

Other dentists of the time paid no attention to the advance. It was not until 1829, when a Scot inventor built a spring-powered drill, that dental technology began to change.

Motor-driven drills appeared in 1854, and from then until the present day, dental drilling has gotten progressively faster, more precise, and much less painful.

---

tion. Not far off the American coast, a British warship, the HMS *Leopard*, overtook the *Chesapeake*. The captain of the *Leopard* ordered the *Chesapeake* to stop for a search for British deserters. Commodore James Barron signaled that he had no deserters on board and would not permit a search. The *Leopard* opened fire, killing three sailors, wounding 18 more, and badly damaging the *Chesapeake*. Then the British searched the *Chesapeake* and dragged four sailors off. The

Background: The British practice of impressment continued until 1815. By that time, an estimated 10,000 sailors had been forcibly removed from American ships.

Discuss: Do you think the United States should have declared war on Great Britain after the *Chesapeake* incident? Why or why not?

Jefferson's home, Monticello, was built near Charlottesville, Virginia.

battered *Chesapeake* returned to Norfolk.

The attack on the *Chesapeake* shocked the American public. This was a direct attack on the United States! Many Americans demanded a declaration of war.

Jefferson Seeks Peace

Thomas Jefferson ordered all British vessels out of American waters. He had to put an end to Great Britain's humiliating treatment of the United States. However, he wished to avoid war. The President looked for a peaceful alternative.

Jefferson decided to apply economic pressure. He would cut off all foreign trade by preventing the export of goods from the United States. On December 22, 1807, Congress passed the **Embargo** Act. The Act forbade all American export trade with foreign nations. Foreign imports were still permitted into the United States. Jefferson was positive that Europeans needed our trade more than we needed theirs. He hoped the embargo would force Europe to recognize our rights.

---

embargo a government order preventing commercial ships from entering or leaving a nation's ports

---

Unfortunately, the embargo hurt the American economy badly. All areas of the country were affected by the loss of European markets. Southern cash crops like tobacco and cotton were hurt because they were mainly sold overseas. New England was especially hard hit because it lived by trade and commerce. The Embargo Act was bitterly resented by many Americans. New England town meetings passed resolutions against the embargo. New England shipowners disobeyed the law. Widespread smuggling and evasion of the law occurred.

Background: In 1979, President Carter placed an embargo on American grain shipments to the Soviet Union. This action was taken in response to the Soviet invasion of Afghanistan. Ask students what groups of Americans were probably hurt by this embargo.

After nearly a year and a half, the President had to admit that the embargo was a failure. In March 1809, the Embargo Act was repealed. Another act replaced it. The new act opened up trade with all countries except France and Great Britain. The United States would resume all trade with any nation that ceased violating its neutral rights. However, the act did not convince Great Britain or France to change their policies. The act expired in the spring of 1810.

In 1808, James Madison was elected President. Thomas Jefferson retired to Monticello, his home in the mountains of Virginia. Jefferson wrote to a friend, "Never did a prisoner, released from his chains, feel such relief as I shall on shaking off the shackles [chains] of power."

Thomas Jefferson kept a busy schedule after leaving the presidency. He worked on inventions and managed his farms. He enjoyed reading and letter writing. Jefferson was flooded with letters. In a single year, he received over 1,000 letters. Each letter received a handwritten reply. The most cherished project of Jefferson's retirement was the founding of the University of Virginia in 1819. Jefferson oversaw the design of the buildings and the arrangement of the campus, which he called an "academic village." From the roof of his home, Monticello, Jefferson would watch the progress of the construction through a telescope. The course of study, as Jefferson wished, was to prepare students to become leaders in politics, the sciences, and the arts.

Thomas Jefferson and John Adams, after years of bitterness, became friends again during the final decade of their lives. They wrote many letters to each other. They discussed a wide variety of topics, from politics to farming to the books they were reading.

These two great patriots died on the fiftieth anniversary of American independence, July 4, 1826. John Adams' last words were: "Thomas Jefferson survives!" Unknown to John Adams, Jefferson had died earlier that afternoon at Monticello. But in other important ways John Adams was correct. Thomas Jefferson still lives in the American spirit. Jefferson believed deeply in democracy. He felt the United States would serve as an example of the benefits of democracy to the world. To his fellow Americans, Thomas Jefferson was a symbol of American liberty.

Section Review

1. What problems did the United States face in foreign affairs with Great Britain and France?
2. Why were Americans angry over the *Chesapeake-Leopard* affair?
3. What were Jefferson's reasons for placing an embargo on all exports? Explain why Americans disliked it.
4. Do you see any connection between Jefferson's embargo of 1807 and the colonist's actions toward Britain in the 1770's? Explain.

CHAPTER REVIEW

Summary

With the election of Thomas Jefferson in 1801, the Republican party controlled the government for the first time. Taxes were lowered, and defense spending was cut in half. The Supreme Court assumed the power of judicial review in 1803 in the case of *Marbury v. Madison*. The Louisiana Purchase in that same year doubled the size of the United States and secured American use of the Mississippi River. The success of Jefferson's programs easily won him a second term as President in 1804.

During his second term, Jefferson's popularity declined dramatically. France and Britain had resumed their war in 1803, and the United States once again declared its neutrality. The issue of free trade brought the United States to the brink of war. To avoid war, Jefferson tried to apply economic pressure through a trade embargo. This hurt the American economy badly and caused great resentment among the American people. In 1809, the problem of foreign affairs passed to the newly elected President, James Madison.

Recalling the Facts

1. What was politically important about the transfer of presidential power from Adams to Jefferson?
2. Who were the "midnight judges"? Why were the Republicans hostile toward them?
3. Why did Napoleon sell the Louisiana Territory to the United States?
4. What did Jefferson ask Lewis and Clark to do on their expedition?
5. Why did France and Britain pass laws restricting foreign trade in Europe in 1806?

Analyzing the Facts

1. Do you think Jefferson was justified in withholding the papers that authorized Adams' appointment of 16 judges? Why or why not?
2. How is the Supreme Court's power of judicial review a check on the power of the other branches of government?

3. Why do you think that the details of the Lewis and Clark expedition are better known than those of the Pike expedition?
4. Why did the British object to the shipment of food and other non-military items to France? How would this kind of trade help their enemy?
5. Why was the British policy of impressment an insult to the honor of the United States?

Time and History

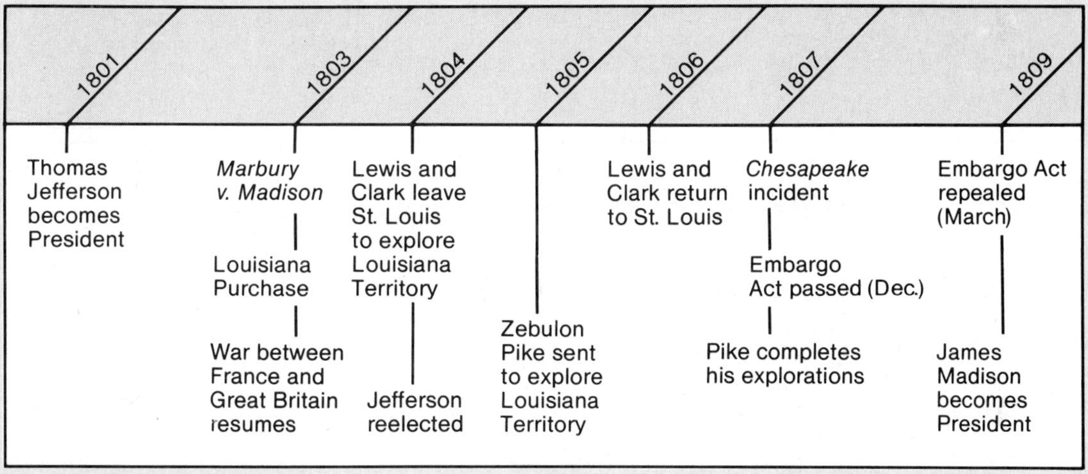

1. How many years did Lewis and Clark spend exploring the Louisiana Territory?
2. Which of the following occurred during Jefferson's first term as President: the Louisiana Purchase, the *Chesapeake* incident, or the return of Lewis and Clark?
3. How many years after war resumed between France and Great Britain was the Embargo Act passed?
4. In what year did the United States buy the Louisiana Territory from France?
5. How many months after the Embargo Act was passed was it repealed by Congress?

Chapter 9 The Republic Survives

Between 1809 and 1812, violations of American neutral rights, impressment, and other matters ruined relations between the United States and Great Britain. In 1812, war was declared. Militarily, the War of 1812 was a disaster for the United States. The Americans lost most of the battles. Washington, D.C., was burned by British troops. Americans were deeply divided over the war. Some felt that the war was unjustified and unwise. However, the Battle of New Orleans gave Americans a victory that wiped away disunity and the feeling of defeat.

The decade following the war began as a time of harmony and unity for America. National pride was never greater. But by the 1820's, this Era of Good Feelings had turned sour. The sections of the nation—West, North, and South—were engaged in bitter disputes.

After you read this chapter, you will be able to:

1. Identify the causes of the War of 1812.
2. Explain why the years 1817–1824 have been called the Era of Good Feelings.

☐ Make and use an outline.

Discuss: How did Napoleon use the United States to get what he wanted? Was he successful? Why or why not?

1. The War of 1812

BEFORE YOU READ: *What were the causes of the War of 1812?*

James Madison became the nation's fourth President in 1809. Madison's experience in government was broad. He had served as secretary of state under Jefferson. He also had served in Congress during the 1790's. Madison had played a key role in writing the Constitution.

James Madison inherited the dangerous state of affairs with Great Britain. Matters like impressment and violations of American neutral rights had badly strained relations between the two nations. Although Madison was well prepared for the presidency, tensions increased during his administration.

Drifting Towards War

Madison was eager to preserve peace with Great Britain and France. In 1810, Congress passed Macon's Bill No. 2. This bill reopened trade with both France and Great Britain. It also said that when either nation recognized America's right to freedom of the seas, Congress would cut off trade with the other.

Napoleon saw this as his chance to drive Great Britain and the United States further apart. On August 10, 1810, France assured the United States that it would stop seizing American merchant ships. But Napoleon secretly still intended to seize American ships in French ports. Madison did not know this, of course. In November 1810, the President announced that all trade with Great Britain would be cut off. Great Britain responded by blockading New York harbor. The British also increased the impressment of American sailors. Relations between the United States and Great Britain worsened.

At the same time, tensions between the United States and American Indians were increasing. Tecumseh, the leader of the Shawnees, wanted to stop Americans from settling on any more Indian land. He also wished to recover the whole Northwest Territory, making the Ohio River the boundary between the United States and Indian Country. Tecumseh and his brother, known as "The Prophet," tried to convince other tribes to join their cause.

In the fall of 1811, Tecumseh visited the southern tribes including the powerful Creeks and Cherokees. He intended to ask them to join him in stopping American expansion. With Tecumseh gone, the Governor of the Indiana Territory, William Henry Harrison, saw his chance to defeat the Indians in the Indiana Territory. In November, Harrison attacked Tecumseh's village along Tippecanoe Creek in western Indiana. When the battle was over, 188 people had been killed. Of these, only 38 were Shawnees; the remainder were Americans. Harrison returned home claiming a great victory. The angry Indians attacked American settlements across the Indiana frontier. Tecumseh offered his help to the British in Canada in the event of war with the United States.

Many Americans were becoming angry at the nation's failure to respond to the aggressive actions of the British and the Indians. They expressed this anger in the congressional election of 1810. A group of young politicians, eager for war with Great Britain, was elected. Many of the

For Extra Interest: Remind students that Tecumseh's desire to recover the whole Northwest Territory for the Indians was the same goal that Pontiac had had in 1763.

Vocabulary Help: War Hawk—a person who favors all-out war or measures designed to provoke or escalate open hostilities. How did the position of the War Hawks differ from Madison's position in 1810?

This painting shows a meeting between the Shawnee chief Tecumseh and William Henry Harrison.

new politicians came from the frontier areas of the South and West. Among them were Henry Clay of Kentucky and John C. Calhoun of South Carolina. The group became known as the "War Hawks." The War Hawks regarded Britain's actions as insults to the nation's honor. They demanded that President Madison declare war.

Madison attempted to maintain peace. He called upon Great Britain to drop its Orders in Council. By early 1812, the British public was feeling the pinch of the American embargo. They asked their government to take action to end the embargo. At last, on June 16, 1812, the British government announced that the Orders in Council had been repealed. But the announcement came too late. Madison had already decided that only war could save America's honor.

On June 1, Madison asked Congress for a declaration of war against Great Britain. On June 18, 1812, Congress voted for war. The members of Congress were unaware that two days earlier Great Britain had recognized America's right to freedom of the seas. News traveled slowly in 1812. Communications between Great Britain and America were carried by ship. The two nations were already at war when the important British announcement reached America.

The War of 1812

In declaring war on Great Britain, the United States hoped to guarantee forever the rights of neutral nations on the high seas. The nation also hoped to defeat and remove the American Indians living in the Northwest and the South. Finally, the United States wanted to restore the nation's honor through victory. Victory, Americans hoped, would come quickly. But the hope was unrealistic. The United States faced enormous problems in waging the war.

The first problem was that the United States Army was unprepared to face the British army. The American army was small, poorly trained, and lacking in discipline. Many of the army's officers were veterans of the War for Independence. They were elderly and lacked the strength needed to be effective leaders. Some younger officers showed promise.

For Extra Interest: Have students write a letter to the editor of an 1812 newspaper expressing either support for or opposition to a declaration of war against Great Britain.

Background: On one invasion of Canada, the New York militia refused to cross the border into Canada on the grounds that it was not obligated to fight outside New York State. The militia watched as the regular troops crossed the Niagara River and were slaughtered by the British.

But it would take time for them to develop their skills.

Another military problem was the size of the American navy. The British navy was more than twice as large as the American navy. The American navy was no match for the powerful British fleet.

The final problem facing the nation was that public opinion was badly divided about the war. Many people felt the war was unnecessary. The war was highly unpopular in New York and New England. The states in these areas refused to allow their militias to fight outside their own boundaries. Their farmers sold food to the British army in Canada. Their state legislatures and town governments condemned the war. Some people in New England talked seriously of leaving the Union. A huge antiwar movement swept across the United States. The Federalist party gained support through its opposition to what it called "Mr. Madison's War."

The war went badly for the United States. Between 1812 and 1814, the United States attempted to invade Canada three times. Each time the American army was defeated. The American navy initially won some battles. But by 1813, the British fleet had most American warships bottled up in port. By 1814, the American navy was left with one major vessel. To make matters worse, the British fleet had blockaded most American harbors.

There were a few bright spots for the American military during the first two years of the war. One came on Lake Erie in 1813. From the beginning of the war, Americans living in the northern part of Ohio near Lake Erie feared that the British would ferry Indians across the lake to raid their settlements. In 1813, Captain Oliver Hazard Perry constructed a naval **squadron** near Erie, Pennsylvania. In the fall of 1813, he sailed out into the lake to meet a British fleet of equal size. The two sides battled at Put-in Bay, near present-day Sandusky, Ohio. Perry destroyed the British fleet in a bloody battle. "We have met the enemy, and they are ours," he reported. Perry's victory in the Battle of Lake Erie gave the United States control of that lake. It also prevented an invasion of Ohio, and it cut British supply lines to Detroit.

---

squadron a naval unit of eight or more ships

The British could no longer hold on to Detroit with the loss of Lake Erie. When the British retreated into Canada, Perry ferried much of William Henry Harrison's army across the lake. Harrison defeated a British and Indian force in a battle at the Thames River. The Shawnee leader Tecumseh lost his life fighting for the British in this battle. Another American victory came early in 1814. Andrew Jackson, commanding the Tennessee militia, defeated the Creek Indians at Horseshoe Bend in eastern Mississippi Territory.

Then in April 1814, Napoleon fell from power, and the war in Europe wound down. Great Britain was free to turn its armies loose against the United States. The British planned to invade the United States from three spots. They would invade the United States from Canada. They would launch an invasion from the sea to capture Washington, D.C. They would invade Louisiana in an attempt to split

Discuss: The British planned to isolate the New England states by pushing south from Canada along Lake Champlain and the Hudson River to the Atlantic Ocean. Do you think this was a good strategy? Why or why not?

Background: By 1814, many of the reasons for fighting the war had simply disappeared. With the defeat of Napoleon, the British no longer needed to impress sailors or seize American ships bound for Europe. Also, the power of the Indians east of the Mississippi River had been broken.

the United States in two along the Mississippi River.

In the fall of 1814, a British army of 11,000 soldiers invaded New York from Canada. In a brutal battle near Lake Champlain, a small American force defeated the British. The invasion was turned back.

At about the same time, a British fleet landed 4,000 soldiers southeast of Washington, D.C. The British marched on the capital. American troops guarding the city fled in panic. Dolley Madison, the President's wife, was in the Executive Mansion. A messenger arrived with news that the British were about to enter Washington. Mrs. Madison fled, taking with her important government papers and a portrait of George Washington. A few hours later, British forces set fire to the President's home. The Executive Mansion had been a creamy yellow color. After the war, it was repainted white to hide the singes from the fire. People began calling it the "White House," and the name stuck. British troops also burned most of the capital's public buildings. Then they moved on to Baltimore. In a desperate battle there, Americans halted the invasion. While watching the battle, Francis Scott Key was inspired to write the "Star-Spangled Banner."

This painting shows British and American warships fighting in the Battle of Lake Erie in 1813.

The British had failed in their first two attempts at invasion. The final invasion did not come until December 1814. By then, other important events had taken place.

The End of the War

American and British diplomats had been meeting in Ghent, Belgium, since August 1814. They were there to discuss peace terms for ending the war. Late in 1814, the talks finally produced results. Both sides agreed to return to the state of affairs that existed before the war. This meant that Britain would return all captured American territory. There would be neither a winner nor a loser. However, the treaty did not address any of the problems that led to the war. The treaty was sent to America for approval.

Before news of the treaty reached the United States, antiwar feelings turned to action in New England. With the war in a **stalemate** and their trade nearly ruined, New Englanders who were against the war met at Hartford, Connecticut. Most of

Background: British imports came to a virtual halt when the embargo was in effect because foreign shippers would have to return to Great Britain with empty holds. As a result the production of manufactured goods in the United States increased.

Famous Americans

DOLLEY PAYNE TODD MADISON

Dolley Madison was one of America's most generous and gracious First Ladies. She was born in North Carolina to a wealthy family of Quakers named Payne. When Dolley Payne was 15, her father decided to free his slaves, sell his land, and move the family to Philadelphia. Dolley Payne met and married a fellow Quaker, John Todd, Jr., in 1790. Three years later, he and one of their sons died of yellow fever. Dolley Payne Todd and her remaining son barely survived.

In time, Dolley Todd began to take part in the social life of Philadelphia, which was then the nation's capital. She and James Madison were married in 1794, only four months after they met. At first, the Madisons lived quietly on James Madison's plantation in Virginia. In 1801, President Jefferson appointed Madison his secretary of state, and the Madisons moved to Washington. Dolley Madison was asked to be the presidential hostess because both President Jefferson and Vice-President Burr were widowers. In 1809, when her husband was elected President, Dolley Madison officially became the First Lady. She opened the executive mansion every Wednesday evening to receive diplomats, members of Congress, and the public. Dolley Madison was skilled at making conversation and putting all kinds of people at ease. She was the first First Lady to make the President's home the center of Washington's social activity.

During the War of 1812, the British captured Washington and burned the President's mansion. Dolley Madison managed to escape with a famous portrait of George Washington as well as important government papers. After the British left Washington, the Madisons lived in a smaller house in the city, but they continued to entertain as generously as before.

these New Englanders were members of the Federalist party. At their meeting, which lasted from December 1814 to January 1815, New Englanders called for a law that would prevent Congress from imposing an embargo that would last for more than a 60-day period. They recommended measures that would make it more difficult for Congress to declare war. The New Englanders also proposed the addition of seven new amendments to the Constitution.

stalemate a deadlock in which neither side seems able to gain an advantage

For Extra Interest: Students might be interested in listening to the song "The Battle of New Orleans" recorded by Johnny Horton.

The Hartford Convention amendments were written to protect New England's interests against the South and West. One amendment, for example, would do away with the three-fifths compromise over slavery. This would reduce the number of southern representatives in the House. Most of the southern representatives were Republicans, and some of these were War Hawks. Another amendment stated that the President could only serve one four-year term. Since 1789, every President except John Adams had served for two four-year terms. Since 1800, all of the Presidents had been Republicans. All of the two-term Presidents had been southerners, too. New Englanders felt these Presidents represented the interests of the South and West more than those of New England.

The New England Federalists headed for Washington in January 1815 to demand that Congress ratify the seven amendments. If Congress refused, the New Englanders threatened that they would meet again to discuss leaving the Union.

At the same time, the British began their final invasion. Neither they nor the Americans knew that a peace treaty had been signed. About 7,500 British troops landed and headed for New Orleans. Andrew Jackson's Tennessee militia was waiting for them. On January 8, 1815, the British attacked. Jackson's cannons and rifles shot them down. The British suffered 2,100 casualties. American casualties totaled 21.

The New England Federalists heard of the peace and Jackson's victory before they reached Washington. They quietly traveled back to New England. Many Americans now regarded them as traitors, not patriots. The Federalist party soon lost much of its support.

Consequences of the War

The United States was a changed nation by 1815. The Battle of New Orleans had restored the nation's honor and pride. The War of 1812 also firmly established American independence. Following the War of 1812, the nations of Europe largely left North America alone. This permitted the United States to devote its energies to westward expansion. The war also destroyed the Federalist party. The Republicans dominated national politics for the next decade. Finally, the war ushered in an "Era of Good Feelings." It was a time when Americans felt great pride in themselves and their nation.

Section Review

1. What were the causes of the War of 1812?
2. Define stalemate. Explain how this term applies to the War of 1812.
3. What was significant about the Battle of New Orleans?
4. Could the United States have avoided war with Great Britain in 1812? Consider the war's causes when explaining your answer.

Background: British respect for the United States increased after the War of 1812. The war ended any lingering British belief that "the colonies" would once again become a part of the British Empire.

Discuss: What are the advantages of having a young President? What are the advantages of having an older President, like James Monroe?

2. The Era of Good Feelings—and Bad

BEFORE YOU READ: *Why was the period of Monroe's presidency called the Era of Good Feelings?*

James Monroe was elected President in 1816. He became the third Virginian in a row to hold the office. The first was Thomas Jefferson. He was followed by James Madison. The three men, called the "Virginia **Dynasty**," led the nation for a total of 24 years.

---

dynasty a succession of rulers who are members of the same family or come from the same geographic region

---

James Monroe was the last of the Revolutionary War leaders to serve as President. He was 61 years old when he took office. Monroe had served in the Continental army. He had been a diplomat for the United States and served as Madison's secretary of state.

The Era of Good Feelings

When Monroe became President in 1817, the bitterness over the War of 1812 had ended. It was a time of harmony and pride for the nation. Americans were proud of the outcome of the War of 1812. They were united in their desire to see the nation grow and prosper. They felt relieved that bitter fighting between political parties was past.

Soon after his inauguration, Monroe made a **goodwill tour** of the country. After Monroe's visit to Boston, a newspaper writer remarked that the nation seemed to be entering an "era of good feelings." This phrase came to describe a brief time when there was a strong sense of unity and harmony in the nation.

---

goodwill tour a trip made throughout a nation for the purpose of showing concern, interest, and friendship

---

During the Era of Good Feelings, the Supreme Court handed down hundreds of decisions aimed at promoting the interests of the nation and the national government. In the case of *McCulloch* v. *Maryland* (1819), the Marshall Court declared that the federal government has the power to create a bank. In *Gibbon* v. *Ogden* (1824), the Court upheld the right of the national government alone to regulate trade among states.

The Era of Good Feelings was a time of improved British-American relations. In charge of foreign affairs was Secretary of State John Quincy Adams, the son of former President John Adams. Under his leadership Great Britain and America resolved a number of old problems. One involved British and American defenses on the Great Lakes. Neither Great Britain nor the United States wanted warships on the lakes. In April 1817, the two nations signed the Rush-Bagot Agreement. Both nations pledged that they would not keep warships on the Great Lakes.

The Convention of 1818 fixed the United States-Canadian border along the 49th parallel. The line extended westward only as far as the Rocky Mountains. Both

Background: When the Supreme Court, or any court, makes a decision, it sets a precedent for all similar cases. Part of the work of a lawyer is to research previous court decisions and select those that will help her or his client.

Background: Spain also laid claim to the Oregon Country in 1818 but relinquished its claim in 1819.

The United States in 1820

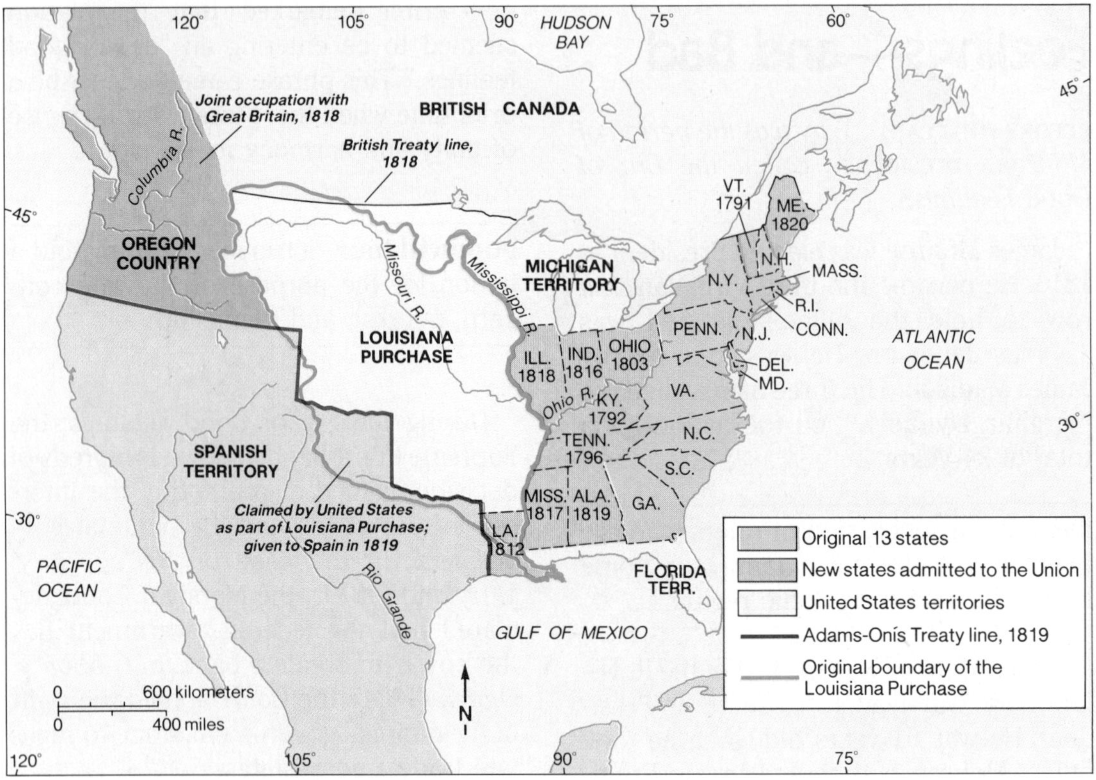

What agreements did the United States make with Great Britain and Spain in the early 1800's that affected the boundaries of the United States?

Great Britain and the United States agreed that the Oregon Country would be under joint American and British control for ten years.

Secretary Adams also worked to ease tensions between the United States and Spain. Spain was supposed to prevent Indians in Florida from raiding American settlements. But the Seminole Indians who lived in northern Florida raided the southern frontier from their villages in Florida, taking horses and slaves from Georgia plantations. The Monroe administration finally took action. John C. Calhoun, Monroe's secretary of war, ordered Andrew Jackson to end this problem. Jackson attacked the Seminoles and then went beyond his orders. He invaded Florida, captured two Spanish forts, and executed two British traders.

Jackson's actions angered the Spanish. Secretary Adams hoped to solve the problem peacefully. He convinced the Spanish that Jackson's raid had demonstrated the United States could take Florida. Spain must give up Florida, or the

Background: West Florida (from the Perido River west to the Mississippi River) had been occupied by the United States from 1810 to 1813. This area, along with East Florida, was formally ceded to the United States by Spain in 1819.

For Extra Interest: Have students look at a map of the Western Hemisphere to find out what, if any, areas remain colonies of European countries today.

United States would seize it. Spain gave in.

In 1819, the two nations signed the Adams-Onís Treaty, which made Florida a part of the United States. Spain was paid $5 million. The treaty also established a boundary line separating the southern United States from Spain's territories in the Southwest. The line extended from the mouth of the Sabine River on the Gulf of Mexico in a northwesterly direction to the 42nd parallel.

The Monroe Doctrine

In 1823, President Monroe announced a new American policy in the area of foreign affairs. Two actions by European powers led to Monroe's announcement. One involved Russia; the other Spain. Russia owned Alaska. By the early 1820's, Russia wished to enlarge its territorial claims. It looked at the lands to the south of Alaska, including Oregon and northern California. At the same time, Spanish colonies in Latin America were gaining their independence. But Spain, backed by other European nations, made plans to recover them militarily.

Secretary of State Adams insisted that the President make it clear to European nations that interference in the affairs of Western Hemisphere nations would not be tolerated. In December 1823, Monroe went before Congress to announce a new policy on foreign affairs. This policy was known as the Monroe **Doctrine**. The Monroe Doctrine stated that the United States would not permit any new European colonization in the Americas. Secondly, any European interference in the affairs of the Americas would be viewed "as dangerous to our peace and safety." Finally, the United States would stay out of the affairs of Europe.

The Monroe Doctrine declared that the United States, not Europe, was the dominant power in the Western Hemisphere.

doctrine a statement of a nation's policy, especially toward other nations

Tensions Mount

In the years following Monroe's election, a spirit of national unity seemed to exist. But by the early 1820's, most Americans realized this was not true. The United States was not a united society.

Tensions were mounting among the nation's three sections—the North, South, and West. One source of tension was the new **protective tariff**. In 1816, Congress set tariffs high to discourage imports and to protect developing American industries. The North, with the exception of New England, solidly approved of a high protective tariff. The tariff would keep foreign competitors' manufactured goods off the American market. New Englanders rejected the tariff for this very reason. By keeping competitors' goods off the American market, the tariff would hurt trade and the people who made their livelihood from it.

protective tariff a high tax placed on imported goods in order to protect domestic manufacturers and industries from foreign competition

The South was also split over the tariff question. Some southerners supported

Background: The Tariff of 1816 placed a tax of from 20 to 30 percent on many foreign manufactured products. The purpose of the tariff was not to raise money but to protect American industries from foreign competition. For this reason it was called a protective tariff.

Discuss: Do you think that sectional disputes are more likely to occur during periods of war or peace? Why?

the tariff because they hoped to establish textile factories in their region. The tariff would keep out competition from European textile manufacturers. Other southerners supported the tariff in the belief that the nation needed to be self-sufficient in the event of another war. Over time, however, most southerners came to oppose the tariff. They feared that the tariff would anger their best cotton customer, Great Britain. A high tariff would hurt the sale of British goods in America. The South feared that Great Britain might strike back. It might place tariffs on southern cotton sold in Great Britain. This would make southern cotton more expensive and sales would decline. Southerners also objected to the tariff because it represented another example of the national government's growing power. A strong government in Washington could someday move to end slavery.

Another question creating divisions across the country was what the government's land-sale policy should be. The federal government still owned huge areas of land. People in the West wanted the land sold in large-sized lots at low prices. This would encourage more settlement. The South was divided over the land-sale issue. Some southerners, particularly southern planters, did not want the government to sell its lands at all. Opening new land would increase the number of cotton growers. Southern planters did not want the competition. Other southerners wanted government land in the South sold cheaply. Such a policy would enable them to buy land and become cotton growers or expand the size of their farms.

The North was also split into two groups. One group, consisting largely of industrial workers, wanted government land sold cheaply. Northern workers were looking for a way to escape factory life. The other group was made up of factory owners. They were afraid of losing workers to the newly opened lands. Factory owners called on the government to refrain from putting its lands up for sale.

The government did not decide the land-sale issue until 1841. Until that time, tensions over this issue remained.

The nation was becoming increasingly divided by the end of the 1810's. Sections of the nation were preoccupied with their own interests. The North, West, and South disagreed more and more over policies of the federal government.

Section Review

1. Why were the years 1817–1824 called the Era of Good Feelings?
2. What did the Monroe Doctrine say?
3. Name the issues that upset national unity by the early 1820's.
4. Both the protective tariff and some Supreme Court decisions strengthened the power of the federal government during the Era of Good Feelings. Why do you think the South objected so strongly to this expansion of federal power?

Outlining

Outlining is a method of organizing information using a set pattern. The pattern distinguishes between topics or main ideas and examples or details that support the topics. The topics are usually expressed in only a few words. Outlining is useful because it helps the reader organize information according to its importance. An outline can be a valuable tool for studying or for preparing reports.

A pattern that is often used in outlining is shown below. It shows the relationship between ideas in a clear, easy-to-read form.

I. Topic or main idea
- **A.** Idea explaining the topic
  - **1.** Example or explanation of idea "A"
  - **2.** Another example of idea "A"
    - **a.** Example or explanation of "2"
    - **b.** Another example of "2"
- **B.** Another idea explaining the topic

II. Topic or another main idea
- **A.** Idea explaining the topic in "II"
- **B.** Another idea explaining the topic in "II"

In this pattern, the topics or main ideas are farthest to the left and are labeled with Roman numerals. Ideas supporting the topic are indented and are labeled with capital letters. The detail of the outline will vary depending on what it will be used for.

1. What is outlining?
2. How can outlines be valuable to a student?
3. How does an outline show the topic or main ideas?
4. How would you show examples or explanations of idea "1" under "A" in outline form?
5. Why would it be helpful to outline a report before writing it?

CHAPTER REVIEW

Summary

On June 18, 1812, President Madison abandoned his efforts to reach a peaceful solution to American differences with Great Britain and asked Congress for a declaration of war. During the War of 1812, the United States saw its capital burned and its ports blockaded. The peace treaty, the Treaty of Ghent, did nothing to resolve the problems that had caused the war. However, the American victory at the Battle of New Orleans restored American pride and honor and ushered in an "Era of Good Feelings."

The "Era of Good Feelings" was a phrase frequently associated with the administration of President James Monroe. During his presidency, he issued the Monroe Doctrine, acquired Florida, and established the 49th parallel as the northern boundary of the United States. However, in 1819 sectional disputes began to threaten the unity of the nation. Many Americans came to believe that the national government was favoring one section of the country at the expense of the others.

Recalling the Facts

1. How did Macon's Bill No. 2 try to force France and Great Britain to recognize America's right to freedom of the seas? Was it successful? Why or why not?
2. What was the cause of increasing tensions between the United States and the American Indians?
3. Why was the Battle of New Orleans fought after the Treaty of Ghent was signed?
4. Why did the Federalist party lose much of its support after the War of 1812?
5. Explain how national opinion divided over the government's land-sale policy.

Analyzing the Facts

1. Tecumseh told other Indian tribes that if all American Indians joined together, they could stop whites from settling on any more Indian land. Do you think the American Indians would have been unsuccessful even if they had joined together? Why or why not?

2. Why did it take so long for news to reach the United States from Europe in the early 1800's? What means of communication do we have today that make it possible for news to travel faster?
3. Why do you think the British chose to destroy Washington, D.C., instead of a large commercial city like New York?
4. Why do you think that Great Britain and the United States were able to solve their problems peacefully after the War of 1812 when they had been unable to do so before the war?

Time and History

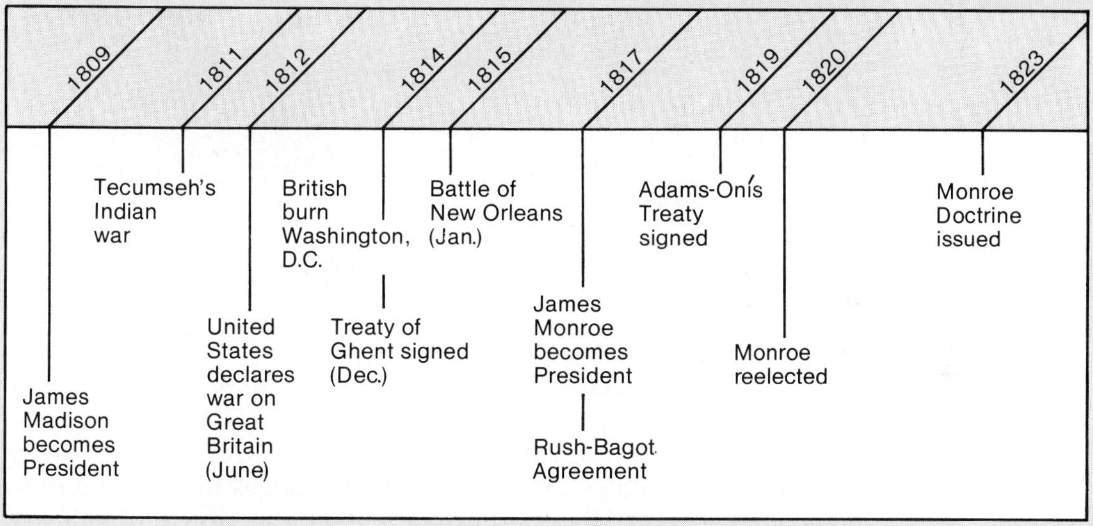

1. How long was the War of 1812: 1 1/2 years, 2 years, 2 1/2 years, or 3 years?
2. Who was President during the War of 1812?
3. Which event occurred last: the Battle of New Orleans, Washington, D.C., burned, or the Treaty of Ghent?
4. How many years after the Americans won the Battle of Lake Erie was the Rush-Bagot Agreement signed?
5. Was the Monroe Doctrine issued during President Monroe's first or second term in office?

Chapter 10 A Changing America

The United States changed dramatically during the early nineteenth century. A major cause for the change was the development of new manufacturing methods and the growth of industry. Changes in manufacturing led to the growth of American cities. During those same years, the United States experienced rapid changes in transportation and communication. Westward expansion and the growth of industry forced the nation to improve its methods of travel. The nation built roads, dug a vast network of canals, and began linking the country together by means of railroads and telegraph lines.

After you read this chapter, you will be able to:

1. Explain the causes of industrial growth in the early 1800's.
2. Identify the major developments in transportation and communication in the early 1800's.

☐ Read a bar graph.

Background: The spinning jenny was operated by a large wheel. When a worker turned the wheel, spools or spindles pulled and twisted the fibers. Arkwright's water frame used water pressure to turn the wheel.

1. The American Industrial Revolution

BEFORE YOU READ: *How did the American Industrial Revolution begin?*

In 1800, the United States was a small nation of 16 states. It had a population of a little more than 5 million people. Most Americans lived in rural areas and led fairly self-sufficient lives.

By 1840, the population of the 26 states of the Union was a little more than 17 million people. Shirts, shoes, tools, and a host of other items were being manufactured in factories. Many Americans had left the countryside for the cities to find jobs in the nation's factories. A revolution was taking place. It altered the United States and changed the lives of Americans forever. This was the American **Industrial Revolution**.

---

industrial revolution the change in a nation's society and economy caused by the replacement of hand tools with machine and power tools and the development of large-scale industrial production

---

The Factory System

The Industrial Revolution began in Great Britain around 1760. Important advances in the development of textile machinery occurred at that time. James Hargreaves invented the spinning jenny. Richard Arkwright improved on it with the water frame, which came to be known as the Arkwright machine. These textile machines made it possible for a worker to spin as many as 80 threads at once.

Hand-operated tools were replaced by power-driven tools and machines. Workers were brought together in factories or mills to run the new machines. This gave rise to what is called the "factory system." Housing was then built near the mills so that travel to and from work was more convenient. Soon towns arose.

Factories produced goods more quickly and cheaply through the use of machines. The **mass production** of goods was now possible. The products turned out by factories also tended to be of higher quality and cheaper than homemade goods.

---

mass production the use of machines to produce goods more quickly and cheaply

---

Great Britain carefully guarded its industrial secrets. The British made it a crime to take information about the design and workings of industrial machinery out of the country. In 1789, however, some British industrial secrets found their way across the Atlantic.

Samuel Slater was a British mechanic who was trained to build and repair highly complicated spinning machines. In 1789, Slater decided to go to America and seek new opportunities. Slater memorized all the intricate details of the spinning machine. Then, disguising himself as a farmer to avoid British authorities, he left Great Britain and sailed for New York.

In 1790, Slater formed a partnership with two cloth makers from Providence, Rhode Island. Slater constructed the

Discuss: Why do you think Great Britain made it a crime to take information about the design and workings of industrial machinery out of the country?

For Extra Interest: Have interested students build a model to demonstrate how a water wheel turns machine parts inside a factory.

British spinning machine from memory. He powered it with water wheels turned by river water. This was the first successful full-time factory in America.

New England was an ideal region for such factories. The region's swift streams made powering the machinery both easy and cheap.

Eli Whitney was one of the first American inventors to contribute to the Industrial Revolution. In 1793, Whitney invented the cotton gin. His "gin," short for engine, was a box containing a wooden cylinder with wire spikes attached to it. By turning a handle connected to the cylinder, cotton fibers were quickly separated from cottonseeds. Eli Whitney also developed a system of interchangeable parts. Whitney first used this system in assembling rifles. By making standard-size parts, the rifles could be assembled more quickly. Whitney's technique was applied to many other goods.

Labor for Industry

The introduction of power-driven machines in factories changed the way people worked in the United States. Some of the factory workers were craftspeople whom the factories had driven out of business. Others were unskilled laborers.

Factory hours were long, and the wages were low. The factories themselves were often dirty and unhealthy places to work. The workers often labored over dangerous machines. Injuries were common.

In southern New England and in the Middle Atlantic states, textile factories used the so-called Fall River system. En-

Winslow Homer's The Morning Bell *gives a romantic view of factory life.*

Background: Some states tried to limit the number of hours that children could work. Massachusetts passed a law in 1842 that said children under 12 could work no more than ten hours per day.

tire families were employed in a mill. Some factories preferred to use as many child laborers as possible. Children could work the same number of hours as adults, but they were paid lower wages. By the early 1820's, about one half of all textile workers in factories were under 16.

Another system of factory employment was used in northern New England. It was called the Lowell system. Francis Cabot Lowell established a textile factory at Waltham, Massachusetts, in 1813. Lowell hired young, unmarried New England farmwomen to work his looms. To persuade young women to come, the company offered high wages and decent housing in dormitories.

Most of the women worked to save money for their marriages or to help their families. Some used their savings for tuition at a "normal" school, in which teachers were trained. Perhaps the most important aspect of the young women's work was that they earned a wage. As one Lowell woman said, "For the first time in this country . . . women had begun to earn and hold her own money, and through its aid had learned to think and to act for herself."

Growth and Change

A few thousand immigrants came to the United States annually in the years immediately following the American Revolution. The number started to increase in the 1820's and peaked in the 1840's and 1850's. Between 1820 and 1860, almost 6 million newcomers arrived in America. The majority were Irish and German. Many of the German immigrants came to America with enough money to buy farmland or settle in the cities of the West.

Immigration, 1820–1840

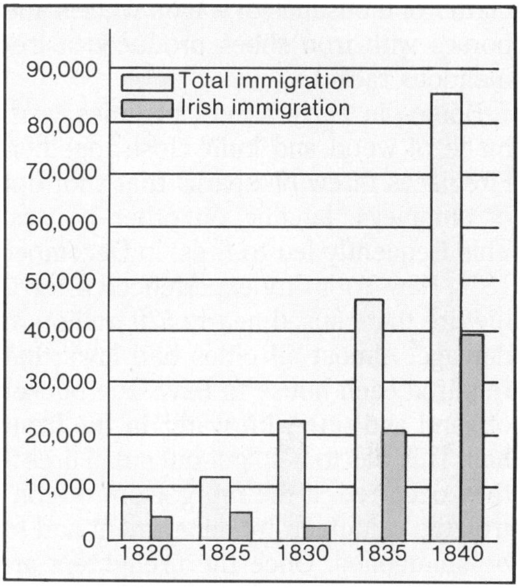

The Irish immigrants were different, however. Most had lived in poverty in their homeland. They had labored as tenant (renter) farmers or landless agricultural workers. In 1845 and 1846, Ireland's potato crop, its chief source of food, had failed. An estimated one million men, women, and children died of starvation. For millions of Irish the United States offered a chance for survival.

The Irish who came to the United States settled in the cities of the Northeast. They became a source of labor for the mill owners.

As American industry and commercial activities grew, so did America's cities. American cities, except for Philadelphia, grew without any planning. They were densely populated, congested, and noisy. People got around in the cities either on

Background: By the 1840's, the Lowell system was changing. The center of town became a depressing slum, wages were cut drastically, and conditions sank to the level of most other factories in the region.

foot, by wagons, or on horseback. The clatter of thousands of wagon wheels and horses with iron shoes produced a tremendous racket.

Homes in early American cities were made of wood and built close together. Fireplaces threw off sparks that shot out of chimneys, landing on other houses. This frequently led to fires. In December 1834, New York City experienced a terrible fire that caused nearly $20 million in damage. Almost all cities had laws that required each house to have one bucket of sand and one with water in the front hall. This was to help put out small fires if they occurred. If the fire got out of control, the volunteer fire department had to be summoned. Once the firefighters arrived, they did not set to work immediately. The homeowner had to offer a fee acceptable to the firefighters before they would put out the fire. Often if a price could not be agreed upon, the house burned down.

Early cities were also dirty and extremely unhealthy. There was no regular garbage collection. Many people simply threw garbage out their doors or windows into the street. The garbage and the lack of sanitary facilities in houses created health problems. Diseases like typhoid, yellow fever, and cholera swept through **urban** areas with tragic results.

urban having to do with a city or cities

Living conditions among the cities' poor were very bad. A physician, Dr. Henry Clark, investigated a run-down house in a **slum** area in Boston. The house had three cellars. "One cellar was reported by police to be occupied nightly as a sleeping-apartment for thirty-nine people," the doctor said. "In another, the tide of water had risen so high that it was necessary to approach the bedside of a patient by means of a plank. . . ."

slum a run-down area of a city in which housing is poor and crowded

Deep social unrest existed in the major cities. It was caused by poverty and low wages. Periodically, the unrest spilled over into destructive riots. Riots took place in many cities. In 1837, a "flour riot" erupted in New York when mobs of unemployed people broke into the city's flour warehouses.

The Industrial Revolution, perhaps more than any other event, altered the United States. It changed forever the way Americans worked and lived.

Section Review

1. How did the American Industrial Revolution begin?
2. What role did Eli Whitney play in the Industrial Revolution?
3. Describe how the Lowell system's labor force was unusual.
4. Is it correct to describe early American cities as an "urban wilderness"? Support your answer with three examples.

Social Studies Skills

Reading a Bar Graph

The invention of the cotton gin in 1793 dramatically changed the economy of the South. Southerners discovered that huge profits could now be made from this crop, and cotton production increased.

One way of showing this increase is on a bar graph. A bar graph illustrates numerical facts with bars of different heights or lengths. It can show changes that occur over a period of time as well as information for a particular year.

To read the bar graph below, first look at its title to see what is being illustrated. Next look at the information on the horizontal (bottom) axis and the vertical (side) axis. The horizontal axis shows that information will be given in ten-year intervals from 1800 to 1850. The vertical axis indicates bales of cotton in hundreds of thousands. To determine how many bales of cotton were produced in a given year, trace an imaginary line from the top of the bar to the vertical axis. The point at which this imaginary line meets the vertical axis provides an estimate of how many cotton bales the bar represents.

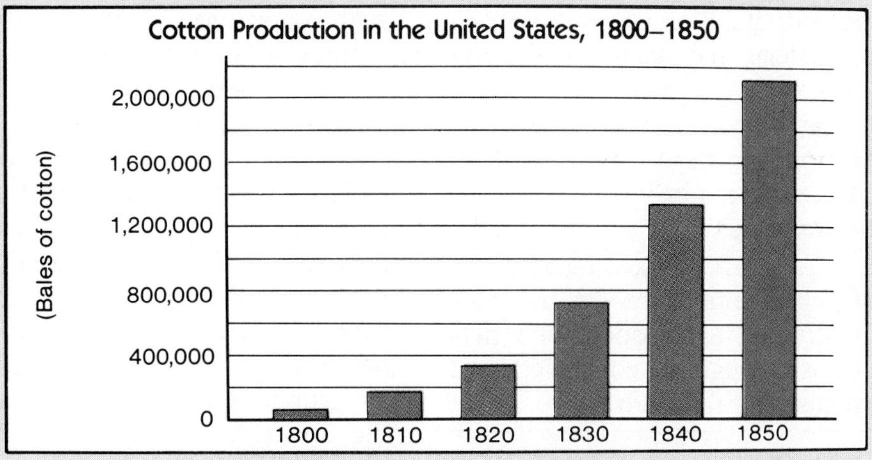

1. What is being illustrated on the bar graph above?
2. What was the approximate amount of cotton produced in 1800?
3. What was the approximate amount of cotton produced in 1850?
4. Between what two years was the increase in cotton production the greatest?

Discuss: Why do you think most of America's industrial growth became concentrated in the northeastern part of the nation in the early 1800's?

2. Transportation and Communication

BEFORE YOU READ: *Why were improvements in transportation needed?*

By 1820, hundreds of thousands of Americans were moving westward. They settled on newly opened lands or found jobs in new western cities like Cincinnati, St. Louis, and Pittsburgh.

At the same time, American industry was growing. Factories were built throughout the northeastern portion of the nation. Western expansion and the Industrial Revolution created a demand for improving America's transportation network. People traveling westward looking for work or new homes wanted better roads. Western farmers wanted faster and better routes to get their crops to eastern markets. Eastern manufacturers wanted better routes to get their products to western markets. Americans called for **internal improvements**. By this they meant the construction of roads, canals, and, later, railroads.

---

internal improvements ways or methods of upgrading a transportation network such as through the construction of roads, canals, and railroads

---

Road Building

A French traveler named Brissot described a trip from Wilmington, Delaware, to Baltimore, Maryland, in the late 1780's.

> The road in general is frightful; it is over a clay soil, full of deep ruts, always in the midst of forests; frequently obstructed by [fallen] trees . . . which obliged us to seek a new passage among the woods.

A traveler on most roads in the nation would have had a similar experience. Roads were in poor shape. Holes, mud, fallen trees, stumps, and rocks made traveling difficult. Roads turned to mud in wet weather. They became clouds of dust in dry seasons.

Techniques for good road building had been developed in Great Britain and France. American engineers quickly adopted these methods. They started to build roads with drainage ditches so that excess water would run off. They topped the roads with tightly packed broken rock or gravel. The first such improved road connected Philadelphia with Lancaster, Pennsylvania. It opened in 1794. Other such roads soon followed.

Many of the new roads were built privately. Owners of these roads were permitted to charge a toll, or a fee. Tolls were collected at various gates, or pikes, built along the length of the road. The gates often consisted of a hinged pole suspended across the roadway. After the travelers paid their tolls, a guard would turn back the gate. These roads came to be called "turnpikes," or simply pikes.

Turnpike construction boomed during the first two decades of the nineteenth century. Up until 1818, however, the nation lacked a good road to connect the region west of the Appalachian Mountains with the eastern portion of the nation. A road of this size was too expensive for the state governments or private builders to construct. The federal government decided to become involved. A

Background: One of the biggest supporters of internal improvements was John C. Calhoun of South Carolina. "Let us, then, bind this republic together with a perfect system of roads and canals," Calhoun urged. "Let us conquer space [distance]."

Background: Cumberland's location on the Potomac River enabled traffic from the road to connect with Washington, D.C., or the Atlantic Ocean. Also, Cumberland was connected to Baltimore by an excellent turnpike.

major road was planned that would eventually connect a point near Washington, D.C., with the Illinois Country.

Construction of the National Road began in 1811 at Cumberland, Maryland. Cumberland is located on the Potomac River. By 1818, the National Road was completed as far as Wheeling, Virginia (now West Virginia), on the Ohio River. By 1833, the road extended to Columbus, Ohio. In 1838, the National Road stretched all the way to Vandalia, Illinois.

This scene shows horses hauling a flat-bottom boat around a bend in the Erie Canal.

The Canal Age

The new improved roads reduced travel times. The new roads speeded mail service and small package delivery. Riding in stagecoaches became more comfortable. But transporting bulky objects or large quantities of goods over the roads was still slow and very expensive. It cost more to ship freight by land than by water even when the water routes were many times longer. The movement of large quantities of heavy freight required waterways. Americans built canals to solve this problem.

Canals were built in both the East and the West. Some of the canals were built to help farmers and travelers reach the Mississippi River more easily. Many of these canals connected the Great Lakes with the Ohio River. The Ohio River would then take travelers or freight to the Mississippi River, on which they could continue down to the port of New Orleans. One of the Great Lakes canals was the Ohio and Erie Canal, built between 1825 and 1832. It stretched a total of 496 kilometers (308 miles) from Cleveland to the Ohio River. The Ohio and Erie Canal was about 12 meters (39 feet) wide at water level, and about one meter (3 feet) deep. It had a path alongside the canal that was 3 meters (10 feet) wide. Mules or horses, walking along the path, hauled flat-bottom boats down the canal.

Another series of canals linked the West with the East. The most famous one was the Erie Canal in New York State. It ran eastward from Buffalo on Lake Erie to Albany on the Hudson River.

The canals reduced the cost of shipping goods dramatically. For example, freight rates between Buffalo and New York City dropped from $100 to $15 per metric ton (one ton). Because shipping costs declined, the prices of the shipped goods fell also. Westerners could now buy goods from eastern commercial centers for a fraction of their former cost.

For Extra Interest: Explain to the class why canals often require locks, and how locks work.

Improvements in Transportation: Canals and the National Road

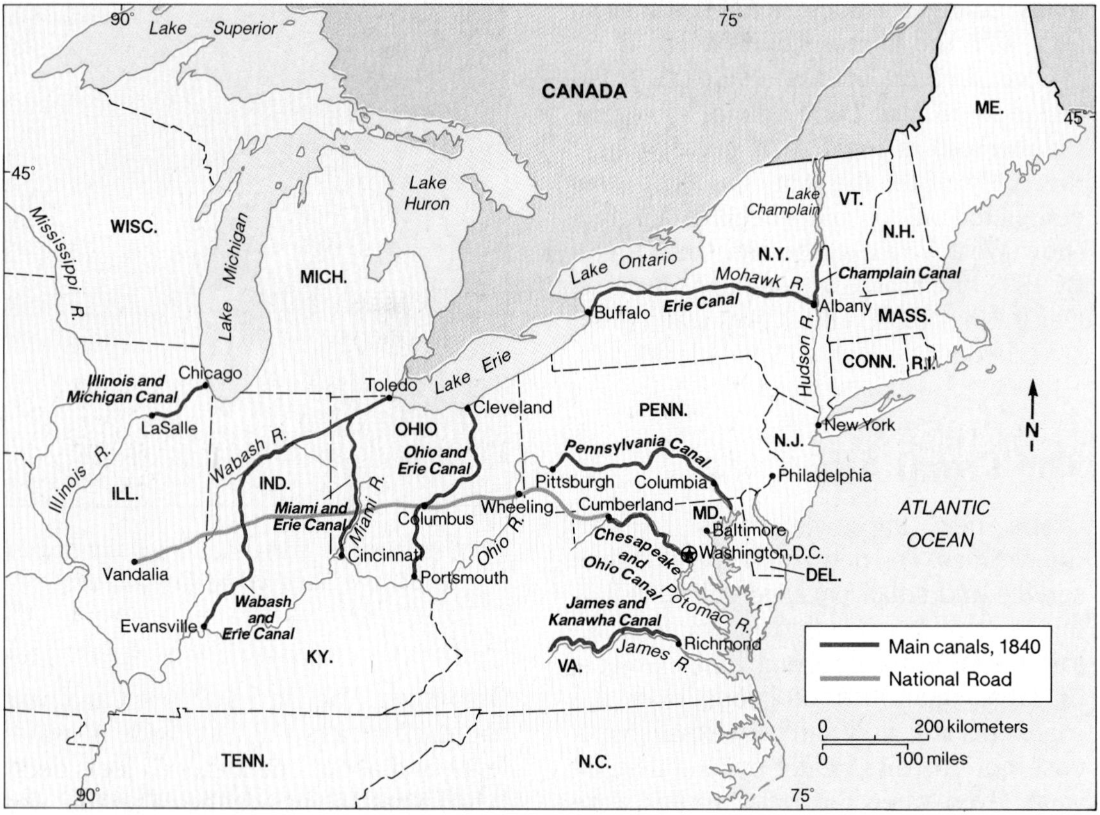

What bodies of water were connected by each of the major canals built by 1840? Through which states did the National Road run?

The canals also stimulated the growth of cities on the Great Lakes. Chicago, Detroit, Cleveland, and Buffalo began to rival the river cities of Pittsburgh, Cincinnati, and St. Louis. The Erie Canal assured New York's position as the biggest commercial center along the Atlantic coast.

Steamboats

Americans traveled by rafts and flatboats on the inland waterways. Flatboats, with a flat bottom and square ends, were used for transportation of people and bulky cargo, especially in shallow water. Rafts and flatboats were adequate when going downstream. But the task of going against the upstream current was difficult. Sometimes, on swift rivers, it was impossible. The invention of a workable steamboat was a major advance in solving this problem.

The first experiments using steam engines to power boats were made in the 1780's and 1790's. However, the major credit for the development of steam-pow-

Discuss: What would be the advantage of using steamboats over flatboats or boats propelled by the wind?

EUREKA!

Vulcanized Rubber

The inventor who turns a bright idea into a million-dollar technological advance is a favorite American folk hero. In many cases, inventors have made millions. But Charles Goodyear was not one of them.

In the early 1830's, Goodyear set out to find a way to make rubber insensitive to changes in temperature. Rubber's usefulness as a waterproofing material and as a cement were well known. But the raw rubber being used would lose its stretch in the cold and melt when heated. Goodyear's first attempt to desensitize rubber failed. The rubber mailbags that he made for the United States government in 1837 became sticky at high temperatures.

The stickiness problem was solved by a rubber-factory worker named Nathaniel Hayward, who treated the rubber with sulfur. Goodyear bought Hayward's process and began trying to improve on it. In 1839, he accidentally dropped some sulfur-treated rubber onto a hot stove. The rubber was "cured" as the result of its exposure to the heat. It now stayed tough and firm in both heat and cold. Goodyear had found what he was looking for. The process he discovered was called vulcanization.

Goodyear patented vulcanization in 1844. But American industry took little notice of his patent and used the process without paying him royalty fees. Goodyear went to England and France, where he tried in vain to set up factories to produce vulcanized rubber. After a French rubber factory failed, Goodyear was sent to prison for his debts.

Vulcanization was an important invention, and it made many people very rich. But Charles Goodyear made not a cent out of it and died $200,000 in debt.

---

ered boats goes to Robert Fulton. Fulton purchased a British boiler and steam engine and had them shipped to New York. He mounted them on his boat, the *Clermont*. This vessel made its first voyage in the summer of 1807. The *Clermont* left New York City on August 17th. It traveled 241 kilometers (150 miles) up the Hudson

Background: On December 25, 1830, the South Carolina Railroad provided the first scheduled steam railway service in the nation when the ***Best Friend of Charleston*** pulled a short passenger train out of Charleston.

River, docking the following day at Albany, New York.

The steamboat was introduced in the West in 1811 by Nicholas J. Roosevelt. Roosevelt built a steamboat in Pittsburgh and named it the *New Orleans*. On its first voyage, the *New Orleans* steamed all the way down the Ohio and Mississippi rivers. After 1815, the use of steamboats increased in the West. The number of steamboats on the Ohio, Mississippi, and other western rivers jumped from 14 in 1817 to 69 in 1821. The steamboats lowered freight and passenger rates. They reduced travel time, and they encouraged more western settlement.

The Railroad Age

The British were the first to begin work on steam locomotion for land travel. A breakthrough came in the 1820's. George Stephenson built a steam locomotive that ran on rails. Stephenson's locomotive, called the *Rocket*, reached 11 kilometers (7 miles) per hour in 1829. A year later, it was running at the fast clip of 43 kilometers (27 miles) per hour.

The first American railroad was the Baltimore and Ohio line. By 1830, the Baltimore and Ohio offered regular passenger service along almost 21 kilometers (13 miles) of track. However, the early carriages of the Baltimore and Ohio were drawn by horses. The line experimented with other means of moving the carriages. Sails on the carriages were tried with little success. Then, during the summer of 1830, another experiment was attempted, one that finally proved to be useful. It was a small steam locomotive called the *Tom Thumb*. The *Tom Thumb* zoomed along the Baltimore and Ohio line at an amazing 16 kilometers (10 miles) per hour!

During the 1830's, railroad construction continued, but the pace was slow. It was hard to raise sufficient money to build long lines. Railroad construction was also blocked in state legislatures by canal and turnpike owners who **lobbied**, or attempted to persuade public officials to vote, against the railroads.

lobby to engage in activities aimed at influencing public officials toward a desired action

Most of the nation's rail lines remained

Early experiments in rail transportation included cars with sails that would catch the wind and move the train.

Background: The cars of early trains were often connected by loose chains. When the engineer applied the brake in the locomotive, each car was stopped by banging into the one in front of it.

For Extra Interest: Have interested students research and report to the class on how the telegraph invented by Morse worked.

short in this era. They radiated out like wheel spokes. Their purpose was to connect major cities to smaller ones in the vicinity. By 1835, Boston had rail connections with Lowell and Worcester, Massachusetts, as well as with Providence, Rhode Island. The longest railroad line in the United States at this time was located in South Carolina. It ran for 219 kilometers (136 miles).

Harriet Martineau of Great Britain recalled trips she took on these early American railroads. "One great inconvenience of the American railroad is that, from wood being used for fuel, there is an incessant [never-ending] shower of large sparks, destructive to dress and comfort, unless all the windows are shut, which is impossible in warm weather." She then continued by describing the trouble caused by flying sparks. "During my last trip, . . . a lady in the car had a shawl burned to destruction on her shoulders; and I found that my own gown had thirteen holes in it."

The canals and railroads were bitter competitors. But in the end, railroads proved to be superior in many ways. Railroads could be built almost anywhere. They were faster than canal travel. They could also operate year-round. Canals had to close down when the water froze during the winter. The future belonged to the railroads.

Samuel Morse and the Telegraph

The early nineteenth century also witnessed changes in the area of communications. The electric telegraph was invented by Samuel F. B. Morse in 1837. Morse's first telegraph line ran from Washington, D.C., to Baltimore. The telegraph used a code made up of dots and dashes that could be interpreted by the receiver. The code became known as Morse code.

By the 1860's, the telegraph was being used widely in this country. The telegraph was used by newspapers to send news stories quickly over long distances. Rail lines used the telegraph to inform stations about arrival times and delays. Election results were spread rapidly across the nation. William F. Channing, a Boston physician, described the importance of the telegraph, saying, "The electric telegraph is the nervous system of this nation." The telegraph and the developments in transportation were changing America rapidly.

Section Review

1. Why did Americans call for improvements in transportation?
2. Define internal improvements and lobby.
3. Identify two effects of the canals on American life and business.
4. What recent developments in transportation and communication have changed the lives of modern Americans?

Discuss: How do improvements in communication help business?

CHAPTER REVIEW

Summary

In the first half of the nineteenth century, the Industrial Revolution spread from Great Britain to the United States. As power-driven tools steadily replaced hand labor, more and cheaper goods became available to the American consumer.

The Industrial Revolution also had a great impact on the way many Americans lived and worked. Men, women, and children worked long hours in the factories for low wages. Millions of immigrants who came to America from 1820 to 1860 also found work in the nation's factories. Cities grew in a haphazard manner, and fires, disease, and filth were common problems.

Improvements in the nation's transportation network were also made during this period. Roads, canals, and railroads were constructed to link manufacturing centers to their markets. The invention of the telegraph in 1837 made it possible to communicate long distances more effectively. By the mid-1800's, industrialization had changed the face of America.

Recalling the Facts

1. Why were early factories frequently built close to rivers or streams?
2. What advantages did machines have over hand labor?
3. Describe living conditions in American cities in the first half of the nineteenth century.
4. How did the growth of industry in the United States create a demand for an improved transportation network?
5. In what ways were railroads superior to canals as a transportation system?

Analyzing the Facts

1. Many of the Irish immigrants who came to America from 1820 to 1860 worked as unskilled laborers in the nation's factories and

often lived in the cities' slums. Do you think they were sorry they had come to America? Why or why not?

2. Which of the internal improvements—roads, canals, steamboats, or railroads—had the greatest impact on western farmers and eastern manufacturers in 1830? Explain your answer.
3. How do you think a canal can be superior to a river?
4. How did the construction of canals and railroad lines stimulate the growth of cities?
5. Briefly describe how America had changed between 1800 and 1840 as a result of the Industrial Revolution.

Time and History

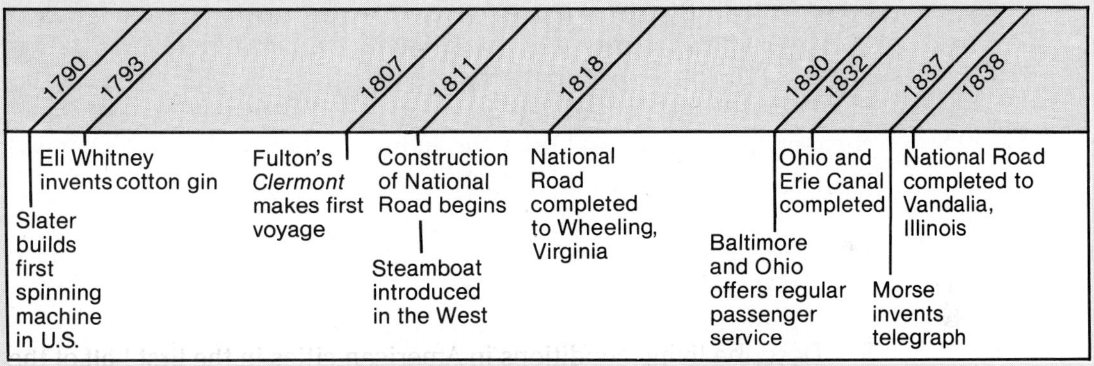

1. Which came first: the cotton gin, the telegraph, Slater's spinning machine, or Fulton's *Clermont*?
2. What was the first improvement made in the nation's transportation system?
3. In what century did the American Industrial Revolution begin?
4. How many years after construction of the National Road began did it reach Wheeling, Virginia?
5. In what year was the first child labor law in the United States passed?

UNIT REVIEW

Summary

The United States entered the nineteenth century with its first Republican President, Thomas Jefferson. Jefferson's first administration was successful largely due to his acquisition of the Louisiana Territory and a temporary halt in the war between France and Great Britain. In 1803, France resumed its war with Great Britain, and Jefferson's second administration was dominated by efforts to maintain American neutrality.

The problems of foreign affairs passed to President Madison in 1809. In 1812, the United States declared war on Great Britain over the issue of America's right to freedom of the seas. The war did little to solve the problems that had started it. However, it brought the United States new respect from European nations and created a feeling of national pride among the American people.

The nineteenth century also saw the beginnings of industrialization in the United States. Factories were built, and the nation's transportation network was improved to move goods to market faster and cheaper than before. By 1840, the Industrial Revolution had changed the way many Americans lived and worked.

Recalling the Facts

1. What was the importance of the Louisiana Purchase to the United States?
2. Why did the Embargo Act hurt President Jefferson's popularity?
3. Why did the United States declare war on Great Britain in 1812?
4. How did industrialization change the way many Americans lived and worked?
5. How was the nation's transportation system improved in the first half of the nineteenth century?

Analyzing the Facts

1. Thomas Jefferson's second term in office was dominated by foreign affairs. What world problems does today's President have to deal with? Do you think the President today is more concerned with foreign affairs or domestic issues?
2. Why was the Rush-Bagot Agreement important?

3. How do you think the European nations would have reacted to the Monroe Doctrine if it had been issued before the War of 1812?
4. Must a nation have a good transportation network for industry to develop? Why or why not?

Vocabulary Review

Define the following terms:

judicial review	goodwill tour	urban
Continental Divide	doctrine	slum
embargo	industrial revolution	internal improvements
stalemate	mass production	lobby

Sharpening Your Skills

1. Outline the section "Growth and Change" in chapter 10, pages 251 to 252.

Answer the next four questions based on the bar graph, "Immigration, 1820–1840," on page 251.

2. In what year was the total immigration to the United States approximately 45,000 people?
3. True or false: The number of Irish immigrants coming to the United States steadily increased from 1820 to 1840.
4. In what year did the number of Irish immigrants first increase significantly?
5. What changes over time does this bar graph show in total immigration to the United States?

Writing and Research

1. The Monroe Doctrine is still an important part of United States foreign policy. Imagine that you are a current presidential adviser, and a South American nation has been threatened with invasion by a European nation. Write a letter to the President advising what action you think the United States should take and explain why.
2. Imagine that the year is 1820, and you have recently moved from your family's farm to the city, where you have gotten a job in a factory. Write a letter home to a friend who is also thinking of moving to the city. Describe your working and living conditions as well as other differences between country and city living.

Unit 4 The Nation Dividing

11 *The division between the North and South deepened in 1819 when Missouri applied for admission as a slave state. More tensions developed between the sections during the presidency of Andrew Jackson, who was elected in 1828. The serious trouble arose when South Carolina threatened to leave the Union. Jackson's presidency also witnessed the forced removal of most American Indians from their homes in the eastern United States.*

12 *In the early 1800's, the South was developing into a society that was very different from Northern society. Southern society was based upon the institution of black slavery. The slave states were governed by a small group of cotton planters who owned most of the South's slaves and controlled most of the region's wealth.*

13 *During the first half of the 1800's, the North became more industrial. Northerners knew that many problems existed in their society. Conditions in Northern prisons and hospitals were poor. Education was not available to all children. Women and blacks lacked many rights. Many people worked hard to find solutions to these and other problems.*

14 *Many Americans believed that the United States should occupy all the land between the Atlantic and Pacific oceans. They called this belief Manifest Destiny. During the 1840's, large numbers of Americans moved to the Far West looking for new opportunities. The United States government gained vast areas of the Far West as a result of a war with Mexico. This led to heated debate between the North and South over the expansion of slavery into the newly conquered areas.*

Chapter
11

The Jacksonian Era

On November 24, 1832, the state of South Carolina demanded that the federal government change its policy on some of its tariffs. If the government did not change, South Carolina announced, the state would leave the Union. This threat raised the possibility of a war between the states. President Andrew Jackson was determined to crush South Carolina, if the crisis came to that. He assured the people of the United States, "The Union will be preserved!" But preserving the Union was becoming more difficult as Northerners and Southerners found themselves disagreeing on many issues.

After you read this chapter, you will be able to:

1. Explain how Missouri's application for statehood led to growing bitterness between the North and the South.
2. Describe Andrew Jackson's rise to political power.
3. Discuss how the tariffs of 1828 and 1832 led to a crisis over the issue of the rights of states.
4. Explain why the eastern Indians were removed to lands west of the Mississippi River.

☐ Interpret an election map.

Discuss: Why was it considered necessary to maintain a balance between the number of free and slave states? Why was this balance especially important in the Senate?

1. Missouri and the Slavery Question

BEFORE YOU READ: *How did the Missouri Compromise resolve the question of slavery in new territories and states?*

The Era of Good Feelings was coming to an end by 1820. Various issues were driving the sections of the nation apart. Northerners, Southerners, and westerners disagreed on tariffs, the Second National Bank of the United States, and the sale of government-owned land. Americans were showing more concern for their section of the nation and its problems. They were increasingly less concerned with the interests of the nation as a whole. This kind of behavior is called **sectionalism**. The sections of the nation were also divided over the slavery issue. In 1819, bitter controversy arose between the free states and the slave states. It involved admitting Missouri to the Union.

---

sectionalism a concern for one's region of the country and its problems that ignores the well-being of the country as a whole

---

The Slavery Dispute

The slavery question had been a major concern of American leaders since the founding of the nation. To satisfy Americans from both free states and slave states, members of Congress used compromise. Each time a slave state was admitted by Congress, a free state was admitted at the same time. For example, Mississippi and Alabama were admitted as slave states between 1815 and 1820. Illinois and Indiana, both free states, were admitted during the same period. In this way, the balance of slave and free states was maintained. In 1819, the nation had 22 states. Eleven of them were free, and an equal number were slave. Compromise had kept both sides, free states and slave states, satisfied.

The balance of free states and slave states was threatened when the people of Missouri applied for statehood in 1818. Missouri wished to enter the Union as a slave state. Congress was faced with the problem of how to solve the Missouri issue to the satisfaction of both Northerners and Southerners.

In February 1819, the House of Representatives began working on a bill to grant statehoood to Missouri. Congressman James Tallmadge of New York added an amendment to the Missouri statehood bill. The Tallmadge amendment stated that bringing any new slaves into Missouri would be a crime. The amendment also said that all slaves born in Missouri *after* it became a state would be freed when they reached the age of 25.

Through his amendment, Tallmadge was trying to guarantee that slavery would eventually disappear in Missouri. Tallmadge wanted to confine slavery to the states where it already existed.

The House voted on the Missouri statehood bill in February 1819. Southern members of Congress who supported slavery were unable to block the bill. The House passed the Missouri statehood bill with the Tallmadge amendment.

The bill was then sent to the Senate for approval. Southerners were able to convince a few Northern senators to vote

For Extra Interest: Remind students of previous compromises, such as the three-fifths compromise, that had been made over the issue of slavery.

Discuss: If the Tallmadge amendment had been passed, do you think slavery would have eventually disappered in Missouri? Why or why not?

against the bill. The Missouri statehood bill with the Tallmadge amendment was rejected by the Senate.

Balance Through Compromise

The failure of the Missouri statehood bill fueled the debate among Americans over the slavery issue. Southerners considered slaves to be property. Northerners seemed to be denying Southerners the right to move to another state with some of their property. They argued that the protection of property was guaranteed by the Constitution. Tallmadge was accused of starting "a fire which only seas of blood could extinguish."

Many in the North were surprised by the South's strong defense of slavery. Many Northerners had incorrectly assumed that many Southerners favored a gradual end to slavery. After all, a Southern President, Thomas Jefferson, had backed the bill to end the foreign slave trade in 1808. All Southern states except South Carolina had abolished the foreign slave trade by 1803. Southerners had also

The Missouri Compromise, 1820

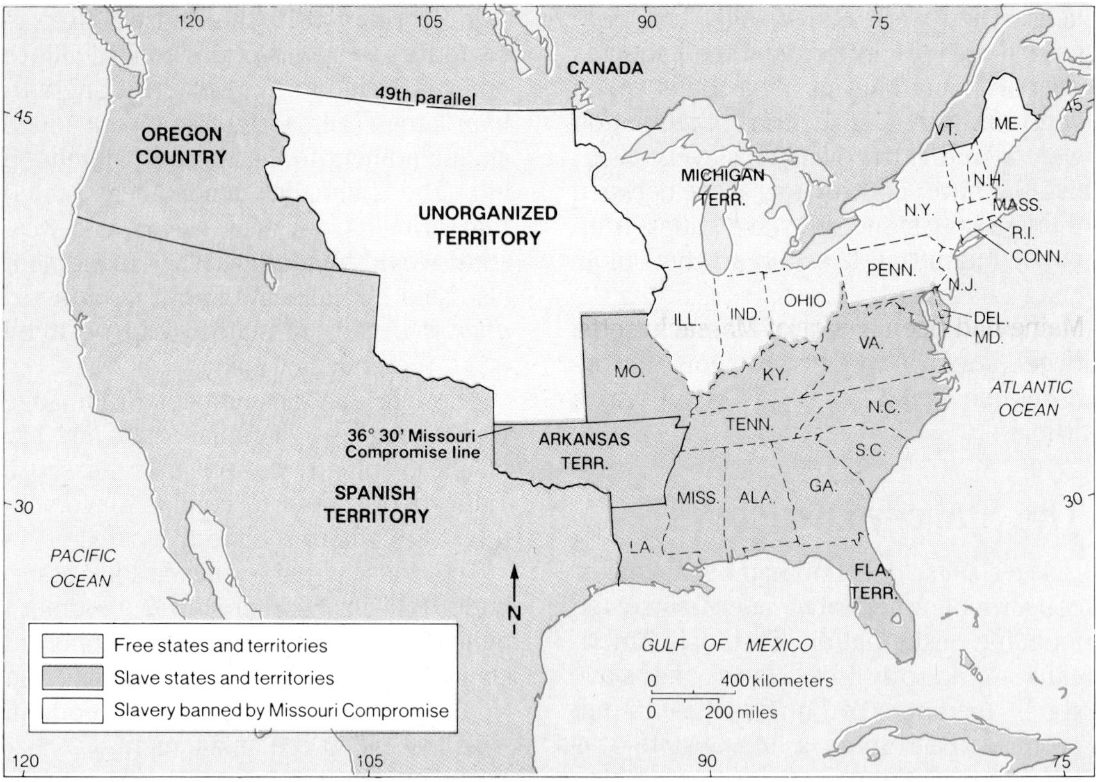

Into which territory could slavery expand according to the terms of the Missouri Compromise? Which territories would remain free?

helped form the American Colonization Society in 1817. This society wanted to return freed slaves to their homeland in Africa. There were even Southern societies that demanded that the slaves be gradually freed, or **emancipated**. In 1820, there were more emancipation societies in the South than in the North. But in spite of these efforts, most Southerners still believed in their right to own slaves.

emancipate to set free or release from slavery

As the debate over Missouri continued, Northern opposition to slavery grew. At the same time, Southern support of slavery increased. It became clear that the nation was deeply divided along sectional lines over the slavery question. The dispute, said the aged Jefferson, "like a fire bell in the night, awakened and filled me with terror."

The debate was further complicated in December 1819, when Maine applied for admission to the Union. Since 1677, Maine had been a part of Massachusetts. Now, Massachusetts had given permission for a separation.

Henry Clay of Kentucky, the speaker of the House, issued a warning to Northern members of Congress. They would have to change their position on Missouri and permit slavery there forever. If they did not, Southerners would reject Maine's petition for statehood. Some Northern members of Congress refused to compromise. Most, however, wanted to see the current slavery dispute settled.

A compromise was at last worked out. To satisfy the South, slavery would be permanently permitted in Missouri. To satisfy the North, Maine was admitted as a free state. In addition, to prevent further conflict, a line was drawn from Missouri's southern border westward across the Louisiana Purchase territories. Slavery was forbidden north of this line, an area that included most of the Louisiana Purchase. It was permitted in territories to the south.

The Missouri Compromise solved the immediate problem. The balance between free and slave states had been maintained. The compromise, however, did not end the slavery debate. Nor did it end sectionalism. The presidential election of 1824 soon made this clear.

Section Review

1. How did the Missouri Compromise solve the question of slavery in new territories and states?
2. Define sectionalism. What did sectionalism have to do with Missouri's statehood?
3. What was the Tallmadge amendment? Did it upset the North or the South more? Why?
4. Thomas Jefferson stated that the debate over Missouri was "like a fire bell in the night." What do you think Jefferson meant by this?

2. The Rise of Andrew Jackson

BEFORE YOU READ: *How did Andrew Jackson rise to political power?*

The campaign and election of 1824 demonstrated the growing sectionalism in the United States. Each section of the nation supported its own candidate for the presidency.

In his almost 50 years of government service, Henry Clay served as both a senator and representative from Kentucky.

The Candidates

Two presidential candidates in 1824 came from the West. One was Henry Clay of Kentucky. Clay called for a new program of vast internal improvements. More roads and canals, paid for by the federal government, would improve the exchange of western farm products and eastern manufactured goods. He also supported a high tariff to protect American manufacturers from foreign competition and favored a national banking system. Clay called his proposal the American System.

The other western candidate was Andrew Jackson of Tennessee. Jackson had become a national military hero as a result of his victory at the battle of New Orleans. For this reason, of all the presidential candidates, only Jackson had nationwide support. Jackson refused to take a stand on Clay's American System or on any of the political issues of the day. He did not want to take a position on any issue that might cost him the support of some voters.

The North's candidate was John Quincy Adams of Massachusetts. He was the son of former President John Adams and a former secretary of state. In the election campaign, Adams strongly supported all measures that would strengthen the country as a whole. He was an enthusiastic supporter of the proposals in Clay's American System.

At the beginning of the election campaign, there were two Southern candidates: John C. Calhoun of South Carolina and William H. Crawford of Georgia. Calhoun's bid for the White House, however, had little appeal outside of South Carolina. Most Southerners supported Crawford. As a result, Calhoun dropped out of the presidential race. He ran for Vice-President instead. Because he was the only candidate for the vice-presidency, Calhoun was assured of victory.

Discuss: Do you think a candidate with only regional support could win a presidential election today? Why or why not?

Background: If this situation had occurred prior to the passage of the 12th Amendment in 1804, Clay would have been considered in the House vote for President. The Constitution had originally specified that the House would choose the President from among the top five candidates.

William H. Crawford had served as Monroe's secretary of the treasury. In the campaign, Crawford received the support of the most powerful Southern politicians. Among these politicians were the last three Presidents—Jefferson, Madison, and Monroe.

The Election of 1824

Adams, Clay, and Crawford were well qualified for the job of President. Jackson was less qualified because he had little experience in government. However, Jackson was the most popular candidate.

On election day, Jackson received the most electoral votes, followed in order by Adams, Crawford, and Clay. But because there were so many candidates running, Jackson failed to receive a majority of the electoral votes cast. For the second time in American history, the House of Representatives had to decide who would be President. The Constitution required that the three candidates receiving the most electoral votes be presented in the House. They were Jackson, Adams, and Crawford.

Clay, who finished fourth, was out of the race. But as speaker of the House, Clay had the power to influence the votes of other representatives. Many members of the House would support Clay's choice for President. The candidate that Henry Clay supported seemed assured of becoming the next President. "It is in fact very much in [Clay's] power," said one politician, "to make the President."

Jackson, Adams, and Crawford each sent supporters to talk with Henry Clay. Jackson's followers demanded that Clay support their candidate. Jackson had won the greatest number of electoral and popular votes. He was the people's choice, they argued. But Clay disliked Jackson. Clay had been the West's leading politician for years. He was not about to help Jackson become more popular in the West than Clay himself was.

Although William Crawford was still a candidate, he was no longer a serious contender. During the election campaign, Crawford had suffered two paralyzing strokes.

John Quincy Adams was the only serious challenger to Jackson. Adams and Clay were not fond of each other personally. But they both supported the American System. Clay decided to support Adams.

John Quincy Adams was selected by the House as the new President on February 9, 1825. When he formed his Cabinet, Adams appointed Henry Clay to be his secretary of state. Jackson was outraged. He was convinced that a "corrupt bargain" had been made between Adams and Clay.

Most historians agree that Adams probably did not make such a bargain. He was too honorable for that. But Jackson was not convinced. He decided to get revenge politically on Adams and Clay.

A New Party Emerges

Andrew Jackson returned to his home in Tennessee to develop his strategy for fighting the Adams administration. With the help of Senator Martin Van Buren of New York, Jackson organized strong opposition to Adams in Congress. As a result, Adams was not very successful in pushing his programs through Congress.

Discuss: Do you think the results of the election of 1824 were fair to Jackson? Why or why not? Did Jackson have a right to protest the results of the election? Why or why not?

Discuss: The campaign leading to the election of 1828 was characterized as dirty. What does this mean? Are there any recent campaigns that you would consider dirty? Explain.

Jackson's tactics made John Quincy Adams look like a weak President.

Andrew Jackson and his supporters also formed a new political party in order to fight Adams. It became known as the Democratic party. The Democratic party attracted the support of wealthy slave owners, farmers from the West and South, wealthy members of the business community, and industrial workers. The Democratic party appealed to those who were dissatisfied with Adams and the Republicans. Andrew Jackson became the leader of the new Democratic party.

The National Republicans and the Democrats readied themselves for the election of 1828. President John Quincy Adams ran as the National Republican presidential candidate. His running mate was Richard Rush. The Democrats nominated Andrew Jackson for President and John C. Calhoun for Vice-President. The Democrats had been preparing for four years. They were well organized and ready for a tough campaign.

Most Americans expected a hard-fought and perhaps dirty campaign. They were not disappointed. The campaign was filled with vicious attacks on each candidate's character and background.

When the votes had been counted, Andrew Jackson received 56 percent of the popular vote. There was little doubt that Americans preferred Andrew Jackson to John Quincy Adams.

Westerners were overjoyed at the news of Jackson's victory. The West was sending a President to the White House for the first time. Jackson's election meant that a person from the frontier could hope to achieve the greatness of Washington or Jefferson. They felt that their new President was a man who cared about them and understood their problems. "It was a proud day for the people," reported one of Jackson's friends. "General Jackson is *their own* President."

On March 4, 1829, thousands of Americans attended Jackson's inauguration. Many were "common people" who had come to see *their* President take the oath of office. After the ceremonies, the noisy crowd followed Jackson to the White House. They hoped to get a chance to shake the new President's hand. Crowds of well-wishers poured into the White House. They stood with muddy boots on the White House chairs and sofas to get a glimpse of Jackson. They spilled punch on the mansion's expensive rugs. They jumped through the windows of the White House to get to refreshments served outside. Mrs. Samuel Smith, a guest at the reception, described the af-

The Election of 1828

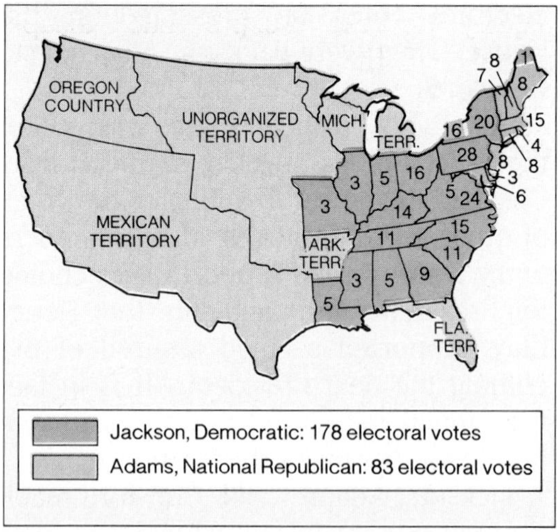

Which states cast electoral votes for both Jackson and Adams in this election?

For Extra Interest: Remind students that John C. Calhoun had served as Vice-President to John Quincy Adams before serving with Andrew Jackson. Ask students why this is unusual considering what they know about Adams and Jackson.

This picture shows the reception following Jackson's inauguration in 1829. What does it suggest about the kind of people who attended?

fair in a letter to her relatives. "But what a scene did we witness!" she wrote. "The majesty of the People had disappeared. . . . [It had become] a mob, scrambling, fighting, romping. . . . Ladies fainted, men were seen with bloody noses." Mrs. Smith concluded, "What a pity, what a pity!"

John Quincy Adams ended his term as President in the same fashion as his father. He left the White House the night before the inauguration. Adams refused to attend the ceremonies for the "barbarian," as he called Jackson. As Jackson began his term as the new President, one Supreme Court justice expressed the fear that this was the beginning of the reign of "King Mob."

Section Review

1. How did Andrew Jackson rise to political power?
2. How was sectionalism demonstrated in the election of 1824?
3. What was Henry Clay's American System?
4. What events led to the establishment of the Democratic party?
5. Why do you think Andrew Jackson won the election of 1828?

Social Studies Skills

Interpreting an Election Map

There were four presidential candidates in the election of 1824. Although Andrew Jackson received more popular and electoral votes than the other three candidates, he did not receive enough electoral votes to win. The map below shows the results of this election.

Like a graph or chart, an election map shows a great deal of information in an easy-to-read manner. Compared to a written description of the election, the map has the advantage of showing visually how electoral votes are distributed. Each candidate is color-coded in the map key. A state casting its electoral votes for a particular candidate is shaded with that candidate's color. The numbers in the states represent the number of electoral votes that candidate received.

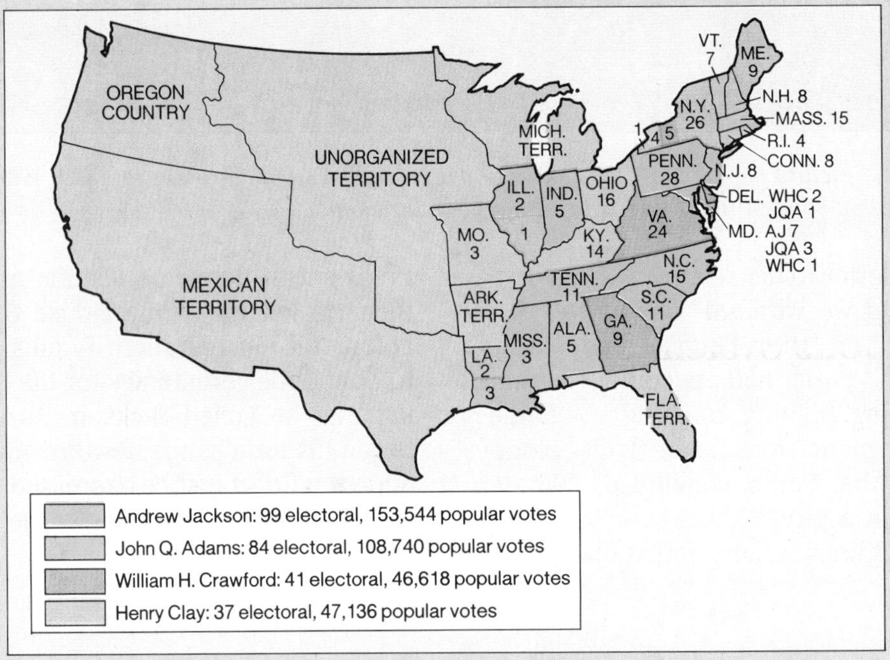

1. What is the advantage of showing election results on a map?
2. Which states cast all their electoral votes for Andrew Jackson?
3. Who received the smallest number of electoral votes? Which states cast all or some of their electoral votes for this candidate?
4. What regional voting patterns do you see in this election?

3. Jackson and the National Crisis

BEFORE YOU READ: *How did the tariffs of 1828 and 1832 lead to crisis over the issue of the rights of states?*

Andrew Jackson was 61 years old when he became President. He had come from a poor background. But Jackson was not one of the common people when he entered the White House. He was a wealthy Tennessee planter and slave owner.

Andrew Jackson was born in 1767 in a log cabin on the South Carolina frontier. Jackson's parents died while he was still a teenager.

Jackson's mother had hoped that he would become a minister. But Jackson was determined to become wealthy and well known. He became a frontier lawyer and then a judge, a military commander, a U.S. senator, and finally President.

The Spoils System

When Jackson took office, he was determined to reward the people who had helped him win the election. Some 20 percent of federal workers, most of whom had not supported Jackson for President, were fired. Their jobs were given to members of the Democratic party. It mattered little whether these people were qualified for the job. In fact, Jackson believed that most government jobs required no special abilities or experience. As long as the job applicants pledged their support to the new President, they were hired. This replacement of government workers by a new President with supporters of his own came to be known as the **spoils system**. It comes from an old expression: "To the victor go the spoils [the prize]."

---

spoils system the practice of rewarding loyal political supporters with government jobs

---

Jackson placed little faith in most of the people he appointed to his official Cabinet. Most of his Cabinet members were not highly qualified people. They had been appointed for political purposes. Jackson relied on their advice so infrequently that he did not even call Cabinet meetings. Instead, Jackson relied on a group of informal advisers. Some happened to be Cabinet members. Others were personal friends whose opinions he trusted. They came to be called the **"Kitchen Cabinet"** because they were an unofficial group that met behind the scenes. Some of the Kitchen Cabinet members included Secretary of State Martin Van Buren; Secretary of War John H. Eaton; Amos Kendall, a western newspaper editor; and Francis Preston Blair, Jr., a Kentucky newspaper reporter.

Kitchen Cabinet a group of informal advisers to the President

---

Trouble Over the Tariff

At the beginning of Jackson's presidency, a serious disagreement developed between the sections of the nation over the issue of tariffs. Between 1789 and 1816, tariffs were used to bring in money to run the national government and pay the national debt. These revenue tariffs

Discuss: Why might Jackson have believed that most government jobs do not require any special abilities or experience? Was there anything in his background that might have influenced this view?

Vocabulary Help: abomination—anything hateful and disgusting. Explain why Southerners would call the tariff of 1828 the "Tariff of Abominations."

had the support of all sections of the nation. After 1816, Congress began to change the nation's tariff policy. **Protective tariffs** were passed to help American industry. High tariffs were placed on foreign manufactured goods so that American industry could become more competitive and expand.

---

protective tariff a high tax placed on imported goods to protect domestic manufacturers from foreign competition

---

In 1828, Congress passed a new protective tariff that raised the tax placed on imports to its highest level yet. Northerners supported the tariff of 1828 because it would protect and promote Northern manufacturing. Southerners, on the other hand, were opposed to it. They called the new tariff the "Tariff of Abominations." Southerners feared that foreign nations would respond with their own protective tariffs. Southern cotton and rice would then become too expensive for foreign customers. The South could lose a great deal of business. To many Southerners, the tariff seemed to prove that Congress was most interested in listening to and supporting Northern concerns.

The planters of South Carolina were determined to fight the new tariff. They turned to the state's most powerful politician, John C. Calhoun, for help and support. Calhoun was then serving as Jackson's Vice-President. The planters hoped that Calhoun could convince Jackson to lower the tariff.

John C. Calhoun found himself in a difficult situation. Calhoun knew that Jackson would enforce the tariff because it was the law. Calhoun had to be careful not to oppose the President. But the Vice-President did not want to lose the support of the planters of South Carolina either. The planters were his base of power in politics.

Calhoun decided that he would not attack the tariff directly. Instead, he proposed a way in which the South could avoid obeying the law. Calhoun's idea was called the doctrine of **nullification**. Calhoun said that the states had created the Union. They had voluntarily surrendered certain powers to it. These powers were stated in the Constitution. If a law passed by Congress gave the national government powers not specifically stated in the Constitution, a state could declare the law not valid, or nullified. The law would not be binding within the borders of that state. Without the right to nullify a law, said Calhoun, the national government could become too strong. It could take too much power away from the states. To the South, Calhoun's reasoning made sense. Southerners saw the tariff as a law that should be nullified.

---

nullification an action taken by a state that declares a law of Congress not valid within the borders of that state

---

The Nullification Crisis

Calhoun's nullification theory stirred debate in the halls of Congress. Senator Robert Y. Hayne of South Carolina supported Calhoun's view and defended the doctrine of nullification. Senator Daniel Webster of Massachusetts defended the power of the federal government. He argued that the Constitution was not a

Background: Calhoun wanted to be the next President. To do this, he needed Jackson's support. He had to be careful not to antagonize Jackson over the tariff issue.

Discuss: Why did Jackson consider nullification a threat to the Union? Which position would you have supported on the nullification issue? Explain your answer.

compact, or agreement, among the states. It was an agreement among the people to set up a federal government.

While Congress debated the nullification issue, President Jackson had refrained from expressing his point of view. In April 1830, all the leaders of the Democratic party attended a dinner in honor of Thomas Jefferson. Plans were made by Calhoun and his supporters to offer toasts supporting the "rights of the states." They expected President Jackson to support the states' rights position. When the dinner was over, Jackson was asked to make the first toast. He lifted his glass, looked straight at Calhoun, and said: "Our Nation: It must be preserved!" The crowd sat in stunned silence. Jackson had challenged Calhoun. Calhoun accepted the challenge and offered the second toast: "The Union, next to our liberty, most dear!" Delaying for a second, Calhoun added, "May we all remember that it [the Union] can only be preserved by respecting the rights of the states. . . ."

The positions were clear. For Calhoun, Hayne, and other Southerners, the Union was a threat to states' rights and American liberty. For Jackson, Webster, and other Americans, the federal government's powers exceeded those of the states. The Union was the best defender of American liberty.

In 1832, Congress passed a new tariff bill. It left most tariff duties at a high level. President Jackson signed it into law. Within a few months, South Carolina nullified the tariffs of 1828 and 1832. It declared that the tariffs were "null, void, and no law, nor binding upon this State, its officers or citizens. . . . " The state of

The painter of this picture attempted to show Jackson as he was seen by the "common people."

Vocabulary Help: insurrection—an act of open rebellion against an established government. Ask students for examples of previous insurrections in American history.

South Carolina also issued a warning to the national government. If the federal government tried to enforce the tariff in South Carolina, the state would withdraw formally from membership in, or **secede** from, the Union.

---

secede to withdraw formally from membership in a group

South Carolina prepared for the federal government's response. Hayne resigned as senator to become governor during the crisis. Calhoun resigned as Vice-President and was elected to replace Hayne as the senator from South Carolina. The state wanted strong leaders to take command in this crisis situation.

President Jackson was determined to enforce the laws that he as President was sworn to defend. In Jackson's view, nullification threatened to bring the government to a standstill. If South Carolina could nullify one law, why could not Virginia nullify another law, and New York still another? "Nullification therefore means insurrection and war," Jackson declared, "and other states have a right to put it down."

President Jackson took two bold actions. First, he ordered the army to prepare 50,000 soldiers to enforce the tariff laws in South Carolina. Second, he issued a "Proclamation to the People of South Carolina." Jackson stated bluntly: "The laws of the United States must be executed. . . . Disunion by armed force is *treason*. Are you really ready to incur its guilt?" To the rest of the nation, the President said, "Union men, fear not. *The Union will be preserved.*"

Jackson also worked behind the scenes to ease the crisis. He called together the leaders of the Democratic party. The President asked them to help convince Congress to lower the tariff. At the same time, South Carolina realized it had gone too far. It had expected help from other Southern states, but none offered any support. Calhoun turned to Henry Clay for help. Clay and the Democratic leaders got Congress to pass a new compromise tariff in 1833. It lowered the tariff gradually over the next decade.

The episode taught South Carolina an important political lesson—that one state alone could not challenge the national government on the issue of states' rights. The support of other states was needed. Beginning in 1833, radicals in South Carolina worked diligently to obtain support from other Southern states.

Section Review

1. How did the tariffs of 1828 and 1832 lead to a crisis over the issue of the rights of states?
2. Define nullification and secede.
3. Why did Andrew Jackson form a "Kitchen Cabinet"?
4. How could the spoils system be used in a corrupt way by elected officials?

Discuss: Why do you think the other Southern states failed to support South Carolina during the nullification crisis?

Discuss: Do you think that white settlers and Indians could have lived together, or do you think, as Jackson did, that their ways of life were too different? Explain your answer.

4. Jackson and Presidential Power

BEFORE YOU READ: *What events led to the "trail of tears" for the Cherokee Indian nation?*

Andrew Jackson chose to run for a second term in 1832. The nullification crisis had turned Jackson against his Vice-President, John C. Calhoun. The President selected Martin Van Buren to run with him as his vice-presidential candidate. The National Republicans picked Henry Clay to run against Jackson. Jackson's popularity still remained high. He easily defeated Clay, winning 56 percent of the votes cast.

Removal of the Eastern Indians

Andrew Jackson, a westerner and an old Indian fighter, did not believe that Indians and whites could live with one another. Their ways of life and customs were too different.

In the early 1800's, the government began forcibly removing eastern tribes to lands west of the Mississippi River. In 1834, Congress marked off land west of the Mississippi River to be reserved for Indian use. It was called the **Indian Country**. Whites were not permitted to settle there.

Indian Country a vast area of land on the Great Plains guaranteed by the American government as the permanent home for American Indians

---

Eastern Indians who refused to move to the Indian Country were bribed or threatened. Sometimes their fate was worse. The Sauk and Fox Indians, for example, tried to return to their homes in northwestern Illinois in 1832. The governor of Illinois called out state troops. Many of the Sauk and Fox were slaughtered.

Other tribes suffered the same mistreatment as the Sauk and Fox. Most tribes realized that they could not stop the flow of white settlers onto their lands. They sadly left their homes and moved

Indian Removal, 1832–1842

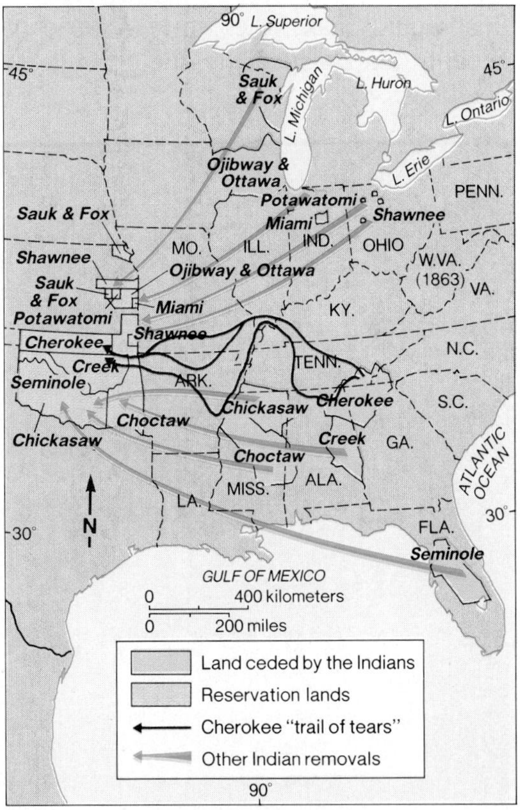

What eastern Indian tribes were removed to land west of the Mississippi River?

Background: Upon being taken prisoner, Black Hawk, leader of the Sauk and Fox, said, "An Indian who is as bad as the white man could not live in our nation. . . . They deal in false actions; they smile in the face of the poor Indian to cheat him. . . . "

Background: Several hundred Cherokees escaped the army's roundup. They hid in the dense forests of North Carolina, north of their old homeland. Today, their descendents still live in North Carolina and are known as the Eastern Cherokees.

westward. The Cherokee Indians of Georgia were an important exception.

The Cherokees sought to hold on to their lands by adopting many of the Americans' ways. The Cherokees lived in houses similar to those of white Americans. They wore American styles of clothing, took up farming and cattle raising, and sent their children, when possible, to white schools. They wrote a constitution and formed their own nation. They published a newspaper, the *Cherokee Phoenix*, in both their own language and English. People as far away as Europe read it. Some Cherokees even owned black slaves. The Cherokees hoped that all this would make the white Americans accept them, especially their Southern neighbors.

Prodded along by soldiers, the Cherokee moved west, making a "trail of tears."

The white people of Georgia were not impressed. They meant to have the Cherokees' homeland for their own, especially after gold was found on the Cherokee nation's land in the 1820's. The Georgia legislature demanded that the Cherokees move westward. President Jackson supported their demand. The Cherokees, however, refused to move. Their government declared, "The Cherokees are not foreigners, but the original inhabitants of America. . . . They now stand on the soil of their own territory."

The Cherokees were determined to save their homeland. They appealed their case in the federal courts. In two decisions, the Supreme Court upheld the rights of the Cherokee nation. But Georgia ignored the court's decisions, and President Jackson refused to use his influence to enforce them.

The Cherokees continued to resist the move for a while longer. But they knew that sooner or later they would have to forfeit their homeland. Criminals from Georgia began to raid their property, driving the Cherokees from their homes. Their homes were burned down and their cattle were stolen. The state of Georgia began selling off the Cherokees' land while they still lived on it. On April 10, 1838, Major General Winfield Scott brought an army into the Cherokees' homeland. His job was to remove the Cherokees to present-day Oklahoma.

More than 16,000 Cherokees were rounded up by the American troops. Young and old, sick and healthy, all were herded along. The troops were rough and unsympathetic. A deaf-mute Indian who turned right instead of left was shot on the spot. Food and water were in short

Discuss: Do you think the government was justified in moving the Cherokees from their homeland to present-day Oklahoma? Why or why not?

Famous Americans

MILLY FRANCIS

Milly Francis was a Creek Indian, born in present-day Alabama. Her father, Josiah Francis, was a successful farmer. He was also a leader of the movement to defend Indian lands from white settlers. In 1813, during the Creek War, General Andrew Jackson defeated many of the Alabama tribes and destroyed their towns. Josiah Francis took his family and many of the other survivors to Spanish Florida.

In 1817, the Indians in Florida captured young Captain Duncan McKrimmon of the Georgia militia. McKrimmon and his troops had been carrying out a raid on Indian territory. The Indians tied McKrimmon to a stake and were about to shoot him. Milly Francis heard the Indians' victory cries. She hurried to the site and persuaded the Indians to spare the soldier's life. McKrimmon's freedom was eventually purchased by the American government.

In the winter of 1818, Andrew Jackson invaded Florida. Josiah Francis was captured by Jackson and hanged. Milly Francis and the rest of her family managed to escape. But a few months later, they were on the verge of starving to death, and they surrendered to the American soldiers in Florida. Milly Francis met McKrimmon again, and he proposed marriage. She rejected his offer, saying that she would have done what she did for any white prisoner. Milly Francis and her family later returned to Creek land in southwest Georgia. When the federal government began to remove all Indians from Georgia, Milly Francis went with the Creek nation to Oklahoma. There she married and raised a family. In 1844, Congress decided to award Milly Francis a Medal of Honor and an annual pension of $96 in recognition of her help in saving McKrimmon's life. A government agent did not notify her until four years later. When the agent found Milly Francis, she was "in a most wretched condition," dying of tuberculosis. It is said that her eyes lit up when she was told of the award. But Milly Francis died before she received either the medal or the pension.

supply. Thousands of the Cherokees died along the way. A reporter for the *New York Observer* traveled along with the Cherokees to Oklahoma. He wrote, "When I passed the last . . . of those suffering exiles and thought that my countrymen had expelled them from their native soil and much beloved homes, . . . I turned from the sight with feelings which language cannot express." Over 4,000

For Extra Interest: Remind students that Thomas Jefferson had opposed the idea of a national bank on the same grounds as Jackson. Ask students what other ideas Jefferson and Jackson had in common.

people, or one quarter of the Cherokee nation, died during the journey. The survivors called the journey a "trail of tears."

The Second Bank

In 1832, the Second Bank of the United States filed an application to be rechartered by Congress. The bank had been chartered by Congress during James Madison's presidency. Its charter ran for a 20-year period, from 1816 to 1836. Under the policies of the bank's president, Nicholas Biddle, the bank had provided a stable money system and economy for the nation in the 1820's. Biddle had wide support among American business leaders.

President Jackson did not approve of the bank because he thought it was unconstitutional. The Constitution, he argued, contained no statement permitting the national government to charter a national bank. Jackson also believed that the bank was too powerful. It controlled the nation's money supply and greatly influenced the economic life of the United States. Jackson believed it was so powerful that it threatened the well-being of average Americans.

Nicholas Biddle, upon the urging of leaders of the National Republican party, decided to apply early for a new charter. Congress passed the bill granting the bank its new charter. President Jackson vetoed it.

Jackson's veto had long-range effects on the role of the presidency. Jackson argued that the President, not Congress, was truly the voice of the people. Members of Congress were elected by only a portion of the public—citizens of a state or a part of a state. The President, however, was elected by the nation. Thus, only Jackson spoke for all Americans. He vetoed the bank charter because he believed it was in the best interest of the American public. No President before Jackson had ever expressed this point of view. All previous Presidents had believed that Congress represented the public. Jackson believed that the President should take a more active role in determining government policies. Through his veto of the bank charter, Jackson strengthened the role of the President. However, Jackson's actions were not supported by all Americans.

Rise of the Whig Party

President Jackson made many political enemies. He had upset many Southerners with his stand on nullification and his treatment of South Carolina. He lost the support of the Northern business community over the bank question. In 1834, people opposed to Jackson formed their own political party. They called it the Whig party. The name was derived from the British Whig party. In Britain, this party opposed the power of the King. In America, the Whig party opposed the administration of "King Andrew I," as they called him.

The Whig party's support came from groups in the North, South, and West. The Whig party favored high protective tariffs, government supported internal improvements, a strong national bank, and government aid to the business community.

Even though the Whigs had nationwide support, they were not united. Several of their leaders were jealous of one another.

Background: Jackson used more vetoes and pocket vetoes (the refusal to sign a bill during the last ten days of a congressional session) than any other previous President. In this way, he exercised greater presidential power.

Discuss: Explain how the divisions within the Whig party would hinder its effectiveness as a political party.

The leaders of the Whig party found it hard to work together.

The greatest conflict among the Whigs arose over the question of slavery in the new territories. The Whigs split into four groups over this issue. The first two groups were called the Northern and Southern "Cotton Whigs." The third group was the Northern "Conscience Whigs." The fourth group was the "Union Whigs."

The Northern Cotton Whigs were bankers and shippers. Their wealth was based on the cotton trade. They supported the extension of slavery into the territories. If more land could be worked by slave labor, more cotton would be available to sell. The extension of slavery would be good for business. The Southern Cotton Whigs were the wealthy planters and major slave owners. They had a monopoly on the production of cotton. They believed that the extension of slavery into the territories would create more cotton growers. They opposed the extension of slavery because the competition would hurt their business.

The Northern Conscience Whigs believed that slavery was wrong. They opposed the extension of slavery into new areas.

How does this cartoon express Whig opposition to Andrew Jackson?

The Union Whigs thought that national prosperity and growth were the most important issues. They wanted to ignore the slavery question because it could lead to severe division within the nation.

Section Review

1. What events led to the "trail of tears" for the Cherokee Indian nation?
2. Explain how Andrew Jackson strengthened the office of the President by his handling of the bank issue.
3. Who were the Whigs? What were the different views of party members on the extension of slavery into new territories?
4. Could the removal of the eastern Indians have been prevented? Explain your answer.

For Extra Interest: Have students make a chart summarizing the positions of the four groups within the early Whig party on the issue of slavery. The chart should also show the issues all Whigs generally supported.

CHAPTER REVIEW

Summary

By 1820, the spirit of unity that had characterized American life following the War of 1812 was disappearing. Sectional disputes arose between 1819 and 1834 over the extension of slavery, protective tariffs, and rechartering the Second Bank of the United States. These disputes threatened to split the nation.

Andrew Jackson dominated American politics during this period. He formed the Democratic party following his defeat for the presidency in 1824. Four years later, Jackson was elected President. As President, Jackson took a firm stand against the right of any state to nullify federal laws or secede from the Union. He supported the forcible removal of thousands of Cherokee Indians from their homelands. Finally, Jackson vetoed the bill granting a new charter to the Second National Bank.

Those who opposed Jackson and his policies formed the Whig party in the 1830's. Although sectional issues divided the Whigs, the formation of this party reestablished the two-party system in United States politics.

Recalling the Facts

1. Why did Southerners who supported slavery object to the Missouri statehood bill in 1819?
2. Andrew Jackson received the most votes for President in 1824, yet he lost the election. Why?
3. What was the "Kitchen Cabinet"? Why did Jackson rely more on his Kitchen Cabinet than on his official Cabinet for advice?
4. Why did Southerners oppose protective tariffs?
5. What did the Cherokee Indians do to try to hold on to their lands in Georgia?
6. Why was the Whig party formed?

Analyzing the Facts

1. How did the election of John Quincy Adams in 1824 affect political parties in the United States?
2. Compare Andrew Jackson to the Presidents who came before him. How was he different? How was he similar?
3. What alternatives did South Carolina have to nullifying the tariffs of 1828 and 1832?

4. Explain the inconsistency in Jackson's enforcement of federal law during the nullification crisis and the case of Cherokee Indian rights.
5. Explain what you consider to be Andrew Jackson's greatest achievement or accomplishment.

Time and History

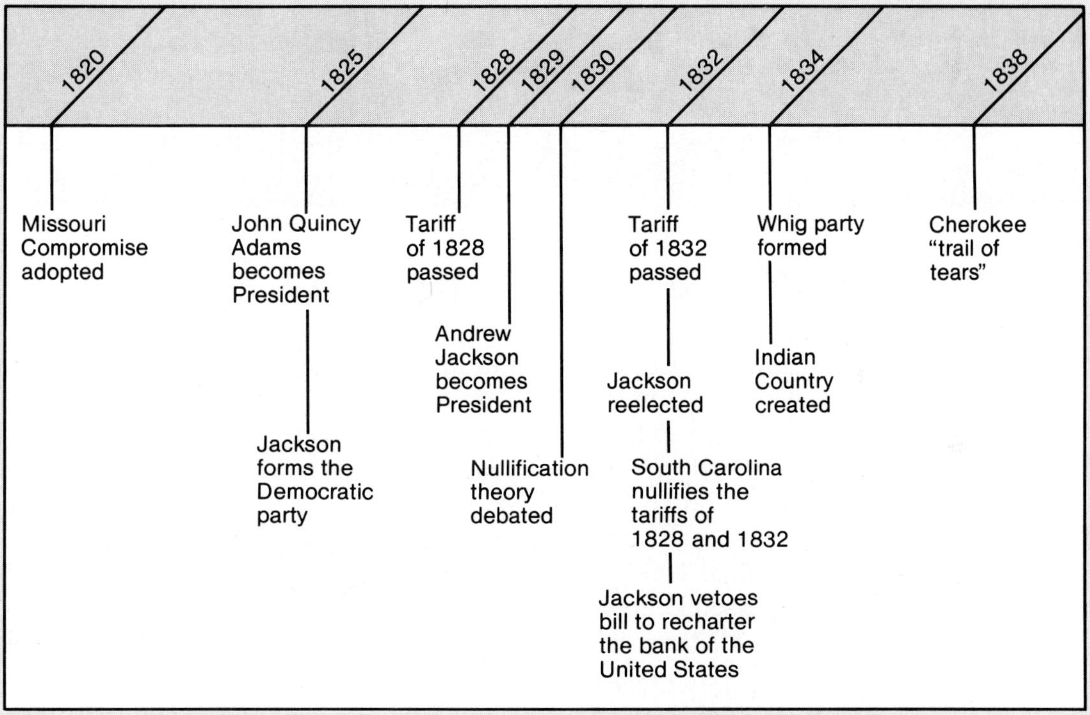

1. Who was President when the Democratic party was formed?
2. How many years after the Democratic party was formed was the Whig party formed?
3. Andrew Jackson served as President for two terms. Was he President when the Cherokees were forced to move west?
4. How many terms in office did John Quincy Adams serve?
5. How long after Andrew Jackson became President did South Carolina nullify the tariffs of 1828 and 1832?

Chapter
12

Slavery and the Old South

"Away, away, away down South in Dixie." So went the chorus to the song "Dixie," a song that became the symbol for the Old South—the South of the years before the Civil War. The Old South was pictured as a land covered by endless fields of white cotton. There, kindly plantation owners sat contentedly on the porches of their mansions. Under the owners' watchful eyes, black slaves worked the owners' fields, cared for their children, cooked their meals, cleaned their homes, and did other useful chores. The slaves' voices filled the air with music as they worked. The society of the Old South was portrayed as peaceful and happy. This picture, however, existed only in people's imaginations. The reality for rich and poor whites, slave owners and non-slave owners, free blacks and slaves was very different.

After you read this chapter, you will be able to:

1. Describe the white class system in the South before the Civil War.
2. Explain what life was like for free blacks and slaves in the Old South.

Vocabulary Help: rural—concerning life in the country and occupations related to farming. Ask students to write two sentences using the word rural.

1. The World of White Southerners

BEFORE YOU READ: *How did the expansion of cotton growing change life in the South?*

The North and the South were developing into very different societies during the first half of the 1800's One society developed in the North. The North was becoming an industrial region. Cities were growing, the population was increasing rapidly, and trains carried people and products to many parts of the North. The North still had a large rural population. But most Northerners welcomed the changes that progress brought to their lives.

A completely different society developed in the South. The South was rural for the most part, and it had a much smaller population than the North. Agriculture, not industry, was the basis of the Southern economy. The South had few factories and still fewer railroads. Most Southerners valued tradition more than change and progress.

However, the greatest difference between the two societies was slavery. The North had started to do away with slavery following the American Revolution. The South had not. This was largely due to the way Southern agriculture developed from the 1790's onward.

Southern Agriculture

Many crops grew well in the South's mild climate. Corn was raised to feed the population and to fatten cattle and hogs for slaughter. Other crops were grown to be sold for profit.

The South had five major cash crops. South Carolina produced rice. Louisiana's cash crop was sugar cane. Tobacco was the cash crop for Virginia, Maryland, North Carolina, and the western part of Kentucky. The people of central Kentucky grew hemp, the fiber used to make rope. In the 1790's, a new cash crop emerged. This was cotton. By the end of the century, cotton was the most important cash crop of the South.

The Industrial Revolution in Great Britain created an enormous demand for Southern cotton. Britain needed great quantities of cotton to keep its textile mills running. Southern farmers wanted to meet this demand, but cotton took too long to clean. Separating the seeds from the fiber by hand took a lot of time. A breakthrough came in 1793. Eli Whitney invented the cotton gin. It was a simple machine that separated the seeds from the cotton by the turn of a handle. Cleaning cotton became faster, easier, and more economical. Before the cotton gin was invented, it took an entire day to clean 0.45 kilogram (1 pound) of cotton by hand. After the cotton gin was developed, 23 kilograms (50 pounds) of cotton could be cleaned in a day.

The cotton gin and the demand for cotton changed the pattern of agriculture in the South. Vast areas of land were converted to cotton production. By 1800, cotton had become the South's most important cash crop.

Cotton was soon growing across a vast stretch of land from the Carolinas to present-day eastern Texas. This area of cotton production came to be known as

Discuss: Why was slavery, which was very popular in the South, not popular in the industrialized North?

Background: The profits from cotton made the South the second richest area of the country. It was second only to New England.

Cash Crops of the South

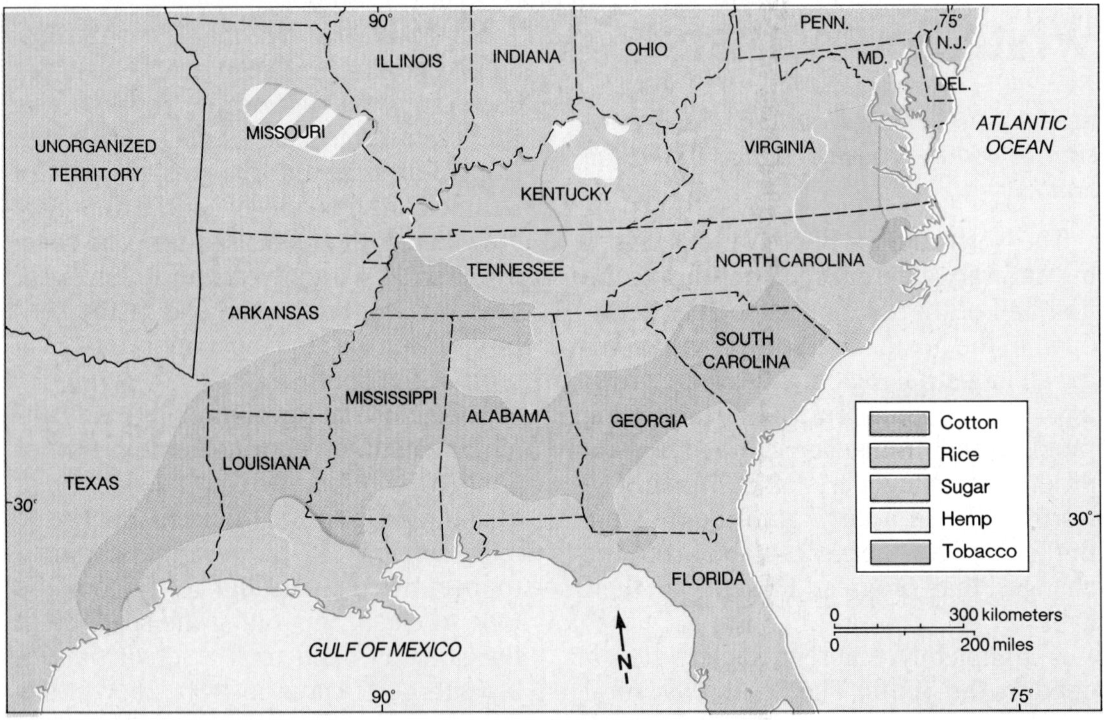

In which states was cotton the principal crop?

the **Cotton Belt**. The owners of the great cotton plantations called this region of the South the "Cotton Kingdom."

Cotton Belt a vast region of the South, stretching from the Carolinas to eastern Texas, where the major cash crop is cotton

---

"King Cotton" and Slavery

The South became the leading producer of raw cotton. By 1860, it was producing 90 percent of the world's cotton. Cotton production brought so much money to planters that it was called "white gold." No one could dispute the importance of cotton to the American economy. A Southern member of Congress declared, "Cotton is King!"

As cotton production expanded, planters needed a steady supply of labor to work the cottonfields. Planters relied on the forced labor of slaves. Black slaves were put to work planting, weeding, and picking the cotton crop. Millions of dollars were spent to purchase more slaves to work in the fields of the Cotton Belt. By 1860, there were some 4 million black slaves in the South. They made up about one third of the Southern population.

Background: As cotton production grew, so did the profits. Planters wanted more land on which to grow cotton. They looked westward. When the War of 1812 ended, Southerners poured into the lands that bordered on the Gulf of Mexico.

Background: Slave labor was the cheapest way to harvest the vast cotton crops. With paid labor, the large profits made by the planters would not have been possible.

EUREKA!

Refrigeration

When you find yourself getting hungry for lunch on a Saturday, what do you do? The chances are good that you open the refrigerator to see what it has to offer. Had you lived before the invention of refrigeration, your meal would likely have been limited to foods produced within a few kilometers (miles) of your home. Before refrigeration, perishable foods could be stored for only short periods of time. More important, these foods could not be shipped from one place to another without spoiling.

As recently as the late nineteenth century, most Americans relied on blocks of ice to keep their perishable foods cold. But ice has the inconvenient habit of melting, and when it does, food spoils.

A Scot named William Cullen is credited with building the first refrigerator in 1748, but it did not work very well. The first practical refrigerator—the ancestor of those in use today—was built by an American inventor who was named Jacob Perkins.

Perkins invented his refrigerator in 1834 while living in England. He produced the effect of cooling by evaporating chemicals such as ether. The ether gas was then compressed and condensed again into a liquid and reused.

Perkins built at least one working refrigerator, with which he made ice. But he did not promote his invention. Another American, Alexander Twinning, made what was probably the first commercial icemaker in 1856. Many other inventors around the world developed similar machines soon after.

By 1900, refrigeration was in wide use. Its impact on society was huge. It made possible the transportation of perishable foods such as meat. It enabled foods to be stored so that shortages could be avoided.

Without this large slave population, the production of cotton and other cash crops would not have prospered.

Only about 25 percent of Southern whites owned slaves. The planters who owned the most slaves dominated society and government in the South.

Southern society was shaped like a pyramid. At the top of the social pyramid were the planters who owned the largest

Background: The wives of the planters managed the home and devoted their spare time to music, literature, and social activities.

plantations and the largest number of slaves—50 to 100 or more. In 1850, there were only about 8,000 planters who owned this many slaves. They made up slightly more than 3 percent of all Southern slave owners. Many of these planters lived in luxury in beautiful mansions. They filled their homes with fine furniture. They hired tutors to teach their children at home or sent their children to boarding schools. Household slaves took care of the personal needs of the planter and the entire family. Field slaves tended to the crops, the animals, the upkeep of the plantation, and many other chores. These planters were the envy of most Southern whites.

Beneath the wealthiest planters were the planters who owned 10 to 50 slaves. In 1850, they numbered about 84,000, making up about 34 percent of Southern slave owners. They imitated many of the customs of the wealthiest planters but led less luxurious lives.

Beneath these two classes was a third group who owned nine or fewer slaves. There were about 154,000 such individuals, making up approximately 63 percent of all slave owners. The members of this group had small farms. Most had bought slaves to ease the burden of back-breaking farm work.

The vast majority of Southern whites owned no slaves at all. They made up about 75 percent of the white population. Many of these Southerners were small farmers who produced food for their own families and raised livestock.

Southern society also included a small group of manufacturers and merchants. Southern manufacturers were engaged in flour milling, textile production, and iron production. Southern merchants made their living by transporting, storing, and selling cotton, tobacco, and other cash crops. Merchants and manufacturers lived comfortable lives.

Cotton is examined by buyers in this scene of the New Orleans Cotton Bureau.

Professionals, such as lawyers and doctors, were another small group in Southern society. Some of the most respected professionals were military officers. According to Southern custom, when a landowner died, his oldest son inherited the property. Younger sons, therefore, often chose careers in the military or other professions.

 Discuss: How do you think daughters of Southern landowners were expected to support themselves?

Background: Poverty-stricken whites made up about 6 percent of the Southern population. Many lived on the least desirable land on the outskirts of towns, in the countryside, or in the mountains. These Southerners lived by hunting and fishing and occasionally grew a few vegetables.

Frontier Life

Southern frontier life could be very lonely. Vast areas of wilderness separated families from their nearest neighbors. Get-togethers often had both a social and a useful function. In the fall, corn had to be husked. A frontier family would harvest the corn and store it in the barn. Then they would invite their neighbors to a "corn shucking." As everyone husked or "shucked" the corn, it gave them an opportunity to socialize. Log rollings were another way of combining work and social activity. After a frontier family cut trees to clear their land, neighbors would come to help move the heavy logs, placing them in great piles for burning.

Many of the small farmers lived in log or frame houses of one or two rooms. Their homes were sparsely furnished. Some had only a table, a chair or two, and a bed.

A Closed Society

Southern society was one of extremes. On one end were the wealthy planters, a small minority of the total population. These planters owned most of the slaves and controlled 90 percent of the South's wealth. They dominated Southern politics and government.

At the other end of Southern society were those who owned few slaves or none. They made up about 98 percent of the white population. Some deeply resented the planters' great wealth and power. They envied the planters' fertile land. But in spite of the differences among whites in Southern society, they were held together by race. White Southerners, whether poor or rich, thought themselves superior to any black person.

Southerners were, for the most part, content with their society as it was. They closed themselves off to ideas that would have brought major change. Anyone who criticized the South was seen as an enemy. Southerners would not tolerate criticism of their society, especially slavery. The Old South was a **closed society**.

closed society a society that will not examine its faults or allow criticism of itself and its institutions

Section Review

1. How did the expansion of cotton growing change life in the Old South?
2. What classes made up Southern society?
3. What factors held Southern society together?
4. Explain why the Old South can be described as a closed society.
5. What regions of the world are heavily dependent on one product or cash crop? How might this dependence affect each region's economy?

Background: Some Southerners attempted to defend their proslavery positions by writing "scientific" essays, which they said proved the need for and inevitability of slavery.

Background: Many free blacks had been given their freedom by their masters. The number of slaves freed voluntarily decreased after 1810 due largely to legal difficulties and opposition from those who feared the increasing number of free blacks.

2. The World of Black Southerners

BEFORE YOU READ: *What was life like for free blacks and slaves in the Old South?*

About 4 million blacks lived in the South by 1860. They held the lowest position in Southern society. There were two groups of Southern blacks—free blacks and slaves.

Free Blacks

There were about 250,000 free blacks in the South. Most had been given their freedom following the American Revolution. Of the free blacks in the slave states, some 215,000 lived in the area called the **Upper South**. This area consisted of the states of Delaware, Virginia, Kentucky, Tennessee, and Missouri. Of these states, Maryland and Virginia had the greatest number of free blacks. Only 35,000 free blacks lived in the states of the **Deep South**. This area comprised the Carolinas, Georgia, Florida, Alabama, Mississippi, Arkansas, Louisiana, and Texas.

Upper South slave states in the northern part of the South: Delaware, Virginia, Kentucky, Tennessee, and Missouri

Deep South slave states in the southern part of the South: the Carolinas, Georgia, Florida, Alabama, Mississippi, Arkansas, Louisiana, and Texas

---

Most free blacks lived in the cities of the South. Many worked in trades dominated by whites, such as carpentry, sailmaking, blacksmithing, and masonry. Some free blacks entered the ministry. A small number became slave owners themselves. Free black women often worked in households or as seamstresses. The majority of free blacks worked at unskilled jobs, as day laborers and farm hands, for example. They were paid very low wages. Life was difficult, but it was much better than the life of a slave. Frederick Douglass wrote, "Life [as a free man], when most oppressive, was a paradise."

Although these blacks were free, their freedom was severely limited. They had very few legal rights. Blacks could not travel freely, they could not testify against whites in court, and they could not vote. Free blacks received much harsher punishment than whites who had committed the same crime. If a free black was convicted of certain crimes, he or she could be punished by being sent temporarily into slavery.

The Institution of Slavery

The demand for slaves grew steadily in the South, especially in the regions where cash crops were grown. About 75 percent of all slaves did agricultural work: 55 percent raised cotton, 10 percent raised tobacco, and the remaining 10 percent of agricultural slaves worked on sugar, rice, or hemp plantations.

In 1808, federal law prohibited the African slave trade. Some illegal trade was carried on after that. But the greatest trade in slaves was within the United States itself. Slave trading flourished between 1815 and 1860 because of the continuing demand for slaves. Professional slave traders carried on the business of

For Extra Interest: Demonstrate how easy it was for a free black to lose his or her freedom. Give imaginary freedom papers to a student in the room. Ask the "free black" to show you, a white Southerner, his or her freedom papers. When the student hands you the papers, tear them up.

Background: Although Congress prohibited the further importation of slaves in 1808, an illicit trade in slaves persisted. Between 1808 and 1860, an estimated 250,000 slaves were imported illegally.

How do you think the people shown in this painting of a slave auction feel about what is taking place?

buying and selling slaves within the United States.

New supplies of slaves came from two main sources. One source was the children of slaves. By law, the children of a woman who was a slave became slaves themselves. Most slave owners felt little guilt in selling the children of their slaves. It was like selling any other piece of property. Another source for slaves was the Upper South. Some areas of the Upper South, especially in Virginia and Maryland, had been farmed by whites for almost 200 years. By the 1800's, the soil was wearing out, and slavery was no longer practical or economical. Slave owners in the Upper South preferred to sell, rather than free, their slaves. They made a handsome profit by selling off their slaves to the slave traders, who resold them in the Deep South. Between 1830 and 1860, Virginia exported nearly 300,000 slaves.

When they arrived in the Deep South, the slaves were usually taken to some central market to be sold. Major slave markets were located in Mobile, Alabama; Charleston, South Carolina; Natchez, Mississippi; Galveston, Texas; and New Orleans, Lousiana.

The slaves were sold at auctions at the central market. William Wells Brown, a former slave, described one scene at a New Orleans slave pen. "In a short time the planters came flocking to the Negro pen to purchase slaves. The slaves were driven out into the yard. Some were set to

Background: Slave traders were usually held in low esteem, but they were tolerated because they performed a service that was of great importance in the South. They scoured the countryside of the Upper South for slaves whom they could buy for resale at a profit in the Deep South.

Background: Some southern states passed laws that prohibited or discouraged the breakup of slave families. These laws were almost entirely ignored and were therefore ineffective.

dancing, some to jumping, some to singing. . . . This was done to make them appear cheerful and happy. . . . " The buyers would check the slaves over carefully. They inspected the slaves' arms, legs, eyes, and teeth. They checked for signs of old age or some kind of physical problem.

Slaves were expensive. A young male slave might cost as much as $1,700 in the Cotton Belt. An adult female slave sold for about $1,000. The average price for a slave was closer to $800.

The slave trade separated children from parents and wives from husbands. For slaves, the breakup of their families was a painful experience. Josiah Henson, a slave, remembered:

> My brothers and sisters were bid off first, and one by one, while my mother, paralyzed by grief, held me by the hand. Her turn came, and she was bought by Isaac Riley. . . . Then I was offered to the purchasers. My mother, with the thought of parting forever from all her children, pushed through the crowd. . . . She fell at [Riley's] feet, and clung to his knees [asking] him in tones that a mother only could command to buy her baby as well as herself, and spare to her one of her little ones.

Isaac Riley refused to purchase Josiah Henson. He even beat and kicked Henson's mother to drive her away. Josiah Henson continued:

> As she crawled away from the brutal man I heard her sob out, "Oh, Lord Jesus, how long, how long shall I suffer this way!" I must have been between five and six years old. I seem to see and hear my poor mother now. . . . [This was] an experience [that I] shared with thousands of my race.

What does this engraving of slaves cutting sugar cane tell you about the conditions under which these slaves worked?

Agricultural Slaves

Most agricultural slaves worked as field hands. Their lives were harsh. They rose before dawn, prepared their meals, fed the livestock, and then went to the fields. If a slave did not reach the fields on time, he or she was often punished by whipping. Field slaves worked long hours planting, hoeing, and picking crops. Field slaves often worked in large gangs. They were under the constant supervision of black "drivers," or bosses. If the slave gangs were large, the slave owner might employ a white boss, or **overseer**. The overseer was responsible for both the

Background: Field slaves worked the longest hours during harvest time, because the planter was eager to get the crops picked before they could be damaged by bad weather. An adult slave was expected to pick 68 kilograms (150 pounds) of cotton a day.

Discuss: How do you think a slave owner decided which slaves to make household servants and which to make field hands? What characteristics would be sought in both cases?

drivers and the gangs. Overseers were permitted to discipline the slaves. They could punish the slaves with beatings or whippings.

overseer a person responsible for supervising the work of other people

After working in the fields until sunset, the weary slaves could not return immediately to their quarters and rest. They had to feed the livestock, put away tools, and cook their meals. All of this had to be completed before a horn sounded, signaling that it was time for bed.

Household slaves received better treatment than field slaves. Household slaves were in contact with the master's family during most of the day. Often a friendly, even close relationship developed between the master's family and the household slaves.

Female household slaves often cooked, sewed, cared for the master's children, and served as maids or nurses. Male household slaves served meals, ran errands, worked as gardeners, butlers, or coach drivers, and cared for the horses and cows.

There was no standard type of housing for slaves on plantations or farms. Some fortunate ones lived in clean, whitewashed cabins. Most slave quarters were miserable. They were poorly built, windowless huts. They gave little protection against bad weather.

Slave huts were often filthy and overcrowded. Many had no furniture. Whatever furniture the slaves used was usually made by the slaves themselves.

Slaves were given a limited amount of clothing. A common supply consisted of shirts or skirts of coarse cotton, a woolen jacket in the winter, a pair of trousers, and perhaps two cotton shirts for the summer. Slaves received one pair of shoes each year.

Because of slavery, stable family life within the black family was very difficult. But slave families did their best to maintain strong bonds of affection. Masters were the ones who determined how much care and freedom a slave child was permitted. Infants were often carried by their mothers to the fields. Young slave children enjoyed a great deal of freedom either to play by themselves or to serve as the playmates of the master's children. Between the ages of seven and ten, children became a part of the work force on the plantation.

Urban Slaves

There were many jobs in Southern cities that white people did not want to perform. Jobs such as cooking or gardening paid too little or were considered too undesirable for whites to do. Slaves provided a source of labor for these jobs.

Slave owners made arrangements with whites in the cities who needed workers. Once a price was set, the slaves were rented. This was called the **hiring-out system**. Most of the money earned by the slave went to the master. A small fraction would sometimes go to the slave. A few slaves were able to save enough money to buy their freedom and freedom for their family.

hiring-out system a system of renting slaves to people in cities who needed workers

Background: Slaves were often hired out during the period between the harvest and the new planting.

Background: Some slaves disguised themselves or forged passes in their effort to escape. Others simply walked off. Southern newspapers carried advertisements for runaway slaves.

On the whole, urban slaves lived under fewer restrictions than slaves in the countryside. The urban slave had more freedom in coming and going. Sometimes urban slaves lived in cabins on the master's property. Frequently, they were permitted to live in their own dwellings. This small freedom was highly prized by urban slaves.

All slaves, both agricultural and urban, had no legal rights. In the first half of the nineteenth century, legal restrictions, called **slave codes**, were passed to keep slaves' activities under tight control. Slaves could not leave their plantation or move about in cities without passes or written permission. Slaves could not make contracts to buy or sell goods. They could not testify in court except against another black person. Slaves were not permitted to own firearms. They could not visit whites or free blacks or receive them as visitors. It was a criminal offense to teach a slave to read or write. Slaves could not hold a meeting or assemble unless a white person was present.

---

slave codes laws placing restrictions on slaves

Slave Reactions

Slaves reacted to slavery in a variety of ways. Some slaves accepted their position even though they resented their lack of freedom. They felt that there was little they could do about it.

Other slaves dreamed of freedom in the North. A small number took the risk of running away. They knew that if they were captured, the punishment would be severe. The owner might whip, beat, or hang them. There were laws in all of the states against killing slaves, but this did not stop some individuals from committing murderous acts. One black child described what happened to a group of captured runaways in Texas: "Massa have a great, long whip . . . of rawhide, and when one [of us fell] behind or give out, he hit him with that whip. Mother, she give out on the way. . . . Massa, he just take out he gun and shot her, and whilst she lay dying he kicks her. . . . "

With so many slaves in the South, the greatest fear of Southern whites was the possibility of a slave revolt. The fear was greatest in states like South Carolina and Mississippi where the slave population was large.

There were a number of small, local slave uprisings during the colonial pe-

In this engraving, Nat Turner is shown discussing plans for his slave revolt with some of his followers.

Discuss: What do you think motivated some blacks to inform white Southerners about planned slave revolts?

riod. More uprisings occurred after the War for Independence. But these did not turn into major disturbances. There were only three large-scale revolts during the period of slavery. In 1800, Gabriel Prosser, a field slave, started a rebellion in Virginia. He dreamed of creating a black state in Virginia over which he would rule. Prosser led a group of 34 slaves on a march toward Richmond, the capital of Virginia. They were armed with guns, knives, and clubs. Two blacks warned the whites in advance. The authorities made numerous arrests and hanged Prosser and all of his followers.

The second revolt took place in 1822. Denmark Vesey (VEE-zee) had purchased his freedom and was a successful carpenter in Charleston, South Carolina. He wanted to end slavery in the South. Vesey and his followers secretly organized a large number of slaves on local plantations. Their plan was to seize weapons from two military arsenals in Charleston. They hoped to free slaves around the city. Again, black informers gave their plans away to whites. Many slaves were punished. Thirty-seven blacks were hanged for plotting the revolt, including Vesey.

The most serious slave revolt occurred nine years later, in 1831. It took place in Southampton County, Virginia. The leader was Nat Turner, a slave and a preacher. Turner believed that God had instructed him to slay the wicked whites. Turner and his followers brutally murdered 57 white men, women, and children. The Nat Turner revolt was put down harshly. Several thousand armed men hunted Turner's followers down. More than 100 slaves, many of them innocent, were killed. After a court trial, 13 slaves and 3 free blacks were hanged. Turner, who avoided capture for nearly two months, was hanged on November 11, 1831.

The Nat Turner revolt frightened many white Southerners. Whites were convinced that Turner had been influenced by Northerners who were against slavery. In the Southerners' eyes, Northerners were endangering the life of every Southern white. In response to the slave revolts, the Southern states strengthened their slave codes. The movements of slaves were restricted even further.

Section Review

1. What was life like for free blacks and slaves in the Old South?
2. What did Frederick Douglass mean when he said that life as a free man, "when most oppressive, was a paradise"?
3. What was the Nat Turner revolt? What effect did it have on white Southerners?
4. Why do you think the slave codes made it illegal for slaves to learn to read and write?

Background: When one participant in a slave revolt was asked what he had to say, he calmly replied, "I have ventured my life in endeavoring to obtain the liberty of my countrymen and am a willing sacrifice to their cause."

CHAPTER REVIEW

Summary

Cotton became the most important cash crop in the South following the invention of Whitney's cotton gin in 1793. Millions of dollars were spent to purchase slaves to plant, weed, and pick the cotton crop. By 1860, black slaves made up about one third of the Southern population.

Only about 25 percent of Southern whites owned slaves. Most of these owned fewer than ten slaves. The wealthiest planters and largest slaveholders, however, controlled 90 percent of the South's wealth and dominated Southern politics. The bulk of the South's white population worked their own farms. A small group of Southerners was engaged in trade and manufacturing.

The lowest position in Southern society was held by the black population. Although some blacks were free, the vast majority were slaves. Many black families were separated at slave auctions. Most slaves lived in miserable huts, were given limited clothing, and were forced to work long hours in the fields. Despite the risk of severe punishment, some slaves ran away or participated in slave revolts.

Recalling the Facts

1. How did the society that developed in the North during the first half of the nineteenth century differ from the society that developed in the South?
2. What percentage of Southern whites owned slaves?
3. How was the freedom of free blacks in the South severely limited?
4. What were the two main sources for new supplies of slaves after 1808?
5. Who determined how much care or freedom a slave child was permitted?
6. What was the result of the three major slave revolts in the South?

Analyzing the Facts

1. Why do you think the population in the North was greater than the population in the South in the first half of the nineteenth century?

2. What caused cotton production to increase in the South? How did this affect slavery?
3. Why do you think that many Southerners valued tradition more than change or progress?
4. How might economic considerations affect the ways in which slaves were disciplined or cared for?
5. Why would a slaveholder go to the trouble of tracking a runaway slave if the intent was to hang the slave once caught?
6. What prevented all slaves from joining together to stage a massive revolt against slavery in the South?

Time and History

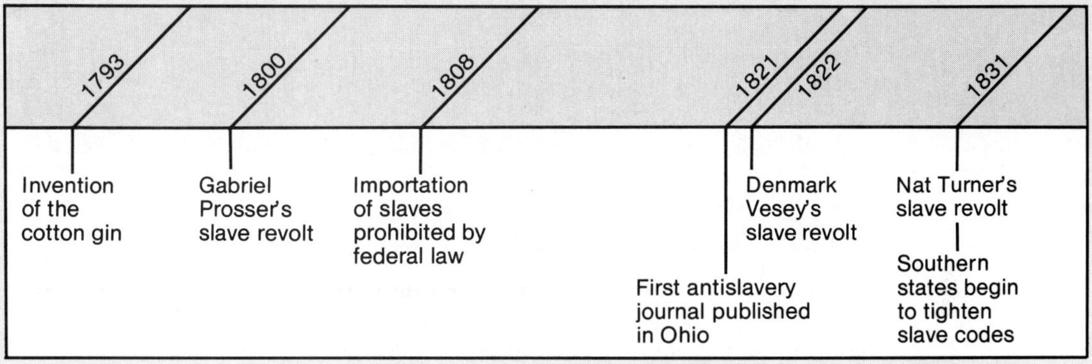

1. In what year was the importation of slaves prohibited by federal law?
2. How many years after the invention of the cotton gin was the importation of slaves prohibited by federal law?
3. How many years separate the first major slave revolt from the last major slave revolt?
4. What event occurred in 1831 that prompted Southern states to begin tightening their slave codes?
5. In what state was the first antislavery journal published? In what year did this occur?

Chapter 13

The Changing North

During the first half of the 1800's, the North was changing. Industry developed and factories were built. Immigrants filled the cities. More people left their farms to find work and a new way of life in the cities. Some Northerners became concerned with the quality of life in America. They worked to improve education, prisons, and care for the mentally ill. They organized to gain more rights for women. They made efforts to bring slavery to an end. The literature produced by American writers emphasized the unique opportunity Americans had to shape their future and that of the nation.

After you read this chapter, you will be able to:

1. Describe the class system that existed in the North.
2. Identify the social problems that concerned Americans.
- Use reference materials.

1. Northern Society Takes Shape

BEFORE YOU READ: *What social classes existed in the North during the first half of the nineteenth century?*

"We are the people of the future," announced a Northern newspaper. Such optimism about Northern society was widespread. The Industrial Revolution was bringing progress, advancement, and improvement. There existed in Northern society a willingness to experiment and an openness to change.

A Growing Population

Between 1840 and 1860, the North experienced a large population increase. Immigration accounted for much of this growth. Over 1.5 million immigrants came to the United States between 1840 and 1850, and 2 million more came between 1850 and 1860. Most immigrants settled in the cities of the North. Many found work in Northern factories.

As the general population grew, so did the size of Northern cities. Between 1830 and 1860, the population of New York City jumped from 200,000 people to nearly one million.

The population of Northern cities was swelled further by thousands of Americans who left their farms in search of better lives. The factory system offered people in the North the chance to improve their standard of living. Wages were increasing. Items like clothing, tools, and household goods were plentiful and more affordable than ever before.

Growth of Cities

CITY	1790	1850
New York City, N.Y.	49,401	696,115
Baltimore, Md.	13,603	169,054
Boston, Mass.	18,320	136,881
Philadelphia, Penn.	28,522	121,376
New Orleans, La.	—	116,375
Cincinnati, Ohio	—	115,435
St. Louis, Mo.	—	77,860
Albany, N.Y.	3,498	50,763
Pittsburgh, Penn.	—	46,601
Louisville, Ky.	200	43,194

Northern society came to place a great emphasis on success. Hundreds of "how to succeed" books were published. The books' main message was that success was possible through hard work, thrift, and a bit of luck.

Changes on the Farm

Cities were not the only area of the North undergoing change. The farms of the North and West were changing, too. New farm tools were developed that greatly aided farmers in the planting and harvesting of crops. One important new tool was the steel plow, invented by John Deere in 1837. It was stronger and more durable than the older iron and wooden plows. The steel plow allowed farmers to plow the hard prairie sod of the West.

Another new farm tool was the mechanical reaper, invented by Cyrus Hall

Vocabulary Help: standard of living—a measure of what necessities and comforts a family's income can buy at a given time. Ask students to identify indicators of the standard of living in present-day American society.

Background: In Boston, New York, and Philadelphia, the upper class owned 80 percent of each city's wealth. By 1860, 5 percent of American families owned more than half the nation's wealth.

McCormick. The McCormick reaper was a horse-drawn machine used for cutting wheat. With this machine, two workers could cut 14 times as much wheat as a dozen workers could with hand tools. During the 1850's, wheat production increased by nearly 75 percent.

These new farm tools changed the nature of farming in the North and West. Farmers with the largest farms benefited the most. The steel plow and the McCormick reaper enabled farmers to grow more crops. Farmers could harvest their crops with greater efficiency. Small farmers had a difficult time competing with the large farmers. Many small farmers were gradually forced out of business. They sold their farms to the larger farmers and went farther west to farm or moved to the cities to look for work.

Of what social classes do you think these skaters in New York's Central Park were members?

The Class System in the North

By the 1800's, the class system of the North was clearly defined. At the top was the upper class. It made up about 10 percent of the Northern population. In 1800, the Northern upper class owned 40 percent of the nation's wealth.

Members of the upper class were bankers, shippers, merchants, and manufacturers. These Northerners lived well. Vacations in Europe were common. The upper class also traveled widely within the United States. They regularly attended lectures and concerts. Members of the upper class sent their children to college. This was a privilege that only about one percent of all Americans could afford.

The Northern middle class was made up of small business people and manufacturers, religious leaders, doctors, lawyers, and farmers who owned their own land. About 35 percent of the Northern population belonged to the middle class. Middle-class Northerners made a good living. They made enough money to educate their children, buy new farm equipment, or expand their businesses. Most middle-class families had only one breadwinner, the father. It was a sign of prestige if the wife and children did not work. It showed that the husband earned enough money from his job to support his entire family.

The Northern middle class lived fairly comfortable lives. Many could purchase the newest conveniences for their homes, items like central heating or indoor

Vocabulary Help: breadwinner—a person whose income helps to support the family. Many middle-class families today have two breadwinners. Ask students to explain why this may be so.

plumbing. Many middle-class parents tried to find a way for their children to rise into the upper class. A common method was to educate their children in the private schools of the rich if the family could afford it.

The lower class made up about 50 percent of Northern society. Lower-class society included rural agricultural workers, and nonagricultural workers who lived in the cities.

Most lower-class agricultural workers could not afford to buy their own land. They drifted from one job to another, never able to settle down. They were very poor. Their diets were bad and many workers were ill or undernourished. Lower-class farm workers tended to live shorter lives than members of the middle and upper classes.

Lower-class workers in the cities made their living as manual laborers and factory workers. These workers had no control over their work conditions, their wages, or their hours. Their work day was long, and the pay was very low. For a 12- to 14-hour work day, they might earn from $0.25 to $1.25. Most lower-class workers worked six days a week.

Most of the jobs lower-class workers held were very dangerous. Industrial accidents were common. If a worker was injured on the job and unable to work, he or she was fired. There were always plenty of other workers ready to fill in.

The children of the lower class were often sent to work at an early age. Lower-class families needed all the money they could get. There was no time for children to go to school and little time for play. Because lower-class children were uneducated, they could not acquire the training or skills that would get them out of the lower class. Most people of the middle and upper classes had little sympathy for the lower class. The poverty of lower-class members was thought to be a reflection on the individuals themselves, not society.

Most Northerners were proud of their society. They believed that the North was a place of great opportunity. Northerners believed that with talent and luck, anyone could rise to the top.

Section Review

1. What social classes existed in the North during the first half of the nineteenth century?
2. Why did Northern cities experience such rapid growth during the first half of the nineteenth century?
3. How did the steel plow and the mechanical reaper change farming in the North and West?
4. Describe what conditions were like for the lower class in the North.
5. Why do you think most immigrants who came to the United States between 1840 and 1860 settled in the cities of the North?

2. A Time of Change

BEFORE YOU READ: *What were some of the social problems that concerned Americans during the first half of the nineteenth century?*

Some Northerners wanted to correct any faults they found in their society. Between the 1830's and the early 1860's, Northerners became preoccupied with improving their society.

Improving Education

Education during the early years of the United States was available only to the very poor and the rich. The poor were educated by charitable groups. The rich sent their children to private schools.

In the early 1800's, many Northerners began working to improve education. They supported the establishment of public schools that would be supported by taxes. These schools would be open to all children at the elementary level. State laws would require all children to attend school.

The modern public education movement began in Massachusetts. The movement's leader was Horace Mann. Mann set up an improved and expanded system of free public education in Massachusetts. Other states soon copied Mann's system. By the 1860's, free public elementary schools existed in all of the Northern states. Southern cities were not far behind. Charleston, South Carolina, for example, set up a system of public schools. But few schools were opened to serve rural Southern children.

Public high schools were still rare outside of Massachusetts, New York, and Ohio. There were only 300 in the United States in 1860. Most secondary education took place in private schools.

The number of colleges grew rapidly between the 1830's and the 1850's. By 1860, there were a total of 186 in the United States. In the 1830's, Horace Mann established the first teacher training schools. They were called normal schools.

The movement for equal education for women made progress in the early 1800's. A number of secondary schools for females were opened in New York, New England, Louisiana, Kentucky, Maryland, and other areas of the nation. One of the most famous pioneers of secondary education for females was Mary Lyon. She founded Mount Holyoke Female Seminary in Massachusetts in 1837. Emma Willard also organized a secondary school for

Many schools in the nineteenth century consisted of only one room where students of all ages were taught by one teacher.

Discuss: Thomas Jefferson stated, "The most [effective] means of preventing [tyranny] would be to illuminate . . . the minds of the people." What does this statement mean? Do you agree or disagree with it? Why?

Background: The prison reforms generally failed to accomplish their primary goal, rehabilitation of the inmates.

women, the Troy Female Seminary in New York. By the 1830's, college education was made available to women. In 1837, Oberlin College in Ohio became the first college to accept both male and female students.

Improving the Prisons

Many Americans became concerned with the harsh conditions in the nation's prisons. These people felt that prisons should be more than places where criminals served their sentences. Prisons should help restore prisoners to useful citizenship. New prison laws were passed. Young offenders were separated from older, hardened criminals. Prisoners were taught trades that would be useful once they were released from prison. Punishments such as whippings were halted. Some prisons were built with separate cells for each prisoner. It was hoped that with time to sit and think in silence, prisoners would see the errors of their ways.

The Mentally Ill

In the 1830's, very few hospitals existed for the mentally ill. Most mental patients were kept in jails, where they were treated harshly. In 1841, a Boston schoolteacher named Dorothea Dix happened to visit a local jail. She was shocked by the treatment of both prisoners and mental patients. "I tell what I have seen," she reported to the state legislature, "insane persons confined in cages, closets, cellars, stalls, pens! Chained, naked, beaten with rods, and lashed into obedience." Dix spent the rest of her life seeking **reform**, or change for the better, for the mentally ill. Her activities led to the construction of a number of hospitals for the care of the mentally ill.

---

reform a change for the better

The Temperance Movement

Many Americans had serious drinking problems in the early 1800's. On an average, each American drank 26 liters (7 gallons) of alcohol in 1810. By 1830, each American was drinking an average of 38 liters (10 gallons) a year. Alcohol abuse was a problem in both the cities and the country. Liquor could be found at funerals, weddings, business meetings, in Congress, in fact, almost everywhere in America.

The reform movement that attacked the drinking problem in America became known as the **temperance** movement. The temperance movement attracted many followers, including a large number of women.

---

temperance moderation in drinking alcoholic beverages or doing without them completely

---

The American Temperance Union was founded in 1826 to coordinate the activities of hundreds of local temperance groups. Reformers were sent out to give lectures about the evils of alcohol. They passed out pamphlets, talked to people, and organized rallies. Some even went into bars to talk directly with the drinkers. One such reformer, John B. Gough, would charge into a bar and scream, "Crawl from the slimy ooze, you drowned

Background: Alcohol was often opposed for moral reasons. "If I be a willing accessory to my brother's death by a pistol or cord, the law holds me guilty," stated one man opposed to alcohol, "but guiltless if I mix his death drink in a cup."

The woman in this picture appears to be giving thanks as her husband "signs the pledge" to give up alcohol forever.

drunkards . . . and speak out against drink." The temperance union hoped to convince Americans to "sign the pledge." By this they meant they hoped to persuade people to stop drinking alcohol forever. Over one million Americans did sign the pledge.

In the 1830's, the reformers demanded that laws be passed outlawing alcohol. In 1851, Maine became the first state to prohibit the manufacture, transportation, and sale of alcohol. A few other states followed suit. But many Americans were strongly opposed to such laws. They claimed that it was one thing to give up alcohol voluntarily, but the government should not force people to give it up. The temperance movement continued its crusade into the twentieth century.

More Rights for Women

American women did not have equal rights with men during the nineteenth century. Women could not vote or hold public office. Higher education was not available to them until the 1830's. In many states, married women could not own property. Women had no power over legal decisions that affected their children. In the event of divorce, the husband gained custody of the children, regardless

Discuss: How do you think the development of greater educational opportunities for women in the early 1800's affected the movement for women's rights in the 1830's?

Background: Women with college degrees began to make some progress in penetrating male-dominated professions. For example, in 1850, Antoinette Brown took a theology degree at Oberlin and became the first woman minister.

of the circumstances. A woman could not sue her husband in court, even in the case of abuse.

In the 1830's, American women began to work for greater equality. Many joined the movement for women's rights. Among those who worked to improve the status of women were Lucretia Mott, Elizabeth Cady Stanton, and Susan B. Anthony.

In 1848, more than 300 supporters of women's rights met at Seneca Falls, New York. They adopted a declaration of independence, which they called the "Declaration of Sentiments." The declaration stated that "all men and women are created equal." It called for equal rights for women in work, in politics, and under the law.

The struggle for equal rights was not an easy one. It was not until 1869 that women won their first victory in the battle to win the right to vote. Wyoming Territory became the first territory or state to grant women the right to vote.

New Directions in Literature

"In the four quarters of the globe, who reads an American book?" asked the British journalist Sydney Smith in 1820. "Or goes to an American play? Or looks at an American picture or statue?" Smith believed the answer was obvious—nobody.

Most Europeans were highly critical of American culture. In the area of literature and the arts, Americans seemed little better than "colonists." Americans read books, plays, and poems by British authors. Americans journeyed to Europe to study painting and music.

In 1820, an American author, James Fenimore Cooper, began to express the American experience in literature. To Cooper, what was unique about America was its newness. America had no ancient past. America was growing and developing with few traditions to hold it back. Americans could change their society, if need be. The future held limitless possibilities for America. Cooper created a character who seemed to express these American qualities. The character's name was Natty Bumppo, or "Hawkeye."

Natty Bumppo was an independent man of the frontier. He was intelligent and resourceful. He was capable of molding the future to his liking. Bumppo was not bound by the rules of the past or of society. James Fenimore Cooper wrote a series of novels called *The Leatherstocking Tales.* They included *The Pioneers, The Prairie, The Pathfinder, The Deerslayer,* and *The Last of the Mohicans.* Natty Bumppo was the main character in each. Cooper's books met with instant success in America and in Europe. They started a new trend in American literature.

Other American writers soon became popular. Nathaniel Hawthorne wrote *The Scarlet Letter* and *The House of the Seven Gables*, books that dealt with the American experience in New England. Herman Melville wrote *Moby Dick.* Other widely read writers were Emily Dickinson, Henry Wadsworth Longfellow, Walt Whitman, and Henry David Thoreau. By 1860, American literature was flourishing.

The Antislavery Movement

The antislavery crusade came to be the most controversial of the nation's reform movements. The drive to **abolish**, or do

For Extra Interest: If students are familiar with the TV character Hawkeye from the old *M*A*S*H* series, explain that this character's nickname was a reference to the Hawkeye character in Cooper's books. Ask students how the two Hawkeyes are similar.

Discuss: Why do you think most Americans rejected the idea of abolishing slavery in the United States during the reform period?

away with, slavery was supported by most reformers. But, it was rejected by most of the American people.

abolish to do away with completely

Efforts to abolish slavery first began before the American Revolution. But the movement never attracted much support. Many early foes of slavery talked of sending blacks, both slave and free, back to Africa. They thought that "colonization," as they called it, was the only possible way to end the problem in America. In 1817, the American Colonization Society was formed. The group raised money to purchase land in Africa. In 1822, the society purchased some West African land, which they named Liberia, for liberty. Only a few thousand blacks were settled there.

The American Colonization Society was unpopular with most white and black Americans. Black Americans strongly objected to colonization in Africa. "We are *natives* of this country," said Peter Williams, a black preacher in New York, " . . . our fathers suffered and bled to purchase its independence." The American Colonization Society ended as a failure in 1834.

Some antislavery reformers tried to convince Southerners that they should voluntarily free their slaves. These reformers believed that slaves should be freed gradually to avoid any great social or economic disturbances. They also felt that slave owners should be compensated, or paid, for the loss of their slave property. This approach to the slavery issue was called **gradualism**. Gradualism never won very wide support.

gradualism a belief in the voluntary freeing of slaves over a long period of time

In the 1830's, the antislavery movement became more radical. Many reformers came to believe that slavery was evil, and like all evil, it must be done away with. These reformers wanted slavery abolished immediately, without compensation. People who had this view became known as **abolitionists**.

abolitionist a person who favors doing away with slavery completely

The best-known abolitionist was William Lloyd Garrison. In 1831, he began publishing a newspaper that demanded an immediate end to slavery by any means necessary. His paper was called *The Liberator*. Garrison strongly criticized slavery and the South. Some people objected to his harshness. He replied, "I will be as harsh as truth. . . . I do not wish to think, or speak, or write with moderation. [Would you] tell a man whose house is on fire to give a moderate alarm?"

Other reformers joined the abolitionist cause. Two wealthy New York business leaders, Arthur and Lewis Tappan, along with Garrison and others, helped form the American Anti-Slavery Society in 1833. They were joined by many church leaders and members. Charles G. Finney, a professor of religion at Oberlin College; Theodore Weld of Cincinnati's Lane Theological Seminary; and the Grimké sisters, Sarah and Angelina, were among those who worked for the abolitionist cause. Black leaders played an important role in

Background: The Grimké sisters were from Charleston, South Carolina. They had to move to the North to express their antislavery beliefs. They were especially active in giving public antislavery lectures.

Background: Although Douglass escaped from slavery in 1838, it was not until 1847 that he purchased his freedom.

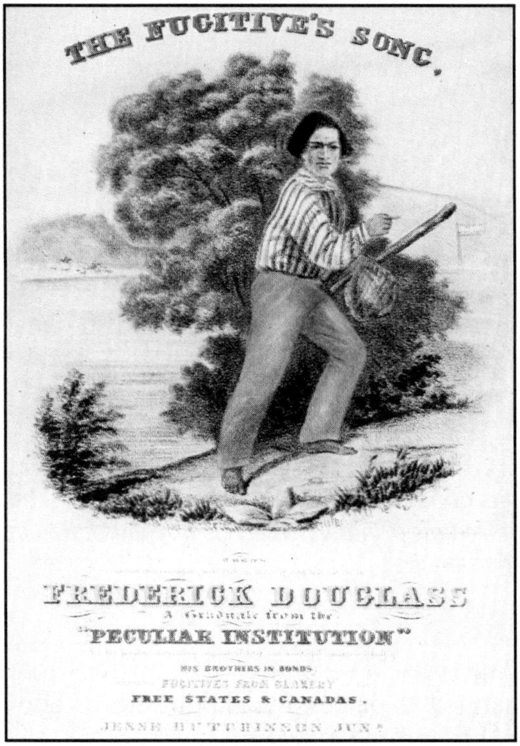

Frederick Douglass is shown on the cover of this abolitionist song sheet published in Boston in 1845.

the abolitionist movement. They published 17 abolitionist newspapers before the Civil War. One of the most famous black leaders of the antislavery movement was Frederick Douglass. Douglass had been born and raised a slave. At about the age of 20, he escaped to freedom in the North. Between 1847 and 1864, Douglass published an abolitionist newspaper called the *North Star.* "The object of the *North Star* will be to attack slavery in all its forms and aspects," stated Douglass, " . . . and to hasten the day of freedom to our three million enslaved fellow-countrymen." Douglass named his newspaper the *North Star* for an important reason. The North Star was the star that guided runaway slaves in their attempts to reach freedom in the North.

The Underground Railroad

Many antislavery Northerners helped slaves to escape from the South. They set up a loose network to smuggle slaves from the South into free states in the North or into Canada. In the 1840's, this network became known as the "Underground Railroad" or "The Liberty Line." Perhaps as many as 60,000 slaves gained their freedom in this way.

The escaping slaves were called "passengers." Most were young adults, male, unmarried, and skilled in a trade. They traveled at night to avoid detection. Usually the runaway slaves sought out farmhouses that were known to be safe as temporary hiding places. These houses were called "stations." Assistance was offered mostly by free blacks, although Quakers and abolitionists helped when they could. Harriet Tubman, a former slave, was one of the most daring leaders on the Underground Railroad. She made 19 trips into the South to bring some 300 slaves to freedom. Runaways who decided not to remain in the United States were taken to the lake ports of Detroit, Michigan; Sandusky, Ohio; Erie, Pennsylvania; and Buffalo, New York. It was a short trip from these ports to Canada and freedom.

The Underground Railroad was illegal. Professional slave catchers and government officials often seized runaways. Southerners condemned the railroad, as did most Northerners.

Discuss: Why do you think so many of the slaves who escaped from the South decided to go to Canada instead of settling in the North?

Discuss: What do you think motivated Southern members of Congress to pass the gag rule? Do you think it was realistic for them to expect the problem of slavery to go away by forcing Congress to ignore it? Why or why not?

The Critics of Abolitionism

White or black, abolitionists often faced violent opposition in the North. William Lloyd Garrison was attacked by a mob in Boston on October 21, 1835. He was dragged through the streets and almost killed. Elijah Lovejoy, who published an antislavery newspaper in Illinois, was shot dead in his office while trying to protect his printing press from destruction by a mob. Antislavery supporters risked their lives pleading their cause. They were beaten and pelted with tomatoes and stones. Sometimes they were tarred and feathered.

Southern reaction to the abolitionists was even harsher. Mail sacks containing abolitionist literature were destroyed. Southerners who spoke out against slavery were often forced to go North or face physical harm. In 1836, Southern members of Congress pushed through a resolution requiring Congress to ignore all antislavery petitions introduced for discussion. This was known as the **gag rule**. The gag rule was not repealed until 1844.

In 1837, a mob set fire to the warehouse where the abolitionist editor Elijah P. Lovejoy had stored his printing press. Lovejoy was killed in the attack.

gag rule a resolution of Congress that banned all discussion of petitions on abolition and the slavery issue

Most Americans feared and disliked the abolitionist movement. The abolitionists' activities increased the tension that existed between the North and the South.

Section Review

1. What were some of the social problems that concerned Americans during the first half of the nineteenth century?
2. What role did Horace Mann play in improving education?
3. What was the "Declaration of Sentiments"? What rights were women fighting for during the nineteenth century?
4. What was the abolitionist movement? How did Southerners react to it?
5. What was there about Northern society that encouraged the growth of so many reform movements? Could the same thing have happened in a closed society like the South? Explain your answer.

Background: Former President John Quincy Adams served as a representative from Massachusetts from 1831 to 1848. He led the fight for the repeal of the gag rule.

Social Studies Skills

Using Reference Books and Card Catalogs

This textbook contains information on the history of the abolitionist movement in the United States. However, to write a report or term paper on this topic would require additional information. Knowing where and how to get additional information make writing a report much easier.

Reference materials, such as encyclopedias, atlases, and almanacs, are good sources of information. The key to using these reference materials effectively is the index or, in the case of many atlases, the table of contents. These guides can help the user locate information more easily than a random search through the materials.

Nonfiction books are another valuable source of information. The quickest way to find a particular book in the library is to use the card catalog. Every book in the library has an author card and a title card. Many books also have subject cards. All the cards are arranged alphabetically. They often contain a brief summary of the book's contents. If a book appears useful, copy the numbers and letters in the upper left corner of its card onto a sheet of paper. This is the call number, and it tells where the book is located on the shelves.

920.073 Bennett, Lerone, 1928–
B Pioneers in protest, by Lerone Bennett, Jr. 1st ed. Chicago, Johnson Pub. Co., 1968 267p.
Contents-Crispus Attucks. . .-Nat Turner.-Wendell Phillips and William Lloyd Garrison.-Harriet Tubman. . . -W.E.B. DuBois.

Author Card

920.073 Pioneers in protest
B Bennett, Lerone
Chicago, Johnson Pub. Co., 1968. 267p.
Contents-Crispus Attucks. . .-Nat Turner.-Wendell Phillips and William Lloyd Garrison.-Harriet Tubman. . . -W.E.B. DuBois.

Title Card

920.073 ABOLITIONISTS
B Bennett, Lerone.
Pioneers in protest. Chicago, Johnson Pub. Co., 1968 267p.
Contents-Crispus Attucks. . .-Nat Turner.-Wendell Phillips and William Lloyd Garrison.-Harriet Tubman. . .-W.E.B. DuBois.

Subject Card

1. What is the key to the effective use of reference books?
2. What is the purpose of the card catalog?
3. What is the call number for the book *Pioneers in Protest*?
4. Do you think the book *Pioneers in Protest* might be a good source of information for a biographical report on William Lloyd Garrison? Why or why not?

CHAPTER REVIEW

Summary

The North developed very differently from the South in the first half of the 1800's. Great changes were occurring as industries expanded and more factories were built. Three social classes developed, reflecting the organization of an industrial society. Bankers, shippers, merchants, and manufacturers made up the small upper class, which controlled most of the region's wealth. The middle class, composed of small business people, religious leaders, professionals, and farmers who owned their own land, also lived fairly comfortable lives. The bulk of the North's population was in the lower class. These people worked long, hard hours for very little pay.

Between the 1830's and the early 1860's, many Northerners became preoccupied with improving their society. Education, the treatment of prisoners and mental patients, and the use of alcohol became targets for reform. Some reformers demanded equal rights for women, while others called for an end to slavery. American literature began to emphasize the opportunity for unlimited change and improvement in American society.

Recalling the Facts

1. About what percentage of the North's population were members of the upper class? the middle class? the lower class?
2. Why did few children in the lower class go to school? How did this affect their future chances to move up in social class?
3. How were prisons and the treatment of prisoners improved during the reform period of the 1800's?
4. What was the purpose of the temperance movement? What progress did temperance groups make toward achieving their goals in the first half of the nineteenth century?
5. What roles did black Americans play in the movement to abolish slavery in the United States?

Analyzing the Facts

1. Compare Northern and Southern society in the first half of the nineteenth century. How were the two societies similar? How were they different?

2. Why were the McCormick reaper and the steel plow of little use to Southern farmers?
3. Compare the life of a slave to that of a lower-class farm laborer in the North. How were their lives similar? How were they different?
4. Why was Northern society more willing to change than Southern society?
5. What were the advantages and disadvantages in the first half of the nineteenth century of requiring all children to attend school? Do you think these same advantages and disadvantages exist today? Explain your answer.

Time and History

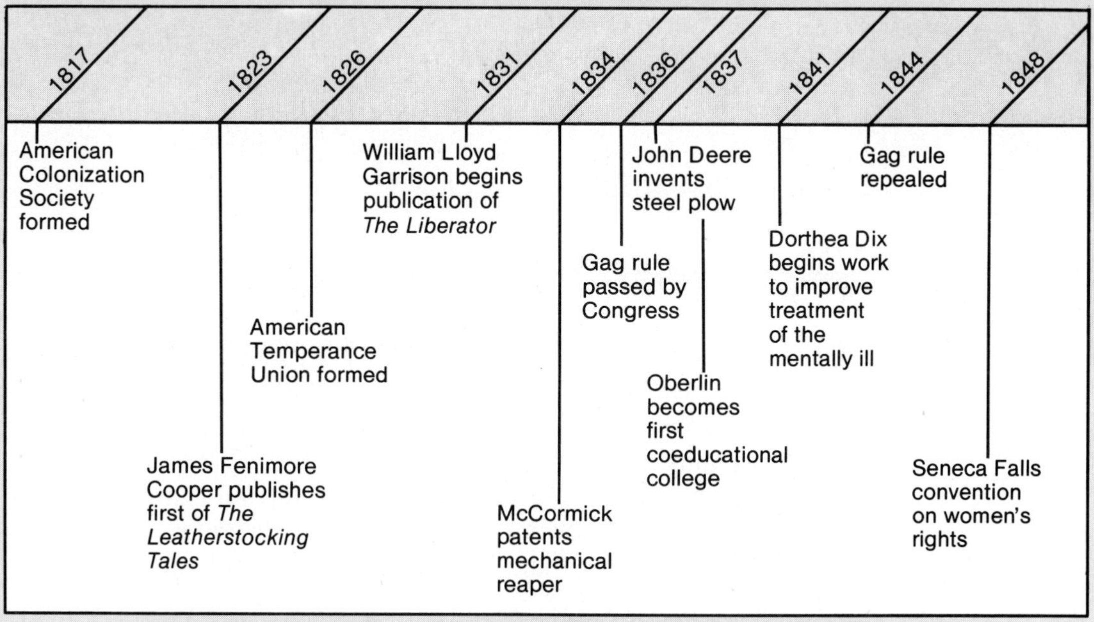
1817
American Colonization Society formed
1823
James Fenimore Cooper publishes first of The Leatherstocking Tales
1826
American Temperance Union formed
1831
William Lloyd Garrison begins publication of The Liberator
1834
McCormick patents mechanical reaper
1836
Gag rule passed by Congress
1837
John Deere invents steel plow
Oberlin becomes first coeducational college
1841
Dorthea Dix begins work to improve treatment of the mentally ill
1844
Gag rule repealed
1848
Seneca Falls convention on women's rights

1. In what decade were two inventions made to improve farming in the North and West? What were these two inventions?
2. In what year was the first organization dedicated to solving the problem of slavery in the United States formed?
3. What evidence is there that women were involved in reform movements between 1830 and 1850?
4. How many years was the gag rule in effect in Congress?
5. What was the first coeducational college in the United States?

Chapter
14

Westward Expansion

Throughout the early nineteenth century, the American frontier moved steadily westward. By 1840, America's western frontier reached the Missouri and Arkansas rivers. Starting in the 1840's, Americans crossed the Great Plains in search of new lands to settle. Thousands of people settled the regions of Oregon, Texas, California, and Utah. This movement of Americans westward caused great tension between the United States and the nations that claimed these western lands.

After you read this chapter, you will be able to:

1. Describe how Americans came to settle the lands of Texas, Oregon, Utah, and California.
2. Explain the causes of the Mexican-American War.
3. Discuss how California's application for statehood triggered a sectional crisis.

Vocabulary Help: frontier—the part of a settled, civilized country that lies next to an unexplored or underdeveloped region. Ask students to compare the frontier line in 1837 to the western boundary of the United States in the same year.

1. Texas and Oregon

BEFORE YOU READ: *How did Americans settle in Texas and Oregon?*

By 1837, America's western frontier was the Missouri River. Beyond it lay the Great Plains. Americans of the 1830's had little interest in the Great Plains. They called it the "Great American Desert." It seemed dry, barren, and inhospitable.

Americans looked farther west for new lands to settle. Eventually, they settled in Oregon, California, Utah, the Southwest, and Texas. The first major settlements were established in the Mexican province of Texas.

Americans in Texas

In 1821, Mexico won its independence from Spain. The population of the Mexican province of Texas was small. Only a few thousand people lived there, many of whom were Americans.

In January 1821, shortly before Mexico became independent, Spanish officials granted land in Texas to Moses Austin. Austin wanted to establish an American settlement in Texas. But before he could establish his settlement, Austin died. His son, Stephen, took over the grant. He led 300 families into Texas in 1821. They settled between the Brazos and Colorado rivers. In return for the right to settle on Mexican land, the Americans promised to recognize Mexican law, to conduct business affairs in Spanish, and to adopt Mexico's Roman Catholic faith. Mexico wanted the American settlers to adopt and blend into the Mexican culture and way of life.

Mexico encouraged other Americans to settle in Texas. The lure of new land brought many Southerners into Texas. Many of the Southern settlers were slaveholders from Tennessee, Mississippi, and Alabama. Most brought their slaves with them. In 1829, Mexico outlawed slavery, but the Amercian settlers ignored the law.

By 1835, there were some 20,000 Americans living in the province of Texas. A large number of the settlers had no intention of letting Mexico tell them what to do. A French visitor observed, "It may be easily foreseen that if Mexico takes no step to check this change, the province of Texas will soon cease to belong to her." Mexico was angered by the behavior of the American settlers. Soon it took strong steps to enforce Mexican law in Texas.

In the early 1830's, Antonio López de Santa Anna became the new president of Mexico. He was determined to tighten control over the Texas province. Santa Anna wanted to enforce the no-slavery law. He prohibited any further American settlement in Texas. Relations between Mexico and the Americans in Texas became strained. In 1835, revolution broke out.

The Republic of Texas

Santa Anna organized an army and marched it northward to crush the rebellion. A small Texas army led by General Sam Houston tried to stop Santa Anna's larger army of 2,400 soldiers, but the Texans had to retreat before the stronger force.

By the end of February 1836, Santa Anna's army had reached the outskirts of San Antonio. Sam Houston and his army

Background: In 1834, Santa Anna granted some requests of the Texans, including the repeal of the anti-immigration decree. He denied, however, the appeal the Texans had made for separation from the Mexican province of Chihuahua.

Background: The Mexicans suffered about 1,550 casualties in the 13-day siege on the Alamo. Today, the Alamo is maintained as a historic site and museum by the Daughters of the Republic of Texas.

retreated once again. However, 187 men chose to stay and fight. They occupied an old Spanish mission-fort called the Alamo. They knew that their chances of victory were small. But they wanted "to make victory worse to the enemy than a defeat."

Between February 26 and March 6, 1836, the Mexican troops made repeated assaults on the Alamo. They suffered heavy losses. Enraged, Santa Anna finally stormed the walls of the Alamo. All of the defenders of the Alamo were killed, including the commanders, Jim Bowie and William Travis, and the Tennessee frontier hero, Davy Crockett. "Remember the Alamo" became the battle cry of the Texas revolution.

While the battle at the Alamo raged, Texans met in a convention at Washington, Texas. On March 2, 1836, they declared their independence from Mexico. A constitution for the Republic of Texas was written. It legalized slavery. It also provided for a president who would serve one three-year term, an elected congress, and a judicial system.

Santa Anna relentlessly pursued Sam Houston. On April 21, 1836, he advanced to the San Jacinto (SAN ha-SEEN-toh) River. This is near the present-day cities of Galveston and Houston. While the

Santa Anna's Mexican forces are shown overwhelming American defenders in this painting of the Battle of the Alamo.

Discuss: Why do you think Texas called itself the "Lone Star Republic"?

In this painting, the wounded victor, Sam Houston, offers his hand to Santa Anna after the Battle of San Jacinto.

Mexican forces rested from the long days of fighting and constant moving about, Houston and his 750 Texas volunteers attacked. Shouting "Remember the Alamo," the Texans killed 630 of the Mexican troops and captured 730 more, including Santa Anna. Santa Anna was forced to sign a treaty recognizing Texas' independence. In October 1836, Sam Houston was installed as the first president of the Republic of Texas.

Once independence was achieved, Texas sought to join the United States. Northern politicians blocked this move. Because slavery already existed in Texas, it would enter the Union as a slave state. That would upset the balance of free and slave states in the Senate. Texas was denied admission to the Union. It remained the Republic of Texas or the "Lone Star Republic."

The Oregon Territory

The Oregon Territory comprised the present-day states of Idaho, Washington, and Oregon, small parts of Montana and Wyoming, and British Columbia in Canada. In 1840, Great Britain and the United States both claimed the Oregon Territory. Under the terms of the Rush-Bagot agreement, negotiated in 1818, both nations agreed to open the Oregon country for settlement for a period of ten years. In 1827, the agreement was extended. This extension favored America's claim on the land because more Americans than Britons were moving into the new territory.

The first Americans to settle Oregon were missionaries. Jason and Daniel Lee were sent out by the Methodist church. They founded a mission near present-day Salem, Oregon. Two other missionaries, Dr. Marcus Whitman and Henry H. Spalding, came to Oregon in 1836 with their wives. The Whitmans and Spaldings were followed by Father Pierre Jean de Smet, a Catholic missionary. These missionaries were interested in converting the American Indians to Christianity. They worked diligently but with little success.

The missionaries described the land and their work in reports and letters. Dr. Whitman worked actively to bring American settlers to Oregon. He even made the long journey back to the East to encourage people to go to Oregon. Whitman spoke of the beauty of the region, the year-round mild temperatures, and the abundant rainfall.

As the reports of Oregon spread, Americans caught "Oregon fever." In 1843, more than 1,000 people met at Independence, Missouri, for the overland journey

Background: The area described by the missionaries is known as the Willamette Valley. It is located between the Coastal Range and the Cascade Mountains in western Oregon. The land east of the Cascades is drier and has more extreme temperatures.

For Extra Interest: Locate points along the Oregon Trail on a wall map so that students can get a general idea of where the trail went.

This painting presents an idealized view of a wagon train approaching Oregon.

to Oregon. The group that met at Independence included people of all ages who hoped for better lives in Oregon. They brought with them nearly 5,000 oxen and cattle. The trip westward would take six months and cover more than 3,200 kilometers (2,000 miles).

The journey began on May 22. The group divided into two columns. Each consisted of 60 covered wagons. The first, or "light column," were those people who had few or no loose cattle. The second, or "cow column," were those with cattle. This group had to proceed at a slower pace. The settlers moved northwest along the trail to the Platte River in present-day Nebraska. From there they followed the Platte and its north forks across the land of the Plains Indians.

The wagon trains traveled seven days a week. The wagons would start moving just after dawn. They would stop only twice a day, at noon and in the evening. At night, the settlers drew the wagons in a circle, or corral. According to Jesse Applegate, the corral was "a circle one hundred yards deep, formed with wagons connected strongly with each other. . . . It is a strong barrier that the most vicious ox cannot break, and in case of attack . . . would be [a good defense]."

The settlers of 1843 learned lessons from which future travelers benefited. They learned that belongings should be kept to a minimum. The Great Plains portion of the trail was strewn with heavy and sometimes valuable furniture and equipment. Such items became too burdensome for such a long and difficult journey. They learned that the stronger oxen were preferable to horses as animals to pull the wagons. They discovered that certain types of clothing—"citified clothing," as they called it—wore out

Background: Another 1,000 settlers traveled the Oregon Trail in 1844, and 3,000 more followed in 1845. These settlers all traveled in small parties, which proved more manageable than large caravans.

Discuss: Do you think the Plains Indians were justified in charging a fee to the settlers who crossed their homelands? Why or why not?

quickly during the difficult trip.

At Fort Laramie, in present-day Wyoming, the trail left the plains for the mountain country. Here the travelers had an opportunity to rest. When they resumed their trip, the settlers passed through treacherous passes in the Rockies. Then they followed the Snake and Columbia rivers westward into the Oregon Territory, arriving in November.

The journey of 1843 was a turning point in the history of Oregon. Many people thought the Oregon settlers would never make it to their destination. The news of their arrival in Oregon removed any doubts that the trip was possible. When the first settlers arrived in 1843, they drew up a constitution for what they called the Republic of Oregon. By 1845, the Oregon settlers demanded that the United States take sole possession of Oregon. The government refused. It did not want a conflict to develop with Great Britain, which also claimed Oregon.

The thousands of travelers who eventually crossed the plains on their way to Oregon had no desire to disturb the Plains Indians. The plains did not appeal to the white settlers. They saw the plains as a vast area to be crossed as quickly as possible. But the simple act of crossing the plains was a major disruption to life there. The travelers frightened the herds of buffalo roaming the Great Plains. The western settlers were frightening the buffalo off some tribes' lands completely. The western settlers also carried new diseases to the Great Plains. These were diseases against which the Indians had no natural defenses. Epidemics of smallpox, for example, swept across the plains. Thousands of American Indians lost their lives from this disease.

At first, the Plains Indians were patient with the settlers crossing their homelands. As more and more Americans moved westward, the Indians began charging a fee to cross their land. Settlers paid the fee but asked the federal government to do something about it. The government sent troops to the plains to punish the Plains Indians. The troops and the Indians engaged in a number of battles during the 1840's and the early 1850's.

Section Review

1. How did Americans settle in Texas and in Oregon?
2. Why did Americans have little interest in settling on the Great Plains before the 1840's?
3. Explain how the admission of Texas into the Union in 1836 might have caused another sectional crisis.
4. What contributed to the growth of Americans' interest in the Oregon Territory?
5. Was the United States government justified in sending troops to punish the Plains Indians for interfering with the settlers moving west? Explain your answer.

For Extra Interest: In all, Henry Clay was defeated three times for the presidency—in 1824, 1832, and 1844. Ask students to identify the candidate who defeated Clay in each instance.

2. Manifest Destiny and the Mexican War

BEFORE YOU READ: *What were the causes of the war between the United States and Mexico?*

In the early 1840's, Americans came to believe that it was America's destiny to rule the continent from ocean to ocean. It did not matter if these western lands belonged to other nations; the United States intended to control them. This belief became known as **Manifest Destiny**.

Manifest Destiny the belief that the United States was intended to spread from the Atlantic to the Pacific oceans

---

Territorial expansion became the major issue in the presidential election of 1844. The Whig party nominated Henry Clay of Kentucky. Clay wanted the nation to expand westward, but he believed it should be done slowly. Rapid expansion might lead to war with Great Britain or Mexico. James K. Polk of Tennessee was the Democratic candidate. He firmly believed in territorial expansion. Polk wanted the United States to gain possession of Oregon. He also wanted Texas brought into the Union. In the election, Polk defeated Clay. His victory meant that America would pursue a course of rapid territorial expansion.

The Oregon Dispute

Texas was admitted to the Union in March 1845, a few days before Polk was inaugurated. Northern Democrats had decided to back the Southern Democrats' desire to bring Texas into the Union as a slave state. They expected Polk and the Southern Democrats to bring Oregon in as a free state in return.

In December 1845, Polk went before Congress to propose the acquisition of the entire Oregon Territory. This included all land from the present-day state of Oregon north to Alaska. Polk proposed that the northern boundary of Oregon be at 54°40′ north latitude. Polk's proposal meant that joint control of Oregon with Great Britain would come to an end. It

Oregon Boundary Dispute

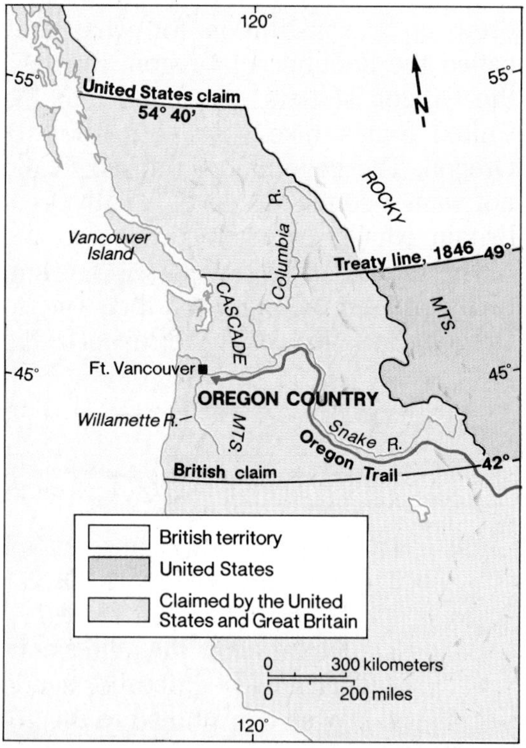

How many kilometers (or miles) north of the 1846 treaty line was the United States claim of 54°40′?

Background: Each degree of latitude can be subdivided into 60 minutes, and each minute can be subdivided into 60 seconds. "Fifty-four forty" in the slogan refers to 54°40′ north latitude.

For Extra Interest: Have students calculate the distance from Nauvoo, Illinois (located on the border of Illinois, near the southeast corner of Iowa), to Salt Lake City, Utah.

was a bold move, one that could have led to war. Democrats supported the President. "Fifty-four forty or fight!" became a popular slogan.

The British did not want to fight a war over a remote wilderness so far from home. The British government offered to negotiate the dispute. It suggested that the 49th parallel become the boundary between Canada and the United States. Polk agreed. The conflict ended without bloodshed.

The Mormons

In the 1840's, a group of American settlers journeyed west into Utah. These settlers were all members of a religious group known as the Church of Jesus Christ of Latter-Day Saints, more commonly called Mormons.

The Mormon religion was founded by Joseph Smith in 1830. In the 1820's, Smith had visions in which he said he was visited by God and an angel. He claimed that one vision led him to the discovery of some ancient writings. The writings were recorded on plates of gold. Smith translated them and published them in 1830 as the *Book of Mormon*. Joseph Smith said they were a continuation of the Old and New Testaments.

The Mormon Church grew slowly. Smith's followers had to move repeatedly to escape persecution—from New York State to Ohio, to Missouri, and to Nauvoo, Illinois. The Mormons found peace for a short time in Illinois. Church membership grew. The larger the Mormon church grew, however, the more non-Mormons were hostile. In 1844, Joseph Smith was arrested and jailed. A mob broke into the jail and shot him. Brigham Young became the Mormons' new leader.

This scene shows Mormons catching quails in Iowa on their way to Utah.

Young decided that the only safe place for his church was outside the United States. Young organized the Mormons for a journey to the West. Young's group of 15,000 people set off in 1846. The Mormons ended their journey when they reached the valley of the Great Salt Lake in Utah. At that time, this area was part of Mexico. The Mormons arrived in Utah in 1847 and established their community. They made the barren wastes of Utah "bloom as the rose," as the Mormons put it.

The Chain Reaction

In 1845, the United States **annexed**, or incorporated, the independent Republic of Texas as a state of the Union. Once Texas became a state, the United States

Background: The Church of Jesus Christ of Latter-day Saints is one of the fastest growing denominations today. It has more than 2 million members. Although most live in the United States, missionary work is conducted worldwide.

Discuss: Why do you think President Polk was willing to fight a war to obtain New Mexico and California? What belief motivated his actions?

inherited Texas' border dispute with Mexico. When Texas had been part of Mexico, its southern border was the Nueces (noo-AY-says) River. Since its independence, Texas claimed the Rio Grande as its southern border. A large strip of land lay between the disputed borders.

---

annex to attach a country or other territory, making it part of a nation

---

In 1845, President Polk sent John Slidell to Mexico. Slidell was instructed to offer up to $30 million for the two Mexican provinces of California and New Mexico. He was also to negotiate the American claim that the Rio Grande was Texas' southern border. The people of Mexico did not want to give up their northern provinces. The Mexican government refused to meet with Slidell.

News of Slidells' rejection reached Washington on January 12, 1846. The following day, President Polk ordered American troops under General Zachary Taylor to occupy the disputed area on the southern boundary of Texas. Taylor moved his troops to the eastern bank of the Rio Grande. At the same time, American ships blockaded the mouth of the river. To Polk, these actions were necessary to defend American territory. To Mexico, the American actions constituted an invasion of their nation.

Polk waited for some incident to occur that would justify declaring war on Mexico, but nothing happened. Finally, in May 1846, he decided to ask Congress to declare war. Polk's flimsy reason was that Mexico had insulted the United States by refusing to meet with John Slidell. Then news arrived that Mexican troops had crossed the Rio Grande and attacked an American mounted patrol. Congress declared war on May 13.

The war with Mexico was highly popular in the South. Southerners hoped that the United States would be able to win vast stretches of land from Mexico. This land could be organized as slave states. Many Southerners also had family ties with people in Texas. Many Northerners questioned whether the war was necessary. Abolitionists convinced many people that it was a war to spread slavery. The Whig party strongly opposed the war. The Massachusetts legislature declared that this "unconstitutional" war was being waged for the purpose of "extending slavery, strengthening slave power, and obtaining control of the free states." Opposition to the Mexican War was strong. It would have been stronger had not the American military been so successful in fighting the war.

The Mexican War

The army's strategy involved a three-pronged attack of Mexican territory. Colonel Stephen Kearney was to secure New Mexico and California from Mexico. General Zachary Taylor was to conquer northern Mexico. General Winfield Scott was to invade central Mexico and capture the capital at Mexico City.

At the war's beginning, Colonel Kearney marched his troops from Fort Leavenworth, Kansas, into New Mexico. Kearney occupied Santa Fe in August 1846 without resistance. From there he headed for California. Kearney helped put down the last Mexican attempts at resistance. By February 1847, New Mexico and Cali-

Discuss: President Polk blamed Mexico for starting the Mexican War. Do you agree that Mexico was to blame? Why or why not?

Famous Americans

JUAN NEPOMUCENO CORTINA

Historians are sharply divided in their opinions of Juan Cortina. One group calls him a "soldier, bandit, murderer, cattle thief, mail robber." Another group considers him to have been "a champion, a hero, and a noble avenger for his people." What is certain is that Juan Nepomuceno Cortina was caught up in one of the most difficult times for the people of the Southwest.

As a result of the war with Mexico, the United States gained a vast area of Mexican territory and 80,000 Mexican people. Some Mexicans were largely untouched by this change in government. Others were treated unfairly by the Americans. Many did not understand the property laws of the United States. They did not register their lands or pay property taxes. As a result, many of them lost their lands. The American courts did little to help protect the rights of Mexicans who were now American citizens. In addition, some were subjected to acts of violence from the Americans who moved onto their lands.

Juan Cortina was born near Brownsville, Texas, in 1830. At that time, Texas was still part of Mexico. As a young man, Juan Cortina was a farm laborer. He strongly resented the way Americans were taking Mexicans' lands from them. In 1859, Cortina organized an army of about 100 men to raid American settlements in Texas. Cortina was eventually chased out of the United States by Texas Rangers and United States Army troops in 1860. He fled to Mexico, where he served as a governor of a Mexican state and as a brigadier general. When he died, he was buried with full military honors in recognition of his devotion to the Mexican-American people.

---

fornia were securely in American hands.

In July 1847, Zachary Taylor, called "Old Rough-and-Ready" by his troops, marched out of Texas. He invaded the northern region of Mexico and defeated the Mexican army at the battle of Monterrey, Mexico. Other Mexican troops swept northward from Mexico City. The Mexican soldiers called themselves the "army of liberation." On February 22, 1847, the Mexicans and the Americans clashed at Buena Vista. A fierce battle raged for two days. Taylor was finally able to shatter the Mexican forces and drove them into retreat.

The third American army was headed by General Winfield Scott. Scott was a tall, strongly built man and a firm believer in the need for following military details and codes precisely. His nickname was

For Extra Interest: Have students research and make a map showing the movement of American forces in the Mexican War.

Discuss: Compare the terms of the Treaty of Guadaloupe Hidalgo to the offer Slidell carried to the Mexican government in 1845. If Mexico had accepted Slidell's offer and a war had not been fought, how would Mexico have benefited?

In this painting, General Zachary Taylor is shown directing American troops at the Battle of Buena Vista.

"Old Fuss-and-Feathers." On March 9, 1847, the navy landed Scott's 10,000 troops on the coast of the Gulf of Mexico, just below Veracruz. By March 29, Scott had occupied Veracruz. Then Scott's troops fought their way westward through the mountains of Mexico. By September 1847, they had reached the outskirts of Mexico City.

The fighting was vicious outside the capital. Scott's troops were finally able to fight their way into the city. The city council sent word to the general that it wished to surrender. The American flag was raised above Mexico City.

The Treaty of Guadalupe Hidalgo

Nicholas Trist was sent by President Polk to negotiate a peace treaty with Mexico. Trist concluded the Treaty of Guadalupe Hidalgo (GWAH-duh-LOOP-ay hih-DAL-goe) in February 1848. According to its terms, Mexico gave up all claims to Texas. Mexico was also forced to sell the entire Southwest—from New Mexico to California—to the United States for $15 million. This included the present-day states of Arizona, New Mexico, California, Nevada, Utah, and parts of Colorado and Wyoming. With the land came responsibility for 80,000 Mexican people who lived on these lands. These people were offered American citizenship.

Section Review

1. What were the causes of the war between the United States and Mexico?
2. Who were the Mormons, and why did they have to flee the United States?
3. Define annex. Why did the United States annex Texas?
4. What lands did the United States gain as the result of the Treaty of Guadalupe Hidalgo?
5. How was the American belief in Manifest Destiny closely related to the beliefs expressed in the Monroe Doctrine?

Discuss: Why do you think Mexico was willing to sell land to the United States in 1853 when it had been unwilling to do so in 1845? What do you think the United States would have done if Mexico had refused to sell the land along the Gila River? Why?

3. California and Sectional Crisis

BEFORE YOU READ: *Why did the application of California for statehood trigger a sectional crisis?*

The Treaty of Guadalupe Hidalgo added 3.1 million square kilometers (1.2 million square miles) of land to the area of the United States. It nearly doubled the size of the nation. America's east–west boundaries now extended from the Atlantic Ocean to the Pacific Ocean. America's Manifest Destiny had been realized.

In 1853, the United States purchased from Mexico an area of land along the Gila River. The purchase, called the Gadsden Purchase, consisted of the southern region of present-day Arizona and New Mexico. It gave the United States its present boundary with Mexico.

Manifest Destiny presented the United States with some difficult decisions. Control of the vast new lands forced the issue of the expansion of slavery to surface once again. Should Congress open these new lands to slavery or should it ban slavery there? Americans looked for a temporary solution at the least, but hoped for a permanent solution.

The United States in 1853

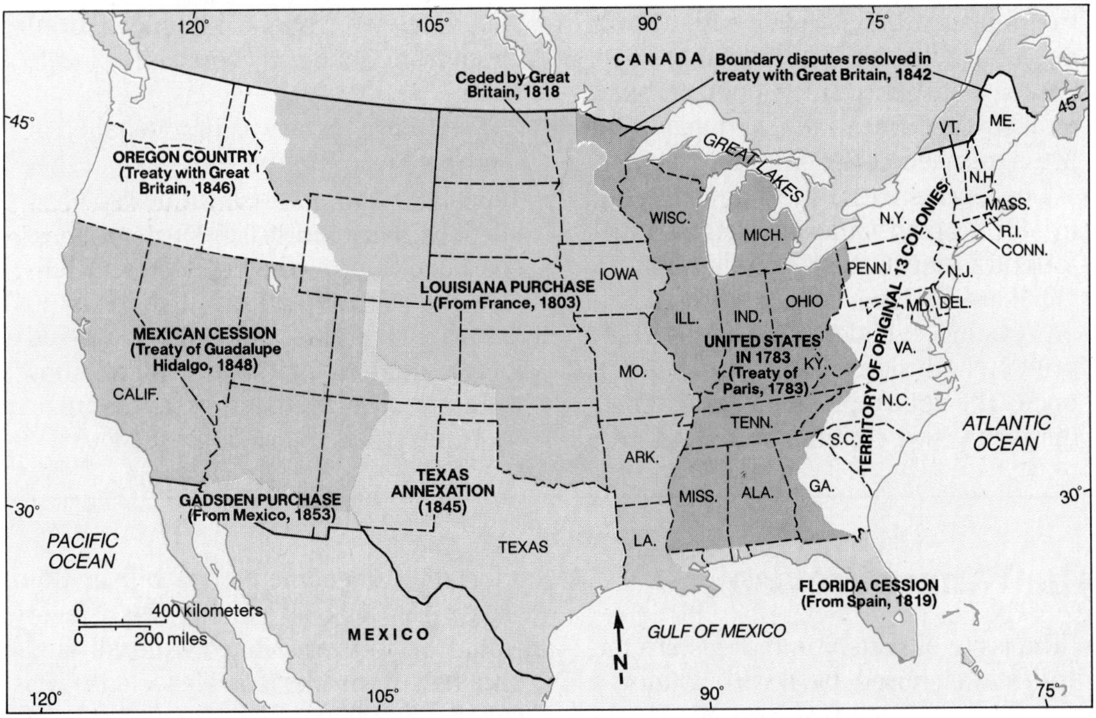

What present-day states were created from the territory acquired from Mexico as a result of the Mexican War? How and when was the land in your state acquired?

EUREKA!

Rotary Press

In this age of rapid technological development, most of today's machines bear little resemblance to their original models. Not so the rotary printing press. The presses used to print newspapers today are essentially the same as those of the nineteenth century.

Before the invention of the rotary press, newspapers were printed on flatbed presses. Sheets of paper were laid one at a time on a plate containing the type. The plate passed under a heavy roller that applied pressure and ink.

In 1846, an American named Richard Hoe replaced the flat plate with a cylinder that held the type and ink. Paper passed between this cylinder and several smaller ones, which applied the pressure needed for printing.

Hoe's press was a great advance, and in 1865, a man named William Bullock took it a step further. In Bullock's machine, paper, type, and ink were all held on rotating cylinders. The press could print on both sides of a piece of paper at once. The rotary press could also handle paper in a continuous roll called a web. The web made it possible to print much faster than had ever been possible before.

The rotary press was first installed at the New York *Tribune*. Very soon, it became the standard press for newspapers all over the country. The rotary press has been improved since Hoe and Bullock first developed it. But there is no doubt that if Hoe and Bullock walked into a modern newspaper plant, they would recognize the presses as their own inventions.

The Wilmot Proviso

The issue of slavery in the western territories was raised by David Wilmot, a Pennsylvania Democrat serving in the House of Representatives. In August 1846, while the Mexican War raged, Wilmot added an amendment to a bill in Congress. His clause stated that slavery would be forever banned from all lands obtained from Mexico. This clause was called the Wilmot **Proviso**. It set off a storm of debate in Congress and in the country.

For Extra Interest: Have students look at a map of the present-day United States. Ask them whether more free or slave states would have been created by extending the Missouri Compromise line to the Pacific and how this might have affected the boundaries of some western states.

proviso a clause that introduces a condition or provision

Southern Whigs and Democrats opposed the Wilmot Proviso because they supported the expansion of slavery. Northern Whigs and Democrats backed the Wilmot Proviso because they did not want to see slavery spreading to the territories conquered from Mexico. Some Southerners suggested extending the Missouri Compromise line of 36°30′ to the Pacific. Northerners objected because this would open most of the new territories to slavery. Northerners argued that since the new territories prohibited slavery under Mexican rule, they should remain that way when they came under American control. Some Americans suggested leaving the slavery decision to the settlers who lived in the new territories.

The Election of 1848

In the presidential election of 1848, the major political parties avoided taking a stand on the slavery expansion issue. The Democratic candidate was Michigan's Senator Lewis Cass. The Democratic party platform avoided any mention of the slavery expansion issue. The Whigs selected the hero of the Mexican War, General Zachary Taylor. Taylor was a Louisiana slave owner, but he had not taken a stand on the slavery expansion issue.

A new political party emerged in August 1848. This third party, called the Free Soil party, was made up of people who supported the Wilmot Proviso. The Free Soil party selected former President Martin Van Buren as its candidate.

On election day, Taylor won. Zachary Taylor entered the White House with little knowledge of politics. He was the first person elected President with no previous political experience.

Taylor viewed the slavery issue as simply a difference of opinions. But shortly after he was elected, Taylor realized the significance of the slavery issue because of events in California.

Gold Fever

California under Mexican control was sparsely settled. One of the settlers was John A. Sutter, who had come to America from Switzerland. He went to California in 1839. Sutter developed a large ranch near Sacramento, in northern California. In August 1847, Sutter hired some workers to build a sawmill. The following January, James Marshall, the supervisor of the workers, spotted some flecks of yellow in the river near where the mill was being built. The flecks were gold. Sutter wanted the gold for himself and tried to keep the discovery a secret. But by spring, the news was out.

Gold hunters from San Francisco swarmed to the area around Sutter's ranch. News of the discovery of gold did not reach the East Coast until fall 1848. Once the news of the gold discovery spread, nothing could stop the gold hunters from heading for California. Some took ships from the East Coast around the tip of South America to California. Another, more popular route was over land. Travelers by the thousands pushed westward across the Great Plains.

Many of the gold hunters of 1849, or **forty-niners**, as they came to be called,

Background: One man, upon boarding a ship for California, threw his last $5 gold piece into the water. He remarked, "I am going where there is plenty more."

This early photograph shows a forty-niner with the tools of his trade.

were not prepared for the difficult cross-country trip. Some wandered off the trails, got lost, and died from starvation. Others drank from unclean waterholes and became very ill.

---

forty-niner a person who took part in the rush to California for gold in 1849

Almost overnight, California was changed. Mining camps had sprung up with colorful names like Poker Flat, Hangtown, Skunk Gulch, and Git-Up-and-Git. Life in these mining camps was expensive. Rooms rented for $1,000 per month, and eggs cost $10 per dozen. Fortunes made in a single day of gold hunting were lost in a single night of gambling. Outlaws ran wild in these towns. Murder was common, as were other forms of lawlessness.

By 1849, nearly 100,000 settlers lived in California. The government was too weak and ineffective to deal with a population of such size. Because of the sharp rise in its population, California qualified for statehood. In March 1850, California requested admission to the Union as a free state.

California's request for admission brought the issue of the expansion of slavery to a head. If California was admitted as a free state, it would upset the balance of free and slave states.

Southern leaders called for a convention of all slaveholding states to meet in June 1850. The purpose of the convention was to discuss how best to protect Southern rights. Southern radicals spoke openly of secession. These radicals became known as the "**Fire-Eaters.**" The convention ended in failure. Delegates agreed on the need to protect Southern rights. However, they could not agree on the method for achieving their goal.

Fire-Eater a Southern radical who wanted the South to secede from the Union

---

The Compromise of 1850

In January 1850, Congress began to debate the issues of California statehood and the extension of slavery into the territory acquired from Mexico. On January 29, Senator Henry Clay suggested a compromise between the North and the South. It became known as the Compromise of 1850. Under the terms of the compromise, California would be admitted as a free state. The question of slavery in the

Background: James Hammond expressed the Fire-Eaters' position when he said, "We should kick them [the Northerners] out of the Capitol and set it on fire."

Background: The new fugitive slave law required that state officials and private citizens help federal authorities capture runaway slaves. Anyone who refused to cooperate could be fined or imprisoned.

territory acquired from Mexico would be decided by the settlers who lived there. In addition, the slave trade in the District of Columbia would be prohibited. However, slavery would still be permitted to exist there. Finally, Congress would pass a new and tougher **fugitive**, or runaway, slave law.

---

fugitive a person who flees or tries to escape

President Zachary Taylor opposed all of the terms of the compromise except for California's entry as a free state. He declared that he would veto the rest of it.

But before Taylor could veto the compromise, he died. His Vice-President, Millard Fillmore, became the new President. Fillmore supported the Compromise of 1850. It became law in September.

Most Americans were pleased with the Compromise of 1850. Members of Congress were convinced that the issues dividing the North and South were settled forever. This belief was shattered within the next few years.

The Compromise of 1850

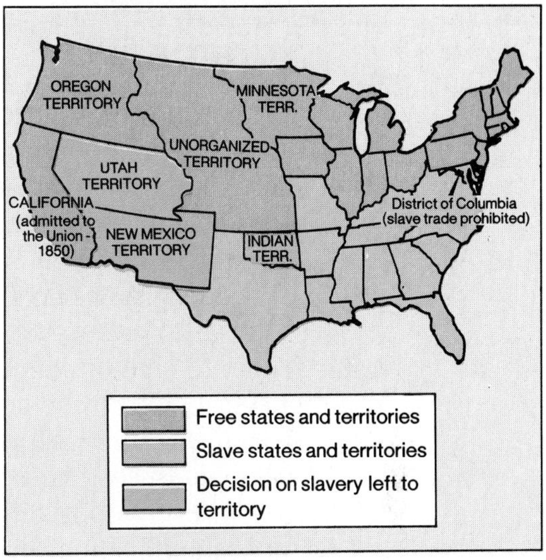

How did the Compromise of 1850 deal with the question of slavery in the lands acquired from Mexico?

Section Review

1. Why did the application of California for statehood trigger a sectional crisis?
2. What specific slavery question was raised by the Treaty of Guadalupe Hidalgo?
3. Define: forty-niner, Fire-Eater, and fugitive.
4. What were the terms of the Compromise of 1850?
5. Why do you think neither major political party took a stand on the slavery expansion issue in the election of 1848?

Background: On July 4, 1850, President Taylor was asked to attend a celebration at Alexandria, Virginia. The day was very hot. At the celebration, President Taylor sat in the hot sun and listened to four hours of speeches. Taylor fell ill, and five days later he died.

CHAPTER REVIEW

Summary

Thousands of Americans moved westward in the 1840's to settle in Texas, Oregon, Utah, and California. Mexico and Great Britain had claims in these areas. As American settlement increased, many Americans came to believe that it was the destiny of the United States to rule the entire continent. This belief was known as Manifest Destiny.

President James Polk was a strong supporter of Manifest Destiny. His proposal to annex the entire Oregon Territory in 1845 forced Great Britain to give up its claims to much of the region. In 1846, Polk persuaded Congress to declare war on Mexico. At the end of the war, Mexico was forced to give up all of its claims to Texas and to sell the entire Southwest to the United States.

Gold fever brought thousands of people to California in 1849. California's application for statehood as a free state in 1850 triggered a crisis over the issue of slavery in the new lands acquired from Mexico. After much debate, Congress accepted a compromise proposed by Senator Henry Clay. Many members of Congress felt that this compromise would settle the issue of slavery forever.

Recalling the Facts

1. What caused the conflict between the Mexican government and American settlers in Texas in the 1830's?
2. How did the westward migrations disturb the life of the Plains Indians?
3. What did the slogan "Fifty-four forty or fight!" refer to?
4. Where did the Mormons establish a community in the West?
5. Why was the Mexican War popular in the South? How did Northerners feel about this war?
6. Why did Northerners object to extending the Missouri Compromise line of 36°30′ as a solution to the question of slavery in the lands acquired from Mexico?

Analyzing the Facts

1. How did the slavery issue affect the admission of Texas and California as states?
2. Why were the Democrats and President Polk willing to risk war

with Great Britain over the issue of Oregon's northern boundary?
3. How were the Mormons similar to the Pilgrims who came to America in 1620?
4. Do you think the Mexican War was justified? Why or why not?
5. What parts of the Compromise of 1850 favored the North? The South? Both sides about equally?

Time and History

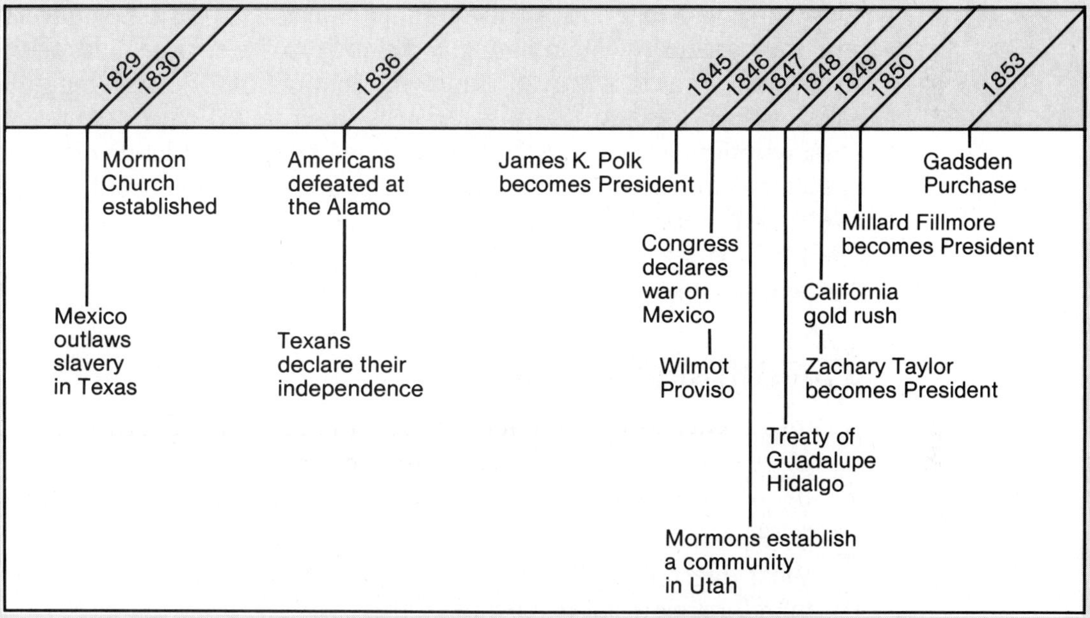

1. When did the Mexican War begin and end? Who was President during this war?
2. How long was the Mormon church in existence before Mormons established a community in Utah?
3. Which event contributed to the outbreak of revolution in Texas: the Wilmot Proviso, the Gadsden Purchase, or Mexico's prohibiton of slavery in its provinces?
4. In what year did thousands of people go to California to look for gold?
5. Who became President when Zachary Taylor died?

UNIT REVIEW

Summary

The years 1820–1850 were years of change and challenge for the United States. The South developed into a closed, agricultural society based on slavery, while the North became industrialized and open to change. Sectional disputes threatened to split the nation apart.

The Union was held together during this period by presidential action and regional compromises. In 1832, President Jackson took a firm stand against the right of any state to nullify federal law. The Missouri Compromise of 1820 and the Compromise of 1850 were adopted in an effort to solve the conflict over the extension of slavery into the territories. Maintaining a balance between free and slave states was seen as a way to avoid the domination of either region's interests in Congress.

Many Americans moved west during this period into lands claimed by Mexico and Great Britain. Prompted by a belief in Manifest Destiny, the United States declared war on Mexico and threatened war with Great Britain. By 1853, the United States was in control of all the land that would make up its 48 continental states.

Recalling the Facts

1. What federal laws did South Carolina nullify in 1832? What did President Jackson do to solve the nullification crisis?
2. What did Andrew Jackson have to do with the formation of the Democratic party in 1824 and the Whig party in 1834?
3. What effect did the invention of the cotton gin have on the demand for slave labor in the South?
4. How was the North changing in the first half of the nineteenth century?
5. What was Manifest Destiny? What role did it play in the Mexican War?

Analyzing the Facts

1. What do you think are the advantages and disadvantages of the spoils system?
2. Why might slaves on one plantation receive better care and treatment than those on another plantation?

3. What alternatives did Southern planters have to slave labor? Why do you think they considered these alternatives unacceptable?
4. What areas of the United States remained unsettled in 1850? What do you think happened to the Indians living in these regions later on, when settlers moved in?

Reviewing Vocabulary

Define the following terms:

emancipate	hiring-out system	abolitionist
spoils system	slave codes	annex
Indian Country	reform	fugitive
Cotton Belt	gag rule	forty-niner

Sharpening Your Skills

1. What are the three types of cards found in a card catalog?
2. What should you do when you find in the card catalog the name of a book that appears useful?

Answer the three questions below based on the election map on page 272.

3. How many electoral votes did New York have in the election of 1828? How did New York cast its electoral votes?
4. What area of the country heavily supported John Quincy Adams in the election of 1828?
5. How many more electoral votes did Jackson receive than Adams?

Writing and Research

1. A press release is a written statement prepared by the President's staff to be given to members of the press. Its purpose is to inform the public and convince them that what the President has done or decided is in the best interests of the nation. Write a press release for President Jackson explaining either his action during the nullification crisis or his decision not to enforce the court's ruling on the land rights of the Cherokee Indians.
2. Research and prepare an oral report on the role of music in the life of the American slaves. Ask the school librarian to help you locate recordings of slave songs that can be played for the class as part of the report.

Unit

5

Division and Reunion

15 *Tensions between the North and the South mounted during the 1850's. The Compromise of 1850 had left the issue of slavery in the western territories up to the settlers who lived there. But this did not stop the proslavery and antislavery forces elsewhere in the country from trying to influence politics in the territories. Pressure from both sides led to violence in Kansas. Events piled up one upon another as the nation headed toward civil war.*

16 *The Civil War began in April 1861. Neither side thought the war would last very long. But it dragged on for four long and bloody years. More than 618,000 soldiers gave their lives to settle the dispute between the North and the South.*

17 *When the war ended, the federal government worked hard to find a plan to reunite the North and the South. The search caused great bitterness between Congress and the Presidents. For the nation, the problems of peace turned out to be as difficult as the war itself.*

Chapter
15

The Breaking of the Union

By the winter of 1860–1861, the United States was coming apart. Seven Southern slave states had already left the Union. No one knew if more would follow. It was rumored that an attempt would be made on Abraham Lincoln's life as he traveled from Illinois to Washington for his inauguration. By late February 1861, Lincoln had reached West Philadelphia. The President-elect was escorted to the train station, where he boarded a train for Washington, D.C. Lincoln was unable to sleep as he headed for the nation's capital. He knew he would have to deal with the seven seceded states in order to prevent a civil war. "My troubles have just begun," he was heard to say.

After you read this chapter, you will be able to:

1. Explain how the Kansas-Nebraska Act renewed the conflict between the North and South over the expansion of slavery into the territories.
2. Discuss the significance of the Dred Scott decision.
3. Show how the election of Abraham Lincoln as President caused some Southern states to leave the Union.

☐ Read a political cartoon.

1. The Calm Is Broken

BEFORE YOU READ: *How did the Kansas-Nebraska Act create a conflict over slavery in the territories?*

The Compromise of 1850 had helped to restore a feeling of calm in the nation. Most Americans hoped the question of the expansion of slavery in the western territories had been settled forever.

In the election of 1852, both the Democrats and the Whigs pledged their support to the Compromise. Democrats selected Franklin Pierce of New Hampshire to run for President. The Whigs chose General Winfield Scott. The only difference between the two parties was that Whig support of the Compromise was milder. The Democrats won the election, and Franklin Pierce became the new President. The Democrats' victory was largely due to their stronger stand in favor of the Compromise of 1850.

Although most Americans supported the Compromise of 1850, there were people who were dissatisfied with parts of it. Some Northerners opposed the Compromise because of the new Fugitive Slave Act. Southern Fire-Eaters objected to it because the Compromise did not permit slavery to expand freely.

The Fugitive Slave Act

The nation's first Fugitive Slave Act was passed in 1793. It permitted slave owners or hired slave catchers to enter any state or territory to capture runaway slaves. Antislavery groups fought the law by aiding the runaways. Many times the antislavery groups hid the slaves from those who wished to capture them. Southern slave owners demanded tougher laws to enable them to capture their runaway slaves.

As part of the Compromise of 1850, Congress passed a new and tougher Fugitive Slave Act. Under this new law, slave catchers could go into court and present evidence that a black person was a runaway. The accused black person had to stand trial before a commissioner. During the trial, the accused was not permitted to speak in his or her own defense. The commissioner received a $10 fee if the accused black was turned over to slavery and only $5 if the person was freed. In addition, the Fugitive Slave Act provided

$200
REWARD
Ranaway from the subscriber, on Sunday night, the 16th of December, negro boy Gusty, who calls himself GustavusSi mms,he is about twenty years of age, five feet six inches high, dark ginger-bread color, large flat nose, which he almost hides with upper lip when he laughs. He carried away with him one black and one grey coat and a brown over-coat and a pair of drab fulled cloth pants and blue comfort, he also had an oil-cloth clothes bag.
I will pay $50 for his apprehension in the state of Maryland or in the District of Columbia, and $200 if taken in a free State.
ANN P. EVERSFIELD.
Bladensburg Po., Prince George's Co., Md.

Advertisements offering rewards for the capture of runaway slaves ran in many newspapers.

Famous Americans

ANTHONY BURNS

Anthony Burns was a slave who escaped from the South after the Compromise of 1850 had been enacted into law. One of the unfortunate aspects of the Compromise was that it strengthened the Fugitive Slave Act. Three months after Burns escaped from Virginia as a stowaway on a ship bound for Boston, he was caught by a Boston marshal and put in jail.

Burns' trial began in the spring of 1854. It attracted an enormous amount of attention, especially among abolitionists. The abolitionists took up his cause, held meetings, and arranged for his defense. But their efforts were to no avail. The trial proceeded very badly for Burns. In a desperate effort to gain Burns' release, the abolitionists attempted to rescue Burns by force from the courthouse. A deputy marshall was killed and a number of people were wounded in the fight. The attempt to free Burns was a failure. The court handed down its decision in the Burns case on June 2, 1854. Burns was convicted and ordered to return to Virginia.

Public reaction to the court decision was swift and angry. People "draped their houses in mourning and hissed the procession that took Burns to his ship." Thousands of people rushed the procession to try to free him. It took 22 military units, including marines, cavalry, and artillery, to hold the people back. Although Burns was forced to return to the South, his trial helped to increase support for the antislavery cause. Within a few months of his return to the South, Burns' freedom was purchased by Northern abolitionists. Burns decided to study for the ministry and attended Oberlin College and the Fairmont Theological Seminary. Anthony Burns eventually left the United States and settled in Canada, where he became a minister.

for a $1,000 fine and a jail term of up to six months for any citizen who prevented the arrest of a fugitive slave or who was found to be hiding a fugitive slave.

The Fugitive Slave Act frightened many black Northerners. Hundreds of former slaves fled to Canada. Of those blacks who stayed in the North, many tried not to draw attention to themselves. Others were prepared to fight to protect themselves from being reenslaved. One such man was Robert Purvis. He told the Pennsylvania Anti-Slavery Society that if a slave catcher entered his house, "I'll seek his life, I'll shed his blood."

Some white Northerners supported the

Background: Militant abolitionists openly defied the Fugitive Slave Act in 1851 when they rescued a slave, Shadrach, from a United States marshal in Boston who was preparing to return him to his owner.

Fugitive Slave Act. To them, slaves were property, and Southerners had a legal right to recover their property. Other white Northerners refused to obey the Fugitive Slave Act. They hid runaways. They joined mobs that freed captured slaves from jails in the North. They tried to block slave catchers from returning blacks to the South. These people were willing to risk stiff punishment for breaking the law. Various Northern states also passed personal liberty laws. These laws were designed to nullify the Fugitive Slave Act and to protect black citizens from kidnapping.

Southern Fire-Eaters supported the Fugitive Slave Act. What they objected to was the rest of the Compromise of 1850. Fire-Eaters wanted slavery to expand without restriction.

The Fire-Eaters came from a number of groups within Southern society. Some were young business people. Others were small farmers. All shared a desire to buy cheap western land and become wealthy planters. The Fire-Eaters demanded that slavery be permitted in all western territories. Their dreams of a prosperous life in the West depended on being able to use slave labor.

The Kansas-Nebraska Act

By 1850, Americans had begun settling the Indian Country. This land, beyond the Mississippi and Missouri rivers, was reserved by federal law for the Indians' sole use. Settlers had discovered that this area, long known as the Great American Desert, was, in fact, good for farming. During the early 1850's, they demanded that the federal government move the Indians off the land. The settlers also wanted this land to be organized into a territory in preparation for statehood.

At the same time, railroad companies, backed by western senators, were making long-range plans to build a railroad across the Great Plains. They wanted to start it at a western city like Chicago, St. Louis, Memphis, or New Orleans. From there, the railroad would go across the plains all the way to California. This line, linking the eastern rail network to the Far West, would be a **transcontinental railroad**. It would speed settlement of the Great Plains and the Far West. It would provide industry with new markets for its products and enable industry to get to needed raw materials more quickly and easily. Railroad planners wanted the government to organize a territory out of the Indians' land so that construction of the railroad could begin.

---

transcontinental railroad a rail line running across an entire continent

---

The demands of both the settlers and the railroads came to rest on the desk of Senator Stephen A. Douglas of Illinois. Douglas was the head of the Senate Committee on Territories. He was also the director of the Illinois Central Railroad and a major **land speculator** in the Chicago area. Douglas realized that if the transcontinental railroad began at Chicago, it would draw settlers to the city. This would increase the value of land he owned, which he could sell for enormous profits. With Douglas' backing, Congress passed the Kansas-Nebraska Act in 1854. The act created two federal territories from that part of the Indian Country north

Discuss: How was the concept of popular sovereignty a direct threat to the power of the federal government? Why do you think many Southerners favored popular sovereignty?

Stephen Douglas

of the Missouri Compromise line of 36°30′. One territory was to be the Nebraska Territory. The other would be the Kansas Territory. Indian landholdings were reduced, and the Indians were required to live on special lands set aside for them.

---

land speculator one who buys land in the hope of selling it later for a profit

---

The Kansas-Nebraska Act stated that the slavery issue would be left to the people of these territories to decide. This was called **popular sovereignty**. By leaving the slavery decision to the territorial settlers, the Kansas-Nebraska Act effectively repealed the Missouri Compromise. Slavery could now exist in a territory or state north of the 36°30′ line if the settlers of that area voted for it.

---

popular sovereignty the belief that the people of a territory should have the right to decide whether their territory would permit slavery

---

The Northern Uproar

Congress passed the Kansas-Nebraska Act believing that few Americans would object to it. The act, however, caused an uproar in the North. Many Northerners did not care if slavery existed in the South, but they felt strongly about free soil. They did not want slavery spreading into territory declared free by the Missouri Compromise.

Some Northerners began to fear that Congress might next do away with the Northwest Ordinance. The Northwest Ordinance of 1787 banned slavery from the part of the nation that became the states of Ohio, Illinois, Indiana, Michigan,

Kansas-Nebraska Act, 1854

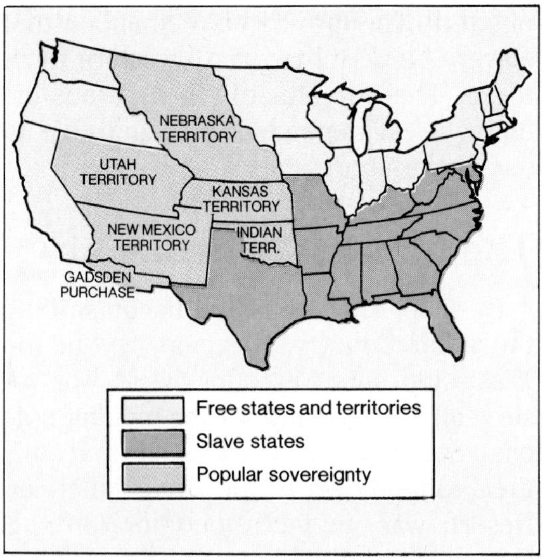

Was your state slave or free in 1854?

Background: An anti-immigration organization, the American party, was also influential in the early 1850's. This party was also known as the Know-Nothings because its members at first kept their purposes secret, answering all questions with the words "I know nothing."

and Wisconsin. Could these free states be turned into slave states by another act of Congress? Northerners believed the answer to be yes. They pointed to the Kansas-Nebraska Act as their evidence.

A storm of protest broke out in the North. At meetings, angry people protested the "Nebraska outrage." Douglas' actions were described as "criminal behavior." Others called the Kansas-Nebraska Act "an atrocious plot" to make these territories into "a dreary region . . . inhabited by masters and slaves."

The Kansas-Nebraska Act produced major changes in America's political parties, too. The Whig party split in half, with Northern Whigs opposing the Kansas-Nebraska Act and Southern Whigs supporting it. The Whig party soon disappeared altogether as members joined forces with other political groups. Southern Whigs joined Douglas and the Democrats because they had supported the opening of western lands to slavery.

Northern Whigs, Democrats who opposed the Kansas-Nebraska Act, abolitionists, and other Northerners joined forces. They created a new political party opposed to the expansion of slavery. They selected the name Republican so that people would identify the new party with Thomas Jefferson and his old party.

The Republicans declared that slavery "was a great moral, social, and political evil." They demanded the repeal of the Kansas-Nebraska Act and the Fugitive Slave Act of 1850. They also agreed to fight the expansion of slavery. In the 1854 elections, the Republicans ran their first candidates. They won a number of state offices and congressional seats. The Republican party then started preparing for the presidential election of 1856.

Southerners continued to form the backbone of the Democratic party. They were very hostile toward the Republican party. They charged that the Republican party wanted to free all slaves and destroy Southern society. They claimed that the Republicans regarded the black race as equal to the white race. For this reason, the Democrats called them "Black Republicans." Southern Democrats saw the Republicans as a threat to the South.

Section Review

1. How did the Kansas-Nebraska Act create a conflict over slavery in the territories?
2. What was the Fugitive Slave Act? How did Northerners react to it?
3. Define popular sovereignty. What groups favored popular sovereignty in the 1850's?
4. What did the new Republican party stand for? Why did Southerners feel threatened by it?
5. Explain how the construction of a transcontinental railroad could have both helped and hurt people living on the Great Plains.

For Extra Interest: Have students investigate how recent controversies have affected the nation's political parties and around what issues third parties have developed in recent years.

Background: The poet John Greenleaf Whittier captured the mood of many Northerners in his 1854 poem: "We cross the prairie as of old/ The Pilgrims crossed the sea,/ To make the West, as they the East,/ the homestead of the Free!"

2. The Crumbling Union

BEFORE YOU READ: *What was the significance of the Supreme Court's decision in the Dred Scott case?*

As a result of the Kansas-Nebraska Act, the center of the slavery controversy shifted to the western plains. The Kansas Territory became the battleground of proslavery Southerners and antislavery Northerners.

Border ruffians moving into Kansas

"Bleeding Kansas"

Thousands of settlers poured into Kansas in 1854, buying land along what they hoped would be the future routes of the railroad. Both Northerners and Southerners wanted to make sure that the people who settled in Kansas held the "right" views on slavery.

Southerners organized groups of proslavery settlers to move into Kansas. Proslavery settlers were joined by lawless individuals, mostly from Missouri, called border ruffians. The border ruffians planned to support the proslavery settlers and "influence" any other settlers with their weapons.

Northerners took action to keep Kansas free. New Englanders organized the Emigrant Aid Society to raise money for settlers to move to Kansas. Various eastern aid societies also sent the New England settlers shipments of rifles. They were called "Beecher's Bibles" because the congregation of the Reverend Henry Ward Beecher, a well-known abolitionist, sent many of them. Beecher himself said that the cause of freedom in Kansas would be won by carrying a rifle rather than a Bible.

By 1856, violence and bloodshed were sweeping across the territory. One armed group of 800 slavery supporters seized the antislavery town of Lawrence on May 21, 1856. They destroyed the offices of two newspapers, robbed the stores, and tried to burn the town to the ground. John Brown, an abolitionist who had settled in Kansas in 1855, made plans to retaliate. It was time to "fight fire with fire," Brown said, to "strike terror in the hearts of the proslavery people." Brown, four of his sons, and two companions seized five proslavery settlers from their cabins along Pottawatomie Creek and murdered them in cold blood.

Bands of armed gangs terrorized the Kansas countryside. People began calling the territory "Bleeding Kansas." But the violence did not stay in Kansas. It spread

Background: Many proslavery Missourians crossed into Kansas to vote unlawfully for proslavery candidates in the territorial elections. The territorial legislature that resulted legalized slavery. In response, free-soilers in Kansas created their own government.

immediately to the halls of Congress.

On May 19 and 20, 1856, Senator Charles Sumner of Massachusetts delivered a harsh speech against the South called "The Crime Against Kansas." Included in his speech were several statements critical of and insulting to Senator Andrew Butler of South Carolina. Two days later, Butler's cousin, Congressman Preston Brooks, entered the floor of the Senate. Sumner was working at his desk. Brooks walked over to Sumner and began beating him over the head with a cane. Sumner finally broke free of his desk, stumbled forward, and collapsed. Sumner was hospitalized and did not return to the Senate for three years. His vacant seat served as a reminder of the crisis within the nation.

Northerners were outraged. Some Southerners expressed deep regret over Brooks' behavior. But they were in the minority. Their voices were drowned out by the sounds of praise. "Every Southern man is delighted," wrote Brooks the day after the event. A Richmond, Virginia, newspaper stated, "The only regret we feel, is that Mr. Brooks did not employ a horsewhip or cowhide . . . instead of a cane."

The Election of 1856

"Bleeding Kansas," "Bleeding Sumner," and the Kansas-Nebraska Act were the main issues in the presidential election of 1856. Stephen A. Douglas was the leading figure in the Democratic party. But he was passed over as a candidate for the presidency because the Kansas-Nebraska Act had made him unpopular in the North. Instead, the Democrats chose James Buchanan of Pennsylvania. Between 1853 and 1856, Buchanan had served as minister to Great Britain under President Pierce. Buchanan had been out of the country during the recent trouble over the Kansas-Nebraska Act. He had not taken a public stand on the law, so he had not made the enemies Douglas had.

The Republicans followed the old Whig practice of selecting a military hero. John C. Frémont was chosen to run for President. It was hoped that his popularity as a hero in the Mexican War would gain the White House for the Republicans. During the campaign, the Republicans pledged that they would not abolish slavery in the

John Frémont and William Dayton were the first Republican party presidential and vice-presidential candidates.

South. But they did promise that they would work to prevent its expansion. They insisted on a free West and a free Kansas. Their slogan was "Free Soil, Free Labor, Free Men, Frémont."

The slogan had great appeal in the North, but it failed to bring victory to Frémont. Frémont won almost no popular votes south of the Ohio River.

By 1857, Democrats and Republicans had taken clear-cut stands on the issue of the expansion of slavery. The Democrats believed that slavery should be allowed to expand outside of the South. They believed that popular sovereignty should determine the issue. The Republicans accepted slavery in the South. They did not want slavery to expand into the territories, however.

At his inauguration, President Buchanan predicted that the entire slavery problem was "approaching its end." He said that the Supreme Court was about to lay the matter to rest. Two days later, on March 6, 1857, the Supreme Court handed down its decision in the Dred Scott case.

Dred Scott

Dred Scott was a slave. He was owned by Dr. John Emerson, an army physician, who lived in the slave state of Missouri. During his career, Emerson had been stationed in the free state of Illinois and in the free Wisconsin Territory. Dred Scott went with Emerson during these tours of service in free territory. Scott became convinced that he should be set free. Having been on free soil made him a free man.

With the aid of white friends, Scott sued to obtain his freedom. He asked the court to set him free on the grounds that he had become free when taken into free territory. If the court agreed, any slave reaching free soil would become free.

The Missouri Supreme Court ruled against Dred Scott, declaring that even in free territory, he was still under Missouri law. Also, his return to Missouri continued his enslavement. From there, Dred Scott's lawyers appealed his case to the United States Supreme Court. The Court ruled that as a slave, Scott was not a citizen of the United States. Therefore, he had no right under the Constitution to sue in a court of law. In addition, the court ruled that the Constitution protected a property owner's right to his or her property. This meant that a slave owner could take a slave (her or his property) to free territory and continue to practice slavery. The Court said the Missouri Compromise was unconstitutional. Congress did not have the right to keep slaves out of a federal territory because that would deprive Americans of their property. This meant that slavery could exist anywhere in the territories.

The Dred Scott decision did not settle the slavery question, as President Buchanan had predicted. Instead of calming the angry mood of the nation, it fueled it. Northerners called the decision "a wicked and false judgment" and the "greatest crime in the [records] of the Republic."

Southerners rejoiced over the decision. "Southern opinion upon the subject of southern slavery . . . is now the supreme law of the land," announced a Georgia newspaper. "Opposition to southern opinion upon this subject is now opposition to the Constitution," it continued.

For Extra Interest: The majority of justices on the Supreme Court were Southerners. They all supported the Dred Scott decision. Only one Northern justice agreed with them. Ask students how this might have affected Northern attitudes on the Dred Scott decision.

The Dred Scott decision caused a split in the Democratic party. Stephen A. Douglas, one of the party's leaders, could not accept the Dred Scott decision. To do so would make his theory of popular sovereignty meaningless. Douglas believed that the people of a territory could prohibit slavery. President Buchanan backed the Court's ruling. He pressured Douglas to support it. When Douglas refused, the Democratic party broke into two groups. One group stood with Douglas and the theory of popular sovereignty. The other group supported President Buchanan and the Dred Scott ruling.

A total of seven debates were held between Abraham Lincoln and Stephen Douglas in the 1858 Illinois senate race.

Lincoln and Douglas

Douglas returned to Illinois in the summer of 1858 to seek reelection as senator. Although President Buchanan used his influence as the head of the Democratic party to crush Douglas' attempts at reelection, Douglas was still very popular in his home state. But he faced a major challenge. The challenge came from the Republican candidate, Abraham Lincoln.

The two candidates had known each other for 20 years. Douglas had been the United States senator from Illinois for more than a decade. He had become one of the most powerful men in the Democratic party. Lincoln, on the other hand, had served a single term as a member of Congress from 1847 to 1849.

Now both men were running for the same seat in the Senate. During the campaign, they engaged in a series of debates across the state of Illinois. In appearance and personality, the two candidates could not have been more different. Douglas was barely 1.5 meters (5 feet) tall, stocky, a forceful speaker, and a confident man. Lincoln was very tall—nearly 1.9 meters (6 1/2 feet), awkward, and slow in speech. Even so, he was an admired speaker and an effective campaigner.

The views expressed by Lincoln in his debates with Douglas alarmed the South. In a speech at Springfield in June 1858, Lincoln declared, "A house divided against itself cannot stand. I believe this government cannot endure permanently half slave and half free. I do not expect the Union to be dissolved—I do not expect the house to fall—but I do expect it will cease to be divided." At Alton, he continued in the same manner. "The real issue in this controversy . . . is the sentiment on the part of one class that looks

Background: *Uncle Tom's Cabin* sold 300,000 copies in its first year of publication (1852). It has been said that when President Lincoln met Stowe during the Civil War, he remarked, "So this is the little lady who wrote the big book that caused the big war!"

upon the institution of slavery *as a wrong*, and of another class that *does not* look upon it as a wrong," stated Lincoln. "[The Republican party] looks upon it as being a moral, social, and political wrong . . . and one method of treating it as a wrong is to make provision that it shall grow no larger."

Stephen Douglas won reelection as the senator from Illinois. However, Lincoln showed the leaders of the Republican party that he could run well as a candidate. He had a quick mind and had impressed his party with his public speaking ability. Lincoln's name began to be considered when the Republican party officials discussed presidential contenders for 1860.

More Attacks on Slavery

The conflict between the North and the South mounted steadily. Two books published in the 1850's added to the controversy and ill feelings.

One book was *Uncle Tom's Cabin*, written by Harriet Beecher Stowe. Her book painted a very harsh picture of slavery. Stowe's book is the story of Simon Legree, a Northerner who became a brutal plantation owner; Uncle Tom, an old black slave who suffers the inhumanity of slavery with dignity; and a slave girl, Eliza, who tries to flee to freedom in the North with her child, Topsy. Southerners claimed that the book was an exaggeration. However, many Northerners accepted it as a true picture of slavery.

The other book was Hinton Rowan Helper's *The Impending Crisis of the South*. Helper was a small farmer from North Carolina. In his book, he attacked slavery, not because it was morally wrong, but because it hurt Southerners who did not own slaves. Helper believed that most Southern farmers would remain in poverty unless slavery was destroyed. Many Southerners called him a traitor. In the North, his book was very popular. It seemed to prove that a free society was superior to a slave society.

In an 1858 speech, William Seward, a senator from New York, described conditions in the nation. He said an "irrepressible conflict" between slavery and freedom had developed. By this, he meant that a battle between the North and the South could no longer be prevented.

Section Review

1. What was the significance of the Supreme Court's decision in the Dred Scott case?
2. Explain how the Kansas Territory came to be called "Bleeding Kansas."
3. Why did James Buchanan win the election of 1856?
4. Why would Lincoln's views toward the Union and slavery worry Southerners?

Social Studies Skills

Reading Political Cartoons

Tensions between the North and the South increased in the 1850's. The issue of slavery in the western territories threatened to split the Union. Political cartoons were published in the North and the South that reflected each section's attitude toward this issue.

Political cartoons are often used to influence public opinion or summarize an existing situation. A cartoonist uses symbols to communicate ideas. For example, cartoonists often use Uncle Sam to stand for the United States, a dove to symbolize peace, a crown to represent royalty, and so on.

To understand a political cartoon, first read the caption or title and any other words that appear in the cartoon. Next, identify all the symbols in the cartoon and the persons or ideas they represent. If any of the symbols are exaggerated, try to determine what the exaggeration means. The cartoonist's message will become clear if all the words and symbols are interpreted correctly.

1. What do the two men in the cartoon symbolize?
2. What does the cannonball represent? Why are the men pushing it?
3. Why did the cartoonist draw the cannonball so large?
4. What is the main idea of this cartoon?

Discuss: Do you think Brown's plan to free Southern slaves would have worked if he had not been captured at Harpers Ferry? Why or why not?

3. "And The War Came"

BEFORE YOU READ: *Why did the election of Abraham Lincoln as President cause the South to secede?*

Abolitionist John Brown was dissatisfied with the setbacks the antislavery movement was experiencing. By early 1859, he had developed a plan to free Southern slaves. His plan was to seize, with a band of followers, the federal arsenal at Harpers Ferry, Virginia (now West Virginia). Brown planned to give the arsenal's guns to thousands of slaves. The slaves would lead a widespread slave revolt to end slavery in the South.

The Raid on Harpers Ferry

Abolitionists had given Brown nearly $4,000 to finance his plan. On the evening of October 16, Brown and 18 followers secretly entered Harpers Ferry and captured the arsenal, seizing thousands of weapons.

Governor Wise of Virginia called out the state militia. He also requested help from the federal government. The state and federal troops stormed the arsenal and captured Brown, who was severely wounded. Brown was put on trial for murder and treason and was found guilty. Before he was sentenced, Brown spoke to the court. "If it is . . . necessary that I should forfeit my life . . . and mingle my blood further . . . with the blood of millions in this slave country whose rights are disregarded by wicked, cruel and unjust [actions]. . . . I submit. Let it be done." John Brown was sentenced to be hanged. On December 2, 1859, Brown was taken to the gallows.

Millions of Northerners came to admire Brown for his dedication to the antislavery cause. Southerners firmly believed they needed protection from Northerners who sympathized with John Brown.

The Election of 1860

In April 1860, the Democrats gathered in Charleston, South Carolina, to decide on their presidential candidate. Northern Democrats backed Stephen Douglas and his stand on popular sovereignty. Southern Democrats rejected Douglas. They insisted that the party come out in support of federal protection for slave owners and their property in all territories. Arguments were heated between Northern and Southern Democrats. When most of the delegates finally agreed to back Douglas as the presidential candidate, the party split in two. Democratic delegates from eight Southern states walked out of the convention.

The Democratic party met again at Baltimore in June 1860. Again the Southern Democrats walked out. The remaining delegates selected Stephen Douglas as their candidate. The Southern Democrats later met at Richmond, Virginia. They selected the nation's Vice-President, John C. Breckinridge, to run for President.

Another political party briefly came into existence in May 1860. The Constitutional Union party was formed by people who opposed the political parties that were driving the nation apart. The party vowed that its members would obey all the laws of the land. Tennessee's John

Background: The Constitutional Union party was made up of former Whigs and Conservatives. Its strength was concentrated in the Upper South.

Discuss: How do you think the split in the Democratic party contributed to Lincoln's victory in 1860?

The Election of 1860

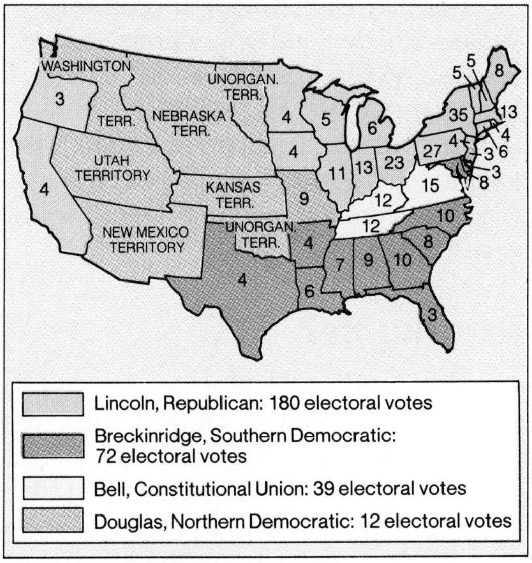

How does the map illustrate that the election of 1860 was a sectional one?

Bell was selected as the Constitutional Union party candidate for President.

At the Republican convention, the leading candidate was William Seward of New York. But many Republicans viewed him as too radical because of his outspoken support of abolitionists. The party turned to Abraham Lincoln. The Republicans promised to respect slavery in the Southern states. But they vowed to fight its expansion into western territories.

The chief issue among candidates in the election of 1860 was the expansion of slavery into western territories. Southern Democrats, supported by the Fire-Eaters, favored the expansion of slavery. Northern Democrats supported the doctrine of popular sovereignty. The Republicans campaigned against the expansion of slavery. The Constitutional Union party recommended that the nation ignore the issue for the sake of the Union.

On election day, Lincoln won an overwhelming number of electoral votes. Lincoln received only 1,866,000 popular votes, or about 40 percent of all votes cast. The total number of votes cast for his three opponents exceeded his total by nearly one million. Abraham Lincoln did not have the support of the majority of Americans.

The Deep South Secedes

The Fire-Eaters and many other Southerners saw Lincoln as a symbol of Northern hostility toward the South. The Fire-Eaters called for state conventions to discuss secession.

South Carolina acted first. On December 20, 1860, South Carolina voted unanimously to secede from the Union. At the same time, South Carolina repealed its approval of the Constitution.

South Carolina did not want to act alone, knowing that the federal government could easily move to crush it. The success of secession depended on other states joining with South Carolina. Representatives from South Carolina were sent to other Southern states. There they spoke with Fire-Eaters and Democratic leaders to organize plans for a Southern nation. By February 1, 1861, six more states had joined South Carolina. Georgia, Mississippi, Alabama, Louisiana, Texas, and Florida had seceded from the Union.

Representatives from the seceded states met on February 4. They announced the formation of a new nation, the Confederate States of America. They also wrote a constitution for their new

Background: In 1861, South Carolina had the highest percentage of blacks (59 percent) in its population, followed by Mississippi (55 percent). Of the free states, New Jersey had the greatest percentage of blacks in its population (4 percent).

nation. Slavery was legalized. The state governments were to be "sovereign and independent" so as to prevent the national government from becoming too powerful.

Leaders of the Confederate States of America were also elected at the Montgomery convention. Jefferson Davis of Mississippi was elected President. His Vice-President was Alexander Stephens of Georgia.

The question of what the states of the Upper South would do still remained. The Upper South had not yet joined the new Southern nation. But the states of the Upper South issued a strong warning to the United States government. If any force was used to bring the seceded states back into the Union, they too would secede.

President Buchanan took a cautious stand. He stated that secession was constitutionally impossible; the Union could not be dissolved. But if any state did secede, there was nothing the federal government could do to stop it. Buchanan was leaving the problem to Lincoln.

Lincoln Takes Office

Abraham Lincoln was sworn into office on March 4, 1861. In his inaugural address, he told Southerners that they should not fear him or the Republicans. Slavery would not be interfered with in the South. Then he declared that no state could leave the Union. Secession, in Lincoln's view, was constitutionally impossible. He did not and would not recognize the Confederate States of America.

Lincoln also spoke about the possibility of civil war. He promised that the federal government would shed no Southern blood—unless it was forced to do so. He ended by saying that if a war broke out, it would start by Southern action. "In *your* hands, my dissatisfied fellow countrymen, and not in *mine*, is the momentous issue of civil war," declared Lincoln. "The government will not [attack] you. You can have no conflict, without being yourselves the aggressors."

Fort Sumter

Lincoln did not want to use force against the seceded states. Such an action would surely drive the states of the Upper South out of the Union. At the same time, Lincoln had to maintain control of federal property in the South.

Two federal forts in the South were still in Union hands. One was Fort Pickens, located at Pensacola, Florida. The other was Fort Sumter, in the Charleston, South Carolina, harbor. The commander of Fort Sumter was Major Robert Anderson. On March 5, Anderson notified the President that his supplies were running out. He also advised Lincoln that Fort Sumter was surrounded by Confederate forces.

Lincoln was in a difficult situation. If he surrendered Fort Sumter, he would be accepting secession. If he defended the fort, it would start a war. Lincoln selected a middle course of action. He decided to send food, not weapons, to Fort Sumter. On April 6, 1861, Lincoln sent a special messenger to Governor Francis Pickens of South Carolina. He informed Pickens that ships carrying food would be arriving to resupply the troops at Fort Sumter.

Lincoln's message was forwarded to President Jefferson Davis. Davis wanted to gain control of Fort Pickens and Fort

For Extra Interest: Have students read the presidential oath of office in article 2, section 8 of the Constitution. Ask students what this oath required Lincoln to do about the seceded states.

Discuss: Why was it advantageous for the North to allow the South to start the fighting?

Fort Sumter

Sumter. He hoped to obtain them peacefully, but he was prepared to take them by force. On April 9, he sent an order to General P. G. T. Beauregard, who commanded Confederate forces at Charleston. Demand Fort Sumter's surrender, he ordered. If it is not surrendered, attack until the fort is in Confederate hands.

Beauregard sent some of his officers to demand that Anderson surrender the fort. Anderson rejected the demand. He said that only when his food ran out would he be forced to vacate the fort.

The Union supply ships were due to arrive at Charleston harbor on April 12. That morning, Confederate guns opened fire on Fort Sumter. Anderson surrendered after 34 hours of bombardment. Fort Sumter was largely destroyed. War had broken out.

Section Review

1. Why did the election of Lincoln cause the South to secede?
2. What did John Brown hope to accomplish in his raid on Harpers Ferry?
3. Explain how events at Fort Sumter led to the Civil War.
4. The United States came into being because the colonies declared their independence from Great Britain. Why would the United States government believe that the South was wrong in declaring its independence?

Background: The Confederates allowed the defeated Union forces at Fort Sumter to sail away on unarmed vessels.

CHAPTER REVIEW

Summary

Tensions between the North and the South mounted during the 1850's. Many Northerners feared that the doctrine of popular sovereignty in the Kansas-Nebraska Act of 1854 would allow slavery to spread into territories north of the old Missouri Compromise line. Northerners who opposed the expansion of slavery formed the Republican party.

The nation moved steadily toward civil war as violence erupted in Kansas among settlers who had come from the North and the South specifically to make that territory free or slave. The Dred Scott decision, antislavery books, and John Brown's raid all divided the country along sectional lines. The election of the Republican candidate, Abraham Lincoln, in 1860 prompted South Carolina to carry out its longstanding threat to secede. Six other states of the Deep South joined with South Carolina to form the Confederate States of America. Fighting broke out when Confederate forces attacked Fort Sumter, a Union fort in South Carolina, in April 1861. The Civil War had begun.

Recalling the Facts

1. What prompted Senator Douglas of Illinois to introduce a bill for organizing the Kansas and Nebraska territories?
2. How did the Kansas-Nebraska Act produce major changes in America's political parties?
3. Why did Dred Scott believe he should be a free man?
4. Who were the presidential candidates in 1860? What position did each political party take on the issue of the expansion of slavery?
5. Why were Presidents Buchanan and Lincoln reluctant to use force to bring the seceded states back into the Union?

Analyzing the Facts

1. The Compromise of 1850 stated that settlers in the territories acquired from Mexico could decide for themselves whether they wanted their territories to be free or slave. Why did this not affect the Kansas and Nebraska territories?

2. Compare the Democratic and Republican stands on the issue of popular sovereignty in 1857.
3. Compare Harriet Beecher Stowe's book, *Uncle Tom's Cabin*, to Hinton Rowan Helper's *The Impending Crisis of the South*. How were the two books similar? How were they different?
4. How do you think Southerners reacted when they learned that many Northerners admired John Brown?
5. Why do you think Lincoln decided to send food to resupply the Union troops at Fort Sumter instead of simply abandoning the fort?

Time and History

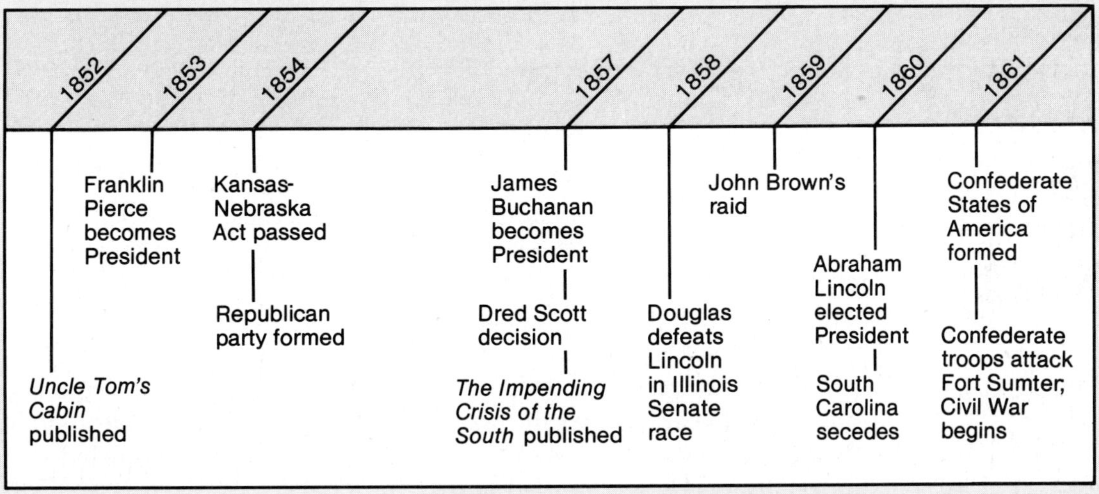

1. Who was President when the Kansas-Nebraska Act was passed?
2. How many years after the Republican party was formed was Lincoln elected President?
3. In what year did the Civil War begin?
4. What two antislavery books were published in the 1850's?
5. What election did Abraham Lincoln lose in the 1850's? Who won that election?

Chapter
16

The Civil War

A wave of war fever swept across the North and the South when people heard the news of the attack on Fort Sumter. There were huge Union rallies in New York. A reporter for the *London Times* witnessed immense crowds in the South. After years of tension, the conflict between North and South had boiled over. People cheered. Bands played. Flags waved. It was as if the arrival of the Civil War called for rejoicing. Americans expected that the war would be no more than a few small but glorious battles. In a short time, however, the terrible knowledge of the reality of the war settled across the land.

After you read this chapter, you will be able to:

1. Describe the advantages, disadvantages, and military strategies of the Union and the Confederacy.
2. Explain how and why Lincoln freed blacks from slavery.
3. Tell what life was like behind the lines during the Civil War.
4. Discuss how General Grant carried out his military strategy.

☐ Write a report.

Discuss: If the border states surrounding Washington, D.C., had seceded, how would this have hurt the Union?

1. The Opening Guns

BEFORE YOU READ: *What were the advantages, disadvantages, and military strategies of the Union and the Confederacy?*

The bombardment of Fort Sumter temporarily united the North. Former foes joined together in support of the Union. Stephen Douglas, for example, paid a call on Lincoln. "There can be no neutrals in this war," said Douglas, "only patriots—and traitors."

Lining Up for Battle

Following Fort Sumter, Abraham Lincoln issued a call for 75,000 volunteer soldiers from the various Northern states. Men rushed to recruiting offices to join the army. They were signed up to serve for 90 days. The government believed that the Southern "rebellion" could be crushed in that amount of time.

Southerners saw Lincoln's call for troops as an act of war. Within two months, the states of the Upper South—Virginia, North Carolina, Tennessee, and Arkansas—left the Union and joined the Confederate States of America. However,

The Union and the Confederacy, 1861

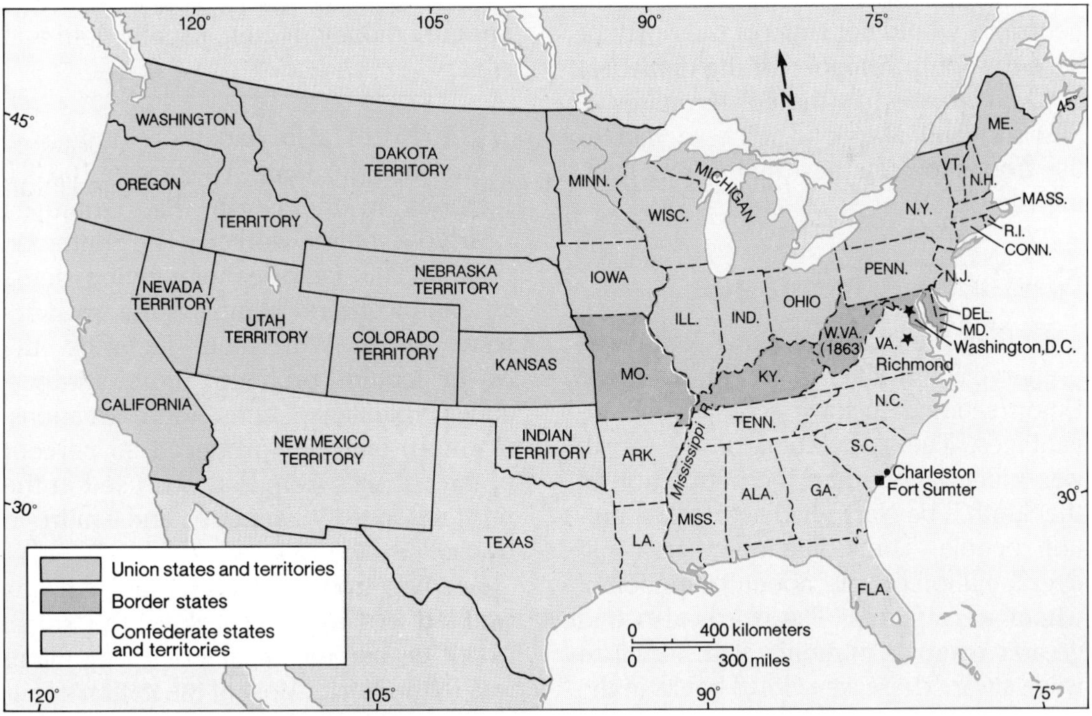

How many states west of the Mississippi River joined the Confederacy? How many states west of the Mississippi remained in the Union?

Background: The governor of Kentucky told Lincoln that his state would furnish no troops "for the wicked purpose of subduing her sister Southern States."

the people of western Virginia and eastern Tennessee sided with the Union. The people of western Virginia formed their own state, West Virginia, and entered the Union in 1863. The eastern region of Tennessee was prevented from joining the Union. Tennessee's Confederate government successfully used force to keep it from breaking away.

Four other slave states that formed the border between the Union and the Confederacy remained in the Union. These states—Delaware, Kentucky, Missouri, and Maryland—came to be called the border states. Delaware, with only 1,800 slaves, fully supported the Union. In fact, on two occasions Delaware's legislature passed statements strongly condemning secession. Kentucky declared that it was neutral. It would not support the North or fight the South. Support for the Confederacy was greatest in the border states of Missouri and Maryland. Lincoln had to use troops to keep these states from leaving the Union.

Northern Advantages

Neither the North nor the South was prepared for a major war. However, the Union seemed to have some major advantages. The population of the North was much larger than the population of the South. The North had nearly 22.5 million people. The Confederacy had just over 9 million people, about 3.6 million of whom were slaves. The North also had greater reserves of money with which to wage a war. There were 1,418 banks in the North but only 224 in the South. Northern banks had greater reserves of **specie**, or gold and silver. They held some $330 million in specie. Southern banks held just $27 million.

Regional Resources in 1861

RESOURCES	NORTH	SOUTH
Population	22,246,000	9,196,800
Railroads (kilometers)	35,100	14,300
Number of Banks	1,418	224
Number of Factories	100,000	18,000
Yearly Value of Manufactures	$1.73 billion	$155 million
Metric Tons of Iron Production	776,563	29,938

specie money in coin, usually gold and silver

The North also had more industrial power than the South. There were 100,000 factories in the North that employed nearly 1.2 million workers. The South had only 18,000 factories employing some 167,000 workers. Many of the workers were slaves. With more factories, the North could produce more clothes, shoes, blankets, tents, and weapons. Northern factories produced 95 percent of the nation's iron. Iron was used in the production of cannons and railroad tracks.

Keeping troops, workers, and citizens well fed was an easier task for the North. About 68 percent of America's farmland was in the North. Most of the nation's railroads were in the North, too. Troops, supplies, and food could be sent along 35,100 kilometers (22,000 miles) of railroad track in the North. The South had only 14,300 kilometers (8,886 miles) of track. The Union had 42 ships available for use in addition to commercial ships owned by Northern merchants. At the outset of the war, the Confederate States of America did not have a navy.

Southern Advantages

The North had the clear advantage in resources, but the South had advantages of its own. For the Confederacy to win the war, it had only to defend itself on its own territory. For the Union to win, it had to conquer the South. The Union would have to invade the South, defeat its armies, conquer its territory, and force its citizens to give up.

A second Southern advantage was the quality of its military leaders. Many of the higher ranking officers in the United States Army were Southerners. When the war started in 1861, most chose to serve the Confederacy. Army officers like Robert E. Lee, J. E. B. Stuart, and Joseph Johnston refused to help the Union army shed Southern blood.

Southerners also anticipated getting support from foreign nations. Foreign textile industries depended heavily on Southern cotton. Southerners predicted that foreign countries, especially Great Britain, needed cotton so badly that they would back the South. To gain foreign support as quickly as possible, the Confederacy cut off all sales of cotton to the world. This was done to force foreign textile factories to shut down. It was hoped that unemployed workers would then demand that their governments aid the Confederacy. With foreign support, the Confederacy would be able to gain its independence.

The Confederacy seemed to have a strong wartime President in Jefferson Davis. Davis had vast military experience. He was trained as a soldier at the U.S. Military Academy at West Point. He was a military hero in the Mexican War. He had served as President Franklin Pierce's secretary of war. In government, Davis had served as the U. S. senator from Mississippi. He seemed to have the background and experience needed to lead the Confederacy to victory.

Abraham Lincoln had almost no military or political experience. He had served for some two months in the Illinois militia during the Black Hawk War, but he saw very little action. In government, he served briefly in Congress and the Illinois state legislature. At the war's beginning, some Northerners—and just about every Southerner—thought that this "backwoods President" from Illinois would never measure up to Jefferson Davis.

Bull Run

By the early summer of 1861, both the North and the South had thousands of volunteer troops. Many were without uniforms. Most were poorly armed and trained. These were amateur armies, full of young men looking for a good fight and a good story to tell their friends, families, and sweethearts. From the beginning, both sides thought one big battle would end the war.

Southern military leaders decided to attack Washington, D. C., to capture the Union capital and end the war quickly. By

Discuss: If foreign countries were not prompted to support the South by the cutoff of cotton sales, how could this policy hurt the South?

Discuss: Why do you think that capturing the enemy capital played such a big part in the early battle plans of both the North and the South?

July 1861, P. G. T. Beauregard had led a Southern army of some 22,000 soldiers toward Washington. They set up camp near the village of Manassas Junction, just south of Washington. They pitched their tents near Bull Run Stream.

Similarly, Northern strategy involved capturing Richmond, Virginia, the new Confederate capital. The first capital at Montgomery, Alabama, had proved to be too small for the Confederate government's needs. The Union general, Irvin McDowell, was ordered to take his 35,000 troops and march southward from Washington. After defeating Beauregard's soldiers, McDowell was supposed to march through Virginia to Richmond. There he was to capture the Confederate capital and bring the war to a close.

In mid-July 1861, McDowell began moving his army slowly toward Manassas. Hundreds of members of Congress, their families, and the curious from Washington tagged along with McDowell's soldiers. They did not want to miss the excitement of the war's single battle.

On July 21, the Union army attacked. At first, the Confederate troops crumbled in disorder. Union troops pressed forward. But on the crest of Henry House Hill, a group of Virginia troops under Thomas J. Jackson refused to retreat further. General Bernard E. Bee told his men to rally behind Jackson, who, he said was standing "like a stone wall." The troops, inspired by "Stonewall" Jackson and aided by fresh Confederate troops, charged ahead.

McDowell's amateur army panicked and began running. They threw down their guns and dashed for the safety of Washington. The people who had come from Washington to watch the battle also fled. As the "Yankees" were driven back, the road from Bull Run was clogged with retreating soldiers, wagons of wounded, and the carriages of civilians.

After their victory at Bull Run—or Manassas, as Southerners called the battle—the Southern army chose not to move against Washington, D.C. Too many Union troops guarded the city. As a result of the battle of Bull Run, each side came to the grim realization that the Civil War would not be ended by one battle.

Section Review

1. What was the military strategy of the Union and the Confederacy at the beginning of the Civil War?
2. List three advantages of the North and three advantages of the South at the start of the Civil War.
3. What important fact did the North and South realize after the battle of Bull Run?
4. Considering the advantages and disadvantages of both sides, which side would have fared better in a short war? A long war? Explain your answers.

Vocabulary Help: During the Civil War, the term "Yankee" was used to refer to a Union soldier or a native or inhabitant of a Northern state. Since the Civil War, the term has become generalized to mean a native or inhabitant of the United States.

Writing a Report

The first step in writing a history report is to choose a topic. An appropriate topic can be chosen by comparing the amount of information available on a particular topic with the desired length of the report. For example, suppose the required length of the report to be written is two to three pages. A topic such as "Civil War Generals" would be too broad in this case because there is just too much information on that topic. Topics that are too narrow, such as "The Color of Civil War Generals' Uniforms," would also be unsatisfactory because there is simply not enough information on that topic. An example of a good topic for such a report would be "Thomas E. 'Stonewall' Jackson in the Civil War."

Once an appropriate topic has been selected, the next step is to locate and record information relevant to the topic. Indexes of reference books and the library's card catalog will be useful in locating materials. When you have found useful information, take notes. Any information to be quoted—such as a passage from a speech—should be copied exactly as it appears. All other information should be expressed in your own words. Copy all the information required to list the source in the report's bibliography.

The key to writing a good report is organization. All information gathered must be organized so that it will be presented in a logical and concise manner. Begin the report with an introductory paragraph that gives the reader some idea of what the report is going to be about. This should be followed by the body of the report, where the main ideas and supporting details are presented and explained. The report should end with a concluding paragraph in which the main ideas are summarized. Sources should be listed in the bibliography, which is the last page of the report.

1. What is the first step in writing a history report? Explain how this would be done.
2. What information should be copied exactly as it appears in a source?
3. Why is organization of information important in writing a good report?
4. What is the purpose of the introductory paragraph in a report?
5. Where should the sources used in preparing a report be listed?

Vocabulary Help: peninsula—a piece of land projecting out into water. Have students locate the peninsula between the York and James rivers.

2. The Tide Shifts

BEFORE YOU READ: *Why did Lincoln issue the Emancipation Proclamation?*

After Bull Run, the North developed a new strategy for winning the war. It was based on a plan proposed by General-in-Chief Winfield Scott. Scott's plan was called the Anaconda Plan, named after the snake that coils around its prey and crushes it to death.

The Anaconda Plan

The Anaconda Plan called for a naval **blockade** of the entire coastline of the Confederacy. This would prevent any ships from coming into or leaving Southern ports. It would block goods like food and weapons from arriving from Europe and cause supply problems for the Confederate army.

---

blockade the isolation of a country at war to prevent the passage and delivery of goods

---

The Anaconda Plan also contained strategies for splitting the South in order to weaken it. One part of the Union army would attempt to gain control of the Mississippi River, cutting the South into eastern and western halves. Another part of the Union army would attempt to capture Richmond, cutting off the northern Confederacy from the southern Confederacy.

As the war continued, a third element was added to the Anaconda Plan. The North would wage a **war of attrition**. The army would not just focus on winning battles but would also try to inflict as many casualties as possible. The North, with a larger population, could easily replace its troops. The less populous South could not.

---

war of attrition a war won by killing as many of the enemy as possible

---

A New Union Commander

Following the humiliating defeat at Bull Run, Lincoln replaced General McDowell with George B. McClellan. McClellan drilled his army in marching, taking battle commands, and firing their weapons. McClellan gave his troops pride and hope.

By the spring of 1862, McClellan had developed a plan to capture Richmond. In April, he sent about 100,000 soldiers and some 300 cannons to a peninsula in Virginia between the York and James rivers. By pushing northwest up this peninsula, the Union army could reach Richmond, the Confederate capital.

Defending the peninsula was a smaller Confederate army of 47,000 troops. It was commanded by Joseph Johnston. McClellan slowly led his troops up the peninsula toward Richmond.

The Union army reached the outskirts of Richmond on May 31. The Confederates lashed out at the Yankees, although the fighting produced no winner. Johnston received a serious wound in the action. General Robert E. Lee was appointed to replace him as commander of the Confederate forces.

Fighting raged for over a month in the area of Richmond. McClellan's caution in battle finally forced the Union troops to fall back toward the James River in July.

For Extra Interest: Remind students that this was the second Battle of Bull Run. Have students compare the two battles at this site in terms of dates, military commanders, and results.

Under the protection of small Union warships called **gunboats**, McClellan's army boarded vessels that returned them to the Potomac River near Washington. The fighting on the peninsula had been more severe than anyone had expected. The Union lost about 15,000 men, while the Confederacy lost some 20,000.

---

gunboat a small warship that is heavily armed and can navigate in shallow river waters

---

Lee Invades the North

While McClellan's troops were sailing back to Washington, Robert E. Lee and Stonewall Jackson marched northward from Richmond. Their troops attacked soldiers under Union General John Pope at Bull Run. In two days of fighting, on August 29 and 30, they completely defeated Pope's men.

Northern morale and Lincoln's popularity declined. The war was costing $2 million a day to fight, and the Union army had achieved nothing. In addition, thousands of Northern men lay dead. Antiwar feeling mounted in the North.

Lee saw how low Northern morale was sinking. He thought that if he acted quickly and boldly, he could end the war. Lee decided to invade the North. On September 4, 1862, Lee's 55,000 troops crossed the Potomac River and entered Maryland.

When the reports reached Washington that Lee was invading the North, McClellan and 85,000 of his troops rushed into Maryland. McClellan did not know the exact location of Lee's troops. But a costly error by one of Lee's messengers led McClellan to Lee. The messenger had dropped Lee's orders and battle plan on the ground. A private in McClellan's army found them wrapped around several cigars. Immediately, McClellan moved to intercept Lee.

The battle at Antietam was the bloodiest day of the Civil War.

The two armies collided on September 17 along Antietam (ann-TEE-tum) Creek, just outside Sharpsburg, Maryland. They battled for 12 hours in the woods and farmland around the creek. The number of casualties on both sides was enormous. Some units of troops were shot down as soon as they began to fight. One group lost 550 men in 10 minutes; another lost 450 troops in 5 minutes.

By nightfall, Union and Confederate casualties totaled 22,719. The tragedy of

Discuss: How do you think the Battle of Antietam affected morale in the North and the South?

Discuss: What effect do you think the Emancipation Proclamation had in the South? Do you think it would strengthen or weaken the South's will to fight? Why?

the battle was that neither side had achieved a victory.

McClellan might have been able to defeat Lee, but he had been too cautious. McClellan was so afraid of losing that he refused to commit his superior forces to the battle. McClellan sent small units into the battle, and they suffered terrible casualties. Soon after, Lincoln removed McClellan from command.

The Emancipation Proclamation

At the beginning of the war, both Congress and Lincoln had stated that the war was being fought to save the Union, not to free the slaves. However, from the beginning of the war, the President came under pressure from some Northerners to free the slaves. Lincoln replied, "My . . . object in this struggle is to save the Union, and is not either to save or destroy Slavery. If I could save the Union without freeing any slave, I would do it; and if I could save it by freeing all the slaves I would do it." Lincoln personally believed that slavery was wrong. But he also knew that many Northerners were not willing to risk their lives to free the slaves.

As the number of battle deaths rose, calls to end the war increased in the North. Lincoln concluded that the only way to weaken the South and bring the war to a quicker end was to attack slavery. Fighting for human freedom would give the Union a moral cause. It might help to keep Great Britain out of the war, too. On May 13, 1861, the British government had announced its neutrality. However, there were members of Parliament who actively supported the South. Lincoln hoped that the British people would not let their government support the South if the war became a fight against slavery. Finally, freed slaves would provide the Union with more troops.

Lincoln told his Cabinet that he planned to free, or emancipate, the slaves. "The moment came," stated the President, "when I felt that slavery must die that the nation might live. . . ." On September 22, 1862, Lincoln made a public declaration that, as of January 1, 1863, "all persons held as slaves within any State or . . . part of a State [in rebellion against the United States] shall be then and . . . forever free." However, Lincoln said he would cancel the Emancipation Proclamation if the South returned to the Union.

The South did not return to the Union. On January 1, 1863, all slaves in the Confederacy were declared free, although virtually no slaves were set free at the time of the proclamation. Only as Union troops captured Confederate territory did emancipation take place. Slaves in Union states were not included in the Emancipation Proclamation for fear that the border states might secede.

As the new year began, the Union army in the East and Lee's army were settled into their winter encampments. The war so far had been a stalemate. Thousands of men had been killed or wounded, but still there was no victor. The war in the West, however, had developed quite differently.

War in the West

The Union army had been victorious in battles fought along the Cumberland, Tennessee, and Mississippi rivers. One

Background: General Burnside, McClellan's replacement, ordered an attack on Lee's Confederate forces near Fredericksburg, Virginia, in December 1862. In this battle, Union casualties totaled 12,653, while Lee lost a little over 5,000 men.

Background: In February 1862, Grant and his troops defeated the Confederates at Fort Henry and Fort Donelson in Tennessee.

part of the Anaconda Plan was working. The Union victories were due, for the most part, to the leadership of Ulysses S. Grant.

Grant was trained at West Point and had served in the Mexican War. He spent six years as a civilian before reentering the U.S. Army as a colonel. Early in 1862, he was made a major-general. Grant had many qualities that made him an excellent general. He was a brave and determined leader who let nothing stand in the way of his goals. Even after experiencing defeat, Grant refused to back off. Grant had the remarkable ability to discover his enemy's weakest position.

By the end of February 1862, Grant and his troops had pushed as far south as Nashville, Tennessee. Mississippi, which lay to the south of Tennessee, was now open to Union attack. Blocking Grant's advance was Albert Sidney Johnston, one of the finest Confederate generals. Grant's army forced the Confederates back to Corinth, Mississippi. In early April 1862, Johnston counterattacked. Grant's men were driven back in vicious fighting.

Rather than retreat, Grant ordered a counterattack. In the bloodiest day of fighting in the West, the two armies battled for ten hours before the Confederates withdrew to their base at Corinth. At the battle of Pittsburg Landing—or Shiloh, as the Northerners called it—Grant lost 13,047 men. The Confederates lost 10,694 men, including General Albert Sidney Johnston.

Northerners were shocked by the large number of casualties. They demanded that Lincoln remove Grant from command. The President replied, "I can't spare this man—he fights!"

The War in the West, 1862–1863

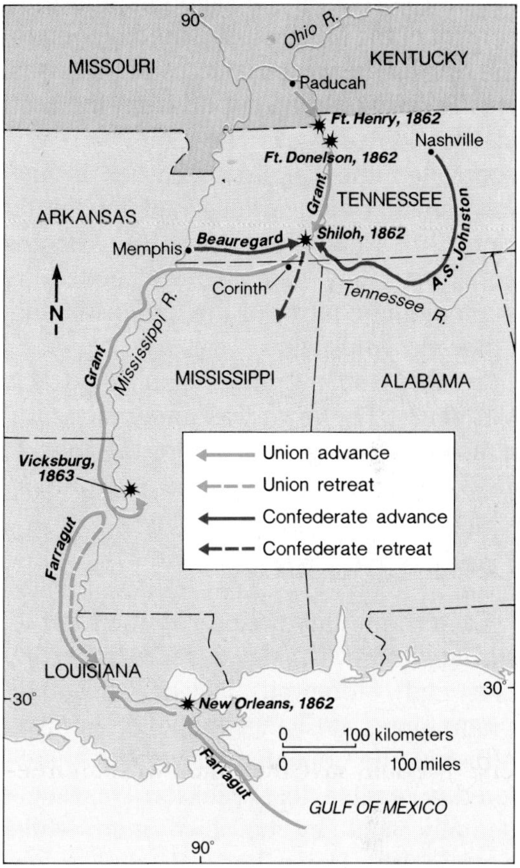

How far did Grant and his troops travel in their march from Shiloh to Vicksburg?

The Union armies continued to advance. Soon Corinth fell, as did Memphis, Tennessee. Then, on April 25, a Union naval fleet, commanded by Admiral David G. Farragut, destroyed most of the Confederate fleet guarding New Orleans and captured the South's largest city.

Tennessee and the northern Mississippi River were now in Union hands, as were New Orleans and the southern end of the Mississippi. Vicksburg, Mississippi,

Background: In the Confederate counterattack, Johnson's forces attacked shortly before six o'clock on Sunday morning, April 6. The Union troops, busy frying bacon and boiling coffee, were taken by surprise.

Background: By moving the war to the North and threatening Washington, perhaps even taking some major Union city like Philadelphia, Lee hoped to shatter Northern morale and force a negotiated peace.

was the last great Confederate fortress left on the river. If the Union captured it, control of the Mississippi would belong to the North. The western states of Arkansas and Texas would be cut off from the rest of the Confederacy. The Union already controlled the Far West. Earlier in the war, small Union armies had fought to victory in New Mexico and the Arizona Territory. They had also succeeded in maintaining control of the California and Colorado gold fields.

In May 1863, Grant began to attack Vicksburg. The town was under siege for almost two months. Finally, on July 4, 1863, Vicksburg surrendered to Grant.

Lee's Bold Move

Eastern military action resumed in the spring of 1863. On May 2, 1863, Robert E. Lee and Stonewall Jackson defeated Union forces at Chancellorsville, Virginia. Although the Confederates won, they suffered a terrible loss. Jackson was accidentally shot by his own men while scouting the Union lines. He died a few days later. Lee had lost one of his ablest generals.

Later in May, the Confederate cabinet and leading generals met to develop a strategy that they hoped would bring victory. Robert E. Lee proposed another invasion of the North. He pointed out that Northern morale was very low. The British House of Commons, aware of Lee's victories, was again discussing a proposal to acknowledge Southern independence. A Southern victory might convince the British to support the Confederacy. The Confederate leaders approved Lee's plan for an invasion.

The War in the East, 1861–1863

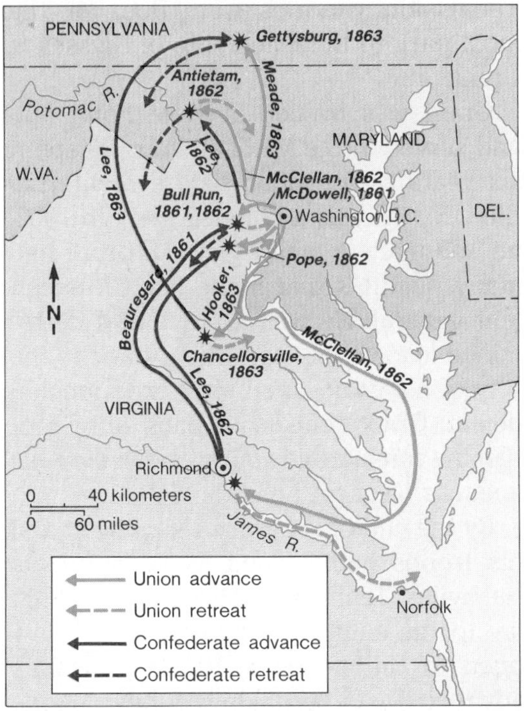

Which battles of the Civil War were fought on Northern territory?

Lee marched northward from Virginia with an army of 76,000 men. On June 15, 1863, Lee's army crossed the Potomac River and headed into Pennsylvania.

The Battle of Gettysburg

News of the Confederate plan for invasion did not cause Northern morale to sink further. It had the opposite effect. Northerners became angry and determined to defend their soil.

General George Meade now commanded the Union army in the East. He moved his forces into position to stop Lee. His army of 80,000 men met Lee's

Background: Burnside was replaced by Joseph Hooker following the Union defeat at Fredericksburg. Five months later, Hooker's army was defeated at Chancellorsville, and Lincoln replaced Hooker with Meade.

Vocabulary Help: flank—the right or left side of a formation or force. What would be the advantage of making a flank attack?

advancing army at the little town of Gettysburg. Between July 1 and July 3, a battle raged in and around the town.

On the first day of the battle, Meade's troops were pushed back through Gettysburg. They finally took up a position on a series of hills, called Cemetery Ridge, just to the south of the town.

On the second day, Lee sent troops to attack the right and left flanks of the Union line. The fighting lasted all day. By dusk, Meade's army still held its ground.

On the third day, after bombarding Union troops for nearly one hour, General Lee ordered his army to charge the center of the Union troops on Cemetery Ridge. The Confederates reached the Union troops but were thrown back. The charge had failed.

The Confederate troops returned to the woods. Some 7,000 Confederates had died during the charge. The battle of Gettysburg was over. It was the bloodiest battle of the Civil War. In the three days of fighting, the two armies suffered more than 51,000 casualties. Lee had lost roughly 28,000 men. Meade had lost some 23,000.

Lee and his troops retreated into Virginia. Lee's invasion of the North had begun with great hopes and had ended in disaster. The Confederate losses at Vicksburg and Gettysburg in early July crushed the South's hopes, especially for assistance from Great Britain.

During Pickett's Charge, Confederate General Lewis Armistead led a brigade that accomplished the farthest penetration of the Union lines. Armistead was mortally wounded in the battle. He is shown on a horse to the right of three Confederate flags.

Discuss: Why do you think the battles of Vicksburg and Gettysburg can be considered turning points in the Civil War?

Vocabulary Help: score—a group of twenty. Have students calculate in scores how many years ago from the current date the Declaration of Independence was written.

Lincoln at Gettysburg

In November 1863, four months after the battle of Gettysburg, a group of Northerners came to Gettysburg to dedicate a national cemetery for the soldiers slain there. Edward Everett, the nation's most famous speaker, was to give a talk. President Abraham Lincoln was also invited to say a few words.

Everett spoke for two hours, Lincoln for only 2 minutes. But Lincoln's words had a greater impact. Lincoln spoke of the sacrifices made at Gettysburg to preserve freedom and democracy:

> Fourscore and seven [87] years ago our fathers brought forth on this continent, a new nation, conceived in liberty, and dedicated to the proposition that all men are created equal.
>
> Now we are engaged in a great civil war, testing whether that nation or any nation so conceived and so dedicated, can long endure. We are met [meeting] on a great battlefield of that war. We have come to dedicate a portion of that field, as a final resting place for those who here gave their lives that that nation might live. It is altogether fitting and proper that we should do this.
>
> But, in a larger sense, we can not dedicate—we can not consecrate—we can not hallow this ground. The brave men, living and dead, who struggled here, have consecrated it, far above our poor power to add or detract. The world will little note, nor long remember what we say here, but it can never forget what they did here. It is for us the living, rather, to be dedicated here to the unfinished work which they who fought here have thus far so nobly advanced. It is rather for us to be here dedicated to the great task remaining before us—that from these honored dead we take increased devotion to that cause for which they gave the last full measure of devotion—that we here highly resolve that these dead shall not have died in vain—that this nation, under God, shall have a new birth of freedom—and that government of the people, by the people, for the people, shall not perish from the earth.

The President returned to Washington by train that evening. Lincoln knew that the terrible slaughter of the nation's young men was not yet over.

Section Review

1. Why did Abraham Lincoln issue the Emancipation Proclamation?
2. What was the Anaconda Plan's strategy for winning the war?
3. What was the outcome of the battle of Gettysburg?
4. What role did General Grant play in securing the West for the Union?
5. Why do you think the British did not clearly favor and support one side during the Civil War?

For Extra Interest: Have students write a paragraph summarizing the main points of Lincoln's Gettysburg Address.

Background: In between the fighting, soldiers often called to each other across the battle lines. Sometimes at night, the soldiers from each side would sneak away to a prearranged spot. There they would exchange stories, chat about life in the army, and swap scarce items.

3. Behind the Battle Lines

BEFORE YOU READ: *What was life like for Union and Confederate soldiers during the Civil War?*

When Confederate and Union soldiers went off to war, very few had any idea of what war really was like. Many of the soldiers were young and inexperienced. They dreamed of heroic acts and victorious battles but faced a much harsher, grimmer reality.

A Soldier's Life

After a soldier had enlisted in the army, he received training in standing at attention, carrying weapons correctly, and marching in formation. Both the Union and Confederate armies distributed single shot rifles to the soldiers. These rifles, called muzzle-loaders, were loaded from the front. The muzzle-loaders were not very accurate, and most troops did not get a great deal of target practice. In fact, some soldiers entered battles without ever having once fired their rifles.

During battles, Northern and Southern soldiers fought each other ferociously. When soldiers were not fighting or marching, they washed clothes, cleaned their weapons, played cards, or wrote letters home. Soldiers especially enjoyed sitting around camp fires at night, singing songs. Food usually consisted of coffee, bacon, and bread baked very hard, called "hardtack."

Casualties were very high in the Civil War. Both the Union and Confederate governments tried to provide good medical care. But little was known at this time about the importance of maintaining sanitary conditions in hospitals. Wounds often became infected, and many soldiers died. Amputations frequently had to be performed to prevent the spread of infection. Diseases like typhoid, dysentery, and pneumonia were frequently contracted and killed thousands of soldiers. No one knew what caused them or how to prevent them.

A Confederate soldier reading a letter from home

The Draft

At the beginning of the Civil War, men rushed to recruiting offices to enlist in the army. By 1862, it became clear that

Background: In the South, "Dixie," written by Dan Emmett, a Northerner, was given new lyrics and became the leading Confederate song. The foremost war song in the North was Julia Ward Howe's "Battle Hymn of the Republic."

Background: In addition to allowing for substitutes, anyone who supervised 20 or more slaves was exempt from military service in the South. The Union draft law allowed a man to avoid service by giving the government $300.

the war would be neither short nor glorious. Men came to know the horrors of war firsthand. The number of volunteers began to dwindle, and the number of desertions increased. In April 1862, the Confederate government enacted the first **draft** law in the nation's history. Men between 18 and 35 years of age were eligible for military service. The draft caused great bitterness. The South had seceded in part because the federal government was becoming too strong. Now the South's own government seemed to be exercising too much authority.

draft the selection of individuals for required military service

The following year, the North also began drafting soldiers. As of March 1863, all males between the ages of 20 and 45 were eligible to serve in the army. In both the North and the South, drafted men had the option of hiring substitutes to serve for them.

Northerners were as bitter as Southerners about the draft. Many Northerners believed that the draft was not in the spirit of the American tradition of freedom. Riots broke out in several Northern cities. The worst riot took place in New York City. Buildings were burned and property was destroyed as bands of youths took to the city's streets. Order was restored only after the draft was temporarily suspended in New York City.

Blacks and the War

Most Northern blacks supported the Union during the Civil War. Many felt that if they fought in the army and helped the

During the Civil War, there were 160 black regiments fighting for the North. Battery "A" of the 2nd U. S. Colored Artillery is pictured here.

Background: Before the Emancipation Proclamation, slaves who fled from their masters to the camps of the Union army were put to work as teamsters, cooks, nurses, carpenters, scouts, and day laborers. Nearly 200,000 escaped slaves performed labor for the Union army.

Background: Black regiments that served in the Northern armies were always led by white officers.

Union win, the government would grant them more rights when the war was over.

When the war first began, the government refused to allow the army to accept blacks who wanted to enlist. Racial prejudice was very strong in the North. Many white Northerners refused to serve with blacks. But by the summer of 1862, the situation had changed. Fewer white Northerners were enlisting. Many white Northerners came to believe that blacks should share the burden of dying for the Union. The government decided to permit blacks to join the army. These black troops fought bravely, even though the army treated them as second-class soldiers. By the end of the war, more than 186,000 black soldiers had served in the army.

The U.S. Navy welcomed black volunteers because it badly needed sailors. Black sailors performed the same jobs as white sailors. However, black sailors received less pay. In addition, black sailors were forced to live in separate quarters aboard ship.

One of the most famous black sailors of the war was Robert Smalls. Smalls was a South Carolina slave who escaped from the South in 1862 by seizing the Confederate ship *Planter*. Smalls turned the ship over to the U.S. Navy and served in the Navy until the end of the war.

The Indians and the War

Five Indian tribes took a direct part in the Civil War. They were the Choctaws, Chickasaws, Creeks, Seminoles, and Cherokees of present-day Oklahoma.

In 1861, the Confederate government sent Albert Pike to talk with these tribes. Pike convinced the Indians to side with the Confederacy. He promised that the South would help them protect their land against the United States. Pike assured them they could keep their land forever. He also said they could keep their black slaves. In return, he asked that the Indians assist the South. Pike and each of the five tribes signed a treaty.

Indians fought with the Confederate army at the battle of Pea Ridge in Arkansas. A Cherokee named Stand Watie became a general in the Confederate army. He led a group called the Cherokee Mounted Rifles. Watie was the last Confederate general to surrender when the Civil War ended.

Not all tribal members wanted to support the South. The Choctaws and Chickasaws were united in their support of the South. But the Creeks, Seminoles, and Cherokees were divided. In November 1861, civil war broke out within these three tribes. The conflict brought death and destruction to these people and their homelands.

Women and the War

The Civil War opened up new opportunities for women. In the North, many factories hired women to replace the men who were off fighting the war. During the war, women made up about a third of the work force. In the South, women took over the running of farms, plantations, and businesses.

In both the North and the South, the most vital role for women was in the field of nursing. Many thousands of women served as nurses in army hospitals. In the South, Phoebe Levy Pember operated a

Background: A bill was introduced in the Confederate senate in 1865 providing for the enlistment of 200,000 blacks and their emancipation if they remained loyal throughout the war. On March 13, 1865, the bill was signed by President Davis.

EUREKA!

Carpet Sweeper

In the nineteenth century, the task of keeping a house clean was more difficult than it is today. The broom was the height of tidiness technology in 1800. It was fairly easy to tackle a dusty floor with a broom. But cleaning rugs and carpets required more work. Rugs were hauled outside, where they were hung and cleaned with a rug beater. It was hard work and raised clouds of dust that made the job a nasty one. Fine carpets called for more delicate treatment. The cleaner got down on hands and knees and brushed the soil away by hand. It is no wonder that when the carpet sweeper was introduced in 1876, it was an instant and overwhelming success.

The carpet sweeper came into being because Melville Bissell was allergic to dust. Bissell ran a china shop in Grand Rapids, Michigan. The merchandise in his store came packed in dusty straw. The straw gave Bissell terrible headaches. During a slow period in his business, Bissell invented a machine that would keep his shop dust-free.

Bissell's sweeper, invented in 1873, was a simple and practical device. Spiral brushes stirred up the dust and swept it into an attached box. A knob allowed the brushes to be adjusted to handle either hard floors or deep rugs.

Bissell patented his invention in 1876 and began manufacturing sweepers. At first, it was a very small business. The parts were made by women who worked out of their homes. Then Bissell and his wife would assemble them. But the sweepers were soon in great demand. Bissell's cottage industry grew into an international business.

huge hospital in Richmond, Virginia. Sally L. Tompkins ran a military hospital in Richmond. She was made a captain by President Davis and became the only woman officer in the Confederate army.

In the North, Dorothea Dix organized a volunteer nursing corps. In June 1861, she was appointed superintendent of female nurses by the Union government. Another Northerner, Clara Barton, started a soldiers' aid society. She and her volunteers performed nursing services and took medical supplies from one Union hospital to another. Many of the hospitals were

Background: By the end of the war, at least 3,200 women in both the North and the South had served as nurses.

Background: After the war, Clara Barton set up an office to find information on thousands of soldiers listed as missing in action. In 1881, Barton founded the American Red Cross Society. She served as its president until 1904.

near battlefields. It took great courage and dedication to go to these areas.

Women like Dix and Barton played an important rule in advancing the nursing profession. Several nursing schools were founded during or soon after the Civil War.

Southern Society at War

Southerners went to war to protect their way of life. But the war itself caused great changes in the South.

Throughout the war, Jefferson Davis and his administration steadily increased the size and power of the Confederate government. The Confederate government regulated industry, directed the economy, and controlled the railroads. It instituted a military draft, increased taxes, and took by force any supplies the army needed. Southerners were alarmed and embittered by this increase in the national government's authority. They wanted their nation to have a weak national government. Great hostility arose against the Confederate government.

The Civil War also changed the South into an industrializing society. Before the war, Southerners looked down on the North because of its factory system. They called Northern workers "slaves without masters." But the war created a need for the products of industry. The Confederate government built up a large factory system in the South to produce shoes, clothing, weapons, and many other vital items. Many Southerners became factory workers.

But the greatest change that the war produced was in many Southerners' views regarding slavery. The Confederacy had gone to war to preserve the right to own slaves. Thousands of Southerners had died to protect this right. However, by March 1865, winning independence came to mean more to some Southerners than slavery. President Davis was willing to free slaves and have them fight as soldiers so that the South could gain its independence. Although the Confederate congress disapproved, Davis put this into effect by executive order. The South of 1861 had largely vanished by 1865.

Section Review

1. What was life like for Union and Confederate soldiers during the Civil War?
2. What changed the Union government's attitude toward black participation in the Civil War?
3. What important contributions did women make to the Civil War?
4. The promises that the Confederate government made to the Indians were similar to promises the United States government had made in the past and broken. Why do you think the Indians would trust the South to fulfill these promises?

Discuss: Many Southerners favored states' rights. What does this mean?

Background: Grant's objective was to attack the South without mercy. He ordered William T. Sherman, the new commander of the Union army in the west, to "get into the interior of the enemy's country as far as you can, inflicting all the damage you can . . . ."

4. The Road to Appomattox

BEFORE YOU READ: *What role did General Grant play in bringing the Civil War to an end?*

By 1864, the South had been severely weakened by the war. It had suffered two major defeats in July 1863 at Vicksburg and at Gettysburg. The Union naval blockade of the South took its toll, too. European goods such as clothing, food, weapons, and railroad equipment could not get through. Southern industry could not provide all that was needed. The people and the Confederate army began to suffer terribly from the shortage of goods.

By 1864, Southern morale had sunk to its lowest point yet. Fewer men joined the army. The draft grew more unpopular. Thousands deserted from the Confederate army.

Grant in Command

General Grant was given command of all Union armies in the West following his victory at Vicksburg. In late November 1863, Grant won a spectacular victory at Chattanooga, Tennessee, forcing the Confederates into a full-scale retreat. Confederate control of lands west of the Appalachian Mountains had been virtually destroyed. In March 1864, Abraham Lincoln made Grant commander of all the Union armies.

Grant's army headed into Virginia in May 1864. On May 5, Grant's and Lee's troops clashed in the dark woods of the Wilderness, an area of thick forests and dense undergrowth west of Fredericksburg. In two days of fighting, Grant suffered 17,666 casualties. Lee lost nearly 11,400 men.

Northerners were horrified by the casualties. But Grant pushed on after Lee. Just to the south of the Wilderness, Grant lost about 18,000 men at Spotsylvania. Early in June, Grant attacked Lee at Cold Harbor, near Richmond. Grant then tried to take the Confederate capital. Lee blocked his path at Petersburg. For the next ten months, until April 1865, the two armies battled there.

The Election of 1864

Antiwar sentiment grew in the North as Union casualties mounted. Between May and June 1864, Grant's army lost some 55,000 men. As the newspapers listed the names of the men wounded or killed, the horror of the war came home to people as never before. Many people began to feel that the price of keeping the South in the Union was too high. Some even suggested that the South should be set free.

Ending the war became the main issue in the presidential election of 1864. The Democrats nominated George B. McClellan, the former Union general, for President. The Democratic platform denounced the war. The Democrats pledged that if they won the election, they would call a halt to the hostilities. The Democrats promised to meet with the South for the purpose of restoring the Union. McClellan, however, rejected the Democratic platform. The Democrats hoped to win the votes of people who were weary of the war.

The Republicans again selected Lin-

Background: Andrew Johnson was chosen as Lincoln's running mate in 1864. Johnson was a Democrat and a Southerner. Some Republicans did not trust him. But he was loyal to the Union. He was the only Southern senator who did not give up his seat when the South seceded in 1861.

Background: One woman described the destruction left by Sherman's army this way: "The fields were trampled down and the road was lined with carcasses of [animals] that the invaders . . . had wantonly shot down to starve our people and prevent them from making their crops . . . ."

coln as their candidate. Lincoln's chances of reelection were uncertain. He was blamed for failing to achieve victory over the South. The high number of casualties was blamed on him also.

Two important Northern victories in August and September of 1864 turned the campaign in Lincoln's favor. First, Admiral Farragut captured Mobile, Alabama. This was the last Confederate stronghold on the Gulf of Mexico. Next, news arrived that General William Tecumseh Sherman had taken Atlanta.

The fall of Atlanta changed the course of the war. It gave a tremendous boost to Northern spirits. People began to believe that the Union could win the war. For the Confederacy, it meant the loss of a valuable railroad and industrial center.

The Union victories assured the reelection of Lincoln. The Republicans also remained in control of Congress. There was little doubt that the North would fight the war to a successful end. In March 1865, Lincoln was inaugurated for his second term as President. In his second inaugural address, Lincoln spoke of the task that lay ahead for the Union: "With malice toward none; with charity for all . . . . Let us strive to finish the work we are in; to bind up the nation's wounds; . . . to do all which may achieve and cherish a just and lasting peace."

The War in Virginia, 1864–1865

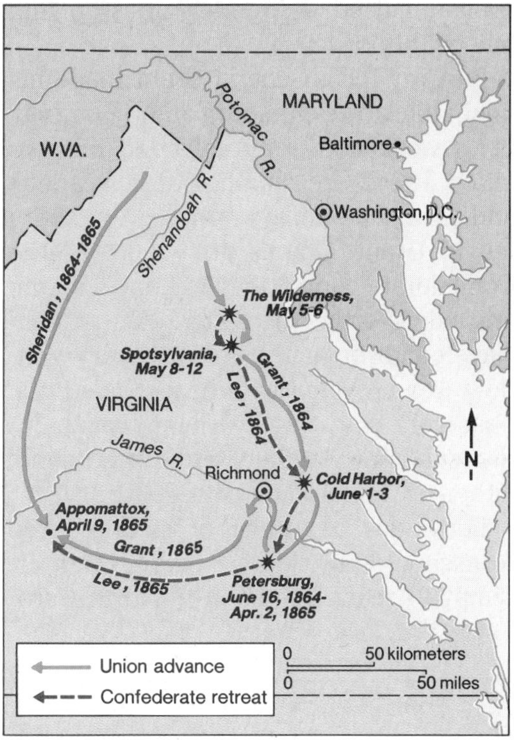

In what direction did Lee's army attempt to escape from Petersburg?

The Confederacy Collapses

On November 15, 1864, General Sherman began a march across Georgia to the Atlantic Ocean. His objective was to make Georgia "an example to rebels" by burning buildings, train depots, and crops. As they headed for the coast, Sherman's army left a path of destruction 65 to 100 kilometers (40 to 60 miles) wide. Sherman's **scorched earth policy** was having its desired effect. Sherman reached Savannah in mid-December. He presented it to President Lincoln as a "Christmas gift."

scorched earth policy a military tactic of burning and destroying everything in an area

From Savannah, Sherman's troops pushed northward through South Carolina. They left the state capital, Columbia, in ashes. Sherman then headed into North

Discuss: Do you think it was necessary for Sherman to follow a scorched earth policy in Georgia? Why or why not? How do you think this policy affected Southerners? Explain your answer.

Background: Word spread quickly through Richmond that the Yankees had broken through Lee's defenses at Petersburg and were on their way. Jefferson Davis left a church service he was attending, collected his papers, and fled Richmond.

Carolina. Confederate General Joseph Johnston tried desperately to stop him but could not.

In April 1865, General Grant made his final attack on Petersburg and Richmond. Lee's weakened army defended the two cities. They were running out of weapons and food. On Sunday, April 2, Petersburg fell to Grant. Grant's army entered the Confederate capital the next day. Lincoln arrived shortly thereafter. As Lincoln traveled through the town, "every window was crowded with heads," said one observer. "But it was a silent crowd, . . . thousands of watchers without a sound, either of welcome or hatred."

Lee and what was left of his army tried to escape. They fled westward, in an attempt to reach Johnston in North Carolina. Lee hoped that he and Johnston would be able to hold off the Union army. But Grant's men pursued Lee. Union General Philip Sheridan's cavalry swept down from the north. Lee was trapped.

On April 7, Grant wrote to Lee, "General, the result of the last week must convince you of the hopelessness of further resistance." Unwilling to risk any more of the lives of his faithful but now small army, Lee asked to surrender.

At approximately 2 P.M. on April 9, Lee and Grant met. The location was the parlor of Wilmer McLean's farmhouse at Appomattox Courthouse, Virginia. The surrender terms offered by Grant were generous. Lee's army had to lay down its weapons, although officers could keep their side arms. Grant permitted every

Members of Lee's army roll up the Confederate flag after the surrender at Appomattox Courthouse.

For Extra Interest: Have interested students do research and report on Robert E. Lee's home, Arlington House, and the beginnings of Arlington National Cemetery in Virginia.

Background: In 1865, President Lincoln, at his last Cabinet meeting, approved creation of the Secret Service in the Treasury Department to fight counterfeiters. The Secret Service was not assigned the function of protecting Presidents until 1901.

Confederate soldier to return home. He would not make them prisoners of war. He also allowed them to take their horses and mules with them "to put in a crop . . . for spring plowing." Lee accepted the terms and thanked General Grant for his generosity.

Lee left the McLean house, bid farewell to his troops, and rode back to Richmond. Grant later said he felt "sad and depressed" at the "downfall of a foe who had fought so long and valiantly."

The news of Lee's surrender was telegraphed throughout the nation. People rejoiced. Soon after, the rest of the Confederate generals surrendered. The Civil War had ended.

The Assassination of Lincoln

Joy over the Northern victory turned to grief less than one week after Appomattox. On the evening of April 14, President Lincoln and his wife Mary went to the theater. The couple took their seats in the presidential box at Ford's Theatre. During the third act, the door of the presidential box silently opened. In stepped John Wilkes Booth, an actor and Confederate sympathizer. He raised a small pistol to the back of Lincoln's head and fired. Mary Lincoln grabbed her husband as he fell. Booth jumped down to the stage and escaped. Lincoln was carried across the street to a boarding house. Early the next morning, Abraham Lincoln died without regaining consciousness.

Lincoln's assassination was part of a larger plot. Several high government officials were targets for assassination that night, including General Grant. But none of the other attempts was successful. Booth was trapped soon afterward in a barn in Virginia. He was shot and killed during the attempt to capture him. Lincoln's body was taken by train to Springfield, Illinois, where he was buried.

The North was torn by grief. Quickly, grief turned to anger. Abraham Lincoln had wanted to treat the defeated South with kindness. It was unlikely that it would now receive such treatment.

Section Review

1. What role did General Grant play in bringing the Civil War to an end?
2. What factors had weakened the Confederacy by 1864?
3. What caused Northern attitudes toward Lincoln's reelection to change in the fall of 1864?
4. What were General Grant's surrender terms at Appomattox?
5. Should armies use the scorched earth policy as a military tactic? Why or why not?

For Extra Interest: Have interested students research and report to the class on John Wilkes Booth and the assassination.

CHAPTER REVIEW

Summary

Both the North and the South entered the Civil War with certain advantages and disadvantages. Both sides also expected the war to be over after one decisive battle. The realization that it would be a long war, however, soon became apparent.

Union forces in the East failed to win a significant victory by 1862. In an attempt to weaken the Confederacy, Lincoln issued the Emancipation Proclamation. Union forces in the West, however, won a series of important battles. By 1863, they controlled the Mississippi River. In that same year, the Union army won its first major victory in the East at Gettysburg.

Both sides suffered heavy casualties in the war. Thousands of soldiers died in battle or from wounds received in battle. Mobile and Atlanta fell to advancing Union armies in 1864. In 1865, General Grant's army captured Richmond, and the Confederacy collapsed. Less than a week later, Northern joy turned to grief over the assassination of President Lincoln.

Recalling the Facts

1. How did the slave states in the Upper South respond to Lincoln's call for volunteer soldiers following the attack on Fort Sumter?
2. Why did Lincoln remove Generals McDowell and McClellan from command?
3. Explain why it became necessary for both the North and the South to begin drafting men into their armies. For what reasons were Northerners and Southerners opposed to the draft?
4. How and why did Northern attitudes toward allowing blacks to serve in the Union army change in 1862?
5. Describe the events that led to Lee's surrender at Appomattox Courthouse. On what date did Lee surrender?

Analyzing the Facts

1. Why would greater reserves of specie be an advantage in fighting a war?
2. What evidence is there to support the idea that Lincoln was less concerned with freeing the slaves for moral reasons than he was

with freeing them to help the Union win the war?

3. Why do you think the Republicans chose Andrew Johnson, a Southerner and a Democrat, as Lincoln's running mate in 1864?
4. During the Civil War, President Lincoln's popularity rose and fell according to the course of the war. In what way is the President responsible for military victories or defeats?

Time and History

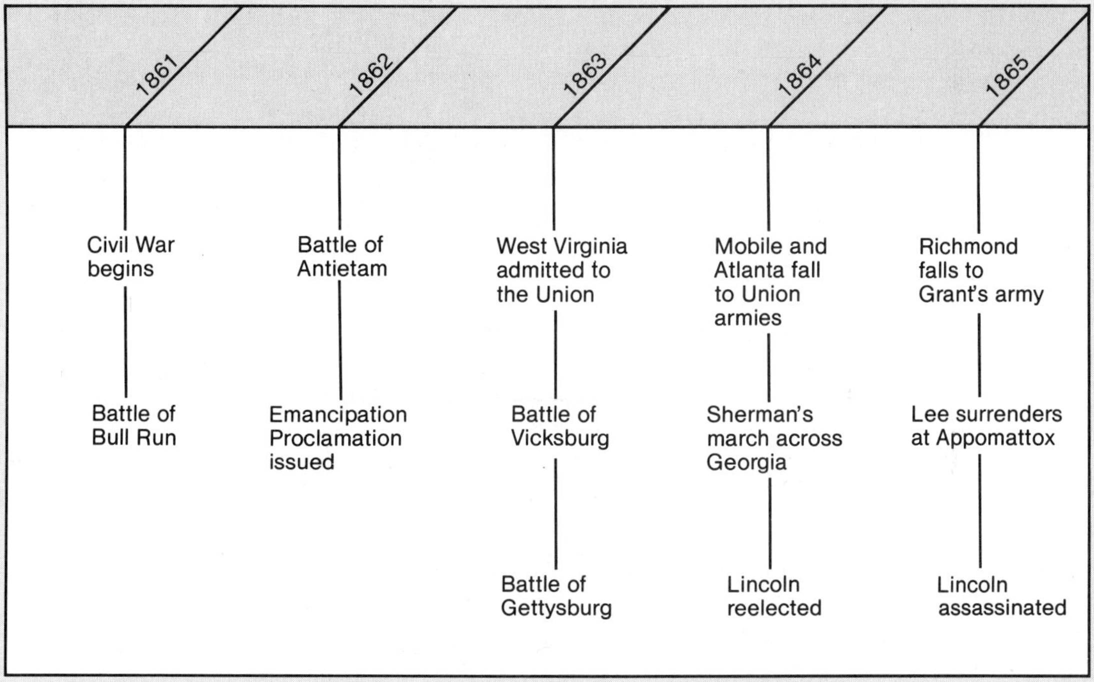

1. Following the fall of Fort Sumter in 1861, what was the first battle of the Civil War?
2. How long did the Civil War last?
3. Put the following battles in the order in which they occurred: Gettysburg, Antietam, Atlanta.
4. What was the last large Southern city to fall to Grant's army?
5. What new state was admitted to the Union during the Civil War? In what year was it admitted?

BEFORE THE WAR AND SINCE THE WAR.
SLAVERY
FREEDOM

Chapter 17 The Problems of Peace

When the Civil War ended in 1865, Northerners and Southerners had to forget past differences and learn to live as one nation again. But the years right after the war were filled with bitter feelings and severe problems. The fate of some 4 million former slaves also had to be addressed. "[The freed slave] had neither money, property, nor friends. He was free from the old plantation, but he had nothing but the dusty road under his feet," declared Frederick Douglass. "He was free from the old quarter that once gave him shelter, but a slave to the rains of summer and the frosts of winter. He was turned loose, naked, hungry, and destitute to the open sky." The problems of peace turned out to be almost as difficult for the nation as the war itself had been.

After you read this chapter, you will be able to:

1. Describe conditions in the South after the Civil War.
2. Explain the differences between the presidential and congressional plans for reuniting the nation.
3. Describe the effects of congressional Reconstruction on the South and Southern blacks.

Background: The Civil War also affected the way in which Americans regarded women and blacks. Women gained great respect for their efforts during the war years. Millions of black people were now freed from slavery.

1. After the Civil War

BEFORE YOU READ: *What were conditions like in the South after the Civil War?*

The Civil War had long-lasting effects on American politics. In the North, the Democratic party came to be viewed as the party that caused the Civil War. The Republican party, on the other hand, was viewed as the party that saved the Union. Until nearly 1900, Republicans waved the "bloody shirt" at each election. The bloody shirt was a symbol to Northern voters of the hundreds of thousands of men who died fighting the "Democratic rebels."

"Age of Hate"

In terms of money spent, the Civil War had been extremely costly. The Union and the Confederate governments had spent billions of dollars to fight the war. A high price was also paid in human lives and suffering. Some 618,000 lives were lost in the conflict. About 4 out of every 100 white Southerners died during the war. More than one out of every 100 Northerners had died. More Americans died during the Civil War than in any other war.

The years immediately following the Civil War have been called the "Age of Hate." The hostility between the North and the South did not die easily. Many Southerners resented being a part of the United States again. Many Northerners blamed the South for causing the Civil War.

In spite of the resentment and hate, the Union did not treat the former Confederates harshly. A small number of Confederate leaders were sent to jail. Their sentences were short. Only President Jefferson Davis was sentenced to a jail term as long as two years. Only one Southern soldier was executed for **war crimes**, or violations of the accepted rules of war. He was Major Henry Wirz. Major Wirz was the commander of the Andersonville prison camp in Georgia. Conditions were so horrible in the prison that nearly 13,000 Union prisoners of war died of hunger or disease.

---

war crime any action during a time of war that violates the accepted rules of war or the assumed standards of humane behavior

---

The South in 1865

Nearly all of the battles of the Civil War had been fought in the South. In 1865, much of the South was in ruins. Richmond, Atlanta, Mobile, and other major cities had been burned to the ground. Most railroad tracks were torn up. Factories were demolished. Farm fields were overgrown with weeds from lack of use. The Southern economy was **bankrupt**, or unable to pay off its war debts. In addition, the Thirteenth Amendment, which abolished slavery, stripped Southerners of some $2.2 billion in slave property. It took decades for the South to recover from the devastation of the war.

---

bankrupt without money or unable to pay off debts

Many of the returning Confederate soldiers were in poor physical condition. Most had eaten poorly during the final

Discuss: The North could have found all Confederate soldiers and their leaders guilty of treason and punished them accordingly. Could the Confederacy have done the same if the South had won the war? Why or why not?

Background: The national government did not help in the task of rebuilding the South, and the resources of the Southern states were inadequate. For example, one fifth of Mississippi's revenue in 1866 was needed to provide artificial limbs for former soldiers.

Richmond, Virginia, was in ruins at the end of the Civil War. Before evacuating the city on April 3, 1865, Confederate troops were ordered to burn any supplies that might fall into enemy hands. Explosions and fire consumed the city as arsenals and armories were blown up.

years of the war. Malnutrition was common. Many were now handicapped, having lost arms, legs, eyes, or hearing. Others suffered from mental and emotional problems caused by the fighting.

Confederate soldiers were shocked and saddened to see how bad conditions were when they returned home. Many homes were burned to the ground. The land was ruined. The returning soldiers wondered how they could ever rebuild their lives and their homeland.

The biggest adjustment that white Southerners had to make was to black freedom. Habits, beliefs, and behavior that had developed over more than 200 years had to be changed.

The Freed Blacks

Times were even harder and more uncertain for the South's black population. Most blacks were penniless and homeless when they were freed. Most could not read or write. Many were unfamiliar with the legal rights they had. They also faced widespread white hostility.

The federal government offered some aid to freed blacks in March 1865 when Congress created the Freedmen's Bureau. "Freedmen" was the term used for all former slaves—men, women, and children. The bureau's primary job was to provide aid to former slaves, although it assisted any Southerner who needed

Discuss: What problems do you think returning Union soldiers faced? Do you think their problems were as great as those facing Confederate veterans? Why or why not?

Famous Americans

CHARLOTTE FORTEN GRIMKÉ

Charlotte Forten was an educator and writer. She was born in Philadelphia in 1837 to a wealthy free black family. During her early years, Forten was tutored at home. Forten's father refused to allow her to attend the separate all-black schools. He was a firm believer in equal educational opportunities. Charlotte Forten was a bright student and eager to prove herself as capable as any white student. When she was 17, Forten was sent to school in Salem, Massachusetts. After completing a teacher-training course, Forten was hired to teach in an all-white Salem school. She was the first black teacher hired by the Salem school system to teach the children of white residents.

The Civil War provided Forten with a great opportunity to help educate freed slaves and to show that they could function as good citizens. In 1861, Union forces captured the sea islands of Port Royal and St. Helena. These islands had been the home of wealthy cotton plantation owners and their slaves. When the Confederate soldiers and white plantation owners fled, thousands of slaves were left behind. A group of Northern reformers, including Charlotte Forten, decided to go to the islands and teach the ex-slaves. They would show the world that the ex-slaves were as worthy as whites of citizenship. These reformers named their plan the Port Royal Experiment. In all, over 70 people volunteered to teach on the islands. Some 2,000 children were educated during the Port Royal Experiment. The program became well known when Forten published an account of her experience in *The Atlantic Monthly* in 1864.

Forten left the islands in 1864 and returned to Philadelphia. For the next several years, she studied, taught, and wrote. In 1878, she married Francis James Grimké, a former slave and a well-known member of the clergy. They both continued to devote their energies to the cause of black Americans.

help. It passed out food, medicine, and supplies. The bureau established some 40 hospitals and set up schools to provide education. By 1870, there were nearly 250,000 blacks in over 4,000 schools established by the Freedmen's Bureau.

The newly freed blacks had a very difficult time finding work. The majority of Southern blacks were poor, uneducated, and unskilled. Jobs were available to them as laborers on the farms of whites. But most blacks turned this work down. Laboring for whites under strict supervision reminded them too much of slavery.

Background: After the war, there was much movement among Southern blacks. Some traveled to Southern cities where the Freedmen's Bureau was issuing rations. Others set out in search of family members, and many moved from the seaboard states to the southwestern frontier in Texas.

Discuss: Compare sharecropping to the crop-lien system. How were the two systems similar? How were they different?

Instead of working for white farmers, many blacks rented land upon which they could farm. These farmers used the profits they made from their crops to pay the rent on the land. This system was called **sharecropping**.

sharecropping a system in which people who cannot afford to buy land can rent land to farm and pay their rent from the profits made from their crops

Another system that developed for farmers who owned no tools, supplies, or seeds was called the **crop-lien system**. Under this system, farmers would borrow money from local bankers and business people to buy tools and seed. In the fall, the farmers would pay off the debt with a portion of the crops they harvested. The value of the crops they grew barely covered their debts. Each year they would need to borrow money again. The cycle kept repeating itself year after year. The crop-lien system kept many farmers deeply in debt.

crop-lien system a system by which farmers borrow money to run their farms and repay the loan with crops

The Era of Rebuilding

The federal government had to develop a plan for rebuilding and reuniting the nation. This process of reorganizing the Southern states and reestablishing them in the Union was called **Reconstruction**. The Reconstruction era lasted from 1865 until 1877.

Reconstruction the process, after the Civil War, of reorganizing the Southern states and readmitting them to the Union

Beginning in 1865, politicians began working on plans to reunite the nation. Democrats and Republicans argued bitterly over Reconstruction policy. But they agreed on certain actions the Southern states would have to take. Each state would have to admit that secession is wrong. It would have to acknowledge that slavery was abolished forever. Each state must behave in a way that indicated they were sorry for the Civil War. Finally, each state had to follow Northern ideas of progress for rebuilding its society.

Americans hoped that once the Civil War ended, it would be an easy task to reunite the nation. They found the job a difficult and trying one.

Section Review

1. What were conditions like in the South after the Civil War?
2. What problems did newly freed blacks face after the war?
3. What was the Freedmen's Bureau?
4. Define sharecropping and crop-lien system.
5. Why do you think the Union did not prosecute more Confederate leaders and army officers for war crimes?

Background: The Reconstruction era was a time of spectacular growth for the United States. The modern oil and steel industries were started. The first transcontinental railroad was built. Construction of the Brooklyn Bridge began in 1871.

Background: Lincoln also wanted the North and the South to be reunited quickly once the war ended. To Lincoln, the Southern states had never left the Union. They had merely been in a state of rebellion.

2. Plans for Reconstruction

BEFORE YOU READ: *What were the differences between the presidential and congressional plans for Reconstruction?*

Developing a Reconstruction program presented Congress and the President with a number of difficult issues to resolve. They had to decide what steps to require for readmitting Southern states. They had to decide whether blacks would be given rights equal to those enjoyed by white citizens. They would also have to settle the issue of who was to be in charge of Reconstruction, the President or Congress.

All these issues provoked debate and argument. But the last one led to a deep crisis within the government. President Lincoln, President Johnson, and Congress each developed very different plans for Reconstruction.

The Presidential Plan

Abraham Lincoln began to plan for Reconstruction during the Civil War. His plan focused on readmitting the South quickly and helping the South recover from the destruction and suffering caused by the war.

In December 1863, President Lincoln announced the details of his plan for Reconstruction. It was called the Ten Percent Plan. Under the plan, a former Confederate state would be readmitted to the Union when 10 percent of those who had voted in the 1860 presidential election had taken an oath of loyalty to the Union. In addition, the state would have to outlaw slavery. The President readmitted Tennessee, Arkansas, and Louisiana to the Union under the Ten Percent Plan before the war ended.

The Congressional Plan

Some members of Congress criticized the presidential plan because they thought it was too lenient. The more radical members of the Republican party also believed it was exclusively Congress' job to organize Reconstruction.

In 1864, Congress passed a harsher program of Reconstruction with legislation called the Wade-Davis Bill. The Wade-Davis Bill required 50 percent of a Southern state's voters to take an oath of loyalty before the state could form a new government and be readmitted to the Union. Lincoln refused to sign this bill into law. He thought the congressional plan was unwise.

For the next year, the President and Congress argued over how to handle the readmission of the South. When the Civil War ended, no final decision had been made. Then, less than a week after Lee surrendered, Lincoln was assassinated. The nation was at peace, but it had no definite plan for Reconstruction.

Johnson's Plan

Vice-President Andrew Johnson became President upon Lincoln's assassination. Johnson was a Southerner from Tennessee. Although he was a Southern Democrat, Johnson had remained loyal to the Union during the war. However, the Republicans, especially its radical members, did not trust him or like him.

Discuss: How do you think you would have reacted to Lincoln's Ten Percent Plan if you had been a Southerner after the Civil War? How do you think you would have reacted if you had been a Northerner?

Background: Lincoln had not required ratification of the Thirteenth Amendment as a condition for readmittance to the Union because Congress did not adopt the amendment until February 1865—almost a year after Lincoln's death.

Andrew Johnson wanted to see the Southern states restored, or returned, to the Union quickly. Johnson's plan for reconstruction was called Presidential Restoration. It lasted from the time he took office in April 1865 until December 1865.

Johnson's plan for restoration was similar to Lincoln's plan, with one major exception. Johnson's plan required the Southern states to ratify the Thirteenth Amendment before they could be permitted to rejoin the Union. The Thirteenth Amendment abolished slavery.

By late 1865, all the former Confederate states had sworn loyalty to the Union and ratified the Thirteenth Amendment. Johnson readmitted the new governments of these states.

The new Southern governments, however, seemed unchanged from the way they had been during the war. Southerners elected many ex-Confederate army officers and government officials to office. In addition, Southern states began passing **black codes**. These were laws that severely limited the freedom of blacks. They prohibited blacks from serving on juries and testifying against whites in court. The state of Mississippi would not permit blacks to buy or rent farmland. This state and others declared that blacks found without employment were to be arrested as vagrants and assigned to landholders to work without pay. The black codes restricted black freedom almost as much as slavery had done.

black code a set of laws passed by the Southern states after the Civil War to limit the rights of blacks

The black man in this engraving was arrested for vagrancy under the black codes. His services are being auctioned off to pay his fine.

Congress Strikes Back

Congressional leaders were furious with what Johnson had allowed to happen in the South. When Congress reconvened in December 1865, its members refused to recognize Johnson's restoration plan. The newly elected Southern senators and representatives were not permitted to take their seats in Congress.

Members of Congress set to work on their own Reconstruction plan. As a first step, Congress authorized the Freedmen's Bureau to continue its work in the South. In June 1866, Congress passed and submitted to the states for ratification a new constitutional amendment. The Fourteenth Amendment granted American citizenship to blacks. It denied ex-Confederate leaders the right to hold state or federal office. It said that if any state pre-

For Extra Interest: Ask the students what previous Supreme Court decision made it necessary to grant American citizenship to blacks. Point out that amending the Constitution is a legislative check on the power of the judicial branch.

Background: The Republicans viewed the election results in 1866 as a command from the public to impose stricter terms on the South's readmission.

vented citizens from voting, that state would lose a number of seats in the House proportionate to the number of voters it excluded. Congress made the Fourteenth Amendment the heart of its Reconstruction plan. Only those Southern states that ratified the Fourteenth Amendment would be readmitted to the Union. Tennessee was the only former Confederate state that ratified the Fourteenth Amendment.

President Johnson believed that the only way he could fight Congress was to take the issue to the American people. Johnson asked Americans to show their support for his program in the upcoming congressional election by voting for candidates who endorsed his plan. Johnson went on a speaking tour around the country. Wherever he went, crowds shouted him down. He, in turn, criticized the crowds harshly. The tour was a failure. The public overwhelmingly elected anti-Johnson politicians to Congress in the election of 1866.

President Andrew Johnson on his speaking tour in 1866

Two thirds of the seats in both houses of Congress were now occupied by Republicans. The Republicans would be able to push their programs through Congress. They had enough votes to override any veto from the President. Congress was now in complete charge of directing the course of Reconstruction.

Section Review

1. What were the major differences between the presidential and congressional plans for Reconstruction?
2. How did President Johnson's plan for restoration differ from the Reconstruction plans of Lincoln and Congress?
3. What rights are protected by the Fourteenth Amendment?
4. How might the period of Reconstruction have been different if President Lincoln had lived? Explain.

Discuss: Why do you think Tennessee was not included in any of the five military districts established by Congress in the Reconstruction Act?

3. The Trials of Reunion

BEFORE YOU READ: *How did congressional Reconstruction affect the role of black Southerners in politics?*

On March 2, 1867, Congress passed the Reconstruction Act, overriding the veto of President Johnson. The Reconstruction Act abolished Southern governments established under Johnson and placed the South under military rule. The old Confederacy, with the exception of Tennessee, was divided into five military districts. Each district was under the complete control of a Union general. The generals were ordered to protect the rights of blacks and guarantee that blacks were permitted to vote in all elections. The generals also supervised the formation of new Southern governments. To gain readmission to the United States, these governments had to ratify the Fourteenth Amendment. In the months that followed, Congress passed more reconstruction acts to strengthen the original act and prevent Southern governments from using delaying tactics.

Impeachment

Andrew Johnson was so strongly opposed to congressional Reconstruction that he did what he could to frustrate the administration of the reconstruction acts. He appointed five military governors who would interpret their powers narrowly so that whites would be favored over blacks. He removed three generals whom he considered too sympathetic to the aims of congressional Reconstruction.

Senators and representatives wanted to stop President Johnson before their Reconstruction program was completely undermined. They decided that Johnson must be removed from office. Said one Republican member of Congress, Johnson had "come to be regarded as an 'obstacle' which must be 'deposed.'" In February 1868, the House of Representatives **impeached** Andrew Johnson, charging him with misconduct in office. Eleven different charges were brought against him. The charges fell into three categories. First, the House charged that he had opposed congressional Reconstruction in general. Second, Johnson was charged with criticizing Congress. Third, the House claimed that Johnson had violated the Tenure of Office Act. This law, passed by Congress in March 1867, forbade any official appointed by the President and confirmed by the Senate to be dismissed by the President without the prior consent of the Senate. Johnson considered this law to be unconstitutional and so had dismissed Secretary of War Edwin Stanton, who strongly supported the radicals in Congress.

---

impeach to charge a public official with misconduct in office

---

It was up to the Senate to determine whether Johnson was innocent or guilty of the impeachment charges. The Senate tried the case from March 30 to May 26, 1868. The vote, 35 to 19, fell one short of the two-thirds majority needed to find Johnson guilty.

Johnson's term in office came to an end within a year of his impeachment trial. At

Discuss: When the President of the United States is tried for impeachment, the Chief Justice of the Supreme Court, instead of the Vice-President, presides over the Senate. Why do you think the Constitution calls for this change?

the end of his term, he returned to Tennessee, an angry and bitter man.

Grant Becomes President

As Johnson's impeachment trial drew to a close, the Republican party met to choose their candidate for the 1868 presidential election. They nominated Ulysses S. Grant. Grant was extremely popular in the North, where he was seen as the military savior of the nation. Grant was nominated in spite of the fact that he had no experience in government.

His opponent in the election was former Governor Horatio Seymour of New York. The electoral vote was not close. Grant won 214 of the 294 electoral votes. However, in the popular vote, Grant won by the narrow margin of 306,000 votes out of a total of 5,715,000 votes cast. Approximately 700,000 Southern blacks had voted for Grant. Without their votes, Grant might have lost.

It was clear to the Republican party that the black vote had to be protected. If it was not protected, the Republicans might not remain in power. Congress, therefore, adopted the last of the three great Reconstruction amendments. The Fifteenth Amendment forbade the states to deny the right to vote to any citizen because of "race, color, or previous condition of servitude [slavery]." It was ratified on March 30, 1870.

This photograph of Ulysses S. Grant was taken during the Civil War.

Reconstruction Governments

Congressional Reconstruction gave Southern blacks many new political rights, such as the right to vote and hold public office. As a result, blacks took an active role in Southern state governments. Blacks helped in drawing up the new state constitutions. They also voted in large numbers. For a while during Reconstruction, black voters even outnumbered white voters in five states—Alabama, Florida, South Carolina, Mississippi, and Louisiana.

Hundreds of blacks were elected to office at all levels of government. Blanche K. Bruce, a former slave, and Hiram Revels were elected as United States senators from Mississippi. Twenty blacks were elected from Southern states to the House of Representatives. Many more blacks served in office at the state and local levels.

By 1870, all 11 Confederate states had

Background: The responsible conduct of the black representatives in Congress moved James G. Blaine, their contemporary, to observe that they "were as a rule studious, earnest, ambitious men, whose public conduct . . . would be honorable to any race."

Vocabulary Help: "Scalawag" had been a term applied by cattle drivers to "the mean, lousy, and filthy kine [cattle] that are not fit for butchers or dogs." Today the term is used as a synonym for rascal.

been readmitted to the Union. Their new governments were under the control of Republicans who had been elected to office. The Republican party in the South drew support from three groups of people. The first group consisted of Southern blacks. The second group was made up of Southern whites who joined the Republican party. They accepted Reconstruction and the changes it brought about in the South. Some joined the Republican party hoping for personal or financial gain. Most Southerners, who still were Democrats, viewed the Southern Republicans as traitors. They called the Southern Republicans **"scalawags."**

---

scalawag a Southern white who joined or supported the Republican party during Reconstruction

---

The third group was made up of thousands of Northerners who had come south following the war. Some came to help the former slaves. They worked as teachers for the Freedmen's Bureau and other similar groups. Some were former Union soldiers who had found the South attractive and decided to reside there after completing their military service. Others came to help the South rebuild. Still others saw a chance to manipulate the governments for greedy purposes.

Southerners disliked these Northerners. They called them **"carpetbaggers"** at first because their traveling bags were made from carpeting material. Soon the term was being used as an insult.

---

carpetbagger a Northerner who moved to the South after the Civil War

---

This cartoon of a carpetbagger shows him as a greedy-looking person with overstuffed bags.

Most of the new Southern governments, or "carpetbagger" governments, had mixed records. Many important reforms were carried out under these governments. Railroads were rebuilt and state-supported school systems were established for the first time. Public spending was increased for prisons, state hospitals, and relief for the poor. But corruption and **graft** were common within the new Southern governments. Officials stole or wasted the public's money. However, such activity was not restricted to the South and its "carpetbagger" governments. Corruption in government existed in all regions and at all levels of government following the Civil War.

Background: Many of the well-to-do Southerners who joined the Republican party were former Whigs who distrusted the Democrats or who felt more at home in a party that supported protective tariffs and subsidies for railroads.

EUREKA!

The Phonograph

Thomas Edison was without question one of the greatest inventive geniuses of all time. Edison received over 1,000 patents in his lifetime. His laboratory in Menlo Park, New Jersey, was the first industrial research lab in the world. It was later copied by corporations everywhere. But of all Thomas Edison's contributions, it was the phonograph that has been called the most original of his inventions.

In 1877, Edison was working on a way to record Morse code messages on waxed paper. Once recorded, they could be sent out later at high speed. In the course of this work, he noticed that a metal spring resting on the paper gave out a musical sound as the paper was pulled under it. Edison connected this phenomenon with the sound made by the recently invented telephone. He combined his observation with the principles used in the telephone. Soon he set his assistant to work building the first phonograph.

The phonograph was a simple invention. The recording was cut into a tinfoil cylinder by a needle. To play the "record" back, a different needle was used, this one attached to a hearing tube.

Edison made the first recording in 1877, a faint, gravelly version of "Mary Had a Little Lamb." Many improvements to the phonograph were made in the years that followed. Before long, households all over the world were showing off this latest technological creation provided by the Wizard of Menlo Park.

---

graft the acquisition of money or favors in dishonest or questionable ways

The End of Reconstruction

By 1870, all of the Southern states were back in the Union. Once this happened, Southern white Democrats began to work to remove the Republican party from control of state and local governments. They wanted **home rule**, by which they meant control of Southern government by the Democrats.

home rule self-government in local and state affairs

Background: Many of the reforms made by "carpetbagger" governments angered Southern Democrats. There was considerable hostility to the idea of educating any children using taxpayers' money, and the idea of educating black children was seen as a foolish extravagance.

Background: Reconstruction did not end abruptly. As ex-Confederates regained their voting rights, the South gained greater home rule. A general amnesty in 1872 restored voting rights to all but about 600 ex-Confederate officials.

Thomas Nast drew this cartoon in 1874 to depict the problems freed blacks faced because of antiblack groups.

In some states, home rule was restored legally through fair elections. In other states, violent methods were used. Groups were organized to prevent blacks from voting. They also hoped to frighten Southern Republicans. These groups used threats, beatings, and even murder to achieve their goal. Over time, they succeeded in preventing whites and blacks from exercising their rights. The best known of these groups was the Ku Klux Klan. It was begun in Tennessee by a former Confederate cavalry leader, General Nathan Bedford Forest.

Northern attitudes aided the growth of the home rule movement. By the middle of the 1870's, many Northerners were tired of fighting the Reconstruction battle. They were no longer committed to helping Southern blacks. Others in the North believed that Southern blacks now had a fair chance to succeed without further help from the federal government. It was up to blacks themselves to see that they prospered.

Between 1872 and 1876, in one Southern state after another, Southern white Democrats steadily returned to power. By 1876, home rule had returned to all but three Southern states. Only in South Carolina, Louisiana, and Florida did Republicans continue to govern.

In the presidential election of 1876, the Republican party nominated Governor Rutherford B. Hayes of Ohio, a former Union general. The Democrats chose Governor Samuel J. Tilden of New York.

To win, one of the candidates had to get at least 185 electoral votes. By election day evening, Hayes had received 165 votes and Tilden had received 184. But there was a problem. The three Southern Republican states had turned in two sets of voting results. One set would have given all their electoral votes to Hayes. The other set contained a majority of votes for Tilden. In addition, one of Oregon's votes was in dispute. In all, 20 electoral votes were in dispute.

A special commission was set up, comprised of five senators, five representatives, and five Supreme Court justices. The commission was to determine who would get the disputed electoral votes. After investigating the matter, the commission, in February 1877, voted along party lines. The eight Republicans voted to give the disputed votes to Hayes, and the seven Democrats voted to award the votes to Tilden. The commission reported to Congress that Rutherford B. Hayes should be President.

In the end, Congress ratified the com-

Background: The Union soldiers in the South during Reconstruction were largely ineffective in dealing with the Klan because its members were sworn to secrecy, disguised themselves and their deeds in many ways, and had the respect and support of the white community.

mission's report because a policital deal had been worked out. The Democrats agreed to accept the commission's report if the Republicans guaranteed that President Hayes would end Reconstruction and remove all federal troops from the South. The Democrats also insisted that Hayes appoint a Southerner to his Cabinet. This deal became known as the Compromise of 1877.

Within a year, the governments in Florida, South Carolina, and Louisiana were controlled by the Democratic party. White Southern rule had been restored in every state of the old Confederacy. The Reconstruction era was over.

Separation for Blacks

Any hope that freedom would also mean equality vanished for blacks following Reconstruction. Blacks found themselves forced to accept many injustices—lower wages than whites, unfair treatment by the legal system, and white violence. The South resumed its practice of **segregation** or separation, of the races. Black Southerners were required by law to attend separate schools, ride in separate railroad cars, use separate public facilities, and eat in separate areas of restaurants.

---

segregation the separation of a race, class, or ethnic group by discriminatory means

---

The Supreme Court, in a number of rulings, gave legal approval to such practices. In 1883, the Supreme Court ruled that the federal government could not protect blacks against discrimination by private individuals. In 1896, segregation became the law of the land as a result of the case *Plessy* v. *Ferguson*. The Supreme Court ruled that the races may be separated as long as facilities provided for each race are equal. This became known as the "separate but equal" doctrine.

The Reconstruction era had laid the foundation for change with the three great Reconstruction amendments. But many years would pass before the change in rights for blacks became a reality.

Section Review

1. How did congressional Reconstruction affect the role of black Southerners in politics?
2. Why did Congress bring impeachment charges against President Andrew Johnson?
3. Who were the "scalawags" and the "carpetbaggers"? What role did they play in Reconstruction?
4. How did the election of 1876 signal the end of the Reconstruction era?
5. Was Reconstruction a success for blacks or a failure? Explain your answer.

CHAPTER REVIEW

Summary

After the Civil War, Americans had to face the challenge of reuniting and adjusting to the changes the war had brought. Returning veterans in both the North and the South had to readjust to civilian life. Organizations, such as the Freedmen's Bureau, were set up to help blacks make the transition from slavery to freedom.

The biggest problem, however, arose over how the states that had seceded would be treated. The relatively lenient presidential plans for Reconstruction were opposed by many Republicans in Congress. They felt that the South should be punished for its actions. In 1867, Congress passed the Reconstruction Act, which sent Union generals to the South to supervise the formation of new governments and protect the rights of blacks.

Under congressional Reconstruction, blacks took an active role in state and local governments in the South. However, when Reconstruction officially ended in 1877, white Southern Democrats quickly regained control of their governments and passed laws to segregate black and white society.

Recalling the Facts

1. What effect did the Civil War have on the way many Americans viewed the two political parties?
2. What issues had to be resolved by the President and the Congress in developing a Reconstruction plan following the Civil War?
3. Although President Andrew Johnson was impeached, he was not removed from office. Why?
4. What role did groups like the Ku Klux Klan play in restoring home rule in the South?
5. How did the position of blacks in the South change when Reconstruction ended?

Analyzing the Facts

1. Who do you think faced the more difficult challenge of readjustment after the Civil War, Confederate veterans or Southern blacks? Explain your answer.

2. Why do you think black voters overwhelmingly supported the Republican party during Reconstruction?
3. Which branch of the federal government exercised the most power during the period of Reconstruction? Give examples to support your answer.
4. Do you think it was reasonable for Northerners to expect blacks to succeed without further help from the federal government in the 1870's? Why or why not?
5. What effect do you think segregation had on the ability of black Americans to achieve racial equality after Reconstruction came to an end?

Time and History

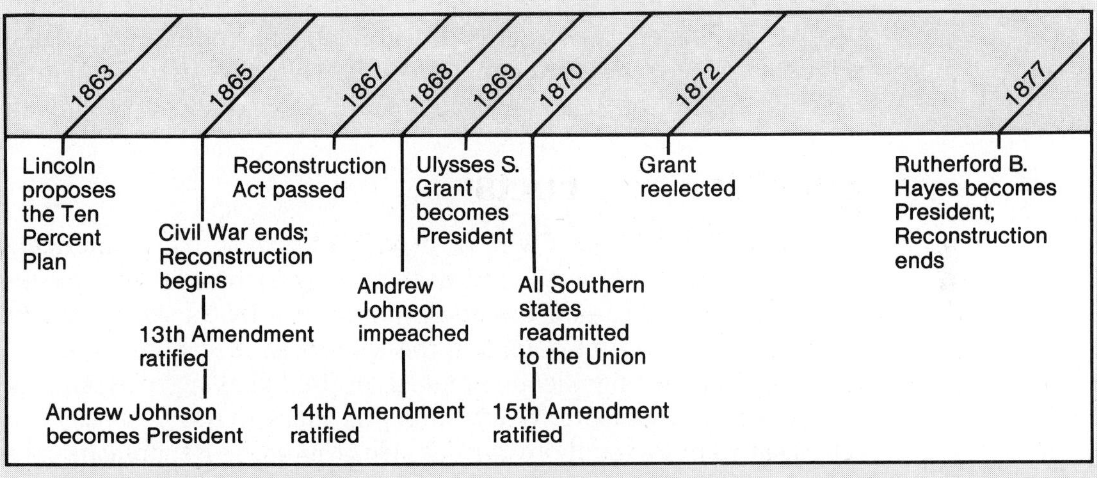

1. How many years passed between the end of the Civil War and the year in which all the Southern states had been readmitted to the Union?
2. How many years did Reconstruction last?
3. Who was President when the Fifteenth Amendment was ratified?
4. What was Lincoln's plan for Reconstruction called?
5. How many years after Andrew Johnson became President was he impeached?

UNIT REVIEW

Summary

Events in the 1850's steadily pushed the nation toward civil war. The sectional dispute over the expansion of slavery into the territories led to violence in Kansas. Following the election of the Republican candidate, Abraham Lincoln, in 1860, seven states of the Deep South seceded from the nation and formed the Confederate States of America. Four states from the upper South joined the new nation in 1861.

The Civil War started in April 1861 with the Confederate attack on Fort Sumter. Hundreds of thousands of soldiers on both sides died as the war dragged on for four long years. During the war, President Lincoln issued the Emancipation Proclamation to free all slaves living in the seceded states. In 1865, Union forces captured Richmond, and the Confederacy collapsed.

President Johnson's plan for reuniting the nation after the war was rejected by Congress as too lenient. Under congressional Reconstruction, blacks made some progress toward achieving equal rights. However, when Reconstruction ended in 1877, white Southern Democrats regained control of their governments and passed laws to segregate the races.

Recalling the Facts

1. Briefly explain how each of the following increased tensions between the North and the South during the 1850's: John Brown's raid, *Uncle Tom's Cabin*, and the Dred Scott decision.
2. What was the significance of each of the following battles in the Civil War: Vicksburg, Gettysburg, and Richmond?
3. What role did the more radical members of the Republican party play in Reconstruction?
4. How did Reconstruction officially end? How did many Northerners feel about Reconstruction by the time it ended?

Analyzing the Facts

1. Why do you think Stephen A. Douglas supported the doctrine of popular sovereignty in Kansas and Nebraska when the issue of slavery in these territories had previously been settled by the Missouri Compromise in 1820?

2. Why do you think more Americans died in the Civil War than in any other war in which the nation has fought?
3. Why have the years immediately following the Civil War been called the "Age of Hate"? What evidence is there to suggest that hatred existed throughout Reconstruction?
4. How was the Fourteenth Amendment an extension of the Bill of Rights?

Reviewing Vocabulary

Define the following terms:

land speculator	draft	black codes
blockade	war crime	impeach
war of attrition	bankrupt	graft
gunboat	Reconstruction	segregation

Sharpening Your Skills

1. What is the key to writing a good report?
2. What is a bibliography, and where should it be placed in a report?
3. What can be found in the body of a good report? What can be found in the concluding paragraph?

Answer the two questions below based on the political cartoon on p. 390.

4. What does the skull over the shield symbolize?
5. What is the main idea of this cartoon?

Writing and Research

1. Prepare a three- to four-page report on some aspect of the Civil War or Reconstruction. Choose a topic suitable for the required length of the report, or ask your teacher for suggested topics.
2. The history of the United States in the years following the Civil War would have been very different if the South had won the war. Write a brief account of what you think would have happened in the ten-year period from 1865 to 1875 if the South had won the Civil War. Write the account in the form of an historical narrative.

Unit 6

The Age of Industry

18 The Great Plains were America's last frontier. These vast lands, in the middle of the continent, had been the home of the American Indians for thousands of years. In the late 1800's, cattle ranchers brought to the plains their herds of longhorn cattle. Pioneer families moved to the plains to farm. The first pioneer families faced great difficulties. By 1900, the days of the frontier were nearly over.

19 America entered a new age in the late 1800's, the Age of Industry. It was a time when factories and mills spread across the continent. There had never before been a time of such rapid industrial growth. American inventors created the marvels of the telephone and the electric light. The products of American industry became the envy of the world. Huge fortunes were made by the leaders of American industry.

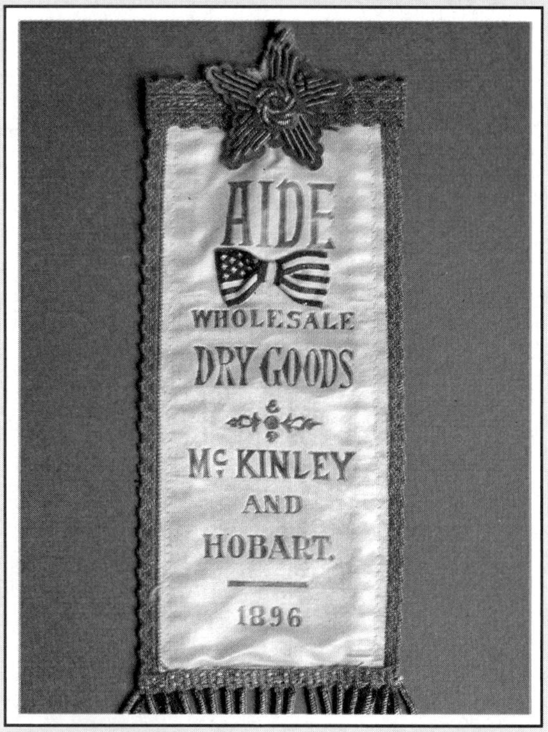

20 *The growth of industry changed the lives of many people. Millions of immigrants, seeking new beginnings, came to the United States. As industry expanded, more people moved to the cities. Workers in American industry organized to improve their lives.*

21 *In the Age of Industry, many local governments were ruled by leaders who were ambitious and dishonest. National elections decided few important issues. The leaders of industry seemed more powerful than the leaders of government.*

22 *In the late 1800's, America began to expand its power abroad. New territories, such as Alaska and Hawaii, were acquired. The United States showed the world its strength in a war with Spain in 1898. During the early 1900's, an American canal was dug through Panama.*

Chapter 18 The Last Frontier

Stretching eastward from the Rocky Mountains is a vast area of low-lying hills and valleys known as the Great Plains. At the end of the Civil War, the Great Plains were the home of thousands of Indians. Whites had passed through this land, heading west on the Oregon Trail or to the California gold fields. But few had settled there.

In the years after the Civil War, settlers began to move onto the Great Plains. Ranchers moved in with herds of longhorn cattle. Pioneer families began to farm. In order to meet the settlers' demands for more land, the Plains Indians were forcibly removed from their lands.

The settlement of the Great Plains was the largest westward migration of people in the history of the United States. More new land was settled in the years 1870 to 1900 than in any other period of history. These vast lands, in the middle of America, were the last frontier.

After you read this chapter, you will be able to:

1. Describe how and why the Plains Indians were removed from their lands.
2. Discuss what life was like for cattle ranchers and cowhands.
3. Explain how the pioneer families solved their problems.

Background: Horses were introduced to North America by the Spanish. Columbus brought horses to Cuba on his second voyage; Cortés introduced them to the mainland in 1519.

1. The Plains Indians

BEFORE YOU READ: *Why were the Plains Indians removed from their lands?*

At the end of the Civil War, more than 100,000 Indians lived on the Great Plains. Some of the tribes of the eastern plains—such as the Santee Dakota and the Wichita of Kansas—spent part of each year farming the land. Most of the Plains Indians—such as the Comanche, Sioux, Cheyenne, and Arapaho—were nomadic. They were skilled riders who hunted the buffalo.

The buffalo provided the Plains Indians with almost everything they needed to survive. The Indians ate fresh buffalo meat and dried what was left. From the buffalo skin they made blankets, moccasins, clothing, and the walls of their tepees. The bones were used as farming tools. The horns became cups and spoons. The stomach was turned into a water bottle. The rough side of the buffalo tongue served as a hairbrush. Dried buffalo manure, called "buffalo chips" by the whites, was used by the Indians as fuel for their cooking fires.

Conflict

Whites first crossed the Great Plains in large numbers during the California Gold Rush. Although the forty-niners feared the worst, conflict with the Indians along the trail was rare.

Later, as white settlers moved onto the plains, conflict between whites and Indians increased. The new settlers wanted to use the land for ranching and farming. The Indians wanted to remain on their lands and to live the nomadic life they had always known. It seemed that conflict between the two groups could not be avoided.

The federal government adopted a policy of removing Indians from their lands. By removing the Indians, the government hoped to reduce chances for conflict and open up more land for settlement. The government required the Indians to remain on special lands set aside for them. These lands were called reservations.

One of the largest tribes of Plains Indians was the people known as the Sioux. The Sioux were placed on a reservation in the Black Hills of South Dakota. The government promised to give the Indians food and other supplies. The government also promised that the reservation land would be the Indians' forever. In 1874, gold was discovered in the Black Hills. Soon thousands of whites were tramping across Indian lands.

The Indians on the reservation resented this invasion of their territory. They were also upset with the food the government gave them. The food was often moldy and spoiled. Many Indians left the reservation.

The government ordered all the Sioux to return to the reservation. Any Indians found off the reservation after February 1, 1876, would be brought back by force. Two Sioux leaders, Sitting Bull and Crazy Horse, decided to fight the army rather than return.

The army sent three units of soldiers to the camp of Sitting Bull and Crazy Horse. The camp was on the banks of the Little Bighorn River in Montana. Among the soldiers was a young colonel, George Armstrong Custer.

Background: The Black Hills are a small group of mountains in western South Dakota and northeastern Wyoming. Dark pines covering the mountain slopes are said to have given the Black Hills their name. The Mount Rushmore National Monument and the largest gold mine in the United States are located there.

American Indian Reservations, 1890

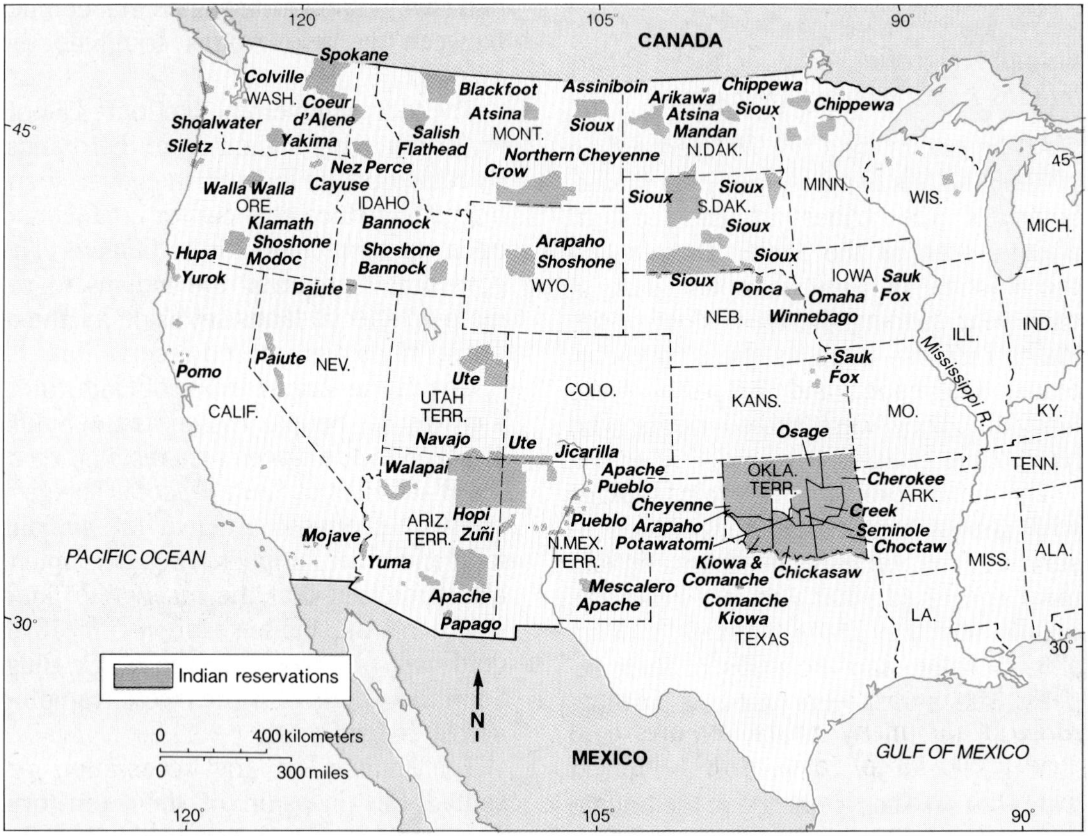

Where were the most reservations located in 1890?

Colonel Custer was the leader of the Seventh Cavalry. On the morning of June 25, 1876, Custer's band of 265 men were the first to reach the Little Bighorn. Instead of waiting for the other units of soldiers to arrive, Custer ordered his men to advance. There were more than 2,500 Sioux at the Little Bighorn that day. A fierce battle began between the soldiers and the Indians.

Within a few hours, the battle was over. Colonel Custer and all of his men lay dead. The Battle of the Little Bighorn—also known as Custer's Last Stand—was a major victory for the Indians.

The victory, however, did the Sioux little good. By October 1876, most of the Sioux had been forced back onto the reservation. Only a small band under Sitting Bull remained at large. Five years later, even this small band, faced with starvation, returned to the reservation.

Background: Fearing that he and his men would be discovered by the Indians, Custer decided to attack the camp without waiting for the rest of the military force to arrive. His advance parties had misinformed him about the strength of the Indian forces.

Background: In 1855, the Nez Perce had a history of peaceful contact with white Americans. They had welcomed Lewis and Clark in 1804 and had offered no resistance to the steady stream of wagons passing through their lands in the 1840's.

Chief Joseph and the Nez Perce

Many other tribes throughout the West were placed on reservations in the late 1800's. One of these tribes was the Nez Perce (NEZZ PURSS). For centuries, the Nez Perce had roamed freely across the grassy hills of Oregon and Idaho.

In 1855, the government set aside a reservation for the Nez Perce in the area where present-day Oregon, Idaho, and Washington meet. The Nez Perce believed the reservation lands would be theirs forever. In 1860, however, gold was discovered on the reservation. White miners swarmed onto the Indian lands.

The government tried to reduce the reservation to less than one fourth its original size. But about 180 of the Indians refused to be confined on the reservation. They remained on their land in northern Oregon for many years. Before their leader, Old Joseph, died in 1871, he gave his son a warning: "A few years more and the white men will be all around you. They have their eyes on this land."

Old Joseph's son became the next leader of the Nez Perce. He was called Chief Joseph. In the early 1870's, whites began to settle the Oregon valley where the Nez Perce lived. Chief Joseph remembered his father's warning.

In 1877, the government ordered all the Nez Perce to move to the small reservation set aside for them. Soldiers were sent to bring the Indians to the reservation. Chief Joseph and a band of Nez Perce men, women, and children fled from them. They hoped to reach safety in Canada. After traveling more than 2,100 kilometers (1,300 miles), the band was overtaken by the soldiers in northern Montana. Following a bloody battle with the soldiers, on a bitterly cold day in September 1877, the Nez Perce put down their weapons.

The surrender of Chief Joseph on October 5, 1877, was a dramatic moment. Snow covered the ground as he came forward to hand over his rifle.

"It is cold and we have no blankets," the chief said. "The little children are freezing to death. My people . . . have run away to the hills, and have no blankets, no food; no one knows where they are—perhaps freezing to death. . . . Hear me, my chiefs. I am tired; my heart is sick and sad. From where the sun now stands, I will fight no more forever."

After their surrender, the Nez Perce were shipped to Oklahoma and placed on a new reservation. The climate in Oklahoma was hot and dry. It was very different from the Oregon valley. Many Nez Perce fell sick and died on their new reservation. In the 1880's, the Nez Perce were moved again to a reservation in eastern Washington. It was there, in 1904, that Chief Joseph died.

The Destruction of the Buffalo

Thirteen million buffalo lived on the Great Plains when the whites first arrived. As railroads were built across the plains, buffalo were killed to feed the railroad workers. After the railroads were built, the killing of the buffalo increased.

In 1871, it was discovered that buffalo hides could be made into leather. A fad for buffalo robes and buffalo coats swept the East. In the early part of the 1870's,

Discuss: Both the Nez Perce and the Sioux came into conflict with the United States government. How were their conflicts similar?

Background: In 1867–1868, William Cody hunted buffalo to feed workers building the Kansas Pacific Railroad. From then on he was known as Buffalo Bill. It is said that he killed more than 4,000 buffalo in less than two years.

Famous Americans

SUSETTE LA FLESCHE TIBBLES

Susette La Flesche was one of the first Americans to speak out for the rights of American Indians. She was the daughter of the famous half-white Omaha chief, Iron Eye. La Flesche was born in 1854. She grew up on the Omahas' reservation near the Missouri River. At the age of eight, she began attending a mission school on the reservation. Her desire for a good education came to the attention of a proprietor of a girls' school in New Jersey. La Flesche was invited to enroll there. After she graduated, La Flesche returned to the reservation to teach. Events on a nearby reservation turned her interests to American Indian rights.

In 1877, the federal government gave away the lands of the Ponca Indians. The Poncas had to move from their home to a reservation in the Indian Territory. One third of the Poncas died there. Their chief, Standing Bear, decided to lead his people back to their homeland in 1879. The United States Army went after them, arrested Standing Bear, and returned the Poncas to the reservation. The Poncas' mistreatment was publicized by a newspaper reporter, Thomas Henry Tibbles. Tibbles helped gain Standing Bear's release from jail. Then Tibbles began a lecture tour, taking with him Standing Bear and Susette La Flesche as Standing Bear's interpreter. It was then that La Flesche began to devote her life to helping the American Indian.

La Flesche lectured and served as an interpreter in the large cities of the East. Her lectures raised money for American Indians to fight for their rights in court. Thomas Henry Tibbles shared the lecture stage with her. The two were married in 1881. They continued to lecture and write, defending the rights of all Americans who were denied equality before the law.

buffalo hunters killed 3 million buffalo *each year*. "Sportsmen" came to the plains to shoot the buffalo from moving railroad cars. By 1883, there were only 200 buffalo left in the West.

With the destruction of the buffalo, the old way of life for the Plains Indians was no longer possible. They had depended upon the buffalo for so many things. But now the buffalo were gone. The time of independence and hunting was over for the Indians of the plains.

The Ghost Dance

By 1890, most of the Indians of the Far West had been placed upon reservations. Many Indians were discouraged and un-

Discuss: By the late nineteenth century, the wild herds of American buffalo were in danger of becoming extinct. What animals are in danger of becoming extinct today? What do you think should be done to protect endangered species?

Discuss: When Black Elk recalls the tragedy at Wounded Knee, he says that "a people's dream died there." What dream is he referring to?

happy with life on these reservations.

In Nevada, a Paiute (pie-YOOT) Indian named Wovoka had a vision that gave new hope to the Indian people. Wovoka dreamed that someday all the white people would disappear from the West and that the Indians who had been killed would come back alive. In his dream, he saw buffalo herds again filling the plains. Wovoka told his people about the dream. He said that if they would dance in a great circle and sing special songs, the dream would come true. The dance was called the Ghost Dance by white Americans.

Soon, Indians from all over the West learned of Wovoka's dream and began dancing the Ghost Dance. The army and government officials became worried. They thought the dance was a "war dance." They were afraid the Indians were preparing for battle.

The Ghost Dance became especially popular among the Sioux. Government officials believed that Sitting Bull was encouraging the dance. They ordered his arrest. In making the arrest, an Indian police officer shot and killed the old Sioux leader.

Some of the believers in the Ghost Dance left the Sioux reservation in South Dakota. Soldiers were sent to bring them back. On December 28, 1890, the soldiers caught up with a group of the Indians at a stream called Wounded Knee. The Indians agreed to surrender their guns. The soldiers placed four powerful cannons on a ridge overlooking the Indian camp.

The next day, someone fired a rifle. The powerful cannons on the ridge opened fire. Shells exploded in the Indian camp, ripping apart the tepees. The Indians screamed and tried to escape.

Of the 350 Indians in the camp, as many as 300 were killed. Those who survived were returned to the reservation. The Battle of Wounded Knee was the last major conflict between whites and Indians on the plains.

The Indians soon abandoned the Ghost Dance. They saw that Wovoka's dream was not going to come true.

Years later, an old Sioux Indian named Black Elk recalled the Battle of Wounded Knee. "When I look back now from this high hill of my old age," Black Elk said, "I can still see the butchered women and children lying heaped and scattered all along the crooked gulch as plain as when I saw them with eyes still young. And I can see that something else died there in the bloody mud, and was buried in the blizzard. A people's dream died there. It was a beautiful dream . . . the nation's hoop is broken and scattered. There is no center any longer, and the sacred tree is dead."

The Dawes Act

Once the Indians were on the reservations, steps were taken to make them become part of the larger American society. Official government policy in the late 1800's was to **assimilate** the Indians.

---

assimilate to make one group of people become part of a larger group

---

In 1887, Congress passed the Dawes Act. This act divided portions of the Indian reservations into individual sections of land. Each head of an Indian family was to be given 65 hectares (160 acres). Any reservation lands left over were to be

Background: Before the arrival of Europeans, there were approximately 2.5 million American Indians living in the New World. By 1890, their numbers had fallen to a low of approximately 250,000.

Discuss: What is the popular image of the American Indians presented in movies and on television? Based on the information in the section you have just read, how realistic an image do you think this is?

This photo of an Indian police officer and his family shows the impact of assimilation on the life of reservation Indians. The younger women have adopted white American styles of clothing, while the older woman clings to her Sioux costume.

sold by the government. The money from the land sales was to be used to support Indian education.

The Dawes Act was passed to help assimilate the Indians. The Indians now could become farmers on their own land. They were supposed to become just like other American farmers in the West. Unfortunately, the major effect of the Dawes Act was that many Indians lost their land. In 1887, Indians had 56 million hectares (139 million acres) of the land in the West. Fifty years later, the Indians had only 19 million hectares (47 million acres). The government had sold much of their land to white ranchers and farmers.

Section Review

1. Why were the Plains Indians removed from their lands?
2. What things did the Plains Indians make from the buffalo?
3. Identify Chief Joseph and Wovoka.
4. How was the Dawes Act supposed to help assimilate the Indians?
5. How do you think the conflicts between the whites and the Indians could have been avoided?

For Extra Interest: Have four students research and give oral reports to the class on the following Apache leaders: Geronimo, Mangas Coloradas (Red Sleeves), Cochise, and Victorio. Ask the class to compare these leaders to Chief Joseph and Sitting Bull.

Background: The average cattle drive employed 16 to 18 cowhands who either rode "point" (front), "flank" (side), or "drag" (rear), plus a cook and a "wrangler" (a person who took care of the horses). They traveled an average of 19 to 25 kilometers (12 to 16 miles) a day.

2. The Cattle Kingdom

BEFORE YOU READ: *What was life like for the cattle ranchers and the cowhands?*

The removal of the Indians from the Great Plains opened a vast area of land for ranching and farming. The grasslands of the plains became pastures for huge herds of longhorn cattle.

Longhorns

The cattle industry had its beginnings in southern Texas. Long before the United States acquired Texas, Mexicans in the Southwest were raising herds of tough and lean cattle. The Mexicans had learned to care for their herds on the open range. A range is a large area of land where cattle graze. The Mexicans were skilled cowhands. They were able to tend their cattle from horseback.

The Mexican cattle herders were the first cowhands of the West. They called themselves **vaqueros** (vah-KAY-roes). The term *vaquero* comes from the Spanish word *vaca*, which means cow. Sometimes American cowhands also called themselves *vaqueros*. When the Americans pronounced the word, it usually sounded more like "buckaroo."

---

vaquero a Mexican cattle herder who was among the first cowhands of the West

---

As the Americans came into Texas, they brought with them their eastern milk cows. Breeding between the American and Mexican cattle produced several new breeds. The most impressive new breed was the famed Texas longhorn. These wiry animals had enormous horns that twisted back toward their bodies. The spread between their horns sometimes reached 3 meters (10 feet). The longhorns were a hardy breed. They were well suited to the harsh conditions of the plains. By the end of the Civil War, 5 million longhorns roamed across the Texas range.

The Long Drive

The nation's supply of beef was greatly reduced during the Civil War. Herds were slaughtered to meet the needs of the two armies. After the war, the demand for beef increased as the population of the United States grew larger. The cattle industry of the Far West grew to meet this demand.

At the end of the Civil War, cattle were selling for $40 to $50 a head on the eastern market. In Texas, meanwhile, longhorn cattle could be bought for $3 or $4 a head. By doing some simple arithmetic, the Texas cattle ranchers soon realized there was an opportunity for making a fortune. Their only problem was how to get their cattle from the Texas plains to the markets of the East.

By the end of the Civil War, railroads had begun to cross the plains. Rail lines reached from the East Coast as far west as Sedalia, Missouri. Sedalia was about 1,100 kilometers (700 miles) from the cattle ranches of southern Texas. If the cattle ranchers could drive their herds overland to Sedalia, then they could ship them by railroad to the East.

Beginning in the spring of 1866, Texas cattle ranchers began making an annual

Background: In 1867, Joseph McCoy, an Illinois cattle rancher, purchased the township of Abilene, Kansas, as a shipping point for cattle from Texas. He laid out a trail from Corpus Christi, Texas, to Abilene. Over 35,000 head of cattle reached Abilene in that year alone.

Cattle Trails of the 1870's

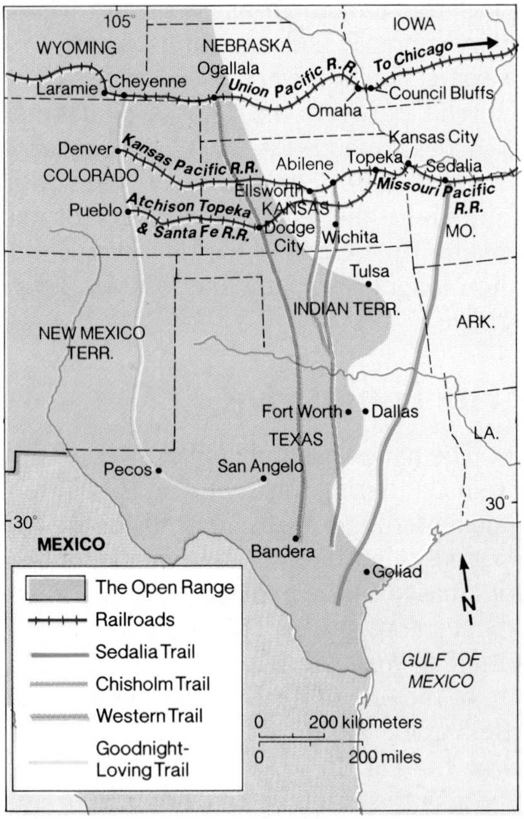

Which cattle trails connected with the Union Pacific Railroad?

"long drive" to the railroad. A thousand or more head of cattle were herded northward by cowhands on horseback. A chuck wagon carried the necessary food and supplies. The drive was headed by a trail boss. By the mid-1880's, 4 million cattle had been driven northward to the railroad.

The first route used by the cattle drivers was the Sedalia Trail. This trail ran northeast from Texas through Oklahoma and Arkansas to Missouri. As railroad lines pushed farther west onto the plains, the Chisholm (CHIZ-um) and Goodnight-Loving trails became more popular.

"Cowtowns" flourished at the end of the trails. Cowtowns such as Abilene and Dodge City, Kansas, were often wild places to live. Cowhands, after months of hard work on the trail, would come to town to drink and gamble. They usually had plenty of money to spend. They were paid for their work at the end of the drive. Sometimes drunken cowhands would shoot up a town. Such cowhands often ended up in "boot hill"—a cemetery for those who died with their boots on.

The Ranchers

By 1880, there were cattle ranches throughout the Great Plains. Once, only buffalo had roamed across the grasslands of Kansas, Colorado, Wyoming, and Montana. Now herds of beef cattle grazed on these same lands. "Cotton was once crowned king," a newspaper editor remarked, "but grass is now." The plains became a vast new empire: the Cattle Kingdom.

The rulers of the new kingdom were the cattle ranchers. These ambitious individuals often got their start by making a claim to free government land. Usually, they grazed their cattle over other public lands as well. Because water was always needed, the ranchers built their homes near a stream or river. If there were a few trees nearby, the rancher would build a log cabin. If there were no trees, the rancher might build a tent of animal skins or a house of sod.

At first, all a rancher had to do was watch the herd graze and fatten, and mul-

Background: Calves that strayed from the herd and could not be identified were called "mavericks." The term was derived from the name of Samuel A. Maverick, a Texas attorney, who once received a herd of cattle as payment and allowed them to graze unbranded.

tiply. When enough cattle were ready for market, they would be taken to the railroad for sale. The rancher would then buy more calves, build a finer ranch house, and hire some cowhands to tend the larger herd. A successful rancher would have a dozen or more cowhands working on the spread.

As other ranchers moved into the area, problems arose. How much land could one rancher claim? How could ranchers keep their cattle separate from those of their neighbors?

The ranchers worked out sensible solutions to these problems. They agreed that each rancher had the right to claim a portion of land along a stream or river. This was only reasonable, since every rancher needed water for the cattle. The claim could extend back away from the water all the way to the nearest ridge. These were "open-range" ranches. An open-range ranch was one on which boundaries were not marked with fences. Some ranches covered as much as 100 square kilometers (38 square miles).

To keep their cattle separate from those of their neighbors, the ranchers used line riding, branding, and the roundup. In line riding, cowhands would camp along the boundary of each ranch. Every morning, the cowhands would ride along the boundary, looking for stray cattle. They would drive any wandering steers back toward the center of each ranch. The cowhands would also brand the young calves. Brands were distinctive marks burned into the calves' hide with a red-hot branding iron. Twice each year, in the spring and fall, roundups would be held. In a roundup, all of the cattle of neighboring ranches would be driven together. The cowhands would then separate the cattle of each ranch by checking the cattle's brands.

The Cowhands

The job of a cowhand was not easy. Cattle herders worked hard for the ranchers. They often lived out on the range for months at a time. Their legs were bowed from spending 12 hours a day in the saddle. Their faces were weather-beaten and wrinkled from the hot sun of the plains.

The job of the cowhands was to keep track of all the cattle. If a cow got lost, the cowhand had to find it and bring it back

Arthur L. Walker was a Colorado cowhand. Do his clothes match the description of cowhand clothing given in your text?

For Extra Interest: Show pictures from books on the American West of cattle brands used by prominent American cattle ranchers in the 1800's.

Background: Most cowhands were small. Carrying too much weight makes it difficult for a horse to work effectively or at top speed for long.

These cowhands are getting ready to go on night guard. What does this photo tell you about the life of a cowhand?

to the herd. "I'll tell you what being a cowpuncher is," one Texas cowhand said. "It ain't roping, and it ain't riding bronc, and it ain't being smart, neither. It's thinking enough about a dumb animal to go out in the rain or snow to try to save that cow."

The cowhands were a varied group. Some of them were as young as 14 or 15 years of age. About one out of every seven cowhands was Mexican. It was from the Mexican *vaqueros* that the other cowhands learned the basic skills of the trade. Also, about one out of seven cowhands was black. Many of the black cowhands once had been slaves on the Texas ranches. There they had learned riding and roping. The black cowhands moved farther west, seeking a new and freer life.

The equipment the cowhands used included a set of special working clothes. On their heads, they wore hats with broad brims. These broad brims shaded their eyes from the blazing sun. Around their necks were large knotted handkerchiefs. These could be pulled over their faces during dust storms. On their hands, they wore thick leather work gloves. "Chaps" were worn over their pants. These leather leggings protected their legs from the dense underbrush known as chapparal. To fit the stirrups of their saddles, they wore boots with narrow toes and high heels. The cowhands' jingling spurs guided their horses while their hands were busy with ropes or whips.

The Last Days of the Open Range

The days of the Cattle Kingdom were numbered. More and more cattle were brought to the plains. The grass was overgrazed, and each year it grew thinner. Also, many of the new cattle brought to the plains did not have the strength to survive the region's harsh conditions.

The summer of 1886 was unusually hot and dry. Much of the grass on the plains withered, and many streams dried up. The following winter was terribly cold. A blizzard left enormous snowdrifts, and the temperature dropped to nearly −57°C (−70°F). Cattle huddled together to keep warm, but thousands starved or froze to death.

Following the winter of 1886–1887, the

Background: Two highly infectious diseases broke out on the Great Plains, killing many cattle during this period. They were hoof and mouth disease and Texas fever.

Discuss: Compare the range wars (cattle ranchers versus sheep ranchers) and the Indian wars (Plains Indians versus white settlers) that were fought on the Great Plains in the 1800's. What caused both conflicts? How was each conflict resolved?

ranchers developed new methods of raising cattle. Herd sizes were reduced. The ranchers fenced in their land and began growing hay to feed the cattle. The days of the open range were over. The life of the cowhand changed, too. Rather than riding the open range, the cowhand became a ranch hand with new jobs to do.

For many cowhands, the passing of the open range meant the end of the "good old days." One cowhand later recalled, "I remember when we sat around the fire the winter through. We didn't do a lick of work for five or six months of the year, except to chop a little wood to build a fire to keep warm by. Now we go to the general roundup, then the calf roundup, then comes haying—something that the old-time cowboy never dreamed of. I tell you, times have changed."

Cattle ranchers also faced competition for grazing land from sheep ranchers. Sheep ranchers began herding sheep on the plains. The sheep ranchers believed that the grass of the plains could support sheep as well as cattle.

The cattle ranchers feared that the sheep would ruin the plains by cropping, or biting off, the grass too close to the ground. Starting in the 1880's, range wars broke out between cattle ranchers and sheep ranchers. At least 20 people were killed and 100 were injured in battles between the two groups. On the plains of Colorado and Wyoming, 600,000 sheep were destroyed. Most of them were driven over cliffs by angry cattle ranchers or cowhands. In spite of this opposition, the sheep were on the plains to stay.

The cattle ranchers' greatest rivals for the grasslands of the plains were not the sheep ranchers. Their greatest rivals were pioneer farmers and their families. The farmers plowed the grasslands under for their crops. They fenced in the old grazing lands of the ranchers. Range wars in the 1880's were also fought between the ranchers and the farmers.

As the days of the open range came to a close, peace returned to the plains. The cattle ranchers, the sheep ranchers, and the farmers all had a share of the land.

Section Review

1. What was life like for the cattle ranchers and the cowhands on the Great Plains?
2. Who were the *vaqueros?* What could the *vaqueros* teach the North American cowhands?
3. How were the ranchers able to get their cattle from the Texas plains to the markets in the East?
4. The life of the cowhands has had a powerful impact on the American imagination. What evidence do you see today of a continuing fascination with the cowhands of the Old West?

For Extra Interest: Have students look at a rainfall map of the United States. Ask students how the amount of rainfall on the Great Plains compares to amounts received in other parts of the country.

3. The Plains Pioneers

BEFORE YOU READ: *How did the pioneers of the plains solve their problems?*

Pioneers came to the Great Plains from many places. Some came from the older states of the Union. They came from Missouri and Illinois, from Tennessee and Kentucky. Pioneers also arrived from other countries. Many Irish settled the plains of Nebraska. Germans came by the thousands to Kansas and to Texas. From the countries of Scandinavia—Norway, Sweden, and Denmark—thousands more moved to the grasslands of Minnesota and the Dakotas.

Problems and Solutions

The pioneer farmers who settled the Great Plains faced many difficult problems. Americans who had crossed the plains earlier had concluded that the land was too dry for farming. The farmers of the plains soon found that their most serious problem was getting enough water for their crops.

Plains farmers at first tried to dig wells. They hoped to raise ground water to the surface by buckets. They soon found that wells on the plains had to be very deep. It was impossible to bring water to the surface in this way.

Although rainfall on the plains was less than in the East, the winds of the plains were stronger. Soon, the farmers realized that they could use these stronger winds to solve their water problem. They built powerful windmills to pump the ground water to the surface. Unfortunately, the windmills were very expensive to build. Most farmers could not afford to build them.

Another solution to the water problem was a new method of farming called "dry farming." In dry farming, fields are plowed more than a foot deep. The deep plowing loosens the soil, helping it to absorb moisture. Also, after each rainfall, farmers rake their fields. The raking covers the fields with a light dust. The dust helps reduce evaporation. More of the precious moisture is thus kept in the soil near the plants' roots.

Because annual rainfall on the plains was less than in the East, the amount of food that could be produced from the land was also less. An eastern farmer could support a family with about 32 hectares (80 acres) of land. On the plains, a farmer needed at least 146 hectares (360 acres). How could a farmer plow, plant, and harvest a farm so large?

Improvements in farm machinery helped solve this problem. Improved plows of steel allowed a farmer to plow the fields much more quickly. Planting was speeded up by mechanical grain drills. The grain drill cut the soil and automatically placed seeds in the ground. Harvesting equipment was also improved by many new inventions. The twine binder, for example, allowed two farmers and a team of horses to harvest 8 hectares (20 acres) of grain in a day.

The combined harvester, or combine, was invented in California in the 1880's. A generation later, its use spread across the plains. The combine could harvest and thresh grain in one operation. Such improvements in farm machinery made

Background: The twine binder, or self-binder, developed from the McCormick reaper. This machine not only cut grain but also tied it into bundles.

For Extra Interest: The total cost of a sod house from an old diary: windows, $1.25 each; door latch, $0.50; pipe for chimney, $0.30; lumber, $0.55; nails, $0.20. Compare this to the cost of building a house today.

farming on the Great Plains easier and more profitable.

Houses, Fuel, and Fences

The forests of the East or Europe had provided farmers with wood for houses, fuel, and fences. But most of the Great Plains was treeless. How could farmers on the plains survive without wood?

The earliest farmhouses on the plains were "dugouts." These houses were little more than holes dug in the sides of a hill. They were dark and dirty.

As pioneer families prospered, they built better homes. Many families on the plains built sod houses. These houses were built out of the turf of the plains. The pioneers cut long strips of sod from the ground and divided the strips into brick-sized pieces. The sod "bricks" were stacked one on top of another to build the walls of the sod house. If any lumber was available, the roof would be made of wood. Otherwise, poles and branches would be placed across the tops of the walls. The roof would be covered with more sod.

It was very hard to keep a sod house clean. Dirt was always falling from the walls or the ceiling. When it rained, muddy water would drip inside the house. Pioneer women sometimes had to cook while holding an umbrella over the stove! The rains made the dirt floors swampy.

The problem of getting enough fuel was more difficult to solve. Fuel was needed for cooking and for heating during the long winter months. Like the Indians, the first pioneers burned dried buffalo manure. This source of fuel disappeared as the buffalo became almost extinct. Later,

This Nebraska family posed proudly in front of their sod house on a sunny day in 1866. What evidence of life on the Great Plains do you see?

Background: There are now more than 600 kinds of barbed wire, which was called "devil's rope" by the cattle ranchers of the late 1800's. Different types are collected by people today as a hobby.

farmers burned dried cow manure. Stoves were invented to burn tightly bound bundles of hay, corncobs, or cornstalks. None of these fuels was very satisfactory. They all burned too rapidly. New fuel had to be added constantly to the fire. The fuel problem was solved only with the building of the railroads. The railroads brought wood or coal from the East to the farmers on the Great Plains.

Fences were needed on the plains to keep cattle and other livestock from the crops. But wood for building fences was very scarce. American inventors helped solve the farmers' fence problem. The best new fence was produced by Joseph F. Glidden in DeKalb, Illinois. Glidden twisted two strands of wire together. At frequent places on the wire, sharp points, or barbs, were attached.

Glidden's "barbed wire" was more effective than smooth wire in keeping livestock away from crops. Barbed wire was cheap and easy to make. And barbed-wire fences needed only a few wooden posts for support.

More Problems

The pioneers had other problems that seemed to have no solution. Each season brought new challenges. In the spring, swollen rivers would flood the plains. Houses and farm equipment were ruined. The summer months could bring unbearable heat. Temperatures might stay as high as 43°C (110°F) for several weeks. Streams would dry up, and farm animals would die.

Swarms of grasshoppers invaded the plains during the summers between 1874 and 1877. The insects arrived without warning, in swarms so large that they blotted out the sun. The grasshoppers ate everything in their path: cornstalks, vegetables, even the handles of pitchforks and plows. The grasshoppers formed a cover on the ground that was 5 centimeters (2 inches) thick. Grasshoppers got inside farmhouses. They ate the curtains from windows and the clothes in closets.

As fall came each year, a new danger arrived. Prairie fires would sweep across the plains, scorching the farmlands. The tinder-dry grasses would be ignited by an untended campfire, a spark from a gun, or a bolt of lightning.

Perhaps the greatest danger to the pioneer farmers came in the winter months. The howling winds would drive snow and ice across the plains. A family might wake up to find snow in their house and their food frozen. To protect their livestock from a blizzard, the pioneers would bring their animals inside their houses. With the temperature at −35°C (−30°F), a family might spend days in their sod house, surrounded by chickens, cows, and pigs.

Pioneer Life

The life of the pioneers was hard. Even the most routine tasks were difficult on the frontier. Clothes had to be washed by hand. Even the soap had to be made. Miriam Davis Colt, a pioneer on the Kansas frontier, complained that scrubbing clothes in a creek never really got them clean. Once they were washed, she said, the clothes looked "clean for brown but awful dirty for white." Having neither starch nor an iron for her clothes, she would press out the wrinkles by a "rub through the hand."

Background: Farmers today can use a machine called a "hopperdozer" to kill grasshoppers. This machine spreads oil on the ground, which makes the grasshoppers jump. When they jump, they hit a canvas and fall into the oil.

Discuss: What problems do American farmers have today? If students are unfamiliar with farm problems, have them look in newspapers and current magazines to find out.

This plains woman is gathering buffalo chips to use as fuel in her home.

Cooking was another time-consuming chore. The fuels that were available for cooking burned very rapidly. A cook had to spend half the time stoking, or feeding fuel to, the fire.

The hard work of the frontier left women with little time for visiting or having fun. One way that women could mix work and play was the quilting bee. A quilting bee was a daylong gathering of women to finish making a quilt. Individual women would work long hours alone making the small pieces of quilt.

Once all the pieces were finished, a woman would invite her neighbors to gather for a quilting bee. The women would sit around a large quilting frame and stitch all the small pieces onto a cloth backing. While they were stitching, the women could visit and enjoy the company of their neighbors.

Pioneer parents were particularly concerned that their children receive an education. Sometimes, it was necessary for women to teach their children at home. Women also helped start schools, and many became teachers and school superintendents for a county or state. The pioneer schools were usually one-room schools. Children of many ages learned from the same teacher.

Teachers were often only a little older than their students. Some were as young as 15 when they took their first job. Although the frontier teachers often had little formal education, many of them were excellent teachers. Between 1870 and 1900, the plains states of Kansas and Nebraska had the highest **literacy rates** in the country. A literacy rate is a measure of the number of people who can read and write.

---

literacy rate the percentage of people in a specific population group who can read and write

---

Frontier teachers often received a higher monthly salary than teachers in the East. But frontier schools were usually only in session for three or four months a year. Children were needed to work on the farm during the rest of the year. Teachers had to find other jobs to support themselves when school was not in session. The pioneer schoolteacher, one writer commented, "works the hardest and gets the nearest to no pay for it of any person I have known. . . ."

For Extra Interest: Invite an antique dealer familiar with quilts to come in and show or describe to the class the many patterns of quilts that were made in the nineteenth century. The dealer might also show other items related to the period.

Discuss: If you had been a settler on the Great Plains at this time, do you think you would have stayed or returned home? Why?

Opportunities

Why did the pioneer families want to move west? They knew they would face many difficult problems on the Great Plains. But the pioneers also knew that the West offered them opportunities to improve their lives.

One of the opportunities of the West was the land itself. The Homestead Act of 1862 invited any citizen to claim 65 hectares (160 acres) of public land. After the citizen had built a dwelling on the land and lived there for five years, the government would give the citizen the land free of charge. The Homestead Act attracted thousands of people west. These people were called **homesteaders**.

---

homesteader a person who settled on government land, built a dwelling on it, and owned it after living on it for five years

---

Unfortunately, the Homestead Act did not take into account the special needs of farmers on the plains. The plains farmers needed more than 65 hectares (160 acres) to make a living.

Also, the Homestead Act was often misused. Some people illegally claimed huge amounts of western land. They expected to sell the land for a great profit. These people were called **speculators**.

---

speculator a person who acquires land in the hopes of selling it later at a great profit

---

The speculators used many tricks to acquire land. They often hired other people to claim land for them. They would then build very small houses on the land. When they reported to the government that they had built a house on their claim, they would describe it as a "twelve by fourteen dwelling." They would fail to say that the size of their "dwelling" was 12 by 14 *inches* rather than 12 by 14 feet! Other speculators would move a small house about on wheels from claim to claim.

Most pioneer farmers never got the free land promised by the Homestead Act. They bought their land from speculators. The land—although not free—was still an opportunity for the pioneers. Once they had their land, they could produce crops to sell.

"Boomers" and "Sooners"

One of the last areas of the West to be opened for settlement was Oklahoma. In the 1870's, most of Oklahoma was called Indian Territory. This territory covered millions of hectares (acres) of land. It contained the reservations of 22 different Indian tribes.

In the 1880's, many white people wanted the government to open Indian Territory for settlement. Those who favored opening the lands were called "Boomers." They said they would come "booming" into the new lands once they were opened.

On March 23, 1889, President Benjamin Harrison announced that a large part of Oklahoma would be opened for settlement. Beginning at noon on April 22, 1889, citizens would be able to claim homesteads in the area. As April 22 neared, thousands of people gathered around the borders of the Oklahoma lands. Soldiers were there to hold back

For Extra Interest: Students might measure their classroom and compare it to the 12 by 14 foot dimension required of a whole house.

Background: Cowhands in the late 1800's had driven thousands of cattle across Indian lands in Oklahoma to reach railroad shipping stations in Kansas.

anyone who crossed the borders too soon. Some did, and these impatient settlers were called "Sooners."

When the noon hour arrived on April 22, there were 50,000 Boomers and Sooners on hand. Guns were fired at exactly 12 o'clock, and the settlers poured across the borders. Men and women rushed forward in wagons and carriages. Some rode horses. Some even rode bicycles. The settlers hurried to make their claims of 65 hectares (160 acres) of free land.

The Dawes Act of 1887 opened more Oklahoma lands for settlement. This act divided reservations into individual sections for each Indian family. It ordered any lands left over to be sold. During the 1890's, many reservations in Indian territory were opened to settlers.

With the settlement of Oklahoma, the frontier had nearly disappeared. The movement of pioneers on the plains had changed forever the great interior of America. Ranchers, cowhands, and pioneer farm families had replaced the Indians and the buffalo. The Indians were confined on reservations. The buffalo were almost extinct. The Old West would continue to stir the imagination—or to haunt the memory—of all Americans. But the days of the frontier were no more.

Sooners cutting wire.

Section Review

1. What problems did the pioneer families have? How did they solve these problems?
2. Define literacy rate. Which states had the highest literacy rates between 1870 and 1900?
3. What problems did pioneer women face as they performed their daily work?
4. Who were the speculators? What tricks did they use to acquire western lands?
5. Did the opportunities of the Great Plains outweigh the hardships faced by the pioneers? Explain your answer.

CHAPTER REVIEW

Summary

After the Civil War, only one frontier remained in the United States. It was the vast, almost flat and treeless area stretching westward from the Mississippi River to the Rocky Mountains. This area, known as the Great Plains, was home to a great many American Indian tribes who primarily hunted to meet their basic needs.

In the late 1800's, miners, farmers, and cattle ranchers moved onto the Great Plains. They put pressure on the government to move the Indians to reservations. The Indians were angry at being pushed from their lands and homes. Numerous conflicts broke out between the American Indians and the white settlers.

Life for the settlers on the Great Plains was very difficult. Cowhands led a rugged and lonely life. Pioneer farmers had to deal with a harsh environment as well as a life filled with very few conveniences. Despite these problems, more and more people came to the Great Plains. By 1890, the last frontier had disappeared from the American landscape.

Recalling the Facts

1. Why did the American Indians have to leave their homes on the Great Plains?

2. How did the mass killing of the buffalo on the Great Plains bring an end to the Indians' way of life?

3. What was the purpose of the Dawes Act? How was it harmful to the Indians?

4. Why did the cattle ranchers resent the coming of sheep ranchers to the Great Plains?

5. What brought an end to open-range ranching?

6. What problems did the pioneers face on the Great Plains?

Analyzing the Facts

1. Horace Greeley, an American editor, wrote, "Go west, young man, and grow with the country." Do you feel this was good advice in the late 1800's? Why or why not?

2. How did the Indian way of life on the Great Plains differ from that of the white newcomers? How did these differences make conflict between the two groups almost unavoidable?

3. Why did the Sioux Indians attack Custer and his men at the Little Bighorn River?
4. Which group of people do you think had a greater effect on forcing the Plains Indians from their land, the buffalo hunter or the army? Explain your answer.
5. In 1961, President Kennedy spoke of a new frontier to "explore the stars, conquer the deserts, eradicate disease, tap the ocean depths, and encourage the arts and commerce." What are new frontiers today? Compare them to the American frontier of the late 1800's in terms of similarities and differences.

Time and History

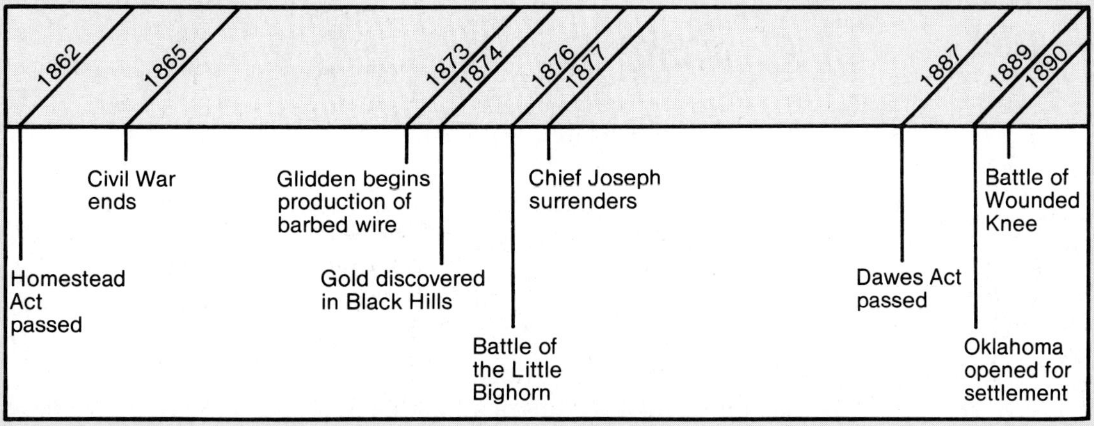

1. In what years on the time line did the United States Army fight the Plains Indians?
2. How long after the Homestead Act was passed was the Oklahoma Territory opened for settlement?
3. In what year was the fencing problem solved for the pioneer settlers on the Great Plains?
4. Which event happened first, the Indian wars on the Great Plains or the Civil War?
5. Which of the following events led to the Battle of the Little Bighorn: gold discovered in the Black Hills, the Dawes Act, or Oklahoma opened for settlement?

Chapter
19

The Rise of Industry

One day, Huckleberry Finn, a character in a book by Mark Twain, saw a mighty steamboat. "She was a big one, and she was coming in a hurry, too. . . . All of a sudden she bulged out, big and scary, with a long row of wide-open furnace doors shining like red-hot teeth."

For many Americans in the late 1800's, their meeting with the Age of Industry was a lot like Huck's meeting with this mighty steamboat. The new industrial age was coming in a hurry, and it was scary. Everything seemed to be changing at once.

Before the Civil War, America had been largely a nation of farmers. By 1900, the United States was the world's leading industrial power. The rapid rise of American industry brought benefits to many people. But the Age of Industry also created serious problems. The benefits of the industrial age were not shared among all the Americans.

After you read this chapter, you will be able to:

1. List the factors that helped American industry grow.
2. Explain why Edison and Bell were heroes of the Age of Industry.
3. Describe how businesses tried to reduce competition.
4. Discuss the attempts of government to regulate business.

☐ Read a circle graph.

For Extra Interest: Have students use an almanac to examine current statistics on goods produced and number of workers employed in American industry. Students can make charts or graphs based on the information they find.

1. Industrial Growth

BEFORE YOU READ: *What factors helped American industry grow?*

Before the Civil War, American factories were making less than $2 billion worth of goods per year. By the early 1900's, factories in the United States were producing goods worth more than $13 billion. American industries were producing more goods than all the industries of Great Britain, France, and Germany combined. In 1900, the United States ranked first among the industrial nations. The world had never seen such rapid industrial growth.

Many factors helped American industry to grow. The nation was rich in natural resources needed by industry. Industrial workers were also available in great numbers. Skilled business leaders contributed their talents to the growth of industry. Big businesses provided the money that was needed for industrial growth. A new method of making goods allowed industries to expand rapidly. The government, in several important ways, also helped industry to grow.

Natural Resources

One of the most important factors in the growth of American industry was the nation's abundant supply of natural resources. Among these resources were coal, iron, and oil.

About half the world's supply of coal is located in the United States. Great beds of coal lay underground in Pennsylvania, West Virginia, Kentucky, and Alabama. Other large deposits were discovered in the Midwest. Coal was used as a major fuel for the nation's growing railroads and factories.

A second important natural resource for industry was iron. Iron is the main ingredient used in making steel. Pennsylvania, Alabama, and Michigan contained large deposits of iron ore. The largest deposit was in the Mesabi Range in northern Minnesota. By 1900, the Mesabi Range was producing one sixth of all the iron ore used in the world. Large ships carried iron ore from the Minnesota mines across the Great Lakes to the steel-making cities of Detroit, Cleveland, and Toledo.

Oil was a third natural resource that was needed by American industry. Oil was needed for the moving parts of trains and factory equipment. Later, oil replaced coal as the primary source of fuel. The first oil wells were drilled in Pennsylvania in 1859. California, Texas, and Oklahoma also became major oil suppliers. By the early 1890's, hundreds of wells were pumping oil in the yards of homes throughout the Los Angeles area.

Many other natural resources helped American industry grow. Gold and silver continued to be mined in California, Nevada, and Colorado. The new mines in the Black Hills of South Dakota added more gold to the nation's supply. In the 1880's, copper mining boomed in Montana and Arizona. Meanwhile, the mines of Missouri, Colorado, and Idaho supplied the nation with great quantities of lead.

Workers

The nation's large work force also helped American industry grow. At the end of the Civil War, more than 2 million

For Extra Interest: Have students look at a natural resources map of the United States and locate deposits of coal, iron, and oil. Ask them if the deposits they located are near centers of industry. Also ask why industrial centers are usually located near these resources.

Vocabulary Help: combine—a farm machine that reaps, threshes, and cleans grain while moving over a field; the grain is poured into sacks, a tank, or a truck, and the stalks are laid on the ground

These women are working in a textile factory. What percentage of the factory's work force appears to be women?

former soldiers were available for work in industry. Many of these individuals were eager to find jobs.

Millions of farm workers left the nation's farms as a result of improvements in farm equipment. Modern farm machines such as mechanical harvesters and combines allowed farmers to increase their production greatly. Using a hand sickle, for instance, a farmer could harvest about 3 hectares (7.5 acres) of grain each year. With a mechanical reaper, a farmer could harvest more than 40 hectares (100 acres). With improvements such as these, fewer farmers were needed to produce the nation's crops. Between 1870 and 1890, more than 4 million men and women left farms for work in factories.

The number of women in the work force was steadily growing. By 1900, about one fifth of all American workers were women. In some industries, such as the manufacture of shoes and garments, women made up as much as 60 percent of the work force.

Immigrants were another important part of the American work force. Between 1860 and 1900, 14 million immigrants came to the United States. Irish immigrants worked in industries in many eastern cities. Irish and Chinese workers helped build the transcontinental railroad. Many immigrants from Germany and Scandinavia found jobs in the factories of Chicago, Cincinnati, and Milwaukee. Italians, Poles, and Russians worked in industries throughout America.

Business Leaders

The growth of American industry also depended on the talents and hard work of business leaders who organized and managed the industries. These business leaders brought together the resources and workers needed for industrial growth. Such organizers and managers were called **entrepreneurs**.

---

entrepreneur a person who organizes and manages a business

Successful entrepreneurs had many talents. They were able to identify the need for new types of goods or services. They knew how to start businesses and to keep them operating. They were able to locate and to obtain needed resources. They knew how to manage the labor of many other people.

Discuss: Whom have you heard of who could be considered an entrepreneur today? If students do not know of anyone, have them look in magazines or newspapers for articles about enterprising business people.

Background: Advantages of a corporation: 1) raises large sums of money quickly to start business, 2) business success will bring profits to investors, and 3) stockholders are not personally responsible for debts of corporation.

One of the most talented American entrepreneurs was a man named Gustavus Swift. Swift saw that as more and more people moved to the cities, there was a growing need for fresh meat. In 1875, he organized a business to meet that need.

Shipping fresh meat over long distances was next to impossible before the Civil War. The meat would spoil. Thousands of cattle were shipped by rail across the country from ranches of the West to the cities of the East. On the journey, many of the cattle lost weight. Others were injured or died.

In the 1870's, refrigerated railroad cars were invented. These cars allowed fresh meat to be shipped long distances without spoiling. Gustavus Swift realized that now it was possible to slaughter cattle much nearer to the western ranches. The fresh meat could then be shipped east in the new refrigerated railroad cars.

Swift built a large slaughterhouse and meat-packing company in Chicago. Swift organized his business very well. He used the latest meat-packing equipment. He reduced the amount of waste by using animal parts that would otherwise have been thrown away. He used animal parts to make medicines, fertilizers, and leather. Swift's meat business was very successful. Other entrepreneurs, such as Philip D. Armour and Michael Cudahy, also developed successful meat-packing companies. Soon fresh meat was being shipped all over the country.

Corporations

To start or run a large business required a lot of money. Money was needed to buy raw materials, buy equipment, and hire workers. Long before the Civil War, a new type of business organization had been developed that could solve the entrepreneurs' money problem. This organization is called a **corporation**. Corporations are formed so that many individuals can pool their money to start a business. Each person who invests money in the business is given a share of **stock**. The more money a person invests in the corporation, the more shares of stock he or she receives. The individual owners of stocks are called stockholders. By providing money, corporations allowed American industries to grow very rapidly.

corporation a business organization formed by individuals who pool their money and become stockholders in the business

stock a share of ownership in a business acquired by a person who invests money in the business

Mass Production

Industries were also able to grow because of a new method of making goods. By the early 1900's, many American products were being made on an **assembly line**. On an assembly line, goods are moved through a factory on a slowly moving belt or track. As the goods pass by, each worker completes one part of the process. In this way, workers could make goods more quickly. Assembly lines made **mass production** possible. Mass production involves using machines to produce goods more quickly and cheaply.

For Extra Interest: Explain how to find a particular stock cost in the newspaper. Have students select a company and calculate how many shares of stock they can buy for $1,000. Have them calculate profits or losses at the end of two weeks.

Background: If one country, such as the United States, places tariffs on foreign goods, other countries feel that they too must have tariffs. Tariffs protect the home market but may make it more difficult for American businesses to sell their goods overseas.

assembly line a method of producing goods in which workers put together a product as it goes past them on a moving belt

mass production the use of machines to produce goods more quickly and cheaply

Government

The government helped industry to grow in several important ways. In the late 1800's, the federal government started many transportation projects. The government built docks and improved harbors. It also provided large grants of land to corporations to build railroads. These projects helped industry by making it easier for businesses to transport their raw materials and to move their products to market.

The federal government also helped industry by placing high taxes on imported goods. These taxes, called tariffs, made foreign goods more expensive than American-made goods. Thus Americans were encouraged to buy goods made in the United States.

In addition, the federal government helped industry in another important way. During most of the 1800's, the federal government followed a "hands-off" policy toward business. A few businesses became very powerful by eliminating competition. Some Americans began to believe that the government should regulate businesses. But under the "hands-off" policy, the government did not interfere with the activities of private businesses. The owners of businesses were left alone. This policy is sometimes called ***laissez-faire*** (LEH-say FAIR). The term *laissez-faire* comes from a French expression that means "let people do as they please."The policy of *laissez-faire* was criticized by many Americans. This policy, however, allowed businesses to expand without government interference.

laissez-faire a government policy of not interfering in the affairs of business

Section Review

1. What factors contributed to the growth of American industry?
2. Describe the kinds of people who made up America's work force in the early 1900's.
3. Who were the entrepreneurs? How did their talents help industry grow?
4. Define the following terms: corporation, assembly line, and *laissez-faire.*
5. Gustavus Swift saw a need and organized a successful business to meet that need. What new opportunities are there today for a person to start a business?

 Discuss: Should the government be involved in regulating businesses? Why or why not?

Social Studies Skills

Reading Circle Graphs

In 1820, most Americans earned their living by farming. However, by 1900, the United States had become an industrial nation, and the majority of its workers held nonagricultural jobs. The circle graphs below show this change. The graphs show percentages by the size of the pieces, or angles, as well as by number. On the first graph below, the nonagricultural wedge is much smaller than the agricultural portion. At the same time, the numbers tell you exactly what percentage of Americans worked in agricultural and nonagricultural jobs in 1820. On the second graph, the size of the nonagricultural wedge is larger.

A circle graph shows percentages, or parts of a whole. The entire circle represents 100 percent. The circle is divided mathematically into as many pieces as are needed to show various percentages. Circle graphs are useful because they show visually how percentages compare to each other and to the whole. This makes the information easier to understand and remember than using numbers alone.

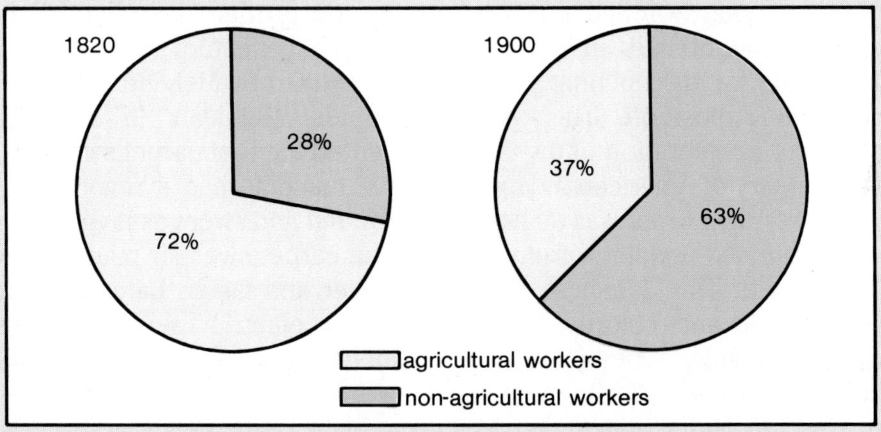

1. Why do you think a circle graph is sometimes called a pie graph?
2. When or why are circle graphs used?
3. In 1900, what percentage of Americans worked in nonagricultural jobs? What percentage made their living by farming?
4. By what percentage did the number of workers in nonagricultural jobs increase from 1820 to 1900? By what percentage did agricultural workers decrease during this same period?

Discuss: What would be shown if an exposition similar to the Centennial Exposition were held today? Do you think that computers, videotape machines, space shuttles, and the like are as impressive to us as the inventions shown in 1876 were to people of that time? Why or why not?

2. A Time of Invention

BEFORE YOU READ: *Why were Thomas Edison and Alexander Graham Bell heroes in the Age of Industry?*

Ideas and inventions flourished in the United States during the late 1800's. Thousands of new products were created by Americans. The heroes of the age were geniuses like Thomas Edison and Alexander Graham Bell. The new inventions improved the lives of people around the world.

Marvels of the New Age

On May 10, 1876, a huge crowd of more than 100,000 people swarmed onto the grounds of Fairmount Park in Philadelphia. They came for the opening day of the Centennial Exposition. This great world's fair was a celebration of the hundredth anniversary of American independence. Even President Grant was on hand.

The fair included exhibits from all around the world. Tiny Japanese dolls, rich Russian furs, and colorful French fabrics were on display. The most exciting exhibits at the fair were the new inventions from the United States. Farmers came to see the new machines that would help them plant and harvest their crops. Business leaders admired the latest advances in factory equipment. Everyone was impressed by the mighty 1500-horsepower Corliss steam engine that provided power for the entire fair.

The inventions on display at the fair were just a small sample of the many products of American genius. Each of the inventions had a special government license. This protected the inventor from having the invention copied. It also gave the inventor the right to make and sell any invention for a certain number of years. This license is called a **patent**. No one else can make or sell a patented invention until the patent runs out.

---

patent a government license that gives someone the right to make and sell an invention for a certain number of years

---

Up until 1860, the government had issued only 36,000 patents for new inventions. Between 1865 and 1900, the government issued 638,000 patents! The late 1800's were truly a "time of invention."

Many of the new inventions helped people in their daily lives. For example, people benefited from a new invention developed by Melville R. Bissell of Grand Rapids, Michigan. In 1876, Bissell invented the first carpet sweeper. This simple machine had a revolving brush that rotated and swept as it was pushed along. The carpet sweeper made housecleaning easier and faster. Later inventions, such as the electric vacuum cleaner and the electric washing machine, made housework even easier.

Many of the new inventions were especially useful to American industry. The typewriter, for instance, was an important invention because it speeded business communications. The first practical typewriter was designed in 1868 by Christopher Sholes in Milwaukee, Wisconsin. Sholes' typewriters were soon made and sold by a New York gun-making firm, E. Remington and Sons.

 Discuss: Why does the government grant patents? Do you think they are necessary? Why or why not?

Background: Granville T. Woods, a black American, made improvements on the automatic air brake. He began inventing in 1885 and received 35 patents for his inventions.

James Ritty invented the cash register in 1879. This machine made it easier for clerks in stores to keep track of their daily sales. The adding machine was patented in 1894 by William S. Burroughs. Business math could now be done much more easily and quickly.

Another new invention improved transportation. This invention was the air brake. Before the air brake was invented, it was very difficult to bring a train to a stop. Hand brakes had to be tightened on each railroad car. A worker would jump from one car to the next, tightening all the brakes to slow down the train.

In 1869, George Westinghouse invented the air brake. The air brake uses compressed air to stop railroad trains or to reduce their speed. The air brake made it possible for an engineer to tighten all the brakes at one time by a control at the front of the train. The air brake made the operation of railroads much safer and easier.

This is a 1912 patent drawing for a new invention, the portable air-withdrawing vacuum. Notice how air is withdrawn by a person's walking on the bellows.

American Heroes

Two of the greatest heroes of the Age of Industry were Thomas Edison and Alexander Graham Bell. Both men were heroes because they had a talent for making useful inventions.

Thomas Edison was the most important inventor in American history. He was born in 1847 in Milan, Ohio. As a child, he enjoyed trying out things he had read about or thought about. Once, when he was six years old, his parents found him sitting on a nest of goose eggs. He explained to his startled parents that he had seen a goose hatch eggs. Now he wanted to find out if he could hatch eggs, too!

In school, young Edison was not a very good student. Most of his education took place at home. His mother became his best teacher. He loved to read, and his father paid him 25 cents for each book that he read.

Edison received his first patent for an invention in 1869, when he was 22 years old. The patent was for an electric vote recorder designed to count votes in Congress. During the next 60 years, Edison received patents for over 1,000 inventions. Among his many inventions was the "autographic press." This device was similar

Background: In 1876, the first telephone line in the United States ran between Boston and Cambridge, Massachusetts, a distance of 3 kilometers (2 miles). By 1915, a transcontinental telephone line was completed.

This is a view of Broadway in New York City around 1880, before the overhead telegraph wires were placed underground.

to the modern mimeograph machine. It could make many copies of a letter or a diagram drawn on a stencil. He also improved the electric motor and battery. Millions of Americans have enjoyed two of Edison's most popular inventions—the phonograph and the motion picture machine.

Edison's most far-reaching invention was the creation of the first economical electrical lighting system. In the early 1800's, Americans worked and played almost entirely during the daylight hours. Other than candles or whale-oil lamps, there was no practical way to light homes or offices at night. By the 1850's, gas lighting was available. Gas, however, was expensive and a fire hazard. Later, kerosene lamps were used, but they too were a fire hazard.

Thomas Edison began experimenting with electricity as a source of light in 1878. In 1879, he invented the first long-burning light bulb. By the early 1880's, he had developed a system for making and sending electricity.

On September 4, 1882, Edison's first electric lighting system began operating in New York. He soon built systems in other cities. By 1900, 2 million electric lights were in use in the United States. Streets, factories, schools, homes, and offices were lit by electricity. People throughout the nation benefited from Edison's genius. They now had more hours each day for reading, visiting, working, and playing.

Another hero of the Age of Industry was Alexander Graham Bell. Bell was born in Edinburgh, Scotland, in 1847. Like Edison, Bell was very curious as a child. He began a small "museum" of minerals, birds' eggs, and wildflowers. He studied his collection with great care. He wanted to

Background: Bell's first message over the telephone was spoken to Thomas Watson, his assistant, who was in another room. He said, "Come here. I want you."

learn all he could about the natural world.

Bell's father was a teacher of the deaf. At an early age, Bell also became interested in the problems of speech and hearing. When Bell was 23 years old, he and his parents moved from Scotland to Canada. The next year, in 1871, Bell was hired as a teacher of the deaf at a school in Massachusetts.

Alexander Graham Bell began experimenting with machines that would help him teach deaf people to speak. He wanted to show deaf people what sound *looked like*. He thought that if they could see the vibrations or movements made by different human tones, they could make similar tones with their own voices.

For several years, Bell worked on the problem. One day in 1875, he made a great discovery. He found a way to send the human voice over a wire. He discovered that sound could be changed into a current of electricity. The current could then be sent through a wire. Bell had discovered the basic idea behind the telephone. In 1876, he was granted a patent for his invention.

The 1876 Centennial Exposition in Philadelphia gave Bell a chance to show the world his new invention. The telephone was one of the many new marvels at the fair. One British scientist said the telephone was "the greatest marvel hitherto achieved." Bell was encouraged by the praise his invention received.

Within a few years, telephones and telphone wires were found all across the country. By 1900, there were 800,000 telephones in the United States. Bell became a famous and wealthy man.

Because of his invention, communication for all Americans was greatly improved. The telephone helped businesses by making it possible for buyers and sellers to communicate over long distances. Also, by using the telephone, families and friends could now visit even when they were far apart. News could travel more rapidly over the telephone. People could find out about important events as soon as they happened. It is easy to see why a man like Alexander Graham Bell became a hero to many Americans.

In later years, Bell worked on many other inventions. He also never gave up his interest in helping the deaf. He established a fund for the study of deafness. Throughout his life, Bell was a leading authority on the education of the deaf.

Section Review

1. Why were Thomas Edison and Alexander Graham Bell heroes to many Americans in the Age of Industry?
2. What is a patent?
3. Which inventions of the late 1800's were especially useful to American industry?
4. Many of the inventions of the late 1800's are still being used today. Which of these inventions are important in your own life? Explain why you think they are important.

Background: Governor Leland Stanford of California missed on his first swing at the gold spike joining the two railroads. His second swing at the spike, made of $20 gold pieces, was successful.

3. Railroads, Steel, and Oil

BEFORE YOU READ: *How did American businesses try to reduce competition?*

The Age of Industry was a time of fierce competition among American businesses. Each business wanted to sell more of its products. More sales would mean more profits.

To sell more of their products, many American businesses lowered their prices. By lowering prices, these businesses hoped to attract customers away from other companies. But other companies lowered their prices to try to keep their customers. As prices dropped, so did businesses' profits.

Competition became a serious problem for American businesses. To solve the problem of competition and maintain profits, many businesses in the late 1800's combined with each other. By combining, businesses would agree on a common price to charge for their products. In this way, both prices and profits could be increased.

Different forms of business combinations were tried in many industries. Combinations became especially common in the three largest American industries: railroads, steel, and oil.

Railroads

By the 1860's, railroads stretched from the East Coast to Omaha, Nebraska. In 1863, construction began on the first railroad to span the continent.

Two companies took up the task of connecting Omaha with the West Coast. The Union Pacific started building westward from Omaha. From Sacramento, California, the Central Pacific Railroad began building eastward.

After six years of construction, the two lines were joined in a lively ceremony at Promontory Point, Utah. On May 10, 1869, a golden spike was hammered in place to complete the new railroad.

This first railroad across the continent was built with special help from the government. Under the Pacific Railroad Acts of 1862 and 1864, the federal government gave to the railroads over 53 million hectares (130 million acres) of land. State governments gave 20 million hectares (49 million acres) to the railroads. This huge gift of land—larger than the entire state of Texas—contained many valuable resources. The government gave the land to the railroad companies to help them pay the costs of building the railroad. The companies later sold their lands to settlers for $435 million.

The railroads helped many American industries to grow. The railroads created a demand for products such as rails and locomotives. The iron and steel industries expanded to meet this demand. By 1875, railroad companies were buying more than half the iron produced in the United States.

The railroads also helped by carrying the raw materials needed by industry. The nation's steel industry was able to expand rapidly because the railroads transported iron ore and supplies of cheap coal.

American industries benefited from the railroads in yet another important way. By expanding America's transportation

Discuss: Why were railroads an improvement over previous methods of transportation? What improvements in transportation have been made in the twentieth century?

Major United States Railroads, 1900

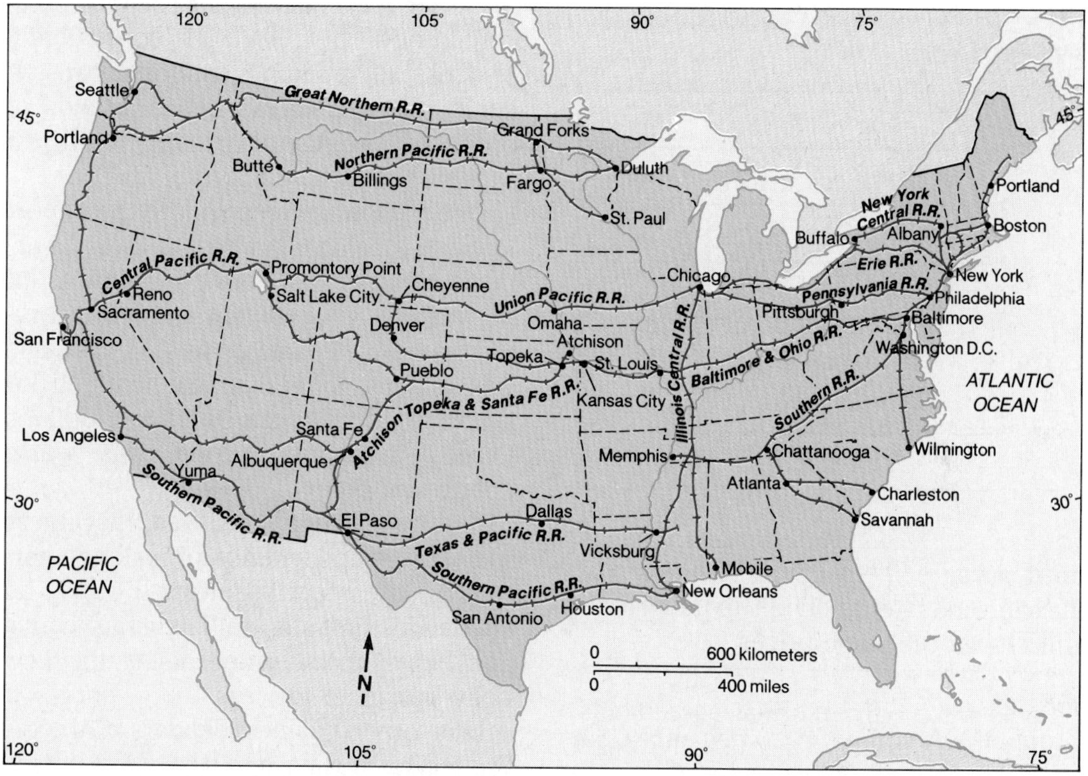

What railroads would be taken in order to get from Baltimore, Maryland, to Yuma, Arizona, in 1900?

network, the railroads created a nationwide market for the products of industry. By 1887, more than 30,000 towns were served by the railroad network. Businesses could now move their products to more customers across the country.

As the number of railroads increased in the United States, the competition for transporting goods increased. Railroads lowered their shipping rates to attract more business. In 1865, for example, it cost 96 cents to ship 45 kilograms (100 pounds) from Chicago to New York. As more railroads were built between the two cities, competition drove prices down. By 1898, the shipping rate had fallen to 20 cents.

To reduce competition, railroads formed "traffic associations" or **pools**. In a pool, several companies agree to charge the same rate for transporting goods. The companies also agree to share the business in a certain area. The pools allowed railroad companies to charge higher rates. The higher rates meant larger profits for the railroads.

Background: Because of the railroads, national time zones were created in 1883 to help in train scheduling. Until that time, each area had its own time. For example, Indiana had 23 local times, and Wisconsin had 38.

Background: In 1880, the tonnage of Bessemer steel exceeded that of wrought iron for the first time. In that year, steel rails accounted for 69 percent of the total annual production of 1.4 million tons of steel.

Iron and Steel Production

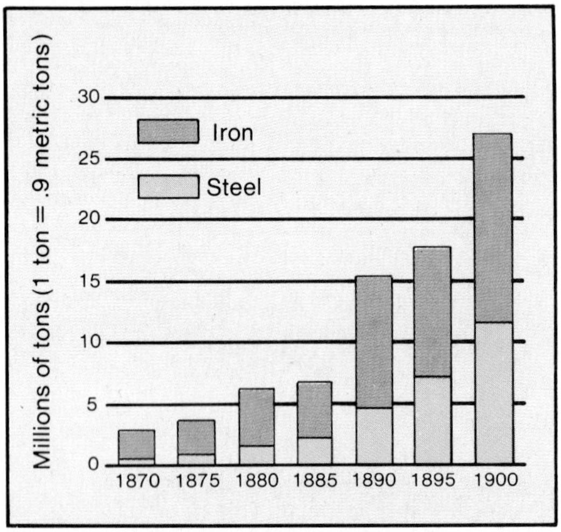

pool an agreement among businesses in the same industry to divide up the market and charge the same prices

Pools were only informal agreements among the railroads. They usually broke down when one railroad would lower its rates to try to attract more business. Competition would begin all over again.

Carnegie and Steel

Steel is an excellent building material. It is strong yet flexible. It can be made into an endless variety of products. Before the 1850's, steel was very difficult and expensive to make.

In the 1850's, two men, working separately, developed a new way to make steel from melted iron. One of the men was a Kentucky kettle maker named William Kelly. The other was Henry Bessemer, an English factory owner. In the new Kelly-Bessemer method, a blast of air was used to burn impurities out of the melted iron. This method allowed steel to be made far more easily and cheaply. Steel could now be used in constructing bridges, tall buildings, and railroads. It could be used in making thousands of products. The Age of Industry could just as well be called the Age of Steel.

One person who recognized the importance of steel was Andrew Carnegie. Carnegie came from a very poor family. But he was a very intelligent and hard-working man. By the time he was 33, Carnegie was making $50,000 a year working for the railroad. In terms of today's dollars, Carnegie's annual income was worth about $350,000.

Andrew Carnegie realized that there was a great opportunity for making a fortune in the steel business. In 1872, he opened his first steel mill in Pennsylvania and began making steel using the new Kelly-Bessemer process.

Like other business leaders, Carnegie wanted his business to grow. He lowered the price of his steel to attract more customers. As the other steel companies lost their customers to Carnegie, he bought them out. Carnegie's steel business eventually became the largest in the United States.

Carnegie was not just an expert at making steel. He was also an expert at making profits. Carnegie looked for ways to lower his costs of making steel. He used the most modern equipment and methods of steelmaking. He also kept his costs down by paying his workers low wages.

Carnegie also reduced his costs by becoming the owner of the raw materials needed to make steel. The materials used in making steel are iron ore, coal, limestone, and coke. Coke is a fuel made from

Background: The Bessemer process was the chief method of making steel until 1907, when it was overtaken by the open-hearth method. By the late 1950's, the Bessemer process accounted for less than 3 percent of the total steel production each year.

Background: The cost of steel rails dropped with new methods of production. In 1873, steel cost $160 a ton, whereas in 1898 it was only $17 a ton.

coal. Carnegie bought his own iron ore mines in the Mesabi Range of Minnesota. To transport the ore to his Pennsylvania steel mills, Carnegie bought ships for crossing the Great Lakes and hundreds of railroad cars. He also bought Pennsylvania coal fields, limestone quarries, and a large coke business.

When Carnegie retired from the steel business, he had made a fortune of $500 million. In today's dollars, Carnegie's fortune would be worth about $6 billion.

Carnegie spent the last years of his life giving money away. In an article called "The Gospel of Wealth," published in 1889, Carnegie wrote that millionaires should be "trustees for the poor." Carnegie believed that millionaires should use their wealth to benefit society. He gave much of his fortune to universities and charities. He also set up a fund to build libraries. More than 2,500 Carnegie libraries were built around the world.

Rockefeller and Oil

John D. Rockefeller was the most successful of all the great entrepreneurs of the late 1800's. He was a pioneer in developing new forms of business combinations. Before he died, he had become the richest person in the world.

Like Carnegie, Rockefeller came from a very poor family. As a boy, he worked at several jobs and saved nearly all the money he earned. In 1862, Rockefeller invested his money in an oil refinery in Cleveland. An oil refinery purifies, or refines, crude oil into useful products such as kerosene.

Rockefeller, like Carnegie, built up his business by using the most modern

John D. Rockefeller, Sr.

equipment and methods of production. By keeping his costs down, he was able to sell his oil at prices lower than other oil companies. In a few years, Rockefeller's refinery was the largest in Cleveland. In 1870, Rockefeller formed the Standard Oil Company of Ohio. Standard Oil was then the largest oil refining company in the world.

As he expanded his business, Rockefeller also used methods that many people considered to be unfair. He made secret agreements with the railroad. He would promise to ship a large amount of oil on a particular railroad, if the railroad company would agree to give him back a part of the shipping rate. The money the railroads secretly gave back to Rockefeller was called a **rebate**. By shipping his oil more cheaply, Rockefeller was able to lower the price of his oil. This allowed him to take more customers away from

Discuss: Carnegie once said that the worst thing that could happen to a young person was to inherit a large fortune. Do you agree or disagree with this idea? Explain your answer.

Discuss: What is the purpose of a rebate? How do rebates offered on products today differ from the rebates Rockefeller got from the railroads?

other oil companies.

rebate a refund of part of the rate charged for goods or services

Rockefeller also used what came to be known as "cut-throat competition." To ruin another oil business in one part of the country, Rockefeller would sell his oil products in that area at a very low price. Soon the other oil business would lose its customers and go out of business. Rockefeller would then buy out the ruined business. Prices for oil in the area would rise again, once Rockefeller had gotten rid of the competition.

To reduce competition further, Rockefeller organized in 1882 the Standard Oil Trust. This was the first **trust** in the United States. In a trust, the owners of several competing businesses allow their companies to be run by a board of trustees. The trustees set prices for all the products of the individual companies. Since there is no longer any competition, prices can be set at a high rate. The high prices mean larger profits for each of the companies.

trust a group of businesses that unite to control production and prices of their goods and make larger profits

The Standard Oil Trust was a combination of 40 different companies. It controlled more than 90 percent of the nation's oil refineries. As the most powerful trustee, Rockefeller had almost total control of the nation's oil business.

Rockefeller's success in the oil industry led to the formation of trusts in many other industries. In the 1880's, more than 5,000 competing firms combined into 300 trusts. Among these were the Whiskey Trust, the Sugar Trust, and the Salt Trust. These trusts were organized to reduce competition. The trusts could then set high prices for their products and make large profits for their owners.

Rockefeller retired from the oil business in 1895. His fortune amounted to more than $800 million ($9.6 billion in today's money). Like Andrew Carnegie, Rockefeller spent his last years giving much of his fortune away. He gave more than $500 million to charities, universities, and other organizations.

Section Review

1. How did American businesses try to reduce competition in the late 1800's?
2. In what ways did the railroads help other American industries grow?
3. How was Andrew Carnegie able to lower the cost of making steel?
4. What is a rebate? How did John D. Rockefeller use rebates to take customers away from other oil companies?
5. Name one advantage and one disadvantage of business trusts.

Background: As Rockefeller's power grew, he was able to force the railroads to give "drawbacks" to the Standard Oil Company. Drawbacks were a portion of what other oil companies had to pay to have their freight transported by rail.

Background: Vanderbilt bought one railroad system after another to form the New York Central. He was ultimately prevented from having a monopoly when Jay Gould would not sell him the Erie Railroad.

4. Regulating Big Business

BEFORE YOU READ: *What attempts were made by the government to regulate business?*

Most Americans had always agreed with the government's "hands-off" policy toward business. They agreed that government should not interfere with the activities of private businesses.

The growth of trusts, however, caused many Americans to change their minds. They saw that "big business" was destroying competition. Many people began to feel that the government should do something to regulate business. Competition somehow should be restored.

The attitudes of big business leaders also angered many people. The attitude of Cornelius Vanderbilt was a good example. Vanderbilt controlled the great New York Central Railroad. He seemed to believe he was above the law. In pursuit of profit, Vanderbilt cared little about what was best for the public. A lawyer once told Vanderbilt that one of his business deals was against the law. "What do I care about the law?" Vanderbilt replied. "Ain't [haven't] I got the power?"

Such an attitude only hurt the business leaders. It caused the public to believe that big business had become too powerful. More and more people came to believe that the government should regulate business. Critics compared business leaders to the mighty lords or barons who ruled in Europe 1,000 years earlier. The critics called the leaders of American industry "robber barons."

The Interstate Commerce Act

In 1886, a committee of the United States Congress reported that many railroads had formed pools to reduce competition. The pools were charging high rates for shipping goods. The committee said that the federal government should regulate the railroads.

The following year, in 1887, Congress passed the Interstate Commerce Act. This act required the railroads to charge shipping rates that were "reasonable and just." The act also said that the railroads could not form pools to reduce competition. Nor could the railroads continue to give rebates to some of their customers.

This cartoon shows the trusts hammering away at the consumer in order to make higher and higher profits.

Vocabulary Help: robber baron—a name given to a nineteenth-century industrialist who accumulated great wealth at the expense of smaller businesses and the public.

EUREKA!

The Adding Machine

The first mechanical calculators were a far cry from the sleek, speedy devices in use today. Their insides held bulky gears and wheels instead of tiny electronic circuits.

Calculating aids such as the abacus, or counting frame, have existed since ancient times. Many inventors tried to improve on these aids by developing a machine that would do arithmetic. The first truly practical adding machine was invented by William S. Burroughs in the early 1880's.

Burroughs came from an inventive family. His father owned a model-making shop in Auburn, New York. There, both father and son created many new gadgets. While working in the shop, Burroughs developed a machine that could do arithmetic problems.

Burroughs tried to market his machine to business, but it did not sell. At the age of 27, he moved to St. Louis, Missouri, where he continued to work on his adding machine. In 1885, he applied for his first patent. He received the patent in 1894.

Burrough's machine contained a set of wheels, each marked off in ten places around its rim. These spots corresponded to numbers from 0 to 9. By positioning the wheels in the proper way, any number could be represented. Calculations were carried out by a gear attached to each wheel. This gear moved the wheel to its new position.

Burroughs founded the American Arithometer Company in 1886 to manufacture and sell his device. Later, he organized the Burroughs Adding Machine Company, which became the Burroughs Corporation. The Burroughs Corporation still makes adding machines. But it is best known today as a maker of more advanced calculating aids: computers.

The act created the Interstate Commerce Commission (ICC) to investigate complaints against the railroads. The rulings of the ICC were to be enforced by the federal courts.

The Interstate Commerce Act was an important act. It showed that the government was willing to regulate the activities of business. However, the railroads challenged the authority of the government to interfere in their activities. They took the government to court to test the legality of the Interstate Commerce Act. In the Maximum Freight Rate Case (1897), the Supreme Court ruled that the ICC could not set shipping rates for the railroads. Other rulings by the Supreme Court further weakened the power of the commisssion.

The Sherman Antitrust Act

In the late 1800's, many Americans came to the conclusion that trusts should be outlawed. Articles in newspapers and magazines urged the government to "break up" the trusts. Small businesses demanded protection from the trusts. Farmers and workers called for antitrust action by the government.

In 1890, Congress passed the Sherman Antitrust Act. It said that trusts and other combinations of businesses "in restraint of trade" were illegal. Combinations "in restraint of trade" were those that restricted or prevented competition. The act provided fines and jail sentences for anyone who violated the act.

In 1892, the Standard Oil Trust was declared illegal. John D. Rockefeller then reorganized his oil business. He formed the Standard Oil Company of New Jersey. This new company was a **holding company**, not a trust. A holding company is a single company that controls other corporations. The holding company owns, or "holds," the majority of stock of the other companies.

---

holding company a corporation that owns enough stock in other companies to control them

---

The Standard Oil Company was the largest holding company in the United States. Following its formation, many other trusts became holding companies.

The Sherman Antitrust Act was not as strong as many people hoped it would be. Corporations found ways to get around the law and continue their unfair business practices. The law was unable to restore competition.

As a result, government attempts to regulate business during this period were ineffective.

Section Review

1. What attempts did the government make to regulate business in the late 1800's?
2. How did the Supreme Court weaken the Interstate Commerce Commission (ICC)?
3. What is a holding company?
4. In what ways does the government regulate business today? Give some examples.

CHAPTER REVIEW

Summary

As the last territorial frontier was disappearing from the American West, another major change was taking place in this country. This was the growth of big business. The United States was particularly fortunate to have everything that was needed to become an industrial giant. These included an abundance of natural resources, a large supply of workers, a lot of money to invest, the means for mass production, and a government that did not interfere in private business affairs. Significant changes in the way Americans lived and worked were achieved through the efforts of inventors and business leaders.

Unfortunately, with this growth came some dishonest business practices. People began asking the government to regulate these large businesses. Two acts were passed—the Interstate Commerce Act and the Sherman Antitrust Act—to control business. These laws were not very effective, and unfair business practices continued.

Recalling the Facts

1. Explain three ways in which the government helped industry to grow in the late 1800's.
2. Describe how products are made on an assembly line.
3. Why was Edison's electric lighting system an improvement over previous methods of lighting?
4. Identify each of the following words as it relates to the growth of business after the Civil War: corporation, rebate, trust, holding company.
5. How did the Interstate Commerce Act attempt to control the railroad business? Why was this law important even though it was ineffective?

Analyzing the Facts

1. Of the six factors that contributed to the growth of American industry, which two do you think were the most important? Why?
2. Explain how interchangeable parts, the assembly line, and mass production relate to each other in the production of manufactured goods.
3. Discuss the impact of electric light and the Kelly-Bessemer process on today's world.

4. Neither the Interstate Commerce Commission nor the Sherman Antitrust Act was effective. Later laws gave government more control over business. How much control do you think government should have over business? Explain your answer.
5. In the late 1800's, many people felt a mixture of excitement and uncertainty about the rapid changes taking place. Compare how people felt then to the way Americans feel today about the changes brought about by rapid advancements and changes in computer technology.

Time and History

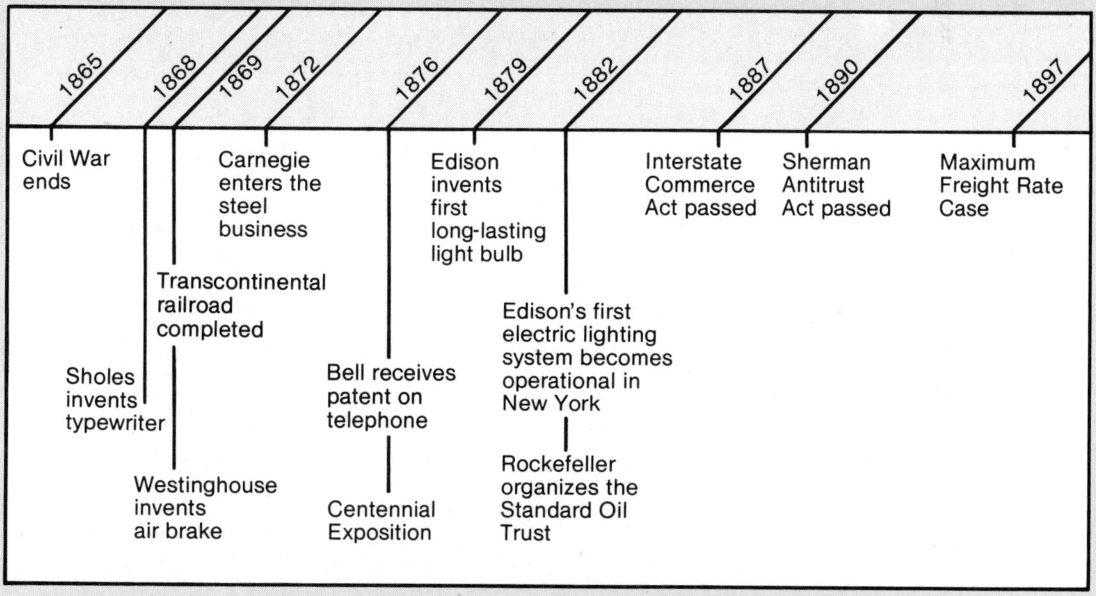

1. Which of the following was invented first: the telephone, the typewriter, the long-lasting light bulb, or the air brake?
2. How long did it take the government to pass legislation controlling trusts after the first trust was formed?
3. In what decade were the telephone and the long-lasting light bulb developed?
4. Was Edison's long-lasting light bulb displayed at the Centennial Exposition? Explain your answer.
5. How many years after the transcontinental railroad was completed did Congress pass the Interstate Commerce Act?

Chapter 20 New Ways of Life Begin

Mary Antin was 13 years old. She had lived all her life in Poland. From her family and friends she had heard many wonderful things about America. She dreamed that someday she would be able to go there. One day in 1894, her parents told Mary that the family was moving to the United States. "So at last I was going to America!" she later wrote. "Really, really going, at last! The boundaries burst. The arch of heaven soared. A million suns shone out for every star. The winds rushed in from outer space, roaring in my ears, 'America! America!'"

Mary Antin and her family were part of a great tide of immigrants who arrived in America during the late 1800's. New ways of life were also beginning for millions of Americans who moved from farms to the nation's cities. The cities were exciting places, but they also had many serious problems. The Age of Industry was also a time of new beginnings for industrial workers.

After you read this chapter, you will be able to:

1. Give reasons why immigrants came to the United States.
2. Discuss the problems of American cities.
3. Trace the rise of organized labor.

For Extra Interest: Before students begin to read this section, ask them under what circumstances they would leave their homeland. Make a list, and later compare the reasons given to those discussed in the text.

1. Immigration

BEFORE YOU READ: *Why did immigrants come to the United States in the late 1800's?*

The United States has always been a nation of immigrants. Between 1860 and 1900, more than 14 million immigrants arrived in America. In the single year of 1882, 788,002 immigrants arrived—more than 2,100 per day.

The immigrants of the late 1800's came for many reasons. They were attracted, or "pulled," to America by a variety of forces. Also, many immigrants were encouraged to leave—or were "pushed"—by conditions in their old countries. A combination of both "pulls" and "pushes" caused the immigrants to come.

The Attractions of America

The United States was known around the world for its democratic way of life. It was the land of liberty. Immigrants had always been attracted to America by the many freedoms it offered.

The United States was also known as the land of opportunity. In the late 1800's, American industries were expanding very rapidly. More and more workers were needed to work in the factories, mines, and mills.

Some immigrants were recruited by employers to work in the United States. The railroads brought over Chinese workers to build the first rail line across the continent. The railroads also recruited Mexicans to work on repair and construction crews.

In 1864, Congress passed the Contract Labor Law. This law permitted employers to recruit foreign workers. Under the terms of this law, employers could make contracts with workers in other countries. Many employers loaned money to foreign workers to pay for their transportation costs. After the workers arrived in the United States, they paid the money back out of their wages.

Groups of immigrants also recruited workers from their old countries. Usually such groups would pay the transportation costs of the new immigrants. They would arrange housing for them and help them get jobs.

Sometimes these groups would take unfair advantage of the newcomers. Many Italian immigrants were recruited to America by a *padrone* (pah-DRO-nee). A *padrone* is a kind of labor contractor. American employers would pay the *padrone* a large fee to supply them with immigrant workers. From this fee, the *padrone* would pay the workers. *Padrones* often paid workers low wages. The *padrones* would thus profit at the expense of their less-experienced fellow immigrants.

Most immigrants, however, did not need to be recruited by anyone. They had learned of the opportunities in America, and they had decided, on their own, to come. Information about America was plentiful. Guidebooks for immigrants were printed in almost every language.

Probably the most important sources of information about life in America were the letters immigrants sent back to their family and friends in the old country. These letters described the wonders of life in the United States.

"We eat here every day," wrote one

Vocabulary Help: In the sense used here, "democratic" means treating persons of all classes in the same way. Why do you think this principle would attract immigrants to America?

Discuss: If you were to write a letter today encouraging a family member or friend to emigrate to the United States, what reasons would you give to encourage this person to come to America?

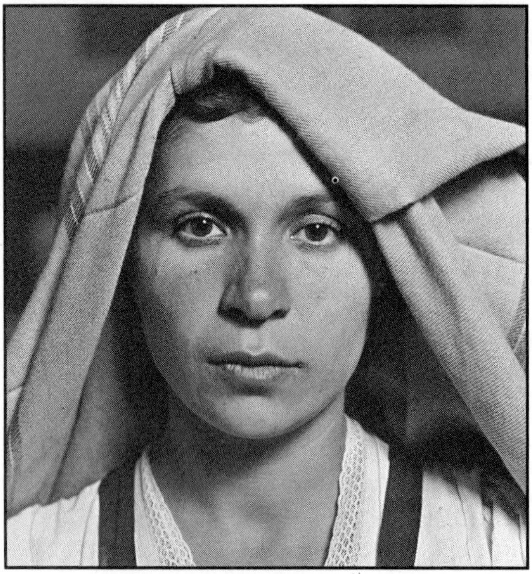

The Albanian woman on the left arrived in the United States in 1905. The woman on the right is a European Jewish immigrant.

immigrant to his family in Poland, "what we get only for Easter in our old country." Life in the United States seemed so much better, the letters said, than life back home. These "America letters" became soiled from the hands of many eager readers. They were the best recruiters the United States ever had.

"The Push"

While conditions in America attracted the immigrants, other conditions in their old countries encouraged them to leave. The most important "push" for the immigrants was hard times at home. Improvements in farming methods reduced the need for farm workers. Many farmers in Europe were forced off lands that they had lived on for years.

A severe drought also struck parts of western Europe in the 1870's and 1880's. These hard times forced thousands of farmers in Great Britain, Germany, and Scandinavia to move. Many of them came to the United States.

In the 1890's, the drought ended in western Europe. New jobs became available in European industries. The hard times were over. Fewer immigrants from northern and western Europe came to the United States. Many of the immigrants of the late 1800's came from other places. They came from southern and eastern Europe. On the West Coast, new immigrants arrived from Asia.

For many years, the rulers of Austria-Hungary, Russia, Turkey, and Japan had not allowed their people to leave their countries. The rulers feared that migration would reduce the country's supply of workers, soldiers, and taxpayers. By the 1890's, however, the rulers of these countries were no longer opposed to their

Background: The words *emigrant* and *immigrant* refer to a person who leaves a country to settle in another. Both words refer to the same person: The emigrant leaves one country and enters and settles in another country as an immigrant.

Background: In 1881, Tsar Alexander III of Russia demanded that everyone living in Russia join the Eastern Orthodox Church and give up their "non-Russian" ways. Most Jews refused to do this and were persecuted. Many left Russia for the United States and Palestine (now Israel).

people's leaving. Immigrants from these countries began coming to the United States in record numbers.

Unfair laws and unfair treatment also encouraged migration. The victims of some of the worst mistreatment were Russian Jews. Since at least 1000 A.D., Jews had lived in Russia. In the 1880's, laws were passed that excluded the Jews from colleges and from various kinds of jobs. They were not allowed to hold positions in government.

Even worse, the Russian government began to sponsor **pogroms** against the Jews. The pogroms were organized attacks or massacres of Jews. Hundreds of Jews were killed by Russian soldiers. To escape the pogroms and other forms of persecution, many Jews came to the United States. Almost 40 percent of the immigrants who came from Russia and Poland were Jews.

---

pogrom an organized persecution and massacre of a minority group

---

Until the 1890's, most immigrants to the United States had come from northern and western Europe. After the 1890's, more southern and eastern European immigrants came to the United States. These newcomers were called the "New Immigrants." The New Immigrants came from Russia, Poland, Italy, Greece, and many other lands.

The change in the pattern of immigration was very great. In the 1880's, southern and eastern Europeans amounted to only 19 percent of the total number of American immigrants. By the early 1900's, they were 66 percent of the total. Only about 200,000 southern and eastern Europeans had come to America before 1880. Between 1880 and 1910, 8.4 million had arrived.

The Passage

Another important reason for the increase in immigration to the United States in the late 1880's was the increased use of the steamship for transoceanic crossings. The steamship made the immigrants' passage to America both easier and cheaper.

The Atlantic passage had taken as long as three months on the old sailing vessels. The new steamships could make it from London to New York in just ten days. The steamships also speeded travel for Asian immigrants across the Pacific Ocean. As more and more steamship companies competed for the business of carrying the immigrants to America, the price of tickets went down to their lowest levels in history.

Conditions on board the steamships were often better than on the old sailing vessels. But there were still many problems. Most immigrants could not afford to travel in regular passenger cabins. They were given rooms below decks in the steerage section of the ships.

The immigrants in steerage could not always come on deck for fresh air. Their quarters were crowded and uncomfortable. Seasickness made the passage difficult. Infectious diseases caused hundreds of deaths.

The majority of all immigrants arrived in New York. Before 1892, the immigrants in New York passed through a reception center called Castle Garden. In 1892, the

Vocabulary Help: steerage—originally referred to the part of the ship closest to the rudder, which steers the ship. A berth in steerage was generally 6 feet long and 2 feet wide. Berths were stacked 2 1/2 feet apart. The fare in steerage was as low as $35 from Europe to the eastern United States.

Background: Between 1820 and 1977, more immigrants have come to the United States from Germany (6,970,000) than any other European or Asian country. Germany is followed by Italy (5,287,000), Great Britain (4,882,000), and Ireland (4,723,000).

federal government built a new reception center. This new center was on Ellis Island in New York harbor.

At Ellis Island, the immigrants were asked about their backgrounds, skills, education, and financial situation. The immigrants were also examined by doctors. They were given advice about transportation, housing, and jobs.

Four out of five of the immigrants chose to settle in the big cities of the Northeast and the Midwest. The immigrants had come to fill America's growing need for labor. It was in the big cities that the demand for labor was greatest.

The experiences of Michael Pupin were typical of many immigrants who arrived in the late 1800's. Michael Pupin was born in eastern Europe, in the kingdom of Austria-Hungary. He arrived in New York at Castle Garden in 1874.

Years later, Michael Pupin became a famous scientist at New York's Columbia University. In his autobiography, *From Immigrant to Inventor*, he described his first day in America. When he arrived at Castle Garden, he was asked by the immigration officials how much money he had. He confessed that he had only 5 cents. Then he was asked if he knew any Americans. He replied that he knew—by their reputations—Benjamin Franklin, Abraham Lincoln, and Harriet Beecher Stowe. He told the officials that he wanted to live in America because it was a land of liberty. He also explained that he was very eager to get a good job. The immigration officials told him of a job opportunity in Delaware. Within 24 hours after his arrival in the United States, Michael Pupin had reached his destination and was ready to begin work.

Immigration, 1820–1925

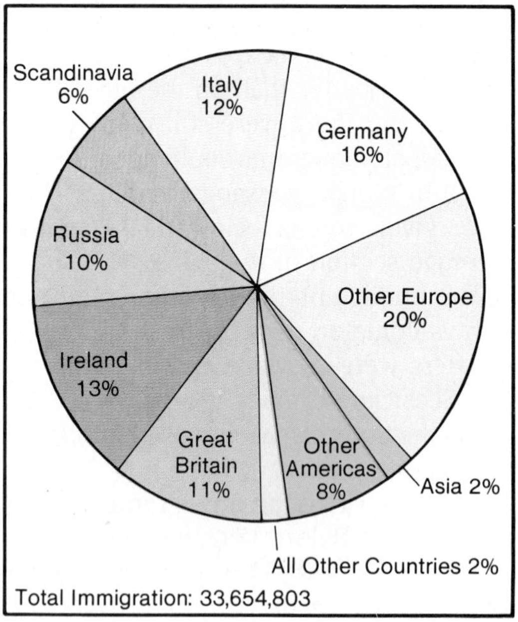

Opposition to Immigration

The increase in immigration in the late 1800's caused many Americans to feel uncomfortable. They feared that too many immigrants were coming. They called for the government to restrict or limit further immigration.

Some churches and charities worried that too many immigrants were being crowded into the big cities. These groups were concerned about the poor living conditions of many of the immigrants. They urged that something be done to improve these conditions. Until improvements could be made, they said, a limit should be placed on the number of immigrants allowed to come in.

Labor leaders also wanted to restrict immigration. Immigrants were often will-

Discuss: From 1971 to 1979, immigrants to the United States came primarily from the Americas (45 percent) and Asia (35 percent). Only 17.7 percent of the immigrants came from Europe. Can you give reasons to explain these statistics?

Discuss: Why do you think that some people feel threatened by the arrival of large numbers of immigrants to the United States?

This photo shows a class of Chinese schoolchildren in San Francisco in 1886. Local laws forced Chinese children to attend their own schools.

ing to work for a lower wage than other American workers. Labor leaders feared that the immigrants would take jobs away from American workers.

Workers on the West Coast were especially opposed to Chinese immigrants. They feared that the Chinese would take their jobs. One group, called the Workingmen's Party of California, demanded an end to Chinese immigration. The leader of this party always ended his speeches by saying, "The Chinese must go!" This party became very powerful in San Francisco. Many unfair laws were passed that applied to the Chinese. The state constitution in 1879 forbade California corporations from hiring Chinese workers.

Other groups were more concerned about the New Immigrants from southern and eastern Europe. The American Protective Association, formed in Iowa in 1887, opposed the New Immigrants. So did a group of New Englanders who organized the Immigration Restriction League in 1894.

These groups wrongly believed that the New Immigrants from Europe and Asia were so "different" that they could never become good Americans. They believed that native-born Americans were superior to the immigrants. They wanted laws passed that would limit the rights of immigrants. They also wanted fewer immigrants to be allowed to come to the United States. The people who joined these groups were **nativists**.

---

nativist one who believes that native-born Americans are superior

---

For Extra Interest: Have students research the contributions made to the United States by immigrants. Figures for research could include: Irving Berlin, Albert Einstein, Mary Anderson, I. M. Pei, Joseph Pulitzer, Martina Navratilova, and Isamu Noguchi.

Discuss: Do you think that immigrants to the United States should have to show that they can read and write in their own language? Why or why not?

The federal government responded to the call for a limit on immigration. In 1882 Congress passed the Chinese Exclusion Act. This law stopped immigration from China for ten years. In 1885, Congress passed the Foran Act. Employers could no longer recruit skilled foreign workers to work in American industry.

In the 1890's, the Immigration Restriction League asked Congress to require that all immigrants take a literacy test. A literacy test measures the ability of a person to read and write. The Immigration Restriction League believed that only immigrants who could read and write in their native language should be allowed to come to the United States. The league believed that many of the New Immigrants would fail the test. Illiteracy rates were higher in southeastern Europe than in northwestern Europe. The nativists hoped the literacy test would keep out many of the immigrants from southern and eastern Europe.

Congress did pass a Literacy Test Act in 1897. However, President Grover Cleveland vetoed the act. President Cleveland said he did not accept the nativists' belief that "the quality of recent immigration is undesirable." The President reminded the nativists that "the same thing was said of immigrants who, with their descendants, are now numbered among our best citizens."

The great symbol of America's welcome to immigrants is the Statue of Liberty, erected in New York harbor in 1886. This magnificent statue was a gift from the people of France. Written on the base of the statue were the words of the poet Emma Lazarus:

Give me your tired, your poor,
Your huddled masses yearning to breathe free,
The wretched refuse of your teeming shore,
Send these, the homeless, tempest-tossed, to me:
I lift my lamp beside the golden door.

The Statue of Liberty would always be a welcome sight for immigrants. The United States, however, was beginning to close the "golden door."

Section Review

1. Why did immigrants come to the United States in the late 1800's?
2. Who were the New Immigrants? How did the pattern of American immigration change in the late 1800's?
3. Who are nativists? Why did some Americans want fewer immigrants to be allowed to come to the United States?
4. Identify the Chinese Exclusion Act and the Foran Act. What is a literacy test?
5. What groups of immigrants are coming to the United States today? What problems do these newest American immigrants have?

Background: The Statue of Liberty has turned a rich green color from exposure to the weather. It is made of large hammered-copper plates that are welded to an iron framework. The entire statue is bolted to a stone pedestal.

Vocabulary Help: urban—characteristic of the city or city life. Have each student write two sentences using the word *urban*.

2. The Promise and Problems of the City

BEFORE YOU READ: *How did Americans solve the problems of the cities in the late 1800's?*

In 1860, only about one in every five Americans lived in a city. Thirty years later, one out of three Americans was a city-dweller. By 1910, the cities of America contained nearly half the nation's people. Between 1860 and 1910, the number of cities in the United States grew from 392 to over 2,200. The United States was becoming an urban nation—a nation of cities.

The cities promised a better life for millions of people. They were filled with many opportunities for work. They had exciting places to go for recreation and entertainment. Libraries, theaters, and museums were located in the cities.

The cities also had many serious problems. They grew so rapidly that they were not able to provide the services needed by their residents.

The Growth of Cities: 1860–1900*

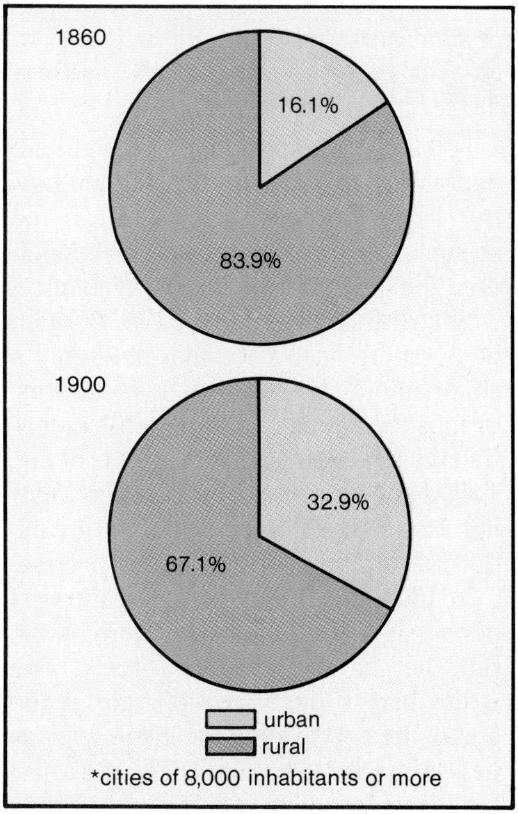

Growth of the Cities

The main reason for the growth of American cities was the expansion of industry. Thousands of new jobs opened up for factory workers, office workers, and salespeople.

The growth of the iron and steel industry brought thousands of new workers to Pittsburgh, Pennsylvania, and Birmingham, Alabama. Chicago grew as its meat-packing industry expanded. The flour mills of Minneapolis, Minnesota, expanded to handle the wheat pouring in from the Great Plains.

Many of the residents of the cities were immigrants. New York had more foreign-born residents than any city in the world. In 1898, four out of five New Yorkers were either foreign-born or were the children of foreign-born parents.

Visitors to American cities were often impressed by the variety of their people. Every large city had its **ethnic** neighborhoods. These were neighborhoods where immigrants who shared the same backgrounds and culture lived. Newspapers, street signs, and advertisements were

For Extra Interest: Have students use a current almanac to see how cities have grown in the United States.

EUREKA!

The Fountain Pen

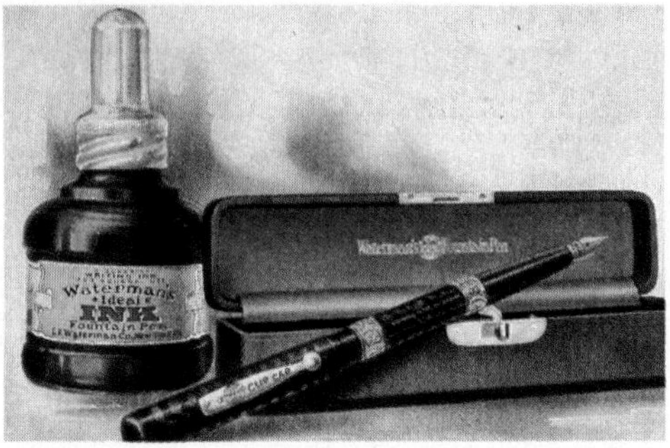

Few people today think of a fountain pen as an example of high technology. But when fountain pens came on the scene in the 1800's, they were considered the height of modern convenience.

Before the invention of the fountain pen, writers used pens that held only a small amount of ink in their metal tips, or nibs. The pens had to be refilled continually by dipping them into pots of ink. This made writing a slow process. Writing was also not very portable. An ink pot was a clumsy item to carry around.

In 1809, the British invented the first pens that carried their own store of ink. But the ink did not flow freely. The writer had to push on a plunger at the end of the pen to keep the ink flowing as he or she wrote. Not until 1884 did fountain pens become widely used. It was then that Lewis Edson Waterman invented a practical ink-feeding device.

Lewis Waterman was born in Massachusetts in 1837. He worked as a teacher, a carpenter, and a lock seller. At the time that he invented his pen, Waterman was selling insurance in Boston.

There was no plunger on the end of Waterman's pen. Instead, the end unscrewed, and ink was squirted in with an eyedropper. The ink flowed freely, much as it does in a modern pen. In fact, although it has been improved, Waterman's design is still the basis for all fountain pens today.

Waterman founded the Ideal Pen Company in 1884 to manufacture his pens. He continued improving them until his death in 1901. He also published a magazine called *Pen Prophet*, which sang the praises of fountain pens.

---

often printed in the language of their neighborhood's residents.

ethnic having to do with a group of people who share the same customs, language, and culture

In addition to immigrants, America's cities attracted Americans from the nation's countryside. The nation's cities in 1910 contained 42 million people. Of that number, 11 million were Americans who had come to the cities from the countryside after 1880.

Americans were attracted to the cities for many reasons. Like the immigrants,

 For Extra Interest: Have student volunteers bring in ethnic foods for the class to sample.

Background: Often housing was so costly and difficult to find that four families would live in a four-room apartment.

the Americans were "pulled" to the cities by the promise of good jobs. Andrew Carnegie, although himself an immigrant, preferred to hire American-born men from the countryside. Carnegie believed these "buckwheats"—as the young men from the countryside were called—made the best workers in the steel mills.

The cities also attracted many Americans because of their promise of excitement. The glitter of the bright lights was hard to resist. Life in the city often seemed far more exciting than life on the farm.

Problems of the Cities

With so many new city-dwellers, there were bound to be problems. The cities were simply growing too fast. There was not enough time to prepare for growth. Many cities were not able to meet the basic needs of their new residents.

Providing housing was perhaps the most serious problem. Older homes in the cities were divided into rooming houses for families. **Tenements**, or poor-quality apartment buildings, were built along the busy streets. Families were crammed into small rooms. Light, air, and privacy were in short supply.

tenement an apartment house that is run-down, very crowded, or poorly built

By 1900, over one million people in New York were living in "dumbbell tenements." The floor plan of these buildings looked like a weight lifter's dumbbell. The dumbbell shape, with its long narrow middle section, allowed a small space of air and light between the apartment buildings. The apartments in the dumbbell tenements were often dark and crowded. The bathrooms for the apartments were in the public hallways. Each bathroom had to serve the needs of 20 residents.

Jacob Riis, a newspaper reporter in New York, wrote a book about life in the crowded cities. His book, *How the Other Half Lives* (1890), includes a revealing account of a New York tenement.

"Be a little careful, please!" Riis wrote. "The hall is dark and you might stumble. . . . Here where the hall turns and dives into utter darkness is . . . a flight of stairs. You can feel your way, if you cannot see it. The sinks are in the hallway, so that all the tenants may have access [use]—and all be poisoned alike by their summer stenches [smells]. . . . Here is a door. Listen! That short, hacking cough, that tiny, helpless wail—what do they mean? . . . The child is dying of measles. With half a chance it might have lived; but it had none. That dark bedroom killed it."

Providing water and getting rid of sewage were other serious problems for the cities. Water was often taken from polluted sources. Epidemics of cholera and typhoid, diseases caused by drinking unclean water, swept through Chicago and Philadelphia in the late 1880's. The Chicago River received so much sewage that it had become, by 1890, a vast open sewer. One newspaper reported an awful truth about the city: "the air stinks."

Transportation was also a major problem. The streets of brick or cobblestone crumbled beneath the traffic. Many of the streets in American cities were nothing more than dirt lanes. Chicago, for example, still had about 2,300 kilometers

Background: Fire was always a problem in the cities. The great Chicago fire in 1871, supposedly started by the O'Learys' cow kicking over a lantern, destroyed 17,000 buildings and killed 250 people.

Discuss: Although living conditions in the cities were bad, most immigrants chose to stay there. Why do you think they did not move to rural areas or return to their homelands?

Subways greatly improved transportation in the nation's cities in the late 1800's. On New York City's subways, certain cars were reserved exclusively for women.

(1,400 miles) of dirt streets in 1890.

Streets were often crowded with a variety of wagons, carriages, handcarts, and pedestrians. Many immigrants sold goods from wagons in the streets. Others set up stands or tables along the city sidewalks. During the day, traffic jams would clog the streets.

Streetcars drawn by horses helped solve some of the problem. But these vehicles were very slow. Their maximum speed was only about 10 kilometers (6 miles) per hour.

Solving Problems

Beginning in the late 1870's, better housing was provided in many cities. Alfred T. White, a New York businessman, built a set of model apartments near the Brooklyn waterfront in 1877. His buildings were attractive and healthful. Good lighting, fresh air, and private bathrooms were provided for each family.

In the 1890's and early 1900's, the cities began to adopt higher standards for public housing. Chicago changed its building code in 1898, requiring builders to follow stricter standards of construction. In 1901, New York outlawed the building of any more dumbbell tenements.

The cities also improved their water systems. Cities began to filter and purify their water. Careful testing of the water reduced the danger of diseases such as typhoid.

Sewage-disposal systems also improved. Many cities developed public

Vocabulary Help: pedestrian—a person who is walking. What are some of the rules that pedestrians must follow?

Background: Frederick Law Olmstead planned parks like Central Park in New York City complete with lakes, zoos, and bridle paths.

sewer systems to replace the private disposal of waste. In the Midwest, several cities began to burn their waste in high-temperature ovens. Other cities developed sewage treatment plants. Los Angeles built one of the nation's first such plants in 1887.

Progress was made in solving the cities' transportation problems. Asphalt paving was introduced in the 1870's. The paving material was cheaper and easier to apply than cobblestone or brick. Most of the dirt streets in the cities were soon covered with asphalt.

Steam railroads, which ran on elevated tracks, were first introduced in New York in the 1870's. They were much faster than the horse-drawn streetcars. Unfortunately, they left a trail of ash and soot on the pedestrians and streets below. In San Francisco, also in the 1870's, the cable car was invented by Andrew Hallidie. The cable cars were moved by a cable that ran beneath the streets. The cars on the surface would "grip" the cable and be pulled along.

A major improvement in transportation was made in the 1880's in Richmond, Virginia. A man named Frank Sprague developed the first electric streetcar system. The streetcar got its power from overhead electric wires. By 1895, over 850 electric streetcar lines were serving American cities.

Subways were also put into service in the late 1800's. The subways provided the fastest transportation yet. Because they traveled underground, the subways did not have to wait for pedestrians crossing the streets or other traffic. Boston put a part of its streetcar line underground in 1897. The first large subway system was built in New York in 1904. The system began with just 24 kilometers (15 miles) of track. Eventually it became the largest system in the world. Early subway systems were also constructed in Philadelphia and Chicago.

The improvements in transportation helped lessen the crowding in the cities. The streetcars and subways allowed workers to live farther from the factories or mills where they worked. New houses and apartments were built far outside of the centers of the cities. "Streetcar suburbs" developed away from the crowded city centers.

By 1900, the cities had not solved all their problems. Important progress, however, had been made.

Section Review

1. How did Americans solve the problems of the nation's cities in the late 1800's?
2. What was the main reason for the growth of American cities?
3. Define ethnic and tenement.
4. American cities still have many problems. What do you think are the most serious problems of the cities today? How could these problems be solved?

Background: Since most people who moved to the "streetcar suburbs" still worked in the cities, only those people who could afford to pay the daily streetcar fares were able to move out of the city centers.

Discuss: Some workers in the late 1800's did piecework. This means that the factory worker was paid a standard amount for each item made. For example, a worker might receive 10 cents per skirt. What are the advantages and disadvantages of this type of payment?

This child is working as a looper in a hosiery mill.

3. The Rise of Organized Labor

BEFORE YOU READ: *What were the major organizations of American workers during the Age of Industry?*

The number of workers in American industry rose rapidly in the late 1800's. At the beginning of the Civil War, there were only 885,000 industrial workers in the United States. By 1890, more than 3.2 million Americans worked in industry.

Conditions and Discontent

Between 1860 and 1900, the average income of American workers rose steadily. Not all workers, however, shared equally in the benefits of employment.

Native-born males usually received higher wages than other workers. Workers with special skills—such as carpenters, masons, or printers—earned far more than unskilled laborers.

Very few women received wages equal to those paid to men. Women who worked in the clothing industry earned less than $1 per day. Even this wage was high, however, compared to what female "domestics" were paid. The domestics washed, cooked, and cleaned in other people's homes for $1 or $2 *per week*.

Black workers also generally earned low wages. Most blacks remained in the South, working on farms. The blacks who did come to the cities were often given the lowest-paying jobs. Immigrants usually earned lower wages than native-born white workers. As the immigrants acquired new skills, however, they increased their earnings.

Working conditions for many American workers were very poor. Many factory workers had to work 60 hours per week. In the steel mills and oil refineries, workers often worked seven days per week.

Illness and accidents on the job were common. Thousands of workers died from diseases caused by poor working conditions. The heavy machinery in the factories and mills was a constant danger. Between 1870 and 1910, there were over 4,000 injuries and deaths at just one of Andrew Carnegie's steel mills.

Some skilled workers were able to provide a decent living for their families. But many unskilled workers were forced to put their children to work to meet expenses. In 1890, more than one million

 Discuss: Why do you think nineteenth-century employers hired children?

Background: Unions started in the early 1800's in the United States. Those who joined were usually skilled in a craft. At that time, the courts usually ruled that strikes were illegal, and unions made little progress in improving working conditions.

girls and boys under age 16 were working. But even this added income was not enough for some families. In 1900, one out of eight American families lived in poverty.

By 1900, the average American worker still earned less than $10 per week. Workers wanted to earn higher wages. They also wanted to work fewer hours per week and in safer workplaces.

Workers were also troubled by the nature of the new industrial work. By the late 1800's, most goods were produced in factories. The new methods of mass production required many workers to repeat over and over, day after day, the same small task. Work on an assembly line was often dull and very boring.

Workers were also discontented by a sense of lost opportunity. In the late 1800's, the possibility of workers' becoming their own bosses was not as great as it once was. Workers could, and did, rise to better-paying jobs. But few workers could ever make enough money to own their own businesses.

Early Organizations

American workers soon realized that they must organize to improve their lives. If they organized—and became united—then they would be much more powerful.

One of the more successful labor organizations was a group called the Knights of Labor. This organization was formed in 1869. The Knights believed that workers could still become business owners. The Knights advised members to pool their resources so that they could form their own businesses. The Knights of Labor welcomed unskilled as well as skilled

The Knights of Labor welcomed women as members. These women were delegates to the 1886 convention of the Knights of Labor.

Discuss: What are the advantages and disadvantages of owning your own business compared to working for someone else?

Background: The founder of the Knights of Labor was Uriah S. Stephens. He coined the slogan, "An injury to one is the concern of all."

workers. It opened its membership to blacks and to women.

The Knights of Labor reached a peak of strength in 1886. In that year, its membership included more than 700,000 workers. An event occurred in 1886, however, that destroyed the Knights.

The Haymarket Bombing

The Knights of Labor and other groups believed that workers should be required to work only eight hours per day. Many employers believed that workers should stay on the job ten or twelve hours each day. The dispute over working hours reached a high point in 1886. By May 1886, several hundred thousand workers had organized to demand an eight-hour workday.

On May 4, 1886, a rally in support of the eight-hour workday was held in Chicago's Haymarket Square. The rally was not sponsored by the Knights of Labor. It was sponsored by a group of **anarchists**. Anarchists are people who believe that any form of organized government is bad because it interferes with individual rights and liberties.

---

anarchist a person who believes that any government interferes with individual liberty and should therefore be replaced by cooperative groups

---

About 3,000 people attended the rally at Haymarket Square. When police began to break up the rally, someone threw a bomb at the police. When the smoke cleared, 70 police officers lay wounded. Seven of the officers were killed.

The anarchists who had sponsored the rally were arrested. Although no one could prove who had thrown the bomb, seven anarchists were sentenced to death. In 1887, four of them were hanged.

The Knights of Labor were blamed for the tragedy of the Haymarket bombing. The Knights had not been involved in the rally. But because they supported the demand for the eight-hour workday, many people blamed them. As a result, the membership of the Knights declined very rapidly.

The American Federation of Labor

As the Knights of Labor declined, a new organization appeared to take its place. This new organization was the American Federation of Labor (AFL). The AFL was a combination of many groups of workers who had joined together to improve their wages and working conditions. The members of each group of workers shared the same craft or skill. There were, for example, groups of carpenters, tailors, bakers, and printers. These groups were called **craft unions**. In 1886, craft unions representing 150,000 workers combined to form the AFL under the leadership of Samuel Gompers.

---

craft union a group of workers sharing the same craft or skill who have joined together to improve their wages and working conditions

---

In a sense, the AFL was the first modern American labor organization. It accepted the fact that most workers would remain workers all their lives. The goals of the AFL were to win higher wages, shorter

Background: In 1882, the Knights of Labor started the tradition of a parade in New York City that came to be called the Labor Day parade. In 1894, Labor Day, the first Monday in September, was made a national holiday.

Background: When bargaining with an employer, unions today may also ask for improved benefits, in addition to higher wages, for the workers. These benefits may include medical and dental insurance, investment opportunities, and paid vacations.

This engraving depicts the violence in Chicago's Haymarket Square.

hours, and better working conditions for skilled workers.

The AFL unions used **collective bargaining** to achieve their goals. In collective bargaining, union members act as a unit in dealing with their employers.

---

collective bargaining discussions between the members of a union and their employer over work-related issues

---

If the employers do not grant the demands of the union, then the union may call a strike or a boycott. In a strike, the employees refuse to work until their demands are granted. In a boycott, the workers and their supporters refuse to buy the products of a business. The boycott ends only when the business owners grant the demands of the employees.

By 1900, the AFL had almost one million members. Like the Knights of Labor, however, the AFL was hurt by the actions of an anarchist, Alexander Berkman.

The Homestead Strike

An AFL union of iron and steel workers called a strike against the Carnegie Steel Company in 1892. The strike was called to protest a cut in wages. Henry Clay Frick, one of Carnegie's top assistants, tried to break the strike and the union.

Frick hired new workers to work at Carnegie's steel plant in Homestead, Pennsylvania. These new workers were called strikebreakers. They were hired to

Discuss: Why do striking workers try to intimidate strikebreakers?

take the place of the striking union members. Frick also hired 300 armed guards to protect the strikebreakers from the angry union members. Violence between the union members and the armed guards left 13 people dead.

During the strike, an anarchist named Alexander Berkman burst into Frick's office. He shot and stabbed Frick several times. Miraculously, Frick recovered from his wounds.

The anarchist was not a member of the AFL. His attack on Frick, however, hurt the strike and the union movement. Public opinion quickly turned against the strikers. The strike was soon over, and the workers had been defeated.

Business Response

Business leaders generally opposed the organization of their workers. If the workers were well organized, they would be able to demand higher wages. Employers, of course, wanted to keep wages as low as possible. For many employers, the cost of labor was like any other production cost. Profits were made by keeping such costs low.

Employers had many methods to use against the unions. They could simply fire workers who joined a union. They could require new employees to sign **yellow-dog contracts**. In these contracts, the new employees would promise never to join a union.

---

yellow-dog contract an agreement a job applicant had to sign promising not to join a union while employed

---

Employers could also **blacklist** workers who were active in union organizing. The names of union organizers were given to other employers, warning them not to hire these workers. Blacklisted workers had a hard time finding jobs.

---

blacklist to put a person's name on a list for the purposes of keeping that person from working in a particular industry

---

If the workers did call a strike, the employers could fight back by bringing in new workers. As in the Homestead strike, the employers could also hire armed guards to protect the strikebreakers.

The Pullman Strike

One of the largest strikes in the late 1800's was a strike of railroad workers. The strike began in 1894 among employees of the Pullman Palace Car Company near Chicago. The Pullman factory made railroad cars that had sleeping compartments. The employees went on strike when the Pullman company tried to lower their wages.

Some of the striking Pullman workers were members of the American Railway Union (ARU). The ARU was an **industrial union**. An industrial union is an organization of all workers in one industry, no matter what kind of skill or craft they have. The ARU voted that all of its members should refuse to work on trains that had Pullman cars. Soon the ARU had shut down all rail traffic to and from Chicago.

---

industrial union an organization of all of the workers in a given industry, regardless of skill or craft

---

 Discuss: Should blacklisting be allowed? Why or why not?

Discuss: How do you think the residents of Chicago felt about the Pullman strike in 1894? Do you think they would have supported the strike or not? Explain your answer.

The railroad companies asked for help from the federal government. President Grover Cleveland responded by sending in soldiers to get the railroads running again. President Cleveland took this action, he said, to assure the movement of the mails. Also, the federal courts issued a special order stopping the union leaders from continuing the strike. This court order was called an **injunction**.

---

injunction an order from a court stopping an individual or group from carrying out some action

---

Eugene V. Debs was the head of the ARU. He refused to obey the court injunction. Debs was arrested and put in prison for six months. Following his arrest, the strikers became disorganized. Soon the railroad strike ended. The workers were defeated. The Pullman company lowered its workers' wages.

The Pullman strike was important because it gave the employers a powerful new tactic. They could now request injunctions to stop strikes.

The Socialist Party

The Pullman strike was also important because it led to the forming of a new labor organization. While Eugene Debs was in prison, he became a socialist. Socialists believe that the government should own the means of producing and distributing the nation's goods. They believe, in other words, that such things as factories and railroads should be owned by the public rather than by private individuals or corporations. The profits of industry should then be given directly to the workers.

In 1897, Debs organized the Socialist party of America. The Socialist party attracted some support among workers in the Northeast and the West. Debs himself ran five times as the Socialist party's candidate for President.

The Socialist party never attracted a large following in the United States. Most American workers did not agree with the ideas of the Socialists. Many workers still hoped someday to become owners of businesses themselves.

Section Review

1. What were some of the major organizations of American workers during the late 1800's?
2. Why were American workers discontented?
3. What are craft unions? What methods did the unions use to achieve their goals?
4. What is an injunction? What other methods did employers use against the unions?
5. What are the advantages and disadvantages of strikes? In your answer, consider how a strike might benefit or hurt a group of workers.

CHAPTER REVIEW

Summary

The need for more workers to fill jobs in expanding American industries was met by a flood of immigration to this country at the end of the nineteenth century. Many people came to America because of difficult conditions in their homelands and the promise of opportunity in America. Unlike those who had come before, many of these "New Immigrants" came from southern and eastern Europe and Asia.

Most newcomers settled in the cities. American cities grew rapidly. Many employment and cultural opportunities were available. However, housing, sanitation, and transportation problems were common.

As more and more immigrants came to this country, some people began to fear that the immigrants would take jobs away from American workers. New organizations sprang up that tried to pressure the government to restrict immigration. Labor unions were also formed that tried to improve the working conditions of the American labor force. By the end of the nineteenth century, Congress had passed laws that limited immigration, and labor unions had made some progress in improving the wages and working conditions in American industries.

Recalling the Facts

1. Name two things that attracted many immigrants to the United States in the late 1800's.
2. Why did labor leaders want restrictions placed on immigration?
3. What problems existed in the cities in the late 1800's? How were they solved?
4. Describe working conditions in the late 1800's.
5. Explain three tactics used by the AFL to achieve their goals.

Analyzing the Facts

1. In the late 1800's, many immigrants were coming to this country, cities were rapidly growing, and labor unions were formed. What connection do you see among these facts? What did one have to do with another?
2. Many people today believe that the problems of the cities mentioned in this chapter (housing, water and sewage, transportation) have not really been solved. Do you agree or disagree with this idea? Explain your answer.

3. How do the ideas expressed in the poem on the base of the Statue of Liberty differ from the demands made by American workers at the turn of the century?
4. Many people today argue that certain groups of workers, such as police officers and firefighters, should not be allowed to strike. Give one reason for this argument and one reason against it. List any other occupational groups that you think should not be allowed to strike and explain your reasoning.

Time and History

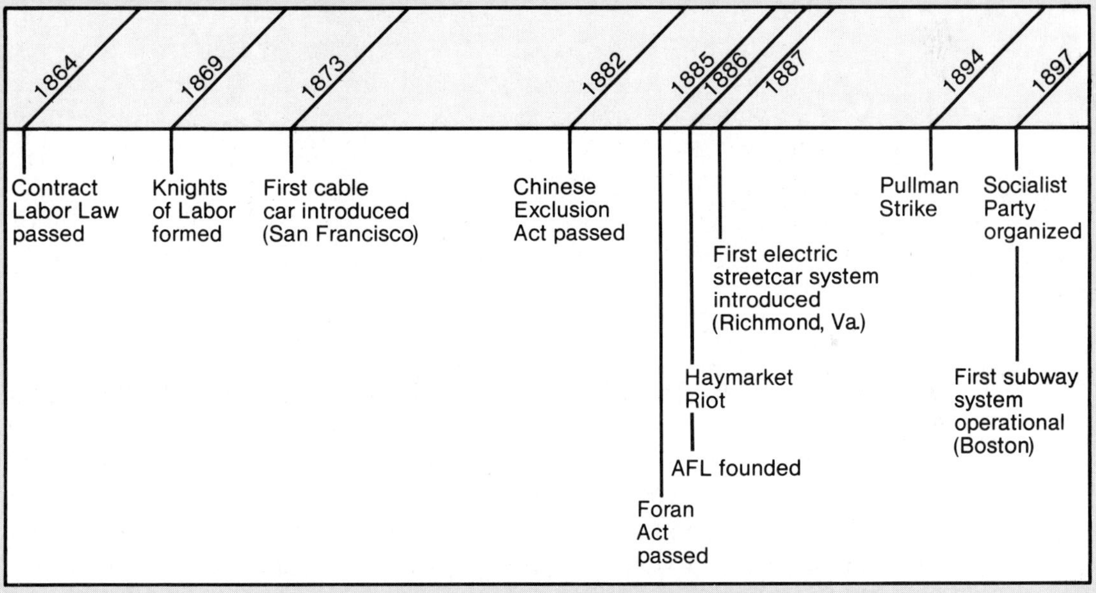

1. What three improvements were made in city transportation systems in the late 1800's?
2. For how many years were American employers allowed to recruit foreign workers?
3. The Haymarket bombing caused the breakup of the Knights of Labor. For how many years did the Knights of Labor exist?
4. When did Congress pass the first law restricting immigration to the United States?
5. The Pullman strike strongly influenced the formation of a new political party. What party was formed, and how many years after the Pullman strike was it organized?

Chapter 21 Political Machines and Parties

"We are here plunged in politics funnier than words can express," Henry Adams wrote during the election of 1884. "Very great issues are involved. . . . But the amusing thing is that no one talks about real interests. . . . Society is torn to pieces. Parties are wrecked from top to bottom. . . . Yet, when I'm not angry, I can do nothing but laugh."

Local politics in America had become hopelessly corrupt. The national parties tried to avoid important issues. Henry Adams' laughter masked a deep disappointment in what politics had become.

After you read this chapter, you will be able to:

1. Discuss the corruption of American city governments.
2. Compare the political parties in the years 1876 to 1896.
3. Trace the rise and fall of the Populist party.

Vocabulary Help: alderman—a member of a city legislative body. Does your city or town have such officials?

1. The Corruption of the Cities

BEFORE YOU READ: *Who benefited from and who was hurt by the corruption of American city governments?*

Many American city governments in the late 1800's were corrupt. "Corrupt" means spoiled or rotten. Public officials accepted bribes and made "shady," or dishonest, deals with local businesses. Votes were bought, and tax money was stolen. A British diplomat said that the government of America's cities was "a failure of democracy."

The Roots of Corruption

American city governments were corrupt for several reasons. The rapid growth of the cities contributed to their corruption. Many city governments failed to provide the basic services needed by their residents. In cities across the country, ambitious and dishonest people took advantage of this failure.

Another cause of corruption was the confusing organization of city government. In New York, for example, there were many different governing boards. The city had a board of supervisors, a board of councilors, a board of aldermen, and a board of education. There were also the police commissioners, the fire commissioners, and the commissioners of Central Park.

City government was a jumble of different groups. The system was so confusing that it could hardly govern at all. This confusion was another opportunity for corruption throughout the entire system.

There was yet another, even more disturbing, cause of city corruption. Many of the honest and industrious residents of the cities took no interest in city government. They failed to accept the responsibilities of good citizenship.

Many wealthier residents of the cities began moving to the suburbs, leaving the crowds and poverty of the city behind. They also left behind any active interest in city government.

Meanwhile, many of the very wealthy residents of the cities also were not interested in local government. They seemed to believe that local politics was not something that a "gentleman" should become involved in.

One wealthy young man in New York considered running for public office in 1880. His well-to-do friends laughed at him. They told him, he later recalled, "that politics were 'low'; that the organizations were not controlled by 'gentlemen'; that I would find them run by saloon-keepers, horse-car conductors, and the like." The young man ignored the advice of his friends. He became a local official, governor, and eventually the President of the United States. His name was Theodore Roosevelt.

The attitude of Roosevelt's friends, however, was a cause of the corruption in city government. If the "good" people would not become active in local government, who would?

Machines and Bosses

Many American cities during the Age of Industry were ruled by **machines**. The machines were corrupt political groups

Discuss: Why do you think that wealthy city residents in the late 1800's considered politics something that a cultured person should not become involved in? Do you think that people today feel the same way? Why or why not?

Background: The ward or precinct was the smallest political division of a machine organization. Each was led by a ward captain, or "ward boss." The various ward captains made up the ward committee, which reported to the boss.

"Big Tim" Sullivan, ward boss of New York's Lower East Side, in 1910.

organized to keep a party in office. They were often led by a strong individual who controlled the city government. The leader of the machine was called a "boss." The boss of the machine, in some cases, was the mayor of the city. Usually, however, the boss held no office at all. The machine included many "ward bosses" or "ward heelers." A ward is a local district of a city. A person could become a ward boss by volunteering to help the boss of the city.

---

machine a political group that organizes to control policy or officials in power

---

The ward bosses provided many services for the people. They helped find jobs for new immigrants and for unemployed workers, and they provided emergency food relief when it was needed.

The ward bosses also helped the cities' residents deal with the confusing system of city government. If a resident had a problem, it was far easier to take the problem to the local boss than to the various boards of the city government.

The bosses also helped people deal with the legal system. If a person was arrested for some minor offense, the ward heeler would "fix" it with the judge. The boss would give the judge a small bribe. A bribe is an illegal payment given in return for an expected favor. The charges would then be dropped.

Typical of the ward bosses were "Hinky Dink" Kenna of Chicago and "Big Tim" Sullivan of New York's Lower East Side. Sullivan was a very popular boss. Every summer, he would provide a free picnic and boat ride for the people of his district. At Christmas, Sullivan gave 5,000 turkey dinners to needy families. And on "Big Tim's" birthday, he would give every poor child in his district a new pair of shoes. When Sullivan died, more than 25,000 people came to his funeral.

Why were the ward bosses doing this? And other than bribing an occasional judge, what did they do that was corrupt? In return for all their services, the ward bosses received something very valuable: votes. The bosses expected the people of their districts to vote exactly as they directed them. If anyone needed extra encouragement, the bosses would buy their votes for $5 or $10 each. To get even more votes from their district, the bosses would "stuff" the ballot boxes with fake votes for the machine's candidates.

The votes from the bosses' districts were needed to keep the machine in power. The machines' candidates were

Background: Another term in the nineteenth century for bribe money was "boodle." The expression "Yankee Boodle—Just Dandy" was a sarcastic sentiment of the day which referred to the practice of making and accepting bribes.

Background: A sarcastic remark frequently heard in nineteenth century American cities was "vote early and vote often."

elected by the votes controlled by the ward bosses.

Why did the machine want power? Why did it want its candidates to be in office? The answer to these questions is money. The city bosses, the ward bosses, and the candidates all were in politics to make money. "To hold one of the principal city offices," a reporter said in 1887, "is equivalent to obtaining a large fortune."

Tammany Hall

The activity of New York's Tammany Hall was the best—or worst—example of how the machines made money. Tammany Hall was the name of the corrupt Democratic machine in New York City. Its boss after the Civil War was William Marcy Tweed.

Boss Tweed required businesses that sold goods to the city to "pad" their bills. This meant that he required the businesses to charge the city more than the goods were really worth. At first, Tweed required businesses to pad their bills by 10 percent. Later, he raised the padding to 85 percent and more.

After the city had paid the padded bills, Tweed required the businesses to return secretly a part of the money. The money they paid back is called a **kickback**. The businesses paid the kickback to Boss Tweed. Tweed, in turn, would divide the money among the various officials and ward bosses of Tammany Hall. The kickbacks were actually thefts of public tax money. The businesses were paid with money from the city treasury. This money had come from the city's taxpayers. The taxpayers were the people hurt most by this system of corruption.

THE BRAINS OF THE TAMMANY RING. (*Harper's Weekly*, October 21st, 1871.)

This cartoon of Boss Tweed is entitled "The Brains of the Tammany Ring." Why is his head depicted as a bag of money?

kickback money, received as payment for goods or services, that is illegally returned to a corrupt public official

Some of the kickback money was used by Tammany Hall to buy shoes for poor children on the birthdays of the ward bosses. A great deal of the money, however, became the personal fortune of Tweed and his followers. These corrupt politicians received the greatest benefits of the system. They became millionaires at the public's expense.

One of Boss Tweed's proudest accomplishments was the construction of the New York Courthouse. This building cost

Background: Boss Tweed and Tammany Hall increased New York City's debt by $70 million.

Background: When construction of the New York County courthouse began in 1868, it was estimated that the building would cost $500,000 to complete.

the taxpayers $12 million. About $9 million of the expense consisted of kickbacks. Corrupt city officials paid enormously padded bills. For example, for one thermometer for the new courthouse, Tammany politicians paid $7,500!

Boss Tweed's activities became so outrageous that a public outcry arose for his arrest. *The New York Times* and *Harper's Weekly* strongly criticized him. Tweed was finally arrested in 1871 and charged with fraud. He was convicted and sentenced to 12 years in prison.

Boss Ruef's San Francisco

Another way that machines made money was by accepting bribes. A local business, for example, might need a license from a city official to operate. Before the city official would issue the license, the official would demand a secret payment of money. This secret payment was a bribe.

Bribery of public officials was common in San Francisco around 1900. San Francisco was ruled by a corrupt machine. The boss of the machine was an attorney named Abraham Ruef. Ruef acted as a go-between between the city officials and local businesses.

Boss Ruef was paid large "attorney's fees" by local businesses that had dealings with the city government. These fees were really bribes. Ruef was hired, for example, by the city's largest streetcar company for $200,000. The company needed permission from the city to convert some of its old cable car lines to electric streetcars. Ruef divided $85,000 of "fees" among the supervisors. The supervisors then voted to permit the streetcar company to change its lines.

Like Tweed, Ruef was brought down by an outraged public. He was convicted of bribery and sent to San Quentin Prison.

Other cities were run by bosses. In Pittsburgh, the boss was Christopher Magee. Chicago had a Republican boss, William Lorimer. In St. Louis, the head of the machine was Ed Butler. The "Santa Fe Ring" was headed by a group of New Mexican bankers, politicians, and lawyers.

The bosses and their machines often provided many services for their cities. They were also corrupt and inefficient. It was not until the early 1900's that many American cities would begin to have honest, effective government.

Section Review

1. Who benefited from and who was hurt by the corruption of American city governments?
2. What were the causes of the corruption in city governments?
3. What are kickbacks? What are bribes?
4. What role did newspapers play in fighting corruption in the city government of New York? What can newspapers do today to expose corruption? Explain your answer.

Discuss: Do you think the bosses of American cities in the late 1800's did more harm or good? Explain your answer.

Background: States were called "swing states" because they did not have a firm pattern of voting for just one party. Ask students how this might affect campaigning in these states.

2. The Political Parade

BEFORE YOU READ: *In what ways were the two major political parties similar and different in the late 1800's?*

National political campaigns during the Age of Industry were exciting affairs. Brass bands marched through the streets. Political rallies included picnics and barbecues. Huge flags and bright banners added to the excitement.

Other than the liveliness of their campaigns, the national political parties offered very little to the American people. Both parties tried to avoid, rather than solve, important problems. The parties were very much like the parades they sponsored. They were noisy and lively, but they accomplished little of lasting value. Nevertheless, Americans were loyal to the party of their choice. Local issues often encouraged party loyalty and voter participation. Each party held strong appeal for the members of certain cultural and ethnic groups.

The Parties

The Democratic and Republican parties were similar in several ways. Each national party depended on local political machines. The machines delivered the votes needed in national as well as local elections. The parties were also similar in their lack of unity. Both parties were divided into different groups, or factions.

The parties had about the same number of supporters. Each presidential election from 1876 through 1896 was very close. In no case was the winner's share of the popular vote more than 51 percent. This near equality in voter support caused both national parties to avoid taking clear stands on the issues. The parties were afraid they might offend voters. If even a few voters were offended, the other party might win the election.

There were also some important differences between the parties. For example, their supporters came from different parts of the country. The Republicans were strongest in New England. They reminded voters that it was the Democrats who had led the South out of the Union. The Democrats, they said, were the party of "rebellion."

The Democrats were strongest in the South. Democratic candidates reminded Southern white voters that the Republicans were responsible for Reconstruction. The Republicans, they said, were the party of "black rule."

In the rest of the country, the vote was split fairly evenly between the two parties. National elections were usually won by whichever party won the "swing states" of Illinois, Indiana, Ohio, New Jersey, and New York. A swing state is a state that provides the winning votes in a national election. The state thus "swings" the election to one party or the other.

The parties also differed in terms of the religious and ethnic backgrounds of their supporters. The Democratic party was more strongly supported by Catholic and Jewish voters. The Republican party found strong support among Protestants. The New Immigrants generally supported the Democratic party. The immigrants benefited from the many services provided by the Democratic machines in

Discuss: Into what occupations do the most talented individuals go today? How do you know? What do we mean by "talented"? How could government attract more talented individuals?

eastern cities. Older American families were likely to be Republicans. There were, of course, many exceptions to these general categories. But religion and national background were important factors in each party's strength.

Both parties received large contributions from businesses, and many people in the late 1800's found this objectionable. They believed that big business was gaining too much control over American politics. Many farmers, workers, and others were unhappy with both parties.

Between 1876 and 1896, a series of weak Presidents occupied the White House. The more ambitious and talented citizens tended to go into business rather than into politics. The political leaders seemed unimpressive in comparison with such giants as Andrew Carnegie and John D. Rockefeller.

Hayes and the Failure of Reform

The corruption that poisoned local politics also affected politics on the national level. One of the worst forms of corruption was the "spoils system." Under this system, people were given government jobs because of their political loyalty instead of their ability.

When a new President was elected, he would give government jobs to his supporters and the supporters of his party. The number of jobs was very large. In 1871, there were 53,000 federal jobs. By 1900, there were 256,000. The government jobs paid good salaries.

Under the spoils system, federal employees often "bought" their jobs by giving money to political candidates. Once in office, the employees had many opportunities for corrupt dealings. Kickbacks and bribes were common.

When Rutherford B. Hayes became President in 1877, he planned to end the spoils system. But when Hayes himself tried to clean up corruption among federal employees, Congress opposed him. He was never able to overcome this opposition. At the end of his first term in office, Hayes was viewed as a failure. He had not ended the spoils system, and he had made many enemies. "I am not liked as President," he wrote in his diary. Hayes was not chosen by the Republicans to run for a second term.

The Tragedy of James A. Garfield

The Republican party in the late 1800's was divided into two main groups, the "Stalwarts" and the "Halfbreeds." The two groups, or factions, did not disagree on important issues. They were rivals for the benefits of the spoils system. Each faction wanted more federal jobs for its members. In 1880, the Republicans nominated James A. Garfield for President and Chester A. Arthur for Vice-President. Garfield belonged to neither faction. Arthur was a leader of the Stalwarts.

Garfield and Arthur narrowly defeated their Democratic opponents in the election of 1880. James A. Garfield was a large and handsome man. Like the two Presidents before him—Grant and Hayes—Garfield had been a Civil War general. Also like Grant and Hayes, Garfield proved to be a weak President.

Garfield disliked the spoils system. But to keep the Republican party united, he

For Extra Interest: Prior to civil service reform, even the job of local postmaster fell under the spoils system. Ask your local postmaster to visit the class to explain the requirements for the job of postmaster and to describe its work responsibilities.

This painting shows President Garfield being shot by Charles Guiteau. Garfield later died from his wounds.

spent much of his time dividing federal jobs between Stalwart and Halfbreed Republicans. "I am considering all day whether A or B shall be appointed to this or that office," Garfield once complained.

One man who failed to get a federal job was a lawyer named Charles Guiteau (gi-TOE). On July 2, 1881, Guiteau met President Garfield in a Washington train station. He shouted, "I am a Stalwart and Arthur is President now!" As he shouted, Guiteau fired two shots from a pistol. One bullet struck Garfield in the back. Guiteau was arrested, tried, and executed. After two months, the President died from his wounds.

Arthur and the Pendleton Act

The assassination of President Garfield caused many people to demand an end to the spoils system. The system must be bad, they thought, if it could lead a person to kill the President.

Following Garfield's death, Chester A. Arthur became President. Arthur was an impressive-looking man, always stylishly dressed. He was known as the "Gentleman Boss." He had been a leader of the Republican machine in New York.

Arthur had long been a defender of the spoils system. Earlier he had served as

Background: In 1880, the Greenback party nominated James Weaver for President. The Greenbacks supported the replacement of gold by paper money, women's right to vote, an end to child labor, a graduated income tax, and federal regulation of interstate commerce.

Background: Under the civil service system today, the names of persons who pass the exams are placed on eligibility lists in order of their grades, plus any points given for veteran preference. The hiring officer may appoint any of the top three persons on the list.

director of the Customs House in New York. The Customs House collected taxes on imported goods. The employees of the Customs House had many opportunities to engage in corrupt practices. In 1878, President Hayes had removed Arthur from his position when Arthur refused to keep out of party politics.

Once Arthur became President, in 1882, he became more sympathetic to those who wanted to end the spoils system. He called for reform, or change, of the system in his first message to Congress.

In January 1883, Congress passed the Pendleton Act. This act said that ability, not political loyalty, would be the basis for federal employment. Many federal jobs would now be filled by persons who had passed competitive public exams for the positions. These jobs were the beginning of the **civil service**.

---

civil service government jobs filled by persons who pass competitive public exams

---

The Pendleton Act was a limited success. Under President Arthur, it applied to only about one out of every ten federal jobs. Later Presidents expanded the civil service. By 1900, almost half of all federal jobs were a part of the civil service.

"Rum, Romanism, and Rebellion"

The election of 1884 was one of the closest in American history. The Republican candidate was James G. Blaine of Maine. Blaine had served in Congress for 20 years. The Democratic nominee was Grover Cleveland, the governor of New York. Cleveland was a courageous opponent of Tammany Hall. He was also a very large man, weighing about 113 kilograms (250 pounds).

There were no real political issues dividing the parties in 1884. But the election illustrated the importance of religion in politics during the late 1800's. In the last days of the campaign, Blaine met with a group of Protestant ministers. At this meeting, one of the ministers called the Democratic party the party of "rum, Romanism, and rebellion." Blaine said nothing to disagree with the remark.

Roman Catholics were greatly offended. They knew that the minister was referring to their church when he said "Romanism." They were insulted that their church had been linked to "rum" and to the "rebellion" of the Civil War.

The remark cost Blaine many votes in New York. Blaine lost New York, and Grover Cleveland became President.

As an opponent of corruption, Cleveland wanted to stop the abuses of veteran's pensions. A veteran's pension is money paid to a person after having served in the armed forces. During the Civil War, Congress had provided pensions for injured Union soldiers. In 1887, Congress passed a new pension bill. This bill would have given pensions to all injured veterans, even if they had been injured long after the war. Cleveland vetoed the measure.

Harrison and the Tariff

At the end of President Cleveland's first term, in 1888, he ran for reelection. He received about 100,000 more votes than

Background: Arthur wanted to be nominated in 1884, but the Republican machine preferred Blaine. The liberal Republicans, who did not support Blaine, left the party and formed the Mugwumps. The Mugwumps eventually joined with the Democrats.

Background: Cleveland's Vice President, Thomas Hendricks, died in 1885. At that time, there was no provision for filling the vacancy. If something had happened to Cleveland, a law passed in 1792 stipulated that the president pro tem of the Senate would assume the presidency.

his Republican opponent, yet he lost the election. The Republican candidate, Benjamin Harrison, was the winner because he received the majority of electoral votes.

Benjamin Harrison was the grandson of Old Tippecanoe, President William Henry Harrison. He had been a corporation lawyer in Indiana. He had little personal charm. One observer called him "the man who never laughs." Another said he was a "human iceberg."

Once again, there were few important issues in the election of 1888. Harrison received strong support from big business. He was given almost unlimited campaign funds from large manufacturers. Harrison rewarded his business supporters by approving the highest tariff yet in American history. This tariff, passed in 1890, was called the McKinley Tariff. It was named for its author, Representative William McKinley of Ohio. The tariff raised the prices of foreign goods so high that the importing of many goods stopped. The tariff was a great victory for Harrison's business supporters.

The McKinley Tariff soon became very unpopular. The prices of goods that were "protected" by the tariff rose quickly. As prices rose, the popularity of President Harrison declined.

President Benjamin Harrison

In 1892, Harrison was defeated for reelection by Grover Cleveland. Harrison's business supporters were disappointed. But they were not alarmed at the thought of having Cleveland as President. Business leaders felt safe that their interests would be protected by either Cleveland or Harrison.

Section Review

1. How were the Democratic and Republican parties similar during the Age of Industry? How were they different?
2. What were the terms of the Pendleton Act? What is civil service?
3. Why did American manufacturers favor high tariffs?
4. Most historians now agree that the Presidents elected between 1876 and 1896 were weak leaders. Which Presidents have been elected during your lifetime? Have these modern Presidents been strong or weak leaders? Explain your answer.

Discuss: Benjamin Harrison is said to have had little personal charm. What is meant by "personal charm?" Do you think this is important for a President to have? Why or why not?

Discuss: Imagine the process of bringing an ear of corn from the farmer's field to your dinner table today. What go-betweens are involved in the process? Which go-betweens do you, the consumer, pay and which does the farmer pay?

3. The Populist Party

BEFORE YOU READ: *How would farmers benefit from inflation?*

In the 1890's, a new political party, the Populist party, was formed. Its support came from farmers and others in the South and West. The Populists forced the two major parties to take a stand on an important issue: the nation's money supply.

Farmers in an Age of Industry

The Age of Industry had brought many benefits to American farmers. The increase in farm production was dramatic. But the Age of Industry brought the farmers new and unexpected problems. The farmers paid high rates to the railroads to ship their goods to market. The farmers also had to pay high fees to "go-betweens." Wheat farmers, for example, had to store their crops in expensive warehouses called grain elevators. Farmers also had to pay high property taxes on the land they owned. In addition, new farm machinery was very expensive.

All these problems—the high shipping rates, fees, taxes, and prices of new machinery—represented production costs to the farmers. Because these costs were very high, the farmers' profits were very small.

To make matters worse, the prices the farmers received for their own products were dropping. Western farmers, for example, had been able to sell their wheat for $1.50 per bushel in 1865. By 1895, the price had dropped to 50 cents. As farm prices dropped, the profits of the farmers became even smaller.

Farmers were forced to borrow money to stay in business. Year after year, the debts of the farmers increased. Many farmers were unable to pay their debts. They eventually lost their land and became renters on land they did not own.

Early Farm Organizations

Farmers in the late 1800's began forming organizations to help them solve their problems. In the 1870's, hundreds of thousands of farmers joined the National Grange of the Patrons of Husbandry. By 1874, the Grange had 1.5 million members. The organization became very powerful in the farm states of Illinois, Wisconsin, Iowa, and Minnesota. The Grange was able to convince the legislatures in these states to pass laws regulating the railroads and grain elevators. The laws set maximum rates that the railroads and the elevator owners could charge. These laws were called the "Granger laws."

The owners of the railroads and grain elevators challenged the Granger laws in federal court. In the case of *Munn* v. *Illinois* (1877), the Supreme Court ruled that the Granger laws were constitutional. Later, however, the Court reversed itself. In the Wabash case of 1886, the Court said that states did not have the power to set rates on railroad shipments traveling between states. This meant that many of the Granger laws were unconstitutional.

The Grange declined in strength. It was soon replaced by another farm organization. By 1890, more than 2 million farmers had joined Farmers' Alliances. The Alliances set up co-ops, or businesses run by

For Extra Interest: Have students look in the business section of the newspaper for the farm commodity prices. Compare today's prices for cotton and wheat to those given in the text for the late 1800's.

Members of the Linwood, Minnesota, Grange posed for this photograph in front of the Crescent Grange Hall around 1880.

groups, to buy supplies and farm equipment for their members. By buying in large quantities, the co-ops could get supplies for their members at lower prices.

The Alliances supported many reforms, such as government ownership of the railroads. They also urged the federal government to set up a warehouse in every county to store farm products. The Alliances favored the lowering of property taxes. A new income tax should be adopted, they said, to replace revenues lost by lowered property taxes.

Candidates endorsed by the Alliances were elected throughout the South and in parts of the West. In the election of 1890, 53 Alliance candidates were elected to Congress.

The Silver Issue

There were two ways that farmers could increase their profits. They could lower their production costs, or they could raise the prices they received for their farm products.

Most of the reforms of the Grange and the Farmers' Alliances were aimed at lowering production costs. Farmers also wanted to find a way to raise the selling price of their crops.

Background: The National Grange also started cooperatives where farmers could buy manufactured goods for less than on the open market. In 1874, the Grange began to stock its cooperatives from Montgomery Ward and Company, a small mail order business.

Background: Today, the Federal Reserve System controls inflation by making money easy or hard to borrow by changing the interest rates. For example, low interest rates encourage people to borrow money. This increases the amount of money in circulation and leads to inflation.

One way that prices could be raised was by increasing the size of the nation's supply of money. The amount of money in circulation in the United States had been steadily declining since the early 1870's. As the money supply had declined, prices also had declined. Each dollar became more valuable. As the years went by, a dollar bought more and more goods.

The nation's money supply could be increased if the federal government decided to print or coin more money. If the federal government put more money into circulation, the value of the money would decrease. Each dollar would become less valuable. It would buy fewer goods. Prices of farm products would rise. Many farmers in the late 1800's, therefore, became supporters of **inflation**.

inflation an increase in the amount of money in circulation that leads to a decrease in its value and a rise in prices

Inflation would benefit the farmers by raising the price of the farmers' crops. It would also lower the value of the farmers' debts. The value of their debts had been steadily increasing for many years. This increase had been caused by the decline in the nation's money supply and the decline in the price of farm products. For example, if a farmer borrowed $500 when wheat was selling for $1 per bushel, the money borrowed would be worth 500 bushels ($500 divided by $1 equals 500). When the price of wheat fell to 50 cents a bushel, by the time the farmer paid back the debt, the money the farmer paid was *worth* 1,000 bushels ($500 divided by 50 cents equals 1,000).

Farmers thus favored inflating the money supply to stop the steady increase in the value of their debts. Bankers and business leaders, however, strongly opposed inflation. Inflation would cause money, which bankers received from debtors, to be worth less than when it was first loaned. Businesses, which sold goods on credit, would also receive money that was worth less than the current value of the goods.

Shortly after the Civil War, many farmers urged the federal government to keep a large supply of paper dollars, called "greenbacks," in circulation. By the late 1800's, farmers had begun to urge the federal government to make more silver dollars. Owners of western silver mines also supported the coinage of more silver money. More greenbacks or more silver money would cause the same thing—inflation. In 1890, Congress passed the Sherman Silver Purchase Act. This act required the government to buy and make a certain amount of silver into coins each month.

The Populist Party

In 1892, leaders of the Farmers' Alliances and other groups formed the People's Party of the U. S. A., better known as the Populist party. The Populists criticized the two major parties for allowing the country to be run by millionaires, trusts, and big businesses.

The Populists called for many reforms. Several of the reforms had been earlier endorsed by the Alliances. They supported, for instance, government ownership of the railroads. They also supported the adoption of a federal income tax.

Discuss: When would it be a good time to borrow money, during a period of rising or declining inflation? Explain your answer.

Background: A declaration of the principles and policies adopted by a political party or a candidate is called a platform. The individual principles of the platform are called planks.

Famous Americans

JACOB S. COXEY

In 1893, the economy took a turn for the worse. Hundreds of thousands of people were out of work.

Jacob Coxey was a wealthy quarry owner from Ohio. As a Populist, he was concerned that the government was not helping the unemployed as it should. He had some ideas he thought would help. A Good Roads Program would hire unemployed workers to fix the roads of the nation for $1.50 per day. A second program would provide money for local public improvements. He decided the way to convince Congress to pass such bills was to show the people in Washington, D.C., how many people were unemployed. Coxey arranged for thousands of unemployed people to meet in Ohio and walk to the nation's capital. Thus was born Coxey's Army.

Coxey started out on Easter Sunday, 1894, with 100 marchers behind him. Coxey's Army reached Washington, D.C., on May 1. By that time, the Army had grown to 500 people. Coxey tried to make a speech on the steps of the Capitol. But the police rushed in and arrested Coxey and others for carrying banners and walking on the grass. His bills were never acted on by the Congress, but the march won wide publicity. Many of Coxey's ideas later became part of the Democratic party's platform. In fact, in May 1944, Coxey was invited to Washington, D.C., to finish the speech he started 50 years earlier.

The Populists believed that big business had gained too much political power and that political power should be returned to the people. They called for the direct election of United States senators. (Senators were still elected by the state legislatures at that time.) The Populists also believed that people should have the right to initiate, or start, laws themselves.

The most controversial reform of the Populists was their support of inflation. The Populists called for the government to increase the money supply by "the free and unlimited coinage of silver."

The Populists hoped to attract support from people in all sections of the country. They counted on the support of the silver-mining states of the Far West. They sought the votes of farmers in the South and on the Great Plains. At first, the Populists actively recruited support from black voters in the South. Nearly 100 black delegates participated in the Populists' first national convention. The Populists also welcomed the support of women, although few women yet had the right to vote. Women served as editors, organizers, and speakers for the party.

Background: Black farmers in the South generally supported the Populists. Populist leaders, like Tom Watson in Georgia, urged the poor white and black farmers to stand and work together for their common good.

The Election of 1896

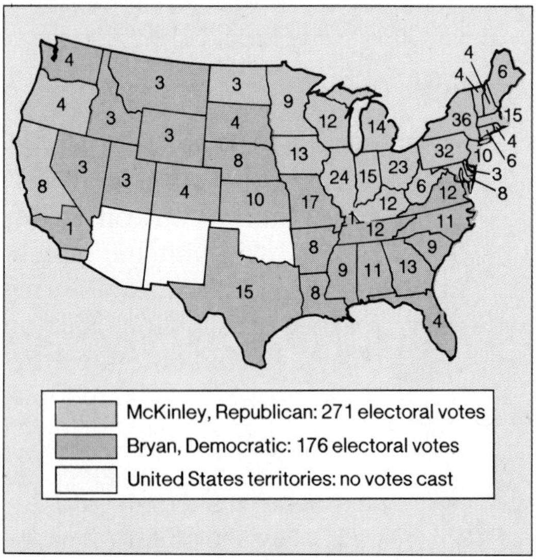

What sections of the nation supported William McKinley in the election of 1896?

One of the most effective Populist speakers was Mary Elizabeth Lease, a Kansas lawyer.

At their 1892 convention in Omaha, Nebraska, the Populists nominated a former Union general, James B. Weaver, for President. In the election of 1892, James Weaver received strong support in the South, the West, and on the plains. Over one million people voted for him. This was a strong showing for a third-party candidate, but it was not enough to win. Grover Cleveland, the Democratic nominee, was the winner.

Hard Times in the 1890's

Following the election of 1892, the United States entered a period of hard times. Prices on the stock market declined rapidly in 1893. More than 15,000 businesses failed. In 1894, about 18 percent of the labor force was unemployed. Over 4 million people were out of work.

One of the causes of the hard times of the 1890's was a growing fear among business leaders that the government was going to give in to the demand for inflation. To end the fear, Congress repealed the Sherman Silver Purchase Act in November 1893. The government would no longer purchase or coin any silver. Therefore, the money supply would not be increased.

The repeal of the Sherman Act angered the farmers. In the Congressional elections of 1894, the Populists made a strong showing. Thirteen members of Congress were elected from the South and West.

The Election of 1896

The election of 1896 was one of the most important elections in American history. The major parties took opposing stands on an important issue.

The Republicans chose William McKinley as their candidate. McKinley was the governor of Ohio. He had served in Congress and was well known as the author of the McKinley Tariff. The Republicans took a stand against inflation, declaring that they were "opposed to the free coinage of silver." They said that "the existing gold standard must be maintained."

The Democratic candidate in 1896 was William Jennings Bryan of Nebraska. Like McKinley, Bryan had served in Congress. At the Democratic convention, Bryan made a powerful speech against the gold standard. "You shall not press down upon the brow of labor this crown of thorns. You shall not crucify mankind upon a

For Extra Interest: Have students research the popularity and the effects of the Populist movement in their state. You may need to help them by referring them to some state history texts.

Discuss: Why do you think the Democrats decided to support the free and unlimited coinage of gold and silver in the election of 1896?

William Jennings Bryan

cross of gold." With these words, Bryan flung his arms wide, as if he were being crucified himself. The speech was a tremendous success. The Democrats voted in favor of "the free and unlimited coinage of both silver and gold." The Populists soon joined the Democrats and nominated Bryan as their candidate too.

During the campaign of 1896, Bryan traveled widely and gave over 600 speeches. McKinley campaigned by staying home. Visitors from all over the country came to see him at his home in Canton, Ohio.

On election day, Bryan won by a large margin in the South, the plains, and in the mining West. McKinley, however, was a bigger winner. He won in all the industrial states of the Northeast. He also won in the northern Midwest.

Why did McKinley win the election of 1896? Banks and big businesses, which were strongly opposed to inflation, gave $3.5 million to McKinley's campaign. Railroads provided special reduced fares for visitors to McKinley's Ohio home. Bryan was able to raise far less money for his campaign.

However, the main reason that McKinley won was that Bryan's support was limited to the South and the West. There were simply not enough voters in those sections to give Bryan a victory.

The defeat of Bryan was a defeat for the farmers and for the Populist party. By 1900, the Populist party was dead. American politics would continue to be dominated by the two major parties. From now on, however, the parties would have a hard time avoiding important issues.

Section Review

1. How would American farmers benefit from inflation?
2. What were the Granger laws?
3. What reforms did the Farmers' Alliances advocate?
4. Who were the candidates for President in 1896? What were the results of this election?
5. During most of American history, there have been two major parties. Sometimes a third party, such as the Populist party, is formed. Why do you suppose people would want to form a new political party?

CHAPTER REVIEW

Summary

In the late 1800's, many city governments in the United States had become corrupt. Powerful political machines led by individuals called bosses controlled the cities. They provided services for city residents in return for votes and favors. Many bosses, like Tweed in New York City and Ruef in San Francisco, became wealthy at the expense of the taxpayers.

The two major political parties, the Democrats and the Republicans, provided little leadership for the country during this period. Both tried to avoid, rather than solve, problems. American politics became dominated by big business. The only significant reform made during this period was the beginning of a civil service system to replace the spoils system.

Just prior to the turn of the century, however, Americans began to demand more government involvement and assistance. Farmers and laborers formed the Populist party in 1892, and working people began to be heard.

Recalling the Facts

1. List and explain three reasons why city governments became corrupt in the late 1800's.
2. What are political machines? How were political machines able to control cities?
3. Why did Democrats and Republicans in the late 1800's avoid taking clear stands on the issues?
4. How did people get government jobs under the spoils system? How did the civil service system change that?
5. What problems did farmers have in the late 1800's?
6. What five specific reforms did the Populists support?

Analyzing the Facts

1. What can citizens do to prevent government corruption today?
2. If you had been living in the United States in the late 1800's, which political party would you probably have supported—the Democratic, Republican, or Populist? Explain your answer.

3. How might the formation of a third political party affect a presidential election?
4. Most Americans would have difficulty naming the Presidents of the late nineteenth century. Why do you think this is so?
5. Do you think a factory worker of the late 1800's would support the free coinage of silver? Explain your answer.

Time and History

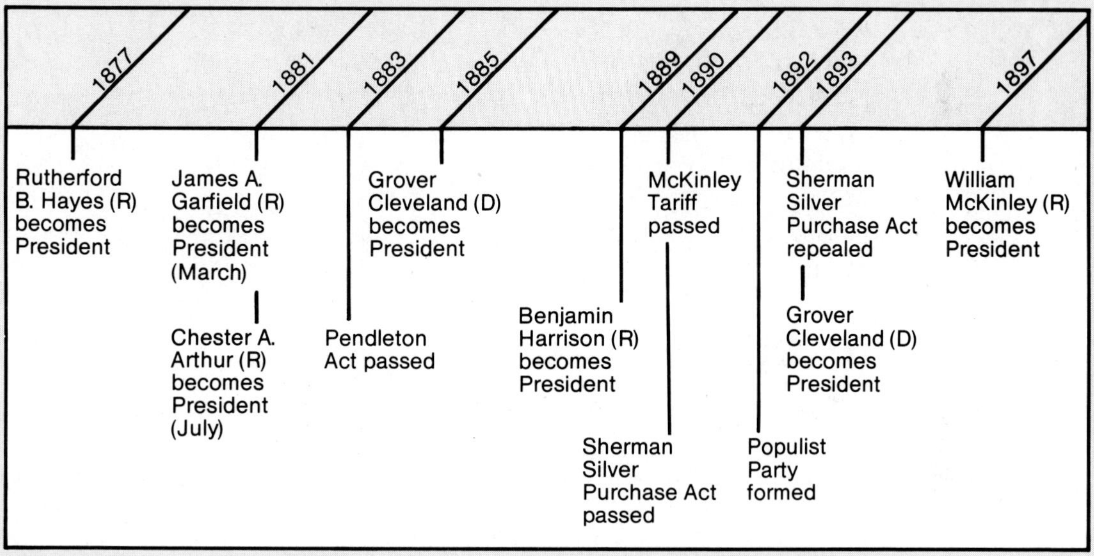

1. From 1876 to 1896, which political party was more successful in getting its candidates elected to the presidency, the Democrats or the Republicans?
2. Which President served the shortest amount of time, and how long did he serve?
3. Who was President when the Sherman Silver Purchase Act was passed?
4. How many years did the U.S. government coin silver before returning to the gold standard?
5. Which President shown on the time line served two four-year terms?

Chapter 22
A Show of Strength

On February 15, 1898, the noise of a terrible explosion startled the city of Havana, Cuba. In the harbor, an American battleship, the *U.S.S. Maine,* was in flames. More than 250 men aboard the ship were killed in the explosion and fire.

By 1898, the United States was on its way to becoming a world power. It was extending its control over new territories. The destruction of the *Maine* led to a war with Spain. It was a war in which the United States showed to the world its new strength.

After you read this chapter, you will be able to:

1. Explain the reasons for American overseas expansion.
2. Identify the results of the Spanish-American War.
3. Describe the contributions of Theodore Roosevelt to American foreign policy.

☐ Recognize propaganda.

Discuss: Is it possible for the United States to remain completely isolated from the rest of the world? Explain your answer.

1. Overseas Expansion

BEFORE YOU READ: *What groups of Americans were interested in American overseas involvement and expansion?*

Americans have always had a divided view of the rest of the world. On the one hand, Americans have wanted to remain separate or isolated from other nations. President Benjamin Harrison said in 1888 that the United States was "an apart nation." Like many Americans, he believed it was in the best interest of our nation to stay out of the affairs of other nations.

On the other hand, Americans have also been interested in other lands. The American people themselves have roots in other countries. Americans have always enjoyed foreign travel. American businesses have been interested in acquiring foreign markets for their goods.

Causes of Expansion

In the Age of Industry, the United States expanded its power and influence around the world. New overseas territories were acquired by the United States. There were groups of Americans who wanted to see America expand its influence overseas.

The most important group of people supporting expansion were owners of America's farms and factories. Farmers and manufacturers were producing more goods than they could sell to American consumers. They needed other outlets for their products. By selling their goods to foreign customers, American farmers and manufacturers found the profitable market they needed. In 1870, Americans sold $450 million worth of goods on foreign markets. By 1900, American foreign trade had increased to $1.5 billion.

"American factories are making more than the American people can use," an Indiana Republican observed in 1898. "American soil is producing more than they can consume. Fate has written our policy for us; the trade of the world must and shall be ours."

American efforts to expand increased further when other nations began to compete for overseas markets. Many other industrial nations—such as Great Britain, France, and Germany—were acquiring new territories in Asia and Africa. Some Americans believed that if the United States wanted to trade with foreign markets, it would have to move quickly.

Overseas expansion was also caused by the closing of the frontier in America. In the late 1800's, the last frontier was being settled. Many Americans feared that the United States was running out of room. The nation, they believed, must now expand overseas.

Early Expansion

Americans remained divided over the issue of overseas expansion. Generally, however, more people believed that the nation should expand its territory or power. These Americans were called **expansionists**.

---

expansionist a person who believes a nation should expand its territory or power

---

Discuss: Compare the attitude of the Indiana Republican in 1898 (quoted in the text) with the attitude of those who supported Manifest Destiny (Chapter 14) in the 1840's. How are they similar and different?

Discuss: How do you think isolated bases scattered around the world can help defend the United States?

William Henry Seward was an expansionist. He served as secretary of state under Abraham Lincoln and Andrew Johnson. Seward believed the United States should acquire naval bases beyond its borders for better defense. Bases would also be useful as America expanded its foreign trade. Naval patrols from the bases could protect American shipping.

Seward had grand plans for acquiring more territory. He believed the United States should purchase islands such as Cuba, Greenland, or Iceland. Seward failed to gain enough support in Congress, and these plans came to nothing.

Seward also failed to get Congress to approve the purchase of the Danish West Indies. These tiny islands in the Caribbean Sea, today called the Virgin Islands, had excellent harbors for naval bases. In 1867, Seward signed a treaty with the Danish government to sell the islands. Congress refused to approve it.

Seward was more successful in acquiring islands halfway around the globe. In 1867, the United States annexed the Midway Islands. These small islands in the Pacific Ocean lay 1,600 kilometers (1,000 miles) northwest of Hawaii. They were "midway" between the United States and Asia. The islands had been discovered by an American naval officer in 1859. They became an important naval base for the United States.

The greatest success of William Henry Seward was his purchase of Alaska. Alaska had been a Russian territory for many years. It had been used as a base for Russian fur traders in the Pacific. The fur traders hunted seals, sea otters, and other marine mammals. As the fur trade declined, Russia became interested in selling Alaska.

On March 30, 1867, Seward and a Russian representative signed a treaty of purchase. Russia agreed to sell Alaska to the United States for $7.2 million. The opponents of the purchase called the scheme "Seward's Folly." One newspaper said the only resources in Alaska were an enormous crop of ice and cows that gave ice cream instead of milk!

Seward pointed out that Alaska had several good sites for naval bases. He explained that Alaska could also serve as a way station to the Far East. In addition, its price was a bargain—less than one cent per hectare (less than 2 cents per acre). After a long debate, Congress approved the treaty. The American flag was raised at Sitka on October 18, 1867. Later, when gold was discovered in Alaska, few Americans criticized the purchase of "Seward's Icebox."

One of the most powerful expansionists was a naval officer named Alfred Thayer Mahan. Mahan argued that the United States must increase the size and strength of its navy. Without a strong navy, he pointed out, the United States could not compete with other nations for foreign markets. Mahan's arguments were very convincing. Congress provided money to construct many new naval ships. In 1893, the United States had the fifth strongest navy in the world. By 1900, it ranked third.

The Hawaiian Islands

The best site in the Pacific for an American naval base was the Hawaiian Islands. The islands had long been settled by Pol-

Background: In 1890, Mahan wrote a book entitled *The Influence of Sea Power Upon History, 1660–1783*. In his book, he argued that all great nations had great navies and depended on sea power for their greatness.

For Extra Interest: Invite a navy officer or recruiter to visit the class and discuss the role of the United States Navy today.

ynesian people. Europeans discovered the islands in 1778. American missionaries first arrived in Hawaii in 1820. They built many missions throughout the islands. Americans also began to acquire land in Hawaii for sugar plantations. Soon many Americans had become wealthy owners of huge sugar plantations.

In 1875, representatives of the Hawaiian government and the United States signed a treaty. The United States agreed to allow the owners of Hawaiian sugar plantations to sell their sugar in the United States without paying any tariff. Hawaii agreed that it would not give or sell any of its territory to a foreign country. In 1887, Hawaii agreed to allow the United States to build a naval base at Pearl Harbor.

The American sugar planters in Hawaii became more and more prosperous. By 1890, Americans controlled most of the plantations in Hawaii. They were selling $20 million worth of sugar in the United States each year. The American sugar planters also had great influence in the Hawaiian government.

In 1890, things began to change. The McKinley Tariff of 1890 changed American policy on imported sugar. If the plantation owners in Hawaii wanted to continue to prosper, Hawaii would have to become part of the United States.

In 1891 a new ruler took over the Hawaiian government. Her name was Queen Lilioukalani (le-LEE-woe-kah-LAH-nee). She believed the Americans had become too powerful in Hawaii. She adopted a policy of "Hawaii for the Hawaiians." The American plantation owners feared Queen Lilioukalani would take away their plantation lands.

Queen Lilioukalani of Hawaii

In 1893, the Americans in Hawaii revolted against the Hawaiian government. The official United States representative in Hawaii, John L. Stevens, helped the revolt to succeed. Stevens ordered 150 United States Marines to the queen's palace. The presence of the marines prompted the queen to surrender.

After the surrender, Stevens wrote to the American government in Washington, D.C. "The Hawaiian pear is now fully ripe," Stevens wrote, "and this is the golden hour to pluck it." He urged the government to make the islands part of the United States. The Americans on the islands proclaimed that Hawaii was an independent republic. In 1894, they elected Sanford B. Dole as president of the Republic of Hawaii.

The actions of the Americans in Hawaii caused debate at home. Expansionists

Background: The McKinley Tariff placed a 2-cents-per-pound tax on sugar imported by the United States. The American sugar planters in Hawaii were eager for the United States to annex the island so they would not have to pay the tariff.

In this cartoon from 1900, Uncle Sam is shown holding the key to China's open door. Why would the United States be at an advantage over its European competitors with the Open Door policy?

urged the United States to take the islands. Other Americans, however, believed that Hawaii should be given back to the Hawaiians. One critic said the Hawaiian revolution was "of sugar, by sugar, and for sugar." Finally, in 1898, Congress voted to add Hawaii to the United States.

The Open Door

Ever since the days of Marco Polo, China had been like a magnet to Europeans. Missionaries and traders from many nations had been drawn to China. By the late 1800's, the Empire of China was very weak. In 1895, Japan easily defeated China in war. Many European nations hurried to acquire territory or influence in China. Great Britain, France, Germany, and Russia obtained naval bases and ports. The European nations began dividing China into **spheres of influence**. Within each sphere, one nation exercised almost complete control. Each nation wanted a larger share of the "China market" for itself.

Discuss: If you had been living in the United States during the 1890's, would you have argued for or against adding Hawaii to the United States? Explain your answer.

Background: The Chinese who killed 231 Europeans during the Boxer Rebellion were members of a group called the Righteous Harmonious Band. The word *band* was mistranslated as "fists," and from this came the name "Boxers."

sphere of influence an area beyond a nation's borders where the nation exercises almost complete control

American missionaries and business leaders became concerned. Missionaries feared they would not be able to continue their work in China. American business leaders worried that they could no longer sell their goods there.

In 1899, the American secretary of state, John Hay, sent a series of notes to the major European powers. These notes asked each nation to keep an "Open Door" within their spheres of influence in China. He meant that Chinese ports should be open to all nations. No special privileges should be granted to any nation. The Open Door notes were intended to keep China open for American traders. The notes were accepted in part by most of the European powers. In 1900, Secretary Hay announced that the Open Door policy was in effect.

The growing European influence in China sparked a Chinese reaction. In 1900, a secret Chinese society captured and killed 231 Europeans. The members of the society, known as "Boxers," wanted to rid China of all foreign influence.

The Europeans fled from the Boxers and hid in their own embassies in Peking. For weeks, the Europeans were cut off from all contact with the outside world. A force of 18,000 soldiers from many nations came to China. The force included 2,500 American soldiers. When the soldiers reached Peking, the Europeans were rescued.

Following the Boxer Rebellion, the United States feared that the Europeans would take revenge on China and tighten their control within their spheres of influence. In July 1900, Secretary of State Hay sent a new set of notes to the Europeans. The notes said that the independence of China must be preserved. The notes also said that the United States supported "the principle of equal and impartial trade with all parts of the Chinese empire."

The Open Door notes of John Hay were a sign of America's new interest in foreign affairs. They revealed the determination of the United States to increase its foreign trade. They showed the willingness of the nation to play a larger role in events far from its shores.

Section Review

1. What groups of Americans were interested in overseas expansion?
2. Define expansionists.
3. What territories did William Henry Seward want to acquire for the United States? How successful was he?
4. What was the purpose of America's Open Door policy in China?
5. Both Alaska and Hawaii were acquired by the United States in the late 1800's. How are these two states important to the nation today?

Background: As a result of the Boxer Rebellion, China had to pay $333 million to compensate for the European losses. The United States never accepted all of its $24 million share.

Background: The revolt in 1895 was not the first attempt by Cubans to gain their independence. Revolts had been occurring since 1868. In 1873, an American ship was captured and the crew executed for bringing weapons to Cuba for a revolution.

2. The Spanish-American War

BEFORE YOU READ: *What were the results of the Spanish-American War?*

The United States went to war against Spain in 1898. The Spanish-American War was one of the shortest wars in American history. The fighting lasted only about ten weeks. One American official called it "a splendid little war." The results of this "little" war were very important. Through the war, the United States gained control over new territories in the Caribbean Sea and the Pacific Ocean.

"Free Cuba!"

Spain once had the largest empire in North and South America. But revolts against Spanish rule began in the early 1800's. By the 1890's, the empire of Spain was very small. The most important colony still under Spanish control was the island of Cuba.

In 1895, Cuba revolted against Spain. The Cubans wanted to be independent, like the other former Spanish colonies. The battle cry of the Cubans was *¡Cuba Libre!* This means "Free Cuba!"

To defeat the Cuban rebels, Spain sent a new governor to Cuba in 1896. The new governor was General Valeriano Weyler. General Weyler used brutal methods to try to defeat the rebels. He believed that many Cuban civilians were helping the rebels. He ordered Spanish soldiers to put tens of thousands of Cuban civilians into **concentration camps**. These camps were surrounded with barbed wire and armed guards. Conditions inside the camps were very poor. Thousands of Cuban civilians, including women and children, died in the camps.

---

concentration camp a prison camp where political enemies or members of minority ethnic groups are confined

---

American newspapers, reporting the events in Cuba, made conditions there seem even worse than they really were. In 1896, for example, newspapers reported the death of a Cuban rebel leader named Antonio Maceo (mah-SAY-oh). Maceo had been killed in battle by Spanish soldiers. The New York papers reported that he had been killed by Spanish trickery. One newspaper claimed that the Spaniards had hired Maceo's doctor to poison him.

These newspapers used exciting but exaggerated news stories to increase the sales of their newspapers. The newspapers were practicing what is called **yellow journalism**.

---

yellow journalism the use of exciting but exaggerated news stories to make a newspaper more popular

---

The newspapers described in gory detail the actions of Spanish soldiers in Cuba. The Spaniards were said to have thrown Cuban prisoners to the sharks. Stories reported that Spanish soldiers dragged wounded Cuban soldiers from their beds and killed them. General Weyler was called "Butcher" Weyler and "Mad Dog" Weyler in colorful American newspaper accounts.

Americans were horrified as they read

Background: Yellow journalism got its name from the Yellow Kid, hero of a comic strip that appeared in the late 1800's. The Yellow Kid was a tough New York City slum-dweller who expressed strong patriotic feelings.

Discuss: Why do you think most Americans thought that Spain was responsible for blowing up the *Maine*? Was this belief based on facts or prejudices?

about the awful events in Cuba. Many Americans believed the United States should do something to stop the bloodshed there.

American business leaders were especially concerned about the events in Cuba. As in Hawaii, many Americans owned sugar plantations on the island. Some of these plantations were being destroyed in the fighting between Spaniards and Cubans.

Remember the *Maine*!

In January 1898, President McKinley ordered the American battleship *Maine* to go to Cuba. Its duty was to protect American lives and property on the war-torn island. The *Maine* steamed into Havana harbor and dropped anchor.

On February 15, 1898, the *Maine* was destroyed by a terrific blast. Over 250 American naval officers and sailors were killed. President McKinley ordered an official investigation. The investigation found that the ship had been destroyed by an underwater explosion.

No one ever discovered who was responsible for blowing up the *Maine*. Most Americans, however, concluded that Spain was to blame. People throughout the nation demanded that war be declared on Spain. The popular rallying cry became "Remember the *Maine*!"

Leaders of American business hoped that war could be avoided. The nation was just recovering from the hard times of the early 1890's. The business leaders feared that war would slow down this recovery.

President McKinley had received strong support from business leaders during his election campaign in 1896. He too hoped to avoid war with Spain. The public pressure for war became more and more powerful. Even members of McKinley's administration came to favor war. His assistant secretary of the navy, Theodore Roosevelt, became impatient with the President's opposition to war. "McKinley has no more backbone," Roosevelt shouted, "than a chocolate éclair!"

McKinley knew that if he continued to oppose war with Spain, he would hurt his chances of reelection. Finally, on April 11, 1898, McKinley asked Congress for a declaration of war against Spain. Eight days later, Congress declared war. The declaration of war stated that the war's only purpose was to free Cuba from Spanish rule.

Added to the declaration of war was an important amendment. This amendment, called the Teller Amendment, said that the United States had no desire to take Cuba for itself. Congress wanted the world to know that this was to be a war to free Cuba, not to add territory to the United States. It was a war, one newspaper agreed, for "the liberty of human beings, for *Cuba Libre*; not for an extension of American territory."

A War on Two Fronts

The first blow to free Cuba was struck in the Philippine Islands. The Philippines are a large group of islands off the southern coast of China, over 12,900 kilometers (8,000 miles) from Cuba. In 1898, the Philippines were still a part of the Spanish empire. Attacking the Philippines was an odd way to free Cuba. But the United States was simply following an old rule of

For Extra Interest: Have students locate Cuba and the Philippine Islands on a wall map of the world. Using the scale in miles, have two students calculate the distance of Cuba from Spain and the Philippines from Spain.

Background: A poem of the day read: "O dewy was the morning / Upon the first of May, / And Dewey was the admiral / Down in Manila Bay, / And dewy were those Spaniards' eyes, / Them orbs of black and blue, / And do we feel discouraged? / I do not think we do."

war: Hit the enemy where it is weakest.

On the evening of April 30, a fleet of six modern American naval vessels approached Manila, the capital city of the Philippine Islands. The fleet was under the command of Commodore George Dewey. Guarding Manila was a Spanish fleet of ten older ships. At dawn on May 1, 1898, the American fleet opened fire on the Spanish vessels. By noon, all the Spanish vessels were destroyed. Not one American ship had been damaged. Only eight American sailors had been wounded.

Commodore Dewey became an instant American hero. Newspapers throughout the United States praised him as a naval genius. The war against Spain, it seemed, was indeed going to be "splendid."

Following the American naval victory, troops were landed in Manila. The American forces were joined by Filipino rebels. The Filipinos, like the Cubans, were fighting to win their independence from Spain. By August 1898, the American and Filipino forces had defeated the Spanish troops in the Philippines.

Meanwhile, in June 1898, American mil-

In the battle of Quasimas, near Santiago, Cuba, the 9th and 10th Colored Cavalry gave much needed support to the Rough Riders.

itary action had begun in Cuba. About 17,000 American soldiers landed near Santiago, a city in southeastern Cuba. To capture the city, the Americans had to defeat the Spanish forces in the hills overlooking Santiago.

On July 1, a major battle was fought at the hilltop village of El Caney. Some 7,000 American soldiers defeated a Spanish force of 600 men. Casualties on both sides were high. Among the soldiers in Cuba was a group of volunteers known as the "Rough Riders." One of the leaders of this group was Theodore Roosevelt. Roosevelt resigned from his position as assistant secretary of the navy to join the fighting in Cuba. On July 1, the same day as the battle at El Caney, Roosevelt and the Rough Riders and other American soldiers charged up San Juan Hill. The charge was a success. The Americans took the hill from the Spanish forces.

Among the first Americans to reach the crest of San Juan Hill were the soldiers of the all-black 9th and 10th Cavalry. Blacks in the armed forces served in separate units from whites. There were four black units in the fighting in Cuba. "The Ninth and Tenth Cavalry regiments fought on either side of me at Santiago," Theodore Roosevelt later recalled, "and I wish no better men beside me in battle." The black soldiers suffered heavy casualties in the battle for San Juan Hill.

The victories at El Caney and San Juan Hill were followed by a naval victory in Santiago Bay. On July 3, 1898, American naval forces attacked and destroyed the Spanish fleet near Santiago. The victory was as complete as the one in Manila Bay. American losses in the battle totaled one killed and one wounded.

Colonel Theodore Roosevelt, one of the leaders of the Rough Riders.

Two weeks later, the Spanish commander in Cuba surrendered to the Americans. Shortly after that, American soldiers landed in Puerto Rico. The Spanish forces there surrendered without a battle.

The Treaty of Paris

The Spanish-American War began as a war to free Cuba. The war ended with the United States in control of several new territories. Americans now faced the question: What should be done with these territories?

The largest and most important territory was the Philippine Islands. Many Americans had never heard of the Philippines before the war. Even President McKinley said he knew nothing about the islands. "When we received the cable [telegram] from Admiral Dewey telling of

Discuss: What advantages do you think the United States had over the Spanish in the Spanish-American War?

United States Possessions, 1899

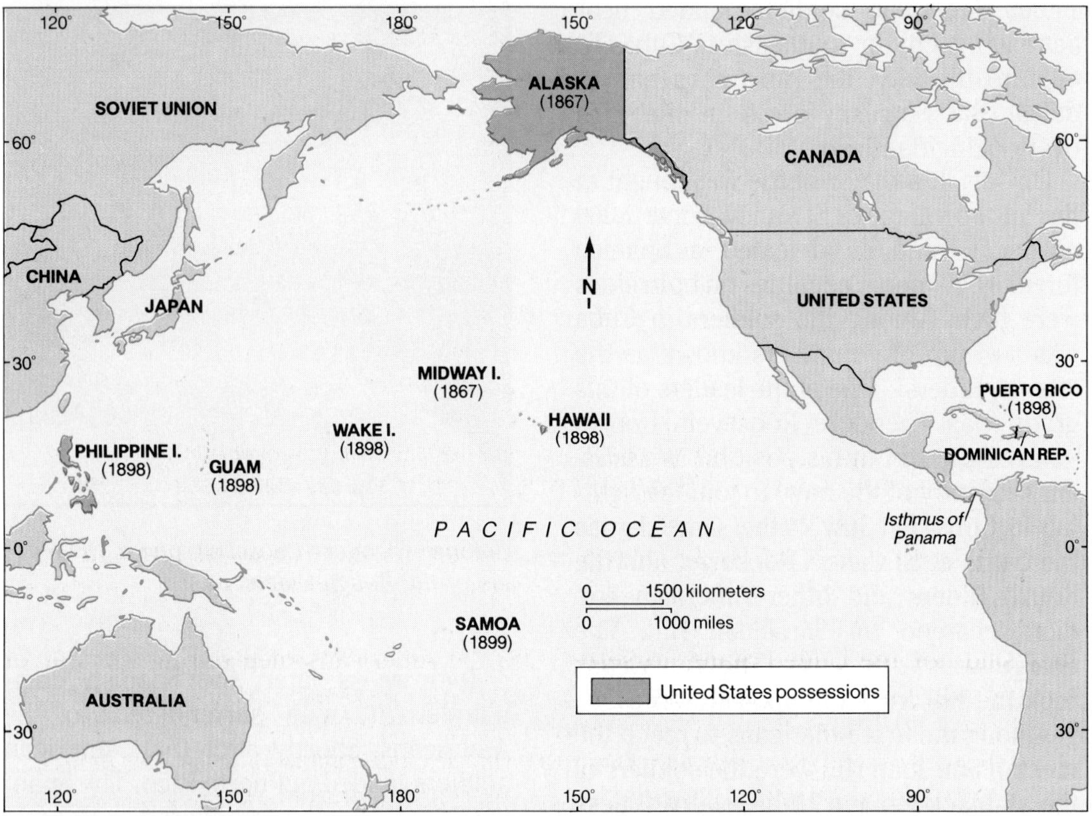

How far was the easternmost American possession from the westernmost American possession?

the taking of the Philippines," McKinley later remarked, "I looked up their location on the globe. I could not have told where those darned islands were within 2,000 miles!"

American business leaders strongly urged the government to keep the Philippines as an American territory. They believed the islands would be very useful in reaching the markets of Asia. Naval bases and fueling stations could be built on the islands.

Some Americans feared that if the United States did not take the Philippines, some other country would. A fleet of German and British ships had come to Manila shortly after Dewey's victory. If the United States pulled out, would the Germans or the British seize the islands?

On December 10, 1898, representatives from Spain and the United States signed a treaty of peace in Paris. Under the terms of the Treaty of Paris, Cuba was to be free of Spanish control. Spain also agreed to give the United States control of the Philippine Islands, Puerto Rico, and Guam. Guam, a tiny island in the Pacific Ocean, had also been captured by the Americans

Background: When American soldiers arrived in Guam, the inhabitants were not even aware that a war was going on between Spain and the United States.

Discuss: If you had been living in 1898, would you have supported independence for the Philippine Islands? Explain your answer.

during the war. The United States agreed to give Spain $20 million.

When news of the Treaty of Paris reached the Philippines, the Filipinos became very angry. They had expected to become independent, like the Cubans. Many Filipinos did not want their country to be controlled by the United States. Fighting soon broke out between the Filipinos and the Americans. Eventually, 70,000 American soldiers were sent to fight in the Philippines. After three years of difficult jungle fighting, the Filipinos surrendered.

The Treaty of Paris set off a great debate in the United States. Expansionists urged Congress to ratify the treaty at once. Opponents of the treaty argued that all of the lands taken from Spain should be made independent. It was not right, they said, for the United States to seize territories against the will of their people. On February 6, 1899, Congress voted to approve the treaty. The vote was very close—just one more vote than was needed.

In 1900, President McKinley ran for reelection. The Republican candidate for Vice President was the popular hero of San Juan Hill, Theodore Roosevelt. The Democrats again chose William Jennings Bryan as their candidate.

Bryan and the Democrats said the main issue in 1900 was expansion. They opposed the American takeover of the Philippines. Bryan said the islands should be made independent. McKinley and the Republicans said the main issue of the election was inflation.

Whatever the main issue was, the Republicans won the election. As in 1896, Bryan was soundly defeated. McKinley believed that his victory meant the American people approved of the results of the Spanish-American War.

The results of the war were impressive. Total American combat deaths in the war were less than 400. However, more than 5,000 Americans died during the war of malaria, typhoid fever, and other diseases. The United States gained control of important territories in the Caribbean, the Pacific, and off the coast of Asia. The "splendid little war" meant that the United States would now have an empire of its own.

Section Review

1. What were the results of the Spanish-American War?
2. What is yellow journalism?
3. Why did the United States declare war on Spain in 1898?
4. Who were two heroes of the Spanish-American War?
5. At the end of the war with Spain, Americans faced a difficult question: What should be done with the territories seized from Spain? If you had been alive in 1898, how would you have answered the question?

Recognizing Propaganda

In 1898, some American journalists tried to arouse public opinion by writing exaggerated and often false accounts of Spanish mistreatment of Cubans. Americans reading these articles were the targets of propaganda. Propaganda is the spreading of information for the purpose of furthering one's own cause or damaging an opposing one. Here are four of the most common propaganda techniques:

1. Bandwagon—tries to convince people that "everybody" uses a certain product or supports a certain cause, so you should, too
2. Name-calling—uses names or labels that call forth negative images and feelings, such as "Communist" or "criminal"
3. Card stacking—uses facts that support one side of an issue
4. Transfer—identifying an idea with a well-known idea or person

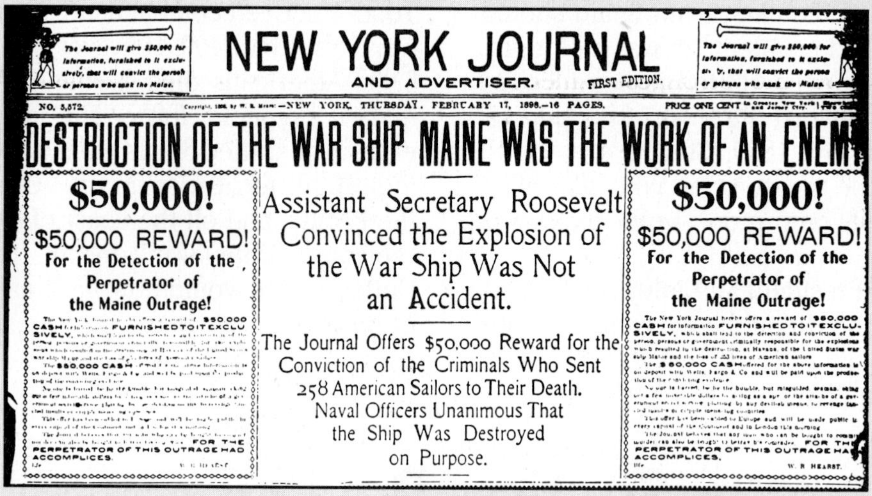
NEW YORK JOURNAL
AND ADVERTISER. FIRST EDITION.
NO. 5,572. —NEW YORK, THURSDAY, FEBRUARY 17, 1898.—16 PAGES. PRICE ONE CENT

DESTRUCTION OF THE WAR SHIP MAINE WAS THE WORK OF AN ENEMY

$50,000!
$50,000 REWARD!
For the Detection of the Perpetrator of the Maine Outrage!

Assistant Secretary Roosevelt Convinced the Explosion of the War Ship Was Not an Accident.

The Journal Offers $50,000 Reward for the Conviction of the Criminals Who Sent 258 American Sailors to Their Death. Naval Officers Unanimous That the Ship Was Destroyed on Purpose.

$50,000!
$50,000 REWARD!
For the Detection of the Perpetrator of the Maine Outrage!

1. Define propaganda.
2. Look at the *New York Journal* of February 17, 1898 above. What types of propaganda do you see? Give examples.
3. The slogan "Remember the Maine!" reminded Americans of another slogan, "Remember the Alamo!" What kind of propaganda technique was being used?
4. Why is it important to be able to recognize propaganda?

Background: Czolgosz confessed a strong urge to kill a "great leader."

3. The Big Stick

BEFORE YOU READ: *What contributions did Theodore Roosevelt make to American foreign policy?*

On September 6, 1901, President McKinley visited the Pan-American Exposition at Buffalo, New York. As McKinley was greeting a crowd of visitors, an anarchist named Leon Czolgosz (CHOLL-gosch) approached him. Czolgosz's hand was wrapped in a handkerchief. In the handkerchief was a pistol. Czolgosz fired two shots at the President. Eight days later, McKinley died of his wounds. Czolgosz was tried and found guilty, and died in the electric chair.

Following McKinley's death, Theodore Roosevelt became President. Roosevelt proved to be the strongest American President since Abraham Lincoln. He made several important contributions to American foreign policy.

Roosevelt was an expansionist. He believed that the United States should expand its power and influence around the world. Roosevelt also believed that the United States should take an active part in helping to solve international problems. In Roosevelt's opinion, the President should be a strong and vigorous leader in the making of foreign policy.

Roosevelt's Personality

Roosevelt's views on foreign policy were partly a result of his own unique personality. He was a person of great energy and ambition. Yet he could also show patience and understanding.

As a young boy, "Teedie" Roosevelt was often sick and very weak. He was called "Teedie" by his family and friends. Later he would be known as "Teddy," though he never liked this nickname. He suffered from asthma, an illness that makes breathing difficult. He also had poor eyesight. After being teased and beaten by some older bullies, Roosevelt decided to build up his strength. He began to lift weights and to learn boxing.

In his twenties, Roosevelt traveled from his native New York to the far western United States. There he worked as a rancher, riding the range and hunting buffalo. In later years, Roosevelt continued to enjoy hunting. He hunted both in the United States and in Africa. Once while on a hunting trip, after he had become President, Roosevelt refused to shoot a young bear cub. When this story was reported in the newspapers, it inspired a toy manufacturer to make some stuffed animals called "Teddy Bears." These were the first teddy bears ever made.

Theodore Roosevelt was an animated speaker who enjoyed talking to the American public.

Vocabulary Help: foreign policy—the way(s) in which one country deals with other countries. What did Theodore Roosevelt think the President's role in making foreign policy should be?

Background: The Spanish-American War pointed out the military need for a direct water passage through the Americas. The U.S.S. *Oregon* took ten weeks at top speed to go from the Puget Sound on the Pacific to Cuba.

Construction of the Panama Canal took ten years and cost the United States $400 million. In the canal's first year of operation, 1,000 ships went through its locks.

The Panama Canal

When Roosevelt became President in 1901, following the death of McKinley, he was irritated by those who referred to him as "His Accidency." He felt the need to show his critics he was worthy of the presidency. The building of the Panama Canal presented Roosevelt with a perfect chance for proving himself a strong leader.

Ever since the days of Columbus, people had dreamed of the advantages to be gained from a direct water passage through the Americas. During the war with Spain, Americans had fought in both the Caribbean and the Pacific. It had become clear that the construction of a canal through Central America would be very useful. A Central American canal would reduce the travel distance from one coast of the United States to the other by more than 11,265 kilometers (7,000 miles)! A canal would also make trade much easier between the eastern United States and Asia.

In 1902, Congress authorized Roosevelt to negotiate with Colombia for the right to build a canal through its northern territory of Panama. At first Colombia seemed willing to allow the United States to build the canal. Representatives of the Colombian government agreed to accept a cash payment of $10 million and an annual lease of $250,000. Later, however, the Colombian government asked the United States for more money.

Roosevelt was furious. He called the Colombians "bandits" and "cutthroats" and ordered the warship *Nashville* to the waters off Panama. The day after the ship arrived, Panama declared its independence from Colombia. The American naval force blocked Colombian troops from landing in Panama.

The revolt of the Panamanians was a success. Within two weeks of the revolt, the new nation of Panama granted the United States a canal zone in exchange for the money earlier promised to Colombia. The canal zone was a strip of land across Panama, from the Atlantic to the Pacific. The zone was 16 kilometers (10 miles) wide.

Construction of the canal proceeded slowly and with great difficulty over the next ten years. Hundreds of lives were

Background: A later President, Woodrow Wilson, expressed "sincere regret" to Colombia for the Panamanian affair. The United States in 1921 agreed to pay Colombia $25 million for its loss of Panama.

lost due to yellow fever and other tropical diseases. Heroic efforts were made to control the diseases. The research of Dr. Walter Reed proved that yellow fever was spread by mosquitoes. Dr. William Gorgas led the fight against insect pests in Panama. Finally, on August 15, 1914, the great canal was opened.

In acquiring the Panama Canal for the United States, Roosevelt proved himself a strong leader. Roosevelt's action, however, made the Colombians feel very bitter toward the United States. They believed that the United States had treated their country unfairly by helping the revolt in Panama to succeed.

Some observers later commented that Roosevelt had used a "big stick" to acquire the Canal Zone. They meant that he had been willing to use military force to win Panama its independence and to gain control of the Canal Zone. The term "big stick" came from one of President Roosevelt's favorite mottoes: "Speak softly, and carry a big stick." Roosevelt felt that it was necessary to back up words with military preparedness.

The Roosevelt Corollary

In the early 1900's, several countries of Central and South America were unable to pay debts owed to merchants and bankers in Europe. The Europeans had sold goods on credit to the Latin Americans and loaned them money. The Europeans threatened to **intervene**, or interfere, in Latin America to collect the money owed to their citizens.

---

intervene to interfere by military force in the internal affairs of another nation

---

President Roosevelt was alarmed by these threats. The United States had opposed European interference in the Americas ever since the Monroe Doctrine of 1823.

The President concluded that the United States should act as an "international police officer" in Latin America. If a Latin American nation owed money to another nation, the United States would see to it that the Latin American nation paid its debts. In 1904, he announced that any "wrongdoing" by a nation in the Western Hemisphere might cause the United States "to intervene in the offending nation's internal affairs."

This announcement became known as the Roosevelt Corollary to the Monroe Doctrine. A corollary is a principle that is based on some already proven statement. The original Monroe Doctrine was intended to prevent Europeans from intervening in the Western Hemisphere. The Roosevelt Corollary stated that the United States reserved the right of intervention for itself.

The first test of the Roosevelt Corollary came in the Dominican Republic. The Dominican Republic owed a great deal of money to several European nations. When it was unable to pay its debts, European business leaders urged their governments to intervene. President Roosevelt persuaded the Dominican government in 1905 to allow American agents to take over the collection of taxes on imported goods. By allowing the Americans to collect taxes, the Dominican Republic was saved from European intervention.

The attitude of the United States toward Latin America was like that of a

Discuss: Why do you think that most Latin Americans have consistently resented the "big brother" attitude adopted by the United States in the Western Hemisphere?

In this cartoon, Uncle Sam is shown as a large rooster "cooping up" the European powers to protect the small roosters that represent Latin American countries. How did the Roosevelt Corollary to the Monroe Doctrine "coop up" the European powers?

strict older brother. The United States would protect the Latin Americans against outsiders. But the United States also insisted that the Latin Americans "behave."

Asian Affairs

In 1904, war broke out between Russia and Japan over Manchuria, a region in northeastern China. Both Russia and Japan sought to establish a sphere of influence in Manchuria. President Roosevelt was concerned that if either Russia or Japan succeeded, other nations would be prevented from trading in the area. Roosevelt called an international conference in 1905 to end the Russo-Japanese War. The two warring nations sent representatives to Roosevelt's conference, and the President succeeded in negotiating a treaty of peace. The following year, in 1906, Roosevelt was awarded the Nobel Peace Prize for his efforts. The Nobel Peace Prize is awarded each year to the person who has made the most important contribution to world peace.

One of the unexpected results of the settlement of the Russo-Japanese War was an increase in Japanese immigration

For Extra Interest: Have students investigate other attempts at world peace during this period, such as the first and second Hague conferences, the Drago Doctrine, and the Carnegie Endowment for International Peace.

Background: Roosevelt did not want the United States to pass laws restricting Japanese immigration. His policy was to cultivate friendly relations with Japan. Friendship, Roosevelt thought, would deter the Japanese from seizing the Philippine Islands.

to the United States. Some Americans on the West Coast, in California especially, held the mistaken view that the Japanese immigrants were an inferior group of people. Several California laws were passed that provided for unfair treatment of, or **discriminated** against, the Japanese people.

---

discriminate to treat a person or a group of people differently from the way all others are treated

---

The San Francisco School Board in 1906 ordered all Japanese students in the city to attend a separate or segregated "Oriental School." This order was an insult to the Japanese. The Japanese government strongly protested to President Roosevelt that the order be dropped.

Roosevelt persuaded the Californians to repeal the segregation order. In return, he promised the Californians that the government would limit further Japanese immigration. In the Gentlemen's Agreement of 1907, Japan agreed to restrict the number of its citizens emigrating to the United States.

Roosevelt's Contributions

Roosevelt's years in the White House were a major turning point in the history of American foreign policy. His forceful actions marked the beginning of a stronger presidential role in making foreign policy.

Possession of the Panama Canal meant that the United States now had a vital interest to defend in Latin America. The Roosevelt Corollary was a clear statement of American intentions. The United States was willing to defend its Latin American neighbors against outside interference, but the United States would not permit "wrongdoing" by the Latin Americans themselves. This "big brother" attitude created a bitterness in Latin America.

Roosevelt asserted that American interests were worldwide. His efforts to settle the Russo-Japanese War were a major break with past American policy. Roosevelt had demonstrated that the United States should no longer remain isolated from the rest of the world. A new era of American responsibilities had begun.

Section Review

1. What contributions did Theodore Roosevelt make to American foreign policy?
2. How would a canal through Central America be useful to the United States?
3. Define intervene. How did the United States prevent European governments from intervening in the Dominican Republic?
4. Roosevelt's personality was shaped, in part, by his early experiences as a child. What connection do you see between Roosevelt's personality and his foreign policy as President?

Discuss: What responsibilities do you think a country characterized as a "world leader" has that other, less powerful countries do not have?

CHAPTER REVIEW

Summary

In the late 1800's, many Americans wanted the United States to expand its influence overseas. These people, called expansionists, included farmers and industrialists who wanted to find new markets for their goods. Other Americans believed that the United States should stay out of the affairs of other nations. As industry boomed and the last American frontier was settled, government policy became expansionist. Between 1867 and 1898, Alaska, the Midway Islands, and the Hawaiian Islands became territories of the United States.

In 1898, the United States fought a short war with Spain. As a result of this war, the United States acquired the Philippine Islands, Puerto Rico, and Guam.

The United States entered the twentieth century with a new President, Theodore Roosevelt. Roosevelt was an aggressive expansionist. He acquired the Panama Canal Zone and let the world know the United States controlled the Western Hemisphere through the Roosevelt Corollary. He brought the United States into the twentieth century as a major world power.

Recalling the Facts

1. What groups of Americans supported overseas expansion? Why did they support it?
2. Why did the United States want to acquire overseas naval bases?
3. Why did the American people pressure the government to declare war on Spain in 1898?
4. How did the United States acquire the Panama Canal Zone?
5. What areas of the world were possessions of the United States at the turn of the century?

Analyzing the Facts

1. Theodore Roosevelt referred to the Spanish-American War as "a splendid little war." Why do you think many Americans in 1898 would have agreed with him?
2. Alaska and Hawaii have become states, and the Midway Islands and Guam remain territories of the United States. How is the importance of these four areas to the United States today similar to their importance at the turn of the century?

3. Theodore Roosevelt's foreign policy was said to be "Speak softly, and carry a big stick." What is meant by this? Do you think this would be a good policy for the United States to have today? Why or why not?
4. How was Roosevelt different from American Presidents of the late 1800's?
5. Since work began in 1904, the United States has been responsible for the construction, operation, maintenance, and defense of the Panama Canal. In 1977, the governments of Panama and the United States signed a treaty that will transfer full control of the canal to Panama on December 31, 1999. Do you think the United States should give up control of the canal? Explain your answer.

Time and History

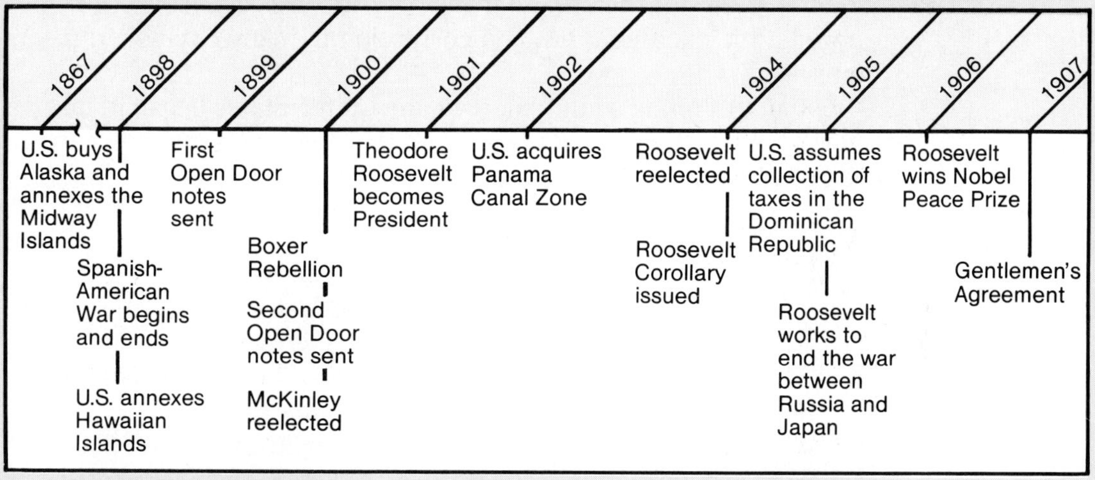

1. What land areas had the United States acquired in the years before the Spanish-American War?
2. Who was President of the United States when the Panama Canal Zone was acquired?
3. Which of the following events did not occur while McKinley was President: the Spanish-American War, the Gentlemen's Agreement, or the Boxer Rebellion?
4. How many years after the Roosevelt Corollary was issued did the United States become involved in the affairs of a Latin American nation?
5. What had President Roosevelt done to earn the Nobel Peace Prize in 1906?

UNIT REVIEW

Summary

From 1865 to the beginning of the twentieth century, changes occurred in all phases of American life. The last frontier, the Great Plains, was settled. This brought an end to the unique life styles of the American Indians and the open range cattle ranchers.

New inventions also changed the country. Two of the most important were the long-lasting light bulb and the telephone. Many other labor-saving devices made life much easier. This technology also changed American industry as the country entered the age of mass production. Simple businesses grew into huge corporations and trusts.

The demand for workers in the new industries brought thousands of people to the United States. Immigrants poured through the "golden door" in hopes of sharing the many opportunities available. The cities in which they settled grew, and corruption in many city governments flourished.

As the turn of the century neared, the United States began to take an interest in lands outside its borders. It was not long before new territories were added to the United States.

Recalling the Facts

1. What caused the disappearance of the last frontier?
2. What factors helped American industry grow?
3. Why did so many immigrants come to the United States in the late 1800's? Where did these immigrants come from?
4. What caused the growth of labor unions in the United States?
5. What groups of Americans were interested in overseas expansion?

Analyzing the Facts

1. Explain how the growth of big business affected small businesses.
2. What similarities are there in the reasons why immigrants in the late 1800's came to the United States and the reasons why the original colonists came?
3. Why are new political parties, like the Populist and Socialist parties of the late 1800's, formed when two major political parties already exist?
4. Explain how the Spanish-American War was a turning point in United States foreign policy.

Reviewing Vocabulary

Define the following terms.

assimilate	laissez-faire	injunction
homesteader	entrepreneur	inflation
speculator	ethnic	sphere of influence
stock	collective bargaining	yellow journalism

Sharpening Your Skills

Answer the first three questions below from the information given in the circle graphs, The Growth of Cities: 1860–1900, on page 445.

1. By what percentage did the population of American cities increase from 1860 to 1900?
2. In what year did the greater percentage of people live in rural areas?
3. What do these graphs tell you about the percentage of people that lived in rural areas in 1860 and 1900?
4. American newspapers in 1896 frequently referred to General Weyler, the Spanish governor of Cuba, as "Butcher" Weyler or "Mad Dog" Weyler. What propaganda technique was being used, and what were the newspapers trying to make their readers believe?
5. Why were the newspaper stories on the death of Antonio Maceo in 1896 propaganda?

Writing and Research

1. Become a pen pal with an American Indian who lives on a reservation. Contacts for establishing pen pals can be obtained by writing to the Bureau of Indian Affairs, Office of Public Information, Room 4627, 18th and "C" Streets N.W., Washington, D.C. 20240, and asking for the addresses of some schools to contact.
2. In the late 1800's, many groups of people had problems that bothered them about this country. Some of these problems resulted from the growth of industry, the growth of the cities, the formation of labor unions, or the expansionist policies of the government. Write a letter to the editor of a newspaper. Pretend you are from one of these groups. Tell the editor about yourself, what the problem is, and what you think should be done to solve it.

Unit

7 Reform, War, Reaction

23 *In the early 1900's, men and women, who called themselves "progressives," worked hard to solve many of the nation's problems. They cleaned up corruption in government and improved the quality of life in America's cities. They increased the power of government over big business. The Presidents during the progressive era were men of vision and high ideals.*

24 *A great war began in Europe in 1914. At first, the United States hoped to stay out of the conflict. In 1917, however, America entered the war. American armed forces helped bring the war to an end. But the peace that followed the war was not lasting.*

25 *By the end of World War I, many Americans had grown tired of the ideals and reforms of the progressives. They were exhausted by the sacrifices of war. America turned in upon itself. For some, the 1920's were years of prosperity and "roaring" good times. Yet this prosperity was built on a shaky foundation.*

Chapter
23

Reform in America

American history has often been viewed as a story of progress. From the earliest colonial times, it had seemed that things in the United States were getting better and better. Around 1900, however, many Americans began to wonder whether the story of progress had come to an end. Was life in America's cities really better than it was 50 years earlier? Were American city and state governments better than they once were? Some Americans reluctantly answered these questions by saying, "No." Others, just as reluctantly, said, "Yes, but not much."

Americans who were concerned about progress organized in the early 1900's. They called themselves "progressives," and they worked to reform American life in many ways.

After you read this chapter, you will be able to:

1. Identify the muckrakers and explain how they contributed to the progressive movement.
2. List the goals of Theodore Roosevelt as President.
3. Discuss the problems that the progressives chose to ignore.
4. Trace the changes in American culture at the turn of the century.

- Use historical photographs to gain information.

Background: Roosevelt likened muckrakers to the character in *Pilgrim's Progress* "who was offered a celestial crown for his muck-rake, but who would neither look up nor regard the crown he was offered, but continued to rake to himself the filth of the floor."

1. The Progressive Movement

BEFORE YOU READ: *What contributions did the muckrakers make to the progressive movement?*

The progressives of the early 1900's had many goals. They wanted to clean up corruption in government, improve conditions in the cities, and control the power of big business.

These reformers were very successful. They were elected to political offices. They helped to elect three Presidents of the United States.

The Roots of Reform

The progressive movement's roots lay in many earlier reform movements. Many progressives had worked to rid the cities of their corrupt bosses and machines. Others had been concerned with the poor living conditions of the cities. Some had been active in the movement to regulate big business.

In the early 1900's, a group of journalists began to write articles that exposed the corruption and poverty in American life. These journalists were given the name **"muckrakers"** by Theodore Roosevelt. He compared their efforts to uncover corruption with those of a person who is raking up filth, or muck.

---

muckraker a journalist who uncovered corruption and poverty in America in the early 1900's

---

By exposing problems, the muckrakers made millions of people aware of the need for reform. Two of the most famous muckrakers were Ida Tarbell and Lincoln Steffens. Ida Tarbell spent four years investigating John D. Rockefeller and the Standard Oil Company. In 1902, *McClure's* magazine began publishing Tarbell's articles. Rockefeller's spectacular success, she reported, had been achieved through the use of rebates, cutthroat competition, and other unfair practices.

Lincoln Steffens traveled to several American cities, investigating corruption in local governments. He found that many local businesses were paying bribes or kickbacks to corrupt city bosses. Steffens' findings appeared in a series of articles in *McClure's*. The articles had titles such as "The Shame of Minneapolis" and "Philadelphia: Corrupt and Contented."

The muckrakers published novels as well as articles. One of the most famous books was *The Jungle* by Upton Sinclair. It described in vivid detail the terrible conditions in the Chicago stockyards and meat-packing industry. Frank Norris published a novel about how the Southern Pacific Railroad was "strangling" the California wheat farmers. Norris called his book *The Octopus*.

The writings of the muckrakers had a great impact on many Americans. People began to demand reform. Readers of *The Jungle*, for example, urged the government to improve conditions in the meatpacking industry.

City Reform

The progressive movement scored its first victories on the local level. Reformers were elected to office in New York,

For Extra Interest: Read to the class selected portions of muckraker books such as *The Jungle* by Upton Sinclair or *How the Other Half Lives* by Jacob Riis.

Chicago, Los Angeles, and many other cities.

In Toledo, Ohio, a reformer named Samuel M. "Golden Rule" Jones was elected mayor in 1897. He ordered an eight-hour workday and set a **minimum wage** for city workers. He built new playgrounds and parks. Jones urged the people of Toledo to take pride in their city.

minimum wage a wage set by law as the least amount employees can be paid for their work

The reformers also improved the organization of city government. In Galveston, Texas, a city commission was formed to govern the city. Members of the commission were elected as independents rather than as candidates of political parties. The new commission also combined the functions of mayor and city council. By eliminating party politics and by combining functions, the commission was more efficient than the old system of city government. By 1914, over 400 cities across the nation were run by commissions.

Jane Addams taking part in one of Hull House's programs for children. Addams headed Hull House until her death in 1935.

Another new form of city government began in Staunton, Virginia. The Staunton city council in 1908 hired a city manager to run the city. The city manager was an expert in solving urban problems. More than 300 cities adopted the city manager form of government by 1923.

One of the most dedicated of the city reformers was Jane Addams. Addams was concerned with helping the poor people of America's cities. In 1889, Jane Addams bought an old Chicago mansion called Hull House. The mansion was in a very poor part of the city. Most of the people who lived in that part of the city were immigrants. Hull House provided services for the immigrants and other poor residents of the city. It was one of the nation's first **settlement houses**. Hull House opened a free clinic for people who could not afford a doctor. It offered classes in everything from literature to cooking. It provided recreation programs for poor children. Soon, settlement houses were being set up in cities throughout the nation.

settlement house a place that provides services for poor residents of a city

State Reform

Another target of the reformers was state governments. Bosses and large corporations practically ran the government

Discuss: What did La Follette mean when he said that "the cure for the ills of democracy is more democracy"?

in many states. In the early 1900's, reform candidates were elected to office in states from New Jersey to California and from Minnesota to Mississippi.

One of the first and most successful state reform movements was in Wisconsin. In 1900, a young Republican reformer named Robert M. La Follette was elected governor. La Follette believed that the "cure for the ills of democracy is more democracy." La Follette wanted to increase the direct participation of the people in state government.

Ever since Andrew Jackson's times, political conventions had nominated candidates for office. The conventions were easily controlled by political bosses and machines. In 1903, Wisconsin adopted a new method for nominating candidates. Candidates were to be chosen in a special public nominating election held before the general election. This nominating election was called a **direct primary**. The direct primary was a more democratic method of choosing candidates than the old convention system. All citizens could vote in this election and thus play a part in the selection of their party's candidate. By 1916, all but three states had adopted the direct primary.

---

direct primary an election to nominate candidates to run in the general election

---

Other methods of increasing the participation of people in state government were instituted. One of these allowed the people of a state to "initiate," or create, their own laws. The people could propose a law and gather signatures in support of it. They could then present the proposal to the voters or to the legislature for approval. If a majority approved the proposal, it became law. This process is called the **initiative**.

---

initiative a process by which people can propose a law and submit it for approval by the voters or the legislature

---

Another method allowed the people to approve or reject a law already passed by the state legislature. If enough signatures were gathered, a law could be "referred" to the people for their approval. If a majority of the voters rejected the law, it was repealed. This process is known as the **referendum**.

---

referendum a process by which people can approve or reject a law

---

Oregon led the way with many government reforms. Oregon was the first state to approve the referendum and the initiative. In 1908, Oregon voters approved the **recall**. The recall allowed the people to challenge any elected official at any time. If enough signatures were gathered, a special election would be held to determine if the official should remain in office.

---

recall a petition signed by voters calling for a special election in which the voters would decide if an official should remain in office

---

The progressives also created many other reforms at the state level. States set up railroad and public utility commissions to regulate these businesses. Laws to forbid employment of young children were passed. States adopted the secret

Background: Most states nominate through a closed primary in which the voter must be registered with a party to participate. In open primary states, the voter may participate in the primary of any party without divulging his or her party affiliation.

Background: Prior to the adoption of the secret ballot, each party or candidate prepared a separate ballot. The ballots were different so they could be easily recognized. The secret ballot was first used in Massachusetts in 1888.

Women's Suffrage Before 1920

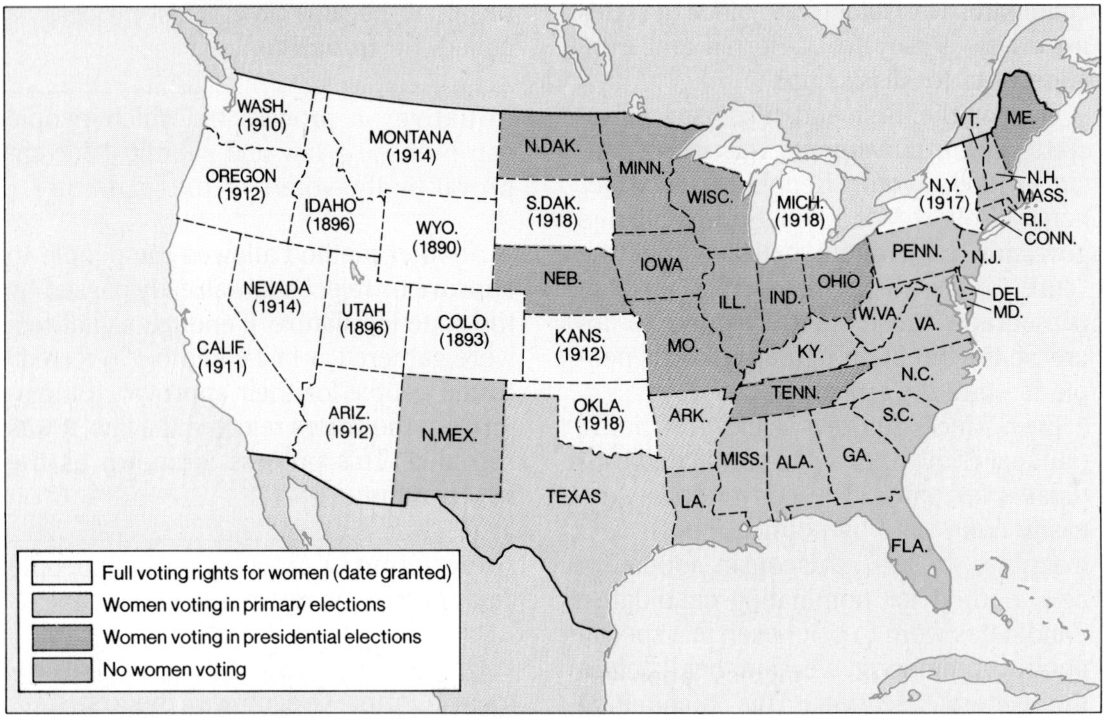

In which area of the country did women gain full voting rights first? Why do you think this was so?

ballot to allow people more freedom to vote as they wished. States also supported an amendment to change the method of electing United States senators. Under the Constitution, senators were chosen by the state legislatures. By 1913, three fourths of the states had approved the 17th Amendment. This amendment provided that senators be elected directly by the people of each state.

Women's Rights

American women played an important role in the progressive movement. One of their major concerns was to win the right to vote, or **suffrage**. Supporters of women's suffrage were known as "suffragists."

suffrage the right to vote

In the late 1800's, women were denied the right to vote in all but a few states. Many people mistakenly believed that women were inferior to men. **Sexism** also made it difficult for many women to enter high-paying professions, such as law and medicine.

sexism the belief that members of one sex are inferior to members of the other

Vocabulary Help: suffragist—anyone who supports women's suffrage. The term suffragette refers to a woman who militantly advocates the right of women to vote.

Background: Wyoming is nicknamed the Equality State because Wyoming women were the first in the nation to vote, hold public office, and serve on juries. They gained these rights in 1869 when Wyoming was organized as a territory.

Women stepped up their efforts in the late 1800's to win the right to vote. In 1890, the National American Woman's Suffrage Association (NAWSA) was organized. NAWSA concentrated on winning the vote on a state-by-state basis. By 1911, Wyoming, Utah, Colorado, Idaho, Washington, and California had granted women the right to vote.

More radical action was taken when Alice Paul organized the Congressional Union for Woman Suffrage in 1914. This group demanded that Congress approve a constitutional amendment granting women suffrage. After some reluctance, NAWSA joined the Congressional Union in support of this demand.

Women marched in dozens of cities, demanding the right to vote. The suffragists were often ridiculed and sometimes arrested. In 1918, Congress approved the 19th Amendment. This amendment stated that citizens shall not be denied the right to vote "on account of sex." Two years later, the amendment was ratified by three fourths of the states. American women had at last won the right to vote.

During the early 1900's, American women also organized to win greater rights as workers. By 1910, nearly 8 million women were in the American labor force. Their wages were low. Their working conditions were often poor—and sometimes unsafe.

In 1911, a fire swept through the Triangle Shirtwaist Factory in New York. The workers at the factory, most of whom were women, rushed to the emergency exits. The exits were locked. Rushing to the windows, they found there were no fire escapes. Many of the workers jumped to their deaths from the windows of the factory. Others were killed by the fire and smoke. In all, 146 people died.

Following this horrible fire, both women and men demanded new laws to protect workers from unsafe conditions. New unions of women workers were formed. New York and other states adopted laws requiring safer workplaces. States also adopted laws that limited the number of hours women could be required to work. Some states set minimum wages for women.

Reformers had scored important victories in cities, states, and factories. The progressives soon took their campaign for reform to the national level. The Presidents of the early 1900's accomplished many of the goals of the progressive movement.

Section Review

1. Who were the muckrakers? How did they make an important contribution to the progressive movement?
2. Define direct primary, initiative, referendum, and recall.
3. Define suffrage. When did American women gain suffrage?
4. What issues today could be subjects for muckraking articles? Name some people who could be called modern-day muckrakers.

Background: Of the 8 million female workers in 1910, only 125,000 were union members. Membership was low because many unions refused to accept women as members.

Using Historical Photographs

At the turn of the century, life was very hard for workers in American factories. Massachusetts textile workers, for example, worked 58 hours per week for very low wages. The newer textile mills in the South paid even lower wages than were paid in the North. The working environment, however, was a little better. In the mills of New England, there was little light or air. Southern mills were large one-story buildings with many windows. Children worked as many as 13 hours a day, often running dangerous machinery.

Sometimes photographs can tell stories even more clearly than words. Being primary source materials, they allow the viewer to make a first-hand interpretation of a scene. Details, which may be missing or overlooked in a written account, are useful in understanding what actually happened or how people felt. In candid photographs facial expressions, gestures, and postures can provide valuable clues about people's feelings. Study the picture below, paying particular attention to details.

1. About how old is the girl in the photograph?
2. In what part of the country do you think she lived? Why?
3. Do you think that this girl came from a poor family? What clues do you see in the photograph to support your answer?
4. What does this photograph add to the written description above on working conditions in textile mills at the turn of the century?

Background: Theodore Roosevelt based his right to interfere in the coal strike in 1902 on the general welfare concept in the Constitution. Roosevelt felt that the public was the third party in the strike.

2. The Progressive Presidents

BEFORE YOU READ: *What were the goals of Theodore Roosevelt as President?*

Three very different Presidents served in the White House between 1901 and 1921: Theodore Roosevelt, William Howard Taft, and Woodrow Wilson. All of these men differed in personal style and effectiveness. Roosevelt and Taft were Republicans. Wilson was a Democrat. Each, however, was a progressive. And they all shared a common commitment to reform.

Roosevelt and the Square Deal

Shortly after Theodore Roosevelt became President in 1901, he delivered his first message to Congress. In his message, Roosevelt set out his goals as President. First, he said, he intended to take action to solve the "serious social problems" facing the nation. Second, he wanted Congress to pass new laws regulating big business. Third, he would work for greater power for the federal government over the railroads. Fourth, he wanted to take action to conserve the nation's natural resources.

Roosevelt's first major action as President was to end a national strike of coal miners. In June 1902, the United Mine Workers union went on strike against the mine owners. The workers demanded higher wages and an eight-hour workday. The mine owners attempted to break the strike by using strikebreakers. One of the strike leaders was Mary Harris Jones. "Mother Jones" and a group of miners' wives, armed with brooms and mops, drove the strikebreakers out of the coalfields.

As the strike dragged on for months, the nation's supply of coal got smaller and smaller. In October, Roosevelt appointed a special commission to settle the strike. In March 1903, the commission announced that it was granting the workers a 10 percent wage increase and a nine-hour work day. To be fair to the mine owners, the commission granted the owners a 10 percent increase in the price of coal.

The settlement, Roosevelt said, was a "square deal" for both sides. The term "square deal"—meaning fair play for all—came to be the slogan of the Roosevelt administration. In solving the coal strike, Roosevelt had taken action to solve one of the nation's problems.

To oversee the activities of business, Congress created a Department of Commerce and Labor in 1903. Within this new department, a Bureau of Corporations was set up to investigate business combinations and practices.

To regulate the railroads, Roosevelt asked Congress to strengthen the Interstate Commerce Commission (ICC). In 1903, Congress passed the Elkins Railroad Act, which made the giving or receiving of rebates illegal.

Roosevelt used the old Sherman Antitrust Act to break up the western railroads. He also took action against other business combinations. Roosevelt soon gained the reputation of being a "trust-buster." Roosevelt, however, did not believe that all business combinations

Background: J. P. Morgan, J. J. Hill, and E. H. Harriman consolidated three large northwestern railroads through a holding company called the Northern Securities Company. In 1904, the Supreme Court ordered this company dissolved on the grounds that it was a restraint of trade.

For Extra Interest: Have students look for government inspection marks on meat and on the packaging for butter, bacon, and eggs.

should be broken up. Most of them should be regulated, he thought, not divided into smaller units.

In 1904, Roosevelt was elected to serve a second term. He took further action to achieve his reform goals. In June 1906, Congress passed the Hepburn Act. This act gave the ICC the power to set maximum shipping rates that could be charged by the railroads.

Among the many social problems identified by the muckrakers were the poor conditions in the nation's food industry. Roosevelt read and was shocked by Upton Sinclair's book on the Chicago meat-packing plants. In 1906, Congress passed the Meat Inspection Act, which set higher standards for the handling of meat. In the same year, Congress passed the Pure Food and Drug Act, which banned the use of harmful drugs or chemicals in food and medicine.

Roosevelt also made progress in achieving his fourth goal, to conserve the nation's natural resources. He set aside 61 million hectares (150 million acres) of forest lands as national forests. Grazing, mining, and lumbering were forbidden or strictly controlled in national forests. In 1908, Roosevelt called a national conference on conservation. More than 40 states created their own conservation commissions.

Taft and the Republican Breakup

At the end of Roosevelt's second term, he suggested that the Republicans choose William Howard Taft as his successor. Taft easily won the Republican nomination. The Democrats nominated William Jennings Bryan once again. In the election of 1908, Taft defeated Bryan by well over one million votes.

Taft was born in Ohio in 1857. He had served as a federal judge and as Roosevelt's secretary of war. He was a very large man, weighing over 135 kilograms (300 pounds). Taft did not have the kind of energy Roosevelt had. He enjoyed long, leisurely meals and an afternoon nap.

Taft won passage of several new reform laws. In 1910, he signed the Mann-Elkins Act, which extended the power of the ICC to regulate telephone and telegraph rates. The act also set up a Commerce Court to speed the settlement of railroad-rate cases. Taft supported a law establishing the eight-hour workday for persons doing work under federal contracts. A new mine safety law was also backed by Taft.

In 1910, Taft got into trouble with Roosevelt's supporters. Taft's secretary of the interior was Richard Ballinger. Ballinger removed from federal protection some lands that Roosevelt had ordered protected. Ballinger opened the lands for development by private businesses. Chief Forester Gifford Pinchot, a dedicated friend of conservation and of Theodore Roosevelt, criticized Ballinger. Taft settled the dispute by firing Gifford Pinchot. Progressives, who supported Roosevelt's goal of protecting natural resources, were upset by the firing of Pinchot.

Roosevelt was in Africa, on a big game hunt, during the Ballinger-Pinchot dispute. In March 1910, he left Africa and was met in Italy by his friend Gifford Pinchot. Pinchot told him of Taft's actions. Roosevelt was disappointed and angry.

Roosevelt and Taft slowly drifted apart. Among other things, the two men differed

Discuss: When Roosevelt returned from his big-game hunt in Africa, he boasted over 3,000 animal trophies. Do you see any inconsistency between this and Roosevelt's desire to conserve the nation's natural resources? Is wildlife a natural resource? Explain your answer.

Background: Republicans who felt that Taft was not doing enough in the way of reform formed the National Republican Progressive League as a part of the Republican party. They supported Robert La Follette for the Republican nomination in 1912—though many hoped Roosevelt would run.

in their approach to big business. Taft was truly a trustbuster. He believed that many large business combinations should be broken up. He sponsored twice as many antitrust suits as Roosevelt ever did. Roosevelt remained convinced that government regulation of big business—*not* antitrust action—was the best idea.

In 1912, Roosevelt announced that he would challenge Taft for the Republican nomination for President. The Taft forces controlled the 1912 Republican convention, and Taft won the nomination.

Roosevelt refused to accept defeat. He and his Republican followers formed a new party, the Progressive party. The Progressives nominated Roosevelt as their candidate. In accepting the nomination, Roosevelt declared that he felt "as strong as a bull moose." The Progressive party itself soon came to be called the "Bull Moose" party. The Progressive platform supported the regulation of corporations, a minimum wage for all workers, and many other reforms.

Meanwhile, the Democrats chose Woodrow Wilson as their candidate. Wilson and the Democratic platform also supported many reforms. On the issue of big business, Wilson said the government should break up the great trusts and monopolies.

With the Republicans divided between Taft and Roosevelt, Wilson won an easy victory in the election of 1912. The Socialist party candidate, Eugene Debs, received almost 900,000 votes and won no electoral votes. The American people—whether they voted for Taft, Roosevelt, Wilson, or Debs—made one thing plain in 1912. They wanted more reforms from the federal government.

The Election of 1912

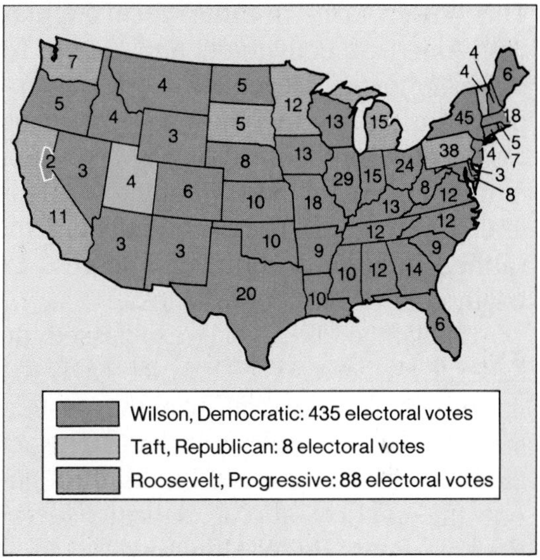

Which states voted for Taft in the election of 1912?

Wilson and the New Freedom

When he became President, Wilson was well prepared for the office. He had been a professor of political science, the president of Princeton University, and governor of New Jersey.

Woodrow Wilson proved to be a strong leader. In April 1913, he called Congress into special session and spoke before its members in person. No President since John Adams had addressed Congress in person. Wilson worked actively with Congress to get laws passed.

In October 1913, Wilson signed the Underwood Tariff. This was the first important reduction of taxes on foreign goods since before the Civil War. The tariff was lowered on more than 100 items,

Background: Wilson practiced law for four years but found it very tedious. He returned to school and received a Ph.D. in 1886. In 1902, he became the president of Princeton University but resigned in 1910 to become the Democratic candidate for governor of New Jersey.

Discuss: Why would American consumers favor lower tariffs? Who benefits from high tariffs? How are lower tariffs consistent with progressive goals?

including food, textiles, iron, and steel. This lower tariff became very popular with American consumers and voters. To make up for lost revenues, Congress approved a federal income tax. Americans would now be required to pay a portion of their annual income directly to the federal government. The 16th Amendment, ratified in 1913, authorized Congress to begin collecting income taxes.

At the end of 1913, Congress passed the Federal Reserve Act. This act gave the nation its first central banking system since the time of Andrew Jackson. The act created Federal Reserve Banks throughout the country and a central Federal Reserve Board in Washington, D.C. The federal banks regulated the activities of private banks. The new system allowed the federal government to control more easily the amount of money in circulation. The federal reserve system provided greater stability and order for the nation's economy.

In 1914, Congress passed two other important laws. One created the Federal Trade Commission (FTC). The FTC was given the power to stop businesses from engaging in unfair methods of competition. Although the FTC was not as strong as some people had hoped, it was able to regulate business. The second important law of 1914 was the Clayton Antitrust Act. This act outlawed business combinations that destroyed competition or controlled an industry. The Clayton Act also gave unions more freedom to organize. It forbade the use of court injunctions to stop strikes, except when necessary to protect property.

As President, Wilson supported other important reforms. In 1915, Congress passed the La Follette Seamen's Act. This act required better working conditions for sailors aboard the nation's ships. The Adamson Act of 1916 established an eight-hour work day for all workers on interstate railroads. The La Follette Act and the Adamson Act were major victories for American workers.

Section Review

1. What four goals did Theodore Roosevelt set out for his presidency in 1901?
2. How did the Elkins Railroad Act, the Hepburn Act, and the Mann-Elkins Act strengthen the Interstate Commerce Commission?
3. What reforms did the Progressive party support in 1912?
4. What two important laws were passed by Congress in 1914? Why were they important?
5. Theodore Roosevelt took forceful action to achieve his goals as President. What are some of the goals of our current President? Do you think the President has achieved any of these goals? Explain your answer.

For Extra Interest: Have students look at dollar bills to find the federal reserve branch that put them in circulation. The branch name and number are located on the front of the bill in a circle.

Background: After the Chinese Exclusion Act, American employers began to use Japanese workers as a source of cheap labor. In 1907, Japan agreed not to issue any more passports to Japanese laborers going to the United States. Many other Japanese, however, continued to come.

3. Progressivism Stops Short

BEFORE YOU READ: *What problems did the progressives choose to ignore?*

The progressive movement had its limits. There were some problems in America that the progressives chose to ignore. Most of the reformers were from middle-class, well-established families. Their ancestors had come to America from northern or western Europe many generations ago. The progressives often had little sympathy for the problems of the New Immigrants. In addition, few progressives were interested in helping black Americans solve their problems.

Immigrants and Black Americans

Many progressives shared the opinion of the nativists that the New Immigrants from southern and eastern Europe were "inferior." Many immigrants, understandably, gave little support to progressive candidates. The immigrants benefited from the services of the city bosses whom the progressives attacked. Many immigrants continued to vote for the bosses' candidates. The city reformers came to view the immigrants as a source of corruption.

In some states, the progressives took an active part in opposing immigration and limiting immigrants' rights. In California, for instance, the progressives passed a state law in 1913 that barred Japanese immigrants from buying land.

One of the deepest and most difficult of American problems has been racial prejudice. The belief that people of one race are, by nature, inferior to people of another race is called **racism**. Many white Americans in the early 1900's, including the progressives, were racists. Some Americans disagreed with racism but did little to fight it. Only a few Americans were actively concerned with the problem of racism in the early 1900's.

---

racism the belief that people of one race are, by nature, inferior to people of another race

---

Theodore Roosevelt was the first President to invite a black American, Booker T. Washington, to visit the White House. Roosevelt's invitation caused a national controversy. In 1912, however, Roosevelt hoped to attract the votes of white southerners by pursuing a "lily-white" policy. He assured southern whites that he was not a supporter of the old Republican policies of Reconstruction. By trusting "[white] men of justice and of vision," Roosevelt promised, "the colored men of the South will ultimately get justice."

Woodrow Wilson was the first southerner to be elected President since the Civil War. President Wilson ordered the employees in many federal departments to be separated by race. Black workers who refused to accept segregation were fired. In Atlanta, Georgia, for example, 35 black postal workers were fired.

In 1914, a group of black leaders met with President Wilson at the White House to protest his racial policies. The President became angered and practically ordered the blacks to leave his office. Progressivism, apparently, was to be for

Discuss: Compare the following words: nativism, sexism, and racism. What do these words have in common? How are they different?

Famous Americans

IDA WELLS-BARNETT

Ida Wells-Barnett was a teacher, journalist, and lecturer who devoted her life to fighting for black rights. Wells was born a slave in Holly Springs, Mississippi. After the Civil War, she attended a freedmen's high school. At the age of 14, she became the sole support of her family when her parents died of yellow fever. Wells became a teacher in a segregated rural school. In 1883, Wells moved to Memphis, Tennessee, where she continued to teach. Wells had always been angered by the inferior educational facilities provided for black children. She began to write articles for small black-owned newspapers. When the Memphis school board learned of the articles, they refused to renew Wells' teaching contract. Wells then became a full-time journalist and part-owner of a newspaper, the *Memphis Free Speech*.

In 1892, three friends of hers were lynched. Wells expressed strong disapproval of the crime in her newspaper. This event led Wells to investigate other lynchings and to publish the facts as they surfaced. She lectured in the United States and abroad for black rights and formed antilynching societies wherever she went.

After Wells' marriage in 1895, she settled in Chicago. It was then that she published *A Red Story*, a history of three years of lynchings in the South. She reported that in 1894, "197 persons were put to death by mobs who gave the victims no opportunity to make a lawful defense."

Ida Wells-Barnett was also concerned with the welfare of Chicago's black population. She helped blacks find jobs and places to live and to get legal aid.

Although Wells-Barnett took part in organizing the National Association for the Advancement of Colored People in 1909, she often criticized it for not speaking out loudly enough. She remained true to her words, "I will never compromise against injustice!"

members of the white race only.

Even worse was the wave of antiblack violence. White racists hoped to keep blacks "in their place" by acts of terror. Race riots broke out in Atlanta, Georgia; St. Louis, Missouri; Springfield, Illinois; and other cities. Many blacks were beaten or killed in these riots. Many blacks who were accused of crimes were hanged by white mobs. Between 1900 and 1914, more than 1,100 blacks were lynched in the United States.

Background: Hampton Institute trained blacks in agricultural, industrial, and mechanical skills. Washington modeled the Tuskegee Institute on Hampton.

Booker T. Washington

Black leaders responded to prejudice and racism in different ways. The most prominent black leader in the 1890's and early 1900's was Booker T. Washington.

Washington was born a slave in Virginia in 1856. When Washington was 16, he walked 800 kilometers (500 miles) to enroll at Hampton Institute, a Virginia school for blacks. He later became a teacher at Hampton. In 1881, he founded a new school for blacks in Alabama, the Tuskegee Institute. Tuskegee provided training in agriculture and industry.

Booker T. Washington believed that blacks should concentrate on learning better agricultural and industrial skills. He believed that it was foolish and dangerous for blacks to try to fight the system of segregation. "Let us, in the future," Washington advised his followers, "spend *less* time talking about the part of the city that we cannot live in, and *more* time in making the part of the city that we can live in beautiful and attractive."

Washington became a powerful figure in black organizations and churches. Many blacks followed his example and accepted segregation while improving their own skills. "Wherever I found a prosperous Negro enterprise, a thriving business place, a good home," one reporter observed, "there I was sure to find Booker T. Washington's picture over the fireplace or a little framed motto expressing his gospel of work and service."

Washington's ideas were also supported by many whites in the North and the South. He offered a way for blacks to improve themselves without directly challenging the racism in white society.

W.E.B. Du Bois

In the early 1900's, a new black leader rose to power. His name was William Edward Burghardt Du Bois (doo BOYSS). Du Bois offered a very different kind of advice to black Americans from that of Booker T. Washington.

W. E. B. Du Bois was born in Massachusetts in 1868. He was a brilliant student and won a scholarship to attend Fisk University in Tennessee. He later attended the University of Berlin and became the first black man to earn a Ph.D. at Harvard University.

Du Bois urged blacks to protest and fight segregation. He believed blacks should demand full equality of opportunity in all things. Du Bois also believed that higher education should be available to black students. Black Americans should be proud of their color, he said, and of their African origins and culture.

In 1903, Du Bois published an essay called "Of Mr. Booker T. Washington and Others." In the essay, he openly criticized Washington for advising blacks to accept second-class citizenship. "The way for a people to gain their reasonable rights is not by voluntarily throwing them away," he wrote.

The differences between Washington and Du Bois were striking. Washington urged blacks to accept segregation and discrimination. Du Bois wanted blacks to demand full equality.

In July 1905, Du Bois and a group of his supporters met in Niagara Falls, Ontario, Canada. They met in Canada because no hotel on the American side of the falls would admit them. At the end of their meeting, the black leaders issued a set of

Discuss: At the Atlanta Exposition in 1895, Washington said: "In all things that are purely social we [blacks] can be as separate as the five fingers, yet one as the hand in all things essential to mutual progress." Ask students to explain this quote.

demands. They called for the removal of all restrictions on black voters in the South, equality of economic opportunity for blacks, higher education for talented black students, and an end to segregation. Du Bois and his followers organized the Niagara Movement to win their demands. The movement, however, failed to attract widespread support. Few Americans, black or white, were even aware of the demands of the Niagara Movement.

The leaders of the Niagara Movement posed for this photograph taken in Canada in 1905.

Black Progress

On the 100th anniversary of the birth of Abraham Lincoln, in 1909, a group of reformers organized the National Association for the Advancement of Colored People (NAACP). The NAACP was dedicated to ending all racial discrimination.

The leadership of the NAACP was mostly white. W. E. B. Du Bois, however, was the guiding spirit and most effective spokesperson for the group. Du Bois served as the editor of the NAACP magazine, *The Crisis*. By 1914, the organization had more than 6,000 white and black members in more than 50 chapters around the country.

The NAACP took legal action to challenge segregation laws. In 1915, it successfully challenged a law that prevented many blacks from voting in Oklahoma. Two years later, the NAACP succeeded in overturning a law in Louisville, Kentucky, that required segregation in housing.

The NAACP was the beginning of the modern movement for racial equality in the United States. The fight to end segregation would be a long one.

Section Review

1. What problems did the progressives choose to ignore?
2. Define racism. How is racism similar to nativism?
3. Compare and contrast the backgrounds and beliefs of Booker T. Washington and W. E. B. Du Bois.
4. The fight to end segregation and racial discrimination is not over in the United States. What problems in race relations still exist today?

 For Extra Interest: Have interested students research and report on the activities of the NAACP today.

Background: Before the Civil War, art and literature were available primarily to the wealthy. After the war, when workers had more leisure time, new libraries and museums made literature and art more accessible to a greater number of people.

4. Cultural Change

BEFORE YOU READ: *In what ways did American literature and painting become more realistic?*

The late 1800's and early 1900's were years of rapid change in American culture. American literature, art, architecture, education, and entertainment were all transformed.

Literature

In the years after the Civil War, many Americans believed that literature should describe only the "smiling aspects of life." Poems and stories should portray the pure and noble things in life. Literature should not describe things as they really were but only as they *should* be.

A few talented authors, however, challenged this view. Bret Harte, for instance, wrote a story called "The Luck of Roaring Camp" about the California gold rush. His characters, rough miners and dance-hall girls spoke as such people really did speak. Mark Twain's *Tom Sawyer* (1876) and *Huckleberry Finn* (1884) described in realistic detail life on the Mississippi River.

Even more realistic was the writing of William Dean Howells, a friend of Mark Twain. Howells declared that novels should be "true to the motives, the impulses, the principles that shape the life of actual men and women." The writing approach of Howells and other authors in Europe and America came to be called **realism**. The realists were the first writers to portray the problems created by the rapid growth of cities and industry. Howells' novel *A Hazard of New Fortunes* (1890) was a model of American realism. It described the greed of business leaders and the poverty of workers in the city.

realism the attempt in art and literature to depict real life as accurately as possible

Other writers went even further in describing "real life." They believed that life for the modern individual was hard and often brutal. Their literature emphasized these harsher aspects of life. The literature produced by these writers was called **naturalism**.

naturalism the approach in literature that emphasizes the observation of life without avoiding the ugly aspects of it

Two of the leading naturalist writers were Stephen Crane and Frank Norris. Crane's *Maggie, A Girl of the Streets* (1893) described the destruction of a young woman in New York by the poverty, drunkenness, and crime of the city. In the *Red Badge of Courage* (1895), Crane portrayed the horror and pain of the Civil War. Frank Norris' *The Octopus* (1901) pictured the struggle of California wheat farmers against the railroad.

The literature that most Americans read appeared in magazines. Some magazines, such as *Harper's* and *Atlantic Monthly*, printed important new fiction by the nation's leading authors. Others, like *Frank Leslie's Jolly Joker*, appealed to a larger audience with simple stories, jokes, and advice columns. *The Ladies' Home Journal* printed many articles on

For Extra Interest: Read passages from Twain's *Tom Sawyer* or *Huckleberry Finn* that reflect realism.

Background: Thomas Eakins was born in Philadelphia in 1844. He studied art in the United States and Europe. His portraits were not popular with the upper class because he painted honestly, not flatteringly.

Winslow Homer's "Crack the Whip" depicts rural life during the 1870's. These boys are playing during a recess from school.

suffrage and other reforms, as well as articles on such subjects as child care and gardening. In 1865, there were only about 700 magazines in the Unites States. By 1900, there were more than 5,000.

Art and Architecture

Many Americans after the Civil War shared the views of Europeans toward art. They accepted the "old masters" of European painting as the standard of artistic quality.

As in literature, some American artists in the late 1800's began to produce a new kind of art. New styles and subjects of painting were introduced. Many American artists wanted to produce paintings that were more realistic. The most important of the realist painters was Thomas Eakins. He was a master of detail. Some of his best paintings portrayed surgeons at work. Every detail was exact.

Winslow Homer was one of the most admired painters of American realism. "When I have selected [a subject]," he once said, "I paint it exactly as it appears." His watercolor paintings of the New England seacoast reveal this great concern for accuracy.

The American painter James A. McNeill Whistler painted in several styles. Some of his paintings were very romantic. Others were masterpieces of realism. Whistler's portrait of his mother became one of the most famous paintings ever done by an American artist.

In the early 1900's, a group of American artists in New York began painting scenes of city life. These realists included Robert Henri, Everett Shinn, and George Luks.

For Extra Interest: Show students pictures of paintings done by Eakins, Homer, and Whistler. Ask them to point out realistic details in these paintings.

For Extra Interest: Arrange for students to take a guided walking tour of your town. Have them note the architectural style of different buildings. When the tour is over, ask students to identify which buildings were designed on the principle of "form follows function."

They pictured such things as crowded streetcars, dirty streets, boxing matches, and laundry hanging from tenement windows. The people they portrayed were often poor and not very attractive. In 1904, a critic called these artists the "Ashcan School."

American architects, like American painters, began experimenting with new styles in the late 1800's. Before the Civil War, architectural design in the United States usually followed European styles. Many banks, churches, and office buildings were designed to look like Greek or Roman temples. Their design appeared unrelated to the building's real purpose.

Louis Sullivan, born in Boston in 1856, suggested a new approach to architecture. He believed that the outward form of a building should express the building's true purpose, or function. Sullivan recommended a guiding principle for all modern architecture: "Form follows function." The office buildings he designed were square, simple, and solid. They had little of the extra decoration that earlier architects had used.

One of Sullivan's followers was Frank Lloyd Wright. Wright designed many homes whose form closely reflected their function and environment. His midwestern "prairie style" houses were long and low, like the plains themselves.

New building materials and inventions also changed architecture. Steel-beam construction and electric elevators made it possible to build taller buildings. The first skyscraper—ten stories high—was built in Chicago in 1885. Its architect was William LeBaron Jenney. In the early 1900's, skyscrapers were built in every major American city.

Education

Before the Civil War, there were only 100 high schools in the United States. By 1915, the number of high schools had risen to more than 11,000. In 1870, only 7 million students were attending school. By 1915, attendance had soared to 20 million. Before the Civil War, many high schools did not admit girls. By 1890, more girls than boys were graduating from high school.

Not only were schools growing in size and attendance, but the quality of education was also changing. Public schools in America had always emphasized the basic skills of reading and writing. Teachers demanded strict discipline. They expected their students to learn by memorizing their lessons. One teacher in Chicago told her class, "Don't stop to think, tell me what you know!"

In the late 1890's and early 1900's, new ideas about education were developed. The most progressive American educator of the time was John Dewey. "Education," Dewey believed, was "the fundamental method of social progress and reform." Children should be taught to be good citizens, he thought, not just good students. A proper education was more than gaining knowledge. It was learning to understand the problems of society and becoming able to solve them. Dewey also believed that children could best "learn by doing." His ideas about teaching and learning were the basis of what was called "progressive education."

Colleges and universities also experienced major changes. Before the Civil War, many state universities admitted only men. By 1900, about 70 percent of

Discuss: Do you think that all buildings should be designed to reflect their function? Why or why not?

the colleges in the United States accepted both men and women. Many of the great business leaders gave money to found new colleges. Vanderbilt University in Tennessee and Stanford University in California were created by railroad millionaires. John D. Rockefeller gave $34 million to the University of Chicago. The federal government also aided the growth of higher education. The number of college students in the nation increased from fewer than 60,000 in 1870 to approximately 400,000 by 1914.

Entertainment

In the days when most Americans lived on farms, there was little interest in organized sports. Most people got plenty of exercise working outside. They could entertain themselves by hunting, fishing, swimming, or playing informal games.

As more people moved to the cities, there were fewer opportunities for outdoor exercise. Bicycling was one of the few ways that city residents could exercise. In the 1890's, a "bicycle fad" swept

The Keystone Kops became film favorites of American moviegoers who loved their slapstick humor.

Background: Vaudeville shows were also a popular form of entertainment at the turn of the century. These shows were performed on stage and consisted of a number of unrelated acts. The cost of entrance ranged from $0.25 to $1.50.

Background: According to the first set of rules drawn up for American baseball in 1845, balls caught on the first bounce constituted an out, pitchers had to throw the ball underhanded, and the first team to score 21 runs was the winner. In addition, no one in the outfield wore a glove.

through many cities. Generally, however, most city residents had to be content with watching other people exercise. Rather than playing games themselves, they became spectators.

The first great spectator sport in America was baseball. By the 1850's, amateur baseball clubs had been formed in many American cities. As early as 1869, a professional team had been organized—the Cincinnati Red Stockings. In the late 1800's, thousands of spectators filled the nation's baseball stadiums to watch their favorite teams. The first World Series was played in 1903. The Boston Red Sox beat the Pittsburgh Pirates, five games to three.

Most large cities in the early 1900's had amusement parks for their residents. The parks were often built by streetcar companies on the edge of town. Some of the most famous parks were Coney Island in New York and Riverview Park near Baltimore. Crowds of people from the city would travel to the parks on Sunday afternoons. They would watch balloon races or circus acts. Children especially enjoyed riding the giant ferris wheels or breathtaking roller coasters.

In the early 1900's, a new form of entertainment brightened the lives of many city dwellers: the motion picture. The earliest movie theaters were called "nickelodeons." They charged 5 cents to watch an eight-minute silent film. The first movie that told a complete story was *The Great Train Robbery*, made in 1903. The film told the story of a mail-train holdup and the pursuit and killing of the robbers.

The film industry began on the East Coast. Thomas Edison, inventor of the motion picture camera and projector, tried to establish a monopoly in the industry. In 1907, the first film company came to California. Soon others followed. California was far from the control of Edison. Also, the climate of California was ideal for shooting outdoor scenes. By 1912, the Los Angeles suburb of Hollywood had become the center of the nation's film industry. More than 10 million people were watching movies in America each year.

Section Review

1. In what ways did American literature and painting become more realistic in the late 1800's and early 1900's?
2. What new approach to architecture did Louis Sullivan suggest?
3. Who was the most progressive American educator? What did he believe was a proper education?
4. What new forms of entertainment did Americans enjoy in the early 1900's?
5. Americans have always enjoyed having fun. Have any new forms of entertainment appeared recently? Can entertainment sometimes be harmful to a person or society? Explain your answers.

CHAPTER REVIEW

Summary

In the early 1900's, attempts were made to solve the problems caused by the rapid growth of American industry. Men and women who called themselves progressives worked hard to bring about reforms in American life. Writers called muckrakers exposed the corruption in city government and the abuses of big business. Under the leadership of three progressive Presidents, the federal government passed laws to regulate business. Efforts were made to break up political machines by allowing people to become more directly involved in the political process. Settlement houses were started to meet the needs of poor city dwellers.

The progressives, however, ignored the needs of black Americans and immigrants. Black leaders like Booker T. Washington and W. E. B. Du Bois tried to help blacks achieve equality. Despite their efforts, blacks continued to suffer racial discrimination.

The United States also experienced many cultural changes in the early 1900's. New forms of literature, art, architecture, education, and entertainment were developing. By 1918, the United States had experienced many changes that would influence its development in the twentieth century.

Recalling the Facts

1. Describe the abuses or corruption exposed by each of the following muckrakers: Ida Tarbell, Lincoln Steffens, Upton Sinclair, Frank Norris.
2. What two new forms of city government began in Galveston, Texas, and Staunton, Virginia?
3. What were two major concerns of women during the progressive era?
4. Why was the Progressive, or "Bull Moose," party formed in 1912?
5. Why did immigrants give little support to progressive candidates?
6. What new developments made it possible to build skyscrapers?

Analyzing the Facts

1. Review the goals of the Populist party in 1892 (Chapter 21). Which of these goals were accomplished in the early 1900's through the efforts of the progressives?

2. Compare the attitudes of Theodore Roosevelt and William Taft on business combinations and the conservation of forest lands.
3. How did the formation of the "Bull Moose" party help Woodrow Wilson become President?
4. Whose methods for achieving racial equality would you have supported, those of Booker T. Washington or W. E. B. Du Bois? Explain your answer.
5. How did Louis Sullivan's idea that "form follows function" in building design fit in with the trend toward realism in art?

Time and History

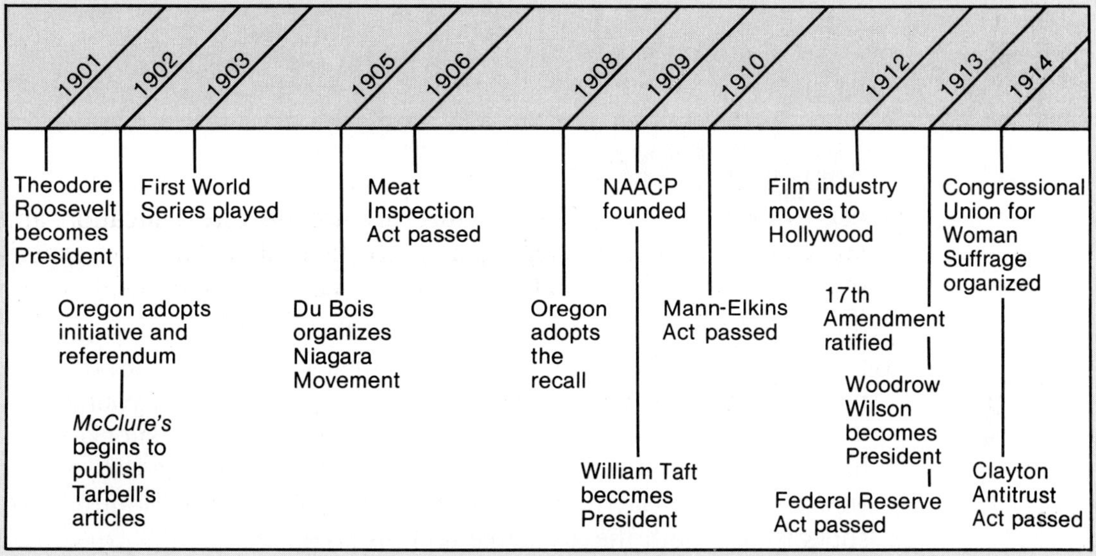

1. How long after Ida Tarbell's articles were published was the Clayton Antitrust Act passed?
2. What state was the first to adopt the initiative, referendum, and recall?
3. Which of the following were passed while Taft was President: Federal Reserve Act, Mann-Elkins Act, Meat Inspection Act?
4. How long after Du Bois organized the Niagara Movement was the NAACP established?
5. What two new forms of entertainment were available to Americans in the early 1900's?
6. Whose term of office was longer, that of President Theodore Roosevelt or President William Taft?

Chapter
24

World War I

In the summer of 1914, Francis Ferdinand, the Archduke of Austria-Hungary, visited the city of Sarajevo (sah-rah-YEA-voe). Sarajevo was the capital of Bosnia, a small province in the kingdom of Austria-Hungary. The archduke and his wife began their visit on June 28, 1914. As they were being driven through the streets of Sarajevo, a young man threw a bomb at their automobile. Francis Ferdinand knocked the bomb away, and it exploded behind the car. Later in the day, an 18-year-old named Gavrilo Princip stepped up to the car. He fired two shots, killing both the archduke and his wife.

These shots were the spark that began World War I. Following the assassination of the archduke, nation after nation declared war. The United States at first hoped to stay out of the war. Eventually, however, it too joined the conflict.

After you read this chapter, you will be able to:

1. Explain the causes of World War I.
2. Describe the American role in the war.
3. List the major proposals of Woodrow Wilson's Fourteen Points.
☐ Compare maps to gain information.

Vocabulary Help: irony—a combination of circumstances or a result that is the opposite of what is expected. Ask students what would be the irony of a fire station burning down. See if they can think of similar ironies.

1. Wilson the Diplomat

BEFORE YOU READ: *What were the reasons for hostility among the European nations?*

When Woodrow Wilson became President in 1913, he had a clear idea of the many reforms he wanted to accomplish. He did not, however, have a clear understanding of world affairs. "It would be the irony of fate," Wilson remarked in 1913, "if my administration had to deal chiefly with foreign affairs."

As it turned out, foreign affairs did become a chief concern of Wilson's administration. In shaping his foreign policy, Wilson combined high ideals with the protection of American interests.

The Cooling-Off Treaties

Woodrow Wilson selected William Jennings Bryan to be his secretary of state. Bryan was opposed to all war and armed conflict. He believed that international disputes should be settled by peaceful means rather than by force or violence. Bryan was a dedicated **pacifist**.

---

pacifist a person who believes that international disputes should be settled by peaceful means rather than by force or violence

---

Bryan's most important accomplishment as secretary of state was a series of "cooling-off" treaties. Between 1913 and 1914, he negotiated 30 treaties among the nations of the world. These treaties provided that disputes among the nations be submitted to an international commission. The commission would study the disputes and recommend solutions. In the meantime, the nations would promise not to go to war. Critics ridiculed the treaties. They thought the treaties would do little good.

Latin American Diplomacy

Woodrow Wilson did not intend to leave all foreign policy matters up to his secretary of state. After only a week in office, President Wilson issued a major foreign policy statement. He denounced the Latin American policy of his predecessor in the White House, William Howard Taft. Taft had acted forcefully to protect American foreign investments and foreign markets. In 1911, for example, the State Department arranged for American bankers to reorganize Nicaragua's finances when revolutionaries threatened to take over the Nicaraguan government. Taft's critics called his policies "dollar diplomacy."

President Wilson strongly denounced dollar diplomacy, but soon he was pursuing a policy very similar to that of Taft. When unrest and disorder threatened American interests or property in Latin America, Wilson ordered armed intervention. In 1915, Wilson landed the Marines in Haiti to put down a revolution. In 1916, American forces landed in the Dominican Republic to end disorder there.

Mexican Interventions

By 1913, American bankers and business leaders had invested over one billion dollars in Mexico. They were very

Background: Dollar diplomacy is the policy of using the economic power or influence of a country to promote the business interests of its private citizens or corporations in another country.

concerned with the unrest they saw there.

Between 1880 and 1911, Mexico was ruled by a **dictator**. During these years, most Mexicans lived in poverty and had no political rights. In 1911, a new leader named Francisco Madero came to power. President Madero began to introduce major reforms in Mexico. In 1913, however, the government was seized by a new military dictator, Victoriano Huerta.

dictator a person who rules a nation with absolute power and authority

President Wilson refused to recognize Huerta's government. Wilson hoped that Huerta would be overthrown and that a more "progressive" president would take over the country.

In April 1914, two crew members from an American naval vessel were briefly arrested in the Mexican port city of Tampico (tam-PEEK-oh). The Americans were arrested for mistakenly entering a restricted area. Wilson responded by ordering the Marines to land at Vera Cruz (VEH-rah CROOS). It seemed that a war was about to begin. The United States and Mexico, however, avoided war by submitting their differences to an international commission.

By August 1914, a new government was in power in Mexico. The new government was headed by Venustiano Carranza. Soon, however, another revolution broke out. The rebel leader had been one of Carranza's own generals, Francisco "Pancho" Villa.

At first, President Wilson supported Villa. Wilson soon became convinced, however, that Villa was little more than a bandit out for personal gain. Wilson switched American support to the Carranza government. Pancho Villa was angered at what he considered a betrayal by the United States. He ordered attacks on American citizens on both sides of the international border. In March 1916, 360 of Villa's men crossed the border and killed 17 Americans in Columbus, New Mexico.

With the permission of the Carranza government, Wilson ordered American forces to pursue and capture Villa. But Villa and his men knew their country well and were always able to escape from the Americans. As the Americans pushed deeper into Mexico, they engaged in battle with the Mexican forces. The Carranza government at last ordered the Americans to withdraw.

President Wilson was frustrated. There seemed to be no end to the unrest in Mexico. In January 1917, Wilson ordered American forces to withdraw from Mexico. The dispute between the two nations was submitted to an international commission for settlement. After six months of debate, the commission could reach no conclusion.

By the time the American forces were withdrawn from Mexico, the attention of the President and the nation had been drawn to the larger crisis in Europe.

The European Crisis

The assassination of Archduke Ferdinand in 1914 was the spark that ignited World War I. Long before the assassination, hostility among the European nations had been building. There were many reasons for this hostility.

For Extra Interest: Have interested students do independent research and prepare reports on Francisco Madero, Victoriano Huerta, Venustiano Carranzo, and Pancho Villa.

Background: In 1914, there were only two independent countries in Africa—Liberia and Ethiopia. The rest of the continent was colonized by European powers.

For years, the nations of Europe had been competing for control of foreign territory and markets in Asia and Africa. They had established empires around the world. The **imperialism** of the European nations had produced many diplomatic crises and several armed conflicts.

---

imperialism the policy and practice of maintaining an empire, a policy marked by competition for control of foreign territory and markets

---

Changing attitudes among the European people also contributed to feelings of hostility. People came to have an intense devotion to their own nation. By the late 1800's, **nationalism** had become almost a second religion for many European people.

---

nationalism an intense devotion by a people to their nation

In the late 1880's and early 1900's, each nation built up its military forces. Armies and navies increased in size. Stockpiles of weapons grew steadily. The military spirit was glorified. This policy of **militarism** added to the feelings of hostility.

---

militarism the policy of building up military strength and glorifying the military spirit

---

The nations of Europe tried to increase their security by forming alliances with other friendly nations. Members of each alliance promised that if one nation was attacked, the other nations in the alliance would go to its defense.

By 1914, there were two major alliances in Europe. Germany, Austria-Hungary, and Turkey were known as the Central Powers. Opposing this alliance were Great Britain, France, Russia, and Italy. These nations were called the Allied Powers, or simply the Allies.

One of the areas where hostility was the greatest was a region in southeastern Europe known as the Balkans. Several Balkan nations, such as Serbia, were independent. Others, like the small province of Bosnia, were controlled by larger European powers. Bosnia was under the control of Austria-Hungary.

Many of the people in Bosnia were Serbians. They wanted Bosnia to be independent of Austria-Hungary so that it could join the neighboring country of Serbia. The Serbians living in Bosnia resented the visit of the archduke of Austria-Hungary to Sarajevo, the capital of Bosnia, in the summer of 1914. The young man who killed the archduke and his wife was a Serbian. Following the assassination, the government of Austria-Hungary issued a set of demands to Serbia. When Serbia did not agree to all of the demands, Austria-Hungary declared war.

The small war between Austria-Hungary and Serbia soon spread to other nations. When Serbia was attacked, the Russians began mobilizing their troops to come to Serbia's defense. Germany, the ally of Austria-Hungary, declared war on Russia and its ally, France. Great Britain entered the conflict and declared war on Germany. By the end of August 1914, the two great European alliances were at war.

Over the next four years, other nations around the world became involved. The conflict became truly a world war.

Background: Great Britain entered the war when Germany marched through neutral Belgium to attack France. Many years earlier, the major European powers, including Germany, had signed an agreement to respect Belgium's neutrality.

European Alliances in 1914

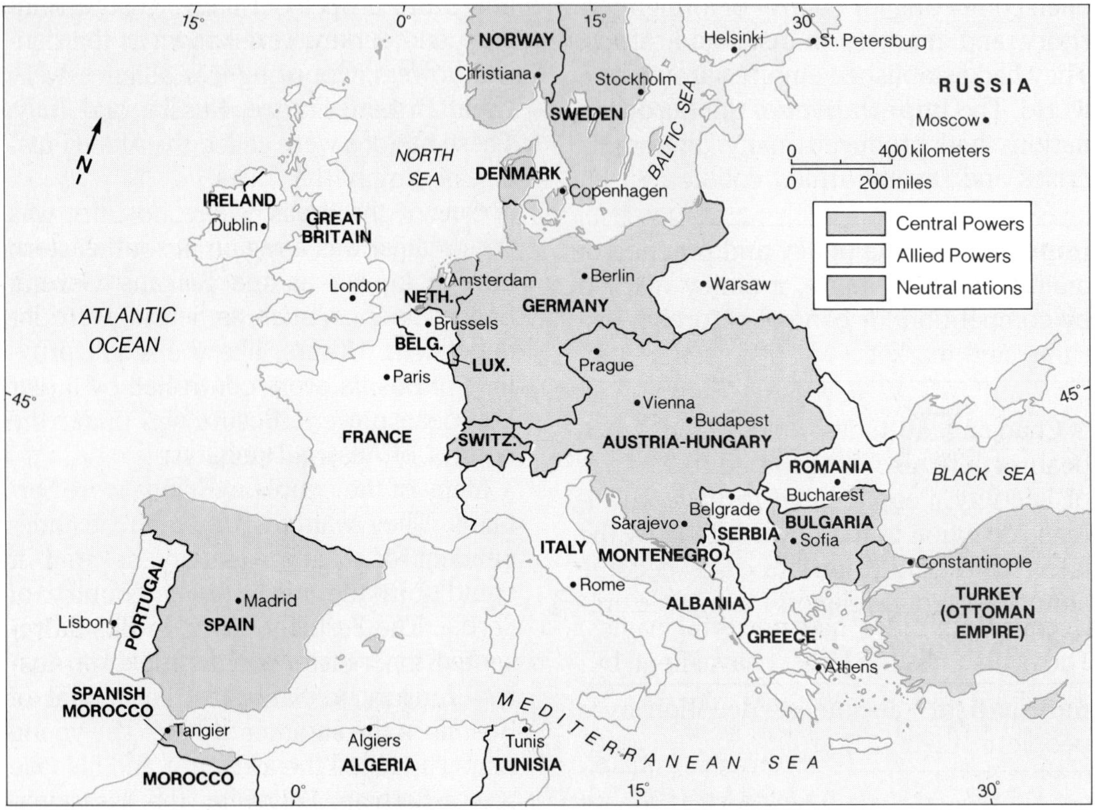

Which nations were neutral in 1914?

The World at War

At the beginning of World War I, the Allied Powers had a great advantage over the Central Powers. The Allies had a larger population and a greater supply of resources than the Central Powers. The Central Powers knew that they would have to win the war quickly if they were to win it at all.

Germany had a plan for a quick victory. The Germans wanted to capture Paris, the capital of France, and quickly defeat the French army. The German plan failed. The French, with the help of the Belgians and the British, stopped the German army outside Paris.

The combat in the western part of Europe became known as the Western Front. By the fall of 1914, the war on the Western Front had bogged down. Hundreds of thousands of soldiers faced each other along a battle line more than 482 kilometers (300 miles) long. It extended from the borders of Switzerland to the North Sea. The armies of each side dug parallel ditches, or trenches, deep enough to conceal soldiers standing up-

Background: Between the trenches was a narrow stretch of land covered with barbed wire called "no-man's-land." Soldiers would go "over the top," cut through the wire, and charge the enemy with fixed bayonets. The defenders would remain in their trenches and fire on the attackers.

Discuss: Why was Germany forced to fight the war on two fronts? Why would this be a disadvantage for Germany?

right. The trenches were muddy, uncomfortable, and very unhealthy. For four years, from 1914 to 1918, the armies of each side fought from their trenches. Small victories were won. But on the whole, the battle lines on the Western Front remained unchanged.

The fighting in eastern Europe was called the Eastern Front. Here the armies of the Central Powers faced Russia. By 1916, the Russians had lost major battles to the Germans. Discontent with the war and disagreement with other policies of the Russian government led to a revolution in Russia in 1917. By the end of the year, Russia had pulled out of the war.

Fighting took place in many other areas during the war. The most important battleground, however, was on the Atlantic Ocean. Both sides had powerful navies. The British had the largest naval fleet, but the Germans had developed a very effective new kind of ship, the U-boat, or submarine. The term "U-boat" comes from the German word *Unterseeboot*, meaning "undersea boat."

Both the Allies and the Central Powers used their navies to try to stop supplies from reaching their enemies. It was the fighting on the Atlantic that ultimately brought the United States into the war.

The American Response

In 1914, when World War I began, Woodrow Wilson called upon all Americans to remain "impartial in thought as well as deed." To be impartial means to be fair to both sides in a dispute. The United States, President Wilson said, would maintain its neutrality.

Most Americans wanted to keep out of the war. Many people, however, found it very hard to remain truly impartial. In 1914, over a third of the American people were immigrants or the children of immigrants. They felt a bond with the lands of their ancestors.

Almost 8 million Americans were of German or Austrian descent. Another 4.5 million were of Irish ancestry, and many Irish-Americans had no love for Great Britain. For centuries, Ireland had fought to be independent of Great Britain. Some Americans of German, Austrian, and Irish descent sympathized with the Central Powers. The majority of America's 92 million people, however, were descendants of immigrants from the Allied Powers. Their sympathies were with Great Britain and the Allies.

American sympathies for the Allies were also aroused by stories of German cruelty that were circulated by the British. The British controlled much of the flow of information about the war to the United States. A great deal of this information was propaganda. Stories favorable to the Allies were passed on to American readers. Favorable accounts of the Central Powers were intercepted.

Economic ties between the United States and the nations of Europe made neutrality even harder to maintain. As a neutral power, the United States had the right to trade with either side in the war. The British navy, however, established a blockade in the Atlantic that shut off the delivery of goods from the United States and other neutral countries to the Central Powers.

British naval vessels stopped American ships on the high seas to inspect their cargoes. They forced American ships into

Background: Great Britain used propaganda to stir up feelings of hatred against the Germans. They reported that Germans tortured innocent children and families in Belgium and that water was denied to dying soldiers by German nurses.

Background: Freedom of the seas did not extend to neutral vessels carrying contraband. Great Britain expanded the definition of contraband to include anything that might aid its enemy, including food and clothing.

American Trade with Europe

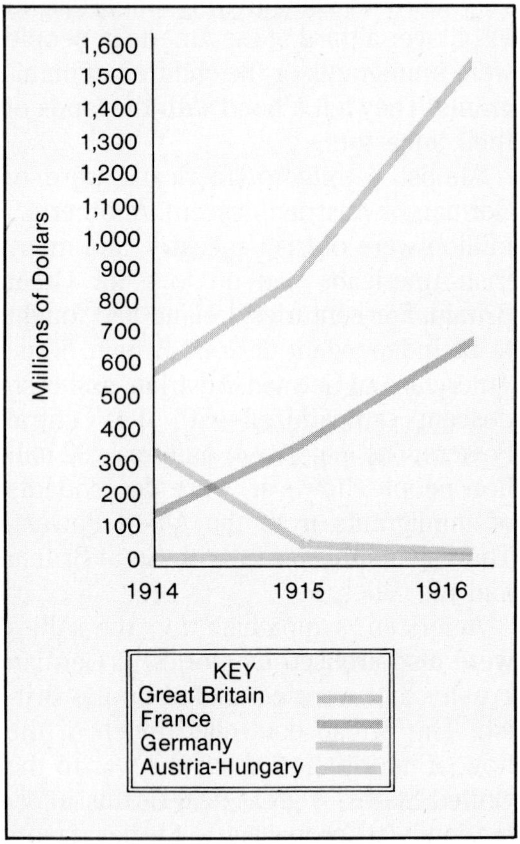

port and seized goods heading for the Central Powers. The British usually, but not always, paid for the goods they seized. These actions were violations of international law.

President Wilson protested the violations, but his protests did little good. The British blockade remained in place. The blockade effectively reduced trade between the United States and the Central Powers. Meanwhile, American trade with Great Britain soared from less than $600 million in 1914 to more than $1.5 billion by 1916. The Allies became heavily dependent upon the United States for food, weapons, ammunition, and other military supplies. By early 1917, the Allies had borrowed over $2 billion from American bankers to pay for their purchases in the United States.

President Wilson's policy of neutrality was weakening. Most Americans still hoped to avoid direct involvement in the conflict. But many were beginning to believe that sooner or later the United States would have to enter the war.

Section Review

1. Why did feelings of hostility develop among the nations of Europe in the years before 1914?
2. What is a pacifist? What was William Jennings Bryan's most important contribution as secretary of state?
3. What effect did the British blockade have on American trade with Europe?
4. Why did Americans find it hard to remain neutral during the European war?
5. Name recent wars that have been fought between other nations. Do you think most Americans were able to feel impartial during these conflicts? Why or why not?

For Extra Interest: Have each student write a letter to the editor of a newspaper in 1917 regarding the sinking of the *Lusitania*. The letters should clearly state how the United States government should respond to this event and why this response is the most appropriate.

2. The United States at War

BEFORE YOU READ: *In what ways did Americans contribute to the Allies' victory in World War I?*

American participation in World War I was brief. Americans in large numbers fought only during the last year of the conflict. But American participation was vitally important. The American forces gave the Allies the added strength they needed to defeat the Central Powers.

Submarine Warfare

In February 1915, the Germans declared the waters around the British Isles a war zone. They announced they would sink any enemy ships in the area.

To enforce their blockade, the Germans used their submarines. Unlike the battleships of the British navy, the U-boats could stop enemy ships only by sinking them. If a submarine came to the surface to inspect or seize another ship, it could be blasted out of the water by the deck guns of the enemy ship. The submarines, therefore, stayed beneath the surface and fired torpedoes into the enemy ships.

On May 7, 1915, a German U-boat fired a torpedo into the British passenger liner *Lusitania*. The *Lusitania* sank. Nearly 1,200 people died. Among the dead were 128 American citizens. President Wilson demanded that Germany apologize for the attack and promise not to attack any more passenger ships. After months of delay, Germany apologized.

In August 1915, a German submarine sank another British passenger ship, the *Arabic*. Two Americans on board were killed. Following the attack on a third passenger ship, the *Sussex*, Germany announced in May 1916 that it would no longer attack without warning any passenger or merchant ships. Germany had abandoned—at least for the time being—its submarine warfare.

1917

On January 31, 1917, Germany announced it was resuming its submarine warfare. Germany proclaimed that its U-boats would sink *all* ships—enemy or neutral, passenger or merchant—heading for Allied nations. Germany could no longer allow the United States to provide its enemies with food and other supplies.

That same month, the British had intercepted a message from the German foreign minister, Arthur Zimmermann, to the government of Mexico. The message proposed that Mexico join Germany in war against the United States. When the war was over, the message explained, Mexico could regain its "lost territory in Texas, New Mexico, and Arizona." When the message was published, the American people were outraged.

In the middle of March, German U-boats sank four American merchant ships. Many Americans were killed. Germany, in effect, had declared war on American shipping. As one Philadelphia newspaper commented, the only difference "between war and what we have now is that now we aren't fighting back."

Woodrow Wilson, on April 2, 1917, called upon Congress to declare war against Germany. "The world must be

Background: The Sussex Pledge contained a qualifying statement. In the pledge, Germany said that it would stop sinking unresisting merchant and passenger liners *if* the United States forced Great Britain to relax its starvation blockade.

Discuss: Why would Mexico be a valuable ally to Germany in a war against the United States? How do you think Mexico would have responded to the Zimmermann message if it had not been intercepted? Explain your answer.

To encourage people to join the army, the government printed up many posters like this one.

made safe for democracy," Wilson declared. The United States should enter the war not for revenge but to defend the basic ideals of all humanity. "We have no selfish ends to serve. We desire no conquest, no dominion [empire]. . . . We are but one of the champions of the rights of mankind. We shall be satisfied when those rights have been made as secure as the faith and the freedom of nations can make them. . . ."

Wilson knew that the United States had already made a tremendous investment in the Allied cause. Billions of dollars' worth of goods had been sold to the Allies, and billions of dollars had been loaned. In defining the goals of American involvement in the war, however, Wilson chose to emphasize the highest of ideals. On April 6, Congress voted to declare war.

The Home Front

As the United States went to war in 1917, its first problem was to raise an army. President Wilson believed that volunteers would not be enough. He believed that young men should be required to serve in the armed forces. In May 1917, Congress passed the Selective Service Act. Under this act, 3 million men were drafted. Another 2 million volunteers joined the various branches of the armed forces.

Another problem for the United States was raising money to pay its new army and to buy needed weapons and supplies. The government urged Americans to buy "Liberty Bonds" to support the war. Citizens who bought the bonds were really loaning money to the government. The government promised to pay the money back after the war was over. Liberty Bonds raised $23 billion. Extra taxes brought in an additional $10 billion.

The government also needed to organize the nation's economy to support the war effort. New boards were set up to manage or regulate business, agriculture, and labor. A food administration directed the activities of American farmers. A powerful war industries board coordinated government purchases of military

Background: Americans on the home front were encouraged to cut their consumption of fuel and certain foods to aid the war effort. Wheatless Mondays and Wednesdays, meatless Tuesdays, gasless Sundays, and heatless Mondays were practiced by patriotic Americans.

EUREKA!

The Zipper

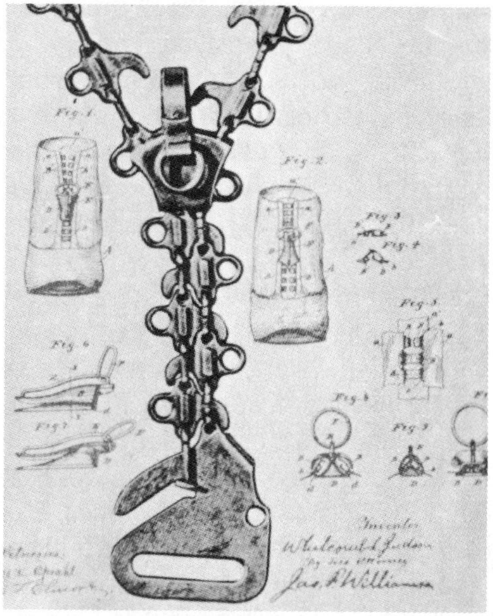

The zipper is one of technology's simplest gadgets. It is hard to believe that it took many attempts to perfect it and make it a part of daily life. But that is exactly what happened.

The first zipper design was dreamed up by Elias Howe, who is better remembered for inventing the sewing machine. Howe patented his zipper design in 1857 but never developed it. The glory of inventing the zipper therefore usually goes to a Chicago engineer named Whitcomb Judson. He patented his design in 1893 and went on to produce zippers for the marketplace.

Judson originally applied his design to shoes. Instead of placing one long zipper along the shoe's tongue, he used several short ones placed across the tongue like buckles. The zippers themselves were made of a series of hooks and eyes that could be joined either singly or by using a slider like those on zippers today.

In 1894, Judson and a lawyer named Lewis Walker founded the Universal Fastener Company. However, zipper sales were slow. The devices had a nasty tendency to pop open at awkward moments. In addition, the sharp hooks tore any cloth they came in contact with.

Despite several tries at improved designs, the company continued to flounder, and competitors with other designs did no better. The world, it seemed, was not yet ready to zip up.

A breakthrough came in 1912, when an engineer at Judson and Walker's company invented a zipper with teeth that meshed when joined together by a slider. Walker changed the company's name to the Hookless Fastener Company and began to sell the new design. This time business was better. When the U.S. Navy ordered 10,000 zip-up flight suits for its pilots during World War I, the zipper was at last on its way.

---

supplies. It decided which factories should produce needed military goods, and it set prices for the goods.

The wartime expansion of the economy opened jobs to new groups of workers. Women were employed in factories

Background: Women made up approximately 20 percent of all workers in the electrical machinery, airplane, and food industries during the war. However, when the war was over, women were pushed aside to provide jobs for returning veterans.

making war goods of all kinds, from ammunition to military uniforms. Black workers also found new opportunities during the war years. Black migration from the South increased rapidly, as blacks came north to work in wartime defense industries. During the 20 years before 1910, only 200,000 blacks had moved to the North. In the five years following 1914, about 500,000 blacks moved to the North.

Government leaders believed that it was important to unite American opinion in favor of the war. The Committee on Public Information printed 75 million pieces of literature urging support of the war. War posters were put on walls of schools, theaters, shops, and offices. Congress also passed laws that made it illegal to express any public opposition to the war. One group that defied these laws and continued to oppose the war was the Socialist party. Its leader, Eugene V. Debs, was sentenced to ten years in prison in 1918. Altogether, more than 1,500 people were arrested for criticizing America's participation in the war.

Ugly incidents took place across the country as immigrants from Germany and Austria-Hungary were attacked. Anti-German feeling was especially strong. Some Americans wanted to rid the country of all things German. Sauerkraut was renamed "liberty cabbage." Hamburger became "liberty sausage."

Over There

George M. Cohan, a popular American songwriter, composed a song in 1917 called "Over There." The song celebrated the arrival of American soldiers in Europe. "The Yanks are coming," Cohan wrote. "The Yanks are coming. And we won't come back till it's over over there."

The first Americans arrived "over there" near the end of June 1917. It was not until the following spring, however, that Americans were in Europe in great numbers. The American Expeditionary Force (AEF) was under the command of General John J. Pershing. The AEF included farmers, laborers, and business executives from every state in the union.

Black Americans served in segregated units, as in earlier wars. Most black units were labor battalions, but some saw combat duty. The all-black 369th Regiment, for example, came under the longest continuous enemy fire of any American unit in the war. During the war, nearly 400,000 black Americans served in the armed forces. Many blacks viewed the war as an opportunity to demonstrate their bravery and patriotism.

Americans in World War I saw or used a variety of new weapons of war. This was the first major war in which airplanes were used. Both sides used them to bomb enemy-held towns, to scout out enemy positions, and to locate enemy warships. American fliers made up about 10 percent of the Allied air force. Seventy-one Americans became "aces," pilots who shot down five or more enemy planes. One of the heroes of the war was Captain Eddie Rickenbacker, an ace who shot down 26 German aircraft.

Other new weapons of war included the rapid firing machine gun and barbed wire. Thousands of soldiers, trying to advance through enemy lines, were caught by strands of barbed wire and shot by enemy gunners. Poison gas was

For Extra Interest: Have students listen to songs that were popular in America during World War I. Suggestions are: "The Caissons Go Rolling Along," "The Marine Hymn," and "Keep the Home Fires Burning."

Background: Airplanes were first used to watch troop movements. The first bombs to fall from airplanes were dropped by hand—the copilot literally threw them out. Eventually, special doors were put in the floors of planes so that bombs could be released automatically.

also introduced during the war. The Germans first used chlorine gas in April 1915. The gas was released from large cylinders fired into the enemy lines. Many soldiers who survived the gas attacks died years later from damaged lungs. To protect the soldiers against poison gas, gas masks were developed.

One of the most impressive new weapons was the tank, a kind of armored land battleship. The tank was a British invention. Tanks provided protection and helped the Allies win several important battles.

The American Contribution

The first important American contribution to the war came on the Atlantic. American warships began attacking German U-boats within weeks of the declaration of war. American naval vessels also provided protection for merchant ships carrying supplies to the Allies. These protective escorts, called **convoys,** proved to be very effective.

convoy a protecting escort for ships or troops

The Western Front, 1918

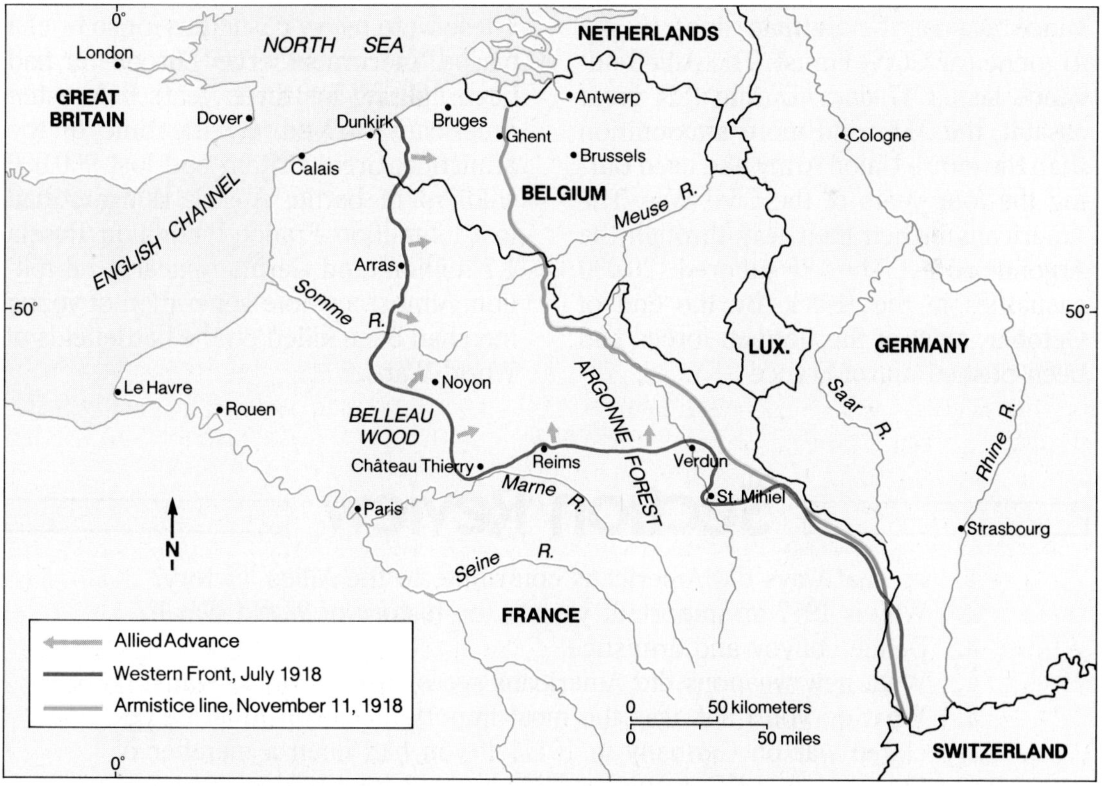

How far was the Western Front from Paris in 1918?

For Extra Interest: Assign an interested student to do research and report to the class on zeppelins.

Background: Shortly before the war ended, a revolution occurred in Germany. Kaiser Wilhelm II fled to the Netherlands, where he stayed until his death in 1941. The new German government that formed was called the Weimar Republic.

The war on the Eastern Front came to an end in March 1918. Following the Russian revolution, the new Russian government signed a separate peace treaty with the Central Powers. German troops, no longer needed in the east, were rushed into battle on the Western Front.

In May and June 1918, the AEF helped turn back a German assault on the Western Front. By late May, the Germans had reached the town of Château-Thierry (sha-TOH-tee-eh-RY), only 80 kilometers (50 miles) from Paris. Early in June, the AEF began driving the Germans back from Château-Thierry and Belleau (BELL-oh) Wood.

Beginning in late September, over one million American soldiers began to advance against the German lines in the Argonne (ar-GON) Forest. The Allied advance lasted 47 days. During this great assault, the AEF used more ammunition than the entire Union Army had used during the four years of the Civil War. The Americans inched their way through the Argonne Forest. The AEF suffered 120,000 casualties in the attack. By the end of October, most of the German forces had been pushed out of France.

The military leaders of the Central Powers now sought to sign an **armistice**, or truce that would stop the fighting. On November 11, 1918, the Germans signed an armistice with the Allied leaders. It went into effect at 11 o'clock that morning. As veterans of the war would always remember, the fighting came to an end at the eleventh hour of the eleventh day of the eleventh month.

---

armistice a truce that stops the fighting of a war

American casualties during the war totaled more than 112,000 dead and 230,000 wounded. More than half of the American deaths were caused by disease. These were heavy casualties for so brief a period of combat. The Europeans had been fighting for three years before the Americans arrived. By the time of the armistice, Great Britain had lost 900,000 soldiers in battle, Austria-Hungary had lost 1.2 million, France 1.4 million, Russia 1.7 million, and Germany nearly 1.8 million. Almost a whole generation of young men had been killed on the battlefields of World War I.

Section Review

1. In what ways did Americans contribute to the Allies' victory?
2. Why is 1917 an important year in the history of World War I?
3. Define convoy and armistice.
4. What new weapons did Americans see or use in World War I?
5. What do you think was the most important reason America declared war on Germany in 1917? If you had been a member of Congress in 1917, would you have voted for the declaration of war? Why or why not?

For Extra Interest: Have students make a bar graph of the casualties suffered by each European nation in World War I.

3. The Elusive Peace

BEFORE YOU READ: *What were the major proposals of Woodrow Wilson's Fourteen Points?*

Following the signing of the armistice in 1918, the leaders of the Allied Powers met to work out the terms of peace. Woodrow Wilson played an important role in these peace negotiations. When the treaty was finished, President Wilson brought it before Congress for approval. After a long and bitter debate, Congress rejected the treaty. The peace established by the treaty proved to be short-lived.

The Fourteen Points

In January 1918, ten months before the war ended, President Wilson addressed Congress to present his program for establishing a lasting peace. Wilson's proposal became known as the Fourteen Points. Wilson proposed that, after the war, all people should be guaranteed the right to live under a government of their own choosing. This right is called the right of **self-determination**.

---

self-determination the right of a people to live under a government of their own choosing

---

Wilson also proposed that the peace treaty guarantee freedom of the seas and the removal of barriers to trade among nations. Treaties should be openly negotiated. Also, each nation should reduce its stockpiles of weapons.

The fourteenth point was the one that Wilson regarded as the most important. It proposed that a "general association of nations" be formed. This association, or league, of nations would guarantee the independence and security of "great and small states alike." If any disputes among nations occurred, they could be peacefully settled by the league.

The Peace Commission

Representatives of the Allied Powers met near Paris for the peace negotiations. The peace conference was held at the Versailles (vehr-SIGH) Palace.

The members of the American Peace Commission were chosen by President Wilson. In making his choices, Wilson made two mistakes. First, he did not choose any senators to serve on the commission. Since the treaty would eventually have to be approved by the Senate, it would have been a good idea to involve senators in the negotiations. Wilson's second mistake was his failure to pick a prominent Republican to be on the commission. Wilson was a Democrat, but the Republicans had a majority in Congress. Wilson would need Republican support to get the treaty approved.

The most important member of the peace commission was to be Woodrow Wilson himself. Wilson was determined to direct the American negotiations for peace. On December 3, 1918, President Wilson left for Europe.

When Wilson arrived in Paris, he was greeted by the largest crowd in the history of France. To millions of Europeans, Woodrow Wilson was a hero. Wilson was the leader whose army had brought an end to the war. Wilson was the one who promised a just and lasting peace.

Background: In 1914, Italy had been part of an alliance with Germany and Austria-Hungary. However, in 1915, Italy entered the war on the side of the Allies after being promised territory in Austria when the war was over. Italy got this land at the peace conference.

The Versailles Treaty

The peace conference began on January 12, 1919. Germany and the other Central Powers were not allowed to participate in the conference. All of the important issues were decided by the leaders of the Allied delegations. These leaders became known as the Big Four: Wilson, Prime Minister David Lloyd George of Great Britain, Premier Georges Clemenceau (kleh-mahn-SOH) of France, and Premier Vittorio Orlando of Italy.

It soon became clear to Wilson that the other Allied leaders did not share his enthusiasm for the Fourteen Points. The Allies had made secret agreements among themselves during the war to divide the spoils of victory. Having fought the Central Powers for four years, they were more interested in revenge than justice.

Negotiations for the peace treaty that ended World War I were held at the Versailles Palace in France. Woodrow Wilson is shown here with the other Allied leaders.

The treaty that was negotiated at Versailles violated many of the Fourteen Points. It ignored the right of self-determination by providing that the boundary of Italy be moved northward into what had been Austria-Hungary. The new boundary placed inside Italy 200,000 people who considered themselves Austrians. The treaty also granted France the right to occupy, for 15 years, a portion of western Germany.

The Fourteen Points had said that colonial matters would be settled in an impartial way. The Treaty of Versailles, however, stripped Germany of its colonies and turned them over to the Allies for administration.

The Allies also demanded that Germany pay for all the damages caused to civilian property during the war. These payments, called **reparations**, amounted to $56 billion. This was a staggering burden, far beyond the ability of Germany to pay.

---

reparations payments by a defeated nation for damages caused during a war

---

The Versailles Treaty was a victor's treaty. The peace terms were very hard on the defeated Central Powers. Only four of Wilson's Fourteen Points were included in the treaty. After protesting the terms of the treaty without success, Germany signed the Versailles Treaty on June 28, 1919.

Discuss: Germany was especially angered and humiliated by the war guilt clause in the Versailles treaty. This clause forced the Germans to accept full responsibility for starting the war. Do you think this clause was fair? Why or why not?

Background: The Constitution states that all treaties made by the President must be approved by two thirds of the Senate.

The Great Debate

Although Wilson was disappointed with some parts of the treaty, there were reasons for him to be proud of it. The newly drawn borders of the European nations left fewer people on "foreign soil" than at any earlier time in history. The former German colonies were to be prepared for independence. And the treaty included the League of Nations.

When Wilson returned from France, he began the job of convincing Congress and the American people to approve the treaty. Although many Americans approved of the treaty, there were also many outspoken critics.

Some Americans opposed the treaty because it violated so many of the Fourteen Points. To them, the treaty seemed designed mainly to destroy Germany.

Other Americans opposed the treaty because it included the League of Nations. They feared that if the United States joined such an organization, it would become permanently involved in the disputes of Europe. They believed the United States should not join any international alliances. People who felt this way were **isolationists**.

---

isolationist a person who believes that his or her nation should not join international alliances or otherwise become involved in foreign affairs

---

Wilson found that the strongest opposition to the treaty and the League of Nations was in the Senate. The leaders of the opposition were all Republican senators.

As required by the Constitution, the treaty signed by the President had to be ratified by the Senate. If the Senate approved the treaty, it would also be approving American membership in the League of Nations. The debate in the Senate over the treaty, therefore, was mainly a debate over whether the United States should join the league.

The senators who opposed the league were divided into several groups. One group was completely opposed to the league. These extreme isolationists were called "irreconcilables." They could not be reconciled, or won over, to support the league. Leaders of this group were Senators William Borah of Idaho and Hiram Johnson of California.

Another group of opponents in the Senate were the "reservationists." They were opposed to the league as it was set up in the Treaty of Versailles. They might support the league, however, if certain changes were made. Senator Henry Cabot Lodge of Massachusetts, leader of this group, drew up a series of proposed changes, or "reservations."

The most important of Senator Lodge's reservations applied to Article 10 of the covenant of the League of Nations. This article required each member nation of the league to take action to protect the territory and independence of all other members. Lodge's reservation to this article said that the United States could not be forced to take any action by the league. Lodge feared that the United States might someday be required to take military action to protect some other member of the league against the will of the American people.

President Wilson regarded Article 10 to be the "heart of the Covenant." Without this article, the League of Nations would

Discuss: Compare the reservationists to the irreconcilables. How were their ideas on the league similar? How were their ideas different?

Discuss: Why do you think that Wilson, who had been willing to compromise with the leaders of other nations at the peace conference, was unwilling to compromise with the Senate on league issues?

not be able to enforce its decisions. The President would not accept Senator Lodge's reservation.

The Versailles Treaty was first submitted to the Senate Foreign Relations Committee. The chairman of the committee was the leader of the reservationists, Henry Cabot Lodge.

Lodge spent two weeks reading aloud to his committee the complete treaty. Then he held six weeks of public hearings on it. Every possible opponent of the treaty was given an opportunity to criticize the treaty and the league.

The Defeat of the Treaty

On September 3, 1919, President Wilson left on a speaking tour of the nation. He wanted to take his case for the League of Nations directly to the American people. He hoped the people would support him and force the Senate to approve the treaty.

Wilson spoke to crowds in the Midwest and the Great Plains. He then toured the West Coast. The climax of Wilson's trip came in a speech before a rally in Pueblo, Colorado, on September 25. As he appeared to make his address, the audience stood and cheered for a full ten minutes. With tears in his eyes, Wilson appealed for support for the League of Nations.

After his speech, the President collapsed. He was exhausted from three weeks of constant traveling and almost nonstop speaking. He returned to Washington where he suffered a stroke that paralyzed the left side of his body. President Wilson never fully recovered from the effects of this stroke.

In November, the Senate voted on the treaty with 14 of Senator Lodge's reservations attached to it. President Wilson urged his Democratic supporters to vote *against* it. The vote was 39 in favor of the treaty and 55 against it. Wilson's loyal Democrats had joined the Republican irreconcilables to defeat the treaty.

The treaty was then presented to the Senate without Lodge's reservations. The Senate rejected it again. The vote was 38 in favor and 53 against. This time the Republican reservationists and irreconcilables had united to defeat the treaty.

The defeat of the Treaty of Versailles was a tragedy for Woodrow Wilson and for the world. The League of Nations was greatly weakened by the failure of the United States to join it.

Section Review

1. What major proposals were contained in the Fourteen Points?
2. What mistakes did Woodrow Wilson make in choosing the members of the American Peace Commission?
3. Define reparations. What reparations were required of Germany?
4. Why did some Americans oppose the Versailles Treaty?
5. Who do you think was most responsible for the failure of the United States to join the League of Nations? Explain your answer.

For Extra Interest: Have interested students research and report to the class on the structure of the League of Nations.

Social Studies Skills

Comparing Maps

The Treaty of Versailles dramatically changed the map of the European mainland. Some nations gained land, and others lost land. New nations were created, and some nations ceased to exist at all.

The map below shows the national borders of Europe as they were drawn at the peace conference in Versailles in 1919. Compare this map to the map of Europe in 1914 on page 526. Each map shows different information. By comparing the two maps, it is possible to answer questions that could not be answered by using either map alone. Using the two maps together makes it possible to see how the political boundaries of Europe changed from 1914 to 1919.

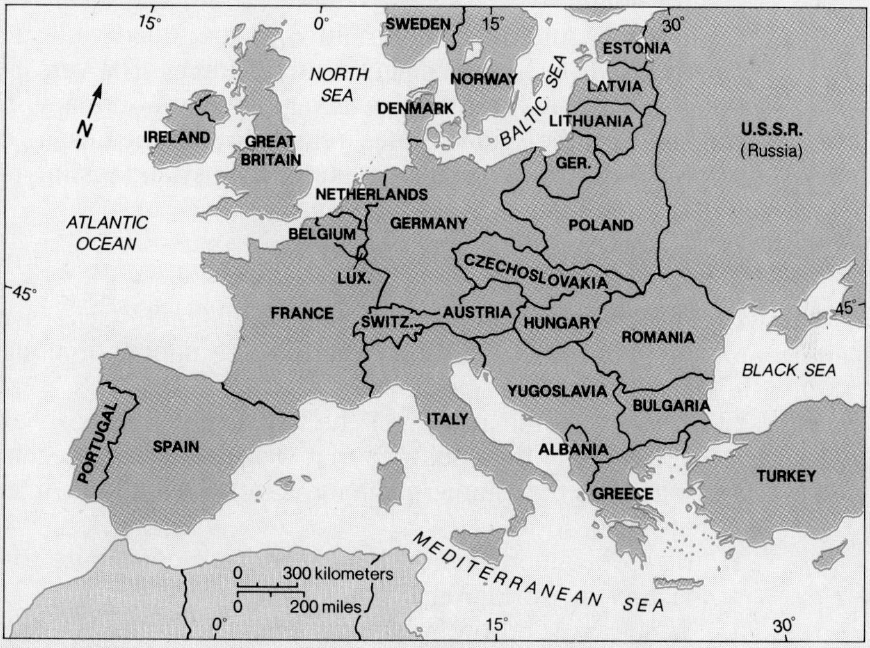

1. What new nations were formed in Europe in 1919?
2. What European nations ceased to exist in 1919?
3. The nation of Poland was formed on land previously controlled by three countries. Name these three countries.
4. Why do you think no changes were made in the national borders of Spain, Switzerland, and the Netherlands?

CHAPTER REVIEW

Summary

When Woodrow Wilson became President in 1913, he hoped to work primarily on progressive reforms. However, as problems developed in Latin America and Europe, foreign affairs became his chief concern. War with Mexico was successfully avoided, but Wilson was unable to keep the United States out of World War I.

Hostility and unrest had been growing in Europe since the late 1800's. Through a system of alliances, the war that started in 1914 as a minor conflict between Austria-Hungary and Serbia spread to most of Europe. Although frequently provoked, the United States managed to avoid military involvement for three years. However, in 1917, Wilson decided that the United States must enter the war to "make the world safe for democracy."

Millions of Americans contributed to the Allied victory by buying Liberty Bonds or by serving in the armed forces. The Versailles Treaty, which ended the war in 1918, was very harsh on Germany. This treaty, coupled with the United States' refusal to join the League of Nations, helped to destroy Wilson's dream for a "just and lasting peace."

Recalling the Facts

1. What was the purpose of the "cooling-off" treaties negotiated by Bryan in 1913–1914? What did the nations that signed them agree to?
2. What were the names of the two major European alliances in 1914? Name the countries that were members of each alliance.
3. What was the Zimmermann message? How did the American people react to it?
4. How did Americans on the home front contribute to the Allied victory in World War I?
5. Why was Woodrow Wilson disappointed in the Versailles Treaty? Why was he proud of it?

Analyzing the Facts

1. Why did such a small spark, the assassination of Archduke Francis Ferdinand, lead to world war?

2. In the 1790's, the United States had almost been drawn into a European war over its belief in the right to freedom of the seas. Why do you think this right was so important to Americans?
3. Do you think the United States should have entered World War I earlier than it did? Why or why not?
4. Which group do you think you would have supported concerning the League of Nations: the group that supported Wilson, the reservationists, or the irreconcilables? Explain your answer.
5. Twenty years after World War I ended, another major war broke out in Europe. Do you think this would have happened if the United States had ratified the Versailles Treaty and joined the League of Nations? Explain your answer.

Time and History

1913	1914	1915	1916	1917	1918	1919
Woodrow Wilson becomes President	World War I begins; United States declares neutrality	Wilson orders Marines to Haiti	Pancho Villa's army kills 17 Americans in New Mexico	Zimmermann message (Jan.)	Russia signs a peace treaty with the Central Powers (March)	Germany signs Versailles Treaty (June)
Huerta takes over the Mexican government		German U-boat sinks *Lusitania*	Wilson reelected	United States declares war on Germany (Apr.)	Armistice signed (Nov.)	United States Senate rejects Versailles Treaty (Nov.)

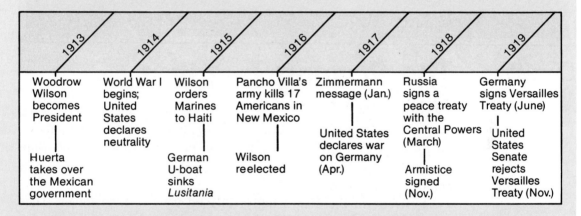

1. How many years after Wilson became President did the United States enter World War I?
2. How many years had Europeans been fighting in World War I before the United States entered the war?
3. What event before 1917 almost brought the United States into World War I? In what year did this happen?
4. Which of the following could *not* have been an issue in Wilson's reelection campaign: the sinking of the Lusitania, the Zimmermann message, or American neutrality in World War I?
5. Why did Russia not sign the Versailles Treaty?

Chapter
25

The Roaring Twenties

On May 21, 1927, a young man named Charles A. Lindbergh became the first person ever to fly alone across the Atlantic Ocean. Lindbergh became a great American hero. To some, he represented the old tradition of individual effort. Others viewed Lindbergh as a symbol of a new age of industry and progress.

Americans in the 1920's had a divided view of themselves. They enjoyed the excitement of prosperous good times. But they were also tired, even frightened, by the changes that had overwhelmed their world.

After you read this chapter, you will be able to:

1. List the causes of American prosperity in the 1920's.
2. Explain the causes of America's postwar mood of isolation and intolerance.
3. Compare the administrations of Harding and Coolidge.
4. Describe American economic problems in the 1920's.

Background: Americans had entered World War I believing they could "make the world safe for democracy." The horrors of the war and the harshness of the Treaty of Versailles caused many Americans to abandon their idealism and to question their ability to right wrongs.

1. Prosperity and Change

BEFORE YOU READ: *What were the causes of American prosperity in the 1920's?*

At the end of World War I, the American people were tired of international crises and war. They were also tired of idealism and reform. Americans longed for security, peace, relaxation, and good times. The 1920's was an era of "roaring" good times, prosperity, and great social and cultural change.

The Election of 1920

The mood of the American people was clearly expressed in the election of 1920. The Democrats nominated Governor James M. Cox of Ohio as their candidate. Cox pledged in his campaign to keep alive the ideals of Woodrow Wilson. He took a strong stand in favor of American participation in the League of Nations.

The Republicans chose as their candidate another Ohioan, Senator Warren G. Harding. Harding avoided taking a clear stand on the league. He offered no new ideals and called for no new reforms. Harding said, rather, that the nation should return to "normalcy." Harding never explained what he meant by the term "normalcy." Most Americans assumed that the term meant a retreat from the reforms and ideals of Woodrow Wilson and the progressives.

Warren G. Harding won the 1920 election in a **landslide** victory. The Republicans carried every state except for the solidly Democratic South.

landslide a large majority of votes for one candidate or party in an election

The Prosperity Decade

The nation's economy boomed in the years after World War I. The output of American manufacturers increased by 60 percent in the 1920's. Only about 2 percent of American workers were unemployed during the decade.

Several factors were responsible for the prosperity of the 1920's. Many European industries had been destroyed during the war. American industries expanded to supply the goods needed by Europe as it recovered from the war. The prosperity was also caused by an increased demand for goods among Americans. During the war years, goods of all sorts had been in short supply. People had saved their money. When the war was over, Americans were eager to buy new homes, household appliances, and other goods.

Government policies also contributed to the prosperity. High tariffs allowed American manufacturers to expand production and to increase profits. Taxes on corporation profits were lowered, leaving businesses more money to expand their operations.

The most important factor in the postwar prosperity of the United States was the growth of new industries. One of the new industries of the 1920's was the production of airplanes. Americans and Europeans had been experimenting with flying machines for many years. The first motor-driven heavier-than-air flight was made at Kitty Hawk, North Carolina, on

Background: The expansion of American industry was aided by the discovery of new oil and coal deposits and by the expanded use of electricity. By 1929, America was producing more electricity than the rest of the world combined.

Background: The price of an early Model T was $950. It was available in "any color you choose so long as it's black." The use of the assembly line method of production reduced the cost of the Model T to $290 in 1925.

December 17, 1903. The pilot was Orville Wright. Orville's flight was in a plane that he and his brother, Wilbur, had built themselves. The flight lasted 12 seconds. The plane traveled 37 meters (120 feet). By 1905, the brothers had succeeded in making a flight of over 39 kilometers (24 miles).

There was little interest in aircraft development until World War I. The use of the airplane as a weapon of war led to a rapid expansion of the aircraft industry. In 1926, Congress passed the Air Commerce Act. This act provided federal aid to private airlines carrying the mail. The act helped make the building and flying of airplanes a big business.

Charles Lindbergh's famous solo flight added to the popularity of flying. In 1928, Amelia Earhart became the first woman to fly across the Atlantic. By 1929, there were 122 commercial airlines in the United States. They carried nearly 500,000 passengers over 80,000 kilometers (50,000 miles) of air routes.

People took their Ford runabouts virtually everywhere, including to their favorite fishing hole.

The single most important new industry in the 1920's was the manufacturing of automobiles. There were many early attempts to build "horseless carriages." The first practical gasoline-powered automobiles were made in the late 1800's. By 1910, there were about 60 companies making autos in the United States.

The most successful early American auto maker was Henry Ford. Ford built his first automobile in 1896. He soon opened an automaking plant, and in 1908 he introduced the Model T. By 1914, Ford was selling 168,000 cars a year.

In the 1920's, Ford faced growing competition from other auto makers who offered the public new models with more appealing styles than the Model T. Ford met the challenge by introducing the Model A, which became one of the most popular cars in America.

The growth of the automobile industry in the 1920's was spectacular. In 1921, Americans purchased 1.5 million automobiles. In 1929, they bought over 5 million. At the end of the decade, there were over 23 million registered automobiles in the United States—an average of nearly one for each family.

Like the railroad of the late 1800's, the automobile contributed to the growth of other industries. The production of steel, rubber, oil, glass, and paint increased. A huge road-building campaign began. The nation's paved roadways increased from 622,800 kilometers (387,000 miles) in 1921 to 1,065,350 kilometers (662,000 miles) by 1929. Restaurants, motels ("*mo*tor ho*tels*"), gas stations, and the tourist industry all expanded to serve the needs of Americans behind the wheel.

Discuss: It has been said that the only things that really changed American life were the automobile and electricity. Do you agree or disagree? Why?

Discuss: Do you think we are a consumer society today? Why or why not? What are necessities today? What are luxuries?

A Changing Society

The 1920's were not only years of prosperity; they were also a time of great social change. The automobile, for example, put an end to the isolation of many rural areas. The automobile also spurred the growth of the suburbs. Workers could live in the suburbs and drive to their jobs in the cities.

Perhaps the most important change in the 1920's was a change in the buying habits of Americans. More people were buying goods for the pleasure of buying them. America in the 1920's was becoming a **consumer society**.

---

consumer society a society in which people buy goods for the pleasure of buying them rather than because of need

---

Many residents of America's cities came to regard as necessities goods that earlier had been luxuries. Vacuum cleaners, electric irons, washing machines, and other household appliances were purchased in great quantities. Advertisers *created* other needs by boosting the virtues of soaps, polishes, cosmetics, and a variety of other "consumer goods."

National tastes were influenced by new or expanded forms of entertainment. The motion picture industry expanded to become the fourth largest industry in the nation. The industry got a special boost in 1927 with the making of the first "talking picture," *The Jazz Singer*. People all across the nation enjoyed the same films in elaborate "movie palaces."

The first radio station in the United States, KDKA in Pittsburgh, began broadcasting in 1920. Two years later, there were over 500 stations in the nation. Radios made it possible for Americans all across the country to listen to the same program at the same time.

This radio drama was acted out in the studio in front of the microphone. The victims of a disaster lie groaning on the floor, while one man narrates and another makes sound effects.

The radio helped increase the popularity of national sporting events. Live broadcasts made national heroes of such sports figures as Babe Ruth, the first great home-run hitter in baseball. The radio also raised national interest in fads such as flagpole sitting and goldfish swallowing. The radio became the center of home entertainment.

New styles of music, such as jazz and ragtime, became popular throughout the nation. Dances like the Charleston and

Discuss: How do you think the new home appliances changed the life of women? What appliances would you like to see invented that would make your life easier?

Famous Americans

ANNIE SMITH PECK

As one of America's most daring mountain climbers, Annie Smith Peck made history. She broke women's and men's climbing records and scaled mountains never climbed before.

Annie Smith Peck became interested in mountain climbing at the age of 35 when she was traveling in Switzerland and saw the Matterhorn for the first time. She made her first important climb in 1888, when she scaled Mt. Shasta in California. In 1895, she climbed the Matterhorn and gained immediate fame. In addition to the climb itself, she attracted attention because of her unusual climbing outfit. Peck wore knickerbockers, a hip-length coat, sturdy boots and woolen hose, and a felt hat tied with a veil. Before this, women had climbed in dresses with less practical shoes and hats.

In 1897, Peck climbed the live volcano, Popocatepetl, and Mount Orizaba in Mexico. Mount Orizaba is 5,285 meters (18,314 feet) high. This was the highest point reached by a woman at that time. Peck's goal was to climb to "some height where no *man* had previously stood." She finally achieved her goal in 1908 when she reached the top of Mt. Huascarán in the Andes. The peak is 6,766 meters (22,198 feet) high. Annie Smith Peck had climbed higher in the Western Hemisphere than any other American woman or man. Peck's feat was covered worldwide.

Peck's expeditions were often underfinanced. She faced extreme danger because she could not afford to buy all the equipment she needed. She also could not afford to hire experienced assistants. Her last climb was made at the age of 82, when she climbed Mount Madison in New Hampshire.

Background: In 1930, Sinclair Lewis became the first American to win a Nobel Prize for literature.

the Black Bottom were enjoyed by Americans in all parts of the country.

Women's roles in society were also changing in the 1920's. More women began to enter the labor force. Women also began to have more social freedom. They started to wear shorter, more comfortable dresses and cut their hair in more practical styles. They spoke and acted more freely than ever before.

The Cultural Reaction

The prosperity of the 1920's caused a strong reaction among many American writers. They believed that American society was becoming too concerned with material wealth and was losing sight of its ideals. The writers of the 1920's, called the Lost Generation, felt separated from their own society, or **alienated**.

---

alienated feeling separated from one's own society

The most popular novelist of the 1920's was Sinclair Lewis. His novel *Main Street* (1920) portrayed the residents of small-town America as conceited and ignorant. *Babbitt* (1922) ridiculed life in the city and presented a very critical portrait of the American business executive.

F. Scott Fitzgerald was another member of the Lost Generation. His novel *This Side of Paradise* (1920) criticized the American dedication to material success. *The Great Gatsby* (1925) presented an account of the empty values of the 1920's.

Some American writers felt so alienated that they left the United States. Ernest Hemingway moved to Paris. There he wrote such books as *A Farewell to Arms* (1929), about the horrors and confusion of World War I.

Black American writers in the 1920's created art and literature that celebrated Afro-American culture. The center of black writing in the 1920's was the district of New York City known as Harlem. The Harlem Renaissance (renaissance means "rebirth") was the result of an outpouring of work by black poets, novelists, artists, and musicians. Langston Hughes, a black poet, expressed the spirit of the Harlem Renaissance. "We young Negro artists," Hughes wrote, "who create now intend to express our individual selves without fear or shame. If white people are pleased, we are glad. If they are not, it doesn't matter. We know we are beautiful. . . ."

Section Review

1. What were the causes of American prosperity during the 1920's?
2. What contribution did the automobile make to the growth of other American industries?
3. Define "consumer society." In what ways was America a consumer society during the 1920's?
4. Why were the writers of the 1920's alienated?
5. Why were many Americans ready for "normalcy" in the 1920's?

For Extra Interest: James Weldon Johnson wrote a beautiful poem called "Lift Every Voice and Sing." This poem, put to music, has often been called the "Black National Anthem." Have students listen to either a reading or a recording of this poem.

2. Isolation and Intolerance

BEFORE YOU READ: *Why did many Americans become isolationists in the 1920's?*

The mood of many Americans after World War I was one of isolation and intolerance. They wanted to be isolated from the affairs of other nations. They also were becoming less tolerant, or accepting, of people who were different from themselves.

Isolation

After World War I, the foremost concern of many Americans was to avoid becoming involved in another war. They wanted the United States to avoid any commitments that might lead to war.

Following the rejection of the Versailles Treaty, Congress passed a joint resolution declaring the war over. Separate peace treaties were then signed with the former Central Powers.

In 1921, the United States invited representatives from Great Britain, Japan, France, Italy, China, and three other nations to come to Washington for a conference. The conference discussed ways of reducing the number of naval weapons, or armaments, in the world. The representatives at the Washington **Disarmament** Conference also discussed mutual concerns in the Pacific and the Far East.

---

disarmament the reduction of weapons

Several major agreements came out of the Washington conference. The Five-Power Treaty was signed by the United States, Great Britain, Japan, France, and Italy. The signers of this treaty agreed to stop building battleships for ten years. They also agreed to limit the number of their other major naval vessels. In the Nine-Power Treaty, all the nations at the conference agreed to respect China's independence and to accept American's Open Door policy. Through these agreements, the United States hoped to preserve the peace. The agreements, however, were actually very weak.

The most impressive—and the weakest—treaty signed by the United States in the 1920's was the Kellogg-Briand Pact. Fifteen nations signed the pact in 1928. Each nation promised not to use war "as an instrument of national policy." The treaty provided no means, however, to enforce the promise. Critics of the pact said it was nothing more than an "international kiss."

The Red Scare

As World War I ended, a new enemy appeared. Many Americans were deeply disturbed by the Russian revolution of 1917. The new Russian government had taken over Russia's factories, railroads, and other means of producing and distributing goods. All property was to be owned in common by the Russian people. The government managed the property for the benefit of the people. This system was called **communism**. Many Americans feared that communists were planning a revolution in the United States. There were probably fewer than 100,000 communists in the United States in 1920. But the fear of revolution was great. In the

Discuss: Why is disarmament so difficult to achieve? What do you think would be a fair proposal for disarmament in today's world?

Background: Although Communists represented only a small percentage of the American population, Americans feared they could take over the government. They had seen how an equally small number of Communists had been able to seize power in Russia in 1917.

years after World War I, there were several major labor strikes around the country. Radicals had been involved in some of the strikes. There also were several bombings and attempted assassinations by radicals. Attempts had been made on the lives of John D. Rockefeller and Attorney General A. Mitchell Palmer.

---

communism an economic system in which all property, in theory, is owned by the people and managed by the national government

---

Radicals of all sorts—communists, socialists, and anarchists—were lumped together. They were all denounced as "reds," or revolutionaries. The nation was gripped by a fear called the "Red Scare."

In 1919, Attorney General A. Mitchell Palmer began a "red hunt" in the United States. Palmer believed that many of the reds were immigrants. He hoped to deport the reds or force them to leave the country. On January 2, 1920, federal agents arrested 6,000 suspected radicals in 33 different cities. Most of those arrested were American citizens. Many were unconnected with any radical group and were innocent of any wrongdoing. Only 556 of the 6,000 could be deported.

One of the most controversial episodes of the Red Scare was the arrest of two Italian radicals. During the robbery of a Massachusetts shoe factory in 1920, a guard and a paymaster had been killed. Nicola Sacco and Bartolomeo Vanzetti were arrested for the crime. Both men were Italian immigrants and anarchists. The evidence against them was weak. But the prejudice against them, because they were immigrants and radicals, was very strong. They were found guilty of the crime in 1921 and sentenced to death.

This painting of the Sacco and Vanzetti case shows demonstrators protesting at the left, Sacco and Vanzetti in the center, and the two men in their coffins at the right.

Background: The name "reds" came from the red flag that had been used by the Communists in Russia as a symbol of their revolution.

Background: Garvey was never able to secure a homeland in Africa for American blacks. His movement collapsed with the failure of his business ventures.

In August 1927, Sacco and Vanzetti were electrocuted. The outcry against their conviction and death helped bring the Red Scare to an end.

Racism and Nativism

The growth of American industry during and after World War I attracted many blacks to the North in search of better jobs. Blacks hoped that by moving north they would escape the rigid segregation of the South. They soon found, however, that segregation and discrimination also existed in the North.

New black leaders emerged in the 1920's. One of these was Marcus Garvey. Garvey urged blacks to leave America and to build a new society in the African "motherland." His slogan was "Back to Africa."

Beginning in 1919, a series of race riots broke out in many American cities. The first, and worst, riot occurred in Chicago. On a hot summer day in 1919, a black child was stoned and drowned as he swam near a "white beach" on Lake Michigan. For more than a week, residents of white and black neighborhoods battled each other. Thirty-eight people were killed. Riots in other cities during the summer of 1919 left 120 people dead.

Organized opposition to blacks also appeared. The Ku Klux Klan was reborn in 1915. The new Klan opposed blacks in all areas of the country. The Klan forced employers to fire blacks from their jobs. It also was responsible for public whippings and lynchings of blacks. By 1925, the Klan had 5 million members.

The Klan of the 1920's was also a nativist organization. It opposed the New Immigrants from southern and eastern Europe. It claimed that Catholics and Jews were a threat to the United States. Klan leaders wanted immigration restricted.

Many Americans shared the Klan's nativist fears. In 1921, Congress passed the Emergency Quota Act. This act limited the number of immigrants who could come to the United States each year. Every nation was given a quota of 3 percent of the number of its immigrants who were in the United States in 1910.

In 1924, Congress passed an even more restrictive act. The National Origins Quota Act reduced each nation's annual quota to 2 percent of the number of its immigrants residing in the United States *in 1890*. By choosing 1890, Congress reduced greatly the total number of immigrants allowed in. It also further discriminated against the New Immigrants. In 1890, there had been few southern and

Black Migration to Northern Cities

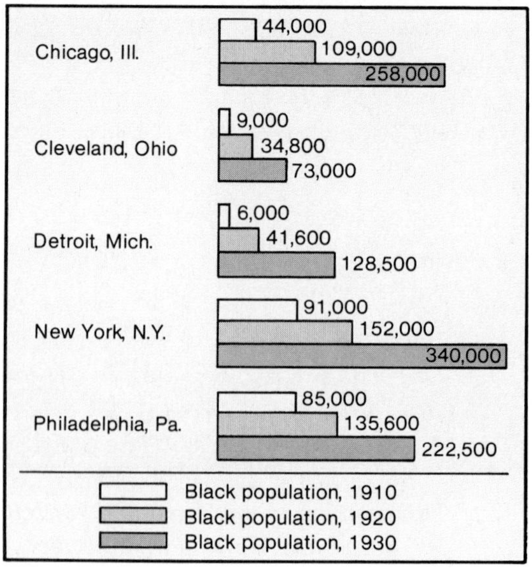

Background: The goal of the new Klan was "Native, white, Protestant supremacy." Klan members in the 1920's wore the same hooded costumes as Klan members had worn during Reconstruction.

Background: Liquor was smuggled over the Canadian and Mexican borders by "bootleggers." It was sold in illegal bars called "speakeasies." By the late 1920's, there were more speakeasies in the country than there had ever been bars.

eastern Europeans in the United States. The 1924 act banned entirely immigration from Japan and other Asian nations.

Country Versus City

By 1920, a majority of Americans lived in cities and towns. Yet many Americans continued to regard city ways with suspicion. They viewed cities as places of evil-doing and dangerous new ideas.

One of the evils identified with city life was alcohol. The movement against alcohol had begun well before the Civil War. By 1919, three-fourths of the states had approved the 18th Amendment to the Constitution. This amendment prohibited the making, transporting, and selling of alcohol. Support for Prohibition was strongest in the countryside. Prohibition had some benefits. It reduced the amount of alcohol consumed by the average American. But the amendment was never totally effective. The worst effect of Prohibition was its contribution to the rise of organized crime. Criminals took over the alcohol business. Gangs fought each other for the right to sell alcohol in the cities. In Chicago, the leading gangster was "Scarface Al" Capone. To run and defend his alcohol business, he hired 1,000 gun-carrying thugs.

The conflict between city and country also played a part in the famous Scopes trial of 1925. The trial centered on the controversial ideas of Charles Darwin. Darwin was a British scientist who argued that all plant and animal life had developed, or evolved, from earlier forms. Many Americans rejected Darwin's ideas because they directly challenged the Biblical account of creation.

In 1925, the state of Tennessee passed a law which forbade public school teachers from teaching "any theory that denies the story of the Divine Creation as taught in the Bible." To test the law, a biology teacher, John T. Scopes, deliberately violated the law and was arrested.

His trial in July 1925 attracted national attention. Most city newspapers ridiculed the Tennessee law. But rural Americans saw the trial as a defense of truth against evil new ideas.

Scopes was convicted of the crime and fined $100. Following the trial, four other states passed laws similar to the one in Tennessee. The Scopes trial deepened the gap between urban America and the American countryside.

Section Review

1. Why did more Americans become isolationists in the 1920's?
2. Define communism. What actions were taken against radicals during the Red Scare?
3. Which groups did the Ku Klux Klan oppose in the 1920's?
4. Identify the good and bad effects of Prohibition.
5. During the 1920's, many Americans who lived in the country had different attitudes from those who lived in the city. Do those differences continue today? Explain your answer.

Discuss: The lawyer for Tennessee was William Jennings Bryan. What connections did Bryan have with the American countryside?

Background: Harding once said, "I am a man of limited talents from a small town; I don't seem to grasp that I am President."

3. Republicans in Power

BEFORE YOU READ: *What scandals occurred during the administration of Warren G. Harding?*

The three Presidents who were elected in the 1920's were all Republicans. Although these Presidents differed in important ways, they shared common attitudes. Warren G. Harding, Calvin Coolidge, and Herbert Hoover firmly believed that government should play a limited role in the nation's affairs.

"A Good Second-Rater"

Warren G. Harding's promise of a return to "normalcy" was welcomed by a majority of American voters in the election of 1920. They were exhausted by the idealism of the progressives and the sacrifices of war.

Harding brought few qualities of leadership to the presidency. His handsome features and friendly personality helped him to be elected to the state legislature in Ohio and then to the United States Senate. When the Republican party picked him as its presidential candidate in 1920, one party leader remarked that Harding was "a good second-rater."

Harding received strong business support during the 1920 campaign. Harding favored a reduction in government regulation of business. And he urged more business leaders to serve in government jobs.

Harding chose many talented people to serve in his administration. Charles Evans Hughes served as secretary of state, Herbert Hoover headed the Commerce Department, Andrew Mellon was the secretary of the treasury, and Henry C. Wallace directed the Department of Agriculture.

The Harding Scandals

Some of the people Harding chose to work in his administration were corrupt. These individuals, known as the Ohio Gang, had served with Harding in state politics.

The leader of the Ohio Gang was a Republican party boss named Harry Daugherty. Harding chose Daugherty to be his attorney general. Unknown to Harding, Daugherty misused his office. He sold pardons and paroles to criminals. Daugherty was later arrested and tried for his crimes.

Harding picked Charles R. Forbes to be director of the Veterans Bureau. Forbes stole millions of dollars from the nation's taxpayers. He demanded and received kickbacks from businesses selling goods to the Veterans Bureau. When his crimes were uncovered, Forbes fled to Europe. Later he returned and was sent to prison for two years.

Another member of the Ohio Gang was Albert B. Fall. Harding chose Fall to be his secretary of the interior. In 1921, Fall arranged for two government oil reserves to be transferred from the Navy Department to the Interior Department. The oil reserves were at Elk Hills, California, and Teapot Dome, Wyoming. Fall then secretly leased these reserves to private oil companies.

The Elk Hills reserve was leased to a company headed by Edward L. Doheny. In

Discuss: How was Harding similar to the Presidents of the late 1900's? How was he different?

Television

No single person invented television. As with many technological achievements, it was the result of many people's efforts. Each scientist built on the work of others.

Crude experiments with television began as early as 1883, when a German scientist invented a mechanical device called a scanner. The scanner broke a picture into a sequence of tiny flashes of light. These flashes varied in brightness corresponding to the shades of gray in the picture being televised. The flashes were converted into electrical signals that transmitted the picture to the receiver or television set.

Similar experiments were done in the United States and Great Britain. The pictures that were produced using the mechanical scanners were only blurry shadows. Scientists realized that to get a good picture, they needed to develop a system that could scan electronically.

Progress toward an electronic scanner was made by the British and the Russians in the early 1900's. However, World War I put a stop to most experimentation with television.

After the war, a Russian scientist named Vladimir Zworykin came to the United States. Zworykin patented a partially electronic TV camera. Commercial interest in television began to build. Zworykin was hired by Westinghouse to develop his ideas further. By 1928, he had developed an improved camera

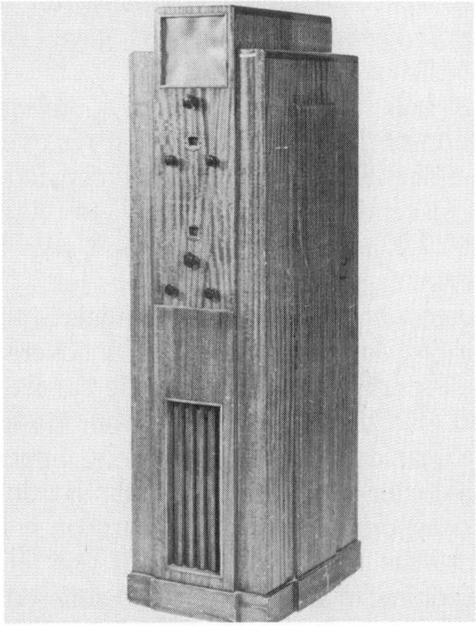

called the iconoscope.

Meanwhile, another approach to electronic television was being pursued by an Idaho inventor named Philo T. Farnsworth. In 1930, he developed an electronic scanning system that made television suitable for home viewing.

In the next ten years, all of these ideas came together, and the development of television flourished. By 1936, RCA was broadcasting experimental programs from the top of the Empire State Building in New York. On February 1, 1940, the National Broadcasting Company transmitted the first official network television broadcast in the United States. Television had begun to penetrate the lives of Americans.

Background: Fall was the first cabinet member ever to be so punished. He served a prison term but evaded the fine by signing a pauper's oath. Sinclair served a short prison term on other charges (jury tampering), and Doheny was acquitted.

return, Secretary Fall received a "loan" of $100,000 from Doheny. The "loan" was really a bribe. The Teapot Dome reserve was leased to an oil company run by Harry F. Sinclair. Sinclair gave Fall $300,000 and a herd of cattle.

In 1923, the Senate ordered an investigation of the leasing of the oil reserves. Secretary Fall was charged and convicted of accepting bribes. He was fined $100,000 and sentenced to one year in prison.

Just months before the scandals in the Harding administration were uncovered, the President took a trip to the Far West and Alaska. While returning from Alaska, the President suffered a painful attack. His doctor—an unqualified man Harding had appointed to serve as surgeon general—assured the President it was food poisoning. In fact, Harding had suffered a heart attack. He traveled on to San Francisco, where he had a second heart attack. On August 2, 1923, Harding died.

"Silent Cal"

The news of Harding's death was sent immediately to the Vice-President, Calvin Coolidge, who was sworn in as President. Coolidge pledged to continue the policies of Harding. Coolidge shared Harding's belief that government should interfere as little as possible with business or other activities of the nation. This style of government matched Coolidge's personality. He was a man of little action and few words. He slept as much as 14 hours a day—including long afternoon naps. He issued few public statements and even tried to avoid private conversations.

Coolidge's nickname, "Silent Cal," was well deserved. According to a popular joke in the 1920's, a woman once sat beside Coolidge at a dinner party. The woman said, "Mr. President, I made a bet with my husband that I could get you to say three words." The President looked at her and replied, "You lose."

In 1924, Calvin Coolidge ran for a second term and won the election with nearly 16 million popular votes. Coolidge's popularity rested largely on the prosperity of the 1920's. The Republicans took full credit for the prosperity. They claimed that the good times had been caused by their probusiness policies. Coolidge was a great admirer of business. He once remarked that "the business of America is business." His able assistants—many of whom had served in the Harding administration—carried out Coolidge's probusiness policies.

Secretary of the Treasury Andrew W. Mellon urged that taxes on corporations and wealthy individuals be lowered. He believed that lower taxes would encourage businesses and their leaders to be more productive. Congress responded by cutting taxes by more than half. At the same time, tariffs were raised to protect industries from foreign competition.

Commerce Secretary Herbert Hoover encouraged businesses to cooperate with each other. Corporations should be allowed, not forbidden, to exchange information about markets and products.

In the 1920's, business leaders were appointed to serve on the Interstate Commerce Commission, the Federal Trade Commission, and the Federal Reserve Board. Rather than controlling business, the commissions themselves came to be controlled *by* business.

Background: Coolidge had attracted national attention in 1919 when, as the governor of Massachusetts, he broke a police strike in Boston by ordering the state militia to keep order. His antiunion stand attracted the support of business and the Republicans.

Discuss: If Calvin Coolidge had decided to run for reelection in 1928, do you think he would have won? Why or why not?

The Supreme Court in the 1920's weakened the power of the federal government to regulate business or to take antitrust action. During the 1920's, 8,000 mining and manufacturing companies combined into larger organizations. Four tobacco companies were making 90 percent of the nation's cigarettes. Three auto companies produced 90 percent of all cars.

The Election of 1928

When Calvin Coolidge decided not to run for reelection in 1928, the Republicans chose his secretary of commerce, Herbert Hoover, as their candidate. Hoover was a very talented man and well qualified to be President.

Before going to work for the government, Hoover had made a fortune as a mining engineer. He worked in many parts of the United States, as well as overseas. He entered public service in 1914. Hoover helped get emergency food supplies to people who had fled their homes or whose homes had been destroyed during World War I. During and after the war, Hoover supervised the feeding of other European **refugees**. His efforts helped save the lives of millions of people.

---

refugee a person who has fled his or her home during a time of war or other emergency

---

Hoover's opponent in the election of 1928 was the governor of New York, Alfred E. Smith. The backgrounds and personalities of the two men were quite different. Whereas Hoover had been born and raised in the Iowa countryside, Al Smith had grown up in New York City. Hoover was Protestant; Smith was a Catholic. The two candidates also differed on an important issue: Prohibition. Hoover supported Prohibition; Smith opposed it.

Herbert Hoover won a landslide victory in the election of 1928. He even received majorities in five states of the Democratic South. Many voters in the countryside rejected Smith because he was a New Yorker and an opponent of Prohibition. Others voted against him because of his religion. The biggest factor in Hoover's victory, however, was the Republican record of prosperity. Hoover, most people expected, would lead the country into many more years of good times.

Section Review

1. What major scandals occurred during the presidency of Warren G. Harding?
2. How did Coolidge's style of government match his personality?
3. What actions did the Republican leaders of the 1920's take that were probusiness?
4. Why did Herbert Hoover win the election of 1928?
5. Which of the three Presidents of the 1920's do you believe was most qualified to be President? Explain your answer.

Background: Smith was the first Catholic to run for the presidency. He had been elected governor of New York four times before running for President.

4. Signs of Trouble

BEFORE YOU READ: *What problems did American industries have in the 1920's?*

The prosperity of the 1920's was built on a shaky foundation. The United States had serious economic problems—problems too many Americans tried to ignore.

Problems of Industry

Although business boomed in the 1920's, some industries experienced hard times. Many factories switched from coal to oil as their primary fuel. As a result, the coal industry went into decline. Also, many Americans began buying clothing made from rayon or other synthetic fabrics. This caused the production of cotton and wool cloth to decline.

An important factor in the prosperity of the 1920's was the expansion of old industries and the development of new ones. Two of the most important industries were construction and automobiles. Even in these industries, however, there were signs of trouble in the 1920's. Both industries expanded too much and too rapidly. More new buildings were constructed and more new automobiles were produced than Americans could buy.

In 1925, over $5 billion worth of new homes and apartments were constructed in the United States. Four years later, only $3 billion worth of new residences were built. The automobile industry continued to expand, but after 1925 it grew at a much slower rate. The auto manufacturers reduced their orders for glass, steel, and rubber. These related industries declined. By 1929, it was clear that the automobile industry had overexpanded. Auto dealers across the nation had a large supply of unsold cars.

Foreign Problems

Americans also became involved in a complex set of economic problems in Europe. During World War I, the Allies had borrowed billions of dollars from the United States. After the war, the victorious Allies demanded heavy reparations from Germany. Germany, however, was unable to pay its debts. As a result, the Allies found it hard to pay back U.S. loans made to them.

In 1924, the United States announced the Dawes Plan to help solve these problems. Under this plan, American bankers would loan money to Germany. Germany would use the money to pay the reparations to the Allies. The Allies would then be able to make payments on their wartime loans.

The United States was thus becoming deeply involved in the economic affairs of Europe. In addition to making loans to Germany, American banks were also loaning money to European businesses. Yet at the same time, the United States was adopting higher tariffs. The tariffs kept many European goods from being sold in the United States. Europeans, unable to sell their goods in America, found it difficult to earn the money they needed to pay back the loans.

In 1928, bankers in the United States reduced the amount they were willing to loan to Germany and to European businesses. The whole system of loans and payments began to fall apart.

 Background: Finland was the only nation to pay its war debt to the United States in full.

Background: The McNary-Haugen bill authorized the government to purchase the surpluses of various commodities. These would either be kept off the market until prices rose or be sold abroad. Coolidge vetoed the bill in 1927 and again in 1929 because it involved price fixing.

Calvin Coolidge was raised on a farm, but he had little sympathy for the problems of American farmers in the 1920's.

The Farmers' Condition

The 1920's were not good years for American farmers. The problems the farmers had faced in the late 1800's had not been solved. In some ways, their problems had only gotten worse.

During World War I, many farms in Europe were destroyed. American farmers expanded their production to meet the needs of the Europeans. When the war ended, European farms resumed production. The demand for American farm products dropped rapidly. In the meantime, the demand for farm products inside the United States grew only very slowly.

The farmers' basic problem in the 1920's was the same as it had been in the 1890's: overproduction. Improvements in farm machinery and farming methods continued to increase the output of the nation's farms. The price of farm products continued to fall. Total farm income fell by nearly 50 percent during the 1920's.

The federal government in the 1920's seemed unwilling to help solve the farmers' problems. Congress passed several bills to aid farmers, but they were vetoed by President Coolidge. "Farmers have never made much money," President Coolidge remarked in 1928. "I don't believe we can do much about it."

Workers in the Twenties

Wages and working conditions for American workers improved in many industries in the 1920's. The wage of the average American worker rose 26 percent between 1919 and 1929. Henry Ford led the way in raising wages and shortening the workweek of his employees. Ford workers were even given paid vacations. Workplaces were made safer, and the number of industrial accidents declined.

In spite of these benefits, American workers were not receiving a fair share of the prosperity of the 1920's. Their increases in wages were far below the increases in profits for the business owners. More than two thirds of all Americans lived at the "minimum comfort level." About one third lived in poverty.

The wealth of the nation was controlled by a few very wealthy families. Rather than trying to divide the wealth more evenly, the government in the

Discuss: Should workers' salaries go up as profits rise? If profits were to rise by 300 percent, should workers' salaries also go up 300 percent? Why or why not?

Discuss: Credit cards are one method of installment buying. What are some advantages of credit card buying to the customer and to the economy? What are some of its disadvantages?

1920's reduced taxes on the income of the wealthy.

The problem of an unfair division of wealth was not just a problem for workers. It was a problem for business as well. The growth and prosperity of business depended on the ability of Americans to buy its products. In the 1920's, workers and farmers were simply not earning enough money to buy the products of American industry.

For a while, this problem was hidden because many Americans were buying goods by paying only a small part of the total price of the items. Each month they paid another small amount, or an installment. This method of buying goods is called the **installment plan**. Each installment also included an extra charge for the unpaid amount, called **interest**. Eventually, many Americans reached the point where they could not afford to add any more payments to their family budget. As more and more American families reached this point, the demand for goods from American industry declined.

---

installment plan a method of buying goods in which a person pays only a small part of the total price and makes regular payments plus interest for the rest of the amount

interest a charge for borrowing money

Unions in the 1920's offered American workers little help. Union membership declined from 5 million in 1920 to about 4.3 million in 1929.

Many of the unions in the 1920's were "company unions." These unions were created by the employers to represent the workers. The company unions were very weak. They were usually forbidden to bargain over such important matters as wages and working hours.

Employers directly attacked the union movement in the 1920's. Unions were branded as un-American by business leaders. Workers were warned to have nothing to do with any unions other than the company unions. Businesses joined a campaign called the American Plan to "protect" workers from the unions. Business leaders said that no worker should be required to join a union. They favored what was known as the **"open shop."**

---

open shop a shop or business in which workers are not required to join a union

---

Government policy in the 1920's also weakened the unions. In 1921, the Supreme Court decided that courts could issue injunctions to stop strikes. This weakened the protection given workers in the Clayton Act of 1914. The Court struck down a federal law regulating child labor in 1922. The following year, it declared unconstitutional a minimum-wage law for women in Washington, D.C.

Wall Street

Another serious problem of the 1920's was the way shares of corporation stocks were bought and sold. Like the other economic problems of the 1920's, many people chose to ignore the problem of the stock market.

The main stock market in the United States is the New York Stock Exchange. Its headquarters are on Wall Street in New York City. The stock market itself is often

Discuss: Why might a stockbrokerage use a bull in its advertisements?

called "Wall Street." The price of a stock being traded on Wall Street depends on business conditions, profits, and other factors. If many people want to buy shares of stock in a company, the price of the stock will rise. If many stockholders want to sell their shares, the price will go down. Prices of stocks on Wall Street rose steadily in the 1920's.

When prices rise on Wall Street, people say it is a "bull market." If prices go down, it is a "bear market." From the spring of 1928 to the fall of 1929, Wall Street experienced the Great Bull Market. The stock of one radio company, for example, rose from $94 per share on March 3, 1928, to $120 on March 10. By March 13, its price had risen to $160. People who bought ten shares of radio stock on March 3 for $940 could sell it 12 days later for $1,600.

More and more people got "in the market" during the 1920's. They paid only a small part of the stock's price and borrowed the rest from an agent who buys and sells stock. The agent is a **stockbroker**. This method of buying stocks—similar to buying goods on the installment plan—is called buying "on margin."

---

stockbroker an agent who buys and sells stock and bonds

Buying stocks on margin became a national craze. People borrowed more and more money to buy stocks. As long as prices continued to go up, people could sell their stocks at a profit and pay off their loans. The Great Bull Market, however, came to a sudden halt in the fall of 1929. People who had bought stocks on margin were suddenly in deep trouble. As the price of stocks fell, hundreds of thousands of Americans were unable to pay their debts.

The Republican leaders of the 1920's had made a serious mistake. They had assumed that the special interests of business and the general well-being of the nation were the same. Many businesses in the 1920's made huge profits. Yet the nation's economy was not healthy. It would take a serious crisis for the nation to recognize and solve its problems. That crisis came in the fall of 1929.

Section Review

1. Which American industries had problems in the 1920's? What were these problems?
2. What basic problem did American farmers have? What was the cause of this problem?
3. Many workers and farmers earned very little money in the 1920's. Why was this a problem for American business? How did the installment plan help hide this problem?
4. How can a person today find out the price of shares of stock on Wall Street? Is today's stock market a "bull market" or a "bear market"?

Background: People buying stock on margin borrowed from 50 to 90 percent of the purchase price from stockbrokers. The brokers borrowed the money they loaned out from banks.

CHAPTER REVIEW

Summary

By 1920, many Americans were tired of the reforms and sacrifices that had marked the previous decade. They wanted to enjoy themselves. Postwar prosperity allowed Americans to buy labor-saving devices and enjoy expanded forms of entertainment. Most Americans adopted an attitude of uninvolvement in domestic reforms and world affairs.

Americans elected three Presidents in the 1920's. Harding, Coolidge, and Hoover all believed that the government should play a limited role in the nation's affairs. They felt that if business prospered, all America would be prosperous.

The 1920's was also a period of intolerance and prejudice. People who were "different" were seen as a threat to American prosperity and security. Efforts were made to rid the country of people who supported revolutionary principles. Blacks, Catholics, Jews, and certain immigrant groups were harassed by nativists and racists.

Caught up in the "good times" and intolerance of the decade, few Americans realized that the prosperity of the 1920's rested on a shaky foundation. They failed to see that prosperity could not continue if the economic problems of the nation remained unsolved.

Recalling the Facts

1. Explain two social changes that occurred in the 1920's as a result of the automobile.
2. How did the prosperity of the 1920's affect women?
3. Give two examples that illustrate American intolerance in the 1920's.
4. How was the division in American life between the country and the city reflected in Prohibition and the Scopes trial?
5. What common attitudes were held by the three Presidents elected in the 1920's?
6. What two groups of people never shared in the prosperity of the 1920's? What caused them to be left out? What did the government do to help them?

Analyzing the Facts

1. Why was Warren G. Harding such a popular candidate in the presidential election of 1920?
2. Why do you think that the peace treaties signed in the 1920's did not prevent future wars?
3. Most black Americans were not interested in going "back to Africa" as Marcus Garvey proposed. Why do you think this was so?
4. People often negatively associate President Harding with the scandals that occurred during his administration. If you were to say something positive about President Harding, what would it be?

Time and History

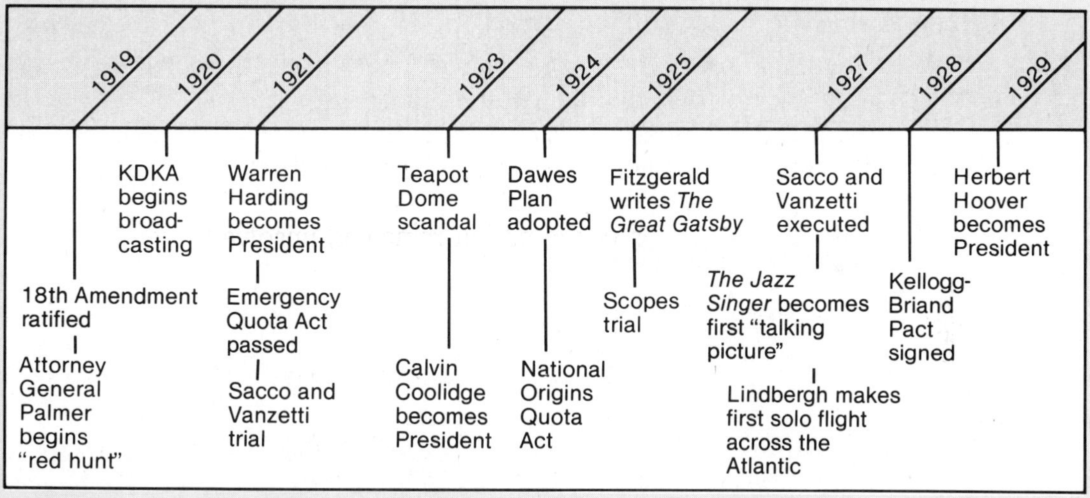

1. When did the Coolidge administration begin and end?
2. How many years passed between the trial and execution of Sacco and Vanzetti?
3. In what year could Americans begin to listen to the radio?
4. In what two years were laws passed that set quotas on the number of immigrants allowed to enter the United States?
5. Who wrote *The Great Gatsby* in 1925?

UNIT REVIEW

Summary

Americans entered the twentieth century full of optimism and hope. Reformers, called progressives, worked hard to solve the many political and social problems that existed in this country in the early 1900's. Changes were made in government to eliminate corruption and give the people a greater role in the political process. Laws were passed to improve working conditions in the nation's factories. The government also attacked the abuses of big business by passing regulations to control them.

By 1914, however, international problems began to demand more attention than domestic reforms. Bitter rivalries among European nations led to the outbreak of a major war. The United States tried to remain neutral, but was eventually drawn into the conflict in 1917. With American military help, the war came to an end in 1918.

After the war, many Americans wanted little to do with domestic reforms or international problems. They soon became caught up in the "good times" of the 1920's. For ten years, Americans ignored the problems that would lead to an economic crisis in 1929.

Recalling the Facts

1. Explain how the direct primary, the initiative, the referendum, and the recall gave people a greater role in the political process.
2. Name and identify two laws that were passed during the progressive period to regulate business.
3. Describe the events that eventually forced the United States to enter World War I.
4. What were Wilson's Fourteen Points? Why did he feel they were so important?
5. What accounted for American prosperity in the 1920's?

Analyzing the Facts

1. Compare the role of government in business affairs during the progressive era to the role that government played in the 1920's.
2. Why was World War I the most destructive that the world had experienced?

3. One of the major reasons Europe went to war in 1914 involved its alliances. The United States today has signed numerous treaties that tie it closely to other world nations. Do you think that alliances are dangerous and lead to war, or do you think that strong alliances can be made that maintain peace?
4. Explain how the intolerance of the 1920's could be viewed as both supportive and destructive of the American way of life.

Reviewing Vocabulary

Define the following terms.

suffrage	armistice	disarmament
racism	self-determination	communism
pacifist	reparations	installment plan
nationalism	alienated	interest

Sharpening Your Skills

Answer the three questions below based on the photograph on page 522.

1. How old do these soldiers appear to be?
2. What does this photograph tell you about how the soldiers felt about one another?
3. What does this photograph add to what you have learned about World War I?

Answer the two questions below, using the maps shown on pages 504 and 509.

4. Which states that had granted full voting rights to women by 1912 cast electoral votes for Theodore Roosevelt?
5. In which state casting electoral votes for Taft were women *not* allowed to vote?

Writing and Research

1. Write a biographical report on one person discussed in this unit. Include a summary of his or her contributions.
2. Write a short story about a person your age who lived during one of the following times: the progressive era, World War I, the 1920's.

Unit

8 Depression and War

26 *The Roaring Twenties came to a sudden halt in 1929. The stock market crashed, many businesses failed, and millions of Americans lost their jobs. The 1930's were the years of the Great Depression. President Franklin D. Roosevelt offered the nation a New Deal of reform, recovery, and relief. During the 1930's, the United States began to recover from the depression.*

O'ER THE RAMPARTS WE WATCH
UNITED STATES
ARMY AIR FORCES

27 *The 1930's were also years of growing international crisis. The leaders of Germany, Italy, and Japan engaged in unprovoked attacks on their neighbors. By 1939, the world was again at war. The United States tried to remain neutral. Eventually, however, the nation provided aid to some of the war's participants.*

28 *On December 7, 1941, the American naval base at Pearl Harbor, Hawaii, was attacked by Japan. Following this, the United States entered World War II. American military forces played a major role in turning the tide against the enemy. The war came to an end in 1945 with the use of a spectacular new weapon, the atomic bomb.*

Chapter
26

The Great Depression

George Turner was riding with his parents in their car when the "black blizzard" struck. A towering black cloud of dust moved across the town of Logan, Oklahoma. "It was an unbelievable darkness," George later recalled. " . . .We seemed to be smothering in dust."

The southern Great Plains in the 1930's became a Dust Bowl. Drought dried the land, and winds blew monstrous dust storms. Farms were ruined. The rest of the country was also suffering from hard times. A new President was elected who promised to bring the hard times to an end.

After you read this chapter, you will be able to:

1. Describe Herbert Hoover's response to the Great Depression.
2. Identify the major programs of Franklin Roosevelt's New Deal.
3. Explain the impact of the New Deal on American life.

For Extra Interest: Invite a stockbroker to class to discuss how the stock market works and what controls are placed on the buying and selling of stock today to prevent another crash.

1. Crash and Depression

BEFORE YOU READ: *What actions did President Herbert Hoover take to end the depression of the 1930's?*

The prosperity of the 1920's came to a sudden halt in the fall of 1929. The nation entered a period of severe economic crisis. Prosperity was replaced by hard times. Thousands of businesses failed, and millions of Americans lost their jobs.

The Stock Market Crash

The great bull market began to weaken in early September 1929. Prices of stocks dropped. Prices of stock on Wall Street are reported as "points." A stock that sells for $18.50 a share, for instance, is listed on the New York Stock Exchange at 18 1/2 points. In late October 1929, prices on Wall Street began dropping rapidly. On Monday, October 28, the price of stock of United States Steel dropped 17 1/2 points. The stock of Westinghouse Electric Company dropped 34 1/2 points.

October 29, 1929, is known as "Black Tuesday." It was the worst day in the history of Wall Street. Prices of industrial stocks dropped an average of 43 points. But that was only the beginning. Stock prices continued to drop further. By mid-November, prices had declined by 228 points. By July 1932, stock prices had fallen by nearly 400 points.

Why did the stock market crash in 1929? Too many people had bought stocks "on margin." As prices began to drop, shareholders feared they would not be able to pay their debts. People rushed to sell their stocks. Their selling of stock only caused prices to drop more rapidly.

If the economy had been strong and healthy, the stock market could have recovered from this decline in prices. But the economy in 1929 was not healthy.

Following the stock market crash, the nation's economy went into a long downward slide. Business activity in the nation slowed. Prices and wages declined. Many workers lost their jobs. The 1930's were the years of the Great **Depression**.

---

depression a period in which business activity slows, prices and wages decline, and many workers lose their jobs

---

The stock market crash was only one of many factors that contributed to the Great Depression. The crash reduced the incomes of American investors. Less money, therefore, was available for investment in corporations. Without new investments, businesses could not expand. The "drying up" of investment money was a major contributor to the depression.

Several basic weaknesses of the American economy also contributed to the depression. The most important of these weaknesses was the poor distribution of the nation's wealth. The incomes of millions of American farmers and workers were too low. Many could no longer afford to buy the products of American industry. At the same time, many American businesses during the 1920's had expanded too rapidly and produced too many goods. The large supply of unsold goods caused prices and profits to decline further.

Discuss: How does business benefit in the long run by giving workers a larger percentage of the profits in wages?

Background: Automobile production fell from 4.5 million vehicles in 1929 to 1.1 million in 1932. In 1931, Ford closed his Detroit plants, and 75,000 workers lost their jobs. The decline in auto production affected thousands of go-betweens and suppliers as well.

Government policy also contributed to the economic collapse. Insufficient regulation of corporations, banks, and industries had led to poor business practices. High tariffs had reduced foreign trade. American manufacturers found it more and more difficult to sell their products overseas.

Hard Times

The slowdown in business activity during the 1930's was astounding. By 1932, the output of the nation's manufacturing plants was about half of what it had been in 1929. Between 1929 and 1932, over 100,000 American companies went out of business.

Especially disturbing was the collapse of many of the nation's banks. Banks had not been properly regulated by the government in the 1920's. Many had made poor use of their depositors' money. In 1929, more than 650 banks went out of business, or "failed." They were unable to pay back the money people had deposited in them. In 1930, over 1,350 banks failed. The next year, nearly 2,300 banks closed their doors.

In the three years after the stock market crash, an average of nearly 100,000 workers lost their jobs each week. By the fall of 1930, 4 million Americans were out of work. Two years later, 11 million were unemployed. Roughly 25 percent of the labor force was jobless in 1933. In the

Scenes such as this were common across the United States as unemployed workers faced the hardships of the depression.

Background: John Steinbeck's *The Grapes of Wrath* is one of the best portrayals of American suffering during the depression. The novel describes an Oklahoma family driven by drought and hard times to abandon their farm and become migrant workers in California.

major industrial cities, the **unemployment rate** was even higher. In Toledo, Ohio, the unemployment rate in 1932 was 80 percent.

unemployment rate the percentage of workers who are jobless

Many workers who were lucky enough to keep their jobs had their wages and hours cut. Between 1929 and 1933, the average wage of workers in American manufacturing plants was cut by 60 percent. Child labor again became a problem. In one factory, 13-year-old girls were paid 50 cents a day to pack goods. Even baseball star Babe Ruth had to take a cut in pay. His salary for 1932 was $10,000 less than it had been the year before.

Middle-class Americans and professionals also faced hard times. Bankers, lawyers, and teachers lost their jobs. Some ended up working as laborers, earning far less than they did before the depression.

Many families were unable to pay their monthly rents or house payments. They had to leave their homes. The fortunate ones found cheaper places to live or moved in with relatives. Others, not so fortunate, had to live in shacks built of scrap lumber. Many simply lived out-of-doors. By 1932, between 1 and 2 million Americans were wandering across the country. They had neither jobs nor homes.

Food was a problem for many. Thousands of people stood in "bread lines," waiting to get a free loaf of bread. "Soup kitchens," offering free bowls of soup, were opened by churches and other charities. In a St. Louis garbage dump, families dug for food. Children and their parents ate weeds and roots in the hills of Pennsylvania. New York hospitals in 1931 admitted 238 persons suffering from starvation. Forty-five of them died.

Farmers were hit especially hard by the depression. Prices for their crops—always pitifully low—dropped to even lower levels. Between 1929 and 1932, wheat prices fell from $1.05 per 35 liters (1 bushel) to 39 cents. Cotton prices dropped from 17 cents to 6 cents per 0.45 kilograms (1 pound). In many areas, farmers could not afford to harvest their crops or bring their livestock to market. Crops were left to rot in the fields. Cattle and pigs were destroyed. Total farm income in the United States dropped from almost $12 billion in 1929 to just $5 billion in 1932.

Hoover's Response

Herbert Hoover was President when the Great Depression began. At first, Hoover hoped that a program of voluntary cooperation would end the depression. He urged business leaders to increase production and not to cut wages. Farmers were encouraged to reduce the size of their crops.

President Hoover also directed the federal government to take action. Congress passed the Agricultural Marketing Act in 1929. This law provided loans to farm "cooperatives" to buy surplus crops. By holding surplus crops off the market, it was hoped that farm prices would rise. In 1930, Congress passed the Hawley-Smoot Tariff. The tariff on most foreign manufactured goods and farm products was

Background: The Hawley-Smoot Tariff was the highest tariff in our nation's history. Within two years of its passage, 25 nations raised their tariffs in retaliation.

Discuss: Why do you think Hoover's program of voluntary cooperation to end the depression did not work?

raised. The higher tariff was intended to protect American businesses and farms from foreign competition.

Hoover's most important program to end the depression was the Reconstruction Finance Corporation (RFC). This agency was created by Congress in 1932. The RFC was set up to loan money to banks, railroads, and other businesses. Hoover hoped that the RFC would save businesses from failing.

Unfortunately, most of Hoover's programs did little to solve the nation's problems. The RFC saved many businesses from failing. But the Agricultural Marketing Act failed because it placed no controls on farm production. Likewise, the Hawley-Smoot Tariff did little good. Other countries soon raised their tariffs, and the United States lost many of its foreign markets.

The nation's most pressing problem was the unemployment and poverty of millions of Americans. President Hoover believed this problem should be solved by private charities and by state and local governments. But these groups soon exhausted their resources. By 1932, more than 100 major cities had no money left for relief payments.

President Hoover strongly opposed any direct federal aid to the poor. He believed that such aid would destroy the character of those who received it. They would become, he feared, permanently dependent on the federal government.

The mood of the country began to turn ugly. In Henryetta, Oklahoma, unemployed workers raided food stores. Nebraska residents armed themselves with pitchforks to stop sheriff's deputies from removing them from their homes.

The largest protest came from a group of World War I veterans. In 1924, Congress had authorized payment of a bonus to all veterans. The bonus was to be paid in 1945. In the spring of 1932, between 15,000 and 20,000 unemployed veterans marched to Washington. They demanded that Congress pay them their bonus immediately. Congress refused. Many of the veterans and their families stayed on in Washington. They lived in shacks along the Potomac River.

The "Bonus Marchers" were an embarassment to President Hoover. He ordered the police to remove them. The veterans' camp was attacked by troops armed with machine guns, tear gas, and tanks. As the soldiers moved through the camp, they burned the veterans' shacks. In the attack, 100 veterans were injured, and one baby died.

The Election of 1932

As the depression worsened, more and more Americans blamed President Hoover. He was criticized, and even ridiculed, across the nation. Communities of homeless people, living in crude shelters, were called "Hoovervilles." Unemployed workers who slept on park benches called their newspaper bedsheets "Hoover blankets." People with no money wore "Hoover flags," empty pockets turned inside out.

The Republicans nominated Herbert Hoover for reelection in 1932. Few, however, believed he had much chance of winning.

The Democrats chose the governor of New York, Franklin Delano Roosevelt, as their candidate. In accepting the nomina-

Background: In February 1930, Congress passed a law authorizing a loan of 50 percent on the veterans' bonus certificates. Democratic leaders later proposed that the entire bonus be paid in cash. Pressure for approval of this measure resulted in the "Bonus March."

Vocabulary Help: polio (short form of poliomyelitis)—an infectious disease caused by virus particles that attack the gray matter of the brain and spinal cord. From 47 to 75 percent of the cases result in paralysis. In 1955, a vaccine was developed by Dr. Jonas E. Salk.

tion, Roosevelt declared to the convention: "I pledge you, I pledge myself, to a new deal for the American people."

Roosevelt's career in politics began in the early 1900's. He served in the New York State legislature and then, during the Wilson administration, was the assistant secretary of the navy.

In 1921, Roosevelt was stricken with polio. His legs were paralyzed. Roosevelt slowly learned to walk with crutches and heavy metal braces on his legs. But he never regained full use of his legs. He spent most of the rest of his life in a wheelchair.

In 1928, Roosevelt was elected governor of New York. He sponsored a variety of reform laws. When the depression began, Governor Roosevelt started the nation's first effective state system of unemployment relief.

During his campaign for the presidency in 1932, Roosevelt offered few specific ideas on how he would end the depression. He spoke with confidence, however, and his personal charm and colorful style attracted many voters.

Roosevelt's greatest advantage in the election of 1932 was the unpopularity of Herbert Hoover. On election day, the voters gave Roosevelt a landslide victory. He carried all but six states.

The Election of 1932

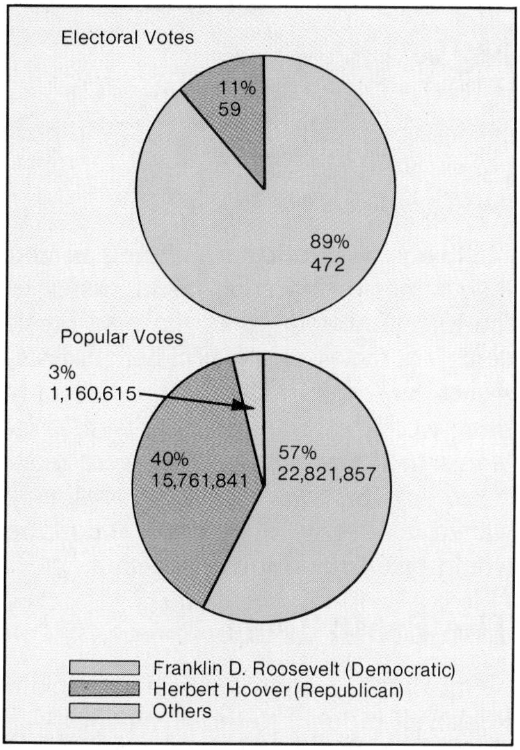

On March 4, 1933, Franklin Roosevelt rode to his inauguration down Pennsylvania Avenue in Washington, D.C. Seated beside him was a glum Herbert Hoover. Also riding in the car that day were the nation's hopes for recovery and relief.

Section Review

1. What actions did President Herbert Hoover take to end the Great Depression?
2. Define depression and unemployment rate.
3. What factors contributed to the Great Depression?
4. Many Americans in 1932 blamed Hoover for the depression. Do you believe this was fair? Explain your answer.

Discuss: What did Roosevelt mean by "the only thing we have to fear is fear itself"? What fears was Roosevelt referring to?

2. Roosevelt and the New Deal

BEFORE YOU READ: *Which New Deal programs provided aid to farmers, businesses, and workers?*

Millions of Americans gathered around their radios on March 4, 1933 to listen to the inaugural address of the new President. "Let me assert my firm belief," President Roosevelt began, "that the only thing we have to fear is fear itself." Listeners to Roosevelt's speech were reassured by his words. They anxiously waited to see what sort of action he would take to end the depression.

The Brain Trust

One of the great strengths that Franklin Roosevelt brought to the presidency was an open mind. He had few fixed ideas on how to attack the problems of the depression. He was willing to experiment. If a program worked, Roosevelt supported it. If not, he would try another approach.

President Roosevelt relied on the advice of a group of very intelligent and talented advisers. The newspapers called these advisers the President's "brain trust." President Roosevelt experimented with the ideas of his brain trust. But his goals never changed. He pledged a New Deal for the nation—a New Deal of reform, recovery, and relief.

The Bank Crisis

Roosevelt's first action as President was to solve the crisis of the nation's banks. Thousands of banks had failed in the depression. Millions of Americans had removed their deposits from the banks that were still open. This massive withdrawal of deposits threatened to destroy the country's entire banking system.

On March 6, 1933, Roosevelt temporarily closed all the nation's banks. He declared a **bank holiday**. Three days later, Congress passed the Emergency Banking Act. Under this act, only sound and healthy banks would be permitted to reopen. The act established federal standards for sound banking practices. Within a few weeks, 12,000 healthy banks were back in business.

---

bank holiday the temporary closing of a nation's banks

To explain his action in the banking crisis, Roosevelt made an informal radio broadcast to the nation. This was the first of many **"Fireside Chats."** The President also met with reporters in press conferences twice a week. By keeping in close touch with the people, Roosevelt boosted the nation's spirits.

Fireside Chat an informal radio talk to the nation by President Roosevelt

---

President Roosevelt took further action to regulate the activities of the banks. The Glass-Steagall Act of 1933 created the Federal Deposit Insurance Corporation (FDIC). This was one of the "alphabet agencies" of the New Deal, federal agencies known by their initials. The FDIC insured bank deposits up to $5,000 for each depositor. People could now deposit their money in banks with confidence.

Background: Some members of Roosevelt's "brain trust" believed that the government should regulate—and not break up—the nation's large business combinations. Others believed in antitrust action. Still others believed in inflation as the way to end the depression.

Background: Another reason for devaluing the dollar was to reduce the value of debts. It was also hoped that exports would increase because foreign currency could buy more products.

Roosevelt also proposed measures to regulate Wall Street. The Securities Act of 1933 required that the public be given greater information about stocks that were offered for sale. The next year, Congress created the Securities and Exchange Commission (SEC). All stock exchanges were required to obtain licenses from the SEC. The SEC was given broad powers to regulate the activities of the stock exchanges. It was hoped that the SEC would prevent another devastating stock market crash.

Currency Reform

In April 1933, President Roosevelt began the process of removing the nation from the gold standard. The President was given the power to reduce the gold content in dollars issued by the United States Mint. This reduction in value, or **devaluation**, of the gold content of the dollar would bring on inflation. Inflation, Roosevelt hoped, would mean higher prices for the products of industry. Higher prices would give American businesses an incentive to be more productive. But, as it turned out, dollar devaluation had little effect on prices.

devaluation a reduction in value

Aid for Farmers

One of the most serious problems facing President Roosevelt was the situation of the nation's farmers. Farm prices and farm income were disastrously low. Farmers were desperate for help.

In May 1933, Congress passed the Agricultural Adjustment Act. This act created the Agricultural Adjustment Administration (AAA) to provide aid to American farmers. The most important help it offered was a plan to raise farm prices by cutting back farm production. The goal of the AAA was to restore the value of farm products to what they had been during the prosperous years of 1909–1914. Once farm products were equal in value to farm products in this earlier period, the AAA announced, they would have achieved **"parity."**

parity the equality of value of current farm products with the value of farm products in another period

This farm family benefited from programs like the AAA, which provided aid to many American farmers during the depression.

For Extra Interest: A good primary-source account of the impact of the depression on American farmers can be found in Studs Terkel's *Hard Times* (New York: Pantheon Books, 1970), pages 252–253. Read the passage by Oscar Heline, an Iowa farmer, aloud to the class.

Discuss: Explain how cutting back on farm production would help farm prices rise.

The AAA paid farmers to reduce the number of hectares (acres) they planted and the size of their herds of livestock. The money to pay the farmers came from new taxes on processors such as mills, cotton gins, and meatpacking plants.

When the AAA was created in 1933, many spring crops had already been planted. The AAA, therefore, paid some farmers to destroy their crops. About 4 million hectares (10 million acres) of cotton were plowed under. Six million pigs were also destroyed.

Following the creation of the AAA, prices for farm products began to rise. By 1936, farm products had reached 90 percent of parity. Farm products, in other words, were worth 90 percent of what they had been worth during 1909–1914. Between 1932 and 1936, the cash income of American farmers nearly doubled. The American farmers' great unsolved problem—low prices caused by overproduction—was at last being solved.

Help for Business and Labor

To help business and labor, Congress passed the National Industrial Recovery Act (NIRA) in June 1933. President Roosevelt called it "the most important and far-reaching legislation ever enacted by the American Congress."

The NIRA created two new federal agencies. The first of these, the National Recovery Administration (NRA), set codes of conduct for the nation's businesses. The NRA allowed businesses to fix common prices for their products. Businesses could also agree among themselves to set limits on production. Antitrust laws, in effect, were suspended. Businesses that were allowed to fix prices, however, had to accept NRA standards for wages and working hours for their employees.

Businesses that cooperated with the NRA were permitted to place on their products the symbol of the NRA, a blue eagle. The director of the NRA hoped that Americans would boycott goods that did not carry this symbol.

The NRA succeeded in raising wages and reducing working hours in many industries. While most wage increases were fairly small, some workers received large raises. Workers in cotton mills, for instance, had their wages raised from $5 a week to $12. Section 7a of the NIRA guaranteed workers the right of collective bargaining. This guarantee encouraged the formation of new labor unions.

The second agency created by the NIRA was the Public Works Administration (PWA). This agency increased federal spending for large construction projects that would benefit the public. The PWA built such things as dams, schools, and hospitals. Thousands of new jobs for American workers were created by the PWA projects. Among the agency's major accomplishments were a new sewage system for Chicago and the Triborough Bridge in New York City.

The housing industry received special assistance from the New Deal. In 1934, Congress created the Federal Housing Administration (FHA). The FHA insured loans for the construction of new homes. Millions of Americans took out FHA loans to build their homes. The construction industry began to recover from the Great Depression.

Background: The farmers who benefited from the AAA were the owners of large and family-sized farms. Small tenant farmers received few benefits. Tenant farmers were often forced off the land by landowners who were reducing the size of their acreage.

EUREKA!

Xerography

If the monks of the thirteenth century could visit a modern office, no doubt they would be most impressed by the office copying machine. Copying a document, which took medieval scribes months of labor, is now done in seconds thanks to a process called xerography.

Xerography was invented by a physicist named Chester Carlson. Carlson's work frequently required him to make copies of drawings and patent specifications. Tired of making the copies by hand, he set to work on a machine that would do the copying for him.

Carlson had very little money for his research. He did all of his experimenting in his apartment, and his neighbors often complained about the smell of the chemicals he used. Nonetheless, he persisted, and after four years of experimentation, he produced the first xerographic copy in 1938.

The xerographic process is based on the fact that opposite electric charges attract each other. In xerography, an electric charge is placed on a light-sensitive plate. When the plate is exposed to light from the image that is being copied, a pattern of positive charge in the shape of the image is created. Then the plate is sprinkled with a negatively charged powder. The powder is attracted to the pattern. Another dose of charge transfers the powder pattern to a piece of paper, where it is fixed in place.

Carlson patented his process in 1940, but he could not get anyone to develop it. At last, in 1947, a small firm called the Haloid Company took xerography on. Eleven years later, the first office copier was introduced. The Haloid Company became the Xerox Corporation, and Chester Carlson became a millionaire.

Relief for the Unemployed

When Franklin Roosevelt became President in 1933, at least 13 million American workers were jobless. Roosevelt believed that the federal government must take direct action to provide relief for the millions of unemployed.

The first New Deal agency to aid the unemployed was the Civilian Conservation Corps (CCC), created in 1933. The CCC recruited young men between the

Background: CCC workers earned $30 a month. Of this, $22 was sent to the young men's families.

ages of 18 and 25 to work in the countryside. At one point, the agency was employing 500,000 young men. They lived in camps in national parks and forests. Many worked on projects to conserve the nation's natural resources. The projects of the CCC were carefully selected so that they would not compete with private businesses. The "CCC boys" planted trees, worked on road construction crews, restored historic buildings, developed parks, improved irrigation systems, and helped control mosquitoes and other pests. They were given their room and board and were paid $30 per month.

Also in 1933, Congress created the Federal Emergency Relief Administration (FERA). Between 1933 and 1935, the FERA provided about $4 billion to the states for aid to the unemployed. Some of the money was given out as cash grants. The states were urged, however, to use the money to pay for useful projects such as repairing roads and improving parks.

The most extensive relief program of the New Deal was the Works Progress Administration (WPA). The WPA built post offices, schools, hospitals, and

The Tennessee Valley Authority

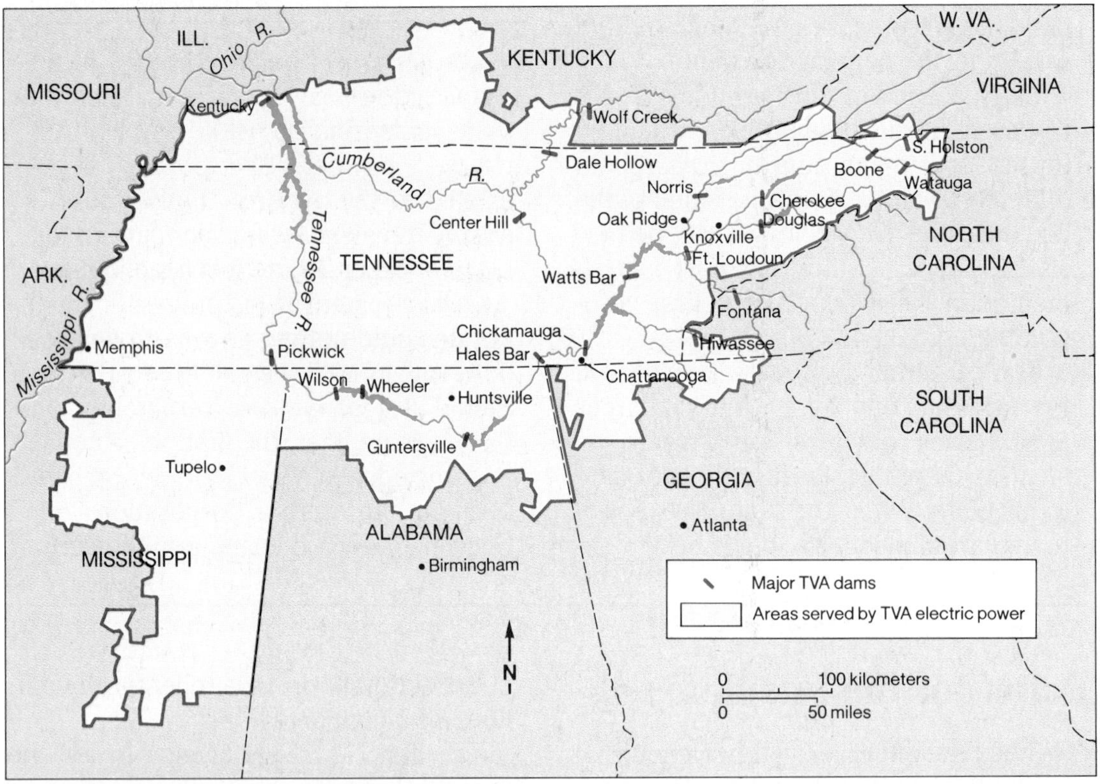

Which states benefited from the improvements made by the Tennessee Valley Authority? In what ways did these states benefit?

Discuss: Do you think the government should sponsor programs like the CCC and the PWA for unemployed workers today? Why or why not? Why do you think some people would oppose such programs today?

Background: The seven states that benefited from TVA projects were North Carolina, Virginia, Tennessee, Georgia, Kentucky, Alabama, and Mississippi.

bridges. At its peak, the WPA provided jobs for nearly 3.3 million workers. More than 250,000 WPA projects were completed across the country.

The WPA also helped unemployed writers, artists, actors, and musicians. The agency hired writers to prepare guidebooks for cities and states. Scholars were hired to record American Indian songs, black spirituals, and country folk tunes. Artists were given jobs painting murals on post office walls. Talented young people were helped by the National Youth Administration (NYA). They were given part-time jobs so that they could stay in school or attend college.

Regional Assistance

Poverty in the United States was not evenly distributed. Some areas were more depressed than others. The Tennessee Valley was one area where conditions were especially bad.

The great Tennessee River, which flowed through the valley, caused frequent flooding. The floods washed away topsoil and destroyed farms. The once-rich forests of the area had been cut for lumber. Many hillsides were barren. The houses and the diet of the people were poor. Electricity was available in only 2 out of every 100 homes. The yearly income in the valley was less than half the national average. More than half the families in the hills of Tennessee were on public relief.

Shortly after his election, President Roosevelt visited the Tennessee Valley. In April 1933, he asked Congress to create a new federal agency to plan improvements for the region. On May 18, 1933, Congress gave its approval to the Tennessee Valley Authority (TVA).

The TVA was given the power to buy, build, and operate dams in the valley. Its authority extended over parts of seven states. It built 16 new dams and took over several older ones. The TVA dams provided flood control and cheap electricity to over 40,000 users. The TVA also replanted forests and restored the soil. Many other programs improved the standard of living in the valley. The TVA was one of the most successful of the New Deal agencies. It transformed the Tennessee Valley, making it more productive and prosperous.

Section Review

1. Which New Deal programs provided aid to American farmers, businesses, and workers?
2. Define bank holiday, devaluation, and parity.
3. Identify the following "alphabet agencies" and explain what they did: FDIC, PWA, CCC, and TVA.
4. As in the 1930's, poverty in the United States today is not evenly distributed. What regions of the country might still need special help from the federal government? Explain your answer.

For Extra Interest: Have students research and report on any "alphabet agency" projects completed in their community or the surrounding area during the depression. Students might contact a local historical society for information.

Background: In 1935, Long was assassinated. He was killed by a young doctor who apparently was outraged by Long's policies as governor.

3. The Second New Deal

BEFORE YOU READ: *What impact did the New Deal have on American life?*

Franklin Roosevelt's goals for the New Deal were economic reform, recovery, and relief. During his first two years in office, Roosevelt's programs had made great headway in easing the effects of the depression.

Yet serious problems remained. Nine million Americans remained unemployed. American factories in 1935 were producing more goods than in 1933, but production was still far below the level of 1929. Full recovery seemed a long way off.

Beginning in 1935, Roosevelt launched a new attack on the problems of the depression. This second New Deal continued many of the programs of the earlier New Deal, such as the CCC and TVA. It also established new programs to attack the depression.

Critics of the New Deal

The second New Deal was prompted by several forceful critics of Roosevelt's policies. Some critics charged that Roosevelt was going too far too fast. The more troublesome critics, however, were those who charged that Roosevelt was not doing enough to end the depression. These critics had their own programs to offer to solve the nation's ills.

One of the most powerful of the critics was the governor of Louisiana, Huey P. Long. Long's program for the nation was called "Share Our Wealth." The government, he believed, should provide every needy family with $2,500, a homestead, and an automobile. To pay for his plan, Long called for a heavy tax on the wealthy. Long's ideas were popular in areas of the South and elsewhere where unemployment was especially high.

Dr. Francis E. Townsend was another critic of the New Deal. He was a retired physician who lived in Long Beach, California. His "Townsend Plan" was a program to help the elderly. The federal government, Townsend believed, should provide a monthly pension of $200 for all Americans over the age of 60. To cover the cost of his program, Townsend proposed a national sales tax. Townsend Clubs sprang up across the nation. By 1935, about 3 million Americans had joined the Townsend movement.

Meanwhile, in Royal Oak, Michigan, a "radio priest" was attracting a large following. In his radio broadcasts, Father Charles E. Coughlin (COG-lihn) called for the federal government to take over the management of the nation's banks, utilities, and natural resources.

New Directions

The second New Deal was also prompted by the actions of the Supreme Court. In 1935, the Court declared several New Deal programs unconstitutional. The most important act that the Court struck down was the National Industrial Recovery Act (NIRA). On May 27, 1935, the Court ruled that the act gave too much lawmaking power to the code authorities of the NRA.

With the defeat of the NIRA, Roosevelt asked his brain trust for a new approach

Background: Two conditions were attached to Townsend's plan. The people receiving the $200-per-month pensions could not hold jobs, and they had to spend the entire $200 within 30 days. Townsend argued that this would pump money into the economy and create jobs.

Background: On December 31, 1936, CIO members staged a sit-down strike at a number of General Motors plants in Flint, Michigan. The strike lasted 44 days and involved 40,000 workers directly and 110,000 indirectly.

to ending the depression. The first New Deal had been based largely on ideas of central, or national, planning. In 1935, Roosevelt began to pay closer attention to people who advised him to promote greater competition in the economy.

The second New Deal got under way in the summer of 1935. Congress passed the Public Utility Holding Company Act in August. This act was designed to break up many of the largest utility holding companies in the nation. Congress also passed heavy new taxes on other holding companies and large corporations. Vigorous antitrust action began.

The second New Deal also expanded direct federal aid to workers and to the unemployed. In 1935, Congress passed the National Labor Relations Act. This law established the National Labor Relations Board (NLRB). The NLRB supervised union elections among employees to make sure the elections were fair and free from interference by employers. It also guaranteed workers the right of collective bargaining and protected workers against a variety of unfair labor practices.

Encouraged by the federal government, new labor unions began to organize. In the 1930's, new unions of industrial workers were formed. These **industrial unions** included all the workers of an industry in a single union. Unions of mine workers, auto workers, and steelworkers gained strength. These unions included many men and women who had never before been organized. In 1938, the Congress of Industrial Organization (CIO) was formed. During the 1930's, CIO unions staged many strikes. In 1937, the auto workers' union won strikes against General Motors and Chrysler.

Roosevelt's warm smile and friendly manner inspired many Americans during the Great Depression.

---

industrial union an organization of all the workers of an industry in a single union

---

One of the most important new laws of the second New Deal was the Social Security Act, passed in August 1935. This act provided federal relief—directly or through the states—to the unemployed. Workers who lost their jobs could collect relief payments of between \$5 and \$15 per week for 15 weeks. The act also provided monthly pensions of \$10 to \$85 for workers who retired at age 65. The money for the relief payments and pensions came from federal payroll taxes.

In January 1936, the Supreme Court

Background: The Social Security Adminstration is in serious financial trouble today because Americans are living longer and the cost of living is going up.

Discuss: Do you think federal judges should be forced to retire at a certain age? Why or why not? Do you think anyone should be forced to retire at a certain age? Why or why not?

declared another part of the New Deal unconstitutional. This time the Court struck down the Agricultural Adjustment Act. The Court ruled that it was unconstitutional to tax processors, such as grain mills, for the purpose of controlling farm production. Two years later, Congress passed a new agricultural act to regulate farm production. The new act did not tax processors, but it did continue to pay farmers to keep their surplus crops off the market.

The Supreme Court Fight

Roosevelt won a tremendous reelection victory in 1936. He carried every state except Maine and Vermont. As he began his second term, President Roosevelt recognized that many serious problems remained unsolved. "I see one-third of a nation ill-housed, ill-clad, ill-nourished," he said in his inaugural speech. The major obstacle blocking further progress, Roosevelt believed, was the Supreme Court.

By the end of 1936, the Court had declared seven major agencies or programs of the New Deal unconstitutional. To protect the programs that remained—and clear the way for new ones—Roosevelt decided to fight the Supreme Court.

In February 1937, Roosevelt asked Congress to reorganize the federal court system. He proposed that for every federal judge who had not retired by age 70, a new judge should be appointed. In 1937, six of the nine justices on the Supreme Court were over 70. Under the Roosevelt plan, six new justices would be appointed. The size of the Court would grow from nine justices to 15.

If Roosevelt's proposal was approved by Congress, he could appoint to the Court six justices sympathetic to the New Deal. Thus his programs would be protected from further court action. Many people, however, thought that Roosevelt's plan to "pack the Court" was an attack on the independence of the judicial branch of the government. Congress rejected the plan in July 1937.

Nevertheless, Roosevelt cleared the Supreme Court obstacle. Within a few years, seven justices retired. Roosevelt filled most of the vacancies with New Deal supporters.

The last major New Deal laws were enacted in 1937 and 1938. In 1937, Congress passed the Farm Tenancy Act. This act provided loans to tenant farmers, sharecroppers, and farm laborers for the purchase of land, equipment, and livestock. The act also created the Farm Security Administration (FSA). The FSA hired photographers such as Dorothea Lange and Walker Evans to record the suffering and the dignity of the American people during the depression.

Congress created the United States Housing Authority (USHA) in September 1937. This agency made loans to cities and states to build new public housing projects. The new USHA residences were made available to people who could not otherwise afford decent housing.

In June 1938, Congress passed the Fair Labor Standards Act. This important law set the first national minimum wage, 40 cents per hour. It also set the length of the maximum work week at 40 hours. The law, however, did not apply to all workers. Farm laborers, for example, were not covered by the provisions of the law.

Background: The New Deal did little to help Mexican Americans. Before the depression, many had worked as migrant farm laborers. By the time the Farm Security Administration was created in 1937, many Mexican Americans had been replaced by white farmers from the "Dust Bowl."

Famous Americans

DOROTHEA LANGE

At the age of 17, Dorothea Lange decided that she wanted to be a photographer. Lange had no camera and had never taken a photograph, but Lange had determination. She decided that the way to start was to apprentice herself to several photographers. When she felt she had learned enough, Lange set up her own portrait studio in California.

Lange was moved by the conditions she saw around her during the Great Depression. She began to photograph the people and places affected by the depression. It was during this period that she became interested in what became known as documentary photography. Her earliest photographs documented the lives of California migrant workers during the depression. In 1935, she was hired by the Farm Security Administration to photograph conditions in the South and Southwest. Her most memorable photograph was taken in 1936 at a pea pickers' camp in Nipomo Valley, California. It is called "Migrant Mother." Lange later described taking the photograph. "I saw and approached the hungry and desperate mother, as if drawn by a magnet. I do not remember how I explained my presence or camera to her, but I do remember she asked me no questions. . . . She told me her age, that she was 32. She said that they had been living on frozen vegetables from the surrounding fields, and birds that the children had killed. She had just sold the tires from the car to buy food. There she sat in that lean-to tent with her children huddled around her, and seemed to know that my pictures might help her, and so she helped me. . . ."

Lange's photographs were so moving that they frequently sparked relief efforts to help the people she photographed. In all of her work, it was Lange's ability to show human suffering and need that made her an extraordinary photographer.

Background: Eleanor Roosevelt strongly urged her husband to appoint black people to important political positions. Black professionals who advised the President on black issues were sometimes called the "Black Cabinet."

An Indian New Deal

In 1934, Congress passed the Indian Reorganization Act (IRA). Under the IRA, the federal government began acquiring more land for American Indians. Between 1935 and 1937, American Indian lands in the United States increased by more than 800,000 hectares (2 million acres). The IRA also gave American Indians a greater role in government on the reservations. Power was gradually transferred from federal officials to local tribal councils.

The federal government reduced its efforts to assimilate the American Indians. American Indians were permitted to live their lives in the old traditional ways, if they desired.

The New Deal also provided many jobs for American Indians. Seventy-two Civilian Conservation Corps (CCC) projects were set aside for unemployed Indians in 15 western states. Other New Deal programs brought work to the reservations.

The New Deal and Black Americans

Black Americans did not share equally in the benefits of the New Deal. The AAA, for example, made most of its payments to owners of large farms. Few black sharecroppers or tenant farmers benefited from the AAA.

President Roosevelt, however, did appoint many black Americans to important positions in his administration. Lawrence A. Oxley was appointed to serve as chief of the Division of Negro Labor in the Department of Labor. Mary McLeod Bethune served as director of the Division of Negro Affairs in the National Youth Administration. The number of black workers on the federal payroll increased from about 50,000 in 1933 to 200,000 by 1947.

Black Americans gave Roosevelt strong political support. Although the New Deal did not provide equal benefits to black Americans, it did provide black Americans with more benefits than had any administration since Reconstruction. Black voters began to vote Democratic.

Significance of the New Deal

The New Deal had a major impact on many aspects of American life. The New Deal, however, did not bring about full recovery from the depression. After all the experiments had been tried and the "alphabet agencies" created, 8.7 million American workers were still unemployed in 1939.

The New Deal expanded the role and responsibilities of the federal government in economic hard times. Many new government agencies were created. The number of permanent federal employees increased from 100,000 in 1932 to more than one million in 1940. The government also assumed many new responsibilities for the general welfare.

To pay for such massive work programs as the PWA and WPA, the government had to borrow huge sums of money. Each year the government spent far more money than it collected in taxes. This policy of **deficit spending** meant an increase in the national debt. The national debt is the total amount of money the government owes to lenders. In 1933, the national debt was less than $22 billion. By

Discuss: Do you think that government should be required to balance its budget or spend only as much as it collects in taxes? Why? What would have to be done to balance the budget?

For Extra Interest: Have students research the voting patterns of the most recent presidential election to determine if the Democratic coalition established during the 1930's is still in operation.

1940, it had increased to $43 billion.

deficit spending the government policy of spending more money each year than is collected in taxes

There were few Americans whose lives were not affected by the New Deal. Farmers, the unemployed, residents of the Tennessee Valley, American Indians, and black Americans all benefited from the New Deal.

President Roosevelt also expanded the role of women in the federal government. He appointed women to important positions in virtually every New Deal agency. He appointed labor leader Rose Schneiderman, for example, to the Labor Advisory Board of the NRA. Frances Perkins, Roosevelt's secretary of labor, was the first woman Cabinet member. Women were also appointed to serve as American representatives in foreign countries.

In politics, Franklin Roosevelt united several groups of supporters behind the Democratic party. The Democratic **coalition** included the solidly Democratic South, the Democratic machines in northern cities, new immigrant groups, black Americans, and other minorities. It also included organized labor, many farmers, and some business leaders. This is the coalition that gave Roosevelt his great reelection victory in 1936. It would be a winning coalition for the Democrats in many elections to come.

Federal Deficit Spending

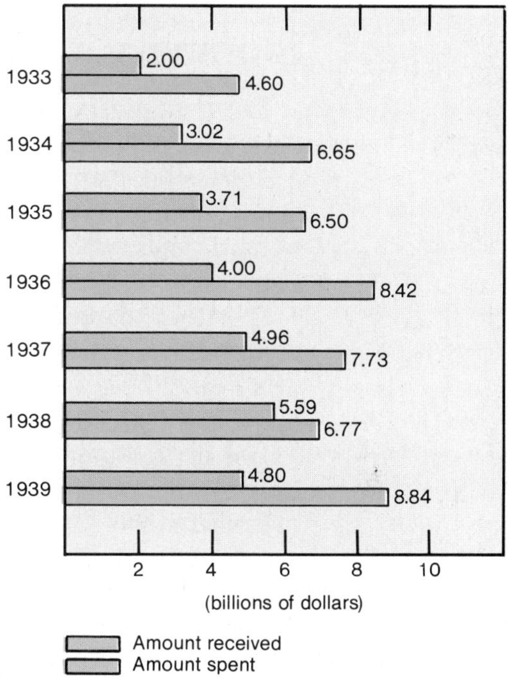

coalition the alliance of several groups of supporters behind a political candidate or party

Section Review

1. What impact did the New Deal have on American life in the 1930's?
2. Define industrial union, deficit spending, and coalition.
3. What benefits did the New Deal provide for American Indians?
4. How important is the New Deal to us today? In what areas of American life can you still see the impact of the New Deal?

CHAPTER REVIEW

Summary

The great prosperity of the 1920's ended with the stock market crash of October 1929. Following the crash, the American economy went into a depression. Many banks and businesses closed. Millions of Americans lost their jobs. Many even lost their homes and farms. This period of hard times, which lasted through the 1930's, was called the Great Depression.

The stock market crash was only one of many factors that contributed to the Great Depression. The uneven distribution of the nation's wealth and the government's failure to regulate business adequately in the 1920's also contributed to the depression.

The depression brought despair to Americans everywhere. Frustrated by Hoover's inability to solve the nation's problems, Americans overwhelmingly supported the Democratic candidate, Franklin D. Roosevelt, in the election of 1932. Roosevelt immediately began a program to bring relief, recovery, and reform to the nation. Numerous federal programs and agencies were started to provide jobs and assistance to unemployed workers. Laws were passed to aid and regulate businesses. Slowly the nation began to recover.

Recalling the Facts

1. How did the practice of buying stock on margin contribute to the stock market crash in 1929?
2. What caused many banks to fail in 1929?
3. What terms were used by Americans to criticize and ridicule President Hoover's inability to solve the nation's problems?
4. How did the Civilian Conservation Corps (CCC) and the Works Progress Administration (WPA) provide relief to unemployed Americans?
5. Why did Roosevelt ask Congress to reorganize the federal court system in 1937?

Analyzing the Facts

1. Why did many Americans lose their jobs as a result of the stock market crash in 1929?

2. Why do you think that charitable organizations were unable to provide the relief needed during the depression?
3. How did Roosevelt's personality help solve the problems of the depression?
4. The New Deal has been criticized for making people dependent on the government and for creating a "welfare state." Do you agree with this, or do you feel that the government has a responsibility to help those who are in need? Explain your answer.

Time and History

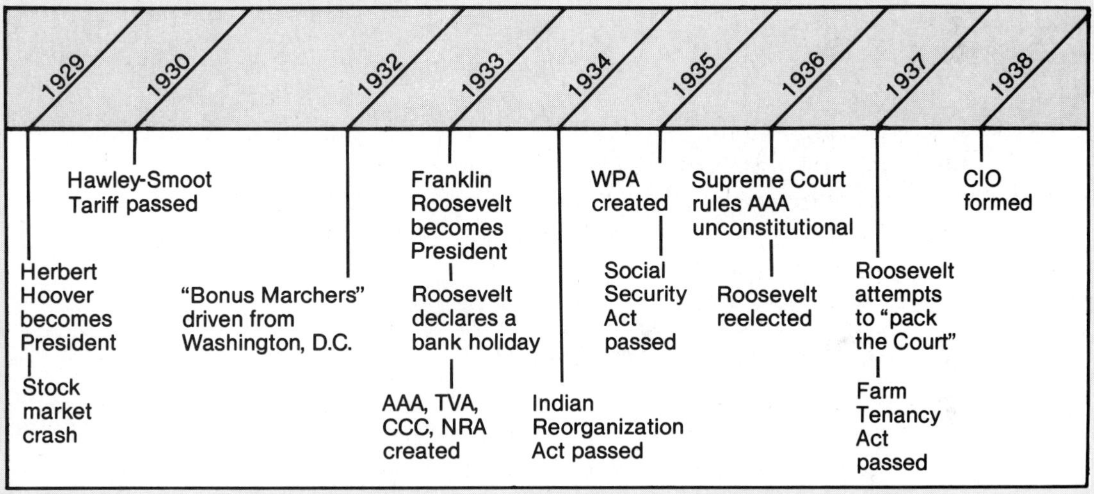

1929
1930
1932
1933
1934
1935
1936
1937
1938
Hawley-Smoot Tariff passed
Herbert Hoover becomes President
Stock market crash
"Bonus Marchers" driven from Washington, D.C.
Franklin Roosevelt becomes President
Roosevelt declares a bank holiday
AAA, TVA, CCC, NRA created
Indian Reorganization Act passed
WPA created
Social Security Act passed
Supreme Court rules AAA unconstitutional
Roosevelt reelected
Roosevelt attempts to "pack the Court"
Farm Tenancy Act passed
CIO formed

1. How long after the stock market crash was the bank holiday called?
2. Which of the following occurred during Hoover's administration: the bank holiday, the Social Security Act, or the Hawley-Smoot Tariff?
3. How many years after the AAA was passed did the Supreme Court rule it unconstitutional?
4. How many years after Roosevelt became President were "alphabet agencies" created to solve the nation's problems?
5. What New Deal legislation was passed during Roosevelt's second term of office?

Chapter **27**

Seeds of Conflict

Anne Frank was born in Germany in 1929. She was a Jew. When Anne was 3, Adolf Hitler became the leader of Germany. Hitler hated the Jews and passed anti-Jewish laws. Anne and her family fled to the Netherlands. Then the Germans invaded the Netherlands. Anne and her family were forced into hiding. They remained in hiding until the Germans discovered them in August 1944. Anne and her family were sent to a concentration camp. It was there that Anne Frank, like millions of other Jews, died. She was 15 years old. The horrors of the concentration camps were one part of the great tragedy of World War II.

After you read this chapter, you will be able to:

1. Trace the rise of the dictators of the 1930's.
2. Describe the aggressive actions of the Axis Powers.
3. Discuss the American response to crises in Europe and Asia.

☐ Compare contrasting points of view.

Background: Germany, Italy, and Japan were all dissatisfied with the Treaty of Versailles. Both the Japanese and the Italians wanted more territory. Germany was humiliated by the loss of its territory in Europe and its colonies overseas.

1. The Rise of the Dictators

BEFORE YOU READ: *In what ways were the dictators of the 1930's similar?*

The peace which had been established in 1919 lasted only 20 years. There were many threats to the peace. The greatest of these was the rise of all-powerful leaders in Europe and Asia.

The Nature of Dictatorship

Strong new leaders rose to power in Germany, Italy, Japan, and elsewhere after World War I. These leaders gained absolute power and authority over their nations. They became dictators.

The dictators of the 1930's shared many common characteristics. The dictators created their own private armed forces or secret police. They used propaganda to build their strength among the people. Opponents were treated brutally. Political parties that opposed the dictators were outlawed. The dictators preached an intense nationalism, glorifying the nation and its people. The dictators launched unprovoked attacks or invasions against their neighbors. They followed a policy of **aggression**.

---

aggression an unprovoked attack, a warlike act, or an invasion

---

One of the reasons the dictators rose to power was the worldwide depression of the 1930's. The new leaders promised that if they were given power, they would restore prosperity.

Another reason for the rise of the dictators was the Treaty of Versailles. The dictators promised to "right the wrongs" of the treaty.

Italy and the Fascists

The years after World War I were a time of great unrest in Italy. The economy was depressed. Unemployment was high, and there were many violent strikes by labor unions. Many Italians feared the government would be overthrown by a Communist revolution. Although there were few Communists in Italy at the time, the fear of communism was great.

In 1919, a new political movement was begun by Benito Mussolini (moos-oh-LEE-nee). Mussolini organized small groups of discontented Italians. His followers were called **fascists**. They were strongly anticommunist. The fascists pledged to defend the nation against revolution. The Italian army supplied the fascists with rifles, trucks, and other military equipment.

---

fascist a person who believes in a government dedicated to glorifying a nation or race; the government is based on centralized, dictatorial rule

---

The fascist movement grew rapidly. By the fall of 1922, the fascists numbered more than 300,000. Mussolini and his followers marched to Rome, the capital of Italy, in October 1922. The Italian king, Victor Emmanuel III, surrendered his power to Mussolini. Mussolini became the Italian premier.

Once in office, Mussolini gained absolute power. He required the members of

Discuss: Italian fascists adopted the ancient Roman fasces as the symbol of their party. A fasces was a bundle of rods tied around an ax. It was carried before Roman magistrates as a symbol of their authority. Why do you think Italian fascists would choose this as their symbol?

Background: Mussolini called himself *Il Duce*, which means "the leader."

the Italian army to take an oath of personal loyalty. He established tight control over the press. Textbooks, movies, and plays were filled with fascist propaganda. In 1925, Mussolini outlawed all political parties except his own Fascist party.

Mussolini's fascist government increased Italy's production of vital crops such as wheat. The government also provided financial aid to many of the nation's businesses. Enormous public works projects reduced unemployment.

Japan

The economy of Japan was also hurt by the depression of the 1930's. The depressed nations of Europe reduced their international trade, and Japan depended on trade for its survival. By 1930, Japan's population reached 60 million people. As the depression deepened, the Japanese became desperate for additional supplies of food and other resources.

New leaders rose to power in Japan during the 1930's. They promised to solve Japan's economic problems by territorial expansion. The new Japanese leaders were officers in the army and navy. Eventually, the most powerful officer was General Hideki Tojo. In 1941, General Tojo became the Japanese premier.

The military leaders also gained control over the Japanese emperor, Hirohito. They told Emperor Hirohito what to say and do.

The rulers of Japan brutally put down anyone who disagreed with their policies. Opponents of the military leaders were terrorized or assassinated. The dictators set up a secret police—called the "thought police"—to expose anyone who had "dangerous thoughts" against the government. Freedom in Japan soon disappeared under the dictatorship.

Germany and the Nazis

The German economy was in chaos after World War I. To pay for its wartime debts and other expenses, the government printed more and more paper money. As the supply of currency increased, the value of German money declined. Inflation skyrocketed. A wheelbarrow full of money was needed to buy a loaf of bread!

This German woman's use of money as kindling for her stove reflects the low value of Germany's currency in the early 1920's.

Background: In October 1922, the German mark stood at 4,500 to the dollar. By November 1923, it stood at 4.2 trillion to the dollar.

In the mid-1920's, the German economy slowly recovered from the disasters of runaway inflation. Then in 1929, Germany was hit by the depression. Political leaders with extreme solutions began to attract many followers.

It was in the midst of the depression of the 1930's that Adolf Hitler came to power in Germany. Adolf Hitler first became active in German politics in 1921 as the leader of a new political party. The official name of the party was the National Socialist German Workers Party. It was better known as the Nazi party. The Nazis were strongly anticommunist and anti-Jewish. They formed their own private army, the SS. Like the fascists in Italy, the Nazis often attacked Communists and other radicals.

During the depression of the 1930's, Hitler and the Nazis gained an immense following. The Nazis promised to restore German prosperity and pride, and to protect the nation from the Communists and the Jews.

By 1932, the Nazi party was the largest political party in Germany. On January 30, 1933, the president of Germany appointed Adolf Hitler to be the nation's chancellor, or premier. When the president died, Hitler assumed his duties as well. He became *Der Führer* (dehr FYOO-ruhr), the all-powerful leader of Germany.

Hitler established a ministry of propaganda to build support for the Nazis. His propaganda minister ordered the burning of books that the Nazis considered to be dangerous. In July 1933, the Nazi party was declared the only legal political party in Germany. The SS killed opponents of Hitler. The Nazi secret police, called the *Gestapo*, also committed murder and acts of brutality to stamp out any opposition.

The Italian dictator Mussolini salutes as Germany's dictator, Adolph Hitler, looks on.

Hitler's most destructive policies were aimed at the Jews. Only about one percent of the German population was Jewish. Yet Hitler blamed the Jews for many of Germany's problems. In 1933, Jews were forbidden to hold political office. After 1935, Jews were denied their German citizenship. They could not teach in any school, work in hospitals, write or publish books, or perform in concerts. Jews were also violently attacked on the streets. Organized mobs looted and destroyed Jewish businesses all over Germany. Jews were forced to wear yellow stars on their clothing to identify themselves as Jews. Even the names of Jewish soldiers who had died in World War I were removed from war memorials.

In spite of Hitler's harsh practices, his

Background: The new Japanese leaders wanted to establish an empire for Japan. They were following the example of earlier Japanese leaders. In 1919, Japan had annexed Korea. During World War I, Japan had tried to control much of the Chinese mainland.

economic policies did help Germany recover from the depression. More land was cultivated, and German farm production increased. The output of raw materials also increased, and many industries resumed full production. By 1936, unemployment in Germany had fallen from about 7 million to 1.5 million.

Acts of Aggression

One of the main similarities among the dictators of the 1930's was that each pursued a policy of aggression.

In September 1931, Japanese forces invaded the Chinese province of Manchuria. The province had rich supplies of coal and iron that Japan wanted. The Chinese forces were quickly defeated. China protested to the League of Nations. The League condemned the Japanese aggression, but it could do nothing to stop the assault. Japan withdrew from the League in 1933. Later, in July 1937, Japan began an invasion of the rest of China.

The second dictatorship to launch an aggressive attack was Italy. In October 1935, Mussolini launched an attack on the

Axis Aggressions in Europe, 1935–1939

Where and when did the major Axis aggressions of the 1930's occur?

Background: In Hitler's racist view of humankind, the Germans were the "master race." He dreamed that someday a vast empire would be ruled by "pure" Germans—men and women who were tall, strong, blond, and attractive.

East African nation of Ethiopia. The League of Nations denounced the Italian invasion of Ethiopia, but no nation came to Ethiopia's defense. Ethiopia fell to the Italians in 1936. In 1937, Italy withdrew from the League of Nations. Two years later, Italy launched an invasion of Albania.

The most serious acts of aggression came from Germany. Adolf Hitler believed that Germany should expand its borders over all territories where German-speaking people lived. These territories included Austria and parts of Czechoslovakia and Poland. Hitler maintained that all lands taken from Germany under the Treaty of Versailles should be restored to Germany.

Furthermore, Hitler believed that the German people should have more living space. Territories that bordered on areas inhabited by Germans should be controlled by Germany. All of Czechoslovakia, Poland, southeastern Europe, and parts of Russia thus should become German territory. The basis of Hitler's plan for Germany's expansion was racism. Because the Germans were a "superior race," Hitler believed, they *deserved* these lands.

Hitler carefully prepared for the expansion of Germany. In 1933, he withdrew from the League of Nations. In defiance of the Treaty of Versailles, he began a massive buildup of German armed forces and ordered German troops to occupy the Rhineland of western Germany. In October 1936, Hitler formed an alliance with Mussolini called the Rome-Berlin Axis. Germany and Italy were known as the Axis Powers.

The stage was now set for Germany's

Armored cars of the German army passed through Prague, Czechoslovakia, in 1939 as bombers flew overhead.

aggression against its neighbors. In March 1938, Hitler moved his troops into Austria. More than 6 million German-speaking people lived in Austria. Many of them welcomed the German forces. Germany and Austria were soon united under Hitler's control.

Next Hitler turned his attention to Czechoslovakia. The northern part of Czechoslovakia, on the southeastern border of Germany, was called the *Sudetenland* (soo-DAY-tin-land). Living there were more than 3 million German-speaking people. Hitler demanded that the Sudetenland be made part of Germany. Czechoslovakia rejected Hitler's demand

Background: The Treaty of Versailles had declared that the Rhineland was to be free of German military forces.

EUREKA!

Synthetic Fibers

For most of human history, people have worn clothing made only from natural fibers such as wool, cotton, and silk. But in 1938, a synthetic, or chemically produced, fiber was developed that freed the textile industry from its dependence on nature. That fiber was nylon.

The notion of artificial fibers is not new. In 1664, British physicist Robert Hooke suggested that it should be possible to make artificial silk. The fiber he described would be stronger than that produced by a silkworm. Hooke's suggestion was not followed up until 225 years later. At that time, several processes for making a silk-like fiber from wood pulp were explored.

In 1889, an artificial silk thread called rayon caught the public's attention. It became the first artificial fiber to be widely used. But because rayon was made from wood pulp, it could not claim to be the first synthetic fiber. That distinction goes to nylon.

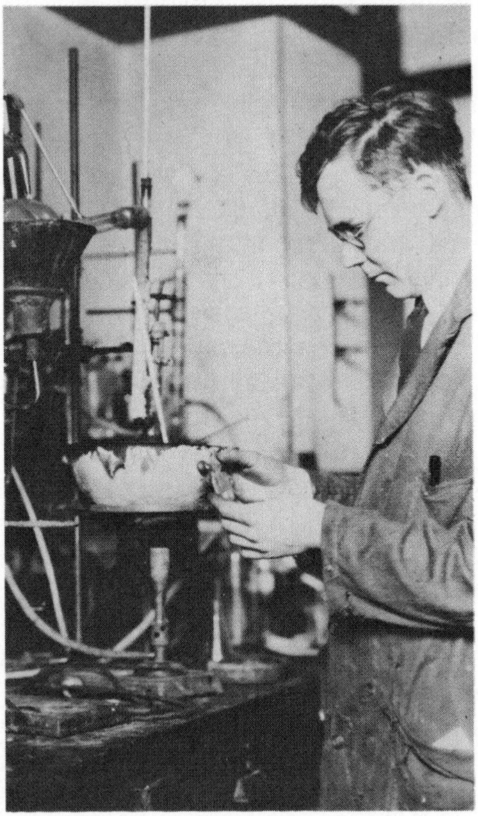

An American chemist named Wallace Carothers developed nylon after ten years of research. In his laboratory at the Du Pont Company, he made fibers from chemicals called polymers. Polymers are made up of molecules consisting of very long chains of atoms. In 1935, Carothers announced that he had made a polymer with all of the qualities needed in a fiber. It was strong and pliable. The polymer could be molded into any shape, and it was inexpensive to produce.

Commercial production of nylon began in 1940, three years after Carothers' death. Today, nylon and the many other synthetic fibers that have followed it are used in everything from underwear to the airplane. They form the basis of one of our nation's largest industries.

Discuss: Why would Hitler want to avoid fighting a war on two fronts?

and appealed to Great Britain and France for help.

In September 1938, Hitler and Mussolini met with the premier of France and the prime minister of Great Britain. The meeting was held at Munich, Germany. The British and French leaders objected to Hitler's demand for the Sudetenland. But they also wanted to avoid going to war over the issue. They decided to give in to Hitler's demands and adopted a policy of **appeasement**. The British prime minister, Neville Chamberlain, was proud of the Munich agreement. Upon returning to Great Britain, he said the agreement meant "peace for our time."

---

appeasement the policy of giving in to the demands of an aggressor in an attempt to avoid further trouble

---

Following the Munich conference, the Sudetenland became part of Germany. Six months later, in March 1939, Hitler seized the rest of Czechoslovakia.

Seeing that appeasement had failed, Great Britain and France pledged to take strong action to stop Hitler's next act of aggression. In April 1939, Great Britain signed an agreement with Poland to defend Poland against any attack. France also committed itself to the defense of Poland. Great Britain and France—and other nations opposed to the Axis—became known as the Allied Powers.

Hitler began making careful plans for an attack on Poland. Before attacking Poland, however, Hitler wanted to make sure that the Soviet Union would not join the Allies in the defense of Poland. He wanted to avoid the possibility of having to fight on two fronts. On August 23, 1939, Germany and the Soviet Union signed a "nonaggression pact." In this pact, the two nations agreed not to attack each other. On September 1, 1939, the German army invaded Poland.

On September 3, 1939, Great Britain and France honored their pledges to defend Poland. They declared war on Germany. The 20-year peace established by the Treaty of Versailles was over. World War II had begun.

Section Review

1. In what ways were the dictators of the 1930's similar?
2. Define aggression and appeasement.
3. How did Adolf Hitler justify his aggressive actions against some of the nations of Europe?
4. The policy of appeasement failed to stop Hitler from further acts of aggression. What other policy could the Allies have followed in 1938? Do you think this policy would have been more effective in stopping Hitler? Explain your answer.

Background: Joseph Stalin was the dictator of the Soviet Union. Under his leadership, the Soviet Union signed nonaggression pacts with Poland and France in 1932 and Italy in 1933. In 1934, the Soviet Union joined the League of Nations.

Background: The dive bombers had ear-splitting whistles mounted on their wings. As they dived down to drop their bombs, the people below were terrified by the whining sound of the oncoming planes.

2. War in Europe

BEFORE YOU READ: *What were the major acts of aggression committed by the Axis Powers in the years 1939 to 1941?*

The war that began in 1939 was the deadliest war in history. Germany, at first, scored many victories. Only slowly were the Allies able to turn the tide.

"Lightning War"

At dawn on the morning of September 1, 1939, the German armed forces began their invasion of western Poland. The Germans called the attack a *blitzkreig* (BLITZ-kreeg), or "lightning war." The blitzkreig was based on two powerful weapons, the airplane and the tank. Its most effective tactic was speed.

The first blow against Poland was struck by the German *Luftwaffe* (LOOFT-vah-fuh), or air force. Using about 1,400 aircraft, the *Luftwaffe* launched surprise attacks on Polish airfields. By September 2, the Polish air force was destroyed.

Next came the German *Panzer* units of armored tanks. As the tanks pushed further into Poland, they branched off in many directions. This made it difficult for the Polish soldiers to concentrate their defenses.

The *Luftwaffe* destroyed the Polish army's communication and transportation systems. The air force also dropped bombs on defenseless cities. Factories, office buildings, homes, and vehicles were destroyed.

In the midst of the German invasion of western Poland, the Soviet Union invaded Poland's eastern border. The world now learned that Germany and the Soviet Union had secretly agreed to divide Poland between them.

When the fighting was over, the western half of Poland was taken over by Germany. The Soviet Union took the eastern half. The lightning war—so far—had proved to be a great success.

The Western Front

Both France and Germany had been preparing for war for a long time. Along their common border, each nation had constructed a long line of armed forts.

When Germany invaded Poland, there was no way that the British and French forces could reach the fighting. The French and British armies sat and waited along the French-German border.

In the spring of 1940, Germany launched a major attack in the west. The attack, however, did not come along the French-German border. German forces struck farther north. In April, Germany invaded Denmark and Norway. Denmark fell almost without a fight. Norway put up more resistance.

While the battle of Norway was still raging, Germany attacked the neutral Low Countries. The Low Countries are Luxembourg, the Netherlands, and Belgium. The attack began on May 10, 1940. It was a blitzkreig. Luxembourg surrendered in a day. The Netherlands fell in five days. In less than three weeks, Belgium had been defeated.

The rapid successes of Germany brought a new leader to power in Great Britain. Neville Chamberlain resigned as prime minister. Winston Churchill, took his place. On May 13, 1940, Prime Minister

Background: On the German side of the French-German border, the Siegfried Line stretched from Switzerland northward to the Netherlands. France's Maginot Line was shorter. It ran from Switzerland to Belgium.

Discuss: In both world wars, Belgium and Switzerland declared their neutrality. Yet in both wars, Belgium was invaded, while Switzerland was not. Look at a physical map of Europe. What geographic features might explain this situation?

Churchill pledged to lead the British to a victory over Germany. "I have nothing to offer but blood, toil, tears, and sweat," he said. "Come, let us go forward together with our united strength."

The Fall of France

With the German victory in Belgium, Germany was in a good position to invade France. The line of French forts ended at the Belgian border. In May 1940, German tanks began pouring out of Belgium into France. The Germans pushed the Allied forces rapidly back across northern France to the English Channel.

To rescue the Allied troops, Prime Minister Churchill ordered every available British ship and boat to sail across the channel. They were to meet at the French coastal town of Dunkirk. From there, the British vessels would bring the Allied soldiers across the Channel to Great Britain.

Nearly 900 vessels went to Dunkirk. The fleet included fishing boats, lifeboats, yachts, barges, tugs, fireboats, and ferries. In the "miracle of Dunkirk," 338,000 men were rescued.

Meanwhile, German forces moved toward Paris. The French army suffered heavy casualties. As the Germans neared Paris, the city panicked. Civilians rushed out of the city. Along the highways leading out of Paris, many civilians were killed by the *Luftwaffe*.

With France near defeat, Mussolini joined the war. On June 10, 1940, Italy declared war on France. Italian troops began invading southern France.

On June 14, the Germans entered Paris. On June 22, 1940, France surrendered. According to the terms of the surrender, northern France was to remain under German occupation. Southern France would be ruled by a pro-German government, with its capital at the city of Vichy (VEE-shee).

Thousands of Allied troops were rescued by a pickup fleet of naval, merchant, and civilian craft at Dunkirk.

Some of the French people organized a secret movement to overthrow the German occupation forces. One leader of the French **underground** was General Charles de Gaulle. General de Gaulle fled to Great Britain shortly before the fall of France. There he became the head of the "Free French." De Gaulle made frequent radio broadcasts to encourage the underground in France.

underground a secret movement organized to overthrow a government or the occupation forces of an enemy

The Battle of Britain

Following the fall of France, Hitler began planning the invasion of Great Britain. German military leaders advised him

Background: Hitler forced France to sign the surrender in the same railway car and in the same place where Germany had been forced to surrender to France in 1918, at the end of World War I.

Discuss: How do you think you would have felt if you had been a British citizen during the battle of Britain?

that the invasion would fail as long as Britain's Royal Air Force (RAF) had control of the skies over Great Britain. Hitler turned to the leader of the *Luftwaffe,* Hermann Goering (GUH-ring), to eliminate the RAF. Goering assured Hitler that the *Luftwaffe* would destroy the RAF.

On July 10, 1940, the battle of Britain began. The Germans began the attack with more planes than the British. But the British had the advantage of an electronic device that could detect objects such as aircraft at long distances. This device, called **radar**, allowed the British to locate and attack the German planes.

---

radar an electronic device that detects objects at long distance

---

In August, Goering ordered his bombers to begin daylight raids on British industrial centers. On August 15, more than 900 German bombers flew over England. It was the largest air battle in history. On that day, the Germans lost 76 planes and the British lost 34. More battles followed, but the results were always the same. German losses were about twice as high as the British.

Goering decided in September to launch terror attacks on London. He hoped to frighten the British people into surrendering. Huge sections of the city were destroyed. Delayed-action bombs fell and then exploded later, killing many people.

By the end of October 1940, it was clear that the Germans were losing the battle of Britain. Germany had lost 1,733 planes, compared to 915 losses for Great Britain. The RAF remained in control of the skies over Great Britain. Hitler had to postpone his invasion plans.

Allied soldiers in London work in the rubble left by the German bombings.

Axis Invasions

The Rome-Berlin Axis gained a new partner in the fall of 1940. On September 27, 1940, Japan joined the alliance of Italy and Germany. Thus was formed the Rome-Berlin-Tokyo Axis. Japan continued its assault on China. The Japanese military leaders made plans to unite all of eastern Asia and the islands of the Pacific under their rule.

The Italians also made plans for further expansion. On October 28, 1940, Italian forces invaded Greece. The Greeks, however, fiercely resisted the Italian forces and pushed them back out of Greece. The Italians also suffered some setbacks in North Africa. For months, the Italians had

Background: The British people were not defeated by the air attacks. They even managed to keep their sense of humor. After the *Luftwaffe* bombed Monkey Hill in the London zoo, one newspaper reported that "the morale of the monkeys remained unaffected."

Discuss: Why do you think General Erwin Rommel was called the "Desert Fox"? What does this name suggest?

been attacking the British in Egypt. In December 1940, the British counterattacked and forced the Italians out of Egypt. British forces moved deep into neighboring Libya, capturing more than 100,000 soldiers.

Hitler was enraged by the poor showing of his Italian ally. He ordered German air and ground forces to North Africa. The leader of the German *Afrika Korps* was a brilliant commander, General Erwin Rommel. He soon earned the name "Desert Fox." On April 3, 1941, Rommel launched an attack on the British in Libya. He pushed the British back into Egypt. Only the Libyan fortress at Tobruk (toe-BROOK) remained under the control of the Allies.

Having recaptured Libya, Hitler then turned to southeastern Europe. On April 6, the blitzkreig struck Greece and Yugoslavia. The Yugoslavs were defeated in 11 days. Greek forces were defeated by the end of April.

Germany was clearly on the attack. Many people wondered what country Germany would invade next. On June 22, 1941, the answer was clear. The blitzkreig was unleashed against the Soviet Union.

The world was stunned by the German attack on the Soviet Union. Less than two years earlier, Hitler and Stalin had signed their nonaggression pact. But the Soviet Union had land and vast supplies of grain, petroleum, and other raw materials desired by Hitler. At the start of the invasion, the German armed forces scored major victories. They pushed deep into Soviet territory. As they neared the capital city of Moscow, however, the Soviet defenses dug in. The Germans were not able to take the capital.

When winter came, the German soldiers were unprepared for the bitter cold. The temperature fell to −17.5°C (0°F). The Germans' light uniforms gave them little protection. Their weapons froze. Their food froze. The Soviet soldiers were better equipped for the cold. They prepared to counterattack.

On December 6, 1941, the Soviets launched their counterattack. The German forces were slowly driven back. In the next five months, the German army suffered 800,000 casualties. The tide had begun to turn against Germany.

Section Review

1. What were the major acts of aggression committed by the Axis Powers in the years 1939–1941?
2. Define underground and radar.
3. Did the Axis forces suffer any defeats during the years 1939–1941? Where did these defeats occur?
4. The German bombing of London only strengthened the British will to resist the Germans. Why do you suppose the British reacted this way? Explain your answer.

Background: The 3-million-soldier German force faced about 2 million Russian troops. The battle line stretched 3,200 kilometers (2,000 miles), from the Arctic to the Black Sea.

Discuss: If you had been one of President Roosevelt's advisers in the 1930's, what course of action would you have suggested the United States take on the debt question? Why?

3. Roosevelt's Foreign Policy

BEFORE YOU READ: *What was the American response to the rise of the dictators overseas?*

During the 1930's, President Roosevelt took an active interest in foreign affairs. He followed very closely the deepening crisis in Europe. Under his direction, American foreign policy moved from neutrality toward greater aid for the victims of Axis aggression.

The Debt Question

One of the first issues that President Roosevelt faced was the question of Allied war debts from World War I. In 1932, the Allied nations of World War I still owed the United States $10 billion. In December 1932, shortly before Roosevelt became President, most of the Allies stopped making payments on their debts. The depression had made it impossible, they said, to pay back the money they had borrowed from the United States during the war.

The Europeans requested that the United States reduce or cancel the debts. Many Americans angrily demanded that the debts be paid in full. Roosevelt tried to steer a middle course through the issue. He did not agree to reduce the debts. Nor did he demand full payment. Rather, he allowed the issue to die. By 1934, all of the Allies had stopped making payments on their debts. With the deepening crisis in Europe, the old debts were largely forgotten.

The Good Neighbor Policy

An important goal of President Roosevelt's foreign policy was to increase American foreign trade. He was especially interested in increasing trade with Latin America. In 1933, the Roosevelt administration adopted the "Good Neighbor policy." The United States signed an agreement in December 1933 with several Latin American nations. "No state has the right to intervene," the United States agreed, "in the internal or external affairs of another." This agreement was a reversal of the Roosevelt Corollary, announced by Theodore Roosevelt in 1904. The Roosevelt Corollary had declared that the United States had the right to intervene in the internal affairs of nations in the Western Hemisphere.

By abandoning the policy of intervention, Franklin Roosevelt hoped to end the bitter feelings of Latin Americans toward the United States. Improved relations would also mean increased trade. The Good Neighbor policy had positive results. Relations did improve between the United States and its Latin American neighbors. Trade also grew. During the 1930's, trade between the United States and Latin America doubled.

Recognition of the Soviet Union

President Roosevelt also hoped to increase trade with the Soviet Union. Ever since the Communist revolution in 1917, the United States and the Soviet Union had not had any official relations. The United States had refused to accept or recognize formally the Communist gov-

Discuss: Why do you think President Roosevelt was interested in increasing American trade during the 1930's?

Discuss: The United States similarly refused to recognize the communist government on mainland China for 30 years (1949–1979). Why do you think the United States withholds diplomatic recognition from governments it does not approve of?

ernment of the Soviet Union. Before trade between the two nations could resume, Roosevelt believed, the United States must extend **diplomatic recognition** to the Soviet government.

---

diplomatic recognition the formal acceptance or recognition by one nation of the government of another

---

The Soviets were eager for diplomatic recognition by the United States. In the early 1930's, the Soviets feared the rising power of their neighbors Germany and Japan. The Soviet government hoped to receive American aid as well as open up trade following diplomatic recognition.

In 1933, the United States officially recognized the Soviet government. In return, the Soviets agreed to stop spreading Communist propaganda in the United States. They also agreed to protect the rights of American citizens traveling in the Soviet Union.

American recognition of the Soviet Union produced few positive results. Trade between the two nations grew only very slowly. The United States did not provide any immediate aid to the Soviets against Germany or Japan. The Soviet Union continued its propaganda campaign inside the United States.

American Neutrality

With the rise of the dictators overseas, the United States had to choose a course of action. The nation could take a more active role in world affairs to stop the dictators and their aggressive foreign policies. Or the United States could try to remain isolated from the growing crises in many countries around the world.

In the early 1930's, it was clear that most Americans wanted to remain isolated. These isolationist feelings were officially expressed in a series of neutrality acts.

In 1935, Congress passed the first Neutrality Act. This act prohibited the sale of military supplies or weapons to any nation engaged in war. The act also warned Americans that if they traveled on the ships of a warring nation, they did so at their own risk.

Congress passed another Neutrality Act in 1937. This act provided that any nation at war could buy nonmilitary goods from the United States only by paying cash. The warring nation would also have to transport the goods from the United States on its own ships. Nonmilitary goods, in other words, could be purchased only on a "cash and carry" basis.

The neutrality acts were designed to keep the United States out of war. Congress remembered well how American trade with the Allied Powers in 1915 and 1916 had led into World War I. By lending money to the Allies and selling them goods on credit, the United States developed a stake in an Allied victory. American ships, carrying goods to the Allies, had been sunk by German U-boats. Those German attacks prompted America to declare war on Germany. Congress in the mid-1930's did not want to repeat the mistakes of 20 years earlier.

Aid for the Allies

President Roosevelt did not agree with those Americans who were isolationists. He believed that the United States should

Discuss: What problem that had occurred during World War I was the United States trying to avoid by warning Americans that if they traveled on the ships of a warring nation, they did so at their own risk?

Discuss: Do you think the United States should have acted to halt the aggression of the dictators during the early 1930's? Why or why not? If so, what action should the United States have taken?

take a more active role to stop the aggressions of the Axis Powers.

In October 1937, Roosevelt delivered a major foreign policy speech in Chicago. He called upon the "peace-loving nations" of the world to "**quarantine**" the aggressor nations. "When an epidemic of physical disease starts to spread," the President explained, "the community approves and joins in a quarantine of the patients in order to protect the health of the community against the spread of the disease."

---

quarantine to separate a diseased person or group from the rest of the population to keep the disease from spreading

---

Roosevelt did not make it clear how he thought the United States should "quarantine" the aggressors. He did make it clear, however, that he thought something should be done to stop the spread of aggression.

The American reaction to Roosevelt's speech was generally negative. The speech reminded many Americans of Woodrow Wilson's call to "make the world safe for democracy." They did not want to follow a similar appeal now. "Americans must not," a Boston newspaper proclaimed, "knowingly or unknowingly, jointly or alone, embark on another attempt to reform the world."

As the dictators increased their aggressive behavior, however, more and more Americans came to support the President's call for action. Following the German attack on Poland in September 1939, Roosevelt asked Congress for an important change in the neutrality acts. He wanted to permit the Allies to buy military supplies from the United States. Congress agreed but said that the supplies would have to be purchased on a "cash and carry" basis.

After Germany invaded Denmark, Norway, and the Low Countries, Roosevelt asked for further action. On May 16, 1940, he asked Congress for $1 billion for a buildup of American defenses. Congress quickly agreed. In September, he asked for a law to draft young men into the armed forces. Congress adopted the Selective Service Act. This was the first peacetime draft in American history.

The National Debate

The fall of France in July 1940 caused even more Americans to support President Roosevelt. By then, two-thirds of the American people believed that Germany posed a direct threat to the United States.

Supporters of President Roosevelt organized the Committee to Defend America by Aiding the Allies. The United States must act now, the committee declared, to defeat the Axis Powers. "Hitler is striking with all the terrible force at his command," a committee spokesperson wrote. "His is a desperate gamble, and the stakes are nothing less than domination of the whole human race . . . . WE CAN HELP—IF WE ACT NOW—before it is too late."

The isolationists also organized themselves. The America First Committee opposed American involvement in the war. Charles Lindbergh, the great American hero of the 1920's, was a leader of the America First Committee. He argued that the United States would only suffer defeat if it tried to halt the Axis Powers.

The national debate between these two

Background: In October 1940, more than 16 million men, ages 21 to 35, reported to their draft boards to register for the draft. Each man was given a number from 1 to 8,500. The numbers were then drawn randomly to determine the order in which the men would be called up for duty.

Vocabulary Help: arsenal—a place for making or storing weapons and other munitions. What did Roosevelt mean when he said that the United States should become the "arsenal of democracy"?

groups continued throughout 1940 and most of 1941. The presidential campaign of 1940 became a part of this debate. The Democrats nominated Franklin Roosevelt for a third term. No President in American history had ever served more than two terms in office. Wendell Willkie, a business executive, was the Republican nominee. Although Willkie generally supported the President's policies, he received the support of many isolationists.

The majority of Americans gave their support to the President. Roosevelt won the election in November 1940 with 499 electoral votes to Willkie's 82.

"Lend-Lease"

In December 1940, Prime Minister Churchill informed President Roosevelt that Great Britain could no longer afford to buy military supplies from the United States. Yet Great Britain desperately needed more supplies.

Roosevelt responded by requesting that Congress drop the "cash and carry" portions of the neutrality acts. He proposed instead that the United States "lend or lease" needed military supplies to the British. America, Roosevelt declared, should become the "arsenal of democracy."

In explaining the lend-lease proposal to the American people, President Roosevelt used a simple illustration. "Suppose my neighbor's home catches fire," Roosevelt said, "and I have a length of garden hose .... If he can take my garden hose and connect it up with his hydrant, I may help him to put out his fire. Now what do I do? I don't say to him before that operation, 'Neighbor, my garden hose cost me $15; you have to pay me $15 for it.'" The hose instead would be loaned to the neighbor, Roosevelt explained. Once the fire was out, the hose could be returned. If the hose was damaged, the neighbor could replace it with a new one.

After long debate, Congress passed the Lend-Lease Act in March 1941. Under the terms of this act, the United States loaned the Allies $50 billion worth of military supplies. In July, American warships began accompanying vessels carrying military supplies to Great Britain. American neutrality was fading fast.

The United States became even more closely tied to Britain in August 1941. President Roosevelt and Prime Minister

This meeting between President Roosevelt and Prime Minister Churchill on a British ship resulted in the Atlantic Charter.

Background: Congress qualified the Lend-Lease Act by stating that materials could only be lent to a nation whose defense was vital to that of the United States.

Background: The sinking of the *Reuben James*, with the loss of 100 American lives, later inspired a popular song: "What were their names? Tell me, what were their names? Did you have a friend on the good *Reuben James*?"

Churchill met aboard a British vessel off the coast of Canada. The two leaders issued a joint statement called the Atlantic Charter. The statement did not contain many details. But both nations pledged themselves to "the final destruction of the Nazi tyranny."

In September 1941, Nazi submarines began attacking American warships. Early that month, a German U-boat fired two torpedoes at the American destroyer *Greer*. Late in October, a German submarine sank an American destroyer, the *Reuben James*. The American people were outraged. By December 1941, the United States seemed on the verge of war with Germany.

Japanese-American Relations

Relations between the United States and Japan also worsened in 1941. President Roosevelt had expressed strong disapproval of the Japanese invasion of China. The United States had placed an embargo on shipments of aviation fuel and scrap metal to Japan. Yet the Japanese army continued to extend its control over more territory.

In July 1941, Japanese forces invaded the French colony of Indochina. This colony occupied a large peninsula south of China. President Roosevelt condemned the invasion and ordered the freezing of Japanese property in the United States and an embargo on all ore shipments to Japan. Trade between the United States and Japan nearly ceased.

The Japanese government now decided on a reckless course of action. They wanted to seize other British, Dutch, and American possessions in the Pacific Ocean. The Japanese wanted the rich oil reserves in the region. But the Japanese feared that American naval forces would try to stop them. The Japanese military government decided to launch a surprise attack on the American forces in the Pacific. In December 1941, the American naval forces were located at a base in Hawaii called Pearl Harbor.

Section Review

1. What was the American response to the rise of the dictators in Europe and Asia?
2. Define diplomatic recognition and quarantine.
3. What were the terms of the neutrality acts of 1935 and 1937? What was the purpose of these acts?
4. Did the United States maintain its neutrality in the period 1939–1941? What aid did America provide to the Allies?
5. The national debate over American foreign policy between 1935 and 1941 was very intense. Which side of the debate do you find most convincing? Explain your answer.

Background: By breaking the Japanese code, the United States learned in November 1941 that Japan planned to declare war on the United States if the oil embargo was not lifted.

Comparing Different Points of View

In 1941, many Americans disagreed over what role the United States should play in World War II. Franklin Roosevelt and Charles Lindbergh held opposing points of view about the most appropriate way to guarantee American security. A viewpoint is the position a person takes on a particular issue. Comparing different viewpoints allows a reader to develop informed opinions based on the different ideas presented.

Examine the different points of view in the quotes below.

The people of Europe who are defending themselves [the Allies] do not ask us to do their fighting. They ask us for the implements of war, the planes, the tanks, the guns, the freighters, which will enable them to fight for their liberty and our security. Emphatically we must get these weapons to them in sufficient volume and quickly enough, so that we and our children will be saved the agony and suffering of war which others have had to endure.

(Franklin Roosevelt, Fireside Chat, December 1940)

I have been forced to the conclusion that we cannot win this war for England, regardless of how much assistance we extend . . . . There is a policy open to this nation that *will* lead to success—a policy that leaves us free to follow our own way of life . . . . It recommends the maintenance of armed forces sufficient to defend this hemisphere from attack by any combination of foreign powers.

(Charles Lindbergh, speech, New York, April 1941)

1. What did Roosevelt think should be done to guarantee American security?
2. Why did Lindbergh disagree with Roosevelt's plan?
3. What did Lindbergh think should be done to guarantee American security?
4. Do you agree with Roosevelt's or Lindbergh's viewpoint? Why? Explain your answer.

CHAPTER REVIEW

Summary

After World War I, dictators came to power in Germany, Italy, and Japan. These strong new leaders promised to "right the wrongs" of the Treaty of Versailles and restore prosperity to their nations' depressed economies. As a means to these ends, Hitler, Mussolini, and Tojo all launched unprovoked attacks on other countries.

Wishing to avoid war, the nations of the world responded to early acts of aggression by attempting to appease the aggressors. Appeasement was not successful. World War II began when Germany invaded Poland in 1939.

In 1940, Italy and Japan entered the war against the Allies. By the end of that year, Germany had conquered almost all of Europe. Great Britain stood alone as the only European country at war with the Axis Powers. After much debate, Congress passed the Lend-Lease Act in 1941 to provide Great Britain with more military supplies. American relations with the Axis Powers steadily worsened through 1941 as the United States was drawn closer to war.

Recalling the Facts

1. Give two reasons for the rise of dictators in Europe and Asia after World War I.
2. What aggressive actions were taken by Japan, Italy, and Germany before World War II began?
3. When and how did World War II begin?
4. Describe the "miracle of Dunkirk."
5. How was the Good Neighbor policy a change from the previous policy of the United States toward Latin American nations?

Analyzing the Facts

1. Do you think it would be difficult for a dictator to rise to power in the United States? Explain your answer.
2. Do you think it was wise for Germany to attack the Soviet Union without first conquering Great Britain? Why or why not?
3. How did Hitler use the Russians to get what he wanted?

4. The League of Nations had been formed after World War I to prevent future wars. Why do you think the league failed to prevent World War II?

Time and History

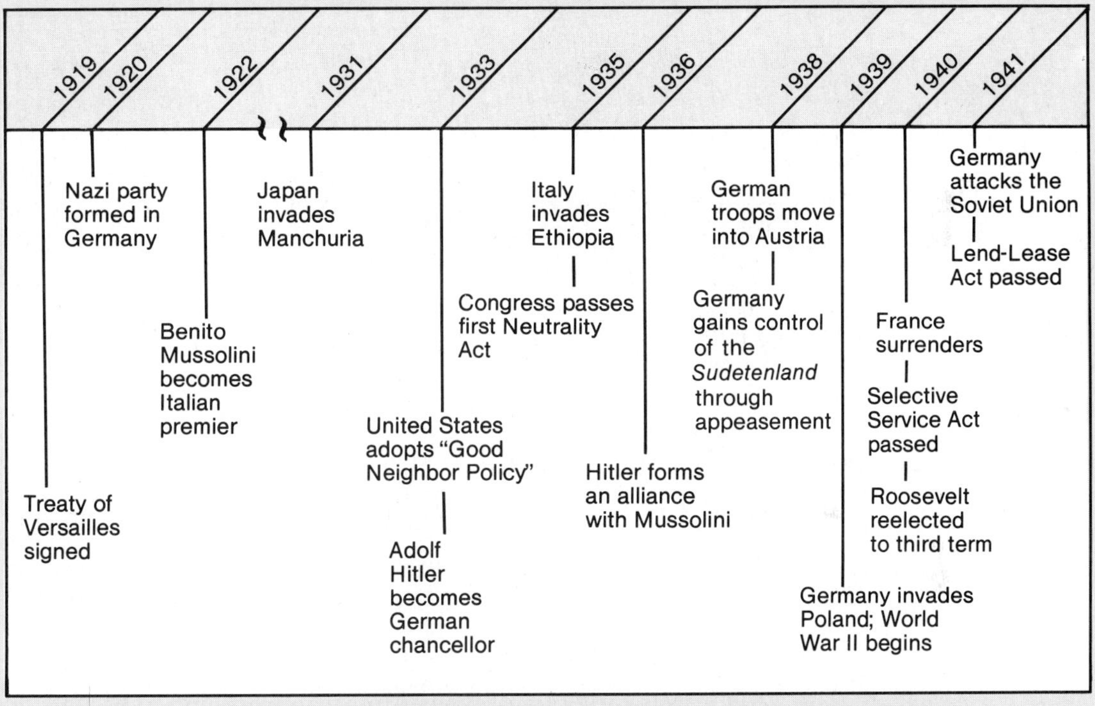
1919
1920
1922
1931
1933
1935
1936
1938
1939
1940
1941
Treaty of Versailles signed
Nazi party formed in Germany
Benito Mussolini becomes Italian premier
Japan invades Manchuria
United States adopts "Good Neighbor Policy"
Adolf Hitler becomes German chancellor
Italy invades Ethiopia
Congress passes first Neutrality Act
Hitler forms an alliance with Mussolini
German troops move into Austria
Germany gains control of the *Sudetenland* through appeasement
Germany invades Poland; World War II begins
France surrenders
Selective Service Act passed
Roosevelt reelected to third term
Germany attacks the Soviet Union
Lend-Lease Act passed

1. How many years after the Treaty of Versailles did World War II begin?
2. Which nation was the first to take aggressive action? Where and when did this occur?
3. How long after the Nazi party was formed did Hitler come to power in Germany?
4. Which came first: the invasion of Ethiopia, the Good Neighbor policy, or the Selective Service Act?
5. How long after World War II began did France fall to the Germans?

Chapter 28
World War II

It was a few minutes before 8:00 A.M. on December 7, 1941. A naval band was playing "The Star-Spangled Banner" aboard the battleship *Nevada* in Pearl Harbor, Hawaii. A color guard was raising the flag.

Suddenly, a Japanese torpedo bomber roared overhead. It began firing at the *Nevada*. At first, no one on board the *Nevada* responded. Then, as more Japanese aircraft appeared, the *Nevada's* guns opened fire. A torpedo slammed into the battleship, and the ship slowly slid aground in shallow water.

The *Nevada* was only one of many American warships to be heavily damaged or sunk. The attack on Pearl Harbor was a brilliant military victory for Japan. Immediately after the attack, however, the United States entered World War II on the Allied side. As in World War I, the American contribution was a decisive factor in the victory of the Allies.

After you read this chapter, you will be able to:

1. Identify the major victories of the Allies during World War II.
2. Describe the impact of the war on American life.
3. Explain how the United States ended the war in Asia.

☐ Compare statistics.

Discuss: Why do you think the United States agreed to a "Europe first" strategy when the United States had been attacked by Japan? Was there anything to be gained by defeating the Axis in Europe before defeating Japan? Explain your answer.

1. America Enters the War

BEFORE YOU READ: *What major victories did the Allied forces achieve in World War II?*

The surprise attack on Pearl Harbor united the nation. The debate over American involvement in the war ended. Few Americans remained isolationists. Support for American entry into the war was almost unanimous.

On Monday, December 8, 1941, President Franklin Roosevelt asked Congress for a declaration of war against Japan. Within four hours, Congress declared war. Only one member of Congress voted against the declaration.

Three days later, on December 11, Germany and Italy declared war on the United States. On the same day, Congress in turn, declared war on them. Not a single member of Congress opposed the war declaration.

The United States was now engaged in a global war. Important questions of strategy had to be decided. The most important question was where America should fight first. British and American leaders agreed on a "Europe first" strategy. Both Great Britain and the Soviet Union were staggering and near collapse. American aid was desperately needed.

Victory at Sea

The Japanese, meanwhile, continued their conquest of lands in the Pacific and Asia. On the day the Japanese attacked Pearl Harbor, they also attacked the Philippine Islands. The Philippines had been an American possession ever since the Spanish-American War. American and Philippine forces bravely fought the Japanese invaders, but they were forced to retreat. The American commander in the Philippines, General Douglas MacArthur, escaped to Australia. General MacArthur promised the Philippine people that someday he would return.

Japanese forces also attacked and captured two American islands in the Pacific, Wake Island and Guam. In February 1942, the Japanese captured the British fortified city of Singapore in Malaya. In March, the Dutch East Indies surrendered to the Japanese. The British colony of Burma fell to Japan in April.

This string of Japanese victories was as impressive as those scored by Germany in Europe. By May 1942, however, the Japanese had become overconfident. They planned to extend their conquests by attempting an invasion of Australia.

The one remaining obstacle to a Japanese attack on Australia was the Allied outpost at Port Moresby, New Guinea. American naval forces intercepted the Japanese fleet as it sailed through the Coral Sea toward Port Moresby. On May 6, 1942, dive bombers from the American aircraft carrier *Lexington* sank the Japanese carrier *Shoho*.

The next day, May 7, Japanese aircraft attacked the *Lexington*. The ship was heavily damaged by bombs and torpedoes and later sank. Nevertheless, the battle of Coral Sea may be considered a victory for the Allies. The Japanese never reached Port Moresby. Australia was saved from invasion.

An even greater American victory was

Background: The island of Singapore, located off the southern tip of the Malay Peninsula, was fortified by the British in the early twentieth century. All guns were permanently aimed toward the sea. The Japanese captured Singapore February 15, 1942, by coming down the Malay Peninsula.

Background: Although the battle of Midway is called a naval battle, it was fought almost entirely in the air by carrier-based aircraft.

scored the next month. The commander of the Japanese fleet, Admiral Isoroku Yamamoto, made plans to capture the Midway Islands. These Pacific islands had been an American possession since 1867. From Midway, the Japanese could launch further raids on the American bases in Hawaii. Unknown to Yamamoto, the United States had broken Japan's secret military code and had learned of his plans.

The battle of Midway was the turning point of the war in the Pacific. Both sides suffered heavy casualties. But all four Japanese aircraft carriers were destroyed. The Allied forces were now on the offensive. The Japanese imperial headquarters ordered that the word "Midway" never be spoken again.

German Assaults

During the first six months of 1942, German submarines sank more than 500 Allied ships in the Atlantic. The German assault on American shipping made it very difficult to get aid to the Allies. Only gradually did the United States develop effective defenses against the submarine attacks.

In Europe, the Germans continued to attack the Soviet Union. "We are attacking Stalingrad," Hitler announced on April 22, 1942, "and we shall take it." For months, the Germans attacked, but the Soviets held out.

When the bitter winter of 1942 set in, the Germans suffered as they had during the attack on Moscow the year before. The Germans were unprepared for the winter. They had not expected the battle for Stalingrad to last so long.

By January 1943, only 80,000 out of 300,000 German soldiers were left to fight. The German commander at Stalingrad surrendered to the Soviets.

Meanwhile, the Germans had resumed their attack on North Africa. After defeating the British at Tobruk, General Rommel advanced eastward into Egypt.

Aid was rushed to the British forces in Egypt. A new British commander, General Bernard L. Montgomery, was placed in charge. Montgomery stopped the German advance at the battle of El Alamein (el ah-lah-MANE) in northern Egypt. On October 23, 1942, the British launched a counterattack. The Germans were driven out of Egypt, across Libya, and into Tunisia.

Operation Torch

On the morning of November 8, 1942, Operation Torch got under way. "Operation Torch" was the code name for the Allied invasion of North Africa. The leader of the Allied forces was General Dwight D. Eisenhower, an American of great military skill. American soldiers landed at Algiers and Oran, where they fought against French forces loyal to the Vichy government. The fiercest fighting occurred on the Atlantic shore, at Casablanca in French Morocco. American forces there were led by General George S. Patton.

On November 10, 1942, the Vichy leader in North Africa ordered his forces to cease fire. In three days, the fighting was over. The American forces marched eastward toward the Germans in Tunisia.

Meanwhile, General Montgomery, the hero of El Alamein, continued to push the

Background: "Before Alamein we never had a victory; after Alamein we never had a defeat," Winston Churchill later remarked.

Famous Americans

BILL MAULDIN

Two of the most popular soldiers during World War II were Willie and Joe, cartoon characters drawn by Bill Mauldin. Willie and Joe were two battle-weary soldiers who represented all American foot soldiers. They were shown putting up with some of the army's foolish regulations and many of the hardships of war. Some of the captions for the cartoons became so well known that they were quoted by many soldiers. "Just gimme th' aspirin," said Willie, "I already got a purple heart." For soldiers who had been wounded in battle, this quote was easy to understand. War was an unpleasant job, but one that had to be done. Soldiers had no time or energy to think of other things, not even glory. When the war finally ended and the soldiers came home, their representative, Willie, appeared on the cover of *Time* magazine.

William Henry Mauldin was born in Mountain Park, New Mexico, in 1921. Much of his art training came from practicing on his own. Mauldin started to attend the Chicago Academy of Fine Arts, but in 1940 he enlisted in the National Guard. In 1943, he was sent to Europe. Mauldin became an artist for the 45th Division *News* and the army newspaper, *Stars and Stripes*. Although his cartoons were popular with the soldiers, some army officers viewed them as unpatriotic. In spite of this criticism, Mauldin won a Pulitzer Prize for his cartoons in 1945. Willie and Joe had made it easier to picture life at the front. They also made Americans realize there was no glamour in war.

Germans westward and northward. The Germans were being caught in the middle. On May 7, 1943, the Allies defeated the remaining German forces in North Africa. About 250,000 Axis soldiers were captured.

Background: Roosevelt said, "It [unconditional surrender] does not mean the destruction of the population of Germany, Italy, or Japan, but it does mean the destruction of the philosophies in those countries, which are based on conquest and the subjugation of other people."

Victory in Europe

North Africa gave the Allies a solid base from which to attack southern Europe. In January 1943, President Roosevelt flew across the Atlantic to Casablanca for a strategy meeting with Prime Minister Churchill. Roosevelt and Churchill made plans for the invasion of Europe. The invasion would begin on the island of Sicily, off the southern coast of Italy. From there, the Allied forces could move onto the Italian peninsula.

At the Casablanca conference, President Roosevelt made a historic declaration of Allied war aims. He declared that the Axis Powers would have to surrender on whatever terms the Allies set. President Roosevelt, in other words, demanded the **unconditional surrender** of the Axis Powers.

unconditional surrender the surrender of a defeated nation on the terms set by the victors

World War II in Europe and North Africa

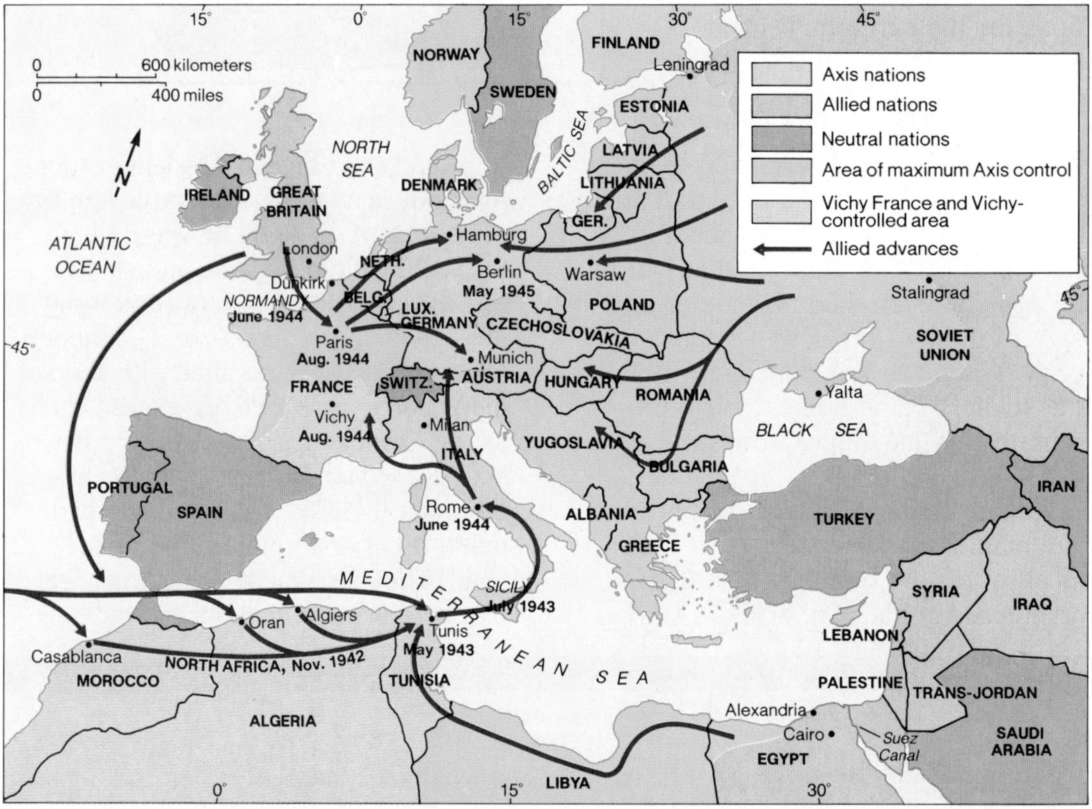

Where did the Allied armies in Africa go after defeating the Axis forces in Tunis? In what direction and through which countries did Soviet forces advance?

For Extra Interest: Invite someone who fought in the D-day invasion to share the experience with the class.

Background: The Battle of the Bulge was the costliest battle in American history. The United States suffered approximately 76,000 casualties.

On the morning of July 10, 1943, American and British forces landed on Sicily. During the fighting in Sicily, Mussolini fell from power. The new Italian leaders began negotiations to sign an armistice with the Allies. But Germany moved its forces into Italy to stop any further Allied advance. On September 3, 1943, Italy surrendered. On the same day, the Allies landed on the Italian peninsula. Heavy fighting between the German and Allied forces continued for months. Finally, on June 4, 1944, the Allied army captured Rome.

The defeat of the German forces in Italy was a major victory for the Allies. An important area of southern Europe was now securely under Allied control.

Just two days after the Allied victory in Rome, the greatest invasion of the war took place. June 6, 1944, was D-Day, the day the Allies landed in France. Over 4,000 vessels brought troops and supplies across the English Channel to the French coast of Normandy. Within two weeks, a million soldiers had been landed. This enormous force began to push eastward through France.

By the middle of December, the Allies had pushed the Germans out of almost all of France and Belgium. The Allies were eager to press on into Germany.

But the Germans were not yet ready to give up. In December 1944, they launched a brave counterattack. In the Battle of the Bulge, the Germans pushed the Allies back across Belgium. This last major offensive, however, was soon stopped.

The American and British forces continued to advance eastward. In March 1945, they crossed the Rhine River onto German soil. Soviet forces by now had also invaded Germany and were pushing westward. By early May, the Soviets had reached Berlin. Adolf Hitler, hiding inside his bomb-proof shelter, committed suicide. On May 7, 1945, German leaders signed an unconditional surrender.

General Eisenhower gives orders to Allied troops before the D-Day invasion.

The Concentration Camps

The joy of victory in Europe was dampened by the knowledge of the terrible suffering the war had caused. Hitler's hatred for the Jews had led to a crime unequaled in the history of the human race. Early in 1942, Hitler put into effect a plan to kill all the Jews of Europe. The "final solution to the Jewish problem," proclaimed the leader of the Nazi SS, would be the extermination, or killing, of the entire Jewish population. The destruction of life that resulted became known as the Holocaust.

The Jews of Germany and the Jews of

Vocabulary Help: Holocaust—the systematic destruction of over 6 million European Jews by the Nazis before and during World War II. This was the first time in history that a plan was organized and carried out to kill so many people of one race or religion.

World War II in the Pacific

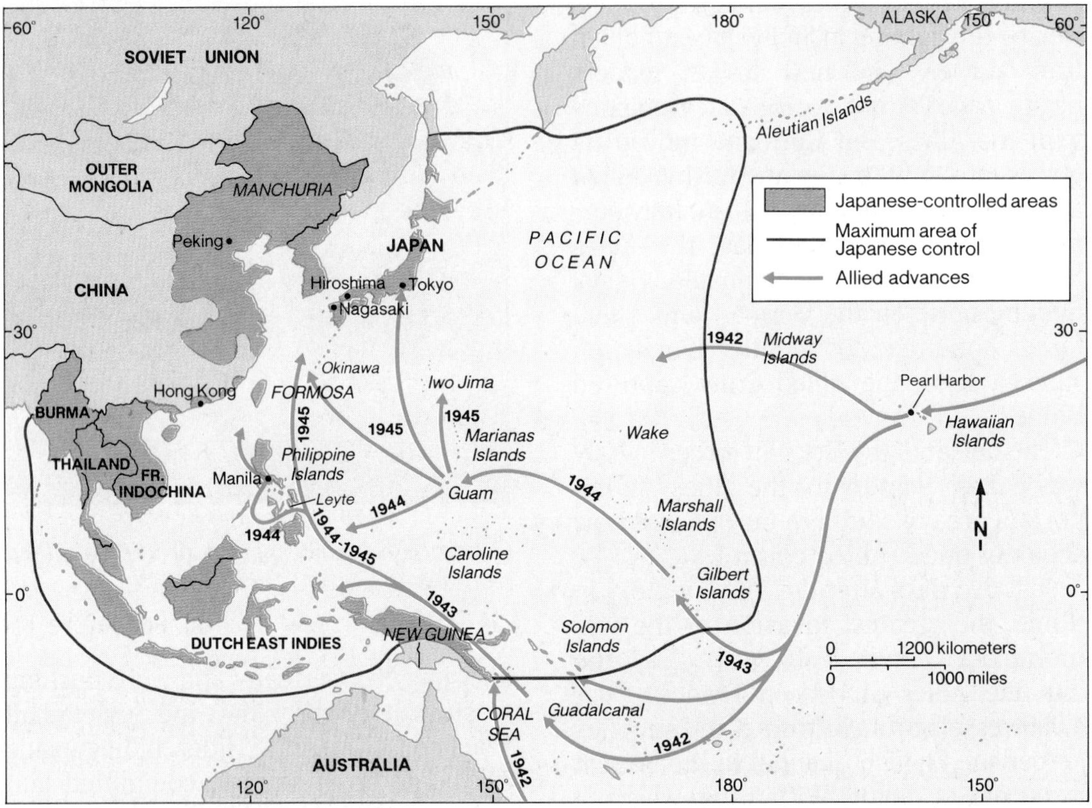

How far is Pearl Harbor from Tokyo? Why do you think the Allied forces used an island-hopping strategy instead of launching an immediate invasion of Japan?

the lands conquered by Germany were herded together. They were taken to concentration camps. Gypsies, radicals, and others whom the Nazis judged undesirable or inferior were also sent to the camps. The inmates of the camps were killed by forced labor, starvation, and poison gas. The bodies of the victims were burned in huge ovens.

No one will ever know for certain how many people were killed in the concentration camps. The German SS destroyed many of the records of the camps. The total number of people killed was probably between 8 and 10 million.

War in the Pacific

Following the battle of Midway in June 1942, American forces began the difficult process of forcing the Japanese to abandon their many conquered islands. In

 Discuss: Why do you think that some Jews today want to keep the memory of the Holocaust alive?

Background: The United States wanted to take Iwo Jima to provide a closer base from which to launch its bombing runs against Japan. American B-29 bombers had previously had to fly 16 hours from the Mariana Islands in the Pacific.

August, the marines landed on Guadalcanal, in the Solomon Islands. After six months of fighting, the Japanese on Guadalcanal were defeated.

Throughout 1943, the **island hopping** continued. In February 1944, the marines defeated the Japanese in the Marshall Islands and moved on to the Marianas and the Carolines. During 1944, American warplanes began attacking Japan itself. American bombers dropped high explosives and fire bombs over Tokyo and other cities.

---

island hopping an American military strategy during World War II to force the Japanese to give up their conquered islands by fighting on each one

---

On October 20, 1944, American forces landed on Leyte Island in the Philippines. General Douglas MacArthur led the American troops. The Japanese counterattacked. In the battle of Leyte Gulf, the American forces defeated the Japanese.

While the fighting continued in the Philippines, American marines landed on the tiny island of Iwo Jima (EE-woe JEE-muh). This island was only about 1,200 kilometers (750 miles) from Tokyo. The battle for Iwo Jima was the bloodiest in the history of the Marine Corps. The marines suffered 20,000 casualties in defeating the Japanese on the island.

The Japanese put up an even more desperate defense against the Allied invasion of Okinawa. This island is just 595 kilometers (370 miles) south of Japan. The invasion began on April 1, 1945. American and British ships around the island were attacked by *Kamikaze* (KAH-mih-KAH-zee) suicide planes. The pilots of these planes deliberately crashed into Allied warships. The Allies suffered 50,000 casualties in the battle for Okinawa. More than 100,000 Japanese were killed before the battle ended in late June 1945.

With the victory on Okinawa, the Allies were now in a position to launch an invasion of the main islands of Japan. Those who had survived the fighting in the Pacific feared that the bloodiest battles of the war were about to begin.

Section Review

1. What major victories did the Allied forces achieve in World War II?
2. Define unconditional surrender and island hopping.
3. Why were the Allied victories in North Africa and Italy important?
4. Identify the following military leaders in World War II: Isoroku Yamamoto, Bernard L. Montgomery, and Douglas MacArthur.
5. Imagine that you had been alive on December 7, 1941. How would you have reacted to the news that Pearl Harbor had been attacked? Explain your answer.

Background: Kamikaze units were formed in various ways. Some commanding officers volunteered their entire squadrons. Some were designated by orders from headquarters. Still others consisted of small groups of fanatical pilots who volunteered for the job.

Discuss: During the depression, farmers had been encouraged to cut production in order to raise prices. Why do you think farmers increased production from 1939 to 1945? What do you think happened to farm prices during the war years? Why?

2. The Home Front

BEFORE YOU READ: *What impact did the war have on the American economy?*

World War II was fought on more than the battlefields overseas. It was also fought in the factories and on the farms back home. America's production capacity was a vital factor in the Allied victory.

The Wartime Economy

At the beginning of World War II, the nation's economy had not yet fully recovered from the depression. As late as June 1940, 8 million people were still unemployed. But by 1945, the number of people in the work force had grown by nearly 7 million. The enormous spending by the federal government for national defense ended the depression.

During the war years, production of military supplies increased steadily. The aircraft industry, for example, greatly expanded its production of warplanes. In 1939, the nation's aircraft industry produced just 6,000 planes of all types. By 1944, the industry was producing 96,000 airplanes per year.

The shipbuilding industry also expanded. In 1939, 215,000 metric tons (237,000 tons) of ships were built. Production increased to over 9 million metric tons (10 million tons) by 1943. A California shipbuilder named Henry J. Kaiser kept his shipyards in operation 24 hours a day. His workers could build entire freighters—called "Liberty ships"—in just 25 days. A new Liberty ship was launched every ten hours at a Kaiser shipyard in 1943.

Overall, the output of America's manufacturing plants nearly doubled between 1939 and 1945. Farm production increased by more than 20 percent. The value of all goods and services produced in the nation was $91 billion in 1939. By 1945, the **gross national product** had reached $167 billion.

gross national product the value of all goods and services produced in a nation

New agencies were created by the federal government to regulate the wartime economy. The Office of Price Administration set prices on many consumer goods. The Office of War Mobilization, established in May 1943, regulated rents, wages, and other parts of the economy.

The government also set limits on the amount of scarce goods that individual families could buy. These goods were needed for the armed forces overseas. The government **rationed** such things as sugar, coffee, meat, and butter and some items of clothing, including shoes. Gasoline was also tightly rationed, and travel was discouraged. Government posters sternly asked, "Is This Trip Necessary?"

ration to limit the portion or share of scarce goods

Paying for the War

World War II was a very expensive war. By mid-1943, the federal government was spending $8 billion *a month* for war costs. The total cost of the war to the United States was about $350 billion. This was ten times the cost of World War I.

To pay for the war, the government

For Extra Interest: Have students make a bar graph showing the gross national product in billions of dollars from 1939 to 1945: 1939, 91; 1940, 100; 1941, 125; 1942, 158; 1943, 192; 1944, 210; 1945, 212.

Background: Employers began withholding taxes from the paychecks of their workers. The employers then turned the tax money over to the federal government. This speeded the collection of income taxes.

borrowed money and raised taxes. As in World War I, the government borrowed money by selling "war bonds" to the American people.

About 40 percent of the war costs were paid by taxation. Taxes were placed on amusements and luxuries. The tax rate was raised on large incomes and on wartime profits of businesses. The income tax was also extended to more Americans. Previously, most white-collar and industrial workers had not had to pay income taxes. During the war they began paying taxes on their incomes.

"Rosie the Riveter"

The need for wartime workers in industry was critical during World War II. Millions of men were being called away from their jobs to serve in the armed forces. American women responded to the call for workers. By 1943, 17 million women were employed. They made up one third of the total American labor force.

Many women moved from low-paying jobs as waitresses and housecleaners to higher-paying jobs as welders and riveters. The wage scale for women workers, however, was usually less than that for men. Also, few women were appointed to supervisory jobs.

Leaders of government and industry actively recruited women. Wartime songs even encouraged women to take up the new jobs. One of the most popular songs was called "Rosie the Riveter."

Raising an Armed Force

When Pearl Harbor was attacked, 1.6 million Americans were serving in the armed forces. Most had been drafted under the 1940 Selective Service Act. During the war, the armed forces expanded rapidly. More than 16 million men were recruited to serve in the army, navy, and marines. Persons who objected to the war, for moral or religious reasons, were not required to fight. During World War II, more than 100,000 Americans became **conscientious objectors**.

conscientious objector a person who refuses to participate in a war for moral or religious reasons

World War II was the first war in which large numbers of women volunteered for the armed forces. Women served as typists, record keepers, machinists, nurses, ambulance drivers, and radio operators. They served in special units such as the

This WAVE officer, designated by the Navy as an Air Navigator, performs duties as part of a military crew.

Background: "If you've sewed on buttons, or made button-holes on a machine," said one wartime poster aimed at women workers, "you can learn to do spot welding on airplane parts. If you've used an electric mixer in your kitchen, you can learn to run a drill press."

Background: Women also enlisted in the Women's Auxiliary Ferrying Squadron (WAFS) of the air force, the *Semper Paratus* Always Ready Service (SPARS) of the coast guard, and the Women's Reserve of the Marine Corps.

army's WACS (Women's Army Corps) or the navy's WAVES (Women Accepted for Voluntary Emergency Service). Altogether, more than 250,000 women joined the armed forces during the war.

More than one million black Americans entered the armed forces during World War II. Segregation and discrimination continued in the armed forces, but blacks were given broader opportunities for service than in World War I. For the first time, black Americans were allowed to join the marines and the army air corps. About 600 black Americans became military pilots. Also, during World War II, the army appointed its first black general, Benjamin Oliver Davis.

Charles Drew, a black doctor, discovered a way to preserve and store blood for use in transfusions. This discovery saved the lives of thousands of American soldiers. Because racial segregation was still practiced during World War II, the blood donated by blacks was kept separate from the blood of white donors.

Other minority groups also made important contributions during the war. About 25,000 American Indians joined the armed forces. The Navajo language was used as a secret code for American military communications. Navajo "code talkers" served both in Europe and in the Pacific. Thousands of other Indians worked in defense industries.

A higher percentage of Mexican Americans volunteered for military service than did any other group of Americans. Mexican Americans also received the highest percentage of Congressional Medals of Honor.

The army unit that received the most medals during World War II was the 442nd Regimental Combat Team. This unit participated in some of the bloodiest fighting during the Allied invasions of Italy in the autumn of 1943. Its members were all Japanese Americans.

Japanese American Relocation

About 112,000 Japanese Americans were living on the West Coast when Pearl Harbor was attacked. Many people on the West Coast opposed the Japanese Americans. They feared that Japanese immigrants would take their jobs. Many also held the mistaken view that the Japanese were an inferior race.

After the attack on Pearl Harbor, opposition to the Japanese Americans increased. Many people imagined that the Japanese Americans were engaged in **espionage**, or spying for Japan. They feared that the Japanese Americans would commit **sabotage**, or destroy bridges, railroads, and power plants, to help Japan. Suspicion was widespread even though there was no evidence of any disloyalty.

espionage spying

sabotage the destruction of railroads, bridges, or other property by enemy agents during war

State and local officials called on the federal government to take action against the Japanese Americans. White farmers who had been competing with Japanese American farmers for years urged the "removal" of the Japanese. Other groups requested that the Japanese Americans be placed in concentration camps.

Background: Congressional Medals of Honor are awarded for heroic acts "at the risk of life above and beyond the call of duty."

Background: Long before Pearl Harbor, laws had been passed against Japanese Americans. Their children had been required to attend segregated schools in San Francisco. Japanese immigrants were prohibited by California law from owning land and by federal law from becoming citizens.

Japanese Americans tried to make conditions in the relocation camps as pleasant as possible by hanging curtains in the windows and planting small gardens.

On February 14, 1942, General John L. DeWitt, the army commander on the West Coast, officially recommended that the Japanese Americans be removed from the West Coast. He admitted that they had not yet committed any disloyal acts. But this only convinced him that they would be disloyal sooner or later.

President Roosevelt signed Executive Order 9066 on February 19, 1942. This order authorized General DeWitt and others to remove the Japanese Americans from the West Coast. During the spring of 1942, all Japanese Americans were placed in "assembly centers." The centers were racetracks, fairgrounds, and livestock halls. Most Japanese Americans were given only a week's notice before they were evacuated to the centers. During this brief period, they had to dispose of their homes, businesses, and personal belongings. Many had to abandon their property or sell it at prices far below its actual value.

During the summer and fall of 1942, the Japanese Americans were moved to "relocation camps." Most of these camps were in parts of the Far West that had harsh weather conditions. The Japanese Americans were housed in tar-paper barracks. The barracks lacked insulation and were terribly hot in the summer and cold in the winter. Families had little privacy. The relocation camps were like prisons.

Discuss: Why do you think Japanese Americans were singled out for removal to relocation centers? Why were German and Italian Americans not moved as well?

They were surrounded by tall barbed-wire fences and armed guards. The Japanese Americans remained in the camps until the end of the war.

The relocation of the Japanese Americans during World War II was a shameful part of American history. The Japanese Americans had committed no crime. Yet they were treated like criminals. Because of relocation, they lost property valued at $400 million.

Wartime Politics

No President before Franklin Roosevelt had ever served three terms in office. As the election of 1944 approached, many Americans wondered if he would run for a fourth term.

In June 1944, the Republicans nominated Thomas E. Dewey for President. Dewey was the governor of New York. At age 42, he was the youngest man ever to be nominated for President. Shortly before the Democratic convention was held, Roosevelt announced that he was willing to run again.

Roosevelt easily won the Democratic nomination. There was, however, a bitter fight over the selection of a vice-presidential nominee. Roosevelt was 62 years old and in poor health. The Democratic convention finally nominated Harry S Truman for Vice-President. Truman was a senator from Missouri.

The campaign of 1944 was hard fought even though Roosevelt and Dewey differed on few issues. The Republicans charged that no one should be allowed to be President four times. The Democrats responded that it was dangerous to "change horses in the middle of the stream." When Dewey emphasized his youth, the Democrats responded that the nation needed someone with experience to lead the nation through the war.

In the election of 1944, Roosevelt carried all of the most populous states except Ohio. His total electoral vote was 432 to Dewey's 99.

Roosevelt's fourth inauguration was a very simple affair. The President believed that elaborate ceremonies were not appropriate for wartime. His inaugural address was one of the briefest in American history. Roosevelt emphasized the grave responsibilities of the United States in war and peace.

Section Review

1. What impact did World War II have on the American economy?
2. Define ration, conscientious objector, and espionage.
3. Why did many people on the West Coast oppose the presence of the Japanese Americans? What action was taken against the Japanese Americans during World War II?
4. Why did Franklin Roosevelt win reelection in 1944? What do you imagine was the most effective Democratic argument for reelecting Roosevelt? Explain your answer.

Discuss: Do you think anyone should be allowed to be President four times? Why or why not? Why do you think Franklin Roosevelt chose to run for a fourth term?

Comparing Statistics

Many American industries expanded during World War II. Thousands of workers who had been unemployed in the 1930's went to work in factories producing planes, tanks, uniforms, guns, and ammunition.

One way of seeing how war affected employment is by comparing statistics. The table below shows what percentage of the American labor force was unemployed between 1930 and 1950. The statistics, or figures, in this table show actual percentages of American workers who were unemployed in particular years. By comparing these statistics, it is possible to see employment trends during this 20-year period.

Unemployment in the United States

Year	Percent Unemployed
1930	8.7
1932	23.6
1934	21.7
1936	16.9
1938	19.0
1940	14.6
1942	4.7
1944	1.2
1946	3.9
1948	3.8
1950	5.3

NOTE: Estimates prior to 1940 are based on sources other than direct enumeration.
Source: Department of Labor, Bureau of Labor Statistics.

1. In what year was unemployment the highest? In what year was it the lowest? What was the percentage of unemployed Americans in each of those years?
2. What was the unemployment trend in the 1930's?
3. The United States entered World War II in 1941. By what percentage did unemployment drop between 1940 and 1942?
4. World War II ended in 1945. What happened to unemployment in the United States after the war?

Discuss: Why do you think the Big Three decided to occupy Germany at the end of the war? Why do you think they decided to divide Germany into occupation zones rather than occupy it as a unit?

3. End of the War

BEFORE YOU READ: *How did the United States bring the war in Asia to an end?*

As the war in Europe neared its end, the Allied leaders began making plans for peace. Conferences were held to work out the peace terms. A new international organization was created to preserve the peace. Dramatic action was taken to hasten the surrender of Japan.

Allied Occupation Zones, 1945

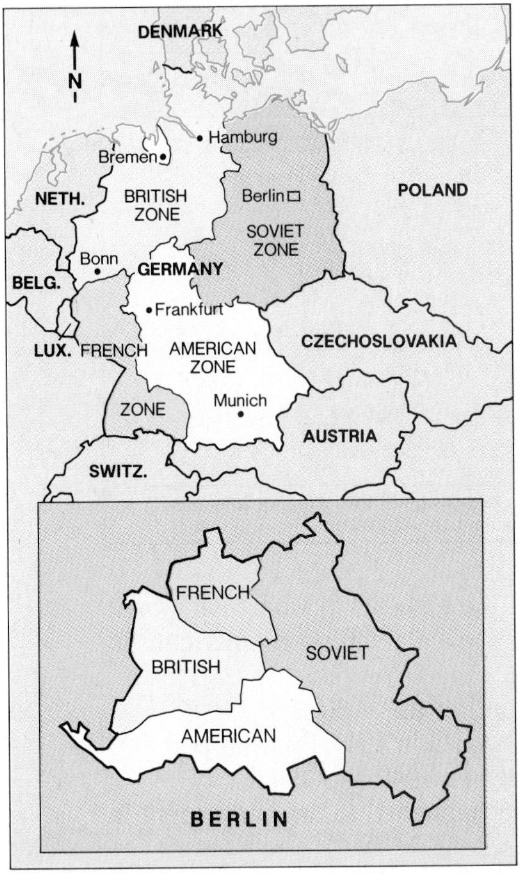

Why do you think Berlin was divided into four occupation zones?

The Yalta Conference

Just two days after his inauguration in 1945, President Roosevelt sailed for Yalta, a Soviet city on the Black Sea. He was traveling to Yalta to meet with other Allied leaders.

The men who met at Yalta were called the Big Three. In addition to Roosevelt, they were Prime Minister Winston Churchill of Great Britain and Premier Joseph Stalin of the Soviet Union. Many important decisions were made at the Yalta conference.

One of the first decisions regarded the terms for Germany's "unconditional surrender." After the war, Germany was to be divided into four zones of occupation. Military forces of the United States, Great Britain, the Soviet Union, and France would each occupy a portion of Germany. Berlin, the capital of prewar Germany, would also be divided into occupation zones. The Big Three decided that Germany would be disarmed and would have to pay reparations for the damage it had caused. Nazi war criminals, such as those responsible for the concentration camps, would be put on trial for their crimes.

The Big Three made decisions about the postwar boundaries of Europe. Poland's boundaries were redrawn. The Allied leaders also agreed that lands freed of German control were to have free elections. These elections would allow the people to choose their own government.

The leaders at Yalta announced that another important conference would be held in San Francisco. The conference, scheduled to open on April 25, 1945, was to create a world organization dedicated to preserving peace.

Background: It was decided at the Yalta Conference that the boundaries of Poland would be shifted westward. About one third of pre-1939 Poland was to become Soviet territory. Former German territory to the west and north of prewar Poland would become Polish.

Background: In 1965, the number of nations serving two-year terms on the UN Security Council was raised from six to ten.

When Franklin Roosevelt returned from Yalta, he was tired and weak. In April 1945, President Roosevelt decided to take a much needed rest. He traveled to the "Little White House" in Warm Springs, Georgia. There, on April 12, Roosevelt suffered a stroke and died.

The nation was shocked and deeply saddened by Roosevelt's death. He had been the President of the United States for more than 12 years.

The United Nations

Immediately after Roosevelt's death, Harry S Truman was sworn in as President. One of President Truman's first official acts was to announce that the international conference at San Francisco would be held on schedule.

The San Francisco conference began on April 25, 1945. In attendance were representatives of 50 nations. Out of the conference came a new international organization, the United Nations (UN). The UN was similar in many ways to the old League of Nations, created after World War I. Like the league, the UN was dedicated to the peaceful settlement of disputes among nations.

The representatives at San Francisco agreed that the United Nations should have two governing bodies. All of the member nations would be represented in the General Assembly. Any member could bring matters before the assembly for debate and action. This body became a kind of giant "town meeting" for the entire world. The assembly would also elect a secretary-general to coordinate the various branches of the UN.

The Security Council would consist of permanent representatives of the Big Five nations—the United States, Great Britain, the Soviet Union, France, and China. Also serving on the council would be representatives of six nations chosen by the assembly for two-year terms. The Security Council would investigate disputes between nations. It also had the power to order action against aggressors. Each of the Big Five nations had the right to veto any action recommended by the council.

The United Nations would also include a Trusteeship Council to oversee various colonial matters. Former colonies of Japan and Germany would be held as "trust territories" by members of the council until their independence had been granted to them.

The United Nations Charter was signed in San Francisco on June 26, 1945. When it was presented to the Senate for approval, there was little opposition.

The Manhattan Project

After Germany surrendered, on May 7, 1945, the United States turned its full attention to the defeat of Japan. President Truman was advised that Japan could be defeated quickly by using a powerful new weapon.

Scientists had begun working on the new weapon shortly after the attack on Pearl Harbor. Among these scientists was a **physicist** named Albert Einstein, a German Jewish refugee. In 1939, Einstein and two other refugee scientists wrote a letter to President Roosevelt. They explained to the President that a powerful new bomb could be made by releasing the energy in the nucleus of an atom. The atomic bomb would not only be more powerful than

For Extra Interest: Write to the UN Bookshop, United Nations, New York, NY 10017, for a film catalog and other information to help in arranging a presentation on the United Nations for the class.

Background: One Manhattan Project scientist who witnessed the first atomic bomb test remarked, "It was as though the earth [had] opened and [the] skies had split."

any previous bomb, it would also release deadly radiation over a wide area. Roosevelt approved a project to begin research and development of this powerful bomb.

---

physicist a scientist who studies the nature of matter and energy

---

The job of developing the bomb was given to a top-secret group of scientists and engineers in May 1943. The code name for this group was the "Manhattan Project." The building of the bomb was done at Los Alamos, New Mexico. On July 16, 1945, an atomic bomb was successfully exploded over the desert sands of south central New Mexico.

The Potsdam Declaration

The day after the atomic blast in New Mexico, President Truman met with Allied leaders in the German city of Potsdam. At the beginning of the conference, Truman told Prime Minister Churchill and Premier Stalin about the new weapon.

On July 26, the American and British leaders issued a declaration setting out the terms for the unconditional surrender of Japan. Portions of Japan would be occupied by Allied military forces. Japanese war criminals would receive "stern justice." Japan would be disarmed and prevented from rearming itself.

At the end of the Potsdam Declaration was a warning to Japan to surrender unconditionally or face "prompt and utter destruction." The declaration did not explain how this "prompt and utter destruction" would be caused.

The military leaders of Japan remained opposed to any negotiations. The Japanese government would not surrender.

Truman's Decision

President Harry Truman faced one of the most difficult and most important decisions in American history. He believed that if the Allies had to invade Japan, hundreds of thousands of lives might be lost. By using the atomic bomb, he had been advised, the war could be ended quickly.

Yet many of the scientists who had developed the bomb now opposed its use. Many of them recommended that the bomb be dropped on a barren island or in a desert. Once the Japanese saw the power of the bomb, they would surely surrender. Some scientists opposed any use of the bomb whatsoever. In June 1945, a group of scientists warned the President that a nuclear arms race would follow the use of the bomb. They recommended that the weapon be placed under strict international control.

President Truman made his final decision as he returned from the Potsdam conference. He ordered the use of atomic weapons against Japan.

On August 6, 1945, an airplane named the *Enola Gay* dropped an atomic bomb on the Japanese city of Hiroshima (hee-roe-SHEE-mah). The blinding flash and heat of the bomb destroyed or damaged 96 percent of the buildings of the city. Some 78,000 people were killed instantly, and another 100,000 were injured. Many of the injured later died from their wounds or from atomic radiation.

In a radio speech, President Truman explained why the bomb had been used. "We have used it in order to shorten the

Background: In the Potsdam Declaration, the Allies also assured the Japanese people that they would not be "enslaved as a race or destroyed as a people." Their "fundamental human rights" would be respected.

agony of war, in order to save the lives of thousands and thousands of young Americans. We shall continue to use it until we completely destroy Japan's power to make war. Only a Japanese surrender will stop us."

The Japanese Surrender

The destruction of Hiroshima did not convince the Japanese to surrender. On August 8, the Soviet Union declared war on Japan. On August 9, an American bomber dropped a second atomic bomb on the city of Nagasaki (nah-gah-SAH-kee). More than 73,000 Japanese were killed.

At last, on August 10, Japan indicated that it was willing to surrender. It asked for only one condition, that Emperor Hirohito be allowed to remain in power. The Allies accepted this condition. Japan surrendered on August 14, 1945.

This view of Hiroshima shows the total destruction that resulted from dropping the atomic bomb.

The most destructive war in history had ended. More than 405,000 Americans had died. Nearly 671,000 were wounded in action. Great Britain and France suffered nearly as many casualties. By comparison, 7.5 million Russians, 3.5 million Germans, and 1.2 million Japanese had died in battle. Millions of additional civilians of many nations were killed.

The final victory in the war came at a very high price. Atomic weapons gave the human race the power to destroy itself. The control of that power would be a major challenge for future generations.

Section Review

1. How did the United States bring the war in Asia to an end?
2. What contribution did physicists make to the war effort?
3. Identify the role of the General Assembly, the Security Council, and the Trusteeship Council in the United Nations.
4. Why do you think Americans so readily accepted the United Nations in 1945, when they had rejected the League of Nations a generation earlier? Explain your answer.

CHAPTER REVIEW

Summary

The United States entered World War II on December 8, 1941, just one day after the Japanese bombed Pearl Harbor. By this time, Germany had captured most of Europe, and Japan was winning victories in the Far East. American forces were badly needed on both fronts.

In Europe, the German advance in Russia had been slowed by the harsh winter. Allied forces invaded Africa and from there moved on to the mainland of Europe. The D-Day invasion of France in 1944 saw the largest landing of troops in history. Germany finally surrendered to the Allies in May 1945.

On the home front, Americans contributed to the war effort by buying war bonds, paying higher taxes, and conserving fuel and food. Factories and farms in the United States produced the huge quantities of supplies needed to win the war.

In the Pacific, American forces slowly pushed the Japanese from the islands they had captured. In April 1945, President Roosevelt died. His successor, Harry Truman, brought the war in the Pacific to an abrupt end by ordering the dropping of two atomic bombs on Japan in August 1945. Japan quickly surrendered, and World War II was over.

Recalling the Facts

1. When and why did the United States enter World War II?
2. Why were the Allied victories in the battle of Coral Sea and the battle of Midway important?
3. Describe the movement of Allied forces in 1944 and 1945 that eventually led to the defeat of Germany.
4. How did the United States raise money to pay for World War II?
5. What important contributions were made by women, blacks, American Indians, Mexican Americans, and Japanese Americans to the war effort?
6. What did the Potsdam Declaration say? How did military leaders in Japan feel about surrender at the time the Potsdam Declaration was issued?

Analyzing the Facts

1. What was the significance of the D-Day invasion?

2. How did World War II bring an end to the Great Depression?
3. Why, of all the major Allied Powers, do you think the United States played the major role in defeating Japan?
4. How do you think the veto power held by the five permanent members of the UN Security Council could affect the effectiveness of that body to preserve peace?
5. Make a list of the pros and cons Truman had to weigh in making his decision to use the atomic bomb against Japan.

Time and History

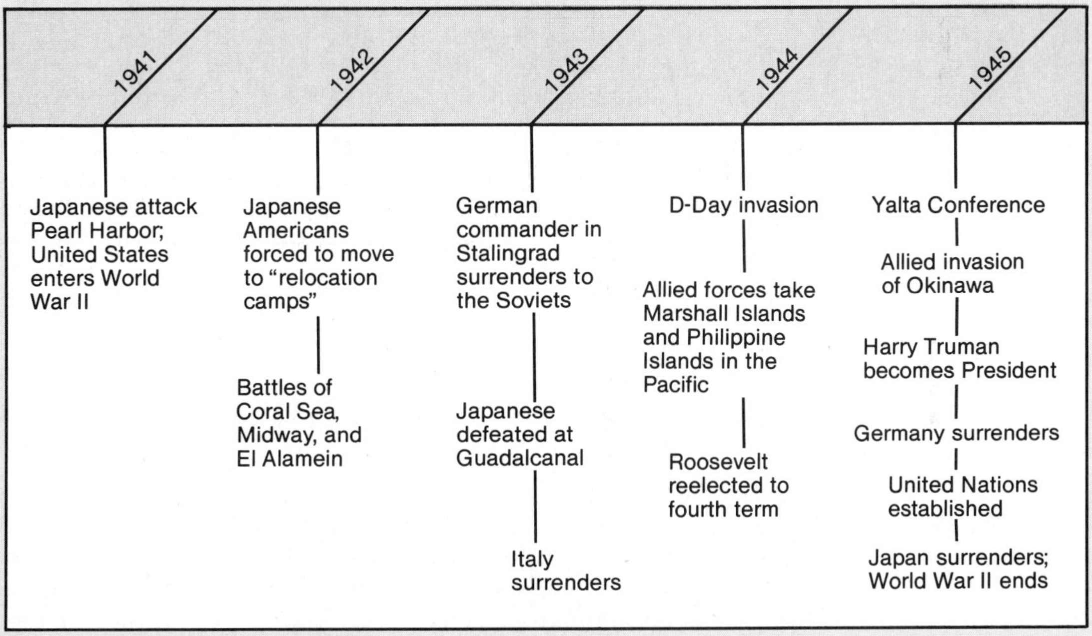

1941
Japanese attack Pearl Harbor; United States enters World War II
1942
Japanese Americans forced to move to "relocation camps"
Battles of Coral Sea, Midway, and El Alamein
1943
German commander in Stalingrad surrenders to the Soviets
Japanese defeated at Guadalcanal
Italy surrenders
1944
D-Day invasion
Allied forces take Marshall Islands and Philippine Islands in the Pacific
Roosevelt reelected to fourth term
1945
Yalta Conference
Allied invasion of Okinawa
Harry Truman becomes President
Germany surrenders
United Nations established
Japan surrenders; World War II ends

1. How many years did the United States fight in World War II?
2. How many years after the D-Day invasion did Germany surrender?
3. In what year was the United Nations established?
4. Japanese Americans were not released from the "relocation camps" until the war ended. How many years did they live in these camps?
5. Which area was captured by the Allies last: the Philippine Islands, Guadalcanal, or Midway?

UNIT REVIEW

Summary

The prosperity of the 1920's ended with the stock market crash in 1929. During the depression that followed, millions of Americans lost their jobs. In 1932, President Franklin D. Roosevelt offered the nation a New Deal. Numerous "alphabet agencies" were created to bring reform, recovery, and relief to the nation. Slowly the United States began to recover from the depression.

In other parts of the world, the depression contributed to the rise of dictators. During the 1930's, dictators in Germany, Italy, and Japan threatened world peace by attacking other nations. Unable to stop Hitler's aggression by peaceful means, France and Great Britain declared war on Germany in 1939.

The United States entered World War II following a Japanese air attack on Pearl Harbor, Hawaii, on December 7, 1941. For almost four years, Americans fought the Axis Powers in Europe, Africa, Asia, and the Pacific. By the time the war ended in 1945, millions of lives had been lost, billions of dollars had been spent, and the responsibility for preventing future wars had been placed in the hands of the newly formed United Nations.

Recalling the Facts

1. What were the causes of the Great Depression?
2. What was the New Deal?
3. How were the dictators who rose to power following World War I similar?
4. Describe where, when, and why World War II broke out. Describe when and why the United States entered the war.
5. What was the Manhattan Project? What role did it play in the outcome of the war?

Analyzing the Facts

1. Why do you think Roosevelt was more successful than Hoover in solving the nation's problems during the depression?
2. How does the New Deal influence our lives today?
3. If the Japanese had not bombed Pearl Harbor, do you think the United States could have avoided military involvement in World War II? Why or why not?

4. Since the end of World War II, much of the responsibility for defending Japan has fallen to the United States. Do you think that Japan should be allowed to build up its military forces now to take over the burden of its defense? Why or why not?

Reviewing Vocabulary

Define the following terms:

depression	fascist	island hopping
Fireside Chat	scapegoat	gross national product
devaluation	appeasement	sabotage
deficit spending	underground	physicist

Sharpening Your Skills

1. Compare Hoover's point of view on direct federal aid to the poor with Roosevelt's.
2. Compare the viewpoints of Manhattan Project scientists on the use of the atomic bomb.

Answer the three questions below by comparing the statistics given in the graph, "Deficit Federal Spending, 1933–1939," on page 583.

3. In what year did the amount of money received by the federal government come closest to the amount it spent?
4. In what years was the amount of money spent by the federal government more than twice what it received?
5. How much money did the federal government spend from 1933 to 1939? How much money did it receive during those years? What was the total federal deficit from 1933 to 1939?

Writing and Research

1. The period from 1929 to 1945 saw many powerful individuals shape history by their deeds and actions. Research and report on one historical figure from this period, and tell how this person helped to shape history.
2. Research and prepare a report on the United Nations. The report should include information on the organization and functions of the General Assembly, the Security Council, the Secretariat, the International Court of Justice, the Economic and Social Council, and the Trusteeship Council.

Unit 9 America's Changing Role

29 Times were good for many Americans in the years following World War II. Prosperity was fueled by a growing demand for consumer goods. Politics reflected the postwar prosperity. Few new reforms were passed by Congress. Not all Americans, however, shared in the good times. Poverty and racial discrimination remained unsolved problems.

30 *The postwar period was also a time of new tensions and dangers. The United States and the Soviet Union became superpowers. Their rivalry affected events around the world. American foreign policy was directed at preventing the spread of communism. The fear of communism also had a powerful effect on events within the United States.*

31 *At the beginning of the 1960's, Americans were filled with a sense of optimism and purpose. Problems at home and abroad, however, weakened this optimism. By the late 1960's, confusion and frustration had replaced the earlier national mood of confidence. For many Americans the 1960's were a bewildering decade.*

Chapter
29

Postwar America

In 1957, Elizabeth Eckford was one of nine black students who were going to attend an all-white high school in Little Rock, Arkansas. A federal court had ordered the school to admit the students. The governor of Arkansas called out the National Guard to keep them from enrolling. As Elizabeth approached the school, angry whites pushed forward. "I looked into the face of an old woman," she recalled, "and it seemed a kind face, but when I looked at her again, she spat on me." Little Rock was one part of the struggle for racial equality.

After you read this chapter, you will be able to:

1. List the causes of American prosperity after World War II.
2. Compare the administrations of Truman and Eisenhower.
3. Describe the major problems of postwar America.
☐ Read a pictograph.

Discuss: What do you think would have been the major concerns of a serviceman or servicewoman at the end of the war?

1. Happy Days

BEFORE YOU READ: *What were the major causes of American prosperity in the years 1945 to 1960?*

The years following World War II were a time of national and personal readjustment. The nation's economy shifted from wartime production to the manufacturing of consumer goods. Millions of Americans who had served in the armed forces returned to civilian life. After years of sacrifice and hardship, the American people were ready to relax and enjoy life again.

The GIs Come Home

Equipment issued to American soldiers during World War II bore two initials: GI. The initials stood for "Government Issue." The term "GI" also came to stand for the men and women who served in the armed forces. At the war's end, there were 12.5 million American GIs.

Following the victory over Japan in August 1945, the armed forces began releasing men and women from the service. The federal government took steps to ease the readjustment to peacetime conditions. In 1944, Congress passed the Servicemen's Readjustment Act, popularly known as the GI Bill of Rights. This act provided many benefits to GIs.

The GI Bill of Rights provided low-interest loans to former GIs who wanted to start their own businesses. "GI loans" were also available for the purchase of homes and farms. The act provided unemployment relief for veterans who had problems finding jobs. They were eligible for weekly payments of $20 for a maximum of 52 weeks. Many veterans became temporary members of the "52–20 Club."

The most important part of the GI Bill was its aid to education. Each former GI was eligible for $500 a year to pay for the cost of attending a college or job-training school. The act also provided up to $75 a month for personal expenses while going to classes. Millions of veterans took advantage of the program.

The goal of most GIs was to return to normal civilian life as quickly as possible. Naturally, there were some problems of personal adjustment. The war had separated many families. Children who had not seen their fathers for several years had to get reacquainted. Many wives who had been "single parents" during the war had to share family leadership with their husbands once again. Other women, who had held high-paying jobs in the wartime defense industries, lost their jobs to returning GIs. These women workers often faced severe problems of economic readjustment. Some veterans had had terrifying experiences during the war. They bore the physical and emotional scars from their wartime service. For them readjustment was especially hard.

However, most GIs succeeded very well in adjusting to civilian life. Many got married and settled down. After 1945, there was a "wedding boom." The average age at which people married dropped sharply, and the birthrate soared in the postwar years. The annual number of births in the United States increased from about 2.5 million in 1940 to more than 4 million in 1955. The children born in these postwar years were members of what was later called the "baby boom" generation.

Background: Besides the GI Bill, the government also gave returning GIs a generous financial bonus when they left the armed services, and it promised GIs that if they had held civil service jobs before the war, they could return to their former positions.

For Extra Interest: Compare postwar prices of new housing with those of today by looking in the real estate section of a local newspaper.

Postwar Prosperity

American prosperity in the postwar years was remarkable. Between 1945 and 1960, the gross national product more than doubled.

One of the causes of the postwar prosperity was the continued spending by the federal government for national defense. Although the armed forces were drastically reduced in size, the government provided huge sums of money for the development of new weapons. Government spending for defense meant millions of jobs for Americans in the defense industries.

Prosperity was also aided by increased foreign trade. The United States was the only major power that emerged from World War II economically stronger than it had been before the war. The farms and factories of other countries were in ruins. The United States became the "workshop of the world." It imported raw materials from around the globe and sold its products in almost every nation. Between 1950 and 1960, the value of American foreign trade doubled.

The most important cause of the postwar prosperity was the increased demand for goods from American consumers. Many goods had been scarce or were rationed during the war. People had little choice but to save their money or buy war bonds. Beginning in 1945, people rushed to buy all the goods that had been unavailable during the war.

There was a huge increase in the demand for new housing. To meet the demand, some people in the housing industry developed a method of mass-producing homes. Builders used standardized parts and automatic equipment to speed construction. Mass production reduced the cost of home construction. The homes sold for about $10,000, an amount far less than the price of a custom-built home.

The entrepreneur who pioneered this new construction was Abraham Levitt. He created the nation's first mass-produced "housing development" on Long Island, New York. The name of the community was Levittown. Levitt's sons, William and Alfred, built other Levittowns in suburban New Jersey and Pennsylvania. Soon imitators were building similar "developments" all across the nation. By the mid-1950's, a million new homes were being built each year.

To fill their new homes, Americans bought many new gadgets and appli-

New Housing Starts

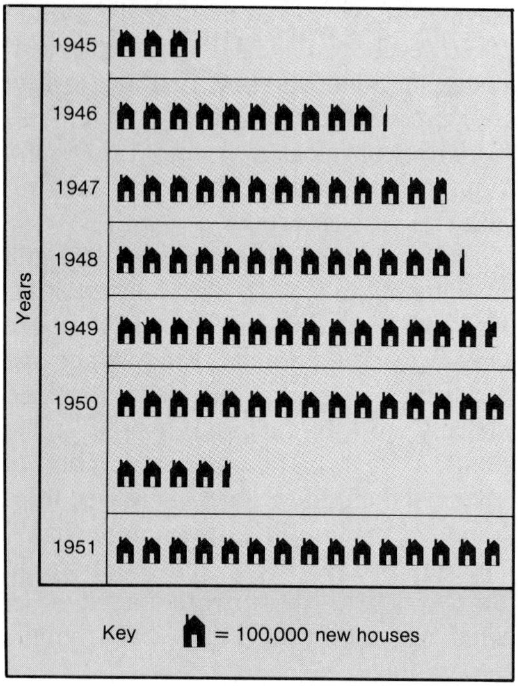

Background: Life in the new suburban communities was centered on the family. The sidewalks and lawns of suburbia were cluttered with the wagons, tricycles, and bicycles of the young "baby boom" generation.

Background: "There's a Ford in your future" was a popular advertisement of the day.

Why do you think the houses in this suburban housing development look so similar?

ances. The first electric clothes dryer appeared on the market in 1946. It was followed by dozens of other conveniences for the home. In 1950, Americans bought 225,000 automatic dishwashers and 750,000 electric garbage disposals.

Automobile production also expanded to meet the postwar demand. In 1946, 2 million autos were produced. Just two years later, nearly 4 million American cars were made.

Work and Play

The American economy not only prospered in the postwar years, it also underwent a basic change. Throughout America's earlier history, most people had worked in such fields as farming, manufacturing, or mining. They had been engaged in the production of goods. In the postwar years, however, more and more Americans held jobs in such fields as advertising, education, sales, and entertainment. Workers in these fields did not produce goods, they produced services. In 1940, only about one third of the American work force held service jobs. By 1960, more than half of all American workers had jobs in service fields.

The basic cause of this change was the increased output of American workers. **Productivity** increased rapidly after 1945. New and improved methods of production reduced the amount of time it took to produce goods. In 1945, for example, it took 310 hours of work to produce an automobile. In 1960, it took only 155 hours, or half as many. This increased productivity meant that fewer workers were needed to produce the nation's goods. More workers were thus available for jobs in service industries.

---

productivity the ability of a worker or business to produce more goods with the same or fewer inputs of land, labor, or capital

---

Increased productivity also allowed businesses to reduce the number of hours they required their employees to work. Paid vacations and holidays became common.

With fewer hours of work and more free time, Americans began looking for new ways to have fun. The most popular form of home entertainment was television. The first television sets were sold in 1939. But production of sets was

Background: Increased leisure time led to the popularity of amusement parks as a form of entertainment. The most successful amusement park was Disneyland in Anaheim, California. Disneyland opened in 1955 and attracted over one million visitors in its first six months.

EUREKA!

The Long-Playing Record

Sound recording and reproduction have changed a great deal since 1877. In that year, Edison made the first sound recording by reciting into a phonograph. One of the most far-reaching changes was the invention of the long-playing record, or LP.

Edison himself introduced a long-playing record in 1927, but it was not a commercial success. The LP as we know it today was developed in the 1940's by a research team at Columbia Records, which is a division of CBS.

The method of sound recording used to make the new LP's was similar to that used for other records. A sharp needle cut a continuous, spiral-shaped groove into a rotating aluminum disc. As the disc turned, the needle vibrated from side to side at a rate determined by the sound being recorded. The wiggly groove "captured" the sound and allowed it to be played back.

The LP was the same size as a standard record, but it held 20 minutes of sound on a side instead of five. This was possible because the LP's grooves were much finer and more closely spaced than those of other records. The LP also played more slowly, turning at 33 1/3 revolutions per minute compared to the rapid 78 rpm of the older discs. This made it possible to record more material on a single disc. The LP's only drawback was that none of the phonographs on the market in 1948 could play it.

Other record companies began developing their own long-playing records, and new phonographs were built to play them. RCA introduced a smaller record that played at 45 rpm. In the 1950's, the 45 soon became the standard for pop music singles, while the LP took over the classical music field. By 1960, no one was recording 78's. The old discs had become collectors' items.

---

interrupted by the war. By 1960, about half of America's homes had one or more sets.

Television had a powerful impact on the American way of life. Families shared an evening's entertainment at home. News from around the world was communicated instantly to television viewers. Advertisers used television to promote their products, and political candidates

 Discuss: What new careers has the television industry made available?

Background: Before the war, there were only three large record companies in the United States: The American Record Company, RCA Victor, and Decca. By 1960, there were dozens of companies producing millions of records.

used it to win votes. Educational programs instructed viewers in everything from how to repair automobiles to how to cook asparagus. Most importantly, television brought shared experiences to Americans across the nation.

The recording industry also expanded in the postwar years. Record players improved in quality, and "hi-fi's" (from "*hi*gh *fi*delity") became as common as television sets. The records themselves became longer playing, more durable, and cheaper to produce.

Jazz increased in popularity in the 1940's and early 1950's. Among the great jazz musicians were Dizzy Gillespie, Duke Ellington, and Charlie Parker.

A new style of popular music also appeared in the mid-1950's—rock and roll. The earliest rock "hits" were "Shake, Rattle, and Roll," recorded in 1954 by Bill Haley and the Comets, and "Rock Around the Clock," recorded the following year. In 1956, a young Mississippi-born singer named Elvis Presley recorded an even bigger hit, "Heartbreak Hotel." Presley was the first of many rock "superstars" to attract a large national audience.

Rock and roll was true teenage music. Its lyrics celebrated teenage romance. It appeared at the time when the oldest members of the "baby boom" generation were reaching adolescence. This new generation had money to spend. They gladly spent it on the music they considered their own.

Young people danced to rock and roll hits on the television show "American Bandstand."

Section Review

1. What were the major causes of American prosperity in the years 1945 to 1960?
2. What benefits were provided by the 1944 GI Bill of Rights?
3. Define productivity. What impact did increased productivity have on the lives of American workers?
4. Do you believe that television has had a positive or negative effect on life in the United States? Explain your answer.

Social Studies Skills

Reading a Pictograph

The post-World War II economic boom contributed to the rapid development of the television industry. The pictograph below shows the increase in American households with television sets.

A pictograph uses symbols to present statistical information. The pictograph key explains how many objects or what amount each symbol represents. Part of a symbol represents a fraction of the number or the amount. For example, in the pictograph below, half of a symbol stands for 5 million, and a quarter of a symbol stands for 2.5 million. To figure the number of households with television sets in any given year, count all the symbols and symbol fractions shown for that year, and multiply the total by 10 million.

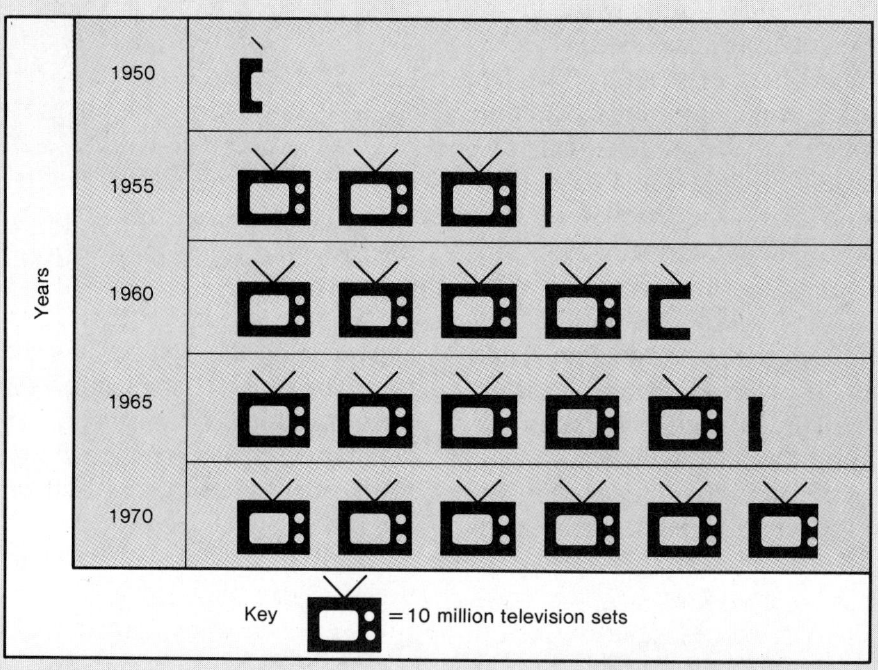

1. Approximately how many households had television sets in 1950?
2. Between what five-year period was the increase in households with television sets the greatest?
3. Why is it difficult to get precise information from a pictograph?
4. In 1967, 55,130,000 households had television sets. How and where would you add this information to the pictograph above?

Discuss: Among Truman's proposals rejected by Congress were federal aid to education and national health insurance. Why do you think Congress failed to approve these proposals?

2. The Politics of Moderation

BEFORE YOU READ: *What proposals were included in Harry Truman's Fair Deal?*

The politics of the postwar years were somewhat similar to those following World War I. There was a desire to return to "normalcy" and a reaction against leaders who called for political or social reforms. Americans seemed to want nothing more than to enjoy their newfound prosperity.

Yet the 1950's were not the 1920's. Following World War II, the nation did not retreat into isolationism. Nor did Americans want to dismantle all the reforms of the New Deal. Postwar politics followed a moderate course.

Harry S Truman

When Vice-President Harry S Truman learned of the death of Franklin Roosevelt, he felt as if "the moon, the stars and all the planets" had fallen upon him. Truman was not well prepared for the presidency. The leaders of the Roosevelt administration had not kept Truman fully informed on many issues.

Truman was a strong supporter of the New Deal. When he became President in 1945, Truman announced that he would continue the policies of Roosevelt. On September 6, 1945, he presented to Congress a 21-point program. He called his program the Fair Deal. He proposed an expanded Social Security program, a higher minimum wage, and continued wage and price controls. He also wanted to guarantee "full employment" for the nation's work force and provide federal aid to education. He supported national health insurance, a public-works program, and new public-housing projects.

Truman did not, however, exert the strong leadership needed to push his program through Congress. He was unable to inspire the kind of loyalty that Roosevelt had enjoyed.

One of the first domestic problems that Truman faced as President was inflation. During the war, prices and wages had been strictly regulated by the federal government. In 1946, the wartime price controls ended. The postwar demand for new products was greater than the supply. Prices rose sharply. Truman favored the continuation of price controls. He was unable, however, to get a strong price-control bill passed by Congress. A weak measure was passed instead. Some prices rose sharply.

The Republicans rallied against Truman in the congressional elections of 1946. The Republican slogan was "Had Enough?" The 1946 elections were a great Republican victory. Republicans were elected to majorities in both houses of Congress.

The Eightieth Congress passed the National Security Act. An investigation of the attack on Pearl Harbor had revealed serious weaknesses in the nation's **intelligence**-gathering system. The National Security Act established an organization to gather and analyze secret information needed for the national defense. This new organization was the Central Intelligence Agency (CIA). The act also created the National Security Council to advise the President.

Background: The National Security Act brought the army, navy, and air force together into one national military establishment. The head of each service became responsible to the secretary of defense, a Cabinet position replacing that of secretary of war.

Discuss: What are the basic differences between liberals and conservatives?

intelligence secret information gathered for the national defense

The 1948 Election

As the presidential election of 1948 approached, Harry Truman found himself criticized by two very different kinds of critics. One group of critics believed that Truman was not doing enough to further the reforms of the New Deal. These critics believed that the government should more actively regulate the economy and promote the greater welfare and greater liberties of all the people. These critics were known as **liberals**.

liberal a person who believes that government should take action to regulate the economy and promote the greater welfare and liberties of the people

Other critics thought that Truman was continuing too much of the New Deal reforms. These critics argued that the economy should be freed from too much government regulation. Social and economic progress, they believed, could best be achieved by allowing business the greatest possible freedom. Such critics were known as **conservatives**.

conservative a person who believes that government regulation of the economy should be kept at a minimum and that progress can best be achieved by allowing business the greatest possible freedom

At their 1948 convention, the Democrats voted to include in their party platform a strong statement in favor of equal rights for blacks. Southern conservatives walked out of the convention and formed their own party, the States' Rights Democratic Party. This party, better known as the "Dixiecrats," nominated Governor J. Strom Thurmond of South Carolina for President. The Democratic coalition that had been carefully built by Franklin D. Roosevelt in the 1930's was coming apart.

Meanwhile, many liberals who were disappointed with Truman's leadership formed a new Progressive party in 1948. The Progressives nominated Henry Wallace for President. Wallace, a former Vice-President during Roosevelt's third term, urged increased American cooperation with the Soviet Union. Some liberals regarded Wallace as too pro-Soviet. They reluctantly supported Truman.

The Election of 1948

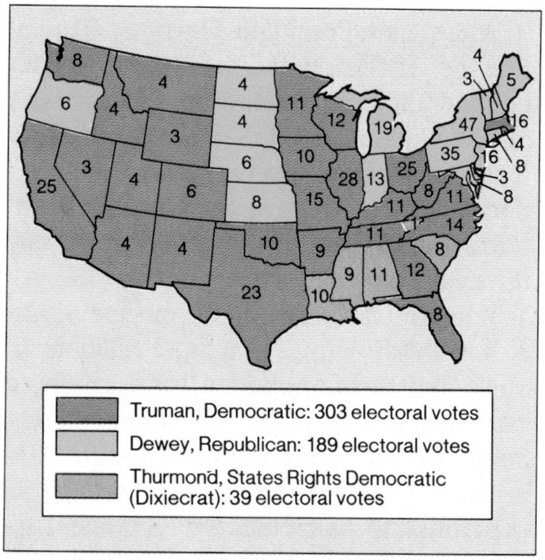

Which regions of the country supported Dewey in the election of 1948?

Background: Henry Wallace, who had served as vice-president during Roosevelt's third term, urged increased American cooperation with the Soviet Union. Some liberals regarded Wallace as too pro-Soviet. They reluctantly supported Truman.

Voters wore these campaign buttons in 1952 to show support for their favorite candidates in the presidential election.

Truman won the Democratic nomination for President in 1948. The prospects for his reelection, however, were not very bright. The Republicans believed that with the Democratic party split apart they had a good chance for victory in 1948. As in 1944, they chose Governor Thomas E. Dewey of New York to be their candidate.

Dewey was confident of victory throughout the campaign. All the public opinion polls indicated that he would win. Yet on election day, Truman scored one of the greatest upsets in American political history. He beat Dewey by more than 2 million votes. The Democrats also won majorities in both the House of Representatives and the Senate.

After the 1948 election, Truman at last was able to get some of his Fair Deal legislation passed. Congress increased the minimum wage from 40 cents to 75 cents per hour. It also extended Social Security coverage to an additional 9 million Americans. Retirement benefits were increased by 75 percent. Congress provided federal funds for the construction of public-housing projects for low-income families. Congress also passed a new immigration law in 1950. The new law doubled the number of southern and eastern Europeans allowed to immigrate to the United States each year.

"I Like Ike"

The success of the Republicans in 1950 caused them to look forward to the presidential election two years later. In 1952, the Republicans chose as their candidate one of the most popular heroes of World War II, General Dwight David Eisenhower.

Truman did not seek reelection in 1952. The Democrats chose Governor Adlai E. Stevenson of Illinois as their candidate.

Background: Eisenhower was a good student and an excellent athlete. He played football and baseball in high school.

Discuss: What qualifications do you think are important for a presidential candidate? What qualifications does the Constitution specify that a President must have?

The campaign of 1952 centered on the personalities of the two presidential candidates and their running mates. Eisenhower, or "Ike" as he was nicknamed, was highly respected and loved by many Americans. His campaign slogan, "I Like Ike," captured the national mood. There were some doubts, however, about the Republican vice-presidential nominee, Senator Richard M. Nixon of California. Nixon was charged with receiving secret campaign funds from a group of supporters. To defend himself against the charge, Nixon, on September 23, 1952, broadcast one of the first nationwide television campaign speeches. He denied all wrongdoing and appealed to the emotions of his viewers by making references to his wife, children, and even his dog, Checkers. The "Checkers speech" proved to be very effective. It helped restore Richard Nixon's reputation.

The Democratic candidate, Adlai Stevenson, was highly intelligent and very witty. To some he seemed almost *too* smart. The Republicans called him an "egghead." Stevenson was also divorced, and this caused many voters to reject him. His running mate was Senator John J. Sparkman of Alabama, a leading Southern Democrat.

The popularity of Eisenhower was too much for the Democrats to overcome. Eisenhower won the election in 1952, receiving 6.6 million more popular votes than Stevenson.

President Eisenhower left most of the routine business of the presidency to his staff. Eisenhower hoped to stay above unimportant political squabbles. Critics, however, charged that the President was losing touch with important issues.

President Eisenhower's domestic policies tended to favor business interests. He appointed people from the business sector to nearly all the important posts in his administration. Eisenhower's policies also provided benefits to the growing suburban middle class. Between 1954 and 1959, Congress passed a series of housing acts that made it easier for Americans to borrow money to buy homes. In 1956, Congress passed the Federal Interstate Highway Act. This act provided $32 billion for a huge interstate highway system. People who commuted from the suburbs to the cities especially welcomed the new highways.

Section Review

1. What were the major proposals of President Truman's Fair Deal?
2. Explain the difference between a liberal and a conservative.
3. Which groups benefited from the domestic policies of the Eisenhower administration?
4. What military leaders other than Eisenhower have been elected President? Do you think it is likely that a military leader will be elected President in the future? Explain your answer.

Discuss: Eisenhower chose the president of General Motors to serve as secretary of defense. What qualifications do you think a secretary of defense should possess?

Discuss: Why do you think minority groups moved to the cities? What groups of people live in inner cities today? Why do you think this is so?

3. Postwar Problems

BEFORE YOU READ: *What major social problems confronted postwar America?*

The prosperity of the postwar years reached more people than prosperous times of earlier periods had. Yet not all Americans shared in the good times. Many residents of the central cities lived in poverty. The wages of workers did not keep up with rising prices, and many unions went on strike. Black Americans demanded—with more force than ever before—an end to racial discrimination.

Urban America

As more and more Americans moved to the suburbs, the central cities became the home of new residents. Some were European immigrants, who were allowed to come in greater numbers by the 1950 immigration law.

Most of the new residents, however, were black Americans from the South and Hispanics from Puerto Rico, Mexico, and other Latin American countries. The black population of Los Angeles, for example, grew from about 25,000 before World War II to nearly 650,000 by 1965. Mexican immigration to Los Angeles also increased rapidly. By 1945, Los Angeles had the largest Mexican population of any city in the world except Mexico City. The migration of blacks and Hispanics also swelled the cities of the East.

The new city residents were often unskilled laborers. They took whatever jobs were available, and these were usually low paying. Moreover, the demand for unskilled labor was declining. Lacking the needed skills, many black and Hispanic workers could not find work. Even those who were skilled found that prejudice often barred them from good jobs. Hispanic workers faced the additional problem of a language barrier. Many workers from Mexico or Puerto Rico spoke little English.

This Puerto Rican family is shown arriving in the United States in 1947.

Labor Problems

As wartime wage and price controls ended in 1946, prices for many goods rose sharply. Wages rose very slowly or not at all. Beginning in January 1946, workers in many industries went on strike for higher wages. President Truman appointed special commissions to help settle the disputes. The commissions

Background: New York's Harlem, formerly a middle-class black district, became an area of severe overcrowding and poverty. Many Puerto Ricans lived in "Spanish," or East, Harlem. By 1960, more Puerto Ricans lived in New York than in San Juan, the capital of Puerto Rico.

Background: In April 1946, 400,000 mine workers went on strike. With the country's supply of coal becoming low, President Truman ordered the federal government to take over the nation's coal mines temporarily. The strike ended when most of the workers' demands were granted.

usually recommended that the workers' demands for higher wages be granted.

Labor received a major setback in 1947. The Republican Congress passed the Labor-Management Relations Act, better known as the Taft-Hartley Act. The Taft-Hartley Act outlawed several union practices. It prohibited agreements between unions and employers to hire only union members to work on particular jobs. **Closed-shop agreements** became illegal under the Taft-Hartley Act. The act also limited the amount of money that unions could contribute to political candidates. The most important part of the act allowed the government to impose a 60-day "cooling-off period" on unions before they could go on strike.

---

closed-shop agreement an agreement between a union and an employer to hire only union members to work on a particular job

---

Labor leaders bitterly criticized the act. President Truman called the act a "slave labor law" and vetoed it. But Congress passed the act over the President's veto.

In spite of its setbacks, the union movement continued to grow in size. Union membership rose from 14.6 million in 1945 to 17 million by 1952. In 1955, the American Federation of Labor (AFL) and the Congress of Industrial Organizations (CIO) combined. The new AFL-CIO had 16 million members. It was the largest labor organization in American history.

By the mid-1950's, labor was becoming more powerful and self-confident. The president of the AFL-CIO, George Meany, boasted in 1955: "American labor never had it so good." Strikes became less common. Leaders of unions and businesses came to share a common outlook. Both hoped to avoid the conflict and expense of strikes.

Racism Under Attack

At the end of World War II, racial segregation by law and custom existed throughout the American South. Discrimination and segregation, though not by law, were also common in much of the North and West.

In the late 1940's, the movement for racial equality scored several victories. In 1946, President Truman appointed a federal commission to determine whether any Americans were being denied the rights guaranteed them by the Constitution. The **Civil Rights** Commission reported in 1947 that black Americans were being denied "the equal protection of the laws" in many southern states. Truman did not have the authority to change state laws. However, he did order an end to racial discrimination in the hiring of federal employees and an end to segregation in the armed forces.

---

civil rights rights guaranteed to individuals by the Constitution

---

There was also progress in breaking the "color line" in American sports. In 1947, Jackie Robinson became a second-base player for the Brooklyn Dodgers. He was the first black baseball player to play in the modern major leagues. By the mid-1960's, blacks were a major force in most professional sports. Blacks were also becoming more prominent in other fields of entertainment. Mahalia Jackson,

For Extra Interest: Have students research and graph the growth in union membership from 1945 to 1960.

For Extra Interest: Have interested students research and report on discrimination against American Indians in the postwar period. Indians were not allowed to vote in some states until a Supreme Court ruling in 1948.

Jackie Robinson was the first black player elected to baseball's Hall of Fame, in 1962.

a gospel singer, made many popular recordings. In 1955, Marian Anderson became the first black member of the New York Metropolitan Opera.

The one area of American life in which racism was the most obvious was education. In the North and West, many schools were segregated. All the states of the South maintained separate schools for black and white students. This system of segregation had been considered constitutional ever since the Supreme Court decision of *Plessy* v. *Ferguson* in 1896. That decision had allowed communities to provide black students with separate facilities as long as they were equal to those of white students. Southern schools for blacks, in fact, were separate but *not* equal. The buildings, textbooks, and other supplies for black students were inferior to those provided to whites.

The National Association for the Advancement of Colored People (NAACP) took legal action to challenge the system of school segregation. In 1954, the Supreme Court issued a historic decision. In the case of *Brown* v. *Board of Education of Topeka*, the court declared that segregation in public schools was unconstitutional. The author of the decision was Chief Justice Earl Warren. "To separate [black children] from others of similar age and qualifications solely because of their race," Warren wrote, "generates a feeling of inferiority . . . that affects their hearts and minds in a way unlikely ever to be undone." The Court ordered the nation's communities to end school segregation "with all deliberate speed."

Many southern communities disobeyed the court's order. By 1957, less than 700 of 3,000 southern school districts were **desegregated**. Some southern states adopted an official policy of "massive resistance." The governors of these states would close any school that the federal courts ordered integrated.

---

desegregate to end racial segregation

The battle over desegregation became a contest between federal authority and state and local governments. In September 1957, Little Rock, Arkansas' all-white Central High School was ordered to be desegregated by a federal court. Arkansas Governor Orval Faubus sent National Guard troops to Little Rock to prevent the order from being carried out. Faubus later withdrew the National Guard, but an

Discuss: Why do you think the Supreme Court reversed its earlier stance of "separate but equal" and ordered an end to segregation "with all deliberate speed"?

Famous Americans

RAY CHARLES

"I was born with music inside me. . . . Music was one of my parts. Like my ribs, my liver, my kidneys, my heart." Ray Charles has said that he cannot remember a time when he was not playing and singing music. Ray Charles Robinson was born in Albany, Georgia, in 1932. Shortly afterward, his family moved to Florida. From the time he was three, Charles was singing in a local church choir. Glaucoma left him blind at the age of six. He was sent to a school for the blind in St. Augustine, Florida, and received his first musical training there in piano and clarinet. Both of Charles' parents died when he was 15. Charles left school to earn his living from music. He played the piano with various bands in Florida. By 1954, Charles had dropped the last name of "Robinson" to avoid confusion with the boxer Sugar Ray Robinson. He had also organized his own rhythm and blues group. His first LP was released in 1957. It consisted of a mixture of pop, gospel, blues, and modern jazz instrumentals. This new sound was widely imitated and soon became a standard type of popular music.

Since 1957, Charles has recorded over 15 albums and won over 11 Grammy awards. He has toured the United States and two-thirds of the other nations of the world. His music has been warmly received everywhere. In 1976, Charles was inducted into the Songwriters Hall of Fame.

Charles sings, writes, and plays his music with great energy and emotion. As he has said, "The important thing in jazz is to feel your music, but *really* feel it and believe it. . . . Soul is when you can take a song and make it part of you—a part that's so true, so real, people think it must have happened to you. I'm not satisfied unless I can make them feel what I feel. . . . " In songs like "Georgia on My Mind," "Hit the Road, Jack," and "Crying Time," one can truly feel the music of Ray Charles.

angry white mob continued to block the black students from entering the school. President Eisenhower responded by sending federal troops to protect the students and to ensure that the court order would be obeyed.

The Movement Widens

The movement for racial equality, known as the civil rights movement, grew stronger in the late 1950's. In 1955, blacks in Montgomery, Alabama, demanded an

For Extra Interest: Refer students back to the introductory paragraphs of this chapter on page 630. Ask students what they would do or how they would feel if they were in Elizabeth's place.

end to segregation on the city's bus system. As in most southern cities, blacks were required to sit in the back of the bus. As the bus filled, blacks were supposed to surrender their seats to white passengers and stand. On December 1, 1955, a black woman named Rosa Parks took a seat in the front of a bus. When a white person asked her to move, she refused. Rosa Parks was arrested and jailed for violating the city's segregation law.

The following day, the city's 50,000 blacks began a boycott of the bus system. They said that they would not ride the buses until they were desegregated. The boycott was a success. A year after Rosa Park's arrest, the Supreme Court ordered the bus system desegregated.

Martin Luther King, Jr., a 26-year-old black Baptist minister, emerged from the Montgomery bus boycott as the national leader of the civil rights movement. While attending college in Boston, King had studied the life of the great Indian leader, Mahatma Gandhi (GAHN-dee). From Gandhi, King learned the philosophy of "nonviolent resistance." He urged blacks to engage in peaceful demonstrations to combat racism. Even if they were attacked or arrested, they should not fight back with violence. Through nonviolence King hoped to arouse the conscience of white Americans. In 1957, King and other black leaders organized the Southern Christian Leadership Conference (SCLC). The SCLC was dedicated to winning full civil rights for black Americans.

In response to the growing demands of black Americans, Congress passed the Civil Rights Act of 1957. In many southern states, local officials denied blacks the right to vote. The Civil Rights Act gave the attorney general the power to obtain court injunctions to stop local officials from interfering with blacks who were seeking to vote. Three years later, a second Civil Rights Act was passed. This act allowed federal officials to appoint special "referees" to register voters.

President Eisenhower was skeptical of the new laws and court decisions. "I don't believe," Eisenhower said, "you can change the hearts of men with laws or decisions." Martin Luther King, Jr., responded: "The law may not change the heart—but it can restrain the heartless."

Section Review

1. List the major social problems that confronted postwar America.
2. What were the terms of the Taft-Hartley Act of 1947?
3. Define civil rights and desegregate.
4. What progress was made between 1945 and 1960 to eliminate racial discrimination and segregation in the United States?
5. What similarities do you see between the movement for civil rights in the twentieth century and the Reconstruction period after the Civil War? What are the differences?

For Extra Interest: Have interested students research the life and work of Dr. Martin Luther King, Jr., and the concept of civil disobedience.

CHAPTER REVIEW

Summary

The years following World War II were "good times" for many Americans. Continued spending by the federal government for national defense, increased foreign trade, and a greater demand by Americans for consumer goods all contributed to the postwar prosperity. Increases in worker productivity resulted in more leisure time for many workers and a rise in the number of Americans holding service jobs.

Political attitudes following World War II were very similar to those that had followed World War I. Americans wanted a return to "normalcy" and generally reacted against calls for further reforms. As a result politics during the Truman and Eisenhower administrations followed a moderate course.

Not all Americans shared in the "good times" following the war. Many inner-city residents lived in poverty. Workers' wages often failed to keep up with inflation, and unions went on strike. Racial discrimination kept many Americans from enjoying the postwar prosperity, and black Americans demanded—with more force than ever before—an end to racial segregation and discrimination.

Recalling the Facts

1. Identify the following terms: GI, 52–20 Club, and baby boom.
2. How did increased worker productivity in the postwar years change the way Americans worked?
3. What industries expanded in the postwar years to provide entertainment for millions of Americans?
4. Why was Truman less effective in getting his Fair Deal programs passed by Congress than Franklin Roosevelt had been with his New Deal?
5. What did the Supreme Court rule in the case of *Brown* v. *Board of Education of Topeka*? What problems followed this decision?
6. Who was Martin Luther King, Jr.? What did he think was the best way for blacks to fight racism?

Analyzing the Facts

1. Do you think the GIs should receive government benefits that other Americans do not receive? Why or why not?

2. Why was Thomas Dewey confident that he would defeat Truman in the presidential election of 1948?
3. If you had been old enough to vote in the presidential election of 1952, for whom would you have voted? Why?
4. Why do you think blacks were able to break the color barrier in professional sports before they were able to do so in other occupational areas?
5. Compare the black boycott of the Montgomery city bus system in 1955–1956 to the colonial boycott of British goods staged to protest the Stamp Act in 1765 (Chapter 4). How were they similar? How were they different?

Time and History

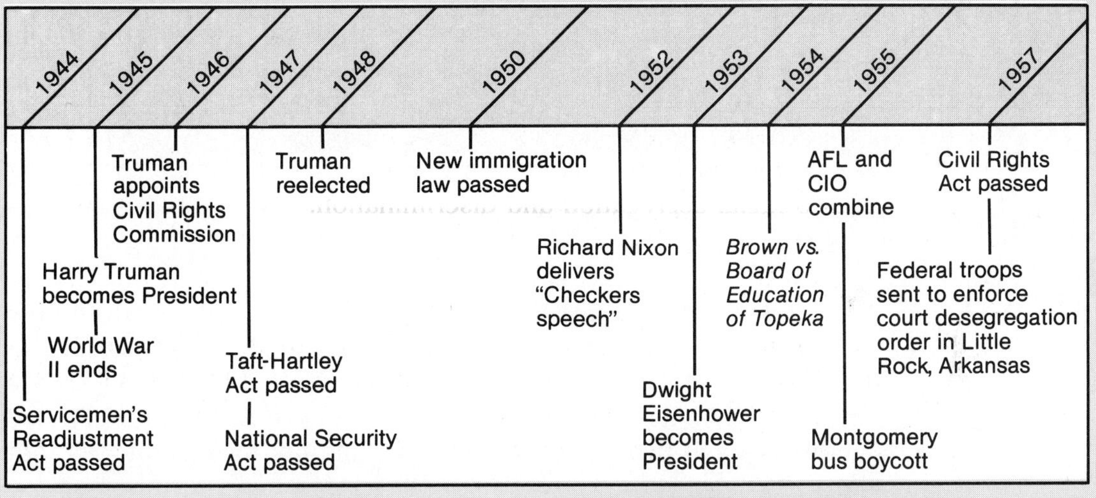

1. How many years was Harry Truman the President of the United States?
2. How many years after the Taft-Hartley Act was passed did the AFL and the CIO combine?
3. Which President ordered federal troops sent to Little Rock, Arkansas, to enforce school desegregation?
4. How many years after Truman appointed the Civil Rights Commission was the Civil Rights Act passed?
5. Which of the following laws was not passed while Truman was President—the Servicemen's Readjustment Act, the Taft-Hartley Act, or the National Security Act?

Chapter
30

The Cold War

On October 5, 1957, a satellite called *Sputnik I* became the first satellite to be launched into space. *Sputnik* had been sent into orbit by a powerful rocket fired from the Soviet Union. The United States had always prided itself on its superior technology. But now the Soviet Union had achieved a feat that the United States could not match—at least not yet.

Sputnik and the reaction it caused were part of a great rivalry between the United States and the Soviet Union. This rivalry affected many other nations around the world. It was the most expensive and most dangerous rivalry the world had ever known.

After you read this chapter, you will be able to:

1. Describe the origins of the Cold War.
2. Trace the American response to Communist expansion.
3. Explain the effects of the Cold War on the United States.
- Distinguish between facts and opinions.

Discuss: Before World War II, the nations of Western Europe had been the most powerful in the world. How had this situation changed after the war?

1. Roots of the Cold War

BEFORE YOU READ: *In what ways do the political and economic systems of the United States and the Soviet Union differ?*

At the end of World War II, the United States was the most powerful nation on earth. Yet Americans did not feel safe. The nation felt threatened by the other great world power to emerge from the war, the Soviet Union. The United States and the Soviet Union had been allies during the war, but grave differences separated the two nations. After the war, the two nations became rivals for power and influence throughout the world.

The Postwar World

The world was a vastly different place after World War II. Europe's power was shattered. Bombing had destroyed cities. Millions of people were homeless, hungry, and living in poverty. The political systems of the European nations had undergone a tremendous strain. Prime Minister Winston Churchill described Europe in 1945 as "a rubble heap" and "a breeding ground of hate."

The old European empires were fast crumbling in Asia, the Middle East, Africa, and elsewhere. The people who lived in Europe's colonies were eager to become independent nations.

It was in this new world that the United States and the Soviet Union emerged as "superpowers." Both the United States and the Soviet Union expected to play leading roles in shaping the postwar world. Both nations were also determined to protect their own vital interests and to ensure the safety of their own people. As the rivalry between the two superpowers increased, each nation viewed the other with growing suspicion and fear.

The two nations differed in their beliefs about government. In theory, the Soviet Union was governed by an elected legislature known as the Supreme Soviet. In fact the government was controlled by a single party, the Communist party. Under Premier Joseph Stalin the Soviet government was a brutal dictatorship. Any criticism of the government was put down. Stalin's secret police arrested hundreds of thousands of Russians who were suspected of being disloyal. Many were either sent to prison camps or executed.

According to communist **ideology**, the means of producing and distributing the nation's goods were owned and managed by the government in the name of the people. Private property under the communist system was limited. The Soviet government owned all industries, natural resources, mines, banks, and the means of communication and transportation. In the **planned economy** of the Soviet Union, the central government directed all types of economic activity.

---

ideology a basic belief or theory of government and society

planned economy a system in which the central government directs all types of economic activity

---

The economic and political systems of the United States, of course, were very different from those of the Soviet Union.

Background: Factories in the Soviet Union produce what the government tells them to produce. Consumer demand does not determine what or how much is produced as it does in the United States.

For Extra Interest: Students should examine a map of the Soviet Union to understand why a warm-water port leading to the Mediterranean was so important to the Soviets. They should understand that Vladivostok is not icefree all year.

In the American system the production and distribution of goods were privately owned and operated for profit. **Capitalism** allowed much greater economic freedom to the individual than the communist system did. In addition, the democratic principles of American government guaranteed political freedoms that the Soviet government did not permit.

capitalism an economic system in which the production and distribution of the nation's goods are privately owned and operated for profit

Soviet Foreign Policy

Two closely related principles guided the foreign policy of the Soviet Union. The first was the principle of self-interest. After the war, Stalin was determined to secure his nation's long western border against future attacks. He believed that it was essential for Russia's security to control the nations that bordered the Soviet Union on the west. Stalin also wanted to be able to get to resources and transportation routes needed by the Soviet Union. This involved securing a warm-water port on the Mediterranean.

The second principle that guided Soviet foreign policy was the belief that the Soviet Union had a historic mission to destroy capitalism and western imperialism. Soviet leaders had a grand vision of their nation's role in promoting communism around the world. Eventually, all the world would be "freed" from both capitalism and imperialism. The Soviet Union would become the dominant power on earth.

The United States, understandably, viewed Soviet foreign policy as aggressive. The United States sought to safeguard its own security. American foreign policy was also directed at promoting capitalism and democratic ideals around the world.

In the postwar period, the United States and the Soviet Union fought a war of propaganda, economic pressure, and military threats. This enormous rivalry between the two nations became known as the **Cold War**. Occasionally, the rivalry became a "hot war," as one of the superpowers engaged in combat with an ally of the other. Fortunately, however, the two superpowers themselves did not go to war directly.

At the end of the war, Russian troops occupied many Eastern European nations. Here Russian tanks are entering Hungary.

Discuss: Why do you think the United States viewed the Soviet Union as aggressive? Why do the Soviets frequently refer to the United States as imperialistic?

Discuss: Why do you think the Allied powers allowed the Soviet Union to dominate the countries of Eastern Europe?

---

cold war a war fought with propaganda, economic pressure, and military threats

---

The First Moves

The first moves in the Cold War came in Eastern Europe. During the last years of World War II, the Russians had driven the German army back across Poland and into Germany. When the war ended, Russian armed forces occupied most of Eastern Europe. At the Yalta Conference in February 1945, Premier Stalin had promised that Poland and other occupied lands would have free elections to determine their new governments. In fact, however, Stalin installed governments in Eastern Europe that were dominated by the Soviet Union. These governments held elections that clearly were not free. **Satellite** governments were established in Poland, Hungary, Rumania, Bulgaria, Albania, and East Germany.

---

satellite a small nation that is dominated by another larger and more powerful nation

---

The expansion of Soviet power alarmed the United States and other western nations. Especially disturbing was the Soviet domination of Poland. The invasion of Poland by the Nazis in 1939 had prompted Great Britain and France to declare war on Germany. Now the freedom of Poland was being threatened again. Furthermore, the Soviet action in Poland was a direct violation of the promise Stalin had made at Yalta. Eleven days before his death, Franklin Roosevelt sent Stalin a message to protest "the lack of progress" in carrying out the Yalta agreement. His protest was ignored.

Stalin also attempted to expand Russian influence in the Near East and southern Europe. In 1945, he demanded that Turkey give several frontier territories to the Soviet Union. The Soviets also sought joint control over the Dardenelles and Bosporus, the narrow straits that connect the Black Sea with the Mediterranean. Meanwhile, the Soviet Union was backing a Communist revolt in Greece. Greek Communists were attempting to overthrow the Greek government. The rebels were receiving supplies from the Soviet Union. The events in Turkey and Greece increased American concern over Soviet foreign policy.

Section Review

1. In what ways do the political and economic systems of the Soviet Union and the United States differ?
2. What were the major goals of Soviet foreign policy after World War II?
3. Define ideology, capitalism, cold war, and satellite.
4. Do you think the Cold War continues today? Explain your answer.

2. The American Response

BEFORE YOU READ: *What did the United States do to prevent the spread of communism in the postwar period?*

In March 1946, Winston Churchill paid a visit to the United States. Churchill was no longer the Prime Minister of Great Britain, but he remained an important world figure. He had been invited to give a speech at a college in Fulton, Missouri. Churchill took the occasion to warn the American people about the danger of Soviet expansion. "An iron curtain," Churchill declared, "has descended across the continent" of Europe. The United States should take strong action, he urged, to stop the further spread of communism and Soviet power.

American Policy

About a year after Winston Churchill's "iron curtain" speech, an American diplomat, George F. Kennan, published an important article. Kennan had spent five years in the Soviet Union. In his article Kennan described Soviet foreign policy as "aggressive." He said that the United States should pursue a policy of **containment** to prevent the expansion of communism and Soviet power.

---

containment the policy of the United States to "contain," or prevent the expansion of, communism and Soviet power

---

The first major expression of the containment policy came in March 1947. President Truman asked Congress for $400 million in aid for Turkey and Greece. Turkey was facing growing pressure from the Soviet Union. Communist-led rebels were fighting the Greek government.

In presenting his request to Congress, President Truman stated, "I believe it must be the policy of the United States to support free peoples who are resisting attempted subjugation [domination] by armed minorities or by outside pressures." In a larger sense, Truman was calling upon Congress to accept the policy of containment. The United States must aid free peoples everywhere, he said, who are resisting communism.

On May 15, 1947, Congress voted to supply the aid to Greece and Turkey. Soon the Soviets dropped their demands on Turkey. The Communist rebels in Greece were defeated. In the eyes of Americans, the containment policy, now known as the Truman Doctrine, had scored its first victories.

The Marshall Plan

After the war, the ruined economies of Western Europe presented the Communists with an excellent opportunity to gain power. Communist parties, in fact, were gaining strength in France and Italy. In 1947, Secretary of State George C. Marshall proposed a massive plan of economic aid for Western Europe.

President Truman submitted Marshall's aid plan to Congress in December 1947. The official name of the plan was the European Recovery Program, but most people called it the Marshall Plan. Congress debated the plan for many weeks. Supporters of the plan argued that it would boost European prosperity, improve American foreign trade, and halt the spread of communism. Opponents charged that the plan was just another "giveaway" program. The critics maintained that the United States should use its limited resources for its own welfare.

As the debate continued, another European nation fell under the control of the Communists. In February 1948, a Communist revolution overthrew the government of Czechoslovakia. Finally, on April 3, 1948, Congress approved $5.3 billion for the first year of Marshall Plan aid. Over the next four years, a total of $12.5 billion in aid was distributed throughout Western Europe.

The Marshall Plan was a great success. The economies of Western Europe were soon restored to health. As poverty in Europe declined, so too did the strength of the European Communist parties.

Berlin and NATO

The Cold War became a dangerous game of moves and countermoves by the two superpowers. Action by one side provoked a reaction from the other.

In 1948, the United States, France, and Great Britain began to unite their zones of occupation in Germany. A new nation, the Federal Republic of Germany, or West Germany, was created out of their three zones.

The Russians were alarmed at the creation of West Germany. They feared the revival of a strong and militant German government. In June 1948, the Soviets blockaded all the roads and highways leading to Berlin. Berlin lies 160 kilometers (100 miles) inside the Soviet occupation zone. After the war, Berlin had been divided into four zones of occupation. The Russians apparently wanted to force the United States, France, and Great Britain to abandon Berlin.

The United States and its allies, however, refused to give up Berlin. American planes began airlifting food and other supplies to the city. From airfields in West Germany, the planes carried thousands of tons of supplies each day to West Berlin's Templehof Airport. The Berlin Airlift was an unprecedented effort to supply an entire city by air. The United States also imposed its own blockade on the Soviet zone in East Berlin. This counterblockade was effective. In May 1949, the Soviets lifted their blockade of Berlin, and the airlift ended.

The Berlin blockade convinced many

United States Foreign Aid

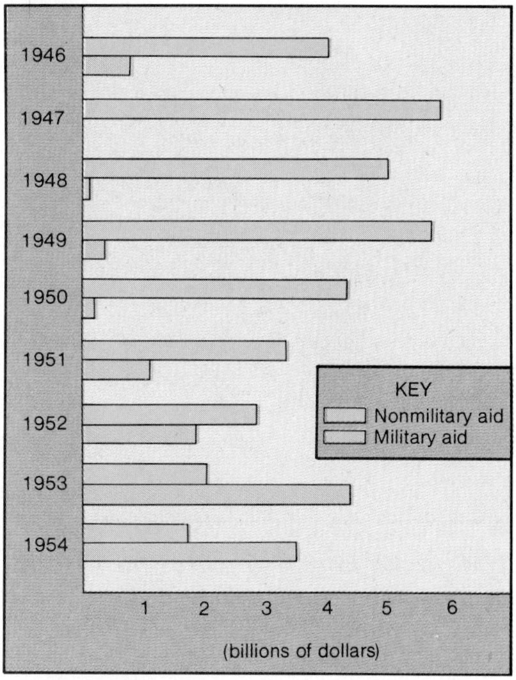

Americans and Western Europeans that Western Europe needed more protection. In April 1949, the United States, Great Britain, France, and nine other nations formed the North Atlantic Treaty Organization (NATO). Each NATO member agreed that an armed attack on any one of them would be regarded as an attack on all.

The Soviet Union reacted to the formation of NATO by creating its own alliance. The alliance, called the Warsaw Pact, included the Soviet Union and its satellite nations in Eastern Europe.

By the early 1950's, Europe was once again divided into two hostile alliances. The NATO allies, led by the United States, were known as "the West." The Warsaw Pact nations, dominated by the Soviet Union, were "the East."

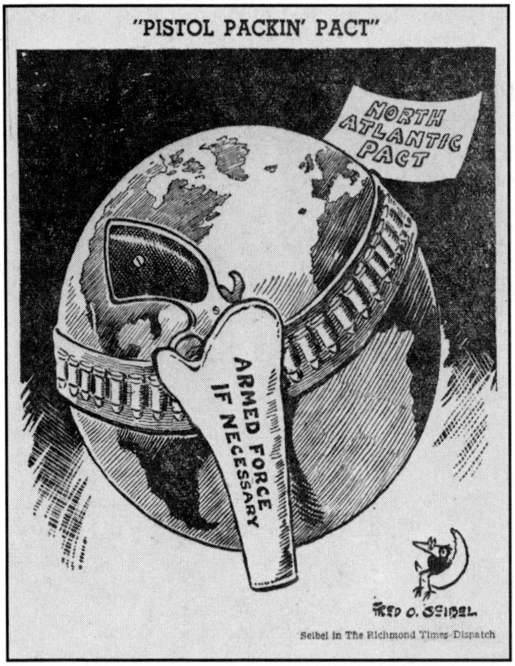

This cartoon from 1949 reflects the need felt by western European nations and the United States to form the defensive alliance called NATO.

Communist Victory in China

After World War II, a civil war resumed in China. The Nationalist government of China was headed by Chiang Kai-shek (chee-AHNG kie-SHEHK). Chiang's government had become very corrupt and had lost the support of many of the Chinese people. Opposing the Nationalist government were Chinese Communists led by Mao Tse-tung (MAH-oe dzuh-DOONG). Mao's forces had won widespread support by seizing the property of wealthy landlords and distributing it to the peasants.

The United States tried to prevent the Chinese civil war from resuming. The American efforts failed. As civil war broke out once again, the United States supplied the forces of Chiang with more than $2 billion in aid. Eventually, however, the Truman administration concluded that the Nationalists had little chance of winning the war. When the Nationalists asked for large-scale military aid, the United States refused.

In December 1949, Chiang Kai-shek and the Nationalist forces retreated to the island of Taiwan (Formosa). The triumphant Communists under Mao Tse-tung established a Communist government, the People's Republic of China.

The United States refused to extend diplomatic recognition to the new government in China. The Soviet Union, on the other hand, promptly recognized the government. On February 14, 1950, the

Discuss: Why would an alliance between the Soviet Union and the People's Republic of China cause concern in the United States?

Background: The UN Security Council was able to vote for UN troops in Korea without a Soviet veto because the Soviet Union was boycotting UN sessions at that time.

Soviet Union formed a defensive alliance with the People's Republic of China.

The Korean Conflict

The conflict on the Asian peninsula of Korea was one of the bloodiest of the Cold War. Korea had been controlled by Japan ever since the early 1900's. After the defeat of the Japanese in World War II, Korea was divided into two zones of occupation. Soviet armed forces occupied Korea north of a line at 38° latitude. The area south of the 38th parallel was occupied by American forces.

In 1948, two rival governments were created in the two occupation zones. South Korea became the Republic of Korea, and the United States promptly recognized the new government. North Korea became the Democratic People's Republic of Korea. The Communist-controlled government in the north was recognized by the Soviet Union. By mid-1949, both of the superpowers had withdrawn their troops from the peninsula.

General Douglas MacArthur and members of his staff view the prelanding bombardment of Inchon, Korea, in 1950.

The Soviet Union encouraged North Korea to unite all of Korea under Communist control. On June 25, 1950, North Korean forces invaded the Republic of Korea. The United Nations Security Council voted immediately to condemn the assault. It also asked all members of the United Nations to help South Korea repel the attack.

The United States and 16 other nations sent armed forces to South Korea. Four out of five of the non-Korean UN soldiers were Americans. The UN forces were placed under the command of an American, General Douglas MacArthur.

During the early stages of the conflict, the North Korean army had nearly driven the South Koreans into the sea at the southern tip of the peninsula. The UN troops then counterattacked, landing at Inchon behind the North Korean lines. By October, MacArthur's forces had pushed the North Koreans back across the 38th parallel. Then MacArthur pushed northward toward the Chinese border.

As the UN forces approached the Yalu River, which separates North Korea and China, Chinese forces joined the fighting. The North Korean and Chinese troops then pushed the UN army back to the 38th parallel. There the fighting continued, with neither side making major gains.

General MacArthur believed that the UN forces should attack China in order to

Background: Technically for the United States, the Korean conflict was not a war at all, for Congress never issued a declaration of war. It was, in President Truman's words, a "police action," in which American forces were fighting as agents of the UN.

Discuss: MacArthur's removal caused great debate at home. Why do you think Truman recalled MacArthur? Do you agree with him? Why or why not?

The Korean War

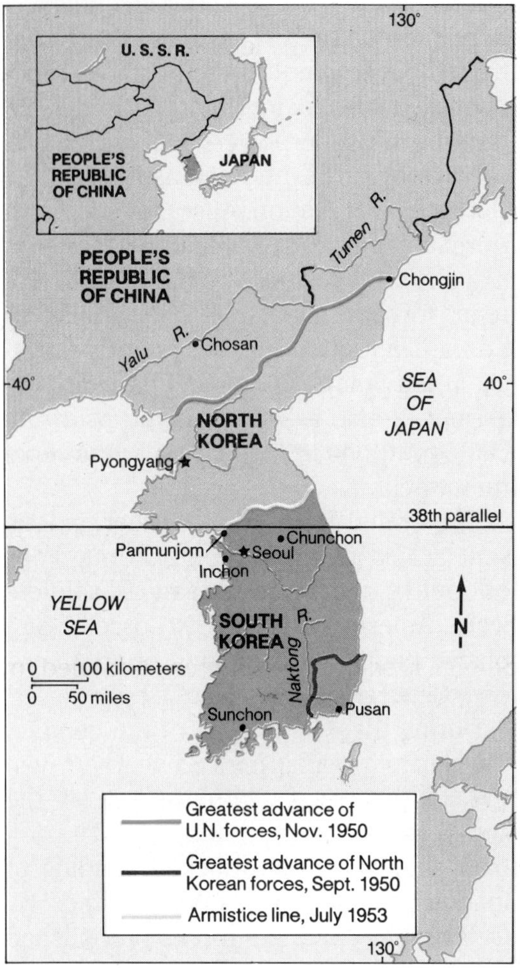

How close did the UN forces get to the Chinese border before retreating to the 38th parallel?

force the Chinese to withdraw from Korea. Other American military leaders, however, cautioned President Truman. General Omar Bradley, the President's top military adviser, believed that an attack on China was likely to prolong the Korean war, not end it.

Truman rejected MacArthur's call for a larger war. MacArthur, however, continued to insist publicly on military action against China. Truman warned MacArthur that he must cease his public disagreement with national policy. MacArthur ignored the President's warning. In April 1951, President Truman dismissed General MacArthur from his command.

Following the removal of MacArthur, the United Nations and North Korea began negotiations in July 1951. At last, on July 27, 1953, an armistice was signed. The armistice divided the peninsula once again near the 38th parallel.

The Arms Race

When Dwight D. Eisenhower became President in 1953, he announced that the United States would respond to any aggressive act by the Soviet Union with a massive counterattack using nuclear weapons. President Eisenhower's secretary of state, John Foster Dulles, called the new policy **"massive retaliation."**

---

massive retaliation the American policy of responding to any aggressive act by launching a counterattack of nuclear weapons

---

On November 1, 1952, just before Eisenhower's election, the United States had successfully tested the first hydrogen bomb (H-bomb). The bomb was almost 3,000 times more destructive than the atomic bomb dropped on Hiroshima. The policy of massive retaliation came to depend upon this powerful weapon.

The massive retaliation policy was intended to discourage the Soviet Union from acts of aggression. But the Soviets

Vocabulary Help: satellite—a humanmade object put into orbit around the earth. Point out to students that this word was defined differently earlier in the chapter, and that the appropriate meaning of this word can be determined by its context.

were also developing nuclear weapons. In September 1949, the Soviet Union had exploded its first atomic bomb. Then in 1953—just ten months after the United States exploded the first hydrogen bomb—the Russians successfully tested their own H-bomb.

In August 1957, the Soviet Union launched the first missile that could carry a nuclear weapon accurately over long distances. The Russians soon gave the world a dramatic demonstration of the power of their new **intercontinental ballistic missile** (ICBM). On October 4, 1957, they used an ICBM rocket engine to launch the first satellite into orbit around the earth. The satellite was *Sputnik I.* A rocket engine powerful enough to launch a satellite into space could also send a nuclear warhead from one continent to another. On February 1, 1958, the first American satellite, *Explorer I,* was launched into space with an ICBM rocket engine.

---

intercontinental ballistic missile a missile capable of carrying a nuclear weapon accurately over long distances

---

The policy of massive retaliation had turned into a nuclear arms race. Both the United States and the Soviet Union built more and more powerful weapons. Each of the superpowers soon became able to destroy the other many times over.

The Limits of Power

President Eisenhower realized that there were limits to what the United States could do to fight communism. If the United States intervened in one of the Warsaw Pact nations, a nuclear war with the Soviet Union was likely to result.

The limits of American power were most clearly revealed in a country named Vietnam. Before World War II, Vietnam was part of the French colony of Indochina. Vietnamese nationalists and Communists, called the Vietminh, began a revolt against the French. The Vietminh wanted to create an independent Vietnam. The leader of the revolution in Vietnam was Ho Chi Minh, a nationalist and Russian-trained Communist.

After the war, the Vietminh resumed their struggle for independence. The Vietminh created the Democratic Republic of Vietnam and selected the northern city of Hanoi as its capital. In southern Vietnam, the French set up a rival government. The capital of this French **protectorate** was Saigon. French armed forces continued to fight the Vietminh.

---

protectorate a dependent nation over which another nation assumes protection and exercises great influence

---

Early in 1950, the People's Republic of China recognized the Hanoi government and began aiding the Vietminh. The United States responded by recognizing the Saigon government and giving it aid.

President Eisenhower believed that it was important to help the Saigon government defend itself against the Communists. If Vietnam fell to communism, he predicted, the other nations of Southeast Asia would fall like "a row of dominoes." By the end of 1953, the United States was providing about $1 billion a year in military aid to the French forces. Yet Eisenhower strongly opposed the sending of

For Extra Interest: Have students compare the definitions of colony, satellite, and protectorate. Ask students to compare these terms for similarities and differences.

American combat troops to Vietnam or to other nations of Southeast Asia. "I cannot conceive of a greater tragedy for America," the President said in February 1954, "than to get heavily involved now in an all-out war in any of those regions."

In May 1954, the French forces suffered a major defeat at the battle of Dien Bien Phu (dee-enn bee-enn FOO). Following this defeat, a peace conference was held in Geneva, Switzerland. Nine nations, including France, Great Britain, the Soviet Union, and China, agreed at Geneva that Vietnam should be divided temporarily into two zones. Ho and the Vietminh would move north of the 17th parallel, and the French would move south of the line. Elections would be held in July 1956 to reunite the country.

The Saigon government feared that if the elections were held, the Communists would win a majority. The proposed elections were put off again and again. Meanwhile, the United States increased its aid to the Saigon government as the French withdrew their forces. Communist rebels from within South Vietnam began to attack the Saigon forces. The rebels were called the National Liberation Front (NLF) or, simply, the Vietcong. They were aided by the Communist government in the north. President Eisenhower sent about 650 military advisers to train the South Vietnamese army. By the end of Eisenhower's administration, in 1961, the Communists were in control of large areas in South Vietnam.

The United States also established a new alliance with other nations in the region. In 1954, the United States and seven other nations established the Southeast Asia Treaty Organization (SEATO). The other members of the alliance were Great Britain, France, Pakistan, Thailand, the Philippines, Australia, and New Zealand. The SEATO members agreed to meet any "common danger" from Communist aggression by taking action according to their own "constitutional processes."

Section Review

1. What did the United States do to prevent the spread of communism in the postwar period?
2. What was the purpose of the Marshall Plan? How successful was the plan?
3. What was the policy of the Eisenhower administration toward events in Vietnam?
4. Define massive retaliation, intercontinental ballistic missile, and protectorate.
5. Why did President Truman remove General MacArthur in 1951 from his command in Korea? What constitutional principle was the President upholding? (See United States Constitution, Article 2, Section 2.)

Discuss: After World War I, the United States returned to a policy of isolationism. After World War II, American foreign policy favored strong involvement in world affairs. What do you think caused this change?

Distinguishing Facts from Opinions

On March 12, 1947, President Truman made an important speech to Congress. He wanted to convince Congress that American aid was needed in countries threatened with Communist takeovers. When reading or listening to a speech, it is important to be able to distinguish facts from opinions. Informed opinions and intelligent decisions are based on facts.

Facts are things known to be true or to have really happened. For example, it is a fact that Truman delivered a speech in Congress on March 12, 1947. Congressional records prove that such an event occurred. Opinions, on the other hand, are beliefs or a person's point of view about something. For example, Truman thought that American aid would stop the spread of communism in Greece. No one knew whether this was true.

Facts are often used to strengthen opinions. However, one must be cautious in accepting others' opinions even though they appear to be based on numerous facts. People can be selective in choosing facts to support their arguments while ignoring those that do not.

Read the paragraphs below, and distinguish what is fact from what is opinion.

The United States has received from the Greek Government an urgent appeal for financial and economic assistance. Preliminary reports from the American Economic Mission now in Greece and reports from the American ambassador in Greece corroborate [support] the statement of the Greek Government that assistance is imperative [necessary] if Greece is to survive as a free nation.

I do not believe that the American people and the Congress wish to turn a deaf ear to the appeal of the Greek Government.

(Truman, March 12, 1947)

1. What is the difference between a fact and an opinion?
2. What facts are given in the paragraphs above?
3. What opinions are given in the paragraphs above?
4. Based on the facts given, would you have favored sending financial and economic assistance to Greece? Why or why not?

Discuss: In what instances might spying be necessary?

3. The Cold War at Home

BEFORE YOU READ: *What caused Americans to fear communism within the United States?*

The tensions of the Cold War were expressed not just in American foreign policy. They also had a powerful impact on events inside the United States. The fear of communism, both at home and abroad, gripped America during the Cold War.

The Fear Within

The fear of communism inside the United States was very widespread in the years after World War II. Several related factors caused the fear. First, there was the expansion of Communist power around the world. The number of countries with Communist governments had greatly increased in the postwar years. Many Americans were concerned that the nation had not been active enough in stopping the expansion of communism. Some began to fear that Communists inside the nation had undermined the effectiveness of American policy.

Second, the fear was caused by Soviet espionage. The Soviet Union had long maintained a network of espionage agents inside the United States and other western nations. Spies in Canada, Great Britain, and the United States had provided the Russians with secrets about the atom bomb. Scholars now believe that the Soviet Union would have developed nuclear weapons even without these secrets. The activities of the Soviet spies, however, raised grave concerns among many Americans.

Third, there was an **irrational** element in the fear. The fear was not entirely based on reasonable or logical grounds. There were actually very few American Communists in the United States. The Communist party in the United States was never able to attract a large following. The peak of its strength came during the Great Depression of the 1930's. Even then, in 1932, the Communist candidate for President received less than 103,000 votes, out of a total vote of more than 39 million cast. The irrational element in the fear of communism was a result of disappointment and frustration. Many Americans were deeply disappointed that the Cold War tensions had emerged so soon after the end of World War II. It seemed that as soon as one war had ended, another had begun. Americans were also frustrated with the failure of the United States to stop the spread of communism abroad. Many clung to the irrational hope that by eliminating the Communists at home, the dangers of international communism would subside.

irrational not reasonable or logical

The Hunt

The first move in the search for Communists in the United States was made by President Truman. In March 1947, Truman ordered a full-scale "loyalty investigation" of government employees. Any federal worker who was a member or even an "associate" of a **subversive** organization was to be fired. Eventually, more

For Extra Interest: Have students review the "red scare" of the 1920's in Chapter 25. Then have them compare and contrast attitudes toward Communist activity within the United States after World War I and World War II.

Discuss: Since most charges were unproved, do you think that it was fair to blacklist people? Why or why not?

than 3 million federal employees were investigated. Only 300 were fired.

---

subversive a person who works from within a nation to undermine and eventually overthrow the government

---

Congress also launched an investigation in 1947. The House Un-American Activities Committee (HUAC) ordered the leaders of the American Communist party to appear before the committee for questioning. The leaders refused. They were later charged with favoring the overthrow of the government of the United States by force. In 1949, 11 Communist party officials were convicted and imprisoned.

Hollywood film stars such as Lauren Bacall and Humphrey Bogart went to Washington, D.C., in 1947 to protest the HUAC investigation of communism in Hollywood.

In October 1947, HUAC began to investigate Communist influence in the Hollywood film industry. Many actors, writers, and directors were asked to give information about the political views of others in the film industry. Some witnesses cooperated fully. Others refused to answer the committee's questions. Many of those who refused to cooperate were later blacklisted from further employment in the film industry. The committee failed to prove any extensive Communist activity in Hollywood.

In 1948, an admitted former Communist, Whittaker Chambers, appeared before the committee. Chambers testified that in the 1930's, he and a man named Alger Hiss had given secret government information to the Soviet Union. Hiss had been an official in the State Department during both the Roosevelt and the Truman administrations.

Hiss appeared before HUAC and denied Chambers' charges. However, evidence was uncovered that indicated that Hiss was guilty of spying. Hiss was charged with lying under oath about his activities. His first trial ended with the jury unable to agree on a verdict. In 1950, Hiss was convicted of **perjury** and sentenced to five years in prison.

---

perjury lying while under an oath to tell the truth

The Hiss case was an important case in American politics. Alger Hiss had been a prominent member of two Democratic administrations. The Republicans could now charge that the Democrats were "soft on communism."

Still more disturbing evidence of

Background: Alger Hiss had been a member of the American delegation to the Yalta conference and had helped organize the United Nations.

Communist activity was revealed in 1950. A physicist named Klaus Fuchs (FYOOKS) admitted in Great Britain that he had been a Soviet spy in the United States in 1944. While working on the atomic bomb project at Los Alamos, New Mexico, Fuchs had given secrets to the Soviet Union. Fuchs was convicted and sentenced to 14 years in prison.

Fuchs revealed the names of Americans who had helped him in the espionage scheme. Fuch's information led to the arrest in the summer of 1950 of Ethel and Julius Rosenberg. The Rosenbergs were charged with giving atomic secrets to the Russians. They pleaded innocent to all charges. The Rosenbergs were convicted of espionage and executed.

McCarthyism

The fear of communism during the Cold War led to the rise of a political leader named Joseph McCarthy. McCarthy stirred the American people to even greater fear by appealing to their worst emotions. He used the fear of communism to boost his own popularity. Joseph McCarthy was a **demagogue**.

---

demagogue a leader who, to boost his or her own popularity, stirs the people by appealing to their worst emotions

---

McCarthy was a Republican Senator from Wisconsin. In planning for his reelection campaign in 1952, McCarthy wanted to do something to increase his popularity. He decided to become a crusader against the danger of communism in the United States.

In a speech on February 9, 1950, McCarthy charged that the State Department was "thoroughly infested with Communists." Waving a piece of paper, he said: "I have here in my hand [the names of] 205 men that were known to the Secretary of State as being members of the Communist party and who nevertheless are still working and shaping the policy of the State Department."

President Truman's secretary of state denied McCarthy's charges. The senator later changed the number of Communists in the state department to 81 and then to 57. In the end, he was unable to prove that a single state department employee was a Communist.

But McCarthy gained enormous publicity by making his unfounded charges. He was elected to a second term by the voters of Wisconsin. He also enjoyed widespread support around the country.

Senator McCarthy used his position as chairperson of the Government Operations Committee to widen his search for Communists. He began an investigation of the Voice of America. This government agency broadcast daily radio programs to foreign countries. McCarthy failed to find any Communists working for the agency.

McCarthy conducted his investigations by holding well-publicized committee hearings. Witnesses were often bullied and insulted by McCarthy. His own statements included both half-truths and outright lies. Many innocent people had their reputations ruined by McCarthy. His wild and unproven charges of Communist activity introduced a new term into the American vocabulary: "McCarthyism."

McCarthy's popularity began to fade in 1954 as he launched an attack on the United States Army. He charged that the army was "coddling" Communists in the service. McCarthy turned his attack on a young associate of the lawyer representing the army before the Senate committee. The attack was totally unfair. The army lawyer, Joseph Welch, asked Senator McCarthy: "Have you no sense of decency, sir, at long last? Have you no sense of decency?"

The lawyer's words brought applause in the Senate hearing room. Millions of Americans, watching on television, saw McCarthy revealed as the bully that he was. In addition, McCarthy failed to prove his charges against the army. In December 1954, the Senate voted to condemn McCarthy for "conduct unbecoming a member." McCarthy fell into disgrace.

Peaceful Coexistence

In the late 1950's, tensions between the two superpowers began to ease. Premier Joseph Stalin died in 1953 and was replaced by several new Soviet leaders. Nikita Khrushchev (kroosh-CHOFF) eventually emerged as the most powerful of the new leaders.

Khrushchev accepted an invitation to visit the United States and arrived in Washington, D.C., on September 14, 1959. He delivered an address to the UN and spoke in many cities across the nation. When Premier Khrushchev and President Eisenhower met, they both expressed the desire of their nations to live together in peace. The two leaders also agreed to hold a formal meeting in Paris.

The Paris **summit conference** was scheduled to begin on May 16, 1960. On May 1, the Russians shot down an American U-2 spy plane flying high over the Soviet Union. At first, the United States denied that the U-2 was a spy plane. President Eisenhower, however, soon admitted the truth. In the midst of the U-2 crisis, the conference began in Paris. Khrushchev demanded that the United States apologize for the spy flight and punish those who were responsible. When President Eisenhower rejected Khrushchev's demand, the summit conference collapsed. The thaw in the Cold War was over.

summit conference a formal meeting of the leaders of nations

Section Review

1. What caused Americans to fear communism within the United States?
2. Who was Alger Hiss? Why was the Hiss case important in American politics?
3. Define subversive, perjury, and demagogue.
4. What do you believe was the most important cause of the fear of communism in the United States during the Cold War? Explain your answer.

CHAPTER REVIEW

Summary

The United States and the Soviet Union emerged from World War II as the world's most powerful nations. However, the political and economic ideologies of these two "superpowers" were very different. Fear and distrust soon led to the outbreak of a "cold war."

During the Cold War, the United States took action to stop the spread of communism. Financial assistance and military personnel were sent to countries threatened with Communist takeovers. In the 1950's, the United States expanded its policy options to include the threat of massive retaliation. However, as the Soviet Union developed and improved its nuclear arsenal, the power of the United States to act in cases of Soviet aggression was limited by the threat of nuclear war.

The fear of communism also led to a widespread search for subversives and spies operating within the United States. Few people were found guilty of the charges leveled against them by Senator Joseph McCarthy and others. However, the actions of the investigating committees harmed the reputations of millions of innocent Americans.

Recalling the Facts

1. Why was the Soviet Union's domination of Poland after World War II disturbing to the United States and other western nations?
2. Why did President Truman relieve General MacArthur of his command during the Korean conflict?
3. What was the result of the Korean conflict?
4. What motivated Joseph McCarthy to become a crusader against the danger of communism in the United States?
5. How did Khrushchev and Eisenhower ease tensions between the United States and the Soviet Union in the late 1950's? Why did tensions between the two countries increase again in 1960?

Analyzing the Facts

1. Why did many Americans fear the Soviet Union after World War II?
2. Germany invaded the Soviet Union in World War I and again in World War II. Do you think the Soviet Union was justified in seizing control of nations in Eastern Europe after World War II to act as a buffer against future attacks? Why or why not?

3. Do you think the United States should have threatened to use nuclear weapons to counterattack acts of Soviet aggression during the Cold War? Why or why not?
4. Do you think foreign aid is an effective weapon against the spread of communism? Why or why not?
5. During the Great Depression, Franklin Roosevelt warned the American people that "the only thing we have to fear is fear itself." Would this quote have been as good a warning during the McCarthy era as it was during the Great Depression? Why or why not?

Time and History

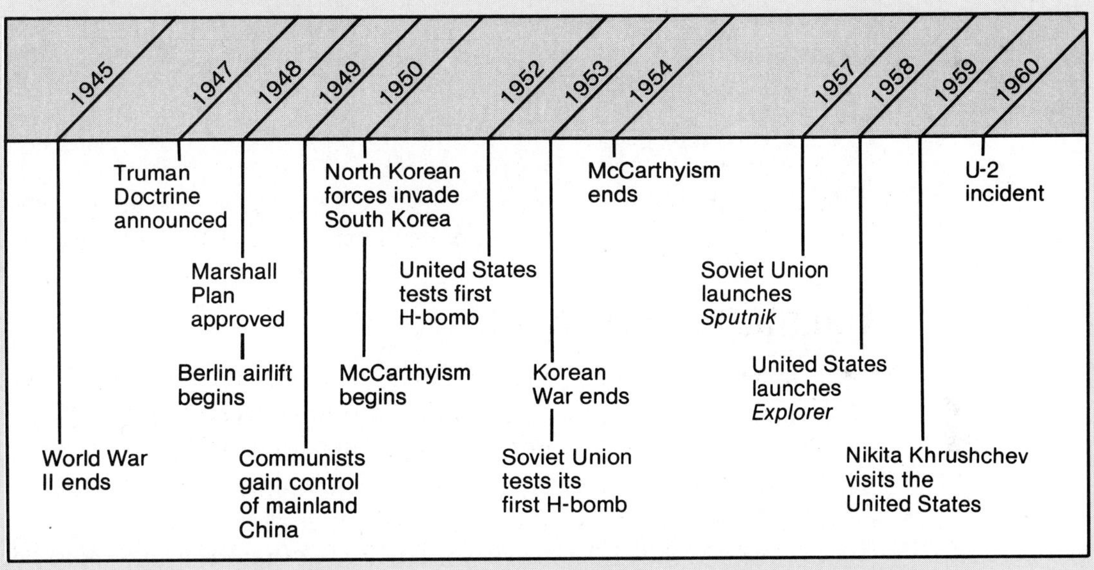

1. How long did the Korean War last? In what years was it fought?
2. In what year was the first satellite launched into space? What country launched it?
3. How long did McCarthyism last?
4. Using the information on the timeline, explain why each statement below must be false:
   a. One reason Khrushchev visited the United States was to protest the U-2 incident.
   b. The United States feared that the Soviet Union would use its hydrogen bomb to help the Communists gain control of mainland China.

Chapter 31

Years of Challenge

At his inauguration, President John F. Kennedy proclaimed America's commitment to the defense of freedom. He declared " . . . that we shall pay any price, bear any burden, meet any hardship, support any friend, oppose any foe to assure the survival and success of liberty."

Americans in the early 1960's were confident that progress could be made in achieving national goals. By the end of the decade, however, confidence had given way to confusion. The 1960's were a time of great change and challenge for the United States.

After you read this chapter, you will be able to:

1. Discuss the major foreign and domestic issues of the Kennedy administration.
2. Trace the civil rights movement during the Johnson years.
3. Identify the difficulties America faced in the Vietnam War.
4. Give reasons why a "counterculture" emerged in the 1960's.

1. The Kennedy Years

BEFORE YOU READ: *What were the major foreign and domestic issues of the Kennedy administration?*

In the twentieth century, the presidency has come to play an ever greater role in American public life. Americans have looked to the President for a sense of national purpose and for a definition of national goals. The two Presidents who served in the White House from 1961 to 1969 were John F. Kennedy and Lyndon B. Johnson. Both men had strong ideas about the nation's goals and purpose.

The Election of 1960

The Republican nomination for President in 1960 went to Dwight Eisenhower's Vice-President, Richard M. Nixon. Nixon focused his campaign on the Eisenhower record. Eisenhower, however, gave Nixon's candidacy only lukewarm support. A reporter asked Eisenhower if he could name the major decisions in which Nixon had participated. The President replied, "If you give me a week, I might think of one."

The Democrats in 1960 chose Senator John F. Kennedy of Massachusetts as their nominee. Kennedy had served as a commander of a naval PT boat during World War II. After the war, he entered politics. Kennedy was first elected to the House of Representatives in 1946 and then to the Senate in 1952.

As the 1960 campaign opened, Nixon led Kennedy in the polls. Nixon was the more experienced candidate and familiar to more voters. Also Kennedy was a Catholic. The only other presidential nominee who had been a Catholic was Al Smith in 1928. Smith's defeat convinced many observers that a Catholic could never be elected. Kennedy had an advantage over Nixon, however, in personal charm and public-speaking ability.

The turning point of the campaign came when the two candidates met in a series of televised debates. No presidential candidates had ever debated on television before. The debates were watched by an estimated 70 million viewers. Kennedy came across as relaxed and confident. Nixon, on the other hand, appeared stiff and nervous. The debates showed that Senator Kennedy could discuss national issues as well as, or better than, Vice-President Nixon.

The election was one of the closest in American history. Kennedy won by a

John F. Kennedy on the campaign trail in Ona, New Hampshire.

Background: John F. Kennedy was 43 years old when he was inaugurated, making him the second youngest President. Theodore Roosevelt became President at age 42 following the assassination of McKinley. Kennedy, therefore, was the youngest person to be elected President.

For Extra Interest: Much has been written about the Green Berets. Have interested students research and report on this unit, or invite a member of the Green Berets to speak to the class.

The Election of 1960

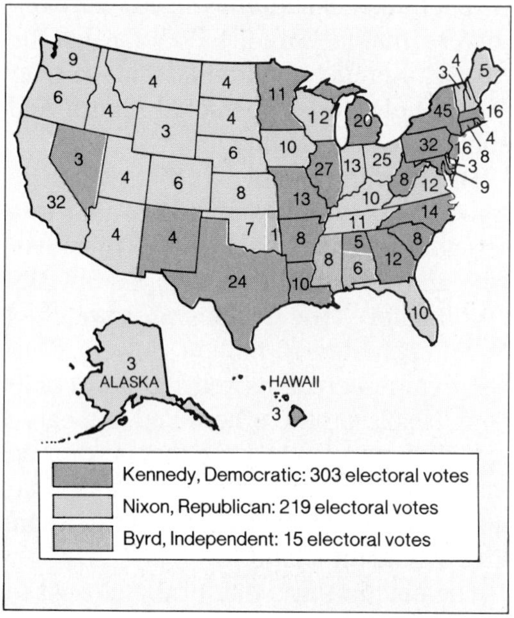

Which candidate won the majority of electoral votes in the Far West? Why do you think this was so?

small margin of the popular vote. He received 303 electoral votes to Nixon's 219.

Kennedy's Foreign Policy

On May 25, 1961, President Kennedy announced a new national goal for the United States. He pledged that America would land a man on the moon and bring him back safely to the earth before the end of the decade. Kennedy was determined to demonstrate the technological superiority of the United States over the Soviet Union.

President Kennedy also wanted the United States to develop a policy flexible enough to respond to Communist threats of all kinds. To combat Communist guerrillas, Kennedy developed a new American fighting unit. The unit was called the Special Forces. Its members were specially trained to fight in guerrilla wars. The President even chose the unit's uniform, including its distinctive green beret. Members of the Special Forces were often called the Green Berets.

President Kennedy created the Peace Corps to improve relations with the "Third World" nations of Africa, Asia, and Latin America. The Peace Corps trained American nurses, teachers, farm advisers, mechanics, and other kinds of helpers to work abroad. It was hoped that the volunteers would help the citizens of these countries improve their way of life. By the mid-1960's, 10,000 Peace Corps volunteers were working overseas.

President Kennedy also took positive steps to improve American relations with Latin America. In 1961, he proposed the formation of the Alliance for Progress. The Alliance provided American aid to Latin America for improvements in housing, health care, and education.

Kennedy's efforts to improve relations with Latin America suffered a setback because of events in Cuba. In 1959, the Cuban government had been overthrown in a revolution led by Fidel Castro. Castro's government began receiving aid from the Soviet Union in 1960. It soon became apparent that Fidel Castro was a Communist.

In early 1961, President Kennedy approved a plan to overthrow the Castro government. On April 17, 1961, a small army of anti-Castro Cubans trained by the Central Intelligence Agency (CIA) invaded Cuba at the Bay of Pigs. The CIA hoped that the Bay of Pigs invasion would cause

Discuss: Why do you think the nations of Asia, Africa, and Latin America are referred to as the "Third World"?

For Extra Interest: Have students ask their parents what they remember about the Cuban missile crisis and how they felt during that time.

the people of Cuba to rise up against Castro. Instead, the invasion was quickly crushed by Castro's armed forces.

Tensions between the United States and the Soviet Union increased further in August 1961 when the Soviets ordered a wall to be built between East and West Berlin. As many as 3 million East Germans had escaped to the West through Berlin. The Berlin Wall made such escapes almost impossible.

The greatest crisis in Soviet-American relations came in October 1962. The United States learned that the Soviets were building missile bases in Cuba. Missiles fired from the bases could strike targets deep inside the United States. On October 22, 1962, President Kennedy announced a naval blockade of Cuba. American warships were ordered to turn back Soviet ships carrying missiles to Cuba. War with the Soviet Union seemed very near. The crisis passed on October 26 when the Soviet Union agreed to remove the missiles. In exchange, the United States promised not to invade Cuba.

When the Berlin Wall was first built, it was hastily constructed of barbed wire. Several years later, concrete slabs were added to make escape more difficult.

The Cuban missile crisis had a positive outcome. Both of the superpowers had seen the grave danger of their rivalry. As a result, tensions between the two nations began to lessen.

Civil Rights

Civil rights became a major concern of the Kennedy administration as the demands of black Americans became impossible to ignore. While Eisenhower was still in office, black college students in Greensboro, North Carolina, organized a protest against discrimination at the local Woolworth's store. The store's lunch counter served whites only. The students occupied seats at the lunch counter until the store agreed to serve blacks. Their **sit-in** received widespread publicity. Soon sit-ins were being staged at lunch counters and other businesses throughout the nation.

sit-in an organized protest in which protesters occupy a business until it agrees to grant their demands

In 1961, northern college students, both black and white, began a series of public demonstrations against segregated bus stations in the South. Southern bus stations maintained separate food counters, waiting rooms, and restrooms for whites and blacks. The demonstrators

Background: In June 1963, President Kennedy expressed his hopes for peaceful coexistence with the Soviet Union. "If we cannot end now our differences," he declared, "at least we can help make the world safe for diversity."

Famous Americans

LOUISE NEVELSON

Louise Nevelson's sculpture emphasizes shape and surface. Her most famous pieces are boxlike constructions filled with bits of wood and all sorts of objects. The boxes are put together to create a wall, tower, or column. Nevelson usually paints the entire sculpture one color. The use of one color has the effect of creating many shadows. The appearance of the sculpture changes as the light falling on it changes.

Nevelson was born in Kiev, Russia, and came to the United States with her family when she was five. When Nevelson was 20, she began to study painting. During the Great Depression, Nevelson began to do sculptures and found that she liked working with clay. Soon, though, she began using wood as her basic material. Nevelson's most successful sculptures have been done in that material.

In 1941, Nevelson had her first show. Critics praised her work, but it was not until the late 1950's that she achieved widespread recognition. In 1959, Nevelson's work was included in a show at the Museum of Modern Art in New York City. She was the first woman and the first sculptor to be asked to join the Sidney Janis Gallery, one of the most highly respected galleries in New York. Nevelson's work has also appeared in many museums and galleries both in the United States and abroad.

traveled by bus throughout the South. They protested the segregated facilities at each bus stop. The students called their demonstrations "freedom rides." They were often met with violence from southern whites. Many students were beaten. One bus in Anniston, Alabama, was set on fire, and 12 "freedom riders" were hospitalized. President Kennedy responded by ordering the desegregation of all bus and train stations.

Some southern states continued to resist the effort to end segregation in their schools. Mississippi, like all southern states, maintained separate universities for blacks and whites. The University of Mississippi at Oxford admitted only white students. In October 1962, a federal court

Discuss: What do you think motivated northern white college students to participate in demonstrations against segregated bus stations in the South in 1961?

For Extra Interest: Obtain a recording of Martin Luther King's "I Have a Dream" speech to play for the class. Ask students whether they think King's dream has been realized.

ordered the university to admit James Meredith, a black student. Whites in Oxford rioted in protest. Mississippi Governor Ross Barnett refused to enforce the order. President Kennedy sent federal troops to the university to enforce the court order and protect Meredith.

In April 1963, Martin Luther King, Jr., launched a campaign to end segregation in all public facilities and improve job opportunities for blacks in Birmingham, Alabama. King and his followers conducted large public demonstrations. Police Chief Eugene "Bull" Conner responded by ordering the police to attack the demonstrators with fire hoses, electric cattle prods, tear gas, and police dogs. Many Americans were horrified by the events in Birmingham.

Segregation at the University of Alabama was also challenged. A federal court ordered the university to desegregate. The governor of Alabama, George Wallace, defied the order. In June 1963, Governor Wallace blocked the entrance of the black students. Only when federal marshals confronted Wallace did the governor step aside.

Within days of the confrontation in Alabama, President Kennedy introduced to Congress a major civil rights act. The proposed act would end segregation in "public accommodations" such as restaurants, theaters, and hotels. It would prohibit racial discrimination in employment. And it would authorize further federal action to end school segregation.

Support for the civil rights act was powerfully demonstrated in August 1963. More than 200,000 Americans gathered at the Lincoln Memorial to demand an end to racial discrimination in the United States. It was the largest civil rights demonstration in the nation's history. Martin Luther King, Jr., made an inspiring address to the crowd. He described his dream of equality for all Americans. "It is a dream," he said, "deeply rooted in the American dream. I have a dream that one day this nation will rise up and live out the true meaning of its creed: 'We hold these truths to be self-evident, that all men are created equal.' " The demonstration in Washington was a sign of the optimism of many Americans that progress toward national goals could be made.

Section Review

1. List the major foreign and domestic issues that faced the Kennedy administration.
2. What did Kennedy do to contain the expansion of communism?
3. Define sit-in. What was the purpose of the sit-in at Greensboro, North Carolina, in February 1960?
4. There were two Cuban crises during the Kennedy administration: The Bay of Pigs invasion and the missile crisis. Do you see any relationship between these two crises? Do you think the second one might have been caused by the first? Explain your answer.

For Extra Interest: In 1983, black leaders staged another march on Washington. Have interested students research and report to the class on who participated in this march and what issues were discussed by the speakers.

For Extra Interest: Questions still exist today about the Kennedy assassination. Have interested students investigate some of the conflicting reports.

2. The Great Society

BEFORE YOU READ: *What major new civil rights laws were enacted during the Johnson administration?*

On November 22, 1963, President Kennedy and his wife were being driven slowly through the streets of Dallas, Texas. Thousands of people waved and cheered as the President passed by. Suddenly shots rang out. Bullets from a high-powered rifle struck the President in the throat and head. Within minutes, he was pronounced dead. His alleged assassin, Lee Harvey Oswald, was quickly arrested. Two days later, Oswald was shot by a Dallas nightclub owner.

The assassination of President Kennedy marked the beginning of a profound shift in the national mood. Feelings of frustration and confusion began to grow.

Lyndon B. Johnson at his ranch in Texas.

Lyndon B. Johnson

Within hours of the assassination, Vice-President Lyndon Baines Johnson was sworn in as President. President Johnson was a native Texan. He had entered Texas politics as a young man and was a great admirer of Franklin Roosevelt. He was first elected to Congress in 1937 and became a United States senator in 1948. Johnson was a master at getting legislation through the Senate.

Johnson shared Kennedy's commitment to liberal reform. Johnson proposed and won passage of many new reform measures. President Johnson called his program the Great Society.

The first year of Johnson's presidency was directed at building support for his upcoming 1964 election. Johnson easily won the Democratic nomination. The Republicans chose as their candidate an extreme conservative, Senator Barry Goldwater of Arizona. The election in November 1964 was a landslide victory for Johnson and the Democrats. Goldwater carried only six states.

War on Poverty

A few weeks after becoming President, Lyndon Johnson declared an "unconditional war on poverty." He was concerned that the nation's great prosperity was not being shared by all Americans. In 1959, 20 percent of the American people were living in poverty. Johnson set as a national goal the elimination of poverty from the nation. It was a very ambitious goal.

The centerpiece of President Johnson's

Discuss: Why do you think an extremely conservative candidate, like Barry Goldwater, would not receive much voter support in 1964?

"war on poverty" was the Economic Opportunity Act. Congress approved the act in August 1964 and provided $950 million for its programs. The act created a powerful new federal agency, the Office of Economic Opportunity (OEO). The OEO coordinated ten antipoverty programs.

Among the OEO programs was a Job Corps to provide training for unemployed young workers. A Neighborhood Youth Corps also helped unemployed young people find work. Volunteers in Service to America (VISTA) was a kind of domestic Peace Corps. VISTA workers provided educational and social services to communities in need. Other OEO programs improved housing, health care, and education for the nation's poor.

Another part of the war on poverty was Medicare. Medicare was a program of federal aid to the elderly for medical care. Congress passed the Medicare program in 1965. In the same year, Congress approved Medicaid. This program extended federal aid for medical care to those who were too young to qualify for Medicare. These two programs guaranteed that no American would be deprived of proper medical care for economic reasons.

President Johnson also convinced Congress of the need to pass the Elementary and Secondary Education Act. This act, passed in 1965, greatly expanded federal aid to the nation's schools, both public and private. Federal aid to education rose from $5 billion in 1964 to $12 billion in 1967.

Urban poverty received special attention from the Johnson administration. In 1965, it established the Department of Housing and Urban Development (HUD). The department directed the nation's efforts to rebuild the decaying cities. Johnson appointed Robert C. Weaver as the first secretary of HUD. Weaver was the first black person ever to serve in a presidential Cabinet. Johnson also created the Model Cities program to provide federal aid for "urban renewal" projects.

The mid-1960's were years of continuing general prosperity. Yet in the midst of this prosperity, poverty did not entirely disappear. Through Johnson's Great Society program, an estimated 4 million people were raised above the poverty level. By 1970, the number of Americans living in poverty had fallen to about 13 percent of the nation's population.

Unfinished Business

When John Kennedy was assassinated in 1963, the most important piece of unfinished business he left behind was his proposed civil rights act. President Johnson applied his powerful legislative skills to win the act's passage in 1964. The Civil Rights Act of 1964 forbade discrimination in public accommodations and employment. It also authorized further federal action against segregation in the schools.

The new law did not, however, eliminate discrimination in voting. Southern states continued to use a variety of devices to keep blacks from voting. One of these was to require blacks to pay a special tax before they were allowed to vote. In January 1964, the Twenty-fourth Amendment abolished **poll taxes** in all federal elections.

---

poll tax a special tax people are required to pay before they can vote

---

EUREKA!

The Laser

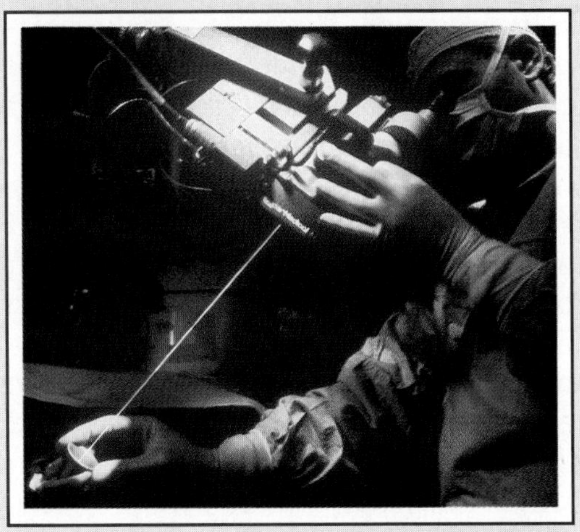

In the less than 30 years since the first experimental laser was built, lasers have already been put to a wide variety of uses. Beams or pulses of laser light serve as precision surgical tools. They can also pinpoint the position of satellites in orbit around the earth and can even transmit telephone communications. The key to the usefulness of the laser lies in the special character of its light. The key to that character lies in the behavior of the atoms that make up a laser light source.

A familiar light source such as the sun emits its light in a haphazard fashion. When one of its atoms is bombarded with the proper amount of energy, some of the energy is absorbed and the atom becomes "excited." Left to its own devices, an excited atom will give off its excess energy at random as a particle of light called a photon. A group of such atoms emits photons in all directions and in every wavelength or color.

But if an already excited atom is hit with still more energy, it can be made to release not one but two photons. They will be of a single color and, most importantly, they will be exactly in step with each other. This orderly and intense release of light is called lasing. A group of Columbia University physicists built the first lasing device in 1954. It produced microwave radiaton rather than visible light. In 1960, Theodore Maiman of Hughes Research Laboratories in Malibu, California, produced the first visible light laser, using a ruby crystal as an emitter.

Lasers are now made from a variety of materials and come in a wide range of sizes. The smallest are the almost microscopic devices that encode telephone conversations as pulses of light. The largest—a huge, room-sized machine—focuses its energy on a tiny pellet of gas to make nuclear fusion.

Southern officials continued to use other ways to keep black Americans from voting. Literacy tests required a voter to be able to read and write to the satisfaction of a local official. Other tests required knowledge of the Constitution. Local officials applied these tests unfairly to blacks.

Background: Many trick questions were used on tests to keep qualified blacks from registering to vote in the South.

Background: On the final day of the march from Selma to Montgomery, Alabama, the 300 demonstrators were joined by over 35,000 supporters from all over the country.

The summer of 1964 was the "freedom summer" of the civil rights movement. Black and white students from around the nation traveled to the South to help southern blacks register to vote. Many of these civil rights workers were beaten. On June 20, 1964, three young civil rights workers were killed in Neshoba County, Mississippi.

Early in 1965, Martin Luther King, Jr., led demonstrations for black voting rights in Alabama. In March, King attempted to lead a march of black and white demonstrators from Selma to the state capital at Montgomery. Alabama police broke up the march with whips, clubs, and tear gas. One minister from the North was beaten to death on a Selma street. President Johnson ordered the National Guard to protect the marchers. The night the march ended, another demonstrator was killed.

The national outrage following the events in Mississippi and Alabama led to the passage of the Voting Rights Act of 1965. This act prohibited literacy tests and other devices used to keep blacks from voting. It also provided federal "examiners" to help blacks register to vote. A major voter registration drive began in the South. Within a few years, blacks were voting in large numbers. Black candidates were elected to public offices in the South for the first time since Reconstruction. By 1969, there were 400 elected black officials in the states of the old Confederacy.

Explosions of Discontent

While progress was being made in the South, discontent was growing in the North. By 1966, 45 percent of the nation's black population lived outside the South. Many blacks lived in segregated sections of the central cities. Life in the black **ghettos** was hard and seemed hopeless. The unemployment rate for blacks was twice that of whites. Half of all black Americans lived in poverty in the 1960's.

A police dog lunges at a black youth during a civil rights demonstration in Birmingham, Alabama.

ghetto a section of a city occupied by members of a single racial or ethnic minority group

Discontent in the ghettos exploded into violence in a series of terrifying riots. Between 1964 and 1967, more than 100 major riots broke out in American cities. The first large riot was in August 1965 in Watts, a nearly all-black district of Los

Background: More than 80 percent of employed blacks worked at the bottom of the economic ladder, as compared to 40 percent of employed whites. Black advancement was greatly restricted by general race bias and discimination in labor unions.

Background: At the time of the riot, one-sixth of Los Angeles' half-million blacks lived in Watts. The area was four times as congested as the rest of the city. More than 30 percent of the potential black wage earners in the area were unemployed.

Angeles. Six hundred buildings were damaged, and 200 were destroyed by fires during the riot. Many stores were looted. Thirty-four people were killed, 31 of whom were black.

In 1966, riots broke out in New York City, Chicago, and San Francisco. In the summer of 1967, rioting in Newark, New Jersey, left 25 people dead. In Detroit, Michigan, 43 people were killed in a riot that lasted a week. Federal troops were sent to Detroit to restore order.

New black leaders and organizations emerged that expressed the discontent of black Americans. The organizations, such as the Student Nonviolent Coordinating Committee (SNCC), tended to be more radical than older groups, such as the NAACP. Some of the new groups supported what came to be called "black power." Black power meant different things to different people. But clearly it was a call for greater control by blacks over their own communities, lives, and destinies.

One of the most powerful of the new black leaders was Malcolm X. The "X," he said, stood for his lost African last name. Malcolm X was a spokesperson for the Nation of Islam, an organization commonly called the Black Muslims. Malcolm X urged blacks to build their own society separate from the white society. He also rejected King's philosophy of nonviolence. "The day of nonviolent resistance," Malcolm X declared, "is over." In 1964, Malcolm X left the Black Muslims to found a new organization. Before he could build up the new organization, he was assassinated in February 1965.

Meanwhile, the leader of nonviolence, Martin Luther King, Jr., led his last demonstration in 1968. King came to Memphis, Tennessee, to support a strike by the city's mostly black garbage collectors. On April 4, 1968, he was assassinated as he stood outside his motel room. As news of King's death was broadcast, riots began again in cities across the country. Americans of all races reacted with shock and anger to the killing of Martin Luther King, Jr. The sense of confusion and frustration in the nation grew deeper.

Section Review

1. What major new civil rights laws were enacted during the Johnson administration?
2. What methods did southern states use to keep blacks from voting?
3. Define ghetto. Where did the major riots of the 1960's occur?
4. Martin Luther King, Jr., was the most highly regarded black leader of the 1960's. Who are the most effective black leaders today? What similarities or differences are there between these leaders and King?

For Extra Interest: The popular song "Abraham, Martin, and John" reflected the bewilderment that many Americans felt in the late 1960's over the assassinations of progressive leaders. Obtain a copy of this song, and play it for the class.

3. Johnson's Foreign Policy

BEFORE YOU READ: *What actions did President Johnson take to expand American involvement in the war in Vietnam?*

President Johnson continued the foreign policy of the Kennedy administration. The major goal of American policy was the containment of communism.

The Dominican Republic

For many years, the Dominican Republic, an island nation in the Caribbean Sea, had been heavily influenced by the United States. In 1961, the dictator of the Dominican Republic, General Rafael Trujillo (troo-HEE-yoh), was assassinated, and his government was overthrown.

Discontent with the new government was strong. In 1965, a revolution began to make Juan Bosch the new leader of the Dominican Republic. President Johnson feared that Bosch would establish a Communist government. The President ordered more than 20,000 American troops to the Dominican Republic to help put down the revolution.

The American forces remained on the island until 1966. They were withdrawn when Bosch was defeated.

President Johnson's forceful action in the Dominican crisis stirred debate. Some critics charged that Johnson had misunderstood the nature of the revolt led by Juan Bosch. The critics argued that Bosch was a Dominican nationalist, not a Communist. The revolt was a civil war, not an act of Communist aggression.

Debate over the American action in the Dominican Republic soon ended. The issues raised by the debate, however, were revived in the greater controversy over American policy in Vietnam.

Vietnam

When Lyndon Johnson became President in November 1963, the war in Vietnam had already been going on for more than 20 years. Since 1954, the Communists controlled the north, and the American-backed government ruled the south. In South Vietnam, the Communist guerrillas, called the Vietcong, continued to fight the South Vietnamese government.

President Eisenhower had authorized American military aid to South Vietnam. President Kennedy had increased the number of American military advisers in South Vietnam from 650 to more than 16,000. At the time of his death, President Kennedy was considering expanding still further the American role in Vietnam.

The head of the South Vietnamese government at Saigon was a corrupt and unpopular leader named Ngo Din Diem (noh din DEE-em). Diem opposed any reforms that he believed would weaken either the position of the Vietnamese upper class or his own power. Diem also opposed Buddhism, the traditional religion of Vietnam. Diem was a Catholic. He ordered demonstrations by Buddhists to be put down with brutal force.

In early November 1963, the military leaders of South Vietnam, secretly encouraged by American officials, overthrew Diem. They executed Diem and members of his administration. Following the overthrow of Diem, South Vietnam

Discuss: Why do you think Congress passed the Tonkin Gulf Resolution instead of declaring war on North Vietnam? How would a declaration of war have affected the United States' allies?

The Vietnam War

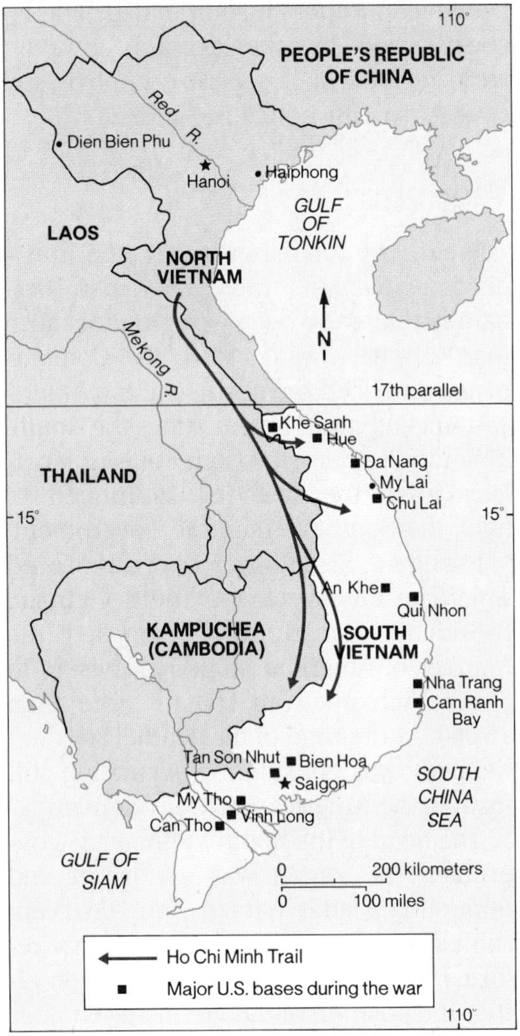

Through what countries did the Ho Chi Minh Trail pass?

was ruled by several military leaders. Eventually, the most powerful leader to emerge was General Nguyen Van Thieu (nwin vahn TYOO).

In August 1964, President Johnson informed the nation that an American warship had been attacked by a North Vietnamese gunboat. The attack took place, the President said, in the Tonkin Gulf off the coast of North Vietnam. Congress responded by passing, almost unanimously, the Tonkin Gulf Resolution. This resolution authorized the President to take "all necessary measures including the use of armed force" to protect the American forces in Vietnam and "to prevent further aggression."

Following the passage of the Tonkin Gulf Resolution, the United States sharply **escalated**, or increased, its role in Vietnam. In February 1965, President Johnson ordered American warplanes to bomb North Vietnam. Eventually, the United States dropped more bombs on Vietnam than in all of World War II and the Korean War combined.

escalate to increase or expand

President Johnson also ordered American combat troops to Vietnam. At the end of 1965, there were 184,000 American troops in Vietnam. By the middle of 1968, more than 538,000 Americans were fighting in Vietnam.

American Difficulties

Total victory in Vietnam was difficult for American armed forces to achieve. The Communist forces in South Vietnam were supported by many people in the South Vietnamese countryside. Native villagers provided food and shelter to the Communists. Some villagers even committed acts of sabotage against American troops. Fighting the Communists was very frustrating. American forces would

Background: In the beginning, the American troops were ordered to protect air bases in South Vietnam. They were then sent into combat to help defend South Vietnamese units from attack. American forces later conducted "search and destroy" missions against the Communist forces.

Discuss: Should the United States have participated in the conflict if the South Vietnamese people were siding with the enemy? Why or why not?

A Vietnamese refugee carrying pots, pans, and a stove walks past United States troops on her way to a refugee camp.

defeat the Communists in a village or town. Then, when Americans left, the Communists would quickly return.

The United States adopted various strategies to overcome this difficulty. A "pacification" program was introduced to win the "hearts and minds" of the people. But the Americans were often unable to win the support of the villagers.

The pacification program gradually was replaced by a strategy of "relocation." Once the Communists were defeated in an area, the villagers would be relocated to refugee camps or to the cities. The deserted villages and countryside would then be destroyed. Bulldozers would flatten the abandoned settlements. American bombers would "saturate" the area with high explosives. Chemicals would be sprayed from airplanes to strip the leaves from trees and other plants. Huge areas of the Vietnamese jungle were **defoliated**.

---

defoliate to strip the leaves from trees and other plants by using a chemical spray

---

The relocation program was no more successful than the pacification program had been. When a village or other area was destroyed, the Communists would simply move their operations elsewhere.

The United States found itself in a very difficult situation in Vietnam. America had to choose between two equally unpleasant alternatives. American leaders were caught in a **dilemma**.

Background: About one-fifth of South Vietnam's extensive forest area was sprayed with herbicides. Chemical herbicides probably destroyed enough food to feed 600,000 persons for a year in South Vietnam, and enough timber to meet the country's needs for 30 years.

Discuss: Who do you think had a stronger argument, the "hawks" or the "doves"? Have students explain their answers.

dilemma a situation in which one has to choose between unpleasant alternatives

On the one hand, the United States could further expand its role in the war. Heavier bombing raids could be made, and more combat units could be sent to Vietnam. President Johnson, however, feared that further escalation of the war would bring direct intervention by China or the Soviet Union.

On the other hand, the United States could reduce its role in Vietnam. The United States could remove its armed forces and leave the fighting to the South Vietnamese. But President Johnson believed that if the United States abandoned Vietnam, the Communists would be encouraged to take over other countries.

For seven years, the United States was caught in this terrible dilemma. The Vietnam conflict remained a "limited war."

Hawks Versus Doves

The war in Vietnam produced a deep division of opinion within the United States. Supporters of the American policy were called "hawks." They believed that the war in Vietnam was caused by Communist aggression. The United States must contain communism, they argued, by defending South Vietnam.

The opponents of American policy were known as "doves." They argued that the war in Vietnam was essentially a civil war between different groups of Vietnamese. The United States, therefore, had no business interfering.

As the war continued, the doves grew in strength. Opposition to the war first appeared on the college campuses. By 1967, student demonstrations against the war had become almost daily occurrences on campuses throughout the nation. The press also gradually became more critical of American policy. By 1968, many leading newspapers and magazines had begun to favor American withdrawal from Vietnam.

Opposition also came from within the government. Many members of Congress and state officials openly criticized government policy. By 1968, the war in Vietnam had become the most important political issue on the minds of many Americans.

Section Review

1. What actions did President Johnson take to escalate American involvement in the Vietnam War?
2. What military difficulties did the United States face in Vietnam?
3. Define defoliate and dilemma.
4. How did the hawks and the doves differ in their view of the war in Vietnam? Which side of the controversy would you have favored? Explain your answer.

Background: In 1968, resistance to the draft erupted nationwide. Many draft evaders went to Canada. Other evaders who refused to serve in the armed forces risked arrest, conviction for draft evasion, and imprisonment.

Discuss: What effect does television have on shaping American opinions? What is the role of advertising on television? What effect does television programming and advertising have on you?

4. Coming Apart

BEFORE YOU READ: *Why did a "counter-culture" emerge in the 1960's?*

American society and culture in the 1960's were entering a period of crisis. The turmoil of the civil rights movement and the war in Vietnam had produced deep divisions among the American people. Some observers concluded that the issues that divided Americans appeared to be more important than the values that held them together.

The Mass Culture

The general prosperity of the postwar period continued into the 1960's. More Americans were buying goods for the pleasure of buying them, rather than because they needed them. Many Americans continued to be fascinated with the newest gadgets, styles, fads, and fashions. The consumer culture of earlier years became so widespread that it was truly a "mass culture." The pursuit of wealth and the enjoyment of material possessions were at the center of the lives of millions of Americans.

The clearest expression of the consumer culture was television. By 1961, there were 55 million television sets in the United States. Americans not only watched the same programs, they also saw the same products being advertised. Millions of Americans instantly recognized advertising "jingles" from television commercials. The products of the mass consumer culture were thus promoted through this powerful medium.

Television also continued to influence the political process. More candidates became skilled at reaching the voters through television. The televised Kennedy-Nixon debates of 1960 inspired similar debates of other candidates in national and state elections. The televising of events in the civil rights movement and the war in Vietnam had a strong impact on public opinion.

Evidence of the mass consumer culture even became apparent in the painting styles of the 1960's. One of the most popular styles of the decade was "pop art."

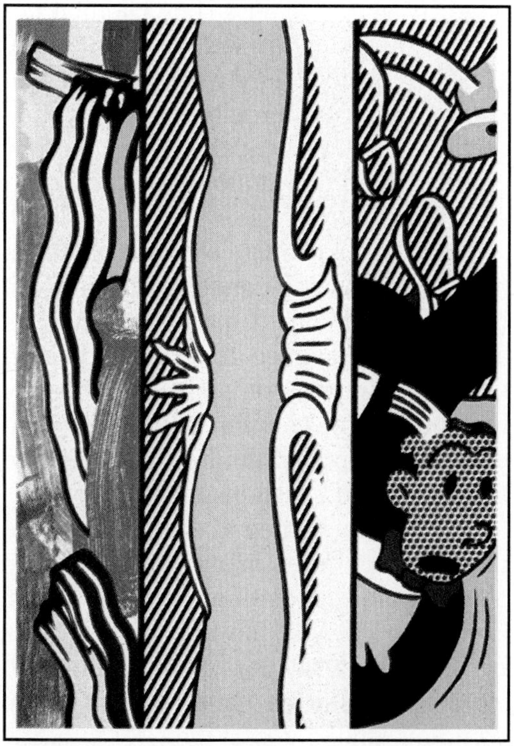

Roy Lichtenstein's paintings are examples of "pop art," a style that became popular in the 1960's. The painting above is called Two Paintings: Dagwood.

For Extra Interest: Have students make a list of ten advertising slogans, leaving out key words. Have students exchange papers and fill in the blanks. You may also wish to have a student hum an advertising jingle for the class to identify.

For Extra Interest: Have students make a bulletin board featuring styles, fads, art, and so on of the 1960's.

The pop artists chose subjects from the mass culture and often portrayed them in large or dramatic paintings. Pop artist Andy Warhol, for example, painted realistic portraits of items such as Campbell's soup cans. Roy Lichtenstein created paintings based on comic strips. The artists seemed to be making fun of the values of the consumer culture.

Some members of the counterculture earned money as street musicians. People enjoyed their music on street corners and in parks.

The Counterculture

Many young people in the 1960's felt alienated from the dominant culture. They formed a "counterculture" that rejected the values and life styles of the majority of Americans. They claimed not to be interested in wealth or material goods. In place of hard work and achievement, the counterculture emphasized "self-fulfillment." Leaders of the counterculture urged their followers to "do their own thing."

There was a genuine element of youthful idealism in the counterculture. Some observers welcomed the new culture as a positive challenge to existing values. Others, however, complained that many members of the counterculture were simply lazy or spoiled chidren who refused to accept adult responsibilities.

As a symbol of their alienation from the dominant culture, many young people adopted unusual clothing and hair styles. Long hair, beads, flowers, and sandals became popular for both men and women. Mustaches and beards were common among young men.

The news media gave the young people a great deal of coverage. Members of the counterculture were called "hippies," "flower children," or "the love generation." The term *hippie* came from the older slang expression "hip," which meant to be aware of the very latest developments. In 1967, the counterculture reached its peak of popularity. The largest concentration of hippies was in the Haight-Ashbury district of San Francisco. There was also a large group on New York City's Lower East Side. Hippies could be found, however, in every major American city.

Popular music became a unifying force of the generation. Folk singers and rock bands often served as spokespeople for the counterculture. Their music expressed themes of alienation and protest. "Where Have All the Flowers Gone?" became a popular antiwar song. Bob Dylan's

For Extra Interest: Obtain recordings of several protest songs popular in the 1960's to play for the class. In addition to those mentioned in the text, "The Eve of Destruction," recorded by Barry Maguire, is a good example.

"The Times They Are a-Changing" described the gap between the younger generation and the older one.

In 1968, a group of young actors and musicians in New York performed a musical called *Hair*. The musical glorified the counterculture. Young people also gathered in huge outdoor "rock festivals." The largest of these was held in 1969 at a farm near Woodstock, New York. Four hundred thousand young people attended the Woodstock festival.

The counterculture was especially strong on college campuses. There the counterculture was closely linked to social and political protest. Students in the 1960's organized to protest racial discrimination, the Vietnam War, the draft, and college policies that restricted their political activities.

This "student movement" began at the University of California at Berkeley in 1964. It soon spread to campuses across the nation. The student protests often led to violent confrontations with local police. Classes were disrupted, and several universities were forced to suspend all classes temporarily. Small groups of radical students bombed or damaged buildings and property on many campuses.

The emergence of the counterculture in the 1960's was the result of several factors. It was, in part, a result of the "baby boom." Young people in the 1960's felt an unusual sense of identity as a generation simply because there were so many of them. The counterculture also represented a direct response to the materialism of the dominant consumer culture. Many young people were sincerely seeking alternative values and ways of life. Others were simply "dropouts" with no sense of purpose.

The counterculture was also a result of the larger issues troubling American society. Young people were alienated because of the slow progress in the movement for racial equality in the United States. The war in Vietnam caused still more powerful feelings of alienation. Many young people opposed the war. For young men, their opposition was especially intense because they were the ones who were being drafted to fight the war. To many young members of the counterculture, the Vietnam War was reason enough to reject the values of the dominant culture.

Section Review

1. Why did a counterculture emerge in the United States in the 1960's?
2. What areas of politics concerned the counterculture?
3. What role did music play in the counterculture?
4. Is the counterculture of the 1960's extinct? Can you think of any ways that the counterculture has affected the values or life styles of today? Explain your answer.

For Extra Interest: Have an interested student research and report to the class on the violence that occurred at Kent State University in 1970.

CHAPTER REVIEW

Summary

Americans entered the 1960's with great hope and optimism. President John F. Kennedy reflected the nation's attitude. His strong stand during the Cuban missile crisis ushered in a period of peaceful coexistence with the Soviet Union. Civil rights became the dominant domestic issue during the Kennedy administration as black Americans staged sit-ins and "freedom rides" to force an end to racial segregation.

Kennedy's assassination in 1963 marked the beginning of a major shift in the national mood. Although President Johnson was very successful in bringing about major social reforms through his "war on poverty," his policy of "limited war" in Vietnam failed to bring an end to the fighting. As the war continued, demonstrations against American involvement in Vietnam increased in size and frequency. Young Americans who felt alienated from the mass culture formed a counterculture that rejected the values and life styles of the majority of Americans. By the late 1960's, feelings of frustration and confusion had replaced the earlier optimism and confidence of the decade.

Recalling the Facts

1. What advantages and disadvantages did the two major candidates, Nixon and Kennedy, have in the 1960 presidential campaign?
2. What support did Kennedy give to the civil rights movement?
3. What was done during President Johnson's administration in an attempt to eliminate poverty in the United States?
4. What two strategies did the United States use in Vietnam in an attempt to keep the Vietnamese villagers from giving aid to the Communist forces? How successful were these strategies?
5. Describe the counterculture that emerged in the late 1960's.

Analyzing the Facts

1. How do you think Lyndon Johnson's many years in Congress helped him get laws passed when he was President?
2. Read the Fifteenth Amendment of the Constitution. How does the wording of this amendment allow racial discrimination in voting to continue?

3. Why do you think it was so important to eliminate racial discrimination in voting?
4. Martin Luther King, Jr., and Malcolm X were both powerful black leaders in the 1960's. How did their philosophies on how black Americans could improve their lives differ?
5. If you had been President Johnson, what would you have done about the American dilemma in Vietnam? Why?
6. The Vietnam War was the first televised war. Every day Americans saw the death and destruction caused by this war in televised newscasts. What impact do you think this had on public opinion?

Time and History

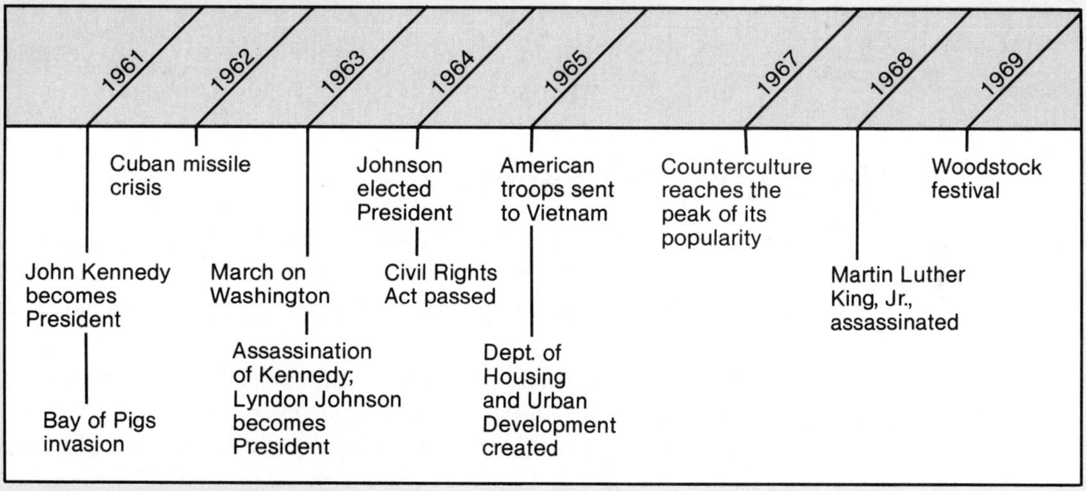

1. How long after he led the march on Washington was Martin Luther King, Jr., assassinated?
2. Which President ordered American combat troops sent to Vietnam? When did this happen?
3. How long after the Bay of Pigs invasion did the Cuban missile crisis occur?
4. Why did Lyndon Johnson become President in 1963?
5. In what year was the Civil Rights Act passed?

UNIT REVIEW

Summary

Americans faced many challenges in the years following World War II. Veterans were eased back into society by the GI Bill, while factories converted to peacetime production. A period of prosperity followed the war, which allowed many Americans to enjoy more leisure time and buy more consumer goods. Not all Americans, however, shared in the good times. Unions called strikes to demand higher wages, and black Americans took action to end racial discrimination.

The postwar period was also a time of new tensions and danger as the Cold War developed between the United States and the Soviet Union. American foreign policy was directed at preventing the spread of communism. Fear of communism also led to a government search for subversives and spies within the United States.

Civil rights issues and American involvement in Vietnam sharply divided the nation in the 1960's. A counterculture that rejected the values of most Americans developed among the nation's young people. For many, the 1960's were years of frustration and confusion.

Recalling the Facts

1. What accounted for the economic prosperity in the United States after World War II?
2. What was the major goal of American foreign policy during the Cold War?
3. How and when was racial segregation outlawed in: (a) the nation's public schools, (b) public accommodations?
4. Why did President Johnson oppose either expanding or reducing America's role in the Vietnam War in the late 1960's?
5. Who was President when each of the following events occurred: Cuban missile crisis, U-2 incident, Berlin airlift, Korean War begins, Bay of Pigs invasion, Tonkin Gulf Resolution, and the civil rights demonstration in Washington? Give the date of each event, and put the events and dates in chronological order.

Analyzing the Facts

1. Why do you think the United States sent Marshall Plan money to the former Axis nations to help them rebuild their economies?

2. Why did the United States become involved in the war in Vietnam?
3. Do you think nuclear weapons guarantee security to the nation that possesses them? Why or why not?
4. How was the way in which Martin Luther King, Jr., died at odds with the philosophy he preached for achieving racial equality?

Reviewing Vocabulary

Define the following terms:

liberal	capitalism	demagogue
conservative	cold war	poll tax
civil rights	massive retaliation	ghetto
ideology	subversive	defoliate

Sharpening Your Skills

1. In 1955, the president of the AFL-CIO, George Meany, said: "American labor never had it so good." Is what Meany said a fact or an opinion? Why?
2. In 1950, Julius and Ethel Rosenberg were arrested. They were later found guilty of espionage and were executed. Are these facts or opinions? Why?

Answer the three questions below based on the pictograph on page 632.

3. Approximately how many new housing starts were made in 1951?
4. Between what two given years was the increase in new housing starts the greatest?
5. In what year did the number of new housing starts peak?

Writing and Research

1. Research and write a front-page news story on a significant event from the Cold War period. Type your story, and design the front page of a newspaper around it. The front-page design should include the name of the newspaper, the news story, a headline, and a picture.
2. Use an almanac or similar source to find statistical information about the United States for the years 1940 to 1960. Make a pictograph from the statistics obtained.

Unit

10 Contemporary America

32 President Richard Nixon worked for world peace by signing a nuclear arms treaty with the Soviet Union in 1972. He also visited China. Nixon's term in office, however, was rocked by a grave constitutional crisis known as "Watergate." Richard Nixon became the first President to resign from office.

33 The United States entered an era of limits in the 1970's. The energy crisis made Americans aware that there were limits to certain sources of energy. Economic problems showed that there were limits to American prosperity. Foreign crises made Americans realize that there were limits to American influence in the affairs of other countries.

34 Ronald Reagan began his term of office in 1981 with a call for national renewal. He took strong action to try to solve the nation's economic problems and to increase America's military strength. The 1980's have witnessed basic changes in the nation's population. New developments in science and technology have also influenced American society.

Chapter **32**

Years of Crisis

July 4, 1976, was America's 200th birthday. The American people celebrated the signing of the Declaration of Independence. The celebration began at the top of Mars Hill Mountain in Maine, where sunlight first touches the United States each day. At 4:33 A.M., members of the national guard fired a 50-gun salute. Later in the day, 15,000 people in Greenville, Ohio, celebrated by joining in a pie-eating contest. In Yuma, Arizona, 6,000 brave people raced down the Colorado River in inner tubes.

The Bicentennial celebration gave the nation a much-needed lift in spirit. The years surrounding 1976 were trying times. They were years of crisis.

After you read this chapter, you will be able to:

1. Explain how the Vietnam War ended.
2. List the new groups that organized for civil rights.
3. Describe President Nixon's actions during the Watergate crisis.

Background: Tet is the first day of the Vietnamese new year, celebrated on January 31. The Tet offensive was particularly upsetting because a cease-fire had been arranged in honor of the new year.

1. Foreign Affairs

BEFORE YOU READ: *How did the war in Vietnam come to an end?*

Except for the Civil War, the Vietnam War divided the country more deeply than any other armed conflict in American history. That division never seemed deeper than it did as the nation entered the election year of 1968.

1968: Year of Decision

On January 31, 1968, the Vietcong launched major attacks on American forces throughout South Vietnam. The attacks were known as the Tet offensive. The strength of the Vietcong assault shocked many Americans. The attacks caused more Americans to question the nation's policy in Vietnam.

Faced with growing opposition to the war in Vietnam, President Johnson made a television address to the nation on March 31, 1968. He reported that he had ordered a limited halt to the bombing of North Vietnam. He also announced that he would not seek reelection.

Johnson's surprise announcements greatly encouraged antiwar Democrats. Many of them gave their support to Senator Robert Kennedy. Senator Kennedy scored his biggest victory in the California primary on June 5, 1968. That night, however, Kennedy was assassinated. When the Democrats met in Chicago in August, Vice-President Hubert Humphrey was chosen as the party's candidate for President. Antiwar demonstrators marched outside the Democratic convention hall to voice their opposition to Humphrey. They identified him with the Vietnam policy of President Johnson.

The increase in antiwar and civil rights demonstrations was deeply disturbing to many Americans. They were ready to vote for conservative leaders who promised to restore order. A new conservative political party, the American Independent party, nominated Alabama governor George Wallace for President. Wallace was an outspoken defender of segregation. He appealed to the fears of Americans who believed that social and political protest had gone too far. The Republicans in 1968 chose former Vice-President Richard Nixon as their candidate. Nixon appealed to what he called the "silent majority" of Americans. These were Americans who had given their largely silent approval to the war in Vietnam. They were Americans who were troubled by the unrest of recent years. Nixon promised to restore order and stability to the nation.

The 1968 election was very close. Nixon won a narrow victory. After the election, Americans eagerly awaited Nixon's promised time of stability and order.

"Peace with Honor"

During the 1968 campaign, Richard Nixon said that he had a secret plan to end the war in Vietnam, a plan that would bring "peace with honor." Once in office President Nixon began to put his plan into effect. By the fall of 1969, he had ordered the withdrawal of 60,000 American troops from Vietnam. Over the next three years, he slowly removed more troops. As American forces withdrew, more of the fighting was left to the Vietnamese.

Background: Over Nixon's veto, Congress passed the War Powers Act in 1973. The act sets a 60-day limit on presidential commitment of American troops to hostilities abroad unless Congress authorizes continued action; 30 days more are allowed for the safe withdrawal of troops.

Discuss: Why do you think American ground forces invading Cambodia led to an increase in antiwar protests? Why do you think that many of these antiwar demonstrations were organized and staged on college campuses?

The Election of 1968

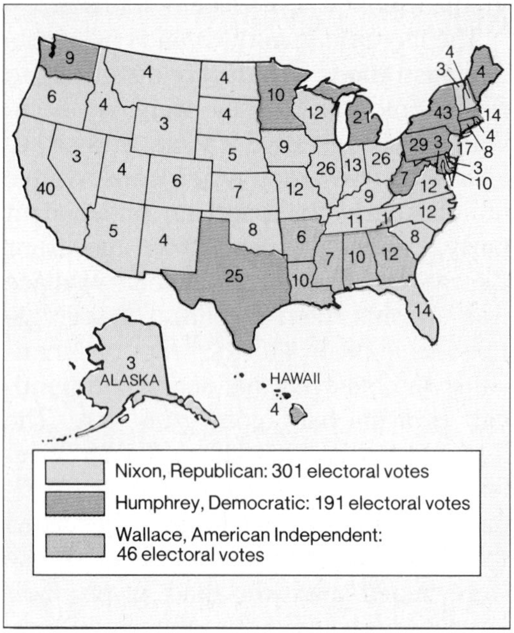

In what area of the country was George Wallace's support the strongest?

Nixon called his plan **Vietnamization**.

Vietnamization the planned withdrawal of American forces from Vietnam with the goal of turning all fighting over to the South Vietnamese

---

Nixon's plan also called for attacks on Communist bases and supply routes in neighboring Cambodia. Beginning in March 1969, Nixon ordered the bombing of Cambodia. On April 30, 1970, the President told the American people that American troops had entered Cambodia.

The bombing and invasion of Cambodia led to more antiwar protests. Hundreds of thousands of demonstrators marched in Washington, D.C. College students across the nation went on strike from their classes to spend all of their time on antiwar activities. The national guard was ordered to the campus of Kent State University in Ohio to help restore order. On May 4, 1970, members of the national guard opened fire on antiwar demonstrators. Four students were killed and nine others injured.

As the election of 1972 neared, Henry Kissinger, President Nixon's top foreign-policy adviser, announced that "peace is at hand." But a few weeks after Nixon was reelected, talks in Paris between the United States and the Vietnamese Communists broke down. The failure of the peace talks led President Nixon to order the heaviest bombing raids of the war. When the bombing raids ended, the Communists returned to the Paris peace talks. On January 27, 1973, a peace agreement was signed. The agreement called for a cease-fire and a return by North Vietnam of several hundred American prisoners of war. It also said that all remaining American forces would leave Vietnam.

Following the return of the prisoners and the removal of the American troops, fighting broke out among the Vietnamese. In April 1975, the Communists took control of Saigon, and the war was over. Many Americans wondered whether the United States had truly achieved "peace with honor."

New Directions

Ending the war in Vietnam was part of a much larger vision that President Nixon and his National Security Adviser Henry Kissinger had for international relations. Nixon and Kissinger believed that the world was becoming a more complex

Background: More than 55,000 Americans died in Vietnam, and over 300,000 were wounded. Vietnamese casualties totaled at least 1.2 million killed. The total number of civilian casualties will probably never be known.

EUREKA!

The Microprocessor

Few inventions have come along that can truly be called revolutionary. The microprocessor, or "computer-on-a-chip," was such an invention. The invention of the microprocessor has led to major changes in the size, power, and performance of computers.

A microprocessor does the work of a computer's central processing unit, or CPU. It is the computer's brain, taking care of all logic and arithmetic operations. It can be programmed to do all sorts of tasks, from turning on a coffeepot to guiding an airplane on its proper course.

A young electronics engineer named Ted Hoff, who was working for the Intel Corporation in California, probably made the first microprocessor. In 1969, Hoff was given the task of making a set of very small electronic parts for a programmable calculator. The plan called for complex circuitry involving many expensive circuit chips. Hoff decided to tackle the problem in a totally new way. He put all of the calculator's logic and arithmetic circuitry on a single silicon chip—a microprocessor.

Intel introduced its microprocessor in 1971. It was about 4.2 millimeters (.2 inches) long and 3.2 millimeters (.1 inch) wide, and it held about 2,300 transistors—the basic elements of the modern electronic devices.

Today's microprocessors contain 20,000 or more transistors. The development of microprocessors has made it possible for today's inexpensive pocket calculator to have more computing power than a $30,000 IBM computer of 1960. As designers find new ways to put more and more circuitry on tiny silicon chips, the microprocessor will change further. It will become even smaller, more powerful, and inexpensive enough to play a more important role in the life of almost everyone.

---

place. They believed that the United States and the Soviet Union were no longer the only superpowers in the world. China, Japan, and Western Europe were now major powers as well. Nixon and Kissinger hoped to establish a new balance among these major powers. The goal of American policy should be to encourage a new international **equilibrium**.

equilibrium a state of balance between opposing forces

Background: Henry Kissinger had come to the United States as a Jewish refugee from Nazi Germany. He was a brilliant professor of government at Harvard University. Kissinger served Nixon as his national security adviser and later as secretary of state.

For Extra Interest: Have interested students research and report on the rivalry that developed between the People's Republic of China and the Soviet Union in the 1960's.

As part of the new equilibrium, President Nixon hoped to establish relations with the People's Republic of China. China and the Soviet Union had become bitter enemies in the 1960's. Nixon hoped that American relations with China would serve as a balance to Soviet power. In February 1972, President Nixon became the first American President to visit China. He held important meetings with Chinese leaders Chou En-Lai (JOE en-LIE) and Mao Tse-tung. The United States and China agreed to set up scientific and cultural exchanges. Plans were made for trade to begin again between the two nations. Steps were taken toward diplomatic recognition of China by the United States.

Nixon and Kissinger also tried to reduce tensions with the Soviet Union. They followed a policy of **détente** (day-TAHNT). Negotiations between the United States and the Soviet Union in 1972 resulted in a treaty limiting nuclear weapons. This was the first Strategic Arms Limitation Treaty (SALT I). President Nixon visited Moscow in May 1972 to sign the agreement. In June 1973, the Soviet Premier Leonid Brezhnev (BREZH-nef) visited the United States.

détente a relaxation of tensions between nations

A reduction of tensions in the Middle East was harder to achieve. The United States had long been a strong supporter of Israel, the Jewish nation created in 1948. Many of the Arab nations in the Middle East were against the creation of Israel. They wanted Israel to be an Arab state, not a Jewish nation.

In 1967 and again in 1973, Israel was attacked by certain Arab countries. In both wars, Israel defeated the Arabs and gained control of Arab territory. In response, the Arab countries placed an embargo on oil sales to America and to other supporters of Israel.

Nixon and Kissinger wanted to maintain support for Israel. They also wanted to ensure continued American access to oil from the Middle East. In the spring of 1974, Kissinger, now the secretary of state, arranged a limited peace agreement in the Middle East. Israel agreed to give up some of the territory seized in the 1967 war. The Arabs lifted their oil embargo. Hostilities, however, continued between Israel and its Arab neighbors.

Section Review

1. How did the war in Vietnam finally come to an end?
2. Define Vietnamization. What were the terms of the Paris peace agreement of 1973?
3. Define equilibrium and détente. How do these terms describe Nixon's foreign policy?
4. Do you believe the United States achieved "peace with honor" in Vietnam? Explain your answer.

Discuss: Do you think that détente is a realistic and workable policy, or will the United States always be at odds with the Soviet Union? Explain your answer.

For Extra Interest: Have interested students research and report to the class on various aspects of the Apollo program or the later Viking missions.

2. Domestic Affairs

BEFORE YOU READ: *What new groups began to organize for their civil rights?*

On July 20, 1969, the American spacecraft *Eagle* landed on the moon. Neil Armstrong, commander of the three-member flight crew, was the first person ever to walk on the moon's surface. His first step, he said, was "one small step for a man, one giant leap for mankind."

The lunar landing was an event that drew the nation together. Other events during the late 1960's and early 1970's, however, emphasized the continuing differences among Americans.

Civil Rights

President Nixon was not a strong supporter of the civil rights movement. The President, for example, opposed **busing**, or the transportation of students to a school to achieve desegregation. Nevertheless, in 1971 the Supreme Court ruled in favor of busing.

busing the transportation of students to a school to achieve desegregation

The continued successes of the black civil rights movement encouraged other minority groups to organize. American Indians were one such group. American Indians are among the nation's poorest people. The unemployment rate among Indians in the 1960's was ten times the national rate. For those Indians living on reservations, housing, health care, and job opportunities were very poor.

In 1968, the American Indian Movement (AIM) was organized. AIM and other American Indian rights groups called for improved conditions and better opportunities for Indian people. To make Americans aware of their situation and demands, the members of AIM staged a number of protests. In 1972, nearly one thousand Indian demonstrators held a six-day sit-in at the Bureau of Indian Affairs in Washington, D. C. At the town of Wounded Knee, South Dakota, Indian protestors clashed with federal officials. One Indian was killed and another wounded.

Indian protests in the late 1960's and early 1970's were successful in bringing about public and government awareness of Indian issues and problems.

Discuss: Do you think busing is a reasonable way to achieve integration? Why or why not?

Vocabulary Help: affirmative action—a policy or program for correcting the effects of discrimination in the employment of certain groups, such as blacks or women. Discuss with the class how affirmative action programs may lead to reverse discrimination.

Indians also went to court to demand payments from the federal government for lost tribal lands.

Another group that gained greater political and economic power was the nation's Hispanic population. The number of Hispanics in the United States had grown to more than 9 million by 1970. Many Hispanics lived in poverty in segregated neighborhoods, or **barrios**. But Hispanics gained greater influence in politics. In the Southwest, Hispanics were elected to public office in several states.

---

barrio a Spanish word meaning district or neighborhood

The largest population of Hispanics lived in California. Most were of Mexican origin. In the 1960's, a Mexican American named Cesar Chavez began to organize farm workers in California. As the leader of the United Farm Workers (UFW), Chavez led many successful strikes for higher wages and better working conditions for farm workers.

Supporters of equal rights for women also organized and called for an end to discrimination. Large public demonstrations were held in cities all over the United States. In 1966, **feminists** organized the National Organization for Women (NOW).

---

feminist a supporter of equal rights for women

Progress was made in breaking down many of the barriers that had long kept women from achieving true equality. Congress passed the Equal Pay Act in 1963. This act barred employers from paying workers of one sex less than they paid workers of the other sex for equal work. The Civil Rights Act of 1964 further prohibited job discrimination based on sex. In 1971, Congress expanded its "affirmative action" standards to include women as well as racial minorities. Employers were to make efforts to seek qualified women for available jobs.

The Economy

The American economy in the post-World War II period was the envy of the world. But in the early 1970's, economic growth slowed. International trade declined. Most disturbing of all, inflation grew at an alarming rate.

Inflation was a problem that hurt all Americans. Higher prices meant that consumers could not get as many goods for their money as they once could. The same goods that cost $100 in 1967 cost $247 in 1980. The price of a pound of rice, for example, rose from $.19 in 1967 to $.51 in 1980. Americans were reminded of inflation every time they went to a store.

The causes of America's economic problems were many and complex. The Vietnam War was partly to blame. The war cost the United States more than $150 billion. During the war, the federal government also continued to spend billions of dollars to fund the many programs of the Great Society. This massive amount of federal spending meant an increased amount of money in the economy and, thus, increased inflation.

The nation's economic problems were also caused by growing international competition from foreign countries. Goods from Western Europe and Japan

Discuss: What is the relationship between wage increases and inflation? How would increased productivity offset wage increases?

Famous Americans

SEIJI OZAWA

Seiji Ozawa, the conductor of the Boston Symphony Orchestra, was born in 1935. His love of music developed early. He learned to enjoy Western music through the hymns he heard in church. Ozawa also enjoyed the Japanese music that surrounded him.

Ozawa's family was very poor, but they did all they could to help develop Seiji's exceptional musical talent. By the age of seven, Ozawa was playing the music of the great nineteenth-century Western composers. His career as a concert pianist seemed certain. But he broke a few fingers playing rugby at school, and his hands never healed properly for piano playing.

For a time, Ozawa decided that composing was the field he should go into. But his teachers at the Toho School of Music in Tokyo thought he would be a good conductor. Ozawa graduated from the Toho School and went to Paris to study conducting.

Ozawa progressed rapidly in his profession. He was engaged as an assistant conductor of the New York Philharmonic for the 1961–1962 season. In 1964, he was invited to return to the New York Philharmonic. During the 1960's, Ozawa served as the conductor of the Toronto Symphony of Canada and music director of the San Francisco Symphony. In 1973, he became the youngest permanent conductor and music director of the Boston Symphony Orchestra.

What makes Ozawa such a great conductor is his ability to conduct classical, romantic, and modern works equally well. He conducts difficult works with ease, and all works are conducted from memory.

In recent years, Ozawa traveled with the Boston Symphony to Japan where he was warmly greeted.

Discuss: How do you think you would have reacted if the company you worked for in 1972 adopted the President's voluntary wage guidelines, while other companies in your area did not? Explain your answer.

were taking more and more markets away from American manufacturers. West German and Japanese automobiles, for example, became popular among American consumers. Increased demand for the world's raw materials also led to a rise in prices. The United States came to rely upon oil supplied by foreign countries. The nation was hard hit in the 1970's when the price of oil rose dramatically.

President Nixon tried to fight inflation by reducing the nation's money supply. In theory, less money in circulation would cause the value of money to rise. The price of goods would decline, and inflation would slow down. Nixon's "tight money" policy, however, had little effect.

On August 15, 1971, President Nixon outlined a bold plan to stop inflation. He ordered a 90-day freeze on all wages and prices. In November, the President announced Phase II of his economic plan. He established standards for future wage and price increases. The standards were enforced by a new federal agency. The President's plan slowed inflation, but it also caused many businesses to cut back production. As production slowed, unemployment increased.

After the November 1972 election, President Nixon announced Phase III of his plan. Wages and prices were allowed to increase or decrease with more flexibility. The new standards were voluntary. The voluntary plan failed, and inflation rose even higher. In 1973, the rate of inflation was 9 percent. The following year, the inflation rate rose to 12 percent. This was the sharpest rise since just after the end of World War II. The average price of consumer goods, as measured by the **consumer price index**, also continued to rise sharply.

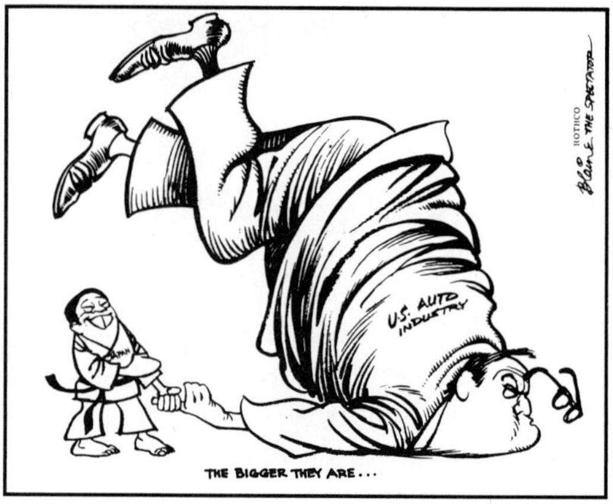

What does this cartoon seem to be saying about the impact of imported Japanese automobiles on the American economy?

consumer price index the average price of a selected group of consumer goods purchased by a typical family

Section Review

1. What new groups began to organize for their civil rights?
2. Define barrio, feminist, and consumer price index.
3. What were some of the causes of America's economic problems?
4. What problems might further inflation cause for the average family? Explain your answer.

Background: George McGovern was an outspoken critic of American policy in Vietnam. Nixon's campaign strategy was to identify McGovern as an "extremist."

3. The Politics of Crisis

BEFORE YOU READ: *What action did President Nixon take after he learned of the break-in at the Watergate office building?*

Richard Nixon had helped to reduce the tensions of the Cold War. Nixon's accomplishments, however, took on less importance in the minds of many Americans when a political scandal known as "Watergate" surfaced. The scandal led to a grave constitutional crisis.

The Election of 1972

Nixon was again chosen to be the Republican candidate for President in 1972. The Democratic party nominated George S. McGovern, a liberal senator from South Dakota.

Richard Nixon's campaign organization in 1972 was known as the Committee to Reelect the President (CREEP). It was directed by members of the White House staff. The committee wanted to make sure that McGovern would be defeated in the election. CREEP hired five men to break into the offices of the Democratic National Committee. The burglars were told to plant electronic "bugs" to spy on the Democrats. On June 17, 1972, the burglars were arrested at Democratic headquarters in the Watergate building in Washington, D.C.

After the arrest of the burglars, President Nixon tried to cover up CREEP's involvement in the planning of the burglary. On June 23, 1972, he secretly ordered the CIA to ask the FBI not to investigate the burglary. By trying to stop the investigation, the President was himself committing a very serious crime.

Nixon's cover-up worked very well—for a while. The election of 1972 was a great Republican victory. Nixon carried every state except Massachusetts, and Washington, D.C. McGovern received only 17 electoral votes to Nixon's 520.

Watergate

Following the 1972 election, a Senate committee was formed to investigate the Watergate burglary. The American people took great interest in the committee's hearings. The involvement of the White House staff in the planning of the Watergate burglary and other illegal campaign activities soon became clear.

Witnesses told the Senate committee that information had been gathered about critics of President Nixon. The critics' mail was opened illegally, and their telephones were illegally "tapped." Illegal campaign contributions had been gathered by CREEP. "Dirty tricks" had been played on Nixon's Democratic opponents. The dirty tricks included the printing of fake campaign literature to embarrass Democratic opponents and to confuse voters.

The evidence of widespread wrongdoing mounted. Many of the President's top White House advisers quit their jobs. Nixon, however, continued to state that he was innocent. "I am not a crook," he said at a news conference.

One witness before the Senate committee reported that President Nixon had a system for tape-recording conversations in the White House. The committee asked

Background: Nixon publicly denounced the Watergate burglary. He denied that his staff was in any way involved. Many Americans did not doubt the President's word.

Background: Amendment 25, ratified in 1967, provides for filling any vacancies that occur in the office of Vice-President. Prior to this amendment, if the office of Vice-President became vacant, it remained vacant until the next presidential election.

The Senate Select Committee on Campaign Practices, headed by Senator Sam Ervin of North Carolina, conducted lengthy hearings to get to the bottom of the Watergate scandal.

Nixon to turn over tapes of his conversations around the time of the Watergate break-in. Nixon, claiming executive privilege, refused.

While the Watergate scandal was growing, Nixon's Vice-President, Spiro Agnew, was charged with accepting kickbacks and bribes while he was governor of Maryland. Agnew resigned as Vice-President in disgrace. President Nixon named Representative Gerald Ford of Michigan to serve as Vice-President.

The Judiciary Committee of the House of Representatives began holding hearings to consider the impeachment of the President. President Nixon was charged with **obstruction of justice** for trying to stop the investigation of the Watergate burglary. He was charged with misusing the powers of the office of President. And he was accused of disobeying Congress by refusing to turn over the White House tapes.

---

obstruction of justice an illegal attempt to stop the investigation of a crime

---

In July 1974, the United States Supreme Court ordered the President to turn over the White House tapes to government investigators. A few days later, the Judiciary Committee voted to recommend that Nixon be impeached. In August, Nixon turned over the White House tapes. These recordings proved that the President had tried to stop the investigation of the Watergate burglary.

The President now faced almost certain impeachment by the House of Representatives and conviction by the Senate. On August 8, 1974, Nixon told the American people that he was resigning from the presidency. The following day, Gerald Ford was sworn in as President.

The Healing

Gerald Ford was unique among American Presidents. Unlike all other Presidents, he had been elected neither President nor Vice-President.

President Ford believed that his most important task was to restore the American people's faith in government. He performed this task well. After three weeks in office, more than 70 percent of the American people approved of his performance as President.

President Ford became less popular, however, when he gave Richard Nixon a

Background: When Gerald Ford became President following the resignation of President Nixon in 1974, he appointed Nelson A. Rockefeller to fill the vice-presidential vacancy.

Background: Ford pardoned Nixon, he said, out of compassion. He also wanted to spare the nation the ordeal of seeing a former President face criminal charges. Nixon's top aides, however, were not pardoned. Many of them were convicted and sentenced to federal prisons.

presidential pardon in September 1974. Ford's pardon meant that Nixon could not be taken to court for any crimes he had committed as President.

In foreign affairs, President Ford continued the Nixon policy of détente. In 1974, Ford and Soviet Premier Leonid Brezhnev signed a new agreement to limit nuclear weapons. In the Middle East, Secretary of State Kissinger arranged a new, limited peace agreement between Israel and Egypt.

In the spring of 1975, the Communist government in Cambodia seized an American merchant ship, the *Mayaguez* (my-ah-GEZZ). President Ford responded to the taking of the *Mayaguez* by ordering the United States Marines to rescue the ship and its crew. The *Mayaguez* and its 39-member crew were released, but 38 marines were killed in the course of the rescue operation.

The nation's economic problems continued to be difficult to solve. Prices were still rising while economic activity remained sluggish or **stagnant**. The strange mixture of economic stagnation and inflation led one observer to diagnose the nation's ills as "stagflation."

---

stagnant sluggish, not flowing or moving about

President Ford hoped that voluntary programs would solve the nation's economic problems. But the economy continued to decline further. This temporary falling off of business activity was the worst **recession** since the Great Depression of the 1930's. In 1975, production fell by more than 10 percent and unemployment rose to nearly 9 percent.

---

recession a temporary decline in production and an increase in the number of unemployed

---

One bright spot in the Ford years was the Bicentennial celebration of 1976. The Bicentennial reminded all Americans that in spite of the nation's problems, the United States still had many reasons to be proud.

Section Review

1. What action did President Nixon take after he learned of the break-in at the Watergate building?
2. What illegal activities were committed by members of the Nixon administration?
3. Why did President Nixon resign from the presidency? Define obstruction of justice.
4. What economic problems confronted President Ford in the 1970's?
5. Do you believe that President Ford made a wise move when he issued a pardon to former President Nixon? Why or why not?

For Extra Interest: Have students make a list of at least five things the United States could be proud of as it celebrated its 200th birthday.

CHAPTER REVIEW

Summary

Richard Nixon was elected President in 1968 on the campaign promise to bring "peace with honor" to Vietnam and restore order and stability in the United States. American forces were gradually withdrawn from Vietnam, and in 1973 a peace agreement was signed that ended direct American involvement in the war. With the aid of Henry Kissinger, President Nixon developed a new American foreign policy designed to establish a worldwide balance of power. Steps were taken to improve relations with the Soviet Union and the People's Republic of China.

Domestic unrest, however, did not end with the withdrawal of American forces from Vietnam. American Indians, Hispanics, and women's groups organized demonstrations to demand an end to injustices and discrimination. Government policies to curb rising inflation were unsuccessful and resulted in increased unemployment. The most serious domestic crisis of the Nixon administration was the Watergate scandal. Rather than risk the possibility of impeachment, President Nixon resigned in 1974. Nixon's successor, Gerald Ford, faced the difficult task of trying to heal the nation's political and economic wounds.

Recalling the Facts

1. What steps did President Nixon take to improve relations with the Soviet Union and the People's Republic of China?
2. What progress was made in the 1960's and 1970's in breaking down the barriers that had long prevented women from achieving equality?
3. Describe the steps taken by President Nixon to try to control inflation. How effective was each phase of the President's program?
4. What evidence was there that President Nixon had tried to stop the investigation of the Watergate burglary?
5. What two events caused many Americans to feel proud of their nation during the years of crisis (1968–1976)?

Analyzing the Facts

1. What problems did minority groups have in common in the 1960's and 1970's? How did they try to solve these problems?

2. In what ways can international trade both hurt and help the American economy?
3. Do you think President Nixon would have been reelected in 1972 if he had fired those members of his staff and campaign organization who had been involved in the Watergate burglary? Why or why not?
4. How did the Watergate scandal produce a serious constitutional crisis?

Time and History

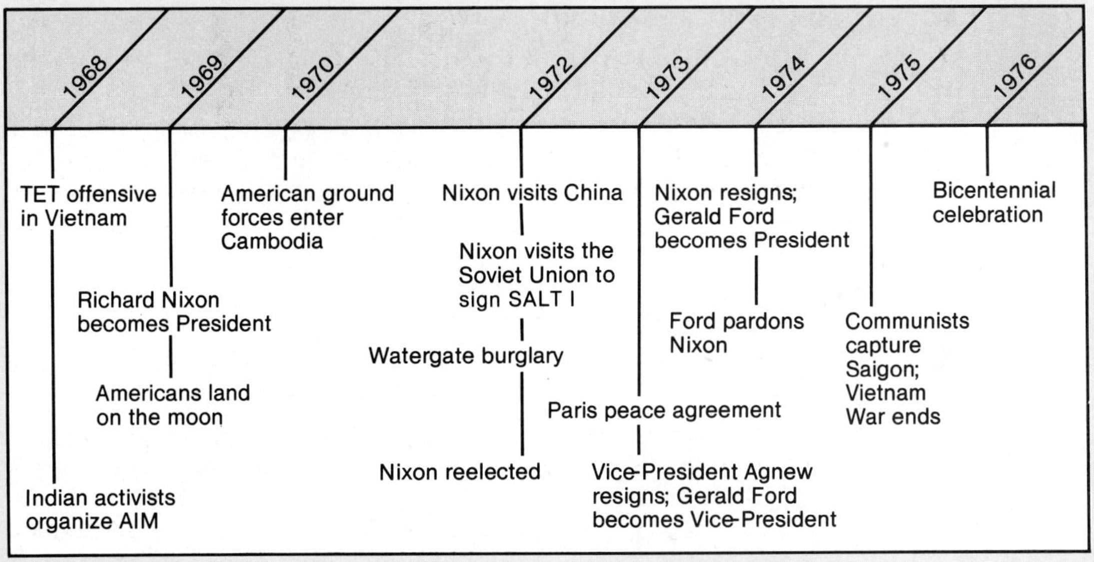

1. How many years did Gerald Ford serve as Vice-President before becoming President?
2. How many years after the American involvement in Vietnam ended did the war end?
3. What two countries did Richard Nixon visit as President?
4. How many years after the Watergate burglary did President Nixon resign?
5. In what year were you born? How many years before you were born did Americans land on the moon?

Chapter 33 The Era of Limits

One of the great joys of summer is going on vacation. Many Americans in the summer of 1979 had to cancel their vacation plans. They feared that they would not be able to buy enough gasoline for their trip. The nation was in the midst of a gasoline shortage. Imports of oil products from the Middle East had been temporarily cut back. Many gasoline stations had customers lined up for blocks waiting to fill their tanks.

The late 1970's became an era of limits. There were limits to what the government could do to solve the nation's economic problems. There were also limits to America's power in the world.

After you read this chapter, you will be able to:

1. Describe President Carter's energy policies.
2. List Carter's accomplishments in foreign affairs.

☐ Make inferences and draw conclusions.

Background: The Carter family was an old one in Georgia, going back eight generations. Carter became an officer in the navy after graduating from the United States Naval Academy. In 1953, he left the navy and took over his family's peanut warehousing business.

1. The Rise of Jimmy Carter

BEFORE YOU READ: *What policies did President Carter support to solve the country's energy crisis?*

Gerald Ford remained a popular President during his years in the White House. Many Americans felt, however, that he had not done enough to improve the nation's economy.

As the election of 1976 neared, many conservative Republicans supported Ronald Reagan, a former California governor. But at the Republican convention, Ford received the nomination.

The Election of 1976

The Democratic candidate in 1976 was the former governor of Georgia, James Earl Carter. Carter had proved to be a good administrator while serving as governor. He was an informal person and always preferred to be called "Jimmy." Carter became well-known when he came out in support of equal rights for blacks in his state. Carter represented the "New South," a South where racial cooperation was replacing racial discrimination.

During the campaign of 1976, Carter turned his inexperience in national affairs into an advantage. The Watergate scandal had caused many Americans to be distrustful of all politicians. Carter ran as an "outsider" to Washington and national politics. Carter also promised to restore honesty to the presidency. During the campaign he pledged, "I'll never lie to you."

The election of 1976 was extremely close. Jimmy Carter won the support of the South, labor unions, and minorities. He received the overwhelming support of black voters. Carter won 297 electoral votes to Ford's 240.

A New Beginning

Jimmy Carter began his term in office by demonstrating his desire for "closeness" to the American people. Following his inaugural address at the Capitol, President Carter walked to the White House, waving to crowds along the way. All other recent Presidents had been driven in an official limousine.

Carter took part in many activities to stay in close touch with the people. He hosted radio "call-in" programs in which Americans could talk to the President. He

The Election of 1976

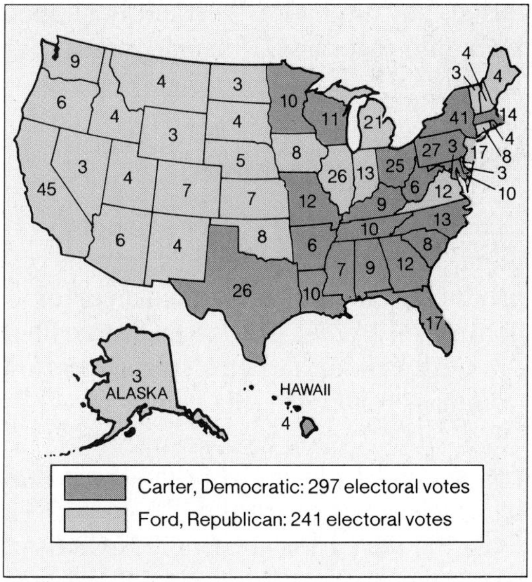

What sectional patterns do you see in the way Americans voted in the election of 1976?

Discuss: What do you think is the best way for the President to stay in touch with the American people? Explain your answer.

Background: Oil production in the United States peaked in 1970. The nation was then importing one fourth of the oil it consumed. By 1980, the United States depended upon foreign oil supplies for nearly half of its annual consumption.

attended town meetings across the country. He even visited with Americans in their homes. These actions won Carter widespread support.

The Economic Dilemma

Americans were eager for the President to show leadership in solving the nation's economic problems. At first, Carter took steps to ease the recession left by Gerald Ford. But as the recession began to disappear, inflation increased. The consumer price index rose by nearly 14 percent in 1980. Carter then moved to fight inflation. The Federal Reserve Board caused bank interest rates to rise to their highest levels in American history. High interest rates led to less borrowing by businesses and individuals. The automobile and housing industries were hit hard by the high interest rates. The demand for goods fell, causing prices to fall as well. Inflation eased, but the nation's economy slipped back into recession. Unemployment rose sharply.

The Energy Crisis

Many years before Carter became President, several of the world's largest oil-producing nations had formed a **cartel** to control oil prices. The cartel was called the Organization of Petroleum Exporting Countries (OPEC). In the winter of 1973–1974, OPEC announced a very large increase in oil prices. The price of a barrel of crude oil rose from $2.41 to $10.95. Over the next several years, OPEC raised prices even higher. By 1981, OPEC oil was selling for $34 a barrel. The total cost of America's imported oil supplies soared.

---

cartel a national or international association of businesses to control production or prices

---

President Carter realized the seriousness of the energy crisis. OPEC oil was costing the United States billions of dollars each year. Carter believed that the solution to the energy crisis lay in the careful use and protection of existing energy sources and the development of new sources. He supported programs that would achieve both of these goals.

In 1977, the President created the Department of Energy. He also recommended that federal controls be removed from the price of domestic oil and natural gas produced in the United States. If energy prices rose, Carter reasoned, people would use less of it. Higher prices would also encourage American oil companies to look for new supplies of oil and gas. In August 1978, Congress approved a plan for the **deregulation** of domestic oil and gas prices.

---

deregulation the removal of controls or regulations

In 1979, President Carter worked to get Congress to approve other energy-related laws. Congress provided tax credits for homeowners who put energy-saving insulation in their homes. Congress also set fuel-efficiency standards for American automakers. The automobile companies had to produce cars that got better gas mileage.

The President proposed the development of new energy sources. He supported the use of energy obtained di-

Discuss: The United States spent $3 billion for foreign oil in 1970 compared with $60 billion in 1980. What do you think accounts for this huge difference?

For Extra Interest: Have interested students research and report on the accident at the Three Mile Island nuclear plant that occurred in 1979.

rectly from sunlight, or **solar energy.** Carter favored the development of wind power as well. The most important alternative source of energy, Carter believed, was liquid fuel made from coal or natural gas. The President asked Congress for $88 billion for the development of these new **synthetic fuels.** In 1980, Congress voted to spend $20 billion on the new fuels.

---

solar energy energy obtained directly from sunlight

synthetic fuels liquid fuels made from coal or natural gas

The source of energy that caused the most debate was that which is released by a nuclear reaction. **Nuclear energy** could be used to generate electricity. Opponents charged that there was no safe way to get rid of deadly wastes from nuclear plants. Opponents also feared the danger of a nuclear plant accident.

---

nuclear energy energy released from an atom in a nuclear reaction or by radioactive decay

---

These solar panels are part of "Solar One," a solar power plant built in Barstow, California.

In March 1979, the Three Mile Island nuclear power plant near Harrisburg, Pennsylvania, had a major accident. Fortunately, the accident caused no deaths or significant radiation leaks. Following the accident, the federal government set stricter safety standards for the nuclear power industry. The building of new nuclear plants in the United States almost came to a halt.

Section Review

1. What policies did President Carter support to solve America's energy crisis?
2. What actions did President Carter take to solve the nation's economic problems? How successful were his efforts?
3. Define solar energy, synthetic fuels, and nuclear energy.
4. During the 1976 campaign, President Carter said to the American people, "I'll never lie to you." What does this statement tell you about American attitudes toward the presidency in the 1970's?

For Extra Interest: Have students debate the use of nuclear energy as a power source in the United States.

Social Studies Skills

Making Inferences and Drawing Conclusions

The factual information just presented on the Carter presidency can be expanded upon by making inferences and drawing conclusions. An inference is an educated guess based on evidence. For example, if the skies begin to darken and loud claps of thunder can be heard, it can be inferred that it is going to rain. Conclusions can also be drawn from facts or inferences. A conclusion may take the form of a judgment, decision, or opinion. The more factual evidence upon which an inference or conclusion is based, the greater the likelihood that it will be valid or correct.

As you read the following paragraph on the role of Rosalynn Carter in her husband's administration, look for evidence that can be used to make inferences and draw conclusions.

> Early in the administration, Rosalynn Carter emerged as a key adviser and personal representative of the President. Not since Jacqueline Kennedy or perhaps even Eleanor Roosevelt had the wife of a President played such an important role. Rosalynn Carter visited Latin America on behalf of the President. She worked hard and successfully for legislation to benefit people suffering from mental illness. In the campaign of 1980, she traveled across the country, making campaign speeches. The partnership forged by America's first family symbolized the increased stature and respect women have earned in American society.

1. What determines the likelihood of an inference or conclusion being valid or correct?
2. From the paragraph above, what can be inferred about Rosalynn Carter's involvement in political affairs during her husband's term in office?
3. What evidence is given to support the inference that Jimmy Carter thought highly of his wife's political abilities?
4. Do you think Rosalynn Carter would make a good ambassador to a foreign country? Why or why not?
5. What is the importance of being able to make inferences and draw conclusions?

Background: President Carter introduced a new moral tone to American relations with other nations. He believed that American foreign policy should be dedicated to the defense of "basic human rights." He established an Office of Human Rights in the State Department.

2. Rights and Realities

BEFORE YOU READ: *What did President Carter accomplish in the area of foreign affairs?*

The foreign policy of President Jimmy Carter combined idealistic intentions and hard realities. Carter was successful in many areas of foreign affairs. Ultimately, however, he was unable to deal with events that were beyond his control.

Carter's Accomplishments

Carter's first major foreign policy success was a pair of treaties worked out with the country of Panama. Control of the Panama Canal by the United States had long been a source of bad feelings in Latin America. The treaties gave control of the canal to Panama.

In September 1978, President Carter invited Premier Menachem Begin (mah-NAH-hem BAY-ginn) of Israel and President Anwar Sadat (ANN-wahr sah-DAHT) of Egypt to come to the United States. The three leaders met at the presidential retreat at Camp David, Maryland. The Camp David Agreement led to a comprehensive peace treaty between Egypt and Israel.

President Carter also improved American relations with the People's Republic of China. Formal diplomatic relations began on January 1, 1979.

In the summer of 1979, Carter signed a new nuclear weapons treaty with the Soviet Union. The treaty was called SALT II. It placed further limits on the strategic arms each country could possess.

Anwar Sadat, Jimmy Carter, and Menachem Begin talk to the press after the signing of the Camp David Agreement.

The Iranian Crisis

The most serious crisis of the Carter administration centered in the oil-rich nation of Iran. The shah, or ruler, of Iran was a close ally of the United States.

Many people in Iran were unhappy with the shah's government. In 1978, a revolution began in Iran. The shah was forced to leave the country. Iran was thrown into chaos. The most powerful figure to emerge from the chaos was a religious leader, the Ayatollah Khomeini (koh-MAY-nee). Khomeini condemned the United States because of its support for the shah. Oil shipments to the United States were cut back. By the summer of 1979, America was suffering from a gasoline shortage.

The shah, meanwhile, was admitted to the United States for medical treatment. A few days later, on November 4, 1979, a mob of Iranian students invaded the United States Embassy in Teheran (tay-RAHN), Iran. The students seized more than 50 diplomats and other Americans

Background: Much of the world's oil supply passes through the Persian Gulf, which borders on Iran. For many years, the United States sent massive economic and military aid to Iran. Those who opposed the shah denounced the United States for supporting his government.

Famous Americans

ALBERTO SALAZAR

In October 1980, a little-known runner by the name of Alberto Salazar predicted that he would beat Bill Rodgers in the upcoming New York Marathon. Rodgers was a four-time winner of the New York Marathon and the New York Marathon record holder. Rodgers responded by saying, "I'm firm on one point, no rookie is going to beat me." Salazar not only won the race and clipped 28 seconds off Rodgers' record, he also became only the second American to run the 26-mile marathon in under 2 hours and 10 minutes. It was the fastest first marathon ever run.

Salazar followed up his spectacular performance in the 1980 New York Marathon with an even more exciting run in the 1981 New York Marathon. Before the race, Salazar predicted he would break the world record held by Australian Derek Clayton. On October 25, Salazar trimmed 20 seconds off the world record and won the New York Marathon in a record time of 2:08:13.

Salazar prepares for a race by running an average of 171 kilometers (106 miles) per week. He stays on a strict schedule, beginning his morning workouts at precisely 9:30. He keeps track of all workouts and keeps a diary of his times and distances. Salazar also records his feelings and sense of commitment to running.

In the Boston Marathon of 1982, Salazar went out in front. But near the end of the race, his lead was shrinking, and he was suffering from dehydration. Salazar managed to find the reserves to keep running and won the race by a mere two seconds. He had done what he claimed must be done. "If I want to win it, it all comes down to 'Can I take more pain than the next guy?'" With his major wins in New York and Boston, Salazar has proved that he can.

Discuss: The United Nations strongly condemned the Soviet invasion of Afghanistan. Do you think the United Nations should have taken stronger action? If so, what action should have been taken? What might have prevented the United Nations from taking this action?

who were in the embassy. They announced that they would hold the Americans as **hostages** until the United States returned the shah to Iran. President Carter refused the students' demand.

---

hostage a person held prisoner until a demand is granted

President Carter was careful in his handling of the hostage crisis. The President tried many forms of diplomacy to free the hostages. When this failed, he ordered a rescue attempt. In April 1980, a small raiding force of marines landed in the Iranian desert. But their helicopters broke down, and two airplanes collided. Eight marines died in the unsuccessful rescue mission. Like so many other events in recent years, the Iranian crisis produced a sense of frustration in the United States.

The Decline of Détente

Just a few weeks after the seizure of the hostages in Iran, Soviet troops invaded Afghanistan in late December 1979. Afghanistan lies along the eastern border of Iran. Afghanistan had been dominated by the Soviet Union since 1978. Afghan guerrillas, however, were battling the country's pro-Soviet government. In 1979, the Soviet troops joined the fighting against the guerrillas.

President Carter declared that the Soviet invasion of Afghanistan was "a stepping-stone to [Russian] control over much of the world's oil supplies." The White House warned that the Soviets might be preparing an attack on Iran or on one of the other oil-rich Middle Eastern nations.

The President took several actions to protest the Soviet invasion. He ordered an embargo on the sale of American grain and other products to the Soviet Union. He refused to allow American athletes to participate in the 1980 Summer Olympic Games to be held in Moscow. He also withdrew the SALT II treaty from debate by the Senate. The President announced that the United States would defend any nation in the Persian Gulf area against Soviet aggression.

Section Review

1. What were the major accomplishments of President Jimmy Carter in foreign affairs?
2. Define hostage. Why did American marines attempt a raid on Iran in 1980?
3. List the actions taken by President Carter to protest the Soviet invasion of Afghanistan.
4. President Carter faced two major foreign crises: the seizure of the Americans in Iran and the Soviet invasion of Afghanistan. Which of these crises do you think presented the more serious threat to world peace? Explain your answer.

Background: Many Americans viewed the invasion of Afghanistan as part of a larger pattern of renewed Soviet aggression. Soviet-backed forces took over Angola in the mid-1970's, and in 1978 a pro-Soviet military leader seized power in South Yemen.

CHAPTER REVIEW

Summary

Disappointed at President Ford's inability to solve the nation's economic problems, the American people elected a new President, James Earl ("Jimmy") Carter, in 1976. The dual problems of inflation and recession, however, proved as frustrating to Carter as they had been to Ford and Nixon. Carter also faced the problem of America's increasing dependence on costly foreign oil. He supported policies to achieve both energy conservation and the development of new energy sources.

President Carter achieved some notable successes in foreign affairs. Through his efforts, a comprehensive peace treaty between Egypt and Israel was signed in March 1979. Carter also improved relations with China and Panama.

Trouble arose in Iran in 1979, when Iranian students seized the American embassy in Teheran and took more than 50 Americans hostage. Diplomatic efforts and a raid by marines in 1980 all failed to secure their release. Further difficulties occurred when the Soviet Union invaded Afghanistan. President Carter protested the move as the spirit of détente began to fade.

Recalling the Facts

1. How did President Carter demonstrate his desire for a "closeness" to the American people during his administration?
2. What did the Federal Reserve Board do to try to reduce inflation? What effect did this have on the nation's economy?
3. Explain the controversy that surrounds nuclear energy. Why do some people support its use, while others oppose it?
4. Why did Khomeini condemn the United States in 1979?
5. Why was the Iranian crisis so frustrating to many Americans?

Analyzing the Facts

1. Why do you think Jimmy Carter received the overwhelming support of black voters in the 1976 presidential election?
2. Why do you think OPEC was able to raise the price of its oil so dramatically? What effect did the high oil prices have on the United States?

3. What do you think are the advantages and disadvantages to the United States of giving up its control of the Panama Canal?
4. Do you think the United States should have returned the shah to the Iranians in order to free the hostages? Why or why not?

Time and History

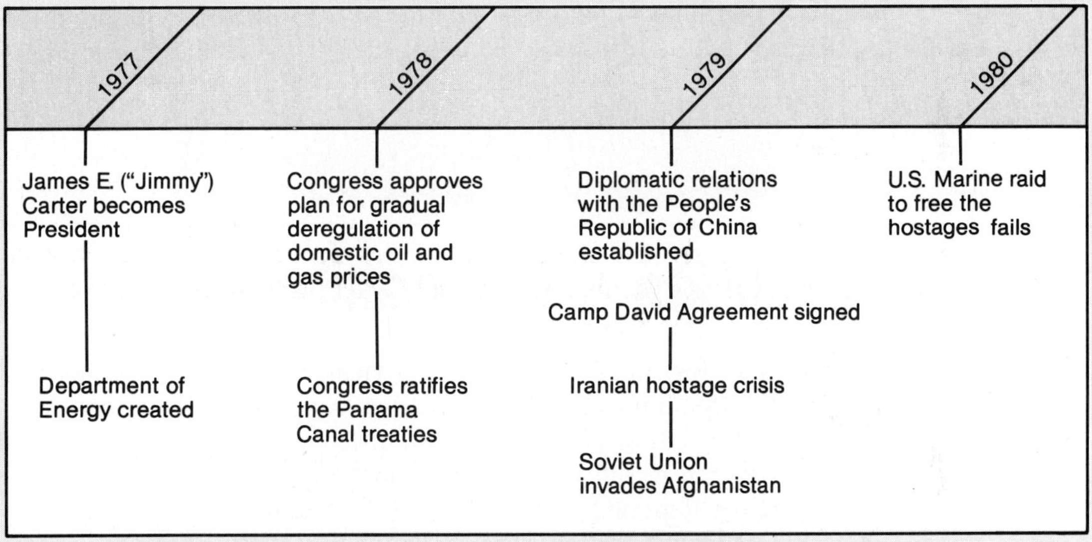

1. In what year did the United States formally recognize the People's Republic of China?
2. How many years after Carter became President did the Iranian hostage crisis occur?
3. What important step toward peace and stability in the Middle East was made in 1979?
4. In what year was a new Cabinet department created? What was it called?
5. To protest the Soviet invasion of Afghanistan, President Carter refused to allow American athletes to participate in the Moscow Olympics the following year. In what year did American athletes not participate in the Olympic Games?

Chapter
34

Realities and Possibilities

One of the most unusual days in American history was January 20, 1981. The Iranian government had at last ordered the American hostages to be freed. At almost the same moment, a new President was taking the oath of office in Washington. Jimmy Carter had been defeated by his Republican opponent, Ronald Reagan.

In his inaugural address, President Reagan spoke about the many frustrations and difficulties the country had faced. "With all the creative energy at our command," the new President stated, "let us begin an era of national renewal. Let us renew our determination, our courage, and our strength. And let us renew our faith and our hope."

After you read this chapter, you will be able to:

1. Discuss the economic policies of the Reagan administration.
2. Trace American involvement in the affairs of Central America.
3. Identify recent changes in the American population.
4. Describe the impact of high technology on American society.

☐ Read a map that shows population changes.

Background: Ronald Reagan was born in the small Illinois town of Tampico on February 6, 1911. He grew up in the nearby town of Dixon. In high school, he enjoyed acting, playing football, and working as a lifeguard.

1. The "Reagan Revolution"

BEFORE YOU READ: *What were the economic policies of President Reagan?*

Politics in the United States tends to swing back and forth. Liberals may be in power for a while. Then conservative leaders are elected. After a while, the country tends to return to liberal leadership. It goes back and forth. In the 1970's and 1980's, the United States swung in a conservative direction. The election of 1980 was clear proof of the renewed strength of American conservatism.

The Election of 1980

The early popularity of Jimmy Carter declined steadily during his first years in office. By 1979, his standing in public opinion polls was lower than any President's in recent history. The Iranian crisis and the Soviet invasion of Afghanistan boosted Jimmy Carter's popularity for a short while. The President was able to win the Democratic nomination for reelection.

The Republican primaries were swept by the former governor of California, Ronald Reagan. At the Republican convention, Reagan won the nomination.

Ronald Reagan began his career as a Hollywood actor. In 1962, he joined the Republican party. In 1966, a group of wealthy California business leaders encouraged him to run for governor of California. Reagan was elected to two terms as California's governor.

In the 1980 campaign, Ronald Reagan said that he would improve the nation's economy by reducing taxes and government spending. Reagan also believed that progress could best be achieved by freeing business from government regulation. During his campaign, he promised "to get the government off the backs of the American people."

Although the international crises in Iran and Afghanistan had helped raise Jimmy Carter's popularity, these crises hurt his chances for reelection in the end. American efforts to free the hostages had failed. Also, many Americans were unhappy with the way Carter was handling the country's economic problems.

The election was held on November 4, 1980, exactly one year after the seizure of the hostages in Iran. Reagan carried all but six states, receiving 489 electoral votes to Carter's 49. Representative John Anderson of Illinois ran as an independent candidate but won no electoral votes. The Republicans won a majority in the Senate for the first time in 26 years. The Democrats remained in control of the House, but the size of their majority was reduced. The Republican victory was so complete that some observers called it the "Reagan revolution."

Promises to Keep

President Reagan began his term in office with wide support among the American people. His personal popularity increased following an assassination attempt on March 30, 1981. The President was shot in the chest as he was leaving a Washington hotel. He quickly recovered from the wound.

The first campaign promises that the

Discuss: President Reagan was 70 years old when he was shot. What inferences can you make about the President's physical condition at the time, considering his rapid recovery?

The Election of 1980

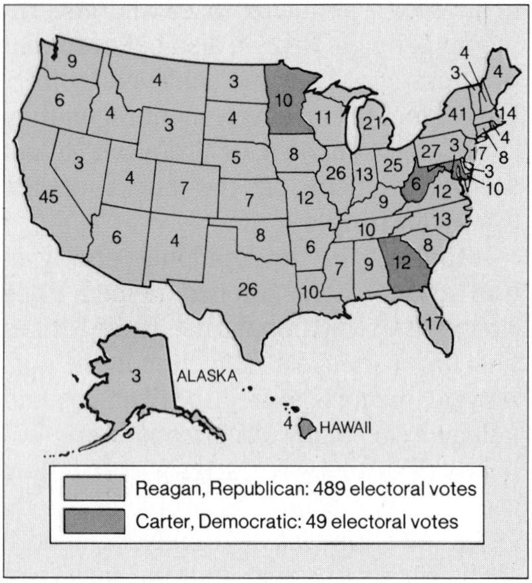

How many states gave their electoral votes to Jimmy Carter in the election of 1980?

President tried to fulfill were in economic policy. He ordered the removal of hundreds of government regulations affecting businesses. In 1981, President Reagan presented Congress with his "Program for Economic Recovery." He asked for cuts in government spending in almost every area of the federal budget except defense. The heaviest cuts were to be made in social welfare programs such as Medicare and student aid. Congress approved most of the President's cuts.

President Reagan also proposed a huge reduction in federal taxes. He asked Congress to lower personal income taxes by 30 percent over a three-year period. He also called for reductions in business taxes. In August 1981, Congress approved a three-year, 25 percent tax cut. It was the largest tax cut in American history.

The theory behind the President's economic policy was fairly simple. If Americans paid less money in taxes, they would have more money left to save. The money they placed in banks would in turn be invested in or loaned to businesses. The businesses would then be able to expand production, hire more workers, and make more profits. Prosperous businesses and workers would pay more taxes, thus making up for the money the government lost through the tax cuts. This economic theory is called "**supply-side**" **economics**.

---

supply-side economics an economic theory that says cutting taxes will lead to economic growth and higher government revenues

---

To lower the inflation rate, the federal government continued to hold down the nation's money supply. Interest rates charged by banks to borrow money rose even higher.

The early effects of the President's policies were not all that he had hoped they would be. Inflation slowed. But the expected burst of new investments did not occur. The nation's economy slipped deeper into recession. By early 1982, the economy slowed down to the lowest levels it had seen since the depression. The unemployment rate reached nearly 10 percent by July 1982.

Recovery from the recession was being prevented in part by the rapid growth of federal deficit spending. The tax cut had decreased government revenues. Yet government spending continued to increase. Even though spending for social welfare programs had been cut, the government had greatly increased spending

FIRST THE GOOD NEWS . . .
©-PLETCHER-1982
YOU ARE LEAVING INFLATIONBURG
WELCOME TO RECESSIONVILLE
ROTHCO

What is this cartoon saying about the early progress of Reagan's economic program?

for national defense. The decrease in revenues and the increase in spending produced a huge **budget deficit.** The budget deficit kept interest rates high. High interest rates discouraged business activity.

---

budget deficit the difference between government spending and revenues when spending exceeds revenues

---

By 1983, the economy had begun to recover from the recession. Many businesses increased production. The unemployment rate dropped slowly, to about 8 percent. The inflation rate was declining. The rise in consumer prices was less than half of what it had been in 1980.

President Reagan received wide support for his economic policies. In the 1984 election, he easily defeated his Democratic opponent, Walter Mondale. President Reagan received 525 electoral votes to Mondale's 13. Reagan won majority support throughout the country, with the exception of Washington, D.C., and Minnesota.

Section Review

1. What were the economic policies of the Reagan administration?
2. What pledges and promises did Ronald Reagan make in his 1980 campaign for President?
3. Define supply-side economics and budget deficit.
4. How might Ronald Reagan's career as an actor have contributed to his success in politics?

Background: Reagan regarded the establishment of martial law in Poland as further evidence of the aggressive nature of the Soviet Union. In the summer of 1982, the President ordered a ban on the sale of equipment to the Soviet Union for construction of a natural gas pipeline.

2. Foreign Affairs

BEFORE YOU READ: *What actions did President Reagan take to increase United States involvement in Central America?*

The spirit of détente declined rapidly during the early 1980's. The foreign policy of the Reagan administration marked a return to the policies of the early days of the Cold War.

Revival of the Cold War

Relations between the United States and the Soviet Union worsened following a crisis in Poland in 1981. Solidarity, an independent Polish labor movement, called for major reforms from the Communist government of Poland. The Soviet Union pressured the Polish government to crack down on Solidarity. In the winter of 1981, the Polish government put the military in charge. Leaders of Solidarity were arrested. President Reagan condemned **martial law** in Poland.

---

martial law temporary military rule over a civilian population

---

One of the major concerns of the Reagan administration was that the United States had been allowed to fall behind the Soviet Union in important areas of national defense. President Reagan took steps to increase spending in many areas of defense. New and more powerful weapons were supplied to each branch of the armed forces. Additional nuclear missiles were installed at American bases in Europe. The President also supported development of the new MX missile. The MX, which President Reagan called the "Peacemaker," carried ten nuclear warheads. The MX completed its first successful test flight in the summer of 1983.

Not everyone agreed with President Reagan's policy on nuclear weapons. Huge demonstrations were held in the early 1980's to protest the President's policy. Communities and states across the nation voted for a "freeze" on the development of nuclear weapons.

Central America

The United States became deeply involved in the affairs of Central America during the presidency of Ronald Reagan. The involvement centered in two countries, Nicaragua and El Salvador.

Until the 1930's, United States Marines had occupied Nicaragua. Dictators then ruled the country. A revolution in 1979 brought to power a government headed by the Sandinist National Liberation Front.

The Sandinista government seized control of the nation's banks and mines. It also **nationalized** Nicaragua's coffee and cotton plantations. Nicaragua became a supply base for Communist-led Salvadoran guerrillas fighting against the American-backed government of nearby El Salvador. In 1981, the United States cut off all aid to Nicaragua. The Soviet Union, Cuba, and other nations began supplying military aid to Nicaragua.

---

nationalize to transfer control of land, resources, or industries to the national government

---

President Reagan responded by order-

Discuss: Do you think that a military build-up in the United States threatens or strengthens our negotiations with the Soviet Union? Explain your answer.

For Extra Interest: Have students locate Nicaragua and El Salvador on a map. Point out that both of these countries have long histories of poverty, illiteracy, and very little freedom.

ing the Central Intelligence Agency (CIA) to train and arm a "secret army" of anti-Sandinista guerrillas. The CIA-backed "secret army" grew from 1,000 in February 1982 to over 12,000 by July 1983.

The other "hot spot" in Central America was El Salvador. Communist-led guerrillas in El Salvador were trying to bring down the American-backed government. Fierce battles were fought between the guerrillas and government troops.

President Reagan ordered increased American military aid to the government of El Salvador. Salvadoran soldiers were brought to the United States for training. American military advisers were sent to Honduras to train other Salvadoran forces and provide further aid.

Congressional debate over El Salvador was intense. The greatest fear of the President's critics was that the United States would become involved in "another Vietnam" in El Salvador. The President told his critics in April 1983 that "there is no thought of sending American combat troops to Central America." But the fear of a deepening American involvement remained.

In this photo, American military personnel are training members of the El Salvadoran army.

Renewed Tensions

Tensions between the United States and the Soviet Union began to build in 1983. On September 1, a Soviet fighter plane shot down a South Korean airliner over the Sea of Japan. The airliner had flown off course into restricted Soviet air space. Among the 269 people aboard the doomed South Korean plane were 60 Americans. President Reagan condemned the Soviet Union for this "barbaric act."

In the Middle East, the President had ordered United States Marines to join an international peacekeeping force in Lebanon. Lebanese Christians and Moslems had been fighting a civil war in Lebanon since the mid-1970's. Lebanon had also become a battleground for the neighboring countries of Israel and Syria. Troops from both Israel and Syria invaded and then controlled portions of Lebanon. On October 23, 1983, 240 United States Marines and other military personnel in Lebanon were killed in a terrorist bombing.

Just two days after the bombing, American fighting forces invaded the island of Grenada in the Caribbean Sea. Grenada had been ruled by a pro-Cuban government since 1979. Cuba had given aid to Grenada for the construction of a modern airport. President Reagan feared that the airport would be used for long-range military aircraft. After the assassination of government leaders on the island, the President was also concerned about the safety of American citizens there.

Discuss: Do you think the United States should have taken stronger action in response to the Soviet downing of a South Korean airliner in 1983? If so, what action do you think should have been taken? Why do you think the United States did not take this action?

Background: Grenada became an independent country in 1974 after more than 200 years of British rule. Grenada is 34 kilometers (21 miles) long and 19 kilometers (12 miles) wide. Its principle export is nutmeg.

The aftermath of the terrorist bombing of marine headquarters in Beirut involved concerted efforts to save the lives of as many marines as possible.

More than 6,000 American troops were sent to Grenada. American citizens were evacuated. Several hundred Cubans on the island were captured and ordered to leave.

Critics of the American action charged that the United States had violated international law. President Reagan strongly defended the action. He blamed the events in Grenada—and in Lebanon—on the Soviet Union. "The events in Lebanon and Grenada, though oceans apart, are closely related," the President said. "Not only has Moscow assisted and encouraged the violence in both countries, but it provides direct support through a network of . . . terrorists." Tensions increased between the two superpowers.

Section Review

1. What actions did President Reagan take to increase American involvement in Central America?
2. How did President Reagan increase the nation's military strength?
3. Define martial law and nationalize.
4. Are there any similarities between American policy toward El Salvador in the early 1980's and American policy toward Vietnam in the early 1960's? Are there any differences? Explain your answer.

Discuss: Under what circumstances do you think the United States has the right to become involved in the affairs of other countries?

Background: Since 1980, the population of the United States has increased by more than one percent a year. In that same year, the Sunbelt as a whole had a larger population than the older industrial regions of the North and East.

3. A Changing People

BEFORE YOU READ: *What areas of the United States have been growing rapidly in recent years?*

The population of the United States has been growing and changing throughout American history. The nation today is far different from what it was in its earliest years.

Growth and Distribution

During the century between 1880 and 1980, the American population more than quadrupled. The 1980 census reported that 226,504,825 people lived in the United States.

The geographic distribution of the population has been changing in recent years. The Southeast and Southwest have been growing much more rapidly than the Northeast and Midwest. People have moved to the **Sunbelt** because of its milder climate and its growing economic opportunities.

Sunbelt the states of the Southeast and Southwest that have experienced large population growth in recent years

---

Many of the central cities of the Northeast and Midwest have continued to decline. Poverty and urban decay are serious problems. But one hopeful sign for the cities has been a change in the flight of people to the suburbs. More people are choosing to remain in the cities.

The "Graying of America"

Another change in the American population has been a growth in the number of older Americans. Improvements in diet and medical care have increased the average number of years that a person can expect to live. **Life expectancy** in the United States increased from about 59 years in 1930 to more than 74 years in 1983.

---

life expectancy the average number of years that a person can expect to live

---

This "graying of America" has created some serious problems. Many older Americans depend upon Social Security payments for their income. That system, however, has become overburdened. Social Security payments have increased from less than $12 billion a year in 1960

The American population is not only growing older, it is also more conscious of the importance of exercise for good health.

For Extra Interest: Have students graph changes in life expectancy patterns in the United States from 1900 to the present. Students may also compare these increases with medical discoveries made in this century.

Discuss: Why do you think the Equal Pay Act of 1963 failed to equalize the average wages earned by men and women?

to $195 billion in 1982. The money for Social Security payments comes from taxes withheld from workers' salaries. The amount of money being put into the system is much less than the money being paid out.

The Social Security crisis will become more serious as the huge "baby boom" generation begins retiring. Twice as many Americans will be receiving Social Security benefits in 2025 than received them in 1981. In March 1983, Congress passed legislation to increase Social Security revenues, largely through higher Social Security taxes and reduced benefits.

American Women

In recent years, major changes have occurred in the status of American women. Only about 30 percent of American women were working outside of the home in 1950. By 1980, 53 percent were part of the paid work force.

Most women continue to work in traditional "women's" jobs such as sales and office work. Their average income remains about 60 percent of the average for working men. Yet women have made progress in entering such fields as law, medicine, and engineering. In 1981, Sandra Day O'Connor became the first woman justice of the Supreme Court. In 1983, Sally K. Ride became the nation's first woman astronaut in space.

In the 1970's and early 1980's, a campaign was conducted to win support for an Equal Rights Amendment (ERA). Supporters of the ERA argued that it would protect women against discrimination in the job market and in laws. Opponents claimed that women's rights were already well protected. They also feared that the ERA might lead to the drafting of women into the armed forces.

Sally K. Ride, America's first woman astronaut

ERA fell three states short of the ratifications needed to become an amendment. Feminists reintroduced the ERA in Congress. But the amendment did not get the votes needed in the House to send it to the states once again for ratification.

Women have made gains in the political arena. The number of elected women officials increased from less than 6,000 in 1975 to 16,500 in 1982. In 1984, Geraldine Ferraro was the Democratic candidate for Vice-President. She was the first woman ever nominated for Vice-President by a major political party.

For Extra Interest: Magazines and advertisements are now depicting men and women in other than traditional roles at home and on the job. Have students prepare a bulletin board of these role changes.

For Extra Interest: Have interested students research and report on the efforts of Jesse Jackson to win the Democratic nomination for President in 1984.

American Diversity

The fastest growing ethnic group in the United States is the nation's Hispanic population. In 1980, there were 14.6 million Hispanic Americans. By the year 2020, the number of Hispanics in the United States is expected to increase to about 47 million. They would be the largest minority in the nation.

The Hispanic population faces problems of low income and high unemployment. One out of four Hispanic families lives in poverty, compared to one out of ten non-Hispanic white families. But Hispanic political power has increased. In 1982, New Mexico elected a Hispanic governor, Toney Anaya. Nine Hispanics were elected to the House. Henry Cisneros was elected mayor of San Antonio, Texas, and Frederico Peña became the chief executive of Denver, Colorado.

Black Americans also continue to face major problems. The average income for black families remains far below that of whites. The unemployment rate among blacks is about twice that of whites.

Many black Americans, however, have made great progress in recent years. Today, one third of all black Americans are part of the American middle class. The percentage of black high-school graduates going on to college is almost the same as that of white graduates.

Black mayors head 30 of the nation's largest cities—in both the North and the South. Among well-known black political leaders are Mayor Andrew Young of Atlanta, Mayor Coleman Young of Detroit, and Mayor Thomas Bradley of Los Angeles. Jesse Jackson, a leader of the civil rights movement, was a candidate for the Democratic presidential nomination in 1984.

Chinese Americans and Japanese Americans have also overcome past discrimination. They have achieved higher average levels of education and income than the nation's population as a whole. Asian Americans have also gained political influence.

New groups of people have come to America in recent years. Following the American withdrawal from Vietnam, thousands of Southeast Asians left South Vietnam. Many settled in the United States. Refugees have also come to the United States from Haiti and Cuba.

Section Review

1. What areas of the United States have been gaining population rapidly in recent years?
2. Define life expectancy. What problems has the increase in life expectancy caused?
3. Identify Sandra Day O'Connor and Sally K. Ride.
4. The rise of the Sunbelt is likely to have a major impact on American politics in the years ahead. How might this shift in the nation's population affect national politics?

Background: Japanese Americans organized to demand payments for their losses suffered during "relocation" in World War II. In 1983, it was recommended that Japanese Americans affected by the relocation be awarded $20,000 each. The recommendation sparked a national debate on the issue.

Social Studies Skills

Mapping Population Change

During the 1970's, many Americans moved to the Sunbelt. This caused the center of population to change. The center of population is calculated from census figures. It is derived by drawing a horizontal line across the country at the point where the number of people living in northern regions equals the number of people living in southern regions. Then a vertical line is drawn indicating where the population in eastern regions equals that of western regions. The point at which the two lines meet is the center of population. When people move from one region of the country to another, the center of population shifts accordingly. For example, if more people move into northern regions than move into southern regions, the population center will shift to the north.

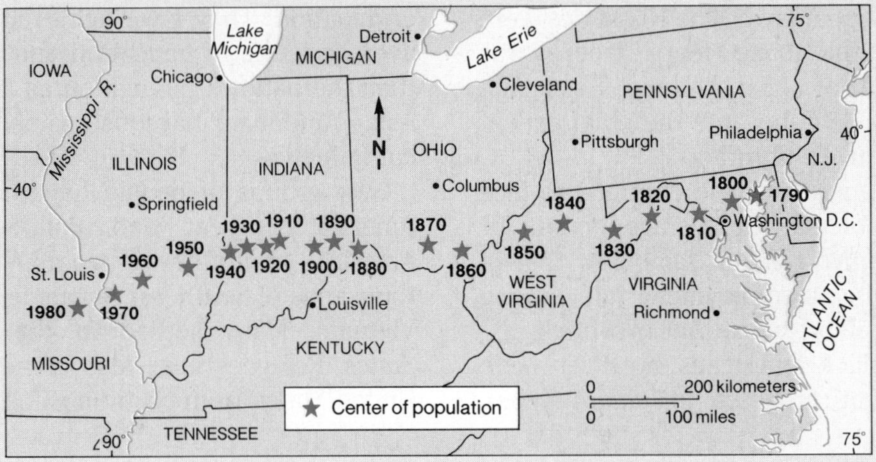

1. In what direction has the center of population primarily moved since it was first established in 1790?
2. In what direction did the center of population move between 1970 and 1980?
3. In what three decades did the population shift the least?
4. In what state was the population center located in 1980?
5. In what two decades was the population shift the greatest?

Discuss: What job skills do you think will be in demand when you graduate from high school? What occupational areas do you think will expand in the future?

4. Toward the Twenty-first Century

BEFORE YOU READ: *What are the distinguishing qualities of a postindustrial society such as the United States?*

The American capacity for invention has been one of the nation's most valuable resources. That genius has produced marvels of technology for the benefit of all Americans.

The Postindustrial Society

The advance of technology in this century has caused a fundamental change in American society. Sociologist Daniel Bell has called the new society of high technology a **postindustrial society.** The term "high technology" refers to highly complex electronic devices such as computers. Computers today play a central role in the making and distributing of the nation's goods. Computers direct robot arms in automobile factories as well as oversee the operation of farms, banks, and countless other enterprises.

---

postindustrial society a modern society based on advanced technology

---

Postindustrial society is also marked by increased productivity in industry and agriculture. But the high level of productivity reduces the number of jobs in certain industries. The number of jobs in such heavy industries as automaking and steel production declines.

Another sign of postindustrial society is the increasing importance of technology in education. Computers assist in the instruction of basic skills at all levels of education. Universities and colleges conduct new research for further technological advances.

Recent breakthroughs in science and technology have been impressive. In 1973, the United States launched *Skylab*, an orbiting space laboratory. *Skylab* was used for many important experiments. On April 12, 1981, the United States launched its first reusable space shuttle, *Columbia*. The space shuttle carried satellites into orbit. In 1983, the second space shuttle, *Challenger*, made its first flight.

Achievements in medicine have been equally as impressive. Genetic research offers the hope of preventing birth defects and other crippling diseases. Organ transplants have become common medical practice. Electronic "pacemakers" inside thousands of Americans help prevent heart attacks.

High technology also has had an impact on American entertainment. Computer-based "video games" have transformed television watching into a more active pastime. Cable television has introduced a broader range of programs. Video-tape and video-disc players have brought to television a variety of new entertainment options.

The Environment and Energy

Americans in recent years have shown a growing awareness of the need to protect the nation's water, land, and air. In 1970, Congress created the Environmental Protection Agency (EPA). Many local communities have also taken action to

For Extra Interest: Have interested students research and report to the class on the current status of cancer research.

EUREKA!

Artificial Intelligence

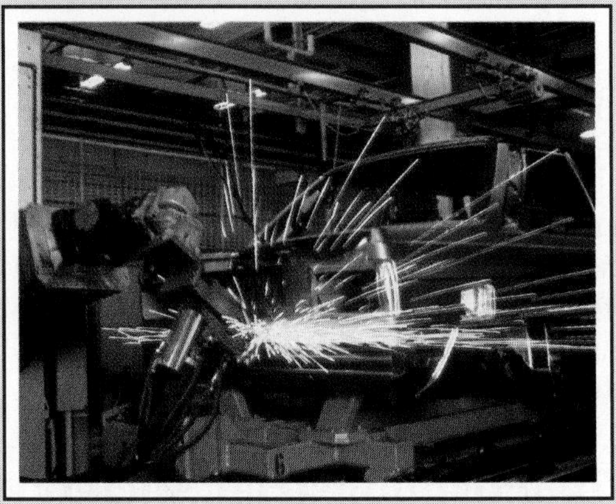

Ever since the first computers were built, scientists have hoped to make machines that could think like human beings, rather than simply calculate very rapidly. But creating artificial intelligence, or AI, has turned out to be a difficult, perhaps impossible task.

One area in which AI is needed is in helping robots to see. Television cameras hooked up to computers give a limited sense of vision to today's robots. The computers that run the robots cannot tell, for example, that an object viewed end-on is the same as an object seen from the side. For a robot working on an assembly line, the ability to make that leap of perception is crucial. It must be able to recognize the parts it is to pick up, no matter from what angle it sees them. Giving robots that power is a task facing scientists working in AI.

Robot vision is only one application of AI. Making computers that can learn and reason is another. American scientists have made great progress toward building AI computers in the 1970's and 1980's. But whether machines that are truly intelligent can be built remains to be seen.

improve the quality of their environment. The residents of the San Francisco area, for example, created a regional agency to protect San Francisco Bay. As a result, the bay's water quality improved, and its wildlife population increased.

For many decades, the waste products from industry have been dumped into open fields or pits. Many of the waste products contained chemicals that were harmful or deadly to humans. In recent years, many Americans have become alarmed at the danger of these **toxic wastes.** The EPA and many state agencies have adopted regulations to control the future dumping of toxic wastes. Action has also been taken to clean up existing dumps.

toxic wastes harmful or deadly waste products from factories or chemical plants

Air pollution is one of the most serious threats to the environment. Technological advances have reduced the amount of pollution caused by industry. The major source of air pollution, however, is the

Background: Concern over toxic wastes has been especially strong in areas where old toxic waste dumps have been found near housing developments.

automobile. In 1970, Congress passed the Clean Air Act. The act required that new automobiles be equipped with antipollution devices.

Progress has also been made in solving the nation's energy crisis. The rise in oil prices in the 1970's led to reduced demand for oil. But the worldwide energy crisis is expected to worsen in the years ahead. As the earth's population continues to grow and more nations become industrialized, the demand for oil will rise sharply.

The best hope for solving the energy crisis remains the conservation of existing energy supplies and the development of new sources. There are many new potential energy sources. High-energy fuels can be produced from organic materials such as wood chips or agricultural wastes. This is called **biomass energy.** Energy from the earth's core can be tapped through hot water or steam near the earth's surface. This **geothermal energy** can be used to generate electricity. Other potential sources of electricity include the sun, the wind, the tides, and ocean currents. Experts predict that these various alternative sources can provide 25 percent of the nation's energy needs in the twenty-first century.

biomass energy energy generated from organic materials

geothermal energy energy from the earth's core, obtained from hot water or steam near the earth's surface

History and the Future

Americans should regard their nation's history with a pride based on knowledge. The United States has faced many difficult times. Its beginnings were filled with danger and hardship. The republic was nearly split apart by a disastrous civil war. New conflicts and dangers have threatened the nation in the twentieth century. Yet the United States has continued to endure.

Today, as always, the nation faces serious problems. The American people can draw strength from their history in attempting to overcome their present difficulties. The record of their past achievements shows Americans that they can regard with confidence the opportunities and challenges of the future.

Section Review

1. What are the major distinguishing features of a postindustrial society such as the United States?
2. What recent achievements have been made in American medical technology?
3. Define toxic wastes, biomass energy, and geothermal energy.
4. How is a knowledge of United States history useful in solving current problems? Explain your answer.

CHAPTER REVIEW

Summary

Ronald Reagan inherited the power and problems of the presidency in 1981. His economic recovery program called for major cuts in government spending and a reduction in federal taxes. By 1983, the economy had begun to recover from the recession, and inflation had declined significantly.

The foreign policy of the Reagan administration marked a return to the early days of the Cold War. American relations with the Soviet Union were strained by events in Poland, the Middle East, and Central America. The President supported the development of new weapon systems as part of a military buildup.

The United States has experienced dramatic changes in its population in recent years. Many Americans have moved to the Sunbelt. The number of older Americans and the percentage of women in the paid labor force have both increased significantly. Hispanics, blacks, and Asian minorities have all made progress toward social and economic equality.

Americans can expect many more advances in technology as they enter the twenty-first century. These advances will bring many changes in the way Americans live and work.

Recalling the Facts

1. What issues hurt President Carter's chances for reelection in 1980?
2. Explain the crisis that occurred in Poland in 1981. How did this crisis affect relations between the United States and the Soviet Union?
3. Why did President Reagan order combat troops to invade Grenada in 1983? How did this invasion affect relations between the Soviet Union and the United States?
4. How has the geographic distribution of the population shifted in recent years? Why has this shift occurred?
5. What is the fastest growing ethnic group in the United States? What problems does this ethnic group face?
6. What impact has high technology had on entertainment in the United States?
7. What efforts have been made by the federal government in recent years to protect the environment?

Analyzing the Facts

1. Because of the time difference, voters in western states cast their votes in a presidential election a few hours later than voters in eastern states. How do you think media reports of early election returns might affect voters in western states?
2. Why do you think President Reagan called the new MX missile the "Peacemaker"?
3. What effect do you think increases in minority populations will have on national politics?
4. How do you think the development of a postindustrial society will affect the importance of education and training?

Time and History

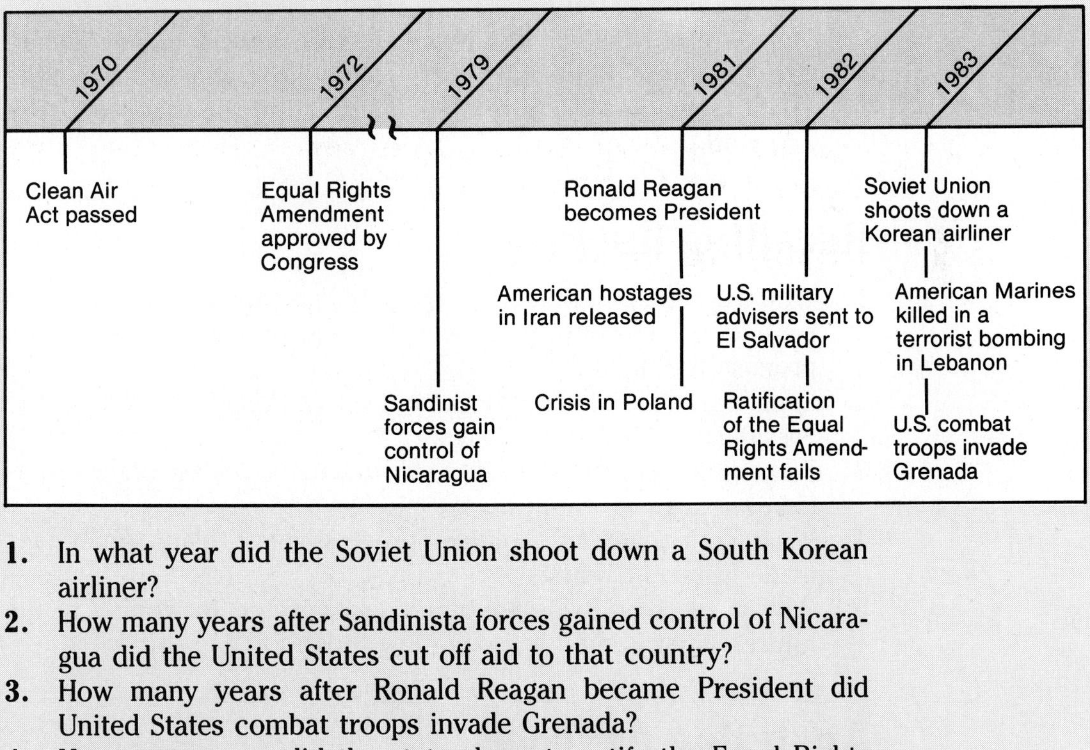

1. In what year did the Soviet Union shoot down a South Korean airliner?
2. How many years after Sandinista forces gained control of Nicaragua did the United States cut off aid to that country?
3. How many years after Ronald Reagan became President did United States combat troops invade Grenada?
4. How many years did the states have to ratify the Equal Rights Amendment?
5. What caused the death of 240 marines in Lebanon in 1983?

UNIT REVIEW

Summary

In recent years, the United States has faced many crises in both domestic and foreign affairs. The progress made by the Nixon administration in foreign affairs was overshadowed by the President's involvement in the Watergate scandal. The popularity of President Nixon's successor, Gerald Ford, suffered from his decision to grant Nixon a full pardon.

Finding solutions to the nation's economic and energy problems challenged America's leaders in the 1970's and 1980's. By the early 1980's, some progress had been made toward solving these problems. International tensions also increased during this period. President Carter directed negotiations for over a year to secure the release of American hostages being held in Iran. Cold War tensions were also renewed during the Carter and Reagan presidencies over events in Afghanistan, the Middle East, Central America, and the Caribbean.

As in the past, the United States can look forward to many challenges in the future. Rapid advances in technology and changes in the American population will have a great impact on the way Americans live and work.

Recalling the Facts

1. Who were the Democratic and Republican candidates in the 1968 presidential election? Who won this election, and what did he promise the nation?
2. Explain how Gerald Ford became the Vice-President and later the President of the United States.
3. What did President Carter do to try to win the release of the American hostages in Iran?
4. What economic and political progress have black Americans made in recent years?
5. Why is the worldwide energy crisis expected to worsen in the future? What is the best long-range hope for its solution?

Analyzing the Facts

1. Why did the Watergate scandal cause many Americans to develop an attitude of suspicion and distrust toward politicians?

2. Why would the housing and automobile industries be particularly hard hit by high interest rates?
3. Of all the problems that the United States must face in the future, which do you feel needs the most attention? Explain your answer.
4. What do you think is the most exciting thing Americans have to look forward to in the future? Explain your answer.

Reviewing Vocabulary

Define the following terms.

détente	cartel	budget deficit
busing	deregulation	nationalize
stagnant	nuclear energy	Sunbelt
recession	supply-side economics	postindustrial society

Sharpening Your Skills

Answer the first two questions based on the information on page 704.

1. What inference can be made about United States dependence on foreign oil in 1979? What evidence supports this inference?
2. What inference can be made about how Americans felt about the gasoline shortage? What evidence supports this inference?

Answer the three questions below based on the election maps on page 692 and page 705.

3. Compare the electoral votes cast by Arizonans in the elections of 1968 and 1976. What does this indicate about population changes in Arizona in the 1960's?
4. What states lost population in the 1960's?
5. What two states experienced the greatest increases in population in the 1960's? In what regions are these states located?

Writing and Research

1. Research and write a report on current efforts to preserve the environment, or attempts at disarmament.
2. Write a news article describing a significant event that you think will occur or you would like to see occur in the future. Write the article as though the event just happened. Include events from the 1970's and 1980's that contributed to this future development.

PRESIDENTS OF THE UNITED STATES

To the right of each portrait are the President's name, his age on taking office, terms of office, party affiliation, the name of the Vice-President, and the name of the President's wife.

1.
George Washington, 57
1789-1797
Federalist
John Adams
Martha Dandridge Washington

2.
John Adams, 61
1797-1801
Federalist
Thomas Jefferson
Abigail Smith Adams

3.
Thomas Jefferson, 57
1801-1809
Democratic-Republican
Aaron Burr
George Clinton
Martha Wayles Jefferson

4.
James Madison, 57
1809-1817
Democratic-Republican
George Clinton
Elbridge Gerry
Dolley Payne Madison

5.
James Monroe, 58
1817-1825
Democratic-Republican
Daniel D. Tompkins
Eliza Kortright Monroe

6.
John Quincy Adams, 57
1825-1829
Democratic-Republican
John C. Calhoun
Louisa Johnson Adams

7.
Andrew Jackson, 61
1829-1837
Democrat
John C. Calhoun
Martin Van Buren
Rachel Donelson Jackson

8.
Martin Van Buren, 54
1837-1841
Democrat
Richard M. Johnson
Hannah Hoes Van Buren

9.
*William Henry Harrison, 68
1841-1841
Whig
John Tyler
Anna Symmes Harrison

10.
John Tyler, 51
1841-1845
Whig
. . . . .
Julia Gardiner Tyler

11.
James K. Polk, 49
1845-1849
Democrat
George M. Dallas
Sarah Childress Polk

12.
*Zachary Taylor, 64
1849-1850
Whig
Millard Fillmore
Margaret Smith Taylor

13.
Millard Fillmore, 50
1850-1853
Whig
. . . . .
Abigail Powers Fillmore

14.
Franklin Pierce, 48
1853-1857
Democrat
William R. King
Jane Appleton Pierce

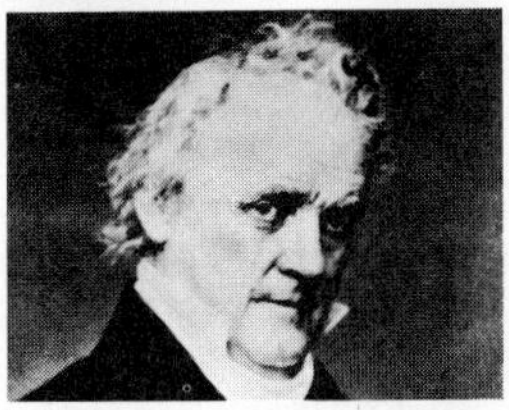

15.
James Buchanan, 65
1857-1861
Democrat
John C. Breckinridge
(unmarried)

16.
**Abraham Lincoln, 52
1861-1865
Republican
Hannibal Hamlin
Andrew Johnson
Mary Todd Lincoln

17.
Andrew Johnson, 56
1865-1869
Democrat
. . . . .
Eliza McCardle Johnson

18.
Ulysses S. Grant, 46
1869-1877
Republican
Schuyler Colfax
Henry Wilson
Julia Dent Grant

19.
Rutherford B. Hayes, 54
1877-1881
Republican
William A. Wheeler
Lucy Webb Hayes

20.
**James A. Garfield, 49
1881-1881
Republican
Chester A. Arthur
Lucretia Rudolph Garfield

21.
Chester A. Arthur, 50
1881-1885
Republican
. . . . .
Ellen Herndon Arthur

22.
Grover Cleveland, 47
1885-1889
Democrat
Thomas A. Hendricks
Frances Folsom Cleveland

23.
Benjamin Harrison, 55
1889-1893
Republican
Levi P. Morton
Caroline Scott Harrison

24.
Grover Cleveland, 55
1893-1897
Democrat
Adlai E. Stevenson
Frances Folsom Cleveland

25.
**William McKinley, 54
1897-1901
Republican
Garret A. Hobart
Theodore Roosevelt
Ida Saxton McKinley

26.
Theodore Roosevelt, 42
1901-1909
Republican
Charles W. Fairbanks
Edith Carow Roosevelt

27.
William H. Taft, 51
1909-1913
Republican
James S. Sherman
Helen Herron Taft

28.
Woodrow Wilson, 56
1913-1921
Democrat
Thomas R. Marshall
Edith Bolling Wilson

29.
*Warren G. Harding, 55
1921-1923
Republican
Calvin Coolidge
Florence Kling Harding

30.
Calvin Coolidge, 51
1923-1929
Republican
Charles G. Dawes
Grace Goodhue Coolidge

31.
Herbert C. Hoover, 54
1929-1933
Republican
Charles Curtis
Lou Henry Hoover

32.
*Franklin D. Roosevelt, 51
1933-1945
Democrat
John N. Garner
Henry A. Wallace
Harry S. Truman
Anna Eleanor Roosevelt

33.
Harry S. Truman, 60
1945-1953
Democrat
Alben Barkley
Bess Wallace Truman

34.
Dwight D. Eisenhower, 62
1953-1961
Republican
Richard M. Nixon
Mamie Doud Eisenhower

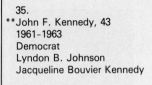

35.
**John F. Kennedy, 43
1961-1963
Democrat
Lyndon B. Johnson
Jacqueline Bouvier Kennedy

36.
Lyndon B. Johnson, 55
1963-1969
Democrat
Hubert H. Humphrey
Claudia (Ladybird) Taylor Johnson

37.
***Richard M. Nixon, 55
1969-1974
Republican
Spiro T. Agnew
Gerald R. Ford
Thelma (Pat) Ryan Nixon

38.
Gerald R. Ford, 61
1974-1977
Republican
Nelson A. Rockefeller
Elizabeth (Betty) Bloomer Ford

39.
James E. Carter, 52
1977-1981
Democrat
Walter F. Mondale
Rosalyn Smith Carter

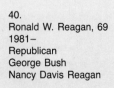

40.
Ronald W. Reagan, 69
1981–
Republican
George Bush
Nancy Davis Reagan

*died while in office
**assassinated
***resigned from office

THE STATES

State	Capital	Order of[1] Entry	Date of[1] Entry	Population[2]	Number of Representatives in the House
Alabama	Montgomery	22	1819	3,890,061	7
Alaska	Juneau	49	1959	400,481	1
Arizona	Phoenix	48	1912	2,717,866	5
Arkansas	Little Rock	25	1836	2,285,513	4
California	Sacramento	31	1850	23,668,562	45
Colorado	Denver	38	1876	2,888,834	6
Connecticut	Hartford	5	1788	3,107,576	6
Delaware	Dover	1	1787	595,225	1
Florida	Tallahassee	27	1845	9,739,992	19
Georgia	Atlanta	4	1788	5,464,265	10
Hawaii	Honolulu	50	1959	965,000	2
Idaho	Boise	43	1890	943,935	2
Illinois	Springfield	21	1818	11,418,461	22
Indiana	Indianapolis	19	1816	5,490,179	10
Iowa	Des Moines	29	1846	2,913,387	6
Kansas	Topeka	34	1861	2,363,208	5
Kentucky	Frankfort	15	1792	3,661,433	7
Louisiana	Baton Rouge	18	1812	4,203,972	8
Maine	Augusta	23	1820	1,124,660	2
Maryland	Annapolis	7	1788	4,216,446	8
Massachusetts	Boston	6	1788	5,737,037	11
Michigan	Lansing	26	1837	9,258,344	18
Minnesota	St. Paul	32	1858	4,077,148	8
Mississippi	Jackson	20	1817	2,520,638	5
Missouri	Jefferson City	24	1821	4,917,444	9
Montana	Helena	41	1889	786,690	2
Nebraska	Lincoln	37	1867	1,570,006	3
Nevada	Carson City	36	1864	799,184	2
New Hampshire	Concord	9	1788	920,610	2
New Jersey	Trenton	3	1787	7,364,158	14
New Mexico	Santa Fe	47	1912	1,299,968	3
New York	Albany	11	1788	17,557,288	34
North Carolina	Raleigh	12	1789	5,874,429	11
North Dakota	Bismarck	39	1889	652,695	1
Ohio	Columbus	17	1803	10,797,419	21
Oklahoma	Oklahoma City	46	1907	3,025,266	6
Oregon	Salem	33	1859	2,632,663	5
Pennsylvania	Harrisburg	2	1787	11,866,728	23
Rhode Island	Providence	13	1790	947,154	2
South Carolina	Columbia	8	1788	3,119,208	6
South Dakota	Pierre	40	1889	690,178	1
Tennessee	Nashville	16	1796	4,590,750	9
Texas	Austin	28	1845	14,228,383	27
Utah	Salt Lake City	45	1896	1,461,037	3
Vermont	Montpelier	14	1791	511,456	1
Virginia	Richmond	10	1788	5,346,279	10
Washington	Olympia	42	1889	4,130,163	8
West Virginia	Charleston	35	1863	1,949,644	4
Wisconsin	Madison	30	1848	4,705,335	9
Wyoming	Cheyenne	44	1890	470,816	1
District of Columbia			1791	637,651	1
Total number of representatives[3]					**435**

[1]For the thirteen original states, the order of entry and the date of entry represent their ratification of the Constitution.
[2]1980 census figures
[3]The total number of representatives in the House does not include the representative from the District of Columbia, who has no vote.

The Declaration of Independence

Preamble

When, in the course of human events, it becomes necessary for one people to dissolve the political bands which have connected them with another, and to assume, among the Powers of the earth, the separate and equal station to which the Laws of Nature and of Nature's God entitle them, a decent respect to the opinions of mankind requires that they should declare the causes which impel them to the separation.

New Principles of Government

We hold these truths to be self-evident: that all men are created equal, that they are endowed by their Creator with certain unalienable Rights, that among these are Life, Liberty, and the pursuit of Happiness.

That to secure these rights, Governments are instituted among Men, deriving their just powers from the consent of the governed. That whenever any Form of Government becomes destructive of these ends, it is the Right of the People to alter or to abolish it, and to institute new Government, laying its foundation on such principles, and organizing its powers in such form, as to them shall seem most likely to effect their Safety and Happiness. Prudence, indeed, will dictate that Governments long established should not be changed for light and transient causes; and accordingly all experience hath shown that mankind are more disposed to suffer while evils are sufferable, than to right themselves by abolishing the forms to which they are accustomed. But when a long train of abuses and usurpations, pursuing invariably the same Object, evinces a design to reduce them under absolute Despotism, it is their right, it is their duty, to throw off such Government, and to provide new Guards for their future security.—

Reasons for Separation

Such has been the patient sufferance of these Colonies; and such is now the necessity which constrains them to alter their former Systems of Government. The history of the present King of Great Britain is a history of repeated injuries and usurpations, all having in direct object the establishment of an absolute Tyranny over these States. To prove this, let facts be submitted to a candid world.

He has refused his Assent to Laws the most wholesome and necessary for the public good.

He has forbidden his Governors to pass Laws of immediate and pressing importance unless suspended in their operation till his Assent should be obtained; and when so suspended, he has utterly neglected to attend to them.

He has refused to pass other Laws for the accommodation of large districts of people, unless those people would relinquish the right of Representation in the Legislature, a right inestimable to them and formidable to tyrants only.

He has called together legislative bodies at places unusual, uncomfortable, and distant from the depository of their Public Records, for the sole purpose of fatiguing them into compliance with his measures.

He has dissolved Representative Houses repeatedly, for opposing with manly firmness, his invasions on the rights of the people.

He has refused for a long time after such dissolutions, to cause others to be elected; whereby the Legislative Powers, incapable of Annihilation, have returned to the people at large for their exercise; the State remaining, in the mean time exposed to all the dangers of invasion from without, and convulsions within.

He has endeavored to prevent the population of these states; for that purpose obstructing the Laws of Naturalization of Foreigners, refusing to pass others to encourage their migration hither, and raising the conditions of new Appropriations of Lands.

He has obstructed the Administration of Justice, by refusing his Assent to Laws for establishing Judiciary Powers.

He has made Judges dependent on his Will alone for the tenure of their offices, and the amount and payment of their salaries.

He has erected a multitude of New Offices, and sent hither swarms of Officers to harass our people and eat out their substance.

He has kept among us, in times of peace, Standing Armies. without the Consent of our legislature.

He has affected to render the Military independent of, and superior to, the Civil Power.

He has combined with others to subject us to a jurisdiction foreign to our constitution and unacknowledged by our laws; giving his Assent to their acts of pretended legislation:

For quartering large bodies of armed troops among us:

For protecting them, by a mock Trial, from Punishment for any Murders which they should commit on the Inhabitants of these States:

For cutting off our Trade with all parts of the World:

For imposing taxes on us without our Consent:

For depriving us, in many cases, of the benefits of Trial by Jury:

For transporting us beyond Seas, to be tried for pretended offenses:

For abolishing the free System of English Laws in a neighboring Province, establishing therein an Arbitrary government, and enlarging its Boundaries so as to render it at once an example and fit instrument for introducing the same absolute rule into these Colonies:

For taking away our Charters, abolishing our most valuable Laws, and altering fundamentally the forms of our governments:

For suspending our own Legislatures, and declaring themselves invested with Power to legislate for us in all cases whatsoever.

He has abdicated government here, by declaring us out of his Protection and waging War against us.

He has plundered our seas, ravaged our Coasts, burned our towns, and destroyed the lives of our people.

He is at this time transporting large armies of foreign mercenaries to complete the works of death, desolation, and tyranny already begun with circumstances of Cruelty & perfidy scarcely paralleled in the most barbarous ages, and totally unworthy the Head of a civilized nation.

He has constrained our fellow Citizens taken Captive on the high Seas to bear Arms against their Country, to become the executioners of their friends and Brethren, or to fall themselves by their Hands.

He has excited domestic insurrections among us, and has endeavored to bring on the inhabitants of our frontiers, the merciless Indian Savages, whose known rule of warfare is an undistinguished destruction of all ages, sexes, and conditions.

In every stage of these Oppressions We have Petitioned for Redress in the most humble terms. Our repeated Petitions have been answered only by repeated injury. A Prince whose character is thus marked by every act which may define a Tyrant, is unfit to be the ruler of a free People.

Nor have We been wanting in attention to our British brethren. We have warned them from time to time of attempts by their legislature to extend an unwarrantable jurisdiction over us. We have reminded them of the circumstances of our emigration and settlement here. We have appealed to their native justice and magnanimity, and we have conjured them by the ties of our common kindred, to disavow these usurpations, which, would inevitably interrupt our connections and correspondence. They, too have been deaf to the voice of justice and of consanguinity. We must, therefore, acquiesce in the necessity, which denounces our Separation, and hold them, as we hold the rest of mankind, Enemies in War, in Peace, Friends.

Formal Declaration of War

We, therefore, the Representatives of the united States of America, in General Congress Assembled, appealing to the Supreme Judge of the world for the rectitude of our intentions, do, in the Name, and by Authority of the good People of these colonies, solemnly publish and declare, That these United Colonies are, and of Right ought to be, Free and Independent States; that they are Absolved from all allegiance to the British Crown, and that all political connection between them and the State of Great Britain is, and ought to be, totally dissolved; and that, as Free and Independent States, they have full Power to levy War, conclude Peace, contract Alliances, establish Commerce, and to do all other Acts and Things which Independent States may of a right do. And, for the support of this Declaration, with a firm reliance on the Protection of Divine Providence, we mutually pledge to each other our Lives, our Fortunes, and our sacred Honor.

Glossary

Page numbers refer to pages in the text where the word is defined.

A

abolish to do away with completely (p. 308)

abolitionist a person who favors doing away with slavery completely (p. 308)

aggression an unprovoked attack or invasion (p. 587)

alienated feeling separated from one's own society (p. 547)

alliance a close association for a common objective (p. 46)

amend to change or add to (p. 161)

anarchist a person who believes that any government interferes with individual liberty and should therefore be replaced by cooperative groups (p. 452)

annex to attach a country or other territory, making it part of a nation (p. 322)

anthropologist a scientist who studies human culture and development (p. 37)

appeasement the policy of giving in to the demands of an aggressor in an attempt to avoid further trouble (p. 593)

archaeologist a scientist who studies the way of life of ancient peoples by examining artifacts and remains (p. 55)

armistice a truce that stops the fighting of a war (p. 534)

assembly line a method of producing goods in which workers put together a product as it goes past them on a moving belt (p. 422)

assimilate to make one group of people become part of a larger group (p. 403)

astrolabe a device used by navigators in the 1400's to determine the position of a ship at sea by locating certain stars (p. 57)

B

bank holiday the temporary closing of a nation's banks (p. 572)

bankrupt without money or unable to pay off debts (p. 379)

barrio a Spanish word meaning district or neighborhood (p. 696)

bill of rights a legal document outlining the rights and privileges of citizens that are to be protected by law (p. 153)

biomass energy energy generated from organic materials (p. 727)

black code a set of laws passed by the Southern states after the Civil War to limit the rights of blacks (p. 384)

blacklist to put a person's name on a list for the purposes of keeping that person from working in a particular industry (p. 454)

blockade the isolation of a country at war to prevent the passage and delivery of goods (p. 360)

boycott a refusal to buy from or deal with a foe so as to punish or bring about change (p. 116)

budget deficit the difference between government spending and revenues when spending exceeds revenues (p. 717)

busing the transportation of students to a school to achieve desegregation (p. 695)

C

capitalism an economic system in which the production and distribution of the nations' goods are privately owned and operated for profit (p. 650)

carpetbagger a Northerner who moved to the South after the Civil War (p. 388)

cartel a national or international association of businesses to control production or prices (p. 706)

cash crop a crop that is grown to be sold, rather than used by the farmer (p. 80)

charter a written grant of rights made by a government or ruler to a person or a company (p. 67)

circumnavigate to sail completely around something (p. 61)

civil liberties rights guaranteed to a person by law or custom, such as freedom of speech (p. 219)

civil rights rights guaranteed to individuals by the Constitution (p. 642)

civil service government jobs filled by persons who pass competitive public exams (p. 466)

closed society a society that will not examine its faults or allow criticism of itself and its institutions (p. 291)

closed-shop agreement an agreement between a union and an employer to hire only union members to work on a particular job (p. 642)

coalition the alliance of several groups of supporters behind a political candidate or party (p. 583)

cold war a war fought with propaganda, economic pressure, and military threats (p. 651)

collective bargaining discussions between the members of a union and their employer over work-related issues (p. 453)

communism an economic system in which all property, in theory, is owned by the people and managed by the national government (p. 549)

compromise a settlement in which each side gives up some demands (p. 157)

concentration camp a prison camp where political enemies or members of minority ethnic groups are confined (p. 482)

confederacy a union of independent groups, societies, or states (p. 43)

confederation a loose union of states in which each member state retains many powers of government (p. 149)

conquistador a Spanish explorer who explored and conquered much of Spain's New World empire (p. 60)

conscientious objector a person who refuses to participate in a war for moral or religious reasons (p. 615)

conservative a person who believes that government regulation of the economy should be kept at a minimum and that progress can best be achieved by allowing business the greatest possible freedom (p. 638)

consumer price index the average price of a selected group of consumer goods purchased by a typical family (p. 698)

consumer society a society in which people buy goods for the pleasure of buying them rather than because of need (p. 545)

containment the policy of the United States to "contain," or prevent the expansion of, communism and Soviet power (p. 652)

Continental Divide a ridge of the Rocky Mountains that separates the rivers flowing in an easterly direction from those flowing in a westerly direction (p. 225)

convoy a protecting escort for ships or troops (p. 533)

corporation a business organization formed by individuals who pool their money and become stockholders in the business (p. 421)

Cotton Belt a vast region of the South, stretching from the Carolinas to eastern Texas, where the major cash crop is cotton (p. 288)

covenant an agreement entered into very seriously, to do a specific thing (p. 82)

craft union a group of workers sharing the same craft or skill who have joined together to improve their wages and working conditions (p. 452)

crop-lien system a system by which farmers borrow money to run their farms and repay the loan with crops (p. 382)

D

Deep South slave states in the southern part of the South: the Carolinas, Georgia, Florida, Alabama, Mississippi, Arkansas, Louisiana, and Texas (p. 292)

deficit spending the government policy of spending more money each year than is collected in taxes (p. 583)

defoliate to strip the leaves from trees and other plants by using a chemical spray (p. 679)

demagogue a leader who, to boost his or her own popularity, stirs the people by appealing to their worst emotions (p. 662)

democratic treating all persons in the same way (p. 43)

depression a period in which business activity slows, prices and wages decline, and many workers lose their jobs (p. 567)

deregulation the removal of controls or regulations (p. 706)

desegregate to end racial segregation (p. 643)

détente a relaxation of tensions between nations (p. 694)

devaluation a reduction in value (p. 573)

dictator a person who rules a nation with absolute power and authority (p. 524)

dilemma a situation in which one has to choose between unpleasant alternatives (p. 680)

diplomatic recognition the formal acceptance or recognition by one nation of the government of another (p. 599)

direct primary an election to nominate candidates to run in the general election (p. 503)

disarmament the reduction of weapons (p. 548)

discriminate to treat a person or a group of people differently from the way all others are treated (p. 493)

doctrine a statement of a nation's policy, especially toward other nations (p. 243)

draft the selection of individuals for required military service (p. 368)

dynasty a succession of rulers who are members of the same family or come from the same geographic region (p. 241)

E

economic warfare the action of waging a war by damaging an enemy's trade, commerce, or economy (p. 227)

emancipate to set free or release from slavery (p. 269)

embargo a government order preventing commercial ships from entering or leaving a nation's ports (p. 230)

emigrate to leave one country and settle in another (p. 67)

entrepreneur a person who organizes and manages a business (p. 420)

equilibrium a state of balance between opposing forces (p. 693)

escalate to increase or expand (p. 678)

espionage spying (p. 616)

ethnic having to do with a group of people who share the same customs, language, and culture (p. 446)

excise tax a tax placed on goods produced within a country (p. 199)

executive having the authority to enforce laws and administer government affairs (p. 157)

expansionist a person who believes a nation should expand its territory or power (p. 477)

extinct no longer living (p. 38)

F

fascist a person who believes in a government dedicated to glorifying a nation or race; the government is based on centralized, dictatorial rule (p. 587)

federal system a system of government that divides power between the national government and individual states (p. 159)

feminist a supporter of equal rights for women (p. 696)

Fire-Eater a Southern radical who wanted the South to secede from the Union (p. 328)

Fireside Chat an informal radio talk to the nation by President Roosevelt (p. 572)

forty-niner a person who took part in the rush to California for gold in 1849 (p. 328)

freedom of the seas the right of any nation's merchant ships to travel in any waters in order to trade with any nation (p. 203)

fugitive a person who flees or tries to escape (p. 329)

G

gag rule a resolution of Congress that banned all discussion of petitions on abolition and the slavery issue (p. 310)

geothermal energy energy from the earth's core, obtained from hot water or steam near the earth's surface (p. 727)

ghetto a section of a city occupied by members of a single racial or ethnic minority group (p. 675)

goodwill tour a trip made throughout a nation for the purpose of showing concern, interest, and friendship (p. 241)

gradualism a belief in the voluntary freeing of slaves over a long period of time (p. 308)

graft the acquisition of money or favors in dishonest or questionable ways (p. 389)

gross national product the value of all goods and services produced in a nation (p. 614)

guerrilla warfare a method of warfare, used by small bands of revolutionary fighters (p. 142)

gunboat a small warship that is heavily armed and can navigate in shallow river waters (p. 361)

H

headright system a system in which land was offered free as a way to bring new settlers to the Virginia colony (p. 80)

hiring-out system a system of renting slaves to people in cities who needed workers (p. 295)

holding company a corporation that owns enough stock in other companies to control them (p. 435)

home rule self-government in local and state affairs (p. 389)

homesteader a person who settled on government land, built a dwelling on it, and owned it after living on it for five years (p. 414)

hostage a person held prisoner until a demand is granted (p. 711)

I

ideology a basic belief or theory of government and society (p. 649)

impeach to charge a public official with misconduct in office (p. 386)

imperialism the policy and practice of maintaining an empire, a policy marked by competition for control of foreign territory and markets (p. 525)

implied powers powers that are not clearly stated in the Constitution but are suggested because of the way the Constitution is worded (p. 200)

impressment the practice of forcing people into public service, especially into a navy (p. 204)

inaugurate to install in office with a formal ceremony (p. 197)

indentured servant a person who worked for someone for a specified period of time to pay off the cost of passage to another country (p. 98)

Indian Country a vast area of land on the Great Plains guaranteed by the American government as the permanent home for American Indians (p. 279)

industrial revolution the change in a nation's society and economy caused by the replacement of hand tools with machine and power tools and the development of large-scale industrial production (p. 249)

industrial union an organization of all the workers of an industry in a single union (p. 579)

inflation an increase in the amount of money in circulation that leads to a decrease in its value and a rise in prices (p. 470)

initiative a process by which people can propose a law and submit it for approval by the voters or the legislature (p. 503)

injunction an order from a court stopping an individual or group from carrying out some action (p. 455)

installment plan a method of buying goods in which a person pays only a small part of the total price and makes regular payments plus interest for the rest of the amount (p. 558)

intelligence secret information gathered for the national defense (p. 638)

intercontinental ballistic missile a missile capable of carrying a nuclear weapon accurately over long distances (p. 657)

interest a charge for borrowing money (p. 558)

internal improvements ways or methods of upgrading a transportation network such as through the construction of roads, canals, and railroads (p. 254)

intervene to interfere by military force in the internal affairs of another nation (p. 491)

irrational not reasonable or logical (p. 660)

island hopping an American military strategy during World War II to force the Japanese to give up their conquered islands by fighting on each one (p. 613)

isolationist a person who believes that his or her nation should not join international alliances or otherwise become involved in foreign affairs (p. 537)

isthmus a narrow neck of land that separates two bodies of water and connects two larger land regions (p. 60)

J

joint-stock company a company that is formed through the pooling of many people's money. Any profits made by the company are shared among those who have invested in it. (p. 73)

judicial having the authority to examine the laws of a government (p. 157).

judicial review the right of the Supreme Court to declare an act of Congress unconstitutional (p. 222)

jurisdiction authority or legal power to hear and decide cases (p. 198)

K

kickback money, received as payment for goods or services, that is illegally returned to a corrupt public official (p. 461)

Kitchen Cabinet a group of informal advisers to the President (p. 275)

kiva a circular room built underground and used for religious ceremonies (p. 41)

L

laissez-faire a government policy of not interfering in the affairs of business (p. 422)

land speculator one who buys land in the hope of selling it later for a profit (p. 340)

landslide a large majority of votes for one candidate or party in an election (p. 543)

legislative having to do with the making of laws (p. 150)

liberal a person who believes that government should take action to regulate the economy and promote the greater welfare and liberties of the people (p. 638)

life expectancy the average number of years that a person can expect to live (p. 721)

literacy rate the percentage of people in a specific population group who can read and write (p. 413)

lobby to engage in activities aimed at influencing public officials toward a desired action (p. 258)

M

machine a political group that organizes to control policy or officials in power (p. 460)

Manifest Destiny the belief that the United States was intended to spread from the Atlantic to the Pacific oceans (p. 320)

martial law temporary military rule over a civilian population (p. 718)

mass production the use of machines to produce goods more quickly and cheaply (p. 249)

massive retaliation the American policy of responding to any aggressive act by launching a counterattack of nuclear weapons (p. 656)

mercantilism an economic system designed to increase the wealth of a country by discouraging imports and encouraging exports. Colonies, with their raw materials, help to serve this purpose. (p. 74)

mercenary a professional soldier hired to serve in a foreign army (p. 131)

militarism the policy of building up military strength and glorifying the military spirit (p. 525)

militia an army made up of citizens rather than professional soldiers (p. 110)

minimum wage a wage set by law as the least amount employees can be paid for their work (p. 502)

minuteman a colonial soldier who could be prepared to fight at a minute's notice (p. 122)

monopoly exclusive control over a product or business (p. 108)

muckraker a journalist who uncovered corruption and poverty in America in the early 1900's (p. 501)

N

nationalism an intense devotion by a people to their nation (p. 525)

nationalize to transfer control of land, resources, or industries to the national government (p. 718)

nativist one who believes native-born persons are superior to immigrants (p. 443)

naturalism the approach in literature that emphasizes the observation of life without avoiding the ugly aspects of it (p. 515)

neutral rights the right of a country at peace to sail on any sea or ocean and trade with any nation (p. 227)

neutrality a position of not participating directly or indirectly in a war between other nations (p. 203)

Northwest Passage an imaginary water passage that early explorers believed would lead through North America to Asia (p. 65)

nuclear energy energy released from an atom in a nuclear reaction or by radioactive decay (p. 707)

nullification an action taken by a state that declares a law of Congress not valid within the borders of that state (p. 276)

O

obstruction of justice an illegal attempt to stop the investigation of a crime (p. 700)

open shop a shop or business in which workers are not required to join a union (p. 558)

ordinance a rule or law of government (p. 152)

overseer a person responsible for supervising the work of other people (p. 295)

P

pacifist a person who believes that international disputes should be settled by peaceful means rather than by force or violence (p. 523)

parity the equality of value of current farm products with the value of farm products in another period (p. 573)

patent a government license that gives someone the right to make and sell an invention for a certain number of years (p. 424)

perjury lying while under an oath to tell the truth (p. 661)

physicist a scientist who studies the nature of matter and energy (p. 622)

planned economy a system in which the central government directs all types of economic activity (p. 649)

pogrom an organized persecution and massacre of a minority group (p. 441)

poll-tax a special tax people are required to pay before they can vote (p. 673)

pool an agreement among businesses in the same industry to divide up the market and charge the same prices (p. 430)

popular sovereignty the belief that the people of a territory should have the right to decide whether their territory would permit slavery (p. 340)

postindustrial society a modern society based on advanced technology (p. 725)

precedent an act or statement that serves as an example for a later one (p. 197)

productivity the ability of a worker or business to produce more goods with the same or fewer inputs of land, labor, or capital (p. 633)

proprietary colony a colony granted by an English king to a person, family, or group of people who governed the colony in the name of the king (p. 95)

protective tariff a high tax placed on imported goods in order to protect domestic manufacturers and industries from foreign competition (p. 243)

protectorate a dependent nation over which another nation assumes protection and exercises great influence (p. 657)

proviso a clause that introduces a condition or provision (p. 327)

Q

quarantine to separate a diseased person or group from the rest of the population to keep the disease from spreading (p. 600)

R

racism the belief that people of one race are, by nature, inferior to people of another race (p. 511)

radar an electronic device that detects objects at long distance (p. 596)

ratify to approve officially (p. 149)

ration to limit the portion or share of scarce goods (p. 614)

realism the attempt in art and literature to depict real life as accurately as possible (p. 515)

rebate a refund of part of the rate charged for goods or services (p. 432)

rebellion armed resistance or opposition to one's government (p. 108)

recall a petition signed by voters calling for a special election in which the voters would decide if an official should remain in office (p. 503)

recession a temporary decline in production and an increase in the number of unemployed (p. 701)

Reconstruction the process, after the Civil War, of reorganizing the Southern states and readmitting them to the Union (p. 382)

referendum a process by which people can approve or reject a law (p. 503)

reform a change for the better (p. 305)

refugee a person who has fled his or her home during a time of war or other emergency (p. 555)

religious toleration recognition of the right to worship according to one's own beliefs (p. 96)

reparations payments by a defeated nation for damages caused during a war (p. 536)

repeal to do away with, take back (p. 117)

revenue tax a tax that raises income for the government (p. 199)

S

sabotage the destruction of railroads, bridges, or other property by enemy agents during war (p. 616)

satellite a small nation that is dominated by another larger and more powerful nation (p. 651)

scalawag a Southern white who joined or supported the Republican party during Reconstruction (p. 388)

scorched earth policy a military tactic of burning and destroying everything in an area (p. 373)

sea dogs English pirates who raided Spanish ships and towns in the late 1500's (p. 72)

secede to withdraw formally from membership in a group (p. 278)

sectionalism a concern for one's region of the country and its problems that ignores the well-being of the country as a whole (p. 267)

sedentary village a settled, permanent village inhabited by people who do not move from place to place (p. 43)

segregation the separation of a race, class, or ethnic group by discriminatory means (p. 391)

self-determination the right of a people to live under a government of their own choosing (p. 535)

settlement house a place that provides services for poor residents of a city (p. 502)

sexism the belief that members of one sex are inferior to members of the other (p. 504)

sharecropping a system in which people who cannot afford to buy land can rent land to farm and pay their rent from the profits made from their crops (p. 382)

sit-in an organized protest in which protesters occupy a business until it agrees to grant their demands (p. 669)

slave codes laws placing restrictions on slaves (p. 296)

slum a run-down area of a city in which housing is poor and crowded (p. 252)

solar energy energy obtained directly from sunlight (p. 707)

specie money in coin, usually gold and silver (p. 356)

speculator a person who acquires land in the hopes of selling it at a great profit (p. 414)

sphere of influence an area beyond a nation's borders where the nation exercises almost complete control (p. 481)

spoils system the practice of rewarding loyal political supporters with government jobs (p. 275)

squadron a naval unit of eight or more ships (p. 237)

stagnant sluggish, not flowing or moving about (p. 701)

stalemate a deadlock in which neither side seems able to gain an advantage (p. 239)

stock a share of ownership in a business acquired by a person who invests money in the business (p. 421)

stockbroker an agent who buys and sells stock and bonds (p. 559)

subversive a person who works from within a nation to undermine and eventually overthrow the government (p. 661)

suffrage the right to vote (p. 504)

summit conference a formal meeting of the leaders of nations (p. 663)

Sunbelt the states of the Southeast and Southwest that have experienced large population growth in recent years (p. 721)

supply-side economies an economic theory that says cutting taxes will lead to economic growth and higher government revenues (p. 716)

surplus an extra supply (p. 49)

synthetic fuels liquid fuels made from coal or natural gas (p. 707)

T

tariff a tax imposed by a government on imported goods (p. 151)

technology knowledge, skills, and objects necessary for human survival and comfort (p. 38)

temperance moderation in drinking alcoholic beverages or doing without them completely (p. 305)

tenement an apartment house that is rundown, very crowded, or poorly built (p. 447)

toxic wastes harmful or deadly waste products from factories or chemical plants (p. 726)

transcontinental railroad a rail line running across an entire continent (p. 339)

trust a group of businesses that unite to control production and prices of their goods and make larger profits (p. 432)

U

unconditional surrender the surrender of a defeated nation on the terms set by the victors (p. 610)

unconstitutional not in agreement with the highest law of the land (p. 200)

underground a secret movement organized to overthrow a government or the occupation forces of an enemy (p. 595)

unemployment rate the percentage of workers who are jobless (p. 569)

Upper South slave states in the northern part of the South: Delaware, Virginia, Kentucky, Tennessee, and Missouri (p. 292)

urban having to do with a city or cities (p. 252)

V

vaquero a Mexican cattle herder who was among the first cowhands of the West (p. 405)

veto refuse to approve (p. 160)

Vietnamization the planned withdrawal of American forces from Vietnam with the goal of turning all fighting over to the South Vietnamese (p. 692)

W

war crime any action during a time of war that violates the accepted rules of war or the assumed standards of humane behavior (p. 379)

war of attrition a war won by killing as many of the enemy as possible (p. 360)

wickiup a brush-covered hut built by the nomadic Indians of the Southwest (p. 45)

Y

yellow journalism the use of exciting but exaggerated news stories to make a newspaper more popular (p. 482)

yellow-dog contract an agreement a job applicant had to sign promising not to join a union while employed (p. 454)

Index

Italic page numbers are pages on which a definition is given.

PHOTO AND ART CREDITS

The following abbreviations will be used: LOC, Library of Congress; MMA, Metropolitan Museum of Art, N.Y.C.; NYPL, New York Public Library.

COVER PHOTO: Courtesy of DPI

UNIT OPENERS

UNIT 1, Chapter 1: 34, "Great Council of The Nez Perces," painting from the journals of Father Nicholas Point (from *Wilderness Kingdom*, Holt, Rinehart & Winston); **Chapter 2:** 35, Colored engraving of ships departing Lisbon to explore New World (Granger); **Chapter 3:** 35, 1756 sampler showing colonial wedding (American Antiquarian Society).

UNIT 2, Chapter 4: 104, Colored engraving of Boston Tea Party (Granger); **Chapter 5:** 104, Painting of Second Battle of Freeman's Farm, Saratoga (Courtesy, Fort Ticonderoga Museum); **Chapter 6:** 105, Banquet pavilion in New York celebrating ratification, July 23, 1788, by David Grim (The New York Historical Society); **Chapter 7:** 105, George Washington (White House Historical Association).

UNIT 3, Chapter 8: 216, "We Owe Allegiance to No Crown," painting by John A. Woodside (Davenport West, Jr.); **Chapter 9:** 217, "Capture of the City of Washington" from Rapin's *History of England* (Anne S. K. Brown Collection, Brown University Library); **Chapter 10:** 217, Engraving of calico printing in a cotton mill, c. 1834 (Granger).

UNIT 4, Chapter 11: 264, "Indian Removal," Choctaw, painting by Valjean Hessing (Philbrook Art Center, Tulsa); **Chapter 12:** 264, "Old Kentucky Home," oil painting by John W. Ehininger (Shelburne Museum, VT); **Chapter 13:** 265, Drawing of Elizabeth Cady Stanton addressing the First Women's Rights Convention at Seneca Falls, N.Y., June 20, 1848 (Granger); **Chapter 14:** 265, Clipper ship card announcing sailing from New York to San Francisco, c. 1850 (Granger).

UNIT 5, Chapter 15: 334, John Brown mural by John S. Curry (Kansas State Capitol, courtesy, Kennedy Galleries, Inc.); **Chapter 16:** 335, "Christmas Eve, 1862," by Thomas Nast (Collection of Col. & Mrs. Edgar Garbisch); **Chapter 17:** 336, "The First Vote," engraving, 1867 (Granger).

UNIT 6, Chapter 18: 396, "End of the Line for The Bison" (Smithsonian Institution); **Chapter 19:** 396, Engraving of President Grant and Brazilian emperor Dom Pedro starting Corliss engine at 1876 Centennial Exhibition (Granger); **Chapter 20:** 397, Immigrants at Ellis Island, c. 1910 (Culver); **Chapter 21:** 397, Campaign banner of McKinley and Hobart, 1896 (Culver, HRW photo by Russell Dian); **Chapter 22:** 397, "Dewey on the bridge of the *Olympic*," painting by Rufus Zogbaum (Courtesy of The State of Vermont).

UNIT 7, Chapter 23: 498, "Hester Street," painting by George Luks, 1905 (Brooklyn Museum); **Chapter 24:** 499, Yanks in the hills near Sedan, Germany, at the end of World War I (Courtesy of The Trustees of the Imperial War Museum); **Chapter 25:** 499, "Spring Lamb," *Life* Magazine cover by Ruth Eastman Rodgers, March 1929 (Culver).

UNIT 8, Chapter 26: 564, "Drought Stricken Area," painting by Alexander Hogue, 1934 (Dallas Museum of Fine Arts); **Chapter 27:** 565, Hitler addressing stormtroopers, Nuremberg, 1936 (Wide World); **Chapter 28:** 565, "O'er the Ramparts We Watch," World War II recruiting poster (Culver).

UNIT 9, Chapter 29: 628, Heavy traffic over the George Washington Bridge (Standard Oil of New Jersey); **Chapter 30:** 629, Khruschev making a speech (Erich Lessing/Magnum); **Chapter 31:** 629, Antiwar protest (Dennis Brack/Black Star).

UNIT 10, Chapter 32: 688, Richard Nixon in China, seated with Sec. of State Rogers, Chou En-Lai and Chiang Ching (Magnum); **Chapter 33:** 689, Iranians protesting at U. S. Embassy (Gianfranco Gorgoni/Contact/Woodfin Camp); **Chapter 34:** 689, Ronald Reagan campaigning in Indiana, 1980 (Michael Evans/Sygma).

CHAPTER OPENERS

Chapter 1: 36, "West Coast Indians Returning from Hunt," painting by Thomas Mower Martin (Courtesy of Glenbow Museum, Calgary, Alberta, Canada); **Chapter 2:** 54, Map showing early view of New World (NYPL, Map Division); **Chapter 3:** 78, "The Hope of Jamestown," painting by John Gadsby, 1841 (Mr. & Mrs. Paul Mellon); **Chapter 4:** 106, "The Fight at Concord Bridge" (A. Lassell Ripley, The Paul Revere Life Insurance Co.); **Chapter 5:** 128, "Declaration of Independence," painting by Edward Hicks, 1845 (Collection of Sotheby Parke-Bernet); **Chapter 6:** 148, "The Signing of The Constitution, 1787," painting by Howard Chandler Christy (Granger); **Chapter 7:** 196, " George Washington Riding to his Inauguration " (Janice E. Chabas); **Chapter 8:** 218, Thomas Jefferson, 1801, painting by Caleb Boyle (Alan P. Kirby Collection of Historical Paintings, Lafayette College); **Chapter 9:** 234, Engraving showing the city of Washington captured by the British forces, 1814 (The New York Historical Society); **Chapter 10:** 248, "Travel by Stagecoach near Trenton, N.J.," watercolor by Pavel Petrovich Svinin, 1811–1813 (MMA, Rogers Fund, 1942); **Chapter 11:** 266, "The Dis-United States," English cartoon, 1856 (Granger); **Chapter 12:** 286, Olivier plantation, Louisiana (Louisiana State Museum); **Chapter 13:** 300, Engraving of Utica, N.Y. in 1850 (NYPL, Print Division); **Chapter 14:** 314, "Emigrants Crossing The Plains," lithograph by Currier & Ives, 1866 (Granger); **Chapter 15:** 336, Lincoln changing trains on the way to his inauguration (Bettmann); **Chapter 16:** 354, Army of the Potomac marching down Pennsylvania Avenue, Washington, D.C. (West Point Museum, Collection of Alexandra McCook Craighead); **Chapter 17:** 378, "Reconstruction: before the war, after the war," lithograph, 1880 (Bettmann); **Chapter 18:** 398, "Crossing, South Platte River," painting by W. H. Jackson (Thomas Gilcrease Institute, Tulsa); **Chapter 19:** 418, "The Big Blow," painting by Aaron Bohrod of the Bessemer converter at Weirton, W. Va. (National Steel Corporation); **Chapter 20:** 438, Immigrants arriving at Ellis Island, 1900 (Culver); **Chapter 21:** 458, President Cleveland, painting titled "The Lost Bet," by Joseph Klir, 1892 (Chicago Historical Society); **Chapter 22:** 476, Cartoon, "The World's Constable" (Culver); **Chapter 23:** 500, City market scene, 1905, Mandrell Street, Chicago (Chicago Historical Society); **Chapter 24:** 522, U. S. Infantry, Argonne, 1918 (Culver); **Chapter 25:** 542, Lindbergh and the Spirit of St. Louis (American Institute of Aeronautics and Astronautics); **Chapter 26:** 566, Migrant workers (Photo by Dorothea Lange, LOC); **Chapter 27:** 586, S. S. Troops rounding up Jews (Culver); **Chapter 28:** 606, Pearl Harbor, 1941 (Navy Department, National Archives); **Chapter 29:** 630, Elizabeth Eckford being jeered by white students, Little Rock High School, 1957 (UPI); **Chapter 30:** 648, May Day parade in front of Lenin's tomb, Moscow (John Launois/Black Star); **Chapter 31:** 666, John F. Kennedy delivering inaugural address (UPI); **Chapter 32:** 690, Tall ship *The Christian Radich* sailing during Bicentennial celebration (Burt Glinn/Magnum); **Chapter 33:** 704, Gas crisis, 1979 (Sepp Seitz/Woodfin Camp); **Chapter 34:** 714, U. S. hostages returning from Iran (David Hume Kennerly/Contact/Woodfin Camp).

PHOTOS WITHIN TEXT

Pg. 4, Courtesy, CBS; 15, Manuel Rodriguez.

UNIT 1, Chapter 1: 39, Arizona State Museum, University of Arizona, Tucson; 41, David Muench; 42, Tony Linck; 44, NYPL, Picture Collection; 45, Courtesy of the Trustees of the British Museum; 47, NYPL, Picture Collection; 48, U.S. National Museum, on deposit with National Collection of Fine Arts, Smithsonian Institution, gift of Mrs. Sarah Harrison. **Chapter 2:** 57, Courtesy of the Trustees, The National Gallery, London; 62, Bibliothèque Nationale; 66, Convent des Ursulines, Quebec; 67, National Gallery of Canada, Ottawa; 69, LOC; 71, Courtesy of Earl of Warwick; 72, Granger. **Chapter 3:** 81, Woolaroc Museum, Bartlesville, OK; 82, Connecticut Historical Society; 84, Historical Picture Service, Chicago; 86, *Book of Trades*, 1807, NYPL, Rare Book Division; 88, Abby Aldrich Rockefeller Folk Art Collection, Colonial Williamsburg; 90, NYPL, Local History and Genealogy; 91, Friends Historical Library of Swarthmore College; 92, NYPL, Prints Division; 93, Library Company of Philadelphia; 94, Philadelphia Museum of Art; 95, Enoch Pratt Free Library, Baltimore; 96, Charleston Library Society, SC.

UNIT 2, Chapter 4: 108, Courtesy, Shelburne Museum, VT; 115, Huntington Library, San Marino, CA; 116, Colonial Williamsburg, Photo National Portrait Gallery, Smithsonian Institution; 119, Courtesy of the Kennedy Galleries, Inc; 123, Delaware Art Museum, Howard Pyle Collection. **Chapter 5:** 131, Electric Boat Division, General Dynamics Corporation; 133, Collection of Nina Fletcher Little and Mrs. Bertram Little; 134, Washington and Lee University; 137, Courtesy, Frick Art Reference Library; 138, New York State Historical Association, Cooperstown; 144, NYPL, Picture Collection. **Chapter 6:** 154, Historical Picture Service, Chicago; 155, Amherst College, Mead Art Museum, Request of Herbert Pratt, 1895; 156, Historical Society of Pennsylvania; 162, Art Commission of New York, HRW Photo by Russell Dian. **Chapter 7:** 199, NYPL, Prints Division, Phelps Stokes Collection; 202, Colt's Patent Fire Arms Mfg. Co. Inc; 204, Courtesy, New York Historical Society; 205, Chicago Historical Society; 207, Courtesy, Howard University, The Fogg Art Museum; 209, NYPL; 210, NYPL.

UNIT 3, Chapter 8: 220, Culver; 222, Washington and Lee University; 226, Amon Carter Museum, Fort Worth; 229, Smithsonian Institution; 230, Thomas Jefferson Coolidge, Jr. **Chapter 9:** 236, Delaware Art Museum, Louisa duPont Copeland Memorial Fund; 238, Irving S. Olds Collection; 239, Courtesy, Greensboro Historical Museum, Greensboro, NC. **Chapter 10:** 250, Yale University Art Gallery, Request of Stephen Carlton Clark, BA 1903; 255, Courtesy, New York Historical Society; 257, NYPL; 258, Culver.

UNIT 4, Chapter 11: 270, The Capitol, Washington, D.C.; 273, White House Collection; 277, Corcoran Gallery of Art; 280, Woolaroc Museum, Bartlesville, OK; 283, Culver. **Chapter 12:** 289, Bettmann; 290, Giraudon/Musee des Beaux Arts, Paris; 293, Courtesy of Museum of Art, Carnegie Institute (Gift of Mrs. W. Fitch Ingersoll); 294, Granger; 296, Granger. **Chapter 13:** 301, Granger; 304, Granger; 306, Granger; 309, Granger; 310, Lincoln Memorial Library. **Chapter 14:** 316, Governor's Mansion, Austin, TX; 317, The State Capitol, Austin, TX; 318, Butler Institute of American Art; 321, Mormon Church, Salt Lake City; 323, NYPL, Picture Collection; 324, San Jacinto Museum of History, TX; 326, Granger; 328, Minnesota Historical Society.

UNIT 5, Chapter 15: 337, Culver; 338, Granger; 340, Bettmann; 342, Culver; 343, Granger; 345, Granger; 347, Marie Dejohn, Courtesy Oxford Press; 351, NYPL, Picture Collection. **Chapter 16:** 361, Granger; 365, Gettysburg National Military Park; 367, Virginia State Library, Courtesy Confederate Museum; 368, Chicago Historical Society; 370, Culver; 374, West Point Museum. **Chapter 17:** 380, LOC; 381, Moorland-Spingarn Research Center, Howard University; 384, Granger; 385, Granger; 387, NYPL, Picture Collection; 388, Bettmann; 389, Culver; 390, LOC.

UNIT 6, Chapter 18: 398, Thomas Gilcrease Institute Tulsa; 402, Nebraska State Historical Society; 404, Photo by James Freeman, Clarke Historical Library, Central Michigan University; 407, Denver Public Library, Western Collection; 408, Kansas State Historical Society; 411, Nebraska State Historical Society, Solomon D. Butcher Collection; 413, Culver; 415, Nebraska State Historical Society, Solomon D. Butcher Collection. **Chapter 19:** 420, Merrimack Valley Textile Museum; 425, Culver; 426, New York Historical Society; 431, Culver; 433, Culver; 434, Burroughs Corp., Dayton, OH. **Chapter 20:** 440 both, Culver; 443, Courtesy of the Bancroft Library, University of California, Berkeley; 446, NYPL, Picture Collection; 448, Culver; 450, National Child Labor Commission; 451, LOC; 453, LOC. **Chapter 21:** 460, Culver; 465, Culver; 467, Culver; 469, Minnesota Historical Society; 471, Culver; 473, Culver. **Chapter 22:** 479, Culver; 480, Culver; 484, LOC; 485, Culver; 488, NYPL; 489, Culver; 490, Culver; 492, Culver.

UNIT 7, Chapter 23: 502, University of Illinois Library at Chicago Circle Campus, Jane Addams Memorial Collection; 506, Lewis W. Hine Photo, George Eastman House; 512, NYPL; 514, LOC; 516, MMA, Gift of Christian A. Zabriskie, 1950; 518, Bettmann. **Chapter 24:** 530, Culver; 531, NYPL, Picture Collection; 536, Courtesy Trustees of the Imperial War Museum. **Chapter 25:** 544, Courtesy of the Ford Archives, Henry Ford Museum, Dearborn, Michigan; 545, Bettmann; 546, Bettmann; 549, Courtesy of the Kennedy Galleries, Inc; 553, Smithsonian Institution; 557, Bettmann.

UNIT 8, Chapter 26: 568, Lewis W. Hine Photo, Historical Picture Service, Chicago; 573, Culver; 575, Xerox Corp.; 579, FDR Library, Hyde Park; 581, Granger. **Chapter 27:** 588, UPI; 589, Culver; 591, UPI; 592, E. I. duPont Nemours & Co; 595, National Gallery of Canada, Massey Collection; 596, UPI; 601, FDR Library, Hyde Park. **Chapter 28:** 609, Culver; 611, U. S. Army Photo; 615, Culver; 617, U. S. Office of War Information; 623, U. S. Air Force Photo.

UNIT 9, Chapter 29: 633, Magnum; 634, CBS Records Archives; 635, Bruce Davidson/Magnum; 639, Culver; 641, Culver; 643, UPI: 644, Chuck Fishman/Contact/Woodfin Camp. **Chapter 30:** 650, UPI; 654, Seibel in the Richmond *Times Dispatch*; 655, UPI; 661, UPI. **Chapter 31:** 667, John F. Kennedy Library; 669, UPI; 670, Pedro E. Guerrero; 672, Wide World; 674, Alexander Tsiaras/Science Source/Photo Researchers; 675, Wide World; 679, P. J. Griffiths/Magnum; 681, © Gemini G. E. L., Courtesy, Castelli Graphics, NY; 682, Cornell Capa/Magnum.

UNIT 10, Chapter 32: 693, Chuck O'Rear/Woodfin Camp; 695, Paul Fusco/Magnum; 697, Costa Manos/Magnum; 698, Blaine in *The Spectator*/Rothco Cartoons; 700, Mack Godfrey/Archive Pictures. **Chapter 33:** 707, T. Zimberoff/Sygma; 709, Sygma; 710, Focus on Sports. **Chapter 34:** 717, Eldon Pletcher/Rothco Cartoons; 719, Eugene Richards/Magnum; 720, Wide World; 721, David Hurn/Magnum; 722, Randy Taylor/Sygma; 726, Diego Goldberg/Sygma.

COVER DESIGN: Heather Gilchrist

MAPS: General Cartography Inc.

CHARTS & GRAPHS: Alice Coxe